THE FIRST AMENDMENT

CASES—COMMENTS—QUESTIONS

Third Edition

By

Steven H. Shiffrin
Professor of Law, Cornell University

Jesse H. Choper
Earl Warren Professor of Public Law,
University of California, Berkeley

AMERICAN CASEBOOK SERIES®

WEST GROUP
A THOMSON COMPANY

ST. PAUL, MINN., 2001

American Casebook Series, and the West Group symbol
are registered trademarks used herein under license.

ISBN 0–314–25201–0

 *TEXT IS PRINTED ON 10% POST CONSUMER RECYCLED PAPER*

2nd Reprint — 2004

Preface

The first amendment is an important cultural symbol in American society, but it is also an important part of American constitutional law. Unfortunately, first amendment law is a growth industry. It has outstripped the capacity of constitutional law books to provide materials that are sufficiently comprehensive for a separate first amendment course.

This book is designed for a two or three unit course in the first amendment. It proceeds on three assumptions:

(1) The body of first amendment law is sufficiently complicated and interconnected that a variety of organizational patterns can usefully be employed in teaching the course. For that reason we present the materials in a way that will permit instructors to depart from the organization of the casebook with relative ease.

(2) Students benefit from notes and questions that force them to come to grips with the diversity of perspectives arrayed in the rich literature of the first amendment. In particular we try to expose students to original perspectives or perspectives they might otherwise tend to slide past.

(3) The first amendment can be characterized as embodying a variety of competing values. In our view, those values are best studied in notes and questions as they emerge from concrete cases rather than from an abstract characterization and classification imposed on the student at the outset of study.

No Supreme Court term passes without further opinions addressing the first amendment. Hence, we will continue to provide annual supplements for recent developments, including one for the 1995–96 term.

Case and statute citations, as well as footnotes, of the Court and commentators have been omitted without so specifying; other omissions are indicated by asterisks or by brackets. Numbered footnotes are from the original materials; lettered footnotes are ours.

In preparing this casebook we have drawn freely from the first amendment materials in the casebooks we have co-authored and continue to co-author with our friends Yale Kamisar, Dick Fallon and the late Bill Lockhart. We owe them many thanks. Finally, thanks to Rose Merendino and Florence D. McKnight for secretarial and administrative assistance far beyond the call of duty.

*

Summary of Contents

Table of Contents

*

Table of Cases

The principal cases are in bold type. Cases cited or discussed in the text are roman type. References are to pages. Cases cited in principal cases and within other quoted materials are not included.

*

Table of Authorities

References are to pages.

THE FIRST AMENDMENT

CASES—COMMENTS—QUESTIONS

Third Edition

*

Part 1

FREEDOM OF EXPRESSION AND ASSOCIATION

Chapter 1

WHAT SPEECH IS NOT PROTECTED?

The first amendment provides that "Congress shall make no law * * * abridging the freedom of speech, or of the press." Some have stressed that no law means NO LAW. For example, Black, J., dissenting in *Konigsberg v. State Bar,* 366 U.S. 36, 81 S.Ct. 997, 6 L.Ed.2d 105 (1961) argued that the "First Amendment's unequivocal command * * * shows that the men who drafted our Bill of Rights did all the 'balancing' that was to be done in this field."

Laws forbidding speech, however, are commonplace. Laws against perjury, blackmail, and fraud prohibit speech.[a] So does much of the law of contracts. Black, J., himself conceded that speech pursued as an integral part of criminal conduct was beyond first amendment protection. Indeed no one contends that citizens are free to say anything, anywhere, at any time. As Holmes, J., observed, citizens are not free to yell "fire" falsely in a crowded theater.[b]

The spectre of a man crying fire falsely in the theater, however, has plagued first amendment theory. The task is to formulate principles that separate the protected from the unprotected. But speech interacts with too many other values in too many complicated ways to expect that a single formula will prove productive.

Are advocates of illegal action, pornographers selling magazines, or publishers of defamation like that person in the theater or are they engaged in freedom of speech? Do citizens have a right to speak on government property? Which property? Is there a right of access to the print or broadcast media? Can government force private owners to grant access for speakers? Does the first amendment offer protection for the wealthy, powerful corporations, and media conglomerates against government attempts to assure greater equality in the intellectual marketplace? Can government demand information about private political associations or reporters' confidential

a. Nonetheless, for a sophisticated defense of Black, J.'s position, see Black, *Mr. Justice Black, the Supreme Court, and the Bill of Rights,* 222 Harper's Mag. 63 (1961).

b. But see fn. b in *Roth v. United States,* p. 103 infra. For the contention that com-

paring the speech clause with other clauses of the Constitution yields insight, see Amar, *Intratextualism,* 112 Harv. L.Rev. 747, 810–17 (1999).

sources without first amendment limits? Does the first amendment require government to produce information it might otherwise withhold?

The Court has approached questions such as these without much attention to the language or history[c] of the first amendment and without a commitment to any general theory.[d] Rather it has sought to develop principles on a case-by-case basis and has produced a complex and conflicting body of constitutional precedent. Many of the basic principles were developed in a line of cases involving the advocacy of illegal action.

I. ADVOCACY OF ILLEGAL ACTION

A. EMERGING PRINCIPLES

SCHENCK v. UNITED STATES, 249 U.S. 47, 39 S.Ct. 247, 63 L.Ed. 470 (1919): Defendants were convicted of a conspiracy to violate the 1917 Espionage Act by causing and attempting to cause insubordination in the armed forces of the United States, and obstruction of the recruiting and enlistment service of the United States, when at war with Germany, by printing and circulating to men accepted for military service approximately fifteen thousand copies of the document described in the opinion. In affirming, HOLMES, J., said for a unanimous Court:

"The document in question upon its first printed side recited the first section of the Thirteenth Amendment, said that the idea embodied in it was

c. See, e.g., Powe, *The Fourth Estate and the Constitution* 22–50 (1991). Perry, *The Constitution, The Courts, and Human Rights,* 63–64 (1982). For a variety of views about the history surrounding the adoption of the first amendment, compare Levy, *Legacy of Suppression* (1960) with Levy, *Emergence of a Free Press* (1985); Levy, *The Legacy Reexamined,* 37 Stan.L.Rev. 767 (1985); Levy, *On the Origins of the Free Press Clause,* 32 U.C.L.A.L.Rev. 177 (1984) and Anastaplo, *Book Review,* 39 N.Y.U.L.Rev. 735 (1964); Anderson, *The Origins of the Press Clause,* 30 U.C.L.A.L.Rev. 455 (1983); Hamburger, *The Development of the Law of Seditious Libel and the Control of the Press,* 37 Stan.L.Rev. 661 (1985); Mayton, *Seditious Libel and the Lost Guarantee of a Freedom of Expression,* 84 Colum.L.Rev. 91 (1984); Mayton, *From a Legacy of Suppression to the 'Metaphor of the Fourth Estate,'* 39 Stan.L.Rev. 139 (1986); Rabban, *The Ahistorical Historian: Leonard Levy on Freedom of Expression in Early American History,* 37 Stan.L.Rev. 795 (1985). But see *McIntyre v. Ohio Election Comm'n,* infra, p. 523. (Thomas, J. concurring) (Scalia, J., dissenting).

For the contention that post-adoption history should play a larger role than philoso-phy in first amendment analysis, see Powe, *Situating Schauer,* 72 Notre D. L.Rev. 1519 (1997). For work focusing on post-adoption periods, see Curtis, *Free Speech, "The People's Darling Privilege"* (2000); Rabban, *Free Speech in its Forgotten Years* (1997). Gibson, *The Supreme Court and Freedom of Expression from 1791 to 1917,* 55 Fordham L.Rev. 263 (1986). See also Chafee, *Free Speech in the United States* (1941); Whipple, *The Story of Civil Liberty in the United States* (1927); Kairys, *Freedom of Speech* in The Politics of Law 160 (Kairys ed. 1982). For an ambitious attempt to marry history, philosophy, and the first amendment, see Richards, *A Theory of Free Speech,* 34 UCLA L.Rev. 1837 (1987).

d. On the difficulties involved in developing general theory, see Alexander & Horton, *The Impossibility of a Free Speech Principle,* 78 Nw.U.L.Rev. 1319 (1983); Farber & Fricky, *Practical Reason and the First Amendment,* 34 UCLA L.Rev. 1615 (1987); Shiffrin, *The First Amendment and Economic Regulation: Away From a General Theory of the First Amendment,* 78 Nw. U.L.Rev. 1212 (1983); Tribe, *Toward A Metatheory of Free Speech,* 10 Sw.U.L.Rev. 237 (1978).

violated by the conscription act and that a conscript is little better than a convict. In impassioned language it intimated that conscription was despotism in its worst form and a monstrous wrong against humanity in the interest of Wall Street's chosen few. It said, 'Do not submit to intimidation,' but in form at least confined itself to peaceful measures such as a petition for the repeal of the act. The other and later printed side of the sheet was headed 'Assert Your Rights.' It stated reasons for alleging that any one violated the Constitution when he refused to recognize 'your right to assert your opposition to the draft,' and went on, 'If you do not assert and support your rights, you are helping to deny or disparage rights which it is the solemn duty of all citizens and residents of the United States to retain.' It described the arguments on the other side as coming from cunning politicians and a mercenary capitalist press, and even silent consent to the conscription law as helping to support an infamous conspiracy. It denied the power to send our citizens away to foreign shores to shoot up the people of other lands, and added that words could not express the condemnation such coldblooded ruthlessness deserves, & c., & c., winding up, 'You must do your share to maintain, support and uphold the rights of the people of this country.' Of course the document would not have been sent unless it had been intended to have some effect, and we do not see what effect it could be expected to have upon persons subject to the draft except to influence them to obstruct the carrying of it out. The defendants do not deny that the jury might find against them on this point.

"But it is said, suppose that that was the tendency of this circular, it is protected by the First Amendment to the Constitution. [We] admit that in many places and in ordinary times the defendants in saying all that was said in the circular would have been within their constitutional rights. But the character of every act depends upon the circumstances in which it is done. The most stringent protection of free speech would not protect a man in falsely shouting fire in a theatre and causing a panic. [The] question in every case is whether the words used are used in such circumstances and are of such a nature as to create a clear and present danger that they will bring about the substantive evils that Congress has a right to prevent. It is a question of proximity and degree.[a] When a nation is at war many things that might be said in time of peace are such a hindrance to its effort that their utterance will not be endured so long as men fight and that no Court could regard them as protected by any constitutional right. It seems to be admitted that if an actual obstruction of the recruiting service were proved, liability

---

a. Although Schenck was convicted for violating a conspiracy statute, Holmes appears to have used the occasion to import the law of criminal attempts into the freedom of expression area. "In *Schenck,* 'clear and present danger,' 'a question of proximity and degree' bridged the gap between the defendant's acts of publication and the [prohibited interferences with the war.] This connection was strikingly similar to the Holmesian analysis of the requirement of 'dangerous proximity to success' [quoting from an earlier Holmes opinion] that, in the law of attempts, bridges the gap between the defendant's acts and the completed crime. In either context, innocuous efforts are to be ignored." Rogat, *Mr. Justice Holmes: Some Modern Views—The Judge as Spectator,* 31 U.Chi.L.Rev. 213, 215 (1964). See also Chafee, *Free Speech in the United States* 81–82 (1941); Shapiro, *Freedom of Speech* 55–58 (1966). But see Holmes, J., dissenting in *Abrams* infra, and fn. b below.

for words that produced that effect might be enforced. The statute of 1917 punishes conspiracies to obstruct as well as actual obstruction. If the act, (speaking, or circulating a paper), its tendency and the intent with which it is done are the same, we perceive no ground for saying that success alone warrants making the act a crime."[b]

———

DEBS v. UNITED STATES, 249 U.S. 211, 39 S.Ct. 252, 63 L.Ed. 566 (1919): Defendant was convicted of violating the Espionage Act for obstructing and attempting to obstruct the recruiting service and for causing and attempting to cause insubordination and disloyalty in the armed services. He was given a ten-year prison sentence on each count, to run concurrently. His criminal conduct consisted of giving the anti-war speech described in the opinion at the state convention of the Socialist Party of Ohio, held at a park in Canton, Ohio, on a June 16, 1918 Sunday afternoon before a general audience of 1,200 persons. At the time of the speech, defendant was a national political figure.[a] In affirming, HOLMES, J., observed for a unanimous Court:

"The main theme of the speech was socialism, its growth, and a prophecy of its ultimate success. With that we have nothing to do, but if a part or the manifest intent of the more general utterances was to encourage those present to obstruct the recruiting service and if in passages such encouragement was directly given, the immunity of the general theme may not be enough to protect the speech. [Defendant had come to the park directly from a nearby jail, where he had visited three socialists imprisoned for obstructing the recruiting service. He expressed sympathy and admiration for these persons and others convicted of similar offenses, and then] said that the master class has always declared the war and the subject class has always fought the battles—that the subject class has had nothing to gain and all to lose, including their lives; [and that] 'You have your lives to lose; you certainly ought to have the right to declare war if you consider a war

---

b. See also *Frohwerk v. United States,* 249 U.S. 204, 39 S.Ct. 249, 63 L.Ed. 561 (1919), where a unanimous Court, per Holmes, J., sustained a conviction for conspiracy to obstruct recruiting in violation of the Espionage Act, by means of a dozen newspaper articles praising the spirit and strength of the German nation, criticizing the decision to send American troops to France, maintaining that the government was giving false and hypocritical reasons for its course of action and implying that "the guilt of those who voted the unnatural sacrifice" is greater than the wrong of those who seek to escape by resistance: "[*Schenck* decided] that a person may be convicted of a conspiracy to obstruct recruiting by words of persuasion. [S]o far as the language of the articles goes there is not much to choose between expressions to be found in them and those before us in *Schenck*." Consider Powe, *The Fourth Estate and the Constitution* 71 (1991): "The case against Frohwerk was [weaker] than that against Schenck on both contested points; the recipients of the writing and the intensity of the writing. [Even] the government attorney who prevailed in *Frohwerk* [concluded that he was] 'one of the clearest examples of the political prisoner.'"

a. Debs had run for the Presidency on the Socialist ticket for the fourth time in 1912. At the 1920 election, while in prison, Debs ran again and received over 900,000 votes as the Socialist candidate, a significant portion of all votes cast in that election.

necessary.' [He next said of a woman serving a ten-year sentence for obstructing the recruiting service] that she had said no more than the speaker had said that afternoon; that if she was guilty so was [he].

"There followed personal experiences and illustrations of the growth of socialism, a glorification of minorities, and a prophecy of the success of [socialism], with the interjection that 'you need to know that you are fit for something better than slavery and cannon fodder.' [Defendant's] final exhortation [was] 'Don't worry about the charge of treason to your masters; but be concerned about the treason that involves yourselves.' The defendant addressed the jury himself, and while contending that his speech did not warrant the charges said 'I have been accused of obstructing the war. I admit it. Gentlemen, I abhor war. I would oppose the war if I stood alone.' The statement was not necessary to warrant the jury in finding that one purpose of the speech, whether incidental or not does not matter, was to oppose not only war in general but this war, and that the opposition was so expressed that its natural and intended effect would be to obstruct recruiting. If that was intended and if, in all the circumstances, that would be its probable effect, it would not be protected by reason of its being part of a general program and expressions of a general and conscientious belief.

"[Defendant's constitutional objections] based upon the First Amendment [were] disposed of in *Schenck*.

"[T]he admission in evidence of the record of the conviction [of various persons he mentioned in his speech was proper] to show what he was talking about, to explain the true import of his expression of sympathy and to throw light on the intent of the address. [Properly admitted, too, was an 'Anti-war Proclamation and Program' adopted the previous year, coupled with testimony that shortly before his speech defendant had stated that he approved it]. Its first recommendation was, 'continuous, active, and public opposition to the war, through demonstrations, mass petitions, and all other means within our power.' Evidence that the defendant accepted this view and this declaration of his duties at the time that he made his speech is evidence that if in that speech he used words tending to obstruct the recruiting service he meant that they should have that effect. [T]he jury were most carefully instructed that they could not find the defendant guilty for advocacy of any of his opinions unless the words used had as their natural tendency and reasonably probable effect to obstruct the recruiting service [and] unless the defendant had the specific intent to do so in his mind."

Notes and Questions

1. *The Man in the Theater.* Consider Kalven, *A Worthy Tradition* 133–34 (1988): "*Schenck*—and perhaps even Holmes himself—are best remembered for the example of the man 'falsely shouting fire' in a crowded theater. Judge Hand said in *Masses* that 'words are not only the keys of persuasion, but the triggers of action.' Justice Holmes makes the same point by means of

the 'fire' example, an image which was to catch the fancy of the culture. But the example has long seemed to me trivial and misleading. It is as if the only conceivable controversy over speech policy were with an adversary who asserts that *all* use of words is absolutely immunized under the First Amendment. The 'fire' example then triumphantly impeaches this massive major premise. Beyond that, it adds nothing to our understanding. If the point were that *only* speech which is a comparable 'trigger of action' could be regulated, the example might prove a stirring way of drawing the line at incitement, but it is abundantly clear that Justice Holmes is not comparing Schenck's leaflet to the shouting of 'fire.' Moreover, because the example is so wholly apolitical, it lacks the requisite complexity for dealing with any serious speech problem likely to confront the legal system. The man shouting 'fire' does not offer premises resembling those underlying radical political rhetoric—premises that constitute criticism of government.''

2. *Reflections.* (a) Consider Kalven, *Ernst Freund and the First Amendment Tradition,* 40 U.Chi.L.Rev. 235, 236–38 (1973): "It has been customary to lavish care and attention on the *Schenck* case, [but *Debs,* argued well before *Schenck* was handed down and decided just one week later,] represented the first effort by Justice Holmes to apply what he had worked out about freedom of speech in *Schenck.* The start of the law of the first amendment is not *Schenck;* it is *Schenck* and *Debs* read together. [Debs' speech] fell into the genre of bitter criticism of government and government policy, sometimes called seditious libel; freedom of such criticism from government marks, we have come to understand, 'the central meaning of the First Amendment' [*New York Times v. Sullivan,* Ch. 1, II, B infra]. During the Vietnam War thousands of utterances strictly comparable in bitterness and sharpness of criticism, if not in literacy, were made; it was pretty much taken for granted they were beyond the reach of government.[b] [*Debs*] raises serious questions as to what the first amendment, and more especially, what the clear and present danger formula can possibly have meant at the time. [Holmes] does not comment on the fact difference between [*Schenck* and *Debs*]: the defendant in *Schenck* had sent his leaflets directly to men who awaited draft call whereas [*Debs*] was addressing a general audience at a public meeting. Holmes offers no discussion of the sense in which Debs' speech presented a clear and present danger. [In fact, *Debs*] did not move [Holmes] to discuss free speech at all; his brief opinion is occupied with two points about admissibility of [evidence]. It was for Holmes a routine criminal appeal.''

3. *Governmental legitimacy.* Consider Solum, *Freedom of Communicative Action,* 83 Nw.U.L.Rev. 54, 122–23 (1989): "Government claims a legitimate monopoly on the use of force. Any fundamental challenge to the legitimacy of this monopoly must include implicit justification or explicit advocacy of illegal action, either of nonviolent civil disobedience or of violent revolution. [S]uch fundamental challenges must be allowed if the government claims that the rightfulness of its monopoly on the use of force would

b. Compare *Debs* with *Bond v. Floyd,* Ch. 1, I, C infra.

be accepted in rational discourse. [I]f a violent revolutionary movement were actually likely to succeed in overthrowing the present government and if we had good reason to believe that the new regime would be worse than the present government, then we would have good reasons to temporarily suspend the right to question fundamental legitimacy in order to avoid this immediate and serious danger. The 'clear and present danger' test operationalizes a qualification of the right to advocate illegal conduct."

4. MASSES PUBLISHING CO. v. PATTEN, 244 Fed. 535 (S.D.N.Y. 1917): The Postmaster of New York advised plaintiff that an issue of his monthly revolutionary journal, *The Masses,* would be denied the mails under the Espionage Act since it tended to encourage the enemies of the United States and to hamper the government in its conduct of the war. The Postmaster subsequently specified as objectionable several cartoons entitled, e.g., "Conscription," "Making the World Safe for Capitalism"; several articles admiring the "sacrifice" of conscientious objectors and a poem praising two persons imprisoned for conspiracy to resist the draft. Plaintiff sought a preliminary injunction against the postmaster from excluding its magazine from the mails. LEARNED HAND, D.J., granted relief:

"[The postmaster maintains] that to arouse discontent and disaffection among the people with the prosecution of the war and with the draft tends to promote a mutinous and insubordinate temper among the troops. This [is] true; men who become satisfied that they are engaged in an enterprise dictated by the unconscionable selfishness of the rich, and effectuated by a tyrannous disregard for the will of those who must suffer and die, will be more prone to insubordination than those who have faith in the cause and acquiesce in the means. Yet to interpret the word 'cause' [in the statutory language forbidding one to 'willfully cause' insubordination in the armed forces] so broadly would [necessarily involve] the suppression of all hostile criticism, and of all opinion except what encouraged and supported the existing policies, or which fell within the range of temperate argument. It would contradict the normal assumption of democratic government that the suppression of hostile criticism does not turn upon the justice of its substance or the decency and propriety of its temper. Assuming that the power to repress such opinion may rest in Congress in the throes of a struggle for the very existence of the state, its exercise is so contrary to the use and wont of our people that only the clearest expression of such a power justifies the conclusion that it was intended.

"The defendant's position, therefore, in so far as it involves the suppression of the free utterance of abuse and criticism of the existing law, or of the policies of the war, is not, in my judgment, supported by the language of the statute. Yet there has always been a recognized limit to such expressions, incident indeed to the existence of any compulsive power of the state itself. One may not counsel or advise others to violate the law as it stands. Words are not only the keys of persuasion, but the triggers of action, and those which have no purport but to counsel the violation of law cannot by any latitude of interpretation be a part of that public opinion which is the final source of government in a democratic state. [To] counsel or advise a man to an act is to urge upon him either that it is his interest or his duty to do it. While, of course, this may be accomplished as well by indirection as expressly, since words carry the meaning that they impart, the definition is exhaustive, I think, and I shall use it. * * * If one stops short of urging upon others that it is their duty or their interest to resist the law, it seems to me one should not be held to have attempted to cause its violation.[c] If that be not the test, I can see no escape from the conclusion that under this section every political agitation which can be shown to be apt to create a seditious temper is illegal. I am confident that by such language Congress had no such revolutionary purpose in view.

"It seems to me, however, quite plain that none of the language and none of the cartoons in this paper can be thought directly to counsel or advise insubordination or mutiny, without a violation of their meaning quite beyond any tolerable understanding. I come, therefore to the [provision of the Act forbidding] any one from willfully obstructing [recruiting or enlistment]. I am not prepared to assent to the plaintiff's position that this only refers to acts other than words, nor that the act thus defined must be shown to have been successful. One may obstruct without preventing, and the mere obstruction is an injury to the service; for it throws impediments in its way. Here again, however, since the question is of the expression of opinion, I construe the sentence, so far as it restrains public utterance, [as] limited to the direct advocacy of resistance to the recruiting and enlistment service. If so, the inquiry is narrowed to the question whether any of the challenged matter may be said to advocate resistance to the draft, taking the meaning of the words with the utmost latitude which they can bear.

"As to the cartoons it seems to me quite clear that they do not fall within such a test. [T]he most that can be said [is that they] may breed such animosity to the draft as will promote resistance and strengthen the determination of those disposed to be recalcitrant. There is no intimation that, however, hateful the draft may be, one is in duty bound to resist it, certainly none that such resistance is to one's interest. I cannot, therefore, even with the limitations which surround the power of the court, assent to the assertion that any of the cartoons violate the act.

"[As for the text], it is plain enough that the [magazine] has the fullest sympathy for [those who resist the draft or obstruct recruiting], that it admires their courage, and that it presumptively approves their conduct. [Moreover,] these passages, it must be remembered, occur in a magazine which attacks with the utmost violence the draft and the war. That such comments have a tendency to arouse emulation in others is clear enough,

c. Fried, *Perfect Freedom, Perfect Justice,* 78 B.U.L.Rev. 717, 725 (1998): "Hand's test both excludes and includes too much. It denies First Amendment protection to pacifist teaching that it is a person's duty peaceably to disobey certain laws, while granting it—to use Mill's example—to the inflammatory denunciation of food speculation to a hungry mob assembled at a corn dealer's house."

but that they counsel others to follow these examples is not so plain. Literally at least they do not, and while, as I have said, the words are to be taken, not literally, but according to their full import, the literal meaning is the starting point for interpretation. One may admire and approve the course of a hero without feeling any duty to follow him. There is not the least implied intimation in these words that others are under a duty to follow. The most that can be said is that, if others do follow, they will get the same admiration and the same approval. Now, there is surely an appreciable distance between esteem and emulation; and unless there is here some advocacy of such emulation, I cannot see how the passages can be said to fall within the [law.] Surely, if the draft had not excepted Quakers, it would be too strong a doctrine to say that any who openly admire their fortitude or even approved their conduct was willfully obstructing the draft.

"When the question is of a statute constituting a crime, it seems to me that there should be more definite evidence of the act. The question before me is quite the same as what would arise upon a motion to dismiss an indictment at the close of the proof: Could any reasonable man say, not that the indirect result of the language might be to arouse a seditious disposition, for that would not be enough, but that the language directly advocated resistance to the draft? I cannot think that upon such language any verdict would stand."[d]

What result if the Court had applied the *Masses* test in *Schenck* or *Debs* ? In *Abrams* or *Gitlow,* infra?

JUSTICE HOLMES—DISSENTING IN ABRAMS v. UNITED STATES
250 U.S. 616, 624, 40 S.Ct. 17, 20, 63 L.Ed. 1173, 1178 (1919).

[In the summer of 1918, the United States sent a small body of marines to Siberia. Although the defendants maintained a strong socialist opposition to "German militarism," they opposed the "capitalist" invasion of Russia, and characterized it as an attempt to crush the Russian Revolution. Shortly thereafter, they printed two leaflets and distributed several thousand copies in New York City. Many of the copies were thrown from a window where one defendant was employed; others were passed around at radical meetings. Both leaflets supported Russia against the United States; one called upon workers to unite in a general strike. There was no evidence that workers responded to the call.

d. In reversing, 246 Fed. 24 (1917), the Second Circuit observed: "If the natural and probable effect of what is said is to encourage resistance to a law, and the words are used in an endeavor to persuade to resistance, it is immaterial that the duty to resist is not mentioned, or the interest of the person addressed in resistance is not suggested. That one may willfully obstruct the enlistment service, without advising in direct language against enlistments, and

without stating that to refrain from enlistment is a duty or in one's interest, seems to us too plain for controversy."

For diverse views concerning Judge Hand's opinion and its importance, see Gunther, *Learned Hand* 151–70, 603 (1994); Schwartz, *Holmes v. Hand,* 1994 S.Ct.Rev. 209; Blasi, *Learned Hand and the Self–Government Theory of the First Amendment,* 61 U.Col.L.Rev. 1 (1990).

[The Court upheld the defendants' convictions for conspiring to violate two provisions of the 1918 amendments to the Espionage Act. One count prohibited language intended to "incite, provoke and encourage resistance to the United States"; the other punished those who urged curtailment of war production. As the Court interpreted the statute, an intent to interfere with efforts against a *declared* war was a necessary element of both offenses. Since the United States had not declared war upon Russia, "the main task of the government was to establish an [*intention*] *to interfere with the war with Germany.*" Chafee, supra, at 115. The Court found intent on the principle that "Men must be held to have intended, and to be accountable for, the effects which their acts were likely to produce. Even if their primary purpose and intent was to aid the cause of the Russian Revolution, the plan of action which they adopted necessarily involved, before it could be realized, defeat of the war program of the United States * * *."

[HOLMES, J., dissented in an opinion with which Brandeis, J., concurred:][a]

[I] am aware of course that the word "intent" as vaguely used in ordinary legal discussion means no more than knowledge at the time of the act that the consequences said to be intended will ensue. [But,] when words are used exactly, a deed is not done with intent to produce a consequence unless that consequence is the aim of the deed. It may be obvious, and obvious to the actor, that the consequence will follow, and he may be liable for it even if he regrets it, but he does not do the act with intent to produce it unless the aim to produce it is the proximate motive of the specific act although there may be some deeper motive behind.

It seems to me that this statute must be taken to use its words in a strict and accurate sense. They would be absurd in any other. A patriot might think that we were wasting money on aeroplanes, or making more cannon of a certain kind than we needed, and might advocate curtailment with success, yet even if it turned out that the curtailment hindered and was thought by other minds to have been obviously likely to hinder the United States in the prosecution of the war, no one would hold such conduct a crime. * * *

I never have seen any reason to doubt that the questions of law that alone were before this Court in the cases of *Schenck, Frohwerk* and *Debs* were rightly decided. I do not doubt for a moment that by the same reasoning that would justify punishing persuasion to murder, the United States constitutionally may punish speech that produces or is intended to produce a clear and imminent danger that it will bring about forthwith certain substantive evils that the United States constitutionally may seek to

---

a. Consider Novick, *Honorable Justice, The Life of Oliver Wendell Holmes* 331 (1989): "The majority did very highly disapprove of Holmes's dissent, and White tried to persuade him to be silent. When Holmes clung to what he thought his duty, three of the justices came to call on him in his library, and [his wife] Fanny joined them in trying to dissuade him from publishing his dissent."

prevent. The power undoubtedly is greater in time of war than in time of peace because war opens dangers that do not exist at other times.

But as against dangers peculiar to war, as against others, the principle of the right to free speech is always the same. It is only the present danger of immediate evil or an intent to bring it about that warrants Congress in setting a limit to the expression of opinion where private rights are not concerned. Congress certainly cannot forbid all effort to change the mind of the country. Now nobody can suppose that the surreptitious publishing of a silly leaflet by an unknown man, without more, would present any immediate danger that its opinions would hinder the success of the government arms or have any appreciable tendency to do so.[b] Publishing those opinions for the very purpose of obstructing, however, might indicate a greater danger and at any rate would have the quality of an attempt.[c] * * *

I do not see how anyone can find the intent required by the statute in any of the defendants' words. The leaflet advocating a general strike is the only one that affords even a foundation for the charge, and [its only object] is to help Russia and stop American intervention there against the popular government—not to impede the United States in the war that it was carrying on. * * *

In this case sentences of twenty years imprisonment have been imposed for the publishing of two leaflets that I believe the defendants had as much right to publish as the Government has to publish the Constitution of the United States now vainly invoked by them. [E]ven if what I think the necessary intent were shown; the most nominal punishment seems to me all

---

b. But cf. Wigmore, *Abrams v. U.S.: Freedom of Speech and Freedom of Thuggery in War–Time and Peace–Time,* 14 Ill. L.Rev. 539, 549–50 (1920): "[The *Abrams* dissent] is dallying with the facts and the law. None know better than judges that what is lawful for one is lawful for a thousand others. If these five men could, without the law's restraint, urge munition workers to a general strike and armed violences then others could lawfully do so; and a thousand disaffected undesirables, aliens and natives alike, were ready and waiting to do so. Though this circular was 'surreptitious,' the next ones need not be so. If such urgings were lawful, every munitions factory in the country could be stopped by them. The relative amount of harm that one criminal act can effect is no measure of its criminality, and no measure of the danger of its criminality. [At a time] when the fate of the civilized world hung in the balance, how could the Minority Opinion interpret law and conduct in such a way as to let loose men who were doing their hardest to paralyze the supreme war efforts of our country?"

c. Would it, if, under the circumstances, the defendant had no reasonable prospect of success? If his efforts were utterly ineffectual? Is bad intention or purpose, without more, an attempt? Or even everything done in furtherance of that bad intention? Or is unlawful "intention" or "purpose" merely one factor in determining whether defendant's conduct comes dangerously near success or stamps the actor as sufficiently dangerous? Cf. Holmes, *The Common Law* 65–66, 68–69 (1881): "Intent to commit a crime is not itself criminal. [Moreover], the law does not punish every act which is done with the intent to bring about a crime. [We] have seen what amounts to an attempt to burn a haystack [lighting a match with intent to start fire to a haystack]; but it was said in the same case, that, if the defendant had gone no further than to buy a box of matches for the purpose, he would not have been liable. [Relevant considerations are] the nearness of the danger, the greatness of the harm and the degree of apprehension felt." See generally Chafee, supra, at 46–47; Linde, *"Clear and Present Danger" Reexamined,* 22 Stan.L.Rev. 1163, 1168–69, 1183–86 (1970); Shapiro, *Freedom of Speech* 55–58 (1966).

that possibly could be inflicted, unless the defendants are to be made to suffer not for what the indictment alleges but for the creed that they avow— [which,] although made the subject of examination at the trial, no one has a right even to consider in dealing with the charges before the Court.

Persecution for the expression of opinions seems to me perfectly logical. If you have no doubt of your premises or your power and want a certain result with all your heart you naturally express your wishes in law and sweep away all opposition. To allow opposition by speech seems to indicate that you think the speech impotent, as when a man says that he has squared the circle, or that you do not care whole-heartedly for the result, or that you doubt either your power or your premises. But when men have realized that time has upset many fighting faiths,[d] they may come to believe even more than they believe the very foundations of their own conduct that the ultimate good desired is better reached by free trade in ideas—that the best test of truth is the power of the thought to get itself accepted in the competition of the market, and that truth is the only ground upon which their wishes safely can be carried out. That at any rate is the theory of our Constitution. It is an experiment, as all life is an experiment. Every year if not every day we have to wager our salvation upon some prophecy based upon imperfect knowledge. While that experiment is part of our system I think that we should be eternally vigilant against attempts to check the expression of opinions that we loathe and believe to be fraught with death, unless they so imminently threaten immediate interference with the lawful and pressing purposes of the law that an immediate check is required to save the country. [Only] the emergency that makes it immediately dangerous to leave the correction of evil counsels to time warrants making any exception to the sweeping command, "Congress shall make no law * * * abridging the freedom of speech." Of course I am speaking only of expressions of opinion and exhortations, which were all that were uttered [here].[e]

Notes and Questions

1.   *"Marketplace of ideas."*

d. "In referring to 'fighting faiths,' Holmes may well have been thinking in part of the abolitionism to which he had been committed in his youth, and which he believed had led to the devastation of the Civil War. In this way, he laid the foundations of modern free speech jurisprudence on the ruins of the natural rights theory which originally supported the First Amendment." Heyman, *Righting the Balance: An Inquiry into the Foundations and Limits of Freedom of Expression*, 78 B.U.L.Rev. 1275, 1303 (1998).

e. Consider Blasi, *Reading Holmes through the Lens of Schauer: The Abrams Dissent*, 72 Notre Dame L. Rev. 1343, 1354–55 (1997): "Nothing [Holmes] says in Abrams by his own injunction, applies to regulations of speech predicated on misstatements of verifiable fact, such as the standard action for defamation. Likewise, disclosures of sensitive information remain outside the ambit of Holmes's argument for free speech, however much such disclosures might contribute to public debate or the checking of government power. The graphic depictions of pornographers, even the soft-core variety, also appear not to be the type of speech that Holmes insists must be tested in the competition of the market."

(a) Consider White, *Justice Holmes and the Modernization of Free Speech Jurisprudence: The Human Dimension,* 80 Calif.L.Rev. 439 (1992): "Holmes' conception of the 'search for truth' was [quite different] from that of Chafee and the other progressive theorists who sought to shift the premises of free speech theory in the early twentieth century. For Chafee and those who emphasized the social interest in free speech, the search for truth was part of a process in which public opinion could become more informed and enlightened. For Holmes, 'truth' was the equivalent of majoritarian prejudice at any point in time. He defined it to Laski as 'the prevailing can't help of the majority,' and to Learned Hand as 'the majority vote of that nation that can lick all others.' The optimistic, democratic vision of Chafee and his progressive contemporaries had resonated with Holmes' skeptical resignation about the primacy of majoritarian sentiment. The 'search for truth' metaphor, embodying both of those perspectives, had arrived in American free speech jurisprudence."

(b) Contrast Holmes' statement of the "marketplace of ideas" argument with John Milton's statement in *Areopagitica:* "And though all the winds of doctrine were let loose to play upon the earth, so Truth be in the field, we do injuriously by licensing and prohibiting to misdoubt her strength. Let her and Falsehood grapple; who ever knew Truth put to the worse, in a free and open encounter?"[f] Holmes claims that the competition of the market is the best test of truth; Milton maintains that truth will emerge in a free and open encounter. How would one verify either hypothesis?

Is the "marketplace of ideas" a "free and open encounter"? Consider Lindblom, *Politics and Markets* 207 (1977): "Early, persuasive, unconscious conditioning—[to] believe in the fundamental politico-economic institutions of one's society is ubiquitous in every society. These institutions come to be taken for granted. Many people grow up to regard them not as institutions to be tested but as standards against which the correctness of new policies and institutions can be tested. When that happens, as is common, processes of critical judgment are short-circuited." Consider also Tribe, *American Constitutional Law* 786 (2d Ed. 1988): "Especially when the wealthy have more access to the most potent media of communication than the poor, how sure can we be that 'free trade in ideas' is likely to generate truth?"

For a specific example, see Shiffrin, *The First Amendment and Economic Regulation: Away From A General Theory of the First Amendment,* 78 Nw.U.L.Rev. 1212, 1281 (1983): "Living in a society in which children and adults are daily confronted with multiple communications that ask them to purchase products inevitably places emphasis on materialistic values. The authors of the individual messages may not intend that general emphasis, but the whole is greater than the sum of the parts. [Advertisers] spend some sixty billion dollars per year. [Those] who would oppose the materialist

f. For commentary explaining Milton's argument, suggesting that Milton's most important contributions to free speech lie elsewhere, see Blasi, *Milton's Areopagitica and the Modern First Amendment*, 13 Communications Lawyer 1 (1996).

message must combat forces that have a massive economic advantage. Any confidence that we will know what is truth by seeing what emerges from such combat is ill placed.''

Do the different market failure considerations offered by Lindblom, Tribe, and Shiffrin add up to a rebuttal of the marketplace argument? Consider *Nimmer on Freedom of Speech* 1–12 (1984): ''If acceptance of an idea in the competition of the market is not the 'best test' [what] is the alternative? It can only be acceptance of an idea by some individual or group narrower than that of the public at large. Thus, the alternative to competition in the market must be some form of elitism. It seems hardly necessary to enlarge on the dangers of that path.'' Is elitism the only alternative to the marketplace perspective? Is elitism always wrong?

(c) Evaluate the following hypothetical commentary: ''Liberals have favored government intervention in the economic marketplace but pressed for laissez-faire in the intellectual marketplace. Conservatives have done the reverse. Liberals and conservatives have one thing in common: inconsistent positions.''

(d) Does the marketplace argument overvalue truth? Consider Schauer, *Free Speech: A Philosophical Enquiry* 23 (1982). Government may seek to suppress opinions ''because their expression is thought to impair the authority of a lawful and effective government, interfere with the administration of justice (such as publication of a defendant's criminal record in advance of a jury trial), cause offence, invade someone's privacy, or cause a decrease in public order. When these are the motives for suppression, the possibility of losing some truth is relevant but hardly dispositive. [In such circumstances] the argument from truth [is] not wholly to the point.'' Is Holmes persuasive when he maintains that before we can suppress opinion we must wait until ''an immediate check is required to save the country''?

(e) Does the marketplace argument threaten first amendment values? Consider Ingber, *The Marketplace of Ideas: A Legitimizing Myth,* 1984 Duke L.J. 1, 4–5 ''[C]ourts that invoke the marketplace model of the first amendment justify free expression because of the aggregate benefits to society, and not because an individual speaker receives a particular benefit. Courts that focus their concern on the audience rather than the speaker relegate free expression to an instrumental value, a means toward some other goal, rather than a value unto itself. Once free expression is viewed solely as an instrumental value, however, it is easier to allow government regulation of speech if society as a whole 'benefits' from a regulated system of expression.''

(f) Does the marketplace argument slight other important free speech values? Consider Wolff, *The Poverty of Liberalism* 18 (1968) ''[I]t is not to assist the advance of knowledge that free debate is needed. Rather, it is in order to guarantee that every legitimate interest shall make itself known and felt in the political [process]. Justice, not truth, is the ideal served by liberty of speech.'' Compare Chevigny, *Philosophy of Language and Free Expression*, 55 N.Y.U.L.Rev. 157 (1980); Leitner, *Liberalism, Separation and*

Speech, 1985 Wis.L.Rev. 79, 89–90 & 103–04. The standard starting place for discussion of free speech values continues to be Emerson, *The System of Freedom of Expression* 6–9 (1970).

(g) Would an emphasis on dissent be preferable to an emphasis on the marketplace metaphor? Consider Shiffrin, *The First Amendment, Democracy, and Romance* (1990): "[A] commitment to sponsoring dissent does not require a belief that what emerges in the 'market' is usually right or that the 'market' is the best test of truth. Quite the contrary, the commitment to sponsor dissent assumes that societal pressures to conform are strong and that incentives to keep quiet are often great. If the marketplace metaphor encourages the view that an invisible hand or voluntaristic arrangements have guided us patiently, but slowly, to Burkean harmony, the commitment to sponsoring dissent encourages us to believe that the cozy arrangements of the status quo have settled on something less than the true or the just. If the marketplace metaphor encourages the view that conventions, habits, and traditions have emerged as our best sense of the truth from the rigorous testing ground of the marketplace of ideas, the commitment to sponsoring dissent encourages the view that conventions, habits, and traditions are compromises open to challenge. If the marketplace metaphor counsels us that the market's version of truth is more worthy of trust than any that the government might dictate, a commitment to sponsoring dissent counsels us to be suspicious of both. If the marketplace metaphor encourages a sloppy form of relativism (whatever has emerged in the marketplace is right for now), the commitment to sponsoring dissent emphasizes that truth is not decided in public opinion polls."[g]

2. *Pragmatism and scientific method.* Consider Blasi, *Reading Holmes through the Lens of Schauer: The Abrams Dissent*, 72 Notre Dame L. Rev. 1343, 1344–45 (1997): "Once the eloquence has been savored (and the false modesty noted), the reader wonders whether Holmes can possibly mean what he seems to be saying about 'the best test of truth.' Is he really so cynical, or fatalistic? Is he asserting a Chicago-school level of faith in markets combined with a willingness both to commodify truth and to ignore the various sources of market failure that operate in the flesh-and-blood society he is supposedly discussing? And even if Holmes wishes to embrace such a mundane conception of truth, how then does truth become 'the only ground' of social organization and aspiration? Furthermore, how does the author of the quip 'the Fourteenth Amendment does not enact Mr. Herbert Spencer's Social Statics' justify the position that the First Amendment

---

g. For a powerful critique of marketplace models, see Baker, *Human Liberty and Freedom of Speech* 6–24, 37–46 (1989). For qualified defenses, see Greenawalt, *Free Speech Justifications*, 89 Colum.L.Rev. 119, 130–41, 153–54 (1989); Schauer, *Language, Truth, and the First Amendment*, 64 Va. L.Rev. 263 (1978). For the proposition that free speech protects the pursuit of knowledge, an intrinsic good, see Garvey, *What are Freedoms For* ch. 4 (1996). For commentary on metaphors in general and the marketplace metaphor in particular, see Winter, *Transcendental Nonsense, Metaphoric Reasoning, and the Cognitive Stakes for Law*, 137 U.Pa.L.Rev. 1105 (1989).

enacts an extreme version of epistemological skepticism and/or moral relativism?

"One possible response is to read Homes as neither a borderline cynic nor a model-building neoclassical economist but rather a pragmatist impressed by how free speech can foster a culture of productive adaptation. In this view, the reference to 'the market'–observe that Holmes never employs the phrase 'marketplace of ideas'–is not meant to evoke anything so elegant and implausible as a fair procedure for determining society's finely calibrated, self-correcting cognitive equilibrium. Rather the claim is simply that the human understanding is eternally fluctuating and incomplete, and constantly in need of inquisitive energy much the way commercial prosperity depends on entrepreneurial energy. In addition, Holmes's allusion to Darwinian forces and his assertion that life is an experiment suggests his embrace of the scientific method, with the implication that the First Amendment represents a commitment by this society to test its truths continually and revise them regularly."[h]

B. STATE SEDITION LAWS

The second main group of cases in the initial development of first amendment doctrine involved state "sedition laws" of two basic types: criminal anarchy laws, typified by the New York statute in *Gitlow,* infra, and criminal syndicalism laws similar to the California statute in *Whitney,* infra. Most states enacted anarchy and syndicalism statutes between 1917 and 1921, in response to World War I and the fear of Bolshevism that developed in its wake, but the first modern sedition law was passed by New York in 1902, soon after the assassination of President McKinley. The law, which prohibited not only actual or attempted assassinations or conspiracies to assassinate, but advocacy of anarchy as well, lay idle for nearly twenty years, until the *Gitlow* prosecution.

GITLOW v. NEW YORK, 268 U.S. 652, 45 S.Ct. 625, 69 L.Ed. 1138 (1925): Defendant was a member of the Left Wing Section of the Socialist Party and a member of its National Council, which adopted a "Left Wing Manifesto," condemning the dominant "moderate Socialism" for its recognition of the necessity of the democratic parliamentary state; advocating the necessity of accomplishing the "Communist Revolution" by a militant and "revolutionary Socialism" based on "the class struggle"; and urging the development of mass political strikes for the destruction of the parliamentary state. Defendant arranged for printing

h. The literature on Holmes' first amendment views and their connection to his larger world view is substantial. See, e.g., White, *Justice Oliver Wendell Holmes* 412–54 (1993); Rogat & O'Fallon, *Mr. Justice Holmes: A Dissenting Opinion—The Speech Cases,* 36 Stan.L.Rev. 1349 (1984); Rabban, *The Emergence of Modern First Amendment Doctrine,* 50 U.Chi.L.Rev. 1205 (1983); Rabban, *Free Speech in Progressive Social Thought,* 74 Texas L.Rev. 951 (1996). For further analysis of the Holmes–Hand correspondence, see Gunther, *Learned Hand and the Origins of Modern First Amendment Doctrine: Some Fragments of History,* 27 Stan.L.Rev. 719 (1975). For illuminating discussion of *Abrams* and the period of which it is a part, see Polenberg, *Fighting Faiths* (1987).

and distributing, through the mails and otherwise, 16,000 copies of the Manifesto in the Left Wing's official organ, The Revolutionary Age. There was no evidence of any effect from the publication and circulation of the Manifesto.

In sustaining a conviction under the New York "criminal anarchy" statutes, prohibiting the "advocacy, advising or teaching the duty, necessity or propriety of overthrowing or overturning organized government by force or violence" and the publication or distribution of such matter, the majority, per SANFORD, J., stated that for present purposes we may and do assume[a] that first amendment freedoms of expression "are among the fundamental personal rights and 'liberties' protected by the due process clause of the Fourteenth Amendment from impairment by the States," but ruled:

"By enacting the present statute the State has determined, through its legislative body, that utterances advocating the overthrow of organized government by force, violence and unlawful means, are so inimical to the general welfare and involve such danger of substantive evil that they may be penalized in the exercise of its police power. That determination must be given great weight. Every presumption is to be indulged in favor of the validity of the statute. And the case is to be considered 'in the light of the principle that the State is primarily the judge of regulations required in the interest of public safety and welfare'; and that its police 'statutes may only be declared unconstitutional where they are arbitrary or unreasonable attempts to exercise authority vested in the State in the public interest.' That utterances inciting to the overthrow of organized government by unlawful means, present a sufficient danger of substantive evil to bring their punishment within the range of legislative discretion, is clear. Such utterances, by their very nature, involve danger to the public peace and to the security of the State. They threaten breaches of the peace and ultimate revolution. And the immediate danger is none the less real and substantial, because the effect of a given utterance cannot be accurately foreseen. The State cannot reasonably be required to measure the danger from every such utterance in the nice balance of a jeweler's scale. A single revolutionary spark may kindle a fire that, smoldering for a time, may burst into a sweeping and destructive conflagration. It cannot be said that the State is acting arbitrarily or unreasonably when in the exercise of its judgment as to the measures necessary to protect the public peace and safety, it seeks to extinguish the spark without waiting until it has enkindled the flame or blazed into the conflagration. It cannot reasonably be required to defer the adoption of measures for its own peace and safety until the revolutionary utterances lead to actual disturbances of the public peace or imminent and immediate danger of its own destruction; but it may, in the exercise of its judgment, suppress the threatened danger in its incipiency.[b]

a. Although *Gitlow* is often cited for the proposition that first amendment freedoms apply to restrict state conduct, its language is dictum. Some would say the first case so holding is *Fiske v. Kansas*, 274 U.S. 380, 47 S.Ct. 655, 71 L.Ed. 1108 (1927) (no evidence to support criminal syndicalism conviction) even though no reference to the first amendment appears in the opinion. See Chafee at 352. Perhaps the honor belongs to *Near v. Minnesota* (1931), Ch. 4, I, B infra.

"[It] is clear that the question in [this case] is entirely different from that involved in those cases where the statute merely prohibits certain acts involving the danger of substantive evil, without any reference to language itself, and it is sought to apply its provisions to language used by the defendant for the purpose of bringing about the prohibited results. There, if it be contended that the statute cannot be applied to the language used by the defendant because of its protection by the freedom of speech or press, it must necessarily be found, as an original question, without any previous determination by the legislative body, whether the specific language used involved such likelihood of bringing about the substantive evil as to deprive it of the constitutional protection. In such cases it has been held that the general provisions of the statute may be constitutionally applied to the specific utterance of the defendant if its natural tendency and probable effect was to bring about the substantive evil which the legislative body might prevent. *Schenck; Debs.* And the general statement in the *Schenck* case that the 'question in every case is whether the words are used in such circumstances and are of such a nature as to create a clear and present danger that they will bring about the substantive evils,' [was] manifestly intended, as shown by the context, to apply only in cases of this class, and has no application to those like the present, where the legislative body itself has previously determined the danger of substantive evil arising from utterances of a specified character."

HOLMES, J., joined by Brandeis, J., dissented: "The general principle of free speech, it seems to me, must be taken to be included in the Fourteenth Amendment, in view of the scope that has been given to the word 'liberty' as there used, although perhaps it may be accepted with a somewhat larger latitude of interpretation than is allowed to Congress by the sweeping language that governs or ought to govern the laws of the United States. If I am right then I think that the criterion sanctioned by the full Court in *Schenck* applies. [It] is true that in my opinion this criterion was departed from in *Abrams,* but the convictions that I expressed in that case are too deep for it to be possible for me as yet to believe that it [has] settled the law. If what I think the correct test is applied it is manifest that there was no

---

b. See also Bork, *Neutral Principles and Some First Amendment Problems,* 47 Ind. L.J. 1, 33 (1971): "To his point that proof of the effect of speech is inherently unavailable and yet its impact may be real and dangerous, Sanford might have added that the legislature is not confined to consideration of a single instance of speech or a single speaker. It fashions a rule to dampen thousands of instances of forcible overthrow advocacy. Cumulatively these may have enormous influence, and yet it may well be impossible to show any effect from any single example. The 'clear and present danger' requirement [is improper] because it erects a barrier to legislative rule where none should exist. The speech concerned has no political value within a republican system of government. Whether or not it is prudent to ban advocacy of forcible overthrow and law violation is a different [question]. Because the judgment is tactical, implicating the safety of the nation, it resembles very closely the judgment that Congress and the President must make about the expediency of waging war, an issue that the Court has wisely thought not fit for judicial determination."

present danger of an attempt to overthrow the government by force on the part of the admittedly small minority who shared the defendant's views. It is said that this manifesto was more than a theory, that it was an incitement. Every idea is an incitement. It offers itself for belief and if believed it is acted on unless some other belief outweighs it or some failure of energy stifles the movement at its birth. The only difference between the expression of an opinion and an incitement in the narrower sense is the speaker's enthusiasm for the result. Eloquence may set fire to reason. But whatever may be thought of the redundant discourse before us it had no chance of starting a present conflagration.[c] If in the long run the beliefs expressed in proletarian dictatorship are destined to be accepted by the dominant forces of the community, the only meaning of free speech is that they should be given their chance and have their way.[d]

"If the publication of this document had been laid as an attempt to induce an uprising against government at once and not at some indefinite time in the future it would have presented a different question. The object would have been one with which the law might deal, subject to the doubt whether there was any danger that the publication could produce any result, or in other words, whether it was not futile and too remote from possible consequences. But the indictment alleges the publication and nothing more."

Notes and Questions

1. The statute in *Schenck* was not aimed directly at expression, but at conduct, i.e., certain actual or attempted interferences with the war effort. Thus, an analysis in terms of proximity between the words and the conduct prohibited (by a concededly valid law) seemed useful. But in *Gitlow* (and in *Dennis,* Ch. 1, I, C infra) the statute was directed expressly against *advocacy* of a certain doctrine. Once the legislature *designates the point at which*

---

c. Consider Kalven, *A Worthy Tradition* 156 (1988): "This famous passage points up the ironies in tradition building. The basic problem of finding an accommodation between speech too close to action and censorship too close to criticism might, we have argued, have been tolerably solved by settling on 'incitement' as the key term. It is a term which came easily to the mind of Learned Hand. But for Holmes it does not resonate as it did for Hand. It strikes his ear as a loose, expansible term. At an inopportune moment in the history of free speech the great master of the common law turns poet: 'Every idea is an incitement.' There is of course a sense in which this is true and in which it is a 'scholastic subterfuge' to pretend that speech can be arrayed in firm categories. But the defendants' proposed instruction had offered a sense in which it was not true, in which incitement required advocacy of some definite and immediate acts of force. The weakness of the

prosecution's case was not that the defendants' radicalism was not dangerous; it was that their manifesto was not concrete enough to be an incitement.

"Justice Holmes's dissent in *Gitlow,* like his *Abrams* peroration, is extraordinary prose to find in a judicial opinion, and I suspect it has contributed beyond measure to the charisma of the First Amendment. But it also carries the disturbing suggestion that the defendants' speech is to be protected precisely because it is harmless and unimportant. It smacks, as will the later protections of Jehovah's Witnesses, of a luxury civil liberty."

d. But see Posner, *Free Speech in an Economic Perspective,* 20 Suff.L.Rev. 1, 7 (1986): "If those beliefs are destined to prevail, free speech is irrelevant. Holmes is not describing a competitive market in ideas but a natural monopoly."

words became unlawful, how helpful is the clear and present danger test? Is the question still how close words come to achieving certain consequences? In *Gitlow,* did Holmes "evade" the difficulty of applying an unmodified *Schenck* test to a different kind of problem? See Rogat, *Mr. Justice Holmes: Some Modern Views—The Judge as Spectator,* 31 U.Chi.L.Rev. 213, 217 (1964). See also Berns, *Freedom, Virtue and the First Amendment* 63 (Gateway ed. 1965); Linde, *"Clear and Present Danger" Reexamined,* 22 Stan.L.Rev. 1163, 1169–79 (1970).

2.   Evaluate the following hypothetical commentary: *"Gitlow's* abandonment of clear and present danger was insignificant because *Schenck's* reference to clear and present danger was toothless. *Schenck* made no effort to prove that the defendant's communication presented a genuine danger. Rather the assumption (followed in *Debs* and *Abrams*) was that any communication intended to encourage resistance to a war was unprotected speech. *Gitlow's* real significance was that it applied a war policy during a time of peace."

3.   Consider Linde, supra, at 1171: "Since New York's law itself defined the prohibited speech, the [*Gitlow*] Court could choose among three positions. It could (1) accept this legislative judgment of the harmful potential of the proscribed words, subject to conventional judicial review; (2) independently scrutinize the facts to see whether a 'danger,' as stated in *Schenck,* justified suppression of the particular expression; or (3) hold that by legislating directly against the words rather than the effects, the lawmaker had gone beyond the leeway left to trial and proof by the holding in *Schenck* and had made a law forbidden by the first amendment." Which course did the *Gitlow* majority choose? The dissenters? Which position should the Court have chosen?

———

Cases such as *Whitney,* infra, raise questions not only about freedom of speech, but also about the right of assembly. In turn, *Whitney* raises the issue of the existence and scope of a right not mentioned in the first amendment: freedom of association. Freedom of association, together with its connections to speech and assembly is explored in Ch. 9 infra. Several of the cases which follow are primarily characterized as speech cases because the assemblies or associations at issue were designed for the purpose of organizing future speech activity.

WHITNEY v. CALIFORNIA

274 U.S. 357, 47 S.Ct. 641, 71 L.Ed. 1095 (1927).

MR. JUSTICE SANFORD delivered the opinion of the Court.

[Charlotte Anita Whitney was convicted of violating the 1919 Criminal Syndicalism Act of California whose pertinent provisions were]:

"Section 1. The term 'criminal syndicalism' as used in this act is hereby defined as any doctrine or precept advocating, teaching or aiding and abetting the commission of crime, sabotage (which word is hereby defined as meaning willful and malicious physical damage or injury to physical property), or unlawful acts of force and violence or unlawful methods of terrorism as a means of accomplishing a change in industrial ownership or control, or effecting any political change.

"Sec. 2. Any person who: * * * 4. Organizes or assists in organizing, or is or knowingly becomes a member of, any organization, society, group or assemblage of persons organized or assembled to advocate, teach or aid and abet criminal syndicalism; * * *

"Is guilty of a felony and punishable by imprisonment."

The first count of the information, on which the conviction was had, charged that on or about November 28, 1919, in Alameda County, the defendant, in violation of the Criminal Syndicalism Act, "did then and there unlawfully, willfully, wrongfully, deliberately and feloniously organize and assist in organizing, and was, is, and knowingly became a member of [a group] organized and assembled to advocate, teach, aid and abet criminal syndicalism." * * *

1. While it is not denied that the evidence warranted the jury in finding that the defendant became a member of and assisted in organizing the Communist Labor Party of California, and that this was organized to advocate, teach, aid or abet criminal syndicalism as defined by the Act, it is urged that the Act, as here construed and applied, deprived the defendant of her liberty without due process of law. [Defendant's] argument is, in effect, that the character of the state organization could not be forecast when she attended the convention; that she had no purpose of helping to create an instrument of terrorism and violence; that she "took part in formulating and presenting to the convention a resolution which, if adopted, would have committed the new organization to a legitimate policy of political reform by the use of the ballot"; that it was not until after the majority of the convention turned out to be "contrary minded, and other less temperate policies prevailed" that the convention could have taken on the character of criminal syndicalism; and that as this was done over her protest, her mere presence in the convention, however violent the opinions expressed therein, could not thereby become a crime. This contention [is in effect] an effort to review the weight of the evidence for the purpose of showing that the defendant did not join and assist in organizing the Communist Labor Party of California with a knowledge of its unlawful character and purpose. This question, which is foreclosed by the verdict of the jury, [is] one of fact merely which is not open to review in this Court, involving as it does no constitutional question whatever. * * *

The essence of the offense denounced by the Act is the combining with others in an association for the accomplishment of the desired ends through the advocacy and use of criminal and unlawful methods. It partakes of the nature of a criminal conspiracy. That such united and joint action involves even greater danger to the public peace and security than the isolated utterances and acts of individuals is clear. We cannot hold that, as here applied, the Act is an unreasonable or arbitrary exercise of the police power of the State, unwarrantably infringing any right of free speech, assembly or association, or that those persons are protected from punishment by the due process clause who abuse such rights by joining and furthering an organization thus menacing the peace and welfare of the State. * * *

Affirmed.

Mr. Justice Brandeis (concurring.) * * *

The felony which the statute created is a crime very unlike the old felony of conspiracy or the old misdemeanor of unlawful assembly. The mere act of assisting in forming a society for teaching syndicalism, of becoming a member of it, or assembling with others for that purpose is given the dynamic quality of crime. There is guilt although the society may not contemplate immediate promulgation of the doctrine. Thus the accused is to be punished, not for attempt, incitement or conspiracy, but for a step in preparation, which, if it threatens the public order at all, does so only remotely. The novelty in the prohibition introduced is that the statute aims, not at the practice of criminal syndicalism, nor even directly at the preaching of it, but at association with those who propose to preach it.

Despite arguments to the contrary which had seemed to me persuasive, it is settled that the due process clause of the Fourteenth Amendment applies to matters of substantive law as well as to matters of procedure. Thus all fundamental rights comprised within the term liberty are protected by the federal Constitution from invasion by the states. The right of free speech, the right to teach and the right of assembly are, of course, fundamental rights. These may not be denied or abridged. But, although the rights of free speech and assembly are fundamental, they are not in their nature absolute. Their exercise is subject to restriction, if the particular restriction proposed is required in order to protect the state from destruction or from serious injury, political, economic or moral. That the necessity which is essential to a valid restriction does not exist unless speech would produce, or is intended to produce,[a] a clear and imminent danger of some substantive evil which the state constitutionally may seek to prevent has been settled. See *Schenck.*

[The] Legislature must obviously decide, in the first instance, whether a danger exists which calls for a particular protective measure. But where a statute is valid only in case certain conditions exist, the enactment of the statute cannot alone establish the facts which are essential to its validity. Prohibitory legislation has repeatedly been held invalid, because unneces-

---

a. Unless speech would produce, *or* is intended to produce? Unless speech *would produce* a clear and imminent danger, although the harm produced was neither advocated nor intended by the speaker? Unless the speaker *intended* to produce a clear and imminent danger, even under extrinsic conditions of actual harmlessness? Compare *Brandenburg v. Ohio,* p. 53 infra. See generally Linde, supra, at 1168–69, 1181, 1185.

sary, where the denial of liberty involved was that of engaging in a particular business. The powers of the courts to strike down an offending law are no less when the interests involved are not property rights, but the fundamental personal rights of free speech and assembly.

This Court has not yet fixed the standard by which to determine when a danger shall be deemed clear; how remote the danger may be and yet be deemed present; and what degree of evil shall be deemed sufficiently substantial to justify resort to abridgment of free speech and assembly as the means of protection. To reach sound conclusions on these matters, we must bear in mind why a state is, ordinarily, denied the power to prohibit dissemination of social, economic and political doctrine which a vast majority of its citizens believes to be false and fraught with evil consequence.

Those who won our independence believed that the final end of the state was to make men free to develop their faculties, and that in its government the deliberative forces should prevail over the arbitrary.[b] They valued liberty both as an end and as a means. They believed liberty to be the secret of happiness and courage to be the secret of liberty. They believed that freedom to think as you will and to speak as you think are means indispensable to the discovery and spread of political truth;[c] that without free speech and assembly discussion would be futile; that with them, discussion affords ordinarily adequate protection against the dissemination of noxious doctrine;[d] that the greatest menace to freedom is an inert people; that public discussion is a political duty; and that this should be a fundamental principle of the American government. They recognized the risks to which all human institutions are subject. But they knew that order cannot be secured merely through fear of punishment for its infraction; that it is hazardous to discourage thought, hope and imagination; that fear breeds repression; that repression breeds hate; that hate menaces stable government; that the path of safety lies in the opportunity to discuss freely supposed grievances and proposed remedies; and that the fitting remedy for evil counsels is good ones.

---

b. For commentary on Brandeis, J.'s use of history, see Bobertz, *The Brandeis Gambit: The Making of America's "First Freedom," 1909–1931,* 40 Wm. & Mary L.Rev. 557 (1999).

c. Consider Blasi, *The First Amendment and the Ideal of Civic Courage,* 29 Wm. & Mary L.Rev. 653, 673–74 (1988): "This is as close as Brandeis gets to the claim that unregulated discussion yields truth. Notice that, in contrast to Holmes, Brandeis never tells us what is 'the best test of truth.' He never employs the metaphor of the marketplace. He speaks only of 'political truth,' and he uses the phrase 'means indispensable' to link activities described in highly personal terms—'think as you will,' 'speak as you think'—with the collective social goal of 'political truth.' I think his emphasis in this passage is on the attitudes and at-

mosphere that must prevail if the ideals of self-government and happiness through courage are to be realized. Brandeis is sketching a good society here, but not, I think, an all-conquering dialectic.'"

d. Consider *Blasi,* supra fn. c, at 674–75: "It is noteworthy that Brandeis never speaks of noxious doctrine being refuted or eliminated or defeated. He talks of societal self-protection and the fitting remedy. He warns us not to underestimate the value of discussion, education, good counsels. To me, his point is that noxious doctrine is most likely to flourish when its opponents lack the personal qualities of wisdom, creativity, and confidence. And those qualities, he suggests, are best developed by discussion and education, not by lazy and impatient reliance on the coercive authority of the state."

Believing in the power of reason as applied through public discussion, they eschewed silence coerced by law—the argument of force in its worst form. Recognizing the occasional tyrannies of governing majorities, they amended the Constitution so that free speech and assembly should be guaranteed.

Fear of serious injury cannot alone justify suppression of free speech and assembly. Men feared witches and burnt women. It is the function of speech to free men from the bondage of irrational fears. To justify suppression of free speech there must be reasonable ground to fear that serious evil will result if free speech is practiced. There must be reasonable ground to believe that the danger apprehended is imminent. There must be reasonable ground to believe that the evil to be prevented is a serious one.[e] Every denunciation of existing law tends in some measure to increase the probability that there will be violation of it. Condonation of a breach enhances the probability. Expressions of approval add to the probability. Propagation of the criminal state of mind by teaching syndicalism increases it. Advocacy of lawbreaking heightens it still further. But even advocacy of violation, however reprehensible morally, is not a justification for denying free speech where the advocacy falls short of incitement and there is nothing to indicate that the advocacy would be immediately acted on. The wide difference between advocacy and incitement, between preparation and attempt, between assembling and conspiracy, must be borne in mind. In order to support a finding of clear and present danger it must be shown either that immediate serious violence was to be expected or was advocated,[f] or that the past conduct furnished reason to believe that such advocacy was then contemplated.

Those who won our independence by revolution were not cowards. They did not fear political change. They did not exalt order at the cost of liberty. To courageous, self-reliant men, with confidence in the power of free and fearless reasoning applied through the processes of popular government, no danger flowing from speech can be deemed clear and present, unless the incidence of the evil apprehended is so imminent that it may befall before there is opportunity for full discussion. If there be time to expose through discussion the falsehood and fallacies, to avert the evil by the processes of education, the remedy to be applied is more speech, not enforced silence.[g] Only an emergency can justify repression. Such must be the rule if authority is to be reconciled with freedom. Such, in my opinion, is the command of the Constitution. It is therefore always open to Americans to challenge a law

e. Does this suffice, regardless of the intent of the speaker? Regardless of the nature of the words he uses?

f. What if violence is advocated, but the advocacy is utterly ineffectual? What if the speaker neither desires nor advocates violence, but, under the circumstances the speech nevertheless is "expected" to produce violence?

g. But see Delgado & Stefanic, *Images of the Outsider in American Law and Culture: Can Free Expression Remedy Systematic Social Ills?*, 77 Corn.L.Rev. 1258 (1992); Lessig, *The Regulation of Social Meaning*, 62 U.Chi.L.Rev. 943, 1036–39 (1995).

abridging free speech and assembly by showing that there was no emergency justifying it.

Moreover, even imminent danger cannot justify resort to prohibition of these functions essential to effective democracy, unless the evil apprehended is relatively serious. Prohibition of free speech and assembly is a measure so stringent that it would be inappropriate as the means for averting a relatively trivial harm to society. A police measure may be unconstitutional merely because the remedy, although effective as means of protection, is unduly harsh or oppressive. Thus, a state might, in the exercise of its police power, make any trespass upon the land of another a crime, regardless of the results or of the intent or purpose of the trespasser. It might, also, punish an attempt, a conspiracy, or an incitement to commit the trespass. But it is hardly conceivable that this court would hold constitutional a statute which punished as a felony the mere voluntary assembly with a society formed to teach that pedestrians had the moral right to cross uninclosed, unposted, waste lands and to advocate their doing so, even if there was imminent danger that advocacy would lead to a trespass. The fact that speech is likely to result in some violence or in destruction of property is not enough to justify its suppression. There must be the probability of serious injury to the State.[h] Among free men, the deterrents ordinarily to be applied to prevent crime are education and punishment for violations of the law, not abridgement of the rights of free speech and assembly.

* * * Whenever the fundamental rights of free speech and assembly are alleged to have been invaded, it must remain open to a defendant to present the issue whether there actually did exist at the time a clear danger, whether the danger, if any, was imminent, and whether the evil apprehended was one so substantial as to justify the stringent restriction interposed by the Legislature. The legislative declaration, like the fact that the statute was passed and was sustained by the highest court of the State, creates merely a rebuttable presumption that these conditions have been satisfied.

Whether in 1919, when Miss Whitney did the things complained of, there was in California such clear and present danger of serious evil, might have been made the important issue in the case. She might have required that the issue be determined either by the court or the jury. She claimed below that the statute as applied to her violated the federal Constitution; but she did not claim that it was void because there was no clear and present danger of serious evil, nor did she request that the existence of these conditions of a valid measure thus restricting the rights of free speech and assembly be passed upon by the court or a jury. On the other hand, there was evidence on which the court or jury might have found that such danger existed. I am unable to assent to the suggestion in the opinion of the court

h. But see Bork, *Neutral Principles and Some First Amendment Problems*, 47 Ind. L.J. 1, 34 (1971): "It is difficult to see how a constitutional court could properly draw the distinction proposed. Brandeis offered no analysis to show that advocacy of law violation merited protection by the Court. Worse, the criterion he advanced is the importance, in the judge's eye, of the law whose violation is urged."

that assembling with a political party, formed to advocate the desirability of a proletarian revolution by mass action at some date necessarily far in the future, is not a right within the protection of the Fourteenth Amendment. In the present case, however, there was other testimony which tended to establish the existence of a conspiracy, on the part of members of the International Workers of the World, to commit present serious crimes, and likewise to show that such a conspiracy would be furthered by the activity of the society of which Miss Whitney was a member. Under these circumstances the judgment of the State court cannot be disturbed. * * *

MR. JUSTICE HOLMES joins in this opinion.

Notes and Questions

1. *"They valued liberty both as an end and as a means."* Should recognition of the value of liberty[i] as an end augment the marketplace perspective or replace it?[j]

i. For literature contending that the related value of autonomy should play a central role in most (or all) aspects of first amendment law, see Baker, *Human Liberty and Freedom of Speech* 47–51 (1989); Richards, *Toleration and the Constitution* 165–77 (1986); Post, *Constitutional Domains* 268–331 (1995); Fried, *The New First Amendment Jurisprudence: A Threat to Liberty,* 59 U.Chi.L.Rev. 225, 233–37 (1992); Post, *Managing Deliberation: The Quandary of Democratic Dialogue,* 103 Ethics 654, 664–66 (1993); Post, *Racist Speech, Democracy, and the First Amendment,* 32 Wm. & Mary L.Rev. 267, 279–85 (1991); Scanlon, *A Theory of Freedom of Expression.* 1 Phil. & Pub.Aff. 204, 215–22 (1972); Strauss, *Persuasion, Autonomy, and Freedom of Expression,* 91 Colum.L.Rev. 334, 353–71 (1991). Wells, *Reinvigorating Autonomy,* 32 Harv. C.R.-C.L. L. Rev. 159 (1997). Cf. Tucker, *Law, Liberalism, and Free Speech* (1985)(qualified endorsement of autonomy from a Rawlsian perspective).

For discussion of the value of autonomy and its connection to the problem of advocacy of illegal action, compare Scanlon, supra, with Scanlon, *Freedom of Expression and Categories of Expression,* 40 U.Pitt. L.Rev. 519 (1979). For commentary on the differences between speaker and listener autonomy, see Sunstein, *Democracy and the Problem of Free Speech* 139–44 (1993); Baker, *Turner Broadcasting: Content–Based Regulation of Persons and Presses,* 1994 Sup.Ct.Rev. 57, 72–80. For the contention that the literature confuses philosophical assumptions of autonomy and empirical claims of autonomy and for doubts about the resolving power of either conception,

see Fallon, *Two Senses of Autonomy,* 46 Stan.L.Rev. 875 (1994). For the suggestion that the value of autonomy depends upon open and rich public discussion, see Sunstein, supra. For the contention that the value of autonomy should be subservient to open and rich discussion, see Fiss, *State Activism and State Censorship,* 100 Yale L.J. 2087 (1991). Fiss, *Why the State,* 100 Harv.L.Rev. 781 (1987); Fiss, *Free Speech and Social Structure,* 71 Iowa L.Rev. 1405 (1986); but see Post, *Equality and Autonomy in First Amendment Discourse,* 95 Mich. L.Rev. 1517 (1997).

j. Compare Baker, *Human Liberty and Freedom of Speech* (1989) (liberty theory should replace marketplace theory); Baker, *Scope of the First Amendment Freedom of Speech,* 25 U.C.L.A.L.Rev. 964 (1978)(accord); Baker, *Harm, Liberty, and Free Speech,* 70 So.Cal.L.Rev. 979 (1997)(harm does not justify invasion of liberty); Heyman, *Righting the Balance: An Inquiry into the Foundations and Limits of Freedom of Expression,* 78 B.U.L.Rev. 1275 (1998)(endorsing natural rights theory of liberty as basis for free speech); and Redish, *The Value of Free Speech,* 130 U.Pa.L.Rev. 591 (1982) (self-realization should be regarded as the first amendment's exclusive value) with Smolla, *Free Speech in an Open Society* 5 (1992) ("There is no logical reason, however, why the preferred position of freedom of speech might not be buttressed by multiple rationales. Acceptance of one rationale need not bump another from the list, as if this were First Amendment musical chairs"); Shiffrin, *The First Amendment and Economic Regulation: Away From a General Theory of the First Amendment,* 78

2. *Brandeis and Republicanism.* Consider Lahav, *Holmes and Brandeis: Libertarian and Republican Justifications for Free Speech,* 4 J.L. & Pol. 451, 460–461 (1987): "[I]n his *Whitney* concurrence, Brandeis tells us, that in the American polity, 'the deliberative forces should prevail over the arbitrary,' that 'public discussion is a political duty,' and that 'the occasional tyranny of governing majorities' should be thwarted. This is radically different from the notion that individuals are free to remain aloof from politics if they so choose (a notion espoused by Holmes), and from the principle of the separation of the state from society. Implied here is the notion of civic virtue—the duty to participate in politics, the importance of deliberation, and the notion that the end of the state is not neutrality but active assistance in providing conditions of freedom which in turn are the 'secret of happiness.' One may even speculate that Brandeis, the progressive leader, believed that the final end of the state was the happiness of mankind.

"These ingredients of the Brandeis position in *Whitney* resonate with republican theory. The theory rests on two central themes: the idea of civic virtue and the idea that the end of politics (or the state) is the common good, which in turn is more than the sum of individual wills. Thus, the state is not separated from society, but rather is committed to the public good, and to a substantive notion of public morality. The members of society are not individuals encased in their autonomous zones, but rather social beings who recognize that they are an integral part of the society. This organic sense of belonging implicitly rejects the notion of combat zones. The republic and its citizens care for the welfare of all. Correctly understood, Brandeis' concurrence in *Whitney* is more than a justification from self-fulfillment or from self-rule. It is a justification from civic virtue."[k]

3. In keeping with the positions of Holmes and Brandeis, is the first amendment best defended as proceeding from a "special kind of argument from character that builds from the claim that a culture that prizes and protects expressive liberty nurtures in its members certain character traits such as inquisitiveness, independence of judgment, distrust of authority, willingness to take initiative, perseverance, and the courage to confront evil"? Vincent Blasi, *Free Speech and Good Character,* 46 UCLA L.Rev. 1567 (1999).

4. Consider Volokh, *Freedom of Speech, Permissible Tailoring, and Transcending Strict Scrutiny,* 144 U.Pa.L.Rev. 2417, 2446 (1996): "Holmes and Brandeis were not condemning the restrictions simply because the

Nw.U.L.Rev. 1212 (1983) (many values including liberty and self-realization underpin the first amendment; single valued orientations are reductionist); Murchison, *Speech and the Self-Realization Value,* 33 Harv. C.R.-C.L. L.Rev. 443 (1998)(emphasizing and illuminating the self-realization value while recognizing other values); But see Schauer, *Must Speech Be Special,* 78 Nw. U.L.Rev. 1284 (1983) (neither liberty nor self-realization should play *any* role in first

amendment theory). See also Cohen, *Freedom of Expression,* 21 Phil. & Pub.Aff. 207 (1993); Raz, *Free Expression and Personal Identification,* 11 Oxford J.Legal St. 311 (1991).

k. For further background comparing the views of Brandeis and Holmes, JJ., see Blasi, fn. c supra; Cover, *The Left, The Right and the First Amendment: 1919–28,* 40 Md.L.Rev. 349 (1981).

government's goals were not important enough, or arguing that the speech-restrictive means were unnecessary. Rather, they were arguing that the means were impermissible (except where a clear and present danger was present). Even if the speech was likely, through its persuasive powers, to undermine the most compelling of interests, the 'meaning of free speech,' 'the theory of our Constitution,' the judgment of '[t]hose who won our independence' about the 'fundamental principle[s] of the American government,' required that the nation run the risk of the compelling interest being undermined."

5. Ten years after *Whitney, De Jonge v. Oregon,* 299 U.S. 353, 57 S.Ct. 255, 81 L.Ed. 278 (1937) held that mere participation in a meeting called by the Communist party could not be made a crime. The right of peaceable assembly was declared to be "cognate to those of free speech and free press and is equally fundamental."

C.   COMMUNISM AND ILLEGAL ADVOCACY

Kent Greenawalt has well described the pattern of decisions for much of the period between *Whitney* and *Dennis* infra: "[T]he clear and present danger formula emerged as the applicable standard not only for the kinds of issues with respect to which it originated but also for a wide variety of other First Amendment problems. If the Court was not always very clear about the relevance of that formula to those different problems, its use of the test, and its employment of ancillary doctrines, did evince a growing disposition to protect expression." *Speech and Crime,* 1980 Am.B.Found.Res.J. 645, 706. By 1951, however, anti-communist sentiment was a powerful theme in American politics. The Soviet Union had detonated a nuclear weapon; communists had firm control of the Chinese mainland; the Korean War had reached a stalemate; Alger Hiss had been convicted of perjury in congressional testimony concerning alleged spying activities for the Soviet Union while he was a State Department official; and Senator Joseph McCarthy of Wisconsin had created a national sensation by accusations that many "card carrying Communists" held important State Department jobs. In this context, the top leaders of the American Communist Party asked the Court to reverse their criminal conspiracy convictions.

DENNIS v. UNITED STATES

341 U.S. 494, 71 S.Ct. 857, 95 L.Ed. 1137 (1951).

Mr. Chief Justice Vinson announced the judgment of the Court and an opinion in which Mr. Justice Reed, Mr. Justice Burton and Mr. Justice Minton join.

Petitioners were indicted in July, 1948, for violation of the conspiracy provisions of the Smith Act during the period of April, 1945, to July, 1948. * * * A verdict of guilty as to all the petitioners was [affirmed by the Second Circuit]. We granted certiorari, limited to the following two questions: (1) Whether either § 2 or § 3 of the Smith Act, inherently or as construed and applied in the instant case, violates the First Amendment and other provisions of the Bill of Rights; (2) whether either § 2 or § 3 of the Act, inherently or as construed and applied in the instant case, violates the First and Fifth Amendments, because of indefiniteness.

Sections 2 and 3 of the Smith Act provide as follows:

"Sec. 2.

"(a) It shall be unlawful for any person—

"(1) to knowingly or willfully advocate, abet, advise, or teach the duty, necessity, desirability, or propriety of overthrowing or destroying any government in the United States by force or violence, or by the assassination of any officer of any such government; * * *

"Sec. 3. It shall be unlawful for any person to attempt to commit, or to conspire to commit, any of the acts prohibited by the provisions [of] this title."

The indictment charged the petitioners with wilfully and knowingly conspiring (1) to organize as the Communist Party of the United States of America a society, group and assembly of persons who teach and advocate the overthrow and destruction of the Government of the United States by force and violence, and (2) knowingly and wilfully to advocate and teach the duty and necessity of overthrowing and destroying the Government of the United States by force and violence. The indictment further alleged that § 2 of the Smith Act proscribes these acts and that any conspiracy to take such action is a violation of § 3 of the Act.

The trial of the case extended over nine months, six of which were devoted to the taking of evidence, resulting in a record of 16,000 pages. Our limited grant of the writ of certiorari has removed from our consideration any question as to the sufficiency of the evidence to support the jury's determination that petitioners are guilty of the offense charged. Whether on this record petitioners did in fact advocate the overthrow of the Government by force and violence is not before us, and we must base any discussion of this point upon the conclusions stated in the opinion of the Court of Appeals, which treated the issue in great detail [and] held that the record supports the following broad conclusions: [that] the Communist Party is a highly disciplined organization, adept at infiltration into strategic positions, use of aliases, and double-meaning language; that the Party is rigidly controlled; that Communists, unlike other political parties, tolerate no dissension from the policy laid down by the guiding [forces]; that the literature of the Party and the statements and activities of its leaders, petitioners here, advocate, and the general goal of the Party was, during the period in question, to achieve a successful overthrow of the existing order by force and violence. * * *

The obvious purpose of the statute is to protect existing Government, not from change by peaceable, lawful and constitutional means, but from change by violence, revolution and terrorism. That it is within the *power* of the Congress to protect the Government of the United States from armed rebellion is a proposition which requires little discussion. Whatever theoretical merit there may be to the argument that there is a "right" to rebellion against dictatorial governments is without force where the existing structure of the government provides for peaceful and orderly change. We reject any principle of governmental helplessness in the face of preparation for revolution, which principle, carried to its logical conclusion, must lead to anarchy. No one could conceive that it is not within the power of Congress to prohibit acts intended to overthrow the Government by force and violence. The question with which we are concerned here is not whether Congress has such *power*, but whether the *means* which it has employed conflict with the First and Fifth Amendments to the Constitution.

One of the bases for the contention that the means which Congress has employed are invalid takes the form of an attack on the face of the statute on the grounds that by its terms it prohibits academic discussion of the merits of Marxism–Leninism, that it stifles ideas and is contrary to all concepts of a free speech and a free press. [This] is a federal statute which we must interpret as well as judge. Herein lies the fallacy of reliance upon the manner in which this Court has treated judgments of state courts. Where the statute as construed by the state court transgressed the First Amendment, we could not but invalidate the judgments of conviction.

The very language of the Smith Act negates the interpretation which petitioners would have us impose on that Act. It is directed at advocacy, not discussion. Thus, the trial judge properly charged the jury that they could not convict if they found that petitioners did "no more than pursue peaceful studies and discussions or teaching and advocacy in the realm of ideas." * * * Congress did not intend to eradicate the free discussion of political theories, to destroy the traditional rights of Americans to discuss and evaluate ideas without fear of governmental sanction. * * *

But although the statute is not directed at the hypothetical cases which petitioners have conjured, its application in this case has resulted in convictions for the teaching and advocacy of the overthrow of the Government by force and violence, which, even though coupled with the intent to accomplish that overthrow, contains an element of speech. For this reason, we must pay special heed to the demands of the First Amendment marking out the boundaries of speech.

[T]he basis of the First Amendment is the hypothesis that speech can rebut speech, propaganda will answer propaganda, free debate of ideas will result in the wisest governmental policies. [An] analysis of the leading cases in this Court which have involved direct limitations on speech, however, will demonstrate that both the majority of the Court and the dissenters in particular cases have recognized that this is not an unlimited, unqualified right, but that the societal value of speech must, on occasion, be subordinated to other values and considerations. * * *

Although no case subsequent to *Whitney* and *Gitlow* has expressly overruled the majority opinions in those cases, there is little doubt that subsequent opinions have inclined toward the Holmes–Brandeis rationale. * * *

In this case we are squarely presented with the application of the "clear and present danger" test, and must decide what that phrase imports.[a] We first note that many of the cases in which this Court has reversed convictions by use of this or similar tests have been based on the fact that the interest which the State was attempting to protect was itself too insubstantial to warrant restriction of speech. * * * Overthrow of the Government by force and violence is certainly a substantial enough interest for the Government to limit speech. Indeed, this is the ultimate value of any society, for if a society cannot protect its very structure from armed internal attack, it must follow that no subordinate value can be protected. If, then, this interest may be protected, the literal problem which is presented is what has been meant by the use of the phrase "clear and present danger" of the utterances bringing about the evil within the power of Congress to punish.

Obviously, the words cannot mean that before the Government may act, it must wait until the putsch is about to be executed, the plans have been laid and the signal is awaited. If Government is aware that a group aiming at its overthrow is attempting to indoctrinate its members and to commit them to a course whereby they will strike when the leaders feel the circumstances permit, action by the Government is required. The argument that there is no need for Government to concern itself, for Government is strong, it possesses ample powers to put down a rebellion, it may defeat the revolution with ease needs no answer. For that is not the question. Certainly an attempt to overthrow the Government by force, even though doomed from the outset because of inadequate numbers or power of the revolutionists, is a sufficient evil for Congress to prevent. The damage which such attempts create both physically and politically to a nation makes it impossible to measure the validity in terms of the probability of success, or the immediacy of a successful attempt. In the instant case the trial judge charged the jury that they could not convict unless they found that petitioners intended to overthrow the Government "as speedily as circumstances would permit." This does not mean, and could not properly mean, that they would not strike until there was certainty of success. What was meant was that the revolutionists would strike when they thought the time was ripe. We must therefore reject the contention that success or probability of success is the criterion.

The situation with which Justices Holmes and Brandeis were concerned in *Gitlow* was a comparatively isolated event, bearing little relation in their minds to any substantial threat to the safety of the community. [They] were

a. Consider Kalven, *A Worthy Tradition* 190–91 (1988): "The [Vinson opinion] acknowledges clear and present danger as the constitutional measure of free speech, but in the process, to meet the political exigencies of the case, it officially adjusts the test, giving it the kiss of death."

not confronted with any situation comparable to the instant one—the development of an apparatus designed and dedicated to the overthrow of the Government, in the context of world crisis after crisis.

Chief Judge Learned Hand, writing for the majority below, interpreted the phrase as follows: "In each case [courts] must ask whether the gravity of the 'evil,' discounted by its improbability, justifies such invasion of free speech as is necessary to avoid the danger." We adopt this statement of the rule. As articulated by Chief Judge Hand, it is as succinct and inclusive as any other we might devise at this time. * * *

Likewise, we are in accord with the court below, which affirmed the trial court's finding that the requisite danger existed. The mere fact that from the period 1945 to 1948 petitioners' activities did not result in an attempt to overthrow the Government by force and violence is of course no answer to the fact that there was a group that was ready to make the attempt. The formation by petitioners of such a highly organized conspiracy, with rigidly disciplined members subject to call when the leaders, these petitioners, felt that the time had come for action, coupled with the inflammable nature of world conditions, similar uprisings in other countries, and the touch-and-go nature of our relations with countries with whom petitioners were in the very least ideologically attuned, convince us that their convictions were justified on this score. And this analysis disposes of the contention that a conspiracy to advocate, as distinguished from the advocacy itself, cannot be constitutionally restrained, because it comprises only the preparation. It is the existence of the conspiracy which creates the danger. * * *

Although we have concluded that the finding that there was a sufficient danger to warrant the application of the statute was justified on the merits, there remains the problem of whether the trial judge's treatment of the issue was correct. He charged the jury, in relevant part, as follows:

"In further construction and interpretation of the statute I charge you that it is not the abstract doctrine of overthrowing or destroying organized government by unlawful means which is denounced by this law, but the teaching and advocacy of action for the accomplishment of that purpose, by language reasonably and ordinarily calculated to incite persons to such action. Accordingly, you cannot find the defendants or any of them guilty of the crime charged unless you are satisfied beyond a reasonable doubt that they conspired to organize a society, group and assembly of persons who teach and advocate the overthrow or destruction of the Government of the United States by force and violence and to advocate and teach the duty and necessity of overthrowing or destroying the Government of the United States by force and violence, with the intent that such teaching and advocacy be of a rule or principle of action and by language reasonably and ordinarily calculated to incite persons to such action, all with the intent to cause the overthrow or destruction of the Government of the United States by force and violence as speedily as circumstances would permit. * * *

"If you are satisfied that the evidence establishes beyond a reasonable doubt that the defendants, or any of them, are guilty of a violation of the statute, as I have interpreted it to you, I find as matter of law that there is sufficient danger of a substantive evil that the Congress has a right to prevent to justify the application of the statute under the First Amendment of the Constitution. This is matter of law about which you have no concern. * * *"

It is thus clear that he reserved the question of the existence of the danger for his own determination, and the question becomes whether the issue is of such a nature that it should have been submitted to the jury.

[When] facts are found that establish the violation of a statute, the protection against conviction afforded by the First Amendment is a matter of law. The doctrine that there must be a clear and present danger of a substantive evil that Congress has a right to prevent is a judicial rule to be applied as a matter of law by the courts. The guilt is established by proof of facts. Whether the First Amendment protects the activity which constitutes the violation of the statute must depend upon a judicial determination of the scope of the First Amendment applied to the circumstances of the case.

[In] *Schenck* this Court itself examined the record to find whether the requisite danger appeared, and the issue was not submitted to a jury. And in every later case in which the Court has measured the validity of a statute by the "clear and present danger" test, that determination has been by the court, the question of the danger not being submitted to the jury. * * * Petitioners intended to overthrow the Government of the United States as speedily as the circumstances would permit. Their conspiracy to organize the Communist Party and to teach and advocate the overthrow of the Government of the United States by force and violence created a "clear and present danger" of an attempt to overthrow the Government by force and violence. They were properly and constitutionally convicted * * *.

Affirmed.

MR. JUSTICE CLARK took no part in the consideration or decision of this case.

MR. JUSTICE FRANKFURTER, concurring in affirmance of the judgment.

[The] demands of free speech in a democratic society as well as the interest in national security are better served by candid and informed weighing of the competing interests, within the confines of the judicial process, than by announcing dogmas too inflexible for the non-Euclidian problems to be solved.

But how are competing interests to be assessed? Since they are not subject to quantitative ascertainment, the issue necessarily resolves itself into asking, who is to make the adjustment?—who is to balance the relevant factors and ascertain which interest is in the circumstances to prevail? Full responsibility for the choice cannot be given to the courts. Courts are not representative bodies. They are not designed to be a good reflex of a democratic society. Their judgment is best informed, and therefore most dependable, within narrow limits. Their essential quality is detachment, founded on independence. History teaches that the independence of the judiciary is jeopardized when courts become embroiled in the passions of the day and assume primary responsibility in choosing between competing political, economic and social pressures.

Primary responsibility for adjusting the interests which compete in the situation before us of necessity belongs to the Congress. [We] are to set aside the judgment of those whose duty it is to legislate only if there is no reasonable basis for [it]. Free-speech cases are not an exception to the principle that we are not legislators, that direct policy-making is not our province. How best to reconcile competing interests is the business of legislatures, and the balance they strike is a judgment not to be displaced by ours, but to be respected unless outside the pale of fair judgment. [A] survey of the relevant decisions indicates that the results which we have reached are on the whole those that would ensue from careful weighing of conflicting interests. The complex issues presented by regulation of speech in public places by picketing, and by legislation prohibiting advocacy of crime have been resolved by scrutiny of many factors besides the imminence and gravity of the evil threatened. The matter has been well summarized by a reflective student of the Court's work. "The truth is that the clear-and-present-danger test is an oversimplified judgment unless it takes account also of a number of other factors: the relative seriousness of the danger in comparison with the value of the occasion for speech or political activity; the availability of more moderate controls than those which the state has imposed; and perhaps the specific intent with which the speech or activity is launched. No matter how rapidly we utter the phrase 'clear and present danger,' or how closely we hyphenate the words, they are not a substitute for the weighing of values. They tend to convey a delusion of certitude when what is most certain is the complexity of the strands in the web of freedoms which the judge must disentangle." Freund, *On Understanding the Supreme Court* 27–28 [1949]. * * *

To make validity of legislation depend on judicial reading of events still in the womb of time—a forecast, that is, of the outcome of forces at best appreciated only with knowledge of the topmost secrets of nations—is to charge the judiciary with duties beyond its equipment. * * *

Even when moving strictly within the limits of constitutional adjudication, judges are concerned with issues that may be said to involve vital finalities. The too easy transition from disapproval of what is undesirable to condemnation as unconstitutional, has led some of the wisest judges to question the wisdom of our scheme in lodging such authority in courts. But it is relevant to remind that in sustaining the power of Congress in a case like this nothing irrevocable is done. The democratic process at all events is not impaired or restricted. Power and responsibility remain with the people and immediately with their representation. All the Court says is that Congress was not forbidden by the Constitution to pass this enactment and that a prosecution under it may be brought against a conspiracy such as the one before us. * * *

Mr. Justice Jackson, concurring.

[E]ither by accident or design, the Communist stratagem outwits the antianarchist pattern of statute aimed against "overthrow by force and violence" if qualified by the doctrine that only "clear and present danger" of accomplishing that result will sustain the prosecution.

The "clear and present danger" test was an innovation by Mr. Justice Holmes in the *Schenck* case, reiterated and refined by him and Mr. Justice Brandeis in later cases, all arising before the era of World War II revealed the subtlety and efficacy of modernized revolutionary techniques used by totalitarian parties. In those cases, they were faced with convictions under so-called criminal syndicalism statutes aimed at anarchists but which, loosely construed, had been applied to punish socialism, pacifism, and left-wing ideologies, the charges often resting on farfetched inferences which, if true, would establish only technical or trivial violations. They proposed "clear and present danger" as a test for the sufficiency of evidence in particular cases.

I would save it, unmodified, for application as a "rule of reason" in the kind of case for which it was devised. When the issue is criminality of a hotheaded speech on a street corner, or circulation of a few incendiary pamphlets, or parading by some zealots behind a red flag, or refusal of a handful of school children to salute our flag, it is not beyond the capacity of the judicial process to gather, comprehend, and weigh the necessary materials for decision whether it is a clear and present danger of substantive evil or a harmless letting off of steam. It is not a prophecy, for the danger in such cases has matured by the time of trial or it was never present. The test applies and has meaning where a conviction is sought to be based on a speech or writing which does not directly or explicitly advocate a crime but to which such tendency is sought to be attributed by construction or by implication from external circumstances. The formula in such cases favors freedoms that are vital to our society, and, even if sometimes applied too generously, the consequences cannot be grave. But its recent expansion has extended, in particular to Communists, unprecedented immunities. Unless we are to hold our Government captive in a judge-made verbal trap, we must approach the problem of a well-organized, nation-wide conspiracy, such as I have described, as realistically as our predecessors faced the trivialities that were being prosecuted until they were checked with a rule of reason.

I think reason is lacking for applying that test to this case.

If we must decide that this Act and its application are constitutional only if we are convinced that petitioner's conduct creates a "clear and present danger" of violent overthrow, we must appraise imponderables, including international and national phenomena which baffle the best informed foreign offices and our most experienced politicians. We would have to foresee and predict the effectiveness of Communist propaganda, opportunities for infiltration, whether, and when, a time will come that they consider propitious for action, and whether and how fast our existing government will deteriorate. And we would have to speculate as to whether an approaching Communist coup would not be anticipated by a nationalistic fascist movement. No doctrine can be sound whose application requires us to make a prophecy of that sort in the guise of a legal decision. The judicial process simply is not adequate to a trial of such far-flung issues. The answers given would reflect our own political predilections and nothing more.

The authors of the clear and present danger test never applied it to a case like this, nor would I. If applied as it is proposed here, it means that the Communist plotting is protected during its period of incubation; its preliminary stages of organization and preparation are immune from the law; the Government can move only after imminent action is manifest, when it would, of course, be too late.

The highest degree of constitutional protection is due to the individual acting without conspiracy. But even an individual cannot claim that the Constitution protects him in advocating or teaching overthrow of government by force or violence. I should suppose no one would doubt that Congress has power to make such attempted overthrow a crime. But the contention is that one has the constitutional right to work up a public desire and will to do what it is a crime to attempt. I think direct incitement by speech or writing can be made a crime, and I think there can be a conviction without also proving that the odds favored its success by 99 to 1, or some other extremely high ratio. * * *

What really is under review here is a conviction of conspiracy, after a trial for conspiracy, on an indictment charging conspiracy, brought under a statute outlawing conspiracy. With due respect to my colleagues, they seem to me to discuss anything under the sun except the law of conspiracy. * * *

The Constitution does not make conspiracy a civil right. [Although] I consider criminal conspiracy a dragnet device capable of perversion into an instrument of injustice in the hands of a partisan or complacent judiciary, it has an established place in our system of law, and no reason appears for applying it only to concerted action claimed to disturb interstate commerce and withholding it from those claimed to undermine our whole Government. * * *

I do not suggest that Congress could punish conspiracy to advocate something, the doing of which it may not punish. Advocacy or exposition of the doctrine of communal property ownership, or any political philosophy unassociated with advocacy of its imposition by force or seizure of government by unlawful means could not be reached through conspiracy prosecution. But it is not forbidden to put down force or violence, it is not forbidden to punish its teaching or advocacy, and the end being punishable, there is no doubt of the power to punish conspiracy for the purpose. * * *

MR. JUSTICE BLACK, dissenting. * * *

So long as this Court exercises the power of judicial review of legislation, I cannot agree that the First Amendment permits us to sustain laws suppressing freedom of speech and press on the basis of Congress' or our own notions of mere "reasonableness." Such a doctrine waters down the First Amendment so that it amounts to little more than an admonition to Congress. The Amendment as so construed is not likely to protect any but those "safe" or orthodox views which rarely need its protection. I must also express my objection to the holding because, as Mr. Justice Douglas' dissent shows, it sanctions the determination of a crucial issue of fact by the judge rather than by the jury. * * *

Public opinion being what it now is, few will protest the conviction of these Communist petitioners. There is hope, however, that in calmer times, when present pressures, passions and fears subside, this or some later Court will restore the First Amendment liberties to the high preferred place where they belong in a free society.

MR. JUSTICE DOUGLAS, dissenting.

If this were a case where those who claimed protection under the First Amendment were teaching the techniques of sabotage, the assassination of the President, the filching of documents from public files, the planting of bombs, the art of street warfare, and the like, I would have no doubts. The freedom to speak is not absolute; the teaching of methods of terror and other seditious conduct should be beyond the pale along with obscenity and immorality. This case was argued as if those were the facts. The argument imported much seditious conduct into the record. That is easy and it has popular appeal, for the activities of Communists in plotting and scheming against the free world are common knowledge. But the fact is that no such evidence was introduced at the trial. There is a statute which makes a seditious conspiracy unlawful. Petitioners, however, were not charged with a "conspiracy to overthrow" the Government. They were charged with a conspiracy to form a party and groups and assemblies of people who teach and advocate the overthrow of our Government by force or violence and with a conspiracy to advocate and teach its overthrow by force and violence. It may well be that indoctrination in the techniques of terror to destroy the Government would be indictable under either statute. But the teaching which is condemned here is of a different character.

So far as the present record is concerned, what petitioners did was to organize people to teach and themselves teach the Marxist–Leninist doctrine contained chiefly in four books: *Foundations of Leninism* by Stalin (1924); *The Communist Manifesto* by Marx and Engels (1848); *State and Revolution* by Lenin (1917); *History of the Communist Party of the Soviet Union* (B.) (1939).

Those books are to Soviet Communism what *Mein Kampf* was to Nazism. If they are understood, the ugliness of Communism is revealed, its deceit and cunning are exposed, the nature of its activities becomes apparent, and the chances of its success less likely. That is not, of course, the reason why petitioners chose these books for their classrooms. They are fervent Communists to whom these volumes are gospel. They preached the creed with the hope that some day it would be acted upon.

The opinion of the Court does not outlaw these texts nor condemn them to the fire, as the Communists do literature offensive to their creed. But if the books themselves are not outlawed, if they can lawfully remain on library shelves, by what reasoning does their use in a classroom become a crime? It would not be a crime under the Act to introduce these books to a class, though that would be teaching what the creed of violent overthrow of the Government is. The Act, as construed, requires the element of intent— that those who teach the creed believe in it. The crime then depends not on what is taught but on who the teacher is. That is to make freedom of speech turn not on *what is said,* but on the *intent* with which it is said. Once we start down that road we enter territory dangerous to the liberties of every citizen. * * *

The vice of treating speech as the equivalent of overt acts of a treasonable or seditious character is emphasized by a concurring opinion, which by invoking the law of conspiracy makes speech do service for deeds which are dangerous to society. [N]ever until today has anyone seriously thought that the ancient law of conspiracy could constitutionally be used to turn speech into seditious conduct. Yet that is precisely what is suggested. I repeat that we deal here with speech alone, not with speech *plus* acts of sabotage or unlawful conduct. Not a single seditious act is charged in the indictment. To make a lawful speech unlawful because two men conceive it is to raise the law of conspiracy to appalling proportions. * * *

There comes a time when even speech loses its constitutional immunity. Speech innocuous one year may at another time fan such destructive flames that it must be halted in the interests of the safety of the Republic. That is the meaning of the clear and present danger test. When conditions are so critical that there will be no time to avoid the evil that the speech threatens, it is time to call a halt. Otherwise, free speech which is the strength of the Nation will be the cause of its destruction.

Yet free speech is the rule, not the exception. The restraint to be constitutional must be based on more than fear, on more than passionate opposition against the speech, on more than a revolted dislike for its contents. There must be some immediate injury to society that is likely if speech is allowed. * * *

I had assumed that the question of the clear and present danger, being so critical an issue in the case, would be a matter for submission to the jury. [The] Court, I think, errs when it treats the question as one of law.

Yet, whether the question is one for the Court or the jury, there should be evidence of record on the issue. This record, however, contains no evidence whatsoever showing that the acts charged viz., the teaching of the Soviet theory of revolution with the hope that it will be realized, have created any clear and present danger to the Nation. The Court, however, rules to the contrary. [The majority] might as well say that the speech of petitioners is outlawed because Soviet Russia and her Red Army are a threat to world peace.

The nature of Communism as a force on the world scene would, of course, be relevant to the issue of clear and present danger of petitioners' advocacy within the United States. But the primary consideration is the strength and tactical position of petitioners and their converts in this country. On that there is no evidence in the record. If we are to take judicial notice of the threat of Communists within the nation, it should not be difficult to conclude that *as a political party* they are of little consequence. Communists in this country have never made a respectable or serious showing in any election. I would doubt that there is a village, let alone a city or county or state, which the Communists could carry. Communism in the world scene is no bogeyman; but Communism as a political faction or party in this country plainly is. Communism has been so thoroughly exposed in this country that it has been crippled as a political force. Free speech has destroyed it as an effective political party. It is inconceivable that those who went up and down this country preaching the doctrine of revolution which petitioners espouse would have any success. In days of trouble and confusion, when bread lines were long, when the unemployed walked the streets, when people were starving, the advocates of a short-cut by revolution might have a chance to gain adherents. But today there are no such conditions. The country is not in despair; the people know Soviet Communism; the doctrine of Soviet revolution is exposed in all of its ugliness and the American people want none of it.

[Unless] and until extreme and necessitous circumstances are shown our aim should be to keep speech unfettered and to allow the processes of law to be invoked only when the provocateurs among us move from speech to action. * * *b

Notes and Questions

1. What was the "substantive evil" in the *Dennis* case, the danger of which was sufficiently "clear and present" to warrant the application of the rule as originally formulated by Holmes and Brandeis? A *successful* revolution? An *attempted* revolution, however futile such an attempt might be? A *conspiracy* to plan the overthrow of the government by force and violence? A "conspiracy *to advocate*" such overthrow? See Gorfinkel & Mack, *Dennis v.*

b. Eighteen years later, concurring in *Brandenburg,* Ch. 1, I, D infra, Douglas, J., declared: "I see no place in the regime of the First Amendment for any 'clear and present danger' test whether strict and tight as some would make it or free-wheeling as the Court in *Dennis* rephrased it. When one reads the opinions closely and sees when and how the 'clear and present danger' test has been applied, great misgivings are aroused. First, the threats were often loud but always puny and made serious only by judges so wedded to the status quo that critical analysis made them nervous. Second, the test was so twisted and perverted in *Dennis* as to make the trial of those teachers of Marxism an all-out political trial which was part and parcel of the cold war that has eroded substantial parts of the First Amendment."

United States and the Clear and Present Danger Rule, 39 Calif.L.Rev. 475, 496–501 (1951); Nathanson, *The Communist Trial and the Clear-and-Present-Danger Test,* 63 Harv.L.Rev. 1167, 1168, 1173–75 (1950). Suppose it were established in *Dennis* that the odds were 99–1 against the Communists attempting an overthrow of the Government until 1961? 1971? Same result?

2. *Suppression of "totalitarian movements".* Consider Auerbach, *The Communist Control Act of 1954,* 23 U.Chi.L.Rev. 173, 188–89 (1956): "[I]n suppressing totalitarian movements a democratic society is not acting to protect the status quo, but the very same interests which freedom of speech itself seeks to secure—the possibility of peaceful progress under freedom. That suppression may sometimes have to be the means of securing and enlarging freedom is a paradox which is not unknown in other areas of the law of modern democratic states. The basic 'postulate,' therefore, which should 'limit and control' the First Amendment is that it is part of the framework for a constitutional democracy and should, therefore, not be used to curb the power of Congress to exclude from the political struggle those groups which, if victorious, would crush democracy and impose totalitarianism."[c]

3. Does the second amendment guarantee individuals (or groups) the right to bear arms for protection including protection against government tyranny?[d] If the second amendment is so construed, does the second amendment shed light on the first?

4. *Dennis distinguished.* In 1954, Senator McCarthy was censured by the United States Senate for acting contrary to its ethics and impairing its dignity. In 1957, when the convictions of 14 "second string" communist leaders reached the Supreme Court in YATES v. UNITED STATES, 354 U.S. 298, 77 S.Ct. 1064, 1 L.Ed.2d 1356 (1957), McCarthy had died, and so had McCarthyism. Although strong anti-communist sentiment persisted, the political atmosphere in *Yates'* 1957 was profoundly different from that of *Dennis'* 1951. Harlan, J., distinguishing *Dennis,* construed the Smith Act narrowly: "[The] essence of the *Dennis* holding was that indoctrination of a group in preparation for future violent action, as well as exhortation to

c. For discussion of the issue, see Rawls, *A Theory of Justice,* 216–21 (1971); Shiffrin, *Racist Speech Outsider Jurisprudence, and the Meaning of America,* 80 Cornell L.Rev. 43, 88 n. 220, 90 n. 232 (1994); Smith, *Radically Subversive Speech and the Authority of Law,* 94 Mich.L.Rev. 348 (1995).

d. Is the second amendment an embarrassment to liberals? See Levinson, *The Embarrassing Second Amendment,* 99 Yale L.J. 637 (1989). For a variety of perspectives on the second amendment, see Symposium, *A Second Amendment Symposium Issue,* 62 Tenn.L.Rev. 443 (1995); Cress, *An Armed Community,* 71 J.Am.Hist. 22 (1984); Cottrol & Diamond, *The Second Amendment: Toward an Afro–Americanist Reconsideration,* 90 Geo.L.Rev. 309 (1991); Hertz, *Gun Crazy,* 75 B.U.L.Rev. 57 (1995);

Kates, *Handgun Prohibition and the Original Meaning of the Second Amendment,* 82 Mich.L.Rev. 204 (1983); Kopel, *The Second Amendment in the Nineteenth Century, I 1998 B.Y.U.L. Rev.* 1359 (1998); Alstyne, *The Second Amendment and the Personal Right to Bear Arms,* 43 Duke L.J. 1236 (1994); Volokh, Cottrol, Levinson, Powe, Jr. & Reynolds, *The Second Amendment as A Teaching Tool in Constitutional Law Classes,* 48 J.Legal Ed. 591 (1998); Williams, *The Constitutional Right to "Conservative" Revolution,* 32 Harv. C.R.-C.L.L.Rev. 413 (1997); Williams, *The Militia Movement and the Second Amendment Revolution,* 81 Cornell L.Rev. 879 (1996); Williams, *Civic Republicanism and the Citizen Militia,* 101 Yale L.J. 551 (1991).

immediate action, by advocacy found to be directed to 'action for the accomplishment' of forcible overthrow, to violence as 'a rule or principle of action,' and employing 'language of incitement,' is not constitutionally protected when the group is of sufficient size and cohesiveness, is sufficiently oriented towards action, and other circumstances are such as reasonably to justify apprehension that action will occur. This is quite a different thing from the view of the District Court here that mere doctrinal justification of forcible overthrow, if engaged in with the intent to accomplish overthrow, is punishable per se under the Smith Act. [T]he trial court's statement that the proscribed advocacy must include the 'urging,' 'necessity,' and 'duty' of forcible overthrow, and not merely its 'desirability' and 'propriety,' may not be regarded as a sufficient substitute for charging that the Smith Act reaches only advocacy of action for the overthrow of government by force and violence. The essential distinction is that those to whom the advocacy is addressed must be urged to *do* something, now or in the future, rather than merely to *believe* in something." Applying this standard, Harlan J., acquitted five defendants and remanded to the lower court for proceedings against the remaining defendants.[e]

5. *The membership clause of the Smith Act.* After *Yates*, the government sought to prosecute communists for being members of an organization advocating the overthrow of the government by force and violence. The Court in *Scales v. United States,* 367 U.S. 203, 81 S.Ct. 1469, 6 L.Ed.2d 782 (1961) and *Noto v. United States,* 367 U.S. 290, 81 S.Ct. 1517, 6 L.Ed.2d 836 (1961) interpreted the membership clause to require that the organization engage in advocacy of the sort described in *Yates* and that the members be active with knowledge of the organization's advocacy and the specific intent to bring about violent overthrow as speedily as circumstances permit.

6. *Spock*. Dr. Spock, Rev. Coffin and others were convicted of conspiring to counsel and abet Selective Service registrants to refuse to have their draft cards in their possession and to disobey other duties imposed by the Selective Service Act of 1967. Spock signed a document entitled "A Call to Resist Illegitimate Authority," which "had 'a double aspect: in part it was a denunciation of governmental policy [in Vietnam] and, in part, it involved a public call to resist the duties imposed by the [Selective Service] Act.' "Several weeks later, Spock attended a demonstration in Washington, D.C., where an unsuccessful attempt was made to present collected draft cards to the Attorney General. *United States v. Spock,* 416 F.2d 165 (1st Cir.1969),

e. Burton, J., concurred. Black, joined by Douglas, dissenting, would have acquitted all defendants. Clark, J., dissenting, would have affirmed the convictions of all defendants. Brennan and Whittaker, JJ., took no part. On remand, the government requested dismissal of the indictments, explaining that it could not meet *Yates'* evidentiary requirements. For commentary, see Gunther, *Learned Hand* 603 (1994); Wells, *Of Communists and Anti–Abortion Protestors: The Consequences of Falling into the Theoretical Abyss,* 33 Ga. L. Rev. 1 (1998); Greenawalt, Speech and Crime, 1980 Am.B.Foun.Res.J. 645, 720 n. 279; Mollan, *Smith Act Prosecutions,* 26 U.Pitt.L. 705 (1965).

per Aldrich, J., ruled that Spock should have been acquitted: "[Spock] was one of the drafters of the Call, but this does not evidence the necessary intent to adhere to its illegal aspects. [H]is speech was limited to condemnation of the war and the draft, and lacked any words or content of counselling. The jury could not find proscribed advocacy from the mere fact [that] he hoped the frequent stating of his views might give young men 'courage to take active steps in draft resistance.' This is a natural consequence of vigorous speech. Similarly, Spock's actions lacked the clear character necessary to imply specific intent under the First Amendment standard. [H]e was at the Washington demonstration, [but took] no part in its planning. [His statements at this demonstration did not extend] beyond the general anti-war, anti-draft remarks he had made before. His attendance is as consistent with a desire to repeat this speech as it is to aid a violation of the law. The dissent would fault us for drawing such distinctions, but it forgets the teaching of [*Bond v. Floyd*]ᶠ that expressing one's views in broad areas is not foreclosed by knowledge of the consequences, and the important lesson of *Noto, Scales* and *Yates* that one may belong to a group, knowing of its illegal aspects, and still not be found to adhere thereto."

D.   A MODERN "RESTATEMENT"

BRANDENBURG v. OHIO

395 U.S. 444, 89 S.Ct. 1827, 23 L.Ed.2d 430 (1969).

PER CURIAM.ᵃ

The appellant, a leader of a Ku Klux Klan group, was convicted under [a 1919] Ohio Criminal Syndicalism statute of "advocat[ing] the duty, necessity, or propriety of crime, sabotage, violence, or unlawful methods of terrorism as a means of accomplishing industrial or political reform" and of "voluntarily assembl[ing] with any society, group or assemblage of persons formed to teach or advocate the doctrines of criminal syndicalism." He was fined $1,000 and sentenced to one to 10 years' imprisonment. * * *

---

f. *Bond v. Floyd*, 385 U.S. 116, 87 S.Ct. 339, 17 L.Ed.2d 235 (1966) found ambiguity in expressions of support for those unwilling to respond to the draft that earlier opinions would have characterized as clear advocacy of illegal action. As Thomas Emerson puts it "the distance traversed [from *Schenck* and *Debs* to *Bond*] is quite apparent." *Freedom of Expression in Wartime*, 116 U.Pa.L.Rev. 975, 988 (1968).

a. See Schwartz, *Holmes Versus Hand: Clear and Present Danger or Advocacy of Unlawful Action?* 1995 S.Ct.Rev. 237: "*Brandenburg* was assigned to Justice Fortas. The draft opinion that he circulated stated a modified version of the Clear and Present Danger test. * * * As it turned out,

Brandenburg did not come down as a Fortas opinion. Though the Justice had circulated his draft opinion in April 1969 and quickly secured the necessary votes, he followed Justice Harlan's suggestion to delay its announcement. Before then, the events occurred that led to Justice Fortas's forced resignation from the Court. The *Brandenburg* opinion was then redrafted by Justice Brennan, who eliminated all references to the Clear and Present Danger test and substituted the present *Brandenburg* language: 'where such advocacy is directed to inciting or producing imminent lawless action and is likely to incite or produce such action.' The Brennan redraft was issued as a per curiam opinion.''

The record shows that a man, identified at trial as the appellant, telephoned an announcer-reporter on the staff of a Cincinnati television station and invited him to come to a Ku Klux Klan "rally" to be held at a farm in Hamilton County. With the cooperation of the organizers, the reporter and a cameraman attended the meeting and filmed the events. Portions of the films were later broadcast on the local station and on a national network.

The prosecution's case rested on the films and on testimony identifying the appellant as the person who communicated with the reporter and who spoke at the rally. The State also introduced into evidence several articles appearing in the film, including a pistol, a rifle, a shotgun, ammunition, a Bible, and a red hood worn by the speaker in the films.

One film showed 12 hooded figures, some of whom carried firearms. They were gathered around a large wooden cross, which they burned. No one was present other than the participants and the newsmen who made the film. Most of the words uttered during the scene were incomprehensible when the film was projected, but scattered phrases could be understood that were derogatory of Negroes and, in one instance, of Jews. Another scene on the same film showed the appellant, in Klan regalia, making a speech. The speech, in full, was as follows:

"This is an organizers' meeting. We have had quite a few members here today which are—we have hundreds, hundreds of members throughout the State of Ohio. I can quote from a newspaper clipping from the Columbus Ohio Dispatch, five weeks ago Sunday morning. The Klan has more members in the State of Ohio than does any other organization. We're not a revengent organization, but if our President, our Congress, our Supreme Court, continues to suppress the white, Caucasian race, it's possible that there might have to be some revengence taken.

"We are marching on Congress July the Fourth, four hundred thousand strong. From there we are dividing into two groups, one group to march on St. Augustine, Florida, the other group to march into Mississippi. Thank you."

The second film showed six hooded figures one of whom, later identified as the appellant, repeated a speech very similar to that recorded on the first film. The reference to the possibility of "revengence" was omitted, and one sentence was added: "Personally, I believe the nigger should be returned to Africa, the Jew returned to Israel." Though some of the figures in the films carried weapons, the speaker did not.

[*Whitney*] sustained the constitutionality of California's Criminal Syndicalism Act, the text of which is quite similar to that of the laws of Ohio. The Court upheld the statute on the ground that, without more, "advocating" violent means to effect political and economic change involves such danger to the security of the State that the State may outlaw it. But *Whitney* has been thoroughly discredited by later decisions [such as *Dennis* which]

Precedent established in Whitney ←

have fashioned the principle that the constitutional guarantees of free speech and free press do not permit a State to forbid or proscribe advocacy of the use of force or of law violation except where such advocacy is directed to inciting or producing imminent lawless action[b] and is likely to incite or produce such action.[2] As we said in *Noto*, "the mere abstract teaching [of] the moral propriety or even moral necessity for a resort to force and violence, is not the same as preparing a group for violent action and steeling it to such action." See also *Bond v. Floyd*. A statute which fails to draw this distinction impermissibly intrudes upon the freedoms guaranteed by the First and Fourteenth Amendments. It sweeps within its condemnation speech which our Constitution has immunized from governmental control. Cf. *Yates* * * *.

Measured by this test, Ohio's Criminal Syndicalism Act cannot be sustained. The Act punishes persons who "advocate or teach the duty, necessity, or propriety" of violence "as a means of accomplishing industrial or political reform"; or who publish or circulate or display any book or paper containing such advocacy; or who "justify" the commission of violent acts "with intent to exemplify, spread or advocate the propriety of the doctrines of criminal syndicalism"; or [who] "voluntarily assemble" with a group formed "to teach or advocate the doctrines of criminal syndicalism." Neither the indictment nor the trial judge's instructions to the jury in any way refined the statute's bald definition of the crime in terms of mere advocacy not distinguished from incitement to imminent lawless action.[3]

Accordingly, we are here confronted with a statute which, by its own words and as applied, purports to punish mere advocacy and to forbid, on pain of criminal punishment, assembly with others merely to advocate the described type of action.[4] Such a statute falls within the condemnation of the

---

b. Consider Wells, *Reinvigorating Autonomy,* 32 Harv. C.R.-C.L. L. Rev. 159, 179 (1997), "The Court's requirement of imminent lawless action is easily justified as based upon concern for autonomy. Speech designed to incite immediate violence or lawless action does not appeal to our thought processes. Rather, it disrespects our rationality and is designed to elicit an unthinking, animalistic response. * * * Speech designed to persuade people to violate the law is not coercive in the same sense as speech designed to incite imminent lawlessness; the former contributes to rather than detracts from our deliberative processes." Compare Dow & Shieldes, *Rethinking the Clear and Present Danger Test,* 73 Indiana L.J. 1217 (1998); Dow, 6 Wm. & Mary Bill of Rts. J. 733 (1998)(clear and present danger test inconsistent with appropriate notions of moral responsibility).

2. It was on the theory that the Smith Act embodied such a principle and that it had been applied only in conformity with it that this Court sustained the Act's constitu-

tionality. That this was the basis for *Dennis* was emphasized in *Yates,* in which the Court overturned convictions for advocacy of the forcible overthrow of the Government under the Smith Act, because the trial judge's instructions had allowed conviction for mere advocacy, unrelated to its tendency to produce forcible action.

3. The first count of the indictment charged that appellant "did unlawfully by word of mouth advocate the necessity, or propriety of crime, violence, or unlawful methods of terrorism as a means of accomplishing political reform * * *." The second count charged that appellant "did unlawfully voluntarily assemble with a group or assemblage of persons formed to advocate the doctrines of criminal syndicalism * * *." The trial judge's charge merely followed the language of the indictment. * * *

4. Statutes affecting the right of assembly, like those touching on freedom of speech, must observe the established dis-

First and Fourteenth Amendments. The contrary teaching of *Whitney* cannot be supported, and that decision is therefore overruled.

Reversed.

MR. JUSTICE BLACK, concurring.

I agree with the views expressed by Mr. Justice Douglas in his concurring opinion in this case that the "clear and present danger" doctrine should have no place in the interpretation of the First Amendment. I join the Court's opinion, which, as I understand it, simply cites *Dennis*, but does not indicate any agreement on the Court's part with the "clear and present danger" doctrine on which *Dennis* purported to rely.

MR. JUSTICE DOUGLAS, concurring.

While I join the opinion of the Court, I desire to enter a caveat.

[Whether] the war power—the greatest leveler of them all—is adequate to sustain [the "clear and present danger"] doctrine is debatable. The dissents in *Abrams* [and other cases] show how easily "clear and present danger" is manipulated to crush what Brandeis called "the fundamental right of free men to strive for better conditions through new legislation and new institutions" by argument and discourse even in time of war. Though I doubt if the "clear and present danger" test is congenial to the First Amendment in time of a declared war, I am certain it is not reconcilable with the First Amendment in days of peace. * * *

Mr. Justice Holmes, though never formally abandoning the "clear and present danger" test, moved closer to the First Amendment ideal when he said in dissent in *Gitlow* [quoting the passage beginning, "Every idea is an incitement."] We have never been faithful to the philosophy of that dissent.

"[In *Dennis,* we distorted] the "clear and present danger" test beyond recognition. [I] see no place in the regime of the First Amendment for any "clear and present danger" test whether strict and tight as some would make it or free-wheeling as the Court in *Dennis* rephrased it.

Notes and Questions

1. What pre-*Brandenburg* decisions, if any, "have fashioned the principle" that advocacy may not be prohibited "except [where] directed to inciting or producing *imminent* lawless action *and * * * likely* to incite or produce such action"? (Emphasis added.) Did *Dennis, Yates* and *Scales* take pains to *deny* that the unlawful action advocated need be "imminent" or that the advocacy must be "likely" to produce the forbidden action? See Linde, *"Clear and Present Danger" Reexamined,* 22 Stan.L.Rev. 1163, 1166–67, 1183–86 (1970).

tinctions between mere advocacy and incitement to lawless action * * * .

2.   Is "the *Brandenburg* version of the clear and present danger test"—as Professor Emerson calls it (is this a misnomer?)—subject to criticism on the ground that "it permits government interference with expression at too early a stage, allowing officials to cut speech off as soon as it shows signs of being effective"? That it is "an ad hoc test" that does not enable the speaker to "know in advance what the limits will be found to be"? That the test is "excessively vague"? See Emerson, *First Amendment Doctrine and the Burger Court*, 68 Calif.L.Rev. 422, 437–38 (1980).

3.   Does *Brandenburg* adopt the *Masses* incitement test as a major part of the required showing? Consider Gunther, *Learned Hand and the Origins of Modern First Amendment Doctrine: Some Fragments of History*, 27 Stan.L.Rev. 719, 754–55 (1975): "An incitement-nonincitement distinction had only fragmentary and ambiguous antecedents in the pre-*Brandenburg* era; it was *Brandenburg* that really 'established' it; and, it was essentially an establishment of the legacy of Learned Hand. [Under] *Brandenburg*, probability of harm is no longer the central criterion for speech limitations. The inciting language of the speaker—the Hand focus on 'objective' words—is the major consideration. And punishment of the harmless inciter is prevented by the *Schenck*–derived requirement of a likelihood of dangerous consequences." (citing *Brandenburg*'s note 4.) But see Shiffrin, *Defamatory Non–Media Speech and First Amendment Methodology*, 25 U.C.L.A.L.Rev. 915, 947 n. 206 (1978): "Several leading commentators assume that *Brandenburg* adopts an incitement requirement. [The] conclusion is apparently based on this line from *Brandenburg*: 'Neither the indictment nor the trial judge's instructions to the jury in any way refined the statute's bald definition of the crime in terms of mere advocacy, not distinguished from incitement to imminent lawless action' [also citing note 4]. The difficulty with attaching significance to this ambiguous statement is that the term 'incitement' is used in the alternative in the Court's statement of its test. Thus, advocacy of imminent lawless action is protected unless it is directed to inciting *or* producing imminent lawless action and is likely to incite *or* produce imminent lawless action. Thus, even assuming that the use of the word incitement refers to express use of language, as opposed to the nature of results (an interpretation which is strained in light of the Court's wording of the test), incitement is not necessary to divorce the speech from first amendment protection. It is enough that the speech is directed to producing imminent lawless action and is likely to produce such action."

If one wants to argue that *Brandenburg* adopted *Masses*, is there anything to be made of the phrase "directed to" in the *Brandenburg* test? Alternatively, did *Yates* adopt the *Masses* test? If so, does its favorable citation in *Brandenburg* constitute an adoption of the *Masses* test?

4.   The *Brandenburg* "inciting or producing imminent lawless action" standard was the basis for reversal of a disorderly conduct conviction in HESS v. INDIANA, 414 U.S. 105, 94 S.Ct. 326, 38 L.Ed.2d 303 (1973) (per

curiam). After antiwar demonstrators on the Indiana University campus had blocked a public street, police moved them to the curbs on either side. As an officer passed him, appellant stated loudly, "We'll take the fucking street later [or again]," which led to his disorderly conduct conviction. His statement, observed the Court, "was not addressed to any person or group in particular" and "his tone, although loud, was no louder than that of the other people in the area. [At] best, [the] statement could be taken as counsel for present moderation; at worst, it amounted to nothing more than advocacy of illegal action at some indefinite future time." This was insufficient, under *Brandenburg,* to punish appellant's words, as the State had, on the ground that they had a "tendency to produce violence." It could not be said that appellant "was advocating, in the normal sense, any action" and there was "no evidence" that "his words were intended to produce, and likely to produce, *imminent* disorder."

REHNQUIST, J., joined by Burger, C.J., and Blackmun, J., dissented: "The simple explanation for the result in this case is that the majority has interpreted the evidence differently from the courts below." The dissenters quarreled with the Court's conclusion that appellant's advocacy "was not directed towards inciting imminent action. [T]here are surely possible constructions of the statement which would encompass more or less immediate and continuing action against the police. They should not be rejected out of hand because of an unexplained preference for other acceptable alternatives."[c]

5. Does *Yates* survive *Brandenburg*'s emphasis on *imminent* lawless action? Consider Kalven, *A Worthy Tradition* 234 (1988): "It is [possible] that [*Brandenburg*] has preserved the group/individual distinction. Under such an approach the *Yates* incitement-to-future-action standard would apply to group speech and the *Brandenburg* incitement-to-immediate-action standard would apply to the individual speaker." Is light shed on the question by *Communist Party of Indiana v. Whitcomb,* 414 U.S. 441, 94 S.Ct. 656, 38 L.Ed.2d 635 (1974), invalidating an Indiana statute denying a political party or its candidates access to the ballot unless the party files an

---

c. See also *NAACP v. Claiborne Hardware Co.,* 458 U.S. 886, 102 S.Ct. 3409, 73 L.Ed.2d 1215 (1982). The Court stated that the remarks of Charles Evers "might have been understood" as inviting violence, but stated that when "such appeals do not incite lawless action, they must be regarded as protected speech." If violent action had followed his remarks, a "substantial question" of liability would have been raised. The Court also observed, however, that the defendant might be held criminally liable for the acts of others if the speeches could be taken as evidence that the defendant gave "other specific instructions to carry out violent acts or threats." Compare *Watts v. United States,* 394 U.S. 705, 89 S.Ct. 1399, 22 L.Ed.2d 664 (1969) (statute prohibiting knowing and wilful threat of bodily harm upon the President is constitutional on its face) (dictum); *Rankin v. McPherson,* p. 540 infra (clerical employee's private expression of desire that Presidential assassination attempt be successful is insufficient justification for dismissal even in a law enforcement agency). For commentary on threats and the first amendment, see Justice Linde's opinion in *State v. Robertson,* 293 Or. 402, 649 P.2d 569 (1982); Baker, *Human Liberty and Freedom of Speech* 54–69 (1989); Gey, *The Nuremberg Files and the First Amendment Value of Threats,* 78 Tex. L.Rev. 541 (2000); Greenawalt, *Criminal Coercion and Freedom of Speech,* 78 Nw.U.L.Rev. 1081 (1984); Note, *United States v. Jake Baker: Revisiting Threats and the First Amendment,* 84 Va. L.Rev. 287 (1998).

affidavit that it "does not advocate the overthrow of local, state or national government by force or violence"? The Court, per Brennan J., maintained that the required oath (which had been interpreted to include advocacy of abstract doctrine) violated the principle of *Brandenburg* and stated that the principle applied not only to attempted denials of public employment, bar licensing, and tax exemption, but also to ballot access denials. The flaw with the state's position was that it furnished access to the ballot "not because the Party urges others 'to *do* something now *or in the future* [but] merely to believe in something,' [*Yates*]" (Second emphasis added).

What happened to the "imminent lawless action" requirement? Does the *Whitcomb* language clarify *Brandenburg*? Modify it?

6.   Does *Brandenburg* apply to the advocacy of trivial crimes? Suppose the advocacy of trespass across a lawn? What result under *Brandenburg*? What result under *Dennis*? Is *Dennis* potentially more speech protective than *Brandenburg*?

7.   Does *Brandenburg* apply to solicitation of crime in private or non-ideological contexts? Consider Shiffrin, note 3 supra, at 950: "How different it might be if the factual context were to involve advocacy of murder in a non-socio-political context. One suspects that little rhetoric about the marketplace of ideas or other first amendment values would be employed and that the serious and explicit advocacy of murder in a concrete way would suffice to divorce the speech from first amendment protection even in the absence of a specific showing of likelihood." Would it matter if it were not explicit or not concrete? For trenchant analysis of the issues raised by the shift in context from public to private or in subject matter from ideological to non-ideological, see Greenawalt, *Speech and Crime,* 1980 Am.B.Found.Res.J. 645.

8.   Nuremberg Files, an anti-abortion Web site included the names, addresses, photographs, and license plate numbers of those who provided abortions or were prominent pro-choice advocates together with their family members. Paladin Press published *Hit Man: A Technical Manual for Independent Contractors.* James Perry relied on the book's instructions to kill three people. Should the Web site and book be protected under *Brandenburg?*[d]

9.   Should the line of cases from *Schenck* to *Brandenburg* fuel cynicism about the binding force of legal doctrine and about the willingness or capacity of the judiciary to protect dissent?[e] To what extent does the focus on Supreme Court cases exaggerate the frailty of legal doctrine?[f]

d. See generally Smolla, *Deliberate Intent* (1999); Sunstein, *One Case at a Time* 191–96 (1999); Malloy & Krotoszynski, Jr., *Recalibrating the Cost of Harm Advocacy,* 41 Wm. & Mary L.Rev. 1159 (2000); Rothchild, *Menacing Speech and the First Amendment: A Functional Approach to Incitement that Threatens,* 8 Tex. J. Women & L. 207 (1999); Note, *Adjusting Absolutism: First Amendment Protection for the Fringe,* 80 B.U.L.Rev. 907 (2000).

e. In fashioning first amendment doctrine, should the overriding objective be at "all times [to] equip the first amendment to do maximum service in those historical periods when intolerance of unorthodox ideas is most prevalent and when governments are most able and most likely to stifle dissent systematically"? Should the first amendment "be targeted for the worst of times"? What impact would such a perspective have on the general development of

II. REPUTATION AND PRIVACY

In an important article, Harry Kalven coined the phrase "two level theory." Kalven, *The Metaphysics of the Law of Obscenity,* 1960 Sup.Ct.Rev. 1, 11. As he described it, *Beauharnais,* infra, and other cases employed a first amendment methodology that classified speech at two levels. Some speech—libel, obscenity, "fighting words"—was thought to be so bereft of social utility as to be beneath first amendment protection. At the second level, speech of constitutional value was thought to be protected unless it presented a clear and present danger of a substantive evil.

In considering libel and privacy, we will witness the collapse of "two level theory." The purpose is not a detailed examination of libel and privacy law. Our interests include the initial exclusion of defamation from first amendment protection, the themes and methods contributing to the erosion of that exclusion, and the articulation of basic first amendment values having implications and applications beyond defamation and the right to privacy.

A. GROUP LIBEL

BEAUHARNAIS v. ILLINOIS, 343 U.S. 250, 72 S.Ct. 725, 96 L.Ed. 919 (1952), per FRANKFURTER, J., sustained a statute prohibiting exhibition in any public place of any publication portraying "depravity, criminality, unchastity, or lack of virtue of a class of citizens, of any race, color, creed or religion [which exposes such citizens] to contempt, derision or obloquy or which is productive of breach of the peace or riots." The Court affirmed a conviction for organizing the distribution of a leaflet which petitioned the Mayor and City Council of Chicago "to halt the further encroachment, harassment and invasion of white people, their property, neighborhoods and persons by the Negro"; called for "one million self respecting white people in Chicago to unite"; and warned that if "the need to prevent the white race from becoming mongrelized by the Negro will not unite us, then the [aggressions], rapes, robberies, knives, guns, and marijuana of the Negro, surely will.":

"Today every American jurisdiction [punishes] libels directed at individuals. '[There] are certain well-defined and narrowly limited classes of speech,

first amendment doctrine? See Blasi, *The Pathological Perspective and the First Amendment,* 85 Colum.L.Rev. 449 (1985).

f. For a comprehensive review and critical analysis of the problems and policies raised by advocacy of illegal action, see Greenawalt, note 7 supra. See generally Greenawalt, *Speech, Crime, and the Uses of*

Language (1989); Kalven, *A Worthy Tradition* (1988). For comparative perspectives, see Zana v. Turkey, 1997–VII Eur. Ct. H.R. 2533; Gavison, *Incitement and the Limits of Law* in *Censorship and Silencing* 43 (Post ed. 1998)(discussing Israeli law and the speech surrounding the assassination of Prime Minister Rabin).

the prevention and punishment of which have never been thought to raise any constitutional problem. These include the lewd and obscene, the profane, the libelous, and the insulting or "fighting" words—those which by their very utterance inflict injury or tend to incite to an immediate breach of the peace. It has been well observed that such utterances are no essential part of any exposition of ideas, and are of such slight social value as a step to truth that any benefit that may be derived from them is clearly outweighed by the social interest in order and morality. "Resort to epithets or personal abuse is not in any proper sense communication of information or opinion safeguarded by the Constitution, and its punishment as a criminal act would raise no question under that instrument." *Cantwell v. Connecticut,* [p. 695 infra].' Such were the views of a unanimous Court in *Chaplinsky v. New Hampshire,* 315 U.S. 568, 62 S.Ct. 766, 86 L.Ed. 1031 (1942).[6]

"No one will gainsay that it is libelous falsely to charge another with being a rapist, robber, carrier of knives and guns, and user of marijuana. The [question is whether the fourteenth amendment] prevents a State from punishing such libels—as criminal libel has been defined, limited and constitutionally recognized time out of mind—directed at designated collectivities and flagrantly disseminated. [I]f an utterance directed at an individual may be the object of criminal sanctions, we cannot deny to a State power to punish the same utterance directed at a defined group, unless we can say that this is a wilful and purposeless restriction unrelated to the peace and well-being of the State.

"Illinois did not have to look beyond her own borders to await the tragic experience of the last three decades to conclude that wilful purveyors of falsehood concerning racial and religious groups promote strife and tend powerfully to obstruct the manifold adjustments required for free, orderly life in a metropolitan, polyglot community. From the murder of the abolitionist Lovejoy in 1837 to the Cicero riots of 1951, Illinois has been the scene of exacerbated tension between races, often flaring into violence and destruction. In many of these outbreaks, utterances of the character here in question, so the Illinois legislature could conclude, played a significant [part.]

"In the face of this history and its frequent obligato of extreme racial and religious propaganda, we would deny experience to say that the Illinois legislature was without reason in seeking ways to curb false or malicious defamation of racial and religious groups, made in public places and by means calculated to have a powerful emotional impact on those to whom it was presented. [I]t would be out of bounds for the judiciary to deny the legislature a choice of policy, provided it is not unrelated to the problem and not forbidden by some explicit limitation on the State's power. That the legislative remedy might not in practice mitigate the evil, or might itself raise new problems, would only manifest once more the paradox of reform. It

---

6. In all but five States, the constitutional guarantee of free speech to every person is explicitly qualified by holding him "responsible for the abuse of that right." * * *

is the price to be paid for the trial-and-error inherent in legislative efforts to deal with obstinate social issues.

"[It would] be arrant dogmatism, quite outside the scope of our authority [for] us to deny that the Illinois Legislature may warrantably believe that a man's job and his educational opportunities and the dignity accorded him may depend as much on the reputation of the racial and religious group to which he willynilly belongs, as on his own merits. This being so, we are precluded from saying that speech concededly punishable when immediately directed at individuals cannot be outlawed if directed at groups with whose position and esteem in society the affiliated individual may be inextricably involved. * * *[18]

"As to the defense of truth, Illinois in common with many States requires a showing not only that the utterance state the facts, but also that the publication be made 'with good motives and for justifiable ends'. Both elements are necessary if the defense is to prevail. [The] teaching of a century and a half of criminal libel prosecutions in this country would go by the board if we were to hold that Illinois was not within her rights in making this combined requirement. Assuming that defendant's offer of proof directed to a part of the defense was adequate, it did not satisfy the entire requirement which Illinois could exact."

The Court ruled that the trial court properly declined to require the jury to find a "clear and present danger": "Libelous utterances not being within the area of constitutionally protected speech, it is unnecessary, either for us or for the State courts, to consider the issues behind the phrase 'clear and present danger.' Certainly no one would contend that obscene speech, for example, may be punished only upon a showing of such circumstances. Libel, as we have seen, is in the same class."

BLACK, J., joined by Douglas, J., dissented: "[The Court] acts on the bland assumption that the First Amendment is wholly irrelevant. [Today's] case degrades First Amendment freedoms to the 'rational basis' level. [We] are cautioned that state legislatures must be left free to 'experiment' and to make legislative judgments. [State] experimentation in curbing freedom of expression is startling and frightening doctrine in a country dedicated to self-government by its people.

"[As] 'constitutionally recognized,' [criminal libel] has provided for punishment of false, malicious, scurrilous charges against individuals, not against huge groups. This limited scope of the law of criminal libel is of no small importance. It has confined state punishment of speech and expression to the narrowest of areas involving nothing more than private feuds. Every expansion of the law of criminal libel so as to punish discussion of matters of public concern means a corresponding invasion of the area dedicated to free expression by the First Amendment.

---

18. [If] a statute sought to outlaw libels of political parties, quite different problems not now before us would be raised. For one thing, the whole doctrine of fair comment as indispensable to the democratic political process would come into play. Political parties, like public men, are, as it were, public property.

"[Whether] the words used in their context here are 'fighting words' in the same sense [as *Chaplinsky*] is doubtful, but whether so or not they are not addressed to or about *individuals*. Moreover, the leaflet used here was also the means adopted by an assembled group to enlist interest in their efforts to have legislation enacted. And the 'fighting' words were but a part of arguments on questions of wide public interest and importance. Freedom of petition, assembly, speech and press could be greatly abridged by a practice of meticulously scrutinizing every editorial, speech, sermon or other printed matter to extract two or three naughty words on which to hang charges of 'group libel.'

"[If] there be minority groups who hail this holding as their victory, they might consider the possible relevancy of this ancient remark: 'Another such victory and I am undone.' "

REED, J., joined by Douglas, J., dissenting, argued that the statute was unconstitutionally vague: "These words—'virtue,' 'derision,' and 'obloquy'— have neither general nor special meanings well enough known to apprise those within their reach as to limitations on speech. Philosophers and poets, thinkers of high and low degree from every age and race have sought to expound the meaning of virtue. * * * Are the tests of the Puritan or the Cavalier to be applied, those of the city or the farm, the Christian or non-Christian, the old or the young?"

DOUGLAS, J., dissented: "Hitler and his Nazis showed how evil a conspiracy could be which was aimed at destroying a race by exposing it to contempt, derision, and obloquy. I would be willing to concede that such conduct directed at a race or group in this country could be made an indictable offense. For such a project would be more than the exercise of free speech. [It] would be free speech plus.

"I would also be willing to concede that even without the element of conspiracy there might be times and occasions when the legislative or executive branch might call a halt to inflammatory talk, such as the shouting of 'fire' in a school or a theatre.

USING CLEAR: PRESENT DANGER TEST

"My view is that if in any case other public interests are to override the plain command of the First Amendment, the peril of speech must be clear and present, leaving no room for argument, raising no doubts as to the necessity of curbing speech in order to prevent disaster."

JACKSON, J., dissenting, argued that the fourteenth amendment does not incorporate the first, as such, but permits the states more latitude than the Congress. He concluded, however, that due process required the trier of fact to evaluate the evidence as to the truth and good faith of the speaker and the clarity and presence of the danger. He was unwilling to assume danger from the tendency of the words and felt that the trial court had precluded the defendant's efforts to show truth and good motives.

DUE PROCESS

Notes and Questions

1. *The right to petition.* Should it make a difference that the leaflet was in the form of a petition to the mayor and city council? Does the right of the people "to petition the Government for a redress of grievances" add anything of substance to Beauharnais' other first amendment arguments? Consider Kalven, *The Negro and the First Amendment* 40 (1965): "If it would make a difference whether the petition was genuine and not just a trick of form, can the Court penetrate the form and appraise the true motivation or must it, as it does with congressional committees accept the official motivation?"[a]

2. *Equality and freedom of speech.* Consider the following hypothetical commentary: "Group libel statutes pose uniquely difficult issues for they involve a clash between two constitutional commitments: the principle of equality and the principle of free speech. They force us to decide what we want to express as a nation: Do we want a powerful symbol of our belief in uninhibited debate or do we want to be the kind of nation that will not tolerate the public calumny of religious, ethnic, and racial groups?"[b] Does the emphasis on equality shortchange the case for prohibiting racist speech? See West, *Progressive Constitutionalism: Reconstructing the Fourteenth Amendment* 147–51 (1994).

3. *Tolerance and freedom of speech.* Should the first amendment be a means of institutionalizing a national commitment to the value of tolerance? By tolerating the intolerable, would we carve out one area of social interaction for extraordinary self-restraint and thereby develop[c] and demonstrate a vital social capacity? See generally Bollinger, *The Tolerant Society: Freedom of Speech and Extremist Speech in America* (1986); Bollinger, *Free Speech and Intellectual Values,* 92 Yale L.J. 438 (1983); Bollinger, *Book Review,* 80 Mich.L.Rev. 617 (1982).

4. *Civility and freedom of speech.* By allowing prosecutions for group libel in the most "odious cases" or cases "so public and offensive that they cannot be avoided" would we "encourage confidence in the discipline of judging itself" and "encourage others to make judgments as well, not simply on group defamation, but on other matters that raise questions about propriety and decency and the obligations that individuals may have to one another"? See Arkes, *Civility and the Restriction of Speech: Rediscovering the Defamation of Groups,* 1974 Sup.Ct.Rev. 281, 331.

a. See *McDonald v. Smith*, 472 U.S. 479, 105 S.Ct. 2787, 86 L.Ed.2d 384 (1985) (denying any special first amendment status for the Petition Clause).

b. See, e.g., *The Price We Pay: The Case Against Racist Speech* (Lederer & Delgado eds. 1995); Matsuda et al., *Words that Wound* (Itzin ed. 1993); Goodpaster, *Equality and Free Speech: The Case Against Sub-* *stantive Equality,* 82 Ia. L.Rev. 645 (1997); Beth, *Group Libel and Free Speech,* 39 Minn.L.Rev. 167, 180–81 (1955) and sources cited in Sec, 1, VI, C.

c. For skepticism about the capacity of courts to achieve any substantial impact in promoting tolerance, see Nagel, *How Useful Is Judicial Review in Free Speech Cases?*, 69 Corn.L.Rev. 302 (1984).

5. *Libel, group libel, and seditious libel.* Consider Kalven, supra, at 15, 16 and 50–51: Seditious libel "is the doctrine that criticism of government officials and policy may be viewed as defamation of government and may be punished as a serious crime. [On] my view, the absence of seditious libel as a crime is the true pragmatic test of freedom of speech. This I would argue is what freedom of speech is about. [The] most revealing aspect of the opinions, and particularly that of Justice Frankfurter, is the absence of any sense of the proximity of the case before them to seditious libel. The case presents almost a perfect instance of that competition among analogies which Edward Levi has emphasized as the essential circumstance of legal reasoning. In the middle we have group libel and Justice Frankfurter's urging its many resemblances to individual libel. [If] the Court's speech theory had been more grounded, as it seems to me it should be, on the relevance of the concept of seditious libel and less on the analogy to the law of attempts found in the slogan 'clear and present danger,' it is difficult to believe that either the debate or the result in *Beauharnais* would have been the same."

B.   PUBLIC OFFICIALS AND SEDITIOUS LIBEL

NEW YORK TIMES CO. v. SULLIVAN

376 U.S. 254, 84 S.Ct. 710, 11 L.Ed.2d 686 (1964).

MR. JUSTICE BRENNAN delivered the opinion of the Court.

[Sullivan, the Montgomery, Ala. police commissioner, sued the New York Times and four black Alabama clergymen for alleged libelous statements in a paid, full-page fund-raising advertisement signed by a "Committee to defend Martin Luther King and the struggle for freedom in the South." The advertisement stated that "truckloads of police armed with shotguns and tear-gas ringed Alabama State College Campus" in Montgomery, and that "the Southern violators [have] bombed [Dr. King's] home, assaulted his person [and] arrested him seven times." In several respects the statements were untrue. Several witnesses testified that they understood the statements to refer to Sullivan because he supervised Montgomery police. Sullivan proved he did not participate in the events described. He offered no proof of pecuniary loss.[3] Pursuant to Alabama law, the trial court submitted the libel issue to the jury, giving general and punitive damages instructions. It returned a $500,000 verdict for Sullivan against all of the defendants.] We hold that the rule of law applied by the Alabama courts is constitutionally deficient for failure to provide the safeguards for freedom of speech and of the press that are required by the First and Fourteenth Amendments in a libel action brought by a public official against critics of his official conduct.[4] We further hold that under the proper safeguards the evidence presented in

3. Approximately 394 copies of the edition of the Times containing the advertisement were circulated in Alabama. Of these, about 35 copies were distributed in Montgomery County. The total circulation of the Times for that day was approximately 650,000 copies.

4. [The] Times contends that the assumption of jurisdiction over its corporate person by the Alabama courts overreaches

this case is constitutionally insufficient to support the judgment for respondent.

I. [The] publication here [communicated] information, expressed opinion, recited grievances, protested claimed abuses, and sought financial support on behalf of a movement whose existence and objectives are matters of the highest public interest and concern. That the Times was paid for publishing the advertisement is as immaterial in this connection as is the fact that newspapers and books are sold. *Smith v. California* [p. 146 infra]. Any other conclusion would discourage newspapers from carrying "editorial advertisements" of this type, and so might shut off an important outlet for the promulgation of information and ideas by persons who do not themselves have access to publishing facilities.

II. Under Alabama law [once] "libel per se" has been established, the defendant has no defense as to stated facts unless he can persuade the jury that they were true in all their particulars. [His] privilege of "fair comment" for expressions of opinion depends on the truth of the facts upon which the comment is based. [Unless] he can discharge the burden of proving truth, general damages are presumed, and may be awarded without proof of pecuniary injury.

[Respondent] relies heavily, as did the Alabama courts, on statements of this Court to the effect that the Constitution does not protect libelous publications. Those statements do not foreclose our inquiry here. None of the cases sustained the use of libel laws to impose sanctions upon expression critical of the official conduct of public officials. [L]ibel can claim no talismanic immunity from constitutional limitations. It must be measured by standards that satisfy the First Amendment.

The First Amendment, said Judge Learned Hand, "presupposes that right conclusions are more likely to be gathered out of a multitude of tongues, than through any kind of authoritative selection. To many this is, and always will be, folly; but we have staked upon it our all." [Thus] we consider this case against the background of a profound national commitment to the principle that debate on public issues should be uninhibited, robust, and wide-open, and that it may well include vehement, caustic, and sometimes unpleasantly sharp attacks on government and public officials. The present advertisement, as an expression of grievance and protest on one of the major public issues of our time, would seem clearly to qualify for the constitutional protection. The question is whether it forfeits that protection

---

the territorial limits of the Due Process Clause. The latter claim is foreclosed from our review by the ruling of the Alabama courts that the Times entered a general appearance in the action and thus waived its jurisdictional objection. * * *

[Since *New York Times* the Court has upheld expansive personal jurisdiction against media defendants. *Calder v. Jones*, 465 U.S. 783, 104 S.Ct. 1482, 79 L.Ed.2d 804 (1984); *Keeton v. Hustler*, 465 U.S. 770, 104 S.Ct. 1473, 79 L.Ed.2d 790 (1984). *Calder* rejected the suggestion that first amendment concerns enter into jurisdictional analysis. It feared complicating the inquiry and argued that because first amendment concerns are taken into account in limiting the substantive law of defamation, "to reintroduce those concerns at the jurisdictional stage would be a form of double counting."]

by the falsity of some of its factual statements and by its alleged defamation of respondent.

Authoritative interpretations of the First Amendment guarantees have consistently refused to recognize an exception for any test of truth—whether administered by judges, juries, or administrative officials—and especially not one that puts the burden of proving truth on the speaker. [E]rroneous statement is inevitable in free debate, and [it] must be protected if the freedoms of expression are to have the "breathing space" that they "need [to] survive."

[Injury] to official reputation affords no more warrant for repressing speech that would otherwise be free than does factual error. Where judicial officers are involved, this Court has held that concern for the dignity and reputation of the courts does not justify the punishment as criminal contempt of criticism of the judge or his decision. This is true even though the utterance contains "half-truths" and "misinformation." Such repression can be justified, if at all, only by a clear and present danger of the obstruction of justice. If judges are to be treated as "men of fortitude, able to thrive in a hardy climate," surely the same must be true of other government officials, such as elected city commissioners. Criticism of their official conduct does not lose its constitutional protection merely because it is effective criticism and hence diminishes their official reputations.

If neither factual error nor defamatory content suffices to remove the constitutional shield from criticism of official conduct, the combination of the two elements is no less inadequate. This is the lesson to be drawn from the great controversy over the Sedition Act of 1798, 1 Stat. 596, which first crystallized a national awareness of the central meaning of the First Amendment. [Although] the Sedition Act was never tested in this Court, the attack upon its validity has carried the day in the court of history. Fines levied in its prosecution were repaid by Act of Congress on the ground that it was unconstitutional. * * * Jefferson, as President, pardoned those who had been convicted and sentenced under the Act and remitted their fines. [Its] invalidity [has] also been assumed by Justices of this Court. [These] views reflect a broad consensus that the Act, because of the restraint it imposed upon criticism of government and public officials, was inconsistent with the First Amendment. * * *

What a State may not constitutionally bring about by means of a criminal statute is likewise beyond the reach of its civil law of libel. The fear of damage awards under a rule such as that invoked by the Alabama courts here may be markedly more inhibiting than the fear of prosecution under a criminal statute. [The] judgment awarded in this case—without the need for any proof of actual pecuniary loss—was one thousand times greater than the maximum fine provided by the Alabama criminal [libel law], and one hundred times greater than that provided by the Sedition Act. And since there is no double-jeopardy limitation applicable to civil lawsuits, this is not the only judgment that may be awarded against petitioners for the same publication.[18] Whether or not a newspaper can survive a succession of such judgments, the pall of fear and timidity imposed upon those who would give voice to public criticism is an atmosphere in which the First Amendment freedoms cannot [survive].

The state rule of law is not saved by its allowance of the defense of truth. A defense for erroneous statements honestly made is no less essential here than was the requirement of proof of guilty knowledge which, in *Smith v. California,* we held indispensable to a valid conviction of a bookseller for possessing obscene writings for [sale].

A rule compelling the critic of official conduct to guarantee the truth of all his factual assertions—and to do so on pain of libel judgments virtually unlimited in amount—leads to a comparable "self-censorship." Allowance of the defense of truth, with the burden of proving it on the defendant, does not mean that only false speech will be deterred.[19] [Under] such a rule, would-be critics of official conduct may be deterred from voicing their criticism, even though it is believed to be true and even though it is in fact true, because of doubt whether it can be proved in court or fear of the expense of having to do so. They tend to make only statements which "steer far wider of the unlawful zone." The rule thus dampens the vigor and limits the variety of public [debate].

The constitutional guarantees require, we think, a federal rule that prohibits a public official from recovering damages for a defamatory falsehood relating to his official conduct unless he proves that the statement was made with "actual malice"—that is, with knowledge that it was false or with reckless disregard of whether it was false or [not].[a]

Such a privilege for criticism of official conduct is appropriately analogous to the protection accorded a public official when *he* is sued for libel by a private citizen. In *Barr v. Matteo,* 360 U.S. 564, 575, 79 S.Ct. 1335, 1341, 3 L.Ed.2d 1434 (1959), this Court held the utterance of a federal official to be absolutely privileged if made "within the outer perimeter" of his duties. The States accord the same immunity to statements of their highest officers, although some differentiate their lesser officials and qualify the privilege

---

18. The Times states that four other libel suits based on the advertisement have been filed against it by [others]; that another $500,000 verdict has been awarded in [one]; and that the damages sought in the other three total $2,000,000.

19. Even a false statement may be deemed to make a valuable contribution to the public debate, since it brings about "the clearer perception and livelier impression of truth, produced by its collision with error." Mill, *On Liberty* 15 (1947).

a. Compare *St. Amant v. Thompson,* 390 U.S. 727, 88 S.Ct. 1323, 20 L.Ed.2d 262 (1968) (publishing while "in fact entertain[ing] serious doubts about the truth of the publication" satisfies standard) with

Garrison v. Louisiana, 379 U.S. 64, 85 S.Ct. 209, 13 L.Ed.2d 125 (1964) (standard requires "high degree of awareness of probable falsity"). See also *Masson v. New Yorker Magazine, Inc.,* 501 U.S. 496, 111 S.Ct. 2419, 115 L.Ed.2d 447 (1991) ("a deliberate alteration of the words uttered by a plaintiff does not equate with knowledge of falsity [unless] the alteration results in a material change of meaning conveyed by the statement"). For discussion of malice and docudrama, see Rodney Smolla, *Harlot's Ghost and JFK: A Fictional Conversation with Norman Mailer, Oliver Stone, Earl Warren and Hugo Black,* 26 Suffolk U.L.Rev. 587 (1992). For discussion of *Masson,* see Bollinger, *The End of New York Times v. Sullivan,* 1991 Sup.Ct.Rev. 1.

they enjoy. But all hold that all officials are protected unless actual malice can be proved. The reason for the official privilege is said to be that the threat of damage suits would otherwise "inhibit the fearless, vigorous, and effective administration of policies of government" and "dampen the ardor of all but the most resolute, or the most irresponsible, in the unflinching discharge of their duties." *Barr*. Analogous considerations support the privilege for the citizen-critic of government. It is as much his duty to criticize as it is the official's duty to administer. [It] would give public servants an unjustified preference over the public they serve, if critics of official conduct did not have a fair equivalent of the immunity granted to the officials themselves. We conclude that such a privilege is required by the First and Fourteenth Amendments.[23]

III. [W]e consider that the proof presented to show actual malice lacks the convincing clarity[b] which the constitutional standard demands, and hence that it would not constitutionally sustain the judgment for respondent under the proper rule of law. [T]here is evidence that the Times published the advertisement without checking its accuracy against the news stories in the Times' own files. The mere presence of the stories in the files does [not] establish that the Times "knew" the advertisement was false, since the state of mind required for actual malice would have to be brought home to the persons in the Times' organization having responsibility for the publication of the advertisement. With respect to the failure of those persons to make the check, the record shows that they relied upon their knowledge of the good reputation of many [whose] names were listed as sponsors of the advertisement, and upon the letter from A. Philip Randolph, known to them as a responsible individual, certifying that the use of the names was authorized. There was testimony that the persons handling the advertisement saw nothing in it that would render it unacceptable under the Times' policy of rejecting advertisements containing "attacks of a personal character"; their failure to reject it on this ground was not unreasonable. We think the evidence against the Times supports at most a finding of negligence in failing to discover the misstatements, and is constitutionally insufficient to show the recklessness that is required for a finding of actual malice.

---

23. We have no occasion here to determine how far down into the lower ranks of government employees the "public official" designation would extend for purposes of this rule, or otherwise to specify categories of persons who would or would not be included. [Nor] need we here determine the boundaries of the "official conduct" concept. * * *

b. Compare *Bose Corp. v. Consumers Union*, 466 U.S. 485, 104 S.Ct. 1949, 80 L.Ed.2d 502 (1984) (appellate courts "must exercise independent judgment and determine whether the record establishes actual malice with convincing clarity."). Accord *Harte–Hanks Communications v. Connaughton*, 491 U.S. 657, 109 S.Ct. 2678, 105 L.Ed.2d 562 (1989). See also *Anderson v. Liberty Lobby, Inc.,* 477 U.S. 242, 106 S.Ct. 2505, 91 L.Ed.2d 202 (1986) (same standard at summary judgment). Should independent appellate judgment be required in all first amendment cases? All constitutional cases? For commentary, see Monaghan, *Constitutional Fact Review,* 85 Colum.L.Rev. 229 (1985); Volokh & McDonnell, *Freedom of Speech and Independent Judgment Review in Copyright Cases,* 107 Yale L.J. 2431 (1998); Volokh, *Freedom of Speech and Appellate Review in Workplace harassment Cases,* 90 Nw. U.L.Rev. 1009 (1996). On the impact of *Bose,* see Gilles, Taking First Amendment Procedure Seriously, 58 Ohio St.L.J. 1752, 1774–79 (1998).

[T]he evidence was constitutionally defective in another respect:[c] it was incapable of supporting the jury's finding that the allegedly libelous statements were made "of and concerning" respondent. [On this point, the Supreme Court of Alabama] based its ruling on the proposition that: "[The] average person knows that municipal agents, such as police and firemen, and others, are under the control and direction of the city governing body, and more particularly under the direction and control of a single commissioner. In measuring the performance or deficiencies of such groups, praise or criticism is usually attached to the official in complete control of the body."

This proposition has disquieting implications for criticism of governmental conduct. [It would transmute] criticism of government, however impersonal it may seem on its face, into personal criticism, and hence potential libel, of the officials of whom the government is composed. [Raising] as it does the possibility that a good-faith critic of government will be penalized for his criticism, the proposition relied on by the Alabama courts strikes at the very center of the constitutionally protected area of free expression. We hold that such a proposition may not constitutionally be utilized to establish that an otherwise impersonal attack on governmental operations was a libel of an official responsible for those operations. Since it was relied on exclusively here, and there was no other evidence to connect the statements with respondent, the evidence was constitutionally insufficient to support a finding that the statements referred to respondent. * * *[d]

MR. JUSTICE BLACK, with whom MR. JUSTICE DOUGLAS joins (concurring).

* * * "Malice," even as defined by the Court, is an elusive, abstract concept, hard to prove and hard to disprove. The requirement that malice be proved provides at best an evanescent protection for the right critically to discuss public affairs and certainly does not measure up to the sturdy safeguard embodied in the First Amendment. Unlike the Court, therefore, I vote to reverse exclusively on the ground that the Times and the individual defendants had an absolute, unconditional constitutional right to publish in the Times advertisement their criticisms of the Montgomery agencies and [officials].

The half-million-dollar verdict [gives] dramatic proof [that] state libel laws threaten the very existence of an American press virile enough to publish unpopular views on public affairs and bold enough to criticize the conduct of public officials. [B]riefs before us show that in Alabama there are

---

c. Implicitly, the Court left open the possibility of a new trial with new evidence. For discussion of the Court's internal debate on the question, see Schwartz, *Super Chief* 531–41 (1983).

d. For a similar ruling that impersonal criticism of a government operation cannot be the basis for defamation "of and concerning" the supervisor of the operation, see *Rosenblatt v. Baer,* 383 U.S. 75, 86 S.Ct. 669, 15 L.Ed.2d 597 (1966): "[T]antamount to a demand for recovery based on libel of government."

now pending eleven libel suits by local and state officials against the Times seeking $5,600,000, and five such suits against the Columbia Broadcasting System seeking $1,700,000. Moreover, this technique for harassing and punishing a free press—now that it has been shown to be possible—is by no means limited to cases with racial overtones; it can be used in other fields where public feelings may make local as well as out-of-state newspapers easy prey for libel verdict seekers.

In my opinion the Federal Constitution has dealt with this deadly danger to the press in the only way possible without leaving the press open to destruction—by granting the press an absolute immunity for criticism of the way public officials do their public duty.

[This] Nation, I suspect, can live in peace without libel suits based on public discussions of public affairs and public officials. But I doubt that a country can live in freedom where its people can be made to suffer physically or financially for criticizing their government, its actions, or its officials. * * *e

———

Professor Kalven observed that the Court in *New York Times* was moving toward "the theory of free speech that Alexander Meiklejohn has been offering us for some fifteen years now." Kalven, *The New York Times Case: A Note On "The Central Meaning of the First Amendment,"* 1964 Sup.Ct.Rev. 191, 221. Indeed Kalven reported Meiklejohn's view that the case was " 'an occasion for dancing in the streets.' "Id. at 221 n. 125. Consider the following excerpts from Meiklejohn's most significant work and Zechariah Chafee's pointed response.

ALEXANDER MEIKLEJOHN—FREE SPEECH AND ITS RELATION TO SELF–GOVERNMENT

3, 26–27, 93–94, 89–91 (1948), reprinted in Meiklejohn,
Political Freedom 9, 27–28, 79–80, 75–77 (1960).
Reprinted with permission of the publisher; copyright
© 1948, 1960 by Harper Collins Publishers

We Americans think of ourselves as politically free. We believe in self-government. If men are to be governed, we say, then that governing must be done, not by others, but by themselves. So far, therefore, as our own affairs are concerned, we refuse to submit to alien control. That refusal, if need be, we will carry to the point of rebellion, of revolution. And if other men, within the jurisdiction of our laws, are denied their right to political freedom, we

---

e. Goldberg, J., joined by Douglas, J., concurring, also asserted for "the citizen and [the] press an absolute unconditional privilege to criticize official conduct," but maintained that the imposition of liability for "[p]urely private defamation" did not abridge the first amendment because it had "little to do with the political ends of a self-governing society." For background on the *New York Times* case, see Lewis, *Make No Law* (1991); Smolla, *Suing The Press* 26–52 (1986). For the Canadian approach, see *Hill v. Church of Scientology of Ontario* [1995], 126 D.L.R.4th 129.

will, in the same spirit, rise to their defense. Governments, we insist, derive their just powers from the consent of the governed. If that consent be lacking, governments have no just powers.

[The] principle of the freedom of speech springs from the necessities of the program of self-government. It is not a Law of Nature or of Reason in the abstract. It is a deduction from the basic American agreement that public issues shall be decided by universal suffrage.[a]

If, then, on any occasion in the United States it is allowable to say that the Constitution is a good document it is equally allowable, in that situation, to say that the Constitution is a bad document. If a public building may be used in which to say, in time of war, that the war is justified, then the same building may be used in which to say that it is not justified. If it be publicly argued that conscription for armed service is moral and necessary, it may likewise be publicly argued that it is immoral and unnecessary. If it may be said that American political institutions are superior to those of England or Russia or Germany, it may, with equal freedom, be said that those of England or Russia or Germany are superior to ours. These conflicting views may be expressed, must be expressed, not because they are valid, but because they are relevant. If they are responsibly entertained by anyone, we, the voters, need to hear them. When a question of policy is "before the house," free men choose to meet it not with their eyes shut, but with their eyes open. To be afraid of ideas, any idea, is to be unfit for self-government. Any such suppression of ideas about the common good, the First Amendment condemns with its absolute disapproval. The freedom of ideas shall not be abridged. * * *

If, however, as our argument has tried to show, the principle of the freedom of speech is derived, not from some supposed "Natural Right," but from the necessities of self-government by universal suffrage, there follows at once a very large limitation of the scope of the principle. The guarantee given by the First Amendment is not, then, assured to all speaking. It is assured only to speech which bears, directly or indirectly, upon issues with which voters have to deal—only, therefore, to the consideration of matters of public interest. Private speech, or private interest in speech, on the other hand, has no claim whatever to the protection of the First Amendment. If men are engaged, as we so commonly are, in argument, or inquiry, or advocacy, or incitement which is directed toward our private interests,

---

a. Consider Cole, *Beyond Unconstitutional Conditions: Charting Spheres of Neutrality in Government–Funded Speech,* 67 N.Y.U.L.Rev. 675, 710 (1992): "If Holmes's 'free trade' metaphor represents the paradigmatic liberal vision of free speech, Meiklejohn's town meeting captures the republican vision of an inclusive public exchange in which ordinary people actively participate as citizens, engaged in an ongoing dialogue about public values and norms. Where the liberal view sees an 'invisible hand' reaching truth through the self-interested behavior of atomistic individuals, the republican vision emphasizes the constitutive role of public dialogue in shaping our collective identity as a community, and the importance of maintaining public institutions for speech to that end." For discussion of the Meiklejohn perspective in the Japanese context, Krotoszynski, Jr., *The Chrysanthemum, the Sword, and the First Amendment,* 1998 Wisc. L.Rev. 905 (1998).

private privileges, private possessions, we are, of course, entitled to "due process" protection of those activities. But the First Amendment has no concern over such protection. * * *

Here, then, are the charges which I would bring against the "clear and present danger" theory. They are all, it is clear, differing forms of the basic accusation that the compact of self-government has been ignored or repudiated.

First, the theory denies or obscures the fact that free citizens have two distinct sets of civil liberties. As the makers of the laws, they have duties and responsibilities which require an absolute freedom. As the subjects of the laws, they have possessions and rights, to which belongs a relative freedom.

Second, the theory fails to keep clear the distinction between the constitutional status of discussions of public policy and the corresponding status of discussions of private policy.

Third, the theory fails to recognize that, under the Constitution, the freedom of advocacy or incitement to action *by the government* may never be abridged. It is only advocacy or incitement to action by individuals or nonpolitical groups which is open to regulation.

Fourth, the theory regards the freedom of speech as a mere device which is to be abandoned when dangers threaten the public welfare. On the contrary, it is the very presence of those dangers which makes it imperative that, in the midst of our fears, we remember and observe a principle upon whose integrity rests the entire structure of government by consent of the governed.

Fifth, the Supreme Court, by adopting a theory which annuls the First Amendment, has struck a disastrous blow at our national education. It has denied the belief that men can, by processes of free public discussion, govern themselves. * * *

The unabridged freedom of public discussion is the rock on which our government stands. With that foundation beneath us, we shall not flinch in the face of any clear and present—or, even, terrific—danger.

ZECHARIAH CHAFEE, JR.—BOOK REVIEW

62 Harv.L.Rev. 891, 894–901 (1949).
Reprinted with permission of the publisher; copyright
© 1949, by the Harvard Law Review Association.

[M]y main objection to Mr. Meiklejohn's book [is that he] places virtually all his argument against current proposals for suppression on a constitutional position which is extremely dubious. Whereas the supporters of these measures are genuinely worried by the dangers of Communism, he refuses to argue that these dangers are actually small. Instead, his constitutional position obliges him to argue that these dangers are irrelevant. No matter how terrible and immediate the dangers may be, he keeps saying, the First

Amendment will not let Congress or anybody else in the Government try to deal with Communists who have not yet committed unlawful [acts.]

Mr. Meiklejohn's basic proposition is that there are two distinct kinds of freedom of speech, protected by quite different clauses of the Constitution. Freedom of speech on matters affecting self-government is protected by the First Amendment and is not open to restrictions by the Government. [By] contrast, private discussion is open to restrictions because it is protected by [fifth amendment due process].

The truth is, I think, that the framers had no very clear idea as to what they meant by "the freedom of speech or of the press," but we can say three things with reasonable assurance. First, these politicians, lawyers, scholars, churchgoers and philosophers, scientists, agriculturalists, and wide readers used the phrase to embrace the whole realm of thought. Second, they intended the First Amendment to give all the protection they desired, and had no idea of supplementing it by the Fifth Amendment. Finally, the freedom which Congress was forbidden to abridge was not, for them, some absolute concept which had never existed on earth. It was the freedom which they believed they already had—what they had wanted before the Revolution and had acquired through independence. In thinking about it, they took for granted the limitations which had been customarily applied in the day-to-day work of colonial courts. Now, they were setting up a new federal government of great potential strength, and (as in the rest of Bill of Rights) they were determined to make sure that it would not take away the freedoms which they then enjoyed in their thirteen sovereign states.

Still, the First Amendment has the power of growing to meet new needs. As Marshall said, it is a *Constitution* which we are interpreting. Although in 1791 the Amendment did not mean what Mr. Meiklejohn says, perhaps it ought to mean that now. But the Supreme Court is unlikely to think so in any foreseeable future. The author condemns the clear and present danger test as "a peculiarly inept and unsuccessful attempt to formulate an exception" to the constitutional protection of public discussion, but he does not realize how unworkable his own views would prove when applied in litigation.

In the first place, although it may be possible to draw a fairly bright line between speech which is completely immune and action which may be punished, some speech on public questions is so hateful that the Court would be very reluctant to protect it from statutory penalties. We are not dealing with a philosopher who can write what he pleases, but with at least five men who are asked to block legislators and prosecutors. The history of the Court Plan in 1937 shows how sure judges have to be of their ground to do that. Take a few examples. A newspaper charges the mayor with taking bribes. Ezra Pound broadcasts from an Italian radio station that our participation in the war is an abominable mistake. A speaker during a very bad food shortage tells a hungry mass of voters that the rationing board is so incompetent and corrupt that the best way to avoid starvation is to demand the immediate death of its members, unless they are ready to resign. Plainly few judges can grant constitutional protection to such speeches.

Even the author begins to hedge. Although his main insistence is on immunity for all speech connected with self-government, as my examples surely are, occasionally he concedes that "repressive action by the government is imperative for the sake of the general welfare," e.g., against libelous assertions, slander, words inciting men to crime, sedition, and treason by words. Here he is diving into very deep water. Once you push punishment beyond action into the realm of language, then you have to say pretty plainly how far back the law should go. You must enable future judges and jurymen to know where to stop. That is just what Holmes did when he drew his line at clear and present danger and the author gives us no substitute test for distinguishing between good public speech and bad public speech. He never faces the problem of Mark Anthony's Oration—discussion which is calculated to produce unlawful acts without ever mentioning them.

At times he hints that the line depends on the falsity of the assertions or the bad motives of the speakers. In the mayor's case, it is no answer to say that false charges are outside the Constitution; the issue is whether a jury shall be permitted to find them false even if they are in fact true. Moreover, in such charges a good deal of truth which might be useful to the voters is frequently mixed with some falsehood, so that the possibility of a damage action often keeps genuine information away from voters. And the low character of speakers and writers does not necessarily prevent them from uttering wholesome truths about politics. Witness the Essays of Francis Bacon. Mr. Meiklejohn has a special dislike for paid "lobbyists for special interests." But if discussing public questions with money in sight is outside the First Amendment, how about speeches by aspirants to a $75,000 job in Washington or editorials in newspapers or books on Free Speech? Dr. Johnson declared that any man who writes except for money is a fool. In short, the trouble with the bad-motive test is that courts and juries would apply it only to the exponents of unpopular views. If what is said happens to be our way, the speaker is as welcome as an ex-revolutionist to the Un–American Committee.

The most serious weakness in Mr. Meiklejohn's argument is that it rests on his supposed boundary between public speech and private speech. That line is extremely blurred. Take the novel *Strange Fruit*, which was lately suppressed in Massachusetts. It did not discuss any question then before the voters, but it dealt thoughtfully with many problems of the relations between whites and Negroes, a matter of great national concern. Was this under the First Amendment or the Fifth? [The] truth is that there are public aspects to practically every subject. [The] author recognizes this when he says that the First Amendment is directed against "mutilation of the thinking process of the community." [This] attitude, however, offers such a wide area for the First Amendment that very little is left for his private speech under the Fifth Amendment. For example, if books and plays are public speech, how can they be penalized for gross obscenity or libels?

On the other hand, if private speech does include scholarship (as the author suggests) and also art and literature, it is shocking to deprive these vital matters of the protection of the inspiring words of the First Amendment. The individual interest in freedom of speech, which Socrates voiced when he said that he would rather die than stop talking, is too precious to be left altogether to the vague words of the due process clause. Valuable as self-government is, it is in itself only a small part of our lives. That a philosopher should subordinate all other activities to it is indeed surprising.

[Even] if Holmes had agreed with Mr. Meiklejohn's view of the First Amendment, his insistence on such absolutism would not have persuaded a single colleague, and scores of men would have gone to prison who have been speaking freely for three decades. After all, a judge who is trying to establish a doctrine which the Supreme Court will promulgate as law cannot write like a solitary philosopher. He has to convince at least four men in a specific group and convince them very soon. The true alternative to Holmes' view of the First Amendment was not at all the perfect immunity for public discussion which Mr. Meiklejohn desires. It was no immunity at all in the face of legislation. Any danger, any tendency in speech to produce bad acts, no matter how remote, would suffice to validate a repressive statute, and the only hope for speakers and writers would lie in being tried by liberal jurymen. * * * Holmes worked out a formula which would invalidate a great deal of suppression, and won for it the solid authority of a unanimous Court. Afterwards, again and again, when his test was misapplied by the majority, Holmes restated his position in ringing words which, with the help of Brandeis and Hughes, eventually inspired the whole Court.[b]

Notes and Questions

1. To what extent does *New York Times* incorporate Meiklejohn's perspective?[c] What is the "central meaning" of the first amendment? Con-

b. Compare Berns, *Freedom, Virtue and the First Amendment* 50–56 (Gateway ed. 1965): "The first thing to be remembered [about the clear and present danger test] is that Schenck was sent to jail with it. The second is that Abrams and Gitlow, with Holmes dissenting in ringing clear and present danger language, were jailed despite it. The third is that [the communists in *Dennis*] were sent to jail with it. [Only *Taylor v. Mississippi*, 319 U.S. 583, 63 S.Ct. 1200, 87 L.Ed. 1600 (1943), reversing the conviction of Jehovah's Witnesses, prosecuted under a wartime state sedition law for publicly urging people not to support the war and for advocating and teaching refusal to salute the flag], can illustrate the use of the [Holmes] doctrine to cause the triumph of free speech over national [security]. Thus, [in] the area in which the rule was first enunciated, the clear and present danger test has been of assistance only to a Jehovah's Witness—not to a Socialist like Debs or a Communist like Gitlow or Dennis, or to anyone else whose opinions are both hated *and* feared. [The test] actually becomes a rationale for avoiding the impossible prohibitions of the First Amendment and for convicting persons for speech that the government has forbidden."

c. For elaboration and modification of Meiklejohn's views, see Meiklejohn, *The First Amendment Is an Absolute*, 1961 Sup. Ct.Rev. 245. For commentary, see Bollinger,

sider Neuborne, *Toward a Democracy–Centered Reading of the First Amendment,* 93 Nw.U.L.Rev. 1055, 1069 (1999): "It is no coincidence that the textual rhythm of the First Amendment moves from protection of internal conscience in the religion clauses, to protection of individual expression in the speech clause, to broad community-wide discussion in the press clause, to concerted action in the assembly (and implied association) clause, and, finally, to formal political activity in the petition clause. Indeed, no rights-bearing document in the Western tradition approximates the precise organizational clarity of the First Amendment as a road map of democracy."

If the first amendment is rooted in a conception of democracy, or even partially rooted in such a conception, does it matter which theory of democracy is entertained? For the suggestion that the particular theory of democracy has implications for a range of first amendment questions, see, Baker, *The Media That Citizens Need,* 147 U.Pa.L.Rev. 317 (1998).

2. *New York Times, definitional balancing, and the two-level theory of the first amendment.* By holding that some libel was within the protection of the first amendment, did the Court dismantle its two-level theory? See Kalven, supra, at 217–218. Or did the Court merely rearrange its conception of what was protected and what was not?

Does *Garrison v. Louisiana,* 379 U.S. 64, 85 S.Ct. 209, 13 L.Ed.2d 125 (1964) shed light on the question? The Court stated: "Calculated falsehood falls into that class of utterances '[of] such slight social value as a step to truth that any benefit that may be derived from them is clearly outweighed by the social interest in order and morality.' *Chaplinsky.*"

Could the judicial process here fairly be called *definitional* classification—defining which categories of libel are to be viewed as "speech" within the first amendment, and which are not? Consider Nimmer, *The Right to Speak from Times to Time, First Amendment Theory Applied to Libel and Misapplied to Privacy,* 56 Calif.L.Rev. 935, 942–43 (1968): "[*New York Times*] points the way to the employment of the balancing process on the definitional rather than the litigation or ad hoc level, [that is,] balancing not for the purpose of determining which litigant deserves to prevail in the particular case, but only for the purpose of defining which forms of speech are to be regarded as 'speech' within the meaning of the first amendment.

Free Speech and Intellectual Values, 92 Yale L.J. 438 (1983); Kalven, supra. For work proceeding from a politically based interpretation of the first amendment, see Amar, *The Bill of Rights* 20–32 (1998); Anastaplo, *The Constitutionalist* (1971); Sunstein, *Democracy and the Problem of Free Speech* (1993); BeVier, *The First Amendment and Political Speech: An Inquiry Into the Substance and Limits of Principle,* 30 Stan. L.Rev. 299 (1978); Bloustein, *The First Amendment and Privacy: The Supreme Court Justice and the Philosopher,* 28 Rutg. L.Rev. 41 (1974); Bork, *Neutral Principles and Some First Amendment Problems,* 47 Ind.L.J. 1 (1971). Farber, *Free Speech Without Romance,* 105 Harv.L.Rev. 554 (1991) (arriving at a politically centered perspective after applying economic analysis); Fiss, *State Activism and State Censorship,* 100 Yale L.J. 2087 (1991); Fiss, *Why the State,* 100 Harv.L.Rev. 781 (1987); Fiss, *Free Speech and Social Structure,* 71 Iowa L.Rev. 1405 (1986). See also Brennan, *The Supreme Court and the Meiklejohn Interpretation of the First Amendment,* 79 Harv. L.Rev. 1 (1965).

[By] in effect holding that knowingly and recklessly false speech was not 'speech' within the meaning of the first amendment, the Court must have implicitly (since no explicit explanation was offered) referred to certain competing policy considerations. This is surely a kind of balancing, but it is just as surely not ad hoc balancing."[d]

3. *The scope of New York Times.* Professor Kalven argued that given the Court's conception of freedom of speech, its holding could not be confined: "the invitation to follow a dialectic progression from public official to government policy to public policy to matters in the public domain, like art, seems * * * overwhelming." Kalven, supra, at 221.

(a) *Public officials. New York Times,* fn. 23 left open "how far down into the lower ranks of governmental employees" the rule would extend, and *Rosenblatt v. Baer,* 383 U.S. 75, 86 S.Ct. 669, 15 L.Ed.2d 597 (1966) suggested the rule might apply to the supervisor of a publicly owned ski resort, saying it applies to those who "appear to the public to [have] substantial responsibility for or control over the conduct of government affairs."[e] Should criticism of the official conduct of *very* high ranking government officials (e.g., the President, the Secretary of State, a general commanding troops in war) be given greater protection than that afforded in *New York Times*?

(b) *Private conduct of public officials and candidates. Garrison,* extended *New York Times* to "anything which might touch on an official's fitness for office," even if the defamation did not concern official conduct in office. Invoking that standard, *Monitor Patriot Co. v. Roy,* 401 U.S. 265, 91 S.Ct.

---

d. The literature about balancing is voluminous. Compare, e.g., Frantz, *The First Amendment in the Balance,* 71 Yale L.J. 1424 (1962); Frantz, *Is the First Amendment Law?—A Reply to Professor Mendelson,* 51 Calif.L.Rev. 729 (1963) with Mendelson, *On the Meaning of the First Amendment: Absolutes in the Balance,* 50 Calif.L.Rev. 821 (1962); Mendelson, *The First Amendment and the Judicial Process: A Reply to Mr. Frantz,* 17 Vand.L.Rev. 479 (1984). For recent criticism of balancing, see Aleinikoff, *Constitutional Law in the Age of Balancing,* 96 Yale L.J. 943 (1987); Nagel, *Constitutional Cultures* (1989); Nagel, *Rationalism in Constitutional Law,* 4 Const.Comm. 9 (1987); Nagel, *The Formulaic Constitution,* 84 Mich.L.Rev. 165 (1985). For a philosophical attack on cost benefit analysis, see Tribe, *Policy Science: Analysis or Ideology?,* 2 Phil. & Pub.Aff. 66 (1972); Tribe, *Technology Assessment and the Fourth Discontinuity: The Limits of Instrumental Rationality,* 46 So.Cal.L.Rev. 617 (1973). For philosophical defenses of balancing, see Schlag, *An Attack on Categorical Approaches to Freedom of Speech,* 30 U.C.L.A.L.Rev. 671 (1983); Shiffrin, *Liberalism, Radicalism, and Legal Scholarship,* 30 U.C.L.A.L.Rev. 1103 (1983) (both resisting any necessary connection between balancing and instrumentalism or cost-benefit analysis). For more doctrinally focused analysis, compare, e.g., Emerson, *First Amendment Doctrine and the Burger Court,* 68 Calif.L.Rev. 422 (1980); Tribe, *Constitutional Calculus: Equal Justice or Economic Efficiency?,* 98 Harv.L.Rev. 592 (1985) with Schauer, *Categories and the First Amendment: A Play in Three Acts,* 34 Vand.L.Rev. 265 (1981); Shiffrin, *The First Amendment and Economic Regulation: Away From a General Theory of the First Amendment,* 78 Nw.U.L.Rev. 1212 (1983); Van Alstyne, *A Graphic Review of the Free Speech Clause,* 70 Calif.L.Rev. 107 (1982).

e. For criticism of *Rosenblatt,* see Note, *The Status/Conduct Continuum: Injecting Rhyme and Reason into Contemporary Public Official Doctrine,* 84 Va.L.Rev 871 (1998).

621, 28 L.Ed.2d 35 (1971) applied *New York Times* to a news column describing a candidate for public office as a "former small-time bootlegger."

(c) *Public figures.* In CURTIS PUB. CO. v. BUTTS and ASSOCIATED PRESS v. WALKER, 388 U.S. 130, 87 S.Ct. 1975, 18 L.Ed.2d 1094 (1967), HARLAN, J., contended that because public figures were not subject to the restraints of the political process, any criticism of them was not akin to seditious libel and was, therefore, a step removed from the central meaning of the first amendment. Nonetheless, he argued that public figure actions should not be left entirely to the vagaries of state defamation law and would have required that public figures show "highly unreasonable conduct constituting an extreme departure from the standards of investigation and reporting ordinarily adhered to by responsible publishers" as a prerequisite to recovery. In response, WARREN, C.J., argued that the inapplicability of the restraints of the political process to public figures underscored the importance for uninhibited debate about their activities since "public opinion may be the only instrument by which society can attempt to influence their conduct." He observed that increasingly "the distinctions between governmental and private sectors are blurred," that public figures, like public officials, "often play an influential role in ordering society," and as a class have a ready access to the mass media "both to influence policy and to counter criticism of their views and activities." He accordingly concluded that the *New York Times* rule should be extended to public figures. Four other justices in *Butts* and *Walker* were willing to go at least as far as Warren, C.J., and subsequent cases have settled on the position that public figures must meet the *New York Times* requirements in order to recover in a defamation action. The critical issues are how to define the concept of public figure and how to apply it in practice. See *Gertz,* infra.

(d) *Private plaintiffs and public issues.* Without deciding whether any first amendment protection should extend to matters not of general or public interest, a plurality led by BRENNAN, J., joined by Burger, C.J., and Blackmun, J., argued in ROSENBLOOM v. METROMEDIA, INC., 403 U.S. 29, 91 S.Ct. 1811, 29 L.Ed.2d 296 (1971), that the *New York Times* rule should be extended to defamatory statements involving matters of public or general interest "without regard to whether the persons involved are famous or anonymous." BLACK, J., would have gone further, opining that the first amendment "does not permit the recovery of libel judgments against the news media even when statements are broadcast with knowledge they are false," and Douglas, J., shared Black, J.'s approach (at least with respect to matters of public interest, although he did not participate in *Rosenbloom.*) WHITE, J., felt that the *New York Times* rule should apply to reporting on the official actions of public servants and to reporting on those involved in or affected by their official action. That principle was broad enough to cover Rosenbloom, a distributor of nudist magazines who had been arrested by the Philadelphia police for distributing obscene materials. The defamatory broadcast wrongly assumed his guilt. Dissenting, Harlan, Stewart and Marshall, JJ., counseled an approach similar to that taken in *Gertz,* infra.

After *Rosenbloom* the lower courts rather uniformly followed the approach taken by the plurality. By 1974, however, the composition of the Court had changed and so had the minds of some of the justices.

C. PRIVATE INDIVIDUALS AND PUBLIC FIGURES

GERTZ v. ROBERT WELCH, INC.

418 U.S. 323, 94 S.Ct. 2997, 41 L.Ed.2d 789 (1974).

MR. JUSTICE POWELL delivered the opinion of the Court.

[Respondent published *American Opinion,* a monthly outlet for the John Birch Society. It published an article falsely stating that Gertz, a lawyer, was the "architect" in a "communist frameup" of a policeman convicted of murdering a youth whose family Gertz represented in resultant civil proceedings, and that Gertz had a "criminal record" and had been an officer in a named "Communist-fronter" organization that advocated violent seizure of our government. In Gertz' libel action there was evidence that *Opinion*'s managing editor did not know the statements were false and had relied on the reputation of the article's author and prior experience with the accuracy of his articles. After a $50,000 verdict for Gertz, the trial court entered judgment n.o.v., concluding that the *New York Times* rule applied to any discussion of a "public issue." The court of appeals affirmed, ruling that the publisher did not have the requisite "awareness of probable falsity." The Court held that *New York Times* did not apply to defamation of private individuals, but remanded for a new trial "because the jury was allowed to impose liability without fault [and] to presume damages without proof of injury."]

II. The principal issue in this case is whether a newspaper or broadcaster that publishes defamatory falsehoods about an individual who is neither a public official nor a public figure may claim a constitutional privilege against liability for the injury inflicted by those statements. * * *

In his opinion for the plurality in *Rosenbloom,* Mr. Justice Brennan took the *Times* privilege one step further [than *Butts* and *Walker*]. He concluded that its protection should extend to defamatory falsehoods relating to private persons if the statements concerned matters of general or public interest. He abjured the suggested distinction between public officials and public figures on the one hand and private individuals on the other. He focused instead on society's interest in learning about certain issues: "If a matter is a subject of public or general interest, it cannot suddenly become less so merely because a private individual is involved or because in some sense the individual did not choose to become involved." Thus, under the plurality opinion, a private citizen involuntarily associated with a matter of general interest has no recourse for injury to his reputation unless he can satisfy the demanding requirements of the *Times* [test].

III.   [Under] the First Amendment there is no such thing as a false idea.[a] However pernicious an opinion may seem, we depend for its correction not on the conscience of the judges and juries but on the competition of other ideas. But there is no constitutional value in false statements of fact. Neither the intentional lie nor the careless error materially advances society's interest in "uninhibited, robust, and wide-open" debate on public issues. * * *

Although the erroneous statement of fact is not worthy of constitutional protection, it is nevertheless inevitable in free debate. [P]unishment of error runs the risk of inducing a cautious and restrictive exercise of the constitutionally guaranteed freedoms of speech and press. [The] First Amendment requires that we protect some falsehood in order to protect speech that matters.

The need to avoid self-censorship by the news media is, however, not the only societal value at issue. [The] legitimate state interest underlying the law of libel is the compensation of individuals for the harm inflicted on them by defamatory falsehoods. We would not lightly require the State to abandon this purpose, for, as Mr. Justice Stewart has reminded us, the individual's right to the protection of his own good name "reflects no more than our basic concept of the essential dignity and worth of every human being—a concept at the root of any decent system of ordered liberty. * * * " *Rosenblatt*.[b]

Some tension necessarily exists between the need for a vigorous and uninhibited press and the legitimate interest in redressing wrongful injury. [In] our continuing effort to define the proper accommodation between these competing concerns, we have been especially anxious to assure to the freedoms of speech and press that "breathing space" essential to their fruitful exercise. To that end this Court has extended a measure of strategic protection to defamatory falsehood.

---

a.   For many years the lower courts took this language seriously and deemed opinion to be absolutely protected (see, e.g., *Ollman v. Evans*, 750 F.2d 970 (D.C.Cir.1984)), but *Milkovich v. Lorain Journal Co.*, 497 U.S. 1, 110 S.Ct. 2695, 111 L.Ed.2d 1 (1990), per Rehnquist, C.J., ultimately denied that there is any "wholesale defamation exception for anything that might be labelled 'opinion.' "For the impact of *Milkovich*, see Sowle, *A Matter of Opinion*, 3 Wm. & Mary L.Rev. 467 (1994); Note, *Eight Years After Milkovich: Applying A Constitutional Privilege for Opinions Under the Wrong Constitution*, 31 Ind. L.Rev. 1107 (1998). On opinion, see Franklin, *Constitutional Libel Law: The Role of Content*, 34 UCLA L.Rev. 1657 (1987); Thomas, *A Pragmatic Approach to Meaning in Defamation Law*, 34 Wake Forest L.Rev. 333 (1999); Shapo, *Editorial: Fact/Opinion = Evidence/Argument*, 91 Nw. U.L. Rev. 1108 (1997).

b.   Stewart, J., continued: "The protection of private personality, like the protection of life itself, is left primarily to the individual States under the Ninth and Tenth Amendments. But this does not mean that the right is entitled to any less recognition by this Court as a basic of our constitutional system." Consider Post, *The Social Foundations of Defamation Law*, 74 Calif.L.Rev. 691, 708 (1986): "[I]t is not immediately clear how reputation, which is social and public, and which resides in the 'common or general estimate of person,' can possibly affect the 'essential dignity' of a person's 'private personality.' The gulf that appears to separate reputation from dignity can be spanned only if defamation law contains an implicit theory of the relationship between the private and public aspects of the self."

The *New York Times* standard defines the level of constitutional protection appropriate to the context of defamation of [public figures and those who hold governmental office]. Plainly many deserving plaintiffs, including some intentionally subjected to injury, will be unable to surmount the barrier of the *New York Times* test. [For] the reasons stated below, we conclude that the state interest in compensating injury to the reputation of private individuals requires that a different rule should obtain with respect to them.

[W]e have no difficulty in distinguishing among defamation plaintiffs. The first remedy of any victim of defamation is self-help—using available opportunities to contradict the lie or correct the error and thereby to minimize its adverse impact on reputation. Public officials and public figures usually enjoy significantly greater access to the channels of effective communication and hence have a more realistic opportunity to counteract false statements than private individuals normally enjoy.[9] Private individuals are therefore more vulnerable to injury, and the state interest in protecting them is correspondingly greater.[c]

More important than the likelihood that private individuals will lack effective opportunities for rebuttal, there is a compelling normative consideration underlying the distinction between public and private defamation plaintiffs. An individual who decides to seek governmental office must accept certain necessary consequences of that involvement in public affairs. He runs the risk of closer public scrutiny than might otherwise be the case. [Those] classed as public figures stand in a similar [position.][d]

9. Of course, an opportunity for rebuttal seldom suffices to undo harm of defamatory falsehood. Indeed, the law of defamation is rooted in our experience that the truth rarely catches up with a lie. But the fact that the self-help remedy of rebuttal, standing alone, is inadequate to its task does not mean that it is irrelevant to our inquiry. [Consider Shiffrin, *Defamatory Non–Media Speech and First Amendment Methodology,* 25 U.C.L.A.L.Rev. 915, 952–53 (1978): "[F]ootnote nine, has seemingly left the first amendment in a peculiar spot. *Gertz* holds that the first amendment offers some protection for defamatory utterances presumably so that our Constitution can continue 'to preserve an uninhibited marketplace of ideas in which truth will ultimately prevail. * * * 'And yet the Court recognizes that 'an opportunity for rebuttal seldom suffices to undo [the] harm of defamatory falsehood,' i.e., truth does not emerge in the marketplace of ideas. Is the Court trapped in an obvious contradiction?"]

c. Suppose otherwise private persons have access to and have freely participated in electronic bulletin boards in which they have been defamed? In this context, should they be regarded as public figures? See Note, *The Gertz Doctrine and Internet Behavior,* 84 Va.L.Rev. 477 (1998); Note, *Defining Cyberlibel: A First Amendment Limit for Libel Suits Against Individuals Arising From Computer Bulletin Board Speech,* 46 Case W.Res.L.Rev. 235 (1995).

d. Consider Bollinger, *Images of a Free Press* 25–26 (1994): "Essentially, the Court has said that, since these individuals have freely chosen a public life, what happens to them is their own doing, just as it is for a man who breaks his leg while hiking in the wilderness. Putting aside for the moment the fact that we also have an interest in encouraging people to enter public affairs, it simply is wrong to suppose that the pain inflicted by defamatory statements about public officials and figures is not our responsibility or concern. It should always be open to people to object to the way the world works under the rules we create, and not be dismissed by the claim that they have chosen to continue living in that world and, therefore, can be taken as having assented to it."

Even if the foregoing generalities do not obtain in every instance, the communications media are entitled to act on the assumption that public officials and public figures have voluntarily exposed themselves to increased risk of injury from defamatory falsehoods concerning them. No such assumption is justified with respect to a private individual. He has not accepted public office nor assumed an "influential role in ordering society." *Butts.* He has relinquished no part of his interest in the protection of his own good name, and consequently he has a more compelling call on the courts for redress of injury inflicted by defamatory falsehood. Thus, private individuals are not only more vulnerable to injury than public officials and public figures; they are also more deserving of recovery.

For these reasons we conclude that the States should retain substantial latitude in their efforts to enforce a legal remedy for defamatory falsehood injurious to the reputation of a private individual. The extension of the *Times* test proposed by the *Rosenbloom* plurality would abridge this legitimate state interest to a degree that we find unacceptable. And it would occasion the additional difficulty of forcing state and federal judges to decide on an ad hoc basis which publications address issues of "general or public interest" and which do not—to determine, in the words of Mr. Justice Marshall, "what information is relevant to self-government." *Rosenbloom.* We doubt the wisdom of committing this task to the conscience of judges. [The] "public or general interest" test for determining the applicability of the *Times* standard to private defamation actions inadequately serves both of the competing values at stake. On the one hand, a private individual whose reputation is injured by defamatory falsehood that does concern an issue of public or general interest has no recourse unless he can meet the rigorous requirements of *Times*. This is true despite the factors that distinguish the state interest in compensating private individuals from the analogous interest involved in the context of public persons. On the other hand, a publisher or broadcaster of a defamatory error which a court deems unrelated to an issue of public or general interest may be held liable in damages even if it took every reasonable precaution to ensure the accuracy of its assertions. And liability may far exceed compensation for any actual injury to the plaintiff, for the jury may be permitted to presume damages without proof of loss and even to award punitive damages.

We hold that, so long as they do not impose liability without fault, the States may define for themselves the appropriate standard of liability for a publisher or broadcaster of defamatory falsehood injurious to a private individual. This approach provides a more equitable boundary between the competing concerns involved here. It recognizes the strength of the legitimate state interest in compensating private individuals for wrongful injury to reputation, yet shields the press and broadcast media from the rigors of strict liability for defamation. At least this conclusion obtains where, as here, the substance of the defamatory statement "makes substantial danger to reputation apparent." *Butts.* This phrase places in perspective the conclusion we announce today. Our inquiry would involve considerations somewhat different from those discussed above if a State purported to condition civil liability on a factual misstatement whose content did not warn a reasonably prudent editor or broadcaster of its defamatory potential. Cf. *Time, Inc. v. Hill* [Part D infra]. Such a case is not now before us, and we intimate no view as to its proper resolution.

IV.   [T]he strong and legitimate state interest in compensating private individuals for injury to reputation [extends] no further than compensation for actual injury. For the reasons stated below, we hold that the States may not permit recovery of presumed or punitive damages, at least when liability is not based on a showing of knowledge of falsity or reckless disregard for the truth.

The common law of defamation is an oddity of tort [law]. Juries may award substantial sums as compensation for supposed damage to reputation without any proof that such harm actually occurred. [This] unnecessarily compounds the potential of any system of liability for defamatory falsehood to inhibit the vigorous exercise of First Amendment freedoms [and] invites juries to punish unpopular opinion rather than to compensate individuals for injury sustained by the publication of a false fact. More to the point, the States have no substantial interest in securing for plaintiffs such as this petitioner gratuitous awards of money damages far in excess of any actual injury.

We would not, of course, invalidate state law simply because we doubt its wisdom, but here we are attempting to reconcile state law with a competing interest grounded in the constitutional command of the First Amendment. It is therefore appropriate to require that state remedies for defamatory falsehood reach no farther than is necessary to protect the legitimate interest involved. It is necessary to restrict defamation plaintiffs who do not prove knowledge of falsity or reckless disregard for the truth to compensation for actual injury. We need not define "actual injury," as trial courts have wide experience in framing appropriate jury instructions in tort action. Suffice it to say that actual injury is not limited to out-of-pocket loss. Indeed, the more customary types of actual harm inflicted by defamatory falsehood include impairment of reputation and standing in the community, personal humiliation, and mental anguish and suffering. Of course, juries must be limited by appropriate instructions, and all awards must be supported by competent evidence concerning the injury, although there need be no evidence which assigns an actual dollar value to the injury.

We also find no justification for allowing awards of punitive damages against publishers and broadcasters held liable under state-defined standards of liability for defamation. In most jurisdictions jury discretion over the amounts awarded is limited only by the gentle rule that they not be excessive. Consequently, juries assess punitive damages in wholly unpredictable amounts bearing no necessary relation to the actual harm caused. And they remain free to use their discretion selectively to punish expressions of unpopular views. [J]ury discretion to award punitive damages unnecessarily exacerbates the danger of media self-censorship; [punitive] damages are wholly irrelevant to the state interest that justifies a negligence standard for private defamation actions. They are not compensation for injury. Instead, they are private fines levied by civil juries to punish reprehensible conduct and to deter its future occurrence. In short, the private defamation plaintiff who establishes liability under a less demanding standard than that stated by *Times* may recover only such damages as are sufficient to compensate him for actual injury.[e]

V.   Notwithstanding our refusal to extend the *New York Times* privilege to defamation of private individuals, respondent contends that we should affirm the judgment below on the ground that petitioner is [a] public figure. [That] designation may rest on either of two alternative bases. In some instances an individual may achieve such pervasive fame or notoriety that he becomes a public figure for all purposes and in all contexts. More commonly, an individual voluntarily injects himself or is drawn into a particular public controversy and thereby becomes a public figure for a limited range of issues. In either case such persons assume special prominence in the resolution of public questions.

Petitioner has long been active in community and professional affairs. He has served as an officer of local civic groups and of various professional organizations, and he has published several books and articles on legal subjects. Although petitioner was consequently well known in some circles, he had achieved no general fame or notoriety in the community. None of the prospective jurors called at the trial had ever heard of petitioner prior to this litigation, and respondent offered no proof that this response was atypical of the local population. We would not lightly assume that a citizen's participation in community and professional affairs rendered him a public figure for all purposes. Absent clear evidence of general fame or notoriety in the community, and pervasive involvement in the affairs of society, an individual should not be deemed a public personality for all aspects of his life. It is preferable to reduce the public-figure question to a more meaningful context by looking to the nature and extent of an individual's participation in the particular controversy giving rise to the defamation.

In this context it is plain that petitioner was not a public figure. He played a minimal role at the coroner's inquest, and his participation related solely to his representation of a private client. He took no part in the criminal prosecution of Officer Nuccio. Moreover, he never discussed either the criminal or civil litigation with the press and was never quoted as having done so. He plainly did not thrust himself into the vortex of this public issue, nor did he engage the public's attention in an attempt to influence its outcome. We are persuaded that the trial court did not err in refusing to characterize petitioner as a public figure for the purpose of this litigation.

---

e. On remand, Gertz was awarded $100,000 in compensatory damages and $300,000 in punitive damages. In the prior trial, he had been awarded only $50,000 in damages.

We therefore conclude that the *New York Times* standard is inapplicable to this case and that the trial court erred in entering judgment for respondent. Because the jury was allowed to impose liability without fault and was permitted to presume damages without proof of injury, a new trial is necessary.[f]

MR. JUSTICE BRENNAN, dissenting.

[I] adhere to my view expressed in *Rosenbloom* that we strike the proper accommodation between avoidance of media self-censorship and protection of individual reputations only when we require States to apply the *New York Times* knowing-or-reckless-falsity standard in civil libel actions concerning media reports of the involvement of private individuals in events of public or general interest. [Although] acknowledging that First Amendment values are of no less significance when media reports concern private persons' involvement in matters of public concern, the Court refuses to provide, in such cases, the same level of constitutional protection that has been afforded the media in the context of defamation of public [persons].

While [the Court's] arguments are forcefully and eloquently presented, I cannot accept them for the reasons I stated in *Rosenbloom:* "The *New York Times* standard was applied to libel of a public official or public figure to give effect to the Amendment's function to encourage ventilation of public issues, not because the public official has any less interest in protecting his reputation than an individual in private life. [In] the vast majority of libels involving public officials or public figures, the ability to respond through the media will depend on the same complex factor on which the ability of a private individual depends: the unpredictable event of the media's continuing interest in the story. Thus the unproved, and highly improbable, generalization that an as yet [not fully defined] class of 'public figures' involved in matters of public concern will be better able to respond through the media than private individuals also involved in such matters seems too insubstantial a reed on which to rest a constitutional distinction."

[Adoption], by many States, of a reasonable care standard in cases where private individuals are involved in matters of public interest—the probable result of today's decision—[will] lead to self-censorship since publishers will be required carefully to weigh a myriad of uncertain factors

---

f. Blackmun, J., concurred: "[Although I joined Brennan, J.'s plurality opinion in *Rosenbloom,* from which the Court's opinion in the present case departs, I join] the Court's opinion and its judgment for two reasons:

"1. By removing the spectres of presumed and punitive damages in the absence of *Times* malice, the Court eliminates significant and powerful motives for self-censorship that otherwise are present in the traditional libel action. By so doing, the Court leaves what should prove to be sufficient and adequate breathing space for a vigorous press. What the Court has done, I believe, will have little, if any, practical effect on the functioning of responsible journalism.

"2. The Court was sadly fractionated in *Rosenbloom.* A result of that kind inevitably leads to uncertainty. I feel that it is of profound importance for the Court to come to rest in the defamation area and to have a clearly defined majority position that eliminates the unsureness engendered by *Rosenbloom's* diversity. If my vote were not needed to create a majority, I would adhere to my prior view. A definitive ruling, however, is paramount."

before publication. The reasonable care standard is "elusive," *Time, Inc. v. Hill;* it saddles the press with "the intolerable burden of guessing how a jury might assess the reasonableness of steps taken by it to verify the accuracy of every reference to a name, picture or portrait." Ibid. Under a reasonable care regime, publishers and broadcasters will have to make pre-publication judgments about juror assessment of such diverse considerations as the size, operating procedures, and financial condition of the news gathering system, as well as the relative costs and benefits of instituting less frequent and more costly reporting at a higher level of accuracy. See 85 Harv.L.Rev. 228 (1971). [And] most hazardous, the flexibility which inheres in the reasonable care standard will create the danger that a jury will convert it into "an instrument for the suppression of those 'vehement, caustic, and sometimes unpleasantly sharp attacks,' [which] must be protected if the guarantees of the First and Fourteenth Amendments are to prevail." *Monitor Patriot Co.*

[A] jury's latitude to impose liability for want of due care poses a far greater threat of suppressing unpopular views than does a possible recovery of presumed or punitive damages. Moreover, the Court's broad-ranging examples of "actual injury" [allow] a jury bent on punishing expression of unpopular views a formidable weapon for doing so. [E]ven a limitation of recovery to "actual injury"—however much it reduces the size or frequency of recoveries—will not provide the necessary elbow room for First Amendment expression. "[The] very possibility of having to engage in litigation, an expensive and protracted process, is threat enough to cause discussion and debate to 'steer far wider of the unlawful zone' thereby keeping protected discussion from public cognizance. * * * " *Rosenbloom.*

[I] reject the argument that my *Rosenbloom* view improperly commits to judges the task of determining what is and what is not an issue of "general or public interest."[3] I noted in *Rosenbloom* that performance of this task would not always be easy. But surely the courts, the ultimate arbiters of all disputes concerning clashes of constitutional values, would only be perform-

---

3. The Court, taking a novel step, would not limit application of First Amendment protection to private libels involving issues of general or public interest, but would forbid the States from imposing liability without fault in any case where the substance of the defamatory statement made substantial danger to reputation apparent. As in *Rosenbloom,* I would leave open the question of what constitutional standard, if any, applies when defamatory falsehoods are published or broadcast concerning either a private or public person's activities not within the scope of the general or public interest.

Parenthetically, my Brother White argues that the Court's view and mine will prevent a plaintiff—unable to demonstrate some degree of fault—from vindicating his reputation by securing a judgment that the publi-

cation was false. This argument overlooks the possible enactment of statutes, not requiring proof of fault, which provide for an action for retraction or for publication of a court's determination of falsity if the plaintiff is able to demonstrate that false statements have been published concerning his activities. Cf. Note, *Vindication of the Reputation of a Public Official,* 80 Harv.L.Rev. 1730, 1739–1747 (1967). Although it may be that questions could be raised concerning the constitutionality of such statutes, certainly nothing I have said today (and, as I read the Court's opinion, nothing said there) should be read to imply that a private plaintiff, unable to prove fault, must inevitably be denied the opportunity to secure a judgment upon the truth or falsity of statements published about him.

ing one of their traditional functions in undertaking this duty. [The] public interest is necessarily broad; any residual self-censorship that may result from the uncertain contours of the "general or public interest" concept should be of far less concern to publishers and broadcasters than that occasioned by state laws imposing liability for negligent falsehood. * * *g

MR. JUSTICE WHITE, dissenting.

[T]he Court, in a few printed pages, has federalized major aspects of libel law by declaring unconstitutional in important respects the prevailing defamation law in all or most of the 50 States. * * *

I. [These] radical changes in the law and severe invasions of the prerogatives of the States [should] at least be shown to be required by the First Amendment or necessitated by our present circumstances. Neither has been [demonstrated.]

The central meaning of *New York Times,* and for me the First Amendment as it relates to libel laws, is that seditious libel—criticism of government and public officials—falls beyond the police power of the State. In a democratic society such as ours, the citizen has the privilege of criticizing his government and its officials. But neither *New York Times* nor its progeny suggest that the First Amendment intended in all circumstances to deprive the private citizen of his historic recourse to redress published falsehoods damaging to reputation or that, contrary to history and precedent, the amendment should now be so interpreted. Simply put, the First Amendment did not confer a "license to defame the citizen." Douglas, *The Right of the People* 38 (1958).

[T]he law has heretofore put the risk of falsehood on the publisher where the victim is a private citizen and no grounds of special privilege are invoked. The Court would now shift this risk to the victim, even though he has done nothing to invite the calumny, is wholly innocent of fault, and is helpless to avoid his injury. I doubt that jurisprudential resistance to liability without fault is sufficient ground for employing the First Amendment to revolutionize the law of libel, and in my view, that body of legal rules poses no realistic threat to the press and its service to the public. The press today is vigorous and robust. To me, it is quite incredible to suggest that threats of libel suits from private citizens are causing the press to refrain from publishing the truth. I know of no hard facts to support that proposition, and the Court furnishes none.

g. Douglas, J., dissented, objecting to "continued recognition of the possibility of state libel suits for public discussion of public issues" as diluting first amendment protection. He added: "Since this case involves a discussion of public affairs, I need not decide at this point whether the First Amendment prohibits all libel actions. 'An unconditional right to say what one pleases about public affairs is what I consider to be *the minimum guarantee* of the First Amendment.' *New York Times* (Black, J., concurring) (emphasis added). But 'public affairs' includes a great deal more than merely political affairs. Matters of science, economics, business, art, literature, etc., are all matters of interest to the general public. Indeed, any matter of sufficient general interest to prompt media coverage may be said to be a public affair. Certainly police killings, 'Communist conspiracies,' and the like qualify."

[I]f the Court's principal concern is to protect the communications industry from large libel judgments, it would appear that its new requirements with respect to general and punitive damages would be ample protection. Why it also feels compelled to escalate the threshold standard of liability I cannot fathom, particularly when this will eliminate in many instances the plaintiff's possibility of securing a judicial determination that the damaging publication was indeed false, whether or not he is entitled to recover money damages. [I] find it unacceptable to distribute the risk in this manner and force the wholly innocent victim to bear the injury; for, as between the two, the defamer is the only culpable party. It is he who circulated a falsehood that he was not required to publish. * * *[h]

V.   [I] fail to see how the quality or quantity of public debate will be promoted by further emasculation of state libel laws for the benefit of the news media.[41] If anything, this trend may provoke a new and radical imbalance in the communications process. Cf. Barron, *Access to the Press—A New First Amendment Right,* 80 Harv.L.Rev. 1641, 1657 (1967). It is not at all inconceivable that virtually unrestrained defamatory remarks about private citizens will discourage them from speaking out and concerning themselves with social problems. This would turn the First Amendment on its head. Note, *The Scope of First Amendment Protection for Good–Faith Defamatory Error,* 75 Yale L.J. 642, 649 (1966). * * *[i]

Notes and Questions

1.   *Gertz and Meiklejohn.* By affording some constitutional protection to all media defamatory speech whether or not it relates to public issues, does the Court squarely reject the Meiklejohn theory of the first amendment? Consider Shiffrin, *Defamatory Non–Media Speech and First Amendment Methodology,* 25 U.C.L.A.L.Rev. 915, 929 (1978): "It may be that the Court has refused to adopt the Meiklejohn 'public issues' test not because it believes that private speech (i.e., speech unrelated to public issues) is as

---

h. White, J., also argued strongly against the Court's rulings on actual and punitive damages.

41. Cf. Pedrick, *Freedom of the Press and the Law of Libel: The Modern Revised Translation,* 49 Cornell L.Q. 581, 601–02 (1964): "A great many forces in our society operate to determine the extent to which men are free in fact to express their ideas. Whether there is a privilege for good faith defamatory misstatements on matters of public concern or whether there is strict liability for such statements may not greatly affect the course of public discussion. How different has life been in those states which heretofore followed the majority rule imposing strict liability for misstatements of fact defaming public figures from life in

the minority states where the good faith privilege held sway?" See also Emerson, *The System of Freedom of Expression* 519 (1970): "[O]n the whole the role of libel law in the system of freedom of expression has been relatively minor and essentially erratic."

i. Burger, C.J., also dissented: "I am frank to say I do not know the parameters of a 'negligence' doctrine as applied to the news media. [I] would prefer to allow this area of law to continue to evolve as it has up to now with respect to private citizens rather then embark on a new doctrinal theory which has no jurisprudential ancestry. [I would remand] for reinstatement of the verdict of the jury and the entry of an appropriate judgment on that verdict."

important as public speech but rather because it doubts its ability to distinguish unerringly between the two. [B]y placing all defamatory media speech within the scope of the first amendment, the Court may believe it has protected relatively little non-public speech. On the other hand, [putting aside comments about public officials and public figures], the Court may fear that if *Gertz* were extended to non-media speech, the result would be to protect much speech having nothing to do with public issues, while safeguarding relatively little that does."[j] For consideration of the distinction between public and private speech and of the media non–media distinction, see *Greenmoss*, p. 297 infra. See also *Philadelphia Newspapers, Inc. v. Hepps,* 475 U.S. 767, 106 S.Ct. 1558, 89 L.Ed.2d 783 (1986) (private figure plaintiff has burden of showing falsity at least when issue is of "public concern" and leaving open the question of what standards apply to non-media defendants).[k]

2. *Public figures.* TIME, INC. v. FIRESTONE, 424 U.S. 448, 96 S.Ct. 958, 47 L.Ed.2d 154 (1976), per REHNQUIST, J., declared that persons who have not assumed a role of especial prominence in the affairs of society are not public figures unless they have " 'thrust themselves to the forefront of particular public controversies in order to influence the resolution of the issues involved.' "It held that a divorce proceeding involving one of America's wealthiest industrial families and containing testimony concerning the extramarital sexual activities of the parties did not involve a "public controversy," "even though the marital difficulties of extremely wealthy individuals may be of interest to some portion of the reading public." Nor was the filing of a divorce suit, or the holding of press conferences ("to satisfy inquiring reporters") thought to be freely publicizing the issues in order to influence their outcome. Recall *Gertz* doubted the wisdom of forcing judges to determine on an ad hoc basis what is and is not of "general or public interest." Is there a basis for distinguishing a public figure test requiring judges to determine on an ad hoc basis what is or is not a "public controversy"?

What does it mean to assume a role of especial prominence in the affairs of society? If Elmer Gertz, a prominent Illinois attorney, does not qualify, does David Letterman? Julia Child? Mr. Rogers? If so, is the slide from

j. For the claim that speech on private matters deserves as much protection as speech on public matters, see id. at 938–42. For discussion of the different meanings of public and private speech, see Schauer, *"Private" Speech and the "Private" Forum: Givhan v. Western Line School District,* 1979 Sup.Ct.Rev. 217. For additional commentary on the question of whether *Gertz* should extend to non-media defendants see, e.g., Hill, *Defamation and Privacy Under the First Amendment,* 76 Colum.L.Rev. 1205 (1976); Lange, *The Speech and Press Clauses,* 23 U.C.L.A.L.Rev. 77 (1975); Nimmer, *Is Freedom of the Press a Redundancy: What Does It Add to Freedom of Speech?,* 26 Hast.L.J. 639 (1975); Van Alstyne, Com-

ment: *The Hazards to the Press of Claiming a "Preferred Position,"* 28 Hast.L.J. 761 (1977); Note, *Mediaocracy and Mistrust: Extending New York Times Defamation Protection to Nonmedia Defendants,* 95 Harv.L.Rev. 1876 (1982).

k. The Communications Decency Act immunizes those who manage electronic bulletin boards and the like from defamation liability for information provided by another. So the *Los Angeles Times* could be liable for defamation published on the letters page of its newspaper, but could not be liable for the same letter if it were published on its web site. Constitutional? See *Zeran v. America Online, Inc.,* 129 F.3d 327 (4th Cir.1997).

public officials to television chefs and personalities too precipitous because the latter "have little, if any effect, on questions of politics, public policy, or the organization and determination of societal affairs"? See Schauer, *Public Figures,* 25 Wm. & Mary L.Rev. 905 (1984). Consider Failinger, *Five Modern Notions in Search of an Author: The Ideology of the Intimate Society in Constitutional Speech Law,* 30 U.Tol. L.Rev. 251, 299 (1999): "[T]he Court merely adds fuel to the cultural fire created by [the] 'star' system—people who want to know intimate details that confirm their trust in those selected by the public to be 'stars,' and yet, they have a secret desire to know 'dirt' on those same persons to justify their beliefs that people just like themselves have been randomly enriched with fame, power, and wealth. [T]his politics of resentment, parlay[s] the shame and envy of those who find themselves in a lower-than-deserved status into a rising backlash against those who have unfairly taken 'their' place. Thus, protection of the cult of personality in the Court's speech doctrine only serves to fuel the fires of self-interested, mean-spirited public life." On the other hand, would a narrow definition of public figures discriminate in favor of orthodox media and discourage attempts "to illuminate previously unexposed aspects of society." Does the negligence concept itself threaten to discriminate "against media or outlets whose philosophies and methods deviate from those of the mainstream"? See generally Anderson, *Libel and Press Self–Censorship,* 53 Tex.L.Rev. 422, 453, 455 (1975).

3. *Taking reputation too seriously?* Consider Smolla, *Suing the Press* 257 (1986): "[I]f we take the libel suit too seriously, we are in danger of raising our collective cultural sensitivity to reputation to unhealthy levels. We are in danger of surrendering a wonderful part of our national identity— our strapping, scrambling, free-wheeling individualism, in danger of becoming less American, less robust, wild-eyed, pluralistic and free, and more decorous, image-conscious, and narcissistic. The media is itself partly to blame for this direction, and it would be dangerous to release it totally from the important check and balance that the libel laws provide. But in the United States, the balance that must be struck between reputation and expression should never be tilted too far against expression, for the right to defiantly, robustly, and irreverently speak one's mind just because it is one's mind is quintessentially what it means to be an American."[1]

1. For historical perspective on the social messages communicated by defamation law, see Rosenberg, *Protecting the Best Men* (1986). For valuable material on how the *Gertz* rules work in practice, Bezanson, *The Developing Law of Editorial Judgment,* 78 Nebraska L.Rev. 754 (1999); Bezanson, Cranberg & Soloski, *Libel Law and the Press: Myth and Reality (1987);* Murchison, Soloski, Bezanson, Cranberg, & Wissler, *Sullivan's Paradox: The Emergence of Judicial Standards of Journalism,* 73 N.C.L.Rev. 7 (1994); Kaufman, *Libel 1980–85: Promises and Realities,* 90 Dick.L.Rev. 545 (1985); Franklin, *Suing Media for Libel: A Litigation Study,* 1981 Am.B.Found. Res.J. 795; Franklin, *Winners and Losers and Why: A Study of Defamation Litigation,* 1980 Am.B.Found.Res.J. 455. For commentary suggesting reforms, see *Annenberg Washington Program, Libel Law* (1988). See also Ackerman, *Bringing Coherence to Defamation Law Through Uniform Legislation: The Search for an Elegant Solution,* 72 N.C.L.Rev. 291 (1994); Anderson, *Is Libel Law Worth Reforming?,* 140 U.Pa.L.Rev. 487 (1991); Bezanson, *The Libel Tort Today,* 45 Wash. & Lee L.Rev. 535 (1988);

D. FALSE LIGHT PRIVACY

TIME, INC. v. HILL, 385 U.S. 374, 87 S.Ct. 534, 17 L.Ed.2d 456 (1967), applied the *New York Times* knowing and reckless falsity standard to a right of privacy action for publishing an erroneous but not defamatory report about private individuals involved in an incident of public interest. In 1952 the Hill family was the subject of national news coverage when held hostage in its home for 19 hours by three escaped convicts who treated the family courteously with no violence. This incident formed part of the basis for a novel, later made into a play, which involved violence against the hostage family. In 1955 *Life* published a picture story that showed the play's cast reenacting scenes from the play in the former Hill home. According to *Life,* the play "inspired by the [Hill] family's experience" "is a heartstopping account of how a family arose to heroism in a crisis." Hill secured a $30,000 judgment for compensatory damages against the publisher under the New York Right to Privacy statute, which, as interpreted, made truth a complete defense to actions based on "newsworthy people or events" but gave a right of action to one whose name or picture was the subject of an article containing "material and substantial falsification." The Court, per BREN-NAN, J., reversed, holding that "the constitutional protections for speech and press preclude the application of the New York statute to redress false reports of matters of public interest in the absence of proof that the defendant published the report with knowledge of its falsity or in reckless disregard of the truth," and that the instructions did not adequately advise the jury that a verdict for Hill required a finding of knowing or reckless falsity: "The guarantees for speech and press are not the preserve of political expression or comment upon public affairs, essential as those are to healthy government. One need only pick up any newspaper or magazine to comprehend the vast range of published matter which exposes persons to public view, both private citizens and public officials. Exposure of the self to others in varying degrees is a concomitant of life in a civilized community. The risk of this exposure is an essential incident of life in a society which places a primary value on freedom of speech and press. [We] have no doubt that the subject of the *Life* article, the opening of a new play linked to an actual incident, is a

Dienes, *Libel Reform: An Appraisal,* 23 U.Mich.J.L.Ref. 1 (1989); Epstein, *Was New York Times v. Sullivan Wrong?,* 53 U.Chi. L.Rev. 782 (1986); Fein, *New York Times v. Sullivan: An Obstacle to Enlightened Public Discourse and Government Responsiveness to the People* (1984); Franklin, *Public Officials and Libel: In Defense of New York Times Co. v. Sullivan,* 5 Cardozo Arts & Ent.L.J. 51 (1986); Franklin, *A Declaratory Judgment Alternative to Current Libel Law,* 74 Calif.L.Rev. 809 (1986); Ingber, *Defamation: A Conflict Between Reason and Decen-* cy, 65 Va.L.Rev. 785 (1979); Leval, *The No–Money, No–Fault Libel Suit: Keeping Sullivan in Its Proper Place,* 101 Harv.L.Rev. 1287 (1988); Levine, *Book Review,* 56 G.W.U.L.Rev. 246 (1987); Lewis, *New York Times v. Sullivan Reconsidered: Time to Return to "The Central Meaning of the First Amendment,"* 83 Colum.L.Rev. 603 (1983); Martin, *The Role of Retraction in Defamation Suits,* 1993 U.Chi.Legal F. 293; Schauer, *Uncoupling Free Speech,* 92 Colum.L.Rev. 1321 (1992); Smolla, *Let the Author Beware: The Rejuvenation of the American Law of Libel,* 132 U.Pa.L.Rev. 1 (1983).

matter of public interest. 'The line between the informing and the entertaining is too elusive for the protection of [freedom of the press.]' Erroneous statement is no less inevitable in such case than in the case of comment upon public affairs, and in both, if innocent or merely negligent, '[it] must be protected if the freedoms of expression are to have the "breathing space" that they "need [to] survive".' [*New York Times*.] We create a grave risk of serious impairment of the indispensable service of a free press in a free society if we saddle the press with the impossible burden of verifying to a certainty the facts associated in news articles with a person's name, picture or portrait, particularly as related to non-defamatory matter. Even negligence would be a most elusive standard, especially when the content of the speech itself affords no warning of prospective harm to another through falsity. A negligence test would place on the press the intolerable burden of guessing how a jury might assess the reasonableness of steps taken by it to verify the accuracy of every reference to a name, picture or [portrait].

"We find applicable here the standard of knowing or reckless falsehood not through blind application of *New York Times,* relating solely to libel actions by public officials, but only upon consideration of the factors which arise in the particular context of the application of the New York statute in cases involving private individuals."

BLACK, J., joined by Douglas, J., concurred in reversal on the grounds stated in the Brennan opinion "in order for the Court to be able at this time to agree on an opinion in this important case based on the prevailing constitutional doctrine expressed in *New York Times,*" but reaffirmed their belief that the "malicious," "reckless disregard of the truth" and "knowing and reckless falsity" exceptions were impermissible "abridgments" of freedom of expression. DOUGLAS, J., also filed a separate concurrence, deeming it "irrelevant to talk of any right of privacy in this context. Here a private person is catapulted into the news by events over which he had no control. He and his activities are then in the public domain as fully as the matters at issue in *New York Times.* Such privacy as a person normally has ceases when his life has ceased to be private."

HARLAN, J., concurring in part and dissenting in part, would have made the test of liability negligence, rather than the *New York Times* "reckless falsity": "It would be unreasonable to assume that Mr. Hill could find a forum for making a successful refutation of the *Life* material or that the public's interest in it would be sufficient for the truth to win out by comparison as it might in that area of discussion central to a free society. Thus the state interest in encouraging careful checking and preparation of published material is far stronger than in *Times.* The dangers of unchallengeable untruth are far too well documented to be summarily dismissed.

"Second, there is a vast difference in the state interest in protecting individuals like Mr. Hill from irresponsibly prepared publicity and the state interest in similar protection for a public official. In *Times* we acknowledged public officials to be a breed from whom hardiness to exposure to charges, innuendos, and criticisms might be demanded and who voluntarily assumed the risk of such things by entry into the public arena. But Mr. Hill came to public attention through an unfortunate circumstance not of his making rather than his voluntary actions and he can in no sense be considered to have 'waived' any protection the State might justifiably afford him from irresponsible publicity. Not being inured to the vicissitudes of journalistic scrutiny such an individual is more easily injured and his means of self-defense are more limited. The public is less likely to view with normal skepticism what is written about him because it is not accustomed to seeing his name in the press and expects only a disinterested report.

"The coincidence of these factors in this situation leads me to the view that a State should be free to hold the press to a duty of making a reasonable investigation of the underlying facts and limiting itself to 'fair comment' on the materials so gathered. Theoretically, of course, such a rule might slightly limit press discussion of matters touching individuals like Mr. Hill. But, from a pragmatic standpoint, until now the press, at least in New York, labored under the more exacting handicap of the existing New York privacy law and has certainly remained robust. Other professional activity of great social value is carried on under a duty of reasonable care and there is no reason to suspect the press would be less hardy than medical practitioners or attorneys."[a]

Notes and Questions

1. Compare ZACCHINI v. SCRIPPS–HOWARD BROADCASTING CO., 433 U.S. 562, 97 S.Ct. 2849, 53 L.Ed.2d 965 (1977): Zacchini performed as a "human cannonball," being shot from a cannon into a net some 200 feet away. Without Zacchini's permission to film or broadcast his act, Scripps–Howard obtained and broadcast the tape of his "shot" on the news. The Ohio Supreme Court held the telecast was protected under *Time, Inc. v. Hill* as a newsworthy event. The Court, per WHITE, J., reversed. *Hill* was distinguishable because Zacchini's claim was based not on privacy or reputation but "in protecting the proprietary interest," an interest "closely analogous to the goals of patent and copyright law." Unlike *Hill,* the issue was not whether Zacchini's act would be available to the public: "[T]he only question is who gets to do the publishing."[b]

2. Does *Hill* survive *Gertz?* Consider the following assertion: "In *Hill* and *Gertz* the same class of plaintiffs have to meet different constitutional

a. Fortas, J., joined by Warren, C.J., and Clark, J., dissented, because "the jury instructions, although [not] a textbook model, satisfied [the *New York Times*] standard." For cogent commentary concerning false light privacy, see Schwartz, *Explaining and Justifying a Limited Tort of False Light Invasion of Privacy,* 41 Case West. L.Rev. 886 (1991).

b. Powell, J., joined by Brennan and Marshall, JJ., dissented, observing that there was no showing that the broadcast was a "subterfuge or cover for private or commercial exploitation." Stevens, J., dissented on procedural grounds.

standards in order to recover. Only the name of the tort has changed. This makes no sense." Is the state interest significantly different in *Gertz* than in *Hill*? Should it matter whether the statement at issue would appear innocuous to a reasonable editor? Offensive? See Zimmerman, *False Light Invasion of Privacy: The Light that Failed,* 64 N.Y.U.L.Rev. 364 (1989).

3. *False news.* Should injury to any particular person be a prerequisite to state regulation of false publications? Consider *Keeton v. Hustler Magazine, Inc.,* 465 U.S. 770, 104 S.Ct. 1473, 79 L.Ed.2d 790 (1984): "False statements of fact harm both the subject of the falsehood *and* the readers of the statement. New Hampshire may rightly employ its libel laws to discourage the deception of its citizens." Could New Hampshire make it a criminal offense to publish false statements with knowledge of their falsity without any requirement of injury to any particular person? See Zimmerman *supra.*

E. EMOTIONAL DISTRESS

HUSTLER MAGAZINE v. FALWELL, 485 U.S. 46, 108 S.Ct. 876, 99 L.Ed.2d 41 (1988), per Rehnquist, C.J., held that public figures and public officials offended by a mass media parody could not recover for the tort of intentional infliction of emotional distress without a showing of *New York Times* malice. Parodying a series of liquor advertisements in which celebrities speak about their "first time," the editors of *Hustler* chose plaintiff Jerry Falwell (a nationally famous minister, host of a nationally syndicated television show, and founder of the Moral Majority political organization) "as the featured celebrity and drafted an alleged 'interview' with him in which he states that his 'first time' was during a drunken incestuous rendezvous with his mother in an outhouse. The *Hustler* parody portrays [Falwell] and his mother[a] 'as drunk and immoral,' and suggests that [Falwell] is a hypocrite who preaches only when he is drunk. In small print at the bottom of the page, the ad contains the disclaimer, 'ad parody—not to be taken seriously.' The magazine's table of contents also lists the ad as 'Fiction; Ad and Personality Parody.' * * *

"This case presents us with a novel question involving First Amendment limitations upon a State's authority to protect its citizens from the intentional infliction of emotional distress.[3] We must decide whether a public figure may recover damages for emotional harm caused by the publication of an ad parody offensive to him, and doubtless gross and repugnant in the eyes of most. [Falwell] would have us find that a State's interest in protecting public figures from emotional distress is sufficient to deny First Amendment

---

a. Falwell's mother was not a plaintiff. What result if she were?

3. Under Virginia law, in an action for intentional infliction of emotional distress a plaintiff must show that the defendant's conduct (1) is intentional or reckless; (2) offends generally accepted standards of decency or morality; (3) is causally connected with the plaintiff's emotional distress; and (4) caused emotional distress that was severe.

protection to speech that is patently offensive and is intended to inflict emotional injury, even when that speech could not reasonably have been interpreted as stating actual facts about the public figure involved. * * *

"In [Falwell's] view, [so] long as the utterance was intended to inflict emotional distress, was outrageous, and did in fact inflict serious emotional distress, it is of no constitutional import whether the statement was a fact or an opinion, or whether it was true or false. It is the intent to cause injury that is the gravamen of the tort, and the State's interest in preventing emotional harm simply outweighs whatever interest a speaker may have in speech of this type.

"Generally speaking the law does not regard the intent to inflict emotional distress as one which should receive much solicitude, and it is quite understandable that most if not all jurisdictions have chosen to make it civilly culpable where the conduct in question is sufficiently 'outrageous.' But in the world of debate about public affairs, many things done with motives that are less than admirable are protected by the First Amendment. '[Debate] on public issues will not be uninhibited if the speaker must run the risk that it will be proved in court that he spoke out of hatred; even if he did speak out of hatred, utterances honestly believed contribute to the free interchange of ideas and the ascertainment of truth.' *Garrison.* Thus while such a bad motive may be deemed controlling for purposes of tort liability in other areas of the law, we think the First Amendment prohibits such a result in the area of public debate about public figures.

"Were we to hold otherwise, there can be little doubt that political cartoonists and satirists would be subjected to damage awards without any showing that their work falsely defamed its subject. * * *

"[Falwell] contends, however, that the caricature in question here was so 'outrageous' as to distinguish it from more traditional political cartoons. There is no doubt that the caricature of [Falwell] and his mother published in Hustler is at best a distant cousin of [traditional] political cartoons * * * and a rather poor relation at that. If it were possible by laying down a principled standard to separate the one from the other, public discourse would probably suffer little or no harm. But we doubt that there is any such standard, and we are quite sure that the pejorative description 'outrageous' does not supply one. 'Outrageousness' in the area of political and social discourse has an inherent subjectiveness about it which would allow a jury to impose liability on the basis of the jurors' tastes or views, or perhaps on the basis of their dislike of a particular expression.

"We conclude that public figures and public officials may not recover for the tort of intentional infliction of emotional distress by reason of publications such as the one here at issue without showing in addition that the publication contains a false statement of fact which was made with 'actual malice,' i.e., with knowledge that the statement was false or with reckless disregard as to whether or not it was true."[b]

Notes and Questions

1.   Does the rationale sweep beyond the holding? If debate on public issues should be uninhibited and if speakers filled with hatred have a place in that debate, why is the holding confined to suits brought by public officials and public figures? Is the holding likely to follow a "dialectic progression" from public official and public figure to all matters in the public domain? Should it? Is that far enough? Should the holding encompass all media speech? All non-media speech? Consider Smolla, *Emotional Distress and the First Amendment,* 20 Ariz.St.L.J. 423, 427 (1988): "The intellectual challenge posed by Falwell's suit is not how to construct a convincing rationale for rejecting his claim, but rather how to articulate limits on that rationale that will permit suits for emotional distress inflicted through speech in other contexts to survive." See generally Smolla, *Jerry Falwell v. Larry Flynt: The First Amendment on Trial* (1988).

2.   Is the problem with the outrageousness standard less its subjectivity than its enabling "a single community to use the authority of the state to confine speech within its own notions of propriety." Does *Falwell* exhibit a need to respect a "marketplace of communities?" Can we respect that marketplace without "blunt[ing the] rules of civility that define the essence of reason and dignity within community life?" Compare Post, *The Constitutional Concept of Public Discourse,* 103 Harv.L.Rev. 601, 632, 643 (1990) with Cohen, *Freedom of Expression,* 21 Phil. and Pub. Aff. 207, 277 n. 62 (1993).

3.   Is there any distinction to be made between persons and trademarks? The Second Circuit permitted an injunction to issue against exhibition of the film *Debbie Does Dallas* on the ground that it infringed on the trademarked uniform of the Dallas Cowboys Cheerleaders. *Dallas Cowboys Cheerleaders, Inc. v. Pussycat Cinema, Ltd.,* 604 F.2d 200 (2d Cir.1979). The movie involves women performing sexual services for a fee so they can go to Dallas to become "Texas Cowgirls." Consistent with *Falwell?* Consider Kravitz, *Trademarks, Speech, and the Gay Olympics Case,* 69 B.U.L.Rev. 131 (1989): "If Rev. Jerry Falwell cannot succeed on a cause of action against an advertising parody suggesting he had a sexual encounter with his mother while drunk in an outhouse, why should an inanimate trademark enjoy greater protection against similar slurs? If Falwell cannot recover, surely Campari, whose trademark was also parodied in the fake ad, should not. [Broadly] interpreted, the holding in *Dallas Cowboys Cheerleaders* suggests that Ford Motor Company might enjoin the distribution of a book or a film

b.   White, J., concurred, but stated that *New York Times* was irrelevant because of the jury's finding that the parody contained no assertion of fact. Kennedy, J., took no part.

that portrayed teenagers having sex in the back of a Ford car." See also Denicola, *Trademarks as Speech,* 1982 Wisc.L.Rev. 158.

F.   DISCLOSURE OF PRIVATE FACTS

FLORIDA STAR v. B.J.F.

491 U.S. 524, 109 S.Ct. 2603, 105 L.Ed.2d 443 (1989).

JUSTICE MARSHALL delivered the opinion of the Court.

Florida Stat. § 794.03 (1987) makes it unlawful to "print, publish, or broadcast * * * in any instrument of mass communication" the name of the victim of a sexual offense. Pursuant to this statute, appellant The Florida Star was found civilly liable for publishing the name of a rape victim which it had obtained from a publicly released police report. The issue presented here is whether this result comports with the First Amendment. We hold that it does not. * * *

[B.J.F.] testified that she had suffered emotional distress from the publication of her name. She stated that she had heard about the article from fellow workers and acquaintances; that her mother had received several threatening phone calls from a man who stated that he would rape B.J.F. again; and that these events had forced B.J.F. to change her phone number and residence, to seek police protection, and to obtain mental health counseling. * * *

The jury awarded B.J.F. $75,000 in compensatory damages and $25,000 in punitive damages. * * *

[We do not] accept appellant's invitation to hold broadly that truthful publication may never be punished consistent with the First Amendment. Our cases have carefully eschewed reaching this ultimate question, mindful that the future may bring scenarios which prudence counsels our not resolving anticipatorily. See, e.g., *Near v. Minnesota,* [p. 335 infra] (hypothesizing "publication of the sailing dates of transports or the number and location of troops"); see also *Garrison v. Louisiana* (endorsing absolute defense of truth "where discussion of public affairs is concerned," but leaving unsettled the constitutional implications of truthfulness "in the discrete area of purely private libels"). Indeed, in [*Cox Broadcasting Corp. v. Cohn,* 420 U.S. 469, 95 S.Ct. 1029, 43 L.Ed.2d 328 (1975)] we pointedly refused to answer even the less sweeping question "whether truthful publications may ever be subjected to civil or criminal liability" for invading "an area of privacy" defined by the State. [We] continue to believe that the sensitivity and significance of the interests presented in clashes between First Amendment and privacy rights counsel relying on limited principles that sweep no more broadly than the appropriate context of the instant case.

In our view, this case is appropriately analyzed with reference to such a limited First Amendment principle. It is the one, in fact, which we articulated in *Smith v. Daily Mail Pub. Co.,* [443 U.S. 97, 99 S.Ct. 2667, 61 L.Ed.2d 399 (1979)] in our synthesis of prior cases involving attempts to punish truthful publication: "[I]f a newspaper lawfully obtains truthful information about a matter of public significance then state officials may not constitutionally punish publication of the information, absent a need to further a state interest of the highest order."[a] * * *

Applied to the instant case, the *Daily Mail* principle clearly commands reversal. The first inquiry is whether the newspaper "lawfully obtain[ed] truthful information about a matter of public significance." It is undisputed that the news article describing the assault on B.J.F. was accurate. In addition, appellant lawfully obtained B.J.F.'s name. Appellee's argument to the contrary is based on the fact that under Florida law, police reports which reveal the identity of the victim of a sexual offense are not among the matters of "public record" which the public, by law, is entitled to inspect. But the fact that state officials are not required to disclose such reports does not make it unlawful for a newspaper to receive them when furnished by the government. Nor does the fact that the Department apparently failed to fulfill its obligation under § 794.03 not to "cause or allow to be * * * published" the name of a sexual offense victim make the newspaper's ensuing receipt of this information unlawful. Even assuming the Constitution permitted a State to proscribe *receipt* of information, Florida has not taken this step. It is, clear, furthermore, that the news article concerned "a matter of public significance[.]" That is, the article generally, as opposed to the specific identity contained within it, involved a matter of paramount public import: the commission, and investigation, of a violent crime which had been reported to authorities.

The second inquiry is whether imposing liability on appellant pursuant to § 794.03 serves "a need to further a state interest of the highest order." Appellee argues that a rule punishing publication furthers three closely related interests: the privacy of victims of sexual offenses; the physical safety of such victims, who may be targeted for retaliation if their names become known to their assailants; and the goal of encouraging victims of such crimes to report these offenses without fear of exposure.

At a time in which we are daily reminded of the tragic reality of rape, it is undeniable that these are highly significant interests, a fact underscored by the Florida Legislature's explicit attempt to protect these interests by enacting a criminal statute prohibiting much dissemination of victim identities. We accordingly do not rule out the possibility that, in a proper case, imposing civil sanctions for publication of the name of a rape victim might be so overwhelmingly necessary to advance these interests as to satisfy the *Daily Mail* standard. For three independent reasons, however, imposing liability for publication under the circumstances of this case is too precipi-

a. Suppose a newspaper publishes the name of a confidential source who it believes has misled it for political reasons and suppose the source sues the newspaper for breach of contract? Should the *Daily Mail* principle apply? See *Cohen v. Cowles Media Co.,* 501 U.S. 663, 111 S.Ct. 2513, 115 L.Ed.2d 586 (1991). Should the *Daily Mail* principle apply in copyright cases?

tous a means of advancing these interests to convince us that there is a "need" within the meaning of the *Daily Mail* formulation for Florida to take this extreme step.

First is the manner in which appellant obtained the identifying information in question. [B.J.F.'s] identity would never have come to light were it not for the erroneous, if inadvertent, inclusion by the Department of her full name in an incident report made available in a press room open to the public. Florida's policy against disclosure of rape victims' identities, reflected in § 794.03, was undercut by the Department's failure to abide by this policy. Where, as here, the government has failed to police itself in disseminating information, it is clear [that] the imposition of damages against the press for its subsequent publication can hardly be said to be a narrowly tailored means of safeguarding anonymity.

That appellant gained access to the information in question through a government news release makes it especially likely that, if liability were to be imposed, self-censorship would result. Reliance on a news release is a paradigmatically "routine newspaper reporting techniqu[e]." The government's issuance of such a release, without qualification, can only convey to recipients that the government considered dissemination lawful, and indeed expected the recipients to disseminate the information further. Had appellant merely reproduced the news release prepared and released by the Department, imposing civil damages would surely violate the First Amendment. The fact that appellant converted the police report into a news story by adding the linguistic connecting tissue necessary to transform the report's facts into full sentences cannot change this result.

A second problem with Florida's imposition of liability for publication is the broad sweep of the negligence per se standard applied under the civil cause of action implied from § 794.03. Unlike claims based on the common law tort of invasion of privacy, civil actions based on § 794.03 require no case-by-case findings that the disclosure of a fact about a person's private life was one that a reasonable person would find highly offensive. On the contrary, under the per se theory of negligence adopted by the courts below, liability follows automatically from publication. This is so regardless of whether the identity of the victim is already known throughout the community; whether the victim has voluntarily called public attention to the offense; or whether the identity of the victim has otherwise become a reasonable subject of public concern—because, perhaps, questions have arisen whether the victim fabricated an assault by a particular person. Nor is there a scienter requirement of any kind under § 794.03, engendering the perverse result that truthful publications challenged pursuant to this cause of action are less protected by the First Amendment than even the least protected defamatory falsehoods: those involving purely private figures, where liability is evaluated under a standard, usually applied by a jury, of ordinary negligence. See *Gertz.* * * *

Third, and finally, the facial underinclusiveness of § 794.03 raises serious doubts about whether Florida is, in fact, serving, with this statute, the significant interests which appellee invokes in support of affirmance. Section 794.03 prohibits the publication of identifying information only if this information appears in an "instrument of mass communication," a term the statute does not define. Section 794.03 does not prohibit the spread by other means of the identities of victims of sexual offenses. An individual who maliciously spreads word of the identity of a rape victim is thus not covered, despite the fact that the communication of such information to persons who live near, or work with, the victim may have consequences equally devastating as the exposure of her name to large numbers of strangers.

When a State attempts the extraordinary measure of punishing truthful publication in the name of privacy, it must demonstrate its commitment to advancing this interest by applying its prohibition evenhandedly, to the small-time disseminator as well as the media giant. Where important First Amendment interests are at stake, the mass scope of disclosure is not an acceptable surrogate for injury. Without more careful and inclusive precautions against alternative forms of dissemination, we cannot conclude that Florida's selective ban on publication by the mass media satisfactorily accomplishes its stated purpose.

Our holding today is limited. We do not hold that truthful publication is automatically constitutionally protected, or that there is no zone of personal privacy within which the State may protect the individual from intrusion by the press, or even that a State may never punish publication of the name of a victim of a sexual offense. We hold only that where a newspaper publishes truthful information which it has lawfully obtained, punishment may lawfully be imposed, if at all, only when narrowly tailored to a state interest of the highest order, and that no such interest is satisfactorily served by imposing liability under § 794.03 to appellant under the facts of this case. * * *

JUSTICE SCALIA, concurring in part and concurring in the judgment.

I think it sufficient to decide this case to rely upon the third ground set forth in the Court's opinion: that a law cannot be regarded as protecting an interest "of the highest order" and thus as justifying a restriction upon truthful speech, when it leaves appreciable damage to that supposedly vital interest unprohibited. In the present case, I would anticipate that the rape victim's discomfort at the dissemination of news of her misfortune among friends and acquaintances would be at least as great as her discomfort at its publication by the media to people to whom she is only a name. Yet the law in question does not prohibit the former in either oral or written form. Nor is it at all clear, as I think it must be to validate this statute, that Florida's general privacy law would prohibit such gossip. Nor, finally, is it credible that the interest meant to be served by the statute is the protection of the victim against a rapist still at large—an interest that arguably would extend only to mass publication. There would be little reason to limit a statute with that objective to rape alone; or to extend it to all rapes, whether or not the felon has been apprehended and confined. In any case, the instructions here did not require the jury to find that the rapist was at large.

This law has every appearance of a prohibition that society is prepared to impose upon the press but not upon itself. Such a prohibition does not protect an interest "of the highest order." For that reason, I agree that the judgment of the court below must be reversed.

JUSTICE WHITE, with whom THE CHIEF JUSTICE and JUSTICE O'CONNOR join, dissenting.

"Short of homicide, [rape] is the 'ultimate violation of self.'" *Coker v. Georgia,* 433 U.S. 584, 97 S.Ct. 2861, 53 L.Ed.2d 982 (1977) (opinion of White, J.). For B.J.F., however, the violation she suffered at a rapist's knife-point marked only the beginning of her ordeal. A week later, while her assailant was still at large, an account of this assault—identifying by name B.J.F. as the victim—was published by The Florida Star. As a result, B.J.F. received harassing phone calls, required mental health counseling, was forced to move from her home, and was even threatened with being raped again. Yet today, the Court holds that a jury award of $75,000 to compensate B.J.F. for the harm she suffered due to the Star's negligence is at odds with the First Amendment. I do not accept this result.

[T]he three "independent reasons" the Court cites for reversing the judgment for B.J.F. [do not] support its result.

The first of these reasons [is] the fact "appellant gained access to [B.J.F.'s name] through a government news release." "The government's issuance of such a release, without qualification, can only convey to recipients that the government considered dissemination lawful," the Court suggests. [But the] "release" of information provided by the government was not, as the Court says, "without qualification." As the Star's own reporter conceded at trial, the crime incident report that inadvertently included B.J.F.'s name was posted in a room that contained signs making it clear that the names of rape victims were not matters of public record, and were not to be published. The Star's reporter indicated that she understood that she "[was not] allowed to take down that information" (i.e., B.J.F.'s name) and that she "[was] not supposed to take the information from the police department." Thus, by her own admission the posting of the incident report did not convey to the Star's reporter the idea that "the government considered dissemination lawful"; the Court's suggestion to the contrary is inapt. * * *

Unfortunately, as this case illustrates, mistakes happen: even when States take measures to "avoid" disclosure, sometimes rape victim's names are found out. As I see it, it is not too much to ask the press, in instances such as this, to respect simple standards of decency and refrain from publishing a victim's name, address, and/or phone number.

Second, the Court complains that appellant was judged here under too strict a liability standard. The Court contends that a newspaper might be found liable under the Florida courts' negligence per se theory without regard to a newspaper's scienter or degree of fault. The short answer to this complaint is that whatever merit the Court's argument might have, it is wholly inapposite here, where the jury found that appellant acted with "reckless indifference towards the rights of others," a standard far higher than the *Gertz* standard the Court urges as a constitutional minimum today. B.J.F. proved the Star's negligence at trial—and, actually, far more than simple negligence; the Court's concerns about damages resting on a strict liability or mere causation basis are irrelevant to the validity of the judgment for appellee.

But even taking the Court's concerns in the abstract, they miss the mark. Permitting liability under a negligence per se theory does not mean that defendants will be held liable without a showing of negligence, but rather, that the standard of care has been set by the legislature, instead of the courts. The Court says that negligence *per se* permits a plaintiff to hold a defendant liable without a showing that the disclosure was "of a fact about a person's private life [that] a reasonable person would find highly offensive." But the point here is that the legislature—reflecting popular sentiment—has determined that disclosure of the fact that a person was raped is categorically a revelation that reasonable people find offensive. And as for the Court's suggestion that the Florida courts' theory permits liability without regard for whether the victim's identity is already known, or whether she herself has made it known—these are facts that would surely enter into the calculation of damages in such a case. In any event, none of these mitigating factors was present here; whatever the force of these arguments generally, they do not justify the Court's ruling against B.J.F. in this case.

Third, the Court faults the Florida criminal statute for being underinclusive: § 794.03 covers disclosure of rape victim's names in "instrument[s] of mass communication," but not other means of distribution, the Court observes. But our cases which have struck down laws that limit or burden the press due to their underinclusiveness have involved situations where a legislature has singled out one segment of the news media or press for adverse treatment. Here, the Florida law evenhandedly covers all "instrument[s] of mass communication" no matter their form, media, content, nature or purpose. It excludes neighborhood gossips because presumably the Florida Legislature has determined that neighborhood gossips do not pose the danger and intrusion to rape victims that "instrument[s] of mass communication" do. Simply put: Florida wanted to prevent the widespread distribution of rape victim's names, and therefore enacted a statute tailored almost as precisely as possible to achieving that end. * * *

At issue in this case is whether there is any information about people, which—though true—may not be published in the press. By holding that only "a state interest of the highest order" permits the State to penalize the publication of truthful information, and by holding that protecting a rape victim's right to privacy is not among those state interests of the highest order, the Court accepts appellant's invitation to obliterate one of the most note-worthy legal inventions of the 20th–Century: the tort of the publication of private facts. W. Prosser, J. Wade, & V. Schwartz, *Torts* 951–952 (8th ed. 1988). Even if the Court's opinion does not say as much today, such obliteration will follow inevitably from the Court's conclusion here. * * *

I do not suggest that the Court's decision today is radical departure from a previously charted course. The Court's ruling has been foreshadowed. In *Time, Inc. v. Hill,* we observed that—after a brief period early in this century where Brandeis' view was ascendant—the trend in "modern" jurisprudence has been to eclipse an individual's right to maintain private any truthful information that the press wished to publish. More recently, in *Cox Broadcasting,* we acknowledged the possibility that the First Amendment may prevent a State from ever subjecting the publication of truthful but private information to civil liability. Today, we hit the bottom of the slippery slope.

I would find a place to draw the line higher on the hillside: a spot high enough to protect B.J.F.'s desire for privacy and peace-of-mind in the wake of a horrible personal tragedy. There is no public interest in publishing the names, addresses, and phone numbers of persons who are the victims of crime—and no public interest in immunizing the press from liability in the rare cases where a State's efforts to protect a victim's privacy have failed. Consequently, I respectfully dissent.[5]

Notes and Questions

1. *Journalistic practice.* Marcus & McMahon, *Limiting Disclosure of Rape Victims' Identities,* 64 S.Cal.L.Rev. 1019, 1046–47 (1991): "The journalists' code of ethics and the policies of most members of the media currently prohibit publication of a rape victim's name. [From] our vantage point, news reporters appear no less aggressive in pursuing their stories. Codifying in a rule of law what is already the prevailing practice would not have a chilling effect on the media."

2. *Outing.* Should the first amendment preclude a privacy cause of action against those who publicly disclose that a private person is gay? What if the person is a public official, e.g., a member of a board of education?[b]

3. *Buying habits.* Suppose government prohibits merchants from disseminating information about the buying habits of their customers. Constitutional?[c]

---

5. The Court does not address the distinct constitutional questions raised by the award of punitive damages in this case. Consequently, I do not do so either. That award is more troublesome than the compensatory award discussed above. Cf. Note, *Punitive Damages and Libel Law,* 98 Harv. L.Rev. 847 (1985).

b. For diverse perspectives, see Smolla, *Free Speech in an Open Society,* 137–39 (1992); Becker, *The Immorality of Publicly Outing Private People,* 73 Ore.L.Rev. 159 (1994); Moretti, *Outing: Justifiable or Unwarranted Invasion of Privacy? The Private Facts Tort As a Remedy for Disclosures of Sexual Orientation,* 11 Cardozo Arts & Ent. L.J. 857 (1993); Comment, *Forced Out of the Closet,* 46 U.Miami L.Rev. 413 (1992); Note, *Outing, Privacy, and the First Amendment,* 102 Yale L.J. 747 (1992); Note, *"Outing" and Freedom of the Press: Sexual Orientation's Challenge to the Supreme Court's Categorical Jurisprudence,* 77 Corn. L.Rev. 103 (1992).

4. *Voyeurism.* Is the direction of television programming less about encouraging democratic dialogue and more about encouraging a nation of voyeurs, people who watch others, but do not engage with them, people who enjoy prying into the affairs of others? Do voyeuristic desires deserve substantial first amendment protection? See Calvert, *The Voyeurism Value in First Amendment Jurisprudence,* 17 Cardoza Arts & Ent.L.J. 273 (1999). Does the casting of privacy as a private value shortchange the interest in the quality of public discourse?[d]

III. OWNERSHIP OF SPEECH

HARPER & ROW v. NATION ENTERPRISES, 471 U.S. 539, 105 S.Ct. 2218, 85 L.Ed.2d 588 (1985): Former President Ford had contracted with Harper & Row and Readers Digest to publish his memoirs and granted them the right to license prepublication excerpts concentrating on his pardon of former President Nixon. Some weeks before a licensed article in Time was to appear, an unknown person presented the editor of The Nation with an unauthorized copy of the 200,000 word Ford manuscript from which the editor wrote a 2,250 word article entitled, "The Ford Memoirs—Behind the Nixon Pardon." The article included 26 verbatim quotations totaling 300 words of Ford's copyrighted expression and was timed to scoop Time. Accordingly, Time cancelled its article and refused to pay the publishers the remaining half of its $25,000 contract price.

In defense against the publishers' copyright claim, The Nation maintained that its publication was protected by the fair use provision of the Copyright Revision Act of 1976, 17 U.S.C. § 107 and by the first amendment. The Court, per O'CONNOR, J., concluded that neither defense was viable and that the fair use provision properly accommodated the relevant first amendment interests: "Article I, § 8, of the Constitution provides that: 'The Congress shall have Power * * * to Promote the Progress of Science and useful Arts, by securing for limited Times to Authors and Inventors the exclusive Right to their respective Writings and Discoveries.' '[This] limited grant is a means by which an important public purpose may be achieved. It is intended to motivate the creative activity of authors and inventors by the provision of a special reward, and to allow the public access to the products of their genius after the limited period of exclusive control has expired.' The

c. See Froomkin, *The Death of Privacy,* 52 Stan. L.Rev. 1049, 1461 (2000); Litman, *Information Privacy/Information Property,* 52 Stan.L.Rev. 1049, 1283 (2000); Cohen, *Examined Lives: Informational Privacy and the Subject as Object,* 52 Stan. L.Rev. 1049 (2000); Volokh, *Freedom of Speech and Information Privacy: The Troubling Implications of a Right to Stop People from Speaking about You,* 52 Stan. L. Rev. 1049 (2000).

d. On the relationship between privacy and public discourse, see Balkin, *How Mass Media Simulate Political Transparency,* 3 Cultural Values 393 (1999); Bollinger, *Images of a Free Press* 34–35 (1991); Levi, *Challenging the Autonomous Press,* 78 Cornell L.Rev. 665, 669–700 (1993); Nagel, *Privacy and Celebrity: An Essay on the Nationalization of Intimacy,* 33 U.Rich.L.Rev. 1121 (2000); Scott, *The Hidden First Amendment Values of Privacy,* 71 Wash.L.Rev. 683 (1996); Volokh, *supra* note c.

monopoly created by copyright thus rewards the individual author in order to benefit the public. This principle applies equally to works of fiction and nonfiction. The book at issue here, for example, was two years in the making, and began with a contract giving the author's copyright to the publishers in exchange for their services in producing and marketing the work. In preparing the book, Mr. Ford drafted essays and word portraits of public figures and participated in hundreds of taped interviews that were later distilled to chronicle his personal viewpoint. It is evident that the monopoly granted by copyright actively served its intended purpose of inducing the creation of new material of potential historical value.

"Section 106 of the Copyright Act confers a bundle of exclusive rights to the owner of the copyright. [T]hese rights—to publish, copy, and distribute the author's work—vest in the author of an original work from the time of its creation. In practice, the author commonly sells his rights to publishers who offer royalties in exchange for their services in producing and marketing the author's work. The copyright owner's rights, however, are subject to certain statutory exceptions. Among these is § 107 which codifies the traditional privilege of other authors to make 'fair use' of an earlier writer's work.[2] In addition, no author may copyright facts or ideas. § 102. The copyright is limited to those aspects of the work—termed 'expression'—that display the stamp of the author's originality.

"[T]here is no dispute that the unpublished manuscript of 'A Time to Heal,' as a whole, was protected by § 106 from unauthorized reproduction. Nor do respondents dispute that verbatim copying of excerpts of the manuscript's original form of expression would constitute infringement unless excused as fair use. Yet copyright does not prevent subsequent users from copying from a prior author's work those constituent elements that are not original—for example, quotations borrowed under the rubric of fair use from other copyrighted works, facts, or materials in the public domain—as long as such use does not unfairly appropriate the author's original contributions. Perhaps the controversy between the lower courts in this case over copyrightability is more aptly styled a dispute over whether The Nation's appropriation of unoriginal and uncopyrightable elements encroached on the originality embodied in the work as a whole. Especially in the realm of factual narrative, the law is currently unsettled regarding the ways in which

2. Section 107 states: "Notwithstanding the provisions of section 106, the fair use of a copyrighted work [for] purposes such as criticism, comment, news reporting, teaching (including multiple copies for classroom use), scholarship, or research, is not an infringement of copyright. In determining whether the use made of a work in any particular case is a fair use the factors to be considered shall include—

"(1) the purpose and character of the use, including whether such use is of a commercial nature or is for nonprofit educational purposes;

"(2) the nature of the copyrighted work;

"(3) the amount and substantiality of the portion used in relation to the copyrighted work as a whole; and

"(4) the effect of the use upon the potential market for or value of the copyrighted work."

uncopyrightable elements combine with the author's original contributions to form protected expression.

"We need not reach these issues, however, as The Nation has admitted to lifting verbatim quotes of the author's original language [constituting] some 13% of The Nation article. [To thereby] lend authenticity to its account of the forthcoming memoirs, The Nation effectively arrogated to itself the right of first publication, an important marketable subsidiary right. For the reasons set forth below, we find that this use of the copyrighted manuscript, even stripped to the verbatim quotes conceded by The Nation to be copyrightable expression, was not a fair use within the meaning of the Copyright Act.

"[The] nature of the interest at stake is highly relevant to whether a given use is fair. [The] right of first publication implicates a threshold decision by the author whether and in what form to release his work. First publication is inherently different from other § 106 rights in that only one person can be the first publisher; as the contract with Time illustrates, the commercial value of the right lies primarily in exclusivity. [Under] ordinary circumstances, the author's right to control the first public appearance of his undisseminated expression will outweigh a claim of fair use.

"Respondents, however, contend that First Amendment values require a different rule under the circumstances of this case. [Respondents] advance the substantial public import of the subject matter of the Ford memoirs as grounds for excusing a use that would ordinarily not pass muster as a fair use—the piracy of verbatim quotations for the purpose of 'scooping' the authorized first serialization. Respondents explain their copying of Mr. Ford's expression as essential to reporting the news story it claims the book itself represents. In respondents' view, not only the facts contained in Mr. Ford's memoirs, but 'the precise manner in which [he] expressed himself was as newsworthy as what he had to say.' Respondents argue that the public's interest in learning this news as fast as possible outweighs the right of the author to control its first publication.

"The Second Circuit noted, correctly, that copyright's idea/expression dichotomy 'strike[s] a definitional balance between the First Amendment and the Copyright Act by permitting free communication of facts while still protecting an author's expression.' No author may copyright his ideas or the facts he narrates.

"Respondents' theory, however, would expand fair use to effectively destroy any expectation of copyright protection in the work of a public figure. Absent such protection, there would be little incentive to create or profit in financing such memoirs and the public would be denied an important source of significant historical information. The promise of copyright would be an empty one if it could be avoided merely by dubbing the infringement a fair use 'news report' of the book. * * *

"In our haste to disseminate news, it should not be forgotten that the Framers intended copyright itself to be the engine of free expression. By establishing a marketable right to the use of one's expression, copyright supplies the economic incentive to create and disseminate ideas. * * *

"Moreover, freedom of thought and expression 'includes both the right to speak freely and the right to refrain from speaking at all.' We do not suggest this right not to speak would sanction abuse of the copyright owner's monopoly as an instrument to suppress facts. But 'The essential thrust of the First Amendment is to prohibit improper restraints on the *voluntary* public expression of ideas; it shields the man who wants to speak or publish when others wish him to be quiet. There is necessarily, and within suitably defined areas, a concomitant freedom *not* to speak publicly, one which serves the same ultimate end as freedom of speech in its affirmative aspect.' *Estate of Hemingway v. Random House, Inc.*, 23 N.Y.2d 341, 348, 296 N.Y.S.2d 771, 776, 244 N.E.2d 250, 255 (1968). * * *

"In view of the First Amendment protections already embodied in the Copyright Act's distinction between copyrightable expression and uncopyrightable facts and ideas, and the latitude for scholarship and comment traditionally afforded by fair use, we see no warrant for expanding the doctrine of fair use to create what amounts to a public figure exception to copyright. Whether verbatim copying from a public figure's manuscript in a given case is or is not fair must be judged according to the traditional equities of fair use."

In assessing the equities, the Court found the purpose of the article to count against fair use, noting that the publication "went beyond simply reporting uncopyrightable information" and made "a 'news event' out of its unauthorized first publication," that the publication was "commercial as opposed to non-profit," that The Nation intended to supplant the "right of first publication," and that it acted in bad faith, for it "knowingly exploited a purloined manuscript." In considering the nature of the copyrighted work, the Court found it significant not only that Ford's work was yet unpublished, but also that The Nation had focused "on the most expressive elements of the work" in a way that exceeded "that necessary to disseminate the facts" and in a "clandestine" fashion that afforded no "opportunity for creative or quality control" by the copyright holder. In evaluating the amount and substantiality of the portion used, the Court cited the district court finding that "The Nation took what was essentially the heart of the book" and pointed to the "expressive value of the excerpts and their key role in the infringing work." Finally, the Court observed that the effect of the use on the market for the copyrighted work was the most important element. It found the Time contract cancellation to be "clear cut evidence of actual damage."

BRENNAN, J., joined by White and Marshall, JJ., dissented: "When The Nation was not quoting Mr. Ford, [its] efforts to convey the historical information in the Ford manuscript did not so closely and substantially track

Mr. Ford's language and structure as to constitute an appropriation of literary form.

"[The] Nation is thus liable in copyright only if the quotation of 300 words infringed any of Harper & Row's exclusive rights under § 106 of the Act. [Limiting] the inquiry to the propriety of a subsequent author's use of the copyright owner's literary form is not easy in the case of a work of history. Protection against only substantial appropriation of literary form does not ensure historians a return commensurate with the full value of their labors. The literary form contained in works like 'A Time to Heal' reflects only a part of the labor that goes into the book. It is the labor of collecting, sifting, organizing and reflecting that predominates in the creation of works of history such as this one. The value this labor produces lies primarily in the information and ideas revealed, and not in the particular collocation of words through which the information and ideas are expressed. Copyright thus does not protect that which is often of most value in a work of history and courts must resist the tendency to reject the fair use defense on the basis of their feeling that an author of history has been deprived of the full value of his or her labor. A subsequent author's taking of information and ideas is in no sense piratical because copyright law simply does not create any property interest in information and ideas.

"The urge to compensate for subsequent use of information and ideas is perhaps understandable. An inequity seems to lurk in the idea that much of the fruit of the historian's labor may be used without compensation. This, however, is not some unforeseen by-product of a statutory scheme intended primarily to ensure a return for works of the imagination. Congress made the affirmative choice that the copyright laws should apply in this way: 'Copyright does not preclude others from using the ideas or information revealed by the author's work. It pertains to the literary [form] in which the author expressed intellectual concepts.' This distinction is at the essence of copyright. The copyright laws serve as the 'engine of free expression,' only when the statutory monopoly does not choke off multifarious indirect uses and consequent broad dissemination of information and ideas. To ensure the progress of arts and sciences and the integrity of First Amendment values, ideas and information must not be freighted with claims of proprietary right.[13]

"In my judgment, the Court's fair use analysis has fallen to the temptation to find copyright violation based on a minimal use of literary form in order to provide compensation for the appropriation of information from a work of history."

---

13. This congressional limitation on the scope of copyright does not threaten the production of history. That this limitation results in significant diminution of economic incentives is far from apparent. In any event noneconomic incentives motivate much historical research and writing. For example, former public officials often have great incentive to "tell their side of the story." And much history is the product of academic scholarship. Perhaps most importantly, the urge to preserve the past is as old as human kind.

Since news reporting is ordinarily conducted for profit and marked by attempts to "scoop" the opposition and by attempts to create "news events," Brennan, J., found the drawing of any negative implications from these factors to be inconsistent with congressional recognition in § 107 that news reporting is a prime example of fair use. He found reliance on bad faith to be equally unwarranted: "No court has found that The Nation possessed the Ford manuscript illegally or in violation of any common law interest of Harper & Row; all common law causes of action have been abandoned or dismissed in this case. Even if the manuscript had been 'purloined' by someone, nothing in this record imputes culpability to The Nation. On the basis of the record in this case, the most that can be said is that The Nation made use of the contents of the manuscript knowing the copyright owner would not sanction the use.

"[T]he Court purports to rely on [the] factual findings that The Nation had taken 'the heart of the book.' This reliance is misplaced, and would appear to be another result of the Court's failure to distinguish between information and literary form. When the District Court made this finding, it was evaluating not the quoted words at issue here but the 'totality' of the information and reflective commentary in the Ford work. The vast majority of what the District Court considered the heart of the Ford work, therefore, consisted of ideas and information The Nation was free to use. It may well be that, as a qualitative matter, most of the value of the manuscript did lie in the information and ideas the Nation used. But appropriation of the 'heart' of the manuscript in this sense is irrelevant to copyright analysis because copyright does not preclude a second author's use of information and ideas.

"At least with respect to the six particular quotes of Mr. Ford's observations and reflections about President Nixon, I agree with the Court's conclusion that The Nation appropriated some literary form of substantial quality. I do not agree, however, that the substantiality of the expression taken was clearly excessive or inappropriate to The Nation's news reporting purpose.

"Had these quotations been used in the context of a critical book review of the Ford work, there is little question that such a use would be fair use within the meaning of § 107 of the Act. The amount and substantiality of the use—in both quantitative and qualitative terms—would have certainly been appropriate to the purpose of such a use. It is difficult to see how the use of these quoted words in a news report is less appropriate.

"The Nation's publication indisputably precipitated Time's eventual cancellation. But that does not mean that The Nation's use of the 300 quoted words caused this injury to Harper & Row. Wholly apart from these quoted words, The Nation published significant information and ideas from the Ford manuscript. [If] The Nation competed with Time, the competition was not for a share of the market in excerpts of literary form but for a share of the market in the new information in the Ford work. * * *

"Because The Nation was the first to convey the information in this case, it did perhaps take from Harper & Row some of the value that publisher sought to garner for itself through the contractual arrangement with Ford and the license to Time. Harper & Row had every right to seek to monopolize revenue from that potential market through contractual arrangements but it has no right to set up copyright [as] a shield from competition in that market because copyright does not protect information. The Nation had every right to seek to be the first to publish that information. * * *

"The Court's exceedingly narrow approach to fair use permits Harper & Row to monopolize information. This holding 'effect[s] an important extension of property rights and a corresponding curtailment in the free use of knowledge and of ideas.' The Court has perhaps advanced the ability of the historian—or at least the public official who has recently left office—to capture the full economic value of information in his or her possession. But the Court does so only by risking the robust debate of public issues that is the 'essence of self-government.' *Garrison.* The Nation was providing the grist for that robust debate. The Court imposes liability upon The Nation for no other reason than that The Nation succeeded in being the first to provide certain information to the public."

Notes and Questions

1. Assume The Nation acquires a "purloined" manuscript of Chief Justice Burger's memoirs. Assume Time is soon to publish exclusive excerpts from his forthcoming book. The editors of The Nation want to run a news story about the book before the Time article appears. They want to know whether they can write a story, whether they can quote from the book, what they should do to reduce the risk in writing the story, and whether their right to quote from the book would be enhanced if they made their story a book review. Advise.

2. Will *Harper & Row* chill freedom of the press? Does it matter? To what extent was the Court influenced by the belief that there was no immediate need for the public to know about the Ford memoirs? Suppose California outlaws broadcast presentations in California of presidential election results (and exit polls or the like) until after the California polls have closed. Constitutional?[a]

3. *Gertz* was reluctant to make ad hoc judgments as to whether statements are or are not of general or public interest.[b] Should the Court be similarly reluctant to make ad hoc judgments as to the bona fide news

---

a. For commentary, see Fischer, *Network "Early Calls" of Elections,* 14 Sw. U.L.Rev. 428 (1984); Note, *Exit Polls and the First Amendment,* 98 Harv.L.Rev. 1927 (1985); Comment, *Restricting the Broadcast of Election Day Projections: A Justifiable Protection of the Right to Vote,* 9 U.Dayton L.Rev. 297 (1984).

b. *But see Greenmoss,* Ch. 3, III infra.

purpose of an article,[c] as to whether expression goes to the "heart of the book," or whether quoted words are "necessary" to communicate the "facts"? Is there an alternative to the making of such judgments?[d]

4. Melville Nimmer had argued that in most cases the idea/expression dichotomy is central to resolving the clash between copyright and the first amendment. *Does Copyright Abridge the First Amendment Guarantees of Free Speech and Press?* 17 U.C.L.A.L.Rev. 1180 (1970). Is the distinction satisfactory?[e] Consider *Cohen v. California,* p. 158 infra, protecting Cohen's use of the phrase "Fuck the Draft": "[W]e cannot indulge the facile assumption that one can forbid particular words without running a substantial risk of suppressing ideas in the process." Cohen's counsel was—Professor Nimmer. Does *Nimmer On Copyright* collide with *Nimmer on Freedom of Speech?* For Nimmer's answer, see id. § 2.05(c), at 72–77; § 3.04, at 28 n. 11.

IV. OBSCENITY

A. EVOLUTION TOWARD A STANDARD

Roth v. United States, infra, contains the Court's first extended discussion of the constitutionality of obscenity laws. The Court's opinion was framed by briefs that proceeded from sharply different visions of first amendment law. Roth argued that no speech including obscenity could be prohibited without meeting the clear and present danger test, that a danger of lustful thoughts was not the type of evil with which a legislature could be legitimately concerned, and that no danger of anti-social conduct had been

c. Compare *Regan v. Time, Inc.,* 468 U.S. 641, 104 S.Ct. 3262, 82 L.Ed.2d 487 (1984): 18 U.S.C. § 474 makes it a crime to photograph United States currency, but exceptions for articles and books for newsworthy purposes are permitted so long as certain size and color requirements are satisfied. 18 U.S.C. § 504. The Court, per White, J., invalidated the purpose requirement: "A determination concerning the newsworthiness [of] a photograph cannot help but be based on the content of the photograph and the message it delivers. [Regulations] which permit the Government to discriminate on the basis of the content of the message cannot be tolerated under the First Amendment. The purpose requirement of § 504 is therefore constitutionally infirm." Stevens, J., dissenting on this point, observed that if the Court's language were applied literally, the constitutionality of the fair use provision of the Copyright Act would be "highly suspect."

d. For a variety of approaches to the fair use issue, see Dratler, *Distilling the Witches' Brew of Fair Use in Copyright Law,* 43 U.Miami L.Rev. 233 (1988); Elkin–Koren, *Cyberlaw* and Social Change, 14 Cardoza Arts & Ent. L.Rev. 215 (1996); Fewer, *Constitutionalizing Copyright: Freedom of Expression and the Limits of Copyright in Canada,* U.Toronto Fac.L.Rev. 175 (1997); Fisher, *Reconstructing the Fair Use Doctrine,* 101 Harv.L.Rev. 1659 (1988); Gordon, *Fair Use as Market Failure: A Structural and Economic Analysis of the Betamax Case and Its Predecessors,* 82 Colum.L.Rev. 1600 (1982); Leval, *Toward a Fair Use Standard,* 103 Harv.L.Rev. 1105 (1990); Nanantel, *Copyright and a Democratic Civil Society,* 106 Yale L.J. 283 (1996); Weinreb, *Fair's Fair: A Comment on the Fair Use Doctrine,* 103 Harv.L.Rev. 1137 (1990).

e. For commentary, see Benkler, *Free as the Air to Common Use, First Amendment Constraints on Enclosure of the Public Domain,* 74 N.Y.U.L. Rev. 354 (1999); Lemley & Volokh, *Freedom of Speech and Injunctions in Intellectual Property Cases,* 48 Duke L.J. 147 (1998); Goldstein, *Copyright and the First Amendment,* 70 Colum.L.Rev. 983 (1970); Patterson & Birch, *Copyright and Free Speech Rights,* 4 J. Intell. Prop.L. 1 (1997); Zimmerman, *Information as Speech, Information as Goods,* 33 Wm. & Mary L.Rev 665 (1992).

shown. On the other hand, the government urged the Court to adopt a balancing test that prominently featured a consideration of the value of the speech involved. The government tendered an illustrative hierarchy of nineteen speech categories with political, religious, economic, and scientific speech at the top; entertainment, music, and humor in the middle; and libel, obscenity, profanity, and commercial pornography at the bottom.

ROTH v. UNITED STATES
ALBERTS v. CALIFORNIA

354 U.S. 476, 77 S.Ct. 1304, 1 L.Ed.2d 1498 (1957).

Mr. Justice Brennan delivered the opinion of the Court. [Roth and Alberts were convicted of violating the federal and California obscenity laws respectively. The issues raised were whether the statutes, *"on their faces and in a vacuum,* violated the freedom of expression and definiteness requirements of the Constitution."[a]]

The dispositive question is whether obscenity is utterance within the area of protected speech and press.[8] Although this is the first time the question has been squarely presented to this Court [expressions] found in numerous opinions indicate that this Court has always assumed that obscenity is not protected by the freedoms of speech and press.

The guaranties of freedom of expression in effect in 10 of the 14 States which by 1792 had ratified the Constitution, gave no absolute protection for every utterance. Thirteen of the 14 States provided for the prosecution of libel, and all of those States made either blasphemy or profanity, or both, statutory crimes. As early as 1712, Massachusetts made it criminal to publish "any filthy, obscene, or profane song, pamphlet, libel or mock sermon" in imitation or mimicking of religious services. * * *

In light of this history, it is apparent that the unconditional phrasing of the First Amendment was not intended to protect every utterance. This phrasing did not prevent this Court from concluding that libelous utterances are not within the area of constitutionally protected speech. *Beauharnais.* At the time of the adoption of the First Amendment, obscenity law was not as fully developed as libel law, but there is sufficiently contemporaneous evidence to show that obscenity, too, was outside the protection intended for speech and press.[b]

---

a. See Lockhart & McClure, *Censorship of Obscenity: The Developing Constitutional Standards,* 45 Minn.L.Rev. 5, 13 (1960).

8. No issue is presented in either case concerning the obscenity of the material involved.

b. The Court here cited three state court decisions (1808 to 1821) recognizing as a common law offense the distribution or display of obscene or indecent materials,

and four state statutes aimed at similar conduct (1800 to 1842). For the contention that obscenity is not "speech" within the meaning of the first amendment (let alone, not *protected* speech), see Schauer, *Free Speech: A Philosophical Enquiry* 181–84 (1982) (a sex aid, not speech). See generally Schauer, *Speech and "Speech"—Obscenity and "Obscenity": An Exercise in the Interpretation of Constitutional Language,* 67

The protection given speech and press was fashioned to assure unfettered interchange of ideas for the bringing about of political and social changes desired by the people. [All] ideas having even the slightest redeeming social importance—unorthodox ideas, controversial ideas, even ideas hateful to the prevailing climate of opinion—have the full protection of the guaranties, unless excludable because they encroach upon the limited area of more important interests. But implicit in the history of the First Amendment is the rejection of obscenity as utterly without redeeming social importance. This rejection for that reason is mirrored in the universal judgment that obscenity should be restrained, reflected in the international agreement of over 50 nations, in the obscenity laws of all of the 48 States, and in the 20 obscenity laws enacted by the Congress from 1842 to 1956. This is the same judgment expressed by this Court in *Chaplinsky* [Ch. 1, V, A infra]: "There are certain well-defined and narrowly limited classes of speech, the prevention and punishment of which have never been thought to raise any Constitutional problem. *These include the lewd and obscene. [It] has been well observed that such utterances are no essential part of any exposition of ideas, and are of such slight social value as a step to truth that any benefit that may be derived from them is clearly outweighed by the social interest in order and morality."* (Emphasis added [by Court].)

We hold that obscenity is not within the area of constitutionally protected speech or press.

It is strenuously urged that these obscenity statutes offend the constitutional guaranties because they punish incitation to impure sexual *thoughts,* not shown to be related to any overt antisocial conduct which is or may be incited in the persons stimulated to such *thoughts.* [It] is insisted that the constitutional guaranties are violated because convictions may be had without proof either that obscene material will perceptibly create a clear and present danger of antisocial conduct, or will probably induce its recipients to such conduct. But, in light of our holding that obscenity is not protected speech, the complete answer to this argument is in the holding of this Court in *Beauharnais:* "Libelous utterances not being within the area of constitutionally protected speech, it is unnecessary, either for us or for the State courts, to consider the issues behind the phrase 'clear and present danger.' Certainly no one would contend that obscene speech, for example, may be punished only upon a showing of such circumstances. * * * "

Geo.L.J. 899 (1979). But see Alexander & Horton, *The Impossibility of a Free Speech Principle,* 78 Nw.U.L.Rev. 1319, 1331–34 (1984). Compare Greenawalt, *Criminal Coercion and Freedom of Speech,* 78 Nw. U.L.Rev. 1081 (1984) (discussing the question of whether all ordinary language should be included within the scope of the first amendment, even if much is ultimately unprotected, and contending that some ordinary language should be wholly outside the scope of the first amendment); Greenawalt, *Speech, Crime, and the Uses of Language* (1989); Post, *Recuperating First Amendment Doctrine,* 47 Stan.L.Rev. 1249 (1995) (speech in its ordinary language sense has no inherent constitutional value and should be defined to include only those social practices which implicate free speech values). But see Haiman, *Comments on Kent Greenawalt's Criminal Coercion and Freedom of Speech, supra* at 1125.

However, sex and obscenity are not synonymous. Obscene material is material which deals with sex in a manner appealing to prurient interest.[20] The portrayal of sex, e.g., in art, literature and scientific works, is not itself sufficient reason to deny material the constitutional protection of freedom of speech and press. Sex, a great and mysterious motive force in human life, has indisputably been a subject of absorbing interest to mankind through the ages; it is one of the vital problems of human interest and public [concern].

The fundamental freedoms of speech and press have contributed greatly to the development and well-being of our free society and are indispensable to its continued growth. [It] is therefore vital that the standards for judging obscenity safeguard the protection of freedom of speech and press for material which does not treat sex in a manner appealing to prurient interest.

The early leading standard of obscenity allowed material to be judged merely by the effect of an isolated excerpt upon particularly susceptible persons. *Regina v. Hicklin,* [1868] L.R. 3 Q.B. 360. Some American courts adopted this standard but later decisions have rejected it and substituted this test: whether to the average person, applying contemporary community standards, the dominant theme of the material taken as a whole appeals to prurient interest. The *Hicklin* test, judging obscenity by the effect of isolated passages upon the most susceptible persons, might well encompass material legitimately treating with sex, and so it must be rejected as unconstitutionally restrictive of the freedoms of speech and press. On the other hand, the substituted standard provides safeguards adequate to withstand the charge of constitutional infirmity. Both trial courts below sufficiently followed the proper standard. Both courts used the proper definition of obscenity.[c]

---

20. I.e., material having a tendency to excite lustful thoughts. *Webster's New International Dictionary* (unabridged, 2d ed., 1949) defines *prurient,* in pertinent part, as follows:

"Itching; longing; uneasy with desire or longing; of persons, having itching, morbid, or lascivious longings; of desire, curiosity, or propensity, lewd * * *."

We perceive no significant difference between the meaning of obscenity developed in the case law and the definition of the A.L.I., *Model Penal Code,* § 207.10(2) (Tent. Draft No. 6, 1957), viz.: "[A] thing is obscene if, considered as a whole, its predominant appeal is to prurient interest, i.e. a shameful or morbid interest in nudity, sex, or excretion, and if it goes substantially beyond customary limits of candor in description or representation of such [matters]." See Comment, id. at 10, and the discussion at page 29 et seq.

c. The opinion quoted with apparent approval from the trial court's instruction in

Roth: "[The] test is not whether it would arouse sexual desires or sexual impure thoughts in those comprising a particular segment of the community, the young, the immature or the highly prudish or would leave another segment, the scientific or highly educated or the so-called worldly-wise and sophisticated indifferent and unmoved. [The] test in each case is the effect of the book, picture or publication considered as a whole, not upon any particular class, but upon all those whom it is likely to reach. In other words, you determine its impact upon the average person in the community. The books, pictures and circulars must be judged as a whole, in their entire context, and you are not to consider detached or separate portions in reaching a conclusion. You judge the circulars, pictures and publications which have been put in evidence by present-day standards of the community. You may ask yourselves does it offend the common conscience of the community by present-day standards.''

[It] is argued that the statutes do not provide reasonably ascertainable standards of guilt and therefore violate the constitutional requirements of due process. *Winters v. New York,* 333 U.S. 507, 68 S.Ct. 665, 92 L.Ed. 840 (1948). The federal obscenity statute makes punishable the mailing of material that is "obscene, lewd, lascivious, or filthy [or] other publication of an indecent character." The California statute makes punishable, inter alia, the keeping for sale or advertising material that is "obscene or indecent." The thrust of the argument is that these words are not sufficiently precise because they do not mean the same thing to all people, all the time, everywhere. Many decisions have recognized that these terms of obscenity statutes are not precise. This Court, however, has consistently held that lack of precision is not itself offensive to the requirements of due process. "[T]he Constitution does not require impossible standards"; all that is required is that the language "conveys sufficiently definite warning as to the proscribed conduct when measured by common understanding and [practices.]" * * *

In summary, then, we hold that these statutes, applied according to the proper standard for judging obscenity, do not offend constitutional safeguards against convictions based upon protected material, or fail to give men in acting adequate notice of what is prohibited. * * *

Affirmed.

Mr. Chief Justice Warren, concurring in the result.

[It] is not the book that is on trial; it is a person. The conduct of the defendant is the central issue, not the obscenity of a book or picture. The nature of the materials is, of course, relevant as an attribute of the defendant's conduct. [The] defendants in both these cases were engaged in the business of purveying textual or graphic matter openly advertised to appeal to the erotic interest of their customers. They were plainly engaged in the commercial exploitation of the morbid and shameful craving for materials with prurient effect. * * *

Mr. Justice Harlan, concurring in the result in [*Alberts*], and dissenting in [*Roth*].

I. [The] Court seems to assume that "obscenity" is a peculiar genus of "speech and press," which is as distinct, recognizable, and classifiable as poison ivy is among other plants. On this basis the *constitutional* question before us simply becomes, as the Court says, whether "obscenity," as an abstraction, is protected by the First and Fourteenth Amendments, and the question whether a *particular* book may be suppressed becomes a mere matter of classification, of "fact," to be entrusted to a fact-finder and insulated from independent constitutional judgment. But surely the problem cannot be solved in such a generalized fashion. Every communication has an individuality and "value" of its own. The suppression of a particular writing or other tangible form of expression is, therefore, an *individual* matter, and in the nature of things every such suppression raises an individual constitutional problem, in which a reviewing court must determine for *itself* whether the attacked expression is suppressible within constitutional [standards].

I do not think that reviewing courts can escape this responsibility by saying that the trier of the facts, be it a jury or a judge, has labeled the questioned matter as "obscene," for, if "obscenity" is to be suppressed, the question whether a particular work is of that character involves not really an issue of fact but a question of constitutional *judgment* of the most sensitive and delicate kind. Many juries might find that Joyce's "Ulysses" or Bocaccio's "Decameron" was obscene, and yet the conviction of a defendant for selling either book would raise, for me, the gravest constitutional problems, for no such verdict could convince me, without more, that these books are "utterly without redeeming social importance." [I] am very much afraid that the broad manner in which the Court has decided these cases will tend to obscure the peculiar responsibilities resting on state and federal courts in this field and encourage them to rely on easy labeling and jury verdicts as a substitute for facing up to the tough individual problems of constitutional judgment involved in every obscenity case.

[In] California the book must have a "tendency to deprave or corrupt its readers"; under the federal statute it must tend "to stir sexual impulses and lead to sexually impure thoughts." [T]he Court compounds confusion when it superimposes on these two statutory definitions a third, drawn from the American Law Institute's *Model Penal Code,* Tentative Draft No. 6: "A thing is obscene if, considered as a whole, its predominant appeal is to prurient interest." The bland assurance that this definition is the same as the ones with which we deal flies in the face of the authors' express rejection of the "deprave and corrupt" and "sexual thoughts" tests.[d] [T]he Court merely assimilates the various tests into one indiscriminate potpourri. * * *

II.   I concur in [*Alberts*]. [T]he [California] legislature has made the judgment that printed words *can* "deprave or corrupt" the reader—that words can incite to anti-social or immoral action. [It] is well known, of course, that the validity of this assumption is a matter of dispute among critics, sociologists, psychiatrists, and penologists. [I]t is not our function to decide this question. That function belongs to the state legislature. [I]t is not irrational, in our present state of knowledge, to consider that pornography

---

d. The opinion quoted the explanation in the Tentative Draft: "Obscenity [in the Tentative Draft] is defined in terms of material which appeals predominantly to prurient interest in sexual matters and which goes beyond customary freedom of expression in these matters. We reject the prevailing test of tendency to arouse lustful thoughts or desires because it is unrealistically broad for a society that plainly tolerates a great deal of erotic interest in literature, advertising, and art, and because regulation of thought or desire, unconnect-ed with overt misbehavior, raises the most acute constitutional as well as practical difficulties. We likewise reject the common definition of obscene as that which 'tends to corrupt or debase.' If this means anything different from tendency to arouse lustful thought and desire, it suggests that change of character or actual misbehavior follows from contact with obscenity. Evidence of such consequences is lacking. [On] the other hand, 'appeal to prurient interest' refers to qualities of the material itself: the capacity to attract individuals eager for a forbidden look.'"

can induce a type of sexual conduct which a State may deem obnoxious to the moral fabric of [society].

Furthermore, even assuming that pornography cannot be deemed ever to cause, in an immediate sense, criminal sexual conduct, other interests within the proper cognizance of the States may be protected by the prohibition placed on such materials. The State can reasonably draw the inference that over a long period of time the indiscriminate dissemination of materials, the essential character of which is to degrade sex, will have an eroding effect on moral standards. And the State has a legitimate interest in protecting the privacy of the home against invasion of unsolicited obscenity.

[I] concur in the judgment because, upon an independent perusal of the material involved, and in light of the considerations discussed above, I cannot say that its suppression would so interfere with the communication of "ideas" in any proper sense of that term that it would offend the Due Process Clause.[e]

MR. JUSTICE DOUGLAS, with whom MR. JUSTICE BLACK concurs, dissenting.

When we sustain these convictions, we make the legality of a publication turn on the purity of thought which a book or tract instills in the mind of the reader. I do not think we can approve that standard and be faithful to the command of the First Amendment * * *.

I would give the broad sweep of the First Amendment full support. I have the same confidence in the ability of our people to reject noxious literature as I have in their capacity to sort out the true from the false in theology, economics, politics, or any other field.

Notes and Questions

1. *Non-obscene advocacy of "sexual immorality."* Two years after *Roth,* KINGSLEY INT'L PICTURES CORP. v. REGENTS, 360 U.S. 684, 79 S.Ct. 1362, 3 L.Ed.2d 1512 (1959), per STEWART, J., underlined the distinction between obscenity and non-obscene "portrayal of sex" in art and literature. *Kingsley* held invalid New York's denial of a license to exhibit the film *Lady Chatterley's Lover* pursuant to a statute requiring such denial when a film "portrays acts of sexual immorality [as] desirable, acceptable or proper patterns of behavior":

"The Court of Appeals unanimously and explicitly rejected any notion that the film is obscene [but] found that the picture as a whole 'alluringly portrays adultery as proper behavior.' [What] New York has done, [is] to prevent the exhibition of a motion picture because that picture advocates an idea—that adultery under certain circumstances may be proper behavior. Yet the First Amendment's basic guarantee is of freedom to advocate ideas.

e. Harlan, J., dissented in *Roth*. He would have limited federal power to reach only "what the Government has termed as 'hard-core' pornography." He stressed both the absence of federal "power over sexual morality" and the danger to free expression of a "blanket ban over the Nation" on such books as *Lady Chatterley's Lover*.

The State, quite simply, has thus struck at the very heart of constitutionally protected liberty.

"[T]he guarantee is not confined to the expression of ideas that are conventional or shared by a majority. It protects advocacy of the opinion that adultery may sometimes be proper, no less than advocacy of socialism or the single tax. And in the realm of ideas it protects expression which is eloquent no less than that which is unconvincing. Advocacy of conduct proscribed by law is not, as Mr. Justice Brandeis long ago pointed out, 'a justification for denying free speech where the advocacy falls short of incitement and there is nothing to indicate that the advocacy would be immediately acted on.' *Whitney.*"[f]

2. *Ideas and the first amendment.* Consider Kalven, *The Metaphysics of the Law of Obscenity,* 1960 Sup.Ct.Rev. 1, 15–16: "The classic defense of John Stuart Mill and the modern defense of Alexander Meiklejohn do not help much when the question is why the novel, the poem, the painting, the drama, or the piece of sculpture falls within the protection of the First Amendment. Nor do the famous opinions of Hand, Holmes, and Brandeis. [The] people do not need novels or dramas or paintings or poems because they will be called upon to vote. Art and belles-lettres do not deal in such ideas—at least not good art or belles-lettres—and it makes little sense here to talk [of] whether there is still time for counter-speech.

"[B]eauty has constitutional status too, [and] the life of the imagination is as important to the human adult as the life of the intellect. I do not think that the Court would find it difficult to protect Shakespeare, even though it is hard to enumerate the important ideas in the plays and poems. I am only suggesting that Mr. Justice Brennan might not have found it so easy to dismiss obscenity because it lacked socially useful ideas if he had recognized that as to this point, at least, obscenity is in the same position as all art and literature."[g]

3. *The moral rationale for prohibition.* Consider Clor, *Obscenity and Public Morality* 41–43 (1969): *Roth* "rejected the government's formula for the decision of obscenity cases, a formula which would have involved it in judgments concerning the importance of public morality and the role of government, as well as judgments concerning the effects of obscenity and the relative value of different forms of speech. The Court preferred to decide the case on the narrow and negative grounds that obscenity is without redeeming social importance. [W]hile the idea of redeeming social importance can be

f. While joining the opinion, Black and Douglas, JJ., also stated that prior censorship of motion pictures violates the first amendment. See discussion of this issue in Ch. 4, II infra. Harlan, J., joined by Frankfurter and Whittaker, JJ., concurred in the result. While "granting that abstract public discussion [of] adultery, unaccompanied by obscene portrayal or actual incitement [may] not constitutionally be proscribed," they concluded that the New York Court of Appeals had found the film obscene, but on viewing the film they concluded it was not obscene. Clark, J., concurred in the result because the statutory standard was too vague.

g. For the relationship between art and the first amendment, see Hamilton, *Art Speech,* 49 Vand.L.Rev. 73 (1996); Nahmod, *Artistic Expression and Aesthetic Theory: The Beautiful, The Sublime and The First Amendment,* 1987 Wisc.L.Rev. 221.

valuable as a definition of what should be protected, it cannot serve as a defense of regulation. Justices Harlan and Douglas can be answered only by a course of reasoning which provides some grounds for government activity in the area of morality, showing that the ends are legitimate and important, which provides some justification for the claims of community conscience, and which explores, more thoroughly than does the Court, the character of the 'thoughts' with which the law is here concerned."

The Court does assert that any value of obscenity as a step to truth is "outweighed by the social interest in order and morality." "But consider Richards, *Free Speech and Obscenity Law: Toward A Moral Theory of the First Amendment,* 123 U.Pa.L.Rev. 45, 81 (1974): "[P]ornography can be seen as the unique medium of a vision of sexuality * * * a view of sensual delight in the erotic celebration of the body, a concept of easy freedom without consequences, a fantasy of timelessly repetitive indulgence. In opposition to the Victorian view that narrowly defines proper sexual function in a rigid way that is analogous to ideas of excremental regularity and moderation, pornography builds a model of plastic variety and joyful excess in sexuality. In opposition to the sorrowing Catholic dismissal of sexuality as an unfortunate and spiritually superficial concomitant of propagation, pornography affords the alternative idea of the independent status of sexuality as a profound and shattering ecstasy."[h]

Even if these characterizations were somewhat overwrought with respect to Roth's publications (e.g., *Wild Passion* and *Wanton By Night*) what of the view that individuals should be able to decide what they want to read and make moral decisions for themselves? Consider John Stuart Mill's statement of the harm principle in *On Liberty:* "[T]he only purpose for which power can be rightfully exercised over any member of a civilized community, against his will is to prevent harm to others."

Does the liberal view overestimate human rational capacity and underestimate the importance of the state in promoting a virtuous citizenry? See generally Clor, supra. Do liberals fail to appreciate the morally corrosive effects of obscenity? Consider the following observation: "Obscenity emphasizes the base animality of our nature, reduces the spirituality of humanity to mere bodily functions, and debases civilization by transforming the private into the public." Consider Kristol, *Reflections of a Neoconservative* 45, 47 (1983): "Bearbaiting and cockfighting are prohibited only in part out of compassion for the suffering animals; the main reason they were abol-

---

h. For the view that pornography can best be defended as a form of anti-social dissent, consider Gey, *The Apologetics of Suppression,* 86 Mich.L.Rev. 1564, 1630 (1988): "Porn exposes a rot in the framework of society, and the great popularity of porn makes the burghers uneasily suspicious that the surface rot may evidence a more deeply rooted degeneration of their moral and political primacy. Thus, the imperative to suppress pornography reveals a much deeper and more insidious insecurity than the moralists will ever acknowledge." Cf. West, *The Feminist–Conservative Anti–Pornography Alliance and the 1986 Attorney General's Commission on Pornography Report,* 1987 Am.B.Found.Res.J. 681, 686–99 (discussing victimizing and liberating aspects of pornography from the perspectives of women while contending that women's experience of pornography, albeit diverse, is different from that of men).

ished was because it was felt that they debased and brutalized the citizenry who flocked to witness such spectacles. And the question we face with regard to pornography and obscenity is whether [they] can or will brutalize and debase our citizenry. We are, after all, not dealing with one passing incident—one book, or one play, or one movie. We are dealing with a general tendency that is suffusing our entire culture. [W]hen men and women make love, as we say, they prefer to be alone—because it is only when you are alone that you can make love, as distinct from merely copulating in an animal and casual way. And that, too, is why those who are voyeurs, if they are not irredeemably sick, also feel ashamed at what they are witnessing. When sex is a public spectacle, a human relationship has been debased into a mere animal connection."[i]

4. *Obscenity and deliberation.* Consider Sunstein, *Words, Conduct, Caste,* 60 U.Chi.L.Rev. 795, 807–08 (1993): "Such materials fall in the same category as misleading commercial speech, libel of private persons, conspiracies, unlicensed medical or legal advice, bribes, perjury, threats, and so forth. These forms of speech do not appeal to deliberative capacities about public matters, or about matters at all—even if this category is construed quite broadly, as it should be, and even if we insist, as we should, that emotive and cognitive capacities are frequently intertwined in deliberative processes and that any sharp split between 'emotion' and 'cognition' would be untrue to political discussion. Many forms of pornography are not an appeal to the exchange of ideas, political or otherwise; they operate as masturbatory aids and do not qualify for top-tier First Amendment protection under the prevailing theories." But see Cole, *Playing by Pornography's Rules: The Regulation of Sexual Expression,* 143 U.Pa.L.Rev. 111, 126–27 (1994): "[T]he argument that sexual speech is 'noncognitive' because it is designed to produce a physical effect is predicated on an impoverished view of sexuality. [Sexual] expression, like human sexuality itself, cannot be 'purely physical.' Rather, it is deeply and inextricably interwoven with our identities, our emotions, our upbringing, our relationships to other human beings, and the ever-changing narratives and images that our community finds stimulating. [Thus,] the argument that sexual expression can be usefully distinguished from political speech because it lacks 'cognitive' appeal is insupportable. Both political and sexual expression work in rational and irrational ways and contribute to our culture, our ideology, and our individual and collective identities through their rational and irrational communicative content."

Compare Sunstein, supra, at 808 & 808 n. 45: "Those who write or read sexually explicit material can often claim important expressive and deliberative interests. Sexually explicit works can be highly relevant to the develop-

---

i. See also Clor, supra; Berns, *Pornography vs. Democracy: The Case for Censorship,* 22 Pub.Int. 13 (1971); George, *Making Children Moral: Pornography, Parents, and the Public Interest,* 29 Ariz.St.L.J. 569 (1997). For the relationship between pornography, commerce, and culture, see Collins & Skover, *The Pornographic State,* 107 Harv.L.Rev. 1374 (1994).

ment of human capacities. [But] no one has set out an approach to free speech based on expression and deliberative value. * * * To be sure, pornography is political in the sense that it has political consequences. But this does not mean that it is political in the First Amendment sense of that word. Much speech that does not belong in the top tier—misleading commercial speech, attempted bribery of public officials—has political consequences. If speech qualified for the top tier whenever it has such consequences, almost all speech would so qualify, and First Amendment doctrine would be made senseless. Instead, the test is whether it is intended and received as a contribution to democratic deliberation—and much pornography fails that test. It is true that the recent attack on pornography has drawn attention to its political character, but this fact does not undermine the First Amendment argument, since the First Amendment conception of 'the political' is properly and importantly different from the conception of 'the political' in popular discussion."

5. *Feminism and pornography.* Does the Court's cryptic recitation of the interests in order and morality obscure the implications of pornography for women in a male-dominated culture? Consider Brownmiller, *Against Our Will: Men, Women & Rape* 442–43, 444 (1976): Pornography is a "systematized commercially successful propaganda machine" encouraging males to get a "sense of power from viewing females as anonymous, panting playthings, adult toys, dehumanized objects to be used, abused, broken and discarded." See also MacKinnon, *Not a Moral Issue*, 2 Yale L. & Pol.Rev. 321, 327 (1984): "[T]he liberal defense of pornography as human sexual liberation, as de-repression—whether by feminists, lawyers, or neo-Freudians—is a defense not only of force and sexual terrorism, but of the subordination of women. Sexual liberation in the liberal sense frees male sexual aggression in the feminist sense. What in the liberal view looks like love and romance looks a lot like hatred and torture to the feminist. Pleasure and eroticism become violation. Desire appears as lust for dominance and submission."

———

STANLEY v. GEORGIA, 394 U.S. 557, 89 S.Ct. 1243, 22 L.Ed.2d 542 (1969), per MARSHALL, J., reversed a conviction for knowing "possession of obscene matter," based on three reels of obscene films found in Stanley's home when police entered under a search warrant for other purposes: "[*Roth*] and the cases following it discerned [an] 'important interest' in the regulation of commercial distribution of obscene material. That holding cannot foreclose an examination of the constitutional implications of a statute forbidding mere private possession of such material. [The constitutional] right to receive information and ideas, regardless of their social worth [*Winters*] is fundamental to our free society. Moreover, in the context of this case—a prosecution for mere possession of printed or filmed matter in the privacy of a person's own home—that right takes on an added dimension. For also fundamental is the right to be free, except in very limited circumstances, from unwanted governmental intrusions into one's privacy.

" 'The makers of our Constitution undertook to secure conditions favorable to the pursuit of happiness. They recognized the significance of man's spiritual nature, of his feelings and of his intellect. [They] sought to protect Americans in their beliefs, their thoughts, their emotions and their sensations. They conferred, as against the government, the right to be let alone—the most comprehensive of rights and the right most valued by civilized man.' *Olmstead v. United States,* 277 U.S. 438, 48 S.Ct. 564, 72 L.Ed. 944 (1928) (Brandeis, J., dissenting). * * *

"These are the rights that appellant is asserting in the case before us. He is asserting the right to read or observe what he pleases—the right to satisfy his intellectual and emotional needs in the privacy of his own home. He is asserting the right to be free from state inquiry into the contents of his library. Georgia contends that appellant does not have these rights, that there are certain types of materials that the individual may not read or even possess. [W]e think that mere categorization of these films as 'obscene' is insufficient justification for such a drastic invasion of personal liberties guaranteed by the First and Fourteenth Amendments. Whatever may be the justifications for other statutes regulating obscenity, we do not think they reach into the privacy of one's own home. If the First Amendment means anything, it means that a State has no business telling a man, sitting alone in his own house, what books he may read or what films he may watch. Our whole constitutional heritage rebels at the thought of giving government the power to control men's minds.

"[I]n the face of these traditional notions of individual liberty, Georgia asserts the right to protect the individual's mind from the effects of obscenity. We are not certain that this argument amounts to anything more than the assertion that the State has the right to control the moral content of a person's thoughts.[8] To some, this may be a noble purpose, but it is wholly inconsistent with the philosophy of the First Amendment. [*Kingsley Pictures.*] Nor is it relevant that obscenity in general, or the particular films before the Court, are arguably devoid of any ideological content. The line between the transmission of ideas and mere entertainment is much too elusive for this Court to draw, if indeed such a line can be drawn at all. [*Winters*]. Whatever the power of the state to control public dissemination of ideas inimical to the public morality, it cannot constitutionally premise legislation on the desirability of controlling a person's private thoughts.

---

8. "Communities believe, and act on the belief, that obscenity is immoral, is wrong for the individual, and has no place in a decent society. They believe, too, that adults as well as children are corruptible in morals and character, and that obscenity is a source of corruption that should be eliminated. Obscenity is not suppressed primarily for the protection of others. Much of it is suppressed for the purity of the community and for the salvation and welfare of the 'consumer.' Obscenity, at bottom, is not crime. Obscenity is sin." Henkin, *Morals and the Constitution: The Sin of Obscenity,* 63 Col.L.Rev. 391, 395 (1963).

"[Georgia] asserts that exposure to obscenity may lead to deviant sexual behavior or crimes of sexual violence. There appears to be little empirical basis for that assertion. But more importantly, if the State is only concerned about literature inducing antisocial conduct, we believe that in the context of private consumption of ideas and information we should adhere to the view that '[a]mong free men, the deterrents ordinarily to be applied to prevent crime are education and punishment for violations of the [law].' *Whitney* (Brandeis, J., concurring). See Emerson, *Toward a General Theory of the First Amendment,* 72 Yale L.J. 877, 938 (1963). Given the present state of knowledge, the State may no more prohibit mere possession of obscenity on the ground that it may lead to antisocial conduct than it may prohibit possession of chemistry books on the ground that they may lead to the manufacture of homemade spirits.

"It is true that in *Roth* this Court rejected the necessity of proving that exposure to obscene material would create a clear and present danger of antisocial conduct or would probably induce its recipients to such conduct. But that case dealt with public distribution of obscene materials and such distribution is subject to different objections. For example, there is always the danger that obscene material might fall into the hands of children, see *Ginsberg,* [fn. d, p. 138 infra], or that it might intrude upon the sensibilities or privacy of the general public. No such dangers are present in this [case.]

"We hold that the First and Fourteenth Amendments prohibit making mere private possession of obscene material a crime. *Roth* and the cases following that decision are not impaired by today's holding. As we have said, the States retain broad power to regulate obscenity; that power simply does not extend to mere possession by the individual in the privacy of his own home."[a]

Notes and Questions

1. *Obscenity and the first amendment.* Is *Stanley* consistent with the constitutional theory of *Roth?* Can the first amendment rationally be viewed as applicable to *private use* but not to *public distribution* of obscenity? Cf. Katz, *Privacy and Pornography,* 1969 Sup.Ct.Rev. 203, 210–11. Might the definitional two-level approach reconcile *Stanley* with *Roth?*

2. *Implications of Stanley.* Could *Stanley*'s recognition of a first amendment right to "receive" and use obscene matter in the home fairly be viewed as implying a right to purchase it from commercial suppliers, or to import it for personal use, or to view it in a theater limited to consenting adults?

PARIS ADULT THEATRE I v. SLATON

413 U.S. 49, 93 S.Ct. 2628, 37 L.Ed.2d 446 (1973).

[The entrance to Paris Adult Theatres I & II was conventional and inoffensive without any pictures. Signs read: "Adult Theatre—You must

---

a. Black, J., concurred separately. Stewart, J., joined by Brennan and White, JJ., concurred in the result on search and seizure grounds.

be 21 and able to prove it. If viewing the nude body offends you, Please Do Not Enter." The District Attorney, nonetheless, had brought an action to enjoin the showing of two films that the Georgia Supreme Court described as "hard core pornography" leaving "little to the imagination." The Georgia Supreme Court assumed that the adult theaters in question barred minors and gave a full warning to the general public of the nature of the films involved, but held that the showing of the films was not constitutionally protected.]

MR. CHIEF JUSTICE BURGER delivered the opinion of the Court. * * *

[We] categorically disapprove the theory [that] obscene, pornographic films acquire constitutional immunity from state regulation simply because they are exhibited for consenting adults only. [Although we have] recognized the high importance of the state interest in regulating the exposure of obscene materials to juveniles and unconsenting adults, this Court has never declared these to be the only legitimate state interests permitting regulation of obscene material. * * *

[W]e hold that there are legitimate state interests at stake in stemming the tide of commercialized obscenity, even assuming it is feasible to enforce effective safeguards against exposure to juveniles and to the passerby.[7] [These] include the interest of the public in the quality of life and the total community environment, the tone of commerce in the great city centers, and, possibly, the public safety itself. The Hill–Link Minority Report of the Commission on Obscenity and Pornography indicates that there is at least an arguable correlation between obscene material and crime. Quite apart from sex crimes, however, there remains one problem of large proportions aptly described by Professor Bickel: "It concerns the tone of the society, the mode, or to use terms that have perhaps greater currency, the style and quality of life, now and in the future. A man may be entitled to read an obscene book in his room, or expose himself indecently there. [We] should protect his privacy. But if he demands a right to obtain the books and pictures he wants in the market, and to foregather in public places—discreet, if you will, but accessible to all—with others who share his tastes, *then to grant him his right is to affect the world about the rest of us, and to impinge on other privacies.* Even supposing that each of us can, if he wishes, effectively avert the eye and stop the ear (which, in truth, we cannot), what

---

7. It is conceivable that an "adult" theatre can—if it really insists—prevent the exposure of its obscene wares to juveniles. An "adult" bookstore, dealing in obscene books, magazines, and pictures, cannot realistically make this claim. The Hill–Link Minority Report of the Commission on Obscenity and Pornography emphasizes evidence (the Abelson National Survey of Youth and Adults) that, although most pornography may be bought by elders, "the heavy users and most highly exposed people to pornography are adolescent females (among women) and adolescent and young males (among men)." *The Report of the Commission on Obscenity* 401 (1970). The legitimate interest in preventing exposure of juveniles to obscene materials cannot be fully served by simply barring juveniles from the immediate physical premises of "adult" bookstores, when there is a flourishing "outside business" in these materials.

is commonly read and seen and heard and done intrudes upon us all, want it or not." 22 *The Public Interest* 25, 25–26 (Winter, 1971). (Emphasis supplied.) [T]here is a "right of the Nation and of the States to maintain a decent [society]," *Jacobellis* (Warren, C.J., dissenting).

But, it is argued, there is no scientific data which conclusively demonstrates that exposure to obscene materials adversely affects men and women or their society. It is urged [that], absent such a demonstration, any kind of state regulation is "impermissible." We reject this argument. It is not for us to resolve empirical uncertainties underlying state legislation, save in the exceptional case where that legislation plainly impinges upon rights protected by the Constitution itself. [Although] there is no conclusive proof of a connection between antisocial behavior and obscene material, the legislature of Georgia could quite reasonably determine that such a connection does or might exist. In deciding *Roth,* this Court implicitly accepted that a legislature could legitimately act on such a conclusion to protect *"the social interest in order and morality."*

From the beginning of civilized societies, legislators and judges have acted on various unprovable assumptions. Such assumptions underlie much lawful state regulation of commercial and business affairs. The same is true of the federal securities, antitrust laws and a host of other federal regulations. [Likewise], when legislatures and administrators act to protect the physical environment from pollution and to preserve our resources of forests, streams and parks, they must act on such imponderables as the impact of a new highway near or through an existing park or wilderness area. [The] fact that a congressional directive reflects unprovable assumptions about what is good for the people, including imponderable aesthetic assumptions, is not a sufficient reason to find that statute unconstitutional.

If we accept the unprovable assumption that a complete education requires certain books, and the well nigh universal belief that good books, plays, and art lift the spirit, improve the mind, enrich the human personality and develop character, can we then say that a state legislature may not act on the corollary assumption that commerce in obscene books,[a] or public exhibitions focused on obscene conduct, have a tendency to exert a corrupting and debasing impact leading to antisocial behavior? [The] sum of experience, including that of the past two decades, affords an ample basis for

---

a. The only case after *Roth* in which the Court upheld a conviction based upon books was in *Mishkin* [p. 138 infra] and most, if not all, of those books were illustrated. *Kaplan v. California,* 413 U.S. 115, 93 S.Ct. 2680, 37 L.Ed.2d 492 (1973) held that books without pictures can be legally obscene "in the sense of being unprotected by the First Amendment." It observed that books are "passed hand to hand, and we can take note of the tendency of widely circulated books of this category to reach the impressionable young and have a continuing impact. A State could reasonably regard the 'hard core' conduct described by *Suite 69* as capable of encouraging or causing antisocial behavior, especially in its impact on young people." Is *Kaplan's* explanation in tension with *Butler v. Michigan* [Ch. 1, III, B infra]? Why should the obscenity standard focus on the average adult if the underlying worry is that books will fall in the hands of children?

legislatures to conclude that a sensitive, key relationship of human existence, central to family life, community welfare, and the development of human personality, can be debased and distorted by crass commercial exploitation of sex. Nothing in the Constitution prohibits a State from reaching such a conclusion and acting on it legislatively simply because there is no conclusive evidence or empirical data.

[Nothing] in this Court's decisions intimates that there is any "fundamental" privacy right "implicit in the concept of ordered liberty" to watch obscene movies in places of public accommodation. [W]e have declined to equate the privacy of the home relied on in *Stanley* with a "zone" of "privacy" that follows a distributor or a consumer of obscene materials wherever he goes.[b]

[W]e reject the claim that Georgia is here attempting to control the minds or thoughts of those who patronize theatres. Preventing unlimited display or distribution of obscene material, which by definition lacks any serious literary, artistic, political, or scientific value as communication, is distinct from a control of reason and the intellect. Cf. Finnis, *"Reason and Passion": The Constitutional Dialectic of Free Speech and Obscenity,* 116 U.Pa.L.Rev. 222, 229–230, 241–243 (1967).

[Finally], petitioners argue that conduct which directly involves "consenting adults" only has, for that sole reason, a special claim to constitutional protection. Our Constitution establishes a broad range of conditions on the exercise of power by the States, but for us to say that our Constitution incorporates the proposition that conduct involving consenting adults only is always beyond state regulation,[14] is a step we are unable to take.[15] [The] issue in this context goes beyond whether someone, or even the majority, considers the conduct depicted as "wrong" or "sinful." The States have the power to make a morally neutral judgment that public exhibition of obscene

---

b. In a series of cases, the Court limited *Stanley* to its facts. It held that *Stanley* did not protect the mailing of obscene material to consenting adults, *United States v. Reidel*, 402 U.S. 351, 91 S.Ct. 1410, 28 L.Ed.2d 813 (1971) or the transporting or importing of obscene materials for private use, *United States v. Orito*, 413 U.S. 139, 93 S.Ct. 2674, 37 L.Ed.2d 513 (1973) (transporting); *United States v. 12 200 Ft. Reels*, 413 U.S. 123, 93 S.Ct. 2665, 37 L.Ed.2d 500 (1973) (importing). Dissenting in *Reels*, Douglas, J., argued that *Stanley* rights could legally be realized "only if one wrote or designed a tract in his attic and printed or processed it in his basement, so as to be able to read it in his study." Do these decisions take the first amendment out of *Stanley*? Are they justified by the rationale in *Paris Adult Theatre*? For example, does importation for personal use intrude "upon us all"? Affect the total community environment?

For the declaration that *Stanley's* "privacy of the home" principle is "firmly ground-

ed" in the first amendment while resisting the principle's expansion to protect consensual adult homosexual sodomy in the home, see *Bowers v. Hardwick*, 478 U.S. 186, 106 S.Ct. 2841, 92 L.Ed.2d 140 (1986). But see Blackmun, J., joined by Brennan, Marshall, and Stevens, JJ., dissenting in *Bowers* ("*Stanley* rested as much on the Court's understanding of the Fourth Amendment as it did on the First").

14. Cf. Mill, *On Liberty* 13 (1955).

15. The state statute books are replete with constitutionally unchallenged laws against prostitution, suicide, voluntary self-mutilation, brutalizing "bare fist" prize fights, and duels, although these crimes may only directly involve "consenting adults." Statutes making bigamy a crime surely cut into an individual's freedom to associate, but few today seriously claim such statutes violate the First Amendment or any other constitutional provision.

material, or commerce in such material, has a tendency to injure the community as a whole, to endanger the public safety, or to jeopardize, in Mr. Chief Justice Warren's words, the States' "right [to] maintain a decent society." *Jacobellis* (dissenting). * * *

MR. JUSTICE BRENNAN, with whom MR. JUSTICE STEWART and MR. JUSTICE MARSHALL join, dissenting.

[I] am convinced that the approach initiated 15 years ago in *Roth* and culminating in the Court's decision today, cannot bring stability to this area of the law without jeopardizing fundamental First Amendment values, and I have concluded that the time has come to make a significant departure from that [approach.]

[The] decision of the Georgia Supreme Court rested squarely on its conclusion that the State could constitutionally suppress these films even if they were displayed only to persons over the age of 21 who were aware of the nature of their contents and who had consented to viewing them. [I] am convinced of the invalidity of that conclusion [and] would therefore vacate the [judgment]. I have no occasion to consider the extent of State power to regulate the distribution of sexually oriented materials to juveniles or to unconsenting [adults.] [*Stanley*] reflected our emerging view that the state interests in protecting children and in protecting unconsenting adults may stand on a different footing from the other asserted state interests. It may well be, as one commentator has argued, that "exposure to [erotic material] is for some persons an intense emotional experience. A communication of this nature, imposed upon a person contrary to his wishes, has all the characteristics of a physical assault * * *. [And it] constitutes an invasion of his [privacy]." [But] whatever the strength of the state interests in protecting juveniles and unconsenting adults from exposure to sexually oriented materials, those interests cannot be asserted in defense of the holding of the Georgia Supreme Court, [which] assumed for the purposes of its decision that the films in issue were exhibited only to persons over the age of 21 who viewed them willingly and with prior knowledge of the nature of their contents. [The] justification for the suppression must be found, therefore, in some independent interest in regulating the reading and viewing habits of consenting [adults].

In *Stanley* we pointed out that "[t]here appears to be little empirical basis for" the assertion that "exposure to obscene materials may lead to deviant sexual behavior or crimes of sexual violence." In any event, we added that "if the State is only concerned about printed or filmed materials inducing antisocial conduct, we believe that in the context of private consumption of ideas and information we should adhere to the view that '[a]mong free men, the deterrents ordinarily to be applied to prevent crime are education and punishment for violations of the [law].' "

Moreover, in *Stanley* we rejected as "wholly inconsistent with the philosophy of the First Amendment," the notion that there is a legitimate state concern in the "control [of] the moral content of a person's thoughts." [The] traditional description of state police power does embrace the regulation of morals as well as the health, safety, and general welfare of the citizenry. [But] the State's interest in regulating morality by suppressing obscenity, while often asserted, remains essentially unfocused and ill-defined. And, since the attempt to curtail unprotected speech necessarily spills over into the area of protected speech, the effort to serve this speculative interest through the suppression of obscene material must tread heavily on rights protected by the First Amendment. * * *

In short, while I cannot say that the interests of the State—apart from the question of juveniles and unconsenting adults—are trivial or nonexistent, I am compelled to conclude that these interests cannot justify the substantial damage to constitutional rights and to this Nation's judicial machinery that inevitably results from state efforts to bar the distribution even of unprotected material to consenting adults.[c]

MR. JUSTICE DOUGLAS, dissenting. * * *

"Obscenity" at most is the expression of offensive ideas. There are regimes in the world where ideas "offensive" to the majority (or at least to those who control the majority) are suppressed. There life proceeds at a monotonous pace. Most of us would find that world offensive. One of the most offensive experiences in my life was a visit to a nation where bookstalls were filled only with books on mathematics and books on religion.

I am sure I would find offensive most of the books and movies charged with being obscene. But in a life that has not been short, I have yet to be trapped into seeing or reading something that would offend me. I never read or see the materials coming to the Court under charges of "obscenity," because I have thought the First Amendment made it unconstitutional for me to act as a censor. * * *

When man was first in the jungle he took care of himself. When he entered a societal group, controls were necessarily imposed. But our society—unlike most in the world—presupposes that freedom and liberty are in a frame of reference that makes the individual, not government, the keeper of his tastes, beliefs, and ideas. That is the philosophy of the First Amendment; and it is the article of faith that sets us apart from most nations in the world.

B.   A REVISED STANDARD

MILLER v. CALIFORNIA

413 U.S. 15, 93 S.Ct. 2607, 37 L.Ed.2d 419 (1973).

MR. CHIEF JUSTICE BURGER delivered the opinion of the Court. [The Court remanded, "for proceedings not inconsistent" with the opinion's obscenity

---

c. For the portion of Brennan, J.'s dissent addressing the difficulties of formulating an acceptable constitutional standard, see *Miller v. California*, p. 135 infra.

standard, Miller's conviction under California's obscenity law for mass mailing of unsolicited pictorial advertising brochures depicting men and women in a variety of group sexual activities.]

This is one of a group of "obscenity-pornography" cases being reviewed by the Court in a re-examination of standards enunciated in earlier cases involving what Mr. Justice Harlan called "the intractable obscenity problem." [I]n this context[a] [we] are called on to define the standards which must be used to identify obscene material that a State may [regulate].

[Nine years after *Roth v. United States*], in *Memoirs v. Massachusetts,* 383 U.S. 413, 16 L.Ed.2d 1, 86 S.Ct. 975 (1966), the Court veered sharply away from the *Roth* concept and, with only three Justices in the plurality opinion, articulated a new test of obscenity. The plurality held that under the *Roth* definition "as elaborated in subsequent cases, three elements must coalesce: it must be established that (a) the dominant theme of the material taken as a whole appeals to a prurient interest in sex; (b) the material is patently offensive because it affronts contemporary community standards relating to the description or representation of sexual matters; and (c) the material is utterly without redeeming social value."

While *Roth* presumed "obscenity" to be "utterly without redeeming social importance," *Memoirs* required that to prove obscenity it must be affirmatively established that the material is "*utterly* without redeeming social value."

Thus, even as they repeated the words of *Roth,* the *Memoirs* plurality produced a drastically altered test that called on the prosecution to prove a negative, i.e., that the material was "*utterly* without redeeming social value"—a burden virtually impossible to discharge under our criminal standards of proof. [Apart] from the initial formulation in *Roth,* no majority of the Court has at any given time been able to agree on a standard to determine what constitutes obscene, pornographic material subject to regulation under the States' police power. See, e.g., *Redrup v. New York,* 386 U.S. 767, 87 S.Ct. 1414, 18 L.Ed.2d 515 (1967).[3] This is not remarkable, for in the area of freedom of speech and press the courts must always remain sensitive to any infringement on genuinely serious literary, artistic, political, or scientific expression. * * *

II. This much has been categorically settled by the Court, that obscene material is unprotected by the First Amendment. [We] acknowledge, howev-

a. The "context" was that in *Miller* "sexually explicit materials have been thrust by aggressive sales action upon unwilling recipients." But nothing in *Miller* limited the revised standard to that context, and the companion case, *Paris Adult Theatre,* applied the same standard to dissemination limited to consenting adults.

3. In the absence of a majority view, this Court was compelled to embark on the practice of summarily reversing convictions for the dissemination of materials that at least five members of the Court, applying their separate tests, found to be protected by the First Amendment. *Redrup.* [Beyond] the necessity of circumstances, however, no justification has ever been offered in support of the *Redrup* "policy." The *Redrup* procedure has cast us in the role of an unreviewable board of censorship for the 50 States, subjectively judging each piece of material brought before us.

er, the inherent dangers of undertaking to regulate any form of expression. State statutes designed to regulate obscene materials must be carefully limited. As a result, we now confine the permissible scope of such regulation to works which depict or describe sexual conduct. That conduct must be specifically defined by the applicable state law, as written or authoritatively construed.[6] A state offense must also be limited to works which, taken as a whole, appeal to the prurient interest in sex, which portray sexual conduct in a patently offensive way, and which, taken as a whole, do not have serious literary, artistic, political, or scientific value.

The basic guidelines for the trier of fact must be: (a) whether "the average person, applying contemporary community standards" would find that the work, taken as a whole, appeals to the prurient interest, (b) whether the work depicts or describes, in a patently offensive way, sexual conduct specifically defined by the applicable state law,[b] and (c) whether the work, taken as a whole, lacks serious literary, artistic, political, or scientific value. We do not adopt as a constitutional standard the "*utterly* without redeeming social value" test of *Memoirs;* that concept has never commanded the adherence of more than three Justices at one time.[7] If a state law that regulates obscene material is thus limited, as written or construed, the First Amendment values applicable to the States [are] adequately protected by the ultimate power of appellate courts to conduct an independent review of constitutional claims when necessary.

We emphasize that it is not our function to propose regulatory schemes for the States. [It] is possible, however, to give a few plain examples of what a state statute could define for regulation under the second part (b) of the standard announced in this opinion, supra:

(a) Patently offensive representations or descriptions of ultimate sexual acts, normal or perverted, actual or simulated.

---

6. See, e.g., Oregon Laws 1971, c. 743, Art. 29, §§ 255–262, and Hawaii Penal Code, Tit. 37, §§ 1210–1216, 1972 Hawaii Session Laws, pp. 126–129, Act 9, Pt. II, as examples of state laws directed at depiction of defined physical conduct, as opposed to expression. [We] do not hold, as Mr. Justice Brennan intimates, that all States other than Oregon must now enact new obscenity statutes. Other existing state statutes, as construed heretofore or hereafter, may well be adequate.

b. On the use of guidelines (a) and (b) against sexual minorities, see Comment, *Behind the Curtain of Privacy: How Obscenity Laws Inhibit the Expression of Ideas About Sex and Gender,* 1998 Wis. L. Rev. 625 (1998).

7. "[We] also reject, as a constitutional standard, the ambiguous concept of 'social importance'." [*Hamling v. United States,* 418 U.S. 87, 94 S.Ct. 2887, 41 L.Ed.2d 590 (1974) upheld a conviction in which the jury had been instructed to find that the material was "utterly without redeeming social value." Defendant argued that the latter phrase was unconstitutionally vague and cited *Miller.* The Court rejected the vagueness challenge: "[O]ur opinion in *Miller* plainly indicates that we rejected the '[social] value' formulation, not because it was so vague as to deprive criminal defendants of adequate notice, but instead because it represented a departure from [*Roth*], and because in calling on the prosecution to 'prove a negative,' it imposed a '[prosecutorial] burden virtually impossible to discharge' and which was not constitutionally required."]

(b) Patently offensive representations or descriptions of masturbation, excretory functions, and lewd exhibition of the genitals.[c]

Sex and nudity may not be exploited without limit by films or pictures exhibited or sold in places of public accommodation any more than live sex and nudity can be exhibited or sold without limit in such public places.[8] At a minimum, prurient,[d] patently offensive depiction or description of sexual conduct must have serious literary, artistic, political, or scientific value to merit First Amendment protection. For example, medical books for the education of physicians and related personnel necessarily use graphic illustrations and descriptions of human anatomy. In resolving the inevitably sensitive questions of fact and law, we must continue to rely on the jury system, accompanied by the safeguards that judges, rules of evidence, presumption of innocence and other protective features [provide].

Mr. Justice Brennan [has] abandoned his former positions and now maintains that no formulation of this Court, the Congress, or the States can adequately distinguish obscene material unprotected by the First Amendment from protected expression, *Paris Adult Theatre I v. Slaton* (Brennan, J., dissenting). Paradoxically, Mr. Justice Brennan indicates that suppression of unprotected obscene material is permissible to avoid exposure to unconsenting adults, as in this case, and to juveniles, although he gives no indication of how the division between protected and nonprotected materials may be drawn with greater precision for these purposes than for regulation of commercial exposure to consenting adults only. Nor does he indicate where in the Constitution he finds the authority to distinguish between a willing "adult" one month past the state law age of majority and a willing "juvenile" one month younger.[e]

---

c. *Jenkins v. Georgia,* 418 U.S. 153, 94 S.Ct. 2750, 41 L.Ed.2d 642 (1974) held the film *Carnal Knowledge* not obscene because it did not " 'depict or describe patently offensive "hard core" sexual conduct' "as required by *Miller:* "[While there] are scenes in which sexual conduct including 'ultimate sexual acts' is to be understood to be taking place, the camera does not focus on the bodies of the actors at such times. There is no exhibition whatever of the actors' genitals, lewd or otherwise, during these scenes. There are occasional scenes of nudity, but nudity alone is not enough to make material legally obscene under the *Miller* standards." *Ward v. Illinois,* 431 U.S. 767, 97 S.Ct. 2085, 52 L.Ed.2d 738 (1977) held that it was not necessary for the legislature or the courts to provide an "exhaustive list of the sexual conduct [the] description of which may be held obscene." It is enough that a state adopt *Miller*'s explanatory examples. Stevens, J., joined by Brennan, Stewart and Marshall, JJ., dissented: "[I]f the statute need only describe the 'kinds' of proscribed sexual conduct, it adds no protection to what the Constitution itself cre-

ates. [The] specificity requirement as described in *Miller* held out the promise of a principled effort to respond to [the vagueness] argument. By abandoning that effort today, the Court withdraws the cornerstone of the *Miller* [structure]."

8. Although we are not presented here with the problem of regulating lewd public conduct itself, the States have greater power to regulate nonverbal, physical conduct than to suppress depictions or descriptions of the same behavior. * * *

d. *Brockett v. Spokane Arcades, Inc.,* 472 U.S. 491, 105 S.Ct. 2794, 86 L.Ed.2d 394 (1985) held that appeals to prurient interest could not be taken to include appeals to "normal" interests in sex. Only appeals to a "shameful or morbid interest in sex" are prurient. Although the Court was resolute in its position that appeals to "good, old fashioned, healthy" interests in sex were constitutionally protected, it did not further specify how "normal" sex was to be distinguished from the "shameful" or "morbid."

Under the holdings announced today, no one will be subject to prosecution for the sale or exposure of obscene materials unless these materials depict or describe patently offensive "hard core" sexual conduct specifically defined by the regulating state law, as written or construed. We are satisfied that these specific prerequisites will provide fair notice to a dealer in such materials that his public and commercial activities may bring prosecution. If the inability to define regulated materials with ultimate, god-like precision altogether removes the power of the States or the Congress to regulate, then "hard core" pornography may be exposed without limit to the juvenile, the passerby, and the consenting adult alike, as indeed, Mr. Justice Douglas contends.

[N]o amount of "fatigue" should lead us to adopt a convenient "institutional" rationale—an absolutist, "anything goes" view of the First Amendment—because it will lighten our burdens. [Nor] should we remedy "tension between state and federal courts" by arbitrarily depriving the States of a power reserved to them under the Constitution, a power which they have enjoyed and exercised continuously from before the adoption of the First Amendment to this day. See *Roth*. "Our duty admits of no 'substitute for facing up to the tough individual problems of constitutional judgment involved in every obscenity case.'" *Jacobellis* (opinion of Brennan, J.).

III. Under a national Constitution, fundamental First Amendment limitations on the powers of the States do not vary from community to community, but this does not mean that there are, or should or can be, fixed, uniform national standards of precisely what appeals to the "prurient interest" or is "patently offensive." These are essentially questions of fact, and our nation is simply too big and too diverse for this Court to reasonably expect that such standards could be articulated for all 50 States in a single formulation, even assuming the prerequisite consensus exists. When triers of fact are asked to decide whether "the average person, applying contemporary community standards" would consider certain materials "prurient," it

---

e. *Butler v. Michigan,* 352 U.S. 380, 77 S.Ct. 524, 1 L.Ed.2d 412 (1957) held that the state could not ban sales to the general public of material unsuitable for children: "The State insists that [by] quarantining the general reading public against books not too rugged for grown men and women in order to shield juvenile innocence, it is exercising its power to promote the general welfare. Surely, this is to burn the house to roast the pig. [The] incidence of this enactment is to reduce the adult population of Michigan to reading only what is fit for children." *Ginsberg v. New York,* 390 U.S. 629, 88 S.Ct. 1274, 20 L.Ed.2d 195 (1968), however, held that the state could bar the distribution to children of books that were suitable for adults, the Court recognizing it was adopting a "variable" concept of ob-

scenity. See also *Ginzburg v. United States,* p. 266 infra ("pandering" method of marketing supports obscenity conviction even though the materials might not otherwise have been considered obscene); *Mishkin v. New York,* 383 U.S. 502, 86 S.Ct. 958, 16 L.Ed.2d 56 (1966) (material designed for and primarily disseminated to deviant sexual group can meet prurient appeal requirement even if the material lacks appeal to an average member of the general public; appeal is to be tested with reference to the sexual interests of the intended and probable recipient group).

The variable obscenity approach had previously been advocated and elaborated by Lockhart and McClure, *Censorship of Obscenity: The Developing Constitutional Standards,* 45 Minn.L.Rev. 5, 77 (1960).

would be unrealistic to require that the answer be based on some abstract formulation. The adversary system, with lay jurors as the usual ultimate fact finders in criminal prosecutions, has historically permitted triers-of-fact to draw on the standards of their community, guided always by limiting instructions on the law. To require a State to structure obscenity proceedings around evidence of a *national* "community standard" would be an exercise in [futility].

We conclude that neither the State's alleged failure to offer evidence of "national standards," nor the trial court's charge that the jury consider state community standards, were constitutional errors. Nothing in the First Amendment requires that a jury must consider hypothetical and unascertainable "national standards" when attempting to determine whether certain materials are obscene as a matter of [fact].

It is neither realistic nor constitutionally sound to read the First Amendment as requiring that the people of Maine or Mississippi accept public depiction of conduct found tolerable in Las Vegas, or New York City. People in different States vary in their tastes and attitudes, and this diversity is not to be strangled by the absolutism of imposed uniformity. As the Court made clear in *Mishkin*, the primary concern with requiring a jury to apply the standard of "the average person, applying contemporary community standards" is to be certain that, so far as material is not aimed at a deviant group, it will be judged by its impact on an average person, rather than a particularly susceptible or sensitive person—or indeed a totally insensitive one.[f] [We] hold the requirement that the jury evaluate the materials with reference to "contemporary standards of the State of California" serves this protective purpose and is constitutionally adequate.[g]

* * *

f. *Pinkus v. United States,* 436 U.S. 293, 98 S.Ct. 1808, 56 L.Ed.2d 293 (1978) upheld a jury instruction stating "you are to judge these materials by the standard of the hypothetical average person in the community, but in determining this average standard you must include the *sensitive and the insensitive,* in other words, [everyone] in the community." On the other hand, in the absence of evidence that "children were the intended recipients" or that defendant "had reason to know children were likely to receive the materials," it was considered erroneous to instruct the jury that children were part of the relevant community. *Butler.* When the evidence would support such a charge, the Court stated that prurient appeal to deviant sexual groups could be substituted for appeal to the average person; moreover, the jury was entitled to take pandering into account. *Ginzburg.*

g. *Jenkins,* fn. b supra, stated that a judge may instruct a jury to apply "contemporary community standards" without any further specification. Alternatively, the state may choose "to define the standards in more precise geographic terms, as was done by California in *Miller.*" *Hamling v. United States,* fn. 7 supra, interpreted a federal obscenity statute to make the relevant community the one from which the jury was drawn. The judge's instruction to consider the "community standards of the 'nation as a whole' delineated a wider geographical area than would be warranted by [*Miller*]" or the Court's construction of the statute, but the error was regarded as harmless under the circumstances. See also *Sable Communications v. FCC,* Ch. 8, II infra ("dial-a-porn" company bears burden of complying with congressional obscenity ban despite diverse local community standards). After these decisions, what advice should lawyers give to publishers who distribute in national markets?

In sum we (a) reaffirm the *Roth* holding that obscene material is not protected by the First Amendment, (b) hold that such material can be regulated by the States, subject to the specific safeguards enunciated above, without a showing that the material is *"utterly* without redeeming social value," and (c) hold that obscenity is to be determined by applying "contemporary community standards," not "national standards." * * *

MR. JUSTICE DOUGLAS, dissenting. * * *

My contention is that until a civil proceeding has placed a tract beyond the pale, no criminal prosecution should be sustained. For no more vivid illustration of vague and uncertain laws could be designed than those we have fashioned. [If] a specific book [or] motion picture has in a civil proceeding been condemned as obscene and review of that finding has been completed, and thereafter a person publishes [or] displays that particular book or film, then a vague law has been made specific. There would remain the underlying question whether the First Amendment allows an implied exception in the case of obscenity. I do not think it does and my views on the issue have been stated over and again. But at least a criminal prosecution brought at that juncture would not violate the time-honored void-for-vagueness test.[8]

No such protective procedure has been designed by California in this case. Obscenity—which even we cannot define with precision—is a hodgepodge. To send men to jail for violating standards they cannot understand, construe, and apply is a monstrous thing to do in a Nation dedicated to fair trials and due process. * * *

MR. JUSTICE BRENNAN, with whom MR. JUSTICE STEWART and MR. JUSTICE MARSHALL join, dissenting.

In my dissent in *Paris Adult Theatre,* decided this date, I noted that I had no occasion to consider the extent of state power to regulate the distribution of sexually oriented material to juveniles or the offensive exposure of such material to unconsenting adults. [I] need not now decide whether a statute might be drawn to impose, within the requirements of the First Amendment, criminal penalties for the precise conduct at issue here. For it is clear that under my dissent in *Paris Adult Theatre,* the statute under which the prosecution was brought is unconstitutionally overbroad, and therefore invalid on its face. * * *

[In his *Paris Adult Theatre* dissent, Brennan, J., joined by Stewart and Marshall, JJ., argued that the state interests in regulating obscenity were not strong enough to justify the degree of vagueness. He criticized not only the Court's standard in *Miller,* but also a range of alternatives:]

II. [The] essence of our problem [is] that we have been unable to provide "sensitive tools" to separate obscenity from other sexually oriented but constitutionally protected speech, so that efforts to suppress the former do not spill over into the suppression of the latter. [The dissent traced the Court's experience with *Roth* and its progeny.]

8. The Commission on Obscenity and Pornography has advocated such a procedure. [See] *Report of the Commission on Obscenity and Pornography* 70–71 (1970).

III.   Our experience with the *Roth* approach has certainly taught us that the outright suppression of obscenity cannot be reconciled with the fundamental principles of the First and Fourteenth Amendments. For we have failed to formulate a standard that sharply distinguishes protected from unprotected speech, and out of necessity, we have resorted to the *Redrup* approach, which resolves cases as between the parties, but offers only the most obscure guidance to legislation, adjudication by other courts, and primary conduct. [T]he vagueness problem would be largely of our own creation if it stemmed primarily from our failure to reach a consensus on any one standard. But after 15 years of experimentation and debate I am reluctantly forced to the conclusion that none of the available formulas, including the one announced today, can reduce the vagueness to a tolerable level while at the same time striking an acceptable balance between the protections of the First and Fourteenth Amendments, on the one hand, and on the other the asserted state interest in regulating the dissemination of certain sexually oriented materials. Any effort to draw a constitutionally acceptable boundary on state power must resort to such indefinite concepts as "prurient interest," "patent offensiveness," "serious literary value," and the like. The meaning of these concepts necessarily varies with the experience, outlook, and even idiosyncracies of the person defining them. Although we have assumed that obscenity does exist and that we "know it when [we] see it," *Jacobellis* (Stewart, J., concurring), we are manifestly unable to describe it in advance except by reference to concepts so elusive that they fail to distinguish clearly between protected and unprotected speech.

[Added to the inherent vagueness of standards] is the further complication that the obscenity of any particular item may depend upon nuances of presentation and the context of its dissemination. See *Ginzburg*. [N]o one definition, no matter how precisely or narrowly drawn, can possibly suffice for all situations, or carve out fully suppressible expression from all media without also creating a substantial risk of encroachment upon the guarantees of the Due Process Clause and the First Amendment.

[The] resulting level of uncertainty is utterly intolerable, not alone because it makes "[b]ookselling [a] hazardous profession," *Ginsberg* (Fortas, J., dissenting), but as well because it invites arbitrary and erratic enforcement of the law. [We] have indicated that "stricter standards of permissible statutory vagueness may be applied to a statute having a potentially inhibiting effect on speech; a man may the less be required to act at his peril here, because the free dissemination of ideas may be the loser." * * *

The problems of fair notice and chilling protected speech are very grave standing alone. But [a] vague statute in this area creates a third [set] of problems. These [concern] the institutional stress that inevitably results where the line separating protected from unprotected speech is excessively vague. [Almost] every obscenity case presents a constitutional question of exceptional difficulty. [As] a result of our failure to define standards with predictable application to any given piece of material, there is no probability of regularity in obscenity decisions by state and lower federal courts. [O]ne cannot say with certainty that material is obscene until at least five members of this Court, applying inevitably obscure standards, have pronounced it [so].

We have managed the burden of deciding scores of obscenity cases by relying on per curiam reversals or denials of certiorari—a practice which conceals the rationale of decision and gives at least the appearance of arbitrary action by this Court. More important, [the] practice effectively censors protected expression by leaving lower court determinations of obscenity intact even though the status of the allegedly obscene material is entirely unsettled until final review here. In addition, the uncertainty of the standards creates a continuing source of tension between state and federal [courts].

The severe problems arising from the lack of fair notice, from the chill on protected expression, and from the stress imposed on the state and federal judicial machinery persuade me that a significant change in direction is urgently required. I turn, therefore, to the alternatives that are now open.

IV.   1. The approach requiring the smallest deviation from our present course would be to draw a new line between protected and unprotected speech, still permitting the States to suppress all material on the unprotected side of the line. In my view, clarity cannot be obtained pursuant to this approach except by drawing a line that resolves all doubts in favor of state power and against the guarantees of the First Amendment. We could hold, for example, that any depiction or description of human sexual organs, irrespective of the manner or purpose of the portrayal, is outside the protection of the First Amendment and therefore open to suppression by the States. That formula would, no doubt, offer much fairer notice [and] give rise to a substantial probability of regularity in most judicial determinations under the standard. But such a standard would be appallingly overbroad, permitting the suppression of a vast range of literary, scientific, and artistic masterpieces. Neither the First Amendment nor any free community could possibly tolerate such a standard.

2. [T]he Court today recognizes that a prohibition against any depiction or description of human sexual organs could not be reconciled with the guarantees of the First Amendment. But the Court [adopts] a restatement of the *Roth-Memoirs* definition of obscenity [that] permits suppression if the government can prove that the materials lack "*serious* literary, artistic, political or scientific value." [In] *Roth* we held that certain expression is obscene, and thus outside the protection of the First Amendment, precisely *because* it lacks even the slightest redeeming social value. [The] Court's approach necessarily assumes that some works will be deemed obscene—even though they clearly have *some* social value—because the State was able to prove that the value, measured by some unspecified standard, was not sufficiently "serious" to warrant constitutional protection. That

result [is] nothing less than a rejection of the fundamental First Amendment premises and rationale of the *Roth* opinion and an invitation to widespread suppression of sexually oriented speech. Before today, the protections of the First Amendment have never been thought limited to expressions of *serious* literary or political value. *Gooding v. Wilson; Cohen v. California; Terminiello v. Chicago* [Sec. V infra].

[T]he Court's approach [can] have no ameliorative impact on the cluster of problems that grow out of the vagueness of our current standards. Indeed, even the Court makes no argument that the reformulation will provide fairer notice to booksellers, theatre owners, and the reading and viewing public. Nor does the Court contend that the approach will provide clearer guidance to law enforcement officials or reduce the chill on protected expression [or] mitigate [the] institutional [problems].

Of course, the Court's restated *Roth* test does limit the definition of obscenity to depictions of physical conduct and explicit sexual acts. And that limitation may seem, at first glance, a welcome and clarifying addition to the *Roth-Memoirs* formula. But just as the agreement in *Roth* on an abstract definition of obscenity gave little hint of the extreme difficulty that was to follow in attempting to apply that definition to specific material, the mere formulation of a "physical conduct" test is no assurance that it can be applied with any greater facility. [The] Court surely demonstrates little sensitivity to our own institutional problems, much less the other vagueness-related difficulties, in establishing a system that requires us to consider whether a description of human genitals is sufficiently "lewd" to deprive it of constitutional protection; whether a sexual act is "ultimate"; whether the conduct depicted in materials before us fits within one of the categories of conduct whose depiction the state or federal governments have attempted to suppress; and a host of equally pointless inquiries. * * *

If the application of the "physical conduct" test to pictorial material is fraught with difficulty, its application to textual material carries the potential for extraordinary abuse. Surely we have passed the point where the mere written description of sexual conduct is deprived of First Amendment protection. Yet the test offers no guidance to us, or anyone else, in determining which written descriptions of sexual conduct are protected, and which are not.

Ultimately, the reformulation must fail because it still leaves in this Court the responsibility of determining in each case whether the materials are protected by the First Amendment. * * *

3. I have also considered the possibility of reducing our own role, and the role of appellate courts generally, in determining whether particular matter is obscene. Thus, [we] might adopt the position that where a lower federal or state court has conscientiously applied the constitutional standard, its finding of obscenity will be no more vulnerable to reversal by this Court than any finding of fact. [E]ven if the Constitution would permit us to

refrain from judging for ourselves the alleged obscenity of particular materials, that approach would solve at best only a small part of our problem. For while it would mitigate the institutional stress, [it] would neither offer nor produce any cure for the other vices of vagueness. Far from providing a clearer guide to permissible primary conduct, the approach would inevitably lead to even greater uncertainty and the consequent due process problems of fair notice. And the approach would expose much protected, sexually oriented expression to the vagaries of jury determinations. Plainly, the institutional gain would be more than offset by the unprecedented infringement of First Amendment rights.

4.   Finally, I have considered the view, urged so forcefully since 1957 by our Brothers Black and Douglas, that the First Amendment bars the suppression of any sexually oriented expression. That position would effect a sharp reduction, although perhaps not a total elimination, of the uncertainty that surrounds our current approach. Nevertheless, I am convinced that it would achieve that desirable goal only by stripping the States of power to an extent that cannot be justified by the commands of the Constitution, at least so long as there is available an alternative approach that strikes a better balance between the guarantee of free expression and the States' legitimate interests.

[I] would hold, therefore, that at least in the absence of distribution to juveniles or obtrusive exposure to unconsenting adults, the First and Fourteenth Amendments prohibit the state and federal governments from attempting wholly to suppress sexually oriented materials on the basis of their allegedly "obscene" contents.[h] Nothing in this approach precludes those governments from taking action to serve what may be strong and legitimate interests through regulation of the manner of distribution of sexually oriented material.

VI.   [I] do not pretend to have found a complete and infallible [answer]. Difficult questions must still be faced, notably in the areas of distribution to juveniles and offensive exposure to unconsenting adults. Whatever the extent of state power to regulate in those areas,[29] it should be clear that the view I espouse today would introduce a large measure of clarity to this troubled area, would reduce the institutional pressure on this Court and the rest of the State and Federal judiciary, and would guarantee fuller freedom of expression while leaving room for the protection of legitimate governmental interests. * * *

Notes and Questions

h. For the portion of Brennan, J.'s dissent addressing the strength and legitimacy of the state interests, see *Paris Adult Theatre,* supra.

29. The Court erroneously states, *Miller,* that the author of this opinion "indicates that suppression of unprotected obscene material is permissible to avoid exposure to unconsenting adults [and] to juveniles * * *." I defer expression of my views as to the scope of state power in these areas until cases squarely presenting these questions are before the Court.

1. *Serious value.* Consider Clor, *Obscenity and the First Amendment: Round Three,* 7 Loy.L.A.L.Rev. 207, 210, 218 (1974): "The *Miller* decision abandons the requirement that a censorable work must be '*utterly* without redeeming social value' and substitutes the rule of 'serious value'—literary, artistic, political, or scientific. This is the most important innovation in the law of obscenity introduced by these decisions. [Serious] literature is to be protected regardless of majority opinions about prurience and offensiveness. *This* is the national principle which is not subject to variation from community to community. If it is to perform this function, the rule will have to be elaborated and the meaning of 'serious value' articulated in some measure. This is the most important item on the legal agenda."

(a) *An independent factor?* Under *Miller* would material found to have "serious artistic value" be entitled to first amendment protection regardless how offensive or prurient? Must each factor in the *Miller* guidelines be independently satisfied, as in *Memoirs? Should* that be so? Would or should that preclude the degree of offensiveness or prurient appeal from affecting the conclusion on the value factor?

(b) *"Serious."* Do you find any guidance for determining when a first amendment value in material depicting sexual conduct is sufficiently "serious" to preclude finding it obscene? Does *Pope v. Illinois,* 481 U.S. 497, 500–501, 107 S.Ct. 1918, 95 L.Ed.2d 439, 445 (1987) assist?: "The proper inquiry is not whether an ordinary member of any given community would find serious literary, artistic, political, or scientific value[,] but whether a reasonable person would find such value in the material, taken as a whole."

(c) *Scope of protected values.* Could the Court consistent with the first amendment exclude serious educational value from those that preclude a finding of obscenity? Serious entertainment value? Could the guidelines be interpreted to include such values? What might explain their omission?

2. *Vagueness and scienter.* Is the *Miller* test intolerably vague? Are there any alternatives that could mitigate the problem? Consider Lockhart, *Escape from the Chill of Uncertainty: Explicit Sex and the First Amendment,* 9 Ga.L.Rev. 533, 563 (1975): "[E]ither legislative action, or constitutional adjudication, could establish as a defense to a criminal obscenity prosecution that the defendant *reasonably believed* that the material involved was not obscene, that is, was constitutionally protected. [Material] that would support such a court or jury finding is not the kind that requires or justifies quick action by the police and prosecutor. The public interest in preventing distribution of borderline material that can reasonably be believed not obscene is not so pressing as to require immediate criminal sanctions and can adequately be protected by a declaratory judgment or injunction action to establish the obscenity of the material."

Smith v. California, 361 U.S. 147, 80 S.Ct. 215, 4 L.Ed.2d 205 (1959) invalidated an ordinance that dispensed with any requirement that a seller of an obscene book have knowledge of its contents, but did not decide what sort of mental element was needed to prosecute. *Hamling v. United States,* supra, stated that it was constitutionally sufficient to show that a distributor of an advertising collage of pictures of sexual acts "had knowledge of the contents of the materials [and] that he knew the character and nature of the materials." Would it be consistent with *Hamling* to afford constitutional protection to a distributor who reasonably believed the material disseminated was not obscene? See Lockhart, supra, at 568.

3. *The practical impact of Miller.* Consider de Grazia, *Girls Lean Back Everywhere: The Law of Obscenity and the Assault on Genius* 561–62, 571 (1992); Until Justice Powell switched his vote, Justice "Brennan and a Court majority were preparing to reverse [Miller's] obscenity conviction * * * [T]he Burger revision of the Brennan doctrine was soon revealed to be a sort of paper tiger[, however]; by and large, there in fact occurred no observable retardation of the country's move during the decade that followed toward nearly absolute freedom for sexual expression in literary and artistic modes, including graphic or pictorial pornography; no increase in lower court convictions for obscenity; and no increase in prosecutorial [activity]."

See also Cole, *Playing by Pornography's Rules: The Regulation of Sexual Expression,* 143 U.Pa.L.Rev. 111, 170, 173 (1994): "Because this prohibition is so narrow, it serves in practice not so much to purge the community of explicit sexually arousing speech as to validate everything that remains as nonoffensive, 'normal,' or socially valuable. In this way, obscenity doctrine collectively assures the community that the pornography it consumes at such a high rate is acceptable. [There] are the few who are actually prosecuted; given the remarkable amount and variety of sexual expression that goes without prosecution, to be prosecuted for obscenity these days is akin to being struck by lightning."

C. VAGUENESS AND OVERBREADTH: AN INTRODUCTION

In *Paris Adult Theatre,* Brennan, J., dissents on the ground that the obscenity statute is unconstitutionally vague. He envisions the possibility that an obscenity statute might overcome his vagueness objection if it were tailored to combat distribution to unconsenting adults or to children. In *Miller,* the materials were in fact distributed to unconsenting adults. There Brennan, J., does not reach the vagueness question but objects on the ground that the statute is overbroad,—i.e., it is not confined to the protection of unconsenting adults and children, but also prohibits distribution of obscene materials to consenting adults. In Brennan, J.'s view, even if the particular conduct at issue in *Miller* might be constitutionally prohibited by a narrower statute, it cannot be reached under a statute that sweeps so much protected speech within its terms.

The doctrines of "vagueness" and "overbreadth" referred to in Brennan, J.'s dissents are deeply embedded in first amendment jurisprudence. At first glance, the doctrines appear discrete. A statute that prohibits the use of the words "kill" and "President" in the same sentence may not be vague, but it is certainly overbroad even though some sentences using those words may be unprotected. Conversely, a vague statute may not be overbroad; it may not pertain to first amendment freedoms at all, or it may clearly be intended to exclude all protected speech from its prohibition but use vague language to accomplish that purpose.

Ordinarily, however, the problems of "vagueness" and "overbreadth" are closely related. An Airport Commissioners resolution banning all "First Amendment activities" in the Los Angeles International Airport was declared overbroad in *Board of Airport Commissioners v. Jews for Jesus,* 482 U.S. 569, 107 S.Ct. 2568, 96 L.Ed.2d 500 (1987). Literally read the statute would have prevented anyone from talking or reading in the airport. But if the language literally covers a variety of constitutionally protected activities, it *cannot be read literally*. If the statute cannot be read according to its terms, however, problems of vagueness will often emerge. To be sure, statutes may be interpreted in ways that will avoid vagueness or overbreadth difficulties. See, e.g., *Scales v. United States,* Ch. 1, I, D supra. It is established doctrine, for example, that an attack based either upon vagueness or overbreadth will be unsuccessful in federal court if the statute in question is "readily subject to a narrowing construction by the state courts." *Young v. American Mini–Theatres, Inc.; Erznoznik v. Jacksonville,* ch. 3, I infra. Moreover, "[f]or the purpose of determining whether a state statute is too vague and indefinite to constitute valid legislation [the Court takes] 'the statute as though it read precisely as the highest court of the State has interpreted it.' " *Wainwright v. Stone,* 414 U.S. 21, 94 S.Ct. 190, 38 L.Ed.2d 179 (1973). Under this policy, a litigant can be prosecuted successfully for violating a statute that by its terms appears vague or overbroad but is interpreted by the state court in the same prosecution to mean something clearer or narrower than its literal language would dictate. *Cox v. New Hampshire,* Ch. 6, I, A infra. The harshness of this doctrine is mitigated somewhat by the fact that "unexpected" or "unforeseeable" judicial constructions in such contexts violate due process. See *Marks v. United States,* 430 U.S. 188, 97 S.Ct. 990, 51 L.Ed.2d 260 (1977).[a]

Somewhat more complicated is the issue of when general attacks on a statute are permitted. Plainly litigants may argue that statutes are vague as to their own conduct or that their own speech is protected. In other words, litigants are always free to argue that a statute is invalid "as applied" to their own conduct. The dispute concerns when litigants can attack a statute

a. For commentary on overbreadth with special focus on the implications of the doctrine mentioned in this paragraph, see Fallon, *Making Sense of Overbreadth,* 100 Yale L.J. 853 (1991).

without reference to their own conduct, an attack sometimes called "on its face."

A separate question is: when should such attacks result in partial or total invalidation of a statute? The terminology here has become as confused as the issues. In the past, the Court has frequently referred to facial attacks on statutes in a way that embraces attempts at either partial or total invalidation. In some recent opinions, however, including those quoted below, it uses the term "facial attack" or "on its face" to refer only to arguments seeking total invalidation of a statute.

Terminology aside, one of the recurrent questions has been the extent to which litigants may argue that a statute is unconstitutionally overbroad even though their own conduct would not otherwise be constitutionally protected. This is often characterized as a standing issue. Ordinarily litigants do not have standing to raise the rights of others. But it has been argued that litigants should have standing to challenge overbroad statutes even if their own conduct would be otherwise unprotected in order to prevent a chilling effect on freedom of speech. Alternatively, it has been argued that no standing problem is genuinely presented because "[u]nder 'conventional' standing principles, a litigant has always had the right to be judged in accordance with a constitutionally valid rule of law." Monaghan, *Overbreadth,* 1981 S.Ct.Rev. 1, 3. On this view, if a statute is unconstitutionally overbroad, it is not a valid rule of law, and any defendant prosecuted under the statute has standing to make that claim.[b] However the issue may be characterized, White, J., contended for many years that a litigant whose own conduct is unprotected should not prevail on an overbreadth challenge without a showing that the statute's overbreadth is "real and substantial." After much litigation, White, J., finally prevailed. The "substantial" overbreadth doctrine now burdens all litigants who argue that a statute should be declared overbroad when their own conduct is unprotected.[c] *Brockett v. Spokane Arcades, Inc.,* Sec. 1, VI, A supra, *New York v. Ferber,* Ch. 1, IV, B infra.

Less clear are the circumstances in which a litigant whose conduct *is* protected can go beyond a claim that the statute is unconstitutional "as applied." Again, litigants are always free to argue that their own conduct is protected. Moreover, the Court has stated that "[t]here is no reason to limit challenges to case-by-case 'as applied' challenges when the statute [in] all its

b. See also Monaghan, *Third Party Standing,* 84 Colum.L.Rev. 277 (1984). See also Sedler, *The Assertion of Constitutional Jus Tertii: A Substantive Approach,* 70 Calif.L.Rev. 1308, 1327 (1982) ("It may be the potential chilling effect upon others' expression that makes the statute invalid, but the litigant has his own right not to be subject to the operation of an invalid statute."). For criticism of the Monaghan position, see Fallon, supra note a, at 871–75; Hill, *The Puzzling Overbreadth Doctrine,* 25 Hofstra L.Rev. 1063 (1997); Sager, *Foreword: State Courts and the Strategic Space Between the Norms and Rules of Constitutional Law,* 63 Tex. L.Rev. 959, 967 & n. 22 (1985).

c. For commentary on the concept of "substantial" overbreadth, see Fallon, supra; Alexander, *Is There an Overbreadth Doctrine,* 22 San Diego L.Rev. 541, 553–54 (1985); Redish, *The Warren Court, The Burger Court and the First Amendment Overbreadth Doctrine,* 78 Nw.U.L.Rev. 1031, 1056–69 (1983).

applications falls short of constitutional demands."[d] *Maryland v. Joseph H. Munson Co.,* 467 U.S. 947, 104 S.Ct. 2839, 81 L.Ed.2d 786 (1984). How far beyond this the Court will go is unclear. In *Brockett v. Spokane Arcades, Inc.,* it referred to the "normal rule that partial, rather than facial invalidation" of statutes is to be preferred and observed that: "[A]n individual whose own speech or expressive conduct may validly be prohibited or sanctioned is permitted to challenge a statute on its face because it also threatens others not before the court—those who desire to engage in legally protected expression but who may refrain from doing so rather than risk prosecution or undertake to have the law declared partially invalid. If the overbreadth is 'substantial,' the law may not be enforced against anyone, including the party before the court, until it is narrowed to reach only unprotected activity, whether by legislative action or by judicial construction or partial invalidation.

"It is otherwise where the parties challenging the statute are those who desire to engage in protected speech that the overbroad statute purports to punish, or who seek to publish both protected and unprotected material. There is then no want of a proper party to challenge the statute, no concern that an attack on the statute will be unduly delayed or protected speech discouraged. The statute may forthwith be declared invalid to the extent that it reaches too far, but otherwise left intact."[e]

Brockett takes the view that it must give standing to the otherwise unprotected to raise an overbreadth challenge, in order to secure the rights of those whose speech should be protected. But it sees no purpose in giving standing to the protected in order to secure rights for those whose speech should not be protected. This position is not without its ironies. In some circumstances, a litigant whose speech is unprotected will be in a better position than one whose speech is protected, at least if the litigant's goal is completely to stop enforcement of a statute.

Finally, what of the cases when it is uncertain whether the litigant's speech is protected? Should courts consider as applied attacks before proceeding to overbreadth attacks? *Board of Trustees v. Fox,* Ch. 3, II infra, declared it "not the usual judicial practice" and "generally undesirable" to proceed to an overbreadth challenge without first determining whether the statute would be valid as applied.[f] Yet the Court has frequently (See, e.g.,

---

d. There is a terminological dispute here. Compare *Los Angeles City Council v. Taxpayers For Vincent,* Ch. 6, II infra (such challenges are not overbreadth challenges) with *Munson,* supra (such challenges are properly called overbreadth challenges).

e. After the Court has declared that the statute is invalid to the extent it reaches too far, the remaining portion of the statute will be examined to determine whether that portion is severable. That is, it could well be the intent of the legislature that the statute stands or falls as a single package. To invalidate a part, then, could be to invalidate the whole. Alternatively, the legislature may

have intended to salvage whatever it might. The question of severability is regarded as one of legislative intent, but, at least with respect to federal legislation, courts will presume that severability was intended. See, e.g., *Regan v. Time, Inc.,* 468 U.S. 641, 104 S.Ct. 3262, 82 L.Ed.2d 487 (1984). The question of whether a provision of a state statute is severable is one of state law.

f. The case arose in the federal courts, and the Court might be less likely to remand to a state court for an as applied determination, but the Court did not address that distinction.

Ch. 1, V, C infra (fighting words cases); *Jews For Jesus,* supra)) declared statutes overbroad without an as applied determination. The Court has yet systematically to detail the considerations relevant to separating the "usual" judicial practice from the unusual.

The issues with respect to vagueness challenges are similar. It remains possible, however, that the Court will resolve them in ways different from the approaches it has fashioned in the law of overbreadth. White, J., clearly argued for a different course. He suggested that vagueness challenges should be confined to "as applied" attacks unless a statute were vague in all of its applications. Accordingly, if a statute clearly proscribed the conduct of a particular defendant, to allow that defendant to challenge a statute for vagueness would in his view "confound vagueness and overbreadth." *Kolender v. Lawson,* 461 U.S. 352, 103 S.Ct. 1855, 75 L.Ed.2d 903 (1983) (White, J., dissenting). In response, the Court stated that a facial attack upon a statute need not depend upon a showing of vagueness in all of a statute's applications: "[W]e permit a facial challenge if a law reaches 'a substantial amount of constitutionally protected conduct,' "*Kolender,* supra. Moreover, the Court has previously allowed litigants to raise the vagueness issue "even though there is no uncertainty about the impact of the ordinances on their own rights." *Young.* But see, e.g., *Broadrick v. Oklahoma,* Ch. 1, VI, A infra, in which White, J., writing for the Court argued that standing to raise the vagueness argument should not be permitted in this situation.

Much less clear are the circumstances in which litigants whose conduct is *not* clearly covered by a statute can go beyond an "as applied" attack.[g] One approach would be to apply the same rule to all litigants, e.g., allowing total invalidation of statutes upon a showing of a "substantial" vagueness. In *Kolender,* the Court made no determination whether the statute involved was vague as to the defendant's own conduct; arguably, the opinion implied that it made no difference. Another approach would analogize to the approach suggested in *Brockett* for overbreadth challenges. Thus, a court might refrain from total invalidation of a statute and confine itself to striking the vague part insofar as the vague part seems to cover protected speech, leaving the balance of the statute intact. *Kolender* itself recites that the Court has "traditionally regarded vagueness and overbreadth as logically related and similar doctrines," but the Court's attitudes toward vagueness remain unclear. The questions of what standards should govern challenges to statutes that go beyond the facts before the Court, who should be able to raise the challenges, and under what circumstances have not been systematically and consistently addressed by the Court.[h]

g. Conceivably, it could make a difference whether the litigants in this class of those "not clearly covered" have engaged in protected or unprotected conduct.

h. For commentary on vagueness and overbreadth, see, e.g., Smolla, *Smolla and* *Nimmer on Freedom of Speech,* 3–121—3–139 (1994); Alexander, *Is There an Overbreadth Doctrine?,* 22 San Diego L.Rev. 541 (1985); Amsterdam, *The Void–For–Vagueness Doctrine in the Supreme Court,* 109 U.Pa.L.Rev. 67 (1960); Bogen, *First Amend-*

V. "FIGHTING WORDS," OFFENSIVE WORDS AND HOSTILE AUDIENCES

A. FIGHTING WORDS

CHAPLINSKY v. NEW HAMPSHIRE, 315 U.S. 568, 62 S.Ct. 766, 86 L.Ed. 1031 (1942): In the course of proselytizing on the streets, appellant, a Jehovah's Witness, denounced organized religion. Despite the city marshal's warning to "go slow" because his listeners were upset with his attacks on religion, appellant continued and a disturbance occurred. At this point, a police officer led appellant toward the police station, without arresting him. While en route, appellant again encountered the city marshal who had previously admonished him. Appellant then said to the marshal (he claimed, but the marshal denied, in response to the marshal's cursing him): "You are a God damned racketeer" and "a damned Fascist and the whole government of Rochester are Fascists or agents of Fascists." He was convicted of violating a state statute forbidding anyone to address "any offensive, derisive or annoying word to any other person who is lawfully in any [public place] [or] call[ing] him by any offensive or derisive name." The Court, per MURPHY, J., upheld the conviction:

"There are certain well-defined and narrowly limited classes of speech, the prevention and punishment of which have never been thought to raise any Constitutional problem.[a] These include the lewd and obscene, the profane, the libelous, and the insulting or 'fighting' words—those which by their very utterance inflict injury or tend to incite an immediate breach of the peace. [S]uch utterances are no essential part of any exposition of ideas, and are of such slight social value as a step to truth that any benefit that may be derived from them is clearly outweighed by the social interest in order and morality. * * *

"On the authority of its earlier decisions, the state court declared that the statute's purpose was to preserve the public peace, no words being

---

ment *Ancillary Doctrines,* 37 Md.L.Rev. 679, 705–26 (1978); Fallon, supra; Monaghan, supra; Redish, supra; Note, *The First Amendment Overbreadth Doctrine,* 83 Harv. L.Rev. 844 (1970).

a. See Haiman, *How Much of Our Speech is Free?,* The Civ.Lib.Rev., Winter, 1975, pp. 111, 123: "[T]his discrimination between two classes of speech made its first U.S. Supreme Court appearance in *Cantwell v. Connecticut* (1940) [p. 695 infra]." Jehovah's Witnesses had been convicted of religious solicitation without a permit and of breach of the peace. The Court set aside both convictions. It invalidated the permit system for "religious" solicitation, because it permitted the licensing official to determine what causes were "religious," thus allowing a "censorship of religion." In setting aside the breach of peace conviction, because the offense covered much protected conduct and left "too wide a discretion in its application," the Court, per Roberts, J., noted: "One may, however, be guilty of [breach of the peace] if he commits acts or makes statements likely to provoke violence and disturbance of good order. [I]n practically all [such decisions to this effect], the provocative language [held to constitute] a breach of the peace consisted of profane, indecent or abusive remarks directed to the person of the hearer. *Resort to epithets or personal abuse is not in any proper sense communication of information or opinion safeguarded by the Constitution,* and its punishment as a criminal act [under a narrowly drawn statute] would raise no question under that instrument." (Emphasis added). For commentary, see Post, *Cultural Heterogeneity and Law,* 76 Calif.L.Rev. 297 (1988).

'forbidden except such as have a direct tendency to cause acts of violence by the person to whom, individually, the remark is addressed'. It was further said: 'The word "offensive" is not to be defined in terms of what a particular addressee thinks. [The] test is what men of common intelligence would understand would be words likely to cause an average addressee to fight. [The] English language has a number of words and expressions which by general consent are "fighting words" when said without a disarming smile. [Such] words, as ordinary men know, are likely to cause a fight. So are threatening, profane or obscene revilings. Derisive and annoying words can be taken as coming within the purview of the statute as heretofore interpreted only when they have this characteristic of plainly tending to excite the addressee to a breach of the peace. [The] statute, as construed, does no more than prohibit the face-to-face words plainly likely to cause a breach of the peace by the addressee, words whose speaking constitute a breach of the peace by the speaker—including "classical fighting words", words in current use less "classical" but equally likely to cause violence, and other disorderly words, including profanity, obscenity and threats.'

"[A] statute punishing verbal acts, carefully drawn so as not unduly to impair liberty of expression, is not too vague for a criminal law. * * *[8]

"Nor can we say that the application of the statute to the facts disclosed by the record substantially or unreasonably impinges upon the privilege of free speech. Argument is unnecessary to demonstrate that the appellations 'damn racketeer' and 'damn Fascist' are epithets likely to provoke the average person to retaliation, and thereby cause a breach of the peace.

"The refusal of the state court to admit evidence of provocation and evidence bearing on the truth or falsity of the utterances is open to no Constitutional objection. Whether the facts sought to be proved by such evidence constitute a defense to the charge or may be shown in mitigation are questions for the state court to determine. Our function is fulfilled by a determination that the challenged statute, on its face and as applied, does not contravene the Fourteenth Amendment."

Notes and Questions

1. *Fighting words and free speech values.* (a) *Self realization.* Does speech have to step toward truth to be of first amendment value? Consider Redish, *The Value of Free Speech,* 130 U.Pa.L.Rev. 591, 626 (1982): "Why not view Chaplinsky's comments as a personal catharsis, as a means to vent his frustration at a system he deemed—whether rightly or wrongly—to be oppressive? Is it not a mark of individuality to be able to cry out at a society

---

8. [Even] if the interpretative gloss placed on the statute by the court below be disregarded, the statute had been previously construed as intended to preserve the public peace by punishing conduct, the direct tendency of which was to provoke the person against whom it was directed to acts of violence.

Appellant need not therefore have been a prophet to understand what the statute condemned.

viewed as crushing the individual? Under this analysis, so-called 'fighting words' represent a significant means of self-realization, whether or not they can be considered a means of attaining some elusive 'truth.' "

(b) *Fighting words and truth.* Are fighting words always false? Should truth be a defense? Always?

(c) *Fighting words and self-government.* Was Chaplinsky's statement *something other than* the expression of an idea? Did he wish to inform the marshal of his opinion of him and did he do so "in a way which was not only unquestionably clear, [but] all too clear"? Loewy, *Punishing Flag Desecrators,* 49 N.C.L.Rev. 48, 82 (1970). How significant is it that Chaplinsky's remarks were not made in the context of a public debate or discussion of political or social issues? Taking into account the events preceding Chaplinsky's remarks, and that the addressee was "an important representative of the Rochester city government," may Chaplinsky's epithets be viewed as "a sharply-expressed form of political protest against indifferent or biased police services in the enforcement of his right to free speech"? Rutzick, *Offensive Language and the Evolution of First Amendment Protection,* 9 Harv.Civ. Rts.—Civ.Lib.L.Rev. 1 (1974). If the speech is directed at a police officer or other official in his representative capacity, is "the real target the government"? Is even the most outrageous abuse in this context "an expression of some opinion concerning governmental policies or practices"? See id.

2. *The social interest in order and morality.* What was the social interest in this case? (a) *The likelihood and immediacy of violent retaliation?* Should the Court have considered whether a *law enforcement officer* so reviled would have been provoked to retaliate? Whatever is assumed about the reaction of an average citizen to offensive words, may it be assumed that police are "trained to remain calm in the face of citizen anger such as that expressed by Chaplinsky"? Rutzick, supra, at 10. See also Powell, J., concurring in *Lewis v. New Orleans,* Ch. 1, V, C infra; Note, 53 B.U.L.Rev. 834, 847 (1973).

(b) *The highly personal nature of the insult, delivered face to face?* Was the marshal "verbally slapped in the face"? May the *Chaplinsky* statute be viewed as "a special type of assault statute"? See Loewy, supra, at 83–84. See also Emerson, *The System of Freedom of Expression* 337–38 (1970). To what extent should the tort of intentional infliction of emotional distress raise constitutional problems? Compare Haiman, *Speech and Law in a Free Society* 148–56 (1981) with Downs, *Skokie Revisited: Hate Group Speech and the First Amendment,* 60 Not.D.Law. 629, 673–85 (1985).

B. HOSTILE AUDIENCES

TERMINIELLO v. CHICAGO, 337 U.S. 1, 69 S.Ct. 894, 93 L.Ed. 1131 (1949): Petitioner "vigorously, if not viciously" criticized various political and racial groups and condemned "a surging, howling mob" gathered in protest outside the auditorium in which he spoke. He called his adversaries "slimy scum," "snakes," "bedbugs," and the like. Those inside the hall could hear those on the outside yell, "Fascists, Hitlers!" The crowd outside tried to tear the clothes off those who entered. About 28 windows were broken; stink bombs were thrown. But in charging the jury, the trial court defined "breach of the peace" to include speech which "stirs the public to anger, *invites dispute,* [or] brings about a condition of unrest" (emphasis added). A 5–4 majority, per DOUGLAS, J., struck down the breach of peace ordinance as thus construed: "[A] function of free speech under our system of government is to invite dispute. It may indeed best serve its high purpose when it induces a condition of unrest, creates dissatisfaction with conditions as they are, or even stirs people to anger. [That] is why freedom of speech, though not absolute, *Chaplinsky,* is nevertheless protected against censorship or punishment, unless shown likely to produce a clear and present danger of a serious substantive evil that rises far above public inconvenience, annoyance, or unrest."

————

FEINER v. NEW YORK, 340 U.S. 315, 71 S.Ct. 303, 95 L.Ed. 295 (1951): Petitioner made a speech on a street corner in a predominantly black residential section of Syracuse, N.Y. A crowd of 75 to 80 persons, black and white, gathered around him, and several pedestrians had to go into the highway in order to pass by. A few minutes after he started, two police officers arrived and observed the rest of the meeting. In the course of his speech, publicizing a meeting of the Young Progressives of America to be held that evening in a local hotel and protesting the revocation of a permit to hold the meeting in a public school auditorium, petitioner referred to the President as a "bum," to the American Legion as "a Nazi Gestapo," and to the Mayor of Syracuse as a "champagne-sipping bum" who "does not speak for the Negro people." He also indicated in an excited manner: "The Negroes don't have equal rights; they should rise up in arms and fight for them."

These statements "stirred up a little excitement." One man indicated that if the police did not get that "S * * * O * * * B * * * " off the stand, he would do so himself. There was not yet a disturbance, but according to police testimony "angry muttering and pushing." In the words of the arresting officer whose testimony was accepted by the trial judge, he "stepped in to prevent it from resulting in a fight." After disregarding two requests to stop speaking, petitioner was arrested and convicted for disorderly conduct. The Court, per VINSON, C.J., affirmed: "The language of *Cantwell* is appropriate here. '[Nobody would] suggest that the principle of freedom of speech sanctions incitement to riot or that religious liberty connotes the privilege to exhort others to physical attack upon those belonging to another sect. When clear and present danger of riot, disorder, interference with traffic upon the public street or other immediate threat to public safety, peace, or order, appears, the power of the State to prevent or punish is obvious.'

"[It] is one thing to say that the police cannot be used as an instrument for the suppression of unpopular views, and another to say that, when as here the speaker passes the bounds of argument or persuasion and undertakes incitement to riot, they are powerless to prevent a breach of the peace. Nor in this case can we condemn the considered judgment of three New York courts approving the means which the police, faced with a crisis, used in the exercise of their power and duty to preserve peace and order.''

BLACK, J., dissented: "The Court's opinion apparently rests on this reasoning: The policeman, under the circumstances detailed, could reasonably conclude that serious fighting or even riot was imminent; therefore he could stop petitioner's speech to prevent a breach of peace; accordingly, it was 'disorderly conduct' for petitioner to continue speaking in disobedience of the officer's request. As to the existence of a dangerous situation on the street corner, it seems far-fetched to suggest that the 'facts' show any imminent threat of riot or uncontrollable disorder. It is neither unusual nor unexpected that some people at public street meetings mutter, mill about, push, shove, or disagree, even violently, with the speaker. Indeed, it is rare where controversial topics are discussed that an outdoor crowd does not do some or all of these things. Nor does one isolated threat to assault the speaker forebode disorder. Especially should the danger be discounted where, as here, the person threatening was a man whose wife and two small children accompanied him and who, so far as the record shows, was never close enough to petitioner to carry out the threat.

"Moreover, assuming that the 'facts' did indicate a critical situation, I reject the implication of the Court's opinion that the police had no obligation to protect petitioner's constitutional right to talk. The police of course have power to prevent breaches of the peace. But if, in the name of preserving order, they ever can interfere with a lawful public speaker, they first must make all reasonable efforts to protect him. Here the policemen did not even pretend to try to protect petitioner. According to the officers' testimony, the crowd was restless but there is no showing of any attempt to quiet it; pedestrians were forced to walk into the street, but there was no effort to clear a path on the sidewalk; one person threatened to assault petitioner but the officers did nothing to discourage this when even a word might have sufficed. Their duty was to protect petitioner's right to talk, even to the extent of arresting the man who threatened to interfere. Instead, they shirked that duty and acted only to suppress the right to speak.

"Finally, I cannot agree with the Court's statement that petitioner's disregard of the policeman's unexplained request amounted to such 'deliberate defiance' as would justify an arrest or conviction for disorderly conduct. On the contrary, I think that the policeman's action was a 'deliberate defiance' of ordinary official duty as well as of the constitutional right of free speech. For at least where time allows, courtesy and explanation of commands are basic elements of good official conduct in a democratic society. Here petitioner was 'asked' then 'told' then 'commanded' to stop speaking, but a man making a lawful address is certainly not required to be silent merely because an officer directs it. Petitioner was entitled to know why he should cease doing a lawful act. Not once was he told."

DOUGLAS, J., joined by Minton, J., dissented: "A speaker may not, of course, incite a riot any more than he may incite a breach of the peace by the use of 'fighting words'. But this record shows no such extremes. It shows an unsympathetic audience and the threat of one man to haul the speaker from the stage. It is against that kind of threat that speakers need police protection. If they do not receive it and instead the police throw their weight on the side of those who would break up the meetings, the police become the new censors of speech. Police censorship has all the vices of the censorship from city halls which we have repeatedly struck down."

Notes and Questions

1. What was the subject of disagreement in *Feiner*? (1) The standard for police interruption of a speech when danger of violence exists and the speaker intends to create disorder rather than to communicate ideas? (2) The standard when such danger exists, but the speaker only desires to communicate ideas? (3) Whether the danger of disorder and violence *was* plain and imminent? (4) Whether the speaker *did* intend to create disorder and violence?

May *Feiner* be limited to the proposition that when a speaker "incites to riot"—but only then—police may stop him without bothering to keep his audience in check? Cf. *Sellers v. Johnson,* 163 F.2d 877 (8th Cir.1947), cert. denied, 332 U.S. 851, 68 S.Ct. 356, 92 L.Ed. 421 (1948). See Stewart, *Public Speech and Public Order in Britain and the United States,* 13 Vand.L.Rev. 625, 632–33 (1960).

Should the speech *always* be prohibitable when the speaker intends to create disorder, rather than communicate ideas? Should the speech be prohibitable *only* under these circumstances? Should a speech *ever* be prohibitable because listeners arrive or will arrive, as they would have in *Sellers,* with a preconceived intent to create disturbance? Is the only really difficult problem in this area posed when *neither* the speaker *nor* the audience which gathers intends to create disorder, but the audience becomes *genuinely* aroused, honestly—whether or not justifiably—enraged? Here, should the police protect the speechmaking to the fullest extent possible? If they are firmly told they must before they can arrest the speaker, what is the likelihood that adequate preventive steps will be taken? See Gellhorn, *American Rights* 55–62 (1960); Note, 49 Colum.L.Rev. 1118, 1123–24 (1949).

Granted that it is undesirable for the continuation of a demonstration to turn on a police judgment whether a crowd is uncontrollable and that frequently, at least, the police will be able to handle the crowd if they are determined to do so, will occasions arise when crowd hostility *is* uncontrollable? May the demonstrators argue that "they have an interest in the publicity value of their own bloodshed or in any event that they have a right to determine their own risks"? See Note, 80 Harv.L.Rev. 1773, 1775 (1967). In such a case, does the ensuing violence pose a danger to innocent bystanders and the police as well as the demonstrators themselves? See id. If and when, despite their best efforts, law enforcement officers simply cannot "quell the mob," must they be allowed to "quell the speaker"?

2. *Edwards v. South Carolina,* 372 U.S. 229, 83 S.Ct. 680, 9 L.Ed.2d 697 (1963) reversed a breach of the peace conviction of civil rights demonstrators who refused to disperse within 15 minutes of a police command. The Court maintained that the 200 to 300 onlookers did not threaten violence and that the police protection was ample. It described the situation as a "far cry from [*Feiner*]." Clark, J., dissenting, pointed to the racially charged atmosphere ("200 youthful Negro demonstrators were being aroused to a 'fever pitch' before a crowd of some 300 people who undoubtedly were hostile.") and concluded that city officials in good faith believed that disorder and violence were imminent. Did *Edwards* miss a golden opportunity to clarify *Feiner*? What if the crowd had been pushing, shoving and pressing more closely around the demonstrators in *Edwards*? Would the case still be a "far cry" from *Feiner* because the demonstrators had not "passed the bounds of argument or persuasion and undertaken incitement to riot"?

3. In the advocacy of illegal action context, the fear of violence arises from audience cooperation with the speaker. In the hostile audience context, the fear of violence arises from audience conflict with the speaker. How do the elements set out in *Brandenburg* relate to those implied in *Feiner*? How should they relate? Should the standard for "fighting words" cases be different from the "hostile audience" cases?

4. Should police be able to prosecute or silence disruptive audiences? Heckling audiences? In what contexts? See generally *In re Kay,* 1 Cal.3d 930, 83 Cal.Rptr. 686, 464 P.2d 142 (1970).

C. OFFENSIVE WORDS

COHEN v. CALIFORNIA

403 U.S. 15, 91 S.Ct. 1780, 29 L.Ed.2d 284 (1971).

Mr. Justice Harlan delivered the opinion of the Court.

[Defendant was convicted of violating that part of a general California disturbing-the-peace statute which prohibits "maliciously and willfully disturb[ing] the peace or quiet of any neighborhood or person" by "offensive conduct." He had worn a jacket bearing the plainly visible words "Fuck the

Draft" in a Los Angeles courthouse corridor, where women and children were present. He testified that he did so as a means of informing the public of the depth of his feelings against the Vietnam War and the draft. He did not engage in, nor threaten, any violence, nor was anyone who saw him violently aroused. Nor was there any evidence that he uttered any sound prior to his arrest. In affirming, the California Court of Appeal construed "offensive conduct" to mean "behavior which has a tendency to provoke *others* to acts of violence or to in turn disturb the peace" and held that the state had proved this element because it was "reasonably foreseeable" that defendant's conduct "might cause others to rise up to commit a violent act against [him] or attempt to forceably remove his jacket."]

In order to lay hands on the precise issue which this case involves, it is useful first to canvass various matters which this record does *not* present.

The conviction quite clearly rests upon the asserted offensiveness of the *words* Cohen used to convey his message to the public. The only "conduct" which the State sought to punish is the fact of communication. Thus, we deal here with a conviction resting solely upon "speech," not upon any separately identifiable conduct which allegedly was intended by Cohen to be perceived by others as expressive of particular views but which, on its face, does not necessarily convey any message and hence arguably could be regulated without effectively repressing Cohen's ability to express himself. Cf. *United States v. O'Brien* [Ch. 2 infra]. Further, the State certainly lacks power to punish Cohen for the underlying content of the message the inscription conveyed. At least so long as there is no showing of an intent to incite disobedience to or disruption of the draft, Cohen could not, consistently with the First and Fourteenth Amendments, be punished for asserting the evident position on the inutility or immorality of the draft his jacket reflected. *Yates.*

Appellant's conviction, then, rests squarely upon his exercise [of] "freedom of speech" [and] can be justified, if at all, only as a valid regulation of the manner in which he exercised that freedom, not as a permissible prohibition on the substantive message it conveys. This does not end the inquiry, of course, for the First and Fourteenth Amendments have never been thought to give absolute protection to every individual to speak whenever or wherever he pleases, or to use any form of address in any circumstances that he chooses. In this vein, too, however, we think it important to note that several issues typically associated with such problems are not presented here.

In the first place, Cohen was tried under a statute applicable throughout the entire State. Any attempt to support this conviction on the ground that the statute seeks to preserve an appropriately decorous atmosphere in the courthouse where Cohen was arrested must fail in the absence of any language in the statute that would have put appellant on notice that certain kinds of otherwise permissible speech or conduct would nevertheless, under California law, not be tolerated in certain places. No fair reading of the phrase "offensive conduct" can be said sufficiently to inform the ordinary person that distinctions between certain locations are thereby created.[3]

In the second place, as it comes to us, this case cannot be said to fall within those relatively few categories of instances where prior decisions have established the power of government to deal more comprehensively with certain forms of individual expression simply upon a showing that such a form was employed. This is not, for example, an obscenity case. Whatever else may be necessary to give rise to the States' broader power to prohibit obscene expression, such expression must be, in some significant way, erotic. *Roth*. It cannot plausibly be maintained that this vulgar allusion to the Selective Service System would conjure up such psychic stimulation in anyone likely to be confronted with Cohen's crudely defaced jacket.

This Court has also held that the States are free to ban the simple use, without a demonstration of additional justifying circumstances, of so-called "fighting words," those personally abusive epithets which, when addressed to the ordinary citizen, are, as a matter of common knowledge, inherently likely to provoke violent reaction. *Chaplinsky*. While the four-letter word displayed by Cohen in relation to the draft is not uncommonly employed in a personally provocative fashion, in this instance it was clearly not "directed to the person of the hearer." No individual actually or likely to be present could reasonably have regarded the words on appellant's jacket as a direct personal insult. Nor do we have here an instance of the exercise of the State's police power to prevent a speaker from intentionally provoking a given group to hostile reaction. Cf. *Feiner; Terminiello*. There is, as noted above, no showing that anyone who saw Cohen was in fact violently aroused or that appellant intended such a result.

[T]he mere presumed presence of unwitting listeners or viewers does not serve automatically to justify curtailing all speech capable of giving offense. While this Court has recognized that government may properly act in many situations to prohibit intrusion into the privacy of the home of unwelcome views and ideas which cannot be totally banned from the public dialogue, we have at the same time consistently stressed that "we are often 'captives' outside the sanctuary of the home and subject to objectionable speech." [a]The ability of government, consonant with the Constitution, to shut off discourse solely to protect others from hearing it is, in other words, dependent upon a showing that substantial privacy interests are being invaded in an essentially intolerable manner. Any broader view of this authority would effectively empower a majority to silence dissidents simply as a matter of personal predilections.

3. It is illuminating to note what transpired when Cohen entered a courtroom in the building. He removed his jacket and stood with it folded over his arm. Meanwhile, a policeman sent the presiding judge a note suggesting that Cohen be held in contempt of court. The judge declined to do so and Cohen was arrested by the officer only after he emerged from the courtroom.

a. For commentary on the captive audience concept, see Balkin, *Free Speech and Hostile Environments*, 99 Colum. L.Rev. 2295, 2306–18 (1999).

[Given] the subtlety and complexity of the factors involved if Cohen's "speech" was otherwise entitled to constitutional protection, we do not think the fact that some unwilling "listeners" in a public building may have been briefly exposed to it can serve to justify this breach of the peace conviction where, as here, there was no evidence that persons powerless to avoid appellant's conduct did in fact object to it, and where [unlike another portion of the same statute barring the use of "vulgar, profane or indecent language within [the] hearing of women or children, in a loud and boisterous manner"], the [challenged statutory provision] evinces no concern [with] the special plight of the captive auditor, but, instead, indiscriminately sweeps within its prohibitions all "offensive conduct" that disturbs "any neighborhood or person."

Against this background, the issue flushed by this case stands out in bold relief. It is whether California can excise, as "offensive conduct," one particular scurrilous epithet from the public discourse, either upon the theory of the court below that its use is inherently likely to cause violent reaction or upon a more general assertion that the States, acting as guardians of public morality, may properly remove this offensive word from the public vocabulary.

The rationale of the California court is plainly untenable. At most it reflects an "undifferentiated fear or apprehension of disturbance [which] is not enough to overcome the right to freedom of expression." *Tinker* [Ch. 7, II infra]. We have been shown no evidence that substantial numbers of citizens are standing ready to strike out physically at whoever may assault their sensibilities with execrations like that uttered by Cohen. There may be some persons about with such lawless and violent proclivities, but that is an insufficient base upon which to erect, consistently with constitutional values, a governmental power to force persons who wish to ventilate their dissident views into avoiding particular forms of expression. The argument amounts to little more than the self-defeating proposition that to avoid physical censorship of one who has not sought to provoke such a response by a hypothetical coterie of the violent and lawless, the States may more appropriately effectuate that censorship themselves.

Admittedly, it is not so obvious that the First and Fourteenth Amendments must be taken to disable the States from punishing public utterance of this unseemly expletive in order to maintain what they regard as a suitable level of discourse within the body politic. We think, however, that examination and reflection will reveal the shortcomings of a contrary viewpoint.

[The] constitutional right of free expression is powerful medicine in a society as diverse and populous as ours. It is designed and intended to remove governmental restraints from the arena of public discussion, putting the decision as to what views shall be voiced largely into the hands of each of us, in the hope that use of such freedom will ultimately produce a more capable citizenry and more perfect polity and in the belief that no other approach would comport with the premise of individual dignity and choice upon which our political system rests.

To many, the immediate consequence of this freedom may often appear to be only verbal tumult, discord, and even offensive utterance. These are, however, within established limits, in truth necessary side effects of the broader enduring values which the process of open debate permits us to achieve. That the air may at times seem filled with verbal cacophony is, in this sense not a sign of weakness but of strength. We cannot lose sight of the fact that, in what otherwise might seem a trifling and annoying instance of individual distasteful abuse of a privilege, these fundamental societal values are truly implicated. * * *

Against this perception of the constitutional policies involved, we discern certain more particularized considerations that peculiarly call for reversal of this conviction. First, the principle contended for by the State seems inherently boundless. How is one to distinguish this from any other offensive word? Surely the State has no right to cleanse public debate to the point where it is grammatically palatable to the most squeamish among us. Yet no readily ascertainable general principle exists for stopping short of that result were we to affirm the judgment below. For, while the particular four-letter word being litigated here is perhaps more distasteful than most others of its genre, it is nevertheless often true that one man's vulgarity is another's lyric. Indeed, we think it is largely because governmental officials cannot make principled distinctions in this area that the Constitution leaves matters of taste and style so largely to the individual.

Additionally, we cannot overlook the fact, because it is well illustrated by the episode involved here, that much linguistic expression serves a dual communicative function: it conveys not only ideas capable of relatively precise, detached explication, but otherwise inexpressible emotions as well. In fact, words are often chosen as much for their emotive as their cognitive force. We cannot sanction the view that the Constitution, while solicitous of the cognitive content of individual speech, has little or no regard for that emotive function which, practically speaking, may often be the more important element of the overall message sought to be communicated. * * *

Finally, and in the same vein, we cannot indulge the facile assumption that one can forbid particular words without also running a substantial risk of suppressing ideas in the process. Indeed, governments might soon seize upon the censorship of particular words as a convenient guise for banning the expression of unpopular views. We have been able [to] discern little social benefit that might result from running the risk of opening the door to such grave results.

It is, in sum, our judgment that, absent a more particularized and compelling reason for its actions, the State may not, consistently with the First and Fourteenth Amendments, make the simple public display here involved of this single four-letter expletive a criminal offense. Because that is the only arguably sustainable rationale for the conviction here at issue, the judgment below must be

Reversed.

[BLACKMUN, J., joined by Burger, C.J., and Black, J., dissented for two reasons: (1) "Cohen's absurd and immature antic [was] mainly conduct and little speech" and the case falls "well within the sphere of *Chaplinsky*"; (2) although it declined to review the state court of appeals' decision in *Cohen,* the California Supreme Court subsequently narrowly construed the breach-of-the-peace statute in another case and *Cohen* should be remanded to the California Court of Appeal in the light of this subsequent construction. White, J., concurred with the dissent on the latter ground.]

Notes and Questions

1. For criticism of *Cohen,* see Bickel, *The Morality of Consent* 72 (1975) (Cohen's speech "constitutes an assault" and this sort of speech "may create [an] environment [in which] actions that were not possible before become possible"); Cox, *The Role of the Supreme Court in American Government* 47–48 (1976) (state has interest in "level at which public discourse is conducted"; state should not have to "allow exhibitionists and [others] trading upon our lower prurient interests to inflict themselves upon the public consciousness and dull its sensibilities"). For a defense (but what not a few would consider a narrow reading) of *Cohen,* see Farber, *Civilizing Public Discourse: An Essay on Professor Bickel, Justice Harlan, and the Enduring Significance of Cohen v. California,* 1980 Duke L.J. 283. See also Ely, *Democracy and Distrust* 114 (1980); Tribe, *American Constitutional Law* 787–88, 851–52, 916–17, 953–54 (2d Ed. 1988). For an overview of Harlan, J.'s approach to the first amendment, see Farber & Nowak, *Justice Harlan and the First Amendment,* 2 Const.Comm. 425 (1985).

2. To what extent, if at all, and in what ways, if any, does *Cohen* restrict the "fighting words" doctrine? Consider Arkes, *Civility and the Restriction of Speech: Rediscovering the Defamation of Groups,* 1974 Sup.Ct. Rev. 281, 316: *Cohen* turned "the presumptions in *Chaplinsky* around: instead of presuming that profane or defamatory speech was beneath constitutional protection, he presumed that the speech was protected and that the burden of proof lay with those who would restrict it." If "one man's vulgarity is another's lyric," how are discriminations to be made in the "fighting words" area?

3. Does the "use of elaborate explanations and high sounding principles to resolve" cases like *Cohen* erect "obstacles to an enhanced public appreciation of free speech?" Does systematic judicial protection of "seemingly silly, unsavory, or dangerous activities" ultimately undermine public support for the idea of free speech? See Nagel, *Constitutional Cultures* 47 (1989).

4. What does *Cohen* decide? Consider Cohen, *A Look Back at Cohen v. California,* 34 UCLA L.Rev. 1595, 1602–03 (1987): "Unless it is overruled or dishonestly distinguished, [*Cohen*] has settled the proposition that a criminal statute is unconstitutional if it punishes all public use of profanity without reference to details such as the nature of the location and audience. The opinion, however, left much to be decided about government controls on the use of profanity based on considerations of time, place, and manner. To what extent can profanity be punished because of the nature of the audience, the nature of the occasion on which it is uttered or displayed, or the manner of its utterance or display?"

5. A series of cases in the early 1970s reversed convictions involving abusive language. *Gooding v. Wilson* invalidated a Georgia ordinance primarily because it had been previously applied to "utterances where there was no likelihood that the person addressed would make an immediate violent response." *Lewis v. New Orleans* ruled that vulgar or offensive speech was protected under the first amendment. Because the statute punished "opprobrious language," it was deemed by the Court to embrace words that do not " 'by their very utterance inflict injury or tend to invite an immediate breach of the peace.' "

Although *Gooding* seemed to require a danger of immediate violence, *Lewis* recited that infliction of injury was sufficient. Dissenting in both cases, Burger, C.J., and Blackmun and Rehnquist, JJ., complained that the majority invoked vagueness and overbreadth analysis "indiscriminately without regard to the nature of the speech in question, the possible effect the statute or ordinance has upon such speech, the importance of the speech in relation to the exposition of ideas, or the purported or asserted community interest in preventing that speech." The dissenters focused upon the facts of the cases (e.g., Gooding to a police officer: "White son of a bitch, I'll kill you," "You son of a bitch, I'll choke you to death," and "You son of a bitch, if you ever put your hands on me again, I'll cut you to pieces."). They complained that the majority had relegated the facts to "footnote status, conveniently distant and in less disturbing focus." In *Gooding, Lewis,* and the other cases, Powell, J., insisted upon the importance of context in decision making. Dissenting in *Rosenfeld v. New Jersey,* 408 U.S. 901, 92 S.Ct. 2479, 33 L.Ed.2d 321 (1972), he suggested that *Chaplinsky* be extended to the "wilful use of scurrilous language calculated to offend the sensibilities of an unwilling audience"; concurring in *Lewis,* he maintained that allowing prosecutions for offensive language directed at police officers invited law enforcement abuse. Finally, he suggested in *Rosenfeld* that whatever the scope of the "fighting words" doctrine, overbreadth analysis was inappropriate in such cases. He doubted that such statutes deter others from exercising first amendment rights.[b]

b. For commentary on Powell, J.'s approach, see Gunther, *In Search of Judicial Quality on a Changing Court: The Case of* *Justice Powell,* 24 Stan.L.Rev. 1001, 1029–35 (1972).

VI. SHOULD NEW CATEGORIES BE CREATED?

Suppose a legislature were to outlaw speech whose dominant theme appeals to a morbid interest in violence, that is patently offensive to contemporary community standards, and that lacks serious literary, artistic, political or scientific value. Constitutional?[a] One approach would be to contend that speech is protected unless it falls into already established categorical exceptions to first amendment protection. Another would be to argue by analogy, e.g., if obscenity is beneath first amendment protection, this speech should (or should not) be beneath such protection. Similarly, one could argue that exceptions to first amendment protection has been fashioned by resort to a balancing methodology and that balancing the relevant interests is the right approach. Alternatively, one could proceed from a particular substantive vision of the first amendment, such as the Meiklejohn view. Which approach has been applied by the Court?[b]

New York v. Ferber, infra, is interesting because it involves the question of whether to create a new category.

A. HARM TO CHILDREN AND THE OVERBREADTH DOCTRINE

NEW YORK v. FERBER, 458 U.S. 747, 102 S.Ct. 3348, 73 L.Ed.2d 1113 (1982), per WHITE, J., upheld conviction of a seller of films depicting young boys masturbating, under N.Y.Penal Law § 263.15, for "promoting[a] a sexual performance," defined as "any performance [which] includes sexual conduct[b] by a child" under 16. The Court addressed the "single question": " 'To prevent the abuse of children who are made to engage in sexual conduct for commercial purposes, could the New York

---

a. See Sanders, *Media Violence and the Obscenity Exception to the First Amendment,* 3 Wm. & Mary Bill Rts. J. 107 (1994); Powe & Krattenmaker, *Televised Violence: First Amendment Principles and Social Science Theory,* 64 Va. L.Rev. 1123 (1978).

b. For commentary on the Court's methodology, see Farber, *The First Amendment* (1998); Redish, *Freedom of Expression: A Critical Analysis* (1984); Shiffrin, *The First Amendment, Democracy, and Romance* (1990); Van Alstyne, *Interpretations of the First Amendment* (1984); Van Alstyne, *A Graphic Review of the Free Speech Clause,* 70 Calif.L.Rev. 107 (1982); Aleinikoff, *Constitutional Law in the Age of Balancing,* 96 Yale L.J. 943 (1987); Bezanson, *The Quality of First Amendment Speech,* 20 Hastings Comm/Ent L.J. 275 (1998); Fallon, *A Constructivist Coherence Theory of Constitutional Interpretation,* 100 Harv. L.Rev. 1189, 1228 n. 191 (1987); Kagan, *Private Speech, Public Purpose: The Role of Governmental Motive in First Amendment*

Doctrine, 63 U. Chi.L.Rev. 413 (1996); Post, *Recuperating First Amendment Doctrine,* 47 Stan.L.Rev. 1249(1995); Schauer, *The Speech of Law and the Law of Speech,* Ark. L.Rev. 687 (1997); Schauer, *Mrs. Palsgraf and the First Amendment,* 47 Wash. & Lee L.Rev. 161 (1990); Schauer, *The Second-Best First Amendment,* 31 Wm. & M.L.Rev. 1 (1989); Schauer, *Categories and the First Amendment: A Play in Three Acts,* 34 Vand. L.Rev. 265 (1981); Schlag, *Rules and Standards,* 33 U.C.L.A.L.Rev. 379 (1985); Stone, *Content Regulation and the First Amendment,* 25 Wm. & Mary L.Rev. 189 (1983); Stone, *Content-Neutral Restrictions,* 54 U.Chi.L.Rev. 46 (1987).

a. "Promote" was defined to include all aspects of production, distribution, exhibition and sale.

b. Sec. 263.3 defined "sexual conduct" as "actual or simulated sexual intercourse, deviate sexual intercourse, sexual bestiality, masturbation, sado-masochistic abuse, or lewd exhibition of the genitals."

State Legislature, consistent with the First Amendment, prohibit the dissemination of material which shows children engaged in sexual conduct, regardless of whether such material is obscene?"[c] * * *

"The *Miller* standard, like its predecessors, was an accommodation between the state's interests in protecting the 'sensibilities of unwilling recipients' from exposure to pornographic material and the dangers of censorship inherent in unabashedly content-based laws. Like obscenity statutes, laws directed at the dissemination of child pornography run the risk of suppressing protected expression by allowing the hand of the censor to become unduly heavy. For the following reasons, however, we are persuaded that the States are entitled to greater leeway in the regulation of pornographic depictions of children.

"First. [The] prevention of sexual exploitation and abuse of children constitutes a government objective of surpassing importance. The legislative findings accompanying passage of the New York laws reflect this concern. * * *

"We shall not second-guess this legislative judgment. Respondent has not intimated that we do so. Suffice it to say that virtually all of the States and the United States have passed legislation proscribing the production of or otherwise combating 'child pornography.' The legislative judgment, as well as the judgment found in the relevant literature, is that the use of children as subjects of pornographic materials is harmful to the physiological, emotional, and mental health of the child. That judgment, we think, easily passes muster under the First Amendment.

"Second. The distribution of photographs and films depicting sexual activity by juveniles is intrinsically related to the sexual abuse of children in at least two ways. First, the materials produced are a permanent record of the children's participation and the harm to the child is exacerbated by their circulation. Second, the distribution network for child pornography must be closed if the production of material which requires the sexual exploitation of children is to be effectively controlled. Indeed, there is no serious contention that the legislature was unjustified in believing that it is difficult, if not impossible, to halt the exploitation of children by pursuing only those who produce the photographs and movies. While the production of pornographic materials is a low-profile, clandestine industry, the need to market the resulting products requires a visible apparatus of distribution. The most expeditious if not the only practical method of law enforcement may be to dry up the market for this material by imposing severe criminal penalties on persons selling, advertising, or otherwise promoting the product. Thirty-five

---

c. The opinion gave the background for such legislation: "In recent years, the exploitive use of children in the production of pornography has become a serious national problem. The federal government and forty-seven States have sought to combat the problem with statutes specifically directed at the production of child pornography. At least half of such statutes do not require that the materials produced be legally obscene. Thirty-five States and the United States Congress have also passed legislation prohibiting the distribution of such materials; twenty States prohibit the distribution of material depicting children engaged in sexual conduct without requiring that the material be legally obscene. New York is one of the twenty."

States and Congress have concluded that restraints on the distribution of pornographic materials are required in order to effectively combat the problem, and there is a body of literature and testimony to support these legislative conclusions.

"[The] *Miller* standard, like all general definitions of what may be banned as obscene, does not reflect the State's particular and more compelling interest in prosecuting those who promote the sexual exploitation of children. Thus, the question under the *Miller* test of whether a work, taken as a whole, appeals to the prurient interest of the average person bears no connection to the issue of whether a child has been physically or psychologically harmed in the production of the work. Similarly, a sexual explicit depiction need not be 'patently offensive' in order to have required the sexual exploitation of a child for its production. In addition, a work which, taken on the whole, contains serious literary, artistic, political, or scientific value may nevertheless embody the hardest core of child pornography. 'It is irrelevant to the child [who has been abused] whether or not the material [has] a literary, artistic, political, or social value.' We therefore cannot conclude that the *Miller* standard is a satisfactory solution to the child pornography problem.

"Third. The advertising and selling of child pornography provides an economic motive for and is thus an integral part of the production of such materials, an activity illegal throughout the nation. 'It rarely has been suggested that the constitutional freedom for speech and press extends its immunity to speech or writing used as an integral part of conduct in violation of a valid criminal statute.' * * *

"Fourth. The value of permitting live performances and photographic reproductions of children engaged in lewd sexual conduct is exceedingly modest, if not de minimis. We consider it unlikely that visual depictions of children performing sexual acts or lewdly exhibiting their genitals would often constitute an important and necessary part of a literary performance or scientific or educational work. As the trial court in this case observed, if it were necessary for literary or artistic value, a person over the statutory age who perhaps looked younger could be utilized. * * *

"Fifth. Recognizing and classifying child pornography as a category of material outside the protection of the First Amendment is not incompatible with our earlier decisions. 'The question whether speech is, or is not protected by the First Amendment often depends on the content of the speech.' *Young v. American Mini Theatres, Inc.* [Ch. 3, I infra]. '[I]t is the content of an utterance that determines whether it is a protected epithet or [an] unprotected "fighting comment" '. Leaving aside the special considerations when public officials are the target, *New York Times Co. v. Sullivan,* a libelous publication is not protected by the Constitution. *Beauharnais.* [It] is not rare that a content-based classification of speech has been accepted because it may be appropriately generalized that within the confines of the given classification, the evil to be restricted so overwhelmingly outweighs the expressive interests, if any, at stake, that no process of case-by-case adjudication is required. When a definable class of material, such as that covered by § 263.15, bears so heavily and pervasively on the welfare of children engaged in its production, we think the balance of competing interests is clearly struck and that it is permissible to consider these materials as without the protection of the First Amendment.

"There are, of course, limits on the category of child pornography which, like obscenity, is unprotected by the First Amendment. As with all legislation in this sensitive area, the conduct to be prohibited must be adequately defined by the applicable state law, as written or authoritatively construed. Here the nature of the harm to be combated requires that the state offense be limited to works that *visually* depict sexual conduct by children below a specified age. The category of 'sexual conduct' proscribed must also be suitably limited and described.

"The test for child pornography is separate from the obscenity standard enunciated in *Miller,* but may be compared to it for purpose of clarity. The *Miller* formulation is adjusted in the following respects: A trier of fact need not find that the material appeals to the prurient interest of the average person; it is not required that sexual conduct portrayed be done so in a patently offensive manner; and the material at issue need not be considered as a whole. We note that the distribution of descriptions or other depictions of sexual conduct, not otherwise obscene, which do not involve live performance or photographic or other visual reproduction of live performances, retains First Amendment protection. As with obscenity laws, criminal responsibility may not be imposed without some element of scienter on the part of the defendant. * * *

"It remains to address the claim that the New York statute is unconstitutionally overbroad because it would forbid the distribution of material with serious literary, scientific, or educational value or material which does not threaten the harms sought to be combated by the State. * * *

"The traditional rule is that a person to whom a statute may constitutionally be applied may not challenge that statute on the ground that it may conceivably be applied unconstitutionally to others in situations not before the Court. *Broadrick v. Oklahoma,* 413 U.S. 601, 93 S.Ct. 2908, 37 L.Ed.2d 830 (1973). In *Broadrick,* we recognized that this rule reflects two cardinal principles of our constitutional order: the personal nature of constitutional rights and prudential limitations on constitutional adjudication.[20] [By] focusing on the factual situation before us, and similar cases necessary for development of a constitutional rule,[21] we face 'flesh-and-blood' legal problems with data 'relevant and adequate to an informed judgment.' This

20. In addition to prudential restraints, the traditional rule is grounded in Art. III limits on the jurisdiction of federal courts to actual cases and controversies. * * *

21. Overbreadth challenges are only one type of facial attack. A person whose activity may be constitutionally regulated nevertheless may argue that the statute under which he is convicted or regulated is invalid on its face. See, e.g., *Terminiello.* See generally Monaghan, *Overbreadth,* 1981 S.Ct.Rev. 1, 10–14.

practice also fulfills a valuable institutional purpose: it allows state courts the opportunity to construe a law to avoid constitutional infirmities.

"What has come to be known as the First Amendment overbreadth doctrine is one of the few exceptions to this principle and must be justified by weighty countervailing policies. The doctrine is predicated on the sensitive nature of protected expression: persons whose expression is constitutionally protected may well refrain from exercising their rights for fear of criminal sanctions by a statute susceptible of application to protected expression. * * *

"In *Broadrick,* we explained [that]: '[T]he plain import of our cases is, at the very least, that facial overbreadth adjudication is an exception to our traditional rules of practice and that its function, a limited one at the outset, attenuates as the otherwise unprotected behavior that it forbids the State to sanction moves from "pure speech" toward conduct and that conduct—even if expressive—falls within the scope of otherwise valid criminal laws that reflect legitimate state interests in maintaining comprehensive controls over harmful, constitutionally unprotected conduct. * * * '

"[*Broadrick*] examined a regulation involving restrictions on political campaign activity, an area not considered 'pure speech,' and thus it was unnecessary to consider the proper overbreadth test when a law arguably reaches traditional forms of expression such as books and films. As we intimated in *Broadrick,* the requirement of substantial overbreadth extended 'at the very least' to cases involving conduct plus speech. This case, which poses the question squarely, convinces us that the rationale of *Broadrick* is sound and should be applied in the present context involving the harmful employment of children to make sexually explicit materials for distribution.

"The premise that a law should not be invalidated for overbreadth unless it reaches a substantial number of impermissible applications is hardly novel.[d] On most occasions involving facial invalidation, the Court has stressed the embracing sweep of the statute over protected expression.[26] Indeed, Justice Brennan observed in his dissenting opinion in *Broadrick*: 'We have never held that a statute should be held invalid on its face merely because it is possible to conceive of a single impermissible application, and in that sense a requirement of substantial overbreadth is already implicit in the doctrine.'

---

d. Scalia, J., dissenting in *Chicago v. Morales,* 527 U.S. 41, 119 S.Ct. 1849, 144 L.Ed.2d 67 (1999), argues that in order to avoid advisory opinions, federal courts should limit themselves to as applied attacks, but that if they insist on considering facial attacks, they should insist that a statute be unconstitutional in all its applications before declaring it unconstitutional. Are either of these positions acceptable?

26. In *Gooding v. Wilson,* the Court's invalidation of a Georgia statute making it a misdemeanor to use " 'opprobrious words or abusive language, tending to cause a breach of the peace' "followed from state judicial decisions indicating that "merely to speak words offensive to some who hear them" could constitute a "breach of the peace." * * *

"The requirement of substantial overbreadth is directly derived from the purpose and nature of the doctrine. While a sweeping statute, or one incapable of limitation, has the potential to repeatedly chill the exercise of expressive activity by many individuals, the extent of deterrence of protected speech can be expected to decrease with the declining reach of the regulation. This observation appears equally applicable to the publication of books and films as it is to activities, such as picketing or participation in election campaigns, which have previously been categorized as involving conduct plus speech. We see no appreciable difference between the position of a publisher or bookseller in doubt as to the reach of New York's child pornography law and the situation faced by the Oklahoma state employees with respect to the State's restriction on partisan political activity.[e] * * *

"Applying these principles, we hold that § 263.15 is not substantially overbroad. We consider this the paradigmatic case of a state statute whose legitimate reach dwarfs its arguably impermissible applications. [While] the reach of the statute is directed at the hard core of child pornography, the Court of Appeals was understandably concerned that some protected expression, ranging from medical textbooks to pictorials in the National Geographic would fall prey to the statute. How often, if ever, it may be necessary to employ children to engage in conduct clearly within the reach of § 263.15 in order to produce educational, medical, or artistic works cannot be known with certainty. Yet we seriously doubt, and it has not been suggested, that these arguably impermissible applications of the statute amount to more than a tiny fraction of the materials within the statute's reach."[f]

---

e. *Brockett v. Spokane Arcades, Inc.*, Ch. 1, IV, B supra, stated: "The Court of Appeals erred in holding that the *Broadrick* substantial overbreadth requirement is inapplicable where pure speech rather than conduct is at issue. *Ferber* specifically held to the contrary." For commentary on the overbreadth discussion in *Broadrick* and *Ferber*, see Redish, *The Warren Court, The Burger Court and the First Amendment Overbreadth Doctrine,* 78 Nw.U.L.Rev. 1031, 1056–69 (1983).

f. Brennan, J., joined by Marshall, J., agreed "with much of what is said in the Court's opinion. [This] special and compelling interest (in protecting the well-being of the State's youth), and the particular vulnerability of children, afford the State the leeway to regulate pornographic material, the promotion of which is harmful to children, even though the State does not have such leeway when it seeks only to protect consenting adults from exposure to such materials. * * * I also agree with the Court that the 'tiny fraction' of material of serious artistic, scientific or educational value that could conceivably fall within the reach of the statute is insufficient to justify strik-

ing the statute on grounds of overbreadth." But the concurrence stated that application of the statute to such materials as "do have serious artistic, scientific or medical value would violate the First Amendment."

On that issue O'Connor, J., wrote a short concurrence: "Although I join the Court's opinion, I write separately to stress that the Court does not hold that New York must except 'material with serious literary, scientific or educational value' from its statute. The Court merely holds that, even if the First Amendment shelters such material, New York's current statute is not sufficiently overbroad to support respondent's facial attack. The compelling interests identified in today's opinion suggest that the Constitution might in fact permit New York to ban knowing distribution of works depicting minors engaged in explicit sexual conduct, regardless of the social value of the depictions. For example, a 12–year-old child photographed while masturbating surely suffers the same psychological harm whether the community labels the photograph 'edifying' or 'tasteless.' The audience's appreciation of the depiction is simply irrelevant to New York's asserted interest in

Notes and Questions

1. Consider Schauer, *Codifying the First Amendment: New York v. Ferber,* 1982 Sup.Ct.Rev. 285, 295: The new category created in *Ferber* "bears little resemblance to the category of obscenity delineated by *Miller.* The Court in *Ferber* explicitly held that child pornography need not appeal to the prurient interest, need not be patently offensive, and need not be based on a consideration of the material as a whole. This last aspect is most important, because it means that the presence of some serious literary, artistic, political, or scientific matter will not constitutionally redeem material containing depictions of sexual conduct by children. The Court referred to the foregoing factors in terms of having 'adjusted' the *Miller* test, but that is like saying a butterfly is an adjusted camel." What precisely is the new category created in *Ferber*?

2. What test or standard of review did the Court use to determine whether the speech should be protected? For general discussion, see Schauer, supra. Did it apply a different test or a standard of review when it formulated its rules in *Gertz*? Are tests or standards of review needed in these contexts? Desirable? Consider Shiffrin, *The First Amendment and Economic Regulation: Away From a General Theory of the First Amendment,* 78 Nw.U.L.Rev. 1212, 1268 (1983): "The complex set of rules produced in *Gertz,* right or wrong, resulted from an appreciation that the protection of truth was important but that the protection of reputation also was important. The Court wisely avoided discussion of levels of scrutiny because any resort to such abstractions would have constitutionalized reductionism." Is "constitutionalized reductionism" desirable because it protects speech and provides guidance to the lower courts?

3. *The absence of children.* SIMON AND SCHUSTER, INC. v. NEW YORK STATE CRIMES BD., 502 U.S. 105, 112 S.Ct. 501, 116 L.Ed.2d 476 (1991), per O'CONNOR, J., struck down a law requiring that income derived from works in which individuals admit to crime involving victims be used to compensate the victims: "[T]he State has a compelling interest in compensating victims from the fruits of the crime, but little if any interest in limiting such compensation to the proceeds of the wrongdoer's speech about the crime."[g]

4. *Overbreadth without a chilling effect?* Massachusetts prohibited adults from posing or exhibiting nude children for purposes of photographs,

protecting children from psychological, emotional, and mental harm."

Stevens, J., also concurred in the judgment in a short opinion that noted his conclusion that the films in the case were not entitled to first amendment protection, and his view that overbreadth analysis should be avoided by waiting until the hypothetical case actually arises.

Blackmun, J., concurred in the result without opinion.

g. Kennedy, J., concurring, would have stricken the statute without reference to the compelling state interest test which he condemned as ad hoc balancing. Blackmun, J., also concurred. Thomas, J., did not participate. For extensive criticism of the strict scrutiny test, see Volokh, *Freedom of Speech, Permissible Tailoring, and Transcending Strict Scrutiny,* 144 U.Pa.L.Rev. 2417, 2446 (1996).

publications, or pictures, moving or otherwise. Bona fide scientific or medical purposes were excepted as were educational or cultural purposes for a bona fide school, museum, or library. Douglas Oakes was prosecuted for taking 10 color photographs of his 14–year–old stepdaughter in a state of nudity covered by the statute. The Massachusetts Supreme Judicial Court declared the statute overbroad. After certiorari was granted in MASSACHUSETTS v. OAKES, 491 U.S. 576, 109 S.Ct. 2633, 105 L.Ed.2d 493 (1989), Massachusetts added a "lascivious intent" requirement to the statute and eliminated the exemptions. O'CONNOR, joined by Rehnquist, C.J., and White and Kennedy, JJ., accordingly refused to entertain the overbreadth challenge and voted to remand the case for determination of the statute's constitutionality as applied: "Because it has been repealed, the former version of [the Massachusetts law] cannot chill protected speech."

SCALIA, J., joined by Blackmun, Brennan, Marshall, and Stevens, JJ., disagreed.[h] "It seems to me strange judicial theory that a conviction initially invalid can be resuscitated by postconviction alteration of the statute under which it was obtained. [Even as a policy matter, the] overbreadth doctrine serves to protect constitutionally legitimate speech not merely *ex post,* that is, after the offending statute is enacted, but also *ex ante,* that is, when the legislature is contemplating what sort of statute to enact. If the promulgation of overbroad laws affecting speech was cost free[,] if *no* conviction of constitutionally proscribable conduct would be lost, so long as the offending statute was narrowed before the final appeal—then legislatures would have significantly reduced incentive to stay within constitutional bounds in the first place.[i] [More] fundamentally, however, [it] seems to me that we are only free to pursue policy objectives through the modes of action traditionally followed by the courts and by the law. [I] have heard of a voidable contract, but never of a voidable law. The notion is bizarre."

5. *How substantial is substantial overbreadth?* Five justices addressed the overbreadth question in *Oakes,* but the substantive issue was not resolved. BRENNAN, J., joined by Marshall and Stevens, JJ., objected that the statute would make it criminal for parents "to photograph their infant children or toddlers in the bath or romping naked on the beach." More generally, he argued that the first amendment "blocks the prohibition of nude posing by minors in connection with the production of works of art not depicting lewd behavior. * * * Many of the world's great artists—Degas,

---

h. Although these five justices agreed that the overbreadth challenge should be entertained, they divided on the merits of the challenge. Scalia, J., joined by Blackmun, J., found no merit in the overbreadth claim (see note 5 infra) and voted to reverse and to remand for determination of the statute's constitutionality as applied. The three remaining justices (see note 5 infra) agreed with the overbreadth challenge and voted to affirm the judgment below. O'Connor, J.'s opinion, therefore, became the plu-

rality opinion, and the Court's judgment was to vacate the judgment below and to remand. In the end, six justices voted against the overbreadth challenge: four because it was moot; two because it did not meet the requirement of substantial overbreadth.

i. For criticism of this point, see Alfred Hill, *The Puzzling First Amendment Overbreadth Doctrine,* 25 Hofstra L.Rev. 1063, 1071 (1997).

Renoir, Donatello, to name but a few—have worked from models under 18 years of age, and many acclaimed photographs have included nude or partially clad minors."

SCALIA, J., joined by Blackmun, J., disagreed: "[G]iven the known extent of the kiddie-porn industry[,] I would estimate that the legitimate scope [of the statute] vastly exceeds the illegitimate. * * * Even assuming that proscribing artistic depictions of preadolescent genitals and postadolescent breasts is impermissible,[2] the body of material that would be covered is, as far as I am aware, insignificant compared with the lawful scope of the statute. That leaves the family photos. [Assuming] that it is unconstitutional (as opposed to merely foolish) to prohibit such photography, I do not think it so common as to make the statute *substantially* overbroad. [My] perception differs, for example, from Justice Brennan's belief that there is an 'abundance of baby and child photographs taken every day' depicting genitals."[b]

————

Subject to exceptions[a] Ohio prohibited the possession of material showing a minor in a state of nudity. Clyde Osborne was convicted for possessing photographs of a nude male adolescent in a variety of sexually explicit poses.[b] The photographs were secured in his home pursuant to a valid search warrant. On appeal the Ohio Supreme Court narrowed the statute to apply only to depictions of nudity involving a lewd exhibition or a graphic focus on the genitals.

OSBORNE v. OHIO, 495 U.S. 103, 110 S.Ct. 1691, 109 L.Ed.2d 98 (1990), per WHITE, J., upheld the statute as construed and remanded for a showing that the photographs possessed by the defendant met the elements fashioned by the Ohio Supreme Court.

White, J., first distinguished *Stanley v. Georgia* [Ch. 1, V, A supra]: "In *Stanley,* we struck down a Georgia law outlawing the private possession of obscene material. We recognized that the statute impinged upon Stanley's

---

2. [Most] adults, I expect, would not hire themselves out as nude models, whatever the intention of the photographer or artist, and however unerotic the pose. There is no cause to think children are less sensitive. It is not unreasonable, therefore, for a State to regard parents' using (or permitting the use) of their children as nude models, or other adults' use of consenting minors, as a form of child exploitation.

b. For the argument that the Court should balance a number of factors including the "state's substantive interest in being able to impose sanctions for a particular kind of conduct under a particular legal standard, as opposed to being forced to rely on other, less restrictive substitutes" instead of trying to determine the number of constitutional and unconstitutional applications, see Fallon, *Making Sense of Overbreadth,* 100 Yale L.J. 853, 894 (1991).

a. Ohio excepted material possessed for "bona fide" purposes (e.g., artistic or scientific) or that showed the possessor's child or ward or where the possessor knew that the parents or guardians had consented in writing to the photography and to the manner in which it had been transferred.

b. Two of the photographs focused on the anus of the boy, one with a plastic object apparently inserted; another on his erect penis with an electric object in his hand.

right to receive information in the privacy of his home, and we found Georgia's justifications for its law inadequate.[3]

"*Stanley* should not be read too broadly. We have previously noted that *Stanley* was a narrow holding and, since the decision in that case, the value of permitting child pornography has been characterized as 'exceedingly modest, if not *de minimis.*' *New York v. Ferber.* But assuming, for the sake of argument, that Osborne has a First Amendment interest in viewing and possessing child pornography, we nonetheless find this case distinct from *Stanley* because the interests underlying child pornography prohibitions far exceed the interests justifying the Georgia law at issue in *Stanley.* * * *

"In *Stanley,* Georgia primarily sought to proscribe the private possession of obscenity because it was concerned that obscenity would poison the minds of its viewers. [The] difference here is obvious: the State does not rely on a paternalistic interest in regulating Osborne's mind. Rather, Ohio has [acted] in order to protect the victims of child pornography; it hopes to destroy a market for the exploitative use of children. * * *

"Osborne contends that the State should use other measures, besides penalizing possession, to dry up the child pornography market. Osborne points out that in *Stanley* we rejected Georgia's argument that its prohibition on obscenity possession was a necessary incident to its proscription on obscenity distribution. This holding, however, must be viewed in light of the weak interests asserted by the State in that case. *Stanley* itself emphasized that we did not 'mean to express any opinion on statutes making criminal possession of other types of printed, filmed, or recorded materials. * * * In such cases, compelling reasons may exist for overriding the right of the individual to possess those materials.'[5]

"Given the importance of the State's interest in protecting the victims of child pornography, we cannot fault Ohio for attempting to stamp out this vice at all levels in the distribution chain. * * *

"Osborne contends that it was impermissible for the Ohio Supreme Court to apply its [narrowed] construction of the statute when evaluating his overbreadth claim.[c] Our cases, however, have long held that a statute as construed 'may be applied to conduct occurring prior to the construction, provided such application affords fair warning to the defendan[t].'[12] [That] Osborne's photographs of adolescent boys in sexually explicit situations

---

3. We have since indicated that our decision in *Stanley* was "firmly grounded in the First Amendment." *Bowers v. Hardwick,* Ch. 1, V, A supra.

5. [T]he *Stanley* Court cited illicit possession of defense information as an example of the type of offense for which compelling state interests might justify a ban on possession. *Stanley,* however, did not suggest that this crime exhausted the entire category of proscribable offenses.

c. Given the statutory limitations and exceptions (see fn. a supra), the Court expressed doubt that the statute was substantially overbroad even without the Ohio Supreme Court's limiting construction although it conceded that the statute by its terms seemed to criminalize some constitutionally protected conduct.

12. This principle, of course, accords with the rationale underlying overbreadth challenges. We normally do not allow a defendant to challenge a law as it is applied to

constitute child pornography hardly needs elaboration. Therefore, although [Ohio's statute] as written may have been imprecise at its fringes, someone in Osborne's position would not be surprised to learn that his possession of the four photographs at issue in this case constituted a crime. * * *

"Finally, despite Osborne's contention to the contrary, we do not believe that *Massachusetts v. Oakes,* supports his theory of this case.

"[F]ive of the *Oakes* Justices feared that if we allowed a legislature to correct its mistakes without paying for them (beyond the inconvenience of passing a new law), we would decrease the legislature's incentive to draft a narrowly tailored law in the first place.

"Legislators who know they can cure their own mistakes by amendment without significant cost may not be as careful to avoid drafting overbroad statutes as they might otherwise be. But a similar effect will not be likely if a judicial construction of a statute to eliminate overbreadth is allowed to be applied in the case before the Court. This is so primarily because the legislatures cannot be sure that the statute, when examined by a court, will be saved by a narrowing construction rather than invalidated for overbreadth. In the latter event, there could be no convictions under that law even of those whose own conduct is unprotected by the First Amendment. Even if construed to obviate overbreadth, applying the statute to pending cases might be barred by the Due Process Clause. Thus, careless drafting cannot be considered to be cost free based on the power of the courts to eliminate overbreadth by statutory construction. * * *

"To conclude, although we find Osborne's First Amendment arguments unpersuasive, we reverse his conviction and remand for a new trial in order to ensure that Osborne's conviction stemmed from a finding that the State had proved each of the elements of the Ohio statute."[d]

BRENNAN, J., joined by Marshall, J., and Stevens, J., dissented: "As written, the Ohio statute is plainly overbroad.[2] * * *

others. In the First Amendment context, however, we have said that "[b]ecause of the sensitive nature of constitutionally protected expression, we have not required that all those subject to overbroad regulations risk prosecution to test their rights. For free expression—of transcendent value to all society, and not merely to those exercising their rights—might be the loser." But once a statute is authoritatively construed, there is no longer any danger that protected speech will be deterred and therefore no longer any reason to entertain the defendant's challenge to the statute on its face.

d. Defendant's attorney did not ask for a scienter instruction (even though Ohio law generally provides for a scienter re-

quirement in criminal cases) and the Court stated that Osborne could be precluded from raising the question on remand. But Osborne did raise the overbreadth issue and was, therefore, entitled to dispute the application of the statute, as construed, to the photographs in his possession even though Osborne's attorney had not specifically objected to the jury instructions.

Blackmun, J., concurring, agreed with the dissent's position that due process entitled the defendant to instructions on "lewd exhibition" and "graphic focus" without regard to whether an objection had been lodged at trial.

2. The Court hints that § 2907.323's exemptions and "proper purposes" provisions might save it from being overbroad. I dis-

"Wary of the statute's use of the 'nudity' standard, the Ohio Supreme Court construed § 2907.323(A)(3) to apply only 'where such nudity constitutes a lewd exhibition or involves a graphic focus on the genitals.' The 'lewd exhibition' and 'graphic focus' tests not only fail to cure the overbreadth of the statute, but they also create a new problem of vagueness. * * *

"The Ohio law is distinguishable [from *Ferber*] for several reasons. First, the New York statute did not criminalize materials with a '*graphic focus*' on the genitals, and, as discussed further below, Ohio's 'graphic focus' test is impermissibly capacious. Even setting aside the 'graphic focus' element, the Ohio Supreme Court's narrowing construction is still overbroad because it focuses on 'lewd exhibitions of *nudity*' rather than 'lewd exhibitions of *the genitals* 'in the context of *sexual conduct,* as in the New York statute at issue in *Ferber*.[e] Ohio law defines 'nudity' to include depictions of pubic areas, buttocks, the female breast, and covered male genitals 'in a discernibly turgid state,' *as well as* depictions of the genitals. On its face, then, the Ohio law is much broader than New York's. * * *

"Indeed, the broad definition of nudity in the Ohio statutory scheme means that 'child pornography' could include any photograph depicting a 'lewd exhibition' of even a small portion of a minor's buttocks or any part of the female breast below the nipple. Pictures of topless bathers at a Mediterranean beach, of teenagers in revealing dresses, and even of toddlers romping unclothed, all might be prohibited.[5]

"It might be objected that many of these depictions of nudity do not amount to 'lewd exhibitions.' But in the absence of *any* authoritative definition of that phrase by the Ohio Supreme Court, we cannot predict which ones. * * *

"The Ohio Supreme Court, moreover, did not specify the perspective from which 'lewdness' is to be determined. A 'reasonable' person's view of 'lewdness'? A reasonable pedophile's? An 'average' person applying contem-

---

agree. The enumerated "proper purposes" (e.g., a "bona fide artistic, medical, scientific, educational * * * or other proper purpose") are simultaneously too vague and too narrow. What is an acceptable "artistic" purpose? Would erotic art along the lines of Robert Mapplethorpe's qualify? What is a valid "scientific" or "educational" purpose? What about sex manuals? What is a permissible "other proper purpose"? What about photos taken for one purpose and recirculated for other, more prurient purposes? The "proper purposes" standard appears to create problems analogous to those this Court has encountered in describing the "redeeming social importance" of obscenity.

At the same time, however, Ohio's list of "proper purposes" is too limited; it excludes such obviously permissible uses as the commercial distribution of fashion photographs or the simple exchange of pictures among family and friends. Thus, a neighbor or grandparent who receives a photograph of an unclothed toddler might be subject to criminal sanctions.

e. The Court read the Ohio Court's opinion to refer to the lewd exhibition of the genitals rather than the lewd exhibition of nudity, but maintained that the distinction was not important anyway.

5. [A] well-known commercial advertisement for a suntan lotion shows a dog pulling down the bottom half of a young girl's bikini, revealing a stark contrast between her suntanned back and pale buttocks. That this advertisement might be illegal in Ohio is an absurd yet altogether too conceivable conclusion under the language of the [statute.]

porary local community standards? Statewide standards? Nationwide standards? In sum, the addition of a 'lewd exhibition' standard does not narrow adequately the statute's reach. If anything, it creates a new problem of vagueness, affording the public little notice of the statute's ambit and providing an avenue for 'policemen, prosecutors, and juries to pursue their personal predilections.'[12] Given the important First Amendment interests at issue, the vague, broad sweep of the 'lewd exhibition' language means that it cannot cure [the overbreadth problem].

"The Ohio Supreme Court also added a 'graphic focus' element to the nudity definition. This phrase, a stranger to obscenity regulation, suffers from the same vagueness difficulty as 'lewd exhibition.' Although the Ohio Supreme Court failed to elaborate what a 'graphic focus' might be, the test appears to involve nothing more than a subjective estimation of the centrality or prominence of the genitals in a picture or other representation. Not only is this factor dependent on the perspective and idiosyncrasies of the observer, it also is unconnected to whether the material at issue merits constitutional protection. Simple nudity, no matter how prominent or 'graphic,' is within the bounds of the First Amendment. Michelangelo's 'David' might be said to have a 'graphic focus' on the genitals, for it plainly portrays them in a manner unavoidable to even a casual observer. Similarly, a painting of a partially clad girl could be said to involve a 'graphic focus,' depending on the picture's lighting and emphasis, as could the depictions of nude children on the friezes that adorn our Courtroom. Even a photograph of a child running naked on the beach or playing in the bathtub might run afoul of the law, depending on the focus and camera angle.

"In sum, the 'lewd exhibition' and 'graphic focus' tests are too vague to serve as any workable limit. Because the statute, even as construed authoritatively by the Ohio Supreme Court, is impermissibly overbroad, I would hold that appellant cannot be retried under it.

"Even if the statute was not overbroad, our decision in *Stanley v. Georgia* forbids the criminalization of appellant's private possession in his home of the materials at issue. [Appellant] was convicted for possessing four photographs of nude minors, seized from a desk drawer in the bedroom of his house during a search executed pursuant to a warrant. Appellant testified that he had been given the pictures in his home by a friend. There was no evidence that the photographs had been produced commercially or distributed. All were kept in an album that appellant had assembled for his personal use and had possessed privately for several years.

"In these circumstances, the Court's focus on *Ferber* rather than *Stanley* is misplaced. [*Ferber*] did nothing more than place child pornography on the same level of First Amendment protection as *obscene* adult pornography, meaning that its production and distribution could be proscribed. The

---

12. The danger of discriminatory enforcement assumes particular importance of the context of the instant case, which involves child pornography with male homosexual overtones. Sadly, evidence indicates that the overwhelming majority of arrests for violations of "lewdness" laws involve male homosexuals.

distinction established in *Stanley* between *what* materials may be regulated and *how* they may be regulated still stands. * * *

"At bottom, the Court today is so disquieted by the possible exploitation of children in the *production* of the pornography that it is willing to tolerate the imposition of criminal penalties for simple *possession*. While I share the majority's concerns, I do not believe that it has struck the proper balance between the First Amendment and the State's interests, especially in light of the other means available to Ohio to protect children from exploitation and the State's failure to demonstrate a causal link between a ban on possession of child pornography and a decrease in its production. * * *

"When speech is eloquent and the ideas expressed lofty, it is easy to find restrictions on them invalid. But were the First Amendment limited to such discourse, our freedom would be sterile indeed. Mr. Osborne's pictures may be distasteful, but the Constitution guarantees both his right to possess them privately and his right to avoid punishment under an overbroad law. I respectfully dissent."

B. HARM TO WOMEN: FEMINISM AND PORNOGRAPHY

Catharine MacKinnon and Andrea Dworkin have drafted an anti-pornography ordinance that has been considered in a number of jurisdictions.[a]

PROPOSED LOS ANGELES COUNTY ANTI–PORNOGRAPHY CIVIL RIGHTS LAW

Section 1. Statement of Policy

Pornography is sex discrimination. It exists in the County of Los Angeles, posing a substantial threat to the health, safety, welfare and equality of citizens in the community. Existing state and federal laws are inadequate to solve these problems in the County of Los Angeles.

Section 2. Findings

Pornography is a systematic practice of exploitation and subordination based on sex which differentially harms women. The harm of pornography includes dehumanization, sexual exploitation, forced sex, forced prostitution, physical injury, and social and sexual terrorism and inferiority presented as entertainment. The bigotry and contempt pornography promotes, with the acts of aggression it fosters, diminish opportunities for equality of rights in employment, education, property, public accommodations and public services; create public and private harassment, persecution and denigration;

a. The ordinance was first considered in Minneapolis. For political, rhetorical, and sociological discussion, see Brest & Vandenberg, *Politics, Feminism, and the Constitution: The Anti–Pornography Movement in Minneapolis,* 39 Stan.L.Rev. 607 (1987). Different versions of the ordinance were passed in Indianapolis, Indiana and Bellingham, Washington (see Baldwin, *Pornography and the Traffic in Women,* 1 Yale J.L. & Fem. 111 (1989)). Both versions were declared unconstitutional.

promote injury and degradation such as rape, battery, child sexual abuse, and prostitution and inhibit just enforcement of laws against these acts; contribute significantly to restricting women in particular from full exercise of citizenship and participation in public life, including in neighborhoods; damage relations between the sexes; and undermine women's equal exercise of rights to speech and action guaranteed to all citizens under the Constitutions and laws of the United States, the State of California and the County of Los Angeles.

Section 3. Definitions

1. *Pornography* is the graphic sexually explicit subordination of women through pictures and/or words that also includes one or more of the following: (i) women are presented dehumanized as sexual objects, things or commodities; or (ii) women are presented as sexual objects who enjoy pain or humiliation; or (iii) women are presented as sexual objects who experience sexual pleasure in being raped; or (iv) women are presented as sexual objects tied up or cut up or mutilated or bruised or physically hurt; or (v) women are presented in postures of sexual submission, servility, or display; or (vi) women's body parts—including but not limited to vaginas, breasts, or buttocks—are exhibited such that women are reduced to those parts; or (vii) women are presented as whores by nature; or (viii) women are presented as being penetrated by objects or animals; or (ix) women are presented in scenarios of degradation, injury, torture, shown as filthy or inferior, bleeding, bruised or hurt in a context that makes these conditions sexual.

2. The use of men,[b] children, or transsexuals in the place of women in (1) above is also pornography for purposes of this law.

Section 4. Unlawful Practices

1. *Coercion into pornography*: It shall be sex discrimination to coerce, intimidate, or fraudulently induce (hereafter, "coerce") any person, including transsexual, into performing for pornography, which injury may date from any appearance or sale of any product(s) of such performance(s). The maker(s), seller(s), exhibitor(s) and/or distributor(s) of said pornography may be sued, including for an injunction to eliminate the product(s) of the performance(s) from the public view.

Proof of one or more of the following facts or conditions shall not, without more, negate a finding of coercion:

(i) that the person is a woman; or

(ii) that the person is or has been a prostitute; or

(iii) that the person has attained the age of majority; or

b. Does this provision wrongly conflate gay pornography with stereotypical heterosexual pornography? See Green, *Pornographies,* 8 J. of Pol. Phil. 27 (2000). For criticism of the ordinance from a lesbian perspective, see Ross, 'It's Merely Designed for Sexual Arousal,' *Feminism & Pornography* 264–317 (Cornell ed. 1999).

(iv) that the person is connected by blood or marriage to anyone involved in or related to the making of the pornography; or

(v) that the person has previously had, or been thought to have had, sexual relations with anyone, including anyone involved in or related to the making of the pornography; or

(vi) that the person has previously posed for sexually explicit pictures with or for anyone, including anyone involved in or related to the making of the pornography at issue; or

(vii) that anyone else, including a spouse or other relative, has given permission on the person's behalf; or

(viii) that the person actually consented to a use of the performance that is changed into pornography; or

(ix) that the person knew that the purpose of the acts or events in question was to make pornography; or

(x) that the person showed no resistance or appeared to cooperate actively in the photographic sessions or in the events that produced the pornography; or

(xi) that the person signed a contract, or made statements affirming a willingness to cooperate in the production of pornography; or

(xii) that no physical force, threats, or weapons were used in the making of the pornography; or

(xiii) that the person was paid or otherwise compensated.

2. *Trafficking in pornography:* It shall be sex discrimination to produce, sell, exhibit, or distribute pornography, including through private clubs.

(i) City, state, and federally funded public libraries or private and public university and college libraries in which pornography is available for study, including on open shelves but excluding special display presentations, shall not be construed to be trafficking in pornography.

(ii) Isolated passages or isolated parts shall not be actionable under this section.

(iii) Any woman has a claim hereunder as a woman acting against the subordination of women. Any man, child, or transsexual who alleges injury by pornography in the way women are injured by it also has a claim.

3. *Forcing pornography on a person:* It shall be sex discrimination to force pornography on a person, including child or transsexual, in any place of employment, education, home, or public place. Only the perpetrator of the force and/or institution responsible for the force may be sued.

4. *Assault or physical attack due to pornography:* It shall be sex discrimination to assault, physically attack or injure any person, including

child or transsexual, in a way that is directly caused by specific pornography. The perpetrator of the assault or attack may be sued. The maker(s), distributor(s), seller(s), and/or exhibitor(s) may also be sued, including for an injunction against the specific pornography's further exhibition, distribution or sale.

Section 5. Defenses

1. It shall not be a defense that the defendant in an action under this law did not know or intend that the materials were pornography or sex discrimination.

2. No damages or compensation for losses shall be recoverable under Sec. 4(2) or other than against the perpetrator of the assault or attack in Sec. 4(4) unless the defendant knew or had reason to know that the materials were pornography.

3. In actions under Sec. 4(2) or other than against the perpetrator of the assault or attack in Sec. 4(4), no damages or compensation for losses shall be recoverable against maker(s) for pornography made, against distributor(s) for pornography distributed, against seller(s) for pornography sold, or against exhibitor(s) for pornography exhibited, prior to the effective date of this law.

Section 6. Enforcement

a. Civil Action: Any person, or their estate, aggrieved by violations of this law may enforce its provisions by means of a civil action. No criminal penalties shall attach for any violation of the provisions of this law. Relief for violations of this law, except as expressly restricted or precluded herein, may include compensatory and punitive damages and reasonable attorney's fees, costs and disbursements.

b. Injunction: Any person who violates this law may be enjoined except that:

(i) In actions under Sec. 4(2), and other than against the perpetrator of the assault or attack under Sec. 4(4), no temporary or permanent injunction shall issue prior to a final judicial determination that the challenged activities constitute a violation of this law.

(ii) No temporary or permanent injunction shall extend beyond such material(s) that, having been described with reasonable specificity by the injunction, have been determined to be validly proscribed under this law.

Section 7. Severability

Should any part(s) of this law be found legally invalid, the remaining part(s) remain valid. A judicial declaration that any part(s) of this law cannot be applied validly in a particular manner or to a particular case or category of cases shall not affect the validity of that part(s) as otherwise applied, unless such other application would clearly frustrate the intent of the Board of Supervisors in adopting this law.

Section 8. Limitation of Action

Actions under this law must be filed within one year of the alleged discriminatory acts.

Notes and Questions

1. *The Ferber analogy.* Consider Sunstein, *Neutrality in Constitutional Law (With Special Reference to Pornography, Abortion, and Surrogacy),* 92 Colum.L.Rev. 1, 24 (1992): "A successful action for rape and sexual assault is difficult enough. The difficulty becomes all the greater when the victims are young women coerced into, and abused during, the production of pornography. Often those victims will be reluctant to put themselves through the experience and possible humiliation and expense of initiating a proceeding. Often prosecutors will be reluctant to act on their behalf. Often they will have extremely little credibility even if they are willing to come forward. In this light, the only realistically effective way to eliminate the practice is to eliminate or reduce the financial benefits." If all women in pornographic films were coerced, would the analogy to *Ferber* be air tight. If not, how much coercion is acceptable? What is the relationship between prostitution and pornography? On the latter, see *Feminism & Pornography* (Cornell ed. 1999).[c]

2. *Relationship between obscenity and pornography.* Consider Andrea Dworkin, *Against the Male Flood: Censorship, Pornography, and Equality,* 8 Harv. Women's L.J. 1, 8–9 (1985): "What is at stake in obscenity law is always erection: under what conditions, in what circumstances, how, by whom, by what materials men want it produced in themselves. Men have made this public policy. Why they want to regulate their own erections through law is a question of endless interest and importance to feminists.
* * *

"The insult pornography offers, invariably, to sex is accomplished in the active subordination of women: the creation of a sexual dynamic in which the putting-down of women, the suppression of women, and ultimately the brutalization of women, *is* what sex is taken to be. Obscenity in law, and in what it does socially, is erection. Law recognizes the act in this. Pornography, however, is a broader, more comprehensive act, because it crushes a whole class of people through violence and subjugation: and sex is the vehicle that does the crushing. The penis is not the test, as it is in obscenity. Instead, the status of women is the issue. Erection is implicated in the subordinating, but who it reaches and how are the pressing legal and social questions. Pornography, unlike obscenity, is a discrete, identifiable system of sexual exploitation that hurts women as a class by creating inequality and abuse."

Consider MacKinnon, *Pornography, Civil Rights, and Speech,* 20 Harv. Civ.Rts.—Civ.Lib.L.Rev. 1, 50–52 & 16–17 (1985): "To reach the magnitude

---

c. See also Chandler, *Feminists as Collaborators and Prostitutes as Autobiographers,* 10 Hastings L.J. 135 (1999).

of this problem on the scale it exists, our law makes trafficking in pornography—production, sale, exhibition, or distribution—actionable. Under the obscenity rubric, much legal and psychological scholarship has centered on a search for the elusive link between pornography defined as obscenity and harm. They have looked high and low—in the mind of the male consumer, in society or in its 'moral fabric,' in correlations between variations in levels of anti-social acts and liberalization of obscenity laws. The only harm they have found has been one they have attributed to 'the social interests in order and morality.' Until recently, no one looked very persistently for harm to women, particularly harm to women through men. The rather obvious fact that the sexes *relate* has been overlooked in the inquiry into the male consumer and his mind. The pornography doesn't just drop out of the sky, go into his head and stop there. Specifically, men rape, batter, prostitute, molest, and sexually harass women. Under conditions of inequality, they also hire, fire, promote, and grade women, decide how much or whether or not we are worth paying and for what, define and approve and disapprove of women in ways that count, that determine our lives.

"In pornography, there it is, in one place, all of the abuses that women had to struggle so long even to begin to articulate, all the *unspeakable* abuse: the rape, the battery, the sexual harassment, the prostitution, and the sexual abuse of children. Only in the pornography it is called something else: sex, sex, sex, sex, and sex, respectively. Pornography sexualizes rape, battery, sexual harassment, prostitution, and child sexual abuse; it thereby celebrates, promotes, authorizes, and legitimizes them. More generally, it eroticizes the dominance and submission that is the dynamic common to them all. It makes hierarchy sexy and calls that 'the truth about sex' or just a mirror of reality." See generally Dworkin, *Pornography: Men Possessing Women* (1981). MacKinnon, *Toward a Feminist Theory of the State* 195–214 (1989); MacKinnon, *Feminism Unmodified* 127–228 (1987).

3. *The trafficking section.* Is the trafficking section constitutional under *Miller?* Consider the following hypothetical commentary: "The Dworkin–MacKinnon proposal focuses on a narrower class of material than *Miller* because it excludes erotic materials that do not involve subordination. That class of material upon which it does focus appeals to prurient interest because it is graphic and sexually explicit. Moreover, the eroticization of dominance in the ways specified in the ordinance is so patently offensive to community standards that it can be said as a matter of law that this class of materials lacks *serious* literary, artistic, political, or scientific value as a matter of law." Do you agree?

Is there a good analogy to *Beauharnais?* To *Ferber?* Did more or less harm exist in *Gertz? Miller? Ferber?* Was there more or less of a threat to first amendment values in *Gertz? Miller? Ferber?* Should this be accepted as a new category? Consider Kaminer, *Pornography and the First Amendment: Prior Restraints and Private Action,* 239, 245 in *Take Back the Night: Women on Pornography* (Lederer ed. 1980): "The Women's Movement is a civil rights movement, and we should appreciate the importance of individual freedom of choice and the danger of turning popular sentiment into law in areas affecting individual privacy.

"Legislative or judicial control of pornography is simply not possible without breaking down the legal principles and procedures that are essential to our own right to speak and, ultimately, our freedom to control our own lives. We must continue to organize against pornography and the degradation and abuse of women, but we must not ask the government to take up our struggle for us. The power it will assume to do so will be far more dangerous to us all than the 'power' of pornography."[d]

4. *Pornography and dissent.* See Langton, *Speech Acts and Unspeakable Acts,* 22 Phil. & Pub.Aff. 293, 311–312 (1993): "What is important here is not whether the speech of pornographers is universally held in high esteem: it is not—hence the common assumption among liberals that in defending pornographers they are defending the underdog. What is important is whether it is authoritative in the domain that counts—the domain of speech about sex—and whether it is authoritative for the hearers that count: people, men, boys, who in addition to wanting 'entertainment,' want to discover the right way to do things, want to know which moves in the sexual game are legitimate. What is important is whether it is authoritative for those hearers who—one way or another—do seem to learn that violence is sexy and

d. Compare Hunter & Law, *Brief Amici Curiae of Feminist Anti–Censorship Taskforce* (on appeal in *Hudnut,* below) 21 U.Mich.J.L.Ref. 69, 109 & 129–30 (1987–88). The ordinance conceivably "would require the judiciary to impose its views of correct sexuality on a diverse community. The inevitable result would be to disapprove those images that are least conventional and privilege those that are closest to majoritarian beliefs about proper sexuality. [Moreover] [b]y defining sexually explicit images of women as subordinating and degrading to them, the ordinance reinforces the stereotypical view that 'good' women do not seek and enjoy sex. [Finally], the ordinance perpetuates a stereotype of women as helpless victims, incapable of consent, and in need of protection." See generally Nadine Strossen, *Defending Pornography* (1995).

For collections of feminist perspectives, see Cornell, ed., *Feminism and* Pornography (2000); *Take Back the Night,* supra; Burstyn, ed., *Women Against Censorship* (1985); Snitow, Stansell & Thompson, etc., *Powers of Desire* 419–67 (1983). For a variety of views (including feminist views), see Weinstein, *Hate Speech, Pornography, and the Radical Attack on Free Speech Doctrine* (1999); Delgado & Stefanic, *Must We Defend Nazis* (1997); Wolfson, *Hate Speech, Sex Speech, Free Speech* (1997); Anderson, *Speaking Freely About Reducing Violence*

Against Women, 10 U.Fla. J.L. & Pub.Pol. 173 (1998); Cohen, *Freedom of Expression,* 21 Phil. & Pub.Aff. 207 (1993); Rhode, *Justice and Gender,* 263–73 (1989); Tushnet, *Red, White, and Blue* 293–312 (1988); Downs, *The Attorney General's Commission and the New Politics of Pornography,* 1987 Am.B.Found.Res.J. 641; Gey, *The Apologetics of Suppression,* 86 Mich.L.Rev. 1564 (1988); Hoffman, *Feminism, Pornography, and the Law,* 133 U.Pa.L.Rev. 497 (1985); Post, *Cultural Heterogeneity and the Law,* 76 Calif.L.Rev. 297 (1988); Richards, *Pornography Commissions and the First Amendment,* 39 Me.L.Rev. 275 (1987); Schauer, *Causation Theory and the Causes of Sexual Violence,* 1987 Am.B.Found.Res.J. 737; Sherry, *An Essay Concerning Toleration,* 71 Minn.L.Rev. 963 (1987); Stone, *Anti–Pornography Legislation as Viewpoint–Discrimination,* 9 Harv.J.Pub.Pol'y 461 (1986); Strossen, *The Convergence of Feminist and Civil Liberties Principles in the Pornography Debate,* 62 N.Y.U.L.Rev. 201 (1987); Sunstein, *Pornography and the First Amendment,* 1986 Duke L.J. 589; West, *The Feminist–Conservative Anti–Pornography Alliance and the 1986 Attorney General's Commission on Pornography Report,* 1987 Am.B.Found.Res.J. 681. For the Canadian approach, see *Regina v. Butler* [1992] 1 S.C.R. 452. For comparative commentary, see Greenawalt, *Fighting Words,* 99–123 (1995).

coercion legitimate: the fifty percent of boys who 'think it is okay for a man to rape a woman if he is sexually aroused by her,' the fifteen percent of male college undergraduates who say they have raped a woman on a date, the eight-six percent who say that they enjoy the conquest part of sex, the thirty percent who rank faces of women displaying pain and fear to be more sexually attractive than faces showing pleasure.''

5. *Subordination.* Is the absence of subordination an appropriate ideal? Consider Meyer, *Sex, Sin, and Women's Liberation: Against Porn–Suppression,* 72 Tex.L.Rev. 1097, 1133 n. 156, 1154–55 (1994): ''I am not suggesting that sex accompanied by intimacy, respect, and caring is not an appropriate ideal. Rather, I mean to argue that the sort of equality in which no one is ever the aggressor in fantasy or in reality is, at best, a 'utopian vision of sexual relations: sex without power, sex without persuasion, sex without pursuit.' [S]exual discourse needs to be free-wheeling and uncontrolled because of the hotly contested nature of issues concerning sexuality. Such issues as what constitutes pleasure for women and its connection to danger, to power, to men, and to aggression and inequality; of what sex is 'good' and 'bad'; and of whether women can escape inequality and coercion within Western sexual culture are debated and dissected with little agreement across boundaries of class, race, and nationality. Allies on other issues disagree about whether all violence is bad, over what constitutes violence or pleasure, and over the meaning of such terms as 'objectified,' 'degraded,' or 'demeaned.' ''See also Keller, *Viewing and Doing: Complicating Pornography's Meaning,* 81 Geo.L.J. 2195, 2231 (1993): ''[R]obin West critiques MacKinnon and Dworkin for their failure to acknowledge the 'meaning and the value, to women, of the pleasure we take in our fantasies of eroticized submission.' Some like Jessica Benjamin and Kate Ellis have attempted to explain psychologically why pleasure can be found by women, as well as men, in submission and power. Of the various meanings pornography could have for a variety of audience members, one meaning for women could be pleasure in depictions of power.''

6. *The pornography definition.* Is the proposed definition too vague? Is it more or less vague than the terminology employed in *Miller?* Is there a core of clear meaning? How would you clarify its meaning? Is the definition overbroad? What revisions, if any, would you suggest to narrow its scope?

Consider Emerson, *Pornography and the First Amendment: A Reply to Professor MacKinnon,* 3 Yale L. & Pol. Rev. 130, 131–32 (1985): ''The sweep of the Indianapolis Ordinance is breathtaking. It would subject to governmental ban virtually all depictions of rape, verbal or pictorial, and a substantial proportion of other presentations of sexual encounters. More specifically, it would outlaw such works of literature as the *Arabian Nights,* John Cleland's *Fanny Hill,* Henry Miller's *Tropic of Cancer,* William Faulkner's *Sanctuary,* and Norman Mailer's *Ancient Evenings,* to name but a few. The ban would extend from Greek mythology and Shakespeare to the millions of copies of 'romance novels' now being sold in the supermarkets. It would embrace much of the world's art, from ancient carvings to Picasso, well-known films too numerous to mention, and a large amount of commercial advertising.

"The scope of the Indianapolis Ordinance is not accidental. * * * As Professor MacKinnon emphasizes, male domination has deep, pervasive and ancient roots in our society, so it is not surprising that our literature, art, entertainment and commercial practices are permeated by attitudes and behavior that create and reflect the inferior status of women. If the answer to the problem, as Professor MacKinnon describes it, is government suppression of sexual expression that contributes to female subordination, then the net of restraint has to be cast on a nearly limitless scale." Would the ordinance inadvertently cover activist anti-pornographic art that uses violent sexual images to make its point. If not, does the intent of the artist excuse any unintended effects? See Adler, *What's Left?: Hate Speech, Pornography, and the Problem of Artistic Expression,* 84 Calif.L.Rev. 1499 (1996).

7. *The assault provision.* Should the maker of a pornographic work be responsible for assaults prompted by the work? Should the maker of non-pornographic works be responsible for imitative assaults. In *Olivia N. v. NBC,* 126 Cal.App.3d 488, 178 Cal.Rptr. 888 (1981), the victim of a sexual assault allegedly imitating a sexual assault in NBC's "Born Innocent" sued the network. Olivia N. claimed that NBC negligently exposed her to serious risk because it knew or should have known that someone would imitate the act portrayed in the movie. Suppose Olivia N. could show that NBC had been advised that such an assault was likely if the movie were shown? Should a court analogize to cases like *Gertz?* The California court ruled that Olivia N. could not prevail unless she met the *Brandenburg* standard.[e]

––––––––

The Indianapolis version of the anti-pornography civil rights ordinance was struck down in AMERICAN BOOKSELLERS ASS'N v. HUDNUT, 771 F.2d 323 (7th Cir.1985), aff'd, 475 U.S. 1001, 106 S.Ct. 1172, 89 L.Ed.2d 291 (1986). The Seventh Circuit, per EASTERBROOK, J., ruled that the definition of pornography infected the entire ordinance (including provisions against trafficking, coercion into pornography, forcing pornography on a person, and assault or physical attack due to pornography) because it impermissibly discriminated on the basis of point of view: "Indianapolis enacted an ordinance defining 'pornography' as a practice that discriminates against women. * * *

" 'Pornography' under the ordinance is 'the graphic sexually explicit subordination of women, whether in pictures or in words, that also includes one or more of the following: (1) Women are presented as sexual objects who

e. For relevant commentary, see Balkin, *The Rhetoric of Responsibility,* 76 Va.L.Rev. 197 (1990); Schauer, *Uncoupling Free Speech,* 92 Colum.L.Rev. 1321 (1992); Schauer, *Mrs. Palsgraf and the First Amendment,* 47 Wash. & Lee L.Rev. 161 (1990).

enjoy pain or humiliation; or (2) Women are presented as sexual objects who experience sexual pleasure in being raped; or (3) Women are presented as sexual objects tied up or cut up or mutilated or bruised or physically hurt, or as dismembered or truncated or fragmented or severed into body parts; or (4) Women are presented as being penetrated by objects or animals; or (5) Women are presented in scenarios of degradation, injury, abasement, torture, shown as filthy or inferior, bleeding, bruised, or hurt in a context that makes these conditions sexual; or (6) Women are presented as sexual objects for domination, conquest, violation, exploitation, possession, or use, or through postures or positions of servility or submission or display.'

"The statute provides that the 'use of men, children, or transsexuals in the place of women in paragraphs (1) through (6) above shall also constitute pornography under this section.' The ordinance as passed in April 1984 defined 'sexually explicit' to mean actual or simulated intercourse or the uncovered exhibition of the genitals, buttocks or anus. An amendment in June 1984 deleted this provision, leaving the term undefined.

"The Indianapolis ordinance does not refer to the prurient interest, to offensiveness, or to the standards of the community. It demands attention to particular depictions, not to the work judged as a whole. It is irrelevant under the ordinance whether the work has literary, artistic, political, or scientific value. The City and many amici point to these omissions as virtues. They maintain that pornography influences attitudes, and the statute is a way to alter the socialization of men and women rather than to vindicate community standards of offensiveness. And as one of the principal drafters of the ordinance has asserted, 'if a woman is subjected, why should it matter that the work has other value?' MacKinnon, *Pornography, Civil Rights, and Speech,* 20 Harv.Civ.Rts.—Civ.Lib.L.Rev. 1, 21 (1985).

"Civil rights groups and feminists have entered this case as amici on both sides. Those supporting the ordinance say that it will play an important role in reducing the tendency of men to view women as sexual objects, a tendency that leads to both unacceptable attitudes and discrimination in the workplace and violence away from it. Those opposing the ordinance point out that much radical feminist literature is explicit and depicts women in ways forbidden by the ordinance and that the ordinance would reopen old battles. It is unclear how Indianapolis would treat works from James Joyce's *Ulysses* to Homer's *Iliad;* both depict women as submissive objects for conquest and domination.

"We do not try to balance the arguments for and against an ordinance such as this. The ordinance discriminates on the ground of the content of the speech. Speech treating women in the approved way—in sexual encounters 'premised on equality' (MacKinnon, supra, at 22)—is lawful no matter how sexually explicit. Speech treating women in the disapproved way—as submissive in matters sexual or as enjoying humiliation—is unlawful no matter how significant the literary, artistic, or political qualities of the work taken as a whole. The state may not ordain preferred viewpoints in this way. The Constitution forbids the state to declare one perspective right and silence opponents.[a] * * *

" 'If there is any fixed star in our constitutional constellation, it is that no official, high or petty, can prescribe what shall be orthodox in politics, nationalism, religion, or other matters of opinion or force citizens to confess by word or act their faith therein.' *West Virginia State Bd. of Educ. v. Barnette.* Under the First Amendment the government must leave to the people the evaluation of ideas. Bald or subtle, an idea is as powerful as the audience allows it to be. A belief may be pernicious—the beliefs of Nazis led to the death of millions, those of the Klan to the repression of millions. A pernicious belief may prevail. Totalitarian governments today rule much of the planet, practicing suppression of billions and spreading dogma that may enslave others. One of the things that separates our society from theirs is our absolute right to propagate opinions that the government finds wrong or even hateful. * * *

"Under the ordinance graphic sexually explicit speech is 'pornography' or not depending on the perspective the author adopts. Speech that 'subordinates' women and also, for example, presents women as enjoying pain, humiliation, or rape, or even simply presents women in 'positions of servility or submission or display' is forbidden, no matter how great the literary or political value of the work taken as a whole. Speech that portrays women in positions of equality is lawful, no matter how graphic the sexual content. This is thought control. It establishes an 'approved' view of women, of how they may react to sexual encounters, of how the sexes may relate to each other. Those who espouse the approved view may use sexual images; those who do not, may not.

"Indianapolis justifies the ordinance on the ground that pornography affects thoughts. Men who see women depicted as subordinate are more likely to treat them so. Pornography is an aspect of dominance.[1] It does not

---

a. But consider Harel, *Bigotry, Pornography, and The First Amendment: A Theory of Unprotected Speech,* 65 S.Cal.L.Rev. 1887, 1889 (1992): "Some ideas and values cannot aid in the process of shaping our political obligations. This is not because these 'values' do not, as a matter of fact, influence the output of the political process but because any influence they do exert does not generate legitimate political obligations. Racist and sexist values cannot participate in the shaping of political obligations because the legal obligations they generate do not have morally binding force."

1. "Pornography constructs what a woman is in terms of its view of what men want sexually. * * * Pornography's world of equality is a harmonious and balanced place. Men and women are perfectly complementary and perfectly bipolar. [All] the ways men love to take and violate women,

women love to be taken and violated. [What] pornography *does* goes beyond its content: It eroticizes hierarchy, it sexualizes inequality. It makes dominance and submission sex. Inequality is its central dynamic; the illusion of freedom coming together with the reality of force is central to its working. [P]ornography is neither harmless fantasy nor a corrupt and confused misrepresentation of an otherwise neutral and healthy sexual situation. It institutionalizes the sexuality of male supremacy, fusing the eroticization of dominance and submission with the social construction of male and female. * * * Men treat women as who they see women as being. Pornography constructs who that is. Men's power over women means that the way men see women defines who women can be. Pornography [is] a sexual reality." MacKinnon, supra, at 17–18 (note omitted, emphasis in original). See also Dworkin, *Pornography: Men Pos-*

persuade people so much as change them. It works by socializing, by establishing the expected and the permissible. In this view pornography is not an idea; pornography is the injury.

"There is much to this perspective. Beliefs are also facts. People often act in accordance with the images and patterns they find around them. People raised in a religion tend to accept the tenets of that religion, often without independent examination. People taught from birth that black people are fit only for slavery rarely rebelled against that creed; beliefs coupled with the self-interest of the masters established a social structure that inflicted great harm while enduring for centuries. Words and images act at the level of the subconscious before they persuade at the level of the conscious. Even the truth has little chance unless a statement fits within the framework of beliefs that may never have been subjected to rational study.

"Therefore we accept the premises of this legislation. Depictions of subordination tend to perpetuate subordination. The subordinate status of women in turn leads to affront and lower pay at work, insult and injury at home, battery and rape on the streets.[2] In the language of the legislature, '[p]ornography is central in creating and maintaining sex as a basis of discrimination. Pornography is a systematic practice of exploitation and subordination based on sex which differentially harms women. The bigotry and contempt it produces, with the acts of aggression it fosters, harm women's opportunities for equality and rights [of all kinds].'

"Yet this simply demonstrates the power of pornography as speech. All of these unhappy effects depend on mental intermediation. Pornography affects how people see the world, their fellows, and social relations. If pornography is what pornography does, so is other speech. Hitler's orations affected how some Germans saw Jews. Communism is a world view, not simply a *Manifesto* by Marx and Engels or a set of speeches. Efforts to suppress communist speech in the United States were based on the belief that the public acceptability of such ideas would increase the likelihood of totalitarian government. [Many] people believe that the existence of televi-

sessing Women (1981). A national commission in Canada recently adopted a similar rationale for controlling pornography. Special Commission on Pornography and Prostitution, 1 *Pornography and Prostitution in Canada* 49–59 (1985).

2. MacKinnon's article collects empirical work that supports this proposition. The social science studies are very difficult to interpret, however, and they conflict. Because much of the effect of speech comes through a process of socialization, it is difficult to measure incremental benefits and injuries caused by particular speech. Several psychologists have found, for example, that those who see violent, sexually explicit films tend to have more violent thoughts. But how often does this lead to actual violence? National commissions on obscenity

here, in the United Kingdom, and in Canada have found that it is not possible to demonstrate a direct link between obscenity and rape or exhibitionism. The several opinions in *Miller v. California* discuss the U.S. commission. See also *Report of the Committee on Obscenity and Film Censorship* 61–95 (Home Office, Her Majesty's Stationery Office, 1979); 1 *Pornography and Prostitution in Canada* 71–73, 95–103. In saying that we accept the finding that pornography as the ordinance defines it leads to unhappy consequences, we mean only that there is evidence to this effect, that this evidence is consistent with much human experience, and that as judges we must accept the legislative resolution of such disputed empirical questions.

sion, apart from the content of specific programs, leads to intellectual laziness, to a penchant for violence, to many other ills. The Alien and Sedition Acts passed during the administration of John Adams rested on a sincerely held belief that disrespect for the government leads to social collapse and revolution—a belief with support in the history of many nations. Most governments of the world act on this empirical regularity, suppressing critical speech. In the United States, however, the strength of the support for this belief is irrelevant. Seditious libel is protected speech unless the danger is not only grave but also imminent. See *New York Times v. Sullivan;* cf. *Brandenburg v. Ohio.*

"Racial bigotry, anti-semitism, violence on television, reporters' biases— these and many more influence the culture and shape our socialization. None is directly answerable by more speech, unless that speech too finds its place in the popular culture. Yet all is protected as speech, however insidious. Any other answer leaves the government in control of all of the institutions of culture, the great censor and director of which thoughts are good for us.

"Sexual responses often are unthinking responses, and the association of sexual arousal with the subordination of women therefore may have a substantial effect. But almost all cultural stimuli provoke unconscious responses. Religious ceremonies condition their participants. Teachers convey messages by selecting what not to cover; the implicit message about what is off limits or unthinkable may be more powerful than the messages for which they present rational argument. Television scripts contain unarticulated assumptions. People may be conditioned in subtle ways. If the fact that speech plays a role in a process of conditioning were enough to permit governmental regulation, that would be the end of freedom of speech. * * *

"Much of Indianapolis's argument rests on the belief that when speech is 'unanswerable,' and the metaphor that there is a 'marketplace of ideas' does not apply, the First Amendment does not apply either. The metaphor is honored; Milton's *Aeropagitica* and John Stewart Mill's *On Liberty* defend freedom of speech on the ground that the truth will prevail, and many of the most important cases under the First Amendment recite this position. The Framers undoubtedly believed it. As a general matter it is true. But the Constitution does not make the dominance of truth a necessary condition of freedom of speech. To say that it does would be to confuse an outcome of free speech with a necessary condition for the application of the amendment.

"A power to limit speech on the ground that truth has not yet prevailed and is not likely to prevail implies the power to declare truth. At some point the government must be able to say (as Indianapolis has said): 'We know what the truth is, yet a free exchange of speech has not driven out falsity, so that we must now prohibit falsity.' If the government may declare the truth, why wait for the failure of speech? Under the First Amendment, however, there is no such thing as a false idea, *Gertz v. Robert Welch, Inc.,* so the government may not restrict speech on the ground that in a free exchange truth is not yet dominant. * * *

"We come, finally, to the argument that pornography is 'low value' speech, that it is enough like obscenity that Indianapolis may prohibit it. Some cases hold that speech far removed from politics and other subjects at the core of the Framers' concerns may be subjected to special regulation. E.g., *FCC v. Pacifica Foundation,* Ch. 8, II infra; *Young v. American Mini Theatres, Inc.* (plurality opinion); *Chaplinsky v. New Hampshire.* These cases do not sustain statutes that select among viewpoints, however. In *Pacifica* the FCC sought to keep vile language off the air during certain times. The Court held that it may; but the Court would not have sustained a regulation prohibiting scatological descriptions of Republicans but not scatological descriptions of Democrats, or any other form of selection among viewpoints.

"At all events, pornography is not low value speech within the meaning of these cases. Indianapolis seeks to prohibit certain speech because it believes this speech influences social relations and politics on a grand scale, that it controls attitudes at home and in the legislature. This precludes a characterization of the speech as low value. True, pornography and obscenity have sex in common. But Indianapolis left out of its definition any reference to literary, artistic, political, or scientific value. The ordinance applies to graphic sexually explicit subordination in works great and small.[3] The Court sometimes balances the value of speech against the costs of its restriction, but it does this by category of speech and not by the content of particular works. See Ely, *Flag Desecration: A Case Study in the Roles of Categorization and Balancing in First Amendment Analysis,* 88 Harv.L.Rev. 1482 (1975); Stone, *Restrictions of Speech Because of its Content: The Strange Case of Subject–Matter Restrictions,* 46 U.Chi.L.Rev. 81 (1978). Indianapolis has created an approved point of view and so loses the support of these cases.

"Any rationale we could imagine in support of this ordinance could not be limited to sex discrimination. Free speech has been on balance an ally of those seeking change. Governments that want stasis start by restricting speech. Culture is a powerful force of continuity; Indianapolis paints pornography as a part of the culture of power. Change in any complex system ultimately depends on the ability of outsiders to challenge accepted views and the reigning institutions. Without a strong guarantee of freedom of speech, there is no effective right to challenge what is."[b]

---

3. Indianapolis briefly argues that *Beauharnais v. Illinois,* which allowed a state to penalize "group libel," supports the ordinance. In *Collin v. Smith,* [Ch. 1, VI, C], we concluded that cases such as *New York Times v. Sullivan* had so washed away the foundations of *Beauharnais* that it could not be considered authoritative. If we are wrong in this, however, the case still does not support the ordinance. It is not clear that depicting women as subordinate in sex-

ually explicit ways, even combined with a depiction of pleasure in rape, would fit within the definition of a group libel. The well received film *Swept Away* used explicit sex, plus taking pleasure in rape, to make a political statement, not to defame. Work must be an insult or slur for its own sake to come within the ambit of *Beauharnais,* and a work need not be scurrilous at all to be pornography under the ordinance.

Notes and Questions

1. In response to the last paragraph, supra, Frank Michelman observes: "[I]t is a fair and obvious question why preservation of 'effective right[s] to challenge what is' does not require protection of a 'freedom of speech' more broadly conceived to protect social critics—'outsiders,' in Judge Easterbrook's phrase—against suppression by nongovernmental as well as by governmental power. It is a fair and obvious question why the assertion that '[g]overnments that want stasis start by restricting speech' does not apply equally to the nongovernmental agencies of power in society. It is a fair and obvious question why our society's openness to challenge does not need protection against repressive private as well as public action." *Conceptions of Democracy in American Constitutional Argument: The Case of Pornography Regulation,* 56 Tenn.L.Rev. 291 (1989), citing MacKinnon, *Feminism Unmodified* 155–58 (1987).

2. *Free speech and silence.* Consider MacKinnon, *Toward a Feminist Theory of the State* 206 (1989): "That pornography chills women's expression is difficult to demonstrate empirically because silence is not eloquent. Yet on no more of the same kind of evidence, the argument that suppressing pornography might chill legitimate speech has supported its protection. [T]he law of the First Amendment comprehends that freedom of expression, in the abstract, is a system but fails to comprehend that sexism (and racism), in the concrete, are also systems."[c] But consider Charles Fried, *Perfect Freedom, Perfect Justice,* 78 B.U. L.Rev. 717, 737 (1998): "[R]acist or sexist speech, if it has the effect attributed to it, produces it through the mind: Potential speakers are persuaded that they are less worthy individuals and so they are less inclined to contribute their voices in debate; and potential listeners are persuaded that these speakers are not worth attending to. But as the argument must concede that the mechanism of the silencing is through persuasion, it must also concede that the government's countermeasures must be directed at silencing the attempt to persuade: The government stops the message because of what it says and the evil the government fears works through the channels of the mind. I do not see how

b. The balance of the opinion suggested ways that parts of the ordinance might be salvaged, if redrafted. It suggested, for example, that the city might forbid coerced participation in any film or in "any film containing explicit sex." If the latter were adopted, would it make a difference if the section applied to persons coerced into participation in such films without regard to whether they were forced into explicit sex scenes? Swygert, J., concurring, joined part of Easterbrook, J.'s opinion for the court, but objected both to the "questionable and broad assertions regarding how human be- havior can be conditioned" and to the "advisory" opinion on how parts of the ordinance might be redrafted.

c. To what extent is discourse inherently empowering and silencing in its effects? To what extent is pornography unique? For rich commentary, see the essays collected in *Censorship and Silencing* (Post ed. 1998); Langton, note 4 supra; Hornsby, *Disempowered Speech,* 23 Philosophical Topics 127 (1997); Jacobson, *Freedom of Speech Acts?,* 24 Phil. & Pub. Aff. 64 (1995); Sadurski, *On Seeing Speech Through An Equality Lens,* 16 Oxford J. of Legal Studies 713 (1996).

we can escape the conclusion that the government is stopping the message because it is afraid that people might believe it. But that is precisely what the First Amendment has consistently identified as what government may not do * * *.''

3. *"We do not try to balance * * *."* Does the existence of point of view discrimination preclude balancing under existing law? Consider Heins, *Viewpoint Discrimination,* 24 Hastings L.Q. 99, 136 (1996) "Judge Easterbrook's point is well-taken, but it reaches beyond the MacKinnon/Dworkin type of ordinance. The First Amendment does not allow the government to dictate 'which thoughts are good for us,' whether it be in the guise of 'feminist' antipornography laws, indecency laws that turn on notions of 'patent offensiveness,' or obscenity laws of the type upheld in *Miller* and *Slaton* because of the lascivious, family-undermining, personality-distorting, and generally immoral thoughts that the Court felt pornography inspires.''

4. Does pornography as defined by Indianapolis (or some part of that category) implicate such little first amendment value as to foreclose constitutional protection? How should such value be assessed? Consider Sunstein, *Pornography and the First Amendment,* 1986 Duke Law Journal 603–04: "First, the speech must be far afield from the central concern of the first amendment, which, broadly speaking, is effective popular control of public affairs. Speech that concerns governmental processes is entitled to the highest level of protection; speech that has little or nothing to do with public affairs may be accorded less protection. Second, a distinction is drawn between cognitive and noncognitive aspects of speech. Speech that has purely noncognitive appeal will be entitled to less constitutional protection.[d] Third, the purpose of the speaker is relevant: if the speaker is seeking to communicate a message, he will be treated more favorably than if he is not. Fourth, the various classes of low-value speech reflect judgments that in certain areas, government is unlikely to be acting for constitutionally impermissible reasons or producing constitutionally troublesome harms.''

How do Sunstein's factors apply to the Indianapolis ordinance?[e]

C. RACIST SPEECH REVISITED

*"What do you want to sell in the marketplace? What idea?
The idea of murder?"*

Erna Gans, a concentration camp survivor and active leader in the Skokie B'nai B'rith.[a]

---

d. For debate about this factor compare Chevigny, *Pornography and Cognition,* 1989 Duke L.J. 420 with Sunstein, *The First Amendment and Cognition,* 1989 Duke L.J. 433. See also Karst, *Boundaries and Reasons: Freedom of Expression and the Subordination of Groups,* 1990 U.Ill. L.Rev. 95.

e. Compare, e.g., Redish, *The Value of Free Speech,* 130 U.Pa.L.Rev. 591, 596–611 (1982) and Alexander, *Low Value Speech,* 83 Nw.U.L.Rev. 547 (1989) with Sunstein, *Low Value Speech Revisited,* 83 Nw. U.L.Rev. 555 (1989). Reconsider the question after completing Section 3.

COLLIN v. SMITH, 578 F.2d 1197 (7th Cir.1978), cert. denied, 439 U.S. 916, 99 S.Ct. 291, 58 L.Ed.2d 264 (1978), per PELL, J., struck down a Village of Skokie *"Racial Slur" Ordinance,* making it a misdemeanor to disseminate any material (defined to include "public display of markings and clothing of symbolic significance") promoting and inciting racial or religious hatred. The Village would apparently apply this ordinance to the display of swastikas and military uniforms by the NSPA, a "Nazi organization" which planned to peacefully demonstrate for some 20–30 minutes in front of the Skokie Village Hall.

Although there was some evidence that some individuals "might have difficulty restraining their reactions to the Nazi demonstration," the Village "does not rely on a fear of responsive violence to justify the ordinance, and does not even suggest that there will be any physical violence if the march is held. This confession takes the case out of the scope of *Brandenburg* and *Feiner.* [It] also eliminates any argument based on the fighting words doctrine of *Chaplinsky,* [which] applied only to words with a direct tendency to cause violence by the persons to whom, individually, the words were addressed."

The court rejected, inter alia, the argument that the Nazi march, with its display of swastikas and uniforms, "will create a substantive evil that it has a right to prohibit: the infliction of psychic trauma on resident holocaust survivors [some 5,000] and other Jewish residents. [The] problem with engrafting an exception on the First Amendment for such situations is that they are indistinguishable in principle from speech that 'invite[s] dispute [or] induces a condition of unrest [or] even stirs people to anger,' *Terminiello.* Yet these are among the 'high purposes' of the First Amendment. [Where,] as here, a crime is made of a silent march, attended only by symbols and not by extrinsic conduct offensive in itself, we think the words of *Street v. New York* [p. 221 infra] are very much on point: '[A]ny shock effect [must] be attributed to the content of the ideas expressed. [P]ublic expression of ideas may not be prohibited merely because the ideas are themselves offensive to some of their hearers.' "

Nor was the court impressed with the argument that the proposed march was "not speech, [but] rather an invasion, intensely menacing no matter how peacefully conducted" (most of Skokie's residents are Jewish): "There *need be* no captive audience, as Village residents may, if they wish, simply avoid the Village Hall for thirty minutes on a Sunday afternoon, which no doubt would be their normal course of conduct on a day when the Village Hall was not open in the regular course of business. Absent such intrusion or captivity, there is no justifiable substantial privacy interest to save [the ordinance], when it attempts, by fiat, to declare the entire Village,

a. Quoted in Friendly & Elliot, *The Constitution: That Delicate Balance* 83 (1984).

at all times, a privacy zone that may be sanitized from the offensiveness of Nazi ideology and symbols."[b]

Notes and Questions

1. Is *Beauharnais,* Ch. 1, II, A supra, still "good law"?

2. *Abstraction and the first amendment.* Consider Schauer, *Harry Kalven and the Perils of Particularism,* 56 U.Chi.L.Rev. 397, 408 (1989): "[O]ne sees in the *Skokie* litigation an available distinction between Nazis and others, an equally available distinction between speech designed to persuade and speech designed to assault, and a decision made by the people rather than a decision designed to interfere with the people's wishes. If doctrinal development under the free speech clause were merely an instance of common law decision making, one might expect to see some or all of these factors treated as relevant, and new distinctions developed in order to make relevant those factors, such as the ones just enumerated, that had been suppressed by previous formulations. Yet we know that this is not what happened. The particular events were abstracted in numerous ways. Nazis became political speakers, a suburban community populated by Holocaust survivors became a public forum, and popularly inspired restrictions became governmental censorship. The resolution of the controversy, therefore, stands not as a monument to the ever-more-sensitive development of common law doctrine, but instead as an embodiment of the way in which the First Amendment operates precisely by the entrenchment of categories whose breadth prevents the consideration of some number of relevant factors, and prevents the free speech decision maker from 'thinking small.' "

3. *The Klan and the Communists.* Are the arguments of those who would prohibit racist speech (or pornography), the same as those would have restricted the speech of the communists (or anarchists). See Gey, *The Case Against Postmodern Censorship Theory,* 145 U.Pa. L.Rev. 193 (1996). But consider Shiffrin, *Dissent, Injustice, and the Meanings of America* 78,79 n. 184 (1999): "Racist speakers seek to persuade people that government (and others)should not treat all persons with equal concern and respect. If our legal system has even a prayer of claiming to be legitimate, however, it must start from the premise that all citizens are worthy of equal concern and respect. * * * In this limited context, the best test of truth is the system's foundational premise of equality, not whether racist speech can emerge in the marketplace of ideas. [To] the extent the communists argue against free

---

b. See also *Skokie v. National Socialist Party,* 69 Ill.2d 605, 14 Ill.Dec. 890, 373 N.E.2d 21 (1978). For commentary relating the Skokie issue to regulation of pornography, and of commercial speech, for the purpose of asking whether there are general principles of freedom of expression and whether freedom of expression should be category-dependent, see Scanlon, *Freedom of Expression and Categories of Expression,* 40 U.Pitt.L.Rev. 519 (1979). For assessment of the complicated connection between Skokie and equality values especially in light of the rest of first amendment law, see Tribe, *Constitutional Choices* 219–20 (1985). Compare Downs, *Skokie Revisited: Hate Group Speech and the First Amendment,* 60 Not.D.Law. 629 (1985). More generally, see Kretzmer, *Freedom of Speech and Racism,* 8 Cardozo L.Rev. 445 (1987).

speech, [they] are in the same position as the Ku Klux Klan, but the harm of that speech is not in the same league as racist speech."

4. *Comparative perspective.* Consider Douglas–Scott, *The Hatefulness of Protected Speech: A Comparison of the American and European Approaches,* 7 Wm. & Mary Bill Rts.J. 305, 343–44 (1999): "There clearly is a radical difference between the German or, more generally, the European and American approach to the regulation of speech. [First], European and, especially, German jurisprudence emphasize particular values-dignity, protection of personal identity, and equality. German judgments stress the potential of racist insults and denials of Nazi atrocities to affect the very core of the identities of members of certain groups, even if those individuals have not been specifically targeted for abuse. [European] case law rejects a conception of individuals as beings who merely should be left to their own devices to make up their own minds about the value of expression in the public domain, to be free to ignore it, or to counter it with more speech. Such an approach isolates human beings by forcing them to take the consequences of painful conduct and ignores the particular susceptibility of certain groups to injury, especially when the offense of the speech seems to be targeted at such groups because of their identity. Under the American model, the individual will be left to his or her less communal and somewhat atomistic existence.

"Second, the European approach is fundamentally more sympathetic to a conception in which the state plays a role in facilitating the realization of freedom, democracy, and equality. Under the European approach, it becomes natural for the state to assume a more affirmative role in actualizing specific constitutional rights. Within the area of freedom of speech this would require the state not only to refrain from violating certain constitutional norms, but also to participate in their realization-an approach which usually is assumed only to be required of socio-economic rights, such as the right to work. Surely it is not enough for societies that claim to be committed to the ideals of social and political equality and respect for individual dignity to remain neutral and passive when threats to these values exist. Sometimes the State must take steps to protect democracy itself, which may involve repressing speech."

For a Canadian perspective, consider Mahoney, *Hate Speech: Affirmation or Contradiction of Freedom of Expression,* 1996 U.Ill.L.Rev. 789, 796 (1996): "[G]enuine democracies that respect the inherent dignity of the [person], social justice, and equality accept the fundamental principle that legislative protection and government regulation are required to protect the vulnerable. It follows that when free speech doctrine is used by more powerful groups to seriously harm less powerful, vulnerable ones, some government action is required."

5. Should the first amendment bar an action for intentional infliction of emotional distress for face to face racial insults?[c] Is it enough that

c. On the relationship between discriminatory speech and the tort of intentional infliction of emotional distress, see Love, *Discriminatory Speech and the Tort of In*

the words in question inflict injury or must the victim show that the words were likely to promote a fight? Suppose a crowd of whites gathers to taunt a young black child on the way to a previously all white school? Suppose short of using violence, they do everything they can to harm the child? Is it the case that "no government that would call itself a decent government would fail to intervene [and] disperse the crowd" and that "the rights of the crowd [cannot] really stand on the same plane" as the child on the way to school? See Arkes, *Civility and the Restriction of Speech: Rediscovering the Defamation of Groups,* 1974 Sup.Ct.Rev. 281, 310–11. Should the first amendment bar state criminal or civil actions precisely tailored to punish racial insults? Insults directed against the handicapped? For the case in favor of a tort action against racial insults, see Delgado, *Words That Wound: A Tort Action for Racial Insults, Epithets, and Name–Calling,* 17 Harv.Civ.Rts.—Civ.Lib. L.Rev. 133 (1982). For a spirited exchange, see Heins, *Banning Words: A Comment on "Words that Wound,"* 18 Har.Civ.Rts.—Civ.Lib.L.Rev. 585 (1983) and *Professor Delgado Replies,* Id. at 593.

6. Is one person's racialist plea another person's act of intimidation? Are these responses patterned? Consider Matsuda, *Public Response to Racist Speech: Considering the Victim's Story,* 87 Mich.L.Rev. 2320, 2326–27 (1989): "[I] am forced to ask why the world looks so different to me from how it looks to many of the civil libertarians whom I consider my allies. [In] advocating legal restriction of hate speech, I have found my most sympathetic audience in people who identify with target groups, while I have encountered incredulity, skepticism, and even hostility from others.

"This split in reaction is also evident in case studies of hate speech. The typical reaction of target-group members to an incident of racist propaganda is alarm and immediate calls for redress. The typical reaction of non-target-group members is to consider the incidents isolated pranks, the product of sick-but-harmless minds. This is in part a defensive reaction: a refusal to believe that real people, people just like us, are racists.[d] This disassociation leads logically to the claim that there is no institutional or state responsibility to respond to the incident.[e] It is not the kind of real and pervasive threat that requires the state's power to quell."[f]

---

tentional Infliction of Emotional Distress, 47 Wash. & Lee L.Rev. 123 (1990).

d. Are victims in a better position to evaluate the truth? Compare Richard Delgado & Jean Stefanic, *Must We Defend Nazis* 86–87 (1997) with Gey, supra at note 3.

e. For the argument that the best interpretation of *Brown v. Board of Education,* 347 U.S. 483, 74 S.Ct. 686, 98 L.Ed. 873 (1954) *requires* government to respond, see Lawrence, infra. For response, see Strossen, infra.

f. For discussion of the extent and character of the harm, see Delgado & Stefanic,

Must We Defend Nazis 4–10 (1997); Matsuda, supra; Lawrence, infra; Delgado, *Campus Antiracism Rules Constitutional Narratives in Collision,* 85 Nw.U.L.Rev. 343, 384 (1991) ("The ubiquity and incessancy of harmful racial depiction are [the] source of its virulence. Like water dripping on sandstone, it is a pervasive harm which only the most hardy can resist. Yet the prevailing first amendment paradigm predisposes us to treat racist speech as individual harm, as though we only had to evaluate the effect of a single drop of water.").

See also Lawrence, *If He Hollers Let Him Go: Regulating Racist Speech on Campus,* 1990 Duke L.J. 431, 474: "If one asks why we always begin by asking whether we can afford to fight racism rather than asking whether we can afford not to, or if one asks why my colleagues who oppose all regulation of racist speech do not feel the burden is theirs (to justify a reading of the first amendment that requires sacrificing rights guaranteed under the equal protection clause), then one sees an example of how unconscious racism operates in the marketplace of ideas. * * * [O]ur unconscious racism causes us (even those of us who are the direct victims of racism) to view the first amendment as the 'regular' amendment—an amendment that works for all people—and the equal protection clause and racial equality as a special interest-amendment important to groups that are less valued."

7. *Effects of regulation.* Consider Shiffrin, *Racist Speech, Outsider Jurisprudence, and the Meaning of America,* 80 Cornell L.Rev. 43, 96–97, 103 (1994): "From the perspective of many millions of Americans, to enact racist speech regulations would be to pass yet another law exhibiting special favoritism for people of color. What makes this kind of law so potentially counterproductive is that its transformation of public racists into public martyrs would tap into widespread political traditions and understandings in our culture. In short, the case of the martyr would be appealingly wrapped in the banner of the American flag. Millions of white Americans already resent people of color to some degree. To fuse that resentment with Americans' love for the first amendment is risky business. [America] would still have a FIRST AMENDMENT and a strong first amendment tradition even if it enacted general racist speech regulations. The problem is not the first amendment; the problem is that racism is now and always has been a central part of the meaning of America." Would hate legislation have the "unfortunate effect of focusing on the individual perpetrator rather than on the victims or on social forces that assist and inform the perpetrator"? Would attention "more fruitfully turn to both the lives and the circumstances of the victims as well as the surrounding social traditions and practices that have made and continue to make that group subject to dehumanization"? Minow, *Regulating Hatred*, 47 UCLA L.Rev. 1253, 1274 (2000).

8. Consider Karst, *Boundaries and Reasons: Freedom of Expression and the Subordination of Groups,* 1990 U.Ill.L.Rev. 95, 140–41: "Group libel and pornography each respond to a sense of inadequacy, but the two types of hate literature are circulated differently. Where the defamation of racial or religious groups is driven by the felt inadequacies of its distributors, today's pornography is largely driven by the inadequacies of its consumers, with most distributors simply profiting from that demand and seeking to increase it. In neither case will elimination of the literature cause the underlying sense of inadequacy to disappear. Anxious hatemongers, thwarted in purveying their racist leaflets, can find plenty of other ways to express their fear and hate, as the Ku Klux Klan and the Nazis have made clear. And anxious men, thwarted in the consumption of pornography, can find substitute

symbols of sexual objectification not just in magazine ads or on television but in every woman they see."

9.   Consider Stanford University's definition of harassment by personal vilification: "Speech or other expression constitutes harassment by personal vilification if it a) is intended to insult or stigmatize an individual or a small number of individuals on the basis of their sex, race, color, handicap, religion, sexual orientation, or national and ethnic origin; and b) is addressed directly to the individual or individuals whom it insults or stigmatizes; and c) makes use of insulting or 'fighting words' or non-verbal symbols." Does this go too far? See Strossen, *Regulating Racist Speech on Campus: A Modest Proposal?* 1990 Duke L.J. 484. Does it not go far enough? See Lawrence, supra at 450 n. 82: "I supported a proposal which would have been broader in scope by prohibiting speech of this nature in all common areas, excepting organized rallies and speeches. It would have been narrower in its protection in that it would not have protected persons who were vilified on the basis of their membership in dominant majority groups." Compare Matsuda, supra at 2357, arguing that speech with a message of racial inferiority, that is directed against a historically oppressed group, and that is persecutorial, hateful, and degrading should be outlawed.[g]

If racial vilification can be prohibited, can religious vilification in the form of blasphemy be outlawed as well?

g. The literature on racist speech is enormous. See, e.g., Weinstein, *Hate Speech, Pornography, and the Radical Attack on Free Speech Doctrine* (1999); Wolfson, *Hate Speech, Sex Speech, Free Speech* (1997); Lederer & Delgado, eds., *The Price We Pay: The Case Against Racist Speech, Hate Propaganda and Pornography* (1995); Greenawalt, *Fighting Words* (1995); Matsuda, Lawrence, Delgado, & Crenshaw, eds., *Words that Wound* (1993); Walker, *Hate Speech: The History of an American Controversy* (1994); Symposium, *Campus Hate Speech and the Constitution in the Aftermath of Doe v. University of Michigan,* 37 Wayne L.Rev. 1309 (1991); Symposium, *Free Speech & Religious, Racial & Sexual Harassment,* 32 Wm. & Mary L.Rev. 207 (1991); Symposium, *Frontiers of Legal Thought: The New First Amendment,* 1990 Duke L.J. 375; Symposium, *Hate Speech and the First Amendment: On A Collision Course?,* 37 Vill.L.Rev. 723 (1992); Symposium, *Hate Speech After R.A.V.: More Conflict Between Free Speech and Equality,* 18 Wm. Mitchell L.Rev. 889 (1992); See also sources cited in connection with *R.A.V. v. City of St. Paul,* p. 313 infra and sources cited in Shiffrin, *Racist Speech, Outsider Jurisprudence, and the Meaning of America,* 80 Corn.L.Rev. 43, 44 n. 6 (1994). For the Canadian perspective, see *Regina v. Keegstra* [1990] 3 S.C.R. 697. For relevant commentary, see Greenawalt, supra; Douglas, *Policing the Past* in *Censorship and Silencing* 67 (Post ed. 1998); Weinreb, *Hate Promotion in a Democratic Society,* 36 McGill L.Rev. 1416 (1991).

Chapter 2

DISTINGUISHING BETWEEN CONTENT REGULATION AND MANNER REGULATION: UNCONVENTIONAL FORMS OF COMMUNICATION

Special first amendment questions are often said to arise by regulation of the time, place, and manner of speech as opposed to regulation of its content. But the two types of regulation are not mutually exclusive. It is possible to regulate time, place, manner, and content in the same regulation. For example, in *Linmark,* Ch. 3, II infra, the township outlawed signs (but not leaflets) advertising a house for sale (but not other advertisements or other messages) on front lawns (but not other places).

Further, the terms, manner and content are strongly contested concepts. Indeed, an issue recurring in this chapter is whether the regulations in question are of manner or content. To the extent this chapter is about manner regulation, it is not exhaustive—much comes later. Most of the cases in this chapter involve unconventional forms of expression. Speakers claim protection for burning draft cards, wearing armbands, mutilating flags, nude dancing, wearing long hair. Fact patterns such as these fix renewed attention on the question of how "speech" should be defined. It may be a nice question as to whether obscenity is not speech within the first amendment lexicon, whether it is such speech but has been balanced into an unprotected state, or whether it is not *freedom* of speech or *the* freedom of speech.[a] But assassinating a public figure, even to send a message, raises no first amendment problem. Robbing a bank does not raise a free speech issue. What does? How do we decide?

The fact patterns in this chapter also invite scrutiny of other issues that appear in succeeding chapters. Should it make a difference if the state's interest in regulating speech is unrelated to what is being said? Suppose the

---

a. See fn. b in *Roth,* p. Ch. 1, VI, A supra.

state's concern arises from the non-communicative impact of the speech act—from its manner. Should that distinction make a constitutional difference, and, if so, how much? These questions become more complicated because in context it is often difficult to determine what the state interest is and sometimes difficult to determine whether there is a meaningful distinction between what is said and how it is said.

Even when the distinction between the manner of the speech and the content of the speech is clear, further doctrinal complications abound. Sometimes the regulation considered by the Court is described as one regulating the "time, place, or manner" of speech, and the Court employs the "time, place, or manner test" which is itself differently phrased in different cases. On other occasions the regulation is described as having an "incidental" impact on freedom of speech, and the Court turns to a different test. These different tests are sometimes described by the Court as functional equivalents. Should there be different tests? In what circumstances?[b]

Finally, in this and succeeding chapters the question arises of the extent to which freedom of speech should require special sensitivity to the methods and communications needs of the less powerful.

UNITED STATES v. O'BRIEN

391 U.S. 367, 88 S.Ct. 1673, 20 L.Ed.2d 672 (1968).

MR. CHIEF JUSTICE WARREN delivered the opinion of the Court.

On the morning of March 31, 1966, David Paul O'Brien and three companions burned their Selective Service registration certificates on the steps of the South Boston Courthouse. A sizable crowd, including several [FBI agents] witnessed the event. Immediately after the burning, members of the crowd began attacking O'Brien [and he was ushered to safety by an FBI agent.] O'Brien stated to FBI agents that he had burned his registration certificate because of his beliefs, knowing that he was violating federal law.

[For this act, O'Brien was convicted in federal court.] He [told] the jury that he burned the certificate publicly to influence others to adopt his antiwar beliefs, as he put it, "so that other people would reevaluate their positions with Selective Service, with the armed forces, and reevaluate their place in the culture of today, to hopefully consider my position."

The indictment upon which he was tried charged that he "wilfully and knowingly did mutilate, destroy, and change by burning [his] Registration Certificate; in violation of [§ 462(b)(3) of the Universal Military Training and Service Act of 1948], amended by Congress in 1965 (adding the words italicized below), so that at the time O'Brien burned his certificate an offense was committed by any person, "who forges, alters, *knowingly de-*

b. See generally Williams, *Content Discrimination and the First Amendment,* 139 U.Pa.L.Rev. 201 (1991).

stroys, knowingly mutilates, or in any manner changes any such certificate * * *." (Italics supplied.)

[On appeal, the] First Circuit held the 1965 Amendment unconstitutional as a law abridging freedom of speech. At the time the Amendment was enacted, a regulation of the Selective Service System required registrants to keep their registration certificates in their "personal possession at all times." Wilful violations of regulations promulgated pursuant to the Universal Military Training and Service Act were made criminal by statute. The Court of Appeals, therefore, was of the opinion that conduct punishable under the 1965 Amendment was already punishable under the nonpossession regulation, and consequently that the Amendment served no valid purpose; further, that in light of the prior regulation, the Amendment must have been "directed at public as distinguished from private destruction." On this basis, the Court concluded that the 1965 Amendment ran afoul of the First Amendment by singling out persons engaged in protests for special treatment. * * *

When a male reaches the age of 18, he is required by the Universal Military Training and Service Act to register with a local draft board. He is assigned a Selective Service number, and within five days he is issued a registration certificate. Subsequently, and based on a questionnaire completed by the registrant, he is assigned a classification denoting his eligibility for induction, and "[a]s soon as practicable" thereafter he is issued a Notice of Classification. * * *

Both the registration and classification certificates bear notices that the registrant must notify his local board in writing of every change in address, physical condition, and occupational, marital, family, dependency, and military status, and of any other fact which might change his classification. Both also contain a notice that the registrant's Selective Service number should appear on all communications to his local board.

[The 1965] Amendment does not distinguish between public and private destruction, and it does not punish only destruction engaged in for the purpose of expressing views.[a] A law prohibiting destruction of Selective Service certificates no more abridges free speech on its face than a motor vehicle law prohibiting the destruction of drivers' licenses, or a tax law prohibiting the destruction of books and records.

O'Brien nonetheless argues [first] that the 1965 Amendment is unconstitutional [as] applied to him because his act of burning his registration certificate was protected "symbolic speech" within the First Amendment. [He claims that] the First Amendment guarantees include all modes of "communication of ideas by conduct," and that his conduct is within this definition because he did it in "demonstration against the war and against the draft."

---

a. But compare Chief Judge Aldrich below, 376 F.2d at 541: "We would be closing our eyes in the light of the prior law if we did not see on the face of the amendment that it was precisely directed at public as distinguished from private destruction. [In] singling out persons engaging in protest for special treatment the amendment strikes at the very core of what the First Amendment protects."

SPEECH IS NOT JUST A DECLARATION OF ONE'S BELIEFS

We cannot accept the view that an apparently limitless variety of conduct can be labelled "speech" whenever the person engaging in the conduct intends thereby to express an idea. However, even on the assumption that the alleged communicative element in O'Brien's conduct is sufficient to bring into play the First Amendment, it does not necessarily follow that the destruction of a registration certificate is constitutionally protected activity. This Court has held that when "speech" and "nonspeech" elements are combined in the same course of conduct, a sufficiently important governmental interest in regulating the nonspeech element can justify incidental limitations on First Amendment freedoms. To characterize the quality of the governmental interest which must appear, the Court has employed a variety of descriptive terms: compelling; substantial; subordinating; paramount; cogent; strong. [W]e think it clear that a government regulation is sufficiently justified if it is within the constitutional power of the government; if it furthers an important or substantial governmental interest; if the governmental interest is unrelated to the suppression of free expression;[b] and if the incidental restriction on alleged First Amendment freedom is no greater than is essential to the furtherance of that interest. We find that the 1965 Amendment meets all of these requirements, and consequently that O'Brien can be constitutionally convicted for violating it. [Pursuant to its power to classify and conscript manpower for military service], Congress may establish a system of registration for individuals liable for training and service, and may require such individuals within reason to cooperate in the registration system. The issuance of certificates indicating the registration and eligibility classification of individuals is a legitimate and substantial administrative aid in the functioning of this system. And legislation to insure the continuing availability of issued certificates serves a legitimate and substantial purpose in the system's administration.

[O'Brien] essentially adopts the position that [Selective Service] certificates are so many pieces of paper designed to notify registrants of their registration or classification, to be retained or tossed in the wastebasket according to the convenience or taste of the registrant. Once the registrant has received notification, according to this view, there is no reason for him to retain the certificates. [However, the registration and classification certificates serve] purposes in addition to initial notification. Many of these purposes would be defeated by the certificates' destruction or mutilation. Among these are [simplifying verification of the registration and classification of suspected delinquents, evidence of availability for induction in the event of emergency, ease of communication between registrants and local boards, continually reminding registrants of the need to notify local boards of changes in status].

Non-speech related purposes

---

b. For the contention that the many tests formulated by the Court are best regarded as prophylactic rules designed to assure that the forbidden purpose of suppressing ideas does not underlie government acts, see Bogen, *Balancing Freedom of Speech*, 38 Md.L.Rev. 387 (1979); Bogen, *The Supreme Court's Interpretation of the Guarantee of Freedom of Speech*, 35 Md. L.Rev. 555 (1976). See generally Bogen, *Bulwark of Liberty: The Court and the First Amendment* (1984).

The many functions performed by Selective Service certificates establish beyond doubt that Congress has a legitimate and substantial interest in preventing their wanton and unrestrained destruction and assuring their continuing availability by punishing people who knowingly and wilfully destroy or mutilate them. And we are unpersuaded that the pre-existence of the nonpossession regulations in any way negates this interest.

In the absence of a question as to multiple punishment, it has never been suggested that there is anything improper in Congress providing alternative statutory avenues of prosecution to assure the effective protection of one and the same interest. Here, the pre-existing avenue of prosecution was not even statutory. Regulations may be modified or revoked from time to time by administrative discretion. Certainly, the Congress may change or supplement a regulation.

[The] gravamen of the offense defined by the statute is the deliberate rendering of certificates unavailable for the various purposes which they may serve. Whether registrants keep their certificates in their personal possession at all times, as required by the regulations, is of no particular concern under the 1965 Amendment, as long as they do not mutilate or destroy the certificates so as to render them unavailable. [The 1965 amendment] is concerned with abuses involving *any* issued Selective Service certificates, not only with the registrant's own certificates. The knowing destruction or mutilation of someone else's certificates would therefore violate the statute but not the nonpossession regulations.

We think it apparent that the continuing availability to each registrant of his Selective Service certificates substantially furthers the smooth and proper functioning of the system that Congress has established to raise armies. * * *

It is equally clear that the 1965 Amendment specifically protects this substantial governmental interest. We perceive no alternative means that would more precisely and narrowly assure the continuing availability of issued Selective Service certificates than a law which prohibits their wilful mutilation or destruction. The 1965 Amendment prohibits such conduct and does nothing more. [The] governmental interest and the scope of the 1965 Amendment are limited to preventing a harm to the smooth and efficient functioning of the Selective Service System. When O'Brien deliberately rendered unavailable his registration certificate, he wilfully frustrated this governmental interest. For this noncommunicative impact of his conduct, and for nothing else, he was convicted. * * *

O'Brien finally argues that the 1965 Amendment is unconstitutional as enacted because what he calls the "purpose" of Congress was "to suppress freedom of speech." We reject this argument because under settled principles the purpose of Congress, as O'Brien uses that term, is not a basis for declaring this legislation unconstitutional.

MOTIVE NOT IMPORTANT

It is a familiar principle of constitutional law that this Court will not strike down an otherwise constitutional statute on the basis of an alleged illicit legislative motive.

[I]f we were to examine legislative purpose in the instant case, we would be obliged to consider not only [the statements of the three members of Congress who addressed themselves to the amendment, all viewing draft-card burning as a brazen display of unpatriotism] but also the more authoritative reports of the Senate and House Armed Services Committees. [B]oth reports make clear a concern with the "defiant" destruction of so-called "draft cards" and with "open" encouragement to others to destroy their cards, [but they] also indicate that this concern stemmed from an apprehension that unrestrained destruction of cards would disrupt the smooth functioning of the Selective Service System. * * *

Reversed.[c]   *REVERSED DECISION OF LOWER COURTS UPHELD RESTRICTIVE LAW*

MR. JUSTICE HARLAN concurring. * * *

I wish to make explicit my understanding that [the Court's analysis] does not foreclose consideration of First Amendment claims in those rare instances when an "incidental" restriction upon expression, imposed by a regulation which furthers an "important or substantial" governmental interest and satisfies the Court's other criteria, in practice has the effect of entirely preventing a "speaker" from reaching a significant audience with whom he could not otherwise lawfully communicate. This is not such a case, since O'Brien manifestly could have conveyed his message in many ways other than by burning his draft card.

MR. JUSTICE DOUGLAS, dissenting.

[Douglas, J., thought that "the underlying and basic problem in this case" was the constitutionality of a draft "in the absence of a declaration of war" and that the case should be put down for reargument on this question. The following Term, concurring in *Brandenburg,* he criticized *O'Brien* on the merits. After recalling that the Court had rejected O'Brien's first amendment argument on the ground that "legislation to insure the continuing availability of issued certificates serves a legitimate and substantial purpose in the [selective service] system's administration," he commented: "But O'Brien was not prosecuted for not having his draft card available when asked for by a federal agent. He was indicted, tried, and convicted for burning the card. And this Court's affirmance [was not] consistent with the First Amendment." He observed, more generally in *Brandenburg:*

["Action is often a method of expression and within the protection of the First Amendment. Suppose one tears up his own copy of the Constitution in eloquent protest to a decision of this Court. May he be indicted? Suppose one rips his own Bible to shreds to celebrate his departure from one 'faith' and his embrace of atheism. May he be indicted? * * *

c.   Marshall, J., took no part.

["The act of praying often involves body posture and movement as well as utterances. It is nonetheless protected by the Free Exercise Clause. Picketing [is] 'free speech plus.' [Therefore], it can be regulated when it comes to the 'plus' or 'action' side of the protest. It can be regulated as to the number of pickets and the place and hours, because traffic and other community problems would otherwise suffer. But none of these considerations are implicated in the symbolic protest of the Vietnam war in the burning of a draft card."]

Notes and Questions

1. *Expression vs. action.* What of the Court's rejection of the idea that conduct is speech "whenever the person engaging in the conduct intends thereby to express an idea." Was it right to question whether O'Brien's conduct was speech? What was it about O'Brien's conduct that made the Court doubt that it was speech? What if O'Brien had burned a copy of the Constitution? Consider Emerson, *The System of Freedom of Expression* 80 & 84 (1970): "To some extent expression and action are always mingled; most conduct includes elements of both. Even the clearest manifestations of expression involve some action, as in the case of holding a meeting, publishing a newspaper, or merely talking. At the other extreme, a political assassination includes a substantial mixture of expression. The guiding principle must be to determine which element is predominant in the conduct under consideration. Is expression the major element and the action only secondary? Or is the action the essence and the expression incidental? The answer, to a great extent, must be based on a common-sense reaction, made in light of the functions and operations of a system of freedom of expression. * * *

"The burning of a draft card is, of course, conduct that involves both communication and physical acts. Yet it seems quite clear that the predominant element in such conduct is expression (opposition to the draft) rather than action (destruction of a piece of cardboard). The registrant is not concerned with secret or inadvertent burning of his draft card, involving no communication with other persons. The main feature, for him, is the public nature of the burning, through which he expresses to the community his ideas and feelings about the war and the draft."

Compare Ely, *Flag Desecration: A Case Study in the Roles of Categorization and Balancing in First Amendment Analysis*, 88 Harv.L.Rev. 1482, 1495 (1975): "[B]urning a draft card to express opposition to the draft is an undifferentiated whole, 100% action and 100% expression. It involves no conduct that is not at the same time communication, and no communication that does not result from conduct. Attempts to determine which element 'predominates' will therefore inevitably degenerate into question-begging judgments about whether the activity should be protected.

"The *O'Brien* Court thus quite wisely dropped the 'speech-conduct' distinction as quickly as it had picked it up."[d]

[handwritten margin note: COURT DIDN'T ADDRESS IT]

2. *Nature of the state interest and first amendment methodology.* Melville Nimmer, *The Meaning of Symbolic Speech under the First Amendment,* 21 U.C.L.A.L.Rev. 29 (1973), followed by John Hart Ely, note 1 supra, and Laurence Tribe, infra, has proposed that the crucial starting point for first amendment methodology is and should be the nature of the state interest. As Ely puts it, at 1497: "The critical question would therefore seem to be whether the harm that the state is seeking to avert is one that grows out of the fact that the defendant is communicating, and more particularly out of the way people can be expected to react to his message, or rather would arise even if the defendant's conduct had no communicative significance whatever."

[handwritten margin note: KIND OF LIKE NEUTRALITY?]

For one view of the difference that the distinction makes, see Tribe, *American Constitutional Law* 791–92 (2d ed. 1988): "The Supreme Court has evolved two distinct approaches to the resolution of first amendment claims; the two correspond to the two ways in which government may 'abridge' speech. If a government regulation is aimed at the communicative impact of an act, analysis should proceed along what we will call *track one*. On that track, a regulation is unconstitutional unless government shows that the message being suppressed poses a 'clear and present danger,' constitutes a defamatory falsehood, or otherwise falls on the unprotected side of one of the lines the Court has drawn to distinguish those expressive acts privileged by the first amendment from those open to government regulation with only minimal due process scrutiny. If a government regulation is aimed at the noncommunicative impact of an act, its analysis proceeds on what we will call *track two*. On that track, a regulation is constitutional, even as applied to expressive conduct, so long as it does not unduly constrict the flow of information and ideas. On track two, the 'balance' between the values of freedom of expression and the government's regulatory interests is struck on a case-by-case basis, guided by whatever unifying principles may be articulated."

[handwritten margin note (vertical left): COMMUNICATIVE V. NONCOMMUNICATIVE]

[handwritten margin note (right): clear & present danger test]

[handwritten margin note (right): CASE BY CASE]

Professor Nimmer, in distinguishing between anti-speech interests (track one) and non-speech interests (track two), would apply definitional balancing (with a presumption in favor of speech) to the former and the *O'Brien* test to the latter. Dean Ely would protect all regulations on track one except for speech that falls "within a few clearly and narrowly defined categories." Ely, *Democracy and Distrust* 110 (1980) (emphasis deleted). On track two, Ely insists that balancing is desirable and unavoidable. Ely, note 1 supra, at 1496–1502.

d. But, as Professor Ely recognizes, the Court picked it up again in *Cohen,* Ch. 1, V, C: "[W]e deal here with a conviction resting solely upon 'speech', cf. *Stromberg,* not upon any separately identifiable conduct which allegedly was intended by Cohen to be perceived by others as expressive of particular views but which, on its face, does not necessarily convey any message and hence arguably could be regulated without effectively repressing Cohen's ability to express himself. Cf. *O'Brien.*"

(a) *Normative value of the distinction.* Is balancing unavoidable on either track? How does one decide what the categories should be without balancing? Does the metaphor of balancing wrongly imply that all values are reduced to a single measure and imply non-existent quantitative capacities? Is the distinction between the tracks important enough to require rules on track one, even if ad hoc procedures are allowable on track two?

Is the distinction between the two tracks at least strong enough to justify a rebuttable presumption that regulation on track one is invalid, but regulation on track two is not? Consider a regulation governing express warranties in commercial advertising. Is much of contract law on track one?[e] Consider "a nationwide ban on *all* posters (intended to conserve paper)." Isn't that on track two? Do these examples suggest that too much emphasis is being placed on a single factor? See Farber, *Content Regulation and the First Amendment: A Revisionist View*, 68 Geo.U.L.Rev. 727, 746–47 (1980).[f]

(b) *Application to O'Brien.* Consider Ely, note 1 supra, at 1498–99: "The interests upon which the government relied were interests, having mainly to do with the preservation of selective service records, that would have been equally threatened had O'Brien's destruction of his draft card totally lacked communicative significance—had he, for example, used it to start a campfire for a solitary cookout or dropped it in his garbage disposal for a lark. (The law prohibited all knowing destructions, public or private)."

Compare Nimmer, note 2 supra, at 41—contending that the *O'Brien* statute was "overnarrow": "[An overnarrow statute] may be said to create a conclusive presumption that in fact the state interest which the statute serves is an anti-rather than a non-speech interest. If the state interest asserted in *O'Brien* were truly the non-speech interest of assuring availability of draft cards, why did Congress choose not to prohibit any knowing conduct which leads to unavailability, rather than limiting the scope of the statute to those instances in which the proscribed conduct carries with it a speech component hostile to governmental policy? The obvious inference to be drawn is that in fact the Congress was completely indifferent to the 'availability' objective, and was concerned only with an interest which the *O'Brien* opinion states is impermissible—an interest in the suppression of free expression."[g]

---

e. For the suggestion that virtually all laws have information effects and that track two embraces virtually all laws not covered by track one, see Alexander, *Trouble on Track Two: Incidental Regulations of Speech and Free Speech*, 44 Hastings L.J. 921 (1993) (arguing that track two countenances an unconstitutional evaluation of the value of speech).

f. See generally Redish, *The Content Distinction in First Amendment Analysis*, 34 Stan.L.Rev. 113 (1981). See notes after *Chicago Police Dept. v. Mosley,* Ch. 6, I, B infra.

g. On the inadequacy of the *O'Brien* methodology to serve as a proxy for problematic motivation, see Bollinger, *The Tolerant Society* 206–12 (1986). On its inadequacy as an organizing principle for first amendment doctrine, see Shiffrin, supra, ch. 1.

(c) *Descriptive value of the distinction.* Does the distinction between the two tracks fully explain the Court's approach in *O'Brien*? Suppose again that an assassin truthfully claims that his or her killing was intended to and did communicate an idea? The assassin's first amendment claim would not prevail, but would it fail because the *O'Brien* test was not met or because no first amendment problem was implicated at all? Is a speech/conduct distinction a necessary prerequisite to the application of the *O'Brien* test?[h]

How different is the *O'Brien* test from the methods used to make decisions on track one? Is the *O'Brien* test as phrased potentially more speech protective than its application in the principal case would suggest? More speech protective than tests sometimes used on track one? Does the application in *O'Brien* offer "little more than the minimal rational-basis test applied in economic due process cases"? See Werhan, *The O'Briening of First Amendment Methodology,* 19 Ariz.St.L.J. 635, 641 (1987): "There is no speech side to the Court's balance. [T]he absence of true balancing within the *O'Brien* methodology can be traced to the origins of the *O'Brien* test. [Having] avoided deciding whether O'Brien's act was protected expression, the Court hardly was in a position to take the next step of incorporating expressive interests into its balance." Id. at 641–42.

3.   Does *O'Brien* shortchange the value of dissent? Consider Shiffrin, *The First Amendment, Democracy, and Romance* 5–6, 81 (1990): "If an organizing symbol makes sense in first amendment jurisprudence, it is not the image of a content-neutral government; it is not a town hall meeting or even a robust marketplace of ideas; still less is it liberty, equality, self-realization, respect, dignity, autonomy, or even tolerance. If the first amendment is to have an organizing symbol, let it be an Emersonian[i] symbol, let it be the image of the dissenter. A major purpose of the first amendment [is] to protect the romantics—those who would break out of classical forms: the dissenters, the unorthodox, the outcasts. [That] Emersonian ideal of freedom of speech has deep roots in the nation's culture, but it has been subtly denigrated in recent first amendment theory and seriously abused in practice.

"[N]either the town hall metaphor nor the marketplace of ideas metaphor [, for example,] is quite apt as a symbol for why *O'Brien* is a first amendment horror story. Town hall meetings can function without the burning of draft cards. And it is hard to claim that truth was kept from the marketplace of ideas. *O'Brien* is one of those not infrequent cases where government prosecutions assist the dissemination of the dissenter's message. Yet, *O'Brien* is perhaps the ultimate first amendment insult. O'Brien is jailed because the authorities find his manner of expression unpatriotic,

h. For commentary on the difficulties in defining speech, see Alexander & Horton, *The Impossibility of a Free Speech Principle,* 78 Nw.U.L.Rev. 1319 (1984).

i. See generally *Ralph Waldo Emerson: Essays and Lectures* (Porte, ed. 1983).

COURT UPHELD RIGHT TO FLAG BURNING

threatening, and offensive. When he complains that his freedom of speech has been abridged, the authorities deny that he has spoken.''

4. *Scope of O'Brien.* Should the *O'Brien* test be confined to unconventional forms of communication? Would a distinction of this type be defensible? See Ely, note 1 supra, at 1489: "The distinction is its own objection."[j]

TEXAS v. JOHNSON

(5–4)

491 U.S. 397, 109 S.Ct. 2533, 105 L.Ed.2d 342 (1989).

23 yrs after O'Brien

JUSTICE BRENNAN delivered the opinion of the Court.

After publicly burning an American flag as a means of political protest, Gregory Lee Johnson was convicted of desecrating a flag in violation of Texas law. This case presents the question whether his conviction is consistent with the First Amendment. We hold that it is not.

1st Amend. Protects flag burning as speech

I

While the Republican National Convention was taking place in Dallas in 1984, respondent Johnson participated in a political demonstration dubbed the "Republican War Chest Tour." As explained in literature distributed by the demonstrators and in speeches made by them, the purpose of this event was to protest the policies of the Reagan administration and of certain Dallas-based corporations. The demonstrators marched through the Dallas streets, chanting political slogans and stopping at several corporate locations to stage "die-ins" intended to dramatize the consequences of nuclear war. On several occasions they spray-painted the walls of buildings and overturned potted plants, but Johnson himself took no part in such activities. He did, however, accept an American flag handed to him by a fellow protestor who had taken it from a flag pole outside one of the targeted buildings.

The demonstration ended in front of Dallas City Hall, where Johnson unfurled the American flag, doused it with kerosene, and set it on fire. While the flag burned, the protestors chanted, "America, the red, white, and blue, we spit on you." After the demonstrators dispersed, a witness to the flag-burning collected the flag's remains and buried them in his backyard. No one was physically injured or threatened with injury, though several witnesses testified that they had been seriously offended by the flag-burning.

Of the approximately 100 demonstrators, Johnson alone was charged with a crime. The only criminal offense with which he was charged was the

j. See also Alfange, *Free Speech and Symbolic Conduct: The Draft–Card Burning Case,* 1968 Sup.Ct.Rev. 1, 23–24; Velvel, *Freedom of Speech and the Draft Card* *Burning Cases,* 16 U.Kan.L.Rev. 149, 153 (1968); Henkin, *On Drawing Lines,* 82 Harv.L.Rev. 63, 79 (1968).

desecration of a venerated object in violation of Tex.Penal Code Ann. § 42.09(a)(3) (1989).[1] * * *

II

Johnson was convicted of flag desecration for burning the flag rather than for uttering insulting words.[2] This fact somewhat complicates our consideration of his conviction under the First Amendment. We must first determine whether Johnson's burning of the flag constituted expressive conduct, permitting him to invoke the First Amendment in challenging his conviction. If his conduct was expressive, we next decide whether the State's regulation is related to the suppression of free expression. *O'Brien.* If the State's regulation is not related to expression, then the less stringent standard we announced in *O'Brien* for regulations of noncommunicative conduct controls. If it is, then we are outside of *O'Brien's* test, and we must ask whether this interest justifies Johnson's conviction under a more demanding standard.[3] A third possibility is that the State's asserted interest is

1. Tex.Penal Code Ann. § 42.09 (1989) provides in full: "§ 42.09. Desecration of Venerated Object

"(a) A person commits an offense if he intentionally or knowingly desecrates:

"(1) a public monument;

"(2) a place of worship or burial; or

"(3) a state or national flag.

"(b) For purposes of this section, 'desecrate' means deface, damage, or otherwise physically mistreat in a way that the actor knows will seriously offend one or more persons likely to observe or discover his action.

"(c) An offense under this section is a Class A misdemeanor."

2. Because the prosecutor's closing argument observed that Johnson had led the protestors in chants denouncing the flag while it burned, Johnson suggests that he may have been convicted for uttering critical words rather than for burning the flag. He relies on *Street v. New York* [394 U.S. 576, 89 S.Ct. 1354, 22 L.Ed.2d 572 (1969)] in which we reversed a conviction obtained under a New York statute that prohibited publicly defying or casting contempt on the flag "either by words or act" because we were persuaded that the defendant may have been convicted for his words alone. Unlike the law we faced in *Street,* however, the Texas flag-desecration statute does not on its face permit conviction for remarks critical of the flag, as Johnson himself admits. Nor was the jury in this case told that it could convict Johnson of flag desecration if it found only that he had uttered words critical of the flag and its referents. Johnson emphasizes, though, that the jury was

instructed—according to Texas' law of parties—that " 'a person is criminally responsible for an offense committed by the conduct of another if acting with intent to promote or assist the commission of the offense, he solicits, encourages, directs, aids, or attempts to aid the other person to commit the offense.' "The State offered this instruction because Johnson's defense was that he was not the person who had burned the flag. Johnson did not object to this instruction at trial, and although he challenged it on direct appeal, he did so only on the ground that there was insufficient evidence to support it. It is only in this Court that Johnson has argued that the law-of-parties instruction might have led the jury to convict him for his words alone. Even if we were to find that this argument is properly raised here, however, we would conclude that it has no merit in these circumstances. The instruction would not have permitted a conviction merely for the pejorative nature of Johnson's words, and those words themselves did not encourage the burning of the flag as the instruction seems to require. Given the additional fact that "the bulk of the State's argument was premised on Johnson's culpability as a sole actor," we find it too unlikely that the jury convicted Johnson on the basis of this alternative theory to consider reversing his conviction on this ground.

3. Although Johnson has raised a facial challenge to Texas' flag-desecration statute, we choose to resolve this case on the basis of his claim that the statute as applied to him violates the First Amendment. Section 42.09 regulates only physical conduct with respect to the flag, not the written or spoken word, and although one violates the

simply not implicated on these facts, and in that event the interest drops out of the picture. * * *

In deciding whether particular conduct possesses sufficient communicative elements to bring the First Amendment into play, we have asked whether "[a]n intent to convey a particularized message was present, and [whether] the likelihood was great that the message would be understood by those who viewed it."[a] [*Spence v. Washington,* 418 U.S. 405, 94 S.Ct. 2727, 41 L.Ed.2d 842 (1974)]. * * *

We have not automatically concluded, however, that any action taken with respect to our flag is expressive. Instead, in characterizing such action for First Amendment purposes, we have considered the context in which it occurred. In *Spence,* for example, we emphasized that Spence's taping of a peace sign to his flag was "roughly simultaneous with and concededly triggered by the Cambodian incursion and the Kent State tragedy." The State of Washington had conceded, in fact, that Spence's conduct was a form of communication, and we stated that "the State's concession is inevitable on this record."

The State of Texas conceded for purposes of its oral argument in this case that Johnson's conduct was expressive conduct and this concession seems to us as prudent as was Washington's in *Spence.* * * *

III

In order to decide whether *O'Brien*'s test applies here * * * we must decide whether Texas has asserted an interest in support of Johnson's conviction that is unrelated to the suppression of expression. [The] State offers two separate interests to justify this conviction: preventing breaches of the peace, and preserving the flag as a symbol of nationhood and national unity. We hold that the first interest is not implicated on this record and that the second is related to the suppression of expression.

A

Texas claims that its interest in preventing breaches of the peace justifies Johnson's conviction for flag desecration.[4] However, no disturbance

---

statute only if one "knows" that one's physical treatment of the flag "will seriously offend one or more persons likely to observe or discover his action," this fact does not necessarily mean that the statute applies only to *expressive* conduct protected by the First Amendment. A tired person might, for example, drag a flag through the mud, knowing that this conduct is likely to offend others, and yet have no thought of expressing any idea; neither the language nor the Texas courts' interpretations of the statute precludes the possibility that such a person would be prosecuted for flag desecration. Because the prosecution of a person who had not engaged in expressive conduct would pose a different case, and because we are capable of disposing of this case on

narrower grounds, we address only Johnson's claim that § 42.09 as applied to political expression like his violates the First Amendment.

a. For criticism of this standard, see Post, *Recuperating First Amendment Doctrine,* 47 Stan. L. Rev. 1249 (1995).

4. Relying on our decision in *Boos v. Barry,* Johnson argues that this state interest is related to the suppression of free expression within the meaning of *O'Brien.* He reasons that the violent reaction to flag-burning feared by Texas would be the result of the message conveyed by them, and that this fact connects the State's interest to the suppression of expression. This view has found some favor in the lower courts.

of the peace actually occurred or threatened to occur because of Johnson's burning of the flag. [The] only evidence offered by the State at trial to show the reaction to Johnson's actions was the testimony of several persons who had been seriously offended by the flag-burning.

The State's position, therefore, amounts to a claim that an audience that takes serious offense at particular expression is necessarily likely to disturb the peace and that the expression may be prohibited on this basis. [W]e have not permitted the Government to assume that every expression of a provocative idea will incite a riot, but have instead required careful consideration of the actual circumstances surrounding such expression, asking whether the expression "is directed to inciting or producing imminent lawless action and is likely to incite or produce such action." *Brandenburg.* To accept Texas' arguments that it need only demonstrate "the potential for a breach of the peace," and that every flag-burning necessarily possesses that potential, would be to eviscerate our holding in *Brandenburg.* This we decline to do.

Nor does Johnson's expressive conduct fall within that small class of "fighting words" that are "likely to provoke the average person to retaliation, and thereby cause a breach of the peace." *Chaplinsky.* No reasonable onlooker would have regarded Johnson's generalized expression of dissatisfaction with the policies of the Federal Government as a direct personal insult or an invitation to exchange fisticuffs.

We thus conclude that the State's interest in maintaining order is not implicated on these facts. * * *

B

The State also asserts an interest in preserving the flag as a symbol of nationhood and national unity. [The] State, apparently, is concerned that such conduct will lead people to believe either that the flag does not stand for nationhood and national unity, but instead reflects other, less positive concepts, or that the concepts reflected in the flag do not in fact exist, that is, we do not enjoy unity as a Nation. These concerns blossom only when a person's treatment of the flag communicates some message, and thus are related "to the suppression of free expression" within the meaning of *O'Brien.* We are thus outside of *O'Brien*'s test altogether.

IV

It remains to consider whether the State's interest in preserving the flag as a symbol of nationhood and national unity justifies Johnson's conviction. [If Johnson] had burned the flag as a means of disposing of it because it was dirty or torn, he would not have been convicted of flag desecration under this Texas law: federal law designates burning as the preferred means of disposing of a flag "when it is in such condition that it is no longer a fitting

Johnson's theory may overread *Boos* insofar as it suggests that a desire to prevent a violent audience reaction is "related to expression" in the same way that a desire to prevent an audience from being offended is "related to expression." Because we find that the State's interest in preventing breaches of the peace is not implicated on these facts, however, we need not venture further into this area.

emblem for display," 36 U.S.C. § 176(k), and Texas has no quarrel with this means of disposal. The Texas law is thus not aimed at protecting the physical integrity of the flag in all circumstances, but is designed instead to protect it only against impairments that would cause serious offense to others.[6] Texas concedes as much: "Section 42.09(b) reaches only those severe acts of physical abuse of the flag carried out in a way likely to be offensive. The statute mandates intentional or knowing abuse, that is, the kind of mistreatment that is not innocent, but rather is intentionally designed to seriously offend other individuals."

Whether Johnson's treatment of the flag violated Texas law thus depended on the likely communicative impact of his expressive conduct. Our decision in *Boos v. Barry* [485 U.S. 312, 108 S.Ct. 1157, 99 L.Ed.2d 333 (1988)] tells us that this restriction on Johnson's expression is content-based. In *Boos,* we considered the constitutionality of a law prohibiting "the display of any sign within 50 feet of a foreign embassy if that sign tends to bring that foreign government into 'public odium' or 'public disrepute.' "Rejecting the argument that the law was content-neutral because it was justified by "our international law obligation to shield diplomats from speech that offends their dignity," we held that "[t]he emotive impact of speech on its audience is not a 'secondary effect' "unrelated to the content of the expression itself.

According to the principles announced in *Boos,* Johnson's political expression was restricted because of the content of the message he conveyed. We must therefore subject the State's asserted interest in preserving the special symbolic character of the flag to "the most exacting scrutiny." *Boos v. Barry.*[8] * * *

According to Texas, if one physically treats the flag in a way that would tend to cast doubt on either the idea that nationhood and national unity are the flag's referents or that national unity actually exists, the message conveyed thereby is a harmful one and therefore may be prohibited.

If there is a bedrock principle underlying the First Amendment, it is that the Government may not prohibit the expression of an idea simply because society finds the idea itself offensive or disagreeable. [We] have not

---

6. *Cf. Smith v. Goguen* [415 U.S. 566, 94 S.Ct. 1242, 39 L.Ed.2d 605 (1974)] (Blackmun, J., dissenting) (emphasizing that lower court appeared to have construed state statute so as to protect physical integrity of the flag in all circumstances); *id.* (Rehnquist, J., dissenting) (same). [In *Goguen,* Blackmun, J., argued that "Goguen's punishment was constitutionally permissible for harming the physical integrity of the flag by wearing it affixed to the seat of his pants" and emphasized that such punishment would not be for "speech—a communicative element."].

8. Our inquiry is, of course, bounded by the particular facts of this case and by the statute under which Johnson was convicted. There was no evidence that Johnson himself stole the flag he burned, nor did the prosecution or the arguments urged in support of it depend on the theory that the flag was stolen. Thus, our analysis does not rely on the way in which the flag was acquired, and nothing in our opinion should be taken to suggest that one is free to steal a flag so long as he later uses it to communicate an idea. We also emphasize that Johnson was prosecuted only for flag desecration—not for trespass, disorderly conduct, or arson.

recognized an exception to this principle even where our flag has been involved. [We] never before have held that the Government may ensure that a symbol be used to express only one view of that symbol or its referents. Indeed, in *Schacht v. United States* [398 U.S. 58, 90 S.Ct. 1555, 26 L.Ed.2d 44 (1970)] we invalidated a federal statute permitting an actor portraying a member of one of our armed forces to " 'wear the uniform of that armed force if the portrayal does not tend to discredit that armed force.' " This proviso, we held, "which leaves Americans free to praise the war in Vietnam but can send persons like Schacht to prison for opposing it, cannot survive in a country which has the First Amendment."

We perceive no basis on which to hold that the principle underlying our decision in *Schacht* does not apply to this case. To conclude that the Government may permit designated symbols to be used to communicate only a limited set of messages would be to enter territory having no discernible or defensible boundaries. Could the Government, on this theory, prohibit the burning of state flags? Of copies of the Presidential seal? Of the Constitution? In evaluating these choices under the First Amendment, how would we decide which symbols were sufficiently special to warrant this unique status? To do so, we would be forced to consult our own political preferences, and impose them on the citizenry, in the very way that the First Amendment forbids us to do.

There is, moreover, no indication—either in the text of the Constitution or in our cases interpreting it—that a separate juridical category exists for the American flag alone. Indeed, we would not be surprised to learn that the persons who framed our Constitution and wrote the Amendment that we now construe were not known for their reverence for the Union Jack. The First Amendment does not guarantee that other concepts virtually sacred to our Nation as a whole—such as the principle that discrimination on the basis of race is odious and destructive—will go unquestioned in the marketplace of ideas. See *Brandenburg.* We decline, therefore, to create for the flag an exception to the joust of principles protected by the First Amendment.

It is not the State's ends, but its means, to which we object. It cannot be gainsaid that there is a special place reserved for the flag in this Nation, and thus we do not doubt that the Government has a legitimate interest in making efforts to "preserv[e] the national flag as an unalloyed symbol of our country." We reject the suggestion, urged at oral argument by counsel for Johnson, that the Government lacks "any state interest whatsoever" in regulating the manner in which the flag may be displayed. Congress has, for example, enacted precatory regulations describing the proper treatment of the flag, see 36 U.S.C. §§ 173–177, and we cast no doubt on the legitimacy of its interest in making such recommendations. To say that the Government has an interest in encouraging proper treatment of the flag, however, is not to say that it may criminally punish a person for burning a flag as a means of political protest. "National unity as an end which officials may foster by persuasion and example is not in question. The problem is whether under our Constitution compulsion as here employed is a permissible means for its achievement.''

We are fortified in today's conclusion by our conviction that forbidding criminal punishment for conduct such as Johnson's will not endanger the special role played by our flag or the feelings it inspires. To paraphrase Justice Holmes, we submit that nobody can suppose that this one gesture of an unknown man will change our Nation's attitude towards its flag. See *Abrams* (Holmes, J., dissenting). Indeed, Texas' argument that the burning of an American flag " 'is an act having a high likelihood to cause a breach of the peace,' '' and its statute's implicit assumption that physical mistreatment of the flag will lead to ''serious offense,'' tend to confirm that the flag's special role is not in danger; if it were, no one would riot or take offense because a flag had been burned.

We are tempted to say, in fact, that the flag's deservedly cherished place in our community will be strengthened, not weakened, by our holding today. Our decision is a reaffirmation of the principles of freedom and inclusiveness that the flag best reflects, and of the conviction that our toleration of criticism such as Johnson's is a sign and source of our strength. Indeed, one of the proudest images of our flag, the one immortalized in our own national anthem, is of the bombardment it survived at Fort McHenry. It is the Nation's resilience, not its rigidity, that Texas sees reflected in the flag—and it is that resilience that we reassert today.

The way to preserve the flag's special role is not to punish those who feel differently about these matters. It is to persuade them that they are wrong. [And,] precisely because it is our flag that is involved, one's response to the flag-burner may exploit the uniquely persuasive power of the flag itself. We can imagine no more appropriate response to burning a flag than waving one's own, no better way to counter a flag-burner's message than by saluting the flag that burns, no surer means of preserving the dignity even of the flag that burned than by—as one witness here did—according its remains a respectful burial. We do not consecrate the flag by punishing its desecration, for in doing so we dilute the freedom that this cherished emblem represents. * * *

JUSTICE KENNEDY, concurring.

I write not to qualify the words Justice Brennan chooses so well, for he says with power all that is necessary to explain our ruling. I join his opinion without reservation, but with a keen sense that this case, like others before us from time to time, exacts its personal toll. * * *

Our colleagues in dissent advance powerful arguments why respondent may be convicted for his expression, reminding us that among those who will be dismayed by our holding will be some who have had the singular honor of carrying the flag in battle. And I agree that the flag holds a lonely place of honor in an age when absolutes are distrusted and simple truths are burdened by unneeded apologetics.

With all respect to those views, I do not believe the Constitution gives us the right to rule as the dissenting members of the Court urge, however painful this judgment is to announce. Though symbols often are what we ourselves make of them, the flag is constant in expressing beliefs Americans share, beliefs in law and peace and that freedom which sustains the human spirit. The case here today forces recognition of the costs to which those beliefs commit us. It is poignant but fundamental that the flag protects those who hold it in contempt.

For all the record shows, this respondent was not a philosopher and perhaps did not even possess the ability to comprehend how repellent his statements must be to the Republic itself. But whether or not he could appreciate the enormity of the offense he gave, the fact remains that his acts were speech, in both the technical and the fundamental meaning of the Constitution. So I agree with the Court that he must go free.

CHIEF JUSTICE REHNQUIST, with whom JUSTICE WHITE and JUSTICE O'CONNOR join, dissenting.

In holding this Texas statute unconstitutional, the Court ignores Justice Holmes' familiar aphorism that "a page of history is worth a volume of logic." *New York Trust Co. v. Eisner,* 256 U.S. 345, 41 S.Ct. 506, 65 L.Ed. 963 (1921). For more than 200 years, the American flag has occupied a unique position as the symbol of our Nation, a uniqueness that justifies a governmental prohibition against flag burning in the way respondent Johnson did here. * * *[b]

The American flag, then, throughout more than 200 years of our history, has come to be the visible symbol embodying our Nation. It does not represent the views of any particular political party, and it does not represent any particular political philosophy. The flag is not simply another "idea" or "point of view" competing for recognition in the marketplace of ideas. Millions and millions of Americans regard it with an almost mystical reverence regardless of what sort of social, political, or philosophical beliefs they may have. I cannot agree that the First Amendment invalidates the Act of Congress, and the laws of 48 of the 50 States, which make criminal the public burning of the flag.

More than 80 years ago in *Halter v. Nebraska* [205 U.S. 34, 27 S.Ct. 419, 51 L.Ed. 696 (1907)], this Court upheld the constitutionality of a Nebraska statute that forbade the use of representations of the American flag for advertising purposes upon articles of merchandise. The Court there said: "For that flag every true American has not simply an appreciation but a deep affection. * * * Hence, it has often occurred that insults to a flag have been the cause of war, and indignities put upon it, in the presence of those

b. Rehnquist, C.J., invoked a legacy of prose, poetry, and law in honor of flags in general and the American flag in particular both in peace and in war, quoting poetry from, among others, Ralph Waldo Emerson and John Greenleaf Whittier. Emerson's poem referred to the Union Jack, but he did not always speak so warmly of the American flag. After passage of the Fugitive Slave Law Emerson wrote, "We sneak about with the infamy of crime in the streets, & cowardice in ourselves and frankly once for all the Union is sunk, the flag is hateful, and shall be hissed." *Emerson in His Journals* 421 (J. Porte ed. 1982).

who revere it, have often been resented and sometimes punished on the spot."

Only two Terms ago, in *San Francisco Arts & Athletics, Inc. v. United States Olympic Committee,* [483 U.S. 522, 107 S.Ct. 2971, 97 L.Ed.2d 427 (1987)], the Court held that Congress could grant exclusive use of the word "Olympic" to the United States Olympic Committee. The Court thought that this "restrictio[n] on expressive speech properly [was] characterized as incidental to the primary congressional purpose of encouraging and rewarding the USOC's activities." As the Court stated, "when a word [or symbol] acquires value 'as the result of organization and the expenditure of labor, skill, and money' by an entity, that entity constitutionally may obtain a limited property right in the word [or symbol]."[c] Surely Congress or the States may recognize a similar interest in the flag.[d]

But the Court insists that the Texas statute prohibiting the public burning of the American flag infringes on respondent Johnson's freedom of expression. Such freedom, of course, is not absolute. [T]he public burning of the American flag by Johnson was no essential part of any exposition of ideas, and at the same time it had a tendency to incite a breach of the peace. Johnson was free to make any verbal denunciation of the flag that he wished; indeed, he was free to burn the flag in private. He could publicly burn other symbols of the Government or effigies of political leaders. He did lead a march through the streets of Dallas, and conducted a rally in front of the Dallas City Hall. He engaged in a "die-in" to protest nuclear weapons. He shouted out various slogans during the march, including: "Reagan, Mondale which will it be? Either one means World War III"; "Ronald Reagan, killer of the hour, Perfect example of U.S. power"; and "red, white and blue, we spit on you, you stand for plunder, you will go under." For none of these acts was he arrested or prosecuted; it was only when he proceeded to burn publicly an American flag stolen from its rightful owner that he violated the Texas statute. * * * As with "fighting words," so with flag burning, for purposes of the First Amendment: It is "no essential part of any exposition of ideas, and [is] of such slight social value as a step to truth that any benefit that may be derived from [it] is clearly outweighed" by the public interest in avoiding a probable breach of the peace. * * *

The result of the Texas statute is obviously to deny one in Johnson's frame of mind one of many means of "symbolic speech." Far from being a case of "one picture being worth a thousand words," flag burning is the

---

c. For criticism, see Boyle, *Shamans, Software, and Spleens* 145–48 (1996); Benkler, *Constitutional Bounds of Database Protection,* 15 Berkeley L.J. 535 (2000); Kravitz, *Trademarks, Speech, and the Gay Olympics Case,* 69 B.U.L.Rev. 131 (1989).

d. In response, Brennan, J., observed that *Halter* was decided "nearly twenty years" before the first amendment was applied to the states and "[m]ore important" that *Halter* involved "purely commercial rather than political speech." Similarly, he stated that the authorization "to prohibit certain commercial and promotion uses of the word 'Olympic' [does not] even begin to tell us whether the Government may criminally punish physical conduct towards the flag engaged in as a means of political protest."

equivalent of an inarticulate grunt or roar that, it seems fair to say, is most likely to be indulged in not to express any particular idea, but to antagonize others. [The] Texas statute deprived Johnson of only one rather inarticulate symbolic form of protest—a form of protest that was profoundly offensive to many—and left him with a full panoply of other symbols and every conceivable form of verbal expression to express his deep disapproval of national policy. Thus, in no way can it be said that Texas is punishing him because his hearers—or any other group of people—were profoundly opposed to the message that he sought to convey. Such opposition is no proper basis for restricting speech or expression under the First Amendment. It was Johnson's use of this particular symbol, and not the idea that he sought to convey by it or by his many other expressions, for which he was punished. * * *

The uniquely deep awe and respect for our flag felt by virtually all of us are bundled off under the rubric of "designated symbols," that the First Amendment prohibits the government from "establishing." But the government has not "established" this feeling; 200 years of history have done that. The government is simply recognizing as a fact the profound regard for the American flag created by that history when it enacts statutes prohibiting the disrespectful public burning of the flag.

The Court concludes its opinion with a regrettably patronizing civics lecture, presumably addressed to the Members of both Houses of Congress, the members of the 48 state legislatures that enacted prohibitions against flag burning, and the troops fighting under that flag in Vietnam who objected to its being burned: "The way to preserve the flag's special role is not to punish those who feel differently about these matters. It is to persuade them that they are wrong." The Court's role as the final expositor of the Constitution is well established, but its role as a platonic guardian admonishing those responsible to public opinion as if they were truant school children has no similar place in our system of government. The cry of "no taxation without representation" animated those who revolted against the English Crown to found our Nation—the idea that those who submitted to government should have some say as to what kind of laws would be passed. Surely one of the high purposes of a democratic society is to legislate against conduct that is regarded as evil and profoundly offensive to the majority of people—whether it be murder, embezzlement, pollution, or flag burning. * * *

Uncritical extension of constitutional protection to the burning of the flag risks the frustration of the very purpose for which organized governments are instituted. The Court decides that the American flag is just another symbol, about which not only must opinions pro and con be tolerated, but for which the most minimal public respect may not be enjoined. The government may conscript men into the Armed Forces where they must fight and perhaps die for the flag, but the government may not prohibit the public burning of the banner under which they fight. I would uphold the Texas statute as applied in this case.[2]

2. In holding that the Texas statute as applied to Johnson violates the First

JUSTICE STEVENS, dissenting. * * *

Even if flag burning could be considered just another species of symbolic speech under the logical application of the rules that the Court has developed in its interpretation of the First Amendment in other contexts, this case has an intangible dimension that makes those rules inapplicable.

A country's flag is a symbol of more than "nationhood and national unity." [T]he American flag * * * is more than a proud symbol of the courage, the determination, and the gifts of nature that transformed 13 fledgling Colonies into a world power. It is a symbol of freedom, of equal opportunity, of religious tolerance, and of goodwill for other peoples who share our aspirations. The symbol carries its message to dissidents both at home and abroad who may have no interest at all in our national unity or survival.

The value of the flag as a symbol cannot be measured. Even so, I have no doubt that the interest in preserving that value for the future is both significant and legitimate. Conceivably that value will be enhanced by the Court's conclusion that our national commitment to free expression is so strong that even the United States as ultimate guarantor of that freedom is without power to prohibit the desecration of its unique symbol. But I am unpersuaded. The creation of a federal right to post bulletin boards and graffiti on the Washington Monument might enlarge the market for free expression, but at a cost I would not pay. Similarly, in my considered judgment, sanctioning the public desecration of the flag will tarnish its value—both for those who cherish the ideas for which it waves and for those who desire to don the robes of martyrdom by burning it. That tarnish is not justified by the trivial burden on free expression occasioned by requiring that an available, alternative mode of expression—including uttering words critical of the flag be employed.

It is appropriate to emphasize certain propositions that are not implicated by this case. [The] statute does not compel any conduct or any profession of respect for any idea or any symbol. [Nor] does the statute violate "the government's paramount obligation of neutrality in its regulation of protected communication." The content of respondent's message has no relevance whatsoever to the case. The concept of "desecration" does not turn on the substance of the message the actor intends to convey, but rather on whether those who view the *act* will take serious offense. Accordingly, one intending to convey a message of respect for the flag by burning it in a public square might nonetheless be guilty of desecration if he knows that others—perhaps simply because they misperceive the intended message—will be seriously offended. Indeed, even if the actor knows that all possible witnesses will

Amendment, the Court does not consider Johnson's claims that the statute is unconstitutionally vague or overbroad. I think those claims are without merit. [By] defining "desecrate" as "deface," "damage" or otherwise "physically mistreat" in a manner that the actor knows will "seriously offend" others, § 42.09 only prohibits flagrant acts of physical abuse and destruction of the flag of the sort at issue here—soaking a flag with lighter fluid and igniting it in public—and not any of the examples of improper flag etiquette cited in Respondent's brief.

understand that he intends to send a message of respect, he might still be guilty of desecration if he also knows that this understanding does not lessen the offense taken by some of those witnesses. The case has nothing to do with "disagreeable ideas." It involves disagreeable conduct that, in my opinion, diminishes the value of an important national asset.

The Court is therefore quite wrong in blandly asserting that respondent "was prosecuted for his expression of dissatisfaction with the policies of this country, expression situated at the core of our First Amendment values." Respondent was prosecuted because of the method he chose to express his dissatisfaction with those policies. Had he chosen to spray paint—or perhaps convey with a motion picture projector—his message of dissatisfaction on the facade of the Lincoln Memorial, there would be no question about the power of the Government to prohibit his means of expression. The prohibition would be supported by the legitimate interest in preserving the quality of an important national asset. Though the asset at stake in this case is intangible, given its unique value, the same interest supports a prohibition on the desecration of the American flag.*

The ideas of liberty and equality have been an irresistible force in motivating leaders like Patrick Henry, Susan B. Anthony, and Abraham Lincoln, schoolteachers like Nathan Hale and Booker T. Washington, the Philippine Scouts who fought at Bataan, and the soldiers who scaled the bluff at Omaha Beach. If those ideas are worth fighting for—and our history demonstrates that they are—it cannot be true that the flag that uniquely symbolizes their power is not itself worthy of protection from unnecessary desecration.

I respectfully dissent.

Notes and Questions

1. *Patriotism*. Consider Fletcher, *Loyalty* 141 (1993): "The [question] is whether the Congress has a sufficiently clear interest in promoting national loyalty to interpret the crime of flag burning as a sanction aimed not at the message of protest, but at the act, regardless of its political slant. Whether

---

* The Court suggested that a prohibition against flag desecration is not content-neutral because this form of symbolic speech is only used by persons who are critical of the flag or the ideas it represents. In making this suggestion the Court does not pause to consider the far-reaching consequences of its introduction of disparate impact analysis into our First Amendment jurisprudence. It seems obvious that a prohibition against the desecration of a gravesite is content-neutral even if it denies some protesters the right to make a symbolic statement by extinguishing the flame in Arlington Cemetery where John F. Kennedy is buried while permitting others to salute the flame by bowing their heads. Few would doubt that a protester who extinguishes the flame has desecrated the gravesite, regardless of whether he prefaces that act with a speech explaining that his purpose is to express deep admiration or unmitigated scorn for the late President. Likewise, few would claim that the protester who bows his head has desecrated the gravesite, even if he makes clear that his purpose is to show disrespect. In such a case, as in a flag burning case, the prohibition against desecration has absolutely nothing to do with the content of the message that the symbolic speech is intended to convey.

Congress and the country possess this interest depends, of course, on what one thinks of loyalty and devotion to country as a value. A high regard for patriotism, for sharing a common purpose in cherishing our people and seeking to solve our problems, leads one easily to perceive the expression of our unity as a value important in itself. The flag is at least as important—to go from the sublime to the ridiculous—as protecting draft cards so that the Selective Service System can function efficiently.''

2. *Dissent.* Consider Shiffrin, *The First Amendment and the Meaning of America,* in *Identities, Politics, and Rights* 318 (Sarat & Kearns eds. 1995): "The flag-burning prohibition is uniquely troubling not because it interferes with the metaphorical marketplace of ideas, not because it topples our image of a content-neutral government (*that* has fallen many times), and not merely because it suppresses political speech. The flag-burning prohibition is a naked attempt to smother dissent. If we must have a 'central meaning' of the first amendment, we should recognize that the dissenters—those who attack existing customs, habits, traditions and authorities—stand at the center of the first amendment and not at its periphery. Gregory Johnson was attacking a symbol which the vast majority of Americans regard with reverence. But that is *exactly* why he deserved first amendment protection. The first amendment has a special regard for those who swim against the current, for those who would shake us to our foundations, for those who reject prevailing authority. In burning the flag, Gregory Johnson rejected, opposed, even blasphemed the Nation's most important political, social, and cultural icon. Clearly Gregory Johnson's alleged act of burning the flag was a quintessential act of dissent. A dissent centered conception of the first amendment would make it clear that *Johnson* was an easy case—rightly decided.''

3. *The meaning of the flag.* Consider Karst, *Law's Promise, Law's Expression, Visions of Power in the Politics of Race, Gender, and Religion* 165 (1993): "According to those opinions the flag stands for our nationhood or national unity (Brennan, paraphrasing the state's lawyers); for principles of freedom or inclusiveness (Brennan); for the nation's resiliency (Brennan); for the nation itself (Rehnquist); for something men will die for in war (Rehnquist); for 'America's imagined past and present' (Rehnquist, in Sheldon Nahmod's apt paraphrase); for courage, freedom, equal opportunity, religious tolerance, and 'goodwill for other peoples who share our aspirations' (Stevens); and for shared beliefs in law and peace and 'the freedom that sustains the human spirit' (Kennedy). So, even within the Supreme Court, the flag stands at once for freedom and for obedience to law, for war and for peace, for unity and for tolerance of difference.''

4. *The Flag's Physical Integrity.* Brennan, J., observes that the Texas law is "not aimed at protecting the physical integrity of the flag in all circumstances * * *." What if it were?[e] In response to *Johnson,*

---

e. For commentary concerning the extent to which a focus on physical integrity can be separated from a concern with content, see Greenawalt, *O'er the Land of the*

Congress passed the Flag Protection Act of 1989 which attached criminal penalties to the knowing mutilation, defacement, burning, maintaining on the floor or ground, or trampling upon any flag of the United States. UNITED STATES v. EICHMAN, 496 U.S. 310, 110 S.Ct. 2404, 110 L.Ed.2d 287 (1990), per BRENNAN, J., invalidated the statute: "Although the Flag Protection Act contains no explicit content-based limitation on the scope of prohibited conduct, it is nevertheless clear that the Government's asserted *interest* is 'related "to the suppression of free expression" 'and concerned with the content of such expression. The Government's interest in protecting the 'physical integrity' of a privately owned flag rests upon a perceived need to preserve the flag's status as a symbol of our Nation and certain national ideals. But the mere destruction or disfigurement of a particular physical manifestation of the symbol, without more, does not diminish or otherwise affect the symbol itself in any way. For example, the secret destruction of a flag in one's own basement would not threaten the flag's recognized meaning. Rather, the Government's desire to preserve the flag as a symbol for certain national ideals is implicated 'only when a person's treatment of the flag communicates [a] message' to others that is inconsistent with those ideals."

STEVENS, J., joined by Rehnquist, C.J., White and O'Connor, JJ., dissenting, argued that the government's "legitimate interest in protecting the symbolic value of the American flag" outweighed the free speech interest. In describing the flag's symbolic value he stated that the flag "inspires and motivates the average citizen to make personal sacrifices in order to achieve societal goals of overriding importance; at all times, it serves as a reminder of the paramount importance of pursuing the ideals that characterize our society. * * * [T]he communicative value of a well-placed bomb in the Capital does not entitle it to the protection of the First Amendment. Burning a flag is not, of course, equivalent to burning a public building. Assuming that the protester is burning his own flag, it causes no physical harm to other persons or to their property. The impact is purely symbolic, and it is apparent that some thoughtful persons believe that impact far from depreciating the value of the symbol, will actually enhance its meaning. I most respectfully disagree."[f]

5. Prior to adopting the Flag Protection Act, the Senate by a vote of 97–3 had passed a resolution expressing "profound disappointment with the [*Johnson*] decision." The House had approved a similar resolution by a vote of 411–5, and President Bush had proposed a constitutional amendment to

Free: Flag Burning as Speech, 37 UCLA L.Rev. 925 (1990); Michelman, Saving Old Glory: On Constitutional Iconography, 42 Stan.L.Rev. 1337 (1990); Stone, *Flag Burning and the Constitution*, 75 Ia.L.Rev. 111 (1989); Tushnet, *The Flag–Burning Episode: An Essay on the Constitution*, 61 U.Col.L.Rev. 39 (1990).

f. But see Loewy, *The Flag–Burning Case: Freedom of Speech When We Need It Most*, 68 N.C.L.Rev. 165, 174 (1989): "Perhaps the ultimate irony is that *Johnson* has done more to preserve the flag as a symbol of liberty than any prior decision, while the decision's detractors would allow real desecration of the flag by making it a symbol of political oppression." Compare West, *Foreword: Taking Freedom Seriously*, 104 Harv. L.Rev. 43. 97–98 (1990) (the militaristic patriotism associated with the flag menaces dissent). See also Greenawalt, fn. e supra.

[Handwritten margin notes: "ONLY REASON ACTION IS BAD IS BECAUSE OF EXPRESSION"; "COURT IS HAVING TO 'WEIGH' OUT THE TWO SIDES"; "☺ HAHA"]

overrule *Johnson*. Opponents argued that a carefully drawn statute might (or would) be upheld by the Court. Suppose you were a member of the House or Senate at that time. Suppose you supported *Johnson* but believed that the statute might be held constitutional, even though you did not think it should be. Suppose you also believed that if a statute were not passed an amendment would.

Consider this exchange during hearings of the House Subcommittee on Civil and Constitutional Rights on *Statutory and Constitutional Responses to the Supreme Court Decision in Texas v. Johnson* (1989): Former Solicitor General Charles Fried: "My good friends and colleagues, Rex Lee and Laurence Tribe, have testified that a statute might be drawn that would pass constitutional muster. [I] hope and urge and pray that we will not act—that no statute be passed and of course that the Constitution not be amended. In short, I believe that *Johnson* is right [in] principle." * * *

Representative Schroeder: "I thought your testimony was eloquent. I think in a purist world, that is where we should go. But [we] are not talking about a purist world. We are talking about a very political world." * * *

Mr. Fried: "There are times when you earn your rather inadequate salary by just doing the right thing, and where you seem to agree with me is that the right thing to do is to do neither one of these. * * * It is called leadership."

Representative Schroeder: "It is called leadership. * * * But I guess what I am saying is if we can't stop a stampede on an amendment without something, isn't it better to try to save the Bill of Rights[g] and the Constitution?"

———

Community for Creative Non–Violence (CCNV) sought to conduct a wintertime demonstration near the White House in Lafayette Park and the Mall to dramatize the plight of the homeless. The National Park Service authorized the erection of two symbolic tent cities for purposes of the demonstration, but denied CCNV's request that demonstrators be permitted to sleep in the tents. National Park Service regulations permit camping (the "use of park land for living accommodation purposes such as sleeping activities") in National Parks only in campgrounds designated for that purpose.

CLARK v. COMMUNITY FOR CREATIVE NON–VIOLENCE, 468 U.S. 288, 104 S.Ct. 3065, 82 L.Ed.2d 221 (1984), per WHITE, J., rejected CCNV's claim that the regulations could not be constitutionally applied against its demonstration: "We need not differ with the view of the Court of Appeals that overnight sleeping in connection with the demonstration is expressive conduct protected to some extent by the First Amendment.[5] We assume for

g. For commentary, compare Michel- man, fn. e, supra with Shiffrin, *Dissent,*   *Injustice, and the Meanings of America* ch. 1 (1999).

present purposes, but do not decide, that such is the case, cf. *O'Brien,* but this assumption only begins the inquiry. Expression, whether oral or written or symbolized by conduct, is subject to reasonable time, place, or manner restrictions. We have often noted that restrictions of this kind are valid provided that they are justified without reference to the content of the regulated speech, that they are narrowly tailored to serve a significant governmental interest, and that they leave open ample alternative channels for communication of the information.

"It is also true that a message may be delivered by conduct that is intended to be communicative and that, in context, would reasonably be understood by the viewer to be communicative. Symbolic expression of this kind may be forbidden or regulated if the conduct itself may constitutionally be regulated, if the regulation is narrowly drawn to further a substantial governmental interest, and if the interest is unrelated to the suppression of free speech. *O'Brien.*

"[That] sleeping, like the symbolic tents themselves, may be expressive and part of the message delivered by the demonstration does not make the ban any less a limitation on the manner of demonstrating, for reasonable time, place, or manner regulations normally have the purpose and direct effect of limiting expression but are nevertheless valid. Neither does the fact that sleeping, arguendo, may be expressive conduct, rather than oral or written expression, render the sleeping prohibition any less a time, place, or manner regulation. To the contrary, the Park Service neither attempts to ban sleeping generally nor to ban it everywhere in the parks. It has established areas for camping and forbids it elsewhere, including Lafayette Park and the Mall. Considered as such, we have very little trouble concluding that the Park Service may prohibit overnight sleeping in the parks involved here.

"The requirement that the regulation be content-neutral is clearly satisfied. The courts below accepted that view, and it is not disputed here that the prohibition on camping, and on sleeping specifically, is content-neutral and is not being applied because of disagreement with the message presented.[a] Neither was the regulation faulted, nor could it be, on the ground that without overnight sleeping the plight of the homeless could not be communicated in other ways. The regulation otherwise left the demon-

---

5. We reject the suggestion of the plurality below, however, that the burden on the demonstrators is limited to "the advancement of a plausible contention" that their conduct is expressive. Although it is common to place the burden upon the Government to justify impingements on First Amendment interests, it is the obligation of the person desiring to engage in assertedly expressive conduct to demonstrate that the First Amendment even applies. To hold otherwise would be to create a rule that all conduct is presumptively expressive. In the absence of a showing that such a rule is necessary to protect vital First Amendment interests, we decline to deviate from the general rule that one seeking relief bears the burden of demonstrating that he is entitled to it.

a. Marshall, J., dissenting, observed that CCNV had held a demonstration the previous winter in which it set up nine tents and slept in Lafayette Park. The D.C. Circuit held that the regulations did not preclude such a demonstration. According to Marshall, J., "The regulations at issue in this case were passed in direct response" to that holding.

stration intact, with its symbolic city, signs, and the presence of those who were willing to take their turns in a day-and-night vigil. Respondents do not suggest that there was, or is, any barrier to delivering to the media, or to the public by other means, the intended message concerning the plight of the homeless.

"It is also apparent to us that the regulation narrowly focuses on the Government's substantial interest in maintaining the parks in the heart of our Capital in an attractive and intact condition, readily available to the millions of people who wish to see and enjoy them by their presence. To permit camping—using these areas as living accommodations—would be totally inimical to these purposes, as would be readily understood by those who have frequented the National Parks across the country and observed the unfortunate consequences of the activities of those who refuse to confine their camping to designated areas.

"It is urged by [CCNV], and the Court of Appeals was of this view, that if the symbolic city of tents was to be permitted and if the demonstrators did not intend to cook, dig, or engage in aspects of camping other than sleeping, the incremental benefit to the parks could not justify the ban on sleeping, which was here an expressive activity said to enhance the message concerning the plight of the poor and homeless. We cannot agree. In the first place, we seriously doubt that the First Amendment requires the Park Service to permit a demonstration in Lafayette Park and the Mall involving a 24-hour vigil and the erection of tents to accommodate 150 people. Furthermore, although we have assumed for present purposes that the sleeping banned in this case would have an expressive element, it is evident that its major value to this demonstration would be facilitative.[b] Without a permit to sleep, it would be difficult to get the poor and homeless to participate or to be present at all. This much is apparent from the permit application filed by respondents: 'Without the incentive of sleeping space or a hot meal, the homeless would not come to the site.' The sleeping ban, if enforced, would thus effectively limit the nature, extent, and duration of the demonstration and to that extent ease the pressure on the parks.

"Beyond this, however, it is evident from our cases that the validity of this regulation need not be judged solely by reference to the demonstration at hand.[c] Absent the prohibition on sleeping, there would be other groups who would demand permission to deliver an asserted message by camping in Lafayette Park. Some of them would surely have as credible a claim in this regard as does CCNV, and the denial of permits to still others would present difficult problems for the Park Service. With the prohibition, however, as is evident in the case before us, at least some around-the-clock demonstrations

---

b. What if it were the exclusive value? For discussion, see Francione, *Experimentation and the Marketplace Theory of the First Amendment,* 136 U.Pa.L.Rev. 417 (1987).

c. For debate about this point and its implications, compare Easterbrook, *Fore-*

word: The Court and the Economic System, 98 Harv.L.Rev. 4, 19–21 (1984) with Tribe, *Constitutional Calculus: Equal Justice or Economic Efficiency?* 98 Harv.L.Rev. 592, 599–603 (1985) and Easterbrook, *Method, Result, and Authority: A Reply,* 98 Harv. L.Rev. 622, 626 (1985).

lasting for days on end will not materialize, others will be limited in size and duration, and the purposes of the regulation will thus be materially served. Perhaps these purposes would be more effectively and not so clumsily achieved by preventing tents and 24–hour vigils entirely in the core areas. But the Park Service's decision to permit nonsleeping demonstrations does not, in our view, impugn the camping prohibition as a valuable, but perhaps imperfect, protection to the parks. If the Government has a legitimate interest in ensuring that the National Parks are adequately protected, which we think it has, and if the parks would be more exposed to harm without the sleeping prohibition than with it, the ban is safe from invalidation under the First Amendment as a reasonable regulation of the manner in which a demonstration may be carried out. [d] * * *

"Contrary to the conclusion of the Court of Appeals, the foregoing analysis demonstrates that the Park Service regulation is sustainable under the four-factor standard of *United States v. O'Brien,* for validating a regulation of expressive conduct, which, in the last analysis is little, if any, different from the standard applied to time, place, or manner restrictions.[8] No one contends that aside from its impact on speech a rule against camping or overnight sleeping in public parks is beyond the constitutional power of the Government to enforce. And for the reasons we have discussed above, there is a substantial Government interest in conserving park property, an interest that is plainly served by, and requires for its implementation, measures such as the proscription of sleeping that are designed to limit the wear and tear on park properties. That interest is unrelated to suppression of expression.

"We are unmoved by the Court of Appeals' view that the challenged regulation is unnecessary, and hence invalid, because there are less speech-restrictive alternatives that could have satisfied the Government interest in preserving park lands. The Court of Appeals' suggestions that the Park Service minimize the possible injury by reducing the size, duration, or frequency of demonstrations would still curtail the total allowable expression in which demonstrators could engage, whether by sleeping or otherwise, and these suggestions represent no more than a disagreement with the Park

---

d. Brownstein, *Alternative Maps for Navigating the First Amendment Maze,* 16 Const. Comm. 101, 117 (1999): "It seems clear that a similar argument could be applied to prohibit leafleting (or all demonstrations for that matter) in Lafayette Park. * * * I do not believe that a ban on leafleting in Lafayette Park would be as cavalierly upheld by the Court as the ban on camping, however."

8. Reasonable time, place, or manner restrictions are valid even though they directly limit oral or written expression. It would be odd to insist on a higher standard for limitations aimed at regulable conduct and having only an incidental impact on speech. Thus, if the time, place, or manner restriction on expressive sleeping, if that is what is involved in this case, sufficiently and narrowly serves a substantial enough governmental interest to escape First Amendment condemnation, it is untenable to invalidate it under *O'Brien* on the ground that the governmental interest is insufficient to warrant the intrusion on First Amendment concerns or that there is an inadequate nexus between the regulation and the interest sought to be served. We note that only recently, in a case dealing with the regulation of signs, the Court framed the issue under *O'Brien* and then based a crucial part of its analysis on the time, place, or manner cases.

Service over how much protection the core parks require or how an acceptable level of preservation is to be attained. We do not believe, however, that either *United States v. O'Brien* or the time, place, or manner decisions assign to the judiciary the authority to replace the Park Service as the manager of the Nation's parks or endow the judiciary with the competence to judge how much protection of park lands is wise and how that level of conservation is to be [attained.]''

BURGER, C.J., concurred "fully in the Court's opinion," but added: "[CCNV's] attempt at camping in the park is a form of 'picketing'; it is conduct, not speech. [It] trivializes the First Amendment to seek to use it as a shield in the manner asserted here."

MARSHALL, J., joined by Brennan, J., dissented: "The majority assumes, without deciding, that the respondents' conduct is entitled to constitutional protection. The problem with this assumption is that the Court thereby avoids examining closely the reality of respondents' planned expression. The majority's approach denatures respondents' asserted right and thus makes all too easy identification of a Government interest sufficient to warrant its abridgment.

"[Missing] from the majority's description is any inkling that Lafayette Park and the Mall have served as the sites for some of the most rousing political demonstrations in the Nation's history.[2] The primary purpose for making *sleep* an integral part of the demonstration was 'to re-enact the central reality of homelessness' and to impress upon public consciousness, in as dramatic a way as possible, that homelessness is a widespread problem, often ignored, that confronts its victims with life-threatening deprivations. As one of the homeless men seeking to demonstrate explained: 'Sleeping in Lafayette Park or on the Mall, for me, is to show people that conditions are so poor for the homeless and poor in this city that we would actually sleep *outside* in the winter to get the point across.' * * * Here respondents clearly intended to protest the reality of homelessness by sleeping outdoors in the winter in the near vicinity of the magisterial residence of the President of the United States. In addition to accentuating the political character of their protest by their choice of location and mode of communication, respondents also intended to underline the meaning of their protest by giving their demonstration satirical names. Respondents planned to name the demonstration on the Mall 'Congressional Village,' and the demonstration in Lafayette Park, 'Reaganville II.'

"Nor can there be any doubt that in the surrounding circumstances the likelihood was great that the political significance of sleeping in the parks would be understood by those who viewed it. Certainly the news media understood the significance of respondents' proposed activity; newspapers

2. At oral argument, the Government informed the Court "that on any given day there will be an average of three or so demonstrations going on" in the Mall–Lafayette Park area. Respondents accurately describe Lafayette Park "as the American analogue to 'Speaker's Corner' in Hyde Park."

and magazines from around the Nation reported their previous sleep-in and their planned display. * * *

"Although sleep in the context of this case is symbolic speech protected by the First Amendment, it is nonetheless subject to reasonable time, place, and manner restrictions. I agree with the standard enunciated by the majority.[6] I conclude, however, that the regulations at issue in this case, as applied to respondents, fail to satisfy this standard. * * *

"[T]here are no substantial Government interests advanced by the Government's regulations as applied to respondents. All that the Court's decision advances are the prerogatives of a bureaucracy that over the years has shown an implacable hostility toward citizens' exercise of First Amendment rights.

"The disposition of this case impels me to make two additional observations. First, in this case, as in some others involving time, place, and manner restrictions, the Court has dramatically lowered its scrutiny of governmental regulations once it has determined that such regulations are content-neutral.[e] The result has been the creation of a two-tiered approach to First Amendment cases: while regulations that turn on the content of the expression are subjected to a strict form of judicial review, regulations that are aimed at matters other than expression receive only a minimal level of scrutiny. The minimal scrutiny prong of this two-tiered approach has led to an unfortunate diminution of First Amendment protection. By narrowly limiting its concern to whether a given regulation creates a content-based distinction, the Court has seemingly overlooked the fact that content-neutral restrictions are also capable of unnecessarily restricting protected expressive activity.[13] * * * The Court [has] transformed the ban against content distinctions from a floor that offers all persons at least equal liberty under the First Amendment into a ceiling that restricts persons to the protection of First Amendment equality—but nothing more.[14] The consistent imposition of silence upon all may fulfill the dictates of an evenhanded content-neutrality. But it offends our 'profound national commitment to the principle that

6. I also agree with the majority that no substantial difference distinguishes the test applicable to time, place, and manner restrictions and the test articulated in *O'Brien.*

e. In support of Marshall, J.'s contention, see generally Lee, *Lonely Pamphleteers, Little People, and the Supreme Court,* 54 G.W.U.L.Rev. 757 (1986).

13. See Redish, *The Content Distinction in First Amendment Analysis,* 34 Stan. L.Rev. 113 (1981).

14. Furthermore, a content-neutral regulation does not necessarily fall with random or equal force upon different groups or different points of view. A content-neutral regulation that restricts an inexpensive mode of communication will fall most heavily upon relatively poor speakers and the points of view that such speakers typically espouse. [See Lee, fn. d supra.] This sort of latent inequality is very much in evidence in this case for respondents lack the financial means necessary to buy access to more conventional modes of persuasion.

A disquieting feature about the disposition of this case is that it lends credence to the charge that judicial administration of the First Amendment, in conjunction with a social order marked by large disparities in wealth and other sources of power, tends systematically to discriminate against efforts by the relatively disadvantaged to convey their political ideas. * * *

debate on public issues should be uninhibited, robust, and wide-open.' *New York Times Co. v. Sullivan.*

"Second, the disposition of this case reveals a mistaken assumption regarding the motives and behavior of Government officials who create and administer content-neutral regulations. The Court's salutary skepticism of governmental decisionmaking in First Amendment matters suddenly dissipates once it determines that a restriction is not content-based. The Court evidently assumes that the balance struck by officials is deserving of deference so long as it does not appear to be tainted by content discrimination. What the Court fails to recognize is that public officials have strong incentives to overregulate even in the absence of an intent to censor particular views. This incentive stems from the fact that of the two groups whose interests officials must accommodate—on the one hand, the interests of the general public and, on the other, the interests of those who seek to use a particular forum for First Amendment activity—the political power of the former is likely to be far greater than that of the latter.[16]"

Notes and Questions

1. Consider Tushnet, *Character as Argument,* 14 Law and Social Inquiry 539, 549 (1989) (reviewing Kalven, *A Worthy Tradition*): "[W]hen political dissidence is in a sense validated by tradition it can lose its political effect. When dissidents use traditional forms of protest, they may be met by [a] kind of indifference—not the considered rejection of their protests but rather resigned acceptance of their actions as the kind of thing we have to put up with every now and then. To capture the attention of a public accustomed to dignified protest, and able to screen it from consciousness, dissidents may have to adopt novel forms of protest, such as sleeping in a national park overnight to draw attention to the disgrace of a national policy that deprives many people of decent shelter. Yet, precisely because their protests take a novel form, they may not be covered by the worthy tradition that Kalven honors. In this sense the dynamics of protest may make the protection of free speech what Kalven tellingly calls a 'luxury civil liberty,' a civil liberty to be enjoyed when nothing of consequence turns on protecting speech and to be abandoned when it really matters."

2. Should the Court have decided whether sleeping in the park in these circumstances was a form of expression entitled to some degree of first amendment protection? Should all forms of expression receive some level of first amendment protection? Is the presence of an "idea" a necessary condition for expression to come within the first amendment's scope? Should nude dancing be excluded from the first amendment's scope because it is not intended to communicate ideas? Should protection for paintings depend upon whether "ideas" are expressed? See *Schad v. Mount Ephraim,* Ch. 3, I infra: "[N]ude dancing is not without its First Amendment protections from

16. See Goldberger, *Judicial Scrutiny in Public Forum Cases: Misplaced Trust in the* Judgment of Public Officials, 32 Buffalo L.Rev. 175, 208 (1983).

CLARK HAS "TIME/PLACE/MANNER"
O'BRIEN HAS 2 PRONG TEST

official regulation." Should hair styles be afforded first amendment protection? Are hair styles distinguishable from nude dancing on the ground that the latter is a form of expressive entertainment? If so, should video games be afforded first amendment protection? See Note, *The First Amendment Side Effects of Curing Pac–Man Fever,* 84 Colum.L.Rev. 744 (1984). But see Schauer, *Free Speech and the Demise of the Soapbox* Book Review, 84 Colum.L.Rev. 558, 565 (1984) ("Maybe there is something I am missing, but the first amendment importance of the messages from an automatic teller to the bank's central computer completely escapes me, as does the first amendment importance of the mutual exchange of electronic and visual symbols between me and the Pac–Man machine.").[f]

3. The "time, place, or manner" test set out in *Clark* is differently stated in different cases. For example, *U.S. Postal Service v. Council of Greenburgh,* 453 U.S. 114, 101 S.Ct. 2676, 69 L.Ed.2d 517 (1981), speaks of "adequate" as opposed to "ample" alternative channels of communication, and *City of Renton v. Playtime Theatres, Inc.,* Ch. 3, I infra, transcends the difference by requiring that the restriction not "unreasonably limit" alternative channels of communication. Beyond these differences, a number of cases state that the regulation must serve a significant government interest without stating that it must be "narrowly tailored" to serve a significant government interest. See e.g., *Heffron v. International Soc. for Krishna Consciousness,* Ch. 6, I, A infra. But see *Ward v. Rock Against Racism,* Ch. 6, I, A infra (reaffirming and defining "narrowly tailored" aspect of the test).

4. Assuming sleeping in the *Clark* context implicates first amendment values, what test should apply?

———

New York Public Health law authorizes the forced closure of a building for one year if it has been used for the purpose of "lewdness, assignation or prostitution." Pursuant to this statute, a civil complaint alleged that prostitution solicitation and sexual activities by patrons were occurring on the premises of an adult bookstore all within the observation of the proprietor. Accordingly, the complaint called for the closure of the building for one year. There was no claim that any books in the store were obscene. The New York Court of Appeals held that the closure remedy violated the first amendment because it was broader than necessary to achieve the restriction against illicit sexual activities. It reasoned that an injunction against the alleged sexual conduct could further the state interest without infringing on first amendment values.

f. See Post, *Recuperating First Amendment Doctrine,* 47 Stan.L.Rev. 1249 (1995) (speech in its ordinary language sense has no inherent constitutional value and should be defined to include only those social practices which implicate free speech values).

Cf. Fish, *There's No Such Thing as Free Speech,* 102 (1994) (" 'Free speech' is just the name we give to verbal behavior that serves the substantive agendas we wish to advance").

ARCARA v. CLOUD BOOKS, INC., 478 U.S. 697, 106 S.Ct. 3172, 92 L.Ed.2d 568 (1986), per BURGER, C.J., reversed, holding that the closure remedy did not violate the first amendment; indeed, that the closure remedy did not require any first amendment scrutiny: "This Court has applied First Amendment scrutiny to a statute regulating conduct which has the incidental effect of burdening the expression of a particular political opinion. *United States v. O'Brien.* * * *

"We have also applied First Amendment scrutiny to some statutes which, although directed at activity with no expressive component, impose a disproportionate burden upon those engaged in protected First Amendment activities. In *Minneapolis Star & Tribune v. Minnesota Commissioner of Revenue,* 460 U.S. 575, 103 S.Ct. 1365, 75 L.Ed.2d 295 (1983), we struck down a tax imposed on the sale of large quantities of newsprint and ink because the tax had the effect of singling out newspapers to shoulder its burden. We imposed a greater burden of justification on the State even though the tax was imposed upon a nonexpressive activity, since the burden of the tax inevitably fell disproportionately—in fact, almost exclusively— upon the shoulders of newspapers exercising the constitutionally protected freedom of the press. Even while striking down the tax in *Minneapolis Star,* we emphasized: 'Clearly, the First Amendment does not prohibit all regulation of the press. It is beyond dispute that the States and the Federal Government can subject newspapers to generally applicable economic regulations without creating constitutional problems.'

"The New York Court of Appeals held that the *O'Brien* test for permissible governmental regulation was applicable to this case because the closure order sought by petitioner would also impose an incidental burden upon respondents' bookselling activities. That court ignored a crucial distinction between the circumstances presented in *O'Brien* and the circumstances of this case: unlike the symbolic draft card burning in *O'Brien,* the sexual activity carried on in this case manifests absolutely no element of protected expression.[a] In *Paris Adult Theatre,* we underscored the fallacy of seeking to use the First Amendment as a cloak for obviously unlawful public sexual conduct by the diaphanous device of attributing protected expressive attributes to that conduct. First Amendment values may not be invoked by merely linking the words 'sex' and 'books.'

"Nor does the distinction drawn by the New York Public Health Law inevitably single out bookstores or others engaged in First Amendment protected activities for the imposition of its burden, as did the tax struck down in *Minneapolis Star.* As we noted in *Minneapolis Star,* neither the press nor booksellers may claim special protection from governmental regulations of general applicability simply by virtue of their First Amendment protected activities. If the city imposed closure penalties for demonstrated

---

a. In an earlier section of the opinion, Burger, C.J., stated that, "petitioners in *O'Brien* had, as respondents here do not, at least the semblance of expressive activity in their claim that the otherwise unlawful burning of a draft card was to 'carry a message' of the actor's opposition to the draft."

Fire Code violations or health hazards from inadequate sewage treatment, the First Amendment would not aid the owner of premises who had knowingly allowed such violations to persist. * * *

"It is true that the closure order in this case would require respondents to move their bookselling business to another location. Yet we have not traditionally subjected every criminal and civil sanction imposed through legal process to 'least restrictive means' scrutiny simply because each particular remedy will have some effect on the First Amendment activities of those subject to sanction. Rather, we have subjected such restrictions to scrutiny only where it was conduct with a significant expressive element that drew the legal remedy in the first place, as in *O'Brien,* or where a statute based on a nonexpressive activity has the inevitable effect of singling out those engaged in expressive activity, as in *Minneapolis Star.* This case involves neither situation, and we conclude the First Amendment is not implicated by the enforcement of a public health regulation of general application against the physical premises in which respondents happen to sell books."[b]

O'CONNOR, J., joined by Stevens, J., concurred: "I agree that the Court of Appeals erred in applying a First Amendment standard of review where, as here, the government is regulating neither speech nor an incidental, nonexpressive effect of speech. Any other conclusion would lead to the absurd result that any government action that had some conceivable speech-inhibiting consequences, such as the arrest of a newscaster for a traffic violation, would require analysis under the First Amendment. If, however, a city were to use a nuisance statute as a pretext for closing down a book store because it sold indecent books or because of the perceived secondary effects of having a purveyor of such books in the neighborhood, the case would clearly implicate First Amendment concerns and require analysis under the appropriate First Amendment standard of review. Because there is no suggestion in the record or opinion below of such pretextual use of the New York nuisance provision in this case, I concur in the Court's opinion and judgment."

BLACKMUN, J., joined by Brennan and Marshall, JJ., dissented: "Despite the obvious role that commercial bookstores play in facilitating free expression, the Court today concludes that a closure order would raise no First Amendment concerns, apparently because it would be triggered, not by respondents' sale of books, but by the nonexpressive conduct of patrons. But the First Amendment, made applicable to the States by the Fourteenth Amendment, protects against all laws 'abridging the freedom of speech'—not

---

b. On remand, the New York Court of Appeals held that, in the absence of a showing that the state had chosen a course no broader than necessary to accomplish its purpose, any forced closure of the bookstore would unduly impair the bookseller's rights of free expression under the New York State constitution. From New York's perspective, the question is not "who is aimed at but who is hit." See *People ex rel. Arcara v. Cloud Books, Inc.,* 68 N.Y.2d 553, 510 N.Y.S.2d 844, 503 N.E.2d 492 (1986). But see *Alexander v. United States,* 509 U.S. 544, 113 S.Ct. 2766, 125 L.Ed.2d 441 (1993)(confiscation and destruction of protected materials for distribution of obscene materials does not violate first amendment).

just those specifically directed at expressive activity. Until today, this Court has never suggested that a State may suppress speech as much as it likes, without justification, so long as it does so through generally applicable regulations that have 'nothing to do with any expressive conduct.' * * *

"At some point, of course, the impact of state regulation on First Amendment rights become so attenuated that it is easily outweighed by the state interest. But when a State directly and substantially impairs First Amendment activities, such as by shutting down a bookstore, I believe that the State must show, at a minimum, that it has chosen the least restrictive means of pursuing its legitimate objectives. The closure of a bookstore can no more be compared to a traffic arrest of a reporter than the closure of a church could be compared to the traffic arrest of its clergyman.

"A State has a legitimate interest in forbidding sexual acts committed in public, including a bookstore. An obvious method of eliminating such acts is to arrest the patron committing them. But the statute in issue does not provide for that. Instead, it imposes absolute liability on the bookstore simply because the activity occurs on the premises. And the penalty—a mandatory 1–year closure—imposes an unnecessary burden on speech. Of course 'linking the words "sex" and "books" 'is not enough to extend First Amendment protection to illegal sexual activity, but neither should it suffice to *remove* First Amendment protection from books situated near the site of such activity. The State's purpose in stopping public lewdness cannot justify such a substantial infringement of First Amendment rights. * * *

"Petitioner has not demonstrated that a less restrictive remedy would be inadequate to abate the nuisance. The Court improperly attempts to shift to the bookseller the responsibility for finding an alternative site. But surely the Court would not uphold a city ordinance banning all public debate on the theory that the residents could move somewhere else. [Because] the statute is not narrowly tailored to further the asserted governmental interest, it is unconstitutional as applied to respondents."

Notes and Questions

1. Should the state's closing of a bookstore *always* trigger heightened judicial scrutiny? Is the first amendment really "not implicated" in *Arcara?* Should fire code regulations trigger first amendment scrutiny? Consider Comment, *Padlock Orders and Nuisance Laws,* 51 Albany L.Rev. 1007, 1026–27 (1987): "Closure penalties for fire code violations or health hazards from inadequate sewage treatment were offered as examples of generally applicable regulations which could constitutionally be applied to bookstores where the owner 'had knowingly allowed such violations to persist.' Few would argue with this conclusion. These generally applicable regulations would be within the state's constitutional power, would further a substantial

governmental interest unrelated to the suppression of free expression, and the incidental restriction on first amendment freedoms, where the owner knowingly allowed the violations to persist, would be no greater than is essential to further the state's interest. Concluding that the *O'Brien* test is satisfied, however, does not support the conclusion that the test does not apply."

2. *Negative theory.* Should the scope of the first amendment be confined to instances in which government may have acted in a biased way? Consider Cass, *Commercial Speech, Constitutionalism, Collective Choice,* 56 U.Cin.L.Rev. 1317, 1352 (1988): "The root concern for first amendment prohibitions on abridgement of speech and press freedom is official bias. There is widespread agreement that limitation of official bias is the principal aim of the first amendment, historically and as amplified over the past half-century by the courts." See generally Cass, *The Perils of Positive Thinking: Constitutional Interpretation and Negative First Amendment Theory,* 34 U.C.L.A. L.Rev. 1405 (1987) (emphasizing official self interest and, to a lesser extent, intolerance as the principal motives of concern).

Professor Schauer has also attempted a justification for freedom of speech not based on any positive aspects of speech,[c] but based on the premise that governments are "less capable of regulating speech than they are of regulating other forms of conduct." Schauer, *Free Speech: A Philosophical Enquiry* 81 (1982). See also Schauer, *Must Speech Be Special?,* 78 Nw. U.L.Rev. 1284 (1983). He suggests that bias, self-interest, and a general urge to suppress that with which one disagrees are significant reasons for this incapability. See *Free Speech,* supra, at 80–86. As he interprets the first amendment, therefore, its "focus * * * is on the motivations of the government." Schauer, *Cuban Cigars, Cuban Books, and the Problem of Incidental Restrictions on Communications,* 26 Wm. & Mary L.Rev. 779, 780 (1985).

Is negative theory consistent with what the Court has *said* about free speech? With the doctrine it has produced? Consider, e.g., *Arcara. O'Brien.* The defamation line of cases. Compare Schauer, *Cuban Cigars,* supra with Shiffrin, *The First Amendment, Democracy, and Romance* (1990). Is the content-based/content-neutral distinction founded exclusively on a concern with government motive? See generally Stone, *Content Regulation and the First Amendment,* 25 Wm. & Mary L.Rev. 189 (1983) (arguing that the basis for the distinction is more complicated). Does an emphasis on motive or content unreasonably downplay the notion that the *effect* of government conduct on the quantity or quality of speech is of independent first amendment value? See generally Redish, *The Content Distinction in First Amendment Analysis,* 34 Stan.L.Rev. 113 (1981); see also Schauer, *The Phenomenology of Speech and Harm,* 103 Ethics 635 (1993)(disputing the hypothesis that the harmful consequences of speech are less than those associated with

c. Compare Williams, *Content Discrimination and the First Amendment,* 139 U.Pa. L.Rev. 201 (1991).

other forms of conduct); Schauer, *The Sociology of the Hate Speech Debate,* 37 Vill.L.Rev. 805 (1992).

3.   Could *Arcara's* failure to find the first amendment implicated be justified without resort to negative theory or motive theory? Consider Tribe, *American Constitutional Law* 978–79 n. 2 (2d ed. 1988): "[W]hen *neither* the law, *nor* the act triggering its enforcement has any significant first amendment dimension,[d] the fact that the law *incidentally* operates to restrict first amendment activity, and that some alternative state measure might offer a less restrictive means of pursuing the state's legitimate objectives, should not serve to condemn what the state has done as unconstitutional." Why not?

d. For relevant commentary, see Dorf, *Incidental Burdens on Fundamental Rights,* 109 Harv. L. Rev. 1175 (1996).

Chapter 3

IS SOME PROTECTED SPEECH LESS EQUAL THAN OTHER PROTECTED SPEECH?

I. NEAR OBSCENE SPEECH

YOUNG v. AMERICAN MINI THEATRES, INC.

427 U.S. 50, 96 S.Ct. 2440, 49 L.Ed.2d 310 (1976).

MR. JUSTICE STEVENS delivered the opinion of the Court.*

[Detroit "Anti–Skid Row" ordinances prohibited "adult motion picture theaters" and "adult book stores" within 1,000 feet of any two other "regulated uses," which included such theaters and book stores, liquor stores, pool halls, pawnshops, and the like. The ordinances defined "adult motion picture theater" as one "presenting material distinguished or characterized by an emphasis on matter depicting, describing or relating to 'Specified Sexual Activities'[a] or 'Specified Anatomical Areas' "[b] and "adult book store" in substantially the same terms. The Court upheld the ordinances, reversing a decision in a federal declaratory judgment action by two theater owners wishing regularly to exhibit "adult" motion pictures.]

I. [R]espondents claim that the ordinances are too vague [because] they cannot determine how much of the ["specified"] activity may be

---

* Part III of this opinion is joined only by The Chief Justice, Mr. Justice White, and Mr. Justice Rehnquist.

a. "Specified Sexual Activities" were defined thus:

"1. Human Genitals in a state of sexual stimulation or arousal;

"2. Acts of human masturbation, sexual intercourse or sodomy;

"3. Fondling or other erotic touching of human genitals, pubic region, buttock or female breast."

b. "Specified Anatomical Areas" were defined thus:

"1. Less than completely and opaquely covered: (a) human genitals, pubic region, (b) buttock, and (c) female breast below a point immediately above the top of the areola, and

"2. Human male genitals in a discernibly turgid state, even if completely and opaquely covered."

---

permissible before the exhibition is "characterized by an emphasis" on such matter. [We] find it unnecessary to consider the validity of [this argument. Both] theaters propose to offer adult fare on a regular basis. [Therefore], the element of vagueness in these ordinances has not affected these respondents. * * *

Because the ordinances affect communication protected by the First Amendment, respondents argue that they may raise the vagueness issue even though there is no uncertainty about the impact of the ordinances on their own rights. On several occasions we have determined that a defendant whose own speech was unprotected had standing to challenge the constitutionality of a statute which purported to prohibit protected speech, or even speech arguably protected. *Broadrick*. The exception is justified by the overriding importance of maintaining a free and open market for the interchange of ideas. Nevertheless, if the statute's deterrent effect of legitimate expression is not "both real and substantial" and if the statute is "readily subject to a narrowing construction by the state courts" the litigant is not permitted to assert the rights of third parties.

We are not persuaded that the Detroit Zoning Ordinances will have a significant deterrent effect on the exhibition of films protected by the First Amendment. [T]he only vagueness in the ordinances relates to the amount of sexually explicit activity that may be portrayed before the material can be said to be "characterized by an emphasis" on such matter. For most films the question will be readily answerable; to the extent that an area of doubt exists, we see no reason why the statute is not "readily subject to a narrowing construction by the state courts." Since there is surely a less vital interest in the uninhibited exhibition of material that is on the border line between pornography and artistic expression than in the free dissemination of ideas of social and political significance,[c] and since the limited amount of uncertainty in the statute is easily susceptible of a narrowing construction, we think this is an inappropriate case in which to adjudicate the hypothetical claims of persons not before the Court. * * *

II.   [T]he ordinances prohibit theaters which are not licensed as "adult motion picture theaters" from exhibiting films which are protected by the First Amendment. Respondents argue that the ordinances are therefore invalid as prior restraints on free speech. The ordinances are not challenged on the ground that they impose a limit on the total number of adult theaters which may operate in the city of Detroit. There is no claim that distributors

---

c. But see Hunter & Law, Ch. 1, VI, B supra, at 119–20: "[S]exual speech is political. One core insight of modern feminism is that the personal is political. The question of who does the dishes and rocks the cradle affects both the nature of the home and the composition of the legislature. The dynamics of intimate relations are likewise political, both to the individuals involved and by their multiplied effects to the wider society. To argue [that] sexually explicit speech is less important than other categories of discourse reinforces the conceptual structures that have identified women's concerns with relationships and intimacy as less significant and valuable precisely because those concerns are falsely regarded as having no bearing on the structure of social and political life."

or exhibitors of adult films are denied access to the market or conversely, that the viewing public is unable to satisfy its appetite for sexually explicit fare. Viewed as an entity, the market for this commodity is essentially unrestrained.

It is true, however, that adult films may only be exhibited commercially in licensed theaters. But that is also true of all motion pictures. The city's general zoning laws require all motion picture theaters to satisfy certain locational as well as other requirements; we have no doubt that the municipality may control the location of theaters as well as the location of other commercial establishments, either by confining them to certain specified commercial zones or by requiring that they be dispersed throughout the city. The mere fact that the commercial exploitation of material protected by the First Amendment is subject to zoning and other licensing requirements is not a sufficient reason for invalidating these ordinances.

Putting to one side for the moment the fact that adult motion picture theaters must satisfy a locational restriction not applicable to other theaters, we are also persuaded that the 1,000–foot restriction does not, in itself, create an impermissible restraint on protected communication. The city's interest in planning and regulating the use of property for commercial purposes is clearly adequate to support that kind of restriction applicable to all theaters within the city limits. In short, apart from the fact that the ordinances treat adult theaters differently from other theaters and the fact that the classification is predicated on the content of material shown in the respective theaters, the regulation of the place where such films may be exhibited does not offend the First Amendment. We turn, therefore, to the question whether the classification is consistent with the Equal Protection Clause.

III. [T]he use of streets and parks for the free expression of views on national affairs may not be conditioned upon the sovereign's agreement with what a speaker may intend to say. [If] picketing in the vicinity of a school is to be allowed to express the point of view of labor, that means of expression in that place must be allowed for other points of view as well. As we said in [*Chicago Police Dep't v. Mosley,* Ch. 6, I, B infra], "The central problem with Chicago's ordinance is that it describes permissible picketing in terms of its subject matter. [A]bove all else, the First Amendment means that government has no power to restrict expression because of its message, its ideas, its subject matter, or its content. [Any] restriction on expressive activity because of its content would completely undercut the 'profound national commitment to the principle that debate on public issues should be uninhibited, robust, and wide-open.' [*New York Times*]. Selective exclusions from a public forum may not be based on content alone, and may not be justified by reference to content alone."

This statement, and others to the same effect, read literally and without regard for the facts of the case in which it was made, would absolutely preclude any regulation of expressive activity predicated in whole or in part on the content of the communication. But we learned long ago that broad statements of principle, no matter how correct in the context in which they are made, are sometimes qualified by contrary decisions before the absolute limit of the stated principle is reached. When we review this Court's actual adjudications in the First Amendment area, we find this to have been the case with the stated principle that there may be no restriction whatever on expressive activity because of its content. * * *

The question whether speech is, or is not, protected by the First Amendment often depends on the content of the speech. Thus, the line between permissible advocacy and impermissible incitation to crime or violence depends, not merely on the setting in which the speech occurs, but also on exactly what the speaker had to say. Similarly, it is the content of the utterance that determines whether it is a protected epithet or an unprotected "fighting comment." * * *.

Even within the area of protected speech, a difference in content may require a different governmental response. [*New York Times*] held that a public official may not recover damages from a critic of his official conduct without proof of "malice" as specially defined in that opinion. Implicit in the opinion is the assumption that if the content of the newspaper article had been different—that is, if its subject matter had not been a public official—a lesser standard of proof would have been adequate. [We] have recently held that the First Amendment affords some protection to commercial speech. [The] measure of [protection] to commercial speech will surely be governed largely by the content of the communication.[32] * * *

More directly in point are opinions dealing with the question whether the First Amendment prohibits the state and federal governments from wholly suppressing sexually oriented materials on the basis of their "obscene character." In *Ginsberg*, the Court upheld a conviction for selling to a minor magazines which were concededly not "obscene" if shown to adults. Indeed, the Members of the Court who would accord the greatest protection to such materials have repeatedly indicated that the State could prohibit the distribution or exhibition of such materials to juveniles and consenting adults. Surely the First Amendment does not foreclose such a prohibition; yet it is equally clear that any such prohibition must rest squarely on an appraisal of the content of material otherwise within a constitutionally protected area.

Such a line may be drawn on the basis of content without violating the Government's paramount obligation of neutrality in its regulation of protected communication. For the regulation of the places where sexually explicit films may be exhibited is unaffected by whatever social, political, or philosophical message the film may be intended to communicate; whether the

---

32. As Mr. Justice Stewart pointed out in *Virginia Pharmacy*, Ch. 3, II infra], the "differences between commercial price and product advertising [and] ideological communication" permits regulation of the former that the First Amendment would not tolerate with respect to the latter (concurring opinion).

motion picture ridicules or characterizes one point of view or another, the effect of the ordinances is exactly the same.

Moreover, even though we recognize that the First Amendment will not tolerate the total suppression of erotic materials that have some arguably artistic value, it is manifest that society's interest in protecting this type of expression is of a wholly different, and lesser, magnitude than the interest in untrammeled political debate that inspired Voltaire's immortal comment.[d] Whether political oratory or philosophical discussion moves us to applaud or to despise what is said, every school-child can understand why our duty to defend the right to speak remains the same. But few of us would march our sons and daughters off to war to preserve the citizen's right to see "Specified Sexual Activities" exhibited in the theaters of our choice. Even though the First Amendment protects communication in this area from total suppression, we hold that the State may legitimately use the content of these materials as the basis for placing them in a different classification from other motion pictures.

The remaining question is whether the line drawn by these ordinances is justified by the city's interest in preserving the character of its neighborhoods. [The] record discloses a factual basis for the Common Council's conclusion that this kind of restriction will have the desired effect.[34] It is not our function to appraise the wisdom of its decision to require adult theaters to be separated rather than concentrated in the same areas. In either event, the city's interest in attempting to preserve the quality of urban life is one that must be accorded high respect. Moreover, the city must be allowed a reasonable opportunity to experiment with solutions to admittedly serious problems.

Since what is ultimately at stake is nothing more than a limitation on the place where adult films may be exhibited,[35] even though the determination of whether a particular film fits that characterization turns on the nature of its content, we conclude that the city's interest in the present and future character of its neighborhoods adequately supports its classification of motion pictures. * * *

MR. JUSTICE POWELL, concurring in the judgment and portions of the opinion.

---

d. The opinion had earlier quoted Voltaire: "I disapprove of what you say, but I will defend to the death your right to say it."

34. The City Council's determination was that a concentration of "adult" movie theaters causes the area to deteriorate and become a focus of crime, effects which are not attributable to theaters showing other types of films. It is this secondary effect which this zoning ordinance attempts to avoid, not the dissemination of "offensive" speech. In contrast, in *Erznoznik v. City of Jacksonville,* 422 U.S. 205, 95 S.Ct. 2268, 45 L.Ed.2d 125 (1975) [holding invalid an ordinance prohibiting drive-in theaters from showing films containing nudity], the justifications offered by the city rested primarily on the city's interest in protecting its citizens from exposure to unwanted, "offensive" speech. * * *

35. The situation would be quite different if the ordinance had the effect of suppressing, or greatly restricting access to, lawful speech. Here, however, the District Court specifically found that "[t]he Ordinances do not affect the operation of existing establishments but only the location of new ones. There are myriad locations in the City of Detroit which must be over 1000 feet from existing regulated establishments. This burden on First Amendment rights is slight." * * *

Although I agree with much of what is said in the plurality opinion, and concur in Parts I and II, my approach to the resolution of this case is sufficiently different to prompt me to write separately.[1] I view the case as presenting an example of innovative land-use regulation, implicating First Amendment concerns only incidentally and to a limited extent. * * *

In this case, there is no indication that the application of the Anti–Skid Row Ordinance to adult theaters has the effect of suppressing production of or, to any significant degree, restricting access to adult movies. Nortown concededly will not be able to exhibit adult movies at its present location, and the ordinance limits the potential location of the proposed Pussy Cat. The constraints of the ordinance with respect to location may indeed create economic loss for some who are engaged in this business. But in this respect they are affected no differently than any other commercial enterprise that suffers economic detriment as a result of land-use regulation. The cases are legion that sustained zoning against claims of serious economic damage.

The inquiry for First Amendment purposes is not concerned with economic impact; rather, it looks only to the effect of this ordinance upon freedom of expression. This prompts essentially two inquiries: (i) does the ordinance impose any content limitation on the creators of adult movies or their ability to make them available to whom they desire, and (ii) does it restrict in any significant way the viewing of these movies by those who desire to see them? On the record in this case, these inquiries must be answered in the negative. At most the impact of the ordinance on these interests is incidental and minimal.[2] Detroit has silenced no message, has invoked no censorship, and has imposed no limitation upon those who wish to view them. The ordinance is addressed only to the places at which this type of expression may be presented, a restriction that does not interfere with content. Nor is there any significant overall curtailment of adult movie presentations, or the opportunity for a message to reach an audience. On the basis of the District Court's finding, it appears that if a sufficient market exists to support them the number of adult movie theaters in Detroit will remain approximately the same, free to purvey the same message. To be sure some prospective patrons may be inconvenienced by this dispersal. But other patrons, depending upon where they live or work, may find it more convenient to view an adult movie when adult theaters are not concentrated in a particular section of the city.

In these circumstances, it is appropriate to analyze the permissibility of Detroit's action under the four-part test of *United States v. O'Brien* [p. 203

---

1. I do not think we need reach, nor am I inclined to agree with, the holding in Part III (and supporting discussion) that nonobscene, erotic materials may be treated differently under First Amendment principles from other forms of protected expression. I do not consider the conclusions in Part I of the opinion to depend on distinctions between protected speech.

2. The communication involved here is not a kind in which the content or effectiveness of the message depends in some measure upon where or how it is conveyed. * * *

supra]. Under that test, a governmental regulation is sufficiently justified, despite its incidental impact upon First Amendment interests, "if it is within the constitutional power of the Government; if it furthers an important government interest; if the government interest is unrelated to the suppression of free expression; and if the incidental restriction [on] First Amendment freedoms is no greater than is essential to the furtherance of that interest." [Powell, J., concluded that the Detroit ordinance satisfied the *O'Brien* test.]

MR. JUSTICE STEWART, with whom MR. JUSTICE BRENNAN, MR. JUSTICE MARSHALL and MR. JUSTICE BLACKMUN join, dissenting.

[This case involves] the constitutional permissibility of selective interference with protected speech whose content is thought to produce distasteful effects. It is elementary that a prime function of the First Amendment is to guard against just such interference. By refusing to invalidate Detroit's ordinance the Court rides roughshod over cardinal principles of First Amendment law, which require that time, place and manner regulations that affect protected expression be content-neutral except in the limited context of a captive or juvenile audience. In place of these principles the Court invokes a concept wholly alien to the First Amendment. Since "few of us would march our sons and daughters off to war to preserve the citizen's right to see 'Specified Sexual Activities' exhibited in the theaters of our choice," the Court implies that these films are not entitled to the full protection of the Constitution. This stands "Voltaire's immortal comment," on its head. For if the guarantees of the First Amendment were reserved for expression that more than a "few of us" would take up arms to defend, then the right of free expression would be defined and circumscribed by current popular opinion. The guarantees of the Bill of Rights were designed to protect against precisely such majoritarian limitations on individual liberty.

The fact that the "offensive" speech here may not address "important" topics—"ideas of social and political significance," in the Court's terminology—does not mean that it is less worthy of constitutional protection. "Wholly neutral futilities [come] under the protection of free speech as fully as do Keats' poems or Donne's sermons." *Winters* (Frankfurter, J., dissenting), accord, *Cohen v. California*. Moreover, in the absence of a judicial determination of obscenity, it is by no means clear that the speech is not "important" even on the Court's terms [*Roth; Kingsley Pictures*].

I can only interpret today's decision as an aberration. The Court is undoubtedly sympathetic, as am I, to the well-intentioned efforts of Detroit to "clean up" its streets and prevent the proliferation of "skid rows." But it is in those instances where protected speech grates most unpleasantly against the sensibilities that judicial vigilance must be at its [height].

The factual parallels between [*Erznoznik* and this case] are striking. There, as here, the ordinance did not forbid altogether the "distasteful" expression but merely required an alteration in the physical setting of the forum. There, as here, the city's principal asserted interest was in minimizing the "undesirable" effects of speech having a particular content. [And] the particular content of the restricted speech at issue in *Erznoznik* precisely parallels the content restricted in [Detroit's] definition of "Specified Anatomical Areas." * * *

The Court must never forget that the consequences of rigorously enforcing the guarantees of the First Amendment are frequently unpleasant. Much speech that seems to be of little or no value will enter the marketplace of ideas, threatening the quality of our social discourse and, more generally, the serenity of our lives. But that is the price to be paid for constitutional freedom. * * *[e]

Notes and Questions

1. *A hierarchy of protected speech.* Stevens, J., contends that as a matter of law some "protected" speech is less worthy than other protected speech. The dissenters and Powell, J., reject that view. Which approach is more likely to preserve first amendment values? Would treating all protected speech equally invite a dilution of the force of the first amendment with respect to the speech that "really" matters? Is the process of allowing judges to pick and choose between types of protected speech too dangerous? Would it be dangerous to protect political speech more than sexually explicit speech? Is sexually explicit speech non-political? If the plaintiff's approach were accepted, would the Court ultimately "rank speech in all its myriad forms, in order of its perceived importance," with new rankings being "created and old ones rejected depending on the Court's view of the worthiness of the speech at issue"? Goldman, *A Doctrine of Worthier Speech: Young v. American Mini Theatres, Inc.,* 21 St. Louis U.L.J. 281, 300–01 (1977).

2. *The exhibitor's free expression.* Did Powell, J., assume that the "first amendment rights [involved] in *Young* were primarily vested in creator and audience"? Note, 42 Mo.L.Rev. 461, 468 (1977); Note, 28 Case W.Res.L.Rev. 456, 482 (1978). Does the plurality opinion and its fn. 35 reflect similar lack of concern for exhibitor's interests? How would a record be built to distinguish *Young* from a similar ordinance in another city?

3. *Exclusionary zoning. Schad v. Mt. Ephraim,* 452 U.S. 61, 101 S.Ct. 2176, 68 L.Ed.2d 671 (1981) invalidated a Borough ordinance that permitted adult theaters and bookstores, but excluded live entertainment from its commercial zone. Even as applied to nude dancing, the Court found that the ordinance was not narrowly drawn to serve a sufficiently substantial state

e. Blackmun, J., joined by the other three dissenters, also filed a dissent that protested the rejection of the vagueness argument, concluding on this issue: "As to the third reason, that 'adult' material is simply entitled to less protection, it certainly explains the lapse in applying settled vagueness principles, as indeed it explains this whole case. In joining Mr. Justice Stewart I have joined his forthright rejection of the notion that First Amendment protection is diminished for 'erotic materials' that only a 'few of us' see the need to protect."

interest.[f] The Court observed that there was no evidence to show that the entertainment at issue was available in reasonably nearby areas. What if it were? Suppose the Borough banned adult theaters and bookstores, but could show they were available nearby?

————

RENTON v. PLAYTIME THEATRES, INC., 475 U.S. 41, 106 S.Ct. 925, 89 L.Ed.2d 29 (1986), per REHNQUIST, J., upheld a zoning ordinance that prohibited adult motion picture theaters from locating within 1,000 feet of any residential zone, church, park, or school. The effect was to exclude such theaters from approximately 94% of the land in the city. Of the remaining 520 acres, a substantial part was occupied by a sewage disposal and treatment plant, a horse racing track and environs, a warehouse and manufacturing facilities, a Mobile Oil tank farm, and a fully-developed shopping center: "[T]he resolution of this case is largely dictated by our decision in *Young*. There, although five Members of the Court did not agree on a single rationale for the decision, we held that the city of Detroit's zoning ordinance, which prohibited locating an adult theater within 1,000 feet of any two other 'regulated uses' or within 500 feet of any residential zone, did not violate the First and Fourteenth Amendments. The Renton ordinance, like the one in *Young*, does not ban adult theaters altogether, but merely provides that such theaters may not be located within 1,000 feet of any residential zone, single-or multiple-family dwelling, church, park, or school. The ordinance is therefore properly analyzed as a form of time, place, and manner regulation.

"Describing the ordinance as a time, place, and manner regulation is, of course, only the first step in our inquiry. This Court has long held that regulations enacted for the purpose of restraining speech on the basis of its content presumptively violate the First Amendment. See *Chicago Police Dept. v. Mosley*, Ch. 6, I, B infra.[a] On the other hand, so-called 'content-neutral' time, place, and manner regulations are acceptable so long as they are designed to serve a substantial governmental interest and do not unreasonably limit alternative avenues of communication.[b]

"At first glance, the Renton ordinance, like the ordinance in *Young*, does not appear to fit neatly into either the 'content-based' or the 'content-

f. But cf. *City of Newport v. Iacobucci*, 479 U.S. 92, 107 S.Ct. 383, 93 L.Ed.2d 334 (1986) (upholding ordinance prohibiting nude or nearly nude dancing in establishments serving liquor).

a. *Mosley* involved an ordinance that banned picketing near a school building except the "peaceful picketing of any school involved in a labor dispute." The Court stated: "The regulation '[slips] from the

neutrality of time, place, and circumstance into a concern about content.' This is never permitted."

b. Compare the statement of the time, place, and manner test in *Clark*, Ch. 2 supra. For commentary, see Day, *The Hybridization of the Content–Neutral Standards for the Free Speech Clause*, 19 Ariz. St.L.J. 195 (1987).

neutral' category. To be sure, the ordinance treats theaters that specialize in adult films differently from other kinds of theaters. Nevertheless, [the] City Council's *'predominate* concerns' were with the secondary effects of adult theaters, and not with the content of adult films themselves. * * *

"[This] finding as to 'predominate' intent is more than adequate to establish that the city's pursuit of its zoning interests here was unrelated to the suppression of free expression.[c] The ordinance by its terms is designed to prevent crime, protect the city's retail trade, maintain property values,[d] and generally 'protec[t] and preserv[e] the quality of [the city's] neighborhoods, commercial districts, and the quality of urban life,' not to suppress the expression of unpopular views. As Justice Powell observed in *Young,* '[i]f [the city] had been concerned with restricting the message purveyed by adult theaters, it would have tried to close them or restrict their number rather than circumscribe their choice as to location.'

"In short, the [ordinance] does not contravene the fundamental principle that underlies our concern about 'content-based' speech regulations: that 'government may not grant the use of a forum to people whose views it finds acceptable, but deny use to those wishing to express less favored or more controversial views.' *Mosley.*

"It was with this understanding in mind that, in *Young,* a majority of this Court decided that at least with respect to businesses that purvey sexually explicit materials,[2] zoning ordinances designed to combat the undesirable secondary effects of such businesses are to be reviewed under the standards applicable to 'content-neutral' time, place, and manner regulations.

"The appropriate inquiry in this case, then, is whether the Renton ordinance is designed to serve a substantial governmental interest and allows for reasonable alternative avenues of communication."

After concluding that the ordinance was designed to serve substantial government interests, the Court ruled that the Renton ordinance allowed "for reasonable alternative avenues of communication": "[W]e note that the

---

c. The court of appeals had held that a finding of predominate intent was inadequate, and would have remanded for the district court to determine whether a "motivating factor" to restrict the exercise of first amendment rights was present. In response, the Court interpreted the court of appeals opinion to require the invalidation of the ordinance if such a motive were found to be present "apparently no matter how small a part this motivating factor may have played in the City Council's decision." This view of the law, the Court continued, "was rejected in *United States v. O'Brien*: 'It is a familiar principle of constitutional law that this Court will not strike down an otherwise constitutional statute on the ba-

sis of an alleged illicit legislative motive. [What] motivates one legislator to make a speech about a statute is not necessarily what motivates scores of others to enact it, and the stakes are sufficiently high for us to eschew guesswork.' "

d. For support, see Clarke, *Freedom of Speech and the Problems of the Lawful Harmful Public Reaction,* 20 Akron L.Rev. 187 (1986).

2. See *Young* (plurality opinion) ("[I]t is manifest that society's interest in protecting this type of expression is of a wholly different, and lesser, magnitude than the interest in untrammeled political debate * * *.").

ordinance leaves some 520 acres, or more than five percent of the entire land area of Renton, open to use as adult theater sites. [Respondents] argue, however, that some of the land in question is already occupied by existing businesses, that 'practically none' of the undeveloped land is currently for sale or lease, and that in general there are no 'commercially viable' adult theater sites within the 520 acres left open by the Renton ordinance. The Court of Appeals accepted these arguments, concluded that the 520 acres was not truly 'available' land, and therefore held that the Renton ordinance 'would result in a substantial restriction' on speech.

"We disagree with both the reasoning and the conclusion of the Court of Appeals. That respondents must fend for themselves in the real estate market, on an equal footing with other prospective purchasers and lessees, does not give rise to a First Amendment violation. And although we have cautioned against the enactment of zoning regulations that have 'the effect of suppressing, or greatly restricting access to, lawful speech,' *Young,* fn. 35 (plurality opinion), we have never suggested that the First Amendment compels the Government to ensure that adult theaters, or any other kinds of speech-related businesses for that matter, will be able to obtain sites at bargain prices. [T]he First Amendment requires only that Renton refrain from effectively denying respondents a reasonable opportunity to open and operate an adult theater within the city, and the ordinance before us easily meets this requirement. * * * [4]"e

BRENNAN, J., joined by Marshall, J., dissented: "The fact that adult movie theaters may cause harmful 'secondary' land use effects may arguably give Renton a compelling reason to regulate such establishments; it does not mean, however, that such regulations are content-neutral. * * *

"The ordinance discriminates on its face against certain forms of speech based on content. Movie theaters specializing in 'adult motion pictures' may not be located within 1,000 feet of any residential zone, single-or multiple-family dwelling, church, park, or school. Other motion picture theaters, and other forms of 'adult entertainment,' such as bars, massage parlors, and adult bookstores, are not subject to the same restrictions. This selective treatment strongly suggests that Renton was interested not in controlling the 'secondary effects' associated with adult businesses, but in discriminating against adult theaters based on the content of the films they exhibit. [Moreover,] many of the City Council's 'findings' do not relate to legitimate land use concerns. As the Court of Appeals observed, '[b]oth the magistrate and the district court recognized that many of the stated reasons for the

---

4. * * * We reject respondents' "vagueness" argument for the same reasons that led us to reject a similar challenge in *Young.* There, the Detroit ordinance applied to theaters "used to present material distinguished or characterized by an emphasis on [sexually explicit matter]." We held that "even if there may be some uncertainty about the effect of the ordinances on other litigants, they are unquestionably applicable to these respondents." We also held that the Detroit ordinance created no "significant deterrent effect" that might justify invocation of the First Amendment "overbreadth" doctrine.

e. Blackmun, J., concurred in the result without opinion.

ordinance were no more than expressions of dislike for the subject matter.'[3] That some residents may be offended by the *content* of the films shown at adult movie theaters cannot form the basis for state regulation of speech. See *Terminiello v. Chicago.*

"Some of the 'findings' [do] relate to supposed 'secondary effects' associated with adult movie theaters[4] [but they were added by the City Council only after this law suit was filed and the Court should not] accept these post-hoc statements at face value. [As] the Court of Appeals concluded, '[t]he record presented by Renton to support its asserted interest in enacting the zoning ordinance is very thin.' * * *[5] * * *[7]

"Even assuming that the ordinance should be treated like a content-neutral time, place, and manner restriction, I would still find it unconstitutional. [T]he ordinance is invalid because it does not provide for reasonable alternative avenues of communication.[f] [R]espondents do not ask Renton to guarantee low-price sites for their businesses, but seek, only a reasonable opportunity to operate adult theaters in the city. By denying them this opportunity, Renton can effectively ban a form of protected speech from its

3. For example, "finding" number 2 states that "[l]ocation of adult entertainment land uses on the main commercial thoroughfares of the City gives an impression of legitimacy to, and causes a loss of sensitivity to the adverse effect of pornography upon children, established family relations, respect for marital relationship and for the sanctity of marriage relations of others, and the concept of non-aggressive, consensual sexual relations."

"Finding" number 6 states that "[l]ocation of adult land uses in close proximity to residential uses, churches, parks, and other public facilities, and schools, will cause a degradation of the community standard of morality. Pornographic material has a degrading effect upon the relationship between spouses."

4. For example, "finding" number 12 states that "[l]ocation of adult entertainment land uses in proximity to residential uses, churches, parks and other public facilities, and schools, may lead to increased levels of criminal activities, including prostitution, rape, incest and assaults in the vicinity of such adult entertainment land uses."

5. As part of the amendment passed after this lawsuit commenced, the City Council added a statement that it had intended to rely on the Washington Supreme Court's opinion in *Northend Cinema, Inc. v. Seattle,* 90 Wash.2d 709, 585 P.2d 1153 (1978), cert. denied, 441 U.S. 946, 99 S.Ct. 2166, 60 L.Ed.2d 1048 (1979), which upheld Seattle's

zoning regulations against constitutional attack. Again, despite the suspicious coincidental timing of the amendment, the Court holds that "Renton was entitled to rely [on] the 'detailed findings' summarized in [the] *Northend Cinema* opinion." In *Northend Cinema,* the court noted that "[t]he record is replete with testimony regarding the effects of adult movie theater locations on residential neighborhoods." The opinion however, does not explain the evidence it purports to summarize, and provided no basis for determining whether Seattle's experience is relevant to Renton's.

7. As one commentator has noted: "[A]nyone with any knowledge of human nature should naturally assume that the decision to adopt almost any content-based restriction might have been affected by an antipathy on the part of at least some legislators to the ideas or information being suppressed. The logical assumption, in other words, is not that there is not improper motivation but, rather, because legislators are only human, that there is a substantial risk that an impermissible consideration has in fact colored the deliberative process." Stone, *Restrictions on Speech Because of its Content: The Peculiar Case of Subject–Matter Restrictions,* 46 U.Chi. L.Rev. 81, 106 (1978).

f. Brennan, J., argued that the ordinance also failed as an acceptable time, place, and manner restriction because it was not narrowly tailored to serve a significant governmental interest.

borders. The ordinance 'greatly restrict[s] access to, lawful speech,' *Young* (plurality opinion), and is plainly unconstitutional."

Notes and Questions

1. Does *Renton*—see fn. 2—endorse a hierarchy of categories among types of protected speech? Consider Tribe, *American Constitutional Law* 939 n. 66 (2d ed. 1988): "[I]t is doubtful that *Renton* can fairly be read as endorsing the concept of a hierarchy of intermediate categories, because the case turned on the majority's characterization of the restriction as content-neutral, and the issue of the relative importance of the speech involved, was, strictly speaking, irrelevant." But cf. Prygoski, *Low Value Speech: From Young to Fraser*, 32 St. Louis Univ.L.J. 317, 345 (1987) (despite the content-neutral language, "antipathy toward the kind of expression involved" swayed the case).

2. Was the ordinance fairly characterized as content-neutral? Is the focus on "secondary effects" convincing? Consider Stone, *Content–Neutral Restrictions*, 54 U.Chi.L.Rev. 46, 115–117 (1987): "[T]he ordinance in *Renton* was not defended in terms of its communicative impact—at least in the sense that the city's concerns did not implicate either of the constitutionally disfavored justifications ordinarily associated with communicative impact. But the Court had never before *Renton* suggested that the absence of a constitutionally disfavored justification is in itself a justification for treating an expressly content-based restriction as if it were content-neutral. To the contrary, with the single exception of *Renton*, the Court in such circumstances has always invoked the stringent standards of content-based review.

"[I]n *New York v. Ferber*[, for example], the Court treated as content-based a law prohibiting 'child pornography,' even though the government defended the law not in terms of communicative impact, but on the ground that the law was necessary to protect children who participate in 'sexual performances.' * * *

"[I]f taken seriously, and extended to other contexts, the Court's transmogrification in *Renton* of an expressly content-based restriction into one that is content-neutral threatens to undermine the very foundation of the content-based/content-neutral distinction. This would in turn erode the coherence and predictability of first amendment doctrine. One can only hope that this aspect of *Renton* is soon forgotten."

But cf. Farber & Frickey, *The Jurisprudence of Public Choice*, 65 Texas L.Rev. 873 (1987): "*[Renton]* appears to adopt the view that the government generally may take into account the content of speech when channeling speech, but may only rarely consider content when the purpose is censorship. We believe that in doing so *Renton* merely states explicitly what was implicit in a long line of prior cases."

Are subject matter restrictions as a class less problematic than other forms of content discrimination in that they often do not discriminate on the basis of point of view? Should *Renton's* secondary effects emphasis be limited to subject-matter-based restrictions? See Note, *The Content Distinction in Free Speech Analysis After Renton,* 102 Harv.L.Rev. 1904 (1989). Even if some subject matter restrictions are less problematic, is the Renton ordinance neutral as to point of view? Consider Stone, *Restrictions of Speech Because of its Content: The Peculiar Case of Subject–Matter Restrictions,* 46 U.Chi.L.Rev. 81, 111–12 (1978): "[T]he speech suppressed by restrictions such as those involved in [cases like *Erznoznik* and *Young*] will almost invariably carry an implicit, if not explicit, message in favor of more relaxed sexual mores. Such restrictions, in other words, have a potent viewpoint-differential impact. [I]n our society, the very presence of sexual explicitness in speech seems ideologically significant, without regard to whatever other messages might be intended. To treat such restrictions as viewpoint-neutral seems simply to ignore reality. Finally, [a] large percentage of citizens apparently feel threatened by nonobscene, sexually-explicit speech and believe it to be morally reprehensible. If it were not for the Court's relatively narrow construction of the obscenity concept, much of this speech would undoubtedly be banned outright. Thus, any restriction along these lines will carry an extraordinarily high risk that its enactment was tainted by this fundamentally illegitimate consideration. Such restrictions, although superficially viewpoint-neutral, pose a uniquely compelling case for content-based scrutiny." Are feminist or neo-conservative objections to near obscene speech both "fundamentally illegitimate." Should all content-based scrutiny be the same? Does *Renton* reconstruct the Court's "narrow construction of the obscenity concept?"

Is the concept of viewpoint neutrality itself problematic? Consider Sunstein, *Pornography and the First Amendment,* 1986 Duke L.J. 589, 615: "One does not 'see' a viewpoint-based restriction when the harms invoked in defense of a regulation are obvious and so widely supported by social consensus that they allay any concern about impermissible government motivation. Whether a classification is viewpoint-based thus ultimately turns on the viewpoint of the decision maker." See generally MacKinnon, *Feminism, Marxism, Method, and the State,* 7 Signs 515, 535–36 (1981).

3. *Renton's* "secondary effects" notion was revisited by several justices in *Boos v. Barry,* Ch. 2 supra. A District of Columbia ordinance banned the display of any sign within 500 feet of a foreign embassy that would tend to bring the embassy into "public odium" or "public disrepute." O'CONNOR, J., joined by Stevens and Scalia, JJ., distinguished *Renton:* "Respondents and the United States do not point to the 'secondary effects' of picket signs in front of embassies. They do not point to congestion, to interference with ingress or egress, to visual clutter, or to the need to protect the security of embassies. Rather, they rely on the need to protect the dignity of foreign diplomatic personnel by shielding them from speech that is critical of their governments. This justification focuses *only* on the content of the speech and the direct impact that speech has on its listeners. The emotive impact of speech on its audience is not a 'secondary effect.'[g] Because the display clause

regulates speech due to its potential primary impact, we conclude it must be considered content-based."[h]

BRENNAN, J., joined by Marshall, J., agreed with the conclusion that the ordinance was content-based, but objected to O'Connor, J.'s "assumption that the *Renton* analysis applies not only outside the context of businesses purveying sexually explicit materials but even to political speech.[i]

———

Five years after *Renton*, the Court held that an Indiana statute prohibiting the knowing or intentional appearing in a public place in a state of nudity could constitutionally be applied to require that any female dancer at a minimum wear "pasties" and a "G-string" when she dances. *Barnes v. Glen Theatre, Inc.*, 501 U.S. 560, 111 S.Ct. 2456, 115 L.Ed.2d 504 (1991). The Justices upholding the ordinance were divided upon the rationale for doing so. Rehnquist, C.J., joined by O'Connor and Kennedy, JJ., applied the *O'Brien* test, characterized the statute as a "public indecency" statute, and concluded that the interests in order and morality justified the statute. Souter, J., concurring, also applied the *O'Brien* test, but concluded that the statute was justified by the "secondary effects" of prostitution, sexual assaults, and other criminal activity even though he recognized that the secondary effects justification had not been articulated by the Indiana legislature or its courts. Scalia, J., argued against the plurality that the interest in morality was not substantial enough to pass muster under *O'Brien*; nonetheless, he voted to uphold the statute by repudiating the *O'Brien* test. He argued that when a general law is directed at conduct, not specifically against expression, it is subject to no first amendment test even

g. See *Forsyth County v. The National-ist Movement*, 505 U.S. 123, 112 S.Ct. 2395, 120 L.Ed.2d 101 (1992)("Listener's reaction to speech is not a content-neutral basis for regulation,"—not secondary effects).

h. In an earlier passage O'Connor, J., responded to the argument that the ordinance was not content-based on the theory that the government was not selecting between viewpoints. The argument was instead that "the permissible message on a picket sign is determined solely by the policies of a foreign government. We reject this contention, although we agree the provision is not viewpoint-based. The display clause determines which viewpoint is acceptable in a neutral fashion by looking to the policies of foreign governments. While this prevents the display clause from being directly viewpoint-based, a label with potential First Amendment ramifications of its own, it does not render the statute content-neutral. Rather, we have held that a regulation that 'does not favor either side of a political

controversy' is nonetheless impermissible because the 'First Amendment's hostility to content-based regulation extends ... to prohibition of public discussion of an entire topic.' Here the government has determined that an entire category of speech—signs or displays critical of foreign governments—is not to be permitted."

For a review of secondary effects doctrine, see Prygoski, *The Supreme Court's "Secondary Effects" Analysis in Free Speech Cases*, 61 Cooley L.Rev. 1 (1989).

i. Rehnquist, J., joined by White and Blackmun, JJ., voted to uphold the ordinance on the basis of Bork, J.'s opinion below in *Finzer v. Barry*, 798 F.2d 1450 (D.C.Cir.1986). Bork, J., stated that the need to adhere to principles of international law might constitute a secondary effect under *Renton* but was not "entirely sure" whether *Renton* alone could dictate that result and did not resolve the issue. Id. at 1469–70 n. 15.

if it is applied against expression. White, joined by Marshall, Blackmun, and Stevens, J., dissenting, argued that the Indiana statute was directed at expression and did not survive close scrutiny.

The fragmented character of the *Barnes* majority created interpretive difficulties for the Pennsylvania Supreme Court in considering an ordinance of Erie, Pennsylvania. Like Indiana, Erie, Pennsylvania, enacted an ordinance making it a offense to knowingly or intentionally appear in public in a "state of nudity." Unlike Indiana, however, the Erie city council made it clear that nude dancing was a special concern in its passage of the ordinance. The preamble to the ordinance stated that "Council specifically wishes to adopt the concept of Public Indecency prohibited by the laws of the State of Indiana, which was approved by the U.S. Supreme Court in *Barnes v. Glen Theatre Inc.,* * * * for the purpose of limiting a recent increase in nude live entertainment within the City" which led to prostitution and other crime.

Pap's A.M., a Pennsylvania corporation, operated "Kandyland," an Erie establishment featuring nude erotic dancing by women. To comply with the ordinance, as written, these dancers had to wear, at a minimum, "pasties" and a "G-string." Pap's filed suit against Erie and city officials, seeking declaratory relief and a permanent injunction against the ordinance's enforcement. The Pennsylvania Supreme Court was unable to find a lowest common denominator uniting the *Barnes* majority; so it felt free to reach an independent judgment, and proceeded to find that the Erie ordinance, although also directed at secondary effects, was primarily directed at expression and did not survive close scrutiny.

ERIE v. PAP'S A.M., 529 U.S. 277, 120 S.Ct. 1382, 146 L.Ed.2d 265 (2000), per O'Connor, J., joined by Rehnquist, C.J., Kennedy, and Breyer, JJ., concluded that the application of the ordinance to prevent nude dancing was constitutional:[a] "Being 'in a state of nudity' is not an inherently expressive condition. As we explained in *Barnes*, however, nude dancing of the type at issue here is expressive conduct, although we think that it falls only within the outer ambit of the First Amendment's protection. * * *

"In *Barnes*, we analyzed an almost identical statute, holding that Indiana's public nudity ban did not violate the First Amendment, although no five Members of the Court agreed on a single rationale for that conclusion. We now clarify that government restrictions on public nudity such as the ordinance at issue here should be evaluated under the framework set forth in *O'Brien* for content-neutral restrictions on symbolic speech. * * *

"The ordinance here, like the statute in *Barnes*, is on its face a general prohibition on public nudity. By its terms, the ordinance regulates conduct alone. It does not target nudity that contains an erotic message; rather, it

a. O'Connor, J., rebuffed a contention that the case was moot. Scalia, J., joined by Thomas, J., would have sustained the moot-ness claim. Stevens, J., joined by Ginsburg, J., did not address the issue.

bans all public nudity, regardless of whether that nudity is accompanied by expressive activity. And like the statute in *Barnes*, the Erie ordinance replaces and updates provisions of an 'Indecency and Immorality' ordinance that has been on the books since 1866, predating the prevalence of nude dancing establishments such as Kandyland. * * *

"Although the Pennsylvania Supreme Court acknowledged that one goal of the ordinance was to combat the negative secondary effects associated with nude dancing establishments, the court concluded that the ordinance was nevertheless content based, relying on Justice White's position in dissent in *Barnes* for the proposition that a ban of this type *necessarily* has the purpose of suppressing the erotic message of the dance. Because the Pennsylvania court agreed with Justice White's approach, it concluded that the ordinance must have another, 'unmentioned' purpose related to the suppression of expression. That is, the Pennsylvania court adopted the dissent's view in *Barnes* that '[s]ince the State permits the dancers to perform if they wear pasties and G-strings but forbids nude dancing, it is precisely because of the distinctive, expressive content of the nude dancing performances at issue in this case that the State seeks to apply the statutory prohibition.'A majority of the Court rejected that view in *Barnes*, and we do so again here.

"Respondent's argument that the ordinance is 'aimed' at suppressing expression through a ban on nude dancing—an argument that respondent supports by pointing to statements by the city attorney that the public nudity ban was not intended to apply to 'legitimate' theater productions—is really an argument that the city council also had an illicit motive in enacting the ordinance. As we have said before, however, this Court will not strike down an otherwise constitutional statute on the basis of an alleged illicit motive. In light of the Pennsylvania court's determination that one purpose of the ordinance is to combat harmful secondary effects, the ban on public nudity here is no different from the ban on burning draft registration cards in *O'Brien*, where the Government sought to prevent the means of the expression and not the expression of antiwar sentiment itself.

"Justice Stevens argues that the ordinance enacts a complete ban on expression. We respectfully disagree with that characterization. The public nudity ban certainly has the effect of limiting one particular means of expressing the kind of erotic message being disseminated at Kandyland. But simply to define what is being banned as the 'message' is to assume the conclusion. We did not analyze the regulation in *O'Brien* as having enacted a total ban on expression. Instead, the Court recognized that the regulation against destroying one's draft card was justified by the Government's interest in preventing the harmful 'secondary effects' of that conduct (disruption to the Selective Service System), even though that regulation may have some incidental effect on the expressive element of the conduct. Because this justification was unrelated to the suppression of O'Brien's antiwar message, the regulation was content neutral. Although there may be cases in which banning the means of expression so interferes with the message that it essentially bans the message, that is not the case here. * * *

"Similarly, even if Erie's public nudity ban has some minimal effect on the erotic message by muting that portion of the expression that occurs when the last stitch is dropped, the dancers at Kandyland and other such establishments are free to perform wearing pasties and G-strings. Any effect on the overall expression is *de minimis*. And as *Justice Stevens* eloquently stated for the plurality in *Young* v. *American Mini Theatres, Inc.,* 'even though we recognize that the First Amendment will not tolerate the total suppression of erotic materials that have some arguably artistic value, it is manifest that society's interest in protecting this type of expression is of a wholly different, and lesser, magnitude than the interest in untrammeled political debate,' and 'few of us would march our sons or daughters off to war to preserve the citizen's right to see' specified anatomical areas exhibited at establishments like Kandyland. If States are to be able to regulate secondary effects, then *de minimis* intrusions on expression such as those at issue here cannot be sufficient to render the ordinance content based.

"This case is, in fact, similar to *O'Brien, Community for Creative Non–Violence,* and *Ward.* The justification for the government regulation in each case prevents harmful 'secondary' effects that are unrelated to the suppression of expression. See, *e.g., Ward* v. *Rock Against Racism* (noting that '[t]he principal justification for the sound-amplification guideline is the city's desire to control noise levels at bandshell events, in order to retain the character of [the adjacent] Sheep Meadow and its more sedate activities,' and citing *Renton* for the proposition that '[a] regulation that serves purposes unrelated to the content of expression is deemed neutral, even if it has an incidental effect on some speakers or messages but not others'). While the doctrinal theories behind 'incidental burdens' and 'secondary effects' are, of course, not identical, there is nothing objectionable about a city passing a general ordinance to ban public nudity (even though such a ban may place incidental burdens on some protected speech) and at the same time recognizing that one specific occurrence of public nudity—nude erotic dancing—is particularly problematic because it produces harmful secondary effects.

"[W]e conclude that Erie's ordinance is justified under *O'Brien.* [E]rie's efforts to protect public health and safety are clearly within the city's police powers. * * * The asserted interests of regulating conduct through a public nudity ban and of combating the harmful secondary effects associated with nude dancing are undeniably important. And in terms of demonstrating that such secondary effects pose a threat, the city need not 'conduct new studies or produce evidence independent of that already generated by other cities' to demonstrate the problem of secondary effects, 'so long as whatever evidence the city relies upon is reasonably believed to be relevant to the problem that the city addresses.' *Renton.* * * * Erie could reasonably rely on the evidentiary foundation set forth in *Renton* and *American Mini Theatres* to the effect that secondary effects are caused by the presence of even one adult entertainment establishment in a given neighborhood. See *Renton* (indicating that reliance on a judicial opinion that describes the evidentiary basis is sufficient). In fact, Erie expressly relied on *Barnes* and its discussion of secondary effects, including its reference to *Renton* and *American Mini Theatres.* * * *

"In any event, Erie also relied on its own findings. The preamble to the ordinance states that 'the Council of the City of Erie *has, at various times over more than a century, expressed its findings* that certain lewd, immoral activities carried on in public places for profit are highly detrimental to the public health, safety and welfare, and lead to the debasement of both women and men, promote violence, public intoxication, prostitution and other serious criminal activity.' The city council members, familiar with commercial downtown Erie, are the individuals who would likely have had first-hand knowledge of what took place at and around nude dancing establishments in Erie, and can make particularized, expert judgments about the resulting harmful secondary effects. * * *

"Justice Souter, however, would require Erie to develop a specific evidentiary record supporting its ordinance[,] and he agrees that the ordinance should therefore be evaluated under *O'Brien*. *O'Brien*, of course, required no evidentiary showing at all that the threatened harm was real. But that case is different, Justice Souter contends, because in *O'Brien* 'there could be no doubt' that a regulation prohibiting the destruction of draft cards would alleviate the harmful secondary effects flowing from the destruction of those cards.

"But whether the harm is evident to our 'intuition,' is not the proper inquiry. If it were, we would simply say there is no doubt that a regulation prohibiting public nudity would alleviate the harmful secondary effects associated with nude dancing. * * * Justice Souter attempts to denigrate the city council's conclusion that the threatened harm was real, arguing that we cannot accept Erie's findings because the subject of nude dancing is 'fraught with some emotionalism,' Yet surely the subject of drafting our citizens into the military is 'fraught' with more emotionalism than the subject of regulating nude dancing.

"As to [whether] the regulation furthers the government interest—it is evident that, since crime and other public health and safety problems are caused by the presence of nude dancing establishments like Kandyland, a ban on such nude dancing would further Erie's interest in preventing such secondary effects. To be sure, requiring dancers to wear pasties and G-strings may not greatly reduce these secondary effects, but *O'Brien* requires only that the regulation further the interest in combating such effects. [It may] be true that a pasties and G-string requirement would not be as effective as, for example, a requirement that the dancers be fully clothed, but the city must balance its efforts to address the problem with the requirement that the restriction be no greater than necessary to further the city's interest.

"[The requirement that the restriction be] no greater than is essential to the furtherance of the government interest—is satisfied as well. The ordinance regulates conduct, and any incidental impact on the expressive element of nude dancing is *de minimis*. The requirement that dancers wear pasties and G-strings is a minimal restriction in furtherance of the asserted government interests, and the restriction leaves ample capacity to convey the dancer's erotic message. Justice Souter points out that zoning is an alternative means of addressing this problem. It is far from clear, however, that zoning imposes less of a burden on expression than the minimal requirement implemented here. In any event, since this is a content-neutral restriction, least restrictive means analysis is not required.

"We hold, therefore, that Erie's ordinance is a content-neutral regulation that is valid under *O'Brien*. Accordingly, the judgment of the Pennsylvania Supreme Court is reversed, and the case is remanded for further proceedings not inconsistent with this opinion."

SCALIA, J., joined by Thomas., J., concurred: "I agree that the decision of the Pennsylvania Supreme Court must be reversed, but disagree with the mode of analysis the Court has applied. The city of Erie self-consciously modeled its ordinance on the public nudity statute we upheld against constitutional challenge in *Barnes*. [In] *Barnes*, I voted to uphold the challenged Indiana statute 'not because it survives some lower level of First Amendment scrutiny, but because, as a general law regulating conduct and not specifically directed at expression, it is not subject to First Amendment scrutiny at all.' Erie's ordinance, too, by its terms prohibits not merely nude dancing, but the act—irrespective of whether it is engaged in for expressive purposes—of going nude in public. The facts that a preamble to the ordinance explains that its purpose, in part, is to 'limi[t] a recent increase in nude live entertainment,' that city councilmembers in supporting the ordinance commented to that effect, and that the ordinance includes in the definition of nudity the exposure of devices simulating that condition, neither make the law any less general in its reach nor demonstrate that what the municipal authorities *really* find objectionable is expression rather than public nakedness. As far as appears (and as seems overwhelmingly likely), the preamble, the councilmembers' comments, and the chosen definition of the prohibited conduct simply reflect the fact that Erie had recently been having a public nudity problem not with streakers, sunbathers or hot-dog vendors, but with lap dancers.

"There is no basis for the contention that the ordinance does not apply to nudity in theatrical productions such as Equus or Hair. Its text contains no such limitation. It was stipulated in the trial court that no effort was made to enforce the ordinance against a production of Equus involving nudity that was being staged in Erie at the time the ordinance became effective. Notwithstanding Justice Stevens' assertion to the contrary, however, neither in the stipulation, nor elsewhere in the record, does it appear that the city was aware of the nudity—and before this Court counsel for the city attributed nonenforcement not to a general exception for theatrical productions, but to the fact that no one had complained. One instance of nonenforcement—against a play already in production that prosecutorial discretion might reasonably have 'grandfathered'—does not render this ordinance discriminatory on its face. To be sure, in the trial court counsel for the city said that '[t]o the extent that the expressive activity that is contained in [such] productions rises to a higher level of protected expression, they would not be [covered],'—but he rested this assertion upon the provision in the preamble that expressed respect for 'fundamental Constitutional guarantees of free speech and free expression.' [What] he was saying there [was] essentially what he said at oral argument before this Court: that the ordinance would not be enforceable against theatrical productions if the Constitution forbade it. Surely that limitation does not cause the ordinance to be not generally applicable, in the relevant sense of being *targeted* against expressive conduct.

"Moreover, even were I to conclude that the city of Erie had specifically singled out the activity of nude dancing, I still would not find that this regulation violated the First Amendment unless I could be persuaded (as on this record I cannot) that it was the communicative character of nude dancing that prompted the ban. When conduct other than speech itself is regulated, it is my view that the First Amendment is violated only '[w]here the government prohibits conduct precisely because of its communicative attributes.' Here, even if one hypothesizes that the city's object was to suppress only nude dancing, that would not establish an intent to suppress what (if anything) nude dancing communicates. I do not feel the need, as the Court does, to identify some 'secondary effects' associated with nude dancing that the city could properly seek to eliminate. (I am highly skeptical, to tell the truth, that the addition of pasties and g-strings will at all reduce the tendency of establishments such as Kandyland to attract crime and prostitution, and hence to foster sexually transmitted disease.) The traditional power of government to foster good morals (bonos mores), and the acceptability of the traditional judgment (if Erie wishes to endorse it) that nude public dancing *itself* is immoral, have not been repealed by the First Amendment."

SOUTER, J., concurred in part and dissented in part: "I [agree] with the analytical approach that the plurality employs in deciding this case. Erie's stated interest in combating the secondary effects associated with nude dancing establishments is an interest unrelated to the suppression of expression under *O'Brien*, and the city's regulation is thus properly considered under the *O'Brien* standards. I do not believe, however, that the current record allows us to say that the city has made a sufficient evidentiary showing to sustain its [regulation].

"[I]ntermediate scrutiny requires a regulating government to make some demonstration of an evidentiary basis for the harm it claims to flow from the expressive activity, and for the alleviation expected from the restriction imposed. That evidentiary basis may be borrowed from the records made by other governments if the experience elsewhere is germane to the measure under consideration and actually relied upon. I will assume, further, that the reliance may be shown by legislative invocation of a judicial opinion that accepted an evidentiary foundation as sufficient for a similar regulation. What is clear is that the evidence of reliance must be a matter of demonstrated fact, not speculative supposition.

"By these standards, the record before us today is deficient in its failure to reveal any evidence on which Erie may have relied, either for the seriousness of the threatened harm or for the efficacy of its chosen remedy. The plurality does the best it can with the materials to hand, but the pickings are slim. [T]he ordinance's preamble assert[s] that over the course of more than a century the city council had expressed 'findings' of detrimental secondary effects flowing from lewd and immoral profitmaking activity in public places. But however accurate the recital may be and however honestly the councilors may have held those conclusions to be true over the years, the recitation does not get beyond conclusions on a subject usually fraught with some emotionalism. [T]he invocation of *Barnes* in one paragraph of the preamble to Erie's ordinance [does not] suffice. The plurality opinion in *Barnes* made no mention of evidentiary showings at all, and though my separate opinion did make a pass at the issue, I did not demand reliance on germane evidentiary demonstrations, whether specific to the statute in question or developed elsewhere. To invoke *Barnes*, therefore, does not indicate that the issue of evidence has been addressed.

"There is one point, however, on which an evidentiary record is not quite so hard to find, but it hurts, not helps, the city. The final *O'Brien* requirement is that the incidental speech restriction be shown to be no greater than essential to achieve the government's legitimate purpose. To deal with this issue, we have to ask what basis there is to think that the city would be unsuccessful in countering any secondary effects by the significantly lesser restriction of zoning to control the location of nude dancing, thus allowing for efficient law enforcement, restricting effects on property values, and limiting exposure of the public. The record shows that for 23 years there has been a zoning ordinance on the books to regulate the location of establishments like Kandyland, but the city has not enforced it. [Even] on the plurality's view of the evidentiary burden, this hurdle to the application of *O'Brien* requires an evidentiary response. * * *

"Careful readers, and not just those on the Erie City Council, will of course realize that my partial dissent rests on a demand for an evidentiary basis that I failed to make when I concurred in *Barnes*. I should have demanded the evidence then, too, and my mistake calls to mind Justice Jackson's foolproof explanation of a lapse of his own, when he quoted Samuel Johnson, 'Ignorance, sir, ignorance.' *McGrath* v. *Kristensen*, 340 U.S. 162, 178, 71 S.Ct. 224, 95 L.Ed. 173 (1950) (concurring opinion). I may not be less ignorant of nude dancing than I was nine years ago, but after many subsequent occasions to think further about the needs of the First Amendment, I have come to believe that a government must toe the mark more carefully than I first insisted.''

STEVENS, J., joined by Ginsburg, J., dissented: ''Far more important than the question whether nude dancing is entitled to the protection of the First Amendment are the dramatic changes in legal doctrine that the Court endorses today. Until now, the 'secondary effects' of commercial enterprises featuring indecent entertainment have justified only the regulation of their location. For the first time, the Court has now held that such effects may justify the total suppression of protected speech. Indeed, the plurality opinion concludes that admittedly trivial advancements of a State's interests may provide the basis for censorship. The Court's commendable attempt to replace the fractured decision in *Barnes* with a single coherent rationale is strikingly unsuccessful; it is supported neither by precedent nor by persuasive reasoning.

''As the preamble to Ordinance No. 75–1994 candidly acknowledges, the council of the city of Erie enacted the restriction at issue 'for the purpose of limiting a recent increase in nude live entertainment within the City.' Prior to the enactment of the ordinance, the dancers at Kandyland performed in the nude. As the Court recognizes, after its enactment they can perform precisely the same dances if they wear 'pasties and G-strings.' In both instances, the erotic messages conveyed by the dancers to a willing audience are a form of expression protected by the First Amendment. Despite the similarity between the messages conveyed by the two forms of dance, they are not identical.

''If we accept Chief Judge Posner's evaluation of this art form, see *Miller* v. *South Bend*, 904 F.2d 1081, 1089–1104 (7th Cir.1990) (en banc), the difference between the two messages is significant. The plurality assumes, however, that the difference in the content of the message resulting from the mandated costume change is '*de minimis.*' Although I suspect that the patrons of Kandyland are more likely to share Chief Judge Posner's view than the plurality's, for present purposes I shall accept the assumption that the difference in the message is small. The crucial point to remember, however, is that whether one views the difference as large or small, nude dancing still receives First Amendment protection, even if that protection lies only in the 'outer ambit' of that Amendment. Erie's ordinance, therefore, burdens a message protected by the First Amendment. If one assumes that the same erotic message is conveyed by nude dancers as by those wearing minuscule costumes, one means of expressing that message is banned;[2] if one assumes that the messages are different, one of those messages is banned. In either event, the ordinance is a total ban.

''The Court relies on the so-called 'secondary effects' test to defend the ordinance. The present use of that rationale, however, finds no support

2. Although nude dancing might be described as one protected ''means'' of conveying an erotic message, it does not follow that a protected message has not been totally banned simply because there are oth- er, similar ways to convey erotic messages. A State's prohibition of a particular book, for example, does not fail to be a total ban simply because other books conveying a similar message are available.

whatsoever in our precedents. Never before have we approved the use of that doctrine to justify a total ban on protected First Amendment expression. On the contrary, we have been quite clear that the doctrine would not support that end. * * *3 * * *4

"The reason we have limited our secondary effects cases to zoning and declined to extend their reasoning to total bans is clear and straightforward: A dispersal that simply limits the places where speech may occur is a minimal imposition whereas a total ban is the most exacting of restrictions. The State's interest in fighting presumed secondary effects is sufficiently strong to justify the former, but far too weak to support the latter, more severe burden. Yet it is perfectly clear that in the present case—to use Justice Powell's metaphor in *American Mini Theatres*—the city of Erie has totally silenced a message the dancers at Kandyland want to convey. The fact that this censorship may have a laudable ulterior purpose cannot mean that censorship is not censorship. For these reasons, the Court's holding rejects the explicit reasoning in *American Mini Theatres* and *Renton* and the express holding in *Schad*. * * *

"The Court's mishandling of our secondary effects cases is not limited to its approval of a total ban. It compounds that error by dramatically reducing the degree to which the State's interest must be furthered by the restriction imposed on speech, and by ignoring the critical difference between secondary effects caused by speech and the incidental effects on speech that may be caused by a regulation of conduct.

"In what can most delicately be characterized as an enormous understatement, the plurality concedes that 'requiring dancers to wear pasties and G-strings may not greatly reduce these secondary effects.' To believe that the mandatory addition of pasties and a G-string will have *any* kind of

3. The Court contends *Ward* shows that we have used the secondary effects rationale to justify more burdensome restrictions than those approved in *Renton* and *American Mini Theatres*. That argument is unpersuasive for two reasons. First, as in the two cases just mentioned, the regulation in *Ward* was as a time, place, and manner restriction. Second, [*Ward*] is not a secondary effects case.

4. We [held] in *Renton* that in enacting its adult theater zoning ordinance, the city of Renton was permitted to rely on a detailed study conducted by the city of Seattle that examined the relationship between zoning controls and the secondary effects of adult theaters. (It was permitted to rely as well on "the 'detailed findings' summarized" in an opinion of the Washington Supreme Court to the same effect.) Renton, having identified the same problem in its own city as that experienced in Seattle, quite logically drew on Seattle's experience

and adopted a similar solution. But if Erie is relying on the Seattle study as well, its use of that study is most peculiar. After identifying a problem in its own city similar to that in Seattle, Erie has implemented a solution (pasties and G-strings) bearing no relationship to the efficacious remedy identified by the Seattle study (dispersal through zoning).

But the city of Erie, of course, has not in fact pointed to any study by anyone suggesting that the adverse secondary effects of commercial enterprises featuring erotic dancing depends in the slightest on the precise costume worn by the performers—it merely assumes it to be so. If the city is permitted simply to assume that a slight addition to the dancers' costumes will sufficiently decrease secondary effects, then presumably the city can require more and more clothing as long as any danger of adverse effects remains.

noticeable impact on secondary effects requires nothing short of a titanic surrender to the implausible. * * * It is one thing to say [that] *O'Brien* is more lenient than the 'more demanding standard' we have imposed in cases such as *Texas* v. *Johnson*. It is quite another to say that the test can be satisfied by nothing more than the mere possibility of *de minimis* effects on the neighborhood.

"The Court is also mistaken in equating our secondary effects cases with the 'incidental burdens' doctrine applied in cases such as *O'Brien*; and it aggravates the error by invoking the latter line of cases to support its assertion that Erie's ordinance is unrelated to speech. The incidental burdens doctrine applies when ' "speech" ' and "nonspeech" elements are combined in the same course of conduct,' and the government's interest in regulating the latter justifies incidental burdens on the former. *O'Brien*. Secondary effects, on the other hand, are indirect consequences of protected speech and may justify regulation of the places where that speech may occur. See *American Mini Theatres*. When a State enacts a regulation, it might focus on the secondary effects of speech as its aim, or it might concentrate on nonspeech related concerns, having no thoughts at all with respect to how its regulation will affect speech—and only later, when the regulation is found to burden speech, justify the imposition as an unintended incidental consequence. But those interests are not the same, and the Court cannot ignore their differences and insist that both aims are equally unrelated to speech simply because Erie might have 'recogniz[ed]' that it could possibly have had either aim in mind. One can think of an apple and an orange at the same time; that does not turn them into the same fruit.

"Of course, the line between governmental interests aimed at conduct and unrelated to speech, on the one hand, and interests arising out of the effects of the speech, on the other, may be somewhat imprecise in some cases. In this case, however, we need not wrestle with any such difficulty because Erie has expressly justified its ordinance with reference to secondary effects. Indeed, if Erie's concern with the effects of the message were unrelated to the message itself, it is strange that the only means used to combat those effects is the suppression of the message. For these reasons, the Court's argument that 'this case is similar to *O'Brien*,'is quite wrong, as are its citations to *Clark* v. *Community for Creative Non–Violence*, and *Ward*, neither of which involved secondary effects. The Court cannot have its cake and eat it too—either Erie's ordinance was not aimed at speech and the Court may attempt to justify the regulation under the incidental burdens test, or Erie has aimed its law at the secondary effects of speech, and the Court can try to justify the law under that doctrine. But it cannot conflate the two with the expectation that Erie's interests aimed at secondary effects will be rendered unrelated to speech by virtue of this doctrinal polyglot. * * *

"The censorial purpose of Erie's ordinance precludes reliance on the judgment in *Barnes* as sufficient support for the Court's holding today. [As] its preamble forthrightly admits, the ordinance's 'purpose' is to 'limi[t]' a protected form of speech; its invocation of *Barnes* cannot obliterate that professed aim.

"Erie's ordinance differs from the statute in *Barnes* in another respect. [In] an earlier proceeding in this case, the Court of Common Pleas asked Erie's counsel 'what effect would this ordinance have on theater ... productions such as Equus, Hair, O[h!] Calcutta[!]? Under your ordinance would these things be prevented * * *?' Counsel responded: 'No, they wouldn't, Your Honor.' Indeed, as *stipulated* in the record, the city permitted a production of Equus to proceed without prosecution, even after the ordinance was in effect, and despite its awareness of the nudity involved in the production. Even if, in light of its broad applicability, the statute in *Barnes* was not aimed at a particular form of speech, Erie's ordinance is quite different. As presented to us, the ordinance is deliberately targeted at Kandyland's type of nude dancing (to the exclusion of plays like Equus), in terms of both its applicable scope and the city's enforcement.[14]

"This narrow aim is confirmed by the expressed views of the Erie City Councilmembers who voted for the ordinance. The four city councilmembers who approved the measure (of the six total councilmembers) each stated his or her view that the ordinance was aimed specifically at nude adult entertainment, and not at more mainstream forms of entertainment that include total nudity, nor even at nudity in general. One lawmaker observed: 'We're not talking about nudity. We're not talking about the theater or art * * * * We're talking about what is indecent and immoral * * * * We're not prohibiting nudity, we're prohibiting nudity when it's used in a lewd and immoral fashion.' * * * In my view, we need not strain to find consistency with more general purposes when the most natural reading of the record reflects a near obsessive preoccupation with a single target of the law.[16]

"It is clear beyond a shadow of a doubt that the Erie ordinance was a response to a more specific concern than nudity in general, namely, nude dancing of the sort found in Kandyland.[18] Given that the Court has not even

---

14. *Justice Scalia* [states] that even if the ordinance singled out nude dancing, he would not strike down the law unless the dancing was singled out because of its message. He opines that here, the basis for singling out Kandyland is morality. But since the "morality" of the public nudity in Hair is left untouched by the ordinance, while the "immorality" of the public nudity in Kandyland is singled out, the distinction cannot be that "nude public dancing *itself* is immoral." Rather, the only arguable difference between the two is that one's message is more immoral than the other's.

16. The Court dismisses this evidence, declaring that it "will not strike down an otherwise constitutional statute on the basis of an alleged illicit motive."*O'Brien* [said] only that we would not strike down a

law "on the *assumption* that a wrongful purpose or motive has caused the power to be exerted," (emphasis added), and that statement was due to our recognition that it is a 'hazardous matter' to determine the actual intent of a body as large as Congress "on the basis of what fewer than a handful of Congressmen said about [a law]," [We] need not base our inquiry on an "assumption," nor must we infer the collective intent of a large body based on the statements of a few, for we have in the re

18. The Court states that Erie's ordinance merely "replaces and updates provisions of an 'Indecency and Immorality' ordinance" from the mid–19th century, just as the statute in *Barnes* did. * * * The record does indicate that Erie's Ordinance No. 75–1994 updates an older ordinance of similar

tried to defend the ordinance's total ban on the ground that its censorship of protected speech might be justified by an overriding state interest, it should conclude that the ordinance is patently invalid."

Notes and Questions

1. Is Scalia, J., correct in arguing that no first amendment test should apply? Suppose a bookstore is closed for one year because the premises were knowingly used for purposes of prostitution. Is his analysis consistent with the language of *O'Brien*? The holding in *Falwell*? Is *Arcara v. Cloud Books, Inc.*, 478 U.S. 697, 106 S.Ct. 3172, 92 L.Ed.2d 568 (1986) (no first amendment scrutiny; statute directed at prostitution and premises used regardless of other uses) consistent with *Barnes* and *Pap's*?

2. *Is nude dancing speech?* Consider Post, *Recuperating First Amendment Doctrine*, 47 Stan.L.Rev. 1249, 1259 (1995): "[T]he outcome in *Barnes* would have been different if Indiana were to have applied its statute to accepted media for the communication of ideas, as for example by attempting to prohibit nudity in movies or in the theater. Any such prohibition would serve interests deemed highly problematic by fully elaborated principles of First Amendment jurisprudence. Crucial to the result in *Barnes,* then, is the distinction between what the Court is prepared to accept as a medium for the communication of ideas, and its implicit understanding of nude dancing in nightclubs, which at least three of the majority Justices explicitly characterized as merely 'expressive conduct.' "

3. *Law and morals.* Consider Blasi, *Six Conservatives in Search of the First Amendment: The Revealing Case of Nude Dancing,* 33 Wm. and Mary L.Rev. 611, 621–22 (1992): "Can a principled conservative approve the enforcement of morals in the context of group vilification? Can a principled liberal argue that topless dancing is protected by the First Amendment but not the shouting of racial epithets? Important differences between the two categories of speech regulation may exist—hate speech ordinarily is not confined to settings in which every member of the audience has made a choice to receive the message, but hate speech also seems more political in character—but the response of many conservatives to the hate speech issue at least suggests that they do not invariably prefer a narrow interpretation

import. Unfortunately, that old regulation is not in the record. [From] statements of one councilmember, it can reasonably be inferred that the old ordinance was merely a residential zoning restriction, not a total ban. If that is so, it leads to the further question why Erie felt it necessary to shift to a total ban in 1994.

But even if the Court's factual contention is correct, it does not undermine the points

I have made in the text. The inference [of motivation] supposedly rebutted in *Barnes* stemmed from the *timing* of the enactment. Here, however, the inferences I draw depend on the text of the ordinance, its preamble, its scope and enforcement, and the comments of the councilmembers. These do not depend on the timing of the ordinance's enactment.

of the First Amendment and do not always take a broad view of the state's power to enforce morality."

II. COMMERCIAL SPEECH

VIRGINIA STATE BOARD OF PHARMACY v. VIRGINIA CITIZENS CONSUMER COUNCIL

425 U.S. 748, 96 S.Ct. 1817, 48 L.Ed.2d 346 (1976).

Mr. Justice Blackmun delivered the opinion of the Court.

[The Court held invalid a Virginia statute that made advertising the prices of prescription drugs "unprofessional conduct," subjecting pharmacists to license suspension or revocation. Prescription drug prices strikingly varied within the same locality, in Virginia and nationally, sometimes by several hundred percent. Such drugs were dispensed exclusively by licensed pharmacists but 95% were prepared by manufacturers, not compounded by the pharmacists.]

[Appellants] contend that the advertisement of prescription drug prices is outside the protection of the First Amendment because it is "commercial speech." There can be no question that in past decisions the Court has given some indication that commercial speech is unprotected.[a]

Last Term, in *Bigelow v. Virginia,* 421 U.S. 809, 95 S.Ct. 2222, 44 L.Ed.2d 600 (1975), the notion of unprotected "commercial speech" all but passed from the scene. We reversed a conviction for violation of a Virginia statute that made the circulation of any publication to encourage or promote the processing of an abortion in Virginia a misdemeanor. The defendant had published in his newspaper the availability of abortions in New York. The advertisement in question, in addition to announcing that abortions were legal in New York, offered the services of a referral agency in that State. [We] concluded that "the Virginia courts erred in their assumptions that advertising, as such, was entitled to no First Amendment protection," and we observed that the "relationship of speech to the marketplace of products or of services does not make it valueless in the marketplace of ideas."

Some fragment of hope for the continuing validity of a "commercial speech" exception arguably might have persisted because of the subject matter of the advertisement in *Bigelow.* We noted that in announcing the availability of legal abortions in New York, the advertisement "did more than simply propose a commercial transaction. It contained factual material of clear 'public interest.'" And, of course, the advertisement related to

---

a. Starting with *Valentine v. Chrestensen,* 316 U.S. 52, 62 S.Ct. 920, 86 L.Ed. 1262 (1942), the opinion summarized the decisions and dicta that gave such "indication." Long after *Chrestensen,* strong arguments against a first amendment exception for commercial speech had appeared. See Redish, *The First Amendment in the Market Place,* 39 Geo.Wash.L.Rev. 429 (1971); Note, 50 Ore.L.Rev. 177 (1971); cf. Note, 78 Harv.L.Rev. 1191 (1965).

activity with which, at least in some respects, the State could not interfere. Indeed, we observed: "We need not decide in this case the precise extent to which the First Amendment permits regulation of advertising that is related to activities the State may legitimately regulate or even prohibit."[b]

Here, [the] question whether there is a First Amendment exception for "commercial speech" is squarely before us. Our pharmacist does not wish to editorialize on any subject, cultural, philosophical, or political. He does not wish to report any particularly newsworthy fact, or to make generalized observations even about commercial matters. The "idea" he wishes to communicate is simply this: "I will sell you the X prescription drug at the Y price." Our question, then, is whether this communication is wholly outside the protection of the First Amendment.

V. [Speech] does not lose its First Amendment protection because money is spent to project it, as in a paid advertisement of one form or another. *New York Times Co. v. Sullivan.* Speech likewise is protected even though it is carried in a form that is "sold" for profit. *Smith v. California.* [Our] question is whether speech which does "no more than propose a commercial transaction," is so removed from any "exposition of ideas," and from "truth, science, morality, and arts in general, in its diffusion of liberal sentiments on the administration of Government", *Roth,* that it lacks all protection. Our answer is that it is not.

Focusing first on the individual parties to the transaction that is proposed in the commercial advertisement, we may assume that the advertiser's interest is a purely economic one. That hardly disqualifies him for protection under the First Amendment. The interests of the contestants in a labor dispute are primarily economic, but it has long been settled that both the employee and the employer are protected by the First Amendment when they express themselves on the merits of the dispute in order to influence its outcome. * * *[17]

As to the particular consumer's interest in the free flow of commercial information, that interest may be as keen, if not keener by far, than his interest in the day's most urgent political debate.[c] Appellees' case in this

---

b. *Bigelow* continued: "Regardless of the particular label asserted by the State— whether it calls speech 'commercial' or 'commercial advertising' or 'solicitation'—a court may not escape the task of assessing the First Amendment interest at stake and weighing it against the public interest allegedly served by the regulation."

17. The speech of labor disputants, of course, is subject to a number of restrictions. The Court stated in *NLRB v. Gissel Packing Co.,* 395 U.S., at 618, 89 S.Ct., at 1942, 23 L.Ed.2d, at 581 (1969), for example, that an employer's threats of retaliation for the labor actions of his employees are "without the protection of the First Amendment." The constitutionality of re-

strictions upon speech in the special context of labor disputes is not before us here. We express no views on that complex subject, and advert to cases in the labor field only to note that in some circumstances speech of an entirely private and economic character enjoys the protection of the First Amendment.

[For the contention that labor speech receives less protection than commercial speech, see Pope, *The Three–Systems Ladder of First Amendment Values: Two Rungs and a Black Hole,* 11 Hast.Con.L.Q. 189 (1984)].

c. "After all. As the National Enquirer likes to observe, "Inquiring Minds Want to Know." They 'want to know' about the

respect is a convincing one. Those whom the suppression of prescription drug price information hits the hardest are the poor, the sick, and particularly the aged. A disproportionate amount of their income tends to be spent on prescription drugs; yet they are the least able to learn, by shopping from pharmacist to pharmacist, where their scarce dollars are best spent. When drug prices vary as strikingly as they do, information as to who is charging what becomes more than a convenience. It could mean the alleviation of physical pain or the enjoyment of basic necessities.

Generalizing, society also may have a strong interest in the free flow of commercial information. Even an individual advertisement, though entirely "commercial," may be of general public interest. The facts of decided cases furnish illustrations: advertisements stating that referral services for legal abortions are available, *Bigelow;* that a manufacturer of artificial furs promotes his product as an alternative to the extinction by his competitors of fur-bearing mammals, see *Fur Information & Fashion Council, Inc. v. E.F. Timme & Son,* 364 F.Supp. 16 (S.D.N.Y.1973); and that a domestic producer advertises his product as an alternative to imports that tend to deprive American residents of their jobs, cf. *Chicago Joint Board v. Chicago Tribune Co.,* 435 F.2d 470 (C.A.7 1970), cert. denied, 402 U.S. 973 (1971). Obviously, not all commercial messages contain the same or even a very great public interest element. There are few to which such an element, however, could not be added. Our pharmacist, for example, could cast himself as a commentator on store-to-store disparities in drug prices, giving his own and those of a competitor as proof. We see little point in requiring him to do so, and little difference if he does not.

Moreover, there is another consideration that suggests that no line between publicly "interesting" or "important" commercial advertising and the opposite kind could ever be drawn. Advertising, however tasteless and excessive it sometimes may seem, is nonetheless dissemination of information as to who is producing and selling what product, for what reason, and at what price. So long as we preserve a predominantly free enterprise economy, the allocation of our resources in large measure will be made through numerous private economic decisions. It is a matter of public interest that those decisions, in the aggregate, be intelligent and well informed. To this end, the free flow of commercial information is indispensable. And if it is indispensable to the proper allocation of resources in a free enterprise system, it is also indispensable to the formation of intelligent opinions as to how that system ought to be regulated or altered. Therefore, even if the First Amendment were thought to be primarily an instrument to enlighten public decision making in a democracy, we could not say that the free flow of information does not serve that goal.[d]

kind of creme rinse Cindi Lauper uses as much as, perhaps even more than, they want to know whether the CIA may have helped bring down the government in South Vietnam." Van Alstyne, *Remembering Melville Nimmer: Some Cautionary Notes on Commercial Speech,* 43 UCLA L.Rev. 1635 (1996); Consider also Tushnet, *Red, White, and Blue* 290 (1988): "The listener's interest in receiving information, a private interest, thus prevails over a more republican vision of politics, in which political discussion is, at least on the level of public norms, 'keener by far' than private interest."

Arrayed against these substantial individual and societal interests are a number of justifications for the advertising ban. These have to do principally with maintaining a high degree of professionalism on the part of licensed pharmacists. [Price] advertising, it is argued, will place in jeopardy the pharmacist's expertise and, with it, the customer's health. It is claimed that the aggressive price competition that will result from unlimited advertising will make it impossible for the pharmacist to supply professional services in the compounding, handling, and dispensing of prescription drugs. Such services are time-consuming and expensive; if competitors who economize by eliminating them are permitted to advertise their resulting lower prices, the more painstaking and conscientious pharmacist will be forced either to follow suit or to go out of business. [It] is further claimed that advertising will lead people to shop for their prescription drugs among the various pharmacists who offer the lowest prices, and the loss of stable pharmacist-customer relationships will make individual [attention] impossible. Finally, it is argued that damage will be done to the professional image of the pharmacist. This image, that of a skilled and specialized craftsman, attracts talent to the profession and reinforces the better habits of those who are in [it].

The strength of these proffered justifications is greatly undermined by the fact that high professional standards, to a substantial extent, are guaranteed by the close regulation to which pharmacists in Virginia are subject. [At] the same time, we cannot discount the Board's justifications entirely. The Court regarded justifications of this type sufficient to sustain the advertising bans challenged on due process and equal protection [grounds].[e]

The challenge now made, however, is based on the First Amendment. This casts the Board's justifications in a different light, for on close inspection it is seen that the State's protectiveness of its citizens rests in large measure on the advantages of their being kept in ignorance. The advertising ban does not directly affect professional standards one way or the other. It affects them only through the reactions it is assumed people will have to the free flow of drug price information. There is no claim that the advertising

d. Consider Shiffrin, *Dissent, Injustice, and the Meaning of America* 40 (1999): "Suppose that the private allocation of resources is a part of public decision making in a democracy. [Government allocation of resources[, however,] is also part of public decision making in a democracy. That one predominates over the other (for many wealthy corporations, of course, free enterprise is the exception, not the rule) seems quite beside the point. Even if we suppose that commercial advertising is political, protection of 'political speech' in this context seems dramatically less important than in others if all that is at stake is the efficient allocation of resources. Moreover, since gov-ernment frequently departs from the enterprise with constitutional blessing, perhaps the proper allocation of resources as seen by the market should not be privileged at all. [Why] should allocation of resources be a First Amendment worry?" Compare Post, *The Constitutional Status of Commercial Speech*, 48 UCLA L.Rev. 1 (2000)(commercial speech provides information necessary for public decision making though it is not as important as "public discourse."

e. The Court referred here to cases upholding bans on advertising prices for eyeglass frames and optometrist and dental services.

ban in any way prevents the cutting of corners by the pharmacist who is so inclined. That pharmacist is likely to cut corners in any event. The only effect the advertising ban has on him is to insulate him from price competition and to open the way for him to make a substantial, and perhaps even excessive, profit in addition to providing an inferior service. The more painstaking pharmacist is also protected but, again, it is a protection based in large part on public ignorance.

It appears to be feared that if the pharmacist who wishes to provide low cost, and assertedly low quality, services is permitted to advertise, he will be taken up on his offer by too many unwitting customers. They will choose the low-cost, low-quality service and drive the "professional" pharmacist out of business. [They] will go from one pharmacist to another, following the discount, and destroy the pharmacist-customer relationship. They will lose respect for the profession because it advertises. All this is not in their best interests, and all this can be avoided if they are not permitted to know who is charging what.

[A]n alternative to this highly paternalistic[f] approach [is] to assume that this information is not in itself harmful, that people will perceive their own best interests if only they are well enough informed, and that the best means to that end is to open the channels of communication rather than to close them. If they are truly open, nothing prevents the "professional" pharmacist from marketing his own assertedly superior product, and contrasting it with that of the low-cost, high-volume prescription drug retailer. But the choice among these alternative approaches is not ours to make or the Virginia General Assembly's. It is precisely this kind of choice, between the dangers of suppressing information, and the dangers of its misuse if it is freely available, that the First Amendment makes for [us].

VI.   In concluding that commercial speech, like other varieties, is protected, we of course do not hold that it can never be regulated in any way. Some forms of commercial speech regulation are surely permissible. We mention a few. [There] is no claim, for example, that the prohibition on prescription drug price advertising is a mere time, place, and manner restriction. We have often approved restrictions of that kind provided that they are justified without reference to the content of the regulated speech, that they serve a significant governmental interest, and that in so doing they leave open ample alternative channels for communication of the information. Whatever may be the proper bounds of time, place, and manner restrictions on commercial speech, they are plainly exceeded by this Virginia statute,

---

f. Consider Schauer, *The Role of the People in First Amendment Theory,* 74 Calif.L.Rev. 761, 788 (1986): "We ought to recognize that popular control over nonpolitical speech may in some circumstances be a bad idea and address directly just why this is so. Perhaps it is time to face up to the paternalism of the first amendment, and maybe much of the rest of the Constitution as well." Is the Court's anti-paternalism paternalistic? For the contention that the Virginia price advertising ban was not paternalistic, see Lowenstein, *"Too Much Puff": Persuasion, Paternalism, and Commercial Speech,* 56 U.Cin.L.Rev. 1205, 1238 (1988).

which singles out speech of a particular content and seeks to prevent its dissemination completely.

Nor is there any claim that prescription drug price advertisements are forbidden because they are false or misleading in any way. Untruthful speech, commercial or otherwise, has never been protected for its own sake. *Gertz.* Obviously much commercial speech is not provably false, or even wholly false, but only deceptive or misleading. We foresee no obstacle to a State's dealing effectively with this problem.[24] The First Amendment, as we construe it today, does not prohibit the State from insuring that the stream of commercial information flows cleanly as well as freely.

Also, there is no claim that the transactions proposed in the forbidden advertisements are themselves illegal in any way. Finally, the special problems of the electronic broadcast media are likewise not in this case.

What is at issue is whether a State may completely suppress the dissemination of concededly truthful information about entirely lawful activity, fearful of that information's effect upon its disseminators and its recipients. Reserving other questions,[25] we conclude that the answer to this one is in the negative. * * *

Mr. Justice Stewart, concurring.[g]

[I] write separately to explain why I think today's decision does not preclude [governmental regulation of false or deceptive advertising]. The Court has on several occasions addressed the problems posed by false statements of fact in libel cases. [Factual] errors are inevitable in free debate, and the imposition of liability for [such errors] can "dampe[n] the

---

24. [C]ommonsense differences between speech that does "no more than propose a commercial transaction," and other varieties [suggest] that a different degree of protection is necessary to insure that the flow of truthful and legitimate commercial information is unimpaired. The truth of commercial speech, for example, may be more easily verifiable by its disseminator than, let us say, news reporting or political commentary, in that ordinarily the advertiser seeks to disseminate information about a specific product or service that he himself provides and presumably knows more about than anyone else. Also, commercial speech may be more durable than other kinds. Since advertising is the sine qua non of commercial profits, there is little likelihood of its being chilled by proper regulation and foregone entirely.

Attributes such as these, the greater objectivity and hardiness of commercial speech, may make it less necessary to tolerate inaccurate statements for fear of silencing the speaker. They may also make it appropriate to require that a commercial message appear in such a form, or include

such additional information, warnings and disclaimers, as are necessary to prevent its being deceptive. They may also make inapplicable the prohibition on prior restraints. Compare *New York Times v. United States* [Ch. 4, III infra] with *Donaldson v. Read Magazine,* 333 U.S. 178, 68 S.Ct. 591, 92 L.Ed. 628 (1948).

25. We stress that we have considered in this case the regulation of commercial advertising by pharmacists. Although we express no opinion as to other professions, the distinctions, historical and functional, between professions, may require consideration of quite different factors. Physicians and lawyers, for example, do not dispense standardized products; they render professional *services* of almost infinite variety and nature, with the consequent enhanced possibility for confusion and deception if they were to undertake certain kinds of advertising.

g. Burger, C.J., separately concurring, stressed the reservation in fn. 25 of the opinion with respect to advertising by attorneys and physicians. Stevens, J., took no part.

vigor and limi[t] the variety of public debate" by inducing "self-censorship." [In] contrast to the press, which must often attempt to assemble the true facts from sketchy and sometimes conflicting sources under the pressure of publication deadlines, the commercial advertiser generally knows the product or service he seeks to sell and is in a position to verify the accuracy of his factual representations before he disseminates them. The advertiser's access to the truth about his product and its price substantially eliminates any danger that governmental regulation of false or misleading price or product advertising will chill accurate and nondeceptive commercial [expression].

Since the factual claims contained in commercial price or product advertisements relate to tangible goods or services, they may be tested empirically and corrected to reflect the truth without in any manner jeopardizing the free dissemination of thought. Indeed, the elimination of false and deceptive claims serves to promote the one facet of commercial price and product advertising that warrants First Amendment protection—its contribution to the flow of accurate and reliable information relevant to public and private decision making.

Mr. Justice Rehnquist, dissenting.

[Under] the Court's opinion the way will be open not only for dissemination of price information but for active promotion of prescription drugs, liquor, cigarettes and other products the use of which it has previously been thought desirable to discourage. Now, however, such promotion is protected by the First Amendment so long as it is not misleading or does not promote an illegal product or [enterprise].

The Court speaks of the consumer's interest in the free flow of commercial information. [This] should presumptively be the concern of the Virginia Legislature, which sits to balance [this] and other claims in the process of making laws such as the one here under attack. The Court speaks of the importance in a "predominantly free enterprise economy" of intelligent and well-informed decisions as to allocation of resources. While there is again much to be said for the Court's observation as a matter of desirable public policy, there is certainly nothing in the United States Constitution which requires the Virginia Legislature to hew to the teachings of Adam Smith in its legislative decisions regulating the pharmacy profession.

[There] are undoubted difficulties with an effort to draw a bright line between "commercial speech" on the one hand and "protected speech" on the other, and the Court does better to face up to these difficulties than to attempt to hide them under labels. In this case, however, the Court has unfortunately substituted for the wavering line previously thought to exist between commercial speech and protected speech a no more satisfactory line of its own—that between "truthful" commercial speech, on the one hand, and that which is "false and misleading" on the other. The difficulty with this line is not that it wavers, but on the contrary that it is simply too Procrustean to take into account the congeries of factors which I believe could, quite consistently with the First and Fourteenth Amendments, properly influence a legislative decision with respect to commercial advertising.

[S]uch a line simply makes no allowance whatever for what appears to have been a considered legislative judgment in most States that while prescription drugs are a necessary and vital part of medical care and treatment, there are sufficient dangers attending their widespread use that they simply may not be promoted in the same manner as hair creams, deodorants, and toothpaste. The very real dangers that general advertising for such drugs might create in terms of encouraging, even though not sanctioning, illicit use of them by individuals for whom they have not been prescribed, or by generating patient pressure upon physicians to prescribe them are simply not dealt with in the Court's opinion. * * *

Notes and Questions

1. As compared to political decision making, is commercial advertising "neither more nor less significant than a host of other market activities that legislatures concededly may regulate."? Is there an "absence of any principled distinction between commercial soliciting and other aspects of economic activity"? Has economic due process been "resurrected, clothed in the ill-fitting garb of the first amendment"? See Jackson & Jeffries, *Commercial Speech: Economic Due Process and the First Amendment*, 65 Va.L.Rev. 1, 18 and 30 (1979). Why may government "be paternalistic regarding the purchase of goods but may not be paternalistic regarding information about those goods"? Alexander, *Speech in the Local Marketplace: Implications of Virginia State Board of Pharmacy v. Virginia Citizens Consumer Council, Inc. for Local Regulatory Power*, 14 San Diego L.Rev. 357, 376 (1977).

2. Does the rationale of *Virginia Pharmacy* extend to image or non-informational advertising? Should such advertising be protected? For relevant discussion, see Lowenstein, *"Too Much Puff": Persuasion, Paternalism, and Commercial Speech*, 56 U.Cin.L.Rev. 1205 (1988); Note, The *"Persuasion Route" of the Law: Advertising and Legal Persuasion*, 100 Colum. L.Rev. 1281 (2000). For the cultural implications of image advertising, see Collins & Skover, *Commerce and Communication*, 71 Tex.L.Rev. 697 (1993).[h] But see Law, *Addiction, Autonomy, and Advertising*, 77 Iowa L.Rev. 909, 932 (1992): "A broad-sweeping principle denying constitutional protection to noninformational commercial speech reinforces a narrow vision of First Amendment values focusing on political participation and rationality. While these plainly are vital First Amendment concerns, the Constitution has been interpreted to protect a wide range of human expression. Film, music, and novels are protected, not because they necessarily provide 'information' or facilitate participation in formal political processes, but because the First

---

h. For the negative implications of advertising (informational or non-informational) for democratic politics and culture, see Baker, *Advertising and a Democratic Press* (1994). See also Collins, *Dictating Content: How Advertising Pressure Can Corrupt A Free Press* (1992).

Amendment protects 'not only ideas capable of relatively precise, detached explication, but otherwise inexpressible emotions as well.' "

3. Footnote 24 suggests that *deceptive* commercial speech may be regulated in ways that would be barred if the speech were political. Sound distinction?

(a) *"Commonsense" differences between commercial speech and other speech.* (1) *Verifiability.* Consider Farber, *Commercial Speech and First Amendment Theory,* 74 Nw.U.L.Rev. 372, 385–86 (1979): "[C]ommercial speech is not necessarily more verifiable than other speech. There may well be uncertainty about some quality of a product, such as the health effect of eggs * * *. On the other hand, political speech is often quite verifiable by the speaker. A political candidate knows the truth about his own past and his present intentions, yet misrepresentations on these subjects are immune from state regulation."

(2) *Durability.* Consider Redish, *The Value of Free Speech,* 130 U.Pa. L.Rev. 591, 633 (1982): "[I]t is also incorrect to distinguish commercial from political expression on the ground that the former is somehow hardier because of the inherent profit motive. It could just as easily be said that we need not fear that commercial magazines and newspapers will cease publication for fear of governmental regulation, because they are in business for profit. Of course, the proper response to this contention is that our concern is not *whether* they will publish, but *what* they will publish: fear of regulation might deter them from dealing with controversial subjects." But see Cass, *Commercial Speech, Constitutionalism, Collective Choice,* 56 U.Cin. L.Rev. 1317, 1368–73 (1988).

(b) *Commercial speech and self-expression.* Is commercial speech distinguishable from political speech because it is unrelated to self-expression? Consider Baker, *Commercial Speech: A Problem in the Theory of Freedom,* 62 Iowa L.Rev. 1, 17 (1976): In commercial speech, the dissemination of the profit motive "breaks the connection between speech and any vision, or attitude, or value of the individual or group engaged in advocacy. Thus the content and form of commercial speech cannot be attributed to individual value allegiances." See generally Baker, *Human Liberty and Freedom of Speech,* chs. 3, 9, 10 (1989). For criticism, see, e.g., Schlag, *An Attack on Categorical Approaches to Freedom of Speech,* 30 U.C.L.A.L.Rev. 671, 710–21 (1983); Shiffrin, *The First Amendment and Economic Regulation: Away From A General Theory of the First Amendment,* 78 Nw.U.L.Rev. 1212 (1983). Even if commercial speech is divorced from self expression (or dignity), should it merit substantial protection. See Estreicher, *Securities Regulation and the First Amendment,* 24 Ga.L.Rev. 223 (1990); Neuborne, *The First Amendment and Government Regulation of Capital Markets,* 55 Brooklyn L.Rev. 5 (1989).

(c) *Contract approach to commercial speech.* Is commercial advertising distinguishable from other forms of speech because of the state interest in regulating contracts? Consider Farber, supra, at 389: "[C]ommercial speech is [more] akin to conduct than are other forms of speech. The unique aspect of commercial speech is that it is a prelude to, and therefore becomes integrated into, a contract, the essence of which is the presence of a promise. Because a promise is an undertaking to ensure that a certain state of affairs takes place, promises obviously have a closer connection with conduct than with self-expression. Second, this approach focuses on the distinctive and powerful state interests implicated by the process of contract formation. In a fundamentally market economy, the government understandably is given particular deference in its enforcement of contractual expectations. Indeed, the Constitution itself gives special protection to contractual expectations in the contract clause. Finally, this approach connects a rather nebulous area of first amendment law with the commonplaces of contract law of which every lawyer has knowledge. Obviously, the technicalities of contract law, with its doctrines of privity, consideration, and the like, should not be blindly translated into first amendment jurisprudence. The basic doctrines of contract law, however, provide a helpful guide in considering commercial speech problems." For discussion, see Alexander & Farber, *Commercial Speech and First Amendment Theory: A Critical Exchange,* 75 Nw.U.L.Rev. 307 (1980).

(d) *Error costs.* Is commercial speech distinguishable because the risks of error are less? Consider Cass, supra at 1360: "[T]he inquiry can be framed as asking four questions: (1) will officials err less systematically or less often in regulation of commercial speech than in regulation of other speech?; (2) will officials err less systematically or less often in regulation of commerce than in regulation of speech?; (3) will the consequences of errors in regulation of one sort of activity generally be less significant than the consequences of errors in the other?; and (4) will the process costs associated with error correction be lower in respect of one activity than the other?" On the risks of error, see generally Cass, supra; McChesney, *A Positive Regulatory Theory of the First Amendment,* 20 Conn.L.Rev. 335 (1988). See also Coase, *Advertising and Free Speech,* 6 J. Legal Stud. 1 (1977); Posner, *Free Speech in an Economic Perspective,* 20 Suffolk U.L.Rev. 1 (1986); Scanlon, *Freedom of Expression and Categories of Expression,* 40 U.Pitt.L.Rev. 519 (1979); Shiffrin, supra at 1275–82.

4. *Limits on regulation of deceptive advertising. Bates v. State Bar,* 433 U.S. 350, 97 S.Ct. 2691, 53 L.Ed.2d 810 (1977), struck down an Arizona Supreme Court rule against a lawyer "publicizing himself" through advertising. It rejected the claim that attorney price advertising was inherently misleading, but left open the "peculiar problems" associated with advertising claims regarding the quality of legal services.[i] Could a lawyer truthfully

i. *Zauderer v. Office of Disciplinary Counsel,* Ch. 9, I infra, held that a state may not discipline attorneys who solicit legal business through newspaper advertisements containing "truthful and nondeceptive information and advice regarding the legal rights of potential clients" or for the advertising use of "accurate and nondeceptive" illustrations. Zauderer had placed illustrated ads in 36 Ohio newspapers publicizing his availability to represent women who had suffered injuries from use of a

advertise that he or she has (1) tried twice as many personal injury cases as any other lawyer in the country? (2) averaged $10,000 more in recoveries per case than any other lawyer in the county? (3) graduated from Harvard Law School in the upper 10% of the class? (4) received "the best legal education this country offers"? Should an advertisement be protected if it is "sufficiently factual to be subject to verification" even if "implications of quality might be drawn from it"? See Canby and Gellhorn, *Physician Advertising: The First Amendment and the Sherman Act,* 1978 Duke L.J. 543, 560–62. Should the Court have deferred to the judgment of the State Bar of Arizona? If not, should it defer to the SEC when it regulates the advertising of securities? The FTC when it regulates automobile advertising? The Virginia Board of Pharmacy when it regulates quality advertising by pharmacists? For deferential treatment of a state ban on the use of tradenames by optometrists, see *Friedman v. Rogers,* 440 U.S. 1, 99 S.Ct. 887, 59 L.Ed.2d 100 (1979).

5. *Paternalism and Democracy.* Is it a part of democratic theory that "individual citizens can be trusted to make *legally valid* life-affecting choices on the basis of an open marketplace of ideas of information and opinion." Redish, *Tobacco Advertising and the First Amendment,* 81 Ia. L.Rev. 589, 604–05 (1996). Consider Shiffrin, *Dissent, Injustice, and the Meanings of America* 143–44 n. 41 (1999): "This argument would seem to prove too much. If democratic theory assumes citizens can be trusted to make such choices in an open marketplace, one would imagine government would be foreclosed not only from fixing prices to discourage consumption, but also from regulating false and misleading advertising. In addition, it would be unclear why government should be permitted to make products illegal for paternalistic reasons—if citizens can truly be trusted. Assuming it were consistent with this version of democratic theory for government to ban products, it would be unclear why its paternalism could not extend to product advertising of legal products. It would not do, for example, to claim that products not made illegal have been certified as safe. To outlaw cigarettes, for example, might create black markets and enormous attendant enforcement problems. The failure to outlaw cigarettes need not suggest that government thinks of them as any less a public health problem than numerous other drugs that are currently outlawed. Whether individual citizens can be 'trusted,' seems to bear no relationship to the legal status of the product. In addition, one could argue that the notion of democracy makes no claims about the quality of *individual* decision making, but makes some relative claims about the quality of *public* decision making."

6. *Truth and commercial advertising.* Should Mercedes Benz be able to truthfully advertise that Elton John drives its car without getting John's

contraceptive device known as the Dalkon Shield Intrauterine Device. In the ad Zauderer stated that he had represented other women in Dalkon Shield litigation. The Court observed that accurate statements of fact cannot be proscribed "merely because it is possible that some readers will infer that he has some expertise in those areas." But it continued to "leave open the possibility that States may prevent attorneys from making non-verifiable claims regarding the quality of their services. *Bates.*"

permission?[j] Should the state be able to prevent homeowners from posting "for sale" signs in order to prevent panic selling in order to maintain an integrated neighborhood? See *Linmark Associates v. Willingboro*, 431 U.S. 85, 97 S.Ct. 1614, 52 L.Ed.2d 155 (1977). May a state regulate the content of contraceptive advertising in order to minimize its offensive character? Cf. *Carey v. Population Services Int'l.*, 431 U.S. 678, 97 S.Ct. 2010, 52 L.Ed.2d 675 (1977) (total ban on contraceptive advertising unconstitutional).[k]

OHRALIK v. OHIO STATE BAR ASS'N, 436 U.S. 447, 98 S.Ct. 1912, 56 L.Ed.2d 444 (1978) upheld the indefinite suspension of an attorney for violating the anti-solicitation provisions of the Ohio Code of Professional Responsibility. Those provisions generally do not allow lawyers to recommend themselves to anyone who has not sought "their advice regarding employment of a lawyer." Albert Ohralik had approached two young accident victims to solicit employment—Carol McClintock in a hospital room where she lay in traction and Wanda Lou Holbert on the day she came home from the hospital. He employed a concealed tape recorder with Holbert, apparently to insure he would have evidence of her assent to his representation. The next day, when Holbert's mother informed Ohralik that she and her daughter did not want to have appellant represent them, he insisted that the daughter had entered into a binding agreement. McClintock also discharged Ohralik, and Ohralik sued her for breach of contract. The Court ruled, per POWELL, J., that a state may forbid in-person solicitation of clients by lawyers for pecuniary gain:

"Expression concerning purely commercial transactions has come within the ambit of the Amendment's protection only recently. In rejecting the notion that such speech is wholly outside the protection of the First Amendment, *Virginia Pharmacy,* we were careful not to hold that it is wholly undifferentiable from other forms of speech.

"We have not discarded the common sense distinction between speech proposing a commercial transaction, which occurs in an area traditionally subject to government regulation, and other varieties of speech. To require a parity of constitutional protection for commercial and noncommercial speech alike could invite dilution, simply by a leveling process, of the force of the Amendment's guarantee with respect to the latter kind of speech. Rather than subject the First Amendment to such a devitalization, we instead have afforded commercial speech a limited measure of protection, commensurate

j. Haemmerli, *Whose Who? The Case for a Kantian Right of Publicity,* 49 Duke L.J. 383 (1999); Liebeler, *A Property Rights Approach to Judicial Decision Making,* 4 Cato J. 783, 802–03 (1985); Shiffrin, supra note 3, at 1257–58 n. 275; Felcher & Rubin, *Privacy, Publicity, and the Portrayal of Real People by the Media,* 88 Yale L.J. 1577 (1979); Treece, *Commercial Exploitation of Names, Likenesses, and Personal Histories,* 51 Tex.L.Rev. 637 (1973).

k. Does protection for commercial speech threaten the tort for interference with contract? See Anderson, *Torts, Speech, and Contracts,* 75 Texas L.Rev. 1499 (1977).

with its subordinate position in the scale of First Amendment values, while allowing modes of regulation that might be impermissible in the realm of noncommercial expression.

"Moreover, 'it has never been deemed an abridgment of freedom of speech or press to make a course of conduct illegal merely because the conduct was in part initiated, evidenced, or carried out by means of language, either spoken, written, or printed.' *Giboney v. Empire Storage & Ice Co.,* 336 U.S. 490, 502, 69 S.Ct. 684, 691, 93 L.Ed. 834 (1949). Numerous examples could be cited of communications that are regulated without offending the First Amendment, such as the exchange of information about securities, *SEC v. Texas Gulf Sulphur Co.,* 401 F.2d 833 (C.A.2 1968), cert. denied, 394 U.S. 976, 89 S.Ct. 1454, 22 L.Ed.2d 756 (1969), corporate proxy statements, *Mills v. Electric Auto–Lite Co.,* 396 U.S. 375, 90 S.Ct. 616, 24 L.Ed.2d 593 (1970), the exchange of price and production information among competitors, *American Column & Lumber Co. v. United States,* 257 U.S. 377, 42 S.Ct. 114, 66 L.Ed. 284 (1921), and employers' threats of retaliation for the labor activities of employees, *NLRB v. Gissel Packing Co.,* 395 U.S. 575, 618, 89 S.Ct. 1918, 1942, 23 L.Ed.2d 547 (1969). Each of these examples illustrates that the State does not lose its power to regulate commercial activity deemed harmful to the public whenever speech is a component of that activity. Neither *Virginia Pharmacy* nor *Bates* purported to cast doubt on the permissibility of these kinds of commercial regulation.

"In-person solicitation by a lawyer of remunerative employment is a business transaction in which speech is an essential but subordinate component. While this does not remove the speech from the protection of the First Amendment, as was held in *Bates* and *Virginia Pharmacy,* it lowers the level of appropriate judicial scrutiny. [A] lawyer's procurement of remunerative employment is a subject only marginally affected with First Amendment concerns. It falls within the State's proper sphere of economic and professional regulation. While entitled to some constitutional protection, appellant's conduct is subject to regulation in furtherance of important state [interests].

" 'The interest of the States in regulating lawyers is especially great since lawyers are essential to the primary function of administering justice and have historically been officers of the courts' [and] act 'as trusted agents of their clients and as assistants to the court in search of a just solution to disputes.'

"[The] substantive evils of solicitation have been stated over the years in sweeping terms: stirring up litigation, assertion of fraudulent claims, debasing the legal profession, and potential harm to the solicited client in the form of overreaching, overcharging, underrepresentation, and misrepresentation." In providing information about the availability and terms of proposed legal services "in-person solicitation serves much the same function as the advertisement at issue in *Bates.* But there are significant differences as well. Unlike a public advertisement, which simply provides information and leaves the recipient free to act upon it or not, in-person solicitation may exert pressure and often demands an immediate response, without providing an opportunity for comparison or reflection. The aim and effect of in-person solicitation may be to provide a one-sided presentation and to encourage speedy and perhaps uninformed decision making; there is no opportunity for intervention or counter-education by agencies of the Bar, supervisory authorities, or persons close to the solicited individual. The admonition that 'the fitting remedy for evil counsels is good ones' is of little value when the circumstances provide no opportunity for any remedy at all. In-person solicitation is as likely as not to discourage persons needing counsel from engaging in a critical comparison of the 'availability, nature, and prices' of legal services; it actually may disserve the individual and societal interest, identified in *Bates,* in facilitating 'informed and reliable decision making.'

"[Appellant's argument that none of the evils of solicitation was found in his case] misconceives the nature of the State's interest. The rules prohibiting solicitation are prophylactic measures whose objective is the prevention of harm before it occurs.[a] The rules were applied in this case to discipline a lawyer for soliciting employment for pecuniary gain under circumstances likely to result in the adverse consequences the State seeks to avert. In such a situation, which is inherently conducive to overreaching and other forms of misconduct, the State has a strong interest in adopting and enforcing rules of conduct designed to protect the public from harmful solicitation by lawyers whom it has [licensed].

"The efficacy of the State's effort to prevent such harm to prospective clients would be substantially diminished if, having proved a solicitation in circumstances like those of this case, the State were required in addition to prove actual injury. Unlike the advertising in *Bates,* in-person solicitation is not visible or otherwise open to public scrutiny. Often there is no witness other than the lawyer and the lay person whom he has solicited, rendering it difficult or impossible to obtain reliable proof of what actually took place. This would be especially true if the lay person were so distressed at the time of the solicitation that he or she could not recall specific details at a later date. If appellant's view were sustained, in-person solicitation would be virtually immune to effective oversight and regulation by the State or by the legal profession, in contravention of the State's strong interest in regulating members of the Bar in an effective, objective, and self-enforcing manner. It therefore is not unreasonable, or violative of the Constitution, for a State to respond with what in effect is a prophylactic rule."[b]

a. But see McChesney, *Commercial Speech in the Professions,* 134 U.Pa.L.Rev. 45 (1985) (anti-solicitation provisions may be motivated by anti-competitive considerations).

b. Marshall and Rehnquist, JJ., each separately concurred in the judgment. Brennan, J., did not participate.

Notes and Questions

1. *Companion case.* IN RE PRIMUS, 436 U.S. 412, 98 S.Ct. 1893, 56 L.Ed.2d 417 (1978), per POWELL, J., held that a state could not constitutionally discipline an ACLU "cooperating lawyer" who, after advising a gathering of allegedly illegally sterilized women of their rights, initiated further contact with one of the women by writing her a letter informing her of the ACLU's willingness to provide free legal representation for women in her situation and of the organization's desire to file a lawsuit on her behalf. "South Carolina's action in punishing appellant for soliciting a prospective litigant by mail, on behalf of ACLU, must withstand the 'exacting scrutiny applicable to limitations on core First Amendment rights.' [Where] political expression or association is at issue, this Court has not tolerated the degree of imprecision that often characterizes government regulation of the conduct of commercial affairs. The approach we adopt today in *Ohralik* that the State may proscribe in-person solicitation for pecuniary gain under circumstances likely to result in adverse consequences, cannot be applied to appellant's activity on behalf of the ACLU. Although a showing of potential danger may suffice in the former context, appellant may not be disciplined unless her activity in fact involved the type of misconduct at which South Carolina's broad prohibition is said to be directed. The record does not support appellee's contention that undue influence, overreaching, misrepresentation, or invasion of privacy actually occurred in this case."

2. *Related cases. Edenfield v. Fane,* 507 U.S. 761, 113 S.Ct. 1792, 123 L.Ed.2d 543 (1993) held that direct personal solicitation of prospective business clients by Certified Public Accountants is protected under the first amendment,[c] but *Florida Bar v. Went For It, Inc.,* 515 U.S. 618, 115 S.Ct. 2371, 132 L.Ed.2d 541 (1995) held that targeted direct-mail solicitations by personal injury attorneys to victims and their relatives for thirty days following an accident were not protected under the first amendment.

3. *A hierarchy of protected speech.* Consider Shiffrin, note 3 supra, at 1218 & 1220–21 (1983). In *Virginia Pharmacy,* "the Court never admitted that commercial speech was less valuable than political speech. The 'commonsense differences' had nothing to do with value. [Although] Justice Blackmun labored to defend the asserted equal relationship between commercial speech and political speech for the *Virginia Pharmacy* majority, Justice Powell in *Ohralik* was content to lead the Court to an opposite position without explanation. In so doing, Justice Powell steered the Court to accept a hierarchy of protected speech for the first time, despite his own stated opposition [in *Young*] to creating any such hierarchy." Does the

c. Blackmun, J., concurred; O'Connor, J., dissented. Compare Ibanez v. Florida Dep't of Business and Professional Regulation, 512 U.S. 136, 114 S.Ct. 2084, 129 L.Ed.2d 118 (1994) (attorney's references in advertising, business cards and stationery to her credentials as a CPA and a Certified Financial Planner are not deceptive or misleading and are protected commercial speech); Accord, Peel v. Attorney Registration and Disciplinary Comm'n, 496 U.S. 91, 110 S.Ct. 2281, 110 L.Ed.2d 83 (1990) (reference on letterhead to prestigious certification is protected speech).

concern that the protection of non-commercial speech would be subject to dilution if it were placed on a par with commercial speech presuppose an unexplained difference between the two types of speech? See id. at 1221 n. 59. For discussion of the dilution argument, see Marshall, *The Dilution of the First Amendment and the Equality of Ideas,* 38 Case W.Res.L.Rev. 566 (1988).

4. *Muddying the hierarchy.* Cincinnati permitted 1,500–2,000 news-racks throughout the city for publications not classified as commercial speech, but refused to allow an additional 62 newsracks that contained two publications classified as commercial speech.

CITY OF CINCINNATI v. DISCOVERY NETWORK, 507 U.S. 410, 113 S.Ct. 1505, 123 L.Ed.2d 99 (1993), per STEVENS, J., held that this discrimination against commercial speech violated the first amendment: The major premise supporting the city's argument is the proposition that commercial speech has only a low value. Based on that premise, the city contends that the fact that assertedly more valuable publications are allowed to use newsracks does not undermine its judgment that its esthetic and safety interests are stronger than the interest in allowing commercial speakers to have similar access to the reading public.

"We cannot agree. In our view, the city's argument attaches more importance to the distinction between commercial and non-commercial speech than our cases warrant and seriously underestimates the value of commercial speech."[20]d

5. *The reach of Discovery Network.* (a) In MARTIN v. STRUTHERS, 319 U.S. 141, 63 S.Ct. 862, 87 L.Ed. 1313 (1943), a city forbade knocking on the door or ringing the doorbell of a resident in order to deliver handbills (in an industrial community where many worked night shifts and slept during the day). In striking down the ordinance, the Court, per BLACK, J., pointed out that the city's objectives could be achieved by means of a law making it

---

20. *Metromedia, Inc. v. San Diego,* 453 U.S. 490, 101 S.Ct. 2882, 69 L.Ed.2d 800 (1981), upon which the city heavily relies, is not to the contrary. In that case, a plurality of the Court found as a permissible restriction on commercial speech a city ordinance that, for the most part, banned outdoor "offsite" advertising billboards, but permitted "onsite" advertising signs identifying the owner of the premises and the goods sold or manufactured on the site. Unlike this case, which involves discrimination between commercial and noncommercial speech, the "offsite-onsite" distinction involved disparate treatment of two types of commercial speech. Only the onsite signs served both the commercial and public interest in guiding potential visitors to their intended destinations; moreover, the plurality concluded that a "city may believe that offsite advertising, with its periodically changing content, presents a more acute problem than does onsite advertising." Neither of these bases has any application to the disparate treatment of newsracks in this case.

The Chief Justice is correct that seven Justices in the *Metromedia* case were of the view that San Diego could completely ban offsite commercial billboards for reasons unrelated to the content of those billboards. Those seven Justices did not say, however, that San Diego could *distinguish* between commercial and noncommercial offsite billboards that cause the same esthetic and safety concerns. That question was not presented in *Metromedia,* for the regulation at issue in that case did not draw a distinction between commercial and noncommercial offsite billboards; with a few exceptions, it essentially banned *all* offsite billboards.

d. Rehnquist, J., joined by White & Thomas, JJ., dissented.

an offense for any person to ring the doorbell of a householder who has "appropriately indicated that he is unwilling to be disturbed. This or any similar regulation leaves the decision as to whether distributors of literature may lawfully call at a home where it belongs—with the homeowner himself."[e] By contrast, *Breard v. Alexandria,* 341 U.S. 622, 71 S.Ct. 920, 95 L.Ed. 1233 (1951) upheld an ordinance forbidding the practice of going door to door to solicit orders for the sale of goods. The commercial element was said to distinguish *Martin.* Does *Breard* survive *Virginia Pharmacy?* Does (should) *Discovery Network* settle the issue? What if, as in *Breard,* the solicitor is selling subscriptions for magazines?

(b) Compare *Schneider,* Ch. 6, I infra (prohibition against leaflet distribution on streets unconstitutional) with *Valentine,* Ch. 3, II (prohibition against distribution of commercial leaflets upheld). Does (should) the holding of *Valentine* survive *Virginia Pharmacy?* Does *Discovery Network* settle the issue?[f]

(c) The Court has held it unconstitutional for a locality to prohibit "For Sale" signs on residential property. *Linmark.* Similarly, the Court has held it unconstitutional to prohibit property owners from displaying political signs at their residences. *City of Ladue v. Gilleo,* 512 U.S. 43, 114 S.Ct. 2038, 129 L.Ed.2d 36 (1994). After *Linmark, Ladue,* and *Discovery Network,* would it be unconstitutional to prohibit signs on residential property that advertise goods and services sold elsewhere?

———

In *Central Hudson Gas & Elec. Corp. v. Public Serv. Comm'n of N.Y.,* 447 U.S. 557, 100 S.Ct. 2343, 65 L.Ed.2d 341 (1980), the Court, per Powell, J., characterized the prior commercial speech cases as embracing a special test: "In commercial speech cases, then, a four-part analysis has developed. At the outset, we must determine whether the expression is protected by the

e. Compare *Lamont v. Postmaster General,* 381 U.S. 301, 85 S.Ct. 1493, 14 L.Ed.2d 398 (1965) (invalidating a federal statute permitting delivery of "communist political propaganda" only if the addressee specifically requested in writing that it be delivered because of the chilling effect on willing recipients) and *Rowan v. U.S. Post Office,* 397 U.S. 728, 90 S.Ct. 1484, 25 L.Ed.2d 736 (1970) (upholding statute authorizing Postmaster General to issue enforceable orders directing senders to refrain from future mailings to addressees who have notified Post Office that they believe mailings to be erotically arousing or sexually provocative ("the mailer's right to communicate is circumscribed only by an affirmative act of the addressee giving notice that he wishes no further mailings from that mailer"). Is *Rowan* problematic because addressees must not only give notice that they want no further mailings, but also that they deem the material to be erotic? Does this implicate impermissible content discrimination? See Stone, *Restrictions of Speech Because of its Content: The Peculiar Case of Subject–Matter Restrictions,* 46 U.Chi.L.Rev. 81, 84–85 (1978).

f. For relevant commentary on the normative issues, see Baker, *Commercial Speech: A Problem in the Theory of Freedom,* 62 Iowa L.Rev. 1 (1976); Redish, *The First Amendment in the Marketplace: Commercial Speech and the Values of Free Expression,* 39 Geo.Wash.L.Rev. 429 (1971); Redish, *The Value of Free Speech,* 130 U.Pa. L.Rev. 591 (1982); Shiffrin, *The First Amendment and Economic Regulation: Away From a General Theory of the First Amendment,* 78 Nw.U.L.Rev. 1212, 1220, 1276–82 (1983).

First Amendment. For commercial speech to come within that provision, it at least must concern lawful activity and not be misleading. Next, we ask whether the asserted governmental interest is substantial. If both inquiries yield positive answers, we must determine whether the regulation directly advances the governmental interest asserted, and whether it is not more extensive than is necessary to serve that interest." Sixteen years later, the members of the Court raised issues about the strength of the test and the circumstances in which it should apply.

44 LIQUORMART, INC. v. RHODE ISLAND

517 U.S. 484, 116 S.Ct. 1495, 134 L.Ed.2d 711 (1996).

JUSTICE STEVENS announced the judgment of the Court and delivered the opinion of the Court with respect to Parts I, II, VII,[a] and VIII,[b] an opinion with respect to Parts III and V, in which JUSTICE KENNEDY, JUSTICE SOUTER, and JUSTICE GINSBURG join, an opinion with respect to Part VI, in which JUSTICE KENNEDY, JUSTICE THOMAS, and JUSTICE GINSBURG join, and an opinion with respect to Part IV, in which JUSTICE KENNEDY and JUSTICE GINSBURG join. * * *

I

In 1956, the Rhode Island Legislature enacted two separate prohibitions against advertising the retail price of alcoholic beverages. The first applies to vendors licensed in Rhode Island as well as to out-of-state manufacturers, wholesalers, and shippers. It prohibits them from "advertising in any manner whatsoever" the price of any alcoholic beverage offered for sale in the State; the only exception is for price tags or signs displayed with the merchandise within licensed premises and not visible from the street. The second statute applies to the Rhode Island news media. It contains a categorical prohibition against the publication or broadcast of any advertisements—even those referring to sales in other States—that "make reference to the price of any alcoholic beverages." * * *

III

Advertising has been a part of our culture throughout our history. Even in colonial days, the public relied on "commercial speech" for vital information about the market. Early newspapers displayed advertisements for goods and services on their front pages, and town criers called out prices in public squares. Indeed, commercial messages played such a central role in public life prior to the Founding that Benjamin Franklin authored his early defense

---

a. Scalia, Kennedy, Souter, Thomas, and Ginsburg, JJ., joined parts I, II, and VII of the Stevens, J., opinion. Section VII concluded that the twenty-first amendment does not qualify the first. The same conclusion was reached in O'Connor, J.'s concurring opinion joined by Rehnquist, C.J., Souter and Breyer, JJ.

b. Scalia, Kennedy, Souter, and Ginsburg, JJ., joined part VIII of the Stevens, J.'s opinion.

of a free press in support of his decision to print, of all things, an advertisement for voyages to Barbados.

In accord with the role that commercial messages have long played, the law has developed to ensure that advertising provides consumers with accurate information about the availability of goods and services. In the early years, the common law, and later, statutes, served the consumers' interest in the receipt of accurate information in the commercial market by prohibiting fraudulent and misleading advertising. It was not until the 1970's, however, that this Court held that the First Amendment protected the dissemination of truthful and nonmisleading commercial messages about lawful products and services. See generally Alex Kozinski & Stuart Banner, *The Anti–History and Pre–History of Commercial Speech*, 71 Texas L.Rev. 747 (1993). * * *

[O]ur early cases uniformly struck down several broadly based bans on truthful, nonmisleading commercial speech, each of which served ends unrelated to consumer protection.[8] Indeed, one of those cases [*Linmark*] expressly likened the rationale that *Virginia Pharmacy Bd.* employed to the one that Justice Brandeis adopted in his concurrence in *Whitney v. California*[:] "the remedy to be applied is more speech, not enforced silence. Only an emergency can justify repression." * * *

At the same time, our early cases recognized that the State may regulate some types of commercial advertising more freely than other forms of protected speech. * * *

In *Central Hudson Gas & Elec. Corp. v. Public Serv. Comm'n of N.Y.*, 447 U.S. 557, 100 S.Ct. 2343, 65 L.Ed.2d 341 (1980), we took stock of our developing commercial speech jurisprudence. In that case, we considered a regulation "completely" banning all promotional advertising by electric utilities. Our decision acknowledged the special features of commercial speech but identified the serious First Amendment concerns that attend blanket advertising prohibitions that do not protect consumers from commercial harms.[c]

Five Members of the Court recognized that the state interest in the conservation of energy was substantial, and that there was "an immediate connection between advertising and demand for electricity." Nevertheless, they concluded that the regulation was invalid because the Commission had failed to make a showing that a more limited speech regulation would not have adequately served the State's interest.

---

8. See *Bates* (ban on lawyer advertising); *Carey* (ban on contraceptive advertising); *Linmark* (ban on "For Sale" signs); *Virginia Bd. of Pharmacy* (ban on prescription drug prices); *Bigelow* (ban on abortion advertising). Although *Linmark* involved a prohibition against a particular means of advertising the sale of one's home, we treated the restriction as if it were a complete ban because it did not leave open "satisfactory" alternative channels of communication.

c. *Central Hudson* referred to commercial speech as "expression related solely to the economic interests of the speaker and its audience." Was the speech in *Central Hudson* solely in the economic interests of the speaker and its audience? Is the *Central Hudson* locution broader or narrower than the category of promoting a commercial transaction? Reconsider this question in connection with the *Greenmoss* case, Ch. 3, III supra.

In reaching its conclusion, the majority explained that although the special nature of commercial speech may require less than strict review of its regulation, special concerns arise from "regulations that entirely suppress commercial speech in order to pursue a nonspeech-related policy." *Id.* n. 9. In those circumstances, "a ban on speech could screen from public view the underlying governmental policy." As a result, the Court concluded that "special care" should attend the review of such blanket bans, and it pointedly remarked that "in recent years this Court has not approved a blanket ban on commercial speech unless the speech itself was flawed in some way, either because it was deceptive or related to unlawful activity."[10]

IV

[W]hen a State entirely prohibits the dissemination of truthful, nonmisleading commercial messages for reasons unrelated to the preservation of a fair bargaining process, there is far less reason to depart from the rigorous review that the First Amendment generally demands. * * *

The special dangers that attend complete bans on truthful, nonmisleading commercial speech cannot be explained away by appeals to the "commonsense distinctions" that exist between commercial and noncommercial speech. Regulations that suppress the truth are no less troubling because they target objectively verifiable information, nor are they less effective because they aim at durable messages. As a result, neither the "greater objectivity" nor the "greater hardiness" of truthful, nonmisleading commercial speech justifies reviewing its complete suppression with added deference. * * *

Precisely because bans against truthful, nonmisleading commercial speech rarely seek to protect consumers from either deception or over-reaching, they usually rest solely on the offensive assumption that the public will respond "irrationally" to the truth. The First Amendment directs us to be especially skeptical of regulations that seek to keep people in the dark for what the government perceives to be their own good.[d]

V

[Although] the record suggests that the price advertising ban may have some impact on the purchasing patterns of temperate drinkers of modest means, the State has presented no evidence to suggest that its speech prohibition will significantly reduce market-wide consumption. Indeed, the District Court's considered and uncontradicted finding on this point is directly to the contrary. Moreover, the evidence suggests that the abusive drinker will probably not be deterred by a marginal price increase, and that

---

10. The Justices concurring in the judgment adopted a somewhat broader view. They expressed "doubt whether suppression of information concerning the availability and price of a legally offered product is ever a permissible way for the State to 'dampen' the demand for or use of the product." Indeed, Justice Blackmun believed that even "though 'commercial' speech is involved, such a regulation strikes at the heart of the First Amendment."

d. See Van Alstyne, *Quo Vadis, Posadas?*, 25 N.Ky.L.Rev. 505 (1998).

the true alcoholic may simply reduce his purchases of other necessities. * * *

As is evident, any conclusion that elimination of the ban would significantly increase alcohol consumption would require us to engage in the sort of "speculation or conjecture" that is an unacceptable means of demonstrating that a restriction on commercial speech directly advances the State's asserted interest. Such speculation certainly does not suffice when the State takes aim at accurate commercial information for paternalistic ends.

The State also cannot satisfy the requirement that its restriction on speech be no more extensive than necessary. It is perfectly obvious that alternative forms of regulation that would not involve any restriction on speech would be more likely to achieve the State's goal of promoting temperance. As the State's own expert conceded, higher prices can be maintained either by direct regulation or by increased taxation. Per capita purchases could be limited as is the case with prescription drugs. Even educational campaigns focused on the problems of excessive, or even moderate, drinking might prove to be more effective.

As a result, even under the less than strict standard that generally applies in commercial speech cases, the State has failed to establish a "reasonable fit" between its abridgment of speech and its temperance goal. *Board of Trustees v. Fox*, 492 U.S. 469, 109 S.Ct. 3028, 106 L.Ed.2d 388 (1989);[e] see also *Rubin v. Coors Brewing Co.*, 514 U.S. 476, 115 S.Ct. 1585, 131 L.Ed.2d 532 (1995)(explaining that defects in a federal ban on alcohol advertising are "further highlighted by the availability of alternatives that would prove less intrusive to the First Amendment's protections for commercial speech").[f] It necessarily follows that the price advertising ban cannot survive the more stringent constitutional review that *Central Hudson* itself concluded was appropriate for the complete suppression of truthful, nonmisleading commercial speech.

e. *Fox*, per Scalia, J., joined by Rehnquist, C.J., White, Stevens, O'Connor, and Kennedy, JJ., in the course of considering a provision that operated to bar commercial organizations from making sales demonstrations in students' dormitory rooms, held that the *Central Hudson* test did not require government to foreclose the possibility of all less restrictive alternatives. The university sought to promote an educational rather than a commercial atmosphere and to prevent commercial exploitation. Scalia, J., characterized these interests as substantial, but stated that it was enough if the fit between means and ends were "reasonable." It did not need to be "perfect." Like time, place, and manner regulations, however, the relationship between means and ends had to be "narrowly tailored to achieve the desired objective." Under that standard, as interpreted, government may not "'burden substantially more speech than is necessary to further the government's legitimate interest,'"but need not foreclose "all conceivable alternatives." Scalia, J., argued that to have a more demanding test in commercial speech than that used for time, place, and manner regulations would be inappropriate because time, place, and manner regulations can apply to political speech.

f. *Rubin* held that a federal provision prohibiting the display of alcoholic content on beer labels violated the first amendment. The Court argued among other things that the overall federal scheme was irrational in that it prohibited alcoholic beverage advertising from mentioning alcoholic content in many circumstances and required disclosures of alcoholic content in the labeling of wines in some circumstances.

VI

The State responds by arguing that it merely exercised appropriate "legislative judgment" in determining that a price advertising ban would best promote temperance. Relying on the *Central Hudson* analysis set forth in *Posadas de Puerto Rico Associates v. Tourism Co. of P. R.*, 478 U.S. 328, 106 S.Ct. 2968, 92 L.Ed.2d 266 (1986), and *United States v. Edge Broadcasting Co.*, 509 U.S. 418, 113 S.Ct. 2696, 125 L.Ed.2d 345 (1993), Rhode Island first argues that, because expert opinions as to the effectiveness of the price advertising ban "go both ways," the Court of Appeals correctly concluded that the ban constituted a "reasonable choice" by the legislature. The State next contends that precedent requires us to give particular deference to that legislative choice because the State could, if it chose, ban the sale of alcoholic beverages outright. See *Posadas*. Finally, the State argues that deference is appropriate because alcoholic beverages are so-called "vice" products. We consider each of these contentions in turn.

The State's first argument fails to justify the speech prohibition at issue. Our commercial speech cases recognize some room for the exercise of legislative judgment. See *Metromedia*. However, Rhode Island errs in concluding that *Edge* and *Posadas* establish the degree of deference that its decision to impose a price advertising ban warrants.

In *Edge*, we upheld a federal statute that permitted only those broadcasters located in States that had legalized lotteries to air lottery advertising. The statute was designed to regulate advertising about an activity that had been deemed illegal in the jurisdiction in which the broadcaster was located. Here, by contrast, the commercial speech ban targets information about entirely lawful behavior.[g]

Posadas is more directly relevant. There, a five-Member majority held that, under the *Central Hudson* test, it was "up to the legislature" to choose to reduce gambling by suppressing in-state casino advertising rather than engaging in educational speech. Rhode Island argues that this logic demonstrates the constitutionality of its own decision to ban price advertising in lieu of raising taxes or employing some other less speech-restrictive means of promoting temperance.

The reasoning in *Posadas* does support the State's argument, but, on reflection, we are now persuaded that *Posadas* erroneously performed the First Amendment analysis. The casino advertising ban was designed to keep

---

g. *Edge* upheld federal legislation prohibiting the broadcast of lottery advertising if the broadcaster were located in a state that does not permit lotteries even in circumstances where 92% of the broadcaster's audience resided in a state that permitted lotteries and where the advertisement was for the lottery in the state where it was legal.

Greater New Orleans Broadcasting v. United States, 527 U.S. 173, 119 S.Ct. 1923, 144 L.Ed.2d 161 (1999), held that the congressional ban on the broadcasting of lottery information could not constitutionally be applied to advertisements of casino gambling when the broadcaster was located in a state where such gambling was legal. In addition, as in *Rubin*, fn. f, the Court objected to the lack of rationale for many of the exceptions to the legislation.

truthful, nonmisleading speech from members of the public for fear that they would be more likely to gamble if they received it. * * *

Because the 5–to–4 decision in *Posadas* marked such a sharp break from our prior precedent, and because it concerned a constitutional question about which this Court is the final arbiter, we decline to give force to its highly deferential approach.

Instead, in keeping with our prior holdings, we conclude that a state legislature does not have the broad discretion to suppress truthful, nonmisleading information for paternalistic purposes that the *Posadas* majority was willing to tolerate. * * *

We also cannot accept the State's second contention, which is premised entirely on the "greater-includes-the-lesser" reasoning endorsed toward the end of the majority's opinion in *Posadas*. * * * The majority concluded that it would "surely be a strange constitutional doctrine which would concede to the legislature the authority to totally ban a product or activity, but deny to the legislature the authority to forbid the stimulation of demand for the product or activity through advertising on behalf of those who would profit from such increased demand." * * *

Although we do not dispute the proposition that greater powers include lesser ones, we fail to see how that syllogism requires the conclusion that the State's power to regulate commercial activity is "greater" than its power to ban truthful, nonmisleading commercial speech. Contrary to the assumption made in *Posadas*, we think it quite clear that banning speech may sometimes prove far more intrusive than banning conduct. As a venerable proverb teaches, it may prove more injurious to prevent people from teaching others how to fish than to prevent fish from being sold.[19] Similarly, a local ordinance banning bicycle lessons may curtail freedom far more than one that prohibits bicycle riding within city limits. In short, we reject the assumption that words are necessarily less vital to freedom than actions, or that logic somehow proves that the power to prohibit an activity is necessarily "greater" than the power to suppress speech about it.

As a matter of First Amendment doctrine, the *Posadas* syllogism is even less defensible. The text of the First Amendment makes clear that the Constitution presumes that attempts to regulate speech are more dangerous than attempts to regulate conduct.

[J]ust as it is perfectly clear that Rhode Island could not ban all obscene liquor ads except those that advocated temperance, we think it equally clear that its power to ban the sale of liquor entirely does not include a power to censor all advertisements that contain accurate and nonmisleading information about the price of the product. As the entire Court apparently now agrees, the statements in the *Posadas* opinion on which Rhode Island relies are no longer persuasive.

19. "Give a man a fish, and you feed him for a day. Teach a man to fish, and you feed him for a lifetime." *The International* *Thesaurus of Quotations* 646 (compiled by R. Tripp 1970).

Finally, we find unpersuasive the State's contention that, under *Posadas* and *Edge*, the price advertising ban should be upheld because it targets commercial speech that pertains to a "vice" activity.

[T]he scope of any "vice" exception to the protection afforded by the First Amendment would be difficult, if not impossible, to define. Almost any product that poses some threat to public health or public morals might reasonably be characterized by a state legislature as relating to "vice activity". Such characterization, however, is anomalous when applied to products such as alcoholic beverages, lottery tickets, or playing cards, that may be lawfully purchased on the open market.[h] The recognition of such an exception would also have the unfortunate consequence of either allowing state legislatures to justify censorship by the simple expedient of placing the "vice" label on selected lawful activities, or requiring the federal courts to establish a federal common law of vice. * * *

VIII

Because Rhode Island has failed to carry its heavy burden of justifying its complete ban on price advertising, we conclude that R.I. Gen. Laws §§ 3–8–7 and 3–8–8.1, as well as Regulation 32 of the Rhode Island Liquor Control Administration, abridge speech in violation of the First Amendment as made applicable to the States by the Due Process Clause of the Fourteenth Amendment. * * *

JUSTICE SCALIA, concurring in part and concurring in the judgment.

I share Justice Thomas's discomfort with the *Central Hudson* test, which seems to me to have nothing more than policy intuition to support it. I also share Justice Stevens' aversion towards paternalistic governmental policies that prevent men and women from hearing facts that might not be good for them. On the other hand, it would also be paternalism for us to prevent the people of the States from enacting laws that we consider paternalistic, unless we have good reason to believe that the Constitution itself forbids them. I will take my guidance as to what the Constitution forbids, with regard to a text as indeterminate as the First Amendment's preservation of "the freedom of speech," and where the core offense of suppressing particular political ideas is not at issue, from the long accepted practices of the American people.

The briefs and arguments of the parties in the present case provide no illumination on that point; understandably so, since both sides accepted *Central Hudson*. The amicus brief on behalf of the American Advertising Federation et al. did examine various expressions of view at the time the First Amendment was adopted; they are consistent with First Amendment

h. For material relevant to the prohibition of tobacco advertising, see Shiffrin, *Dissent, Injustice, and the Meanings of America* ch. 2 (1999); Sullivan, *Cheap Spirits, Cigarettes, and Free Speech: The Implications of 44 Liquormart*, 1996 Sup.Ct. Rev. 123 (1996); Redish, *Tobacco Advertising and the First Amendment*, 81 Ia. L.Rev. 589 (1996); Law, *Addiction, Autonomy, and Advertising*, 77 Iowa L.Rev. 909, 932 (1992); Lowenstein, *"Too Much Puff": Persuasion, Paternalism, and Commercial Speech*, 56 U.Cin.L.Rev. 1205, 1238 (1988).

protection for commercial speech, but certainly not dispositive. I consider more relevant the state legislative practices prevalent at the time the First Amendment was adopted, since almost all of the States had free-speech constitutional guarantees of their own, whose meaning was not likely to have been different from the federal constitutional provision derived from them. Perhaps more relevant still are the state legislative practices at the time the Fourteenth Amendment was adopted, since it is most improbable that that adoption was meant to overturn any existing national consensus regarding free speech. Indeed, it is rare that any nationwide practice would develop contrary to a proper understanding of the First Amendment itself—for which reason I think also relevant any national consensus that had formed regarding state regulation of advertising after the Fourteenth Amendment, and before this Court's entry into the field. The parties and their amici provide no evidence on these points.

Since I do not believe we have before us the wherewithal to declare *Central Hudson* wrong—or at least the wherewithal to say what ought to replace it—I must resolve this case in accord with our existing jurisprudence, which [would] prohibit the challenged regulation. * * * [A]ccordingly [I] join Parts I, II, VII, and VIII of Justice Stevens' opinion.

JUSTICE THOMAS, concurring in Parts I, II, VI, and VII, and concurring in the judgment.

In cases such as this, in which the government's asserted interest is to keep legal users of a product or service ignorant in order to manipulate their choices in the marketplace, the balancing test adopted in *Central Hudson* should not be applied, in my view. Rather, such an "interest" is per se illegitimate and can no more justify regulation of "commercial" speech than it can justify regulation of "noncommercial" speech. * * *

Although the Court took a sudden turn away from *Virginia Pharmacy Bd.* in *Central Hudson*, it has never explained why manipulating the choices of consumers by keeping them ignorant is more legitimate when the ignorance is maintained through suppression of "commercial" speech than when the same ignorance is maintained through suppression of "noncommercial" speech. * * *

Justice O'Connor, with whom THE CHIEF JUSTICE, JUSTICE SOUTER, and JUSTICE BREYER join, concurring in the judgment. * * *

I agree with the Court that Rhode Island's price-advertising ban is invalid. I would resolve this case more narrowly, however, by applying our established *Central Hudson* test to determine whether this commercial-speech regulation survives First Amendment scrutiny. * * *

The fit between Rhode Island's method and [its goal of reducing consumption] is not reasonable. If the target is simply higher prices generally to discourage consumption, the regulation imposes too great, and unnecessary, a prohibition on speech in order to achieve it. The State has other methods at its disposal—methods that would more directly accomplish this stated goal without intruding on sellers' ability to provide truthful, nonmisleading information to customers. * * * A tax, for example, is not normally very difficult to administer and would have a far more certain and direct effect on prices, without any restriction on speech. The principal opinion suggests further alternatives, such as limiting per capita purchases or conducting an educational campaign about the dangers of alcohol consumption. The ready availability of such alternatives—at least some of which would far more effectively achieve Rhode Island's only professed goal, at comparatively small additional administrative cost—demonstrates that the fit between ends and means is not narrowly tailored. Too, this regulation prevents sellers of alcohol from communicating price information anywhere but at the point of purchase. No channels exist at all to permit them to publicize the price of their products.

Respondents point for support to *Posadas*. The closer look that we have required since *Posadas* comports better with the purpose of the analysis set out in *Central Hudson*, by requiring the State to show that the speech restriction directly advances its interest and is narrowly tailored. Under such a closer look, Rhode Island's price-advertising ban clearly fails to pass muster.

Because Rhode Island's regulation fails even the less stringent standard set out in *Central Hudson*, nothing here requires adoption of a new analysis for the evaluation of commercial speech regulation. [Because] we need go no further, I would not here undertake the question whether the test we have employed since *Central Hudson* should be displaced. * * *

Notes and Questions

1. Consider Kathleen M. Sullivan, *Cheap Spirits, Cigarettes, and Free Speech: The Implications of 44 Liquormart,* 1996 Sup.Ct. Rev. 123, 160 (1996): "A plurality [is] willing to move commercial speech somewhat closer to the core of the First Amendment applying strict scrutiny to paternalistic interventions between speaker and listener for the listener's own good. It remains to be seen whether this group of Justices would extend that approach to all content-based commercial speech regulations, whether a fifth or more will join them, and whether such a move would prompt any change in the Court's currently exceptional treatment of false and misleading commercial speech." Should the category "commercial speech" be abandoned altogether?

2. Consider Akhil Reed Amar, *Intratextualism,* 112 Harv. L.Rev. 747, 810 (1999): "The Justices are beginning to detach the First Amendment from democracy and graft it onto property, moving from free speech to free markets."

III. PRIVATE SPEECH

Before studying *Dun & Bradstreet,* below, review *Gertz,* Ch. 1, II, C supra.

Dun & Bradstreet, Inc., a credit reporting agency, falsely and negligently reported to five of its subscribers that Greenmoss Builders, Inc. had filed a petition for bankruptcy and also negligently misrepresented Greenmoss' assets and liabilities. In the ensuing defamation action, Greenmoss recovered $50,000 in compensatory damages and $300,000 in punitive damages. Dun & Bradstreet argued that, under *Gertz,* its first amendment rights had been violated because presumed and punitive damages had been imposed without instructions requiring a showing of *New York Times* malice. Greenmoss argued that the *Gertz* protections did not extend to non-media defendants and, in any event, did not extend to commercial speech.

DUN & BRADSTREET, INC. v. GREENMOSS BUILDERS, INC., 472 U.S. 749, 105 S.Ct. 2939, 86 L.Ed.2d 593 (1985), rejected Dun & Bradstreet's contention, but there was no opinion of the Court. The common theme of the five justices siding with Greenmoss was that the first amendment places less value on "private" speech than upon "public" speech.

POWELL, J., joined by Rehnquist and O'Connor, JJ., noted that the Vermont Supreme Court below had held "as a matter of federal constitutional law" that "the media protections outlined in *Gertz* are inapplicable to nonmedia defamation actions." In affirming, Powell, J., stated that his reasons were "different from those relied upon by the Vermont Supreme Court": "Like every other case in which this Court has found constitutional limits to state defamation laws, *Gertz* involved expression on a matter of undoubted public concern. * * *

"We have never considered whether the *Gertz* balance obtains when the defamatory statements involve no issue of public concern. To make this determination, we must employ the approach approved in *Gertz* and balance the State's interest in compensating private individuals for injury to their reputation against the First Amendment interest in protecting this type of expression. This state interest is identical to the one weighed in *Gertz.* * * *

"The First Amendment interest, on the other hand, is less important than the one weighed in *Gertz.* We have long recognized that not all speech is of equal First Amendment importance.[5] It is speech on 'matters of public

---

5. This Court on many occasions has recognized that certain kinds of speech are less central to the interests of the First Amendment than others. Obscene speech and "fighting words" long have been accorded no protection. *Roth; Chaplinsky.* In the area of protected speech, the most prominent example of reduced protection for certain kinds of speech concerns commercial speech. Such speech, we have noted, occupies a "subordinate position in the scale of First Amendment values." *Ohralik.* * * *

concern' that is 'at the heart of the First Amendment's protection.' [In] contrast, speech on matters of purely private concern is of less First Amendment concern. As a number of state courts, including the court below, have recognized, the role of the Constitution in regulating state libel law is far more limited when the concerns that activated *New York Times* and *Gertz* are absent.[6] In such a case, '[t]here is no threat to the free and robust debate of public issues; there is no potential interference with a meaningful dialogue of ideas concerning self-government; and there is no threat of liability causing a reaction of self-censorship by the press. The facts of the present case are wholly without the First Amendment concerns with which the Supreme Court of the United States has been struggling.' *Harley-Davidson Motorsports, Inc. v. Markley,* 279 Or. 361, 366, 568 P.2d 1359, 1363 (1977).

"While such speech is not totally unprotected by the First Amendment, see *Connick,* its protections are less stringent. [In] light of the reduced constitutional value of speech involving no matters of public concern, we hold that the state interest adequately supports awards of presumed and punitive damages—even absent a showing of 'actual malice.'[7]

"The only remaining issue is whether petitioner's credit report involved a matter of public concern. In a related context, we have held that '[w]hether [speech] addresses a matter of public concern must be determined by [the expression's] content, form, and context [as] revealed by the whole record.' *Connick v. Myers* [Ch. 9, II infra]. These factors indicate that petitioner's credit report concerns no public issue.[8] It was speech solely in the individual

Other areas of the law provide further examples. In *Ohralik* we noted that there are "[n]umerous examples [of] communications that are regulated without offending the First Amendment, such as the exchange of information about securities, * * * corporate proxy statements, [the] exchange of price and production information among competitors, [and] employers' threats of retaliation for the labor activities of employees." Yet similar regulation of political speech is subject to the most rigorous scrutiny. Likewise, while the power of the State to license lawyers, psychiatrists, and public school teachers—all of whom speak for a living—is unquestioned, this Court has held that a law requiring licensing of union organizers is unconstitutional under the First Amendment. *Thomas v. Collins*, [Ch. 4, I, A infra]; see also *Rosenbloom v. Metromedia* (opinion of Brennan, J.) ("the determinant whether the First Amendment applies to state libel actions is whether the utterance involved concerns an issue of public or general concern").

6. As one commentator has remarked with respect to "the case of a commercial supplier of credit information that defames a person applying for credit"—the case before us today—"If the first amendment requirements outlined in *Gertz* apply, there is something clearly wrong with the first amendment or with *Gertz*." Shiffrin, *The First Amendment and Economic Regulation: Away From a General Theory of the First Amendment,* 78 Nw.L.Rev. 1212, 1268 (1983).

7. The dissent, purporting to apply the same balancing test that we do today, concludes that even speech on purely private matters is entitled to the protections of *Gertz.* * * *

The dissent's "balance" [would] lead to the protection of all libels—no matter how attenuated their constitutional interest. If the dissent were the law, a woman of impeccable character who was branded a "whore" by a jealous neighbor would have no effective recourse unless she could prove "actual malice" by clear and convincing evidence. This is not malice in the ordinary sense, but in the more demanding sense of *New York Times.* The dissent would, in effect, constitutionalize the entire common law of libel.

8. The dissent suggests that our holding today leaves all credit reporting subject to

interest of the speaker and its specific business audience. Cf. *Central Hudson.* This particular interest warrants no special protection when—as in this case—the speech is wholly false and clearly damaging to the victim's business reputation. Moreover, since the credit report was made available to only five subscribers, who, under the terms of the subscription agreement, could not disseminate it further, it cannot be said that the report involves any 'strong interest in the free flow of commercial information.' *Virginia Pharmacy.* There is simply no credible argument that this type of credit reporting requires special protection to ensure that 'debate on public issues [will] be uninhibited, robust, and wide-open.' *New York Times.*

"In addition, the speech here, like advertising, is hardy and unlikely to be deterred by incidental state regulation. See *Virginia Pharmacy.* It is solely motivated by the desire for profit, which, we have noted, is a force less likely to be deterred than others. Arguably, the reporting here was also more objectively verifiable than speech deserving of greater protection. In any case, the market provides a powerful incentive to a credit reporting agency to be accurate, since false credit reporting is of no use to creditors. Thus, any incremental 'chilling' effect of libel suits would be of decreased significance.

"We conclude that permitting recovery of presumed and punitive damages in defamation cases absent a showing of 'actual malice' does not violate the First Amendment when the defamatory statements do not involve matters of public concern."

Although expressing the view that *Gertz* should be overruled and that the *New York Times* malice definition should be reconsidered, BURGER, C.J., concurring, stated that: "The single question before the Court today is whether *Gertz* applies to this case. The plurality opinion holds that *Gertz* does not apply because, unlike the challenged expression in *Gertz,* the alleged defamatory expression in this case does not relate to a matter of public concern. I agree that *Gertz* is limited to circumstances in which the alleged defamatory expression concerns a matter of general public importance, and that the expression in question here relates to a matter of essentially private concern. I therefore agree with the plurality opinion to the extent that it holds that *Gertz* is inapplicable in this case for the two reasons indicated. No more is needed to dispose of the present case."

WHITE, J., who had dissented in *Gertz,* was prepared to overrule that case or to limit it, but he disagreed with Powell, J.'s, suggestion that the plurality's resolution of the case was faithful to *Gertz:*

reduced First Amendment protection. This is incorrect. The protection to be accorded a particular credit report depends on whether the report's "content, form, and context" indicate that it concerns a public matter. We also do not hold, as the dissent suggests we do, that the report is subject to reduced constitutional protection because it constitutes economic or commercial speech. We discuss such speech, along with advertising, only to show how many of the same concerns that argue in favor of reduced constitutional protection in those areas apply here as well.

"It is interesting that Justice Powell declines to follow the *Gertz* approach in this case. I had thought that the decision in *Gertz* was intended to reach cases that involve any false statements of fact injurious to reputation, whether the statement is made privately or publicly and whether or not it implicates a matter of public importance. Justice Powell, however, distinguishes *Gertz* as a case that involved a matter of public concern, an element absent here. Wisely, in my view, Justice Powell does not rest his application of a different rule here on a distinction drawn between media and non-media defendants. On that issue, I agree with Justice Brennan that the First Amendment gives no more protection to the press in defamation suits than it does to others exercising their freedom of speech. None of our cases affords such a distinction; to the contrary, the Court has rejected it at every turn. It should be rejected again, particularly in this context, since it makes no sense to give the most protection to those publishers who reach the most readers and therefore pollute the channels of communication with the most misinformation and do the most damage to private reputation. If *Gertz* is to be distinguished from this case, on the ground that it applies only where the allegedly false publication deals with a matter of general or public importance, then where the false publication does not deal with such a matter, the common-law rules would apply whether the defendant is a member of the media or other public disseminator or a non-media individual publishing privately. Although Justice Powell speaks only of the inapplicability of the *Gertz* rule with respect to presumed and punitive damages, it must be that the *Gertz* requirement of some kind of fault on the part of the defendant is also inapplicable in cases such as this. * * *

"The question before us is whether *Gertz* is to be applied in this case. For either of two reasons, I believe that it should not. First, I am unreconciled to the *Gertz* holding and believe that it should be overruled. Second, as Justice Powell indicates, the defamatory publication in this case does not deal with a matter of public importance."

BRENNAN, J., joined by Marshall, Blackmun and Stevens, JJ., dissented:

"This case involves a difficult question of the proper application of *Gertz* to credit reporting—a type of speech at some remove from that which first gave rise to explicit First Amendment restrictions on state defamation law— and has produced a diversity of considered opinions, none of which speaks for the Court. Justice Powell's plurality opinion affirming the judgment below would not apply the *Gertz* limitations on presumed and punitive damages [because] the speech involved a subject of purely private concern and was circulated to an extremely limited audience. * * * Justice White also would affirm; he would not apply *Gertz* to this case on the ground that the subject matter of the publication does not deal with a matter of general or public importance. The Chief Justice apparently agrees with Justice White. The four who join this opinion would reverse the judgment of the Vermont Supreme Court. We believe that, although protection of the type of expression at issue is admittedly not the 'central meaning of the First

Amendment,' *Gertz* makes clear that the First Amendment nonetheless requires restraints on presumed and punitive damage awards for this expression. * * *

"[Respondent urged that *Gertz* be restricted] to cases in which the defendant is a 'media' entity. Such a distinction is irreconcilable with the fundamental First Amendment principle that '[t]he inherent worth [of] speech in terms of its capacity for informing the public does not depend upon the identity of its source, whether corporation, association, union, or individual.' *First National Bank v. Bellotti* [Ch. X infra]. First Amendment difficulties lurk in the definitional questions such an approach would generate. And the distinction would likely be born an anachronism.[7] Perhaps most importantly, the argument that *Gertz* should be limited to the media misapprehends our cases. We protect the press to ensure the vitality of First Amendment guarantees. This solicitude implies no endorsement of the principle that speakers other than the press deserve lesser First Amendment protection. * * *

"The free speech guarantee gives each citizen an equal right to self-expression and to participation in self-government. [Accordingly,] at least six Members of this Court (the four who join this opinion and Justice White and The Chief Justice) agree today that, in the context of defamation law, the rights of the institutional media are no greater and no less than those enjoyed by other individuals or organizations engaged in the same activities.[10] * * *

"Purporting to 'employ the approach approved in *Gertz*,' Justice Powell balances the state interest in protecting private reputation against the First Amendment interest in protecting expression on matters not of public concern.[11]

"The five Members of the Court voting to affirm the damage award in this case have provided almost no guidance as to what constitutes a protected 'matter of public concern.' Justice White offers nothing at all, but his opinion does indicate that the distinction turns on solely the subject matter of the expression and not on the extent or conditions of dissemination of that expression. Justice Powell adumbrates a rationale that would appear to focus primarily on subject matter.[12] The opinion relies on the fact that the speech

7. Owing to transformations in the technological and economic structure of the communications industry, there has been an increasing convergence of what might be labeled "media" and "nonmedia."

10. Justice Powell's opinion does not expressly reject the media/nonmedia distinction, but does expressly decline to apply that distinction to resolve this case.

11. One searches *Gertz* in vain for a single word to support the proposition that limits on presumed and punitive damages obtained only when speech involved matters of public concern. *Gertz* could not have been grounded in such a premise. Distrust of placing in the courts the power to decide

what speech was of public concern was precisely the rationale *Gertz* offered for rejecting the *Rosenbloom* plurality approach. * * *

12. Justice Powell also appears to rely in part on the fact that communication was limited and confidential. Given that his analysis also relies on the subject matter of the credit report, it is difficult to decipher exactly what role the nature and extent of dissemination plays in Justice Powell's analysis. But because the subject matter of the expression at issue is properly understood as a matter of public concern, it may well be that this element of confidentiality is crucial to the outcome as far as Justice

at issue was 'solely in the individual interest of the speaker and its *business* audience.' Analogizing explicitly to advertising, the opinion also states that credit reporting is 'hardy' and 'solely motivated by the desire for profit.' These two strains of analysis suggest that Justice Powell is excluding the subject matter of credit reports from 'matters of public concern' because the speech is predominantly in the realm of matters of economic concern."

Brennan, J., pointed to precedents (particularly labor cases) protecting speech on economic matters and argued that, "the breadth of this protection evinces recognition that freedom of expression is not only essential to check tyranny and foster self-government but also intrinsic to individual liberty and dignity and instrumental in society's search for truth."

Moreover, he emphasized the importance of credit reporting: "The credit reporting of Dun & Bradstreet falls within any reasonable definition of 'public concern' consistent with our precedents. Justice Powell's reliance on the fact that Dun & Bradstreet publishes credit reports 'for profit' is wholly unwarranted. Time and again we have made clear that speech loses none of its constitutional protection 'even though it is carried in a form that is "sold" for profit.' *Virginia Pharmacy*. More importantly, an announcement of the bankruptcy of a local company is information of potentially great concern to residents of the community where the company is [located]. And knowledge about solvency and the effect and prevalence of bankruptcy certainly would inform citizen opinions about questions of economic regulation. It is difficult to suggest that a bankruptcy is not a subject matter of public concern when federal law requires invocation of judicial mechanisms to effectuate it and makes the fact of the bankruptcy a matter of public record. * * *

"Even if the subject matter of credit reporting were properly considered—in the terms of Justice White and Justice Powell—as purely a matter of private discourse, this speech would fall well within the range of valuable expression for which the First Amendment demands protection. Much expression that does not directly involve public issues receives significant protection. Our cases do permit some diminution in the degree of protection afforded one category of speech about economic or commercial matters. 'Commercial speech'—defined as advertisements that 'do no more than propose a commercial transaction'—may be more closely regulated than other types of speech. [Credit] reporting is not 'commercial speech' as this Court has defined the term.

Powell's opinion is concerned. In other words, it may be that Justice Powell thinks this particular expression could not contribute to public welfare because the public generally does not receive it. This factor does not suffice to save the analysis. See n. 18 infra.

[In fn. 18, Brennan, J., indicated that, "Dun & Bradstreet doubtless provides thousands of credit reports to thousands of subscribers who receive the information pursuant to the same strictures imposed on the recipients in this case. As a systemic matter, therefore, today's decision diminishes the free flow of information because Dun & Bradstreet will generally be made more reticent in providing information to all its subscribers."]

"[In] *every* case in which we have permitted more extensive state regulation on the basis of a commercial speech rationale—the speech being regulated was pure advertising—an offer to buy or sell goods and services or encouraging such buying and selling. Credit reports are not commercial advertisements for a good or service or a proposal to buy or sell such a product. We have been extremely chary about extending the 'commercial speech' doctrine beyond this narrowly circumscribed category of advertising because often vitally important speech will be uttered to advance economic interests and because the profit motive making such speech hardy dissipates rapidly when the speech is not advertising."[a]

Finally, Brennan, J., argued that even if credit reports were characterized as commercial speech, "unrestrained" presumed and punitive damages would violate the commercial speech requirement that "the regulatory means chosen be narrowly tailored so as to avoid any unnecessary chilling of protected expression. [Accordingly,] Greenmoss Builders should be permitted to recover for any actual damage it can show resulted from Dun & Bradstreet's negligently false credit report, but should be required to show actual malice to receive presumed or punitive damages."

Notes and Questions

1. Which of the following are "private" according to the opinions of Powell, J., Burger, C.J., and White, J.? (a) a report in the *Wall Street Journal* that Greenmoss has gone bankrupt; (b) a confidential report by Dun & Bradstreet to a bank that a famous politician has poor credit. Would the answer be different if the subject of the report were an actor? (c) a statement in the campus newspaper or by one student to another that a law professor is an alcoholic. Would it make a difference if the law professor was being considered for a Supreme Court appointment?

Consider the relationship between the public/private focus of the *Greenmoss* decision and the "public controversy" aspect of the public figure definition. If the speech does not relate to a "public" controversy, can it be "public" within the terms of *Greenmoss*? See Smolla, *Law of Defamation* 3–15 (1986). Reconsider *Time, Inc. v. Firestone,* Ch. 1, II, C supra.[b]

a. Brennan, J., cited *Consolidated Edison,* Ch. 10 infra, which invalidated a regulation that prohibited a utility company from inserting its views on "controversial issues of public policy" into its monthly electrical bill mailings. The mailing that prompted the regulation advocated nuclear power.

b. For discussion of the different meanings of public and private speech, see Schauer, *"Private" Speech and the "Private" Forum: Givhan v. Western Line School District,* 1979 Sup.Ct.Rev. 217. Compare Perry, *Freedom of Expression: An Es-* *say on Theory and Doctrine,* 78 Nw. U.L.Rev. 1137 (1983) (denying any meaningful distinction between personal and political decisions). See generally Symposium, *The Public/Private Distinction,* 130 U.Pa. L.Rev. 1289 (1982); Drechsel, *Defining "Public Concern" in Defamation Cases Since Dun & Bradstreet v. Greenmoss Builders,* 43 Fed.Com.L.J. 1 (1990); Lieberwitz, *Freedom of Speech in Public Sector Employment: The Deconstitutionalization of the Public Sector Workplace,* 19 U.C.Davis L.Rev. 597 (1986); Massaro, *Significant Silences: Freedom of Speech in the Public Sector Workplace,* 61 S.Cal.L.Rev. 1, 68–76

Finally, does it matter why the D & B subscribers received the information about Greenmoss? Suppose, for investment or insurance purposes, the subscribers had asked for reports on all aspects of the construction industry in Vermont? Compare *Lowe v. SEC*, Ch. 4, III infra.

2.   What standard should apply to employers who make negative statements about former employees? Should employers be liable to a subsequently injured person if they fail to disclose an individual's sexual or violent misconduct? Should they be required to disclose such conduct? If they are required to disclose such conduct, is a "good faith" standard appropriate? See Oliver, *Opening the Channels of Communication Among Employers*, 33 Valparaiso U.L.Rev. 687 (1999); Verkerke, *Legal Regulation of Employment Reference Practices*, 65 U.Chi.L.Rev. 111 (1998).

3.   What standard should be applied to publicly disseminated defamatory comments made about apples or eggs?[c]

4.   Should the focus of the decision have been commercial speech instead of private speech? Would an expansion of the commercial speech definition have been preferable to the promotion of ad hoc decision making about the nature of "private" speech? Consider Shiffrin, *The First Amendment and Economic Regulation: Away From A General Theory of the First Amendment*, 78 Nw.U.L.Rev. 1212, 1269 n. 327 (1983): "[D]rawing lines based on underlying first amendment values is a far cry from sending out the judiciary on a general ad hoc expedition to separate matters of general public interest from matters that are not. A commitment to segregate certain commercial speech from *Gertz* protection is not a commitment to general ad hoc determinations."

5.   According to Powell, J., in fn. 5, are the *Ohralik* examples, i.e., exchange of information about securities, corporate proxy statements and the like, examples of protected speech subject to regulation? In what sense, are those examples of communication protected? What is the significance of Powell, J.'s suggestion that they are something other than commercial speech?[d] Where do those examples fit into Brennan, J.'s view of the first amendment? For general discussion, see Shiffrin, note 2 supra; Wolfson, *The First Amendment and the SEC*, 20 Conn.L.Rev. 265 (1988). See also Comment, *A Political Speech Exception to the Regulation of Proxy Solicitations*, 86 Colum.L.Rev. 1453 (1986).

(1987). Comment, *A Conflict in the Public Interest*, 31 Santa Clara L.Rev. 997 (1991). For commentary on the question of whether Gertz should extend to non-media defendants see e.g. sources cited in note 1 after *Gertz*, Ch. 1, II, C supra.

   c. Collins, *Free Speech, Food Libel, & The First Amendment * * * in Ohio*, 26 Ohio N.U. L.Rev. 1 (2000); Wasserman, *Two Degrees of Speech Protection: Free Speech Through the Prism of Agricultural Disparagement Laws* , 8 Wm. & Mary Bill Rts. J. 323 (2000).

   d. Consider *Board of Trustees v. Fox*, Sec. 3, II supra (dictum stating that attorneys or tutors dispensing advice for a fee is not commercial speech and strongly suggesting that regulations prohibiting such speech in college dormitories may be unconstitutional).

IV.   LABOR SPEECH

DEBARTOLO CORP. v. FLORIDA GULF COAST BLDG. AND CONST. TRADES COUNCIL

485 U.S. 568, 108 S.Ct. 1392, 99 L.Ed.2d 645 (1988).

JUSTICE WHITE delivered the opinion of the Court.

This case centers around the respondent union's peaceful handbilling of the businesses operating in a shopping mall in Tampa, Florida, owned by petitioner, the Edward J. DeBartolo Corporation (DeBartolo). The union's primary labor dispute was with H.J. High Construction Company (High) over alleged substandard wages and fringe benefits. High was retained by the H.J. Wilson Company (Wilson) to construct a department store in the mall, and neither DeBartolo nor any of the other 85 or so mall tenants had any contractual right to influence the selection of contractors.

The union, however, sought to obtain their influence upon Wilson and High by distributing handbills asking mall customers not to shop at any of the stores in the mall "until the Mall's owner publicly promises that all construction at the Mall will be done using contractors who pay their employees fair wages and fringe benefits." The handbills' message was that "[t]he payment of substandard wages not only diminishes the working person's ability to purchase with earned, rather than borrowed, dollars, but it also undercuts the wage standard of the entire community." The handbills made clear that the union was seeking only a consumer boycott against the other mall tenants, not a secondary strike by their employees. At all four entrances to the mall for about three weeks in December 1979, the union peacefully distributed the handbills without any accompanying picketing or patrolling.

[DeBartolo] [filed] a complaint with the National Labor Relations Board (Board), charging the union with engaging in unfair labor practices under § 8(b)(4) of the National Labor Relations Act (NLRA), 61 Stat. 141, as amended, 29 U.S.C. § 158(b)(4).[2] [T]he Board held that the union's handbilling was proscribed by § 8(b)(4)(ii)(B).

---

2. That section provides in pertinent part: "§ 158. Unfair labor practices * * *

"(b) Unfair labor practices by [a] labor organization[.] It shall be an unfair labor practice for a labor organization or its agents—* * *

"(4)(i) to engage in, or to induce or encourage any individual employed by any person engaged in commerce or in an industry affecting commerce to engage in, a strike or a refusal in the course of his employment to use, manufacture, process, transport, or otherwise handle or work on any goods, articles, materials, or commodities or to perform any services;

or (ii) to threaten, coerce, or restrain any person engaged in commerce or in an industry affecting commerce, where in either case an object thereof is—* * *

"(B) forcing or requiring any person to cease using, selling, handling, transporting, or otherwise dealing in the products of any other producer, processor, or manufacturer, or to cease doing business with any other person, or forcing or requiring any other employer to recognize or bargain with a labor organization as the representative of his employees unless such labor organization has been certified as the representative of such employees

[T]he Board has construed § 8(b)(4) of the Act to cover handbilling at a mall entrance urging potential customers not to trade with any retailers in the mall, in order to exert pressure on the proprietor of the mall to influence a particular mall tenant not to do business with a nonunion construction contractor. [T]he Board's construction of the statute, as applied in this case, poses serious questions of the validity of § 8(b)(4) under the First Amendment. The handbills involved here truthfully revealed the existence of a labor dispute and urged potential customers of the mall to follow a wholly legal course of action, namely, not to patronize the retailers doing business in the mall. The handbilling was peaceful. No picketing or patrolling was involved. On its face, this was expressive activity arguing that substandard wages should be opposed by abstaining from shopping in a mall where such wages were paid. Had the union simply been leafletting the public generally, including those entering every shopping mall in town, pursuant to an annual educational effort against substandard pay, there is little doubt that legislative proscription of such leaflets would pose a substantial issue of validity under the First Amendment. The same may well be true in this case, although here the handbills called attention to a specific situation in the mall allegedly involving the payment of unacceptably low wages by a construction contractor.

That a labor union is the leafletter and that a labor dispute was involved does not foreclose this analysis. We do not suggest that communications by labor unions are never of the commercial speech variety and thereby entitled to a lesser degree of constitutional protection. The handbills involved here, however, do not appear to be typical commercial speech such as advertising the price of a product or arguing its merits, for they pressed the benefits of unionism to the community and the dangers of inadequate wages to the economy and the standard of living of the populace. Of course, commercial speech itself is protected by the First Amendment, *Virginia Pharmacy,* and however these handbills are to be classified, [we] must independently inquire whether there is another interpretation, not raising these serious constitutional concerns, that may fairly be ascribed to § 8(b)(4)(ii). * * *

The case turns on whether handbilling such as involved here must be held to "threaten, coerce, or restrain any person" to cease doing business with another, within the meaning of § 8(b)(4)(ii)(B). We note first that

under the provisions of section 159 of this title: Provided, That nothing contained in this clause (B) shall be construed to make unlawful, where not otherwise unlawful, any primary strike or primary picketing; * * *

"Provided further, [the 'publicity proviso'] That for the purposes of this paragraph (4) only, nothing contained in such paragraph shall be construed to prohibit publicity, other than picketing, for the purpose of truthfully advising the public, including consumers and members of a labor organization, that a product or products are produced by an employer with whom the labor organization has a primary dispute and are distributed by another employer, as long as such publicity does not have an effect of inducing any individual employed by any person other than the primary employer in the course of his employment to refuse to pick up, deliver, or transport any goods, or not to perform any services, at the establishment of the employer engaged in such distribution."

"induc[ing] or encourag[ing]" employees of the secondary employer to strike is proscribed by § 8(b)(4)(i). But more than mere persuasion is necessary to prove a violation of § 8(b)(4)(ii): that section requires a showing of threats, coercion, or restraints. Those words, we have said, are "nonspecific, indeed vague," and should be interpreted with "caution" and not given a "broad sweep"; and in applying § 8(b)(1)(A) they were not to be construed to reach peaceful recognitional picketing. Neither is there any necessity to construe such language to reach the handbills involved in this case. There is no suggestion that the leaflets had any coercive effect on customers of the mall. There was no violence, picketing, or patrolling and only an attempt to persuade customers not to shop in the mall.

The Board nevertheless found that the handbilling "coerced" mall tenants and explained in a footnote that "[a]ppealing to the public not to patronize secondary employers in an attempt to inflict economic harm on the secondary employers by causing them to lose business. [S]uch appeals constitute 'economic retaliation' and are therefore a form of coercion." Our decision in *NLRB v. Fruit and Vegetable Packers, Local 760,* 377 U.S. 58, 84 S.Ct. 1063, 12 L.Ed.2d 129 (1964) (*Tree Fruits*),[a] however, makes untenable the notion that *any* kind of handbilling, picketing, or other appeals to a secondary employer to cease doing business with the employer involved in the labor dispute is "coercion" within the meaning of § 8(b)(4)(ii)(B) if it has some economic impact on the neutral. In that case, the union picketed a secondary employer, a retailer, asking the public not to buy a product produced by the primary employer. We held that the impact of this picketing was not coercion within the meaning of § 8(b)(4) even though, if the appeal succeeded, the retailer would lose revenue.[4]

NLRB v. Retail Store Employees, Local 1001, 447 U.S. 607, 100 S.Ct. 2372, 65 L.Ed.2d 377 (1980) (*Safeco*), in turn, held that consumer picketing urging a general boycott of a secondary employer aimed at causing him to sever relations with the union's real antagonist was coercive and forbidden by § 8(b)(4).[b] It is urged that *Safeco* rules this case because the union sought a general boycott of all tenants in the mall. But "picketing is qualitatively

---

a. *Tree Fruits* involved union picketing and handbilling urging consumers not to buy Washington apples from Safeway markets. The union's dispute was with those who supplied apples to Safeway, not with Safeway. In finding no violation, the Court observed that if the union's appeal succeeds, "the secondary employers' purchases from the struck firms are decreased only because the public has diminished its purchases of the struck product. On the other hand, when consumer picketing is employed to persuade customers not to trade at all with the secondary employer, the latter stops buying the struck product, not because of a falling demand, but in response to pressure designed to inflict injury on his

business generally. In such case, the union does more than merely follow the struck product; it creates a separate dispute with the secondary employer."

4. The Board points out that *Tree Fruits* indicates urging customer boycotts can be coercion within the meaning of § 8(b)(4). But the Court was there talking about picketing and not mere handbilling.

b. *Safeco* involved union picketing (and handbilling that was not challenged) urging consumers to cancel their Safeco insurance policies. The union's dispute was with Safeco, not with the title companies, but 90% of the title companies' income was derived from the sale of Safeco insurance.

'different from other modes of communication,' "and *Safeco* noted that the picketing there actually threatened the neutral with ruin or substantial loss. As Justice Stevens pointed out in his concurrence in *Safeco,* picketing is "a mixture of conduct and communication" and the conduct element "often provides the most persuasive deterrent to third persons about to enter a business establishment." Handbills containing the same message, he observed, are "much less effective than labor picketing" because they "depend entirely on the persuasive force of the idea."[c] Similarly, the Court stated in *Hughes v. Superior Court,* 339 U.S. 460, 70 S.Ct. 718, 94 L.Ed. 985 (1950): "Publication in a newspaper, or by distribution of circulars, may convey the same information or make the same charge as do those patrolling a picket line. But the very purpose of a picket line is to exert influences, and it produces consequences, different from other modes of communication."[d]

In *Tree Fruits,* we could not discern with the "requisite clarity" that Congress intended to proscribe all peaceful consumer picketing at secondary sites. There is even less reason to find in the language of § 8(b)(4)(ii), standing alone, any clear indication that handbilling, without picketing, "coerces" secondary employers. The loss of customers because they read a handbill urging them not to patronize a business, and not because they are intimidated by a line of picketers, is the result of mere persuasion, and the neutral who reacts is doing no more than what its customers honestly want it to do. * * *

The Board's reading of § 8(b)(4) would make an unfair labor practice out of any kind of publicity or communication to the public urging a consumer boycott of employers other than those the [publicity] proviso specifically deals with.[e] On the facts of this case, newspaper, radio, and

---

c. The *Safeco* plurality, per Powell, J., argued that legislative prohibition of the concededly truthful picketing was justified because such picketing "spreads labor discord by coercing a neutral party to join the fray." The prohibition of picketing in pursuit of such "unlawful objectives" was said to impose "no impermissible restrictions upon constitutionally protected speech." See St. Antoine, *Free Speech or Economic Weapon? The Persisting Problem of Picketing,* 16 Suffolk U.L.Rev. 883, 901 (1982): "[*Safeco*] was the first time the Supreme Court had ever clearly sustained a ban on peaceful and orderly picketing addressed to, and calling for seemingly lawful responses by, individual consumers acting on their own." Contrast *Claiborne Hardware,* p. 521 infra.

d. *Hughes* involved picketing of a grocery store with placards reading "Lucky Won't Hire Negro Clerks in Proportion to Negro Trade—Don't Patronize." California enjoined the picketing on the ground that the picketing was for an unlawful purpose,

i.e., it encouraged racial discrimination: if the picketing were permitted, "then other races, white, yellow, brown, and red, would have equal rights to demand discriminatory hiring on a racial basis." Concurring with California's assessment that the picketers' objective was unlawful (even though an employer could "voluntarily" have adopted racial quotas without violating any law), the Court, per Frankfurter, J., stated that "The Constitution does not demand that the element of communication in picketing prevail over the mischief furthered by its use in these situations." Moreover, picketing was declared to be "more than free speech, since it involves patrol and [the] loyalties and responses evoked and exacted by picket lines are unlike those flowing from appeals by printed word." Finally, Frankfurter, J., referred to the "compulsive features in picketing, beyond the aspect of mere communication as an appeal to [reason]."

e. Earlier in the litigation, the Court held (*Edward J. DeBartolo Corp. v. NLRB,* 463 U.S. 147, 103 S.Ct. 2926, 77 L.Ed.2d

television appeals not to patronize the mall would be prohibited; and it would be an unfair labor practice for unions in their own meetings to urge their members not to shop in the mall. * * *

In our view, interpreting § 8(b)(4) as not reaching the handbilling involved in this case is not foreclosed either by the language of the section or its legislative history. That construction makes unnecessary passing on the serious constitutional questions that would be raised by the Board's understanding of the statute. * * *[f]

Notes and Questions

1. *The problem of categorization.* What is the relationship between labor publicity handbilling and commercial speech? Public speech? Private speech? Should it be separately categorized?[g] Should there be different categories for speech by employers and speech by employees? Consider *NLRB v. Gissel Packing Co.*, 395 U.S. 575, 89 S.Ct. 1918, 23 L.Ed.2d 547 (1969) (discussing anti-union statements by employer during union organizational drive): "Any assessment of the precise scope of employer expression [must] be made in the context of its labor relations setting. Thus, an employer's rights cannot outweigh the equal right of the employees to associate [freely]. And any balancing of those rights must take into account the economic dependence of the employees on their employers, and the necessary tendency of the former, because of that relationship, to pick up intended implications of the latter that might be more readily dismissed by a more disinterested ear. Stating these obvious principles is but another way of recognizing that what is basically at stake is the establishment of a nonpermanent, limited relationship between the employer, his economically dependent employee, and his union agent, not the election of legislators or the enactment of legislation whereby that relationship is ultimately defined and where the independent voter may be freer to listen more objectively and employers as a class freer to talk. Compare *New York Times Co. v. Sullivan.*"

2. *The speech-conduct distinction.* Does the Court's speech-conduct distinction adequately distinguish handbilling from picketing? Consider

---

535 (1983)), that the publicity proviso did not protect the union's handbilling because the proviso is limited to publicity "intended to inform the public that the primary employer's product is 'distributed by' the secondary employer" and the cotenants did not distribute any product produced by High.

f. O'Connor and Scalia, JJ., concurred in the judgment without opinion; Kennedy, J., took no part.

g. See Cox, *Foreword: Freedom of Expression in the Burger Court,* 94 Harv. L.Rev. 1 (1980); Getman, *Labor Speech and Free Speech: The Curious Policy of Limited*

Expression, 43 Md.L.Rev. 4 (1984); Goldman, *The First Amendment and Nonpicketing Labor Publicity,* 36 Vand.L.Rev. 1469 (1983); Harper, fn. h, infra; Kohler, *Setting the Conditions for Self–Rule: Unions, Associations, Our First Amendment Discourse and the Problem of DeBartolo,* 1990 Wisc. L.Rev. 149. Pope, *The First Amendment, The Thirteenth Amendment, and the Right to Organize in the Twenty–First Century,* 51 Rutgers L.Rev. 941 (1999); Pope, *Labor and the Constitution: From Abolition to Deindustrialization,* 65 Texas L.Rev. 1071 (1987); Pope, fn. h infra; St. Antoine, fn. c supra; Tribe, note 2 infra.

Tribe, *Constitutional Choices,* 200 (1985): "In a significant number of labor cases, the speech-conduct distinction has been employed to justify restrictions directed specifically at the communicative impact of expressive activity. [As] articulated by Justice Stevens in [*Safeco*], the 'signal' doctrine mandates a lowered level of protection for expression 'that calls for an automatic response to a signal, rather than a reasoned response to an idea.' Though generally mentioned in the same breath as coercion, the idea of a signal by itself does not carry any implication of physical or economic coercion. The idea appears to be rather that by triggering deeply held sentiments, picketing bypasses viewers' faculties of reason and, thus, in a sense brainwashes them into compliance with the boycott.[h]

"Yet this aspect of labor picketing is common to other kinds of picketing, to most effective political communication, and to virtually all advertising—political or commercial—carried in the electronic media.[i] Thus, the speech-conduct distinction, with or without the 'signal' wrinkle, adds nothing to the underlying logic of the cases but does provide another superficially neutral facade to cover the Court's consistent denial of protection to labor picketing."

3. *The determination of truth.* The Court notes that the handbills "truthfully revealed the existence of a labor dispute." What if the existence of a labor dispute were concealed? Consider *Hospital & Service Employees Union Local 399 v. NLRB,* 743 F.2d 1417 (9th Cir.1984). The union distributed handbills and published advertisements in labor newspapers urging a boycott of Delta Airlines and detailing facts about Delta's safety record. The union opined that, "It takes more than money to fly Delta. It takes nerve. Let's look at the accident record."

Although the NLRB did not question the underlying facts about Delta's safety record, it maintained that the union materials were not true, but

---

h. In an influential article, Archibald Cox had employed the signal concept somewhat differently. Signal picketing was characterized as that directed primarily, if not exclusively to union members, not the general public. Picketing was the "signal" by which the discipline and organized economic power of unions was invoked. Picketing directed primarily to the general public ("publicity picketing"), he argued, depended upon the persuasiveness of the message rather than the sanctions inherent in the discipline and power of unions. See Cox, *Strikes, Picketing and the Constitution,* 4 Vand.L.Rev. 574, 592–602 (1951). See Harper, *The Consumer's Emerging Right to Boycott,* 93 Yale L.J. 409, 442 (1984) (Stevens' *Safeco* opinion "distorted" Cox's distinction; but recommending a distinction between consumer boycotts and producer boycotts). Compare Pope, *The Three Systems Ladder of First Amendment Values,* 11 Hastings Con.L.Q. 189, 243–45 (criticizing

Harper's distinction as unreasonably denying labor the use of employee boycotts) with Gregory, *Constitutional Limitations on the Regulation of Union and Employer Conduct,* 49 Mich.L.Rev. 191, 206–07 (1950) (criticizing Cox's distinction as recommending judicial favoritism for labor) ("All picketing is obviously intended to coerce.") and Jones, *Picketing and Coercion: A Jurisprudence of Epithets,* 39 Va.L.Rev. 1023, 1050–52 (1953) (distinguishing between coercion and causing economic loss for picketed business).

i. See also St. Antoine, supra fn. c, at 902: "To the extent that Justice Stevens' emphasis is on an automatic response to a cryptic 'unfair,' as distinct from a reasoned response to a long list of particularized grievances, I can only restate my belief that a political party's two-word bumper sticker is as much protected by the first amendment as the elaborate platform adopted at its national convention."

misleading in that they did not reveal the primary dispute.[j] The NLRB sought to prohibit not only the handbills, but also the ads. What result? What if the facts about safety were inaccurate? Should the NLRB be able to sanction the making of false and misleading statements in union representation elections? To set such elections aside because of materially misleading statements? See *Midland Nat'l Life Ins.*, 263 N.L.R.B. 127, 1982 WL 23832 (1982).

4. Should boycotts be distinguished from advocating boycotts? FTC v. SUPERIOR COURT TRIAL LAWYERS ASSOCIATION, 493 U.S. 411, 110 S.Ct. 768, 107 L.Ed.2d 851 (1990), per STEVENS, J., held that a trial lawyers' group refusal to accept appointments representing indigent defendants until adequate compensation was provided could be prosecuted under the antitrust laws without first amendment violation: "The lawyers' association argues that if its conduct would otherwise be prohibited by the Sherman Act and the Federal Trade Act, it is nonetheless protected by the First Amendment rights recognized in *NAACP v. Claiborne Hardware Co.*, 458 U.S. 886, 102 S.Ct. 3409, 73 L.Ed.2d 1215 (1982). That case arose after black citizens boycotted white merchants in Claiborne County, Miss. The white merchants sued under state law to recover losses from the boycott. We found that the 'right of the States to regulate economic activity could not justify a complete prohibition against a nonviolent, politically motivated boycott designed to force governmental and economic change and to effectuate rights guaranteed by the Constitution itself.' We accordingly held that 'the nonviolent elements of petitioners' activities are entitled to the protection of the First Amendment.'

"The lawyers' association contends that because it, like the boycotters in *Claiborne Hardware,* sought to vindicate constitutional rights, it should enjoy a similar First Amendment protection. It is, of course, clear that the association's efforts to publicize the boycott, to explain the merits of its cause, and to lobby District officials to enact favorable legislation—like similar activities in *Claiborne Hardware*—were activities that were fully protected by the First Amendment. But nothing in the FTC's order would curtail such activities, and nothing in the FTC's reasoning condemned any of those activities.

"The activity that the FTC order prohibits is a concerted refusal by CJA lawyers to accept any further assignments until they receive an increase in their compensation; the undenied objective of their boycott was an economic advantage for those who agreed to participate. It is true that the *Claiborne Hardware* case also involved a boycott. That boycott, however, differs in a decisive respect. Those who joined the *Claiborne Hardware* boycott sought no special advantage for themselves. They were black citizens in Port Gibson, Mississippi, who had been the victims of political, social, and economic discrimination for many years. They sought only the equal respect and equal treatment to which they were constitutionally entitled. They

j. Other handbills discussed the primary dispute along with the safety record. The NLRB also sought to prohibit these as "coercive." Constitutional?

struggled 'to change a social order that had consistently treated them as second class citizens.' As we observed, the campaign was not intended 'to destroy legitimate competition.' Equality and freedom are preconditions of the free market, and not commodities to be haggled over within it.

"The same cannot be said of attorney's fees."

In response to the argument that *United States v. O'Brien* required that courts abandon per se rules and apply the antitrust laws with attention to the individual case, the Court argued that the expressive aspects of boycotts were ordinarily not significant and that the need for per se rules was acute (particularly with respect to price fixing arrangements): "For these reasons, it is at least possible that the *Claiborne Hardware* doctrine, which itself rests upon *O'Brien,* exhausts *O'Brien* 's application to the antitrust statutes."

BRENNAN, J., joined by Marshall, J., concurring in part and dissenting in part, agreed that if a boycott used economic power in an unlawful way to send a message, no first amendment protection should be afforded. But, he maintained: "When a boycott seeks to generate public support for the passage of legislation, it may operate on a *political* rather than *economic* level, especially when the Government is the [target.] The majority today permits the FTC to find an expressive boycott to violate the antitrust laws, without even requiring a showing that the participants possessed market power or that their conduct triggered any anticompetitive effects. * * *

"Expressive boycotts have been a principal means of political communication since the birth of the Republic. [From] the colonists' protest of the Stamp and Townsend Acts to the Montgomery bus boycott and the National Organization for Women's campaign to encourage ratification of the Equal Rights Amendment, boycotts have played a central role in our Nation's political discourse. In recent years there have been boycotts of supermarkets, meat, grapes, iced tea in cans, soft drinks, lettuce, chocolate, tuna, plastic wrap, textiles, slacks, animal skins and furs, and products of Mexico, Japan, South Africa, and the Soviet Union. * * *

"The role of boycotts in political speech is too central, and the effective alternative avenues open to the Trial Lawyers were too few, to permit the FTC to invoke the *per se* rule in this case."

———

V. CONCEIVING AND RECONCEIVING THE STRUCTURE OF FIRST AMENDMENT DOCTRINE: HATE SPEECH REVISITED—AGAIN

R.A.V. v. ST. PAUL

505 U.S. 377, 112 S.Ct. 2538, 120 L.Ed.2d 305 (1992).

JUSTICE SCALIA delivered the opinion of the Court.

In the predawn hours of June 21, 1990, petitioner and several other teenagers allegedly assembled a crudely-made cross by taping together broken chair legs. They then allegedly burned the cross inside the fenced yard of a black family that lived across the street from the house where petitioner was staying. Although this conduct could have been punished under any of a number of laws, one of the two provisions under which respondent city of St. Paul chose to charge petitioner (then a juvenile) was the St. Paul Bias–Motivated Crime Ordinance, St. Paul, Minn.Legis.Code § 292.02 (1990), which provides:

> "Whoever places on public or private property a symbol, object, appellation, characterization or graffiti, including, but not limited to, a burning cross or Nazi swastika, which one knows or has reasonable grounds to know arouses anger, alarm or resentment in others on the basis of race, color, creed, religion or gender commits disorderly conduct and shall be guilty of a misdemeanor." * * *

I

In construing the St. Paul ordinance, we are bound by the construction given to it by the Minnesota court. Accordingly, we accept the Minnesota Supreme Court's authoritative statement that the ordinance reaches only those expressions that constitute "fighting words" within the meaning of *Chaplinsky*. Petitioner and his *amici* urge us to modify the scope of the *Chaplinsky* formulation, thereby invalidating the ordinance as "substantially overbroad," *Broadrick v. Oklahoma*. We find it unnecessary to consider this issue. Assuming, *arguendo*, that all of the expression reached by the ordinance is proscribable under the "fighting words" doctrine, we nonetheless conclude that the ordinance is facially unconstitutional in that it prohibits otherwise permitted speech solely on the basis of the subjects the speech addresses.

[From] 1791 to the present, our society, like other free but civilized societies, has permitted restrictions upon the content of speech in a few limited areas, which are "of such slight social value as a step to truth that any benefit that may be derived from them is clearly outweighed by the social interest in order and morality." *Chaplinsky*. * * *

We have sometimes said that these categories of expression are "not within the area of constitutionally protected speech," *Roth; Beauharnais; Chaplinsky;* or that the "protection of the First Amendment does not extend" to them, *Bose Corp. v. Consumers Union of United States, Inc.;*

Sable Communications of Cal., Inc. v. FCC. Such statements must be taken in context, however, and are no more literally true than is the occasionally repeated shorthand characterizing obscenity "as not being speech at all," Sunstein, *Pornography and the First Amendment,* 1986 Duke L.J. 589, 615, n. 146. What they mean is that these areas of speech can, consistently with the First Amendment, be regulated *because of their constitutionally proscribable content* (obscenity, defamation, etc.)—not that they are categories of speech entirely invisible to the Constitution, so that they may be made the vehicles for content discrimination unrelated to their distinctively proscribable content. Thus, the government may proscribe libel; but it may not make the further content discrimination of proscribing *only* libel critical of the government. * * *

Our cases surely do not establish the proposition that the First Amendment imposes no obstacle whatsoever to regulation of particular instances of such proscribable expression, so that the government "may regulate [them] freely," (White, J., concurring in judgment). That would mean that a city council could enact an ordinance prohibiting only those legally obscene works that contain criticism of the city government or, indeed, that do not include endorsement of the city government. Such a simplistic, all-or-nothing-at-all approach to First Amendment protection is at odds with common sense and with our jurisprudence as well.[4] It is not true that "fighting words" have at most a "de minimis" expressive content or that their content is *in all respects* "worthless and undeserving of constitutional protection"; sometimes they are quite expressive indeed. We have not said that they constitute "*no* part of the expression of ideas," but only that they constitute "no *essential* part of any exposition of ideas." *Chaplinsky.*

The proposition that a particular instance of speech can be proscribable on the basis of one feature (e.g., obscenity) but not on the basis of another (e.g., opposition to the city government) is commonplace, and has found application in many contexts. We have long held, for example, that nonverbal expressive activity can be banned because of the action it entails, but not because of the ideas it expresses—so that burning a flag in violation of an ordinance against outdoor fires could be punishable, whereas burning a flag in violation of an ordinance against dishonoring the flag is not. See *Johnson.* See also *Barnes v. Glen Theatre, Inc.* (Scalia, J., concurring in judgment) (Souter, J., concurring in judgment); *United States v. O'Brien.* Similarly, we have upheld reasonable "time, place, or manner" restrictions, but only if they are "justified without reference to the content of the regulated speech." *Ward v. Rock Against Racism;* see also *Clark v. Community for Creative Non–Violence* (noting that the *O'Brien* test differs little from the standard

---

4. Justice White concedes that a city council cannot prohibit only those legally obscene works that contain criticism of the city government, but asserts that to be the consequence, not of the First Amendment, but of the Equal Protection Clause. Such content-based discrimination would not, he asserts, "be rationally related to a legitimate government interest." But of course the only *reason* that government interest is not a "legitimate" one is that it violates the First Amendment. This Court itself has occasionally fused the First Amendment into the Equal Protection Clause in this fashion, but at least with the acknowledgment (which Justice White cannot afford to make) that the First Amendment underlies its analysis. * * *

applied to time, place, or manner restrictions). And just as the power to proscribe particular speech on the basis of a noncontent element (e.g., noise) does not entail the power to proscribe the same speech on the basis of a content element; so also, the power to proscribe it on the basis of *one* content element (e.g., obscenity) does not entail the power to proscribe it on the basis of *other* content elements.

In other words, the exclusion of "fighting words" from the scope of the First Amendment simply means that, for purposes of that Amendment, the unprotected features of the words are, despite their verbal character, essentially a "nonspeech" element of communication. Fighting words are thus analogous to a noisy sound truck: Each is, as Justice Frankfurter recognized, a "mode of speech," *Niemotko v. Maryland,* 340 U.S. 268, 71 S.Ct. 325, 95 L.Ed. 267 (1951) (Frankfurter, J., concurring in result); both can be used to convey an idea; but neither has, in and of itself, a claim upon the First Amendment. As with the sound truck, however, so also with fighting words: The government may not regulate use based on hostility—or favoritism— towards the underlying message expressed.

The concurrences describe us as setting forth a new First Amendment principle that prohibition of constitutionally proscribable speech cannot be "underinclusiv[e]" (White, J., concurring in judgment)—a First Amendment "absolutism" whereby "within a particular 'proscribable' category of expression, * * * a government must either proscribe *all* speech or no speech at all" (Stevens, J., concurring in judgment). That easy target is of the concurrences' own invention. In our view, the First Amendment imposes not an "underinclusiveness" limitation but a "content discrimination" limitation upon a State's prohibition of proscribable speech. There is no problem whatever, for example, with a State's prohibiting obscenity (and other forms of proscribable expression) only in certain media or markets, for although that prohibition would be "underinclusive," it would not discriminate on the basis of content. See, e.g., *Sable Communications* (upholding 47 U.S.C. § 223(b)(1) (1988), which prohibits obscene *telephone* communications).

Even the prohibition against content discrimination that we assert the First Amendment requires is not absolute. It applies differently in the context of proscribable speech than in the area of fully protected speech. The rationale of the general prohibition, after all, is that content discrimination "rais[es] the specter that the Government may effectively drive certain ideas or viewpoints from the marketplace," *Simon & Schuster,* [Sec. 1, VI, A infra]. But content discrimination among various instances of a class of proscribable speech often does not pose this threat.

When the basis for the content discrimination consists entirely of the very reason the entire class of speech at issue is proscribable, no significant danger of idea or viewpoint discrimination exists. Such a reason, having been adjudged neutral enough to support exclusion of the entire class of speech from First Amendment protection, is also neutral enough to form the basis of distinction within the class. To illustrate: A State might choose to prohibit only that obscenity which is the most patently offensive *in its prurience*—i.e., that which involves the most lascivious displays of sexual activity. But it may not prohibit, for example, only that obscenity which includes offensive *political* messages. And the Federal Government can criminalize only those threats of violence that are directed against the President, see 18 U.S.C. § 871—since the reasons why threats of violence are outside the First Amendment (protecting individuals from the fear of violence, from the disruption that fear engenders, and from the possibility that the threatened violence will occur) have special force when applied to the person of the President. See *Watts v. United States* (upholding the facial validity of § 871 because of the "overwhelmin[g] interest in protecting the safety of [the] Chief Executive and in allowing him to perform his duties without interference from threats of physical violence"). But the Federal Government may not criminalize only those threats against the President that mention his policy on aid to inner cities. And to take a final example (one mentioned by Justice Stevens), a State may choose to regulate price advertising in one industry but not in others, because the risk of fraud (one of the characteristics of commercial speech that justifies depriving it of full First Amendment protection) is in its view greater there. Cf. *Morales v. Trans World Airlines, Inc.*, 504 U.S. 374, 112 S.Ct. 2031, 119 L.Ed.2d 157 (1992) (state regulation of airline advertising); *Ohralik v. Ohio State Bar Assn.* (state regulation of lawyer advertising). But a State may not prohibit only that commercial advertising that depicts men in a demeaning fashion, see, e.g., L.A. Times, Aug. 8, 1989, section 4, p. 6, col. 1.

Another valid basis for according differential treatment to even a content-defined subclass of proscribable speech is that the subclass happens to be associated with particular "secondary effects" of the speech, so that the regulation is *"justified* without reference to the content of the * * * speech," *Renton v. Playtime Theatres, Inc.* A State could, for example, permit all obscene live performances except those involving minors. Moreover, since words can in some circumstances violate laws directed not against speech but against conduct (a law against treason, for example, is violated by telling the enemy the nation's defense secrets), a particular content-based subcategory of a proscribable class of speech can be swept up incidentally within the reach of a statute directed at conduct rather than speech. Thus, for example, sexually derogatory "fighting words," among other words, may produce a violation of Title VII's general prohibition against sexual discrimination in employment practices. Where the government does not target conduct on the basis of its expressive content, acts are not shielded from regulation merely because they express a discriminatory idea or philosophy.

These bases for distinction refute the proposition that the selectivity of the restriction is "even arguably 'conditioned upon the sovereign's agreement with what a speaker may intend to say.' "There may be other such bases as well. Indeed, to validate such selectivity (where totally proscribable speech is at issue) it may not even be necessary to identify any particular "neutral" basis, so long as the nature of the content discrimination is such that there is no realistic possibility that official suppression of ideas is afoot. (We cannot think of any First Amendment interest that would stand in the way of a State's prohibiting only those obscene motion pictures with blue-eyed actresses.) Save for that limitation, the regulation of "fighting words," like the regulation of noisy speech, may address some offensive instances and leave other, equally offensive, instances alone. See *Posadas de Puerto Rico*.[6]

II

Applying these principles to the St. Paul ordinance, we conclude that, even as narrowly construed by the Minnesota Supreme Court, the ordinance is facially unconstitutional. Although the phrase in the ordinance, "arouses anger, alarm or resentment in others," has been limited by the Minnesota Supreme Court's construction to reach only those symbols or displays that amount to "fighting words," the remaining, unmodified terms make clear that the ordinance applies only to "fighting words" that insult, or provoke violence, "on the basis of race, color, creed, religion or gender." Displays containing abusive invective, no matter how vicious or severe, are permissible unless they are addressed to one of the specified disfavored topics. Those who wish to use "fighting words" in connection with other ideas—to express hostility, for example, on the basis of political affiliation, union membership, or homosexuality—are not covered. The First Amendment does not permit St. Paul to impose special prohibitions on those speakers who express views on disfavored subjects.

In its practical operation, moreover, the ordinance goes even beyond mere content discrimination, to actual viewpoint discrimination.[a] Displays containing some words—odious racial epithets, for example—would be prohibited to proponents of all views. But "fighting words" that do not themselves invoke race, color, creed, religion, or gender—aspersions upon a person's mother, for example—would seemingly be usable ad libitum in the placards of those arguing *in favor* of racial, color, etc. tolerance and equality, but could not be used by that speaker's opponents. One could hold up a sign saying, for example, that all "anti-Catholic bigots" are misbegotten; but not that all "papists" are, for that would insult and provoke violence "on the basis of religion." St. Paul has no such authority to license one side of a

---

6. Justice Stevens cites a string of opinions as supporting his assertion that "selective regulation of speech based on content" is not presumptively invalid. [A]ll that their contents establish is what we readily concede: that presumptive invalidity does not mean invariable invalidity, leaving room for such exceptions as reasonable and viewpoint-neutral content-based discrimination in nonpublic forums, or with respect to certain speech by government employees.

a. Consider Brownstein, *Alternative Maps for Navigating the First Amendment Maze*, 16 Const. Comm. 101, 105 (1999): "Even an ostensibly innocuous subject matter regulation that prohibits speech about dogs, for example, may directly restrict at least one of the viewpoints that might be expressed in a debate about what constitutes the best household pet."

debate to fight freestyle, while requiring the other to follow Marquis of Queensbury Rules.

What we have here, it must be emphasized, is not a prohibition of fighting words that are directed at certain persons or groups (which would be *facially* valid if it met the requirements of the Equal Protection Clause); but rather, a prohibition of fighting words that contain (as the Minnesota Supreme Court repeatedly emphasized) messages of "bias-motivated" hatred and in particular, as applied to this case, messages "based on virulent notions of racial supremacy." One must wholeheartedly agree with the Minnesota Supreme Court that "[i]t is the responsibility, even the obligation, of diverse communities to confront such notions in whatever form they appear," but the manner of that confrontation cannot consist of selective limitations upon speech. St. Paul's brief asserts that a general "fighting words" law would not meet the city's needs because only a content-specific measure can communicate to minority groups that the "group hatred" aspect of such speech "is not condoned by the majority." The point of the First Amendment is that majority preferences must be expressed in some fashion other than silencing speech on the basis of its content. * * *

[T]he reason why fighting words are categorically excluded from the protection of the First Amendment is not that their content communicates any particular idea, but that their content embodies a particularly intolerable (and socially unnecessary) *mode* of expressing *whatever* idea the speaker wishes to convey. St. Paul has not singled out an especially offensive mode of expression—it has not, for example, selected for prohibition only those fighting words that communicate ideas in a threatening (as opposed to a merely obnoxious) manner. Rather, it has proscribed fighting words of whatever manner that communicate messages of racial, gender, or religious intolerance. Selectivity of this sort creates the possibility that the city is seeking to handicap the expression of particular ideas.[b]

b. Consider Shiffrin, *Racist Speech, Outsider Jurisprudence, and the Meaning of America,* 80 Corn.L.Rev. 43, 59, 57 (1994): "If the argument is that a particular subject matter implicates the very risks the category was designed to cover, but in a more severe way, what difference does it make that the category of speech involved is not the most offensive *mode* of speech? The question is whether it causes the most serious form of injury. Since when is the mere possibility of idea discrimination in regulating less than fully protected speech of such enormous constitutional import? [Scalia, J.'s] description of the case law breathes new life into the expression about ostriches hiding their heads in the sand. When the government outlaws threats against the President, advertisements for casino gambling or alcoholic beverages, or the burning of draft cards, or when it engages in a campaign of zoning adult theaters out of neighborhoods, no one but a person wearing a black robe with a strong will to believe or befuddle could possibly suppose that 'there is no realistic possibility that official suppression of ideas is afoot.' Point-of-view discrimination permeates these categories. If point-of-view discrimination were as major an evil as the Court often supposes, one would think that a demanding test would have been applied in some of these cases. But many of the justices presumably share the governmental view that advertisements for casino gambling or alcoholic beverages, the burning of draft cards, and the kind of films shown in adult theaters are not worth much. They either do not look for point-of-view discrimination or devise tests that command them not to look. Perhaps they cannot see the ways in which they themselves discriminate."

[St.] Paul argues that the ordinance comes within another of the specific exceptions we mentioned, the one that allows content discrimination aimed only at the "secondary effects" of the speech, see *Renton v. Playtime Theatres, Inc.* According to St. Paul, the ordinance is intended, "not to impact on [sic] the right of free expression of the accused," but rather to "protect against the victimization of a person or persons who are particularly vulnerable because of their membership in a group that historically has been discriminated against." Even assuming that an ordinance that completely proscribes, rather than merely regulates, a specified category of speech can ever be considered to be directed only to the secondary effects of such speech, it is clear that the St. Paul ordinance is not directed to secondary effects within the meaning of *Renton.* As we said in *Boos v. Barry,* "[l]isteners' reactions to speech are not the type of 'secondary effects' we referred to in *Renton.*" * * *[7]

Finally, St. Paul and its *amici* defend the conclusion of the Minnesota Supreme Court that, even if the ordinance regulates expression based on hostility towards its protected ideological content, this discrimination is nonetheless justified because it is narrowly tailored to serve compelling state interests. Specifically, they assert that the ordinance helps to ensure the basic human rights of members of groups that have historically been subjected to discrimination, including the right of such group members to live in peace where they wish. We do not doubt that these interests are compelling, and that the ordinance can be said to promote them. But the "danger of censorship" presented by a facially content-based statute requires that that weapon be employed only where it is "*necessary* to serve the asserted [compelling] interest." The existence of adequate content-neutral alternatives thus "undercut[s] significantly" any defense of such a statute, casting considerable doubt on the government's protestations that "the asserted justification is in fact an accurate description of the purpose and effect of the law." The dispositive question in this case, therefore, is whether content discrimination is reasonably necessary to achieve St. Paul's compelling interests; it plainly is not. An ordinance not limited to the favored topics, for example, would have precisely the same beneficial effect. In fact the only interest distinctively served by the content limitation is that of displaying the city council's special hostility towards the particular biases thus singled out. That is precisely what the First Amendment forbids. The politicians of St. Paul are entitled to express that hostility—but not through the means of imposing unique limitations upon speakers who (however benightedly) disagree. * * *

7. St. Paul has not argued in this case that the ordinance merely regulates that subclass of fighting words which is most likely to provoke a violent response. But even if one assumes (as appears unlikely) that the categories selected may be so described, that would not justify selective regulation under a "secondary effects" theory. The only reason why such expressive conduct would be especially correlated with violence is that it conveys a particularly odious message; because the "chain of causation" thus *necessarily* "run[s] through the persuasive effect of the expressive component" of the conduct, it is clear that the St. Paul ordinance regulates on the basis of the "primary" effect of the speech—i.e., its persuasive (or repellent) force.

Let there be no mistake about our belief that burning a cross in someone's front yard is reprehensible. But St. Paul has sufficient means at its disposal to prevent such behavior without adding the First Amendment to the fire. * * *

JUSTICE WHITE, with whom JUSTICE BLACKMUN and JUSTICE O'CONNOR join, and with whom JUSTICE STEVENS joins except as to Part I(A), concurring in the judgment. * * *

Today [the] Court announces that earlier Courts did not mean their repeated statements that certain categories of expression are "not within the area of constitutionally protected speech." *Roth.* The present Court submits that such clear statements "must be taken in context" and are not "literally true."

To the contrary, those statements meant precisely what they said: The categorical approach is a firmly entrenched part of our First Amendment jurisprudence. * * * Nevertheless, the majority holds that the First Amendment protects those narrow categories of expression long held to be undeserving of First Amendment protection—at least to the extent that lawmakers may not regulate some fighting words more strictly than others because of their content. The Court announces that such content-based distinctions violate the First Amendment because "the government may not regulate use based on hostility—or favoritism—towards the underlying message expressed." Should the government want to criminalize certain fighting words, the Court now requires it to criminalize all fighting words.

To borrow a phrase, "Such a simplistic, all-or-nothing-at-all approach to First Amendment protection is at odds with common sense and with our jurisprudence as well." It is inconsistent to hold that the government may proscribe an entire category of speech because the content of that speech is evil, but that the government may not treat a subset of that category differently without violating the First Amendment; the content of the subset is by definition worthless and undeserving of constitutional protection.

The majority's observation that fighting words are "quite expressive indeed," is no answer. Fighting words are not a means of exchanging views, rallying supporters, or registering a protest; they are directed against individuals to provoke violence or to inflict injury. Therefore, a ban on all fighting words or on a subset of the fighting words category would restrict only the social evil of hate speech, without creating the danger of driving viewpoints from the marketplace.

Therefore, the Court's insistence on inventing its brand of First Amendment underinclusiveness puzzles me.[3] [T]he Court's new "underbreadth" creation serves no desirable function. Instead, it permits, indeed invites, the continuation of expressive conduct that in this case is evil and worthless in First Amendment terms until the city of St. Paul cures the underbreadth by

---

3. The assortment of exceptions the Court attaches to its rule belies the majority's claim that its new theory is truly concerned with content discrimination. See Part I(C), infra (discussing the exceptions).

adding to its ordinance a catch-all phrase such as "and all other fighting words that may constitutionally be subject to this ordinance."

Any contribution of this holding to First Amendment jurisprudence is surely a negative one, since it necessarily signals that expressions of violence, such as the message of intimidation and racial hatred conveyed by burning a cross on someone's lawn, are of sufficient value to outweigh the social interest in order and morality that has traditionally placed such fighting words outside the First Amendment.[4] Indeed, by characterizing fighting words as a form of "debate" the majority legitimates hate speech as a form of public discussion. * * *

B

* * * The majority appears to believe that its doctrinal revisionism is necessary to prevent our elected lawmakers from prohibiting libel against members of one political party but not another and from enacting similarly preposterous laws. The majority is misguided.

Although the First Amendment does not apply to categories of unprotected speech, such as fighting words, the Equal Protection Clause requires that the regulation of unprotected speech be rationally related to a legitimate government interest. A defamation statute that drew distinctions on the basis of political affiliation or "an ordinance prohibiting only those legally obscene words that contain criticism of the city government" would unquestionably fail rational basis review.[9]

Turning to the St. Paul ordinance and assuming arguendo, as the majority does, that the ordinance is not constitutionally overbroad (but see Part II, infra), there is no question that it would pass equal protection review. The ordinance proscribes a subset of "fighting words," those that injure "on the basis of race, color, creed, religion or gender." This selective regulation reflects the City's judgment that harms based on race, color, creed, religion, or gender are more pressing public concerns than the harms caused by other fighting words. In light of our Nation's long and painful experience with discrimination, this determination is plainly reasonable. Indeed, as the majority concedes, the interest is compelling.

---

4. This does not suggest, of course, that cross burning is always unprotected. Burning a cross at a political rally would almost certainly be protected expression. Cf. *Brandenburg v. Ohio.* But in such a context, the cross burning could not be characterized as a "direct personal insult or an invitation to exchange fisticuffs," *Texas v. Johnson,* to which the fighting words doctrine, see Part II, infra, applies.

9. The majority is mistaken in stating that a ban on obscene works critical of government would fail equal protection review only because the ban would violate the First Amendment. While decisions such as *Police Dept. of Chicago v. Mosley,* 408 U.S. 92, 92 S.Ct. 2286, 33 L.Ed.2d 212 (1972), recognize that First Amendment principles may be relevant to an equal protection claim challenging distinctions that impact on protected expression, there is no basis for linking First and Fourteenth Amendment analysis in a case involving unprotected expression. Certainly, one need not resort to First Amendment principles to conclude that the sort of improbable legislation the majority hypothesizes is based on senseless distinctions.

C

The Court has patched up its argument with an apparently nonexhaustive list of ad hoc exceptions, in what can be viewed as an attempt to confine the effects of its decision to the facts of this case, or as an effort to anticipate some of the questions that will arise from its radical revision of First Amendment law.

For instance, if the majority were to give general application to the rule on which it decides this case, today's decision would call into question the constitutionality of the statute making it illegal to threaten the life of the President. Surely, this statute, by singling out certain threats, incorporates a content-based distinction; it indicates that the Government especially disfavors threats against the President as opposed to threats against all others.[10] But because the Government could prohibit all threats and not just those directed against the President, under the Court's theory, the compelling reasons justifying the enactment of special legislation to safeguard the President would be irrelevant, and the statute would fail First Amendment review.

To save the statute, the majority has engrafted the following exception onto its newly announced First Amendment rule: Content-based distinctions may be drawn within an unprotected category of speech if the basis for the distinctions is "the very reason the entire class of speech at issue is proscribable." Thus, the argument goes, the statute making it illegal to threaten the life of the President is constitutional, "since the reasons why threats of violence are outside the First Amendment (protecting individuals from the fear of violence, from the disruption that fear engenders, and from the possibility that the threatened violence will occur) have special force when applied to the person of the President."

The exception swallows the majority's rule. Certainly, it should apply to the St. Paul ordinance, since "the reasons why [fighting words] are outside the First Amendment * * * have special force when applied to [groups that have historically been subjected to discrimination]."

To avoid the result of its own analysis, the Court suggests that fighting words are simply a mode of communication, rather than a content-based category, and that the St. Paul ordinance has not singled out a particularly objectionable mode of communication. Again, the majority confuses the issue. A prohibition on fighting words is not a time, place, or manner restriction; it is a ban on a class of speech that conveys an overriding message of personal injury and imminent violence, a message that is at its ugliest when directed against groups that have long been the targets of discrimination. Accordingly, the ordinance falls within the first exception to the majority's theory.

As its second exception, the Court posits that certain content-based regulations will survive under the new regime if the regulated subclass

---

10. Indeed, such a law is content based in and of itself because it distinguishes between threatening and nonthreatening speech.

"happens to be associated with particular 'secondary effects' of the speech
* * *'' which the majority treats as encompassing instances in which
"words can * * * violate laws directed not against speech but against
conduct * * *.''[11] Again, there is a simple explanation for the Court's
eagerness to craft an exception to its new First Amendment rule: Under the
general rule the Court applies in this case, Title VII hostile work environment claims would suddenly be unconstitutional.

Title VII makes it unlawful to discriminate "because of [an] individual's
race, color, religion, sex, or national origin," 42 U.S.C. § 2000e–2(a)(1), and
the regulations covering hostile workplace claims forbid "sexual harassment," which includes "[u]nwelcome sexual advances, requests for sexual
favors, and other verbal or physical conduct of a sexual nature" which
creates "an intimidating, hostile, or offensive working environment." The
regulation does not prohibit workplace harassment generally; it focuses on
what the majority would characterize as the "disfavored topi[c]" of sexual
harassment. In this way, Title VII is similar to the St. Paul ordinance that
the majority condemns because it "impose[s] special prohibitions on those
speakers who express views on disfavored subjects." Under the broad principle the Court uses to decide the present case, hostile work environment
claims based on sexual harassment should fail First Amendment review;
because a general ban on harassment in the workplace would cover the
problem of sexual harassment, any attempt to proscribe the subcategory of
sexually harassing expression would violate the First Amendment.

Hence, the majority's second exception, which the Court indicates would
insulate a Title VII hostile work environment claim from an underinclusiveness challenge because "sexually derogatory 'fighting words' * * * may
produce a violation of Title VII's general prohibition against sexual discrimination in employment practices." But application of this exception to a
hostile work environment claim does not hold up under close examination.

First, the hostile work environment regulation is not keyed to the
presence or absence of an economic quid pro quo, but to the impact of the
speech on the victimized worker. Consequently, the regulation would no
more fall within a secondary effects exception than does the St. Paul
ordinance. Second, the majority's focus on the statute's general prohibition
on discrimination glosses over the language of the specific regulation governing hostile working environment, which reaches beyond any "incidental"
effect on speech. If the relationship between the broader statute and specific
regulation is sufficient to bring the Title VII regulation within *O'Brien,* then
all St. Paul need do to bring its ordinance within this exception is to add
some prefatory language concerning discrimination generally.

---

11. The consequences of the majority's
conflation of the rarely-used secondary effects standard and the *O'Brien* test for conduct incorporating "speech" and "non-
speech" elements, see generally *United*
States v. O'Brien, present another question
that I fear will haunt us and the lower
courts in the aftermath of the majority's
opinion.

As the third exception to the Court's theory for deciding this case, the majority concocts a catchall exclusion to protect against unforeseen problems. * * * This final exception would apply in cases in which "there is no realistic possibility that official suppression of ideas is afoot." As I have demonstrated, this case does not concern the official suppression of ideas. The majority discards this notion out-of-hand.

As I see it, the Court's theory does not work and will do nothing more than confuse the law. Its selection of this case to rewrite First Amendment law is particularly inexplicable, because the whole problem could have been avoided by deciding this case under settled First Amendment principles.

II

Although I disagree with the Court's analysis, I do agree with its conclusion: The St. Paul ordinance is unconstitutional. However, I would decide the case on overbreadth grounds. * * *

In construing the St. Paul ordinance, the Minnesota Supreme Court drew upon the definition of fighting words that appears in *Chaplinsky*— words "which by their very utterance inflict injury or tend to incite an immediate breach of the peace." However, the Minnesota court was far from clear in identifying the "injur[ies]" inflicted by the expression that St. Paul sought to regulate. Indeed, the Minnesota court emphasized (tracking the language of the ordinance) that "the ordinance censors only those displays that one knows or should know will create anger, alarm or resentment based on racial, ethnic, gender or religious bias." I therefore understand the court to have ruled that St. Paul may constitutionally prohibit expression that "by its very utterance" causes "anger, alarm or resentment."

Our fighting words cases have made clear, however, that such generalized reactions are not sufficient to strip expression of its constitutional protection. The mere fact that expressive activity causes hurt feelings, offense, or resentment does not render the expression unprotected. See *United States v. Eichman,* 496 U.S. 310, 319, 110 S.Ct. 2404, 2410, 110 L.Ed.2d 287 (1990); *Texas v. Johnson,* 491 U.S. 397, 409, 414, 109 S.Ct. 2533, 2541, 2544, 105 L.Ed.2d 342 (1989); *Hustler Magazine, Inc. v. Falwell,* 485 U.S. 46, 55–56, 108 S.Ct. 876, 882, 99 L.Ed.2d 41 (1988). * * * Although the ordinance reaches conduct that is unprotected, it also makes criminal expressive conduct that causes only hurt feelings, offense, or resentment, and is protected by the First Amendment. Cf. *Lewis,* supra, at 132.[13] The ordinance is therefore fatally overbroad and invalid on its face.

---

13. Although the First Amendment protects offensive speech, it does not require us to be subjected to such expression at all times, in all settings. We have held that such expression may be proscribed when it intrudes upon a "captive audience." And expression may be limited when it merges into conduct. *United States v. O'Brien,* 391 U.S. 367, 88 S.Ct. 1673, 20 L.Ed.2d 672 (1968). However, because of the manner in which the Minnesota Supreme Court construed the St. Paul ordinance, those issues are not before us in this case.

JUSTICE BLACKMUN, concurring in the judgment.

I regret what the Court has done in this case. The majority opinion signals one of two possibilities: it will serve as precedent for future cases, or it will not. Either result is disheartening.

In the first instance, by deciding that a State cannot regulate speech that causes great harm unless it also regulates speech that does not (setting law and logic on their heads), the Court seems to abandon the categorical approach, and inevitably to relax the level of scrutiny applicable to content-based laws. [T]his weakens the traditional protections of speech. If all expressive activity must be accorded the same protection, that protection will be scant. The simple reality is that the Court will never provide child pornography or cigarette advertising the level of protection customarily granted political speech. If we are forbidden from categorizing, as the Court has done here, we shall reduce protection across the board. It is sad that in its effort to reach a satisfying result in this case, the Court is willing to weaken First Amendment protections.

In the second instance is the possibility that this case will not significantly alter First Amendment jurisprudence, but, instead, will be regarded as an aberration—a case where the Court manipulated doctrine to strike down an ordinance whose premise it opposed, namely, that racial threats and verbal assaults are of greater harm than other fighting words. I fear that the Court has been distracted from its proper mission by the temptation to decide the issue over "politically correct speech" and "cultural diversity," neither of which is presented here. If this is the meaning of today's opinion, it is perhaps even more regrettable.

I see no First Amendment values that are compromised by a law that prohibits hoodlums from driving minorities out of their homes by burning crosses on their lawns, but I see great harm in preventing the people of Saint Paul from specifically punishing the race-based fighting words that so prejudice their community.

I concur in the judgment, however, because I agree with Justice White that this particular ordinance reaches beyond fighting words to speech protected by the First Amendment.

JUSTICE STEVENS, with whom JUSTICE WHITE and JUSTICE BLACKMUN join as to Part I, concurring in the judgment.

Conduct that creates special risks or causes special harms may be prohibited by special rules. Lighting a fire near an ammunition dump or a gasoline storage tank is especially dangerous; such behavior may be punished more severely than burning trash in a vacant lot. Threatening someone because of her race or religious beliefs may cause particularly severe trauma or touch off a riot, and threatening a high public official may cause substantial social disruption; such threats may be punished more severely than threats against someone based on, say, his support of a particular athletic team. There are legitimate, reasonable, and neutral justifications for such special rules.

This case involves the constitutionality of one such ordinance. * * *

I

* * * Our First Amendment decisions have created a rough hierarchy in the constitutional protection of speech. Core political speech occupies the highest, most protected position; commercial speech and nonobscene, sexually explicit speech are regarded as a sort of second-class expression; obscenity and fighting words receive the least protection of all. Assuming that the Court is correct that this last class of speech is not wholly "unprotected," it certainly does not follow that fighting words and obscenity receive the *same* sort of protection afforded core political speech. Yet in ruling that proscribable speech cannot be regulated based on subject matter, the Court does just that. Perversely, this gives fighting words *greater* protection than is afforded commercial speech. If Congress can prohibit false advertising directed at airline passengers without also prohibiting false advertising directed at bus passengers and if a city can prohibit political advertisements in its buses while allowing other advertisements, it is ironic to hold that a city cannot regulate fighting words based on "race, color, creed, religion or gender" while leaving unregulated fighting words based on "union membership or homosexuality." The Court today turns First Amendment law on its head: Communication that was once entirely unprotected (and that still can be wholly proscribed) is now entitled to greater protection than commercial speech—and possibly greater protection than core political speech. See *Burson v. Freeman*, Ch. 6, III infra.

Perhaps because the Court recognizes these perversities, it quickly offers some ad hoc limitations on its newly extended prohibition on content-based regulations.[c]

[T]he Court recognizes that a State may regulate advertising in one industry but not another because "the risk of fraud (one of the characteristics that justifies depriving [commercial speech] of full First Amendment protection * * *)" in the regulated industry is "greater" than in other industries. [T]he same reasoning demonstrates the constitutionality of St. Paul's ordinance. "[O]ne of the characteristics that justifies" the constitutional status of fighting words is that such words "by their very utterance inflict injury or tend to incite an immediate breach of the peace." *Chaplinsky*. Certainly a legislature that may determine that the risk of fraud is greater in the legal trade than in the medical trade may determine that the

---

c. In an earlier passage and footnote of his opinion, Stevens, J., argued: "[W]hile the Court rejects the 'all-or-nothing-at-all' nature of the categorical approach, it promptly embraces an absolutism of its own: within a particular 'proscribable' category of expression, the Court holds, a government must either proscribe all speech or no speech at all. The Court disputes this characterization because it has crafted two exceptions, one for 'certain media or markets' and the other for content discrimination based upon 'the very reason that the entire class of speech at issue is proscribable.' These exceptions are, at best, ill-defined. The Court does not tell us whether, with respect to the former, fighting words such as cross-burning could be proscribed only in certain neighborhoods where the threat of violence is particularly severe, or whether, with respect to the second category, fighting words that create a particular risk of harm (such as a race riot) would be proscribable. The hypothetical and illusory category of these two exceptions persuades me that either my description of the Court's analysis is accurate or that the Court does not in fact mean much of what it says in its opinion."

risk of injury or breach of peace created by race-based threats is greater than that created by other threats.

Similarly, it is impossible to reconcile the Court's analysis of the St. Paul ordinance with its recognition that "a prohibition of fighting words that are directed at certain persons or groups * * * would be facially valid." A selective proscription of unprotected expression designed to protect "certain persons or groups" (for example, a law proscribing threats directed at the elderly) would be constitutional if it were based on a legitimate determination that the harm created by the regulated expression differs from that created by the unregulated expression (that is, if the elderly are more severely injured by threats than are the nonelderly). Such selective protection is no different from a law prohibiting minors (and only minors) from obtaining obscene publications. St. Paul has determined—reasonably in my judgment—that fighting-word injuries "based on race, color, creed, religion or gender" are qualitatively different and more severe than fighting-word injuries based on other characteristics. Whether the selective proscription of proscribable speech is defined by the protected target ("certain persons or groups") or the basis of the harm (injuries "based on race, color, creed, religion or gender") makes no constitutional difference: what matters is whether the legislature's selection is based on a legitimate, neutral, and reasonable distinction.

In sum, the central premise of the Court's ruling—that "[c]ontent-based regulations are presumptively invalid"—has simplistic appeal, but lacks support in our First Amendment jurisprudence. To make matters worse, the Court today extends this overstated claim to reach categories of hitherto unprotected speech and, in doing so, wreaks havoc in an area of settled law. Finally, although the Court recognizes exceptions to its new principle, those exceptions undermine its very conclusion that the St. Paul ordinance is unconstitutional. Stated directly, the majority's position cannot withstand scrutiny. * * *

III

* * * Unlike the Court, I do not believe that all content-based regulations are equally infirm and presumptively invalid; unlike Justice White, I do not believe that fighting words are wholly unprotected by the First Amendment. To the contrary, I believe our decisions establish a more complex and subtle analysis, one that considers the content and context of the regulated speech, and the nature and scope of the restriction on speech. * * *

* * * Whatever the allure of absolute doctrines, it is just too simple to declare expression "protected" or "unprotected" or to proclaim a regulation "content-based" or "content-neutral."

In applying this analysis to the St. Paul ordinance, I assume arguendo— as the Court does—that the ordinance regulates *only* fighting words and therefore is *not* overbroad. Looking to the content and character of the regulated activity, two things are clear. First, by hypothesis the ordinance bars only low-value speech, namely, fighting words. By definition such expression constitutes "no essential part of any exposition of ideas, and [is] of such slight social value as a step to truth that any benefit that may be derived from [it] is clearly outweighed by the social interest in order and morality." *Chaplinsky.* Second, the ordinance regulates "expressive conduct [rather] than * * * the written or spoken word."

Looking to the context of the regulated activity, it is again significant that the statute (by hypothesis) regulates *only* fighting words. Whether words are fighting words is determined in part by their context. Fighting words are not words that merely cause offense; fighting words must be directed at individuals so as to "by their very utterance inflict injury." By hypothesis, then, the St. Paul ordinance restricts speech in confrontational and potentially violent situations. The case at hand is illustrative. The cross-burning in this case—directed as it was to a single African–American family trapped in their home—was nothing more than a crude form of physical intimidation. That this cross-burning sends a message of racial hostility does not automatically endow it with complete constitutional protection.

Significantly, the St. Paul ordinance regulates speech not on the basis of its subject matter or the viewpoint expressed, but rather on the basis of the *harm* the speech causes. * * * Contrary to the Court's suggestion, the ordinance regulates only a subcategory of expression that causes *injuries based on* "race, color, creed, religion or gender," not a subcategory that involves *discussions* that concern those characteristics.[9] The ordinance, as construed by the Court, criminalizes expression that "one knows * * * [by its very utterance inflicts injury on] others on the basis of race, color, creed, religion or gender." * * *

Finally, it is noteworthy that the St. Paul ordinance is, as construed by the Court today, quite narrow. The St. Paul ordinance does not ban all "hate speech," nor does it ban, say, all cross-burnings or all swastika displays. Rather it only bans a subcategory of the already narrow category of fighting words. Such a limited ordinance leaves open and protected a vast range of expression on the subjects of racial, religious, and gender equality. As construed by the Court today, the ordinance certainly does not " 'raise the specter that the Government may effectively drive certain ideas or view-

---

9. The Court contends that this distinction is "wordplay," reasoning that "[w]hat makes [the harms caused by race-based threats] distinct from [the harms] produced by other fighting words is * * * the fact that [the former are] caused by a *distinctive idea.*" In this way, the Court concludes that regulating speech based on the injury it causes is no different from regulating speech based on its subject matter. This analysis fundamentally miscomprehends the role of "race, color, creed, religion [and] gender" in contemporary American society. One need look no further than the recent social unrest in the Nation's cities to see that race-based threats may cause more harm to society and to individuals than other threats. Just as the statute prohibiting threats against the President is justifiable because of the place of the President in our social and political order, so a statute prohibiting race-based threats is justifiable because of the place of race in our social and political order. Although it is regrettable that race occupies such a place and is so incendiary an issue, until the Nation matures beyond that condition, laws such as St. Paul's ordinance will remain reasonable and justifiable.

points from the marketplace.' " Petitioner is free to burn a cross to announce a rally or to express his views about racial supremacy, he may do so on private property or public land, at day or at night, so long as the burning is not so threatening and so directed at an individual as to "by its very [execution] inflict injury." Such a limited proscription scarcely offends the First Amendment.

In sum, the St. Paul ordinance (as construed by the Court) regulates expressive activity that is wholly proscribable and does so not on the basis of viewpoint, but rather in recognition of the different harms caused by such activity. Taken together, these several considerations persuade me that the St. Paul ordinance is not an unconstitutional content-based regulation of speech. Thus, were the ordinance not overbroad, I would vote to uphold it.[d]

Notes and Questions

1.   At the capital sentencing phase of a murder case, the prosecution sought to introduce evidence that the defendant was a member of the Aryan Brotherhood which was stipulated to be a "white racist gang." DAWSON v. DELAWARE, 503 U.S. 159, 112 S.Ct. 1093, 117 L.Ed.2d 309 (1992), per Rehnquist, C.J., held that the admission of the evidence was irrelevant and concluded that its admission violated the first amendment: "Even if the Delaware group to which Dawson allegedly belongs is racist, those beliefs, so far as we can determine, had no relevance to the sentencing proceeding in this case. For example, the Aryan Brotherhood evidence was not tied in any way to the murder of Dawson's [white] victim. * * * Whatever label is given to the evidence presented, however, we conclude that Dawson's First Amendment rights were violated by the admission of the Aryan Brotherhood evidence in this case, because the evidence proved nothing more than Dawson's abstract beliefs. [Delaware] might have avoided this problem if it had presented evidence showing more than mere abstract beliefs on Dawson's part, but on the present record one is left with the feeling that the Aryan Brotherhood evidence was employed simply because the jury would find these beliefs morally reprehensible. Because Delaware failed to do more, we cannot find the evidence was properly admitted as relevant character evidence."

THOMAS, J., dissented: "Dawson introduced mitigating character evidence that he had acted kindly toward his family. The stipulation tended to undercut this showing by suggesting that Dawson's kindness did not extend to members of other racial groups. Although we do not sit in judgment of the morality of particular creeds, we cannot bend traditional concepts of relevance to exempt the antisocial."

d. For background on *R.A.V.,* see Cleary, *Beyond the Burning Cross* (1994). For additional commentary, see Symposium, *Hate Speech After R.A.V.: More Conflict Between Free Speech and Equality,* 18 Wm. Mitchell L.Rev. 889 (1992); Amar, *The Case of the Missing Amendments,* 106 Harv. L.Rev. 124 (1992); Kagan, *The Changing Faces of First Amendment Neutrality,* 1992 Sup.Ct.Rev. 29; Kagan, *Regulation of Hate Speech and Pornography After R.A.V.,* 60 U.Chi.L.Rev. 873 (1993); Lawrence, *Crossburning and the Sound of Silence,* 37 Vill. L.Rev. 787 (1992); Shiffrin, supra.

WISCONSIN v. MITCHELL, 508 U.S. 476, 113 S.Ct. 2194, 124 L.Ed.2d 436 (1993), per REHNQUIST, C.J., held no first amendment violation was present when Wisconsin permitted a sentence for aggravated battery to be enhanced on the ground that the white victim had been selected because of his race. The Court observed that, unlike *R.A.V.,* the Wisconsin statute was aimed at conduct, not speech, that a chilling effect on speech was unlikely, that the focus on motive was no different than that employed in federal and state anti-discrimination statutes, and that bias-inspired conduct is more likely "to provoke retaliatory crimes, inflict distinct emotional harms on their victims, and incite community unrest." Consistent with *R.A.V.?*[e] After *Mitchell,* could the state "enact a general regulation against the use of fighting words, and then have a sentence enhancement based on racial motivation." See Farber, *The First Amendment* 115 (1998): "There seems to be a reasonable argument for distinguishing R.A.V. even when the enhancement is applied to a speech-based regulation."[f]

2.   Consider Shiffrin, *Racist Speech, Outsider Jurisprudence, and the Meaning of America,* 80 Cornell L.Rev. 43, 65 (1994): "Justice Scalia [maintains] that the rationale of the prohibition against content discrimination is the 'specter that the Government may effectively drive certain ideas of viewpoints from the marketplace.' That concern, however, is difficult to take seriously in the context of *R.A.V.* St. Paul prohibited only a small class of 'fighting words,' words which make a slight contribution to truth—just a particular socially unacceptable *mode* of presentation in Justice Scalia's view. It is hard to see how that raises the 'specter that the Government may effectively drive certain ideas or viewpoints from the marketplace.' Even more telling is Justice Scalia's 'content-neutral' alternative to the St. Paul ordinance: a 'pure' fighting words statute, which, he maintains, could serve the valid government interests in protecting basic human rights of members of groups historically subject to discrimination. But this content-neutral alternative would drive the very same ideas and viewpoints (along with others) from the marketplace. Thus, Justice Scalia cannot plausibly claim to be concerned about this result." Is there a better rationale?

3.   Consider Kagan, *Private Speech, Public Purpose: The Role of Governmental Motive in First Amendment Doctrine,* 63 U.Chi.L.Rev. 413 (1996): "[H]alf hidden beneath a swirl of doctrinal formulations, the crux of the dispute between the majority and the concurring opinions concerned the proper understanding of St. Paul's motive in enacting its hate-speech law.

---

e.   See Lawrence, *Punishing Hate: Bias Crimes Under American Law* (1999); Jacobs & Potter, *Hate Crimes, Criminal Law and Identity Politics* (1998); Herel & Parchomovsky, *On Hate and Equality,* 109 Yale L.J 507 (1999); Brownstein, *Rules of Engagement for Cultural Wars,* 29 U.C. Davis L.Rev. 553 (1996); Gellman, *Sticks and Stones Can Put You in Jail, But Can Words Increase Your Sentence?,* 39 U.C.L.A. L.Rev.

333 (1991); See generally Tribe, *The Mystery of Motive, Private and Public: Some Notes Inspired by the Problems of Hate Crime and Animal Sacrifice,* 1993 Sup.Ct. Rev. 1.

f.   California's anti-paparazzi legislation provides stiffer penalties for trespass if the purpose is to photograph or videotape someone without their permission. Constitutional?

The majority understood this motive as purely censorial—a simple desire to blot out ideas of which the government or a majority of its citizens disapproved. The concurring Justices saw something different: an effort by the government, divorced from mere hostility toward ideas, to counter a severe and objectively ascertainable harm caused by (one form of) an idea's expression.''

4. In distinguishing Title VII law, Scalia, J., states that if government does not target discriminatory conduct on the basis of its expressive content, government may regulate, apparently without first amendment scrutiny, even if the conduct expresses a discriminatory idea or philosophy. Is this consistent with *O'Brien?* The opinions in *Barnes* other than Scalia, J.'s? Suppose St. Paul outlawed all conduct that tended to create a racially or sexually hostile environment. Consider Fallon, *Sexual Harassment, Content Neutrality, and the First Amendment Dog That Didn't Bark,* 1994 Sup.Ct. Rev. 1, 16: "A statute of this kind, which would restrict the press, political orators, and private citizens engaged in conversation in their homes, would surely offend the First Amendment. Certainly Justice Scalia [does] not believe otherwise." Could St. Paul outlaw racial harassment under Scalia, J.'s rationale and apply it to the facts of *R.A.V.* without first amendment scrutiny?

Are many applications of sexual harassment law problematic under the first amendment?[g]

g. For a variety of views, see Greenawalt, *Fighting Words* 77–96 (1995); Balkin, *Free Speech and Hostile Environments,* 99 Colum. L.Rev. 2295 (1999); Mary Becker, *How Free is Speech at Work?,* 29 U.C. Davis L.Rev. 815 (1996); Browne, *Title VII as Censorship: Hostile–Environment Harassment and the First Amendment,* 52 Ohio St.L.J. 481 (1991); Estlund, *Freedom of Expression in the Workplace and the Problem of Discriminatory Harassment,* 75 Texas L.Rev. 687 (1997); Estlund, *The Architecture of the First Amendment and the Case of Workplace Harassment,* 72 Notre Dame L.Rev. 1361 (1997); Fallon, supra; Gerard, *The First Amendment in a Hostile Environment: A Primer on Free Speech and Sexual Harassment,* 68 Notre D.L.Rev. 579 (1995); Greene, *Sexual Harassment Law and the First Amendment,* 71 Chi.-Kent L.Rev. 729 (1995); Sangree, *Title VII Prohibitions Against Hostile Environment Sexual Harassment and the First Amendment: No Collision in Sight,* 47 Rutgers L.Rev. 461 (1995); Strauss, *Sexist Speech in the Workplace,* 25 Harv.C.R.–C.L.L.Rev. 1 (1990); Strossen, *Regulating Workplace Sexual Harassment and Upholding the First Amendment—Avoiding a Collision,* 37 Vill. L.Rev. 757 (1992); Volokh, *Freedom of Speech and Workplace Harassment,* 39 U.C.L.A.L.Rev. 1791 (1992); Volokh, *How Harassment Law Restricts Free Speech,* 47 Rutgers L.Rev. 563 (1995); Volokh, *What Speech Does "Hostile Work Environment" Harassment Law Restrict?,* 85 Geo. L.J. 627, 647 (1997). See also *Davis v. Monroe County Board of Educ.,* 526 U.S. 629, 119 S.Ct. 1661, 143 L.Ed.2d. 839 (1999) (Kennedy, J., dissenting).

Chapter 4

PRIOR RESTRAINTS

Prior restraint is a technical term in first amendment law. A criminal statute prohibiting all advocacy of violent action would *restrain* speech and would have been enacted *prior* to any restrained communication. The statute would be overbroad, but it would not be a prior restraint. A prior restraint refers only to closely related, distinctive methods of regulating expression that are said to have in common their own peculiar set of evils and problems, in addition to those that accompany most any governmental interference with free expression. "The issue is not whether the government may impose a particular restriction of substance in an area of public expression, such as forbidding obscenity in newspapers, but whether it may do so by a particular method, such as advance screening of newspaper copy. In other words, restrictions which could be validly imposed when enforced by subsequent punishment are, nevertheless, forbidden if attempted by prior restraint." Emerson, *The Doctrine of Prior Restraint,* 20 Law and Contemp. Prob. 648 (1955).

The classic prior restraints were the English licensing laws which required a license in advance to print any material or to import or to sell any book.[a] One of the questions raised in this chapter concerns the types of government conduct beyond the classic licensing laws that should be characterized as prior restraints. Another concerns the question of when government licensing of speech, press, or assembly should be countenanced. Perhaps, most important, the chapter explores the circumstances in which otherwise protected speech may be restrained on an ad hoc basis.

I. FOUNDATION CASES

A. LICENSING

LOVELL v. GRIFFIN, 303 U.S. 444, 58 S.Ct. 666, 82 L.Ed. 949 (1938), per HUGHES, C.J., invalidated an ordinance prohibiting the distri-

a. For a persuasive chronicling of the abuses in a modern licensing system, see generally Powe, *American Broadcasting and the First Amendment* (1987).

bution of handbooks, advertising or literature within the city of Griffin, Georgia without obtaining written permission of the City Manager: "[T]he ordinance is invalid on its face. Whatever the motive which induced its adoption, its character is such that it strikes at the very foundation of the freedom of the press by subjecting it to license and censorship. The struggle for the freedom of the press was primarily directed against the power of the licensor. It was against that power that John Milton directed his assault by his 'Appeal for the Liberty of Unlicensed Printing.' And the liberty of the press became initially a right to publish '*without* a license what formerly could be published only *with* one.' While this freedom from previous restraint upon publication cannot be regarded as exhausting the guaranty of liberty, the prevention of that restraint was a leading purpose in the adoption of the constitutional provision. Legislation of the type of the ordinance in question would restore the system of license and censorship in its baldest form.

"The liberty of the press is not confined to newspapers and periodicals. It necessarily embraces pamphlets and leaflets. These indeed have been historic weapons in the defense of liberty, as the pamphlets of Thomas Paine and others in our own history abundantly attest. The press in its historic connotation comprehends every sort of publication which affords a vehicle of information and opinion. * * *

"The ordinance cannot be saved because it relates to distribution and not to publication. 'Liberty of circulating is as essential to that freedom as liberty of publishing; indeed, without the circulation, the publication would be of little value.' *Ex parte Jackson,* 96 U.S. (6 Otto) 727, 733, 24 L.Ed. 877 (1877).

"[As] the ordinance is void on its face, it was not necessary for appellant to seek a permit under it. She was entitled to contest its validity in answer to the charge against her.

"[Reversed and] remanded."[a]

Notes and Questions

1. *First amendment procedure.* Notice that Lovell would get the benefit of the prior restraint doctrine even if the material she distributed was obscene or otherwise unprotected. In that respect, the prior restraint doctrine is similar to the doctrines of overbreadth and vagueness. For particular concerns that underlie the prior restraint doctrine, consider Emerson, *The System of Freedom of Expression* 506 (1970):

"A system of prior restraint is in many ways more inhibiting than a system of subsequent punishment: It is likely to bring under government scrutiny a far wider range of expression; it shuts off communication before it takes place; suppression by a stroke of the pen is more likely to be applied than suppression through a criminal process; the procedures do not require attention to the safeguards of the criminal process; the system allows less

---

a.   Cardozo, J., took no part.

opportunity for public appraisal and criticism; the dynamics of the system drive toward excesses, as the history of all censorship shows."[b]

2. *Scope and character of the doctrine.* What is the vice of the licensing scheme in *Lovell?* Is the concern that like vague statutes it affords undue discretion and potential for abuse? Is the real concern the uncontrolled power of the licensor to deny licenses? Suppose licenses were automatically issued to anyone who applied?

To what extent should the prior restraint doctrine apply to non-press activities? To a licensing ordinance that otherwise forbids soliciting membership in organizations that exact fees of their members? See *Staub v. Baxley,* 355 U.S. 313, 78 S.Ct. 277, 2 L.Ed.2d 302 (1958) (yes). To a licensing ordinance that otherwise prohibits attempts to secure contributions for charitable or religious causes? See *Cantwell v. Connecticut,* 310 U.S. 296, 60 S.Ct. 900, 84 L.Ed. 1213 (1940) (yes).

Should the prior restraint doctrine apply to all aspects of newspaper circulation? See *Lakewood v. Plain Dealer Publishing Co.,* 486 U.S. 750, 108 S.Ct. 2138, 100 L.Ed.2d 771 (1988) (invalidating ordinance granting Mayor power to grant or deny annual permits to place newsracks on public property).[c]

Suppose, in the above cases, that the authority of the licensor were confined by narrow, objective, and definite standards or that licenses were automatically issued to anyone who applied. *Hynes v. Mayor,* 425 U.S. 610, 96 S.Ct. 1755, 48 L.Ed.2d 243 (1976), per Burger, C.J., stated in dictum that a municipality could regulate house to house soliciting by requiring advance notice to the police department in order to protect its citizens from crime and undue annoyance: "A narrowly drawn ordinance, that does not vest in municipal officials the undefined power to determine what messages residents will hear, may serve these important interests without running afoul of the First Amendment." But cf. *Thomas v. Collins,* 323 U.S. 516, 65 S.Ct. 315, 89 L.Ed. 430 (1945) (registration requirement for paid union organizers invalid prior restraint); *Talley v. California,* 362 U.S. 60, 80 S.Ct. 536, 4 L.Ed.2d 559 (1960) (ban on anonymous handbills "void on its face," noting that the "obnoxious press licensing law of England, which was also enforced on the Colonies was due in part to the knowledge that exposure of the names of printers, writers and distributors would lessen the circulation of literature critical of the government").

b. But see Posner, *Free Speech in an Economic Perspective,* 20 Suff.L.Rev. 1, 13 (1986): "The conventional arguments for why censorship is worse than criminal punishment are little better than plausible (though I think there is at least one good argument)" [observing that speech ordinarily does not produce sufficient damage to justify sifting through massive materials].

c. WHITE, J., joined by Stevens and O'Connor, JJ., dissenting, contended that *Lovell* should apply only if the newspaper had a constitutional right to place newsracks on public sidewalks. Otherwise, the newspaper should be required to show that a denial was based on improper reasons.

B. INJUNCTIONS

NEAR v. MINNESOTA

283 U.S. 697, 51 S.Ct. 625, 75 L.Ed. 1357 (1931).

Mr. Chief Justice Hughes delivered the opinion of the Court.

[The *Saturday Press* published articles charging that through graft and incompetence named public officials failed to expose and punish gangsters responsible for gambling, bootlegging, and racketeering in Minneapolis. It demanded a special grand jury and special prosecutor to deal with the situation and to investigate an alleged attempt to assassinate one of its publishers. Under a statute that authorized abatement of a "malicious, scandalous and defamatory newspaper" the state secured, and its supreme court affirmed, a court order that "abated" the Press and perpetually enjoined the defendants from publishing or circulating "any publication whatsoever which is a malicious, scandalous or defamatory newspaper." The order did not restrain the defendants from operating a newspaper "in harmony with the general welfare."]

The object of the statute is not punishment, in the ordinary sense, but suppression of the offending newspaper. [In] the case of public officers, it is the reiteration of charges of official misconduct, and the fact that the newspaper [is] principally devoted to that purpose, that exposes it to suppression. [T]he operation and effect of the statute [is] that public authorities may bring the owner or publisher of a newspaper or periodical before a judge upon a charge of conducting a business of publishing scandalous and defamatory matter—in particular that the matter consists of charges against public officers of official dereliction—and, unless the owner or publisher is able and disposed to bring competent evidence to satisfy the judge that the charges are true and are published with good motives and for justifiable ends, his newspaper or periodical is suppressed and further publication is made punishable as a contempt. This is of the essence of censorship.

The question is whether a statute authorizing such proceedings [is] consistent with the conception of the liberty of the press as historically conceived and guaranteed. [I]t has been generally, if not universally, considered that it is the chief purpose of the guaranty to prevent previous restraints upon publication. The struggle in England, directed against the legislative power of the licenser, resulted in renunciation of the censorship of the press. The liberty deemed to be established was thus described by Blackstone: "The liberty of the press is indeed essential to the nature of a free state; but this consists in laying no *previous* restraints upon publications, and not in freedom from censure for criminal matter when published. Every freeman has an undoubted right to lay what sentiments he pleases before the public; to forbid this, is to destroy the freedom of the press; but if he publishes what is improper, mischievous or illegal, he must take the consequence of his own temerity." [The] criticism upon Blackstone's statement has not been because immunity from previous restraint upon publication has not been regarded as deserving of special emphasis, but chiefly because that immunity cannot be deemed to exhaust the conception of the liberty guaranteed by State and Federal Constitutions.

[T]he protection even as to previous restraint is not absolutely unlimited. But the limitation has been recognized only in exceptional cases. [N]o one would question but that a government might prevent actual obstruction to its recruiting service or the publication of the sailing dates of transports or the number and location of troops. On similar grounds, the primary requirements of decency may be enforced against obscene publications. The security of the community life may be protected against incitements to acts of violence and the overthrow by force of orderly [government].[a]

The exceptional nature of its limitations places in a strong light the general conception that liberty of the press, historically considered and taken up by the Federal Constitution, has meant, principally although not exclusively, immunity from previous restraints or censorship. The conception of liberty of the press in this country had broadened with the exigencies of the colonial period and with the efforts to secure freedom from oppressive administration. That liberty was especially cherished for the immunity it afforded from previous restraint of the publication of censure of public officers and charges of official [misconduct].

The fact that for approximately one hundred and fifty years there has been almost an entire absence of attempts to impose previous restraints upon publications relating to the malfeasance of public officers is significant of the deep-seated conviction that such restraints would violate constitutional right. Public officers, whose character and conduct remain open to debate and free discussion in the press, find their remedies for false accusations in actions under libel laws providing for redress and punishment, and not in proceedings to restrain the publication of newspapers and periodicals. [The] fact that the liberty of the press may be abused by miscreant purveyors of scandal does not make any the less necessary the immunity of the press from previous restraint in dealing with official misconduct. Subsequent punishment for such abuses as may exist is the appropriate remedy, consistent with constitutional [privilege].

The statute in question cannot be justified by reason of the fact that the publisher is permitted to show, before injunction issues, that the matter published is true and is published with good motives and for justifiable ends. If such a statute, authorizing suppression and injunction on such a basis, is constitutionally valid, it would be equally permissible for the Legislature to provide that at any time the publisher of any newspaper could be brought

---

a. For critical commentary on the concessions in *Near,* see Linde, *Courts and Censorship,* 66 Minn.L.Rev. 171 (1981); Smith, *Prior Restraint: Original Intentions and Modern Interpretations,* 28 Wm. & M.L.Rev. 439, 462 (1987). For criticism of the overuse of preliminary injunctions in a variety of intellectual property contexts, see Lemley & Volokh, *Freedom of Speech and Injunctions in Intellectual Property Cases,* 48 Duke L.J. 147 (1998).

before a court, or even an administrative officer (as the constitutional protection may not be regarded as resting on mere procedural details), and required to produce proof of the truth of his publication, or of what he intended to publish and of his motives, or stand enjoined. If this can be done, the Legislature may provide machinery for determining in the complete exercise of its discretion what are justifiable ends and restrain publication accordingly. And it would be but a step to a complete system of censorship.

[For] these reasons we hold the statute, so far as it authorized the proceedings in this action, [to] be an infringement of the liberty of the press guaranteed by the Fourteenth Amendment. * * *

MR. JUSTICE BUTLER (dissenting).

[T]he *previous restraints* referred to by [Blackstone] subjected the press to the arbitrary will of an administrative officer. [The] Minnesota statute does not operate as a *previous* restraint on publication within the proper meaning of that phrase. It does not authorize administrative control in advance such as was formerly exercised by the licensers and censors, but prescribes a remedy to be enforced by a suit in equity. In this case [t]he business and publications unquestionably constitute an abuse of the right of free press. [A]s stated by the state Supreme Court [they] threaten morals, peace, and good order. [The] restraint authorized is only in respect of continuing to do what has been duly adjudged to constitute a nuisance. [It] is fanciful to suggest similarity between the granting or enforcement of the decree authorized by this statute to prevent *further* publication of malicious, scandalous, and defamatory articles and the *previous restraint* upon the press by licensers as referred to by Blackstone and described in the history of the times to which he alludes. * * *

It is well known, as found by the state supreme court, that existing libel laws are inadequate effectively to suppress evils resulting from the kind of business and publications that are shown in this case. The doctrine [of this decision] exposes the peace and good order of every community and the business and private affairs of every individual to the constant and protracted false and malicious assaults of any insolvent publisher who may have purpose and sufficient capacity to contrive and put into effect a scheme or program for oppression, blackmail or extortion. * * *

MR. JUSTICE VAN DEVANTER, MR. JUSTICE MCREYNOLDS, and MR. JUSTICE SUTHERLAND concur in this opinion.[b]

Notes and Questions

1. *Near and seditious libel: a misuse of prior restraint?* *Near* was decided three decades before *New York Times v. Sullivan,* p. 64 supra.

---

b. For background on the *Near* case, see Friendly, *Minnesota Rag* (1981); Murphy, *Near v. Minnesota in the Context of Histori-* *cal Developments,* 66 Minn.L.Rev. 95, 133–60 (1981).

Should the Court have looked to the substance of the regulation rather than its form? Consider Jeffries, *Rethinking Prior Restraint,* 92 Yale L.J. 409, 416–17 (1983): "In truth, *Near* involved nothing more or less than a repackaged version of the law of seditious libel, and this the majority rightly refused to countenance. Hence, there was pressure, so typical of this doctrine, to cram the law into the disfavored category of prior restraint, even though it in fact functioned very differently from a scheme of official licensing. Here there was no license and no censor, no ex parte determination of what was prohibited, and no suppression of publication based on speculation about what somebody might say. Here the decision to suppress was made by a judge (not a bureaucrat), after adversarial (not ex parte) proceedings, to determine the legal character of what had been (and not what might be) published. The only aspect of prior restraint was the incidental fact that the defendants were commanded not to repeat that which they were proved to have done.

"[I]f *Near* reached the right result, does it really matter that it gave the wrong reason? The answer, I think, is that it does matter, at least that it has come to matter as *Near* has become a prominent feature of the First Amendment landscape—a landmark, as the case is so often called, from which we chart our course to future decisions. [T]he Court has yet to explain (at least in terms that I understand) what it is about an injunction that justifies this independent rule of constitutional disfavor.''

Should a court be able to enjoin the continued distribution of material it has finally adjudicated to be unprotected defamation under existing law? Suppose it enjoins the publication of any material that does not comply with the mandates of *New York Times* and *Gertz*?

2. *The collateral bar rule.* Does the collateral bar rule shed light on the relationship between prior restraints and injunctions? That rule insists "that a court order must be obeyed until it is set aside, and that persons subject to the order who disobey it may not defend against the ensuing charge of criminal contempt on the ground that the order was erroneous or even unconstitutional." Barnett, *The Puzzle of Prior Restraint,* 29 Stan.L.Rev. 539, 552 (1977). WALKER v. BIRMINGHAM, 388 U.S. 307, 87 S.Ct. 1824, 18 L.Ed.2d 1210 (1967) upheld the rule against a first amendment challenge in affirming the contempt conviction of defendants for violating an ex parte injunction issued by an Alabama court enjoining them from engaging in street parades without a municipal permit issued pursuant to the city's parade ordinance. The Court, per STEWART, J., (Warren, C.J., Brennan, Douglas, and Fortas, JJ., dissenting) held that because the petitioners neither moved to dissolve the injunction nor sought to comply with the city's parade ordinance, their claim that the injunction and ordinance were unconstitutional[c] did not need to be considered: "This Court cannot hold that the petitioners were constitutionally free to ignore all the procedures of the law

---

c. Indeed, the ordinance in question was declared unconstitutional two years later. *Shuttlesworth v. Birmingham,* 394 U.S. 147, 89 S.Ct. 935, 22 L.Ed.2d 162 (1969) (ordinance conferring unbridled discretion to prohibit any parade or demonstration is unconstitutional prior restraint).

and carry their battle to the streets. [R]espect for judicial process is a small price to pay for the civilizing hand of law, which alone can give abiding meaning to constitutional freedom." Although *Walker* suggested that its holding might be different if the court issuing the injunction lacked jurisdiction or if the injunction were "transparently invalid or had only a frivolous pretense to validity," it held that Alabama's invocation of the collateral bar rule was not itself unconstitutional.

Cf. *Poulos v. New Hampshire,* 345 U.S. 395, 73 S.Ct. 760, 97 L.Ed. 1105 (1953) (claim of arbitrary refusal to issue license for open air meeting need not be entertained when a licensing statute is considered to be valid on its face in circumstance where speaker fails to seek direct judicial relief and proceeds without a license).[d] Does *Poulos* pose considerable danger to first amendment interests because the low visibility of the administrative decision permits easy abridgement of free expression? See Monaghan, *First Amendment "Due Process,"* 83 Harv.L.Rev. 518, 543 (1970). Do *Lovell, Walker,* and *Poulos* fit easily together? Consider Blasi, *Prior Restraints on Demonstrations,* 68 Mich.L.Rev. 1482, 1555 (1970): "A refuses to apply for a permit; he undertakes a march that could have been prohibited in the first place; he is prosecuted for parading without a permit under a statute that is defective for overbreadth. B applies for a permit; he is rudely rebuffed by a city official in clear violation of the state permit statute (which is not invalid on its face); he marches anyway in a manner that would be protected by the first amendment, he is prosecuted for parading without a permit. C applies for a permit; he is rudely rebuffed; he notifies city officials that he will march anyway; the officials obtain an injunction against the march; the injunction is overbroad and is also based on a state statute that is overbroad; C marches in a manner ordinarily within his constitutional rights; he is prosecuted for contempt. Under the law as it now stands, A wins, but B and C lose!"

3. *Time, place, and manner regulations.* Should injunctions that impose time, place, or manner regulations in response to proven wrongdoing be subjected to more stringent examination than that ordinarily applied to general regulations imposed by legislative or executive action? See *Madsen v. Women's Health Center,* 512 U.S. 753, 114 S.Ct. 2516, 129 L.Ed.2d 593 (1994).

4. *The commentators, injunctions, and prior restraint.* Should the link between prior restraint doctrine and injunctions depend upon the collateral bar rule? Does the analogy between licensing systems and injunctions hold only in that event? See Fiss, *The Civil Rights Injunction* 30, 69–74 (1978); Barnett, note 2 supra, at 553–54. Should the prior restraint doctrine be wholly inapplicable to injunctions so long as "expedited appellate review allows an immediate opportunity to test the validity of an injunction against speech and only so long as that opportunity is genuinely effective to allow

---

d. For consideration of when licensing statutes for assemblies are valid, see *Cox v. New Hampshire,* Ch. 6, I, A infra.

timely publication should the injunction ultimately be adjudged invalid"? Jeffries, note 1 supra, at 433.[e] Indeed should the whole concept of prior restraint be abandoned? Consider id. at 433–34: "In the context of administrative preclearance, talking of prior restraint is unhelpful, though not inapt. A more informative frame of reference would be overbreadth, the doctrine that explicitly identifies why preclearance is specially objectionable. In the context of injunctions, however, the traditional doctrine of prior restraint is not merely unhelpful, but positively misleading. It focuses on a constitutionally inconsequential consideration of form and diverts attention away from the critical substantive issues of First Amendment coverage. The result is a two-pronged danger. On the one hand, vindication of First Amendment freedoms in the name of prior restraint may exaggerate the legitimate reach of official competence to suppress by subsequent punishment. On the other hand, insistence on special disfavor for prior restraints outside the realm of substantive protection under the First Amendment may deny to the government an appropriate choice of means to vindicate legitimate interests. In my view, neither risk is justified by any compelling reason to continue prior restraint as a doctrinally independent category of contemporary First Amendment analysis."[f]

For a nuanced argument that the prior restraint doctrine should apply to injunctions even in those jurisdictions that reject the applicability of the collateral bar rule to first amendment arguments, see Blasi, *Toward a Theory of Prior Restraint: The Central Linkage,* 66 Minn.L.Rev. 11 (1981). Except in particular contexts, Professor Blasi does not claim that the chilling effect of injunctions on speech is more severe than those associated with criminal laws and civil liability rules. He does argue that unlike criminal laws and civil liability rules, regulation of speech by licensing and injunctions requires abstract and unduly speculative adjudication, stimulates overuse by regulatory agents, can to some extent distort the way in which audiences perceive the message at issue, and unreasonably implies that the activity of disseminating controversial communications is "a threat to, rather than an integral feature of, the social order." Id. at 85. He argues that many of these factors are aggravated if the collateral bar rule applies and that other undesirable features are added. For example, speakers are forced to reveal planned details about their communication. He concludes that the "concept of prior restraint is coherent at the core." Id. at 93.[g]

e. For the argument that regulation by injunction is generally more speech protective than regulation via subsequent punishment, see Mayton, *Toward A Theory of First Amendment Process: Injunctions of Speech, Subsequent Punishment, and the Costs of the Prior Restraint Doctrine,* 67 Corn.L.Rev. 245 (1982). For the contention that this should count in favor of subsequent punishment in many contexts, see Redish, *The Proper Role of the Prior Restraint Doctrine in First Amendment Theory,* 70 Va.L.Rev. 53, 92–93 (1984).

f. See also Scordato, *Distinction Without a Difference,* 68 N.C.L.Rev. 1 (1989) (generally agreeing with Jeffries but arguing that a small part of prior restraint doctrine should be salvaged).

g. See also Farber, *The First Amendment* 48–49 (1998). For detailed criticism of

II. PRIOR RESTRAINTS, OBSCENITY, AND COMMERCIAL SPEECH

KINGSLEY BOOKS, INC. v. BROWN, 354 U.S. 436, 77 S.Ct. 1325, 1 L.Ed.2d 1469 (1957), per FRANKFURTER, J., upheld a state court decree, issued pursuant to a New York statute, enjoining the publisher from further distribution of 14 booklets the state court found obscene. On appeal to the Supreme Court the publisher challenged only the prior restraint, not the obscenity finding:

"The phrase 'prior restraint' is not a self-wielding sword. Nor can it serve as a talismatic test. The duty of closer analysis and critical judgment in applying the thought behind the phrase has thus been authoritatively put by one who brings weighty learning to his support of constitutionally protected liberties: 'What is needed,' writes Professor Paul A. Freund, 'is a pragmatic assessment of its operation in the particular circumstances. The generalization that prior restraint is particularly obnoxious in civil liberties cases must yield to more particularistic analysis.' *The Supreme Court and Civil Liberties,* 4 Vand.L.Rev. 533, 539.

"Wherein does § 22–a differ in its effective operation from the type of statute upheld in *Alberts,* [p. 112 supra]. One would be bold to assert that the in terrorem effect of [criminal] statutes less restrains booksellers in the period before the law strikes than does § 22–a. Instead of requiring the bookseller to dread that the offer for sale of a book may, without prior warning, subject him to a criminal prosecution with the hazard of imprisonment, the civil procedure assures him that such consequences cannot follow unless he ignores a court order specifically directed to him for a prompt and carefully circumscribed determination of the issue of obscenity. Until then, he may keep the book for sale and sell it on his own judgment rather than steer 'nervously among the treacherous shoals.'[a]

"Criminal enforcement and the proceeding under § 22–a interfere with a book's solicitation of the public precisely at the same stage. In each situation the law moves after publication; the book need not in either case have yet passed into the hands of the public. [H]ere as a matter of fact copies of the booklets whose distribution was enjoined had been on sale for several weeks when process was served. In each case the bookseller is put on notice by the complaint that sale of the publication charged with obscenity in the period before trial may subject him to penal consequences. In the one case he may suffer fine and imprisonment for violation of the criminal statute, in the other, for disobedience of the temporary injunction. The bookseller may of course stand his ground and confidently believe that in any judicial proceed-

---

Blasi's position, all in defense of a different core, see Redish, fn. e, at 59–75.

a. In fact, § 22–a did not require a civil adjudication before criminal prosecution, as

intimated by the opinion. The feasibility of such a requirement is considered in Lockhart, *Escape from the Chill of Uncertainty,* 9 Ga.L.Rev. 533, 569–86 (1975).

ing the book could not be condemned as obscene, but both modes of procedure provide an effective deterrent against distribution prior to adjudication of the book's content—the threat of subsequent penalization.[2] "

The Court pointed out that in both criminal misdemeanor prosecutions and injunction proceedings a jury could be called as a matter of discretion, but that defendant did not request a jury trial and did not attack the statute for its failure to require a jury.

"Nor are the consequences of a judicial condemnation for obscenity under § 22–a more restrictive of freedom of expression than the result of conviction for a misdemeanor. In *Alberts,* the defendant was fined $500, sentenced to sixty days in prison, and put on probation for two years on condition that he not violate the obscenity statute. Not only was he completely separated from society for two months but he was also seriously restrained from trafficking in all obscene publications for a considerable time. Appellants, on the other hand, were enjoined from displaying for sale or distributing only the particular booklets theretofore published and adjudged to be obscene. Thus, the restraint upon appellants as merchants in obscenity was narrower than that imposed on *Alberts.*

"Section 22–a's provision for the seizure and destruction of the instruments of ascertained wrongdoing expresses resort to a legal remedy sanctioned by the long history of Anglo–American law. See Holmes, *The Common Law,* 24–26.

"[It] only remains to say that the difference between *Near* and this case is glaring in fact. The two cases are no less glaringly different when judged by the appropriate criteria of constitutional law. Minnesota empowered its courts to enjoin the dissemination of future issues of a publication because its past issues had been found offensive. In the language of Mr. Chief Justice Hughes, 'This is of the essence of censorship.' As such, it was enough to condemn the statute wholly apart from the fact that the proceeding in *Near* involved not obscenity but matters deemed to be derogatory to a public officer. Unlike *Near,* § 22–a is concerned solely with obscenity and, as authoritatively construed, it studiously withholds restraint upon matters not already published and not yet found to be offensive."[b]

---

2. This comparison of remedies takes note of the fact that we do not have before us a case where, although the issue of obscenity is ultimately decided in favor of the bookseller, the State nevertheless attempts to punish him for disobedience of the interim injunction. For all we know, New York may impliedly condition the temporary injunction so as not to subject the bookseller to a charge of contempt if he prevails on the issue of obscenity.

b. Warren, C.J., dissented, objecting that the New York law "places the book on trial" without any consideration of its "manner of use." Black and Douglas, JJ., dissented, objecting to a state-wide decree depriving the publisher of separate trials in different communities, and to substituting "punishment by contempt for punishment by jury trial." Brennan, J., dissenting, contended that a jury trial is required to apply properly the *Roth* standard for obscenity.

TIMES FILM CORP. v. CHICAGO

365 U.S. 43, 81 S.Ct. 391, 5 L.Ed.2d 403 (1961).

MR. JUSTICE CLARK delivered the opinion of the Court.

Petitioner challenges on constitutional grounds the validity on its face of that portion of § 155–4[a] of the Municipal Code of the City of Chicago which requires submission of all motion pictures for examination prior to their public exhibition. Petitioner is a New York corporation owning the exclusive right to publicly exhibit in Chicago the film known as "Don Juan." It applied for a permit, as Chicago's ordinance required, and tendered the license fee but refused to submit the film for examination. The appropriate city official refused to issue the permit and his order was made final on appeal to the Mayor. The sole ground for denial was petitioner's refusal to submit the film for examination as required. Petitioner then brought this suit seeking injunctive relief ordering the issuance of the permit without submission of the [film] * * *. Its sole ground is that the provision of the ordinance requiring submission of the film constitutes, on its face, a prior restraint[2] * * * [Admittedly,] the challenged section of the ordinance imposes a previous restraint, and the broad justiciable issue is therefore present as to whether the ambit of constitutional protection includes complete and absolute freedom to exhibit, at least once, any and every kind of motion picture. It is that question alone which we decide.

[T]here is not a word in the record as to the nature and content of "Don Juan." We are left entirely in the dark in this regard, as were the city officials and the other reviewing courts. Petitioner claims that the nature of the film is irrelevant, and that even if this film contains the basest type of pornography, or incitement to riot, or forceful overthrow of orderly government, it may nonetheless be shown without prior submission for examination. The challenge here is to the censor's basic authority; it does not go to any statutory standards employed by the censor or procedural requirements as to the submission of the film. * * *

Petitioner would have us hold that the public exhibition of motion pictures must be allowed under any circumstances. The State's sole remedy,

---

a. The portion of the section here under attack is as follows: "Such permit shall be granted only after the motion picture film for which said permit is requested has been produced at the office of the commissioner of police for examination or censorship. * * *"

2. That portion of § 155–4 of the Code providing standards is as follows: "If a picture or series of pictures, for the showing or exhibition of which an application for a permit is made, is immoral or obscene, or portrays, depravity, criminality, or lack of virtue of a class of citizens of any race, color, creed, or religion and exposes them to contempt, derision, or obloquy, or tends to produce a breach of the peace or riots, or purports to represent any hanging, lynching, or burning of a human being, it shall be the duty of the commissioner of police to refuse such permit; otherwise it shall be his duty to grant such permit.

"In case the commissioner of police shall refuse to grant a permit as hereinbefore provided, the applicant for the same may appeal to the mayor. Such appeal shall be presented in the same manner as the original application to the commissioner of police. The action of the mayor on any application for a permit shall be final." * * *

it says, is the invocation of criminal process under the Illinois pornography statute and then only after a transgression. But this position [is] founded upon the claim of absolute privilege against prior restraint under the First Amendment—a claim without sanction in our cases. To illustrate its fallacy, we need only point to one of the "exceptional cases" which Chief Justice Hughes enumerated in *Near,* namely, "the primary requirements of decency [that] may be enforced against obscene publications." Moreover, we later held specifically "that obscenity is not within the area of constitutionally protected speech or press." *Roth.* Chicago emphasizes here its duty to protect its people against the dangers of obscenity in the public exhibition of motion pictures. [It] is not for this Court to limit the State in its selection of the remedy it deems most effective to cope with such a problem, absent, of course, a showing of unreasonable strictures on individual liberty resulting from its application in particular circumstances. * * *

As to what may be decided when a concrete case involving a specific standard provided by this ordinance is presented, we intimate no opinion. [At] this time we say no more than this—that we are dealing only with motion pictures and, even as to them, only in the context of the broadside attack presented on this record.

Affirmed.

MR. CHIEF JUSTICE WARREN, with whom MR. JUSTICE BLACK, MR. JUSTICE DOUGLAS and MR. JUSTICE BRENNAN join, dissenting. * * *

I hesitate to disagree with the Court's formulation of the issue before us, but, with all deference, I must insist that the question presented in this case is *not* whether a motion picture exhibitor has a constitutionally protected, "complete and absolute freedom to exhibit, at least once, any and every kind of motion picture." [The] question here presented is whether the City of Chicago—or, for that matter, any city, any State or the Federal Government—may require all motion picture exhibitors to submit all films to a police chief, mayor or other administrative official, for licensing and censorship prior to public exhibition within the jurisdiction.

The booklets enjoined from distribution in *Kingsley* were concededly obscene. There is no indication that this is true of the moving picture here. This was treated as a particularly crucial distinction. Thus, the Court has suggested that, in times of national emergency, the Government might impose a prior restraint upon "the publication of the sailing dates of transports or the number and location of troops." *Near.* But, surely this is not to suggest that the Government might require that all newspapers be submitted to a censor in order to assist it in preventing such information from reaching print. Yet in this case the Court gives its blessing to the censorship of all motion pictures in order to prevent the exhibition of those it feels to be constitutionally unprotected.

[E]ven if the impact of the motion picture is greater than that of some other media, that fact constitutes no basis for the argument that motion pictures should be subject to greater suppression. This is the traditional argument made in the censor's behalf; this is the argument advanced against newspapers at the time of the invention of the printing press. The argument was ultimately rejected in England, and has consistently been held to be contrary to our Constitution.[a] No compelling reason has been predicated for accepting the contention now. * * *[b]

Notes and Questions

1. Should the producers of *Bambi* be forced to submit their film to show it in a particular city? Should they be forced to pay a license fee? Suppose hundreds of cities adopted the Chicago system? If films must be submitted before exhibition, can a city constitutionally require that books be submitted before distribution? What are the "peculiar problems" associated with films?

2. *Procedural safeguards.* FREEDMAN v. MARYLAND, 380 U.S. 51, 85 S.Ct. 734, 13 L.Ed.2d 649 (1965), per BRENNAN, J., set out procedural safeguards designed to reduce the dangers associated with prior restraints of films. It required that the procedure must "assure a prompt final judicial decision, to minimize the deterrent effect of an interim and possibly errone- ous denial of a license," that the censor must promptly institute the proceedings, that the burden of proof to show that the speech in question is unprotected must rest on the censor, and that the proceedings be adversari- al. The *Freedman* standards have been applied in other contexts. *Blount v. Rizzi,* 400 U.S. 410, 91 S.Ct. 423, 27 L.Ed.2d 498 (1971) (postal stop orders of obscene materials); *United States v. Thirty–Seven Photographs,* 402 U.S. 363, 91 S.Ct. 1400, 28 L.Ed.2d 822 (1971) (customs seizure of obscene materials); *Southeastern Promotions, Ltd. v. Conrad,* 420 U.S. 546, 95 S.Ct. 1239, 43 L.Ed.2d 448 (1975) (denial of permit to use municipal theater for the musical, Hair); *Carroll v. President and Commissioners of Princess Anne,* 393 U.S. 175, 89 S.Ct. 347, 21 L.Ed.2d 325 (1968) (10 day restraining order against particular rallies or meetings invalid because *ex parte*). But cf. *FW/PBS v. Dallas,* 493 U.S. 215, 110 S.Ct. 596, 107 L.Ed.2d 603 (1990) (suggesting that partial application of *Freedman* standards (dispensing with burden of going to court and burden of proof, but retaining assurance of timely decision making by licensor and prompt judicial review) to ordinance licensing sexually oriented businesses ostensibly without regard to content of films or books would be appropriate). Should the collateral bar rule apply to *Carroll*? Do the *Freedman* standards make the *Times Film* decision palat- able?[c] For thorough discussion of the procedural issues, see Monaghan, *First Amendment "Due Process,"* 83 Harv.L.Rev. 518 (1970).

a. For the contention that the argument has in fact received a warm reception in the twentieth century, see Lively, *Fear and the Media: A First Amendment Horror Show,* 69 Minn.L.Rev. 1071 (1985).

b. Douglas, J., joined by Warren, C.J., and Black, J., dissenting, elaborated on the evils connected with systems of censorship.

c. For the contention that *Freedman* procedures fail to address the main concern of the prior restraint doctrine, see Redish, *The Proper Role of the Prior Restraint Doc- trine in First Amendment Theory,* 70 Va. L.Rev. 53, 75–89 (1984).

3. *Informal prior restraints.* BANTAM BOOKS, INC. v. SULLIVAN, 372 U.S. 58, 83 S.Ct. 631, 9 L.Ed.2d 584 (1963), per BRENNAN, J., (Harlan, J. dissenting) held unconstitutional the activities of a government commission that would identify "objectionable" books (some admittedly not obscene), notify the distributor in writing, inform the distributor of the Commission's duty to recommend obscenity prosecutions to the Attorney General and that the Commission's list of objectionable books was distributed to local police departments. The Commission thanked distributors in advance for their "cooperation," and a police officer usually visited the distributor to learn what action had been taken. In characterizing these practices as a system of prior administrative restraints, rather than mere legal advice, the Court observed that it did not mean to foreclose private consultation between law enforcement officers and distributors so long as such consultations were "genuinely undertaken with the purpose of aiding the distributor to comply" with the laws and avoid prosecution. What if the Commission circulated its list to distributors, police and prosecutors without mentioning prosecution? What if the prosecutor circulates a list of sixty books he or she regards as obscene and subject to prosecution?

4. *Comparing obscenity and commercial speech.* To combat deception, could commercial advertising be constitutionally subjected to a *Times Film* regime? Would such a scheme be permissible for advertising via some media, but not others? Reconsider fn. 24 in *Virginia Pharmacy,* p. 266 supra. Should the prohibition on prior restraints be inapplicable to injunctions against commercial advertising? Should *Freedman* standards be required? Should injunctions be permitted against a newspaper that carries unprotected advertising in addition to the advertiser? PITTSBURGH PRESS CO. v. PITTSBURGH COMM'N ON HUMAN RELATIONS, 413 U.S. 376, 93 S.Ct. 2553, 37 L.Ed.2d 669 (1973), per POWELL, J., upheld an order forbidding Pittsburgh Press to carry sex-designated "help wanted" ads, except for exempt jobs: "As described by Blackstone, the protection against prior restraint at common law barred only a system of administrative censorship. [While] the Court boldly stepped beyond this narrow doctrine in *Near* [it] has never held that all injunctions are impermissible. See *Lorain Journal Co. v. United States,* 342 U.S. 143, 72 S.Ct. 181, 96 L.Ed. 162 (1951).[d] The special vice of a prior restraint is that communication will be suppressed, either directly or by inducing excessive caution in the speaker, before an adequate determination that it is unprotected by the First Amendment.

"The present order does not endanger arguably protected speech. Because the order is based on a continuing course of repetitive conduct, this is not a case in which the Court is asked to speculate as to the effect of publication. Moreover, the order is clear and sweeps no more broadly than necessary. And because no interim relief was granted, the order will not have

d. *Lorain* upheld a Sherman Act injunction restraining a newspaper from seeking to monopolize commerce by refusing to carry advertising from merchants who advertised through a competing radio station.

gone into effect until it was finally determined that the actions of Pittsburgh Press were unprotected."

STEWART, J., joined by Douglas, J., dissented: Putting to one side "the question of governmental power to prevent publication of information that would clearly imperil the military defense of our Nation," "no government agency can tell a newspaper in advance what it can print and what it cannot."[e]

Does *Pittsburgh Press* indicate the Court will not limit permissible prior restraints to the *Near* "exceptional" areas? Does it mean that when a "continuing course of repetitive conduct" enables a court to make an "adequate determination that [a publication] is unprotected by the First Amendment" the policy against prior restraints does not apply when the restraint will not go "into effect until it [is] finally determined [judicially] that the actions [were] unprotected"? If so, what are the implications for the future of the prior restraint doctrine? Or can *Pittsburgh Press* be narrowly limited as applicable only to repetitive conduct in commercial advertising?

III. LICENSING "PROFESSIONALS": A DICHOTOMY BETWEEN SPEECH AND PRESS?

LOWE v. SEC, 472 U.S. 181, 105 S.Ct. 2557, 86 L.Ed.2d 130 (1985): The Investment Advisors Act of 1940 provides for injunctions and criminal penalties against anyone using the mails in conjunction with the advisory business who is not registered with the SEC or otherwise exempt from registration. An investment advisor includes "any person who, for compensation, engages in the business of advising others, either directly or through publications or writings, as to the value of securities or as to the advisability of investing in, purchasing, or selling securities, or who, for compensation and as part of a regular business, issues or promulgates analyses or reports concerning securities; but does not include [the] publisher of any bona fide newspaper, news magazine or business or financial publication of general and regular [circulation]." The SEC sought an injunction against Lowe and his affiliated businesses primarily alleging that Lowe's registration with the SEC had been properly revoked because of various fraudulent activities,[a] and that by publishing investment newsletters, Lowe was using the mails as an investment advisor. The SEC did not claim that any information in the newsletters had been false or materially misleading or that Lowe had yet profited from the advice tendered. The SEC did contend that Lowe's prior criminal conduct showed his "total lack of fitness" to remain in an

---

e. Blackmun, J., dissented "for substantially the reasons stated by" Stewart, J. Burger, C.J., dissenting, argued that the majority had mischaracterized the character and interim effect of the Commission's order.

a. For example, during the period that he was giving personal investment advice, Lowe had been convicted of misappropriating funds of a client, tampering with evidence to cover up fraud of a client, and stealing from a bank.

occupation with "numerous opportunities for dishonesty and self-dealing." Lowe admitted that his registration had been properly revoked, but denied that his newsletters were covered by the act and argued that, in any event, they were protected against registration and restraint under the first amendment.

The Court, per STEVENS, J., denied that Lowe's publication of financial newsletters made him an investment advisor under the act. The Court's interpretation was strongly influenced by first amendment considerations. It stated that Congress was "undoubtedly aware of two major First Amendment [cases] decided before the enactment of the Act." Citing *Near* and *Lovell,* the Court pointed to the maxim that "It is always appropriate to assume that our elected representatives, like other citizens, know the law." The doctrine against prior restraints and the notion that freedom of the press includes everything from distributing leaflets to mass circulation of magazines was said to support a "broad reading" of the exclusion for bona fide publishers of regular and general circulation:

"The exclusion itself uses extremely broad language that encompasses any newspaper, business publication, or financial publication provided that two conditions are met. The publication must be 'bona fide,' and it must be 'of regular and general circulation.' Neither of these conditions is defined, but the two qualifications precisely differentiate 'hit and run tipsters' and 'touts' from genuine publishers. Presumably a 'bona fide' publication would be genuine in the sense that it would contain disinterested commentary and analysis as opposed to promotional material disseminated by a 'tout.' Moreover, publications with a 'general and regular' circulation would not include 'people who send out bulletins from time to time on the advisability of buying and selling stocks' or 'hit and run tipsters.' Because the content of petitioners' newsletters was completely disinterested, and because they were offered[b] to the general public on a regular schedule, they are described by the plain language of the exclusion. * * *

"The dangers of fraud, deception, or overreaching that motivated the enactment of the statute are present in personalized communications but are not replicated in publications that are advertised and sold in an open market.[57] To the extent that the chart service contains factual information about past transactions and market trends, and the newsletters contain commentary on general market conditions, there can be no doubt about the

---

b. Lowe's newsletters in fact did not appear according to schedule. White, J., concurring, remarked: "As is evident from the Court's conclusion that petitioner's publications meet the regularity requirement, the Court's construction of the requirement adopts the view of our major law reviews on the issue of regular publication: good intentions are enough."

57. Cf. *Ohralik.* It is significant that the Commission has not established that petitioners have had authority over the funds of subscribers; that petitioners have been delegated decisionmaking authority to handle subscribers' portfolios or accounts; or that there have been individualized, investment-related interactions between petitioners and subscribers.

protected character of the communications,[58] a matter that concerned Congress when the exclusion was drafted. The content of the publications and the audience to which they are directed in this case reveal the specific limits of the exclusion. As long as the communications between petitioners and their subscribers remain entirely impersonal and do not develop into the kind of fiduciary, person-to-person relationships that were discussed at length in the legislative history of the Act and that are characteristic of investment adviser-client relationships, we believe the publications are, at least presumptively, within the exclusion and thus not subject to registration under the Act.[59]"c

WHITE, J., joined by Burger, C.J., and Rehnquist, J., concurring, argued that the Court's statutory interpretation was "improvident" and "based on a thinly disguised conviction" that the Act was unconstitutional as applied to prohibit publication by unregistered advisors: "Indeed the Court tips its hand when it discusses [*Lovell*] and *Near*. [While] purporting not to decide the question, the Court bases its statutory holding in large measure on the assumption that Congress already knew the answer to it when the statute was enacted. The Court thus attributes to the 76th Congress a clairvoyance the Solicitor General and the Second Circuit apparently lack—that is, the ability to predict our constitutional holdings 45 years in advance of our declining to reach them."

Finding it necessary to reach the constitutional question, White, J., argued that an injunction against Lowe's publications would violate the first amendment: "The power of government to regulate the professions is not lost whenever the practice of a profession entails speech. The underlying principle was expressed by the Court in *Giboney v. Empire Storage & Ice Co.,* [336 U.S. 490, 69 S.Ct. 684, 93 L.Ed. 834 (1949)]: 'it has never been deemed an abridgment of freedom of speech or press to make a course of conduct illegal merely because the conduct was in part initiated, evidenced, or carried out by means of language, either spoken, written, or printed.'

"Perhaps the most obvious example of a 'speaking profession' that is subject to governmental licensing is the legal profession. Although a lawyer's work is almost entirely devoted to the sort of communicative acts that, viewed in isolation, fall within the First Amendment's protection, we have never doubted that '[a] State can require high standards of qualification, such as good moral character or proficiency in its law, before it admits an applicant to the [bar].' [To] protect investors, the Government insists, it may

58. Moreover, because we have squarely held that the expression of opinion about a commercial product such as a loudspeaker is protected by the First Amendment, *Bose Corp.,* Ch. 1, II, B supra, it is difficult to see why the expression of an opinion about a marketable security should not also be protected.

59. The Commission suggests that an investment adviser may regularly provide,

in newsletterform, advice to several clients based on recent developments, without tailoring the advice to each client's individual needs, and that this is the practice of investment advising. However, the Commission does not suggest that this "practice" is involved here; thus, we have no occasion to address this concern.

c. Powell, J., took no part.

require that investment advisers, like lawyers, evince the qualities of truth-speaking, honor, discretion, and fiduciary responsibility.

"But the principle that the government may restrict entry into professions and vocations through licensing schemes has never been extended to encompass the licensing of speech per se or of the press. At some point, a measure is no longer a regulation of a profession but a regulation of speech or of the press; beyond that point, the statute must survive the level of scrutiny demanded by the First Amendment.

"[It] is for us, then, to find some principle by which to answer the question whether the Investment Advisers Act as applied to petitioner operates as a regulation of speech or of professional conduct.

"This is a problem Justice Jackson wrestled with in his concurring opinion in *Thomas v. Collins* [Ch. 4, I, A supra]. His words are instructive: '[A] rough distinction always exists, I think, which is more shortly illustrated than explained. A state may forbid one without its license to practice law as a vocation, but I think it could not stop an unlicensed person from making a speech about the rights of man or the rights of labor, or any other kind of right, including recommending that his hearers organize to support his views. Likewise, the state may prohibit the pursuit of medicine as an occupation without its license, but I do not think it could make it a crime publicly or privately to speak urging persons to follow or reject any school of medical thought. So the state to an extent not necessary now to determine may regulate one who makes a business or a livelihood of soliciting funds or memberships for unions. But I do not think it can prohibit one, even if he is a salaried labor leader, from making an address to a public meeting of workmen, telling them their rights as he sees them and urging them to unite in general or to join a specific union.'

"Justice Jackson concluded that the distinguishing factor was whether the speech in any particular case was 'associat[ed] [with] some other factor which the state may regulate so as to bring the whole within its official control.' If 'in a particular case the association or characterization is a proven and valid one,' he concluded, the regulation may stand.

"These ideas help to locate the point where regulation of a profession leaves off and prohibitions on speech begin. One who takes the affairs of a client personally in hand and purports to exercise judgment on behalf of the client in the light of the client's individual needs and circumstances is properly viewed as engaging in the practice of a profession. Just as offer and acceptance are communications incidental to the regulable transaction called a contract, the professional's speech is incidental to the conduct of the profession. [Where] the personal nexus between professional and client does not exist, and a speaker does not purport to be exercising judgment on behalf of any particular individual with whose circumstances he is directly acquainted, government regulation ceases to function as legitimate regulation of professional practice with only incidental impact on speech; it becomes regulation of speaking or publishing as such, subject to the First Amendment's [command].

"I do not believe it is necessary to the resolution of this case to determine whether petitioner's newsletters contain fully protected speech or commercial speech. [E]ven where mere 'commercial speech' is concerned, the First Amendment permits restraints on speech only when they are narrowly tailored to advance a legitimate governmental interest. The interest here is certainly legitimate: the Government wants to prevent investors from falling into the hands of scoundrels and swindlers. The means chosen, however, is extreme. [Our] commercial speech cases have consistently rejected the proposition that such drastic prohibitions on speech may be justified by a mere possibility that the prohibited speech will be fraudulent. See *Zauderer; Bates.*
* * *

"I emphasize the narrowness of the constitutional basis on which I would decide this case. I see no infirmity in defining the term 'investment adviser' to include a publisher like petitioner, and I would by no means foreclose the application of, for example, the Act's antifraud or reporting provisions to investment advisers (registered or unregistered) who offer their advice through publications. Nor do I intend to suggest that it is unconstitutional to invoke the Act's provisions for injunctive relief and criminal penalties against unregistered persons who, for compensation, offer personal investment advice to individual clients. I would hold only that the Act may not constitutionally be applied to prevent persons who are unregistered (including persons whose registration has been denied or revoked) from offering impersonal investment advice through publications such as the newsletters published by petitioner."

Notes and Questions

1.   Is White, J.'s speech/profession dichotomy persuasive? Should the existence of a "profession" justify prior restraints?

2.   Does White, J., suggest an element of special privilege for the press? Consider Shiffrin, *The First Amendment and Economic Regulation: Away From a General Theory of the First Amendment,* 78 Nw.U.L.Rev. 1212, 1276 (1983): "The doctrine of prior restraint may have been designed to put the press on an equal footing. People could speak or write without a license and that ought not to change merely because they used a printing press. Yet we now license a good deal of speech (for example, of lawyers), and those licenses are clearly prior restraints. So we have turned the law upside down. To speak you sometimes need a license; to use the press you almost never do. A doctrine designed to create equality for the press has evolved into one that gives it a special place."

3.   If lawyers, psychiatrists, and investment advisors can be licensed, what about fortune tellers? Union organizers? Journalists?

4.   Does *Lowe* threaten the "foundations of SEC financial disclosure regulation [and cast] a pall on the validity of government regulation of the professions." See generally Wolfson, *The First Amendment and the SEC,* 20 Conn.L.Rev. 265 (1988) (arguing that much securities and professional regulation violates the first amendment). See also Estreich-

er, *Securities Regulation and the First Amendment*, 24 Ga.L.Rev. 223 (1990) (arguing against restrictions of securities' advertising). For general commentary, see Symposium, *The First Amendment and Federal Securities Regulation,* 20 Conn.L.Rev. 261 (1988).

———

RILEY v. NATIONAL FEDERATION OF THE BLIND, 487 U.S. 781, 108 S.Ct. 2667, 101 L.Ed.2d 669 (1988), per BRENNAN, J., invalidated a scheme for licensing professional fundraisers who were soliciting on behalf of charitable organizations: "[North Carolina's] provision requires professional fundraisers to await a determination regarding their license application before engaging in solicitation, while volunteer fundraisers, or those employed by the charity, may solicit immediately upon submitting an application. [It] is well settled that a speaker's rights are not lost merely because compensation is received; a speaker is no less a speaker because he or she is paid to speak. [Generally,] speakers need not obtain a license to speak. However, that rule is not absolute. For example, states may impose valid time, place, or manner restrictions. North Carolina seeks to come within the exception by alleging a heightened interest in regulating those who solicit money. Even assuming that the State's interest does justify requiring fundraisers to obtain a license before soliciting, such a regulation must provide that the licensor 'will, within a specified brief period, either issue a license or go to court.' *Freedman.* That requirement is not met here * * *. The statute on its face does not purport to require when a determination must be made, nor is there an administrative regulation or interpretation doing so."

REHNQUIST, C.J., joined by O'Connor, J., dissented: "It simply is not true that [fundraisers] are prevented from engaging in any protected speech on their own behalf by the State's licensing requirements; the requirements only restrict their ability to engage in the profession of 'solicitation' without a license. We do not view bar admission requirements as invalid because they restrict a prospective lawyer's 'right' to be hired as an advocate by a client. So in this case we should not subject to strict scrutiny the State's attempt to license a business—professional fundraising—some of whose members might reasonably be thought to pose a risk of fraudulent activity."[a]

IV. PRIOR RESTRAINTS AND NATIONAL SECURITY

NEW YORK TIMES CO. v. UNITED STATES [THE PENTAGON PAPERS CASE]

403 U.S. 713, 91 S.Ct. 2140, 29 L.Ed.2d 822 (1971).

PER CURIAM.

We granted certiorari in these cases in which the United States seeks to enjoin the *New York Times* and the *Washington Post* from

---

a. Stevens, J., also dissented from the Court's treatment of the licensing issue.   For other aspects of the case, see p. 516 infra.

publishing the contents of a classified study entitled "History of U.S. Decision–Making Process on Viet Nam Policy."ᵃ

"Any system of prior restraints of expression comes to this Court bearing a heavy presumption against its constitutional validity." *Bantam Books;* see also *Near.* The Government "thus carries a heavy burden of showing justification for the enforcement of such a restraint." [The district court in the *Times* case and both lower federal courts] in the *Post* case held that the Government had not met that burden. We agree. [T]he stays entered [by this Court five days previously] are vacated. * * *

Mᴿ. Jᴜsᴛɪᴄᴇ Bʟᴀᴄᴋ, with whom Mᴿ. Jᴜsᴛɪᴄᴇ Dᴏᴜɢʟᴀs joins, concurring.

I adhere to the view that the Government's case against the *Post* should have been dismissed and that the injunction against the *Times* should have been vacated without oral argument when the cases were first presented to this Court. I believe that every moment's continuance of the injunctions against these newspapers amounts to a flagrant, indefensible, and continuing violation of the First Amendment. Furthermore, after oral arguments, I agree [with] the reasons stated by my Brothers Douglas and Brennan. In my view it is unfortunate that some of my Brethren are apparently willing to hold that the publication of news may sometimes be enjoined. Such a holding would make a shambles of the First Amendment.

[F]or the first time in the 182 years since the founding of the Republic, the federal courts are asked to hold that the First Amendment does not mean what it says, but rather means that the Government can halt the publication of current news of vital importance to the people of this country.

[Both] the history and language of the First Amendment support the view that the press must be left free to publish news, whatever the source, without censorship, injunctions, or prior restraints.

In the First Amendment the Founding Fathers gave the free press the protection it must have to fulfill its essential role in our democracy. The press was to serve the governed, not the governors. The Government's power to censor the press was abolished so that the press would remain forever free to censure the Government. The press was protected so that it could bare the secrets of government and inform the people. Only a free and unrestrained press can effectively expose deception in government. * * *

---

a. On June 12–14, 1971 the *New York Times* and on June 18 the *Washington Post* published portions of this "top secret" Pentagon study. Government actions seeking temporary restraining orders and injunctions progressed through two district courts and two courts of appeals between June 15–23. After a June 26 argument, ten Supreme Court opinions were issued on June 30, 1971.

The Government does not even attempt to rely on any act of Congress. Instead it makes the bold and dangerously far-reaching contention that the courts should take it upon themselves to "make" a law abridging freedom of the press in the name of equity, presidential power and national security, even when the representatives of the people in Congress have adhered to the command of the First Amendment and refused to make such a law. To find that the President has "inherent power" to halt the publication of news by resort to the courts would wipe out the First Amendment and destroy the fundamental liberty and security of the very people the Government hopes to make "secure." [The] word "security" is a broad, vague generality whose contours should not be invoked to abrogate the fundamental law embodied in the First Amendment. * * *

MR. JUSTICE DOUGLAS, with whom MR. JUSTICE BLACK joins, concurring.

While I join the opinion of the Court I believe it necessary to express my views more fully.

[The First Amendment leaves] no room for governmental[b] restraint on the press.

There is, moreover, no statute barring the publication by the press of the material which the *Times* and *Post* seek to use. * * *

These disclosures may have a serious impact. But that is no basis for sanctioning a previous restraint on the press * * *.

The dominant purpose of the First Amendment was to prohibit the widespread practice of governmental suppression of embarrassing information. [A] debate of large proportions goes on in the Nation over our posture in Vietnam. That debate antedated the disclosure of the contents of the present documents. The latter are highly relevant to the debate in progress.

Secrecy in government is fundamentally anti-democratic, perpetuating bureaucratic errors. Open debate and discussion of public issues are vital to our national health. * * *

The stays in these cases that have been in effect for more than a week constitute a flouting of the principles of the First Amendment as interpreted in *Near*.

MR. JUSTICE BRENNAN, concurring.

I write separately [to] emphasize what should be apparent: that our judgment in the present cases may not be taken to indicate the propriety, in the future, of issuing temporary stays and restraining orders to block the publication of material sought to be suppressed by the Government. So far as I can determine, never before has the United States sought to enjoin a newspaper from publishing information in its possession. * * *

---

b. But see Denbeaux, *The First Word of the First Amendment,* 80 Nw.U.L.Rev. 1156 (1986).

The entire thrust of the Government's claim throughout these cases has been that publication of the material sought to be enjoined "could," or "might," or "may" prejudice the national interest in various ways. But the First Amendment tolerates absolutely no prior judicial restraints of the press predicated upon surmise or conjecture that untoward consequences may result.* Our cases, it is true, have indicated that there is a single, extremely narrow class of cases in which the First Amendment's ban on prior judicial restraint may be overridden. Our cases have thus far indicated that such cases may arise only when the Nation "is at war," [*Schenck*]. Even if the present world situation were assumed to be tantamount to a time of war, or if the power of presently available armaments would justify even in peace-time the suppression of information that would set in motion a nuclear holocaust, in neither of these actions has the Government presented or even alleged that publication of items from or based upon the material at issue would cause the happening of an event of that nature. [Thus,] only governmental allegation and proof that publication must inevitably, directly and immediately cause the occurrence of an event kindred to imperiling the safety of a transport already at sea can support even the issuance of an interim restraining order. In no event may mere conclusions be sufficient: for if the Executive Branch seeks judicial aid in preventing publication, it must inevitably submit the basis upon which that aid is sought to scrutiny by the judiciary. And therefore, every restraint issued in this case, whatever its form, has violated the First Amendment—and not less so because that restraint was justified as necessary to afford the courts an opportunity to examine the claim more thoroughly. Unless and until the Government has clearly made out its case, the First Amendment commands that no injunction may issue.

Mr. Justice Stewart, with whom Mr. Justice White joins, concurring.

[I]n the cases before us we are asked neither to construe specific regulations nor to apply specific laws. [We] are asked, quite simply, to prevent the publication by two newspapers of material that the Executive Branch insists should not, in the national interest, be published. I am convinced that the Executive is correct with respect to some of the documents involved. But I cannot say that disclosure of any of them will surely result in direct, immediate, and irreparable damage to our Nation or its people. That being so, there can under the First Amendment be but one judicial resolution of the issues before us. I join the judgments of the Court.

Mr. Justice White, with whom Mr. Justice Stewart joins, concurring.

---

* *Freedman* and similar cases regarding temporary restraints of allegedly obscene materials are not in point. For those cases rest upon the proposition that "obscenity is not protected by the freedoms of speech and press." *Roth.* Here there is no question but that the material sought to be suppressed is within the protection of the First Amendment; the only question is whether, notwithstanding that fact, its publication may be enjoined for a time because of the presence of an overwhelming national interest. * * *

I concur in today's judgments, but only because of the concededly extraordinary protection against prior restraints enjoyed by the press under our constitutional system. I do not say that in no circumstances would the First Amendment permit an injunction against publishing information about government plans or operations. Nor, after examining the materials the Government characterizes as the most sensitive and destructive, can I deny that revelation of these documents will do substantial damage to public interests. Indeed, I am confident that their disclosure will have that result. But I nevertheless agree that the United States has not satisfied the very heavy burden which it must meet to warrant an injunction against publication in these cases, at least in the absence of express and appropriately limited congressional authorization for prior restraints in circumstances such as these.

The Government's position is simply stated: The responsibility of the Executive for the conduct of the foreign affairs and for the security of the Nation is so basic that the President is entitled to an injunction against publication of a newspaper story whenever he can convince a court that the information to be revealed threatens "grave and irreparable" injury to the public interest; and the injunction should issue whether or not the material to be published is classified, whether or not publication would be lawful under relevant criminal statutes enacted by Congress and regardless of the circumstances by which the newspaper came into possession of the information.

At least in the absence of legislation by Congress, based on its own investigations and findings, I am quite unable to agree that the inherent powers of the Executive and the courts reach so far as to authorize remedies having such sweeping potential for inhibiting publications by the press. [To] sustain the Government in these cases would start the courts down a long and hazardous road that I am not willing to travel at least without congressional guidance and direction.

* * * Prior restraints require an unusually heavy justification under the First Amendment; but failure by the Government to justify prior restraints does not measure its constitutional entitlement to a conviction for criminal publication. That the Government mistakenly chose to proceed by injunction does not mean that it could not successfully proceed in another way.

* * * Congress has addressed itself to the problems of protecting the security of the country and the national defense from unauthorized disclosure of potentially damaging information. It has not, however, authorized the injunctive remedy against threatened publication. It has apparently been satisfied to rely on criminal sanctions and their deterrent effect on the responsible as well as the irresponsible press. * * *

Mr. Justice Harlan, with whom The Chief Justice and Mr. Justice Blackmun join, dissenting. * * *

With all respect, I consider that the Court has been almost irresponsibly feverish in dealing with these cases.

Both [the] Second Circuit and [the] District of Columbia Circuit rendered judgment on June 23. [This] Court's order setting a hearing before us on June 26 at 11 a.m., a course which I joined only to avoid the possibility of even more peremptory action by the Court, was issued less than 24 hours before. The record in the *Post* case was filed with the Clerk shortly before 1 p.m. on June 25; the record in the *Times* case did not arrive until 7 or 8 o'clock that same night. The briefs of the parties were received less than two hours before argument on June 26.

This frenzied train of events took place in the name of the presumption against prior restraints created by the First Amendment. Due regard for the extraordinarily important and difficult questions involved in these litigations should have led the Court to shun such a precipitate timetable. In order to decide the merits of these cases properly, some or all of the following questions should have been faced: * * *

2.   Whether the First Amendment permits the federal courts to enjoin publication of stories which would present a serious threat to national security. See *Near* (dictum). * * *

4.   Whether the unauthorized disclosure of any of these particular documents would seriously impair the national security.

5.   What weight should be given to the opinion of high officers in the Executive Branch of the Government with respect to [question] 4. * * *

7.   Whether the threatened harm to the national security or the Government's possessory interest in the documents justifies the issuance of an injunction against publication in light of—

a.   The strong First Amendment policy against prior restraints on publication; b. The doctrine against enjoining conduct in violation of criminal statutes; and c. The extent to which the materials at issue have apparently already been otherwise disseminated.

These are difficult questions of fact, of law, and of judgment; the potential consequences of erroneous decision are enormous. The time which has been available to us, to the lower courts, and to the parties has been wholly inadequate for giving these cases the kind of consideration they deserve. It is a reflection on the stability of the judicial process that these great issues—as important as any that have arisen during my time on the Court—should have been decided under the pressures engendered by the torrent of publicity that has attended these litigations from their inception.

Forced as I am to reach the merits of these cases, I dissent from the opinion and judgments of the Court. Within the severe limitations imposed by the time constraints under which I have been required to operate, I can only state my reasons in telescoped form, even though in different circumstances I would have felt constrained to deal with the cases in the fuller sweep indicated above.

[It] is plain to me that the scope of the judicial function in passing upon the activities of the Executive Branch of the Government in the field of foreign affairs is very narrowly restricted. This view is, I think, dictated by the concept of separation of powers upon which our constitutional system [rests.] I agree that, in performance of its duty to protect the values of the First Amendment against political pressures, the judiciary must review the initial Executive determination to the point of satisfying itself that the subject matter of the dispute does lie within the proper compass of the President's foreign relations power. Constitutional considerations forbid "a complete abandonment of judicial control." Moreover, the judiciary may properly insist that the determination that disclosure of the subject matter would irreparably impair the national security be made by the head of the Executive Department concerned—here the Secretary of State or the Secretary of Defense—after actual personal consideration by that officer.[c] This safeguard is required in the analogous area of executive claims of privilege for secrets of state.

But in my judgment the judiciary may not properly go beyond these two inquiries and redetermine for itself the probable impact of disclosure on the national security. "[T]he very nature of executive decisions as to foreign policy is political, not judicial. Such decisions are wholly confided by our Constitution to the political departments of the government, Executive and Legislative. They are delicate, complex, and involve large elements of prophecy. They are and should be undertaken only by those directly responsible to the people whose welfare they advance or imperil. They are decisions of a kind for which the judiciary has neither aptitude, facilities nor responsibility and which has long been held to belong in the domain of political power not subject to judicial intrusion or inquiry." *Chicago & S. Air Lines v. Waterman S.S. Corp.* (Jackson, J.), 333 U.S. 103, 68 S.Ct. 431, 92 L.Ed. 568 (1948).

Even if there is some room for the judiciary to override the executive determination, it is plain that the scope of review must be exceedingly narrow. I can see no indication in the opinions of either the District Court or the Court of Appeals in the *Post* litigation that the conclusions of the Executive were given even the deference owing to an administrative agency, much less that owing to a co-equal branch of the Government operating within the field of its constitutional prerogative. * * *

Pending further hearings in each case conducted under the appropriate ground rules, I would continue the restraints on publication. I cannot believe that the doctrine prohibiting prior restraints reaches to the point of prevent-

c. Consider Godofsky & Rogatnick, *Prior Restraints: The Pentagon Papers Case Revisited*, 18 Cum.L.Rev. 527, 536–37 (1988): "Ironically, Justice Harlan's view of the Constitution might, ultimately, have presented more problems for the Government than those of most of the other Justices. Realistically, how often can the Secretary of State or Secretary of Defense devote 'actual personal consideration' to the question of whether material about to be pub- lished should be suppressed? And of what does 'actual personal consideration' consist? Must the Secretary himself read the documents? Is it sufficient 'consideration' by a Cabinet officer to act on the advice of his subordinates? If so, is not the 'actual personal consideration' test substantially meaningless? Could a Cabinet officer be required to testify as to the basis for his decision in order to test his 'bona fides'?"

ing courts from maintaining the status quo long enough to act responsibly in matters of such national importance as those involved here.

Mr. Justice Blackmun, dissenting.

[The First Amendment] is only one part of an entire Constitution. Article II of the great document vests in the Executive Branch primary power over the conduct of foreign affairs and places in that branch the responsibility for the Nation's safety. Each provision of the Constitution is important, and I cannot subscribe to a doctrine of unlimited absolutism for the First Amendment at the cost of downgrading other provisions. First Amendment absolutism has never commanded a majority of this Court. What is needed here is a weighing, upon properly developed standards, of the broad right of the press to print and of the very narrow right of the Government to prevent. Such standards are not yet developed. The parties here are in disagreement as to what those standards should be. But even the newspapers concede that there are situations where restraint is in order and is constitutional. Mr. Justice Holmes gave us a suggestion when he said in *Schenck,* "It is a question of proximity and degree. When a nation is at war many things that might be said in time of peace are such a hindrance to its effort that their utterance will not be endured so long as men fight and that no Court could regard them as protected by any constitutional right."

I therefore would remand these cases to be developed expeditiously, of course, but on a schedule permitting the orderly presentation of evidence from both sides [and] with the preparation of briefs, oral argument and court opinions of a quality better than has been seen to this point. [T]hese cases and the issues involved and the courts, including this one, deserve better than has been produced thus far. * * *[d]

Notes and Questions

1. *What did the case decide?* Do you agree that "the case [did] not make any law at all, good or bad"? That on the question "whether injunctions against the press are permissible, it is clear that [the case] can supply no precedent?" See Junger, *Down Memory Lane: The Case of the Pentagon Papers,* 23 Case W.Res.L.Rev. 3, 4–5 (1971). Or do you find in several concurring opinions a discernible standard that must be satisfied before a majority of the Court would permit an injunction against the press on national security grounds? Cf. 85 Harv.L.Rev. 199, 205–06 (1971). Do you find guidance as to the outcome if Congress were to authorize an injunction in narrow terms to protect national security? Cf. id. at 204–05. Might it

d. Marshall, J., concurring, did not deal with first amendment issues but only with separation of powers—the government's attempt to secure through the Court injunctive relief that Congress had refused to authorize.

Burger, C.J., dissenting, complained that because of "unseemly haste," "we do not know the facts of this case. [W]e literally do not know what we are acting on." He expressed no views on the merits, apart from his joinder in Harlan, J.'s opinion, and a statement that he would have continued the temporary restraints in effect while returning the cases to the lower courts for more thorough exploration of the facts and issues.

fairly be said that this is a separation of powers decision, like the *Steel Seizure* case, as well as a first amendment decision? See Junger, supra, at 19.

2. *"De facto" prior restraint.* One difficulty with viewing the prior restraint doctrine as "simply creat[ing] a 'presumption' against the validity of the restraint" (Emerson's characterization of the current approach) rather than as "a prohibition on all restraints subject to certain categorical exceptions," observes Emerson, *First Amendment Doctrine and the Burger Court,* 68 Calif.L.Rev. 422, 457–58 (1980), is that "the requirement of ad hoc scrutiny of prior restraints is itself likely to result in a 'de facto' prior restraint." Pointing to Brennan, J.'s comment in *Pentagon Papers* that "every restraint issued in this case [has] violated the First Amendment—and not less so because that restraint was justified as necessary to afford the courts an opportunity to examine the claim more thoroughly," Emerson notes that "[t]his is exactly what happened when the government sought to enjoin *The Progressive* magazine from publishing an article on the manufacture of the hydrogen bomb. The Supreme Court refused to order an expedited appeal from the [federal district court] injunction against publication [and, although the case was ultimately dismissed by the Seventh Circuit,] *The Progressive* remained under effective prior restraint for nearly seven months."

Compare *Near* and *Pentagon Papers* with UNITED STATES v. PROGRESSIVE, INC., 467 F.Supp. 990 (W.D.Wis.1979) (preliminary injunction issued Mar. 28, 1979), request for writ of mandamus den. sub nom. *Morland v. Sprecher,* 443 U.S. 709, 99 S.Ct. 3086, 61 L.Ed.2d 860 (1979), case dismissed, 610 F.2d 819 (7th Cir.1979).[e] *The Progressive* planned to publish an article entitled, "The H–Bomb Secret—How We Got It, Why We're Telling It," maintaining that the article would contribute to informed opinion about nuclear weapons and demonstrate the inadequacies of a system of secrecy and classification. Although the government conceded that at least some of the information contained in the article was "in the public domain" or had been "declassified," it argued that "national security" permitted it to censor information originating in the public domain "if when drawn together, synthesized and collated, such information acquires the character of presenting immediate, direct and irreparable harm to the interests of the United States." The Secretary of State stated that publication would increase thermonuclear proliferation and that this would "irreparably impair the national security of the United States." The Secretary of Defense maintained that dissemination of the Morland article would lead to a substantial increase in the risk of thermonuclear proliferation and to use or threats that would "adversely affect the national security of the United States."

e. The government's action against *The Progressive* was abandoned after information similar to that it sought to enjoin was published elsewhere.

Although recognizing that this constituted "the first instance of prior restraint against a publication in this fashion in the [nation's history]," the district court enjoined defendants, pending final resolution of the litigation, from publishing or otherwise disclosing any information designated by the government as "restricted data" within the meaning of The Atomic Energy Act of 1954: "What is involved here is information dealing with the most destructive weapon in the history of mankind, information of sufficient destructive potential to nullify the right to free speech and to endanger the right to life itself. [Faced] with a stark choice between upholding the right to continued life and the right to freedom of the press, most jurists would have no difficulty in opting for the chance to continue to breathe and function as they work to achieve perfect freedom of expression.

"[A] mistake in ruling against *The Progressive* will seriously infringe cherished First Amendment rights. [A] mistake in ruling against the United States could pave the way for thermonuclear annihilation for us all. In that event, our right to life is extinguished and the right to publish becomes moot.

"[W]ar by foot soldiers has been replaced in large part by machines and bombs. No longer need there be any advance warning or any preparation time before a nuclear war could be commenced. [In light of these factors] publication of the technical information on the hydrogen bomb contained in the article is analogous to publication of troop movements or locations in time of war and falls within the extremely narrow exception to the rule against prior restraint [recognized in *Near*].[f]

"The government has met its burden under § 2274 of The Atomic Energy Act [which authorizes injunctive relief against one who would communicate or disclose restricted data 'with reason to believe such data will be utilized to injure the United States or to secure an advantage to any foreign nation.'] [I]t has also met the test enunciated by two Justices in *Pentagon Papers,* namely grave, direct, immediate and irreparable harm to the United States."

The court distinguished *Pentagon Papers* as follows: "[T]he study involved [there] contained historical data relating to events some three to twenty years previously. Secondly, the Supreme Court agreed with the lower court that no cogent reasons were advanced by the government as to why the article affected national security except that publication might cause some embarrassment to the United States. A final and most vital difference between these two cases is the fact that a specific statute is involved here [§ 2274 of The Atomic Energy Act]."

f. One of the reasons the court gave for finding that the objected-to technical portions of the article fell within the *Near* exception was that it was "unconvinced that suppression of [these portions] would in any plausible fashion impede the defendants in their laudable crusade to stimulate public knowledge of nuclear armament and bring about enlightened debate on national policy questions." Should this have been a factor in the decision to issue the preliminary injunction?

3. *CIA secrecy agreement.* The Central Intelligence Agency requires employees to sign a "secrecy agreement" as a condition of employment, an agreement committing the employee not to reveal classified information nor to publish any information obtained during the course of employment without prior approval of the Agency. In SNEPP v. UNITED STATES, 444 U.S. 507, 100 S.Ct. 763, 62 L.Ed.2d 704 (1980), Snepp had published a book called *Decent Interval* about certain CIA activities in South Vietnam based on his experiences as an agency employee without seeking prepublication review. At least for purposes of the litigation, the government conceded that Snepp's book divulged no confidential information. The Court, per curiam (Stevens, J., joined by Brennan and Marshall, JJ., dissenting) held that Snepp's failure to submit the book was a breach of trust and the government was entitled to a constructive trust on the proceeds of the book: "[E]ven in the absence of an express agreement, the CIA could have acted to protect substantial government interests by imposing reasonable restrictions on employee activities that in other contexts might be protected by the First Amendment. The Government has a compelling interest in protecting both the secrecy of information important to our national security and the appearance of confidentiality so essential to the effective operation of our foreign intelligence service."[g] When employees or past employees do submit publications for clearance, should *Freedman* standards apply? Can former CIA employees be required to submit all public speeches relating to their former employment for clearance? Are extemporaneous remarks permitted? To what extent can secrecy agreements be required of public employees outside the national security area?[h]

g. Compare *Haig v. Agee,* 453 U.S. 280, 101 S.Ct. 2766, 69 L.Ed.2d 640 (1981), stating that "repeated disclosures of intelligence operations and names of intelligence personnel" for the "purpose of obstructing intelligence operations and the recruiting of intelligence personnel" are "clearly not protected by the Constitution." What if the publisher of the information merely has "reason to believe that such activities would impair or impede the foreign intelligence activities of the United States"? See 50 U.S.C. § 421.

h. For criticism of *Snepp,* see Cheh, *Judicial Supervision of Executive Secrecy,* 69 Corn.L.Rev. 690 (1984); Easterbrook, *Insider Trading, Secret Agents, Evidentiary Privileges, and the Production of Information,* 1981 Sup.Ct.Rev. 309, 339–53; Godofsky & Rogatnick, *Prior Restraints: The Pentagon Papers Case Revisited,* fn. c supra, at 543–54 (1988); Koffler & Gershman, *The New Seditious Libel,* 69 Corn.L.Rev. 816 (1984); Medow, *The First Amendment and the Secrecy State: Snepp v. United States,* 130 U.Pa.L.Rev. 775 (1982). For a thorough exploration of the occasions in which secrecy has been preferred over public knowledge, see DuVal, *The Occasions of Secrecy,* 47 U.Pitt.L.Rev. 579 (1986).

Chapter 5

JUSTICE AND NEWSGATHERING

This section explores four problems, problems which are connected with the fair administration of justice or with newsgathering or with both. The first problem involves publicity about trials. The government seeks to deter or punish speech by the press that it fears will threaten the fair administration of justice, but speech of that character falls into no recognized category of unprotected speech. Thus, the courts must consider whether absolute protection is called for, or, alternatively, whether new categories or ad hoc determinations are appropriate, and whether prior restraints are permissible. Alternatively, if the press cannot be prevented from speaking about trials, can prosecutors, defense attorneys, litigants and potential witnesses be prevented from speaking to the press?

In the second problem the government seeks to fairly administer the justice system by forcing reporters to reveal their confidential sources. The press maintains that any such authorized compulsion would have a chilling effect on its ability to gather the news.

The third problem also involves newsgathering. The press engages in fraud to gain access to private sources and succeeds in uncovering evidence of substantial public interest. May the press be successfully sued for fraud in these circumstances? Should it be liable for the damages caused by its truthful publication? For punitive damages?

In the final problem, government seeks not to punish speech, but to administer justice in private. It refuses to let the public or press witness its handling of prisoners, or its conduct of trial or pre-trial proceedings. The question is whether the first amendment can serve as a sword allowing the press or citizen-critics to gather information. Assuming it can, what are its limits within the justice system? Does any right of access reach beyond the justice system? Does the first amendment require that the press be granted access not afforded the public? Does the first amendment permit differential access? If so, what are the limits on how government defines the press?

I. PUBLICITY ABOUT TRIALS

In a number of cases, defendants have asserted that their rights to a fair trial have been abridged by newspaper publicity. SHEPPARD v. MAXWELL, 384 U.S. 333, 86 S.Ct. 1507, 16 L.Ed.2d 600 (1966), is probably the most notorious "trial by newspaper" case. The Court, per CLARK, J., (Black, J. dissenting) agreed with the "finding" of the Ohio Supreme Court that the atmosphere of defendant's murder trial was that of a " 'Roman holiday' for the news media." The courtroom was jammed with reporters. And in the corridors outside the courtroom, "a host of photographers and television personnel" photographed witnesses, counsel and jurors as they entered and left the courtroom. Throughout the trial, there was a deluge of publicity, much of which contained information never presented at trial, yet the jurors were not sequestered until the trial was over and they had begun their deliberations.

The Court placed the primary blame on the trial judge. He could "easily" have prevented "the carnival atmosphere of the trial" since "the courtroom and courthouse premises" were subject to his control. For example, he should have provided privacy for the jury, insulated witnesses from the media, instead of allowing them to be interviewed at will, and "made some effort to control the release of leads, information, and gossip to the press by police officers, witnesses, and the counsel for both sides." No one "coming under the jurisdiction of the court should be permitted to frustrate its function."

The Court recognized that "there is nothing that proscribes the press from reporting events that transpire in the courtroom. But where there is a reasonable likelihood that prejudicial news prior to trial will prevent a fair trial, the judge should continue the case until the threat abates, or transfer it to another county not so permeated with publicity. In addition, sequestration of the jury was something the judge should have raised sua sponte with counsel. If publicity during the proceedings threatens the fairness of the trial, a new trial should be ordered. But we must remember that reversals are but palliatives; the cure lies in those remedial measures that will prevent the prejudice at its inception."

The Court, however, reiterated its extreme reluctance "to place any direct limitations on the freedom traditionally exercised by the news media for '[w]hat transpires in the courtroom is public property.' "The press "does not simply publish information about trials but guards against the miscarriage of justice by subjecting the police, prosecutors, and judicial processes to extensive public scrutiny and criticism."

In anticipation of the trial of Simants for a mass murder which had attracted widespread news coverage, the county court prohibited everyone in attendance from, inter alia, releasing or authorizing for publication "any testimony given or evidence adduced." Simants' preliminary hearing (open to the public) was held the same day, subject to the restrictive order. Simants was bound over for trial. Respondent Nebraska state trial judge then entered an order which, as modified by the state supreme court, restrained the press and broadcasting media from reporting any confessions or incriminating statements made by Simants to law enforcement officers or third parties, except members of the press, and from reporting other facts "strongly implicative" of the defendant. The order expired when the jury was impaneled.

NEBRASKA PRESS ASS'N v. STUART, 427 U.S. 539, 96 S.Ct. 2791, 49 L.Ed.2d 683 (1976), per Burger, C.J., struck down the state court order: "To the extent that the order prohibited the reporting of evidence adduced at the open preliminary hearing, it plainly violated settled principles: 'There is nothing that proscribes the press from reporting events that transpire in the courtroom.' *Sheppard*."[a] To the extent that the order prohibited publication "based on information gained from other sources, [the] heavy burden imposed as a condition to securing a prior restraint was not met." The portion of the order regarding "implicative" information was also "too vague and too broad" to survive scrutiny of restraints on first amendment rights.

"[P]retrial publicity—even pervasive, adverse publicity—does not inevitably lead to an unfair trial. The capacity of the jury eventually impaneled to decide the case fairly is influenced by the tone and extent of the publicity, which is in part, and often in large part, shaped by what attorneys, police and other officials do to precipitate news coverage. [T]he measures a judge takes or fails to take to mitigate the effects of pretrial publicity—the measures described in *Sheppard*—may well determine whether the defendant receives a trial consistent [with] due process.

"[The] Court has interpreted [first amendment] guarantees to afford special protection against orders that prohibit the publication or broadcast of particular information or commentary—orders that impose [a] 'prior' restraint on speech. None of our decided cases on prior restraint involved restrictive orders entered to protect a defendant's right to a fair and impartial jury, but [they] have a common thread relevant to this case. * * *

"The thread running through [*Near* and *Pentagon Papers*], is that prior restraints on speech and publication are the most serious and the least tolerable infringement on First Amendment rights. A criminal penalty or a judgment in a defamation case is subject to the whole panoply of protections afforded by deferring the impact of the judgment until all avenues of appellate review have been exhausted. [But] a prior restraint [has] an immediate and irreversible sanction. If it can be said that a threat of

a. The Court added, however, that the county court "could not know that closure of the preliminary hearing was an alterna- tive open to it until the Nebraska Supreme Court so construed state law."

criminal or civil sanctions after publication 'chills' speech, prior restraint 'freezes' it at least for the time.

"[I]f the authors of [the first and sixth amendments], fully aware of the potential conflicts between them, were unwilling or unable to resolve the issue by assigning to one priority over the other, it is not for us to rewrite the Constitution by undertaking what they declined. [Yet] it is nonetheless clear that the barriers to prior restraint remain high unless we are to abandon what the Court has said for nearly a quarter of our national existence and implied throughout all of [it.]

"We turn now to the record in this case to determine whether, as Learned Hand put it, 'the gravity of the "evil," discounted by its improbability, justifies such invasion of free speech as is necessary to avoid the danger,' *Dennis* [2d Cir.], aff'd. To do so, we must examine the evidence before the trial judge when the order was entered to determine (a) the nature and extent of pretrial news coverage; (b) whether other measures would be likely to mitigate the effects of unrestrained pretrial publicity; (c) how effectively a restraining order would operate to prevent the threatened danger. The precise terms of the restraining order are also important. We must then consider whether the record supports the entry of a prior restraint on publication, one of the most extraordinary remedies known to our jurisprudence."

As to (a), although the trial judge was justified in concluding there would be extensive pretrial publicity concerning this case, he "found only 'a clear and present danger that pretrial publicity *could* impinge upon the defendant's right to a fair trial.' [Emphasis added by the Court]. His conclusion as to the impact of such publicity on prospective jurors was of necessity speculative, dealing as he was with factors unknown and unknowable."

As to (b), "there is no finding that alternative means [e.g., change of venue, postponement of trial to allow public attention to subside, searching questions of prospective jurors] would not have protected Simants' rights, and the Nebraska Supreme Court did no more than imply that such measures might not be adequate. Moreover, the record is lacking in evidence to support such a finding."

As to (c), in view of such practical problems as the limited territorial jurisdiction of the trial court issuing the order, the difficulties of predicting what information "will in fact undermine the impartiality of jurors," the problem of drafting an order that will "effectively keep prejudicial information from prospective jurors," and that the events "took place in a community of only 850 people"—throughout which, "it is reasonable to assume," rumors that "could well be more damaging than reasonably accurate news accounts" would "travel swiftly by word of mouth"—"it is far from clear that prior restraint on publication would have protected Simants' rights."

"[It] is significant that when this Court has reversed a state conviction because of prejudicial publicity, it has carefully noted that some course of action short of prior restraint would have made a critical difference. However difficult it may be, we need not rule out the possibility of showing the kind of threat to fair trial rights that would possess the requisite degree of certainty to justify restraint. [We] reaffirm that the guarantees of freedom of expression are not an absolute prohibition under all circumstances, but the barriers to prior restraint remain high and the presumption against its use continues intact. We hold that, with respect to the order entered in this case [the] heavy burden imposed as a condition to securing a prior restraint was not [met]."

BRENNAN, J., joined by Stewart and Marshall, JJ., concurring, would hold that "resort to prior restraints on the freedom of the press is a constitutionally impermissible method for enforcing [the right to a fair trial by a jury]; judges have at their disposal a broad spectrum of devices for ensuring that fundamental fairness is accorded the accused without necessitating so drastic an incursion on the equally fundamental and salutary constitutional mandate that discussion of public affairs in a free society cannot depend on the preliminary grace of judicial censors": "Commentary and reporting on the criminal justice system is at the core of First Amendment values, for the operation and integrity of that system is of crucial import to citizens concerned with the administration of Government. Secrecy of judicial action can only breed ignorance and distrust of courts and suspicion concerning the competence and impartiality of judges; free and robust reporting, criticism, and debate can contribute to public understanding of the rule of law and to comprehension of the functioning of the entire criminal justice system, as well as improve the quality of that system by subjecting it to the cleansing effects of exposure and public accountability.

"[In] effect, we are now told by respondents that the [first and sixth amendments] can no longer coexist when the press possesses and seeks to publish 'confessions and admissions against interest' and other information 'strongly implicative' of a criminal defendant as the perpetrator of a crime, and that one or the other right must therefore be subordinated. I disagree. Settled case law concerning the impropriety and constitutional invalidity of prior restraints on the press compels the conclusion that there can be no prohibition on the publication by the press of any information pertaining to pending judicial proceedings or the operation of the criminal justice system, no matter how shabby the means by which the information is obtained.[15] This does not imply, however, any subordination of Sixth Amendment rights, for an accused's right to a fair trial may be adequately assured through methods that do not infringe First Amendment values.

"[The narrow national security exception mentioned in *Near* and *Pentagon Papers*] does not mean, as the Nebraska Supreme Court assumed, that prior restraints can be justified on an ad hoc balancing approach that

---

15. Of course, even if the press cannot be enjoined from reporting certain information, that does not necessarily immunize it from civil liability for libel or invasion of privacy or from criminal liability for transgressions of general criminal laws during the course of obtaining that information.

concludes that the 'presumption' must be overcome in light of some perceived 'justification.' Rather, this language refers to the fact that, as a matter of procedural safeguards and burden of proof, prior restraints even within a recognized exception to the rule against prior restraints will be extremely difficult to justify; but as an initial matter, the purpose for which a prior restraint is sought to be imposed 'must fit within one of the narrowly defined exceptions to the prohibition against prior restraints.' Indeed, two Justices in [*Pentagon Papers*] apparently controverted the existence of even a limited 'military security' exception to the rule against prior restraints on the publication of otherwise protected material. (Black, J., concurring); (Douglas, J., concurring). And a majority of the other Justices who expressed their views on the merits made it clear that they would take cognizance only of a 'single, extremely narrow class of cases in which the First Amendment's ban on prior judicial restraint may be overridden.' (Brennan, J., concurring). * * *

"The only exception that has thus far been recognized even in dictum to the blanket prohibition against prior restraints against publication of material which would otherwise be constitutionally shielded was the 'military security' situation addressed in [*Pentagon Papers*]. But unlike the virtually certain, direct, and immediate harm required for such a restraint [the] harm to a fair trial that might otherwise eventuate from publications which are suppressed pursuant to orders such as that under review must inherently remain speculative.

"[O]nce the jury is impaneled, the techniques of sequestration of jurors and control over the courtroom and conduct of trial should prevent prejudicial publicity from infecting the fairness of judicial proceedings. Similarly, judges may stem much of the flow of prejudicial publicity at its source, before it is obtained by representatives of the press. But even if the press nevertheless obtains potentially prejudicial information and decides to publish that information, the Sixth Amendment rights of the accused may still be adequately protected. In particular, the trial judge should employ the voir dire to probe fully into the effect of publicity. [We] have indicated that even in a case involving outrageous publicity and a 'carnival atmosphere' in the courtroom, 'these procedures would have been sufficient to guarantee [the defendant] a fair trial.' [For] this reason, the one thing *Sheppard* did not approve were 'any direct limitations on the freedom traditionally exercised by the news media.' Indeed, the traditional techniques approved in *Sheppard* for ensuring fair trials would have been adequate in every case in which we have found that a new trial was required due to lack of fundamental fairness to the accused. * * *

"There are additional, practical reasons for not starting down the path urged by respondents. The ['military security' exception] involves no judicial weighing of the countervailing public interest in receiving the suppressed information; the direct, immediate, and irreparable harm that would result from disclosure is simply deemed to outweigh the public's interest in knowing, for example, the specific details of troop movements during wartime. [H]owever, any attempt to impose a prior restraint on the reporting of information concerning the operation of the criminal justice system will inevitably involve the courts in an ad hoc evaluation of the need for the public to receive particular information that might nevertheless implicate the accused as the perpetrator of a crime. [T]he press may be arrogant, tyrannical, abusive, and sensationalist, just as it may be incisive, probing, and informative. But at least in the context of prior restraints on publication, the decision of what, when, and how to publish is for editors, not judges. Every restrictive order imposed on the press in this case was accordingly an unconstitutional prior restraint * * *."

Although they joined the Court's opinion, White and Powell, JJ., also filed brief concurrences. WHITE, J., expressed "grave doubts" that these types of restrictive orders "would ever be justifiable." POWELL, J., "emphasize[d] the unique burden" resting upon one who "undertakes to show the necessity for prior restraint on pretrial publicity." In his judgment, a prior restraint "requires a showing that (i) there is a clear threat to the fairness of trial, (ii) such a threat is posed by the actual publicity to be restrained, and (iii) no less restrictive alternatives are available. Notwithstanding such a showing, a restraint may not issue unless it also is shown that previous publicity or publicity from unrestrained sources will not render the restraint inefficacious. [A]ny restraint must comply with the standards of specificity always required in the First Amendment context."

STEVENS, J., concurred in the judgment. For the reasons articulated by Brennan, J., he "agree[d] that the judiciary is capable of protecting the defendant's right to a fair trial without enjoining the press from publishing information in the public domain, and that it may not do so." But he reserved judgment, until further argument, on "[w]hether the same absolute protection would apply no matter how shabby or illegal the means by which the information is obtained, no matter how serious an intrusion on privacy might be involved, no matter how demonstrably false the information might be, no matter how prejudicial it might be to the interests of innocent persons, and no matter how perverse the motivation for publishing it." He indicated that "if ever required to face the issue squarely" he "may well accept [Brennan, J.'s] ultimate conclusion."[b]

Notes and Questions

1. *Why the prior restraint reliance?* Does "the reasoning used by all of the justices premised solely on the traditional aversion to prior restraints, insufficiently" protect the press? Sack, *Principle and Nebraska Press Association v. Stuart*, 29 Stan.L.Rev. 411, 411 (1977). Would the *Nebraska Press* order have been "equally objectionable" if "framed as a statutory sanction punishing publication after it had occurred"?

b. For background on *Nebraska Press,* see Friendly & Elliot, *The Constitution: That Delicate Balance* 148–58 (1984).

2. *Why the Dennis citation?* Consider Schmidt, *Nebraska Press Association: An Expansion of Freedom and Contraction of Theory,* 29 Stan.L.Rev. 431, 459–60 (1977): Burger, C.J.'s reliance on *Dennis* "is remarkable, almost unbelievable, because that test is both an exceedingly odd means of determining the validity of a prior restraint and a controversial and recently neglected technique of first amendment adjudication. [If] the [*Dennis*] test is the right one for prior restraints, what tests should govern a subsequent punishment case resting on legislation?" See also Barnett, note 1 supra, at 542–44. Burger, C.J.'s citation to *Dennis* should be read in conjunction with dictum in his majority opinion in *Landmark Communications, Inc. v. Virginia,* note 6 infra. There he questioned reliance upon the clear and present danger standard but observed: "Properly applied, the test requires a court to make its own inquiry into the imminence and magnitude of the danger said to flow from the particular utterance and then to balance the character of the evil, as well as its likelihood, against the need for free and unfettered expression. The possibility that other measures will serve the State's interests should also be weighed."

3. *Future press restraints.* Was *Nebraska Press* a strong case for restraint? Is it "difficult to believe that any other case will provide an exception to the rule against prior restraints in fair trial/free press cases"? Goodale, *The Press Ungagged: The Practical Effect on Gag Order Litigation of Nebraska Press Association v. Stuart,* 29 Stan.L.Rev. 497, 504 (1977). If so, does the dispute between the justices over the right standard make a difference? Does the collateral bar rule shed light on that question? See id. at 511–12; Barnett, note 1 supra, at 553–58. Should the collateral bar rule apply in this situation?

4. *Application to non-press defendants.* Should *Nebraska Press* standards apply to court orders preventing prosecutors, witnesses, potential witnesses, jurors,[c] defendants, or defense attorneys from talking to the press about the case? Should different standards apply to each category—e.g., do defense attorneys deserve as much protection as the press? See *Gentile v. State Bar,* 501 U.S. 1030, 111 S.Ct. 2720, 115 L.Ed.2d 888 (1991) (less stringent standard ("substantial likelihood of material prejudice") applies to defense attorneys, not clear and present danger).[d]

5. *Obstructing justice.* A series of cases have held that the first amendment greatly restricts contempt sanctions against persons whose comments on pending cases were alleged to have created a danger of obstruction of the judicial process. "Such repression can be justified, if at all, only by a clear

---

c. Strauss, *Juror Journalism,* 12 Yale L. & Pol'y Rev. 389 (1994); Comment, *Checkbook Journalism, Free Speech, and Fair Trials,* 143 U.Pa.L.Rev. 1739 (1995).

d. For commentary, see Chemerinsky, *Silence is Not Golden,* 47 Emory L.Rev. 859 (1998); Strauss, *Why It's Not Free Speech versus Fair Trial,* 1998 U.Chi.Legal F. 109; Weinreb, *Speaking Out Outside the Courtroom,* 47 Emory L.J. 889 (1998); Freedman & Starwood, *Prior Restraints on Freedom of Expression by Defendants and Defense Attorneys: Ratio Decidendi v. Obiter Dictum,* 29 Stan.L.Rev. 607 (1977); Comment, *First Amendment Protection of Criminal Defense Attorneys' Extrajudicial [Statements],* 8 Whittier L.Rev. 1021 (1987).

and present danger of the obstruction of justice." *New York Times Co. v. Sullivan,* p. 64 supra. In *Bridges v. California,* 314 U.S. 252, 62 S.Ct. 190, 86 L.Ed. 192 (1941), union leader Bridges had caused publication or acquiesced in publication of a telegram threatening a strike if an "outrageous" California state decision involving Bridges' dock workers were enforced. The Court reversed Bridges' contempt citation. Consider Tribe, *American Constitutional Law* 624 (1978): "If Bridges' threat to cripple the economy of the entire West Coast did not present danger enough, the lesson of the case must be that almost nothing said outside the courtroom is punishable as contempt."[3]

Would it make a difference if a petit jury were impaneled? Suppose Bridges published an open letter to petit jurors? What if copies were sent by Bridges to each juror? Cf. *Wood v. Georgia,* 370 U.S. 375, 82 S.Ct. 1364, 8 L.Ed.2d 569 (1962) (open letter to press and grand jury—contempt citation reversed). But cf. *Cox v. Louisiana,* 379 U.S. 559, 85 S.Ct. 476, 13 L.Ed.2d 487 (1965) infra (statute forbidding parades near courthouse with intent to interfere with administration of justice upheld): ("[W]e deal not with the contempt power [but] a statute narrowly drawn to punish" not a pure form of speech but expression mixed with conduct "that infringes a substantial state interest in protecting the judicial process.").

6. *Confidentiality and privacy.* A series of cases has rebuffed state efforts to protect confidentiality or privacy by prohibiting publication. *Cox Broadcasting Corp. v. Cohn,* Ch. 1, II, F supra (state could not impose liability for public dissemination of the name of rape victim derived from public court documents); *Oklahoma Pub. Co. v. District Court,* 430 U.S. 308, 97 S.Ct. 1045, 51 L.Ed.2d 355 (1977) (pretrial order enjoining press from publishing name or picture of 11–year-old boy accused of murder invalid when reporters had been lawfully present at a prior public hearing and had photographed him en route from the courthouse); *Landmark Communications, Inc. v. Virginia,* 435 U.S. 829, 98 S.Ct. 1535, 56 L.Ed.2d 1 (1978) (statute making it a crime to publish information about particular confidential proceedings invalid as applied to non-participant in the proceedings, at least when the information had been lawfully acquired); *Smith v. Daily Mail Pub. Co.,* 443 U.S. 97, 99 S.Ct. 2667, 61 L.Ed.2d 399 (1979) (statute making it a crime for newspapers (but not broadcasters) to publish the name of any youth charged as a juvenile offender invalid as applied to information lawfully acquired from private sources). But cf. *Seattle Times Co. v. Rinehart,* 467 U.S. 20, 104 S.Ct. 2199, 81 L.Ed.2d 17 (1984) (order enjoining newspaper from disseminating information acquired as a litigant in pretrial discovery valid so long as order is entered on a showing of good cause and does not restrict the dissemination of the information if gained from other sources).

3. Compare Rieger, *Lawyers' Criticism of Judges: Is Freedom of Speech A Figure of Speech?,* 2 Const.Comm. 69 (1985).

II. NEWSGATHERING

A. PROTECTION OF CONFIDENTIAL SOURCES

BRANZBURG v. HAYES

408 U.S. 665, 92 S.Ct. 2646, 33 L.Ed.2d 626 (1972).

MR. JUSTICE WHITE delivered the opinion of the Court.

[Branzburg, a Kentucky reporter, wrote articles describing his observations of local hashish-making and other drug violations. He refused to testify before a grand jury regarding his information. The state courts rejected his claim of a first amendment privilege.

[Pappas, a Massachusetts TV newsman-photographer, was allowed to enter and remain inside a Black Panther headquarters on condition he disclose nothing. When an anticipated police raid did not occur, he wrote no story. Summoned before a local grand jury, he refused to answer any questions about what had occurred inside the Panther headquarters or to identify those he had observed. The state courts denied his claim of a first amendment privilege.

[Caldwell, a N.Y. Times reporter covering the Black Panthers, was summoned to appear before a federal grand jury investigating Panther activities. A federal court issued a protective order providing that although he had to divulge information given him "for publication," he could withhold "confidential" information "developed or maintained by him as a professional journalist." Maintaining that absent a specific need for his testimony he should be excused from attending the grand jury altogether, Caldwell disregarded the order and was held in contempt. The Ninth Circuit reversed, holding that absent "compelling reasons" Caldwell could refuse even to attend the grand jury, because of the potential impact of such an appearance on the flow of news to the public.]

[Petitioners' first amendment claims] may be simply put: that to gather news it is often necessary to agree either not to identify [sources] or to publish only part of the facts revealed, or both; that if the reporter is nevertheless forced to reveal these confidences to a grand jury, the source so identified and other confidential sources of other reporters will be measurably deterred from furnishing publishable information, all to the detriment of the free flow of information protected by the First Amendment. Although petitioners do not claim an absolute privilege [they] assert that the reporter should not be forced either to appear or to testify before a grand jury or at trial until and unless sufficient grounds are shown for believing that the reporter possesses information relevant to a crime the grand jury is investigating, that the information the reporter has is unavailable from other sources, and that the need for the information is sufficiently compelling to override the claimed invasion of First Amendment interests occasioned by the disclosure. [The] heart of the claim is that the burden on news gathering resulting from compelling reporters to disclose confidential information outweighs any public interest in obtaining the information.

[We agree] that news gathering [qualifies] for First Amendment protection; without some protection for seeking out the news, freedom of the press could be eviscerated. But this case involves no intrusions upon speech [and no] command that the press publish what it prefers to withhold. [N]o penalty, civil or criminal, related to the content of published material is at issue here. The use of confidential sources by the press is not forbidden or restricted; reporters remain free to seek news from any source by means within the law. No attempt is made to require the press to publish its sources of information or indiscriminately to disclose them on request.

The sole issue before us is the obligation of reporters to respond to grand jury subpoenas as other citizens do and to answer questions relevant to an investigation into the commission of crime.

[T]he First Amendment does not guarantee the press a constitutional right of special access to information not available to the public generally. [Although] news gathering may be hampered, the press is regularly excluded from grand jury proceedings, our own conferences, the meetings of other official bodies gathered in executive session, and the meetings of private organizations. Newsmen have no constitutional right of access to the scenes of crime or disaster when the general public is excluded, and they may be prohibited from attending or publishing information about trials if such restrictions are necessary to assure a defendant a fair trial before an impartial tribunal. [It] is thus not surprising that the great weight of authority is that newsmen are not exempt from the normal duty of appearing before a grand jury and answering questions relevant to a criminal investigation.

[Because] its task is to inquire into the existence of possible criminal conduct and to return only well-founded indictments, [the grand jury's] investigative powers are necessarily broad. [T]he long standing principle that "the public has a right to every man's evidence," except for those persons protected by a constitutional, common law, or statutory privilege, is particularly applicable to grand jury proceedings.

A [minority] of States have provided newsmen a statutory privilege of varying breadth, [but] none has been provided by federal statute. [We decline to create one] by interpreting the First Amendment to grant newsmen a testimonial privilege that other citizens do not enjoy. [On] the records now before us, we perceive no basis for holding that the public interest in law enforcement and in ensuring effective grand jury proceedings is insufficient to override the consequential, but uncertain, burden on news gathering which is said to result from insisting that reporters, like other citizens, respond to relevant questions put to them in the course of a valid grand jury investigation or criminal trial.

This conclusion [does not] threaten the vast bulk of confidential relationships between reporters and their sources. Grand juries address themselves to the issues of whether crimes have been committed and who committed them. Only where news sources themselves are implicated in crime or possess information relevant to the grand jury's task need they or the reporter be concerned about grand jury subpoenas. Nothing before us indicates that a large number or percentage of *all* confidential news sources fall into either category and would in any way be deterred by [our holding]. * * * 33

Accepting the fact, however, that an undetermined number of informants not themselves implicated in crime will nevertheless, for whatever reason, refuse to talk to newsmen if they fear identification by a reporter in an official investigation, we cannot accept the argument that the public interest in possible future news about crime from undisclosed, unverified sources must take precedence over the public interest in pursuing and prosecuting those crimes reported to the press by informants and in thus deterring the commission of such crimes in the future.

[The] privilege claimed here is conditional, not absolute; given the suggested preliminary showings and compelling need, the reporter would be required to testify. [If] newsmen's confidential sources are as sensitive as they are claimed to be, the prospect of being unmasked whenever a judge determines the situation justifies it is hardly a satisfactory solution to the problem. For them, it would appear that only an absolute privilege would suffice.

We are unwilling to embark the judiciary on a long and difficult journey to such an uncertain destination. The administration of a constitutional newsman's privilege would present practical and conceptual difficulties of a high order. Sooner or later, it would be necessary to define those categories of newsmen who qualified for the privilege, a questionable procedure in light of the traditional doctrine that liberty of the press is the right of the lonely pamphleteer who uses carbon paper or a mimeograph just as much as of the large metropolitan publisher who utilizes the latest photocomposition methods. [The] informative function asserted by representatives of the organized press in the present cases is also performed by lecturers, political pollsters, novelists, academic researchers, and dramatists. Almost any author may quite accurately assert that he is contributing to the flow of information to the public, that he relies on confidential sources of information, and that these sources will be silenced if he is forced to make disclosures before a grand jury.

In each instance where a reporter is subpoenaed to testify, the courts would also be embroiled in preliminary factual and legal determinations with respect to whether the proper predicate had been laid for the reporters'

33. In his *Press Subpoenas: An Empirical and Legal Analysis* 6–12 (1971), Prof. Blasi found that slightly more than half of the 975 reporters questioned said that they relied on regular confidential sources for at least 10% of their stories. Of this group of reporters, only 8% were able to say with some certainty that their professional functioning had been adversely affected by the threat of subpoena; another 11% were not certain whether or not they had been adversely affected. [See also Blasi, *The Newsman's Privilege: An Empirical Study,* 70 Mich.L.Rev. 229 (1971).]

appearance. [I]n the end, by considering whether enforcement of a particular law served a "compelling" governmental interest, the courts would be inextricably involved in distinguishing between the value of enforcing different criminal laws. By requiring testimony from a reporter in investigations involving some crimes but not in others, they would be making a value judgment which a legislature had declined to [make.]

At the federal level, Congress has freedom to determine whether a statutory newsman's privilege is necessary and desirable and to fashion standards and rules as narrow or broad as deemed necessary [and], equally important, to re-fashion those rules as experience from time to time may dictate. There is also merit in leaving state legislatures free, within First Amendment limits, to fashion their own standards in light of the conditions and problems with respect to the relations between law enforcement officials and press in their own areas. * * *

[G]rand jury investigations if instituted or conducted other than in good faith, would pose wholly different issues for resolution under the First Amendment. Official harassment of the press undertaken not for purposes of law enforcement but to disrupt a reporter's relationship with his news sources would have no justification. Grand juries are subject to judicial control and subpoenas to motions to quash. We do not expect courts will forget that grand juries must operate within the limits of the First Amendment as well as the Fifth.

We turn, therefore, to the disposition of the cases before us. [*Caldwell*] must be reversed. If there is no First Amendment privilege to refuse to answer the relevant and material questions asked during a good-faith grand jury investigation, then it is a fortiori true that there is no privilege to refuse to appear before such a grand jury until the Government demonstrates some "compelling need" for a newsman's testimony. [*Branzburg*] must be affirmed. Here, petitioner refused to answer questions that directly related to criminal conduct which he had observed and written about. [If] what petitioner wrote was true, he had direct information to provide the grand jury concerning the commission of serious crimes. [In *Pappas,* we] affirm [and] hold that petitioner must appear before the grand jury to answer the questions put to him, subject, of course, to the supervision of the presiding judge as to "the propriety, purposes, and scope of the grand jury inquiry and the pertinence of the probable testimony."

MR. JUSTICE POWELL, concurring in the opinion of the Court.

I add this brief statement to emphasize what seems to me to be the limited nature of the Court's holding. The Court does not hold that newsmen, subpoenaed to testify before a grand jury, are without constitutional rights with respect to the gathering of news or in safeguarding their sources. [As] indicated in the concluding portion of the opinion, the Court states that no harassment of newsmen will be tolerated. If a newsman believes that the grand jury investigation is not being conducted in good faith he is not without remedy. Indeed, if the newsman is called upon to give information bearing only a remote and tenuous relationship to the subject of the investigation, or if he has some other reason to believe that his testimony implicates confidential source relationships without a legitimate need of law enforcement, he will have access to the Court on a motion to quash and an appropriate protective order may be entered. The asserted claim to privilege should be judged on its facts by the striking of a proper balance between freedom of the press and the obligation of all citizens to give relevant testimony with respect to criminal conduct. The balance of these vital constitutional and societal interests on a case-by-case basis accords with the tried and traditional way of adjudicating such questions.*

In short, the courts will be available to newsmen under circumstances where legitimate First Amendment interests require protection.

Mr. Justice Douglas, dissenting. * * *

It is my view that there is no "compelling need" that can be shown [by the Government] which qualifies the reporter's immunity from appearing or testifying before a grand jury, unless the reporter himself is implicated in a crime. His immunity in my view is therefore quite complete, for absent his involvement in a crime, the First Amendment protects him against an appearance before a grand jury and if he is involved in a crime, the Fifth Amendment stands as a barrier. Since in my view there is no area of inquiry not protected by a privilege, the reporter need not appear for the futile purpose of invoking one to each [question.]

Two principles which follow from [Alexander Meiklejohn's] understanding of the First Amendment are at stake here. One is that the people, the ultimate governors, must have absolute freedom of and therefore privacy of their individual opinions and beliefs regardless of how suspect or strange they may appear to others. Ancillary to that principle is the conclusion that an individual must also have absolute privacy over whatever information he may generate in the course of testing his opinions and beliefs. In this regard, Caldwell's status as a reporter is less relevant than is his status as a student who affirmatively pursued empirical research to enlarge his own intellectual viewpoint. The second principle is that effective self-government cannot succeed unless the people are immersed in a steady, robust, unimpeded, and uncensored flow of opinion and reporting which are continuously subjected

---

* It is to be remembered that Caldwell asserts a constitutional privilege not even to appear before the grand jury unless a court decides that the government has made a showing that meets the three preconditions specified in [Stewart, J.'s dissent]. To be sure, this would require a "balancing" of interests by the Court, but under circumstances and constraints significantly different from the balancing that will be appropriate under the Court's decision. The newsman witness, like all other witnesses, will have to appear; he will not be in a position to litigate at the threshold the State's very authority to subpoena him. Moreover, absent the constitutional preconditions that [the dissent] would impose as heavy burdens of proof to be carried by the State, the court—when called upon to protect a newsman from improper or prejudicial questioning—would be free to balance the competing interests on their merits in the particular case. The new constitutional rule endorsed by [the dissent] would, as a practical matter, defeat such a fair balancing and the essential societal interest in the detection and prosecution of crime would be heavily subordinated.

to critique, rebuttal, and re-examination. In this respect, Caldwell's status as a newsgatherer and an integral part of that process becomes critical. * * *

Sooner or later any test which provides less than blanket protection to beliefs and associations will be twisted and relaxed so as to provide virtually no protection at all. [A] compelling interest test may prove as pliable as did the clear and present danger test. Perceptions of the worth of state objectives will change with the composition of the Court and with the intensity of the politics of the [times.]

Today's decision will impede the wide open and robust dissemination of ideas and counterthought which a free press both fosters and protects and which is essential to the success of intelligent self-government. Forcing a reporter before a grand jury [will lead] dissidents to communicate less openly to trusted reporters [and] cause editors and critics to write with more restrained pens. * * *

MR. JUSTICE STEWART, with whom MR. JUSTICE BRENNAN and MR. JUSTICE MARSHALL join, dissenting.

The Court's crabbed view of the First Amendment reflects a disturbing insensitivity to the critical role of an independent press in our society. [While] Mr. Justice Powell's enigmatic concurring opinion gives some hope of a more flexible view in the future, the Court in these cases holds that a newsman has no First Amendment right to protect his sources when called before a grand jury. The Court thus invites state and federal authorities to undermine the historic independence of the press by attempting to annex the journalistic profession as an investigative arm of government. Not only will this decision impair performance of the press' constitutionally protected functions, but it will, I am convinced, in the long run, harm rather than help the administration of justice.

[As] private and public aggregations of power burgeon in size and the pressures for conformity necessarily mount, there is obviously a continuing need for an independent press to disseminate a robust variety of information and opinion through reportage, investigation and criticism, if we are to preserve our constitutional tradition of maximizing freedom of choice by encouraging diversity of expression. * * *

A corollary of the right to publish must be the right to gather news. [This right] implies, in turn, a right to a confidential relationship between a reporter and his source. This proposition follows as a matter of simple logic once three factual predicates are recognized: (1) newsmen require informants to gather news; (2) confidentiality—the promise or understanding that names or certain aspects of communications will be kept off-the-record—is essential to the creation and maintenance of a news-gathering relationship with informants; and (3) the existence of an unbridled subpoena power—the absence of a constitutional right protecting, in *any* way, a confidential relationship from compulsory process—will either deter sources from divulging information or deter reporters from gathering and publishing information. * * *

After today's decision, the potential informant can never be sure that his identity or off-the-record communications will not subsequently be revealed through the compelled testimony of a newsman. A public spirited person inside government, who is not implicated in any crime, will now be fearful of revealing corruption or other governmental wrong-doing, because he will now know he can subsequently be identified by use of compulsory process. The potential source must, therefore, choose between risking exposure by giving information or avoiding the risk by remaining silent.

The reporter must speculate about whether contact with a controversial source or publication of controversial material will lead to a subpoena. In the event of a subpoena, under today's decision, the newsman will know that he must choose between being punished for contempt if he refuses to testify, or violating his profession's ethics[10] and impairing his resourcefulness as a reporter if he discloses confidential information. * * *

The impairment of the flow of news cannot, of course, be proven with scientific precision, as the Court seems to demand. [But] we have never before demanded that First Amendment rights rest on elaborate empirical studies demonstrating beyond any conceivable doubt that deterrent effects exist; we have never before required proof of the exact number of people potentially affected by governmental action, who would actually be dissuaded from engaging in First Amendment activity. * * *

Surely the analogous claim of deterrence here is as securely grounded in evidence and common sense as the claims in [such cases as *NAACP v. Alabama*], although the Court calls the claim "speculative." [To] require any greater burden of proof is to shirk our duty to protect values securely embedded in the Constitution. We cannot await an unequivocal—and therefore unattainable—imprimatur from empirical studies. We can and must accept the evidence developed in the record, and elsewhere, that overwhelmingly supports the premise that deterrence will occur with regularity in important types of newsgathering relationships. Thus, we cannot escape the conclusion that when neither the reporter nor his source can rely on the shield of confidentiality against unrestrained use of the grand jury's subpoena power, valuable information will not be published and the public dialogue will inevitably be impoverished.

[A]ny exemption from the duty to testify before the grand jury "presupposes a very real interest to be protected." Such an interest must surely be the First Amendment protection of a confidential relationship. [This protection] functions to insure nothing less than democratic decision making

---

10. The American Newspaper Guild has adopted the following rule as part of the newsman's code of ethics: "Newspaper men shall refuse to reveal confidences or disclose sources of confidential information in court or before other judicial or investigative bodies."

through the free flow of information to the public, and it serves, thereby, to honor the "profound national commitment to the principle that debate on public issues should be uninhibited, robust and wide-open." *New York Times v. Sullivan.*

[W]hen an investigation impinges on First Amendment rights, the government must not only show that the inquiry is of "compelling and overriding importance" but it must also "convincingly" demonstrate that the investigation is "substantially related" to the information sought. Governmental officials must, therefore, demonstrate that the information sought is *clearly* relevant to a *precisely* defined subject of governmental inquiry. They must demonstrate that it is reasonable to think the witness in question has that information. And they must show that there is not any means of obtaining the information less destructive of First Amendment liberties. * * *

I believe the safeguards developed in our decisions involving governmental investigations must apply to the grand jury inquiries in these cases. Surely the function of the grand jury to aid in the enforcement of the law is no more important than the function of the legislature, and its committees, to make the law. [T]he vices of vagueness and overbreadth which legislative investigations may manifest are also exhibited by grand jury inquiries, since grand jury investigations are not limited in scope to specific criminal acts.

[Thus,] when a reporter is asked to appear before a grand jury and reveal confidences, I would hold that the government must (1) show that there is probable cause to believe that the newsman has information which is clearly relevant to a specific probable violation of law; (2) demonstrate that the information sought cannot be obtained by alternative means less destructive of First Amendment rights; and (3) demonstrate a compelling and overriding interest in the information. * * *

The crux of the Court's rejection of any newsman's privilege is its observation that only "where news sources themselves are implicated in crime or possess information *relevant* to the grand jury's task need they or the reporter be concerned about grand jury subpoenas." (emphasis supplied). But this is a most misleading construct. [G]iven the grand jury's extraordinarily broad investigative powers and the weak standards of relevance and materiality that apply during such inquiries, reporters, if they have no testimonial privilege, will be called to give information about informants who have neither committed crimes nor have information about crime. It is to avoid deterrence of such sources and thus to prevent needless injury to First Amendment values that I think the government must be required to show probable cause that the newsman has information which is clearly relevant to a specific probable violation of criminal law. * * *

Both the "probable cause" and "alternative means" requirements [would] serve the vital function of mediating between the public interest in the administration of justice and the constitutional protection of the full flow of information. These requirements would avoid a direct conflict between these competing concerns, and they would generally provide adequate protection for newsmen. No doubt the courts would be required to make some delicate judgments in working out this accommodation. But that, after all, is the function of courts of law. Better such judgments, however difficult, than the simplistic and stultifying absolutism adopted by the Court in denying any force to the First Amendment in these cases.[36] * * *

[I]n the name of advancing the administration of justice, the Court's decision, I think, will only impair the achievement of that goal. People entrusted with law enforcement responsibility, no less than private citizens, need general information relating to controversial social problems. [W]hen a grand jury may exercise an unbridled subpoena power, and sources involved in sensitive matters become fearful of disclosing information, the newsman will not only cease to be a useful grand jury witness; he will cease to investigate and publish information about issues of public import.

[In Stewart, J.'s view, the Ninth Circuit correctly ruled that in the circumstances of the case, Caldwell need not divulge confidential information and, moreover, that in this case Caldwell had established that "his very appearance [before] the grand jury would jeopardize his relationship with his sources, leading to a severance of the news gathering relationship and impairment of the flow of news to the public." But because "only in very rare circumstances would a confidential relationship between a reporter and his source be so sensitive [as to preclude] his mere appearance before the grand jury," Stewart, J., would confine "*this* aspect of the *Caldwell* judgment [to] its own facts." Thus, he would affirm in *Caldwell* and remand the other cases for further proceedings not inconsistent with his views.]

Notes and Questions

1. *The role of the press.* Consider Blasi, *The Checking Value in First Amendment Theory,* 1977 Am.B.Found.Res.J. 521, 593: The White, J., opinion "characterized the press as a private-interest group rather than an institution with a central function to perform in the constitutional system of checks and balances [and] labeled the source relationships that the reporters sought to maintain 'a private system of informers operated by the press to report on criminal conduct' [cautioning] that this system would be 'unaccountable to the public' were a reporter's privilege to be recognized." In contrast to White, J.'s perspective, consider the remarks of Stewart, J., in a much-discussed address, *"Or of the Press,"* 26 Hast.L.J. 631, 634 (1975): "In setting up the three branches of the Federal Government, the Founders deliberately created an internally competitive[a] system. [The] primary purpose[b] of [the Free Press Clause] was a similar one: to create a fourth

---

36. The disclaimers in Mr. Justice Powell's concurring opinion leave room for the hope that in some future case the Court may take a less absolute position in this area.

a. For commentary on how the "cozy connections" between press and govern-

institution outside the Government as an additional check on the three official branches.''[c] Proceeding from variations of this fourth estate view of the press, most commentators endorse a reporter's privilege. See, e.g.,[d] Baker, *Press Rights and Government Power to Structure the Press,* 34 U.Miami L.Rev. 819, 858 (1980) (absolute protection). But see Bezanson, *The New Free Press Guarantee,* 63 Va.L.Rev. 731, 759–62 (1977) (press clause prevents special governmental assistance for press). Claims for an independent press-clause, however, need not interpret the press clause along fourth estate lines, see *Nimmer on Freedom of Speech* 2–104—2–129 (1984).

2. *Evaluating Powell, J.'s concurrence.* Did five justices—or only four— hold that grand juries may pursue their goals by any means short of bad faith? May one conclude that the information sought bears "only a remote and tenuous relationship to the subject of investigation" on grounds falling short of demonstrating "bad faith"? Does Powell, J.'s suggested test—the privilege claim "should be judged on its facts by [balancing the] vital constitutional and societal interests on a case-by-case basis"—resemble Stewart, J.'s dissenting approach more than White, J.'s? Extrajudicially, Stewart, J., has referred to *Branzburg* as a case which rejected claims for a journalist's privilege "by a vote of 5–4, or, considering Mr. Justice Powell's concurring opinion, perhaps by a vote of 4½–4½." Stewart, *"Or of the Press,"* 26 Hast.L.J. 631, 635 (1975). The majority of courts applying *Branzburg* have concluded that Powell, J.'s opinion read together with the dissents affords the basis for a qualified privilege. Among the issues litigated are whether the privilege should be confined to journalists (or extended e.g. to academics) and the related question of how to define journalists and whether the privilege belongs to the source, the reporter, or both. For an exhaustive

ment demonstrate that the relationship is often more cooperative than adversarial, see Soifer, *Freedom of the Press in the United States* in Press Law in Modern Democracies 79, 108–110 (Lahav, ed., 1985).

b. For spirited debate about the historical evidence, compare Anderson, *The Origins of the Press Clause,* 30 U.C.L.A.L.Rev. 455 (1983) with Levy, *On the Origins of the Free Press Clause,* 32 U.C.L.A.L.Rev. 177 (1984). See generally Levy, *Emergence of a Free Press* (1985).

c. For Brennan, J.'s views, see *Address,* 32 Rutg.L.Rev. 173 (1979).

d. For criticism of the notion of an independent press clause, see Lange, *The Speech and Press Clauses,* 23 U.C.L.A.L.Rev. 77 (1975); Lewis, *A Preferred Position for Journalism?,* 7 Hof. L.Rev. 595 (1979); Van Alstyne, *The First Amendment and the Free Press: A Comment on Some New Trends and Some Old Theories,* 9 Hof.L.Rev. 1 (1980); Van Alstyne, *The Hazards to the Press of Claiming a "Preferred Position",* 28 Hast.L.J. 761

(1977). But see Abrams, *The Press is Different: Reflections on Justice Stewart and the Autonomous Press,* 7 Hof.L.Rev. 563 (1979). For an effort to transcend the issues involved, see generally Sack, *Reflections on the Wrong Question: Special Constitutional Privilege for the Institutional Press,* 7 Hof. L.Rev. 629 (1979). Finally, for commentary on the "tension between journalism as the political, sometimes partisan fourth estate and journalism as a profession" purporting to operate as a "neutral and objective medium," see Lahav, *An Outline for a General Theory of Press Law in Democracy* in Press Law in Modern Democracies 339, 352–54 (Lahav ed. 1985). See also Bollinger, *The Press and the Public Interest: An Essay on the Relationship Between Social Behavior and the Language of First Amendment Theory,* 82 Mich.L.Rev. 1447, 1457 (1984) (commenting generally on the pitfalls connected with justifying a free press by arguing that it serves the public interest: "More than most groups (compare lawyers, for example) the press is in conflict over its relationship to the world on which it regularly reports.").

survey, see Goodale, Moodhe & Imes, *Reporter's Privilege Cases* in Communications Law 1984, at 339 (1984).

The Court's most recent expression on the subject unanimously refuses, at least in the absence of bad faith, to extend a qualified first amendment privilege to "confidential" tenure files and, in dictum, confines *Branzburg* to the recognition that the " 'bad faith' exercise of grand jury powers might raise First Amendment concerns." *University of Pennsylvania v. EEOC*, 493 U.S. 182, 110 S.Ct. 577, 107 L.Ed.2d 571 (1990) (gender discrimination claim). For relevant commentary, see Byrne, *Academic Freedom: A "Special Concern of the First Amendment*," 99 Yale L.J. 251 (1989).

3. *Other contexts.* Does *Branzburg's* emphasis on the grand jury's special role in the American criminal justice system warrant different treatment of the journalist's privilege when a prosecutor seeks disclosure? See Murasky, *The Journalist's Privilege: Branzburg and Its Aftermath*, 52 Tex.L.Rev. 829, 885 (1974). Are the interests of civil litigants in compelling disclosure of a journalist's confidences significantly weaker than those of criminal litigants? Should there be an absolute journalist's privilege in civil discovery proceedings? See id. at 898–903. What if the journalist is a party to the litigation? Should journalists have greater protection for non-confidential information than other potential witnesses? See *Gonzales v. National Broadcasting Co.*, 155 F.3d 618 (2d Cir.1998).

4. *State "shield laws" and a criminal defendant's right to compulsory process.* As of 1984, 26 states had enacted "shield" laws.[e] Some protect only journalists' sources; some (including New Jersey) protect undisclosed information obtained in the course of a journalist's professional activities as well as sources. See Goodale, Moodhe & Imes, note 3 supra.

In re Farber, 78 N.J. 259, 394 A.2d 330 (1978), cert. denied, 439 U.S. 997, 99 S.Ct. 598, 58 L.Ed.2d 670 (1978): *New York Times* investigative reporter Myron Farber wrote a series of articles claiming that an unidentified "Doctor X" had caused the death of several patients by poisoning. This led to the indictment and eventual prosecution of Dr. Jascalevich for murder. (He was ultimately acquitted.) In response to the defendant's request, the trial court demanded the disclosure of Farber's sources and the production of his interview notes and other information for his in camera inspection. Relying on the first amendment and the state shield law, Farber refused to comply with the subpoenas. After White, J., and then Marshall, J., had

---

e. Consider Uelmen, *Leaks, Gags and Shields: Taking Responsibility*, 37 Santa Clara L.Rev. 943, 945 (1997): "Current 'shield laws' encourage the leaking of information by protecting the leaker from any consequences for his breach of confidentiality, and place no responsibility on reporters for lack of restraint in promising confidentiality to their sources. Somehow the irony has escaped us, that we encourage irresponsible breaches of confidentiality by guaranteeing to violators that we will protect the confidentiality of their breach! Those who have no respect for confidentiality that protects others are rewarded by our guarantee of absolute confidentiality for their treachery."

denied stays, each deeming it unlikely that four justices would grant certiorari at this stage of the case, Farber was jailed for civil contempt and the *Times* heavily fined.

The state supreme court (5–2) upheld civil and criminal convictions of the *Times* and Farber. Under the circumstances, it ruled, the first amendment did not protect Farber against disclosure. Nor did the New Jersey shield law, for Farber's statutory rights had to yield to Dr. Jascalevich's sixth amendment right "to have compulsory process for obtaining witnesses in his favor."[f]

ZURCHER v. STANFORD DAILY, 436 U.S. 547, 98 S.Ct. 1970, 56 L.Ed.2d 525 (1978), again declined to afford the press special protection—dividing very much as in *Branzburg*.[a] A student newspaper that had published articles and photographs of a clash between demonstrators and police brought this federal action, claiming that a search of its offices for film and pictures showing events at the scene of the police-demonstrators clash (the newspaper was not involved in the unlawful acts) had violated its first and fourth amendment rights. A 5–3 majority, per WHITE, J., held that the fourth amendment does not prevent the government from issuing a search warrant (based on reasonable cause to believe that the "things" to be searched for are located on the property) simply because the owner or possessor of the place to be searched is not reasonably suspected of criminal involvement. The Court also rejected the argument that "whatever may be true of third-party searches generally, where the third party is a newspaper, there are additional [first amendment factors justifying] a nearly per se rule forbidding the search warrant and permitting only the subpoena duces tecum. The general submission is that searches of newspaper offices for evidence of crime reasonably believed to be on the premises will seriously threaten the ability of the press to gather, analyze, and disseminate news.

"[Although] [a]ware of the long struggle between Crown and press and desiring to curb unjustified official intrusions, [the Framers] did not forbid warrants where the press was involved, did not require special showing that subpoenas would be impractical, and did not insist that the owner of the place to be searched, if connected with the press, must be shown to be implicated in the offense being investigated. Further, the prior cases do no

f. For an exhaustive analysis of the case, see Note, 32 Rutg.L.Rev. 545 (1979). The case is also discussed at length by *New York Times* columnist Anthony Lewis, *A Preferred Position for Journalism?*, 7 Hof. L.Rev. 595, 610–18 (1979). See also Nowak, Rotunda & Young, *Constitutional Law* 912–13 (2d ed. 1983); Tribe, *American Constitutional Law* 975 n. 35 (2d ed. 1988).

a. In both cases, White, J., joined by Burger, C.J., Blackmun, Powell and Rehn-

quist, JJ., delivered the opinion of the Court and in both cases the "fifth vote"—Powell, J.,—also wrote a separate opinion which seemed to meet the concerns of the dissent part way. In both cases Stewart, J., dissented, maintaining that the Court's holding would seriously impair "newsgathering." Stevens, J., who had replaced Douglas, J., also dissented in *Zurcher,* as had Douglas in *Branzburg.* Brennan, J., who had joined Stewart, J.'s dissent in *Branzburg,* did not participate in *Zurcher.*

more than insist that the courts apply the warrant requirements with particular exactitude when First Amendment interests would be endangered by the search. [N]o more than this is required where the warrant requested is for the seizure of criminal evidence reasonably believed to be on the premises occupied by a newspaper. Properly administered, the preconditions for a warrant—probable cause, specificity [as to] place [and] things to be seized and overall reasonableness—should afford [the press] sufficient protection * * *.

"[R]espondents and amici have pointed to only a very few instances [since] 1971 involving [newspaper office searches]. This reality hardly suggests abuse, and if abuse occurs, there will be time enough to deal with it. Furthermore, the press [is] not easily intimidated—nor should it be."

POWELL, J., concurring, rejected Stewart, J.'s dissenting view that the press is entitled to "a special procedure, not available to others," when the government requires evidence in its possession, but added: "This is not to say [that a warrant] sufficient to support the search of an apartment or an automobile would be reasonable in supporting the search of a newspaper office. [While] there is no justification for the establishment of a separate Fourth Amendment procedure for the press, a magistrate asked to issue a warrant for the search of press offices can and should take cognizance of the independent values protected by the First Amendment—such as those highlighted by [Stewart, J., dissenting]—when he weighs such factors."[b]

STEWART, joined by Marshall, J., dissented: "A search warrant allows police officers to ransack the files of a newspaper, reading each and every document until they have found the one named in the warrant, while a subpoena would permit the newspaper itself to produce only the specific documents requested. A search, unlike a subpoena, will therefore lead to the needless exposure of confidential information completely unrelated to the purpose of the investigation. The knowledge that police officers can make an unannounced raid on a newsroom is thus bound to have a deterrent effect on the availability of confidential news sources. [The result] will be a diminishing flow of potentially important information to the public.

"[Here, unlike *Branzburg,* the newspaper does] not claim that any of the evidence sought was privileged[, but] only that a subpoena would have served equally well to produce that evidence. Thus, we are not concerned with the principle, central to *Branzburg,* that ' "the public [has] a right to everyman's evidence," ' but only with whether any significant social interest would be impaired if the police were generally required to obtain evidence from the press by means of a subpoena rather than a search. * * *

b. Powell, J., noted that his *Branzburg* concurrence may "properly be read as supporting the view expressed in the text above, and in the Court's [*Zurcher*] opinion," that under the warrant requirement "the magistrate should consider the values of a free press as well as the societal interest in enforcing the criminal laws."

"Perhaps as a matter of abstract policy a newspaper office should receive no more protection from unannounced police searches than, say, the office of a doctor or the office of a bank. But we are here to uphold a Constitution. And our Constitution does not explicitly protect the practice of medicine or the business of banking from all abridgement by government. It does explicitly protect the freedom of the press."[c]

Notes and Questions

1. The distinctions between search and subpoena are underscored in Tribe, *American Constitutional Law* 973 (2d ed. 1988): "When a subpoena is served on a newspaper, it has the opportunity to assert constitutional and statutory rights [such as 'shield laws,' enacted in many states, protecting reporters from divulging information given them in confidence] to keep certain materials confidential. Such protection is circumvented when officials can proceed *ex parte,* by search warrant. And the risk of abuse may be greatest exactly when the press plays its most vital and creative role in our political system, the role of watchdog on official corruption and abuse. Officials who find themselves the targets [of] media investigations may well be tempted to conduct searches to find out precisely what various journalists have discovered, and to retaliate against reporters who have unearthed and reported official wrongdoing."

B. ACCESS TO PRIVATE SOURCES

Two ABC television reporters used false resumes to get jobs at Food Lion, Inc. supermarkets and, using concealed mini-cameras, secretly video-taped food handling practices during a brief period of employment. Six months later some of the video footage was used by ABC during sweeps week in a *PrimeTime Live* broadcast that was sharply critical of Food Lion. The broadcast included, for example, videotape appearing to show "Food Lion employees repackaging and redating fish that had passed the expiration date, grinding expired beef with fresh beef, and applying barbeque sauce to chicken past its expiration date in order to mask the smell and sell it as fresh in the gourmet food section. The program included statements by former Food Lion employees alleging even more serious mishandling of meat at Food Lion stores across several states."

Food Lion sued Capital Cities/ABC, Inc., [the producers of] *PrimeTime Live,* and Lynne Dale and Susan Barnett, two reporters for the program * * *. Food Lion did not sue for defamation, but challenged ABC's methods of gathering information, alleging among other things fraud, breach of duty of loyalty, and trespass. In federal district court, Food Lion won a judgment for compensatory damages of $1,400 on its fraud claim, $1 against each of

c. Stevens, J., dissented on the general fourth amendment issue.

the reporters on the duty of loyalty and trespass claims, and $315,000 in punitive damages on the fraud claim against the producers and ABC.

On appeal, FOOD LION, INC. v. CAPITAL CITIES/ABC, INC., 194 F.3d 505 (4th Cir.1999), per MICHAEL, J., found no actionable fraud under the relevant state law, but affirmed the judgments for breach of duty of loyalty and trespass against a first amendment attack. The court found no actionable fraud because of the lack of injury resulting from its employment of the two reporters other than damages from the publication which it found were not cognizable under the first amendment. The other claims gave rise to nominal damages, not damages arising from the publication: "Because Dale and Barnett did not compete with Food Lion, misappropriate any of its profits or opportunities, or breach its confidences, ABC argues that the reporters did not engage in any disloyal conduct that is tortious under existing law. * * * The interests of the employer (ABC) to whom Dale and Barnett gave complete loyalty were adverse to the interests of Food Lion, the employer to whom they were unfaithful. ABC and Food Lion were not business competitors but they were adverse in a fundamental way. ABC's interest was to expose Food Lion to the public as a food chain that engaged in unsanitary and deceptive practices. Dale and Barnett served ABC's interest, at the expense of Food Lion, by engaging in the taping for ABC while they were on Food Lion's payroll. In doing this, Dale and Barnett did not serve Food Lion faithfully, and their interest (which was the same as ABC's) was diametrically opposed to Food Lion's. In these circumstances, we believe that the highest courts of North and South Carolina would hold that the reporters—in promoting the interests of one master, ABC, to the detriment of a second, Food Lion—committed the tort of disloyalty against Food Lion. * * *

"ABC argues that it was error to allow the jury to hold Dale and Barnett liable for trespass * * *. We turn first to whether Dale and Barnett's consent to be in non-public areas of Food Lion property was void from the outset because of the resume misrepresentations. '[C]onsent to an entry is often given legal effect' even though it was obtained by misrepresentation or concealed intentions. Without this result, 'a restaurant critic could not conceal his identity when he ordered a meal, or a browser pretend to be interested in merchandise that he could not afford to buy. Dinner guests would be trespassers if they were false friends who never would have been invited had the host known their true character, and a consumer who in an effort to bargain down an automobile dealer falsely claimed to be able to buy the same car elsewhere at a lower price would be a trespasser in a dealer's showroom.'

"Of course, many cases on the spectrum become much harder than these examples, and the courts of North and South Carolina have not considered the validity of a consent to enter land obtained by misrepresentation. Further, the various jurisdictions and authorities in this country are not of one mind in dealing with the issue. Compare *Restatement (Second) of Torts*, § 892B(2) (1965) ('[i]f the person consenting to the conduct of another ... is induced [to consent] by the other's misrepresentation, the consent is not effective for the unexpected invasion or harm') and *Shiffman v. Empire Blue Cross and Blue Shield,* 256 A.D.2d 131, 681 N.Y.S.2d 511, 512 (App. Div.1998) (reporter who gained entry to medical office by posing as potential patient using false identification and insurance cards could not assert consent as defense to trespass claim 'since consent obtained by misrepresentation or fraud is invalid'), with *Desnick v. American Broadcasting Companies,* 44 F.3d 1345 (7th Cir.1995)(ABC agents with concealed cameras who obtained consent to enter an ophthalmic clinic by pretending to be patients were not trespassers because, among other things, they 'entered offices open to anyone').

"We like *Desnick*'s thoughtful analysis about when a consent to enter that is based on misrepresentation may be given effect. In *Desnick,* ABC sent persons posing as patients needing eye care to the plaintiffs' eye clinics, and the test patients secretly recorded their examinations. Some of the recordings were used in a PrimeTime Live segment that alleged intentional misdiagnosis and unnecessary cataract surgery. *Desnick* held that although the test patients misrepresented their purpose, their consent to enter was still valid because they did not invade 'any of the specific interests [relating to peaceable possession of land] the tort of trespass seeks to protect:' the test patients entered offices 'open to anyone expressing a desire for ophthalmic services' and videotaped doctors engaged in professional discussions with strangers, the testers; the testers did not disrupt the offices or invade anyone's private space; and the testers did not reveal the 'intimate details of anybody's life.' *Desnick* supported its conclusion with the following comparison:

> ' "Testers" who pose as prospective home buyers in order to gather evidence of housing discrimination are not trespassers even if they are private persons not acting under color of law. The situation of [ABC's] "testers" is analogous. Like testers seeking evidence of violation of anti-discrimination laws, [ABC's] test patients gained entry into the plaintiffs' premises by misrepresenting their purposes (more precisely by a misleading omission to disclose those purposes). But the entry was not invasive in the sense of infringing the kind of interest of the plaintiffs that the law of trespass protects; it was not an interference with the ownership or possession of land.' * * *

"Although the consent cases as a class are inconsistent, we have not found any case suggesting that consent based on a resume misrepresentation turns a successful job applicant into a trespasser the moment she enters the employer's premises to begin work. Moreover, if we turned successful resume fraud into trespass, we would not be protecting the interest underlying the tort of trespass—the ownership and peaceable possession of land. Accordingly, we cannot say that North and South Carolina's highest courts would hold that misrepresentation on a job application alone nullifies the consent given to an employee to enter the employer's property, thereby turning the employee into a trespasser. The jury's finding of trespass therefore cannot be sustained on the grounds of resume misrepresentation.

"There is a problem, however, with what Dale and Barnett did after they entered Food Lion's property. The jury also found that the reporters committed trespass by breaching their duty of loyalty to Food Lion 'as a result of pursuing [their] investigation for ABC.' We affirm the finding of trespass on this ground because the breach of duty of loyalty—triggered by the filming in non-public areas, which was adverse to Food Lion—was a wrongful act in excess of Dale and Barnett's authority to enter Food Lion's premises as employees.

"The Court of Appeals of North Carolina has indicated that secretly installing a video camera in someone's private home can be a wrongful act in excess of consent given to enter. In the trespass case of *Miller v. Brooks*, 123 N.C.App. 20, 472 S.E.2d 350, 355 (N.C.Ct.App.1996), the (defendant) wife, who claimed she had consent to enter her estranged husband's (the plaintiff's) house, had a private detective place a video camera in the ceiling of her husband's bedroom. The court noted that '[e]ven an authorized entry can be trespass if a wrongful act is done in excess of and in abuse of authorized entry.' [We] recognize that *Miller* involved a private home, not a grocery store, and that it involved some physical alteration to the plaintiff's property (installation of a camera). Still, we believe the general principle is applicable here, at least in the case of Dale, who worked in a Food Lion store in North Carolina. Although Food Lion consented to Dale's entry to do her job, she exceeded that consent when she videotaped in non-public areas of the store and worked against the interests of her second employer, Food Lion, in doing so. * * *

"Here, both Dale and Barnett became employees of Food Lion with the certain consequence that they would breach their implied promises to serve Food Lion faithfully. They went into areas of the stores that were not open to the public and secretly videotaped, an act that was directly adverse to the interests of their second employer, Food Lion. Thus, they [committed] trespass because Food Lion's consent for them to be on its property was nullified when they tortiously breached their duty of loyalty to Food Lion. * * *

"ABC argues that even if state tort law covers some of Dale and Barnett's conduct, the district court erred in refusing to subject Food Lion's claims to any level of First Amendment scrutiny. ABC makes this argument because Dale and Barnett were engaged in newsgathering for *PrimeTime Live*. It is true that there are 'First Amendment interests in newsgathering.' *Branzburg* ("without some protection for seeking out the news, freedom of the press could be eviscerated."). However, the Supreme Court has said in no uncertain terms that 'generally applicable laws do not offend the First Amendment simply because their enforcement against the press has incidental effects on its ability to gather and report the news.' *Cohen v. Cowles Media Co.*, 501 U.S. 663, 669, 111 S.Ct. 2513, 115 L.Ed.2d 586 (1991).[a]

a. For commentary, see Barron, *Cohen v. Cowles Media and its Significance for* *First Amendment Law and Journalism,* 3 Wm. & Mary Bill Rts. J. 419 (1994); Easton,

"In *Cowles,* Cohen, who was associated with a candidate for governor of Minnesota, gave damaging information about a candidate for another office to two reporters on their promise that his (Cohen's) identity would not be disclosed. Because editors at the reporters' newspapers concluded that the source was an essential part of the story, it was published with Cohen named as the origin.[b] Cohen was fired from his job as a result, and he sued the newspapers for breaking the promise. The question in the Supreme Court was whether the First Amendment barred Cohen from recovering damages under state promissory estoppel law. The newspapers argued that absent 'a need to further a state interest of the highest order,' the First Amendment protected them from liability for publishing truthful information, lawfully obtained, about a matter of public concern. The Supreme Court disagreed, holding that the press 'has no special immunity from the application of general laws' and that the enforcement of general laws against the press 'is not subject to stricter scrutiny than would be applied to enforcement against other persons or organizations.'

"The key inquiry in *Cowles* was whether the law of promissory estoppel was a generally applicable law. The Court began its analysis with some examples of generally applicable laws that must be obeyed by the press, such as those relating to copyright, labor, antitrust, and tax. More relevant to us, '[t]he press may not with impunity break and enter an office or dwelling to gather news.' In analyzing the doctrine of promissory estoppel, the Court determined that it was a law of general applicability because it 'does not target or single out the press,' but instead applies 'to the daily transactions of all the citizens of Minnesota.' * * * The Court thus refused to apply any heightened scrutiny to the enforcement of Minnesota's promissory estoppel law against the newspapers.

"The torts Dale and Barnett committed, breach of the duty of loyalty and trespass, fit neatly into the *Cowles* framework. Neither tort targets or singles out the press. Each applies to the daily transactions of the citizens of North and South Carolina. If, for example, an employee of a competing grocery chain hired on with Food Lion and videotaped damaging information in Food Lion's non-public areas for later disclosure to the public, these tort laws would apply with the same force as they do against Dale and Barnett here. Nor do we believe that applying these laws against the media will have more than an 'incidental effect' on newsgathering.

"ABC argues that *Cowles* is not to be applied automatically to every 'generally applicable law' because the Supreme Court has since said that 'the enforcement of [such a] law may or may not be subject to heightened

Two Wrongs Mock a Right: Overcoming the Cohen Maledicta that Bar First Amendment Protection for Newsgathering, 58 Ohio St. L.J. 1135 (1997); Levi, *Dangerous Liaisons: Seduction and Betrayal in Confidential Press–Source Relations,* 43 Rutgers L.Rev. 609 (1991).

b. The newspaper contended that the information provided (which reflected badly upon a political candidate) was misleading and that the source's name was newsworthy because he was associated with the other side in the political campaign.

scrutiny under the First Amendment.' *Turner Broadcasting System, Inc. v. FCC,* 512 U.S. 622, 640, 114 S.Ct. 2445, 129 L.Ed.2d 497 (1994) (contrasting *Barnes v. Glen Theatre, Inc.,* 501 U.S. 560, 111 S.Ct. 2456, 115 L.Ed.2d 504 (1991), and *Cowles*). In *Glen Theatre* nude dancing establishments and their dancers challenged a generally applicable law prohibiting public nudity. Because the general ban on public nudity covered nude dancing, which was expressive conduct, the Supreme Court applied heightened scrutiny. * * * There is [an] arguable tension between [*Glen Theatre* and *Cowles*]. The cases are consistent, however, if we view the challenged conduct in *Cowles* to be the breach of promise and not some form of expression. In *Glen Theatre,* on the other hand, an activity directly covered by the law, nude dancing, necessarily involved expression, and heightened scrutiny was applied. Here, as in *Cowles,* heightened scrutiny does not apply because the tort laws (breach of duty of loyalty and trespass) do not single out the press or have more than an incidental effect upon its work.

"For the foregoing reasons, we affirm the judgment that Dale and Barnett breached their duty of loyalty to Food Lion and committed trespass. We likewise affirm the damages award against them for these torts in the amount of $2.00. We have already indicated that the fraud claim against all of the ABC defendants must be reversed. Because Food Lion was awarded punitive damages only on its fraud claim, the judgment awarding punitive damages cannot stand.

"We do not reach the [question whether publication damages were proximately caused by the fraud] because an overriding (and settled) First Amendment principle precludes the award of publication damages in this case * * *.[c] Food Lion attempted to avoid the First Amendment limitations on defamation claims by seeking publication damages under non-reputational tort claims, while holding to the normal state law proof standards for these torts. This is precluded by *Hustler Magazine v. Falwell.*

"Food Lion argues that *Cowles,* and not *Hustler* governs its claim for publication damages. According to Food Lion, *Cowles* allowed the plaintiff to recover—without satisfying the constitutional prerequisites to a defamation action—economic losses for publishing the plaintiff's identity in violation of a legal duty arising from generally applicable law. Food Lion says that its claim for damages is like the plaintiff's in *Cowles,* and not like Falwell's in *Hustler.* This argument fails because the Court in *Cowles* distinguished the damages sought there from those in Hustler in a way that also distinguishes Food Lion's case from *Cowles*:

'Cohen is not seeking damages for injury to his reputation or his state of mind. He sought damages ... for breach of a promise that caused him to lose his job and lowered his earning capacity. Thus, this is not a case like Hustler ... where we held that the constitutional libel standards apply to a

c. Food Lion closed 80 stores and laid off more than 1,000 employees as a result of the broadcast.

claim alleging that the publication of a parody was a state-law tort of intentional infliction of emotional distress.'

"Food Lion, in seeking compensation for matters such as loss of good will and lost sales, is claiming reputational damages from publication, which the *Cowles* Court distinguished by placing them in the same category as the emotional distress damages sought by Falwell in *Hustler*. In other words, according to *Cowles*, 'constitutional libel standards' apply to damage claims for reputational injury from a publication such as the one here.

"Food Lion also argues that because ABC obtained the videotapes through unlawful acts, that is, the torts of breach of duty of loyalty and trespass, it (Food Lion) is entitled to publication damages without meeting the *New York Times* standard. The Supreme Court has never suggested that it would dispense with the *Times* standard in this situation, and we believe *Hustler* indicates that the Court would not. In *Hustler* the magazine's conduct would have been sufficient to constitute an unlawful act, the intentional infliction of emotional distress, if state law standards of proof had applied. [Notwithstanding] the nature of the underlying act, the Court held that satisfying *New York Times* was a prerequisite to the recovery of publication damages.

"In sum, Food Lion could not bypass the *New York Times* standard if it wanted publication damages. * * * The district court therefore reached the correct result when it disallowed these damages, although we affirm on a different ground.[d]

Notes and Questions

1. *Civil disobedience?* Consider Bezanson, *Means and Ends and Food Lion: The Tension Between Exemption and Independence in Newsgathering By the Press*, 47 Emory L.J. 895 (1998): "The law's normal response when an individual violates the society's rules for a moral or just end is to give the act a decent name–civil disobedience–and then to hold the law violator to account, on the theory that if the 'end' is very important, it must be important enough to achieve at the price the law exacts. A jury [in *Food Lion*] decided that ABC violated the law, perhaps for a just cause, but the price of doing so is the jury's damage award. Jesse Jackson recently went to jail overnight, a price he was willing to pay for taking the law into his own hands in service of his own ends. Whether we agree with him or not, we should respect him for that. We would discount the importance of Jackson's act by ignoring it or excusing it."

2. *A newsgather's privilege?* Suppose a reporter has probable cause to believe that a person or institution's conduct poses a significant threat to the health, safety, or financial well-being of others and that his or her methods

---

d. Niemeyer, J., concurring in part and dissenting in part, maintained that the fraud claim implicated damages other than the publication damages that were sufficient to justify the punitive damages award.

of newsgathering were not substantially more intrusive than necessary to obtain documentation of the wrongdoing. Should fraud or trespass be privileged? Would the facts in *Food Lion* meet the test?[e] Should the press be liable for publication damages?[f] Punitive damages?[g]

3. *Anti-paparazzi legislation.* California Civil Code § 1708.8 provides that: "A person is liable for physical invasion of privacy when the defendant knowingly enters onto the land of another without permission or otherwise committed a trespass, in order to physically invade the privacy of the plaintiff with the intent to capture any type of visual image, sound recording, or other physical impression of the plaintiff engaging in a personal or familial activity and the physical invasion occurs in a manner that is offensive to a reasonable person. A person is liable for constructive invasion of privacy when the defendant attempts to capture, in a manner that is offensive to a reasonable person, any type of visual image, sound recording, or other physical impression of the plaintiff engaging in a personal or familial activity under circumstances in which the plaintiff had a reasonable expectation of privacy, through the use of a visual or auditory enhancing device, regardless of whether there is a physical trespass, if this image, sound recording, or other physical impression could not have been achieved without a trespass unless the visual or auditory enhancing device was used.

"A person who commits physical invasion of privacy or constructive invasion of privacy, or both, is liable for up to three times the amount of any general and special damages that are proximately caused by the violation of this section.

"This section shall not be construed to impair or limit any otherwise lawful activities of law enforcement personnel or employees of governmental agencies or other entities, either public or private who, in the course and scope of their employment, and supported by an articulable suspicion, attempt to capture * * * evidence of suspected illegal activity, the suspected violation of any administrative rule or regulation, a suspected fraudulent insurance claim, or any other suspected fraudulent conduct or activity involving a violation of law or pattern of business practices adversely affecting the public health or safety. * * *

" 'Personal and familial activity' includes, but is not limited to, intimate details of the plaintiff's personal life, interactions with the plaintiff's family or significant others, or other aspects of plaintiff's private affairs or concerns. Personal and familial activity does not include illegal or otherwise criminal activity[, but] shall include the activities of victims of crime * * *."

e. See generally Lidsky, *Prying, Spying, and Lying: Intrusive Newsgathering and What the Law should do about it,* 73 Tulane L.Rev 173 (1998). See also Zimmerman, *I Spy: The Newsgatherer Under Cover,* 33 U.Rich.L.Rev. 1185 (2000).

f. See Epstein, *Privacy, Publication, and the First Amendment,* 52 Stan. L.Rev. 1003 (2000).

g. See Sims, *Food for the Lions: Excessive Damages for Newsgathering Torts and the Limitations of first Amendment Doctrines,* 78 B.U.L.Rev. 507 (1998); Comment, *Balancing, Press Immunity, and the Compatibility of Tort Law with the First Amendment,* 82 Minn.L.Rev. 1695 (1998).

Constitutional?[h] Consider Recent Legislation, *Anti-Paparazzi Legislation,* 36 Harv. J. on Legis. 250 (1999): "Public figures will continue to paint the press as evil and mercenary, but until history unfolds, it can be hard to tell a paparazzo from an investigative news journalist. In order to inform the public, the press needs to be able to behave in a way that is contrary to the wishes of its subjects."

4. *Media ride-alongs.* WILSON v. LAYNE, 526 U.S. 603, 119 S.Ct. 1692, 143 L.Ed.2d 818 (1999), per REHNQUIST, C.J., held that privacy considerations outweighed the interests served by having *Washington Post* reporters accompany police in executing an arrest warrant in the home: "Respondents argue that the presence of the *Washington Post* reporters in the Wilsons' home [served] a number of legitimate law enforcement purposes. They first assert that officers should be able to exercise reasonable discretion about when it would 'further their law enforcement mission to permit members of the news media to accompany them in executing a warrant.' But this claim ignores the importance of the right of residential privacy at the core of the Fourth Amendment. It may well be that media ride-alongs further the law enforcement objectives of the police in a general sense, but that is not the same as furthering the purposes of the search. Were such generalized 'law enforcement objectives' themselves sufficient to trump the Fourth Amendment, the protections guaranteed by that Amendment's text would be significantly watered down.

"Respondents next argue that the presence of third parties could serve the law enforcement purpose of publicizing the government's efforts to combat crime, and facilitate accurate reporting on law enforcement activities. There is certainly language in our opinions interpreting the First Amendment which points to the importance of 'the press' in informing the general public about the administration of criminal justice. *Cox Broadcasting Corp.* * * * No one could gainsay the truth of these observations, or the importance of the First Amendment in protecting press freedom from abridgement by the government. But the Fourth Amendment also protects a very important right, and in the present case it is in terms of that right that the media ride-alongs must be judged.

"Surely the possibility of good public relations for the police is simply not enough, standing alone, to justify the ride-along intrusion into a private home.

h. O'Neill, *Privacy and Press Freedom: Paparazzi and other Intruders,* 1999 U.Ill. Rev 703; Comment, *Much Ado About Newsgathering: Personal Privacy, Law Enforcement, and the Law of Unintended Consequences for Anti–Paparazzi Legislation,* 147 U.Pa.L.Rev. 1435 (1999);Comment, *Paparazzi Legislation: Policy Arguments and Legal Analysis in Support of their Constitutionality,* 46 UCLA L.Rev. 1633 (1999); Note, *Privacy, Technology, and the California "Anti–Paparazzi Statute,"* 112 Harv. L.Rev. 1367 (1999).

C.   ACCESS TO TRIALS AND OTHER GOVERNMENTALLY CONTROLLED INSTITUTIONS AND INFORMATION

By 1978, no Supreme Court holding contradicted Burger, C.J.'s contention for a plurality in *Houchins v. KQED,* 438 U.S. 1, 98 S.Ct. 2588, 57 L.Ed.2d 553 (1978) that, "neither the First Amendment nor the Fourteenth Amendment mandates a right of access to government information or sources of information within the government's control." Or as Stewart, J., put it in an often-quoted statement, "The Constitution itself is neither a Freedom of Information Act nor an Official Secrets Act." *"Or of the Press,"* 26 Hast.L.J. 631, 636 (1975). *Richmond Newspapers,* infra, constitutes the Court's first break with its past denials of first amendment rights to information within governmental control.

RICHMOND NEWSPAPERS, INC. v. VIRGINIA
448 U.S. 555, 100 S.Ct. 2814, 65 L.Ed.2d 973 (1980).

[At the commencement of his fourth trial on a murder charge (his first conviction having been reversed and two subsequent retrials having ended in mistrials), defendant moved, without objection by the prosecutor or two reporters present, that the trial be closed to the public—defense counsel stating that he did not "want any information being shuffled back and forth when we have a recess as [to] who testified to what." The trial judge granted the motion, stating that "the statute gives me that power specifically." He presumably referred to Virginia Code § 19.2–266, providing that in all criminal trials "the court may, in its discretion, exclude [any] persons whose presence would impair the conduct of a fair trial, provided that the [defendant's right] to a public trial shall not be violated." Later the same day the trial court granted appellants' request for a hearing on a motion to vacate the closure order. At the closed hearing, appellants observed that prior to the entry of its closure order the court had failed to make any evidentiary findings or to consider any other, less drastic measures to ensure a fair trial. Defendant stated that he "didn't want information to leak out," be published by the media, perhaps inaccurately, and then be seen by the jurors. Noting inter alia that "having people in the Courtroom is distracting to the jury" and that if "the rights of the defendant are infringed in any way [and if his closure motion] doesn't completely override all rights of everyone else, then I'm inclined to go along with" the defendant, the court denied the motion to vacate the closure order. Defendant was subsequently found not guilty.]

MR. CHIEF JUSTICE BURGER announced the judgment of the Court and delivered an opinion in which MR. JUSTICE WHITE and MR. JUSTICE STEVENS joined.

[T]he precise issue presented here has not previously been before this Court for decision. [*Gannett Co. v. DePasquale,* 443 U.S. 368, 99 S.Ct. 2898, 61 L.Ed.2d 608 (1979)] was not required to decide whether a right of access to *trials,* as distinguished from hearings on *pre*trial motions, was constitutionally guaranteed. The Court held that the Sixth Amendment's guarantee to the accused of a public trial gave neither the public nor the press an enforceable right of access to a *pretrial* suppression hearing. One concurring opinion specifically emphasized that "a hearing on a motion before trial to suppress evidence is not a *trial*." (Burger, C.J., concurring). Moreover, the Court did not decide whether the First and Fourteenth Amendments guarantee a right of the public to attend trials; nor did the dissenting opinion reach this issue. [H]ere for the first time the Court is asked to decide whether a criminal trial itself may be closed to the public upon the unopposed request of a defendant, without any demonstration that closure is required to protect the defendant's superior right to a fair trial, or that some other overriding consideration requires closure.

[T]he historical evidence demonstrates conclusively that at the time when our organic laws were adopted, criminal trials both here and in England had long been presumptively open[, thus giving] assurance that the proceedings were conducted fairly to all concerned, [and] discourag[ing] perjury, the misconduct of participants, and decisions based on secret bias or partiality. [Moreover, the] early history of open trials in part reflects the widespread acknowledgment [that] public trials had significant therapeutic value. [When] a shocking crime occurs, a community reaction of outrage and public protest often follows. Thereafter the open processes of justice serve an important prophylactic purpose, providing an outlet for community concern, hostility, and emotion.

[The] crucial prophylactic aspects of the administration of justice cannot function in the dark; no community catharsis can occur if justice is "done in a corner [or] in any covert manner." [To] work effectively, it is important that society's criminal process "satisfy the appearance of justice," and the appearance of justice can best be provided by allowing people to observe it.

[From] this unbroken, uncontradicted history, supported by reasons as valid today as in centuries past, we are bound to conclude that a presumption of openness inheres in the very nature of a criminal trial under our system of criminal justice. [Nevertheless,] the State presses its contention that neither the Constitution nor the Bill of Rights contains any provision which by its terms guarantees to the public the right to attend criminal trials. Standing alone, this is correct, but there remains the question whether, absent an explicit provision, the Constitution affords protection against exclusion of the public from criminal trials.

[The] expressly guaranteed [first amendment] freedoms share a common core purpose of assuring freedom of communication on matters relating to the functioning of government. Plainly it would be difficult to single out any aspect of government of higher concern and importance to the people than the manner in which criminal trials are conducted * * *.

The Bill of Rights was enacted against the backdrop of the long history of trials being presumptively open. [In] guaranteeing freedoms such as those of speech and press, the First Amendment can be read as protecting the right of everyone to attend trials so as to give meaning to those explicit guarantees. * * * Free speech carries with it some freedom to listen. "In a variety of contexts this Court has referred to a First Amendment right to 'receive information and ideas.' " *Kleindienst v. Mandel,* 408 U.S. 753, 762, 92 S.Ct. 2576, 2581, 33 L.Ed.2d 683 (1972).[a] What this means in the context of trials is that the First Amendment guarantees of speech and press, standing alone, prohibit government from summarily closing courtroom doors which had long been open to the public at the time that amendment was adopted.

[It] is not crucial whether we describe this right to attend criminal trials to hear, see, and communicate observations concerning them as a "right of access," cf. *Gannett* (Powell, J., concurring); *Saxbe v. Washington Post Co.,* 417 U.S. 843, 94 S.Ct. 2811, 41 L.Ed.2d 514 (1974); *Pell v. Procunier,* 417 U.S. 817, 94 S.Ct. 2800, 41 L.Ed.2d 495 (1974),[11] or a "right to gather information," for we have recognized that "without some protection for seeking out the news, freedom of the press could be eviscerated." *Branzburg v. Hayes.* The explicit, guaranteed rights to speak and to publish concerning what takes place at a trial would lose much meaning if access to observe the trial could, as it was here, be foreclosed arbitrarily.

The right of access to places traditionally open to the public, as criminal trials have long been, may be seen as assured by the amalgam of the First Amendment guarantees of speech and press; and their affinity to the right of assembly is not without relevance. From the outset, the right of assembly was regarded not only as an independent right but also as a catalyst to augment the free exercise of the other First Amendment rights with which it was deliberately linked by the draftsmen. * * * Subject to the traditional time, place, and manner restrictions, streets, sidewalks, and parks are places traditionally open, where First Amendment rights may be exercised [see generally Ch. 6 infra]; a trial courtroom also is a public place where the people generally—and representatives of the media—have a right to be present, and where their presence historically has been thought to enhance the integrity and quality of what takes place.

* * * Notwithstanding the appropriate caution against reading into the Constitution rights not explicitly defined, the Court has acknowledged that certain unarticulated rights are implicit in enumerated guarantees [referring, inter alia, to the rights of association and of privacy and the right to travel]. [T]hese important but unarticulated rights [have] been found to share constitutional protection in common with explicit guarantees. The concerns expressed by Madison and others have thus been [resolved].[b]

a. *Mandel* held that the Executive had plenary power to exclude a Belgium journalist from the country, at least so long as it operated on the basis of a facially legitimate and bona fide reason for exclusion. Although the Court decided ultimately not to balance the government's particular justification against the first amendment interest, it recognized that those who sought personal communication with the excluded alien did have a first amendment interest at stake. The Court apparently assumed that the excluded speaker had no rights at stake, and none were asserted on his behalf.

11. *Procunier* and *Saxbe* are distinguishable in the sense that they were concerned with penal institutions which, by definition, are not "open" or public places. * * * See also *Greer v. Spock* (military bases) [Ch. 6, II infra].

We hold that the right to attend criminal trials[17] is implicit in the guarantees of the First Amendment; without the freedom to attend such trials, which people have exercised for centuries, important aspects of freedom of speech and "of the press could be eviscerated." *Branzburg.*

[In the present case,] the trial court made no findings to support closure; no inquiry was made as to whether alternative solutions would have met the need to ensure fairness; there was no recognition of any right under the Constitution for the public or press to attend the trial. In contrast to the pretrial proceeding dealt with in *Gannett,* there exist in the context of the trial itself various tested alternatives to satisfy the constitutional demands of fairness. [For example, there was nothing] to indicate that sequestration of the jurors would not have guarded against their being subjected to any improper information.[c] * * * Absent an overriding interest articulated in findings, the trial of a criminal case must be open to the public. * * *

Reversed.[d]

MR. JUSTICE BRENNAN, with whom MR. JUSTICE MARSHALL joins, concurring in the judgment.

[*Gannett*] held that the Sixth Amendment right to a public trial was personal to the accused, conferring no right of access to pretrial proceedings that is separately enforceable by the public or the press. [This case] raises the question whether the First Amendment, of its own force and as applied to the States through the Fourteenth Amendment, secures the public an independent right of access to trial proceedings. Because I believe that [it does secure] such a public right of access, I agree [that], without more, agreement of the trial judge and the parties cannot constitutionally close a trial to the public.[1]

---

b. The Chief Justice noted "the perceived need" of the Constitution's draftsmen "for some sort of constitutional 'saving clause' [which] would serve to foreclose application to the Bill of Rights of the maxim that the affirmation of particular rights implies a negation of those not expressly defined. Madison's efforts, culminating in the Ninth Amendment, served to allay the fears of those who were concerned that expressing certain guarantees could be read as excluding others."

17. Whether the public has a right to attend [civil trials is] not raised by this case, but we note that historically both civil and criminal trials have been presumptively open.

c. Once the jurors are selected, when, if ever, will their sequestration *not* be a satisfactory alternative to closure?

d. Powell, J., took no part. In *Gannett,* he took the position that a first amendment right of access applied to courtroom proceedings, albeit subject to overriding when justice so demanded or when confidentiality was necessary.

1. Of course, the Sixth Amendment remains the source of the *accused's* own right to insist upon public judicial proceedings. *Gannett.*

That the Sixth Amendment explicitly establishes a public trial right does not impliedly foreclose the derivation of such a right from other provisions of the Constitution. The Constitution was not framed as a work of carpentry, in which all joints must fit snugly without overlapping. * * *

While freedom of expression is made inviolate by the First Amendment, and with only rare and stringent exceptions, may not be suppressed, the First Amendment has not been viewed by the Court in all settings as providing an equally categorical assurance of the correlative freedom of access to information.[2] Yet the Court has not ruled out a public access component to the First Amendment in every circumstance. Read with care and in context, our decisions must therefore be understood as holding only that any privilege of access to governmental information is subject to a degree of restraint dictated by the nature of the information and countervailing interests in security or confidentiality. [Cases such as *Houchins, Saxbe* and *Pell*] neither comprehensively nor absolutely deny that public access to information may at times be implied by the First Amendment and the principles which animate it.

The Court's approach in right of access cases simply reflects the special nature of a claim of First Amendment right to gather information. Customarily, First Amendment guarantees are interposed to protect communication between speaker and listener. When so employed against prior restraints, free speech protections are almost insurmountable. See generally Brennan, *Address,* 32 Rutg.L.Rev. 173, 176 (1979). But the First Amendment embodies more than a commitment to free expression and communicative interchange for their own sakes; it has a *structural* role to play in securing and fostering our republican system of self-government. Implicit in this structural role is not only "the principle that debate on public issues should be uninhibited, robust, and wide-open," but the antecedent assumption that valuable public debate—as well as other civic behavior—must be informed. The structural model links the First Amendment to that process of communication necessary for a democracy to survive, and thus entails solicitude not only for communication itself, but for the indispensable conditions of meaningful communication.

[A]n assertion of the prerogative to gather information must [be] assayed by considering the information sought and the opposing interests invaded. This judicial task is as much a matter of sensitivity to practical necessities as it is of abstract reasoning. But at least two helpful principles may be sketched. First, the case for a right of access has special force when drawn from an enduring and vital tradition of public entree to particular proceedings or information. Such a tradition commands respect in part because the Constitution carries the gloss of history. More importantly, a tradition of accessibility implies the favorable judgment of experience. Second, the value of access must be measured in specifics. Analysis is not advanced by rhetorical statements that all information bears upon public

---

2. A conceptually separate, yet related, question is whether the media should enjoy greater access rights than the general public. But no such contention is at stake here. Since the media's right of access is at least equal to that of the general public, this case is resolved by a decision that the state statute unconstitutionally restricts public access to trials. As a practical matter, however, the institutional press is the likely, and fitting, chief beneficiary of a right of access because it serves as the "agent" of interested citizens, and funnels information about trials to a large number of individuals.

issues; what is crucial in individual cases is whether access to a particular government process is important in terms of that very process.

[This Court has] persistently defended the public character of the trial process. *In re Oliver,* 333 U.S. 257, 68 S.Ct. 499, 92 L.Ed. 682 (1948), established that [fourteenth amendment due process] forbids closed criminal trials [and] acknowledged that open trials are indispensable to First Amendment political and religious freedoms.

By the same token, a special solicitude for the public character of judicial proceedings is evident in the Court's rulings upholding the right to report about the administration of justice. While these decisions are impelled by the classic protections afforded by the First Amendment to pure communication, they are also bottomed upon a keen appreciation of the structural interest served in opening the judicial system to public inspection. So, in upholding a privilege for reporting truthful information about judicial misconduct proceedings, *Landmark* emphasized that public scrutiny of the operation of a judicial disciplinary body implicates a major purpose of the First Amendment—"discussion of governmental affairs." Again, *Nebraska Press* noted that the traditional guarantee against prior restraint "should have particular force as applied to reporting of criminal proceedings." And *Cox Broadcasting* instructed that "[w]ith respect to judicial proceedings in particular, the function of the press serves to guarantee the fairness of trials and to bring to bear the beneficial effects of public scrutiny upon the administration of justice."

* * * Open trials play a fundamental role in furthering the efforts of our judicial system to assure the criminal defendant a fair and accurate adjudication of guilt or innocence. But, as a feature of our governing system of justice, the trial process serves other, broadly political, interests, and public access advances these objectives as well. To that extent, trial access possesses specific structural significance.

[For] a civilization founded upon principles of ordered liberty to survive and flourish, its members must share the conviction that they are governed equitably. That necessity * * * mandates a system of justice that demonstrates the fairness of the law to our citizens. One major function of the trial is to make that demonstration.

Secrecy is profoundly inimical to this demonstrative [purpose]. Public access is essential, therefore, if trial adjudication is to achieve the objective of maintaining public confidence in the administration of justice. But the trial [also] plays a pivotal role in the entire judicial process, and, by extension, in our form of government. Under our system, judges are not mere umpires, but, in their own sphere, lawmakers—a coordinate branch of *government.* [Thus], so far as the trial is the mechanism for judicial fact finding, as well as the initial forum for legal decision making, it is a genuine governmental proceeding.

[More] importantly, public access to trials acts as an important check, akin in purpose to the other checks and balances that infuse our system of government. "The knowledge that every criminal trial is subject to contemporaneous review in the forum of public opinion is an effective restraint on possible abuse of judicial power," *Oliver*—an abuse that, in many cases, would have ramifications beyond the impact upon the parties before the court. * * *

Popular attendance at trials, in sum, substantially furthers the particular public purposes of that critical judicial proceeding.[22] In that sense, public access is an indispensable element of the trial process itself. Trial access, therefore, assumes structural importance in our "government of laws."

As previously noted, resolution of First Amendment public access claims in individual cases must be strongly influenced by the weight of historical practice and by an assessment of the specific structural value of public access in the circumstances. With regard to the case at hand, our ingrained tradition of public trials and the importance of public access to the broader purposes of the trial process, tip the balance strongly toward the rule that trials be open.[23] What countervailing interests might be sufficiently compelling to reverse this presumption of openness need not concern us now,[24] for the statute at stake here authorizes trial closures at the unfettered discretion of the judge and parties.[25] [Thus it] violates the First and Fourteenth Amendments * * *.

MR. JUSTICE STEWART, concurring in the judgment.

Whatever the ultimate answer [may] be with respect to pretrial suppression hearings in criminal cases, the First and Fourteenth Amendments clearly give the press and the public a right of access to trials themselves, civil as well as criminal.[2] * * *

In conspicuous contrast to a military base, *Greer v. Spock*; a jail, *Adderley v. Florida*, 385 U.S. 39, 87 S.Ct. 242, 17 L.Ed.2d 149 (1966)]; or a prison, *Pell*, a trial courtroom is a public place. Even more than city streets, sidewalks, and parks as areas of traditional First Amendment activity, a trial courtroom is a place where representatives of the press and of the public are not only free to be, but where their presence serves to assure the integrity of what goes on.

22. In advancing these purposes, the availability of a trial transcript is no substitute for a public presence at the trial itself. As any experienced appellate judge can attest, the "cold" record is a very imperfect reproduction of events that transpire in the courtroom. * * *

23. The presumption of public trials is, of course, not at all incompatible with reasonable restrictions imposed upon courtroom behavior in the interests of decorum. Thus, when engaging in interchanges at the bench, the trial judge is not required to allow public or press intrusion upon the huddle. Nor does this opinion intimate that judges are restricted in their ability to conduct conferences in chambers, inasmuch as such conferences are distinct from trial proceedings.

24. For example, national security concerns about confidentiality may sometimes warrant closures during sensitive portions of trial proceedings, such as testimony about state secrets.

25. Significantly, closing a trial lacks even the justification for barring the door to pretrial hearings: the necessity of preventing dissemination of suppressible prejudicial evidence to the public before the jury pool has become, in a practical sense, finite and subject to sequestration.

2. [The] right to speak implies a freedom to listen, *Kleindienst v. Mandel.* The right to publish implies a freedom to gather information, *Branzburg.* See concurring opinion of Justice Brennan, supra.

But this does not mean that the First Amendment right of members of the public and representatives of the press to attend civil and criminal trials is absolute. Just as a legislature may impose reasonable time, place and manner restrictions upon the exercise of First Amendment freedoms, so may a trial judge impose reasonable limitations upon the unrestricted occupation of a courtroom by representatives of the press and members of the public. Moreover, [there] may be occasions when not all who wish to attend a trial may do so.[3] And while there exist many alternative ways to satisfy the constitutional demands of a fair trial, those demands may also sometimes justify limitations upon the unrestricted presence of spectators in the courtroom.[5]

Since in the present case the trial judge appears to have given no recognition to the right [of] the press and [the] public to be present at [the] murder trial over which he was presiding, the judgment under review must be reversed. * * *

MR. JUSTICE WHITE, concurring.

This case would have been unnecessary had *Gannett* construed the Sixth Amendment to forbid excluding the public from criminal proceedings except in narrowly defined circumstances. But the Court there rejected the submission of four of us to this effect, thus requiring that the First Amendment issue involved here be addressed. On this issue, I concur in the opinion of the Chief Justice.

MR. JUSTICE BLACKMUN, concurring in the judgment.

My opinion and vote in partial dissent [in] *Gannett* compels my vote to reverse the judgment. [It] is gratifying [to] see the Court now looking to and relying upon legal history in determining the fundamental public character of the criminal trial. * * *

The Court's ultimate ruling in *Gannett,* with such clarification as is provided by the opinions in this case today, apparently is now to the effect that there is no *Sixth* Amendment right on the part of the public—or the press—to an open hearing on a motion to suppress. I, of course, continue to believe that *Gannett* was in error, both in its interpretation of the Sixth Amendment generally, and in its application to the suppression hearing, for I remain convinced that the right to a public trial is to be found where the Constitution explicitly placed it—in the Sixth Amendment.

[But] with the Sixth Amendment set to one side in this case, I am driven to conclude, as a secondary position, that the First Amendment must provide some measure of protection for public access to the trial. The opinion in partial dissent in *Gannett* explained that the public has an intense need and

---

3. In such situations, representatives of the press must be assured access, *Houchins* (concurring opinion).

5. This is not to say that only constitutional considerations can justify such restrictions. The preservation of trade secrets, for example, might justify the exclusion of the public from at least some segments of a civil trial. And the sensibilities of a youthful prosecution witness, for example, might justify similar exclusion in a criminal trial for rape, so long as the defendant's Sixth Amendment right to a public trial were not impaired.

a deserved right to know about the administration of justice in general; about the prosecution of local crimes in particular; about the conduct of the judge, the prosecutor, defense counsel, police officers, other public servants, and all the actors in the judicial arena; and about the trial itself. It is clear and obvious to me, on the approach the Court has chosen to take, that, by closing this criminal trial, the trial judge abridged these First Amendment interests of the public. * * *

Mr. Justice Stevens, concurring.

This is a watershed case. Until today the Court has accorded virtually absolute protection to the dissemination of information or ideas, but never before has it squarely held that the acquisition of newsworthy matter is entitled to any constitutional protection whatsoever. An additional word of emphasis is therefore appropriate.

Twice before, the Court has implied that any governmental restriction on access to information, no matter how severe and no matter how unjustified, would be constitutionally acceptable so long as it did not single out the press for special disabilities not applicable to the public at large. In a dissent joined by [Brennan and Marshall, JJ.] in *Saxbe,* Justice Powell unequivocally rejected [that conclusion.] And in *Houchins,* I explained at length why [Brennan, Powell, JJ.] and I were convinced that "[a]n official prison policy of concealing * * * knowledge from the public by arbitrarily cutting off the flow of information at its source abridges [first amendment freedoms]." Since [Marshall and Blackmun, JJ.] were unable to participate in that case, a majority of the Court neither accepted nor rejected that conclusion or the contrary conclusion expressed in the prevailing opinions. Today, however, for the first time, the Court unequivocally holds that an arbitrary interference with access to important information is an abridgment of the freedoms of speech and of the press protected by the First Amendment.

It is somewhat ironic that the Court should find more reason to recognize a right of access today than it did in *Houchins.* For *Houchins* involved the plight of a segment of society least able to protect itself, an attack on a longstanding policy of concealment, and an absence of any legitimate justification for abridging public access to information about how government operates. In this case we are protecting the interests of the most powerful voices in the community, we are concerned with an almost unique exception to an established tradition of openness in the conduct of criminal trials, and it is likely that the closure order was motivated by the judge's desire to protect the individual defendant from the burden of a fourth criminal trial.[2]

---

2. Neither that likely motivation nor facts showing the risk that a fifth trial would have been necessary without closure of the fourth are disclosed in this record, however. The absence of any articulated reason for the closure order is a sufficient basis for distinguishing this case from *Gan-* *nett.* The decision today is in no way inconsistent with the perfectly unambiguous holding in *Gannett* that the rights guaranteed by the Sixth Amendment are rights that may be asserted by the accused rather than members of the general public. * * *

In any event, for the reasons stated [in] my *Houchins* opinion, as well as those stated by the Chief Justice today, I agree that the First Amendment protects the public and the press from abridgment of their rights of access to information about the operation of their government, including the Judicial Branch; given the total absence of any record justification for the closure order entered in this case, that order violated the First Amendment * * *.

MR. JUSTICE REHNQUIST, dissenting.

[For] the reasons stated in my separate concurrence in *Gannett,* I do not believe that [anything in the Constitution] require[s] that a State's reasons for denying public access to a trial, where both [the prosecution and defense] have consented to [a court-approved closure order], are subject to any additional constitutional review at our hands.

[The] issue here is not whether the "right" to freedom of the press * * * overrides the defendant's "right" to a fair trial, [but] whether any provision in the Constitution may fairly be read to prohibit what the [trial court] did in this case. Being unable to find any such prohibition in the First, Sixth, Ninth, or any other Amendments to [the] Constitution, or in the Constitution itself, I dissent.

Notes and Questions

1. *Beyond the justice system.* May (should) "public access to information about how government operates" (to use Stevens, J.'s phrase) be denied, as the Chief Justice suggests, simply on the ground that the place at issue has not been *traditionally* open to the public (recall how the Chief Justice distinguishes penal institutions from criminal trials) or should the government also have to advance, as Stevens, J., suggests, "legitimate justification" for "abridging" public access? Compare the controversy over whether "the right to a public forum" should turn on whether the place at issue has *historically* been dedicated to the exercise of first amendment rights or on whether the manner of expression is *basically incompatible* with the normal activity of the place at a particular time. See generally the materials on the Public Forum: New Forums, Ch. 6, II infra. See also Note, *The First Amendment Right to Gather State–Held Information,* 89 Yale L.J. 923, 933–39 (1979). Consider, too, Blasi, *The Checking Value in First Amendment Theory,* 1977 Am.B.Found.Res.J. 521, 609–10:

"[S]ince, under the checking value [the value that first amendment freedoms can serve in checking the abuse of power by public officials], the dissemination of information about the behavior of government officials is the paradigm First Amendment activity, policies and practices that reduce the amount and quality of information disseminated to the public should not be upheld simply because they serve the convenience, or embody traditional prerogatives, of the government. At a minimum, restrictions on press coverage of official activities should be upheld only if it can be shown that the restrictions substantially promote an important governmental objective that cannot be promoted sufficiently by alternative policies having a less restrictive impact on what interested outsiders can learn about official conduct. For example, under this standard all journalists could not be excluded from a police inspection of the scene of a recent crime if a single pool reporter and/or photographer could be admitted without disrupting the investigation.

"Second, under the checking value, the interest of the press (and ultimately the public) in learning certain information relevant to the abuse of official power would sometimes take precedence over perfectly legitimate and substantial government interests such as efficiency and confidentiality. Thus, the First Amendment may require that journalists have access as a general matter to some records, such as certain financial documents, which anyone investigating common abuses of the public trust would routinely want to inspect, even though the granting of such access would undoubtedly entail some costs and risks. Also, the balance might be tilted even more in the direction of access if a journalist could demonstrate that there are reasonable grounds to believe that certain records contain evidence of misconduct by public officials."

But cf. Kamisar, *Right of Access to Information Generated or Controlled by the Government: Richmond Newspapers Examined and Gannett Revisited* in Choper, Kamisar & Tribe, The Supreme Court: Trends and Developments, 1979–80 145, 166 (1981): "I am sure I am not alone when I say that these law review commentaries go quite far. But *someday* the views they advance may be the law of the land. In the meantime, however, many more battles will have to be fought. *Someday* we may look back on *Richmond Newspapers* as the '*Powell v. Alabama*' of the right of access to government-controlled information—but it was a long, hard road from *Powell* to *Gideon*."[e]

2. *Within the justice system.* How far does (should) *Richmond Newspapers* extend within the justice system? To criminal pre-trial proceedings?[f] How is a trial defined? Should it extend to conferences in chambers or at the bench? To grand jury hearings? To civil trials? To depositions? To records of any or all of the above? Should it apply outside judicial proceedings? Should wardens be permitted to completely preclude access by the public and press to prisons? To executions? What if the prisoner wants to close the execution? For wide-ranging discussion of these and related questions, see Choper, Kamisar, and Tribe, note 1 supra, at 145–206 (Professor Tribe was winning counsel in *Richmond Newspapers*). See also Fenner & Koley, *Access to*

e. For endorsements of generous access, see Haiman, *Speech and Law in a Free Society* 108–14, 368–97 (1981); Yudof, *When Government Speaks* 246–55 (1983); Emerson, *Legal Foundations of the Right to Know*, 1976 Wash.U.L.Q. 1, 14–17; Lewis, *A Public Right to Know about Public Institutions: The First Amendment as Sword*, 1980 Sup.Ct.Rev. 1. But see Bevier, *An Informed Public, an Informing Press: The Search for a Constitutional Principle*, 68 Calif.L.Rev. 482 (1980).

f. See *Press-Enterprise Co. v. Superior Court*, 478 U.S. 1, 106 S.Ct. 2735, 92 L.Ed.2d 1 (1986) ("California preliminary hearings are sufficiently like a trial" to implicate *Richmond Newspapers'* "qualified First Amendment right of access"); *El Vocero de Puerto Rico v. Puerto Rico*, 508 U.S. 147, 113 S.Ct. 2004, 124 L.Ed.2d 60 (1993) (reaching same conclusion as to Puerto Rican preliminary hearings).

Judicial Proceedings: To Richmond Newspapers and Beyond, 16 Harv.Civ. Rts.—Civ.Lib.L.Rev. 415 (1981).

3. *Closing trials.* After *Richmond Newspapers,* what showing should suffice to justify closure of a criminal trial? See *Globe Newspaper Co. v. Superior Court,* 457 U.S. 596, 102 S.Ct. 2613, 73 L.Ed.2d 248 (1982) (routine exclusion of press and public during testimony of minor victim of sex offense unconstitutional); *Press-Enterprise Co. v. Superior Court,* 464 U.S. 501, 104 S.Ct. 819, 78 L.Ed.2d 629 (1984) (extending *Richmond Newspapers* to voir dire examination of jurors). To overcome either the first amendment or the sixth amendment right to a public trial, the Court has required that the party seeking to close the proceedings "must advance an overriding interest that is likely to be prejudiced, the closure must be no broader than necessary to protect that interest, the trial court must consider reasonable alternatives to closing the proceeding, and it must make findings adequate to support the closure." *Waller v. Georgia,* 467 U.S. 39, 104 S.Ct. 2210, 81 L.Ed.2d 31 (1984).

4. *Special access rights for the press.* Is a press section in public trials required when the seating capacity would be exhausted by the public? Is a press section permitted? What limits attach to government determinations of who shall get press passes? See, e.g., *Sherrill v. Knight,* 569 F.2d 124 (D.C.Cir.1977) (denial of White House press pass infringes upon first amendment guarantees in the absence of adequate process); *Borreca v. Fasi,* 369 F.Supp. 906 (D.Haw.1974) (preliminary injunction against denial of access of a reporter to Mayor's press conferences justified when basis for exclusion is allegedly "inaccurate" and "irresponsible" reporting); *Los Angeles Free Press, Inc. v. Los Angeles,* 9 Cal.App.3d 448, 88 Cal.Rptr. 605 (1970) (exclusion of weekly newspaper from scenes of disaster and police press conferences upheld when newspaper did not report policy and fire events "with some regularity"). Cf. *Los Angeles Police Department v. United Reporting Publishing Corp.,* 528 U.S. 32, 120 S.Ct. 483, 145 L.Ed.2d 451 (1999)(law mandating release of arrest records for a scholarly, journalistic, political, or governmental purpose, but not to sell a product or service, may not be challenged on its face; remanded for as applied attack).

When access is required, may the press be prevented from taking notes? Is the right to bring tape recorders into public trials protected under *Richmond Newspapers?* What about "unobtrusive" television cameras? Consider Ares, *Chandler v. Florida: Television, Criminal Trials, and Due Process,* 1981 Sup.Ct.Rev. 157, 174: "Television in the courtroom expands public access to public institutions both qualitatively, because of its immediacy, and quantitatively, because of its reach. It is reported that a majority of Americans acquire their news primarily from television rather than from newspapers. To exclude the most important source of information about the working of courts without some compelling reason cannot be squared with the First Amendment." Cf. *Chandler v. Florida,* 449 U.S. 560, 101 S.Ct. 802, 66 L.Ed.2d 740 (1981) (subject to certain safeguards a state may *permit* electronic media and still photography coverage of public criminal proceedings over the objection of the accused).

Does *Chandler's* holding demean the interest in fair trials? Consider Griswold, *The Standards of the Legal Profession: Canon 35 Should Not Be Surrendered,* 48 A.B.A.J. 615, 617 (1962): "The presence of cameras and television [has] an inhibiting effect on some people, and an exhilarating effect on others. In either event, there would be distortion, and an inevitable interference with the administration of justice. With all the improved techniques in the world, the introduction of radio and television to the courtroom will surely and naturally convert it into a stage for those who can act, and into a place of additional burden for those who cannot."[g] Do these objections apply with the same force to appellate proceedings?[h] Suppose first amendment attorney, Mary McDermott, plans a test case. Consider Kamisar, *Chandler v. Florida: What Can Be Said for a "Right of Access" to Televise Judicial Proceedings?* in Choper, Kamisar, & Tribe, The Supreme Court: Trends and Developments 1980–81, at 149, 168 (1982): "At the present time, no federal court allows TV coverage. *The place to begin* may well be the place that is likely to be the last holdout—the United States Supreme Court."

g. Compare Arenella, *Televising High Profile Trials: Are We Better Off Pulling the Plug,* 37 Santa Clara L. Rev. 879 (1997)(suggesting that most high profile trials should not be televised). But see Sager & Frederikson, *Televising the Judicial Branch: In Furtherance of the Public's First Amendment Rights,* 69 S. Cal. L.Rev. 1519 (1996).

h. See Ares, supra, at 189–90.

Chapter 6

THE PUBLIC FORUM

The case law treating the question of when persons can speak on public property has come to be known as public forum doctrine. But "[t]he public forum saga began, and very nearly ended," Stone, *Fora Americana: Speech in Public Places,* 1974 Sup.Ct.Rev. 233, 236, with an effort by Holmes, J., then on the Supreme Judicial Court of Massachusetts, "to solve a difficult first amendment problem by simplistic resort to a common-law concept," Blasi, *Prior Restraints on Demonstrations,* 68 Mich.L.Rev. 1482, 1484 (1970). For holding religious meetings on the Boston Common, a preacher was convicted under an ordinance prohibiting "any public address" upon publicly-owned property without a permit from the mayor. In upholding the permit ordinance Holmes, J., observed: "For the legislature absolutely or conditionally to forbid public speaking in a highway or public park is no more an infringement of rights of a member of the public than for the owner of a private house to forbid it in the house." *Massachusetts v. Davis,* 162 Mass. 510, 511, 39 N.E. 113, 113 (1895). On appeal, a unanimous Supreme Court adopted the Holmes position, 167 U.S. 43, 17 S.Ct. 731, 42 L.Ed. 71 (1897): "[T]he right to absolutely exclude all right to use [public property], necessarily includes the authority to determine under what circumstances such use may be availed of, as the greater power contains the lesser."

This view survived until *Hague v. CIO,* 307 U.S. 496, 59 S.Ct. 954, 83 L.Ed. 1423 (1939), which rejected Jersey City's claim that its ordinance requiring a permit for an open air meeting was justified by the "plenary power" rationale of *Davis.* In rejecting the implications of the *Davis* dictum, Roberts, J., in a plurality opinion, uttered a famous "counter dictum," which has played a central role in the evolution of public forum theory: "Wherever the title of streets and parks may rest, they have immemorially been held in trust for the use of the public and, time out of mind, have been used for purposes of assembly, communicating thoughts between citizens, and discussing public questions. Such use of the streets and public places has, from ancient times, been a part of the privileges, immunities, rights, and liberties of citizens. [This privilege of a citizen] is not absolute, but relative, and must be exercised in subordination to the general comfort and convenience, and in consonance with peace and good order; but it must not, in the guise of regulation, be abridged or denied." Eight months later, the *Hague* dictum was given impressive content by Roberts, J., for the Court, in *Schneider*, infra.

I. FOUNDATION CASES

A. MANDATORY ACCESS

SCHNEIDER v. NEW JERSEY, 308 U.S. 147, 60 S.Ct. 146, 84 L.Ed. 155 (1939), per ROBERTS, J., invalidated several ordinances prohibiting leafleting on public streets or other public places: "Municipal authorities, as trustees for the public, have the duty to keep their communities' streets open and available for movement of people and property, the primary purpose to which the streets are dedicated. So long as legislation to this end does not abridge the constitutional liberty of one rightfully upon the street to impart information through speech or the distribution of literature, it may lawfully regulate the conduct of those using the streets. For example, a person could not exercise this liberty by taking his stand in the middle of a crowded street, contrary to traffic regulations, and maintain his position to the stoppage of all traffic; a group of distributors could not insist upon a constitutional right to form a cordon across the street and to allow no pedestrian to pass who did not accept a tendered leaflet; nor does the guarantee of freedom of speech or of the press deprive a municipality of power to enact regulations against throwing literature broadcast in the streets. Prohibition of such conduct would not abridge the constitutional liberty since such activity bears no necessary relationship to the freedom to speak, write, print or distribute information or opinion. * * *

"In *Lovell* [Ch. 4, I, A supra] this court held void an ordinance which forbade the distribution by hand or otherwise of literature of any kind without written permission from the city manager. [Similarly] in *Hague v. C.I.O.*, an ordinance was held void on its face because it provided for previous administrative censorship of the exercise of the right of speech and assembly in appropriate public places.

"The [ordinances] under review do not purport to license distribution but all of them absolutely prohibit it in the streets and, one of them, in other public places as well.

"The motive of the legislation under attack in Numbers 13, 18 and 29 is held by the courts below to be the prevention of littering of the streets and, although the alleged offenders were not charged with themselves scattering paper in the streets, their convictions were sustained upon the theory that distribution by them encouraged or resulted in such littering. We are of opinion that the purpose to keep the streets clean and of good appearance is insufficient to justify an ordinance which prohibits a person rightfully on a public street from handing literature to one willing to receive it. Any burden imposed upon the city authorities in cleaning and caring for the streets as an indirect consequence of such distribution results from the constitutional protection of the freedom of speech and press. This constitutional protection does not deprive a city of all power to prevent street littering. There are obvious methods of preventing littering. Amongst these is the punishment of those who actually throw papers on the streets.

"It is suggested that [the] ordinances are valid because their operation is limited to streets and alleys and leaves persons free to distribute printed matter in other public places. But, as we have said, the streets are natural and proper places for the dissemination of information and opinion; and one is not to have the exercise of his liberty of expression in appropriate places abridged on the plea that it may be exercised in some other place."

McReynolds, J., "is of opinion that the judgment in each case should be affirmed."

Notes and Questions

1. *Leaflets and the streets as public forum.* Consider Kalven, *The Concept of the Public Forum: Cox v. Louisiana,* 1965 S.Ct.Rev. 1, 18 & 21: "Leaflet distribution in public places in a city is a method of communication that carries as an inextricable and expected consequence substantial littering of the streets, which the city has an obligation to keep clean. It is also a method of communication of some annoyance to a majority of people so addressed; that its impact on its audience is very high is doubtful. Yet the constitutional balance in *Schneider* was struck emphatically in favor of keeping the public forum open for this mode of communication.

"[The] operative theory of the Court, at least for the leaflet situation, is that, although it is a method of communication that interferes with the public use of the streets, the right to the streets as a public forum is such that leaflet distribution cannot be prohibited and can be regulated only for weighty reasons."

2. *Litter prevention as a substantial interest.* Does the interest in distributing leaflets always outweigh the interest in preventing littering? Suppose helicopters regularly dropped tons of leaflets on the town of Irvington?

3. *Beyond leaflets.* COX v. NEW HAMPSHIRE, 312 U.S. 569, 61 S.Ct. 762, 85 L.Ed. 1049 (1941), per Hughes, C.J., upheld convictions of sixty-eight Jehovah's Witnesses for parading without a permit. They had marched in four or five groups (with perhaps twenty others) along the sidewalk in single file carrying signs and handing out leaflets: "[T]he state court considered and defined the duty of the licensing authority and the rights of the appellants to a license for their parade, with regard only to consideration of time, place and manner so as to conserve the public convenience." The licensing procedure was said to "afford opportunity for proper policing" and " 'to prevent confusion by overlapping parades, [to] secure convenient use of the streets by other travelers, and to minimize the risk of disorder.' "A

municipality "undoubtedly" has "authority to control the use of its public streets for parades or processions." But see Baker, *Unreasoned Reasonableness: Mandatory Parade Permits and Time, Place, and Manner Regulations,* 78 Nw.U.L.Rev. 937, 992 (1984): Approximately 26,000 people walked on the same sidewalks during the same hour the defendants in *Cox* "marched." "This single difference in what [the defendants] did—'marching in formation,' which they did for expressive purposes and which presumably is an 'assembly' that the first amendment protects—turned out to have crucial significance. This sole difference, engaging in first amendment protected conduct, made them guilty of a criminal offense. [Surely] something is wrong with this result."

4. *Charging for use of public forum.* Cox said there was nothing "contrary to the Constitution" in the exaction of a fee " 'incident to the administration of the [licensing] Act and to the maintenance of public order in the matter licensed.' "But see *Forsyth County v. The Nationalist Movement,* 505 U.S. 123, 112 S.Ct. 2395, 120 L.Ed.2d 101 (1992)(speech cannot be financially burdened for expenses associated with hostile audience in a licensing context).

5. *Reasonable time, place, and manner regulations.* As *Cox* reveals, a right of access to a public forum does not guarantee immunity from reasonable time, place, and manner regulations. In HEFFRON v. INTERNATIONAL SOC. FOR KRISHNA CONSCIOUSNESS, 452 U.S. 640, 101 S.Ct. 2559, 69 L.Ed.2d 298 (1981), for example, the Court, per WHITE, J., upheld a state fair rule prohibiting the distribution of printed material or the solicitation of funds except from a duly licensed booth on the fairgrounds. The Court noted that consideration of a forum's special attributes is relevant to the determination of reasonableness, and the test of reasonableness is whether the restrictions "are justified without reference to the content of the regulated speech, that they serve a significant governmental interest, and that in doing so they leave open ample alternative channels for communication of the information"[a]

WARD v. ROCK AGAINST RACISM, 491 U.S. 781, 109 S.Ct. 2746, 105 L.Ed.2d 661 (1989), per KENNEDY, J., observes that "[E]ven in a public forum the government may impose reasonable restrictions on the time, place, or manner of protected speech, provided the restrictions 'are justified without reference to the content of the regulated speech, that they are narrowly tailored to serve a significant governmental interest, and that they leave open ample alternative channels for communication of the information.' " The case reasserts that the *O'Brien* test is little different from the time, place, and manner test, and then states: "Lest any confusion on the point remain, we reaffirm today that a regulation of the time, place, or manner of protected speech must be narrowly tailored to serve the government's legitimate content-neutral interests but that it need not be the least-restrictive or least-intrusive means of

a. Brennan, J., joined by Marshall and Stevens, JJ., dissented in part as did Blackmun, J., in a separate opinion. Their dispute was not with the Court's test, but its application.

doing so. Rather, the requirement of narrow tailoring is satisfied 'so long as [the] regulation promotes a substantial government interest that would be achieved less effectively absent the regulation.' To be sure, this standard does not mean that a time, place, or manner regulation may burden substantially more speech than is necessary to further the government's legitimate interests. Government may not regulate expression in such a manner that a substantial portion of the burden on speech does not serve to advance its goals."[g] MARSHALL, J., dissenting, joined by Brennan and Stevens, JJ., complains of the Court's "serious distortion of the narrowly tailoring requirement" and states that the Court's rejection of the less restrictive alternative test relies on "language in a few opinions * * * taken out of context."

Should the time, place, and manner test be different from the *O'Brien* test? Is there any difference between those tests and the approach employed in *Schneider?*

B. EQUAL ACCESS

CHICAGO POLICE DEP'T v. MOSLEY, 408 U.S. 92, 92 S.Ct. 2286, 33 L.Ed.2d 212 (1972), invalidated an ordinance banning all picketing within 150 feet of a school building while the school is in session and one half-hour before and afterwards, except "the peaceful picketing of any school involved in a labor dispute."

The suit was brought by a federal postal employee who, for seven months prior to enactment of the ordinance, had frequently picketed a high school in Chicago. "During school hours and usually by himself, Mosley would walk the public sidewalk adjoining the school, carrying a sign that read: 'Jones High School practices black discrimination. Jones High School has a black quota.' His lonely crusade was always peaceful, orderly, and [quiet]." The Court, per MARSHALL, J., viewed the ordinance as drawing "an impermissible distinction between labor picketing and other peaceful picketing": "The central problem with Chicago's ordinance is that it describes permissible picketing in terms of its subject matter. Peaceful picketing on the subject of a school's labor-management dispute is permitted, but all other peaceful picketing is prohibited. The operative distinction is the message on a picket sign. But, above all else, the First Amendment means that government has no power to restrict expression because of its message, its ideas, its subject matter, or its content.

"[U]nder the Equal Protection Clause, not to mention the First Amendment itself,[a] government may not grant the use of a forum to people whose

---

g. A ban on handbilling, of course, would suppress a great quantity of speech that does not cause the evils that it seeks to eliminate, whether they be fraud, crime, litter, traffic congestion, or noise. For that reason, a complete ban on handbilling would be substantially broader than necessary to achieve the interests justifying it.

a. *Consolidated Edison Co. v. Public Service Comm'n,* Ch. 10 infra, abandoned equal protection and cited *Mosley* as a first amendment case: "The First Amendment's

views it finds acceptable, but deny use to those wishing to express less favored or more controversial views. And it may not select which issues are worth discussing or debating in public facilities. There is an 'equality of status in the field of ideas,' and government must afford all points of view an equal opportunity to be heard. Once a forum is opened up to assembly or speaking by some groups, government may not prohibit others from assembling or speaking on the basis of what they intend to say. Selective exclusions from a public forum may not be based on content alone, and may not be justified by reference to content alone.

"[Not] all picketing must always be allowed. We have continually recognized that reasonable 'time, place and manner' regulations of picketing may be necessary to further significant governmental interests. Similarly, under an equal protection analysis, there may be sufficient regulatory interests justifying selective exclusions or distinctions among picketers. [But] [b]ecause picketing plainly involves expressive conduct within the protection of the First Amendment, discriminations among picketers must be tailored to serve a substantial governmental interest. In this case, the ordinance itself describes impermissible picketing not in terms of time, place and manner, but in terms of subject matter. The regulation 'thus slip[s] from the neutrality of time, place and circumstance into a concern about content.' This is never permitted.[b] * * *

"Although preventing school disruption is a city's legitimate concern, Chicago itself has determined that peaceful labor picketing during school hours is not an undue interference with school. Therefore, under the Equal Protection clause, Chicago may not maintain that other picketing disrupts the school unless that picketing is clearly more disruptive than the picketing Chicago already permits. If peaceful labor picketing is permitted, there is no justification for prohibiting all nonlabor picketing, both peaceful and nonpeaceful. 'Peaceful' labor picketing, however the term 'peaceful' is defined, is obviously no less disruptive than 'peaceful' nonlabor picketing. But Chicago's ordinance permits the former and prohibits the latter.

"[We also] reject the city's argument that, although it permits peaceful labor picketing, it may prohibit all nonlabor picketing because, as a class, nonlabor picketing is more prone to produce violence than labor picketing. Predictions about imminent disruption from picketing involve judgments appropriately made on an individualized basis, not by means of broad classifications, especially those based on subject matter. Freedom of expres-

hostility to content-based regulation extends not only to restrictions on particular viewpoints, but also to prohibition of public discussion of an entire topic." But see, e.g., *Minnesota State Board v. Knight,* 465 U.S. 271, 104 S.Ct. 1058, 79 L.Ed.2d 299 (1984) (stating that *Mosley* is an equal protection case).

b. Farber, *The First Amendment* 23 (1998): "[T]he Court never really explained the basis for its rule. On the face of things, it is not clear that distinctions based on subject matter should always be considered particularly troublesome. For instance, there seems to be nothing suspicious about the decisions of the drafters of the National Labor Relations Act and the Taft–Hartley Act to regulate labor picketing but not antiwar picketing."

sion, and its intersection with the guarantee of equal protection, would rest on a soft foundation indeed if government could distinguish among picketers on such a wholesale and categorical basis. '[I]n our system, undifferentiated fear or apprehension of disturbance is not enough to overcome the right to freedom of expression.' *Tinker.* Some labor picketing is peaceful, some disorderly; the same is true for picketing on other themes. No labor picketing could be more peaceful or less prone to violence than Mosley's solitary vigil. In seeking to restrict nonlabor picketing which is clearly more disruptive than peaceful labor picketing, Chicago may not prohibit all nonlabor picketing at the school forum."[c]

Notes and Questions

1. Consider Karst, *Equality as a Central Principle in the First Amendment,* 43 U.Chi.L.Rev. 20, 28 (1975): "*Mosley* is a landmark first amendment decision. It makes two principal points: (1) the essence of the first amendment is its denial to government of the power to determine which messages shall be heard and which suppressed * * *. (2) Any 'time, place and manner' restriction that selectively excludes speakers from a public forum must survive careful judicial scrutiny to ensure that the exclusion is the minimum necessary to further a significant government interest. Taken together, these statements declare a principle of major importance. The Court has explicitly adopted the principle of equal liberty of expression. [The] principle requires courts to start from the assumption that all speakers and all points of view are entitled to a hearing, and permits deviation from this basic assumption only upon a showing of substantial necessity."[d]

2. What if the *Mosley* ordinance had not excepted labor picketing, but had banned *all* picketing within 150 feet of a school during school hours? Consider Karst 37–38: "The burden of this restriction would fall most heavily on those who have something to communicate to the school [population]. Student picketers presenting a grievance against a principal, or striking custodians with a message growing out of a labor dispute, would be affected more seriously by this ostensibly content-neutral ordinance than would, say the proponents of a candidate for Governor [who could just as effectively carry their message elsewhere]. This differential impact amounts to de facto content discrimination, presumptively invalid under the first amendment equality principle.

"[The city faces] an apparent dilemma. [If it] bars all picketing within a certain area, it will effectively discriminate against those groups that can communicate to their audience only by picketing within that area. But if the city adjusts its ordinance to this differential impact, as by providing a

---

c. Consider Burger, C.J., joined the Court's opinion, but also concurred. Blackmun and Rehnquist, JJ., concurred in the result.

d. For commentary on the relationship between equality and freedom of speech

borrowing and adapting the theory of Jurgen Habermas, see Solum, *Freedom of Communicative Action,* 83 Nw.U.L.Rev. 54 (1989).

student-picketing or labor-picketing exemption, [it runs] afoul of *Mosley* itself. The city can avoid the dilemma by amending the ordinance to ban not all picketing but only noisy picketing."[e]

3.   Does equality fully explain the special concern with content regulation? Consider Stone, *Content Regulation and the First Amendment*, 25 Wm. & Mary L.Rev. 189, 207 (1983): "The problem, quite simply, is that restrictions on expression are rife with 'inequalities,' many of which have nothing whatever to do with content. The ordinance at issue in *Mosley*, for example, restricted picketing near schools, but left unrestricted picketing near hospitals, libraries, courthouses, and private homes. The ordinance at issue in *Erznoznik* restricted drive-in theaters that are visible from a public street, but did not restrict billboards. [Whatever] the effect of these content-neutral inequalities on first amendment analysis, they are not scrutinized in the same way as content-based inequalities. Not all inequalities, in other words, are equal. And although the concern with equality may support the content-based/content-neutral distinction, it does not in itself have much explanatory power."

Is the concern with content discrimination explainable because of concerns about communicative impact, distortion of public debate, or government motivation? See generally Stone, supra. See also sources cited in notes 1 & 2 after *O'Brien,* Ch. 4 supra and Cass, *First Amendment Access to Government Facilities,* 65 Va.L.Rev. 1287, 1323–25 (1979); Stephan, *The First Amendment and Content Discrimination,* 68 Va.L.Rev. 203 (1982); Stone, *Restrictions of Speech Because of its Content: The Peculiar Case of Subject–Matter Restrictions,* 46 U.Chi.L.Rev. 81 (1978).

4.   An Illinois statute prohibited picketing residences or dwellings—except when the dwelling is "used as a place of business," or is "a place of employment involved in a labor dispute or the place of holding a meeting [on] premises commonly used to discuss subjects of general public interest," or when a "person is picketing his own [dwelling]. Can a conviction for picketing the Mayor of Chicago's home be upheld? Is *Mosley* distinguishable? See *Carey v. Brown,* 447 U.S. 455, 100 S.Ct. 2286, 65 L.Ed.2d 263 (1980).

II.   NEW FORUMS

Are first amendment rights on government property confined to streets and parks? "[W]hat about other publicly owned property, ranging from the grounds surrounding a public building, to the inside of a welfare office, publicly run bus, or library, to a legislative gallery?" Stone, *Fora Americana,* supra, at 245.

e. As Karst notes, such an ordinance was upheld in *Grayned v. Rockford,* 408 U.S. 104, 92 S.Ct. 2294, 33 L.Ed.2d 222 (1972), the companion case to *Mosley.*

INTERNATIONAL SOCIETY FOR KRISHNA CONSCIOUSNESS, INC. v. LEE

505 U.S. 672, 112 S.Ct. 2701, 120 L.Ed.2d 541 (1992).

CHIEF JUSTICE REHNQUIST delivered the opinion of the Court.

In this case we consider whether an airport terminal operated by a public authority is a public forum and whether a regulation prohibiting solicitation in the interior of an airport terminal violates the First Amendment.

The relevant facts in this case are not in dispute. Petitioner International Society for Krishna Consciousness, Inc. (ISKCON) is a not-for-profit religious corporation whose members perform a ritual known as sankirtan. The ritual consists of " 'going into public places, disseminating religious literature and soliciting funds to support the religion.' " The primary purpose of this ritual is raising funds for the movement.

Respondent Walter Lee, now deceased, was the police superintendent of the Port Authority of New York and New Jersey and was charged with enforcing the regulation at issue. The Port Authority owns and operates three major airports in the greater New York City area: John F. Kennedy International Airport (Kennedy), La Guardia Airport (La Guardia), and Newark International Airport (Newark). The three airports collectively form one of the world's busiest metropolitan airport complexes. By decade's end they are expected to serve at least 110 million passengers annually. * * *

The Port Authority has adopted a regulation forbidding within the terminals the repetitive solicitation of money or distribution of literature. The regulation states: "1. The following conduct is prohibited within the interior areas of buildings or structures at an air terminal if conducted by a person to or with passers-by in a continuous or repetitive manner: (a) The sale or distribution of any merchandise, including but not limited to jewelry, food stuff, candles, flowers, badges and clothing. (b) The sale or distribution of flyers, brochures, pamphlets, books or any other printed or written material. (c) Solicitation and receipt of funds."

The regulation governs only the terminals; the Port Authority permits solicitation and distribution on the sidewalks outside the terminal buildings. The regulation effectively prohibits petitioner from performing sankirtan in the terminals. * * *

It is uncontested that the solicitation at issue in this case is a form of speech protected under the First Amendment.[3] But it is also well settled that the government need not permit all forms of speech on property that it owns and controls.

United States Postal Service v. Council of Greenburgh Civic Assns., 453 U.S. 114, 129, 101 S.Ct. 2676, 2685, 69 L.Ed.2d 517 (1981);[a] *Greer v. Spock,*

---

3. We deal here only with ISKCON's petition raising the permissibility of solicitation. Respondent's cross-petition concerning the leafletting ban is disposed of in the companion case, *Lee v. International Society for Krishna Consciousness, Inc.*

a. *Greenburgh* held that the post office could prevent individuals from placing unstamped material in residential mail boxes.

424 U.S. 828, 96 S.Ct. 1211, 47 L.Ed.2d 505 (1976).[b] Where the government is acting as a proprietor, managing its internal operations, rather than acting as lawmaker with the power to regulate or license, its action will not be subjected to the heightened review to which its actions as a lawmaker may be subject. Thus, we have upheld a ban on political advertisements in city-operated transit vehicles, *Lehman v. City of Shaker Heights,* 418 U.S. 298, 94 S.Ct. 2714, 41 L.Ed.2d 770 (1974), even though the city permitted other types of advertising on those vehicles. Similarly, we have permitted a school district to limit access to an internal mail system used to communicate with teachers employed by the district. *Perry Education Assn. v. Perry Local Educators' Ass'n,* 460 U.S. 37, 103 S.Ct. 948, 74 L.Ed.2d 794 (1983).[c]

"These cases reflect, either implicitly or explicitly, a 'forum-based' approach for assessing restrictions that the government seeks to place on the use of its property. *Cornelius v. NAACP Legal Defense and Educational Fund, Inc.,* 473 U.S. 788, 800, 105 S.Ct. 3439, 3448, 87 L.Ed.2d 567 (1985)[d] Under this approach, regulation of speech on government property that has traditionally been available for public expression is subject to the highest scrutiny. Such regulations survive only if they are narrowly drawn to achieve a compelling state interest. *Perry.* The second category of public property is the designated public forum, whether of a limited or unlimited character— property that the state has opened for expressive activity by part or all of the

b. *Greer* held that the military could bar a presidential candidate from speaking on a military base even though members of the public were free to visit the base, the President had spoken on the base, and other speakers (e.g., entertainers and anti-drug speakers) had spoken by invitation on the base.

c. *Perry* held it permissible to deny access to the mailboxes for a competing union despite permitting access for the duly elected union and access for various community groups such as the cub scouts, the YMCA, and other civic and church organizations. *Mosley* and *Carey* were distinguished: "[The] key to those decisions [was] the presence of a public forum." Compare Lamb's Chapel v. Center Moriches Union Free School Dist., 508 U.S. 384, 113 S.Ct. 2141, 124 L.Ed.2d 352 (1993) (school could not exclude religious groups from access to school property for after school meetings so long as it held the property generally open for meetings by social, civic, and recreation groups).

d. *Cornelius* upheld an executive order that included organizations providing direct health and welfare services to individuals or their families in a charity drive in the federal workplace while excluding legal defense and political advocacy organizations.

A 4–3 majority, per O'Connor, J., determined that "government does not create a public forum by inaction or by permitting limited discourse, but only by intentionally opening a non-traditional forum for public discourse." Observing that the Court will look to the policy and practice of the government, the nature of the property and its compatibility with expressive activity in discerning intent, O'Connor, J., insisted that "we will not find that a public forum has been created in the face of clear evidence of a contrary intent, nor will we infer that the Government intended to create a public forum when the nature of the property is inconsistent with expressive activity."

Blackmun, J., dissented in *Cornelius v. NAACP Legal Defense and Educational Fund, Inc.,* 473 U.S. 788, 105 S.Ct. 3439, 87 L.Ed.2d 567 (1985): "If the Government does not create a limited public forum unless it intends to provide an 'open forum' for expressive activity, and if the exclusion of some speakers is evidence that the Government did not intend to create such a forum, no speaker challenging denial of access will ever be able to prove that the forum is a limited public forum. The very fact that the Government denied access to the speaker indicates that the Government did not intend to provide an open forum for expressive activity, and [that] fact alone would demonstrate that the forum is not a limited public forum."

public. [*Id.*]e Regulation of such property is subject to the same limitations as that governing a traditional public forum. Finally, there is all remaining public property. Limitations on expressive activity conducted on this last category of property must survive only a much more limited review. The challenged regulation need only be reasonable, as long as the regulation is not an effort to suppress the speaker's activity due to disagreement with the speaker's view. * * *

[Our] precedents foreclose the conclusion that airport terminals are public fora. Reflecting the general growth of the air travel industry, airport terminals have only recently achieved their contemporary size and character. But given the lateness with which the modern air terminal has made its appearance, it hardly qualifies for the description of having "immemorially * * * time out of mind" been held in the public trust and used for purposes of expressive activity. Moreover, even within the rather short history of air transport, it is only "[i]n recent years [that] it has become a common practice for various religious and non-profit organizations to use commercial airports as a forum for the distribution of literature, the solicitation of funds, the proselytizing of new members, and other similar activities." 45 Fed.Reg. 35314 (1980). Thus, the tradition of airport activity does not demonstrate that airports have historically been made available for speech activity. Nor can we say that these particular terminals, or airport terminals generally, have been intentionally opened by their operators to such activity; the frequent and continuing litigation evidencing the operators' objections belies any such claim. In short, there can be no argument that society's time-tested judgment, expressed through acquiescence in a continuing practice, has resolved the issue in petitioner's favor.

Petitioner attempts to circumvent the history and practice governing airport activity by pointing our attention to the variety of speech activity that it claims historically occurred at various "transportation nodes" such as rail stations, bus stations, wharves, and Ellis Island. Even if we were inclined to accept petitioner's historical account describing speech activity at these locations, an account respondent contests, we think that such evidence is of little import for two reasons. First, much of the evidence is irrelevant to *public* fora analysis, because sites such as bus and rail terminals traditionally have had *private* ownership. The development of privately owned parks that ban speech activity would not change the public fora status of publicly held parks. But the reverse is also true. The practices of privately held transportation centers do not bear on the government's regulatory authority over a publicly owned airport.

---

e. In interpreting this approach, *Perry* also stated in footnote 7 that: "A public forum may be created for a limited purpose such as use by certain groups, e.g., *Widmar v. Vincent* [Ch. 11, III, infra] (student groups), or for the discussion of certain subjects, e.g., *City of Madison Joint School District v. Wisconsin Employ. Relat. Com'n,* 429 U.S. 167, 97 S.Ct. 421, 50 L.Ed.2d 376 (1976) (school board business)."

Second, the relevant unit for our inquiry is an airport, not "transportation nodes" generally. When new methods of transportation develop, new methods for accommodating that transportation are also likely to be needed. And with each new step, it therefore will be a new inquiry whether the transportation necessities are compatible with various kinds of expressive activity. To make a category of "transportation nodes," therefore, would unjustifiably elide what may prove to be critical differences of which we should rightfully take account. The "security magnet," for example, is an airport commonplace that lacks a counterpart in bus terminals and train stations. And public access to air terminals is also not infrequently restricted—just last year the Federal Aviation Administration required airports for a 4-month period to limit access to areas normally publicly accessible. To blithely equate airports with other transportation centers, therefore, would be a mistake. * * *

As commercial enterprises, airports must provide services attractive to the marketplace. In light of this, it cannot fairly be said that an airport terminal has as a principal purpose "promoting the free exchange of ideas." To the contrary, the record demonstrates that Port Authority management considers the purpose of the terminals to be the facilitation of passenger air travel, not the promotion of expression. Even if we look beyond the intent of the Port Authority to the manner in which the terminals have been operated, the terminals have never been dedicated (except under the threat of court order) to expression in the form sought to be exercised here: i.e., the solicitation of contributions and the distribution of literature. * * * Thus, we think that neither by tradition nor purpose can the terminals be described as satisfying the standards we have previously set out for identifying a public forum.

The restrictions here challenged, therefore, need only satisfy a requirement of reasonableness. * * *

We have on many prior occasions noted the disruptive effect that solicitation may have on business. "Solicitation requires action by those who would respond: The individual solicited must decide whether or not to contribute (which itself might involve reading the solicitor's literature or hearing his pitch), and then, having decided to do so, reach for a wallet, search it for money, write a check, or produce a credit card." Kokinda. Passengers who wish to avoid the solicitor may have to alter their path, slowing both themselves and those around them. The result is that the normal flow of traffic is impeded. This is especially so in an airport, where "air travelers, who are often weighted down by cumbersome baggage * * * may be hurrying to catch a plane or to arrange ground transportation." Delays may be particularly costly in this setting, as a flight missed by only a few minutes can result in hours worth of subsequent inconvenience.

In addition, face-to-face solicitation presents risks of duress that are an appropriate target of regulation. The skillful, and unprincipled, solicitor can target the most vulnerable, including those accompanying children or those suffering physical impairment and who cannot easily avoid the solicitation.

The unsavory solicitor can also commit fraud through concealment of his affiliation or through deliberate efforts to shortchange those who agree to purchase. Compounding this problem is the fact that, in an airport, the targets of such activity frequently are on tight schedules. This in turn makes such visitors unlikely to stop and formally complain to airport authorities. As a result, the airport faces considerable difficulty in achieving its legitimate interest in monitoring solicitation activity to assure that travelers are not interfered with unduly.

The Port Authority has concluded that its interest in monitoring the activities can best be accomplished by limiting solicitation and distribution to the sidewalk areas outside the terminals. This sidewalk area is frequented by an overwhelming percentage of airport users. Thus the resulting access of those who would solicit the general public is quite complete. In turn we think it would be odd to conclude that the Port Authority's terminal regulation is unreasonable despite the Port Authority having otherwise assured access to an area universally traveled. * * *

Moreover, "the justification for the Rule should not be measured by the disorder that would result from granting an exemption solely to ISKCON." For if petitioner is given access, so too must other groups. "Obviously, there would be a much larger threat to the State's interest in crowd control if all other religious, nonreligious, and noncommercial organizations could likewise move freely." As a result, we conclude that the solicitation ban is reasonable. * * *

JUSTICE O'CONNOR, concurring in 91–155 [on the solicitation issue] and concurring in the judgment in 91–339 [on the distribution of literature issue]. * * *

In the decision below, the Court of Appeals upheld a ban on solicitation of funds within the airport terminals operated by the Port Authority of New York and New Jersey, but struck down a ban on the repetitive distribution of printed or written material within the terminals. I would affirm both parts of that judgment.

I concur in the Court's opinion in No. 91–155 and agree that publicly owned airports are not public fora. * * *

* * * That airports are not public fora, however, does not mean that the government can restrict speech in whatever way it likes. * * *

"The reasonableness of the Government's restriction [on speech in a nonpublic forum] must be assessed in light of the purpose of the forum and all the surrounding circumstances." *Cornelius.* " '[C]onsideration of a forum's special attributes is relevant to the constitutionality of a regulation since the significance of the governmental interest must be assessed in light of the characteristic nature and function of the particular forum involved.' " In this case, the "special attributes" and "surrounding circumstances" of the airports operated by the Port Authority are determinative. Not only has the Port Authority chosen *not* to limit access to the airports under its control, it has created a huge complex open to traveler and nontravelers alike. The airports house restaurants, cafeterias, snack bars, coffee shops, drug stores, food stores, nurseries, barber shops, currency exchanges, art exhibits, commercial advertising displays, bookstores, newsstands, dental offices and private clubs. The International Arrivals Building at JFK Airport even has two branches of Bloomingdale's.

We have said that a restriction on speech in a nonpublic forum is "reasonable" when it is "consistent with the [government's] legitimate interest in 'preserv[ing] the property * * * for the use to which it is lawfully dedicated.'" *Perry.* * * * In my view, the Port Authority is operating a shopping mall as well as an airport. The reasonableness inquiry, therefore, is not whether the restrictions on speech are "consistent with * * * preserving the property" for air travel, but whether they are reasonably related to maintaining the multipurpose environment that the Port Authority has deliberately created.

Applying that standard, I agree with the Court in No. 91–155 that the ban on solicitation is reasonable. * * *

In my view, however, the regulation banning leafletting—or, in the Port Authority's words, the "continuous or repetitive * * * distribution of * * * printed or written material"—cannot be upheld as reasonable on this record. I therefore concur in the judgment in No. 91–339 striking down that prohibition. While the difficulties posed by solicitation in a nonpublic forum are sufficiently obvious that its regulation may "rin[g] of common-sense," the same is not necessarily true of leafletting. To the contrary, we have expressly noted that leafletting does not entail the same kinds of problems presented by face-to-face solicitation. Specifically, "[o]ne need not ponder the contents of a leaflet or pamphlet in order mechanically to take it out of someone's hand * * *. 'The distribution of literature does not require that the recipient stop in order to receive the message the speaker wishes to convey; instead the recipient is free to read the message at a later time.'" With the possible exception of avoiding litter, it is difficult to point to any problems intrinsic to the act of leafletting that would make it naturally incompatible with a large, multipurpose forum such as those at issue here. * * *

Of course, it is still open for the Port Authority to promulgate regulations of the time, place, and manner of leafletting which are "content-neutral, narrowly tailored to serve a significant government interest, and leave open ample alternative channels of communication." For example, during the many years that this litigation has been in progress, the Port Authority has not banned sankirtan completely from JFK International Airport, but has restricted it to a relatively uncongested part of the airport terminals, the same part that houses the airport chapel. In my view, that regulation meets the standards we have applied to time, place, and manner restrictions of protected expression.

I would affirm the judgment of the Court of Appeals in both No. 91–155 and No. 91–339.

JUSTICE KENNEDY, with whom JUSTICE BLACKMUN, JUSTICE STEVENS, and JUSTICE SOUTER join as to Part I, concurring in the judgment.

While I concur in the judgment affirming in this case, my analysis differs in substantial respects from that of the Court. In my view the airport corridors and shopping areas outside of the passenger security zones, areas operated by the Port Authority, are public forums, and speech in those places is entitled to protection against all government regulation inconsistent with public forum principles. The Port Authority's blanket prohibition on the distribution or sale of literature cannot meet those stringent standards, and I agree it is invalid under the First and Fourteenth Amendments. The Port Authority's rule disallowing in-person solicitation of money for immediate payment, however, is in my view a narrow and valid regulation of the time, place, and manner of protected speech in this forum, or else is a valid regulation of the nonspeech element of expressive conduct. I would sustain the Port Authority's ban on solicitation and receipt of funds.

I

[The Court's] analysis is flawed at its very beginning. It leaves the government with almost unlimited authority to restrict speech on its property by doing nothing more than articulating a non-speech-related purpose for the area, and it leaves almost no scope for the development of new public forums absent the rare approval of the government. The Court's error lies in its conclusion that the public-forum status of public property depends on the government's defined purpose for the property, or on an explicit decision by the government to dedicate the property to expressive activity. In my view, the inquiry must be an objective one, based on the actual, physical characteristics and uses of the property. * * *

The First Amendment is a limitation on government, not a grant of power. Its design is to prevent the government from controlling speech. Yet under the Court's view the authority of the government to control speech on its property is paramount, for in almost all cases the critical step in the Court's analysis is a classification of the property that turns on the government's own definition or decision, unconstrained by an independent duty to respect the speech its citizens can voice there. The Court acknowledges as much, by reintroducing today into our First Amendment law a strict doctrinal line between the proprietary and regulatory functions of government which I thought had been abandoned long ago. *Schneider; Grayned v. City of Rockford,* 408 U.S. 104, 92 S.Ct. 2294, 33 L.Ed.2d 222 (1972).[f]

The Court's approach is contrary to the underlying purposes of the public forum doctrine. The liberties protected by our doctrine derive from

f. *Grayned* stated that: "The crucial question is whether the manner of expression is basically incompatible with the normal activity of a particular place at a particular time." Applying that test, the Court held constitutional an ordinance forbidding the making of noise which disturbs or tends to disturb the peace or good order of a school session.

the Assembly, as well as the Speech and Press Clauses of the First Amendment, and are essential to a functioning democracy. See Kalven, *The Concept of the Public Forum: Cox v. Louisiana,* 1965 S.Ct.Rev. 1, 14, 19. Public places are of necessity the locus for discussion of public issues, as well as protest against arbitrary government action. At the heart of our jurisprudence lies the principle that in a free nation citizens must have the right to gather and speak with other persons in public places. The recognition that certain government-owned property is a public forum provides open notice to citizens that their freedoms may be exercised there without fear of a censorial government, adding tangible reinforcement to the idea that we are a free people. * * *

The Court's analysis rests on an inaccurate view of history. The notion that traditional public forums are property which have public discourse as their principal purpose is a most doubtful fiction. The types of property that we have recognized as the quintessential public forums are streets, parks, and sidewalks. It would seem apparent that the principal purpose of streets and sidewalks, like airports, is to facilitate transportation, not public discourse. [Similarly,] the purpose for the creation of public parks may be as much for beauty and open space as for discourse. Thus under the Court's analysis, even the quintessential public forums would appear to lack the necessary elements of what the Court defines as a public forum.

The effect of the Court's narrow view of the first category of public forums is compounded by its description of the second purported category, the so-called "designated" forum. The requirements for such a designation are so stringent that I cannot be certain whether the category has any content left at all. In any event, it seems evident that under the Court's analysis today few if any types of property other than those already recognized as public forums will be accorded that status. * * *

One of the places left in our mobile society that is suitable for discourse is a metropolitan airport. It is of particular importance to recognize that such spaces are public forums because in these days an airport is one of the few government-owned spaces where many persons have extensive contact with other members of the public. Given that private spaces of similar character are not subject to the dictates of the First Amendment, it is critical that we preserve these areas for protected speech. In my view, our public forum doctrine must recognize this reality, and allow the creation of public forums which do not fit within the narrow tradition of streets, sidewalks, and parks. Under the proper circumstances I would accord public forum status to other forms of property, regardless of its ancient or contemporary origins and whether or not it fits within a narrow historic tradition. If the objective, physical characteristics of the property at issue and the actual public access and uses which have been permitted by the government indicate that expressive activity would be appropriate and compatible with those uses, the property is a public forum. * * * The possibility of some theoretical inconsistency between expressive activities and the property's uses should not bar a finding of a public forum, if those inconsistencies can be avoided through simple and permitted regulations.

The second category of the Court's jurisprudence, the so-called designated forum, provides little, if any, additional protection for speech. Where government property does not satisfy the criteria of a public forum, the government retains the power to dedicate the property for speech, whether for all expressive activity or for limited purposes only. I do not quarrel with the fact that speech must often be restricted on property of this kind to retain the purpose for which it has been designated. And I recognize that when property has been designated for a particular expressive use, the government may choose to eliminate that designation. But this increases the need to protect speech in other places, where discourse may occur free of such restrictions. In some sense the government always retains authority to close a public forum, by selling the property, changing its physical character, or changing its principal use. Otherwise the State would be prohibited from closing a park, or eliminating a street or sidewalk, which no one has understood the public forum doctrine to require. The difference is that when property is a protected public forum the State may not by fiat assert broad control over speech or expressive activities; it must alter the objective physical character or uses of the property, and bear the attendant costs, to change the property's forum status.

Under this analysis, it is evident that the public spaces of the Port Authority's airports are public forums. First, the District Court made detailed findings regarding the physical similarities between the Port Authority's airports and public streets. These findings show that the public spaces in the airports are broad, public thoroughfares full of people and lined with stores and other commercial activities. An airport corridor is of course not a street, but that is not the proper inquiry. The question is one of physical similarities, sufficient to suggest that the airport corridor should be a public forum for the same reasons that streets and sidewalks have been treated as public forums by the people who use them.

Second, the airport areas involved here are open to the public without restriction. Plaintiffs do not seek access to the secured areas of the airports, nor do I suggest that these areas would be public forums. And while most people who come to the Port Authority's airports do so for a reason related to air travel, either because they are passengers or because they are picking up or dropping off passengers, this does not distinguish an airport from streets or sidewalks, which most people use for travel. * * *

Third, and perhaps most important, it is apparent from the record, and from the recent history of airports, that when adequate time, place, and manner regulations are in place, expressive activity is quite compatible with the uses of major airports. The Port Authority's primary argument to the contrary is that the problem of congestion in its airports' corridors makes expressive activity inconsistent with the airports' primary purpose, which is to facilitate air travel. The First Amendment is often inconvenient. But that is besides the point. Inconvenience does not absolve the government of its obligation to tolerate speech. * * *

The danger of allowing the government to suppress speech is shown in the case now before us. A grant of plenary power allows the government to tilt the dialogue heard by the public, to exclude many, more marginal voices. The first challenged Port Authority regulation establishes a flat prohibition on "[t]he sale or distribution of flyers, brochures, pamphlets, books or any other printed or written material," if conducted within the airport terminal, "in a continuous or repetitive manner." We have long recognized that the right to distribute flyers and literature lies at the heart of the liberties guaranteed by the Speech and Press Clauses of the First Amendment. The Port Authority's rule, which prohibits almost all such activity, is among the most restrictive possible of those liberties. The regulation is in fact so broad and restrictive of speech, Justice O'Connor finds it void even under the standards applicable to government regulations in nonpublic forums. I have no difficulty deciding the regulation cannot survive the far more stringent rules applicable to regulations in public forums. The regulation is not drawn in narrow terms and it does not leave open ample alternative channels for communication. * * *

II

It is my view, however, that the Port Authority's ban on the "solicitation and receipt of funds" within its airport terminals should be upheld under the standards applicable to speech regulations in public forums. The regulation may be upheld as either a reasonable time, place, and manner restriction, or as a regulation directed at the non-speech element of expressive conduct. The two standards have considerable overlap in a case like this one. * * *

I am in full agreement with the statement of the Court that solicitation is a form of protected speech. If the Port Authority's solicitation regulation prohibited all speech which requested the contribution of funds, I would conclude that it was a direct, content-based restriction of speech in clear violation of the First Amendment. The Authority's regulation does not prohibit all solicitation, however; it prohibits the "solicitation and receipt of funds." I do not understand this regulation to prohibit all speech that solicits funds. It reaches only personal solicitations for immediate payment of money. Otherwise, the "receipt of funds" phrase would be written out of the provision. The regulation does not cover, for example, the distribution of preaddressed envelopes along with a plea to contribute money to the distributor or his organization. As I understand the restriction it is directed only at the physical exchange of money, which is an element of conduct interwoven with otherwise expressive solicitation. In other words, the regulation permits expression that solicits funds, but limits the manner of that expression to forms other than the immediate receipt of money.

So viewed, I believe the Port Authority's rule survives our test for speech restrictions in the public forum. * * *

[T]he government interest in regulating the sales of literature[, however,] is not as powerful as in the case of solicitation. The danger of a fraud arising from such sales is much more limited than from pure solicitation, because in the case of a sale the nature of the exchange tends to be clearer to both parties. Also, the Port Authority's sale regulation is not as narrowly drawn as the solicitation rule, since it does not specify the receipt of money as a critical element of a violation. And perhaps most important, the flat ban on sales of literature leaves open fewer alternative channels of communication than the Port Authority's more limited prohibition on the solicitation and receipt of funds. Given the practicalities and ad hoc nature of much expressive activity in the public forum, sales of literature must be completed in one transaction to be workable. Attempting to collect money at another time or place is a far less plausible option in the context of a sale than when soliciting donations, because the literature sought to be sold will under normal circumstances be distributed within the forum. * * *

Against all of this must be balanced the great need, recognized by our precedents, to give the sale of literature full First Amendment protection. We have long recognized that to prohibit distribution of literature for the mere reason that it is sold would leave organizations seeking to spread their message without funds to operate. "It should be remembered that the pamphlets of Thomas Paine were not distributed free of charge." *Murdock v. Pennsylvania,* 319 U.S. 105, 63 S.Ct. 870, 87 L.Ed. 1292 (1943). The effect of a rule of law distinguishing between sales and distribution would be to close the marketplace of ideas to less affluent organizations and speakers, leaving speech as the preserve of those who are able to fund themselves. One of the primary purposes of the public forum is to provide persons who lack access to more sophisticated media the opportunity to speak. A prohibition on sales forecloses that opportunity for the very persons who need it most. And while the same arguments might be made regarding solicitation of funds, the answer is that the Port Authority has not prohibited all solicitation, but only a narrow class of conduct associated with a particular manner of solicitation. * * *g

Justice Souter, with whom Justice Blackmun and Justice Stevens join, concurring in the judgment in No. 91–339 [on the distribution of literature issue] and dissenting in No. 91–155 [on the solicitation issue].

I join in Part I of Justice Kennedy's opinion and the judgment of affirmance in No. 91–339. I agree with Justice Kennedy's view of the rule that should determine what is a public forum and with his conclusion that the public areas of the airports at issue here qualify as such. * * *

g. For commentary on Kennedy, J.'s perspective, see Gey, *Reopening the Public Forum–From Sidewalks to Cyberspace,* 58 Ohio St. L.J. 1535 (1998); Comment, *"Objective" Approaches to the Public Forum Doctrine,* 90 Nw. U.L.Rev. 1185 (1996).

From the Court's conclusion in No. 91–155, however, sustaining the total ban on solicitation of money for immediate payment, I respectfully dissent.

[T]he respondent comes closest to justifying the restriction as one furthering the government's interest in preventing coercion and fraud.[1] The claim to be preventing coercion is weak to start with. While a solicitor can be insistent, a pedestrian on the street or airport concourse can simply walk away or walk on. * * * Since there is here no evidence of any type of coercive conduct, over and above the merely importunate character of the open and public solicitation, that might justify a ban, the regulation cannot be sustained to avoid coercion.

As for fraud, our cases do not provide government with plenary authority to ban solicitation just because it could be [fraudulent.] The evidence of fraudulent conduct here is virtually nonexistent. It consists of one affidavit describing eight complaints, none of them substantiated, "involving some form of fraud, deception, or larceny" over an entire 11–year period between 1975 and 1986, during which the regulation at issue here was, by agreement, not enforced. Petitioners claim, and respondent does not dispute, that by the Port Authority's own calculation, there has not been a single claim of fraud or misrepresentation since 1981. * * *

Even assuming a governmental interest adequate to justify some regulation, the present ban would fall when subjected to the requirement of narrow tailoring. Thus, in *Schaumburg v. Citizens for a Better Environment,* 444 U.S. 620, 100 S.Ct. 826, 63 L.Ed.2d 73 (1980), we said: "The Village's legitimate interest in preventing fraud can be better served by measures less intrusive than a direct prohibition on solicitation. Fraudulent misrepresentations can be prohibited and the penal laws used to punish such conduct directly. * * * "

[Finally,] I do not think the Port Authority's solicitation ban leaves open the "ample" channels of communication required of a valid content-neutral time, place and manner restriction. A distribution of preaddressed envelopes is unlikely to be much of an alternative. The practical reality of the regulation, which this Court can never ignore, is that it shuts off a uniquely powerful avenue of communication for organizations like the International Society for Krishna Consciousness, and may, in effect, completely prohibit

---

1. Respondent also attempts to justify its regulation on the alternative basis of "interference with air travelers," referring in particular to problems of "annoyance," and "congestion." The First Amendment inevitably requires people to put up with annoyance and uninvited persuasion. Indeed, in such cases we need to scrutinize restrictions on speech with special care. In their degree of congestion, most of the public spaces of these airports are probably more comparable to public streets than to the fairground as we described it in *Heffron v. International Society for Krishna Consciousness, Inc.* Consequently, the congestion argument, which was held there to justify a regulation confining solicitation to a fixed location, should have less force here. Be that as it may, the conclusion of a majority of the Court today that the Constitution forbids the ban on the sale [Ed. Does the majority of the Court conclude that the Constitution forbids the ban on the *sale* of literature?], as well as the distribution, of leaflets puts to rest respondent's argument that congestion justifies a total ban on solicitation. While there may, of course, be congested locations where solicitation could severely compromise the efficient flow of pedestrians, the proper response would be to tailor the restrictions to those choke points.

unpopular and poorly funded groups from receiving funds in response to protected solicitation. * * *

Accordingly, I would reverse the judgment of the Court of Appeals in No. 91–155, and strike down the ban on solicitation.

LEE v. INTERNATIONAL SOCIETY FOR KRISHNA CONSCIOUSNESS, INC.

505 U.S. 830, 112 S.Ct. 2709, 120 L.Ed.2d 669 (1992).

PER CURIAM.

For the reasons expressed in the opinions of Justice O'Connor, Justice Kennedy, and Justice Souter in *International Society for Krishna Consciousness, Inc. v. Lee,* the judgment of the Court of Appeals holding that the ban on distribution of literature in the Port Authority airport terminals is invalid under the First Amendment is

Affirmed.

CHIEF JUSTICE REHNQUIST, with whom JUSTICE WHITE, JUSTICE SCALIA and JUSTICE THOMAS join, dissenting.

Leafletting presents risks of congestion similar to those posed by solicitation. It presents, in addition, some risks unique to leafletting. And of course, as with solicitation, these risks must be evaluated against a backdrop of the substantial congestion problem facing the Port Authority and with an eye to the cumulative impact that will result if all groups are permitted terminal access. Viewed in this light, I conclude that the distribution ban, no less than the solicitation ban, is reasonable. I therefore dissent from the Court's holding striking the distribution ban.

I will not trouble to repeat in detail all that has been stated in No. 91–155, *International Society for Krishna Consciousness, Inc. v. Lee,* describing the risks and burdens flowing to travelers and the Port Authority from permitting solicitation in airport terminals. Suffice it to say that the risks and burdens posed by leafletting are quite similar to those posed by solicitation. The weary, harried, or hurried traveler may have no less desire and need to avoid the delays generated by having literature foisted upon him than he does to avoid delays from a financial solicitation. And while a busy passenger perhaps may succeed in fending off a leafletter with minimal disruption to himself by agreeing simply to take the proffered material, this does not completely ameliorate the dangers of congestion flowing from such leafletting. Others may choose not simply to accept the material but also to stop and engage the leafletter in debate, obstructing those who follow. Moreover, those who accept material may often simply drop it on the floor once out of the leafletter's range, creating an eyesore, a safety hazard, and additional cleanup work for airport staff. See *City Council of Los Angeles v. Taxpayers for Vincent,* 466 U.S. 789, 104 S.Ct. 2118, 80 L.Ed.2d 772 (1984) (aesthetic interests may provide basis for restricting speech).[h]

h. *Vincent* upheld a city ordinance prohibiting the placing of signs on public property as applied to the signs of a political candidate on the cross-arms of utility poles.

In addition, a differential ban that permits leafletting but prohibits solicitation, while giving the impression of permitting the Port Authority at least half of what it seeks, may in fact prove for the Port Authority to be a much more Pyrrhic victory. Under the regime that is today sustained, the Port Authority is obliged to permit leafletting. But monitoring leafletting activity in order to ensure that it is *only* leafletting that occurs, and not also soliciting, may prove little less burdensome than the monitoring that would be required if solicitation were permitted. At a minimum, therefore, I think it remains open whether at some future date the Port Authority may be able to reimpose a complete ban, having developed evidence that enforcement of a differential ban is overly burdensome. Until now it has had no reason or means to do this, since it is only today that such a requirement has been announced. * * *

Notes and Questions

1. *The First amendment and geography.* Consider Farber & Nowak, *The Misleading Nature of Public Forum Analysis: Content and Context in First Amendment Adjudication,* 70 Va.L.Rev., 1219, 1234–35 (1984): "Classification of public places as various types of forums has only confused judicial opinions by diverting attention from the real first amendment issues involved in the cases. Like the fourth amendment, the first amendment protects people, not places. Constitutional protection should depend not on labeling the speaker's physical location but on the first amendment values and governmental interests involved in the case. Of course, governmental interests are often tied to the nature of the place. [To] this extent, the public forum doctrine is a useful heuristic [device]. But when the heuristic device becomes the exclusive method of analysis, only confusion and mistakes can result." Compare Post, *Between Governance and Management: The History and Theory of the Public Forum,* 34 U.C.L.A.L.Rev. 1713, 1777 (1987): "*Grayned's* 'incompatibility' test takes into account only the specific harm incident to a plaintiff's proposed speech; it does not recognize the generic damage to managerial authority flowing from the very process of independent judicial review of institutional decision making. [The] Court's present focus 'on the character of the property at issue' is a theoretical dead end, because there is no satisfactory theory connecting the classification of government property with the exercise of first amendment rights. But there is great potential for a rich and principled jurisprudence if the Court were to focus instead on the relationship between judicial review and the functioning of institutional authority."

2. Would the Arlington National Cemetery be open to solicitation and the distribution of literature under Kennedy, J.'s approach? Consider Comment, *"Objective" Approaches to the Public Forum Doctrine,* 90 Nw. U.L.Rev. 1185, 1240 (1996): "The only differences between the Cemetery and the typical park might be concrete tombstones instead of bird baths and the

increased likelihood of solemn expressions on the faces of Cemetery visitors.''

3. *Footnote 7 forums.* What is the relationship between the Court's second category of property in *Perry* and its fn. 7 (see fn. e. supra)? Is the discretion to create forums limited? Is it necessary to show that restrictions on such forums are necessary to achieve a compelling state interest? If a restriction (to certain speakers or subjects) is challenged, can the restrictions be used to show that that the property is not a public forum of the second category? Is this inadmissible circularity? See Tribe, *Equality as a First Amendment Theme: The ''Government-as-Private Actor'' Exception* in Choper, Kamisar & Tribe, The Supreme Court: Trends and Developments 1982–1983, at 221, 226 (1984); Post, supra at 1752–56. In any event, does fn. 7 create a fourth category of property without setting guiding stands? Are the *Perry* mailboxes fn. 7 forums?

LEHMAN v. SHAKER HEIGHTS, 418 U.S. 298, 94 S.Ct. 2714, 41 L.Ed.2d 770 (1974), held that a public transit system could sell commercial advertising space for cards on its vehicles while refusing to sell space for ''political'' or ''public issue'' advertising. BLACKMUN, J., joined by Burger, C.J., White and Rehnquist, JJ., ruled the bus cards not be a public forum and found the city's decision reasonable because it minimized ''chances of abuse, the appearance of favoritism, and the risk of imposing upon a captive audience.''

DOUGLAS, J., concurring, maintained that political messages and commercial messages were both offensive and intrusive to captive audiences, noted that the commercial advertising policy was not before the court, and voted to deny a right to spread a political message to a captive audience.

BRENNAN, J., joined by Stewart, Marshall, and Powell, JJ., dissenting, observed that the ''city's solicitous regard for 'captive riders' [has] a hollow ring in the present case where [it] has opened its rapid transit system as a forum for communication.''

Is *Lehman* a fn. 7 forum?

4. *The relationship between the public forum tests and other tests.* In *Vincent,* a political candidate had placed signs on publicly owned utility poles, and the Court assessed the constitutionality of an ordinance that prohibited the placing of signs on public property. What test applies? A public forum test? A time, place, and manner test? The *O'Brien* test?[i]

i. For additional commentary on public forum issues, see Berger, *Pruneyard Revisited: Political Activity on Private Lands,* 66 N.Y.U.L.Rev. 650 (1991); Buchanan, *The Case of the Vanishing Public Forum,* 1991 U.Ill.L.Rev. 949 (1991); Day, *The End of the Public Forum Doctrine,* 78 Iowa L.Rev. 143 (1992); Gey, *Reopening the Public Forum– From Public Sidewalks to Cyberspace,* 58 Ohio St.L.J. 1535 (1998); Goldstone, *The Public Forum Doctrine in the Age of the Information Superhighway (Where Are the Public Forums on the Information Superhighway?),* 46 Hastings L.J. 335 (1995); Krotoszynski, Jr., *Celebrating Selma: The Importance of Context in Public Forum Analysis,* 104 Yale L.J. 1411 (1995); Naughton, *Is Cyberspace A Public Forum? Computer Bulletin Boards, Free Speech, and State Action,* 81 Geo.L.J. 409 (1992); Note,

5. In order to prevent voter intimidation and election fraud, Tennessee prohibits either the soliciting of votes or the display or distribution of campaign materials within 100 feet of the entrance to a polling place. Is the campaign-free zone a public forum? Is the permitting of charitable or religious speech (including solicitation) or commercial speech while banning election speech (but not exit polling) impermissible content discrimination?

BURSON v. FREEMAN, 504 U.S. 191, 112 S.Ct. 1846, 119 L.Ed.2d 5 (1992) upheld the statute. BLACKMUN, J., joined by Rehnquist, C.J., and White and Kennedy, JJ., argued that the 100 foot zone was a public forum, that the regulation was based on the content of the speech, that the state was required to show that its statute was necessary to achieve a compelling state interest and narrowly drawn to achieve that end, and determined that this was the "rare case" in which strict scrutiny against content regulation could be satisfied: "There is [ample evidence] that political candidates have used campaign workers to commit voter intimidation or electoral fraud. In contrast, there is simply no evidence that political candidates have used other forms of solicitation or exit polling to commit such electoral abuses. States adopt laws to address the problems that confront them. The First Amendment does not require States to regulate for problems that do not exist. * * *

"Here, the State, as recognized administrator of elections, has asserted that the exercise of free speech rights conflicts with another fundamental right, the right to cast a ballot in an election free from the taint of intimidation and fraud. A long history, a substantial consensus, and simple common sense shows that some restricted zone around polling places is necessary to protect that fundamental right. Given the conflict between those two rights, we hold that requiring solicitors to stand 100 feet[j] from the entrances to polling places does not constitute an unconstitutional compromise."[k]

SCALIA, J., agreed with Blackmun, J., that the regulation was justified, but maintained that the area around a polling place is not a public forum: "If the category of 'traditional public forum' is to be a tool of analysis rather than a conclusory label, it must remain faithful to its name and derive its content from *tradition*. Because restrictions on speech around polling places are as venerable a part of the American tradition as the secret ballot, [Tennessee's statute] does not restrict speech in a traditional public forum, and the 'exacting scrutiny' that the Court purports to apply is inappropriate.

46 Okla.L.Rev. 155 (1993). For commentary on speaker-based restrictions, see Stone, *Content Regulation and the First Amendment*, 25 Wm. & Mary L.Rev. 189, 244–51 (1983).

j. Blackmun, J., argued that the question of whether the state should be required to set a smaller zone, perhaps 25 feet, would put the state to an unreasonable burden of proof, and that the difference between such zones was not of constitutional moment.

k. Kennedy, J., concurring, objected to the compelling state interest test as a form of ad hoc balancing that wrongly imperilled first amendment rights, but noted that the first amendment must appropriately give way in some cases where other constitutional rights are at stake. Thomas, J., took no part.

Instead, I believe that the [statute] though content-based, is constitutional because it is a reasonable, viewpoint-neutral regulation of a non-public forum."

STEVENS, J., joined by O'Connor and Souter, J., did not address the question of whether the area around a polling place was a public forum, but agreed with Blackmun, J., that the regulation could not be upheld without showing that it was necessary to serve a compelling state interest by means narrowly tailored to that end. He contended that the existence of the secret ballot was a sufficient safeguard against intimidation[1] and that the fear of fraud from last minute campaigning could not be reconciled with *Mills v. Alabama* (prohibition on election day editorials unconstitutional). In addition, Stevens, J., argued that the prohibition disproportionately affects candidates with "fewer resources, candidates from lesser visibility offices, and 'grassroots' candidates" who specially profit from "last-minute campaigning near the polling place. * * * The hubbub of campaign workers outside a polling place may be a nuisance, but it is also the sound of a vibrant democracy."

III.   THE PUBLIC FORUM, PRIVACY AND PRIVATE PROPERTY RIGHTS

A.   THE PUBLIC FORUM AND PRIVACY

A Colorado statute regulates speech-related conduct within 100 feet of the entrance to any health care facility. Colo. Rev. Stat. § 18–9–122(3) (1999)makes it unlawful within the regulated areas for any person to "knowingly approach" within eight feet of another person, without that person's consent, "for the purpose of passing a leaflet or handbill to, displaying a sign to, or engaging in oral protest, education, or counseling with such other person * * * ." HILL v. COLORADO, 530 U.S. 703, 120 S.Ct. 2480, 147 L.Ed.2d 597 (2000), per STEVENS, J., upheld the statute: "Although the statute [prohibits] speakers from approaching unwilling listeners, it does not require a standing speaker to move away from anyone passing by. Nor does it place any restriction on the content of any message that anyone may wish to communicate to anyone else, either inside or outside the regulated areas. It does, however, make it more difficult to give unwanted advice, particularly in the form of a handbill or leaflet, to persons entering or leaving medical facilities.

"The question is whether the First Amendment rights of the speaker are abridged by the protection the statute provides for the unwilling listener. * * * The First Amendment interests of petitioners are clear and undisputed. As a preface to their legal challenge, petitioners emphasize three propositions. First, they accurately explain that the areas protected by the statute

---

1. Stevens, J., argued that the record showed no evidence of intimidation or abuse, nor did it offer a basis for denying election advocacy, while permitting other forms of political advocacy, e.g., environ- mental advocacy. He maintained that the plurality had shifted the strict scrutiny standard from the state to the candidate who wished to speak.

encompass all the public ways within 100 feet of every entrance to every health care facility everywhere in the State of Colorado. There is no disagreement on this point, even though the legislative history makes it clear that its enactment was primarily motivated by activities in the vicinity of abortion clinics. Second, they correctly state that their leafletting, sign displays, and oral communications are protected by the First Amendment. The fact that the messages conveyed by those communications may be offensive to their recipients does not deprive them of constitutional protection. Third, the public sidewalks, streets, and ways affected by the statute are 'quintessential' public forums for free speech. Finally, although there is debate about the magnitude of the statutory impediment to their ability to communicate effectively with persons in the regulated zones, that ability, particularly the ability to distribute leaflets, is unquestionably lessened by this statute.

"On the other hand, petitioners do not challenge the legitimacy of the state interests that the statute is intended to serve. It is a traditional exercise of the States' 'police powers to protect the health and safety of their citizens.' That interest may justify a special focus on unimpeded access to health care facilities and the avoidance of potential trauma to patients associated with confrontational protests. See *Madsen*, Ch. 4, I, B supra. Moreover, as with every exercise of a State's police powers, rules that provide specific guidance to enforcement authorities serve the interest in even-handed application of the law. Whether or not those interests justify the particular regulation at issue, they are unquestionably legitimate.

"It is also important when conducting this interest analysis to recognize the significant difference between state restrictions on a speaker's right to address a willing audience and those that protect listeners from unwanted communication. This statute deals only with the latter. * * *

"The unwilling listener's interest in avoiding unwanted communication has been repeatedly identified in our cases. It is an aspect of the broader 'right to be let alone' that one of our wisest Justices characterized as 'the most comprehensive of rights and the right most valued by civilized men.' *Olmstead v. United States* (Brandeis, J., dissenting). The right to avoid unwelcome speech has special force in the privacy of the home, *Rowan v. Post Office Dept.*, 397 U.S. 728, 90 S.Ct. 1484, 25 L.Ed.2d 736 (1970), and its immediate surroundings, *Frisby v. Schultz*, 487 U.S. 474, 108 S.Ct. 2495, 101 L.Ed.2d 420 (1988),[a] but can also be protected in confrontational settings. * * *

---

a. Anti-abortion demonstrators picketed on a number of occasions outside a doctor's home. In response, the Town Board passed an ordinance that was interpreted to prohibit picketing taking place solely in front of a residence and directed at a residence. *Frisby*, per O'Connor, J., upheld the ordinance: "The state's interest in protecting the well-being, tranquility, and privacy of the home is certainly of the highest order in a free and civilized society." Brennan, joined by Marshall, dissenting, would have permitted the town to regulate the number of residential picketers, the hours, and the

"The dissenters argue that we depart from precedent by recognizing a 'right to avoid unpopular speech in a public forum,' We, of course, are not addressing whether there is such a 'right.' Rather, we are merely noting that our cases have repeatedly recognized the interests of unwilling listeners in situations where 'the degree of captivity makes it impractical for the unwilling   viewer   or   auditor   to   avoid   exposure. * * *[25]

"As we explained in *Ward v. Rock Against Racism*:

'The principal inquiry in determining content neutrality, in speech cases generally and in time, place, or manner cases in particular, is whether the government has adopted a regulation of speech because of disagreement with the message it conveys.' * * *

"Theoretically, of course, cases may arise in which it is necessary to review the content of the statements made by a person approaching within eight feet of an unwilling listener to determine whether the approach is covered by the statute. But that review need be no more extensive than a determination of whether a general prohibition of 'picketing' or 'demonstrating' applies to innocuous speech. The regulation of such expressive activities, by definition, does not cover social, random, or other everyday communications. See *Webster's Third New International Dictionary* 600, 1710 (1993) (defining 'demonstrate' as 'to make a public display of sentiment for or against a person or cause' and 'picket' as an effort 'to persuade or otherwise influence'). Nevertheless, we have never suggested that the kind of cursory examination that might be required to exclude casual conversation from the coverage of a regulation of picketing would be problematic. * * *

"The Colorado statute's regulation of the location of protests, education, and counseling [places] no restrictions on—and clearly does not prohibit—either a particular viewpoint or any subject matter that may be discussed by a speaker. Rather, it simply establishes a minor place restriction on an extremely broad category of communications with unwilling listeners. Instead of drawing distinctions based on the subject that the approaching speaker may wish to address, the statute applies equally to used car salesmen, animal rights activists, fundraisers, environmentalists, and missionaries. Each can attempt to educate unwilling listeners on any subject, but without consent may not approach within eight feet to do so. * * *

noise level of the pickets. Stevens, J., dissenting, would have limited the ban to conduct that "unreasonably interferes with the privacy of the home and does not serve a reasonable communicate purpose." He worried that a sign such as "GET WELL CHARLIE—OUR TEAM NEEDS YOU," would fall within the sweep of the ordinance.

25. Furthermore, whether there is a 'right' to avoid unwelcome expression is not before us in this case. The purpose of the Colorado statute is not to protect a potential listener from hearing a particular message. It is to protect those who seek medical treatment from the potential physical and emotional harm suffered when an unwelcome individual delivers a message (whatever its content) by physically approaching an individual at close range, i.e., within eight feet. In offering protection from that harm, while maintaining free access to health clinics, the State pursues interests constitutionally distinct from the freedom from unpopular speech to which Justice Kennedy refers.

"Here, the statute's restriction seeks to protect those who enter a health care facility from the harassment, the nuisance, the persistent importuning, the following, the dogging, and the implied threat of physical touching that can accompany an unwelcome approach within eight feet of a patient by a person wishing to argue vociferously face-to-face and perhaps thrust an undesired handbill upon her. The statutory phrases, 'oral protest, education, or counseling,' distinguish speech activities likely to have those consequences from speech activities (such as Justice Scalia's 'happy speech' that are most unlikely to have those consequences. The statute does not distinguish among speech instances that are similarly likely to raise the legitimate concerns to which it responds. Hence, the statute cannot be struck down for failure to maintain 'content neutrality,' or for 'underbreadth.'

"Also flawed is Justice Kennedy's theory that a statute restricting speech becomes unconstitutionally content based because of its application 'to the specific locations where that discourse occurs,' A statute prohibiting solicitation in airports that was motivated by the aggressive approaches of Hari–Krishnas does not become content based solely because its application is confined to airports—'the specific location where that discourse occurs.' A statute making it a misdemeanor to sit at a lunch counter for an hour without ordering any food would also not be 'content based' even if it were enacted by a racist legislature that hated civil rights protesters (although it might raise separate questions about the State's legitimate interest at issue).

"Similarly, the contention that a statute is 'viewpoint based' simply because its enactment was motivated by the conduct of the partisans on one side of a debate is without support. The antipicketing ordinance upheld in *Frisby v. Schultz*, a decision in which both of today's dissenters joined, was obviously enacted in response to the activities of antiabortion protesters who wanted to protest at the home of a particular doctor to persuade him and others that they viewed his practice of performing abortions to be murder. We nonetheless summarily concluded that the statute was content neutral."

Stevens, J., maintained that the statute was a reasonable place regulation: "The three types of communication regulated by § 18–9–122(3) are the display of signs, leafletting, and oral speech. The 8–foot separation between the speaker and the audience should not have any adverse impact on the readers' ability to read signs displayed by demonstrators. In fact, the separation might actually aid the pedestrians' ability to see the signs by preventing others from surrounding them and impeding their view. Furthermore, the statute places no limitations on the number, size, text, or images of the placards. And, as with all of the restrictions, the 8–foot zone does not affect demonstrators with signs who remain in place.

"With respect to oral statements, the distance certainly can make it more difficult for a speaker to be heard, particularly if the level of background noise is high and other speakers are competing for the pedestrian's attention. Notably, the statute places no limitation on the number of speakers or the noise level, including the use of amplification equipment, although we have upheld such restrictions in past cases. [T]he statute allows the speaker to remain in one place, and other individuals can pass within eight feet of the protester without causing the protester to violate the statute. Finally, here there is a 'knowing' requirement that protects speakers 'who thought they were keeping pace with the targeted individual' at the proscribed distance from inadvertently violating the statute.

"It is also not clear that the statute's restrictions will necessarily impede, rather than assist, the speakers' efforts to communicate their messages. The statute might encourage the most aggressive and vociferous protesters to moderate their confrontational and harassing conduct, and thereby make it easier for thoughtful and law-abiding sidewalk counselors like petitioners to make themselves heard. But whether or not the 8–foot interval is the best possible accommodation of the competing interests at stake, we must accord a measure of deference to the judgment of the Colorado Legislature. Once again, it is worth reiterating that only attempts to address unwilling listeners are affected.

"The burden on the ability to distribute handbills is more serious because it seems possible that an 8–foot interval could hinder the ability of a leafletter to deliver handbills to some unwilling recipients. The statute does not, however, prevent a leafletter from simply standing near the path of oncoming pedestrians and proffering his or her material, which the pedestrians can easily accept. And, as in all leafletting situations, pedestrians continue to be free to decline the tender. * * *

"Justice Kennedy [argues] that the statute leaves petitioners without adequate means of communication. This is a considerable overstatement. The statute seeks to protect those who wish to enter health care facilities, many of whom may be under special physical or emotional stress, from close physical approaches by demonstrators. In doing so, the statute takes a prophylactic approach; it forbids all unwelcome demonstrators to come closer than eight feet. We recognize that by doing so, it will sometimes inhibit a demonstrator whose approach in fact would have proved harmless. But the statute's prophylactic aspect is justified by the great difficulty of protecting, say, a pregnant woman from physical harassment with legal rules that focus exclusively on the individual impact of each instance of behavior, demanding in each case an accurate characterization (as harassing or not harassing) of each individual movement within the 8–foot boundary. Such individualized characterization of each individual movement is often difficult to make accurately. A bright-line prophylactic rule may be the best way to provide protection, and, at the same time, by offering clear guidance and avoiding subjectivity, to protect speech itself.* * *

"Petitioners argue that § 18–9–122(3) is invalid because it is 'overbroad.' There are two parts to petitioners' 'overbreadth' argument. On the one hand, they argue that the statute is too broad because it protects too many people in too many places, rather than just the patients at the facilities where confrontational speech had occurred. Similarly, it burdens all speakers, rather than just persons with a history of bad conduct. On the other hand, petitioners also contend that the statute is overbroad because it 'bans virtually the universe of protected expression, including displays of signs, distribution of literature, and mere verbal statements.'

"The first part of the argument does not identify a constitutional defect. The fact that the coverage of a statute is broader than the specific concern that led to its enactment is of no constitutional significance. What is important is that all persons entering or leaving health care facilities share the interests served by the statute. It is precisely because the Colorado Legislature made a general policy choice that the statute is assessed under the constitutional standard set forth in *Ward*, rather than a more strict standard. See *Madsen* * * * In this case, it is not disputed that the regulation affects protected speech activity, the question is thus whether it is a 'reasonable restrictio[n] on the time, place, or manner of protected speech.' * * *

"The second part of the argument is based on a misreading of the statute and an incorrect understanding of the overbreadth doctrine. As we have already noted, § 18–9–122(3) simply does not 'ban' any messages, and likewise it does not 'ban' any signs, literature, or oral statements. It merely regulates the places where communications may occur. [Petitioners] have not persuaded us that the impact of the statute on the conduct of other speakers will differ from its impact on their own sidewalk counseling. Like petitioners' own activities, the conduct of other protesters and counselors at all health care facilities are encompassed within the statute's 'legitimate sweep.' Therefore, the statute is not overly broad.

"Petitioners also claim that § 18–9–122(3) is unconstitutionally vague. * * * [This] concern is ameliorated by the fact that § 18–9–122(3) contains a scienter requirement. The statute only applies to a person who 'knowingly' approaches within eight feet of another, without that person's consent, for the purpose of engaging in oral protest, education, or counseling. The likelihood that anyone would not understand any of those common words seems quite remote. * * *

"The judgment of the Colorado Supreme Court is affirmed."

Souter, J., joined by O'Connor, Ginsburg, & Breyer, JJ., concurred: "I join the opinion of the Court and add this further word. The key to determining whether Colo. Rev. Stat. § 18–9–122(3) (1999), makes a content-based distinction between varieties of speech lies in understanding that content-based discriminations are subject to strict scrutiny because they place the weight of government behind the disparagement or suppression of some messages, whether or not with the effect of approving or promoting others. * * *

"Concern about employing the power of the State to suppress discussion of a subject or a point of view is not, however, raised in the same way when a law addresses not the content of speech but the circumstances of its delivery.

The right to express unpopular views does not necessarily immunize a speaker from liability for resorting to otherwise impermissible behavior meant to shock members of the speaker's audience, see *United States v. O'Brien* (burning draft card), or to guarantee their attention, see *Kovacs v. Cooper*, 336 U.S. 77, 69 S.Ct. 448, 93 L.Ed. 513 (1949) (sound trucks); *Frisby v. Schultz* (residential picketing); *Heffron v. International Soc. for Krishna Consciousness, Inc.*, Ch. 6, I, B (soliciting). Unless regulation limited to the details of a speaker's delivery results in removing a subject or viewpoint from effective discourse (or otherwise fails to advance a significant public interest in a way narrowly fitted to that objective), a reasonable restriction intended to affect only the time, place, or manner of speaking is perfectly valid. * * *

"It is important to recognize that the validity of punishing some expressive conduct, and the permissibility of a time, place, or manner restriction, does not depend on showing that the particular behavior or mode of delivery has no association with a particular subject or opinion. Draft card burners disapprove of the draft, see *O'Brien*, and abortion protesters believe abortion is morally wrong, *Madsen*.[b] There is always a correlation with subject and viewpoint when the law regulates conduct that has become the signature of one side of a controversy. But that does not mean that every regulation of such distinctive behavior is content based as First Amendment doctrine employs that term. The correct rule, rather, is captured in the formulation that a restriction is content based only if it is imposed because of the content of the speech. * * *

"No one disputes the substantiality of the government's interest in protecting people already tense or distressed in anticipation of medical attention (whether an abortion or some other procedure) from the unwanted intrusion of close personal importunity by strangers. The issues dividing the Court, then, go to the content neutrality of the regulation, its fit with the interest to be served by it, and the availability of other means of expressing the desired message (however offensive it may be even without physically close communication).

"Each of these issues is addressed principally by the fact that subsection (3) simply does not forbid the statement of any position on any subject. It does not declare any view as unfit for expression within the 100–foot zone or

---

b. *Madsen v. Women's Health Center*, per Rehnquist, C.J., struck down an injunction creating a 300–foot buffer zone around the homes of those who worked in abortion clinics: "The 300–foot zone around the residence is much larger than the zone approved in *Frisby*. [The] 300–foot zone would ban '[g]eneral marching through residential neighborhoods, or even walking a route in front of an entire block of houses.' The record before us does not contain sufficient justification for this broad a ban on picketing; it appears that a limitation on the time, duration of picketing, and number of pick-ets outside a smaller zone could have accomplished the desired result." In separate opinions Stevens, J., Souter, J., and Scalia, J., joined by Kennedy and Thomas, JJ., joined in the judgment of the Court on this issue. For commentary, see Wells, *Of Communists and Anti–Abortion Protestors: The Consequences of Falling into the Theoretical Abyss*, 33 Ga. L. Rev. 1 (1998); Brownstein, *Rules of Engagement for Cultural Wars: Regulating Conduct, Unprotected Speech, and Protected Expression in Anti–Abortion Protests–Section II*, 29 U.C.Davis L.Rev. 1163 (1996).

beyond it. What it forbids, and all it forbids, is approaching another person closer than eight feet (absent permission) to deliver the message. * * *

"This is not to say that enforcement of the approach restriction will have no effect on speech; of course it will make some difference. The effect of speech is a product of ideas and circumstances, and time, place, and manner are circumstances. The question is simply whether the ostensible reason for regulating the circumstances is really something about the ideas. Here, the evidence indicates that the ostensible reason is the true reason."

SCALIA, J., joined by Thomas, J., dissented: "What is before us [is] a speech regulation directed against the opponents of abortion, and it therefore enjoys the benefit of the 'ad hoc nullification machine' that the Court has set in motion to push aside whatever doctrines of constitutional law stand in the way of that highly favored practice. Having deprived abortion opponents of the political right to persuade the electorate that abortion should be restricted by law, the Court today continues and expands its assault upon their individual right to persuade women contemplating abortion that what they are doing is wrong. Because, like the rest of our abortion jurisprudence, today's decision is in stark contradiction of the constitutional principles we apply in all other contexts, I dissent.* * *

"Whatever may be said about the restrictions on the other types of expressive activity, the regulation as it applies to oral communications is obviously and undeniably content-based. A speaker wishing to approach another for the purpose of communicating any message except one of protest, education, or counseling may do so without first securing the other's consent. Whether a speaker must obtain permission before approaching within eight feet—and whether he will be sent to prison for failing to do so— depends entirely on *what he intends to say* when he gets there. I have no doubt that this regulation would be deemed content-based *in an instant* if the case before us involved antiwar protesters, or union members seeking to 'educate' the public about the reasons for their strike. * * *

"The Court asserts that this statute is not content-based for purposes of our First Amendment analysis because it neither (1) discriminates among viewpoints nor (2) places restrictions on 'any subject matter that may be discussed by a speaker.' But we have never held that the universe of content-based regulations is limited to those two categories, and such a holding would be absurd. Imagine, for instance, special place-and-manner restrictions on all speech except that which 'conveys a sense of contentment or happiness.' This 'happy speech' limitation would not be 'viewpoint-based'— citizens would be able to express their joy in equal measure at either the rise or fall of the NASDAQ, at either the success or the failure of the Republican Party—and would not discriminate on the basis of subject matter, since gratification could be expressed about anything at all. Or consider a law restricting the writing or recitation of poetry—neither viewpoint-based nor limited to any particular subject matter. Surely this Court would consider such regulations to be 'content-based' and deserving of the most exacting scrutiny.

" 'The vice of content-based legislation—what renders it deserving of the high standard of strict scrutiny—is not that it is always used for invidious, thought-control purposes, but that it lends itself to use for those purposes.' A restriction that operates only on speech that communicates a message of protest, education, or counseling presents exactly this risk. When applied, as it is here, at the entrance to medical facilities, it is a means of impeding speech against abortion. The Court's confident assurance that the statute poses no special threat to First Amendment freedoms because it applies alike to 'used car salesmen, animal rights activists, fundraisers, environmentalists, and missionaries,' is a wonderful replication (except for its lack of sarcasm) of Anatole France's observation that '[t]he law, in its majestic equality, forbids the rich as well as the poor to sleep under bridges * * *' This Colorado law is no more targeted at used car salesmen, animal rights activists, fund raisers, environmentalists, and missionaries than French vagrancy law was targeted at the rich. We know what the Colorado legislators, by their careful selection of content ('protest, education, and counseling'), were taking aim at, for they set it forth in the statute itself: the 'right to protest or counsel against certain medical procedures' on the sidewalks and streets surrounding health care facilities.

"The Court is unpersuasive in its attempt to equate the present restriction with content-neutral regulation of demonstrations and picketing—as one may immediately suspect from the opinion's wildly expansive definitions of demonstrations as 'public display[s] of sentiment for or against a person or cause,' and of picketing as an effort 'to persuade or otherwise influence.' (On these terms, Nathan Hale was a demonstrator and Patrick Henry a picket.) When the government regulates 'picketing,' or 'demonstrating,' it restricts a particular manner of expression that is, as the author of today's opinion has several times explained, 'a mixture of conduct and communication.' [Today], of course, Justice Stevens gives us an opinion restricting not only handbilling but even one-on-one conversation of a particular content. * * *

"The Court makes too much of the statement in *Ward* that '[t]he principal inquiry in determining content neutrality ... is whether the government has adopted a regulation of speech because of disagreement with the message it conveys.' That is indeed 'the *principal* inquiry'—suppression of uncongenial ideas is the worst offense against the First Amendment—but it is not the *only* inquiry. Even a law that has as its purpose something unrelated to the suppression of particular content cannot irrationally single out that content for its prohibition. An ordinance directed at the suppression of noise (and therefore 'justified without reference to the content of regulated speech') cannot be applied only to sound trucks delivering messages of 'protest.' Our very first use of the 'justified by reference to content' language made clear that it is a prohibition *in addition to*, rather than in place of, the prohibition of facially content-based restrictions. 'Selective exclusions from a public forum' we said, 'may not be based on content alone, and may not be justified by reference to content alone.' *Mosley*."[2]

Scalia, J., argued that the statute could not pass muster even if it were content neutral: "Just three Terms ago, in upholding an injunction against antiabortion activities, the Court refused to rely on any supposed 'right of the people approaching and entering the facilities to be left alone.' *Schenck v. Pro–Choice Network of Western N.Y.*[c] It expressed 'doubt' that this 'right . . . accurately reflects our First Amendment jurisprudence.' Finding itself in something of a jam (the State here has passed a regulation that is obviously not narrowly tailored to advance any other interest) the Court today neatly re-packages the repudiated 'right' as an 'interest' the State may decide to protect and then places it onto the scales opposite the right to free speech in a traditional public forum.

"To support the legitimacy of its self-invented state interest, the Court relies upon a bon mot in a 1928 dissent (which we evidently overlooked in *Schenck*). It characterizes the 'unwilling listener's interest in avoiding unwanted communication' as an 'aspect of the broader 'right to be let alone' Justice Brandeis coined in his dissent in *Olmstead v. United States*. The amusing feature is that even this slim reed contradicts rather than supports the Court's position. The right to be let alone that Justice Brandeis identified was a right the Constitution 'conferred, *as against the government*'; it was *that* right, not some generalized 'common-law right' or 'interest' to be free from hearing the unwanted opinions of one's fellow citizens, which he called the 'most comprehensive' and 'most valued by civilized men.' To the extent that there can be gleaned from our cases a 'right to be let alone' in the sense that Justice Brandeis intended, it is the right of the *speaker* in the

---

2. The Court's contention that the statute is content-neutral because it is not a 'regulation of speech' but a 'regulation of the places where some speech may occur,' is simply baffling. First, because the proposition that a restriction upon the places where speech may occur is not a restriction upon speech is both absurd and contradicted by innumerable cases. And second, because the fact that a restriction is framed as a 'regulation of the places where some speech may occur' has nothing whatever to do with whether the restriction is content-neutral—which is why *Boos* held to be content-based the ban on displaying, within 500 feet of foreign embassies, banners designed to "bring into public odium any foreign government."

c. *Schenck*, per Rehnquist, C.J., maintained that an injunction ordering abortion protesters to cease and desist from "counseling" women entering abortion clinics, who indicate they do not wish to be counseled, could not be sustained in order to protect privacy: "As [a] general matter, we have indicated that in public debate our own citizens must tolerate insulting, and often outrageous, speech in order to provide adequate breathing space to the freedoms protected by the First Amendment." This portion of the injunction was sustained on other grounds. Demonstrators had previously engaged in physical intimidation against women and their escorts. The lower court ordered demonstrators to stay 15 feet away from doorways, driveways, and driveway entrances except for two sidewalk counselors in order to accommodate free speech rights. The Court observed that the counselors, if ordered to desist, and other demonstrators could present their messages outside the 15–foot buffer zone and that their consignment to that area was a result of their own previous intimidation.

public forum to be free from government interference of the sort Colorado has imposed here.

"In any event, the Court's attempt to disguise the 'right to be let alone' as a 'governmental interest in protecting the right to be let alone' is unavailing for the simple reason that this is not an interest that may be legitimately weighed against the speakers' First Amendment rights (which the Court demotes to the status of First Amendment 'interests') We have consistently held that 'the Constitution does not permit the government to decide which types of otherwise protected speech are sufficiently offensive to require protection *for the unwilling listener or viewer.' Erznoznik.* * * *

"The Court nonetheless purports to derive from our cases a principle limiting the protection the Constitution affords the speaker's right to direct 'offensive messages' at 'unwilling' audiences in the public forum. There is no such principle. We have upheld limitations on a speaker's exercise of his right to speak on the public streets *when that speech intrudes into the privacy of the home. Frisby.* * * * As the universally understood state of First Amendment law is described in a leading treatise: 'Outside the home, the burden is generally on the observer or listener to avert his eyes or plug his ears against the verbal assaults, lurid advertisements, tawdry books and magazines, and other 'offensive' intrusions which increasingly attend urban life.' Tribe, *American Constitutional Law* § 12–19, p. 948 (2d ed. 1988). The Court today elevates the abortion clinic to the status of the home.* * *

"The burdens this law imposes upon the right to speak are substantial, despite an attempt to minimize them that is not even embarrassed to make the suggestion that they might actually 'assist * * * the speakers' efforts to communicate their messages.' (Compare this with the Court's statement in a nonabortion case, joined by the author of today's opinion: 'The First Amendment mandates that we presume that speakers, not the government, know best both what they want to say and how to say it.' *Riley.* The Court displays a willful ignorance of the type and nature of communication affected by the statute's restrictions. It seriously asserts, for example, that the 8–foot zone allows a speaker to communicate at a 'normal conversational distance.' I have certainly held conversations at a distance of eight feet seated in the quiet of my chambers, but I have never walked along the public sidewalk— and have not seen others do so—'conversing' at an 8–foot remove. The suggestion is absurd. So is the suggestion that the opponents of abortion can take comfort in the fact that the statute 'places no limitation on the number of speakers or the noise level, including the use of amplification equipment.' That is good enough, I suppose, for 'protesting'; but the Court must know that most of the 'counseling' and 'educating' likely to take place outside a health care facility cannot be done at a distance and at a high-decibel level. The availability of a powerful amplification system will be of little help to the woman who hopes to forge, in the last moments before another of her sex is to have an abortion, a bond of concern and intimacy that might enable her to persuade the woman to change her mind and heart. The counselor may wish to walk alongside and to say, sympathetically and as softly as the circumstances allow, something like: 'My dear, I know what you are going through. I've been through it myself. You're not alone and you do not have to do this. There are other alternatives. Will you let me help you? May I show you a picture of what your child looks like at this stage of her human development?' The Court would have us believe that this can be done effectively—yea, perhaps even *more* effectively—by shouting through a bullhorn at a distance of eight feet.

"The Court seems prepared, if only for a moment, to take seriously the magnitude of the burden the statute imposes on simple handbilling and leafletting. That concern is fleeting, however, since it is promptly assuaged by the realization that a leafletter may, without violating the statute, stand 'near the path' of oncoming pedestrians and make his 'proffe[r] * * * which the pedestrians can easily accept.' It does not take a veteran labor organizer to recognize—although surely any would, see Brief for American Federation of Labor and Congress of Industrial Organization as Amicus Curiae—that leafletting will be rendered utterly ineffectual by a requirement that the leafletter obtain from each subject permission to approach, or else man a stationary post (one that does not obstruct access to the facility, lest he violate subsection (2) of statute) and wait for passersby voluntarily to approach an outstretched hand. That simply is not how it is done, and the Court knows it—or should. A leafletter, whether he is working on behalf of Operation Rescue, Local 109, or Bubba's Bar-B–Que, stakes out the best piece of real estate he can, and then walks a few steps toward individuals passing in his vicinity, extending his arm and making it *as easy as possible* for the passerby, whose natural inclination is generally not to seek out such distributions, to simply accept the offering. Few pedestrians are likely to give their 'consent' to the approach of a handbiller (indeed, by the time he requested it they would likely have passed by), and even fewer are likely to walk over in order to pick up a leaflet. In the abortion context, therefore, ordinary handbilling, which we have in other contexts recognized to be a 'classic for[m] of speech that lie[s] at the heart of the First Amendment,' will in its most effective locations be rendered futile, the Court's implausible assertions to the contrary notwithstanding."

Scalia, J., also questioned the breadth of the statute: " 'The fact,' the Court says, 'that the coverage of a statute is broader than the specific concern that led to its enactment is of no constitutional significance.' That is true enough ordinarily, but it is not true with respect to restraints upon speech, which is what the doctrine of overbreadth is all about. [Again], the Court says that the overbreadth doctrine is not applicable because this law simply 'does not 'ban' any signs, literature, or oral statements,' but 'merely regulates the places where communications may occur.' I know of no precedent for the proposition that time, place, and manner restrictions are not subject to the doctrine of overbreadth. Our decision in *United States v. Grace*, 461 U.S. 171, 103 S.Ct. 1702, 75 L.Ed.2d 736 (1983), demonstrates the contrary: Restriction of speech on the sidewalks around the Supreme

Court was invalidated because it went further than the needs of security justified. Surely New York City cannot require a parade permit and a security bond for any individual who carries a sign on the sidewalks of Fifth Avenue. * * *

"The foregoing discussion of overbreadth was written before the Court, in responding to Justice Kennedy, abandoned any pretense at compliance with that doctrine, and acknowledged—indeed, boasted—that the statute it approves 'takes a prophylactic approach,' and adopts '[a] bright-line prophylactic rule.'[5] I scarcely know how to respond to such an unabashed repudiation of our First Amendment doctrine. Prophylaxis is the antithesis of narrow tailoring. [If] the Court were going to make this concession, it could simply have dispensed with its earlier (unpersuasive) attempt to show that the statute was narrowly tailored. So one can add to the casualties of our whatever-it-takes proabortion jurisprudence the First Amendment doctrine of narrow tailoring and overbreadth. * * *

"Before it effectively threw in the towel on the narrow-tailoring point, the Court asserted the importance of taking into account 'the place to which the regulations apply in determining whether these restrictions burden more speech than necessary.' A proper regard for the 'place' involved in this case should result in, if anything, a commitment by this Court to adhere to and rigorously enforce our speech-protective standards. The public forum involved here—the public spaces outside of health care facilities—has become, by necessity and by virtue of this Court's decisions, a forum of last resort for those who oppose abortion. [For] those who share an abiding moral or religious conviction (or, for that matter, simply a biological appreciation) that abortion is the taking of a human life, there is no option but to persuade women, one by one, not to make that choice. And as a general matter, the most effective place, if not the only place, where that persuasion can occur, is outside the entrances to abortion facilities. By upholding these restrictions on speech in this place the Court ratifies the State's attempt to make even that task an impossible one.

"Those whose concern is for the physical safety and security of clinic patients, workers, and doctors should take no comfort from today's decision. Individuals or groups intent on bullying or frightening women out of an abortion, or doctors out of performing that procedure, will not be deterred by Colorado's statute; bullhorns and screaming from eight feet away will serve their purposes well. But those who would accomplish their moral and religious objectives by peaceful and civil means, by trying to persuade individual women of the rightness of their cause, will be deterred; and that is not a good thing in a democracy."

5. Of course the Court greatly understates the scope of the prophylaxis, saying that 'the statute's prophylactic aspect is justified by the great difficulty of protecting, say, a pregnant woman from physical harassment with legal rules that focus exclusively on the individual impact of each instance of behavior.' But the statute prevents the 'physically harassing' act of (shudder!) approaching within closer than eight feet not only when it is directed against pregnant women, but also (just to be safe) when it is directed against 300–pound, male, and unpregnant truck drivers—surely a distinction that is not 'difficult to make accurately.'

KENNEDY, J., dissented: "The Court's holding contradicts more than a half century of well-established First Amendment principles. For the first time, the Court approves a law which bars a private citizen from passing a message, in a peaceful manner and on a profound moral issue, to a fellow citizen on a public sidewalk. If from this time forward the Court repeats its grave errors of analysis, we shall have no longer the proud tradition of free and open discourse in a public forum. * * *

"The Court errs in asserting the Colorado statute is no different from laws sustained as content neutral in earlier cases. The prohibitions against 'picketing' and/or 'leafleting' upheld in *Frisby*, *Grace*, and *Mosley*, the Court says are no different from the restrictions on 'protest, education, or counseling' imposed by the Colorado statute. The parallel the Court sees does not exist. No examination of the content of a speaker's message is required to determine whether an individual is picketing, or distributing a leaflet, or impeding free access to a building. Under the Colorado enactment, however, the State must review content to determine whether a person has engaged in criminal 'protest, education, or counseling.' When a citizen approaches another on the sidewalk in a disfavored-speech zone, an officer of the State must listen to what the speaker says. If, in the officer's judgment, the speaker's words stray too far toward 'protest, education, or counseling'—the boundaries of which are far from clear—the officer may decide the speech has moved from the permissible to the criminal. The First Amendment does not give the government such power.

"The statute is content based for an additional reason: It restricts speech on particular topics. [If] oral protest, education, or counseling on every subject within an 8–foot zone present a danger to the public, the statute should apply to every building entrance in the State. It does not. It applies only to a special class of locations: entrances to buildings with health care facilities. We would close our eyes to reality were we to deny that 'oral protest, education, or counseling' outside the entrances to medical facilities concern a narrow range of topics—indeed, one topic in particular. [If], just a few decades ago, a State with a history of enforcing racial discrimination had enacted a statute like this one, regulating 'oral protest, education, or counseling' within 100 feet of the entrance to any lunch counter, our predecessors would not have hesitated to hold it was content based or viewpoint based. [To] say that one citizen can approach another to ask the time or the weather forecast or the directions to Main Street but not to initiate discussion on one of the most basic moral and political issues in all of contemporary discourse, a question touching profound ideas in philosophy and theology, is an astonishing view of the First Amendment. For the majority to examine the statute under rules applicable to content-neutral regulations is an affront to First Amendment teachings. * * *

"In a further glaring departure from precedent we learn today that citizens have a right to avoid unpopular speech in a public forum. [*Rowan*] did not hold, contrary to statements in today's opinion that the First Amendment permits the government to restrict private speech in a public forum. Indeed, the Court in Rowan recognized what everyone, before today, understood to be true: "[W]e are often 'captives' outside the sanctuary of the home and subject to objectionable speech and other sound...." * * *

"[A]nd *Lehman v. Shaker Heights* [did] not, contrary to the majority's assertions, suggest that government is free to enact categorical measures restricting traditional, peaceful communications among citizens in a public forum. Instead, the Court admonished that citizens usually bear the burden of disregarding unwelcome messages. Today's decision is an unprecedented departure from this Court's teachings respecting unpopular speech in public fora.

"The Colorado statute offends settled First Amendment principles in another fundamental respect. It violates the constitutional prohibitions against vague or overly broad criminal statutes regulating speech." Kennedy, J., argued that the terms "protest," "counseling," "education," and "consent" were undefined and unduly vague. "The statute's vagueness [becomes] as well one source of its overbreadth. The only sure way to avoid violating the law is to refrain from picketing, leafleting, or oral advocacy altogether. Scienter cannot save so vague a statute as this."

Kennedy, J., also argued that the statute burdened more speech than necessary under the *Ward* test: "Both the State and the Court attempt to sidestep the enactment's obvious content-based restriction by praising the statute's breadth, by telling us all topics of conversation, not just discourse on abortion, are banned within the statutory proscription. The saving feature the Court tries to grasp simply creates additional free speech infirmity. Our precedents do not permit content censoring to be cured by taking even more protected speech within a statute's reach. The statute before us, as construed by the majority, would do just that. If it indeed proscribes 'oral protest, education, or counseling' on all subjects across the board, it by definition becomes 'substantially broader than necessary to achieve the government's interest.' *Ward*.

"The whimsical, arbitrary nature of the statute's operation is further demonstration of a restriction upon more speech than necessary. The happenstance of a dental office being located in a building brings the restricted-speech zone into play. If the same building also houses an organization dedicated, say, to environmental issues, a protest against the group's policies would be barred. Yet if, on the next block there were a public interest enterprise in a building with no health care facility, the speech would be unrestricted. The statute is a classic example of a proscription not narrowly tailored and resulting in restrictions of far more speech than necessary to achieve the legislature's object. * * *

"The majority insists the statute aims to protect distraught women who are embarrassed, vexed, or harassed as they attempt to enter abortion clinics. If these are punishable acts, they should be prohibited in those terms. In the course of praising Colorado's approach, the majority does not pause to tell us why, in its view, substantially less restrictive means cannot be employed to ensure citizens access to health care facilities or to prevent physical contact between citizens. The Court's approach is at odds with the rigor demanded by *Ward*. * * *

"The means of expression at stake here are of controlling importance. Citizens desiring to impart messages to women considering abortions likely do not have resources to use the mainstream media for their message, much less resources to locate women contemplating the option of abortion. Lacking the aid of the government or the media, they seek to resort to the time honored method of leafleting and the display of signs. Nowhere is the speech more important than at the time and place where the act is about to occur. As the named plaintiff, Leila Jeanne Hill, explained, 'I engage in a variety of activities designed to impart information to abortion-bound women and their friends and families. . . .' 'In my many years of sidewalk counseling I have seen a number of [these] women change their minds about aborting their unborn children as a result of my sidewalk counseling, and God's grace.' * * *

"The Court now strikes at the heart of the reasoned, careful balance I had believed was the basis for the joint opinion in *Casey*. The vital principle of the opinion was that in defined instances the woman's decision whether to abort her child was in its essence a moral one, a choice the State could not dictate. Foreclosed from using the machinery of government to ban abortions in early term, those who oppose it are remitted to debate the issue in its moral dimensions. In a cruel way, the Court today turns its back on that balance. It in effect tells us the moral debate is not so important after all and can be conducted just as well through a bullhorn from an 8–foot distance as it can through a peaceful, face-to-face exchange of a leaflet. The lack of care with which the Court sustains the Colorado statute reflects a most troubling abdication of our responsibility to enforce the First Amendment."

B. THE PUBLIC FORUM AND ACCESS
TO "PRIVATE" PROPERTY

MARSH v. ALABAMA

326 U.S. 501, 66 S.Ct. 276, 90 L.Ed. 265 (1946).

MR. JUSTICE BLACK delivered the opinion of the Court.

[The Gulf Shipbuilding Corporation owned all the property of a thickly settled "company town," known as Chickasaw, a suburb of Mobile, Alabama. Chickasaw had "all the characteristics of any other American town": streets, houses, a "business block" with stores rented by merchants and used for shopping by the residents and with a U.S. postoffice from which mail deliveries were made. A public highway ran thirty feet parallel to the "business block," and highway travelers used the town's facilities as if they belonged to any other town.

Appellant, a Jehovah's Witness, undertook to distribute religious literature on the "business block," despite Gulf-posted signs in the stores that

"This Is Private Property" and that written permission was required for street solicitations. After being warned by Chickasaw's policeman, a deputy of the Mobile County sheriff, paid by Gulf, appellant was arrested and convicted under an Alabama trespass statute.]

* * * Under our decision in Lovell v. Griffin [Ch. 4, I supra], and others which have followed that case, neither a state nor a municipality can completely bar the distribution of literature containing religious or political ideas on its streets, sidewalks and public places or make the right to distribute dependent on a flat license tax or permit to be issued by an official who could deny it at will. * * * From these decisions it is clear that had the people of Chickasaw owned all the homes, and all the stores, and all the streets, and all the sidewalks, all those owners together could not have set up a municipal government with sufficient power to pass an ordinance completely barring the distribution of religious literature. * * * Can those people who live in or come to Chickasaw be denied freedom of press and religion simply because a single company has legal title to all the town? * * *

We do not agree that the corporation's property interests settle the question. * * * Ownership does not always mean absolute dominion. The more an owner, for his advantage, opens up his property for use by the public in general, the more do his rights become circumscribed by the statutory and constitutional rights of those who use it. * * * Thus, the owners of privately held bridges, ferries, turnpikes and railroads may not operate them as freely as a farmer does his farm. Since these facilities are built and operated primarily to benefit the public and since their operation is essentially a public function, it is subject to state regulation. * * *

When we balance the Constitutional rights of owners of property against those of the people to enjoy freedom of press and religion, as we must here, we remain mindful of the fact that the latter occupy a preferred position. * * * In our view the circumstance that the property rights to the premises where the deprivation of liberty, here involved, took place, were held by others than the public, is not sufficient to justify the State's permitting a corporation to govern a community of citizens so as to restrict their fundamental liberties and the enforcement of such restraint by the application of a State statute. Insofar as the State has attempted to impose criminal punishment on appellant for undertaking to distribute religious literature in a company town, its action cannot stand.[a] * * *

Mr. Justice Reed, dissenting.

* * * What the present decision establishes as a principle is that one may remain on private property against the will of the owner and contrary to the law of the state so long as the only objection to his presence is that he is exercising an asserted right to spread there his religious views. * * * Of course, such principle may subsequently be restricted by this Court to the precise facts of this case—that is to private property in a company town

---

a. Frankfurter, J., concurred. Jackson, J., took no part.

where the owner for his own advantage has permitted a restricted public use by his licensees and invitees. Such distinctions are of degree and require new arbitrary lines, judicially drawn, instead of those hitherto established by legislation and precedent. * * *

We do not understand from the record that there was objection to appellant's use of the nearby public highway and under our decisions she could rightfully have continued her activities a few feet from the spot she insisted upon using. * * * The passway here in question was not put to any different use than other private passways that lead to privately owned areas, amusement places, resort hotels or other businesses. There had been no dedication of the sidewalk to the public use, express or implied. * * *

We cannot say that Jehovah's Witnesses can claim the privilege of a license, which has never been granted, to hold their meetings in other private places, merely because the owner has admitted the public to them for other limited purposes. Even though we have reached the point where this Court is required to force private owners to open their property for the practice there of religious activities or propaganda distasteful to the owner, because of the public interest in freedom of speech and religion, there is no need for the application of such a doctrine here. Appellant, as we have said, was free to engage in such practices on the public highways. * * *

THE CHIEF JUSTICE and MR. JUSTICE BURTON join in this dissent.

———

In AMALGAMATED FOOD EMPLOYEES UNION v. LOGAN VALLEY PLAZA, INC., 391 U.S. 308, 88 S.Ct. 1601, 20 L.Ed.2d 603 (1968), a state court had enjoined peaceful picketing of the Weis supermarket located within the Logan Valley Mall shopping center on the sole ground that it constituted a trespass on the property of the owners of the center. The union picketing, objecting to the fact that the market was nonunion, was in the parcel pickup area alongside the market and in the adjacent portion of the shopping center parking lot. The injunction's effect was to limit picketing to earthen berms separating the shopping center property from the public roads outside it.

The Court, per MARSHALL, J., noting that the limitation would "substantially hinder" petitioners' communications efforts, reversed: "The shopping center here is clearly the functional equivalent to the business district of Chickasaw involved in *Marsh.*

"It is true that * * * petitioners are free to canvass the neighborhood with their message about the nonunion status of Weis Market, just as they have been permitted by the state courts to picket on the berms outside the mall. Thus, unlike the situation in *Marsh,* there is no power on respondents' part to have petitioners totally denied access to the community for which the mall serves as a business district. This fact, however, is not determinative. In

Marsh itself the precise issue presented was whether the appellant therein had the right, under the First Amendment, to pass out leaflets in the business district, since there was no showing made there that the corporate owner would have sought to prevent the distribution of leaflets in the residential areas of the town. * * * Here the roadways provided for vehicular movement within the mall and the sidewalks leading from building to building are the functional equivalents of the streets and sidewalks of a normal municipal business district. The shopping center premises are open to the public to the same extent as the commercial center of a normal town.

"[I]t may well be that respondents' ownership of the property here in question gives them various rights, under the laws of Pennsylvania, to limit the use of that property by members of the public in a manner that would not be permissible were the property owned by a municipality. All we decide here is that because the shopping center serves as the community business block 'and is freely accessible and open to the people in the area and those passing through,' *Marsh,* the State may not delegate the power, through the use of its trespass laws, wholly to exclude those members of the public wishing to exercise their First Amendment rights on the premises in a manner and for a purpose generally consonant with the use to which the property is actually put."[9]

BLACK, J. dissented: "It seems clear to me, in light of the customary way that supermarkets now must operate, that pick-up zones are as much a part of these stores as the inside counters where customers select their goods or the check-out and bagging sections where the goods are paid for. I cannot conceive how such a pick-up zone, even by the wildest stretching of *Marsh v. Alabama,* could ever be considered dedicated to the public or to pickets. * * *

"I would go further, however, and hold that the entire injunction is valid. * * * I believe that whether this Court likes it or not the Constitution recognizes and supports the concept of private ownership of property. The Fifth Amendment provides that 'no person shall * * * be deprived of life, liberty, or property, without due process of law; nor shall private property be taken for public use, without just compensation.' This means to me that there is no right to picket on the private premises of another to try to convert the owner or others to the views of the pickets. It also means, I think, that if this Court is going to arrogate to itself the power to act as the Government's agent to take a part of Weis' property to give to the pickets for their use, the Court should also award Weis just compensation for the property taken.

9. The picketing carried on by petitioners was directed specifically at patrons of the Weis Market located within the shopping center and the message sought to be conveyed to the public concerned the manner in which that particular market was being operated. We are, therefore, not called upon to consider whether respondents' property rights could, consistently with the First Amendment, justify a bar on picketing which was not thus directly related in its purpose to the use to which the shopping center property was being put.

" * * * The question is under what circumstances can private property be treated as though it were public? The answer that *Marsh* gives is when that property has taken on *all* the attributes of a town, i.e., 'residential buildings, streets, a system of sewers, a sewage disposal plant and a "business block" on which business places are situated.' I can find nothing in *Marsh* which indicates that if one of these features is present, e.g., a business district, this is sufficient for the Court to confiscate a part of an owner's private property and give its use to people who want to picket on it.

"In allowing the trespass here, the majority opinion indicates that Weis and Logan invited the public to the shopping center's parking lot. This statement is contrary to common sense. Of course there was an implicit invitation for customers of the adjacent stores to come and use the marked off places for cars. But the whole public was no more wanted there than they would be invited to park free at a pay parking lot. Is a store owner or several of them together less entitled to have a parking lot set aside for customers than other property owners? To hold that store owners are compelled by law to supply picketing areas for pickets to drive store customers away is to create a court-made law wholly disregarding the constitutional basis on which private ownership of property rests in this country."[a]

———

LLOYD CORP. v. TANNER, 407 U.S. 551, 92 S.Ct. 2219, 33 L.Ed.2d 131 (1972): Respondents had been threatened with arrest for peacefully distributing antiwar handbills in the Lloyd Center "Mall"—a 25–acre, privately owned shopping complex in Portland, Ore., which contained over 60 commercial tenants as well as an auditorium, skating rink, gardens, benches, etc. The lower federal courts had granted respondents an injunction against the Center, finding that, under *Marsh* and *Logan Valley,* "the Mall is the functional equivalent of a public business district."

The Court, per POWELL, J., reversed: In *Logan Valley,* "the picketing was 'directly related in its purpose to the use to which the shopping center property was being put' [whereas here, respondents' message] was directed to all members of the public, not solely to patrons of Lloyd Center or of any of its operations. Respondents could have distributed these handbills on any public street, on any public sidewalk, in any public park, or in any public building in the city of Portland. [Furthermore, in *Logan Valley,* the picketers] would have been deprived of all reasonable opportunity to convey their message to patrons of the Weis store had they been denied access to the shopping center [whereas here], adequate alternative avenues of communication exist. * * * The central building complex was surrounded by public sidewalks, totaling 66 linear blocks. All persons who enter or leave the

a. White, J., also dissented. Douglas, J., wrote a separate concurring opinion. Harlan, J., would have dismissed the writ as improvidently granted because of petitioner's failure properly to present the issue of preemption by the federal labor statutes.

private areas within the complex must cross public streets and sidewalks, either on foot or in automobiles. When moving to and from the privately owned parking lots, automobiles are required by law to come to a complete stop. * * * Indeed, respondents moved to these public areas and continued distribution of their handbills after being requested to leave the interior malls.

"Although accommodations between the values protected by [the first amendment, the due process clause, and the fifth amendment just compensation clause] are sometimes necessary, and the courts properly have shown a special solicitude for the guarantees of the First Amendment, this Court has never held that a trespasser or an uninvited guest may exercise general rights of free speech on property privately owned and used nondiscriminatorily for private purposes only. Even where public property is involved, the Court has recognized that it is not necessarily available for speech, pickets or other communicative activities. * * * It is true that facilities at the Center are used for certain meetings and for various promotional activities. The obvious purpose, recognized widely as legitimate and responsible business activity, is to bring potential shoppers to the Center, to create a favorable impression, and to generate goodwill. There is no open-ended invitation to the public to use the Center for any and all purposes, however incompatible with the interests of both the stores and the shoppers whom they serve."

The argument "that the property of a large shopping center is 'open to the public,' serves the same purposes as a 'business district' of a municipality, and therefore has been dedicated to certain types of public use * * * reaches too far." In *Marsh,* "the owner of the company town was performing the full spectrum of municipal powers and stood in the shoes of the State. In the instant case there is no comparable assumption or exercise of municipal functions or power."

MARSHALL, J., joined by Douglas, Brennan and Stewart, JJ., dissented, finding "no valid distinction" from *Logan Valley.* "From its inception," Portland depended on Lloyd Center "to supply much needed employment opportunities. To insure the success of the Center, the city carefully integrated it into the pattern of streets already established and planned future development of streets around the Center. It is plain, therefore, that Lloyd Center is the equivalent of a public 'business district' within the meaning of *Marsh* and *Logan Valley.* In fact, the Lloyd Center is much more analogous to the company town in *Marsh* than was the Logan Valley Plaza."

As for the contention that the handbilling was unrelated "to the use to which the shopping center was being put," because Lloyd Center allowed parades on Veterans Day, speeches by presidential candidates and solicitations by the American Legion, "the property of Lloyd Center is generally open to First Amendment activity [and] respondents cannot be excluded." But even if it were "never opened to First Amendment activity * * * I would not reach a different result in this case." When "a balance between the freedom to speak, a freedom that is given a preferred place in our hierarchy of values, and the freedom of a private property-owner to control his property" is "fairly weighted, the balance can only be struck in favor of speech." On the one side, "for many Portland citizens, Lloyd Center will so completely satisfy their wants that they will have no reason to go elsewhere for goods or services. If speech is to reach these people, it must reach them in Lloyd Center." On the other side, "there is no evidence to indicate that speech directed to topics unrelated to the shopping center would be more likely to impair the motivation of customers to buy than speech directed to the uses to which the Center is put, which petitioner concedes is constitutionally protected under *Logan Valley*. On the contrary, common sense would indicate that speech that is critical of a shopping center or one or more of its stores is more likely to deter consumers from purchasing goods or services than speech on any other subject." Further, "even assuming that the litter might have increased, that is not a sufficient reason for barring First Amendment activity. See, e.g., *Schneider v. State*. If petitioner is truly concerned about litter, it should * * * prosecute those who throw handbills away, not those who use them for communicative purposes."

As for respondents' access to the public, "the District Court found that certain stores in the Center could only be reached by using the private walkways of the Mall" and that hence "the Mall was the only place where respondents had reasonable access to all of Lloyd Center's patrons.[7] * * * It would not be surprising in the future to see cities rely more and more on private businesses to perform functions once performed by governmental agencies. The advantage of reduced expenses and an increased tax base cannot be overstated. As governments rely on private enterprise, public property decreases in favor of privately owned property. It becomes harder and harder for citizens to find means to communicate with other citizens. Only the wealthy may find effective communication possible unless we adhere to *Marsh* and continue to hold that '[t]he more an owner, for his advantage, opens up his property for use by the public in general, the more do his rights become circumscribed by the statutory and constitutional rights of those who use it.' "

HUDGENS v. NLRB, 424 U.S. 507, 96 S.Ct. 1029, 47 L.Ed.2d 196 (1976), per STEWART, J., overruled *Logan Valley* and held that picketing

7. * * * The record plainly shows that it was impossible to reach many of the shoppers in the Center without using the Mall unless respondents were willing to approach cars as they were leaving the center. The District Court and the Court of Appeals took the view that requiring respondents to run from the sidewalk, to knock on car windows, to ask that the windows be rolled down so that a handbill could be distributed, to offer the handbill, run back to the sidewalk, and to repeat this gesture for every automobile leaving Lloyd Center involved hazards not only to respondents but also to other pedestrians and automobile passengers. Having never seen Lloyd Center, except in photographs contained in the record, and having absolutely no idea of the amount of traffic entering or leaving the Center, the Court cavalierly overturns the careful findings of facts below. This, in my opinion, exceeds even the most expansive view of the proper appellate function of this Court.

of a store in a shopping center by a union with a grievance against the store's warehouse (located elsewhere) was not entitled to first amendment protection: "The Court in its *Lloyd* opinion did not say that it was overruling the *Logan Valley* decision. Indeed, a substantial portion of the Court's opinion in *Lloyd* was devoted to pointing out the differences between the two cases, noting particularly that, in contrast to the handbilling in *Lloyd,* the picketing in *Logan Valley* had been specifically directed to a store in the shopping center and the pickets had had no other reasonable opportunity to reach their intended audience. But the fact is that the reasoning of the Court's opinion in *Lloyd* cannot be squared with the reasoning of the Court's opinion in *Logan Valley.*"

The Court then observed that constitutional free speech protections apply to governmental actions, not to the actions by owners of private property, and pointed to the language which *Lloyd* had used to distinguish *Marsh,* namely that there was no comparable assumption or exercise of municipal functions or power:

"If a large self-contained shopping center *is* the functional equivalent of a municipality, as *Logan Valley* held, then the First and Fourteenth Amendments would not permit control of speech within such a center to depend upon the speech's content. For while a municipality may constitutionally impose reasonable time, place, and manner regulations on the use of its streets and sidewalks for First Amendment purposes and may even forbid altogether such use of some of its facilities, what a municipality may *not* do under the First and Fourteenth Amendments is to discriminate in the regulation of expression on the basis of the content of that expression. *Mosley.*[9] It conversely follows, therefore, that if the respondents in the *Lloyd* case did not have a First Amendment right to enter that shopping center to distribute handbills concerning Vietnam, then the pickets in the present case did not have a First Amendment right to enter this shopping center for the purpose of advertising their strike against the Butler Shoe Co.

"We conclude, in short, that under the present state of the law the constitutional guarantee of free expression has no part to play in a case such as this."[a]

MARSHALL, J., joined by BRENNAN, J., dissented: "In *Logan Valley* we recognized what the Court today refuses to recognize—that the owner of the modern shopping center complex, by dedicating his property to public use as a business district, to some extent displaces the 'State' from control of historical First Amendment forums, and may acquire a virtual monopoly of places suitable for effective communication. The roadways, parking lots, and walkways of the modern shopping center may be as essential for effective

---

9. The Court has in the past held that some expression is not protected "speech" within the meaning of the First Amendment. *Roth; Chaplinsky.*

a. Powell, J., joined by Burger, C.J., concurred. White, J., concurred in the re- sult but argued that *Lloyd* should be followed without overruling *Logan Valley.* He noted that the picketing was addressed to conduct that involved a warehouse off the center's premises. Stevens, J., did not participate.

speech as the streets and sidewalks in the municipal or company-owned town. I simply cannot reconcile the Court's denial of any role for the First Amendment in the shopping center with *Marsh*'s recognition of a full role for the First Amendment on the streets and sidewalks of the company-owned town.

"My reading of *Marsh* admittedly carried me farther than the Court in *Lloyd*, but the *Lloyd* Court remained responsive in its own way to the concerns underlying *Marsh*. *Lloyd* retained the availability of First Amendment protection when the picketing is related to the function of the shopping center, and when there is no other reasonable opportunity to convey the message to the intended audience. Preserving *Logan Valley* subject to *Lloyd*'s two related criteria guaranteed that the First Amendment would have application in those situations in which the shopping center owner had most clearly monopolized the forums essential for effective communication. This result, although not the optimal one in my view, *Lloyd Corp. v. Tanner* (Marshall, J., dissenting), is nonetheless defensible.

"In *Marsh*, the private entity had displaced the 'state' from control of all the places to which the public had historically enjoyed access for First Amendment purposes, and the First Amendment was accordingly held fully applicable to the private entity's conduct. The shopping center owner, on the other hand, controls only a portion of such places, leaving other traditional public forums available to the citizen. But the shopping center owner may nevertheless control all places essential for the effective undertaking of some speech-related activities—namely, those related to the activities of the shopping center. As for those activities, then, the First Amendment ought to have application under the reasoning of *Marsh*, and that was precisely the state of the law after *Lloyd*.

"The Court's only apparent objection to this analysis is that it makes the applicability of the First Amendment turn to some degree on the subject matter of the speech. But that in itself is no objection, and the cases cited by the Court to the effect that government may not 'restrict expression because of its message, its ideas, its subject matter, or its content,' *Mosley*, are simply inapposite. In those cases, it was clearly the government that was acting, and the First Amendment's bar against infringing speech was unquestionably applicable; the Court simply held that the government, faced with a general command to permit speech, cannot choose to forbid some speech because of its message. The shopping center cases are quite different; in these cases the primary regulator is a private entity whose property has 'assume[d] to some significant degree the functional attributes of public property devoted to public use.' The very question in these cases is whether, and under what circumstances, the First Amendment has any application at all. The answer to that question, under the view of *Marsh* described above, depends to some extent on the subject of the speech the private entity seeks to regulate, because the degree to which the private entity monopolizes the effective channels of communication may depend upon what subject is involved. This limited reference to the subject matter of the speech poses none of the dangers of government suppression or censorship that lay at the heart of the cases cited by the Court. It is indeed ironic that those cases whose obvious concern was the promotion of free speech, are cited today to require its surrender. * * *

"The interest of members of the public in communicating with one another on subjects relating to the businesses that occupy a modern shopping center is substantial. Not only employees with a labor dispute, but also consumers with complaints against business establishments, may look to the location of a retail store as the only reasonable avenue for effective communication with the public.[b] As far as these groups are concerned, the shopping center owner has assumed the traditional role of the state in its control of historical First Amendment forums. *Lloyd* and *Logan Valley* recognized the vital role the First Amendment has to play in such cases, and I believe that this Court errs when it holds otherwise."[c]

Notes and Questions

1.   On remand, the NLRB held in SCOTT HUDGENS, 230 NLRB 414 (1977) that the picketers' speech was protected under the National Labor Relations Act: "[W]e find that, under the circumstances here, Hudgens property right to exclude certain types of activity on his Mall must yield to the Section 7 right of primary economic picketing directed against an employer doing business on that Mall."

The labor act protects speech related to union organizing, but does not protect speech unconcerned with labor such as consumer speech or most speech concerning public affairs. Does this state of affairs raise any problems under *Mosley*?

2.   *Migrant labor camps.* A company that has a large commercial farm owns a "residential community" adjacent to it that is several miles from the nearest municipality. The "community" has duplex homes and apartments for about half of the 300 farmworkers (and their families) who work on the farm either seasonally or year-round. It also has a store that sells food, a cafeteria, and a recreation center. Does *Marsh* or *Hudgens* govern the

---

b. *Logan Valley* noted: "It has been estimated that by the end of 1966 there were between 10,000 and 11,000 shopping centers in the United States and Canada, accounting for approximately 37% of the retail sales in those two countries. These figures illustrate the substantial consequences for workers seeking to challenge substandard working conditions, consumers protesting shoddy or overpriced merchandise, and minority groups seeking nondiscriminatory hiring policies that a contrary decision here would have. Business enterprises located in downtown areas would be subject to on-the-spot public criticism for their practices, but businesses situated in the suburbs could largely immunize themselves from similar criticism by creating a *cordon sanitaire* of parking lots around their stores. Neither precedent nor policy compels a result so at variance with [the] first amendment."

c. For a decision that the free speech and petition provisions of the California constitution require that "shopping center owners permit expressive activity on their property," see *Robins v. Pruneyard Shopping Center,* 23 Cal.3d 899, 153 Cal.Rptr. 854, 592 P.2d 341 (1979). For rejection of the argument that such a decision violates the shopping center owner's free speech or property rights, see *PruneYard Shopping Center v. Robins,* Ch. 9, I infra.

question of whether the company may exclude union organizers from the "residential community"? See Note, *First Amendment and the Problem of Access to Migrant Labor Camps,* 67 Corn.L.Rev. 560 (1976).

3. *Residential communities.* A company owns a "residential community, covering 129 acres and housing 12,000 family units made up of some 35,000 people, in 171 adjoining and 'interrelated' apartment houses." Does *Marsh* or *Hudgens* govern the question of whether the company may refuse to rent to blacks? May refuse to permit nonresidents to distribute political pamphlets in the apartment houses? On the privately owned "sidewalks" within the community? See *Watchtower Bible & Tract Society v. Metropolitan Life Ins. Co.,* 297 N.Y. 339, 79 N.E.2d 433 (1948), cert. denied, 335 U.S. 886, 69 S.Ct. 232, 93 L.Ed. 425 (1948).

Chapter 7

GOVERNMENT SUPPORT OF SPEECH

Public forum doctrine recognizes that government is obligated to permit some of its property to be used for communicative purposes without content discrimination, but public forum doctrine also allows other government property to be restricted to some speakers or for talk about selected subjects. In short, in some circumstances government can provide resources for some speech while denying support for other speech. Indeed, government is a significant actor in the marketplace of ideas. Sometimes the government speaks as government; sometimes it subsidizes speech without purporting to claim that the resulting message is its own. It supports speech in many ways: official government messages; statements of public officials at publicly subsidized press conferences; artistic, scientific, or political subsidies, even the classroom communications of public school teachers.

If content distinctions are suspect when government acts as censor, they are the norm when government speaks or otherwise subsidizes speech. Government makes editorial judgments; it decides that some content is appropriate for the occasion and other content is not. The public museum curator makes content decisions in selecting exhibits; the librarian in selecting books; the public board in selecting recipients for research grants; the public official in composing press releases.

The line between support for speech and censorship of speech is not always bright, however. In any event, the Constitution limits the choices government may make in supporting speech. For example, government support of religious speech is limited under the establishment clause. See Part 2. This chapter explores the extent to which the speech clause or constitutional conceptions of equality should limit government discretion in supporting speech.

I. SUBSIDIES OF SPEECH

RUST v. SULLIVAN

500 U.S. 173, 111 S.Ct. 1759, 114 L.Ed.2d 233 (1991).

CHIEF JUSTICE REHNQUIST delivered the opinion of the Court.

These cases concern a facial challenge to Department of Health and Human Services (HHS) regulations which limit the ability of Title X fund recipients to engage in abortion-related activities. * * *

A

In 1970, Congress enacted Title X of the Public Health Service Act (Act), 84 Stat. 1506, as amended, 42 U.S.C. §§ 300–300a–41, which provides federal funding for family-planning services. The Act authorizes the Secretary to "make grants to and enter into contracts with public or nonprofit private entities to assist in the establishment and operation of voluntary family planning projects which shall offer a broad range of acceptable and effective family planning methods and services." 42 U.S.C. § 300(a). Grants and contracts under Title X must "be made in accordance with such regulations as the Secretary may promulgate." 42 U.S.C. § 300a–4. Section 1008 of the Act, however, provides that "[n]one of the funds appropriated under this subchapter shall be used in programs where abortion is a method of family planning." 42 U.S.C. § 300a–6. * * *

In 1988, the Secretary promulgated new regulations designed to provide " 'clear and operational guidance' " to grantees about how to preserve the distinction between Title X programs and abortion as a method of family planning." 53 Fed.Reg. 2923–2924 (1988). * * *

The regulations attach three principal conditions on the grant of federal funds for Title X projects. First, the regulations specify that a "Title X project may not provide counseling concerning the use of abortion as a method of family planning or provide referral for abortion as a method of family planning." 42 CFR § 59.8(a)(1) (1989). Because Title X is limited to preconceptional services, the program does not furnish services related to childbirth. Only in the context of a referral out of the Title X program is a pregnant woman given transitional information. § 59.8(a)(2). Title X projects must refer every pregnant client "for appropriate prenatal and/or social services by furnishing a list of available providers that promote the welfare of the mother and the unborn child." Id. The list may not be used indirectly to encourage or promote abortion, "such as by weighing the list of referrals in favor of health care providers which perform abortions, by including on the list of referral providers health care providers whose principal business is the provision of abortions, by excluding available providers who do not provide abortions, or by 'steering' clients to providers who offer abortion as a method of family planning." § 59.8(a)(3). The Title X project is expressly prohibited from referring a pregnant woman to an abortion provider, even upon specific request. One permissible response to such an inquiry is that "the project does not consider abortion an appropriate method of family planning and therefore does not counsel or refer for abortion." § 59.8(b)(5).

Second, the regulations broadly prohibit a Title X project from engaging in activities that "encourage, promote or advocate abortion as a method of family planning." § 59.10(a). Forbidden activities include lobbying for legislation that would increase the availability of abortion as a method of family planning, developing or disseminating materials advocating abortion as a method of family planning, providing speakers to promote abortion as a method of family planning, using legal action to make abortion available in any way as a method of family planning, and paying dues to any group that advocates abortion as a method of family planning as a substantial part of its activities. Id.

Third, the regulations require that Title X projects be organized so that they are "physically and financially separate" from prohibited abortion activities. § 59.9. To be deemed physically and financially separate, "a Title X project must have an objective integrity and independence from prohibited activities. Mere bookkeeping separation of Title X funds from other monies is not sufficient." Id. The regulations provide a list of nonexclusive factors for the Secretary to consider in conducting a case-by-case determination of objective integrity and independence, such as the existence of separate accounting records and separate personnel, and the degree of physical separation of the project from facilities for prohibited activities. Id.

[Petitioners] are Title X grantees and doctors who supervise Title X funds suing on behalf of themselves and their patients. Respondent is the Secretary of the Department of Health and Human Services. [Petitioners] contend that the regulations violate the First Amendment by impermissibly discriminating based on viewpoint because they prohibit "all discussion about abortion as a lawful option—including counseling, referral, and the provision of neutral and accurate information about ending a pregnancy—while compelling the clinic or counselor to provide information that promotes continuing a pregnancy to term." They assert that the regulations violate the "free speech rights of private health care organizations that receive Title X funds, of their staff, and of their patients" by impermissibly imposing "viewpoint-discriminatory conditions on government subsidies" and thus "penaliz[e] speech funded with non-Title X monies." Because "Title X continues to fund speech ancillary to pregnancy testing in a manner that is not even-handed with respect to views and information about abortion, it invidiously discriminates on the basis of viewpoint." Relying on *Regan v. Taxation with Representation of Washington,* 461 U.S. 540, 103 S.Ct. 1997, 76 L.Ed.2d 129 (1983)[a] and *Arkansas Writers' Project, Inc. v. Ragland,* 481 U.S. 221, 107 S.Ct. 1722, 95 L.Ed.2d 209 (1987),[b] petitioners

a. *Regan* upheld tax code provisions that permitted contributions to veteran's organizations to be deductible even if they engaged in substantial lobbying while deny-

also assert that while the Government may place certain conditions on the receipt of federal subsidies, it may not "discriminate invidiously in its subsidies in such a way as to 'ai[m] at the suppression of dangerous ideas.'" *Regan.*

There is no question but that the statutory prohibition contained in § 1008 is constitutional. [The] Government can, without violating the Constitution, selectively fund a program to encourage certain activities it believes to be in the public interest, without at the same time funding an alternate program which seeks to deal with the problem in another way.[c] In so doing, the Government has not discriminated on the basis of viewpoint; it has merely chosen to fund one activity to the exclusion of the other. "[A] legislature's decision not to subsidize the exercise of a fundamental right does not infringe the right." *Regan.* * * *

The challenged regulations implement the statutory prohibition by prohibiting counseling, referral, and the provision of information regarding abortion as a method of family planning. They are designed to ensure that the limits of the federal program are observed. The Title X program is designed not for prenatal care, but to encourage family planning. A doctor who wished to offer prenatal care to a project patient who became pregnant could properly be prohibited from doing so because such service is outside the scope of the federally funded program. The regulations prohibiting abortion counseling and referral are of the same ilk; "no funds appropriated for the project may be used in programs where abortion is a method of family planning," and a doctor employed by the project may be prohibited in the course of his project duties from counseling abortion or referring for abortion. This is not a case of the Government "suppressing a dangerous idea," but of a prohibition on a project grantee or its employees from engaging in activities outside of its scope.

To hold that the Government unconstitutionally discriminates on the basis of viewpoint when it chooses to fund a program dedicated to advance certain permissible goals, because the program in advancing those goals necessarily discourages alternate goals, would render numerous government programs constitutionally suspect. When Congress established a National

---

ing deductions for contributions to other religious, charitable, scientific, or educational organizations if they engaged in substantial lobbying.

b. *Arkansas Writers' Project, Inc. v. Ragland,* held it unconstitutional to impose a sales tax on general interest magazines while exempting newspapers, religious, professional, trade, and sports journals. Discriminatory taxation against the press or segments of it has generally been invalidated. *Minneapolis Star & Tribune v. Minnesota Comm. of Rev.,* 460 U.S. 575, 103 S.Ct. 1365, 75 L.Ed.2d 295 (1983) (some press treated more favorably and press treated differently from other enterprises); *Grosje-*

an v. American Press Co., 297 U.S. 233, 56 S.Ct. 444, 80 L.Ed. 660 (1936) (same). But see *Leathers v. Medlock,* 499 U.S. 439, 111 S.Ct. 1438, 113 L.Ed.2d 494 (1991) (upholding general sales tax extension to cable that was not applicable to the print media on the grounds that it did not suppress ideas and that the tax did not target a small group of speakers).

c. The Court cited *Maher v. Roe,* 432 U.S. 464, 97 S.Ct. 2376, 53 L.Ed.2d 484 (1977) (constitutional for government to subsidize childbirth without subsidizing abortions) and *Harris v. McRae,* 448 U.S. 297, 100 S.Ct. 2671, 65 L.Ed.2d 784 (1980) (accord).

Endowment for Democracy to encourage other countries to adopt democratic principles, 22 U.S.C. § 4411(b), it was not constitutionally required to fund a program to encourage competing lines of political philosophy such as Communism and Fascism. Petitioners' assertions ultimately boil down to the position that if the government chooses to subsidize one protected right, it must subsidize analogous counterpart rights. But the Court has soundly rejected that proposition. Within far broader limits than petitioners are willing to concede, when the government appropriates public funds to establish a program it is entitled to define the limits of that program.

We believe that petitioners' reliance upon our decision in *Arkansas Writers' Project* is misplaced. That case involved a state sales tax which discriminated between magazines on the basis of their content. Relying on this fact, and on the fact that the tax "targets a small group within the press," contrary to our decision in *Minneapolis Star,* the Court held the tax invalid. But we have here not the case of a general law singling out a disfavored group on the basis of speech content, but a case of the Government refusing to fund activities, including speech, which are specifically excluded from the scope of the project funded.

Petitioners rely heavily on their claim that the regulations would not, in the circumstance of a medical emergency, permit a Title X project to refer a woman whose pregnancy places her life in imminent peril to a provider of abortions or abortion-related services. This case, of course, involves only a facial challenge to the regulations, and we do not have before us any application by the Secretary to a specific fact situation. On their face, we do not read the regulations to bar abortion referral or counseling in such circumstances. * * *

Petitioners also contend that the restrictions on the subsidization of abortion-related speech contained in the regulations are impermissible because they condition the receipt of a benefit, in this case Title X funding, on the relinquishment of a constitutional right, the right to engage in abortion advocacy and counseling.

[H]ere the government is not denying a benefit to anyone, but is instead simply insisting that public funds be spent for the purposes for which they were authorized. The Secretary's regulations do not force the Title X grantee to give up abortion-related speech; they merely require that the grantee keep such activities separate and distinct from Title X activities. Title X expressly distinguishes between a Title X *grantee* and a Title X *project*. The grantee, which normally is a health care organization, may receive funds from a variety of sources for a variety of purposes. The grantee receives Title X funds, however, for the specific and limited purpose of establishing and operating a Title X project. 42 U.S.C. § 300(a). The regulations govern the scope of the Title X *project's* activities, and leave the grantee unfettered in its other activities. The Title X *grantee* can continue to perform abortions, provide abortion-related services, and engage in abortion advocacy; it simply is required to conduct those activities through programs that are separate and independent from the project that receives Title X funds.

In contrast, our "unconstitutional conditions" cases involve situations in which the government has placed a condition on the *recipient* of the subsidy rather than on a particular program or service, thus effectively prohibiting the recipient from engaging in the protected conduct outside the scope of the federally funded program. [By] requiring that the Title X grantee engage in abortion-related activity separately from activity receiving federal funding, Congress has, consistent with our teachings in *League of Women Voters* and *Regan,* not denied it the right to engage in abortion-related activities. Congress has merely refused to fund such activities out of the public fisc, and the Secretary has simply required a certain degree of separation from the Title X project in order to ensure the integrity of the federally funded program.

The same principles apply to petitioners' claim that the regulations abridge the free speech rights of the grantee's staff. Individuals who are voluntarily employed for a Title X project must perform their duties in accordance with the regulation's restrictions on abortion counseling and referral. The employees remain free, however, to pursue abortion-related activities when they are not acting under the auspices of the Title X project. The regulations, which govern solely the scope of the Title X project's activities, do not in any way restrict the activities of those persons acting as private individuals. The employees' freedom of expression is limited during the time that they actually work for the project; but this limitation is a consequence of their decision to accept employment in a project, the scope of which is permissibly restricted by the funding authority.

This is not to suggest that funding by the Government, even when coupled with the freedom of the fund recipients to speak outside the scope of the Government-funded project, is invariably sufficient to justify government control over the content of expression. For example, this Court has recognized that the existence of a Government "subsidy," in the form of Government-owned property, does not justify the restriction of speech in areas that have "been traditionally open to the public for expressive activity," or have been "expressly dedicated to speech activity." Similarly, we have recognized that the university is a traditional sphere of free expression so fundamental to the functioning of our society that the Government's ability to control speech within that sphere by means of conditions attached to the expenditure of Government funds is restricted by the vagueness and overbreadth doctrines of the First Amendment, *Keyishian v. Board of Regents* Ch. 9, II. It could be argued by analogy that traditional relationships such as that between doctor and patient should enjoy protection under the First Amendment from government regulation, even when subsidized by the Government. We need not resolve that question here, however, because the Title X program regulations do not significantly impinge upon the doctor-patient relationship. Nothing in them requires a doctor to represent as his own any opinion that he does not in fact hold. Nor is the doctor-patient relationship established by the Title X program sufficiently all-encompassing so as to justify an expectation on the part of the patient of comprehensive medical advice. The program does not provide post-conception medical care, and therefore a doctor's silence with regard to abortion cannot reasonably be thought to mislead a client into thinking that the doctor does not consider abortion an appropriate option for her. The doctor is always free to make clear that advice regarding abortion is simply beyond the scope of the program. In these circumstances, the general rule that the Government may choose not to subsidize speech applies with full force. * * *

JUSTICE BLACKMUN, with whom JUSTICE MARSHALL joins, with whom JUSTICE STEVENS joins as to Parts II[d] and III,[e] and with whom JUSTICE O'CONNOR joins as to Part I,[f] dissenting. * * *

II

A

Until today, the Court never has upheld viewpoint-based suppression of speech simply because that suppression was a condition upon the acceptance of public funds. Whatever may be the Government's power to condition the receipt of its largess upon the relinquishment of constitutional rights, it surely does not extend to a condition that suppresses the recipient's cherished freedom of speech based solely upon the content or viewpoint of that speech. * * *

It cannot seriously be disputed that the counseling and referral provisions at issue in the present cases constitute content-based regulation of speech. Title X grantees may provide counseling and referral regarding any of a wide range of family planning and other topics, save abortion.

The Regulations are also clearly viewpoint-based. While suppressing speech favorable to abortion with one hand, the Secretary compels anti-abortion speech with the other. For example, the Department of Health and Human Services' own description of the Regulations makes plain that "Title X projects are *required* to facilitate access to prenatal care and social services, including adoption services, that might be needed by the pregnant client to promote her well-being and that of her child, while making it abundantly clear that the project is not permitted to promote abortion by facilitating access to abortion through the referral process." 53 Fed.Reg. 2927 (1988) (emphasis added).

Moreover, the Regulations command that a project refer for prenatal care each woman diagnosed as pregnant, irrespective of the woman's expressed desire to continue or terminate her pregnancy. 42 CFR § 59.8(a)(2) (1990). If a client asks directly about abortion, a Title X physician or

---

d. Part II discussed freedom of speech and portions of it are set out below.

e. Part III argued that the regulations violated the fifth amendment due process clause.

f. Part I contended that the regulations were not authorized by the statute. O'Connor, and Stevens, JJ., each filed separate dissents advancing the same contention.

counselor is required to say, in essence, that the project does not consider abortion to be an appropriate method of family planning. § 59.8(b)(4). Both requirements are antithetical to the First Amendment. See *Wooley v. Maynard* [Ch. 9, I infra].

The Regulations pertaining to "advocacy" are even more explicitly viewpoint-based. These provide: "A Title X project may not *encourage, promote or advocate* abortion as a method of family planning." § 59.10 (emphasis added). They explain: "This requirement prohibits actions to *assist* women to obtain abortions or *increase* the availability or accessibility of abortion for family planning purposes." § 59.10(a) (emphasis added). The Regulations do not, however, proscribe or even regulate anti-abortion advocacy. These are clearly restrictions aimed at the suppression of "dangerous ideas."

Remarkably, the majority concludes that "the Government has not discriminated on the basis of viewpoint; it has merely chosen to fund one activity to the exclusion of another." But the majority's claim that the Regulations merely limit a Title X project's speech to preventive or preconceptional services rings hollow in light of the broad range of nonpreventive services that the Regulations authorize Title X projects to provide.[2] By refusing to fund those family-planning projects that advocate abortion *because* they advocate abortion, the Government plainly has targeted a particular viewpoint. The majority's reliance on the fact that the Regulations pertain solely to funding decisions simply begs the question. Clearly, there are some bases upon which government may not rest its decision to fund or not to fund. For example, the Members of the majority surely would agree that government may not base its decision to support an activity upon considerations of race. As demonstrated above, our cases make clear that ideological viewpoint is a similarly repugnant ground upon which to base funding decisions.

The majority's reliance upon *Regan* in this connection is [misplaced]. That case stands for the proposition that government has no obligation to subsidize a private party's efforts to petition the legislature regarding its views. Thus, if the challenged Regulations were confined to non-ideological limitations upon the use of Title X funds for lobbying activities, there would exist no violation of the First Amendment. The advocacy Regulations at issue here, however, are not limited to lobbying but extend to all speech having the effect of encouraging, promoting, or advocating abortion as a method of family planning. § 59.10(a). Thus, in addition to their impermissible focus upon the viewpoint of regulated speech, the provisions intrude upon a wide range of communicative conduct, including the very words spoken to a woman by her physician. By manipulating the content of the doctor/patient dialogue, the Regulations upheld today force each of the petitioners "to be an instrument for fostering public adherence to an

2. In addition to requiring referral for prenatal care and adoption services, the Regulations permit general health services such as physical examinations, screening for breast cancer, treatment of gynecological problems, and treatment for sexually transmitted diseases. 53 Fed.Reg. 2927 (1988). None of the latter are strictly preventive, preconceptional services.

ideological point of view [he or she] finds unacceptable." *Wooley v. Maynard.* This type of intrusive, ideologically based regulation of speech goes far beyond the narrow lobbying limitations approved in *Regan,* and cannot be justified simply because it is a condition upon the receipt of a governmental benefit.[3]

B

The Court concludes that the challenged Regulations do not violate the First Amendment rights of Title X staff members because any limitation of the employees' freedom of expression is simply a consequence of their decision to accept employment at a federally funded project. Ante, at 22. But it has never been sufficient to justify an otherwise unconstitutional condition upon public employment that the employee may escape the condition by relinquishing his or her job.

The majority attempts to circumvent this principle by emphasizing that Title X physicians and counselors "remain free * * * to pursue abortion-related activities when they are not acting under the auspices of the Title X project." "The regulations," the majority explains, "do not in any way restrict the activities of those persons acting as private individuals." Under the majority's reasoning, the First Amendment could be read to tolerate *any* governmental restriction upon an employee's speech so long as that restriction is limited to the funded workplace. This is a dangerous proposition, and one the Court has rightly rejected in the past.

In *Abood,* it was no answer to the petitioners' claim of compelled speech as a condition upon public employment that their speech outside the workplace remained unregulated by the State.[g] Nor was the public employee's First Amendment claim in *Rankin v. McPherson,* derogated because the communication that her employer sought to punish occurred during business hours.[h] At the least, such conditions require courts to balance the speaker's

---

3. The majority attempts to obscure the breadth of its decision through its curious contention that "the Title X program regulations do not significantly impinge upon the doctor-patient relationship." That the doctor-patient relationship is substantially burdened by a rule prohibiting the dissemination by the physician of pertinent medical information is beyond serious dispute. This burden is undiminished by the fact that the relationship at issue here is not an "all-encompassing" one. A woman seeking the services of a Title X clinic has every reason to expect, as do we all, that her physician will not withhold relevant information regarding the very purpose of her visit. To suggest otherwise is to engage in un-informed fantasy. Further, to hold that the doctor-patient relationship is somehow incomplete where a patient lacks the resources to seek comprehensive healthcare

from a single provider is to ignore the situation of a vast number of Americans. As Justice Marshall has noted in a different context: "It is perfectly proper for judges to disagree about what the Constitution requires. But it is disgraceful for an interpretation of the Constitution to be premised upon unfounded assumptions about how people live." *United States v. Kras,* 409 U.S. 434, 93 S.Ct. 631, 34 L.Ed.2d 626 (1973) (dissenting opinion).

g. *Abood v. Detroit Board of Education* (compelled funding of ideological activities of union violates freedom of speech).

h. *Rankin v. McPherson* (expressed hope that assassination attempt of president be successful is protected speech when uttered in private to fellow employee during working hours).

interest in the message against those of government in preventing its dissemination.

In the cases at bar, the speaker's interest in the communication is both clear and vital. In addressing the family-planning needs of their clients, the physicians and counselors who staff Title X projects seek to provide them with the full range of information and options regarding their health and reproductive freedom. Indeed, the legitimate expectations of the patient and the ethical responsibilities of the medical profession demand no less. "The patient's right of self-decision can be effectively exercised only if the patient possesses enough information to enable an intelligent choice. * * * The physician has an ethical obligation to help the patient make choices from among the therapeutic alternatives consistent with good medical practice." Current Opinions, the Council on Ethical and Judicial Affairs of the American Medical Association ¶ 8.08 (1989). * * *

The Government's articulated interest in distorting the doctor/patient dialogue—ensuring that federal funds are not spent for a purpose outside the scope of the program—falls far short of that necessary to justify the suppression of truthful information and professional medical opinion regarding constitutionally protected conduct.[4] Moreover, the offending Regulation is not narrowly tailored to serve this interest. For example, the governmental interest at stake could be served by imposing rigorous bookkeeping standards to ensure financial separation or adopting content-neutral rules for the balanced dissemination of family-planning and health information. By failing to balance or even to consider the free speech interests claimed by Title X physicians against the Government's asserted interest in suppressing the speech, the Court falters in its duty to implement the protection that the First Amendment clearly provides for this important message.

C

Finally, it is of no small significance that the speech the Secretary would suppress is truthful information regarding constitutionally protected conduct of vital importance to the listener. One can imagine no legitimate governmental interest that might be served by suppressing such information. * * *

Notes and Questions

1. *Free speech?* Is the problem in *Rust* one of free speech or of the right to secure an abortion? Consider Greene, *Government of the Good,* 53 Vand. L.Rev. 1, 5 (2000): "Should it be improper as a matter of political theory, or unconstitutional, for government to condition the funding of health clinics on their advocating condom use by teens?"

2. *Political Speech.* Are there first amendment limits on the extent to which government can subsidize political speech. Suppose government itself

---

4. It is to be noted that the Secretary has made no claim that the Regulations at issue reflect any concern for the health or welfare of Title X clients.

enters the political fray. Should a city government be able to buy media time to speak on behalf of candidates? To influence the outcome of initiative campaigns?[i]

3. *Managerial domains.* Consider Post, *Subsidized Speech,* 106 Yale L.J. 151, 164 (1996): "Public discourse must be distinguished from ['manage-rial'] domains * * * Within managerial domains, the state organizes its resources so as to achieve specified ends. The constitutional value of manage-rial domains is that of instrumental rationality, a value that conceptualizes persons as means to an end rather than as autonomous agents. * * * Within managerial domains, therefore, ends may be imposed upon persons.

"Managerial domains are necessary so that a democratic state can actually achieve objectives that have been democratically agreed upon. * * * Thus the state can regulate speech within public educational institutions so as to achieve the purposes of education; it can regulate speech within the judicial system so as to attain the ends of justice; it can regulate speech within the military so as to preserve the national defense; it can regulate the speech of government employees so as to promote ' "the efficiency of the public services [the government] performs through its employees" '; and so forth.

"As a result of this instrumental orientation, viewpoint discrimination occurs frequently within managerial domains. To give but a few obvious examples: the president may fire cabinet officials who publicly challenge rather than support Administration policies; the military may discipline officers who publicly attack rather than uphold the principle of civilian control over the armed forces; public defenders who prosecute instead of defend their clients may be sanctioned; prison guards who encourage instead of condemn drug use may be chastised. Viewpoint discrimination occurs within managerial domains whenever the attainment of legitimate manageri-al objectives requires it.

"[Clearly], First Amendment doctrine within managerial domains differs fundamentally from First Amendment doctrine within public discourse."[j]

---

i. For relevant commentary, see Yudof, *When Government Speaks: Politics, Law, and Government Expression in America* (1983); Cole, *Beyond Unconstitutional Conditions: Charting Spheres of Neutrality in Government–Funded Speech,* 67 N.Y.U.L.Rev. 675 (1992). Delgado, *The Language of the Arms Race,* 64 B.U.L.Rev. 961 (1984); Emerson, *The Affirmative Side of the First Amendment,* 15 Ga.L.Rev. 795 (1981); Kamenshine, *The First Amendment's Implied Political Establishment Clause,* 67 Calif.L.Rev. 1104 (1979); Shiffrin, *Government Speech,* 27 U.C.L.A.L.Rev. 565 (1980); Redish & Kessler, *Government Subsidies and Free Expression,* 80 Minn. L.Rev. 543 (1996); Schauer, *Book Review,*

35 Stan.L.Rev. 373 (1983); Yudof, *When Governments Speak: Toward A Theory of Government Expression and the First Amendment,* 57 Tex.L.Rev. 863 (1979); Ziegler, *Government Speech and the Constitution: The Limits of Official Partisanship,* 21 B.C.L.Rev. 578 (1980); Note, *The Constitutionality of Municipal Advocacy in Statewide Referendum Campaigns,* 93 Harv. L.Rev. 535 (1980).

j. For similar first amendment perspectives, see Baker, *Campaign Expenditures and Free Speech,* 33 Harv. C.R.-C.L.Rev. 1 (1998)(referring to bounded contexts); Halberstam, *Commercial Speech, Professional Speech, and the Constitutional Status of*

Is the *Rust* situation an appropriate instance to invoke the managerial domain perspective? Or does it matter that the speakers whose speech is limited are not bureaucrats, but professionals who "must always qualify their loyalty and commitment to the vertical hierarchy of an organization by their horizontal commitment to general professional norms and standards." See id. at 172.

4. *Private speakers.* Consider Gey, *Reopening the Public Forum—From Sidewalks to Cyberspace,* 58 Ohio St. L. J. 1535, 1601 (1998), "[C]ertainly the government may express its point of view on any matter of public policy. Indeed, creating public policy, informing the public about the policy's content, and defending the policy against political opponents is the central purpose of a democratic government. But extending the capacity of the government to control speech beyond the narrow confines of the government itself—that is, beyond the agencies of government, individuals who are elected members of the government, or employees of the government speaking on the government's behalf—is neither necessary to the process of governing nor consistent with the democratic premise that no government can use its general policymaking authority to suppress or overwhelm its opposition and thereby perpetuate its control of the government indefinitely.

"It is crucial to remember that references to speech by 'the government' are really references to the speech of whatever political faction happened to capture control of the government at the last election. One of the primary purposes of the First Amendment is to ensure that the political faction that won the last election does not abuse the legitimate power it obtains from that victory to manipulate the results of the next election. Therefore, it is necessary to impose strict limits on any victorious faction's ability to 'speak' on behalf of the government."

5. *Deception.* Consider Roberts, *Rust v. Sullivan and the Control of Knowledge,* 61 Geo.Wash.L.Rev. 587, 594–95 (1993): "[P]regnancy may accelerate the progression of certain serious medical conditions, such as heart disease, hypertension, diabetes, sickle cell anemia, cancer and AIDS. For example, a woman with diabetic retinopathy who becomes pregnant may go blind. The regulations prohibited doctors from advising women suffering from these conditions that abortion may reduce the long-term risks to their health. Moreover, the recommendation of prenatal care may give the false impression that pregnancy does not jeopardize these women's health."

6. *Domination.* Note, *Unconstitutional Conditions as "Nonsubsidies": When is Deference Inappropriate?* 80 Geo.L.J. 131, 135 (1991): "*Rust* was wrongly decided because the government's domination of the entire family

Social Institutions, 147 U.Pa.L.Rev. 771 (1991)(referring to bounded speech institutions). For sympathetic criticism, see Tushnet, *The Possibilites of Comparative Constitutional Law,* 108 Yale L.J. 1225 (1999). On the other hand, are their circumstances in which the problem of government sup-

ported speech should be regarded as outside the managerial domain and inside the realm of distributive justice where individuals are not treated as a means to an end? See Heyman, *State-Supported Speech,* 1999 Wisc. L.Rev. 1119, 1139–40.

planning dialogue for many of those who seek such information has made private alternatives unavailable. Poor women have a right to this information because the Constitution respects the interests of those who want to receive a particular message, not just the interests of those who speak. In the limited context of the exchange between the family planning counselor and the poor pregnant woman who wants information concerning a range of options, government has gone far toward creating a monopoly. By contrast, a broad portion of government's speech-related subsidies, such as those for the Kennedy Center, do not involve 'crowding out' of private alternatives and thus do not raise analogous First Amendment concerns."

7. *Rust distinguished.* The University of Virginia subsidized the printing costs of a wide variety of student organizations, but refused to fund religious publications (those that "primarily promote or manifest a particular belief in or about a deity or an ultimate reality"). ROSENBERGER v. RECTOR OF THE UNIVERSITY OF VIRGINIA, 515 U.S. 819, 115 S.Ct. 2510, 132 L.Ed.2d 700 (1995), per KENNEDY, J., held that the refusal to fund religious speech violated the free speech clause: "[In *Rust*] the government did not create a program to encourage private speech but instead used private speakers to transmit specific information pertaining to its own program. We recognized that when the government appropriates public funds to promote a particular policy of its own it is entitled to say what it wishes.

"It does not follow, however, * * * that viewpoint-based restrictions are proper when the University does not itself speak or subsidize transmittal of a message it favors but instead expends funds to encourage a diversity of views from private speakers."[k]

Souter, J., joined by Stevens, Ginsburg and Breyer, JJ., dissented: "If the Guidelines were written or applied so as to limit only such Christian advocacy and no other evangelical efforts that might compete with it, the discrimination would be based on viewpoint. But that is not what the regulation authorizes; it applies to Muslim and Jewish and Buddhist advocacy as well as to Christian. And since it limits funding to activities promoting or manifesting a particular belief not only "in" but "about" a deity or ultimate reality, it applies to agnostics and atheists as well as it does to deists and theists. The Guidelines * * * thus do not skew debate by funding one position but not its competitors. [T]hey simply deny funding for hortatory speech that 'primarily promotes or manifests' any view on the merits of religion; they deny funding for the entire subject matter of religious apologetics."[l]

---

k. O'Connor, J., and Thomas, J., filed concurring opinions.

l. For commentary on whether the Virginia practice constitutes viewpoint discrimination, see Greenawalt, *Viewpoints From Olympus,* 96 Colum. L.Rev. 697 (1996).

In 1989 the National Endowment for the Arts ("NEA") supported two artists whose work sparked controversy: Robert Mapplethorpe's exhibit, *The Perfect Moment*, included homoerotic photographs; Andres Serrano's photograph, *Piss Christ*, showed a crucifix immersed in urine. In reaction, Congress reduced appropriations in 1990 by the amount that had been granted to the two recipients and took a number of steps leading up to the passage of Title 20 U.S.C. § 954(d) which provided that, "No payment shall be made under this section except upon application therefor which is submitted to the National Endowment for the Arts in accordance with regulations issued and procedures established by the Chairperson. In establishing such regulations and procedures, the Chairperson shall ensure that (1) artistic excellence and artistic merit are the criteria by which applications are judged, taking into consideration general standards of decency and respect for the diverse beliefs and values of the American public; and (2) applications are consistent with the purposes of this section. Such regulations and procedures shall clearly indicate that obscenity is without artistic merit, is not protected speech, and shall not be funded."

The National Council on the Arts which advises the NEA Chairperson resolved to implement the provision by ensuring that the panels conducting initial reviews of grant applications represent geographic, ethnic, and aesthetic diversity, and the Chairperson agreed. Several artists, whose grant applications had been approved before the passage of § 954(d), but reconsidered and denied afterwards, brought suit, challenging § 954(d)(1) on its face. The district court and the court of appeals declared § 954(d)(1) unconstitutional.

NATIONAL ENDOWMENT FOR THE ARTS v. FINLEY, 524 U.S. 569, 118 S.Ct. 2168, 141 L.Ed.2d 500 (1998), per O'CONNOR, J., joined by Rehnquist, C.J., and Stevens, Kennedy, and Breyer, JJ.,[a] upheld § 954(d)(1) maintaining that it did not impermissibly discriminate on the basis of point of view and was not unconstitutionally vague: "Respondents argue that the provision is a paradigmatic example of viewpoint discrimination because it rejects any artistic speech that either fails to respect mainstream values or offends standards of decency. The premise of respondents' claim is that § 954(d)(1) constrains the agency's ability to fund certain categories of artistic expression. The NEA, however, reads the provision as merely hortatory, and contends that it stops well short of an absolute restriction. Section 954(d)(1) adds 'considerations' to the grant-making process; it does not preclude awards to projects that might be deemed 'indecent' or 'disrespectful,' nor place conditions on grants, or even specify that those factors must be given any particular weight in reviewing an application. Indeed, the agency asserts that it has adequately implemented § 954(d)(1) merely by ensuring the representation of various backgrounds and points of view on the advisory panels that analyze grant applications. We do not decide wheth-

a. Ginsburg, J., also joined O'Connor, J.'s opinion except for the paragraph accompanying footnote b infra.

er the NEA's view—that the formulation of diverse advisory panels is sufficient to comply with Congress' command—is in fact a reasonable reading of the statute. It is clear, however, that the text of § 954(d)(1) imposes no categorical requirement. The advisory language stands in sharp contrast to congressional efforts to prohibit the funding of certain classes of speech. When Congress has in fact intended to affirmatively constrain the NEA's grant-making authority, it has done so in no uncertain terms. See § 954(d)(2) ('[O]bscenity is without artistic merit, is not protected speech, and shall not be funded').

"Furthermore, like the plain language of § 954(d), the political context surrounding the adoption of the 'decency and respect' clause is inconsistent with respondents' assertion that the provision compels the NEA to deny funding on the basis of viewpoint discriminatory criteria. The legislation was a bipartisan proposal introduced as a counterweight to amendments aimed at eliminating the NEA's funding or substantially constraining its grant-making authority. [B]efore the vote on § 954(d)(1), one of its sponsors stated: 'If we have done one important thing in this amendment, it is this. We have maintained the integrity of freedom of expression in the United States.'

"That § 954(d)(1) admonishes the NEA merely to take 'decency and respect' into consideration, and that the legislation was aimed at reforming procedures rather than precluding speech, undercut respondents' argument that the provision inevitably will be utilized as a tool for invidious viewpoint discrimination.

"Respondents' claim that the provision is facially unconstitutional may be reduced to the argument that the criteria in § 954(d)(1) are sufficiently subjective that the agency could utilize them to engage in viewpoint discrimination. Given the varied interpretations of the criteria and the vague exhortation to 'take them into consideration,' it seems unlikely that this provision will introduce any greater element of selectivity than the determination of 'artistic excellence' itself. * * *

"Any content-based considerations that may be taken into account in the grant-making process are a consequence of the nature of arts funding. The NEA has limited resources and it must deny the majority of the grant applications that it receives, including many that propose 'artistically excellent' projects. The agency may decide to fund particular projects for a wide variety of reasons, 'such as the technical proficiency of the artist, the creativity of the work, the anticipated public interest in or appreciation of the work, the work's contemporary relevance, its educational value, its suitability for or appeal to special audiences (such as children or the disabled), its service to a rural or isolated community, or even simply that the work could increase public knowledge of an art form.'

"Respondent's reliance on our decision in *Rosenberger v. Rector and Visitors of Univ. of Va.*, 515 U.S. 819, 115 S.Ct. 2510, 132 L.Ed.2d 700 (1995), is therefore misplaced. In *Rosenberger*, a public university declined to authorize disbursements from its Student Activities Fund to finance the

ROSENBERGER

printing of a Christian student newspaper. We held that by subsidizing the Student Activities Fund, the University had created a limited public forum, from which it impermissibly excluded all publications with religious editorial viewpoints. Although the scarcity of NEA funding does not distinguish this case from *Rosenberger*, the competitive process according to which the grants are allocated does. In the context of arts funding, in contrast to many other subsidies, the Government does not indiscriminately 'encourage a diversity of views from private speakers.' The NEA's mandate is to make aesthetic judgments, and the inherently content-based 'excellence' threshold for NEA support sets it apart from the subsidy at issue in *Rosenberger*—which was available to all student organizations that were 'related to the educational purpose of the University'—and from comparably objective decisions on allocating public benefits, such as access to a school auditorium or a municipal theater, see *Lamb's Chapel v. Center Moriches Union Free School Dist.*, 508 U.S. 384, 386, 113 S.Ct. 2141, 124 L.Ed.2d 352 (1993); *Southeastern Promotions, Ltd. v. Conrad*, 420 U.S. 546, 555, 95 S.Ct. 1239, 43 L.Ed.2d 448 (1975), or the second class mailing privileges available to 'all newspapers and other periodical publications,' see *Hannegan v. Esquire, Inc.*, 327 U.S. 146, 148, n. 1, 66 S.Ct. 456, 90 L.Ed. 586 (1946).

"Respondents do not allege discrimination in any particular funding decision. * * * Thus, we have no occasion here to address an as-applied challenge in a situation where the denial of a grant may be shown to be the product of invidious viewpoint discrimination. If the NEA were to leverage its power to award subsidies on the basis of subjective criteria into a penalty on disfavored viewpoints, then we would confront a different case. We have stated that, even in the provision of subsidies, the Government may not 'ai[m] at the suppression of dangerous ideas,' and if a subsidy were 'manipulated' to have a 'coercive effect,' then relief could be appropriate. * * * Unless and until § 954(d)(1) is applied in a manner that raises concern about the suppression of disfavored viewpoints, however, we uphold the constitutionality of the provision.

"Finally, although the First Amendment certainly has application in the subsidy context, we note that the Government may allocate competitive funding according to criteria that would be impermissible were direct regulation of speech or a criminal penalty at stake. So long as legislation does not infringe on other constitutionally protected rights, Congress has wide latitude to set spending priorities. See *Regan v. Taxation with Representation of Wash.*, 461 U.S. 540, 549, 103 S.Ct. 1997, 76 L.Ed.2d 129 (1983). In the 1990 Amendments that incorporated § 954(d)(1), Congress modified the declaration of purpose in the NEA's enabling act to provide that arts funding should 'contribute to public support and confidence in the use of taxpayer funds,' and that '[p]ublic funds ... must ultimately serve public purposes the Congress defines.' § 951(5). And as we held in *Rust*, Congress may 'selectively fund a program to encourage certain activities it believes to be in the public interest, without at the same time funding an alternative program which seeks to deal with the problem in another way.' In doing so, 'the Government has not discriminated on the basis of viewpoint; it has merely chosen to fund one activity to the exclusion of the other.'[b]

"The lower courts also erred in invalidating § 954(d)(1) as unconstitutionally vague. * * * The terms of the provision are undeniably opaque, and if they appeared in a criminal statute or regulatory scheme, they could raise substantial vagueness concerns. It is unlikely, however, that speakers will be compelled to steer too far clear of any 'forbidden area' in the context of grants of this nature. But when the Government is acting as patron rather than as sovereign, the consequences of imprecision are not constitutionally severe.

"In the context of selective subsidies, it is not always feasible for Congress to legislate with clarity. Indeed, if this statute is unconstitutionally vague, then so too are all government programs awarding scholarships and grants on the basis of subjective criteria such as 'excellence.' To accept respondents' vagueness argument would be to call into question the constitutionality of these valuable government programs and countless others like them.

"Section 954(d)(1) merely adds some imprecise considerations to an already subjective selection process. It does not, on its face, impermissibly infringe on First or Fifth Amendment rights."

SCALIA, J., joined by Thomas, J., concurred in the judgment: " 'The operation was a success, but the patient died.' What such a procedure is to medicine, the Court's opinion in this case is to law. It sustains the constitutionality of 20 U.S.C. § 954(d)(1) by gutting it. The most avid congressional opponents of the provision could not have asked for more. I write separately because, unlike the Court, I think that § 954(d)(1) must be evaluated as written, rather than as distorted by the agency it was meant to control. By its terms, it establishes content-and viewpoint-based criteria upon which grant applications are to be evaluated. And that is perfectly constitutional.

"[The statute means what it says. Under the statute, the] application reviewers must take into account 'general standards of decency' and 'respect for the diverse beliefs and values of the American public' when evaluating artistic excellence and merit. One can regard this as either suggesting that decency and respect are elements of what Congress regards as artistic excellence and merit, or as suggesting that decency and respect are factors to be taken into account in addition to artistic excellence and merit. But either way, it is entirely, 100% clear that decency and respect are to be taken into account in evaluating applications.

"This is so apparent that I am at a loss to understand what the Court has in mind (other than the gutting of the statute) when it speculates that the statute is merely 'advisory.' General standards of decency and respect for Americans' beliefs and values *must* (for the statute says that the Chairper-

b. Ginsburg, J., joined O'Connor, J.'s opinion with the exception of the paragraph accompanying this footnote.

son 'shall ensure' this result) be taken into account [in] evaluating all applications. This does not mean that those factors must always be dispositive, but it *does* mean that they must always be considered. The method of compliance proposed by the National Endowment for the Arts (NEA)— selecting diverse review panels of artists and nonartists that reflect a wide range of geographic and cultural perspectives—is so obviously inadequate that it insults the intelligence. A diverse panel membership increases the odds that, *if and when* the panel takes the factors into account, it will reach an accurate assessment of what they demand. But it in no way increases the odds that the panel *will* take the factors into consideration—much less *ensures* that the panel will do so, which is the Chairperson's duty under the statute. Moreover, the NEA's fanciful reading of § 954(d)(1) would make it wholly superfluous. Section 959(c) already requires the Chairperson to 'issue regulations and establish procedures ... to ensure that all panels are composed, to the extent practicable, of individuals reflecting ... diverse artistic and cultural points of view.'

"I agree with the Court that § 954(d)(1) 'imposes no categorical requirement' in the sense that it does not require the denial of all applications that violate general standards of decency or exhibit disrespect for the diverse beliefs and values of Americans. Compare § 954(d)(2) ('[O]bscenity ... shall not be funded'). But the factors need not be conclusive to be discriminatory. To the extent a particular applicant exhibits disrespect for the diverse beliefs and values of the American public or fails to comport with general standards of decency, the likelihood that he will receive a grant diminishes. In other words, the presence of the 'tak[e] into consideration' clause 'cannot be regarded as mere surplusage; it means something.' And the 'something' is that the decision maker, all else being equal, will favor applications that display decency and respect, and disfavor applications that do not.

"This unquestionably constitutes viewpoint discrimination.[1] That conclusion is not altered by the fact that the statute does not 'compe[l]' the denial of funding any more than a provision imposing a five-point handicap on all black applicants for civil service jobs is saved from being race discrimination by the fact that it does not compel the rejection of black applicants. If viewpoint discrimination in this context is unconstitutional (a point I shall address anon), the law is invalid unless there are some situations in which the decency and respect factors *do not constitute viewpoint discrimination*. And there is none. [T]he conclusion of viewpoint discrimination is not affected by the fact that what constitutes 'decency' or 'the diverse beliefs and values of the American people' is difficult to pin down—any more than a civil-service preference in favor of those who display 'Republican-party values' would be rendered nondiscriminatory by the fact

---

1. [O]ne might argue that the decency and respect factors constitute content discrimination rather than viewpoint discrimination, which would render them easier to uphold. Since I believe this statute must be upheld in either event, I pass over this conundrum and assume the worst.

that there is plenty of room for argument as to what Republican-party values might be.

"The 'political context surrounding the adoption of the "decency and respect" clause,' [does] not change its meaning or affect its constitutionality. All that is proved by the various statements [from] the floor debates is (1) that the provision was not meant categorically to exclude any particular viewpoint (which I have conceded, and which is plain from the text), and (2) that the language was not meant to do anything that is unconstitutional. That in no way propels the Court's leap to the countertextual conclusion that the provision was merely 'aimed at reforming procedures,' and cannot be 'utilized as a tool for invidious viewpoint discrimination.' It is evident in the legislative history that § 954(d)(1) was prompted by, and directed at, the public funding of such offensive productions as Serrano's 'Piss Christ,' the portrayal of a crucifix immersed in urine, and Mapplethorpe's show of lurid homoerotic photographs. Thus, even if one strays beyond the plain text it is perfectly clear that the statute was meant to disfavor—that is, to discriminate against—such productions. Not to ban their funding absolutely, to be sure (though as I shall discuss, that also would not have been unconstitutional); but to make their funding more difficult.

"More fundamentally, of course, all this legislative history has no valid claim upon our attention at all. It is a virtual certainty that very few of the Members of Congress who voted for this language both (1) knew of, and (2) agreed with, the various statements that the Court has culled from * * * the floor debate (probably conducted on an almost empty floor). And it is wholly irrelevant that the statute was a 'bipartisan proposal introduced as a 'counterweight' to an alternative proposal that would directly restrict funding on the basis of viewpoint. We do not judge statutes as if we are surveying the scene of an accident; each one is reviewed, not on the basis of how much worse it could have been, but on the basis of what it says. It matters not whether this enactment was the product of the most partisan alignment in history or whether, upon its passage, the Members all linked arms and sang, 'The more we get together, the happier we'll be.' It is 'not consonant with our scheme of government for a court to inquire into the motives of legislators.' The law at issue in this case is to be found in the text of § 954(d)(1), which passed both Houses and was signed by the President. And that law unquestionably disfavors—discriminates against—indecency and disrespect for the diverse beliefs and values of the American people. * * *

"With the enactment of § 954(d)(1), Congress did not *abridge* the speech of those who disdain the beliefs and values of the American public, nor did it *abridge* indecent speech. Those who wish to create indecent and disrespectful art are as unconstrained now as they were before the enactment of this statute. Avant-garde artists such as respondents remain entirely free to epater les bourgeois; they are merely deprived of the additional satisfaction of having the bourgeoisie taxed to pay for it. * * *

"As we noted in *Rust,* when Congress chose to establish the National Endowment for Democracy it was not constitutionally required to fund programs encouraging competing philosophies of government—an example of funding discrimination that cuts much closer than this one to the core of political speech which is the primary concern of the First Amendment. It takes a particularly high degree of chutzpah for the NEA to contradict this proposition, since the agency itself discriminates—and is required by law to discriminate—in favor of artistic (as opposed to scientific, or political, or theological) expression. Not all the common folk, or even all great minds, for that matter, think that is a good idea. In 1800, when John Marshall told John Adams that a recent immigration of Frenchmen would include talented artists, 'Adams denounced all Frenchmen, but most especially "schoolmasters, painters, poets, & C." He warned Marshall that the fine arts were like germs that infected healthy constitutions.' J. Ellis, *After the Revolution: Profiles of Early American Culture* 36 (1979). Surely the NEA itself is nothing less than an institutionalized discrimination against that point of view. Nonetheless it is constitutional, as is the congressional determination to favor decency and respect for beliefs and values over the opposite.[3]

"The nub of the difference between me and the Court is that I regard the distinction between 'abridging' speech and funding it as a fundamental divide, on this side of which the First Amendment is inapplicable. The Court, by contrast, seems to believe that the First Amendment, despite its words, has some ineffable effect upon funding, imposing constraints of an indeterminate nature which it announces (without troubling to enunciate any particular test) are not violated by the statute here—or, more accurately, are not violated by the quite different, emasculated statute that it imagines."

Souter, J., dissented: "The decency and respect proviso mandates viewpoint-based decisions in the disbursement of government subsidies, and the Government has wholly failed to explain why the statute should be afforded an exemption from the fundamental rule of the First Amendment that viewpoint discrimination in the exercise of public authority over expressive activity is unconstitutional. * * *[2]

"[An argument] for avoiding unconstitutionality that the Court appears to regard with some favor is the Government's argument that the NEA may comply with § 954(d) merely by populating the advisory panels that analyze grant applications with members of diverse backgrounds. Would that it were

3. I suppose it would be unconstitutional for the government to give money to an organization devoted to the promotion of candidates nominated by the Republican party—but it would be just as unconstitutional for the government itself to promote candidates nominated by the Republican party, and I do not think that that unconstitutionality has anything to do with the First Amendment.

2. [Congress] has no obligation to support artistic enterprises that many people detest. The First Amendment speaks up only when Congress decides to participate in the Nation's artistic life by legal regulation, as it does through a subsidy scheme like the NEA. If Congress does choose to spend public funds in this manner, it may not discriminate by viewpoint in deciding who gets the money.

so easy; this asserted implementation of the law fails even to 'reflec[t] a plausible construction of the plain language of the statute.' *Rust*.

"The Government notes that § 954(d) actually provides that '[i]n establishing ... regulations and procedures, the Chairperson [of the NEA] shall ensure that (1) artistic excellence and artistic merit are the criteria by which applications are judged, taking into consideration general standards of decency and respect for the diverse beliefs and values of the American public.' According to the Government, this language requires decency and respect to be considered not in judging applications, but in making regulations. If, then, the Chairperson takes decency and respect into consideration through regulations ensuring diverse panels, the statute is satisfied. But it would take a great act of will to find any plausibility in this reading. The reference to considering decency and respect occurs in the subparagraph speaking to the 'criteria by which applications are judged,' not in the preamble directing the Chairperson to adopt regulations; it is in judging applications that decency and respect are most obviously to be considered. * * *

"[Another] try at avoiding constitutional problems is the Court's disclaimer of any constitutional issue here because '[s]ection 954(d)(1) adds "considerations" to the grant-making process; it does not preclude awards to projects that might be deemed "indecent" or "disrespectful," nor place conditions on grants, or even specify that those factors must be given any particular weight in reviewing an application.' * * *

"That is not a fair reading. Just as the statute cannot be read as anything but viewpoint based, or as requiring nothing more than diverse review panels, it cannot be read as tolerating awards to spread indecency or disrespect, so long as the review panel, the National Counsel on the Arts, and the Chairperson have given some thought to the offending qualities and decided to underwrite them anyway. That, after all, is presumably just what prompted the congressional outrage in the first place, and there was nothing naive about the Representative who said he voted for the bill because it does 'not tolerate wasting Federal funds for sexually explicit photographs [or] sacrilegious works.'

"But even if I found the Court's view of 'consideration' plausible, that would make no difference at all on the question of constitutionality. What if the statute required a panel to apply criteria 'taking into consideration the centrality of Christianity to the American cultural experience,' or 'taking into consideration whether the artist is a communist,' or 'taking into consideration the political message conveyed by the art,' or even 'taking into consideration the superiority of the white race'? Would the Court hold these considerations facially constitutional, merely because the statute had no requirement to give them any particular, much less controlling, weight? I assume not.

"A second basic strand in the Court's treatment of today's question and the heart of Justice Scalia's in effect assumes that whether or not the statute mandates viewpoint discrimination, there is no constitutional issue here because government art subsidies fall within a zone of activity free from

First Amendment restraints. The Government calls attention to the roles of government-as-speaker [in] which the government is of course entitled to engage in viewpoint discrimination: if the Food and Drug Administration launches an advertising campaign on the subject of smoking, it may condemn the habit without also having to show a cowboy taking a puff on the opposite page; and if the Secretary of Defense wishes to buy a portrait to decorate the Pentagon, he is free to prefer George Washington over George the Third.

"The Government freely admits, however, that it neither speaks through the expression subsidized by the NEA,[6] nor buys anything for itself with its NEA grants. On the contrary, believing that '[t]he arts ... reflect the high place accorded by the American people to the nation's rich cultural heritage,' § 951(6), and that '[i]t is vital to a democracy ... to provide financial assistance to its artists and the organizations that support their work,' § 951(10), the Government acts as a patron, financially underwriting the production of art by private artists and impresarios for independent consumption. Accordingly, the Government would have us liberate government-as-patron from First Amendment strictures not by placing it squarely within the categories of government-as-buyer or government-as-speaker, but by recognizing a new category by analogy to those accepted ones. The analogy is, however, a very poor fit, and this patronage falls embarrassingly on the wrong side of the line between government-as-buyer or-speaker and government-as-regulator-of-private-speech.

"[*Rosenberger*] controls here. The NEA, like the student activities fund in *Rosenberger*, is a subsidy scheme created to encourage expression of a diversity of views from private speakers. Congress brought the NEA into being to help all Americans 'achieve a better understanding of the past, a better analysis of the present, and a better view of the future.' § 951(3). The NEA's purpose is to 'support new ideas' and 'to help create and sustain ... a climate encouraging freedom of thought, imagination, and inquiry.' §§ 951(10),(7). Given this congressional choice to sustain freedom of expression, *Rosenberger* teaches that the First Amendment forbids decisions based on viewpoint popularity. So long as Congress chooses to subsidize expressive endeavors at large, it has no business requiring the NEA to turn down funding applications of artists and exhibitors who devote their 'freedom of thought, imagination, and inquiry' to defying our tastes, our beliefs, or our values. It may not use the NEA's purse to 'suppres[s] ... dangerous ideas.' *Regan v. Taxation with Representation.*

"The Court says otherwise, claiming to distinguish *Rosenberger* on the ground that the student activities funds in that case were generally available to most applicants, whereas NEA funds are disbursed selectively and competitively to a choice few. But the Court in *Rosenberger* anticipated and

---

6. Here, the "communicative element inherent in the very act of funding itself," *Rosenberger* (Souter, J., dissenting), is an endorsement of the importance of the arts collectively, not an endorsement of the individual message espoused in a given work of art.

specifically rejected just this distinction when it held in no uncertain terms that '[t]he government cannot justify viewpoint discrimination among private speakers on the economic fact of scarcity.'[8] Scarce money demands choices, of course, but choices 'on some acceptable [viewpoint] neutral principle,' like artistic excellence and artistic merit;[9] 'nothing in our decision[s] indicate[s] that scarcity would give the State the right to exercise viewpoint discrimination that is otherwise impermissible.'[10]."

Notes and Questions

1. Consider Bezanson, *The Government Speech Forum: Forbes and Finley and Government Speech Selection Judgments*, 83 Iowa L.Rev. 953, 969 (1998): "How can we know when government acts only to subsidize the expression of others with no communicative design of its own, as in *Rosenberger*, and when government's subsidy of others' speech is simply an efficient means of communicating the government's own expressive design? Are the answers to these questions important, as the Court's majority and Justice Souter in dissent believed, or are they irrelevant, as Justices Scalia and Thomas believed? These are the central questions posed by the *Finley* case."

2. Consider Cole, *Symposium: Art, Distribution & the State: Perspectives in the National Endowment for the Arts*, 17 Cardoza Arts & Ent.L.J. 705, 721 (1999): "[If] as Justice Scalia says, when the government funds rather than directly regulates speech, the First Amendment is simply irrelevant, then the public debate would be greatly impoverished * * *. The print press is subsidized by mailing privileges. The broadcast media is subsidized by free access to the air waves. Public broadcasting is also subsidized by tax payer dollars. Political organizations are subsidized by free access to public property for demonstrations. Non-profit organizations and advocacy groups are subsidized through tax exemptions. Public universities are subsidized through the public payroll. Private universities are subsidized through tax

8. The Court's attempt to avoid *Rosenberger* by describing NEA funding in terms of competition, not scarcity, will not work. Competition implies scarcity, without which there is no exclusive prize to compete for; the Court's 'competition' is merely a surrogate for 'scarcity.'

9. While criteria of 'artistic excellence and artistic merit' may raise intractable issues about the identification of artistic worth, and could no doubt be used covertly to filter out unwanted ideas, there is nothing inherently viewpoint discriminatory about such merit-based criteria. [Decency] and respect, on the other hand, are inherently and facially viewpoint based, and serve no legitimate and permissible end. The Court's assertion that the mere fact that grants must be awarded according to artistic merit precludes 'absolute neutrality'

on the part of the NEA is therefore misdirected. It is not to the point that the government necessarily makes choices among competing applications, or even that its judgments about artistic quality may be branded as subjective to some greater or lesser degree; the question here is whether the government may apply patently viewpoint-based criteria in making those choices.

10. [Leaving] aside the proper application of forum analysis to the NEA and its projects, I cannot agree that the holding of *Rosenberger* turned on characterizing its metaphorical forum as public in some degree. Like this case, *Rosenberger* involved viewpoint discrimination, and we have made it clear that such discrimination is impermissible in all forums, even non-public [ones].

subsidies, grants, and financial aid for students. That is where the public debate takes place—in the press, in the universities, and in political organizations. Every one of those organizations is ultimately speaking with government funds. If the government could impose whatever restrictions it wants on who gets funding to speak, we would have a much less free public debate."

3. If the government consistently with the first amendment can impose a point of view on bureaucrats or on doctors when they are subsidized with government funds (*Rust*), is it nonetheless barred from telling academics the point of view they can advance in the classroom? If so, should artists on panels be considered more like bureaucrats and doctors or more like academics. Is there a problem with giving special protection for some institutions and not others or some professionals and not others? How does one decide which actors favor some speech over other speech? See Schauer, *The Ontology of Censorship* in *Censorship and Silencing* 147 (Post ed. 1998). See generally Schauer, *Principles, Institutions, and the First Amendment,* 112 Harv. L.Rev. 84 (1998).[c]

4. Suppose the Endowment refuses to fund a work of considerable artistic merit on the ground that it is racist. Constitutional? If so, could one consistently argue that the Endowment could not constitutionally refuse to fund art on the ground that it is indecent? Consider also Heyman, *State-Supported Speech,* 1999 Wisc. L.Rev. 1119, 1139–40: "Suppose [a] state legislature becomes concerned about violence in popular culture and the impact it may have on young people. Instead of attempting to regulate violent entertainment, the legislature decides to create a program to support art and culture, with the proviso that no funds should be awarded to works that glorify violence. There can be little doubt that this would constitute viewpoint discrimination. Yet it seems highly implausible to suggest that if the government chooses to support non-violent art, it must support violent art as well. Instead, the proviso should be upheld on the same ground that Souter offers in defending criteria of artistic merit—that it serves a 'perfectly legitimate' governmental goal."[d]

II.　GOVERNMENT AS EDUCATOR
AND EDITOR

Oregon's Compulsory Education Act of 1922 required all students to attend public schools through the eighth grade.[a] Two operators of private

c. Are the issues involved in supporting some speech over other speech different in the sciences than the arts? See Wasserman, *Public Funding for Science and Art* in *Censorship and Silencing* 169 (Post ed. 1998).

d. For additional commentary, see Shiffrin, *Dissent, Injustice, and the Meanings of America* ch.1 (1999); Fiss, *State Activism*

and State Censorship, 100 Yale L.J. 2087, 2101 (1991); Sabrin, *Thinking About Content: Can It Play An Appropriate Role in Government Funding of the Arts?* 102 Yale L.J. 1209 (1993).

a. The statute provided exemptions for children with disabilities, or who had completed the eighth grade, or who lived con-

schools, the Society of the Sisters of the Holy Names of Jesus and Mary and the Hill Military Academy sought and secured an injunction against the act's enforcement. The governor of Oregon appealed.

PIERCE v. SOCIETY OF SISTERS, 268 U.S. 510, 45 S.Ct. 571, 69 L.Ed. 1070 (1925), per McREYNOLDS, J., held that the law violated the substantive due process rights of the parents and the schools: "The manifest purpose is to compel general attendance at public schools by normal children, between 8 and 16, who have not completed the eighth grade. * * * No question is raised concerning the power of the state reasonably to regulate all schools, to inspect, supervise and examine them, their teachers and pupils; to require that all children of proper age attend some school, that teachers shall be of good moral character and patriotic disposition, that certain studies plainly essential to good citizenship must be taught, and that nothing be taught which is manifestly inimical to the public welfare.

"The inevitable practical result of enforcing the act under consideration would be destruction of appellees' primary schools, and perhaps all other private primary schools for normal children within the state of Oregon. Appellees are engaged in a kind of undertaking not inherently harmful, but long regarded as useful and meritorious. Certainly there is nothing in the present records to indicate that they have failed to discharge their obligations to patrons, students, or the state. And there are no peculiar circumstances or present emergencies which demand extraordinary measures relative to primary education.

"Under the doctrine of *Meyer v. Nebraska*, 262 U.S. 390, 43 S.Ct. 625, 67 L.Ed. 1042, (1923), we think it entirely plain that the Act of 1922 unreasonably interferes with the liberty of parents and guardians to direct the upbringing and education of children under their control. * * * The fundamental theory of liberty upon which all governments in this Union repose excludes any general power of the state to standardize its children by forcing them to accept instruction from public teachers only. The child is not the mere creature of the state; those who nurture him and direct his destiny have the right, coupled with the high duty, to recognize and prepare him for additional obligations.

"Appellees are corporations, and therefore, it is said, they cannot claim for themselves the liberty which the Fourteenth Amendment guarantees. [But] they have business and property for which they claim protection. These are threatened with destruction through the unwarranted compulsion which appellants are exercising over present and prospective patrons of their schools. * * * Generally, it is entirely true, as urged by counsel, that no person in any business has such an interest in possible customers as to enable him to restrain exercise of proper power of the state upon the ground that he will be deprived of patronage. But the injunctions here sought are not against the exercise of any proper power. Appellees asked protection against arbitrary, unreasonable, and unlawful interference with their pa-

siderable distances from a public school, or who held a special permit from the county superintendent. The Court did not believe these exemptions were especially important.

trons and the consequent destruction of their business and property. Their interest is clear and immediate * * * ."

Notes and Questions

1. Apart from due process, did the Oregon law violate the free speech rights of the affected parents? The schools? The children?

2. Can a law like that in *Pierce* be defended on the ground that private schools siphon off the wealthy and the academically talented from the public schools while undermining a strong base of political support for generous financing of the schools?[b] On the ground that democratic education depends on schools that are integrated in terms of race, class, and religion?

3. If parents have a right to send their children to private schools, do they also have a right to have their children excused from instruction they find objectionable? If so, what limits, if any, accompany that right?[c] Do captive audiences of government speech have a first amendment right not to be propagandized? Do children educated in public schools have such a right? See Gottlieb, *In The Name of Patriotism: The Constitutionality of "Bending" History in Public Secondary Schools,* 62 N.Y.U.L.Rev. 497 (1987). If ad hoc methods of separating education from propaganda are unreliable, are any institutional structures or processes required? Should this be a constitutional right without a remedy?[d]

4. Is public education itself objectionable? Consider Mill, *On Liberty* 98 (Spitz ed. 1975): "A general State education is a mere contrivance for moulding people to be exactly like one another * * * . An education established and controlled by the State should only exist, if it exist at all, as one of many competing experiments carried on for the purpose of example and stimulus, to keep the others up to a certain standard of excellence."

5. Consider Yudof, *When Government Speaks: Politics, Law, and Government Expression in America* 229–230 (1983): "*Pierce* may be construed (whatever the original motivations of the justices) as telling governments that they are free to establish their own public schools and to make education compulsory for certain age groups, but not free to eliminate competing, private-sector educational institutions that may serve to create heterogeneity and to counter the state's dominance over the education of the young. * * * *Pierce* represents a reasonable, if imperfect, accommodation of

b. Is the empirical assumption correct, see Gutmann, *Democratic Education* 117 (1987).

c. See generally Stolzenberg, *"He Drew a Circle that Shut Me Out": Assimilation, Indoctrination, and the Paradox of a Liberal Education,* 106 Harv. L. Rev. 581 (1993). On parental free speech rights, see generally Gilles, *On Educating Children; a Parentalist Manifesto,* 63 U.Chi.L.Rev. 93 (1996).

d. Consider also captive audiences of prisoners, soldiers, or workers in public institutions. Do "informed consent" provisions concerning abortion raise first amendment captive audience issues? Cf. Public Utilities Comm'n v. Pollak, 343 U.S. 451, 72 S.Ct. 813, 96 L.Ed. 1068 (1952)(city transit company's playing of radio programs does not violate Constitution).

conflicting pressures. The state may promulgate its messages in the public school, while parents are free to choose private schools with different orientations. The state must tolerate private education, but need not fund it. The state may make some demands of private schools to satisfy compulsory schooling laws, but those demands may not be so excessive as to turn private schools into public schools managed and funded by the public sector. The integrity of the communications and socialization processes in private schools and families remains intact, while the state's interest in producing informed, educated, and productive citizens is not sacrificed.''

But consider Greene, *Why Vouchers are Constitutional and Why They are Not,* 13 Notre Dame J. of L.Ethics & Pub. Policy 397, 407 (1999): "[T]he *Pierce* assumption—although, in one view, assuring multiple repositories of power by counteracting the state's school monopoly—in fact assures that children will get their basic education not from multiple sources, but rather from their parents or their parent's agents alone. [Overruling] *Pierce* would free up funds used for private schooling and would direct parental energies at improving the private schools. Different public schools would, of course, focus on different values, and parents would still therefore have significant input into the curriculum of their local public schools. But we would remove some children from the monopoly of their parents and substitute a plural system of education.''

6.   A Nebraska law that outlawed the teaching of languages other than English[e] in any school to students who had yet to pass the eighth grade. The Nebraska Supreme Court upheld the conviction of an instructor who taught reading in the German language in a private elementary school. The Nebraska Supreme Court thought the law had a defensible purpose: "The Legislature had seen the baneful effects of permitting foreigners, who had taken residence in this country, to rear and educate their children in the language of their native land. The result of that condition was found to be inimical to our own safety. To allow the children of foreigners, who had emigrated here, to be taught from early childhood the language of the country of their parents was to rear them with that language as their mother tongue. It was to educate them so that they must always think in that language, and, as a consequence, naturally inculcate in them the ideas and sentiments foreign to the best interests of this country. The statute, therefore, was intended not only to require that the education of all children be conducted in the English language, but that, until they had grown into that language and until it had become a part of them, they should not in the schools be taught any other language. * * * The hours which a child is able to devote to study in the confinement of school are limited. It must have ample time for exercise or play. Its daily capacity for learning is comparatively small.''

MEYER v. NEBRASKA, supra, per McREYNOLDS, J., held that the statute violated due process: "While this court has not attempted to

e. The teaching of Latin, Greek, and Hebrew was permitted.

DECIDED UNDER DUE PROCESS RATHER THAN FIRST AMEND.?

define with exactness the liberty [guaranteed under the fourteenth amendment], the term has received much consideration and some of the included things have been definitely stated. Without doubt, it denotes not merely freedom from bodily restraint but also the right of the individual to contract, to engage in any of the common occupations of life, to acquire useful knowledge, to marry, establish a home and bring up children, to worship God according to the dictates of his own conscience, and generally to enjoy those privileges long recognized at common law as essential to the orderly pursuit of happiness by free men. [Corresponding] to the right of control, it is the natural duty of the parent to give his children education suitable to their station in life; and nearly all the states, including Nebraska, enforce this obligation by compulsory laws. Practically, education of the young is only possible in schools conducted by especially qualified persons who devote themselves thereto. The calling always has been regarded as useful and honorable, essential, indeed, to the public welfare. Mere knowledge of the German language cannot reasonably be regarded as harmful. Heretofore it has been commonly looked upon as helpful and desirable. Plaintiff in error taught this language in school as part of his occupation. His right thus to teach and the right of parents to engage him so to instruct their children, we think, are within the liberty of the amendment. * * *

"It is said the purpose of the legislation was to promote civic development by inhibiting training and education of the immature in foreign tongues and ideals before they could learn English and acquire American ideals, and 'that the English language should be and become the mother tongue of all children reared in this state.' It is also affirmed that the foreign born population is very large, that certain communities commonly use foreign words, follow foreign leaders, move in a foreign atmosphere, and that the children are thereby hindered from becoming citizens of the most useful type and the public safety is imperiled.

"For the welfare of his Ideal Commonwealth, Plato suggested a law which should provide: 'That the wives of our guardians are to be common, and their children are to be common, and no parent is to know his own child, nor any child his parent. * * * The proper officers will take the offspring of the good parents to the pen or fold, and there they will deposit them with certain nurses who dwell in a separate quarter; but the offspring of the inferior, or of the better when they chance to be deformed, will be put away in some mysterious, unknown place, as they should be.' In order to submerge the individual and develop ideal citizens, Sparta assembled the males at seven into barracks and intrusted their subsequent education and training to official guardians. Although such measures have been deliberately approved by men of great genius their ideas touching the relation between individual and state were wholly different from those upon which our institutions rest; and it hardly will be affirmed that any Legislature could impose such restrictions upon the people of a state without doing violence to both letter and spirit of the Constitution.

. . . QUOTING REPUBLIC

"The desire of the Legislature to foster a homogeneous people with American ideals prepared readily to understand current discussions of civic matters is easy to appreciate. Unfortunate experiences during the late war and aversion toward every character of truculent adversaries were certainly enough to quicken that aspiration. But the means adopted, we think, exceed the limitations upon the power of the state and conflict with rights assured to plaintiff in error.[f] The interference is plain enough and no adequate reason therefor in time of peace and domestic tranquility has been shown.

"As the statute undertakes to interfere only with teaching which involves a modern language, leaving complete freedom as to other matters, there seems no adequate foundation for the suggestion that the purpose was to protect the child's health by limiting his mental activities. It is well known that proficiency in a foreign language seldom comes to one not instructed at an early age, and experience shows that this is not injurious to the health, morals or understanding of the ordinary child."[g]

TINKER v. DES MOINES IND. COMMUNITY SCHOOL DISTRICT

393 U.S. 503, 89 S.Ct. 733, 21 L.Ed.2d 731 (1969).

MR. JUSTICE FORTAS delivered the opinion of the Court.

[Petitioners, two high school students and one junior high student, wore black armbands to school to publicize their objections to the Vietnam conflict and their advocacy of a truce. They refused to remove the armbands when asked to do so. In accordance with a ban on armbands which the city's school principals had adopted two days before in anticipation of such a protest, petitioners were sent home and suspended from school until they would return without the armbands. They sought a federal injunction restraining school officials from disciplining them, but the lower federal courts upheld the constitutionality of the school authorities' action on the ground that it was reasonable in order to prevent a disturbance which might result from the wearing of the armbands.]

[T]he wearing of armbands in the circumstances of this case was entirely divorced from actually or potentially disruptive conduct by those

---

f. Are statutes mandating English as the only language of government constitutional? See Cornell & Bratton, *Deadweight Costs and Intrinsic Wrongs of Nativism,* 84 Cornell L.Rev. 595 (1999).

g. Holmes and Sutherland, JJ., dissented, arguing, that the Court should defer to the state's interest. In addition, to studying *Pierce* and *Meyer* in connection with due process, the student may wish to reconsider them in the course of studying freedom of religion. In that connection, consider the argument that the law in *Pierce* was sub-

stantially motivated by anti-Catholic sentiment, that the law in *Meyer* was substantially motivated by anti-German sentiment and that the purpose of teaching German in *Meyer* was to help children participate in Lutheran services which were taught in German. For rich discussion of the other purposes present in *Pierce* and *Meyer,* see Barbara Bennett Woodhouse, *"Who Owns the Child?": Meyer and Pierce and the Child as Property,* 33 Wm. & Mary L. Rev. 995 (1992); See generally Ross, *Nativism, Education, and the Constitution, 1917–1927* (1994).

participating in it. It was closely akin to "pure speech" which, we have repeatedly held, is entitled to comprehensive protection under the First Amendment. * * *

First Amendment rights, applied in light of the special characteristics of the school environment, are available to teachers and students. It can hardly be argued that either students or teachers shed their constitutional rights to freedom of speech or expression at the schoolhouse gate. This has been the unmistakable holding of this Court for almost 50 years. In *Meyer v. Nebraska,* [262 U.S. 390, 43 S.Ct. 625, 67 L.Ed. 1042 (1923)], this Court [held that fourteenth amendment due process] prevents States from forbidding the teaching of a foreign language to young students. Statutes to this effect, the Court held, unconstitutionally interfere with the liberty of teacher, student, and parent. * * *

The problem presented by the present case does not relate to regulation of the length of skirts or the type of clothing, to hair style or deportment. [It] does not concern aggressive, disruptive action or even group demonstrations. Our problem involves direct, primary First Amendment rights akin to "pure speech."

The school officials banned and sought to punish petitioners for a silent, passive, expression of opinion, unaccompanied by any disorder or disturbance on the part of petitioners. There is here no evidence whatever of petitioners' interference, actual or nascent, with the school's work or of collision with the rights of other students to be secure and to be let alone. Accordingly, this case does not concern speech or action that intrudes upon the work of the school or the rights of other students.

Only a few of the 18,000 students in the school system wore the black armbands. Only five students were suspended for wearing them. There is no indication that the work of the school or any class was disrupted. Outside the classrooms, a few students made hostile remarks to the children wearing armbands, but there were no threats or acts of violence on school premises.

[I]n our system, undifferentiated fear or apprehension of disturbance [the District Court's basis for sustaining the school authorities' action] is not enough to overcome the right to freedom of expression. Any departure from absolute regimentation may cause trouble. Any variation from the majority's opinion may inspire fear. Any words spoken, in class, in the lunchroom or on the campus, that deviates from the views of another person, may start an argument or cause a disturbance. But our Constitution says we must take this risk [and] our history says that it is this sort of hazardous freedom—this kind of openness—that is the basis of our national strength and of the independence and vigor of Americans who grow up and live in this relatively permissive, often disputatious society.

In order for the State in the person of school officials to justify prohibition of a particular expression of opinion, it must be able to show that its action was caused by something more than a mere desire to avoid the discomfort and unpleasantness that always accompany an unpopular viewpoint. Certainly where there is no finding and no showing that the exercise of the forbidden right would "materially and substantially interfere with the requirements of appropriate discipline in the operation of the school," the prohibition cannot be sustained. *Burnside v. Byars.*

In the present case, the District Court made no such finding, and our independent examination of the record fails to yield evidence that the school authorities had reason to anticipate that the wearing of the armbands would substantially interfere with the work of the school or impinge upon the rights of other students. Even an official memorandum prepared after the suspension that listed the reasons for the ban on wearing the armbands made no reference to the anticipation of such disruption.

On the contrary, the action of the school authorities appears to have been based upon an urgent wish to avoid the controversy which might result from the expression, even by the silent symbol of armbands, of opposition to this Nation's part in the conflagration in Vietnam. * * *

It is also relevant that the school authorities did not purport to prohibit the wearing of all symbols of political or controversial significance. The record shows that students in some of the schools wore buttons relating to national political campaigns, and some even wore the Iron Cross, traditionally a symbol of Naziism. The order prohibiting the wearing of armbands did not extend to these. Instead, a particular symbol—black armbands worn to exhibit opposition to this Nation's involvement in Vietnam—was singled out for prohibition. Clearly, the prohibition of expression of one particular opinion, at least without evidence that it is necessary to avoid material and substantial interference with school work or discipline, is not constitutionally permissible.

In our system, state-operated schools may not be enclaves of totalitarianism. School officials do not possess absolute authority over their students. Students in school as well as out of school are "persons" under our Constitution. They are possessed of fundamental rights which the State must respect, just as they themselves must respect their obligations to the State. In our system, students may not be regarded as closed-circuit recipients of only that which the State chooses to communicate. They may not be confined to the expression of those sentiments that are officially approved. In the absence of a specific showing of constitutionally valid reasons to regulate their speech, students are entitled to freedom of expression of their views.

[The principle of prior cases underscoring the importance of diversity and exchange of ideas in the schools,] is not confined to the supervised and ordained discussion which takes place in the classroom. The principal use to which the schools are dedicated is to accommodate students during prescribed hours for the purpose of certain types of activities. Among those activities is personal intercommunication among the students. This is not only an inevitable part of the process of attending school. It is also an important part of the educational process.

A student's rights therefore, do not embrace merely the classroom hours. When he is in the cafeteria, or on the playing field, or on the campus during the authorized hours, he may express his opinions, even on controversial subjects like the conflict in Vietnam, if he does so "[without] materially and substantially interfering [with] appropriate discipline in the operation of the school" and without colliding with the rights of others. *Burnside.* But conduct by the student, in class or out of it, which for any reason—whether it stems from time, place, or type of behavior—materially disrupts classwork or involves substantial disorder or invasion of the rights of others is, of course, not immunized by the [first amendment].

We properly read [the first amendment] to permit reasonable regulation of speech-connected activities in carefully restricted circumstances. But we do not confine the permissible exercise of First Amendment rights to a telephone booth or the four corners of a pamphlet, or to supervised and ordained discussion in a school classroom. * * *

Reversed and remanded.[a]

Mr. Justice Stewart, concurring.

Although I agree with much of what is said in the Court's opinion, and with its judgment in this case, I cannot share the Court's uncritical assumption that, school discipline aside, the First Amendment rights of children are co-extensive with those of adults. Indeed, I had thought the Court decided otherwise just last Term in *Ginsberg v. New York* [Ch. 1, IV, II supra.] I continue to hold the view I expressed in that case: "[A] State may permissibly determine that, at least in some precisely delineated areas, a child—like someone in a captive audience—is not possessed of that full capacity for individual choice which is the presupposition of First Amendment guarantees." (concurring opinion).

Mr. Justice White, concurring.

While I join the Court's opinion, I deem it appropriate to note, first, that the Court continues to recognize a distinction between communicating by words and communicating by acts or conduct which sufficiently impinge on some valid state interest; and, second, that I do not subscribe to everything the Court of Appeals said about free speech in its opinion in *Burnside,* a case relied upon by the Court in the matter now before us.

Mr. Justice Black, dissenting. * * *

Assuming that the Court is correct in holding that the conduct of wearing armbands for the purpose of conveying political ideas is protected by the First Amendment [the] crucial remaining questions are whether students and teachers may use the schools at their whim as a platform for the

a. See also Amar, *A Tale of Three Wars: Tinker in Constitutional Context,* 48 Drake L.Rev. 507 (2000); Chemerinsky, *Students Do Leave Their First Amendment Rights at the Schoolhouse Door: What's Left of Tinker?,* 48 Drake L.Rev. 527 (2000); Strossen, Keeping the Constitution inside the Schoolhouse Gate, 48 Drake L.Rev. 445 (2000; Yudof, *When Governments Speak: Toward a Theory of Government Expression and the First Amendment,* 57 Tex.L.Rev. 863, 884–85 (1979).

exercise of free speech—"symbolic" or "pure"—and whether the Courts will allocate to themselves the function of deciding how the pupils' school day will be spent. * * *

While the record does not show that any of these armband students shouted, used profane language, or were violent in any manner, detailed testimony by some of them shows their armbands caused comments, warnings by other students, the poking of fun at them, and a warning by an older football player that other, nonprotesting students had better let them alone. There is also evidence that the professor of mathematics had his lesson period practically "wrecked" chiefly by disputes with Beth Tinker, who wore her armband for her "demonstration." Even a casual reading of the record shows that this armband did divert students' minds from their regular lessons, and that talk, comments, etc., made John Tinker "self-conscious" in attending school with his armband. While the absence of obscene or boisterous and loud disorder perhaps justifies the Court's statement that the few armband students did not actually "disrupt" the classwork, I think the record overwhelmingly shows that the armbands did exactly what the elected school officials and principals foresaw it would, that is, took the students' minds off their classwork and diverted them to thoughts about the highly emotional subject of the Vietnam war.

[E]ven if the record were silent as to protests against the Vietnam war distracting students from their assigned class work, members of this Court, like all other citizens, know, without being told, that the disputes over the wisdom of the Vietnam war have disrupted and divided this country as few other issues ever have. Of course students, like other people, cannot concentrate on lesser issues when black armbands are being ostentatiously displayed in their presence to call attention to the wounded and dead of the war, some of the wounded and the dead being their friends and neighbors. It was, of course, to distract the attention of other students that some students insisted up to the very point of their own suspension from school that they were determined to sit in school with their symbolic armbands. * * *

MR. JUSTICE HARLAN, dissenting.

I certainly agree that state public school authorities in the discharge of their responsibilities are not wholly exempt from the requirements of the Fourteenth Amendment respecting the freedoms of expression and association. At the same time I am reluctant to believe that there is any disagreement between the majority and myself on the proposition that school officials should be accorded the widest authority in maintaining discipline and good order in their institutions. To translate that proposition into a workable constitutional rule, I would, in cases like this, cast upon those complaining the burden of showing that a particular school measure was motivated by other than legitimate school concerns—for example, a desire to prohibit the expression of an unpopular point of view, while permitting expression of the dominant opinion.

Finding nothing in this record which impugns the good faith of respondents in promulgating the arm band regulation, I would affirm the judgment below.

Notes and Questions

1. Should the government's interest in education trump the school child's interest in speaking in the classroom? Are the two interests compatible in this case? May students be prohibited from voicing their opinions of the Vietnam War in the middle of a math class? If so, why can't they be prevented from expressing their views on the same issue in the same class by means of "symbolic speech"? Cf. Nahmod, *Beyond Tinker: The High School as an Educational Public Forum,* 5 Harv.Civ.Rts. & Civ.Lib.L.Rev. 278 (1970).

2. Could school authorities adopt a regulation forbidding *teachers* to wear black armbands in the classroom? Or prohibiting teachers from wearing *all* symbols of political or controversial significance in the classroom or anywhere on school property? Are students a "captive" group? Do the views of a teacher occupying a position of authority carry much more influence with a student than would those of students inter sese? Consider *James v. Board of Educ.,* 461 F.2d 566 (2d Cir.1972), holding that school officials violated a high school teacher's constitutional rights by discharging him because he had worn a black armband in class in symbolic protest of the Vietnam War. But the court stressed that "the armband did not disrupt classroom activities [nor] have any influence on any students and did not engender protest from any student, teacher or parent." What if it had? By implication, did the court confirm the potency of the "heckler's veto"? See Note, 39 Brook.L.Rev. 918 (1973). Same result if appellant had been a 3rd grade teacher rather than an 11th grade teacher? See Shiffrin, *Government Speech,* 27 U.C.L.A.L.Rev. 565, 647–53 (1980).

3. Consider Chemerinsky, supra note a, at 529: "[I]n the three decades since *Tinker,* the courts have made it clear that students leave most of their constitutional rights at the schoolhouse gate. The judiciary's unquestioning acceptance of the need for deference to school authority leaves relatively little room for protecting student's constitutional rights. The decisions over the past thirty years are far closer to Justice Black's dissent in *Tinker* than they are to Justice Fortas's majority opinion."

HAZELWOOD SCHOOL DISTRICT v. KUHLMEIER

484 U.S. 260, 108 S.Ct. 562, 98 L.Ed.2d 592 (1988).

JUSTICE WHITE delivered the opinion of the Court.

This case concerns the extent to which educators may exercise editorial control over the contents of a high school newspaper produced as part of the school's journalism curriculum.

I

Petitioners are the Hazelwood School District in St. Louis County, Missouri; various school officials; Robert Eugene Reynolds, the principal of Hazelwood East High School, and Howard Emerson, a teacher in the school district. Respondents are three former Hazelwood East students who were staff members of Spectrum, the school newspaper. They contend that school officials violated their First Amendment rights by deleting two pages of articles from the May 13, 1983, issue of Spectrum.

Spectrum was written and edited by the Journalism II class at Hazelwood East. The newspaper was published every three weeks or so during the 1982–1983 school year. More than 4,500 copies of the newspaper were distributed during that year to students, school personnel, and members of the community.

The Board of Education allocated funds from its annual budget for the printing of Spectrum. [The] Journalism II course was taught by Robert Stergos for most of the 1982–1983 academic year. Stergos left Hazelwood East to take a job in private industry on April 29, 1983, when the May 13 edition of Spectrum was nearing completion, and petitioner Emerson took his place as newspaper adviser for the remaining weeks of the term.

The practice at Hazelwood East during the spring 1983 semester was for the journalism teacher to submit page proofs of each Spectrum issue to Principal Reynolds for his review prior to publication. On May 10, Emerson delivered the proofs of the May 13 edition to Reynolds, who objected to two of the articles scheduled to appear in that edition. One of the stories described three Hazelwood East students' experiences with pregnancy; the other discussed the impact of divorce on students at the school.

Reynolds was concerned that, although the pregnancy story used false names "to keep the identity of these girls a secret," the pregnant students still might be identifiable from the text. He also believed that the article's references to sexual activity and birth control were inappropriate for some of the younger students at the school. In addition, Reynolds was concerned that a student identified by name in the divorce story had complained that her father "wasn't spending enough time with my mom, my sister and I" prior to the divorce, "was always out of town on business or out late playing cards with the guys," and "always argued about everything" with her mother. Reynolds believed that the student's parents should have been given an opportunity to respond to these remarks or to consent to their publication. He was unaware that Emerson had deleted the student's name from the final version of the article.

Reynolds believed that there was no time to make the necessary changes in the stories before the scheduled press run and that the newspaper would not appear before the end of the school year if printing were delayed to any significant extent. He concluded that his only options under the circumstances were to publish a four-page newspaper instead of the planned six-page newspaper, eliminating the two pages on which the offending stories appeared, or to publish no newspaper at all. Accordingly, he directed Emerson to withhold from publication the two pages containing the stories on pregnancy and divorce.[1] He informed his superiors of the decision, and they concurred. * * *

II

Students in the public schools do not "shed their constitutional rights to freedom of speech or expression at the schoolhouse gate." *Tinker.* They cannot be punished merely for expressing their personal views on the school premises—whether "in the cafeteria, or on the playing field, or on the campus during the authorized hours"—unless school authorities have reason to believe that such expression will "substantially interfere with the work of the school or impinge upon the rights of other students." *Tinker.*

We have nonetheless recognized that the First Amendment rights of students in the public schools "are not automatically coextensive with the rights of adults in other settings," *Bethel School District No. 403 v. Fraser,* 478 U.S. 675, 106 S.Ct. 3159, 92 L.Ed.2d 549 (1986) and must be "applied in light of the special characteristics of the school environment." *Tinker.* A school need not tolerate student speech that is inconsistent with its "basic educational mission," *Fraser,* even though the government could not censor similar speech outside the school. Accordingly, we held in *Fraser* that a student could be disciplined for having delivered a speech that was "sexually explicit" but not legally obscene at an official school assembly, because the school was entitled to "disassociate itself" from the speech in a manner that would demonstrate to others that such vulgarity is "wholly inconsistent with the 'fundamental values' of public school education." We thus recognized that "[t]he determination of what manner of speech in the classroom or in school assembly is inappropriate properly rests with the school board," rather than with the federal courts. It is in this context that respondents' First Amendment claims must be considered.

A

We deal first with the question whether Spectrum may appropriately be characterized as a forum for public expression. [T]he evidence relied upon by the Court of Appeals fails to demonstrate the "clear intent to create a public forum," *Cornelius,* that existed in cases in which we found public forums to have been created. School [officials] "reserve[d] the forum for its intended purpos[e]," *Perry,* as a supervised learning experience for journalism students. Accordingly, school officials were entitled to regulate the contents of

---

1. The two pages deleted from the newspaper also contained articles on teenage marriage, runaways, and juvenile delinquents, as well as a general article on teenage pregnancy. Reynolds testified that he had no objection to these articles and that they were deleted only because they appeared on the same pages as the two objectionable articles.

Spectrum in any reasonable manner. It is this standard, rather than our decision in *Tinker,* that governs this case.

B SCHOOL'S ROLE

The question whether the First Amendment requires a school to tolerate particular student speech—the question that we addressed in *Tinker*—is different from the question whether the First Amendment requires a school affirmatively to promote particular student speech. The former question addresses educators' ability to silence a student's personal expression that happens to occur on the school premises. The latter question concerns educators' authority over school-sponsored publications, theatrical productions, and other expressive activities that students, parents, and members of the public might reasonably perceive to bear the imprimatur of the school. These activities may fairly be characterized as part of the school curriculum, whether or not they occur in a traditional classroom setting, so long as they are supervised by faculty members and designed to impart particular knowledge or skills to student participants and audiences.[3]

[A] school may in its capacity as publisher of a school newspaper or producer of a school play "disassociate itself," *Fraser,* not only from speech that would "substantially interfere with [its] work * * * or impinge upon the rights of other students," *Tinker,* but also from speech that is, for example, ungrammatical, poorly written, inadequately researched, biased or prejudiced, vulgar or profane, or unsuitable for immature audiences.[4] A school must be able to set high standards for the student speech that is disseminated under its auspices—standards that may be higher than those demanded by some newspaper publishers or theatrical producers in the "real" world—and may refuse to disseminate student speech that does not meet those standards. [Otherwise,] the schools would be unduly constrained from fulfilling their role as "a principal instrument in awakening the child to cultural values, in preparing him for later professional training, and in helping him to adjust normally to his environment." *Brown v. Board of Education.*

Accordingly, we conclude that the standard articulated in *Tinker* for determining when a school may punish student expression need not also be the standard for determining when a school may refuse to lend its name and

3. The distinction that we draw between speech that is sponsored by the school and speech that is not is fully consistent with *Papish v. Board of Curators* [410 U.S. 667, 93 S.Ct. 1197, 35 L.Ed.2d 618 (1973)] which involved an off-campus "underground" newspaper that school officials merely had allowed to be sold on a state university campus.

4. The dissent perceives no difference between the First Amendment analysis applied in *Tinker* and that applied in *Fraser.* We disagree. The decision in *Fraser* rested on the "vulgar," "lewd," and "plainly of-

fensive" character of a speech delivered at an official school assembly rather than on any propensity of the speech to "materially disrupt classwork or involve substantial disorder or invasion of the rights of others." Indeed, the *Fraser* Court cited as "especially relevant" a portion of Justice Black's dissenting opinion in *Tinker* "disclaim[ing] any purpose * * * to hold that the Federal Constitution compels the teachers, parents and elected school officials to surrender control of the American public school system to public school students." Of course, Justice Black's observations are equally relevant to the instant case.

resources to the dissemination of student expression. Instead, we hold that educators do not offend the First Amendment by exercising editorial control over the style and content of student speech in school-sponsored expressive activities so long as their actions are reasonably related to legitimate pedagogical concerns.[7] * * *a

JUSTICE BRENNAN, with whom Justice Marshall and Justice Blackmun join, dissenting.

* * *

The Court is certainly correct that the First Amendment permits educators "to assure that participants learn whatever lessons the activity is designed to teach. * * *" That is, however, the essence of the *Tinker* test, not an excuse to abandon it. Under *Tinker,* school officials may censor only such student speech as would "materially disrup[t]" a legitimate curricular function. Manifestly, student speech is more likely to disrupt a curricular function when it arises in the context of a curricular activity—one that "is designed to teach" something—than when it arises in the context of a noncurricular activity. Thus, under *Tinker,* the school may constitutionally punish the budding political orator if he disrupts calculus class but not if he holds his tongue for the cafeteria. That is not because some more stringent standard applies in the curricular context. (After all, this Court applied the same standard whether the Tinkers wore their armbands to the "classroom" or the "cafeteria.") It is because student speech in the noncurricular context is less likely to disrupt materially any legitimate pedagogical purpose.

I fully agree with the Court that the First Amendment should afford an educator the prerogative not to sponsor the publication of a newspaper article that is "ungrammatical, poorly written, inadequately researched, biased or prejudiced," or that falls short of the "high standards [for] student speech that is disseminated under [the school's] auspices * * *." But we need not abandon *Tinker* to reach that conclusion; we need only apply it. The enumerated criteria reflect the skills that the curricular newspaper "is designed to teach." The educator may, under *Tinker,* constitutionally "censor" poor grammar, writing, or research because to reward such expression would "materially disrup[t]" the newspaper's curricular purpose. * * *

---

7. A number of lower federal courts have similarly recognized that educators' decisions with regard to the content of school sponsored newspapers, dramatic productions, and other expressive activities are entitled to substantial deference. We need not now decide whether the same degree of deference is appropriate with respect to school-sponsored expressive activities at the college and university level.

a. White, J., concluded that Principal Reynolds acted reasonably in requiring de-
letion of the pages from the newspaper. In addition to concerns about privacy and failure to contact persons discussed in the stories, White, J., found that it was "not unreasonable for the principal to have concluded that [frank talk about sexual histories, albeit not graphic, with comments about use or nonuse of birth control] was inappropriate in a school-sponsored publication distributed to 14–year–old freshmen and presumably taken home to be read by students' even younger brothers and sisters."

The Court relies on bits of testimony to portray the principal's conduct as a pedagogical lesson to Journalism II students who "had not sufficiently mastered those portions of [the] curriculum that pertained to the treatment of controversial issues and personal attacks, the need to protect the privacy of individuals [and] 'the legal, moral, and ethical restrictions imposed upon journalists * * *.' " In that regard, the Court attempts to justify censorship of the article on teenage pregnancy on the basis of the principal's judgment that (1) "the [pregnant] students' anonymity was not adequately protected," despite the article's use of aliases; and (2) the judgment "that the article was not sufficiently sensitive to the privacy interests of the students' boyfriends and parents * * *." Similarly, the Court finds in the principal's decision to censor the divorce article a journalistic lesson that the author should have given the father of one student an "opportunity to defend himself" against her charge that (in the Court's words) he "chose 'playing cards with the guys' over home and family * * *."

But the principal never consulted the students before censoring their work. [T]hey learned of the deletions when the paper was released. [Further,] he explained the deletions only in the broadest of generalities. In one meeting called at the behest of seven protesting Spectrum staff members (presumably a fraction of the full class), he characterized the articles as " 'too sensitive' for 'our immature audience of readers,' " and in a later meeting he deemed them simply "inappropriate, personal, sensitive and unsuitable for the newspaper." The Court's supposition that the principal intended (or the protesters understood) those generalities as a lesson on the nuances of journalistic responsibility is utterly incredible. If he did, a fact that neither the District Court nor the Court of Appeals found, the lesson was lost on all but the psychic Spectrum staffer.

The Court's second excuse for deviating from precedent is the school's interest in shielding an impressionable high school audience from material whose substance is "unsuitable for immature audiences." [Tinker] teaches us that the state educator's undeniable, and undeniably vital, mandate to inculcate moral and political values is not a general warrant to act as "thought police" stifling discussion of all but state-approved topics and advocacy of all but the official position.

[The] mere fact of school sponsorship does not, as the Court suggests, license such thought control in the high school, whether through school suppression of disfavored viewpoints or through official assessment of topic sensitivity. [Moreover, the] State's prerogative to dissolve the student newspaper entirely (or to limit its subject matter) no more entitles it to dictate which viewpoints students may express on its pages, than the State's prerogative to close down the schoolhouse entitles it to prohibit the nondisruptive expression of antiwar sentiment within its gates.

Official censorship of student speech on the ground that it addresses "potentially sensitive topics" is, for related reasons, equally impermissible. I would not begrudge an educator the authority to limit the substantive scope of a school-sponsored publication to a certain, objectively definable topic, such as literary criticism, school sports, or an overview of the school year. Unlike those determinate limitations, "potential topic sensitivity" is a vaporous nonstandard [that] invites manipulation to achieve ends that cannot permissibly be achieved through blatant viewpoint discrimination and chills student speech to which school officials might not object. * * *[b]

Notes and Questions

1. Consider Hafen, *Hazelwood School District and the Role of First Amendment Institutions,* 1988 Duke L.J. 685, 701, 704–05: "[T]he question whether authoritarian or anti-authoritarian approaches will best develop the minds and expressive powers of children is more a matter of educational philosophy and practice than of constitutional law. For that reason alone, first amendment theories applied by courts largely on the basis of anti-authoritarian assumptions are at best a clumsy and limited means of ensuring optimal educational development, whether the goal is an understanding of democratic values or a mastery of basic intellectual skills. Thus, one of *Hazelwood's* major contributions is its reaffirmation of schools' institutional role—and their accountability to the public for fulfilling it responsibly—in nurturing the underlying values of the first amendment. * * *

"The first amendment must [protect] not only individual writers, but newspapers; not only religious persons, but churches; not only individual students and teachers, but schools. These 'intellectual and moral associations' form a crucial part of the constitutional structure, for they help teach the peculiar and sometimes paradoxical blend of liberty and duty that sustains both individual freedom and the entire culture from one generation to the next.'

2. Consider Minow & Spellman, *Passion For Justice,* 10 Cardozo L.Rev. 37, 69 (1988): "The majority does not acknowledge the power it is exercising in the act of deferring to the 'reasonable' judgments of the [principal:] the power to signal to school officials all around the country, that it is all right to err on the side of eliminating student speech, it is all right to indulge your paternalistic attitudes toward the students; you do not need to guard against your own discomfort with what students want to discuss, for the 'rights' really lie within your own judgment about what they need." See also id. at 68 n. 108: "The dissent is acutely sensitive to the impact of censorship on students, but less attentive to the impact of judicial review on the school officials. Although equal attention to competing sides may make a decision more difficult, refraining from seeing the power of competing arguments itself may lead to tragic blindness."

---

b. Brennan, J., further argued that the material deleted was not conceivably tortious and that less restrictive alternatives, such as more precise deletions, were readily available.

3. Does *Kuhlmeier* apply to high school teacher's educational judgments? Is a school board's action against classroom speech sufficient if it is reasonably related to legitimate pedagogical concerns or do considerations of academic freedom require a more demanding standard? See *Boring v. Buncombe County Board of Education*, 136 F.3d 364 (4th Cir.1998)(drama teacher selects play involving a dysfunctional divorced single parent family including a lesbian daughter and an unmarried pregnant daughter); *Ward v. Hickey*, 996 F.2d 448 (1st Cir.1993)(teacher discusses abortion of Down's Syndrome fetus in ninth grade biology class). Should *Kuhlmeier* have any application at the college level?[c]

(5-4) KIND OF

BOARD OF EDUCATION v. PICO, 457 U.S. 853, 102 S.Ct. 2799, 73 L.Ed.2d 435 (1982): Several members of the Island Trees Board of Education attended a conference sponsored by Parents of New York United (PONYU), a politically conservative organization. At the conference these board members obtained lists of books they described as "objectionable" and "improper fare for school students." On ascertaining that its school libraries contained eleven of the books,[a] the Board informally directed, over the objection of the school superintendent, that the books be delivered to the Board's offices so that Board members could read them. The Board justified its action by characterizing the listed books as "anti-American, anti-Christian, anti-Semitic, and just plain filthy" and concluding that it had a "duty" and a "moral obligation" "to protect the children in our school from this moral danger as surely as from physical and medical dangers." The Board then appointed a parent-teacher "Book Review Committee" to recommend to the board which books should be retained. The Committee recommended that only two books be removed and a third be available to students only with parental approval. But the Board, without giving any reasons, decided that

c. See Sorenson & LaManque, *The Application of v. Kuhlmeier in College Litigation*, 22 J. of College & Univ. Law 971 (1996). For a range of views on academic freedom, consider Dworkin, *Freedom's Law* ch. 11 (1996); Gutmann, Democratic Education (rev. ed. 1999); Buss, *Academic Freedom and Freedom of Speech: Communicating the Curriculum*, 2 J. of Gender, Race & Justice 213 (1999); Byrne, *Academic Freedom: A "Special Concern of the First Amendment,"* 99 Yale L.J. 251 (1989); Weiner, *Dirty Words in the Classroom: Teaching the Limits of the First Amendment*, 66 Tenn.L.Rev. 597 (1999); Van Alstyne, *Academic Freedom and the First Amendment in the Supreme Court of the United States: An Unhurried Historical Review*, 53 Law & Contemp. Probs. 79 (1990); Van Alstyne, *The Constitutional Rights of Teachers and Professors*, 1970 Duke L.J. 841.

a. As the plurality opinion noted: "The nine [listed] books in the High School library were: *Slaughter House Five*, by Kurt Vonnegut, Jr.; *The Naked Ape*, by Desmond Morris; *Down These Mean Streets*, by Piri Thomas; *Best Short Stories of Negro Writers*, edited by Langston Hughes; *Go Ask Alice*, of anonymous authorship; *Laughing Boy*, by Oliver LaFarge; *Black Boy*, by Richard Wright; *A Hero Ain't Nothin' But A Sandwich*, by Alice Childress; and *Soul On Ice*, by Eldridge Cleaver. The [listed] book in the Junior High School library was *A Reader for Writers*, edited by Jerome Archer. Still another listed book, *The Fixer*, by Bernard Malamud, was found to be included in the curriculum of a twelfth grade literature course."

The Board subsequently decided that only *Laughing Boy* should be returned to the library without restriction, and that *Black Boy* should be made available subject to parental approval.

nine books should be removed and that another should be made available subject to parental approval. Respondent students then brought an action for declaratory and injunctive relief under 42 U.S.C. § 1983, contending that the Board's actions had violated their first amendment rights. The district court granted summary judgment for the Board, stating that the Board had "restricted access only to certain books which [it] believed to be, in essence, vulgar." A 2–1 majority of the Second Circuit reversed. One member of the majority concluded that at least at the summary judgment stage, the Board had not offered sufficient justification for its action. A second member of the majority "viewed the case as turning on the contested factual issue of whether [the Board's] removal decision was motivated by a justifiable desire to remove books containing vulgarities and sexual explicitness, or rather by an impermissible desire to suppress ideas." The Supreme Court (5–4) upheld reversal of the summary dismissal of the suit, but there was no opinion of the Court. BRENNAN, J., announced the judgment of the Court in an opinion joined by Marshall and Stevens, JJ., and in part by Blackmun, J.:

"We emphasize at the outset the limited nature of the substantive question presented by the case before us. [T]his case [does] not involve textbooks, or indeed any books that Island Trees students would be required to read. Respondents do not seek in this Court to impose limitations upon their school Board's discretion to prescribe the curricula of the Island Trees schools. On the contrary, the only books at issue in this case are *library* books, books that by their nature are optional rather than required reading. [Furthermore,] even as to library books, the action before us does not involve the *acquisition* of books. Respondents have not sought to compel their school Board to add to the school library shelves any books that students desire to read. Rather, the only action challenged in this case is the *removal* from school libraries of books originally placed there by the school authorities, or without objection from them.

"[We] think that the First Amendment rights of students may be directly and sharply implicated by the removal of books from the shelves of a school library. * * * [W]e have held that in a variety of contexts 'the Constitution protects the right to receive information and ideas.' *Stanley v. Georgia.* [W]e do not deny that local school boards have a substantial legitimate role to play in the determination of school library content. [But] that discretion may not be exercised in a narrowly partisan or political manner. If a Democratic school board, motivated by party affiliation, ordered the removal of all books written by or in favor of Republicans, few would doubt that the order violated the constitutional rights of the students denied access to those books. The same conclusion would surely apply if an all-white school board, motivated by racial animus, decided to remove all books authored by blacks or advocating racial equality and integration. Our Constitution does not permit the official suppression of *ideas.* Thus whether petitioners' removal of books from their school libraries denied respondents

MOTIVE

their First Amendment rights depends upon the motivation behind petitioners' actions. If petitioners *intended* by their removal decision to deny respondents access to ideas with which petitioners disagreed, and if this intent was the decisive factor in petitioners' decision,[22] then petitioners have exercised their discretion in violation of the Constitution. On the other hand, respondents implicitly concede that an unconstitutional motivation would *not* be demonstrated if it were shown that petitioners had decided to remove the books at issue because those books were pervasively vulgar. And again, respondents concede that if it were demonstrated that the removal decision was based solely upon the 'educational suitability' of the books in question, then their removal would be 'perfectly permissible.' In other words, in respondents' view such motivations if decisive of petitioners' actions, would not carry the danger of an official suppression of ideas, and thus would not violate respondents' First Amendment rights. * * *

"This would be a very different case if the record demonstrated that petitioners had employed established, regular, and facially unbiased procedures for the review of controversial materials. But [respondents'] allegations and some of the evidentiary materials presented below do not rule out the possibility that petitioners' removal procedures were highly irregular and ad hoc—the antithesis of those procedures that might tend to allay suspicions regarding petitioners' motivations.

"Construing these claims, affidavit statements, and other evidentiary materials in a manner favorable to respondents, we cannot conclude that petitioners were 'entitled to a judgment as a matter of law.' The evidence plainly does not foreclose the possibility that petitioners' decision to remove the books rested decisively upon disagreement with constitutionally protected ideas in those books, or upon a desire on petitioners' part to impose upon the students of the Island Trees High School and Junior High School a political orthodoxy to which petitioners and their constituents adhered."[b]

In the view of BLACKMUN, J., concurring, "the principle involved here is both narrower and more basic than 'the right to receive information' identified by the plurality. I do not suggest that the State has any affirmative obligation to provide students with information or ideas, something that may well be associated with a 'right to receive.' And I do not believe, as the plurality suggests, that the right at issue here is somehow associated with the peculiar nature of the school library; if schools may be used to inculcate ideas, surely libraries may play a role in that process. Instead, I suggest that certain forms of state discrimination *between* ideas are improper. In particular, our precedents command the conclusion that the State may not act to deny access to an idea simply because state officials disapprove of that idea for partisan or political reasons.[2] * * *

---

22. By "decisive factor" we mean a "substantial factor" in the absence of which the opposite decision would have been reached.

b. For criticism of Brennan, J.'s opinion, see Lee, *The Supreme Court and the Right to Receive Expression*, 1987 Sup.Ct. Rev. 303, 323–27.

"[S]chool officials may seek to instill certain values 'by persuasion and example,' or by choice of emphasis. That sort of positive educational action, however, is the converse of an intentional attempt to shield students from certain ideas that officials find politically distasteful. Arguing that the majority in the community rejects the ideas involved, does not refute this principle: 'The very purpose of a Bill of Rights was to withdraw certain subjects from the vicissitudes of political controversy, to place them beyond the reach of majorities and officials * * *.' *Barnette.*"

WHITE, J., who concurred in the judgment, noted that although the District Court found that the books were removed because the school board believed them "to be, in essence, vulgar," both Court of Appeals judges in the majority concluded that there was a material issue of fact that precluded summary judgment for petitioners. As White, J., understood it, "[t]he unresolved factual issue [is] the reason or reasons underlying the school board's removal of the books" and he was "not inclined to disagree with the Court of Appeals on such a fact-bound issue. [The] Court seems compelled to go further and issue a dissertation on the extent to which the First Amendment limits the discretion of the school board to remove books from the school library. I see no necessity for doing so at this point. When findings of fact and conclusions of law are made by the District Court, that may end the case."

BURGER, C.J., joined by Powell, Rehnquist, and O'Connor, JJ., dissented:

"[The] plurality concludes that under the Constitution school boards cannot choose to retain or dispense with books if their discretion is exercised in a 'narrowly partisan or political manner.' The plurality concedes that permissible factors are whether the books are 'pervasively vulgar' or educationally unsuitable. 'Educational suitability,' however, is a standardless phrase. This conclusion will undoubtedly be drawn in many—if not most—instances because of the decision maker's content-based judgment that the ideas contained in the book or the idea expressed from the author's method of communication are inappropriate for teenage pupils. * * *

"Further, there is no guidance whatsoever as to what constitutes 'political' factors. [V]irtually all educational decisions necessarily involve 'political' determinations.

"What the plurality views as valid reasons for removing a book at their core involve partisan judgments. Ultimately the federal courts will be the judge of whether the motivation for book removal was 'valid' or 'reasonable.' Undoubtedly the validity of many book removals will ultimately turn on a

2. In effect, my view presents the obverse of the plurality's analysis: while the plurality focuses on the failure to provide information, I find crucial the State's decision to single out an idea for disapproval and then deny access to it.

judge's evaluation of the books. Discretion must be used, and the appropriate body to exercise that discretion is the local elected school board, not judges."

Powell, J., also dissented: "In different contexts and in different times, the destruction of written materials has been the symbol of despotism and intolerance. But the removal of nine vulgar or racist books from a high school library by a concerned local school board does not raise this specter. For me, today's decision symbolizes a debilitating encroachment upon the institutions of a free people."[c]

Rehnquist, J., joined by Burger, C.J., and Powell, J., "disagree[d] with Justice Brennan's opinion because it is largely hypothetical in character, failing to take account of the facts as admitted by the parties [and] because it is analytically unsound and internally inconsistent":

"I can cheerfully concede [that a Democratic school board could not, for political reasons, remove all books by or in favor of Republicans, and that an all-white school board, motivated by racial animus, could not remove all books authored by blacks or advocating racial equality], but as in so many other cases the extreme examples are seldom the ones that arise in the real world of constitutional litigation. In *this case* the facts taken most favorably to respondents suggest that nothing of this sort happened. The nine books removed undoubtedly did contain 'ideas,' but in the light of the excerpts from them found in the dissenting opinion [in the court below], it is apparent that eight of them contained demonstrable amounts of vulgarity and profanity and the ninth contained nothing that could be considered partisan or political. [R]espondents admitted as much. Petitioners did not, for the reasons stated hereafter, run afoul of the First and Fourteenth Amendments by removing these particular books from the library in the manner in which they did. I would save for another day—feeling quite confident that that day will not arrive—the extreme examples posed in Justice Brennan's opinion.

"Considerable light is shed on the correct resolution of the constitutional question in this case by examining the role played by petitioners. Had petitioners been the members of a town council, I suppose all would agree that, absent a good deal more than is present in this record, they could not have prohibited the sale of these books by private booksellers within the municipality. But we have also recognized that the government may act in other capacities than as sovereign, and when it does the First Amendment may speak with a different voice * * *. By the same token, expressive conduct which may not be prohibited by the State as sovereign may be proscribed by the State as property owner [quoting from *Adderley*, Ch. 6, II supra].

"With these differentiated roles of government in mind, it is helpful to assess the role of government as educator, as compared with the role of government as sovereign. When it acts as an educator, at least at the elementary and secondary school level, the government is engaged in inculcating social values and knowledge in relatively impressionable young peo-

---

c. Powell, J., appended a summary of excerpts from the books at issue collected in the opinion of Judge Mansfield dissenting below.

ple. Obviously there are innumerable decisions to be made as to what courses should be taught, what books should be purchased, or what teachers should be employed. In every one of these areas the members of a school board will act on the basis of their own personal or moral values, will attempt to mirror those of the community, or will abdicate the making of such decisions to so-called 'experts.' [In] the very course of administering the many-faceted operations of a school district, the mere decision to purchase some books will necessarily preclude the possibility of purchasing others. The decision to teach a particular subject may preclude the possibility of teaching another subject. A decision to replace a teacher because of ineffectiveness may by implication be seen as a disparagement of the subject matter taught. In each of these instances, however, the book or the exposure to the subject matter may be acquired elsewhere. The managers of the school district are not proscribing it as to the citizenry in general, but are simply determining that it will not be included in the curriculum or school library. In short, actions by the government as educator do not raise the same First Amendment concerns as actions by the government as sovereign. * * *

"Education consists of the selective presentation and explanation of ideas. The effective acquisition of knowledge depends upon an orderly exposure to relevant information. Nowhere is this more true than in elementary and secondary schools, where, unlike the broad-ranging inquiry available to university students, the courses taught are those thought most relevant to the young students' individual development. Of necessity, elementary and secondary educators must separate the relevant from the irrelevant, the appropriate from the inappropriate. Determining what information *not* to present to the students is often as important as identifying relevant material. This winnowing process necessarily leaves much information to be discovered by students at another time or in another place, and is fundamentally inconsistent with any constitutionally required eclecticism in public education.

"[Unlike] university or public libraries, elementary and secondary school libraries are not designed for free-wheeling inquiry; they are tailored, as the public school curriculum is tailored, to the teaching of basic skills and ideas. Thus, Justice Brennan cannot rely upon the nature of school libraries to escape the fact that the First Amendment right to receive information simply has no application to the one public institution which, by its very nature, is a place for the selective conveyance of ideas."

In a brief separate dissent, O'CONNOR, J., observed: "If the school board can set the curriculum, select teachers, and determine initially what books to purchase for the school library, it surely can decide which books to discontinue or remove from the school library so long as it does not also interfere with the right of students to read the material and to discuss it. As Justice Rehnquist persuasively argues, the plurality's analysis overlooks the fact that in this case the government is acting in its special role as educator.

"I do not personally agree with the board's action with respect to some of the books in question here, but it is not the function of the courts to make the decisions that have been properly relegated to the elected members of school boards. It is the school board that must determine educational suitability, and it has done so in this case. I therefore join the Chief Justice's dissent."

Notes and Questions

1. Consider Yudof, *Tinker Tailored: Good Faith, Civility, and Student Expression,* 69 St. John's L.Rev. 365, 371 (1965): "[Justice Brennan's] application of a right to know in the context of public schooling is not coherent. * * * The problem with Justice Brennan's rationale is that it indicates that there are good and bad reasons to remove books from the library. In either instance, however, the right to know has been violated because the book has been removed. * * * In one scenario [a] book is excised from the library for poor grammar, and in another, [because] it is ideologically repugnant. [Regardless] of the reason for its removal, the same book is gone."

2. Consider Yudof, *Library Book Selection and Public Schools: The Quest for the Archimedean Point,* 59 Ind.L.J. 527, 530 (1984): The critical questions in *Pico* are "who will control socialization of the young, what are the values to which they will be socialized, and how will cultural grounding and critical reflection be accommodated." On the latter point, see Mendelson, *The Habermas–Gadamer Debate,* New German Critique 18 (1979).[d]

3. Should librarians have a first amendment right to select and retain books against the objections of a school board? Against a city council in a non-school context?[e] Should elementary school teachers have a first amendment right to resist interference with their teaching by "politically" motivated administrators or school boards? At secondary levels? Should student

d. For a range of views on the scope and propriety of government promotion of particular values, see sources collected in fn. i after *Rust* supra. See also Dworkin, *A Matter of Principle* 181–204, 221–33 (1985); Moshman, *Children, Education, and the First Amendment* (1989); Tussman, *Government and the Mind* (1977); Bitensky, *A Contemporary Proposal for Reconciling the Free Speech Clause With Curricular Values Inculcation in the Public Schools,* 70 Notre Dame L.Rev. 769 (1995); Diamond, *The First Amendment and Public Schools: The Case Against Judicial Intervention,* 59 Tex. L.Rev. 477 (1981); Garvey, *Children and the First Amendment,* 57 Tex.L.Rev. 321 (1979); Greene, *Government of the Good,* 53 Vand.L.Rev. 1 (2000); Goldstein *The Asserted Constitutional Right of Public School Teachers to Determine What They Teach,* 124 U.Pa.L.Rev. 1293 (1976); Gottlieb, *In*

The Name of Patriotism: The Constitutionality of "Bending" History in Public Secondary Schools, 62 N.Y.U.L.Rev. 497 (1987); Levinson, *The Tutelary State* in *Censorship and Silencing* 169 (Post ed. 1998). Nahmod, *Controversy in the Classroom: The High School Teacher and Freedom of Expression,* 39 Geo.Wash.L.Rev. 1032 (1971); Sherry, *Responsible Republicanism: Educating for Citizenship,* 62 U.Chi.L.Rev. 131 (1995); van Geel, *The Search for Constitutional Limits on Governmental Authority to Inculcate Youth,* 62 Tex.L.Rev. 197 (1983).

e. See O'Neil, *Libraries, Librarians and First Amendment Freedoms,* 4 Hum.Rts. 295 (1975); O'Neil, *Libraries, Liberties and the First Amendment,* 42 U.Cin.L.Rev. 209 (1973). But see Greene, *Government of the Good,* 53 Vand.L.Rev. 1 (2000).

newspapers have a first amendment right to resist ad hoc intervention by administrators? See Canby, *The First Amendment and the State as Editor: Implications for Public Broadcasting,* 52 Tex.L.Rev. 1123 (1974). What of an approach that allows (requires?) administrators to set policies and procedures but prohibits ad hoc intervention?

4.   Every Justice recognizes that some content discrimination is permitted in selecting books and making curricular decisions. The line between a public forum and a facility subject to the government's editorial discretion, however, may be hard to draw. SOUTHEASTERN PROMOTIONS, LTD. v. CONRAD, 420 U.S. 546, 95 S.Ct. 1239, 43 L.Ed.2d 448 (1975), reacting to reports that the musical *Hair* included nudity and was obscene, a publicly-appointed board denied *Hair's* producers a permit to use a theater dedicated for "cultural advancement and for clean, healthful, entertainment which will make for the upbuilding of a better citizenship." The Court, per BLACKMUN, J., held that the theater was a public forum "designed for and dedicated to expressive activities" and that the board's procedures amounted to a prior restraint in violation of *Freedman* requirements, Ch. 4, II supra. One of the dissenters, REHNQUIST, J., asked: "May a municipal theater devote an entire season to Shakespeare, or is it required to book any potential producer on a first come, first served basis? [T]he Court's opinion [seems] to give no constitutionally permissible role in the way of selection to the municipal authorities." For commentary, see Karst, *Public Enterprise and the Public Forum: A Comment on Southeastern Promotions, Ltd. v. Conrad,* 37 Ohio St.L.J. 247 (1976); Shiffrin, fn. i after *Regan,* supra, at 581–88; Comment, *Access to State–Owned Communications Media—The Public Forum Doctrine,* 26 U.C.L.A.L.Rev. 1410, 1440–44 (1979).

5.   Blackmun, J., states in fn. 2 that the crucial point is the state's decision to "single out an idea for disapproval and then deny access to it." Suppose the government does not deny access to speech but officially denounces it. Constitutional?[f] LAMONT v. POSTMASTER GENERAL, 381 U.S. 301, 85 S.Ct. 1493, 14 L.Ed.2d 398 (1965), per DOUGLAS, J., invalidated a federal statute permitting delivery of "communist political propaganda" only if the addressee specifically requested in writing that it be delivered: "We rest on the narrow ground that the addressee in order to receive his mail must request in writing that it be delivered. [The] addressee carries an affirmative obligation which we do not think the Government may impose on him. This requirement is almost certain to have a deterrent effect, especially as respects those who have sensitive positions. [Public] officials, like school teachers who have no tenure, might think they would invite disaster if they read what the Federal Government says contains the seeds of treason. Apart

f. Consider Professor Lawrence's suggestion that segregation's "*only* purpose is to label or define blacks as inferior." Lawrence, " 'One More River to Cross'—Recognizing the Real Injury in Brown," in *Shades of Brown* 49, 50 (Bell ed. 1980). See also Lawrence, *If He Hollers Let Him Go: Regulating Racist Speech on Campus,* 1990 Duke L.J. 431. When should governmental denunciation of persons or groups be considered a violation of the first amendment?

from them, any addressee is likely to feel some inhibition in sending for literature which federal officials have condemned as 'communist political propaganda.' " But cf. Meese v. Keene, 481 U.S. 465, 107 S.Ct. 1862, 95 L.Ed.2d 415 (1987)(government could label a film as "political propaganda" over the objection of an exhibitor without violating the first amendment).[g]

g. Would an objection from the producer of a film present a stronger case?

Chapter 8

THE ELECTRONIC MEDIA

The mass media are not invariably the most effective means of communication. For example, the right to place messages on utility poles concerning a lost dog may be more important than access to a radio or a television station. In some circumstances, picketing outside a school or placing leaflets in teachers' mailboxes may be the most effective communications medium. Nonetheless, the law regulating access to the mass media is of vital societal importance. This chapter considers first, cases in which government seeks to force newspapers and broadcasters to grant access and cases in which the first amendment is claimed to demand access. Second, this section considers cases involving regulation of the electronic media, particularly those where government seeks to regulate "indecency" in broadcasting, cable, and on the internet.

I. ACCESS TO THE MASS MEDIA

MIAMI HERALD PUB. CO. v. TORNILLO, 418 U.S. 241, 94 S.Ct. 2831, 41 L.Ed.2d 730 (1974), per BURGER, C.J., unanimously struck down a Florida "right of reply" statute, which required any newspaper that "assails" the personal character or official record of a candidate in any election to print, on demand, free of cost, any reply the candidate may make to the charges, in as conspicuous a place and the same kind of type, provided the reply takes up no more space than the charges. The opinion carefully explained the aim of the statute to "ensure that a wide variety of views reach the public" even though "chains of newspapers, national newspapers, national wire and news services, and one-newspaper towns, are the dominant features of a press that has become noncompetitive and enormously powerful and influential in its capacity to manipulate popular opinion and change the course of events," placing "in a few hands the power to inform the American people and shape public opinion."[a] Nonetheless, the Court concluded that to require the printing of a reply violated the first amendment: "Compelling editors or publishers to publish that which" "reason" tells them should not be published' is what is at issue in this case. The Florida statute operates as a command in the same sense as a statute or regulation forbidding

a. The opinion developed these views at greater length, citing "generally" Barron, *Access to the Press—A New First Amendment Right,* 80 Harv.L.Rev. 1641 (1967); Lange, *The Role of the Access Doctrine in the Regulation of the Mass Media: A Critical Review and Assessment,* 52 N.C.L.Rev. 1, 8 (1973). For historical background and a spirited criticism of the statute, see Powe, *Tornillo,* 1987 Sup.Ct.Rev. 345.

appellant from publishing specified matter. [The] Florida statute exacts a penalty on the basis of the content of a newspaper. The first phase of the penalty resulting from the compelled printing of a reply is exacted in terms of the cost in printing and composing time and materials and in taking up space that could be devoted to other material the newspaper may have preferred to print. It is correct, as appellee contends, that a newspaper is not subject to the finite technological limitations of time that confront a broadcaster but it is not correct to say that, as an economic reality, a newspaper can proceed to infinite expansion of its column space to accommodate the replies that a government agency determines or a statute commands the readers should have available.

"Faced with the penalties that would accrue to any newspaper that published news or commentary arguably within the reach of the right of access statute, editors might well conclude that the safe course is to avoid controversy and that, under the operation of the Florida statute, political and electoral coverage would be blunted or reduced. Government enforced right of access inescapably 'dampens the vigor and limits the variety of public debate,' *New York Times*.

"Even if a newspaper would face no additional costs to comply with a compulsory access law and would not be forced to forego publication of news or opinion by the inclusion of a reply, the Florida statute fails to clear the barriers of the First Amendment because of its intrusion into the function of editors. A newspaper is more than a passive receptacle or conduit for news, comment, and advertising. The choice of material to go into a newspaper, and the decisions made as to limitations on the size of the paper, and content, and treatment of public issues and public officials–whether fair or unfair–constitutes the exercise of editorial control and judgment. It has yet to be demonstrated how governmental regulation of this crucial process can be exercised consistent with First Amendment guarantees of a free press as they have evolved to this time."[b]

---

b. Brennan, J., joined by Rehnquist, J., joined the Court's opinion in a short statement to express the understanding that the opinion "implies no view upon the constitutionality of 'retraction' statutes affording plaintiffs able to prove defamatory falsehoods a statutory action to require publication of a retraction. See generally Note, *Vindication of the Reputation of a Public Official*, 80 Harv.L.Rev. 1730, 1739–1747 (1967)."

White, J., concurred. After agreeing that "prior compulsion by government in matters going to the very nerve center of a newspaper—the decision as to what copy will or will not be included in any given edition-collides with the First Amendment," he returned to his attack on *Gertz*,

decided the same day: "Reaffirming the rule that the press cannot be forced to print an answer to a personal attack made by it [throws] into stark relief the consequences of the new balance forged by the Court in the companion case also announced today. *Gertz* goes far toward eviscerating the effectiveness of the ordinary libel action, which has long been the only potent response available to the private citizen libeled by the press. [To] me it is a near absurdity to so deprecate individual dignity, as the Court does in *Gertz,* and to leave the people at the complete mercy of the press, at least in this stage of our history when the press, as the majority in this case so well documents, is steadily becoming more powerful

The Federal Communications Commission has long imposed on radio and television broadcasters the "fairness doctrine"—requiring that stations (1) devote a reasonable percentage of broadcast time to discussion of public issues and (2) assure fair coverage for each side.[a] At issue in RED LION BROADCASTING CO. v. FCC, 395 U.S. 367, 89 S.Ct. 1794, 23 L.Ed.2d 371 (1969), were the application of the fairness doctrine to a particular broadcast[b] and two specific access regulations promulgated under the doctrine: (1) the "political editorial" rule, requiring that when a broadcaster, in an editorial, "endorses or opposes" a political candidate, it must notify the candidate opposed, or the rivals of the candidate supported, and afford them a "reasonable opportunity" to respond; (2) the "personal attack" rule, requiring that "when, during the presentation of views on a controversial issue of public importance, an attack is made on the honesty, character [or] integrity [of] an identified person or group," the person or group attacked must be given notice, a transcript of the attack, and an opportunity to respond.[5] "[I]n view of [the] scarcity of broadcast frequencies, the Government's role in allocating those frequencies, and the legitimate claims of those unable without government assistance to gain access to those frequencies for expression of their views," a 7–0 majority, per WHITE, J., upheld both access regulations:[c]

"[The broadcasters] contention is that the First Amendment protects their desire to use their allotted frequencies continuously to broadcast whatever they choose, and to exclude whomever they choose from ever using that frequency. No man may be prevented from saying or publishing what he thinks, or from refusing in his speech or other utterances to give equal weight to the views of his opponents. This right, they say, applies equally to broadcasters.

"Although broadcasting is clearly a medium affected by a First Amendment interest, differences in the characteristics of new media justify differences in the First Amendment standards applied to [them]. Just as the Government may limit the use of sound-amplifying equipment potentially so noisy that it drowns out civilized private speech, so may the Government limit the use of broadcast equipment. The right of free speech of a broadcast-

---

and much less likely to be deterred by threats of libel suits."

a. For helpful background on the origins, justification and administration of the fairness doctrine, see Barrow, *The Fairness Doctrine: A Double Standard for Electronic and Print Media*, 26 Hast.L.J. 659 (1975); Schmidt, *Freedom of the Press vs. Public Access* 157–98 (1976).

b. *Red Lion* grew out of a series of radio broadcasts by fundamentalist preacher Billy James Hargis, who had attacked Fred J. Cook, author of an article attacking Hargis and "hate clubs of the air." When Cook heard about the broadcast, he demanded that the station give him an opportunity to reply. Cook refused to pay for his "reply

time" and the FCC ordered the station to give Cook the opportunity to reply whether or not he would pay for it. The Supreme Court upheld the order of free reply time. See Schmidt, fn. a supra, at 161–63.

5. Excepted were "personal attacks [by] legally qualified candidates [on] other such candidates" and "bona fide newscasts, bona fide news interviews, and on-the-spot coverage of a bona fide news event."

c. Surprisingly, none of the justices joining White, J.'s opinion felt the need to make additional remarks, but Douglas, J., who did not participate in *Red Lion*, expressed his disagreement with it in the *CBS* case, infra.

er, the user of a sound truck, or any other individual does not embrace a right to snuff out the free speech of [others].

"Where there are substantially more individuals who want to broadcast than there are frequencies to allocate, it is idle to posit an unabridgeable First Amendment right to broadcast comparable to the right of every individual to speak, write, or publish. [It] would be strange if the First Amendment, aimed at protecting and furthering communications, prevented the Government from making radio communication possible by requiring licenses to broadcast and by limiting the number of licenses so as not to overcrowd the spectrum. * * *

"By the same token, as far as the First Amendment is concerned those who are licensed stand no better than those to whom licenses are refused. A license permits broadcasting, but the licensee has no constitutional right [to] monopolize a radio frequency to the exclusion of his fellow citizens. There is nothing in the First Amendment which prevents the Government from requiring a licensee to share his frequency with others and to conduct himself as a proxy or fiduciary with obligations to present those views and voices which are representative of his community and which would otherwise, by necessity, be barred from the airwaves.

"[The] people as a whole retain their interest in free speech by radio and their collective right to have the medium function consistently with the ends and purposes of the First Amendment. It is the right of the viewers and listeners, not the right of the broadcasters, which is paramount. [It] is the purpose of the First Amendment to preserve an uninhibited marketplace of ideas in which truth will ultimately prevail, rather than to countenance monopolization of that market, whether it be by the Government itself or a private licensee. [It] is the right of the public to receive suitable access to social, political, esthetic, moral, and other ideas and experiences which is crucial [here.]

"In terms of constitutional principle, and as enforced sharing of a scarce resource, the personal attack and political editorial rules are indistinguishable from the equal-time provision of § 315 [of the Communications Act], a specific enactment of Congress requiring [that stations allot equal time to qualified candidates for public office] and to which the fairness doctrine and these constituent regulations are important complements. [Nor] can we say that it is inconsistent with the First Amendment goal of producing an informed public capable of conducting its own affairs to require a broadcaster to permit answers to personal attacks occurring in the course of discussing controversial issues, or to require that the political opponents of those endorsed by the station be given a chance to communicate with the public. Otherwise, station owners and a few networks would have unfettered power to make time available only to the highest bidders, to communicate only their own views on public issues, people and candidates, and to permit on the air only those with whom they agreed. There is no sanctuary in the First Amendment for unlimited private censorship operating in a medium not open to all.

"[It is contended] that if political editorials or personal attacks will trigger an obligation in broadcasters to afford the opportunity for expression to speakers who need not pay for time and whose views are unpalatable to the licensees, then broadcasters will be irresistibly forced to self-censorship and their coverage of controversial public issues will be eliminated or at least rendered wholly ineffective. Such a result would indeed be a serious matter, [but] that possibility is at best speculative. [If these doctrines turn out to have this effect], there will be time enough to reconsider the constitutional implications. The fairness doctrine in the past has had no such overall effect. That this will occur now seems unlikely, however, since if present licensees should suddenly prove timorous, the Commission is not powerless to insist that they give adequate and fair attention to public issues. It does not violate the First Amendment to treat licensees given the privilege of using scarce radio frequencies as proxies for the entire community, obligated to give suitable time and attention to matters of great public concern. To condition the granting or renewal of licenses on a willingness to present representative community views on controversial issues is consistent with the ends and purposes of those constitutional provisions forbidding the abridgment of freedom of speech and freedom of the press."[7]

Notes and Questions

1. *Tension between Miami Herald and Red Lion.* Consider Bollinger, *Freedom of the Press and Public Access: Toward a Theory of Partial Regulation of the Mass Media,* 75 Mich.L.Rev. 1, 4–6, 10 (1976): "What seems so remarkable about the unanimous *Miami Herald* opinion is the complete absence of any reference to the Court's unanimous decision five years earlier in *Red Lion*[, upholding] the so-called personal attack rule, [which] is almost identical in substance to the Florida statute declared unconstitutional in *Miami Herald.* That omission, however, is no more surprising than the absence of any discussion in *Red Lion* of the cases in which the Court expressed great concern about the risks attending government regulation of the print media.

"[The] scarcity rationale [articulated in *Red Lion* does not] explain why what appears to be a similar phenomenon of natural monopolization within the newspaper industry does not constitute an equally appropriate occasion for access regulation. A difference in the cause of concentration—the exhaus-

---

7. The Court noted that it "need not deal with the argument that even if there is no longer a technological scarcity of frequencies limiting the number of broadcasters, there nevertheless is an economic scarcity in the sense that the Commission could or does limit entry to the broadcasting market on economic grounds and license no more stations than the market will support. Hence, it is said, the fairness doctrine or its equivalent is essential to satisfy the claims of those excluded and of the public generally. A related argument, which we also put side, is that quite apart from scarcity of frequencies, technological or economic, Congress does not abridge freedom of speech or press by legislation directly or indirectly multiplying the voices and views presented to the public through time sharing, fairness doctrines, or other devices which limit or dissipate the power of those who sit astride the channels of communication with the general public." For background and discussion of *Red Lion,* see Friendly, *The Good Guys, The Bad Guys and the First Amendment* (1975).

tion of a physical element necessary for communication in broadcasting as contrasted with the economic constraints on the number of possible competitors in the print media—would seem far less relevant from a first amendment standpoint than the fact of concentration itself.

"[Instead] of exploring the relevance for the print media of the new principle developed in broadcasting, the Court merely reiterated the opposing, more traditional, principle that the government cannot tell editors what to publish. It thus created a paradox, leaving the new principle unscathed while preserving tradition."

2. *The absence of balancing in Miami Herald.* Did *Miami Herald* present a confrontation between the rights of speech and press? "Nowhere does [*Miami Herald*] explicitly acknowledge [such a confrontation], but implicit recognition of the speech interest," observes Nimmer, *Is Freedom of the Press a Redundancy? What Does it Add to Freedom of Speech?*, 26 Hast.L.J. 639, 645, 657 (1975), "may be found in the Court's reference to the access advocates' argument that, given the present semimonopolistic posture of the press, speech can be effective and therefore free only if enhanced by devices such as a right of reply statute. The Court in accepting the press clause argument in effect necessarily found it to be superior to any competing speech clause claims. [But] the issue cannot be resolved merely by noting, as did [*Miami Herald*], that a right of reply statute 'constitutes the [state] exercise of editorial control and judgment.' This is but one half of the equation. [*Miami Herald*] ignored the strong conflicting claims of 'speech.' Perhaps on balance the press should still prevail, but those who doubt the efficacy of such a result are hardly persuaded by an approach that apparently fails to recognize that any balancing of speech and press rights is required."[8]

3. *Scope of Miami Herald.* Consider Schmidt, supra, note a, at 233–35: "From the perspective of First Amendment law generally, *Miami Herald* would be a stark and unexplained deviation if one were to read the decision as creating absolute prohibitions on access obligations.[9] [The] fact the Court offers no discussion as to why First Amendment rules respecting access should be absolute, while all other rules emanating from that Amendment are relative, suggests that the principle of *Miami Herald* probably is destined for uncharted qualifications and exceptions." But see Powe, *Tornillo,* 1987 Sup.Ct.Rev. 345, 391, 390: "Quite frankly I do not believe that a twenty page Supreme Court opinion meeting all the standards of craft (all considerations

---

8. Does *Miami Herald* demonstrate, as Professor Nimmer believes, at 644B46, that free speech and press can be distinct, even conflicting interests? Lewis, *A Preferred Position for Journalism?*, 7 Hof.L.Rev. 595, 603 (1979), thinks not: "[T]he vice of the [Florida right of reply] law lay in the compulsion to publish; and I think the result would be no different if the case involved a compulsion to speak. If a state statute re-

quired any candidate who spoke falsely about another to make a corrective speech, would it survive challenge under the first amendment?"

9. "Even in the area of 'the central freedom of the First Amendment,' which is criticism of the governmental acts of public officials," recalls Professor Schmidt, fn. a supra, at 232, "there is no absolute protection for expression."

are ventilated fully and the opinion be of publishable quality for a good legal journal) can as effectively protect the right of press autonomy as the blunt rejection in *Tornillo*.

"Chief Justice Burger's failure to engage, so annoying to Schmidt and other commentators, is in fact a great strength of the opinion."

Would a statute requiring nondiscriminatory access to the classified ads section of a newspaper pass muster under *Miami Herald?* A requirement that legal notices be published?

4. *Absolute editorial autonomy—some of the time.* Is it ironic that *Gertz* was decided the same day as *Miami Herald?* Which poses a greater threat to editorial autonomy—a negligence standard in defamation cases or the guaranteed access contemplated by the Florida statute? Whose autonomy is important—the editors or the owners? May government protect editors from ad hoc intervention by corporate owners? See generally Baker, *Press Rights and Government Power to Structure the Press,* 34 U.Miami L.Rev. 819 (1980).

5. *Why was the Court so averse to a limited right of access to the print media?* "One possible explanation," suggests Blasi, 1977 Am.B.Found.Res.J. 521, 621–22, and one "consistent with the checking value," is that even "such a narrow right of reply could have the effect of shifting newspaper coverage away from topics that are central to the checking function—discussions of the fitness of candidates, particularly those with records in office—and toward less valued subjects for which the reply right would be inapplicable. A more likely reason is that the Justices perceived the print media as having historically enjoyed an adversary relationship with government which could only be compromised, symbolically as well as materially, if officials could dictate, for whatever reason, what the content of a particular publication must be. It is significant in this respect that the only Justice who elaborated on the concept of journalistic discretion as it relates to newspapers, [concurring] Justice White, stressed the role of the press as a watchdog over government. It is even possible that the Court responded more favorably to the print journalists' claim to be free from access legislation than to the similar claim of broadcast journalists precisely because the Justices viewed the electronic media as fulfilling, historically as well as currently, a somewhat different and less significant role in the checking process. The Court may well have been influenced by the fact that the networks have never really had an I.F. Stone or a Seymour Hersh or a Woodward and Bernstein."

6. *The threat to editorial autonomy in Red Lion.* Consider Schmidt, fn. a supra, at 166: *Red Lion* "left broadcaster autonomy almost entirely at the mercy of the FCC." See also Van Alstyne, *The Möbius Strip of the First Amendment: Perspectives on Red Lion,* 29 S.C.L.Rev. 539, 571 (1978): "Indeed, if one continues to be troubled by *Red Lion,* I think it is not because one takes lightly the difficulty of forum allocation in a society of scarce resources. Rather, it is because one believes that the technique of the

fairness doctrine in particular may represent a very trivial egalitarian gain and a major first amendment loss; that a twist has been given to the equal protection idea by a device the principal effect of which is merely to level down the most vivid and versatile forum we have, to flatten it out and to render it a mere commercial mirror of each community. What may have been lost is a willingness to risk the partisanship of licensees as catalysts and as active advocates with a freedom to exhort, a freedom that dares to exclaim 'Fuck the draft,' and not be made to yield by government at once to add, 'but on the other hand there is also the view, held by many.' "

Is the right of reply portion of the fairness doctrine less threatening than general fairness requirements? Consider Blasi, note 5 supra, at 627: "I do not believe that loss of editorial control requested by [narrowly] defined rights of reply is likely to undercut journalistic autonomy to such a degree as to dissipate the ethos that makes news organizations view themselves as guardians of the public welfare. And if one's conception of journalistic autonomy derives from the checking value, the preservation of this ethos is the appropriate measure, not some notion of total control analogous to that which an individual must enjoy within a certain sphere if he is to be truly autonomous." But see Karst, *Equality as a Central Principle in the First Amendment,* 43 U.Chi.L.Rev. 20, 49 (1975): "Even though the right-of-reply portion of the fairness doctrine upheld in *Red Lion* is less threatening than the doctrine's more general insistence on fair coverage of issues, a right of reply will give added encouragement to an editorial blandness already promoted by the broadcasters' commercial advertisers; broadcasters will simply minimize the number of newscasts to which a fairness doctrine obligation will attach." Did similar reasoning lead *Miami Herald* to invalidate the state right-of-reply statute directed at newspapers?

7. *The best of both worlds.* "[T]he critical difference between what the Court was asked to do in *Red Lion* and what it was asked to do in *Miami Herald,*" maintains Professor Bollinger note 1 supra, at 27, "involved choosing between a partial regulatory system and a universal one. Viewed from that perspective, the Court reached the correct result in both cases." Continues Bollinger at 27, 32–33, 36–37: "[T]here are good first amendment reasons for being both receptive to and wary of access regulation. This dual nature of access legislation suggests the need to limit carefully the intrusiveness of the regulation in order safely to enjoy its remedial benefits. Thus, a proper judicial response is one that will permit the legislature to provide the public with access *somewhere* within the mass media, but not throughout the press. The Court should not, and need not, be forced into an all-or-nothing position on this matter; there is nothing in the first amendment that forbids having the best of both worlds."[10]

---

10. Does the existence of the threat of regulation or the Court's rhetoric about the press have a substantial impact on press decisions? Compare Bollinger, *Images of a* *Free Press* (1991) with Levi, *Challenging the Autonomous Press,* 78 Cornell L.Rev. 665 (1993).

For a powerful critique of the regulated world, see Powe, *American Broadcasting and the First Amendment* (1987). For a powerful critique of the unregulated world, see Baker, *The First Amendment in Modern Garb,* 58 Ohio St.L.J. 311 (1997).

———

"Like many equal protection issues," observes Karst, note 6 supra, at 45, "the media-access problem should be approached from two separate constitutional directions. First, what does the Constitution *compel* government to do in the way of equalizing? Second, what does the Constitution *permit* government to do in equalizing by statute?" *Red Lion* and *Miami Herald* presented the second question; the first is raised by COLUMBIA BROADCASTING SYSTEM, INC. v. DEMOCRATIC NAT'L COMMITTEE, 412 U.S. 94, 93 S.Ct. 2080, 36 L.Ed.2d 772 (1973) (*CBS*): The FCC rejected the claims of Business Executives' Move for Vietnam Peace (BEM) and the Democratic National Committee (DNC) that "responsible" individuals and groups are entitled to purchase advertising time to comment on public issues, even though the broadcaster has complied with the fairness doctrine. The District of Columbia Circuit held that "a flat ban on paid public issue announcements" violates the first amendment "at least when other sorts of paid announcements are accepted,"[a] and remanded to the FCC to develop "reasonable procedures and regulations determining which and how many 'editorial advertisements' will be put on the air." The Supreme Court, per Burger, C.J., reversed, holding that neither the "public interest" standard of the Communications Act (which draws heavily from the first amendment) nor the first amendment itself—assuming that refusal to accept such advertising constituted "governmental action" for first amendment purposes[b]— requires broadcasters to accept paid editorial announcements. As pointed out in Blasi, note 5 supra, at 613–14, although the Chief Justice "built to some extent" on *Red Lion,* his opinion "evinced a most important change of emphasis. For whereas Justice White based his argument in *Red Lion* on the premise that broadcasters are mere 'proxies' or 'fiduciaries' for the general public, the Chief Justice's opinion [in *CBS*] invoked a concept of 'journalistic independence' or 'journalistic discretion,' the essence of which is that broadcasters do indeed have special First Amendment interests which have to be considered in the constitutional calculus."

a. Compare the access claim advanced in the city bus advertising context in *Lehman v. Shaker Heights,* 418 U.S. 298, 94 S.Ct. 2714, 41 L.Ed.2d 770 (1974) (public transit system permitted to sell commercial advertising for cards on its vehicles while refusing to sell space for political advertising).

b. Burger, C.J., joined by Stewart and Rehnquist, JJ., concluded that a broadcast licensee's refusal to accept an advertisement was not "governmental action" for first amendment purposes. Although White, Blackmun and Powell, JJ., concurred in other parts of the Chief Justice's opinion, they did not decide this question for, *assuming* governmental action, they found that the challenged ban did not violate the first amendment. Douglas, J., who concurred in the result, assumed *no* governmental action. Dissenting, Brennan, J., joined by Marshall, J., found that the challenged ban did constitute "governmental action."

Observed the Chief Justice: "[From various provisions of the Communications Act of 1934] it seems clear that Congress intended to permit private broadcasting to develop with the widest journalistic freedom consistent with its public obligations. Only when the interests of the public are found to outweigh the private journalistic interests of the broadcasters will government power be asserted within the framework of the Act. License renewal proceedings, in which the listening public can be heard, are a principal means of such regulation.

"[W]ith the advent of radio a half century ago, Congress was faced with a fundamental choice between total Government ownership and control of the new medium—the choice of most other countries—or some other alternative. Long before the impact and potential of the medium was realized, Congress opted for a system of private broadcasters licensed and regulated by Government. The legislative history suggests that this choice was influenced not only by traditional attitudes toward private enterprise, but by a desire to maintain for licensees, so far as consistent with necessary regulation, a traditional journalistic [role.]

"The regulatory scheme evolved slowly, but very early the licensee's role developed in terms of a 'public trustee' charged with the duty of fairly and impartially informing the public audience. In this structure the Commission acts in essence as an 'overseer,' but the initial and primary responsibility for fairness, balance, and objectivity rests with the licensee. This role of the Government as an overseer and ultimate arbiter and guardian of the public interest and the role of the licensee as a journalistic 'free agent' call for a delicate balancing of competing interests. The maintenance of this balance for more than 40 years has called on both the regulators and the licensees to walk a 'tightrope' to preserve the First Amendment values written into the Radio Act and its successor, the Communications Act.

"The tensions inherent in such a regulatory structure emerge more clearly when we compare a private newspaper with a broadcast licensee. The power of a privately owned newspaper to advance its own political, social, and economic views is bounded by only two factors: first, the acceptance of a sufficient number of readers—and hence advertisers—to assure financial success; and, second, the journalistic integrity of its editors and publishers. A broadcast licensee has a large measure of journalistic freedom but not as large as that exercised by a newspaper. A licensee must balance what it might prefer to do as a private entrepreneur with what it is required to do as a 'public trustee.' To perform its statutory duties, the Commission must oversee without censoring. This suggests something of the difficulty and delicacy of administering the Communications Act—a function calling for flexibility and the capacity to adjust and readjust the regulatory mechanism to meet changing problems and needs.

"The licensee policy challenged in this case is intimately related to the journalistic role of a licensee for which it has been given initial and primary responsibility by Congress. The licensee's policy against accepting editorial advertising cannot be examined as an abstract proposition, but must be viewed in the context of its journalistic role. It does not help to press on us the idea that editorial ads are 'like' commercial ads, for the licensee's policy against editorial spot ads is expressly based on a journalistic judgment that 10–to 60–second spot announcements are ill-suited to intelligible and intelligent treatment of public issues; the broadcaster has chosen to provide a balanced treatment of controversial questions in a more comprehensive form. Obviously, the licensee's evaluation is based on its own journalistic judgment of priorities and newsworthiness.

"Moreover, the Commission has not fostered the licensee policy challenged here; it has simply declined to command particular action because it fell within the area of journalistic discretion. [The] Commission's reasoning, consistent with nearly 40 years of precedent, is that so long as a licensee meets its 'public trustee' obligation to provide balanced coverage of issues and events, it has broad discretion to decide how that obligation will be met. We do not reach the question whether the First Amendment or the Act can be read to preclude the Commission from determining that in some situations the public interest requires licensees to re-examine their policies with respect to editorial advertisements.[c] The Commission has not yet made such a determination; it has, for the present at least, found the policy to be within the sphere of journalistic discretion which Congress has left with the licensee.

"[I]t must constantly be kept in mind that the interest of the public is our foremost concern. With broadcasting, where the available means of communication are limited in both space and time, [Meiklejohn's admonition] that '[w]hat is essential is not that everyone shall speak, but that everything worth saying shall be said' is peculiarly appropriate.

"[Congress] has time and again rejected various legislative attempts that would have mandated a variety of forms of individual access. [It] has chosen to leave such questions with the Commission, to which it has given the flexibility to experiment with new ideas as changing conditions require. In this case, the Commission has decided that on balance the undesirable effects of the right of access urged by respondents would outweigh the asserted [benefits.]

---

c. *Columbia Broadcasting System, Inc. v. FCC,* 453 U.S. 367, 101 S.Ct. 2813, 69 L.Ed.2d 706 (1981) upheld FCC administration of a statutory provision guaranteeing "reasonable" access to the airwaves for federal election candidates. The Court, per Burger, C.J., observed that "the Court has never approved a *general* right of access to the media. *Miami Herald; CBS v. DNC.* Nor do we do so today." But it found that the limited right of access "properly balances the First Amendment rights of federal candidates, the public, and broadcasters." White, J., joined by Rehnquist and Stevens, JJ., dissented on statutory grounds. For criticism on constitutional grounds, see Polsby, *Candidate Access to the Air: The Uncertain Future of Broadcaster Discretion,* 1981 Sup.Ct.Rev. 223.

"The Commission was justified in concluding that the public interest in providing access to the marketplace of 'ideas and experiences' would scarcely be served by a system so heavily weighted in favor of the financially affluent, or those with access to wealth. Even under a first-come-first-served system [the] views of the affluent could well prevail over those of others, since they would have it within their power to purchase time more frequently. Moreover, there is the substantial danger [that] the time allotted for editorial advertising could be monopolized by those of one political persuasion.

"These problems would not necessarily be solved by applying the Fairness Doctrine, including the *Cullman* doctrine [requiring broadcasters to provide free time for the presentation of opposing views if a paid sponsor is unavailable], to editorial advertising. If broadcasters were required to provide time, free when necessary, for the discussion of the various shades of opinion on the issue discussed in the advertisement, the affluent could still determine in large part the issues to be discussed. Thus, the very premise of the Court of Appeals' holding—that a right of access is necessary to allow individuals and groups the opportunity for self-initiated speech—would have little meaning to those who could not afford to purchase time in the first instance.

"If the Fairness Doctrine were applied to editorial advertising, there is also the substantial danger that the effective operation of that doctrine would be jeopardized. To minimize financial hardship and to comply fully with its public responsibilities a broadcaster might well be forced to make regular programming time available to those holding a view different from that expressed in an editorial advertisement. [The] result would be a further erosion of the journalistic discretion of broadcasters in the coverage of public issues, and a transfer of control over the treatment of public issues from the licensees who are accountable for broadcast performance to private individuals who are not. The public interest would no longer be 'paramount' but rather subordinate to private whim especially since, under the Court of Appeals' decision, a broadcaster would be largely precluded from rejecting editorial advertisements that dealt with matters trivial or insignificant or already fairly covered by the broadcaster. If the Fairness Doctrine and the *Cullman* doctrine were suspended to alleviate these problems, as respondents suggest might be appropriate, the question arises whether we would have abandoned more than we have gained. Under such a regime the congressional objective of balanced coverage of public issues would be seriously threatened.

"Nor can we accept the Court of Appeals' view that every potential speaker is 'the best judge' of what the listening public ought to hear or indeed the best judge of the merits of his or her views. All journalistic tradition and experience is to the contrary. For better or worse, editing is what editors are for; and editing is selection and choice of material. That editors—newspaper or broadcast—can and do abuse this power is beyond doubt, but that is not reason to deny the discretion Congress provided. Calculated risks of abuse are taken in order to preserve higher values. The presence of these risks is nothing new; the authors of the Bill of Rights accepted the reality that these risks were evils for which there was no acceptable remedy other than a spirit of moderation and a sense of responsibility—and civility—on the part of those who exercise the guaranteed freedoms of expression.

"It was reasonable for Congress to conclude that the public interest in being informed requires periodic accountability on the part of those who are entrusted with the use of broadcast frequencies, scarce as they are. In the delicate balancing historically followed in the regulation of broadcasting Congress and the Commission could appropriately conclude that the allocation of journalistic priorities should be concentrated in the licensee rather than diffused among many. This policy gives the public some assurance that the broadcaster will be answerable if he fails to meet their legitimate needs. No such accountability attaches to the private individual, whose only qualifications for using the broadcast facility may be abundant funds and a point of view. To agree that debate on public issues should be 'robust, and wide-open' does not mean that we should exchange 'public trustee' broadcasting, with all its limitations, for a system of self-appointed editorial commentators.

"[T]he risk of an enlargement of Government control over the content of broadcast discussion of public issues [is] inherent in the Court of Appeals' remand requiring regulations and procedures to sort out requests to be heard–a process involving the very editing that licensees now perform as to regular programming. [Under] a constitutionally commanded and government supervised right-of-access system urged by respondents and mandated by the Court of Appeals, the Commission would be required to oversee far more of the day-to-day operations of broadcasters' conduct, deciding such questions as whether a particular individual or group has had sufficient opportunity to present its viewpoint and whether a particular viewpoint has already been sufficiently aired. Regimenting broadcasters is too radical a therapy for the ailment respondents complain of.

"Under the Fairness Doctrine the Commission's responsibility is to judge whether a licensee's overall performance indicates a sustained good faith effort to meet the public interest in being fully and fairly informed. The Commission's responsibilities under a right-of-access system would tend to draw it into a continuing case-by-case determination of who should be heard and when. Indeed, the likelihood of Government involvement is so great that it has been suggested that the accepted constitutional principles against control of speech content would need to be relaxed with respect to editorial advertisements. To sacrifice First Amendment protections for so speculative a gain is not warranted, and it was well within the Commission's discretion to construe the Act so as to avoid such a result.

"The Commission is also entitled to take into account the reality that in a very real sense listeners and viewers constitute a 'captive audience.' [It] is no answer to say that because we tolerate pervasive commercial advertisement [we] can also live with its political counterparts.

"The rationale for the Court of Appeals' decision imposing a constitutional right of access on the broadcast media was that the licensee impermissibly discriminates by accepting commercial advertisements while refusing editorial advertisements. The court relied on [lower court cases] holding that state-supported school newspapers and public transit companies were forbidden by the First Amendment from excluding controversial editorial advertisements in favor of commercial advertisements.[d] The court also attempted to analogize this case to some of our decisions holding that States may not constitutionally ban certain protected speech while at the same time permitting other speech in public areas [citing e.g., *Grayned* and *Mosley,* Ch. 6, I supra].

"These decisions provide little guidance, however, in resolving the question whether the First Amendment required the Commission to mandate a private right of access to the broadcast media. In none of those cases did the forum sought for expression have an affirmative and independent statutory obligation to provide full and fair coverage of public issues, such as Congress has imposed on all broadcast licensees. In short, there is no 'discrimination' against controversial speech present in this case. The question here is not whether there is to be discussion of controversial issues of public importance on the broadcast media, but rather who shall determine what issues are to be discussed by whom, and when."

DOUGLAS, J., concurred in the result, but "for quite different reasons." Because the Court did not decide whether a broadcast licensee is "a federal agency within the context of this case," he assumed that it was not. He "fail[ed] to see," then "how constitutionally we can treat TV and the radio differently than we treat newspapers"[e]:

"I did not participate in [*Red Lion* and] would not support it. The Fairness Doctrine has no place in our First Amendment regime. It puts the head of the camel inside the tent and enables administration after administration to toy with TV or radio in order to serve its sordid or its benevolent ends. [The uniqueness of radio and TV] is due to engineering and technical problems. But the press in a realistic sense is likewise not available to all. [T]he daily newspapers now established are unique in the sense that it would be virtually impossible for a competitor to enter the field due to the financial exigencies of this era. The result is that in practical terms the newspapers and magazines, like the TV and radio, are available only to a select few. [That] may argue for a redefinition of the responsibilities of the press in First Amendment terms. But I do not think it gives us carte blanche to design systems of supervision and control nor empower [the government to] make 'some' laws 'abridging' freedom of the press.

d. But see *Lehman v. Shaker Heights.*

e. Cf. *Miami Herald;* Barrow, supra, at 683–91.

"[O]ne hard and fast principle which [the First Amendment] announces is that government shall keep its hands off the press. [That means] that TV and radio, as well as the more conventional methods for disseminating news, are all included in the concept of 'press' as used in the First Amendment and therefore are entitled to live under the laissez faire regime which the First Amendment [sanctions].

"Licenses are, of course, restricted in time and while, in my view, Congress has the power to make each license limited to a fixed term and nonreviewable, there is no power to deny renewals for editorial or ideological reasons [for] the First Amendment gives no preference to one school of thought over the others.

"The Court in today's decision by endorsing the Fairness Doctrine sanctions a federal saddle on broadcast licensees that is agreeable to the traditions of nations that never have known freedom of press and that is tolerable in countries that do not have a written constitution containing prohibitions as absolute as those in the First Amendment."[f]

BRENNAN, J., joined by Marshall, J., dissented, viewing "the *absolute* ban on the sale of air time for the discussion of controversial issues" as "governmental action"[g] violating the first amendment: "As a practical matter, the Court's reliance on the Fairness Doctrine as an 'adequate' alternative to editorial advertising seriously overestimates the ability—or willingness—of broadcasters to expose the public to the 'widest possible dissemination of information from diverse and antagonistic sources.' [Indeed,] in light of the strong interest of broadcasters in maximizing their audience, and therefore their profits, it seems almost naive to expect the majority of broadcasters to produce the variety and controversiality of material necessary to reflect a full spectrum of viewpoints. Stated simply, angry customers are not good customers and, in the commercial world of mass communications, it is simply 'bad business' to espouse—or even to allow others to espouse—the heterodox or the controversial. As a result, even under the Fairness Doctrine, broadcasters generally tend to permit only established—or at least moderated—views to enter the broadcast world's 'marketplace of ideas.'[24]

"Moreover, the Court's reliance on the Fairness Doctrine as the *sole* means of informing the public seriously misconceives and underestimates the public's interest in receiving ideas and information directly from the advocates of those ideas without the interposition of journalistic middlemen. Under the Fairness Doctrine, broadcasters decide what issues are 'important,' how 'fully' to cover them, and what format, time and style of coverage are 'appropriate.' The retention of such *absolute* control in the hands of a few government licensees is inimical to the First Amendment, for vigorous, free debate can be attained only when members of the public have at least *some* opportunity to take the initiative and editorial control into their own hands.

f. Noting that his views "closely approach those expressed by Mr. Justice Douglas," Stewart, J., also concurred.

g. See fn. b supra.

24. [Citing many secondary sources to support this statement.]

"[S]tanding alone, [the Fairness Doctrine] simply cannot eliminate the need for a further, complementary airing of controversial views through the limited availability of editorial advertising. Indeed, the availability of at least *some* opportunity for editorial advertising is imperative if we are ever to attain the 'free and general discussion of public matters [that] seems absolutely essential to prepare the people for an intelligent exercise of their rights as citizens.'

"Moreover, a proper balancing of the competing First Amendment interests at stake in this controversy must consider, not only the interests of broadcasters and of the listening and viewing public, but also the independent First Amendment interest of groups and individuals in effective self-expression. [I]n a time of apparently growing anonymity of the individual in our society, it is imperative that we take special care to preserve the vital First Amendment interest in assuring 'self-fulfillment [of expression] for each individual.' For our citizens may now find greater than ever the need to express their own views directly to the public, rather than through a governmentally appointed surrogate, if they are to feel that they can achieve at least some measure of control over their own destinies.

"[F]reedom of speech does not exist in the abstract. [It] can flourish only if it is allowed to operate in an effective forum—whether it be a public park, a schoolroom, a town meeting hall, a soapbox, or a radio and television frequency. For in the absence of an effective means of communication, the right to speak would ring hollow indeed. And, in recognition of these principles, we have consistently held that the First Amendment embodies not only the abstract right to be free from censorship, but also the right of an individual to utilize an appropriate and effective medium for the expression of his views.

"[W]ith the assistance of the Federal Government, the broadcast industry has become what is potentially the most efficient and effective 'marketplace of ideas' ever devised. [Thus], although 'full and free discussion' of ideas may have been a reality in the heyday of political pamphleteering, modern technological developments in the field of communications have made the soapbox orator and the leafleteer virtually obsolete. And, in light of the current dominance of the electronic media as the most effective means of reaching the public, any policy that *absolutely* denies citizens access to the airwaves necessarily renders even the concept of 'full and free discussion' practically meaningless.

"[T]he challenged ban can be upheld only if it is determined that such editorial advertising would unjustifiably impair the broadcaster's assertedly overriding interest in exercising *absolute* control over 'his' frequency. Such an analysis, however, hardly reflects the delicate balancing of interests that this sensitive question demands. Indeed, this 'absolutist' approach wholly disregards the competing First Amendment rights of all 'nonbroadcaster' citizens, ignores the teachings of our recent decision in *Red Lion,* and is not supported by the historical purposes underlying broadcast regulation in this Nation. [T]here is simply no overriding First Amendment interest of broadcasters that can justify the *absolute* exclusion of virtually all of our citizens from the most effective 'marketplace of ideas' ever devised.

"[T]his case deals *only* with the allocation of *advertising* time—airtime that broadcasters regularly relinquish to others without the retention of significant editorial control. Thus, we are concerned here not with the speech of broadcasters themselves but, rather, with their 'right' to decide which *other* individuals will be given an opportunity to speak in a forum that has already been opened to the public.

"Viewed in this context, the *absolute* ban on editorial advertising seems particularly offensive because, although broadcasters refuse to sell any airtime whatever to groups or individuals wishing to speak out on controversial issues of public importance, they make such airtime readily available to those 'commercial' advertisers who seek to peddle their goods and services to the public. [Yet an] individual seeking to discuss war, peace, pollution, or the suffering of the poor is denied this right to speak. Instead, he is compelled to rely on the beneficence of a corporate 'trustee' appointed by the Government to argue his case for him.

"It has been long recognized, however, that although access to public forums may be subjected to reasonable 'time, place, and manner' regulations, '[s]elective exclusions from a public forum, may not be based on *content* alone.' *Mosley* (emphasis added). Here, of course, the differential treatment accorded 'commercial' and 'controversial' speech clearly violates that principle. Moreover, and not without some irony, the favored treatment given 'commercial' speech under the existing scheme clearly reverses traditional First Amendment priorities. For it has generally been understood that 'commercial' speech enjoys *less* First Amendment protection than speech directed at the discussion of controversial issues of public importance."[h]

Notes and Questions

1. *"Elitism" and the CBS case?* Consider Bollinger, *Elitism, The Masses and the Idea of Self–Government,* in Constitutional Government in America 99, 104–05 (Collins ed. 1980): "[CBS] seemed to rely on the problems of administration and the need for journalistic discretion as the primary reasons for its result. It was this latter theory of the case that caused the decision to be hailed by the press [as] representing a substantial shift in the Court's thinking from that found in *Red Lion.* [But], the opinion is deceptive on that score; for the emphasis on journalistic discretion did not arise from a pure belief in the wisdom of journalists but rather from a perceived need to maintain control of the content of broadcasting in the hands of those who live under the aegis of government scrutiny.

"[The] difficulty with the claim of BEM and DNC was that it opened the broadcast doors to people who were not made 'responsible' through the

h. Cf. Brennan, J.'s dissent in *Lehman* v. Shaker Heights.

subtle processes of government selection and oversight. And the possibilities of exploitation of mass public opinion on such vital matters as the war effort, through techniques of distortion and emotional appeals, was a more pressing danger than any commercial speech * * *.

"All of this is to suggest that [an] elitist view colored the thinking of the Court in *CBS,* as it has in other areas of broadcast regulation. The phenomenon cannot be explained away as simply the reactionary stance of conservative justices to anti-war speech. Whatever one thinks of the outcome of the *CBS* case, the fear of manipulation as a motivating factor in our thinking is not a distinctive characteristic of any particular ideological group. It also supports the position, advocated by many liberals, that something ought to be done to remove or lessen the amount of violence on television."

2. *Confronting scarcity.* Consider Tribe, *American Constitutional Law* 1005 (2d ed. 1988): "*CBS* took a step away from *Red Lion* by its treatment of broadcasters as part of the 'press' with an important editorial function to perform rather than as analogous to the postal or telephone systems, but *CBS* was firmly in the *Red Lion* tradition when it refused to consider the possibility that either the technologically scarce radio and television channels, or the finite time available on such channels, might be allocated much as economically scarce newspaper opportunities are allocated: by a combination of market mechanisms and chance rather than by government design coupled with broadcaster autonomy."

Suppose the government sold the airwaves to the highest bidder and allowed subsequent exchange according to property and contract law. Consider Note, *Reconciling Red Lion and Tornillo: A Consistent Theory of Media Regulation,* 28 Stan.L.Rev. 563, 583 (1976): "This regulatory strategy would remove the government from direct determination of the particular individuals who are allowed to broadcast, leaving this decision to market forces, and would avoid the need for specific behavioral commands and sanctions now necessary to secure compliance by broadcasters with the various obligations imposed by the public interest standard. [Under] strict scrutiny, then, the existence of this clearly identifiable less restrictive alternative indicates that the Communications Act is unconstitutional."

But see Van Alstyne, "Congress may indeed be free to 'sell off' the airwaves, and it may be wholly feasible to allocate most currently established broadcast signals by competitive bidding that, when done, may well produce private licensees operating truly without subsidy. But only a singularly insensitive observer would believe that this choice is not implicitly also a highly speech-restrictive choice by Congress. It is fully as speech-restrictive as though, in the case of land, government were to withdraw from *all* ownership and all subsidized maintenance of all land, including parks, auditoriums, and streets and to remain in the field exclusively as a policeman to enforce the proprietary decisions of all private landowners."[i]

Should it be constitutional for the government to exercise "ownership" over the entire broadcast spectrum?[j]

3. *The "fairness" doctrine criticized.* The Court's assumption that the fairness doctrine works tolerably well has been roasted by the commentators. See, e.g., Rowan, *Broadcast Fairness: Doctrine, Practice, Prospects* (1984); Simmons, *The Fairness Doctrine and the Media* (1978); Johnson & Dystel, *A Day in the Life: The Federal Communications Commission,* 82 Yale L.J. 1575 (1973). Consider Krattenmaker & Powe, *The Fairness Doctrine Today: A Constitutional Curiosity and an Impossible Dream,* 1985 Duke L.J. 151, 175: "If the doctrine is to be taken seriously then suspected violations lurk everywhere and the FCC should undertake continuous oversight of the industry. If the FCC will not—or cannot—do that, then the doctrine must be toothless except for the randomly-selected few who are surprised to feel its bite after the fact." For a vigorous defense of the fairness doctrine, see Ferris & Kirkland, *Fairness—The Broadcaster's Hippocratic Oath,* 34 Cath. U.L.Rev. 605 (1985).

4. *The fairness doctrine repealed.* The FCC concluded a 15 month administrative proceeding with an official denunciation of the fairness doctrine, pointing in particular to the marked increase in the information services marketplace since *Red Lion* and the effects of the doctrine in application. FCC, *[General] Fairness Doctrine Obligations of Broadcast Licensees,* 102 F.C.C.2d 142 (1985). *Syracuse Peace Council,* 2 FCC Rcd 5043 (1987) held that "under the constitutional standard established by *Red Lion* and its progeny, the fairness doctrine contravenes the First Amendment and its enforcement is no longer in the public interest."[k]

5. *The worst of both worlds.* Evaluate the following hypothetical commentary: "*CBS v. DNC* allows government to grant virtually exclusive

---

i. For detailed, but traditional, criticism of the scarcity argument, see Spitzer, *Controlling the Content of Print and Broadcast,* 58 S.Cal.L.Rev. 1349 (1985). But see Metro Broadcasting v. FCC, 497 U.S. 547, 110 S.Ct. 2997, 111 L.Ed.2d 445 (1990)(reaffirming the government's power to regulate the "limited number" of broadcast licensees in the context of upholding minority ownership policies designed to effectuate more diverse programming and to safeguard the "rights of the viewing and listening audiences"). For criticism of the scarcity argument in light of new technology, see Lessig, *Code* 182–85 (1999).

j. See Robinson, *The Electronic First Amendment: An Essay for the New Age,* 47 Duke L.J. 899, 933–39 (1998); Spitzer, *The Constitutionality of Licensing Broadcasters,* 64 N.Y.U.L.Rev. 990 (1989); Shiffrin, *Gov-*

ernment Speech, 27 UCLA L.Rev. 565, 587 n. 122, 644–45 (1980).

k. *Syracuse Peace Council v. FCC,* 867 F.2d 654 (D.C.Cir.1989) affirmed the FCC's determination that the fairness doctrine no longer serves the public interest without reaching constitutional issues. On June 20, 1987 President Reagan had vetoed congressional legislation designed to preserve the fairness doctrine on the ground that the legislation was unconstitutional. Radio–Television News Directors Assoc. v. FCC, 229 F.3d 269 (D.C.Cir.2000) ordered the FCC to vacate the personal attack rules with the understanding that the rules might be reinstated if the Commission conducted a new rule-making proceeding to determine whether the public interest, consistent with the first amendment, required them.

control over American's most valuable communication medium to corporations who regard it as their mission to 'deliver' audiences to advertisers. The system gives us the worst of both worlds: the world of profit-seeking—without a free market; the world of regulation—without planning." For discussion of alternatives, see Cass, *Revolution in the Wasteland* (1981); Owen, *Economics and Freedom of Expression: Media Structure and the First Amendment* (1975); Firestone & Jacklin, *Deregulation and the Pursuit of Fairness* in Telecommunications Policy and the Citizen 107 (Haight ed. 1979); Nader & Riley, *Oh Say Can You See: A Broadcast Network for the Audience,* 5 J.L. & Pol. 1 (1988); Owen, *Structural Approaches to the Problem of Television Network Economic Dominance,* 1979 Duke L.J. 191.

6.   Do access proposals miss the central problem? Is television at the heart of an "amusement-centered culture" that substitutes images and sound bites for serious public discourse while encouraging a privatized nonengaged citizenry? Consider Collins and Skover, *The First Amendment in an Age of Paratroopers,* 68 Tex.L.Rev. 1087, 1088–89 (1990): "With entertainment as the paradigm for most public discourse, traditional first-amendment values—which stress civic restraint and serious dialogue—are overshadowed. Given these core values and the anticensorial direction of first-amendment theory, is there anything that could (or should) be done to thwart, rather than to feed, an amusement-centered culture?

"In attempting to answer this question, we confront a paradox: by saving itself, the first amendment destroys itself. On the one hand, to preserve its anticensorial ideals, the first amendment must protect both the old and new media cultures. Accordingly, it must constrain most governmental controls over expression, including those over the commercial use of electronic media. On the other hand, if the first amendment's protections do not differentiate between the old and new media cultures, the modern obsession with self-amusement will trivialize public discourse and undermine the traditional aim of the first amendment."[1]

7.   Consider Geller, *The Transformation of Television News: Articles and Comments: Fairness and the Public Trustee Concept: Time to Move On,* 47 Fed.Com.L.J. 79, 83–84 (1994): "It makes no sense to try to impose effective, behavioral regulation [when] conventional television faces such fierce and increasing competition, and viewership is declining rather than growing. It would be much sounder to truly deregulate broadcasting by eliminating the public trustee requirement and in its place substituting a reasonable spectrum fee imposed on existing stations (and an auction for all new frequency assignments), with the sums so obtained dedicated to public telecommunications. * * * For the first time, we would have a structure that works to accomplish explicit policy goals. The commercial system would continue to do what it already does—deliver a great variety of entertainment and news-type programs. The noncommercial system would have the funds

---

1. For discussion of the Collins–Skover paradox by Max Lerner, David M. O'Brien, Martin Redish, Edward Rubin, Herbert Schiller, and Mark Tushnet, see Colloquy: *The First Amendment and the Paratroopers Paradox,* 68 Texas L.Rev. 1087 (1990).

to accomplish its goals—to supply needed public service such as educational programming for children, cultural fare, minority presentations, and in-depth informational programs.''

8. *Cable television.* Can government require cable operators to grant an access channel for the public, for the government, and for educational institutions? Which is the better analogy: *Red Lion* or *Miami Herald?* Need government lease space or otherwise afford access to utility poles under its control (and grant rights of way) to all competing cable companies. Is the appropriate analogy to *Schneider? Perry? Vincent? Red Lion? Miami Herald?*

———

The Cable Television and Consumer Protection and Competition Act of 1992 required cable television systems to devote a portion of their channels to local broadcast channels including commercial stations and public broad-cast stations.[a] The Congress was concerned about the monopolistic character of cable operations in most localities and the economic incentives for cable operators to favor their own programming. It also pointed to the importance of maintaining local broadcasting. TURNER BROADCASTING SYSTEM, INC. v. FCC, 512 U.S. 622, 114 S.Ct. 2445, 129 L.Ed.2d 497 (1994), per KENNEDY, J., joined by Rehnquist, C.J., and Blackmun, Souter, JJ., upheld the requirement so long as the Government could demonstrate on remand that in the absence of legislation, a large number of broadcast stations would not be carried or would be adversely repositioned, that such stations would be at serious risk of financial difficulty, that the impact on cable operators would not excessively impact on cable operator's programming selections (as opposed to using unused channel capacity), and that no effective alternative less restrictive means existed. The plurality, joined by Stevens, J., argued that the antitrust interests of government were content neutral, but con-cluded that ''some measure of heightened First Amendment scrutiny'' was appropriate because the act was not a generally applicable law but directed at cable operators. ''The scope and operation of the challenged provisions make clear [that] Congress designed the must-carry provisions not to pro-mote speech of a particular content, but to prevent cable operators from exploiting their economic power to the detriment of broadcasters, and

---

a. It also required that they be placed in the same numerical position as when broad-cast over the air. For pre-*Turner* commen-tary, see Brenner, *Cable Television and the Freedom of Expression,* 1988 Duke L.J. 329. See also Powe, supra, at 216–47; Saylor, *Municipal Ripoff: The Unconstitutionality of Cable Television Franchise Fees and Ac-cess Support Payments,* 35 Cath.U.L.Rev. 671 (1986); Pool, *Technologies of Freedom* 151–88 (1983); Price, *Taming Red Lion: The First Amendment and Structural Ap-proaches to Media Regulation,* 31 Fed.

Comm.L.J. 215 (1979); Comment, *Access to Cable Television: A Critique of the Affirma-tive Duty Theory of the First Amendment,* 70 Calif.L.Rev. 1393 (1982). For discussion of other technologies, see *Special Issue, Vi-deotex,* 36 Fed.Comm.L.J. 119 (1984); For valuable commentary on the implications for the first amendment in cyberspace, see Symposium: *Emerging Media Technology and the First Amendment,* 104 Yale L.J. 1611 (1995); Price, *Free Expression and Di-gital Dreams: The Open and Closed Terrain of Speech,* 22 Critical Inquiry 64 (1995).

thereby to ensure that all Americans, especially those unable to subscribe to cable, have access to free television programming—whatever its content."[b]

O'CONNOR, J., joined by Scalia, Ginsburg, & Thomas, JJ., concurring in part and dissenting in part, would have held the requirements unconstitutional without a remand. They argued that strict scrutiny was appropriate because the preference for broadcasters over cable programmers on many channels was justified with reference to content (referring to findings about local public affairs programming and public television).[c] Although the interest in public affairs programming was said to be weighty, O'Connor, J., observed that public affairs cable-programming could be displaced: "In the rare circumstances where the government may draw content-based distinctions to serves its goals, the restrictions must serve the goals a good deal more precisely than this." O'Connor, J., also argued that the requirements should fail content neutral scrutiny as well because the act disadvantaged cable operators with no anti-competitive motives and favored broadcasters who could financially survive even if dropped from a cable system.[d]

Notes and Questions

1. Has the United States "consistently and properly engaged in content-motivated structuring of the communications realm" in ways that have usually "benefitted the nation." See Baker, *Turner Broadcasting: Content–Based Regulation of Persons and Presses,* 1994 Sup.Ct.Rev. 57, 94. Does the dissent's emphasis on content discrimination shortchange the government's interest in assuring a robust communications system? Would such an emphasis lead to the conclusion that commercial broadcasters deserved no preference but public broadcasters did? Consider Hawthorne and Price, *Rewiring the First Amendment: Meaning, Content and Public Broadcasting* 12 Cardozo Arts & Ent.L.J. 499, 504 (1994): "If the absence of a meaningful content basis for preferring commercial broadcasters should impair their entitlement to 'must-carry' treatment, precisely the converse is true for noncommercial broadcasters. These entities have been mandated to carry on government's historic responsibility to educate the citizenry and more recent undertaking to subsidize the arts."[e]

---

b. Blackmun, J., concurring, emphasized the importance of deferring to Congress during the new proceedings. Stevens, J., concurring, reluctantly joined the order to remand; he would have preferred to affirm the must-carry legislation without further proceedings. Ginsburg, J., concurred in parts of the Court's opinion (including the section arguing for intermediate first amendment scrutiny regarding the antitrust interest), filed a separate concurring opinion, and joined O'Connor, J.'s opinion.

c. Kennedy, J., argued that such findings showed "nothing more than the recognition that the services provided by broadcast television have some intrinsic value and, thus, are worth preserving against the threats posed by cable."

d. Thomas, J., did not join this section of the opinion.

e. For additional commentary, see Sunstein, *One Case at a Time* 172–82 (1999); Robinson, *The Electronic First Amendment: An Essay for the New Age,* 47 Duke L.J.

2. After remand, TURNER BROADCASTING SYSTEM, INC. v. FCC, 520 U.S. 180, 117 S.Ct. 1174, 137 L.Ed.2d 369 (1997), per KENNEDY, J., joined by Rehnquist, C.J., Stevens, and Souter, JJ., upheld the must-carry provisions. Applying the *O'Brien* test, he emphasized the importance of deferring to Congress so long as it had "drawn reasonable inferences based upon substantial evidence." He found that the legislation was narrowly tailored to preserve the benefits of local broadcast television, to promote widespread dissemination of information from a multiplicity of sources, and to promote fair competition.

BREYER, J., concurring, joined Kennedy, J.'s opinion except for his discussion and conclusion regarding the fair competition rationale.[f]

O'CONNOR, J., joined by Scalia, Thomas, and Ginsburg, JJ., dissenting, argued again that strict scrutiny should apply, agreed that deference was owed to Congress "in its predictive judgments and its evaluation of complex economic questions," but maintained that even under intermediate scrutiny, the Court had an independent duty to examine with care the Congressional interests, the findings, and the fit between the goals and consequences. She criticized the Court for being too deferential even on the assumption that the legislation was content neutral.

On O'Connor, J.'s analysis, the record did not support either the conclusion that cable posed a significant threat to local broadcast markets or that the act was narrowly tailored to deal with anti-competitive conduct.[g]

––––––––

ARKANSAS EDUCATIONAL TELEVISION COMMISSION v. FORBES, 523 U.S. 666, 118 S.Ct. 1633, 140 L.Ed.2d 875 (1998), per KENNEDY, J., concluded that a candidate debate sponsored by a state-owned public television broadcaster was a nonpublic forum subject to constitutional restraints, but that the broadcaster's decision to exclude a candidate was reasonable: "A state-owned public television broadcaster [Arkansas Educational Television Commission 'AETC'] sponsored a candidate debate from which it excluded an independent congressional candidate [Ralph Forbes] with little popular support. The issue before us is whether, by reason of its state ownership, the station had a constitutional obligation to allow every candidate access to the debate. We conclude that, unlike most other public television programs, the candidate debate was subject to constitutional constraints applicable to nonpublic fora under our forum prece-

899, 911–13 (1998); Barron, *Reading Turner through a Tornillo Lens,* 13 Comm. Lawyer (1995); Price & Hawthorne, *Saving Public Television,* Hast. Comm./Ent.L.J. 65 (1994); *The First Amendment in Cyberspace,* 104 Yale L.J. 1757 (1995).

f. Stevens, J., also filed a concurring opinion.

g. Would *Turner* justify the application of "must carry" rules to segments of the Internet such as Netscape. See Chin, *Making the World Wide Web Safe for Democracy: A Medium–Specific First Amendment Analysis,* 19 Hastings Comm/Ent L.J. 309 (1997).

dents. Even so, the broadcaster's decision to exclude the candidate was a reasonable, viewpoint-neutral exercise of journalistic discretion. * * *

"Although public broadcasting as a general matter does not lend itself to scrutiny under the forum doctrine, candidate debates present the narrow exception to the rule. For two reasons, a candidate debate like the one at issue here is different from other programming. First, unlike AETC's other broadcasts, the debate was by design a forum for political speech by the candidates. Consistent with the long tradition of candidate debates, the implicit representation of the broadcaster was that the views expressed were those of the candidates, not its own. The very purpose of the debate was to allow the candidates to express their views with minimal intrusion by the broadcaster. In this respect the debate differed even from a political talk show, whose host can express partisan views and then limit the discussion to those ideas.

"Second, in our tradition, candidate debates are of exceptional significance in the electoral process. [Deliberation] on the positions and qualifications of candidates is integral to our system of government, and electoral speech may have its most profound and widespread impact when it is disseminated through televised debates. * * *

"Under our precedents, the AETC debate was not a designated public forum. * * * [T]he government creates a designated public forum when it makes its property generally available to a certain class of speakers, as the university made its facilities generally available to student groups in *Widmar*. On the other hand, the government does not create a designated public forum when it does no more than reserve eligibility for access to the forum to a particular class of speakers, whose members must then, as individuals, 'obtain permission,' to use it. For instance, the Federal Government did not create a designated public forum in Cornelius when it reserved eligibility for participation in the CFC drive to charitable agencies, and then made individual, non-ministerial judgments as to which of the eligible agencies would participate.

"The [distinction] between general and selective access furthers First Amendment interests. By recognizing the distinction, we encourage the government to open its property to some expressive activity in cases where, if faced with an all-or-nothing choice, it might not open the property at all.[a] That this distinction turns on governmental intent does not render it

---

a. In a later section, the Court stated: "In each of the 1988, 1992, and 1996 Presidential elections, for example, no fewer than 22 candidates appeared on the ballot in at least one State. In the 1996 congressional elections, it was common for 6 to 11 candidates to qualify for the ballot for a particular seat. In the 1993 New Jersey gubernatorial election, to illustrate further, sample ballot mailings included the written statements of 19 candidates. On logistical grounds alone, a public television editor might, with reason, decide that the inclusion of all ballot-qualified candidates would

'actually undermine the educational value and quality of debates.'

"Were it faced with the prospect of cacophony, on the one hand, and First Amendment liability, on the other, a public television broadcaster might choose not to air candidates' views at all.

"These concerns are more than speculative. As a direct result of the Court of Appeals' decision in this case, the Nebraska Educational Television Network canceled a scheduled debate between candidates in Nebraska's 1996 United States Senate race. A

unprotective of speech. Rather, it reflects the reality that, with the exception of traditional public fora, the government retains the choice of whether to designate its property as a forum for specified classes of speakers.

"Here, the debate did not have an open-microphone format. [AETC] did not make its debate generally available to candidates for Arkansas' Third Congressional District seat. Instead, just as the Federal Government in *Cornelius* reserved eligibility for participation in the CFC program to certain classes of voluntary agencies, AETC reserved eligibility for participation in the debate to candidates for the Third Congressional District seat (as opposed to some other seat). At that point, just as the Government in *Cornelius* made agency-by-agency determinations as to which of the eligible agencies would participate in the CFC, AETC made candidate-by-candidate determinations as to which of the eligible candidates would participate in the debate. 'Such selective access, unsupported by evidence of a purposeful designation for public use, does not create a public forum.' Thus the debate was a nonpublic forum.

"The debate's status as a nonpublic forum, however, did not give AETC unfettered power to exclude any candidate it wished. [To] be consistent with the First Amendment, the exclusion of a speaker from a nonpublic forum must not be based on the speaker's viewpoint and must otherwise be reasonable in light of the purpose of the property. *Cornelius.* * * *

"There is no substance to Forbes' suggestion that he was excluded because his views were unpopular or out of the mainstream. * * * Nor did AETC exclude Forbes in an attempted manipulation of the political process. The evidence provided powerful support for the jury's express finding that AETC's exclusion of Forbes was not the result of 'political pressure from anyone inside or outside [AETC].' There is no serious argument that AETC did not act in good faith in this case. AETC excluded Forbes because the voters lacked interest in his candidacy, not because AETC itself did. The broadcaster's decision to exclude Forbes was a reasonable, viewpoint-neutral exercise of journalistic discretion consistent with the First Amendment."

STEVENS, J., joined by Souter & Ginsburg, JJ., dissented: "The official action that led to the exclusion of respondent Forbes from a debate with the two major-party candidates for election to one of Arkansas' four seats in Congress does not adhere to well-settled constitutional principles. The ad hoc decision of the staff of [AETC] raises precisely the concerns addressed by 'the many decisions of this Court over the last 30 years, holding that a law subjecting the exercise of First Amendment freedoms to the prior restraint of a license, without narrow, objective, and definite standards to guide the licensing authority, is unconstitutional.' *Shuttlesworth v. Birmingham.*

First Amendment jurisprudence yielding these results does not promote speech but represses it."

"Given the fact that the Republican winner in the Third Congressional District race in 1992 received only 50.22% of the vote and the Democrat received 47.20%, it would have been necessary for Forbes, who had made a strong showing in recent Republican primaries, to divert only a handful of votes from the Republican candidate to cause his defeat. Thus, even though the AETC staff may have correctly concluded that Forbes was 'not a serious candidate,' their decision to exclude him from the debate may have determined the outcome of the election in the Third District.

"If a comparable decision were made today by a privately owned network, it would be subject to scrutiny under the Federal Election Campaign Act unless the network used 'pre-established objective criteria to determine which candidates may participate in [the] debate.' 11 CFR § 110.13(c) (1997). No such criteria governed AETC's refusal to permit Forbes to participate in the debate. Indeed, whether that refusal was based on a judgment about 'newsworthiness'—as AETC has argued in this Court— or a judgment about 'political viability'—as it argued in the Court of Appeals—the facts in the record presumably would have provided an adequate basis either for a decision to include Forbes in the Third District debate or a decision to exclude him * * *.

"The apparent flexibility of AETC's purported standard suggests the extent to which the staff had nearly limitless discretion to exclude Forbes from the debate based on ad hoc justifications. Thus, the Court of Appeals correctly concluded that the staff's appraisal of 'political viability' was 'so subjective, so arguable, so susceptible of variation in individual opinion, as to provide no secure basis for the exercise of governmental power consistent with the First Amendment.' * * *

"The reasons that support the need for narrow, objective, and definite standards to guide licensing decisions apply directly to the wholly subjective access decisions made by the staff of AETC.[18] The importance of avoiding arbitrary or viewpoint-based exclusions from political debates militates strongly in favor of requiring the controlling state agency to use (and adhere to) pre-established, objective criteria to determine who among qualified candidates may participate. A constitutional duty to use objective standards—i.e., 'neutral principles'—for determining whether and when to adjust a debate format would impose only a modest requirement that would fall far short of a duty to grant every multiple-party request. Such standards would also have the benefit of providing the public with some assurance that state-owned broadcasters cannot select debate participants on arbitrary grounds."

18. Ironically, it is the standardless character of the decision to exclude Forbes that provides the basis for the Court's conclusion that the debates were a nonpublic forum rather than a limited public forum. [T]he Court explains that '[a] designated public forum is not created when the government allows selective access for individual speakers rather than general access for a class of speakers.' If, as AETC claims, it did invite either the entire class of 'viable' candidates, or the entire class of 'newsworthy' candidates, under the Court's reasoning, it created a designated public forum.

Notes and Questions

1. Consider Schauer, *Principles, Institutions, and the First Amendment*, 112 Harv. L. Rev. 84 (1998): "Beyond designated public forums, [it] is hard to see the point of forum analysis in government enterprise cases. In the typical case, the complaint is not about access, but about discriminatory treatment. And at the heart of this issue is the seemingly banal but quite important point that content-based discriminatory treatment is appropriate in some contexts, but not in others. Yet once we recognize this idea, the point of combining the determination of which contexts permit content discrimination and which do not with public forum analysis is elusive. If access is mandatory, then the focus on content discrimination is redundant. But if access is not mandatory, then the existence (or not) of a public forum is superfluous. What is not superfluous is the question whether this is one of the government enterprises which may control for content or viewpoint, and as to this question public forum doctrine offers no assistance. * * * That forum analysis plays no role at all in *Finley*, and that the conclusory distinction between a nonpublic forum and a not-forum does all of the work in *Forbes*, serves only to underscore the point."

2. *No point of view discrimination?* Consider Schauer & Pildes, *Electoral Exceptionalism and the First Amendment*, 77 Texas L.Rev. 1803, 1804 n. 5 (1999): "[A] standard of electoral viability serves to entrench accepted views against the challenge of non-accepted views * * *. The role of challenges is not to displace the two-party system, as that is unlikely for many reasons, but precisely to shift the terms of electoral debate." Does that amount to point of view discrimination? See generally Raskin, *The Debate Gerrymander*, 77 Texas L.Rev. 1943 (1999). If not, should the exclusion of Forbes have been invalidated anyway on the ground that the exclusion skews public debate? Should the state's purpose matter? See Fiss, *The Censorship of Television*, 93 Nw.U.L.Rev. 1215, 1233 (1999).

3. *Congressional action.* Suppose Congress required state owned broadcast stations to admit all official candidates to televised debates. Constitutional?

II.   THE ELECTRONIC MEDIA AND CONTENT REGULATION

FCC v. PACIFICA FOUNDATION

438 U.S. 726, 98 S.Ct. 3026, 57 L.Ed.2d 1073 (1978).

[Mr. Justice Stevens delivered the opinion of the Court (Parts I, II, III, and IV–C) and an opinion in which Chief Justice Burger and Mr. Justice Rehnquist joined (Parts IV–A and IV–B).

[In an early afternoon weekday broadcast in October 1973, respondent's New York radio station aired a 12–minute selection called "Filthy Words,"

510 FREEDOM OF EXPRESSION & ASSOCIATION Pt. 1

from a comedy album by a satiric humorist, George Carlin. The monologue, which had evoked frequent laughter from a live theater audience before whom it had originally been delivered, began by referring to Carlin's thought about the seven words you can't say on the public airwaves, "the ones you definitely wouldn't say ever." He then listed the words ("shit," "piss," "fuck," "motherfucker," "cocksucker," "cunt," and "tits"), "the ones that will curve your spine, grow hair on your hands and (laughter) maybe, even bring us, God help us, peace without honor (laughter) um, and a bourbon (laughter)," and repeated them over and over in a variety of colloquialisms. The monologue was played as part of the station's regular program, which was devoted that day to contemporary attitudes toward the use of language. Immediately prior to the broadcast of the Carlin monologue, listeners were advised that it included sensitive language which some might regard as offensive. Those who might be offended were advised to change the station and return in fifteen minutes.

[The FCC received a complaint from a man in New York stating that while driving in his car with his young son he had heard the broadcast of the Carlin monologue. In response, the FCC issued a Declaratory Order granting the complaint and holding that Pacifica "could have been the subject of administrative sanctions," but that this order would only be "associated with the station's license file, and in the event that subsequent complaints are received, the Commission will then decide whether it should utilize any of the available sanctions it has been granted by Congress."][a]

The Commission characterized the language used in the Carlin monologue as "patently offensive," though not necessarily obscene, and expressed the opinion that it should be regulated by principles analogous to those found in the law of nuisance where the "law generally speaks to *channeling* behavior more than actually prohibiting it. [T]he concept of 'indecent' is intimately connected with the exposure of children to language that describes, in terms patently offensive as measured by contemporary community standards for the broadcast medium, sexual or excretory activities and organs, at times of the day when there is a reasonable risk that children may be in the audience."[5]

Applying these considerations to the language used in the monologue as broadcast by respondent, the Commission concluded that certain words depicted sexual and excretory activities in a patently offensive manner, noted that they "were broadcast at a time when children were undoubtedly in the audience (i.e., in the early afternoon)," and that the prerecorded language, with these offensive words "repeated over and over," was "deliberately broadcast." In summary, the Commission stated: "We therefore hold that

---

a. The FCC's action is placed in the context of other similar actions in Powe, *American Broadcasting and the First Amendment* 162–90 (1987).

5. Thus, the Commission suggested, if an offensive broadcast had literary, artistic,

political or scientific value, and were preceded by warnings, it might not be indecent in the late evening, but would be so during the day, when children are in the audience.

the language as broadcast was indecent and prohibited by 18 U.S.C. 1464 [forbidding the use of 'any obscene, indecent or profane language' by means of radio communications.]"[6] [The Commission subsequently clarified its opinion, pointing out] that it "never intended to place an absolute prohibition on the broadcast of this type of language, but rather sought to channel it to times of day when children most likely would not be exposed to it." * * *

I.   The general statements in the Commission's memorandum opinion do not change the character of its order. Its action was an adjudication under 5 U.S.C. § 554(e); it did not purport to engage in formal rulemaking or in the promulgation of any regulations. The order "was issued in a special factual context"; questions concerning possible action in other contexts were expressly reserved for the future. The specific holding was carefully confined to the monologue "as broadcast." * * *

II.   The relevant statutory questions are whether the Commission's action is forbidden "censorship" within the meaning of 47 U.S.C. § 326 and whether speech that concededly is not obscene may be restricted as "indecent" under the authority of 18 U.S.C. § 1464. [The] prohibition against censorship unequivocally denies the Commission any power to edit proposed broadcasts in advance [but] has never been construed to deny the Commission the power to review the content of completed broadcasts in the performance of its regulatory duties. * * *

III.   The only other statutory question presented by this case is whether the afternoon broadcast of the "Filthy Words" monologue was indecent within the meaning of § 1464.[13] Even that question is narrowly confined by the arguments of the parties.

* * * Pacifica's claim that the broadcast was not indecent within the meaning of the statute rests entirely on the absence of prurient appeal.

The plain language of the statute does not support Pacifica's argument. The words "obscene, indecent, or profane" are written in the disjunctive, implying that each has a separate meaning. Prurient appeal is an element of the obscene, but the normal definition of "indecent" merely refers to nonconformance with accepted standards of morality.

---

6.   Chairman Wiley concurred in the result without joining the opinion. Commissioners Reid and Quello filed separate statements expressing the opinion that the language was inappropriate for broadcast at any time. Commissioner Robinson, joined by Commissioner Hooks filed a concurring statement expressing the opinion that "we can regulate offensive speech to the extent it constitutes a public nuisance. [The] governing idea is that 'indecency' is not an inherent attribute of words themselves; it is rather a matter of context and conduct. [If] I were called on to do so, I would find that Carlin's monologue, if it were broadcast at an appropriate hour and accompanied by suitable warning, was distinguished by sufficient literary value to avoid being 'indecent' within the meaning of the statute."

13.   [The] statutes authorizing civil penalties incorporate § 1464, a criminal statute. But the validity of the civil sanctions is not linked to the validity of the criminal penalty. [Thus,] we need not consider any question relating to the possible application of § 1464 as a criminal statute.

Pacifica argues, however, that this Court has construed the term "indecent" in related statutes to mean "obscene," as that term was defined in *Miller* [Ch. 1, IV, B supra]. Pacifica relies most heavily on the construction this Court gave to 18 U.S.C. § 1461 [prohibiting the mailing of "obscene, lewd, lascivious, indecent, filthy or vile" material] in *Hamling v. United States* [Ch. 1, IV, B supra].

Because neither our prior decisions nor the language or history of § 1464 supports the conclusion that prurient appeal is an essential component of indecent language, we reject Pacifica's construction of the statute. When that construction is put to one side, there is no basis for disagreeing with the Commission's conclusion that indecent language was used in this broadcast.

IV. Pacifica makes two constitutional attacks on the Commission's order. First, it argues that the Commission's construction of the statutory language broadly encompasses so much constitutionally protected speech that reversal is required even if Pacifica's broadcast of the "Filthy Words" monologue is not itself protected by the First Amendment. Second, Pacifica argues that inasmuch as the recording is not obscene, the Constitution forbids any abridgment of the right to broadcast it on the radio.

A. The first argument fails because our review is limited to the question whether the Commission has the authority to proscribe this particular broadcast. As the Commission itself emphasized, its order was "issued in a specific factual context." That approach is appropriate for courts as well as the Commission when regulation of indecency is at stake, for indecency is largely a function of context—it cannot be adequately judged in the abstract.

The approach is also consistent with *Red Lion*. In that case the Court rejected an argument that the Commission's regulations defining the fairness doctrine were so vague that they would inevitably abridge the broadcasters' freedom of speech. * * *

It is true that the Commission's order may lead some broadcasters to censor themselves. At most, however, the Commission's definition of indecency will deter only the broadcasting of patently offensive references to excretory and sexual organs and activities.[18] While some of these references may be protected, they surely lie at the periphery of First Amendment concern. The danger dismissed so summarily in *Red Lion,* in contrast, was that broadcasters would respond to the vagueness of the regulations by refusing to present programs dealing with important social and political controversies. Invalidating any rule on the basis of its hypothetical application to situations not before the Court is "strong medicine" to be applied "sparingly and only as a last resort." *Broadrick* [Ch. 1, 6 supra]. We decline to administer that medicine to preserve the vigor of patently offensive sexual and excretory speech.

18. A requirement that indecent language be avoided will have its primary effect on the form, rather than the content, of serious communication. There are few, if any, thoughts that cannot be expressed by the use of less offensive language.

B.   When the issue is narrowed to the facts of this case, the question is whether the First Amendment denies government any power to restrict the public broadcast of indecent language in any circumstances. For if the government has any such power, this was an appropriate occasion for its exercise.

The words of the Carlin monologue are unquestionably "speech" within the meaning of the First Amendment. It is equally clear that the Commission's objections to the broadcast were based in part on its content. The order must therefore fall if, as Pacifica argues, the First Amendment prohibits all governmental regulation that depends on the content of speech. Our past cases demonstrate, however, that no such absolute rule is mandated * * *.

The question in this case is whether a broadcast of patently offensive words dealing with sex and excretion may be regulated because of its content.[20] Obscene materials have been denied the protection of the First Amendment because their content is so offensive to contemporary moral standards. *Roth.* But the fact that society may find speech offensive is not a sufficient reason for suppressing it. Indeed, if it is the speaker's opinion that gives offense, that consequence is a reason for according it constitutional protection. For it is a central tenet of the First Amendment that the government must remain neutral in the marketplace of ideas. If there were any reason to believe that the Commission's characterization of the Carlin monologue as offensive could be traced to its political content—or even to the fact that it satirized contemporary attitudes about four letter words[22]— First Amendment protection might be required. But that is simply not this case. These words offend for the same reasons that obscenity offends. Their place in the hierarchy of First Amendment values was aptly sketched by Mr. Justice Murphy when he said, "such utterances are no essential part of any exposition of ideas, and are of such slight social value as a step to truth that any benefit that may be derived from them is clearly outweighed by the social interest in order and morality." *Chaplinsky.*

Although these words ordinarily lack literary, political, or scientific value, they are not entirely outside the protection of the First Amendment. Some uses of even the most offensive words are unquestionably protected. Indeed, we may assume, arguendo, that this monologue would be protected in other contexts. Nonetheless, the constitutional protection accorded to a communication containing such patently offensive sexual and excretory language need not be the same in every context. It is a characteristic of

20.   Although neither Justice Powell nor Justice Brennan directly confronts this question, both have answered it affirmatively, the latter explicitly, at fn. 3, infra, and the former implicitly by concurring in a judgment that could not otherwise stand.

22.   The monologue does present a point of view; it attempts to show that the words it uses are "harmless" and that our atti-

tudes toward them are "essentially silly." The Commission objects, not to this point of view, but to the way in which it is expressed. The belief that these words are harmless does not necessarily confer a First Amendment privilege to use them while proselytizing just as the conviction that obscenity is harmless does not license one to communicate that conviction by the indiscriminate distribution of an obscene leaflet.

speech such as this that both its capacity to offend and its "social value," to use Mr. Justice Murphy's term, vary with the circumstances. Words that are commonplace in one setting are shocking in another. To paraphrase Mr. Justice Harlan, one occasion's lyric is another's vulgarity. Cf. *Cohen v. California.*[25]

In this case it is undisputed that the content of Pacifica's broadcast was "vulgar," "offensive," and "shocking." Because content of that character is not entitled to absolute constitutional protection under all circumstances, we must consider its context in order to determine whether the Commission's action was constitutionally permissible.

C.   We have long recognized that each medium of expression presents special First Amendment problems. And of all forms of communication, it is broadcasting that has received the most limited First Amendment [protection.]

The reasons for these distinctions are complex, but two have relevance to the present case. First, the broadcast media have established a uniquely pervasive presence in the lives of all Americans. Patently offensive, indecent material presented over the airwaves confronts the citizen, not only in public, but also in the privacy of the home, where the individual's right to be let alone plainly outweighs the First Amendment rights of an intruder. *Rowan v. Post Office Dept.,* 397 U.S. 728, 90 S.Ct. 1484, 25 L.Ed.2d 736. Because the broadcast audience is constantly tuning in and out, prior warnings cannot completely protect the listener or viewer from unexpected program content. To say that one may avoid further offense by turning off the radio when he hears indecent language is like saying that the remedy for an assault is to run away after the first blow. One may hang up on an indecent phone call, but that option does not give the caller a constitutional immunity or avoid a harm that has already taken place.[27]

Second, broadcasting is uniquely accessible to children, even those too young to read. Although Cohen's written message might have been incomprehensible to a first grader, Pacifica's broadcast could have enlarged a child's vocabulary in an instant. Other forms of offensive expression may be withheld from the young without restricting the expression at its source. Bookstores and motion picture theaters, for example, may be prohibited from making indecent material available to children. We held in *Ginsberg*

---

25. The importance of context is illustrated by the *Cohen* case. [So] far as the evidence showed no one in the courthouse was offended by [Cohen's jacket.]

In holding that criminal sanctions could not be imposed on Cohen for his political statement in a public place, the Court rejected the argument that his speech would offend unwilling viewers; it noted that "there was no evidence that persons powerless to avoid [his] conduct did in fact object to it." In contrast, in this case the Commission was responding to a listener's strenuous complaint, and Pacifica does not ques-

tion its determination that this afternoon broadcast was likely to offend listeners. It should be noted that the Commission imposed a far more moderate penalty on Pacifica than the state court imposed on Cohen. Even the strongest civil penalty at the Commission's command does not include criminal prosecution.

27. Outside the home, the balance between the offensive speaker and the unwilling audience may sometimes tip in favor of the speaker, requiring the offended listener to turn away. See *Erznoznik.* * * *

[Ch. 1, IV, B supra] that the government's interest in the "well being of its youth" and in supporting "parents' claim to authority in their own household" justified the regulation of otherwise protected expression.[28] The ease with which children may obtain access to broadcast material, coupled with the concerns recognized in *Ginsberg,* amply justify special treatment of indecent broadcasting.

It is appropriate, in conclusion, to emphasize the narrowness of our holding. This case does not involve a two-way radio conversation between a cab driver and a dispatcher, or a telecast of an Elizabethan comedy. We have not decided that an occasional expletive in either setting would justify any sanction or, indeed, that this broadcast would justify a criminal prosecution. The Commission's decision rested entirely on a nuisance rationale under which context is all-important. The concept requires consideration of a host of variables. The time of day was emphasized by the Commission. The content of the program in which the language is used will also affect the composition of the audience, and differences between radio, television, and perhaps closed-circuit transmissions, may also be relevant. As Mr. Justice Sutherland wrote, a "nuisance may be merely a right thing in the wrong place–like a pig in the parlor instead of the barnyard." We simply hold that when the Commission finds that a pig has entered the parlor, the exercise of its regulatory power does not depend on proof that the pig is obscene.

[R]eversed.

MR. JUSTICE POWELL, with whom MR. JUSTICE BLACKMUN joins, concurring.

I join Parts I, II, III, and IV(C) of Justice Stevens' opinion. The Court today reviews only the Commission's holding that Carlin's monologue was indecent "as broadcast" at two o'clock in the afternoon, and not the broad sweep of the Commission's opinion. In addition to being consistent with our settled practice of not deciding constitutional issues unnecessarily, this narrow focus also is conducive to the orderly development of this relatively new and difficult area of law, in the first instance by the Commission, and then by the reviewing courts.

I also agree with much that is said in Part IV of Justice Stevens' opinion, and with its conclusion that the Commission's holding in this case does not violate the First Amendment. Because I do not subscribe to all that is said in Part IV, however, I state my views separately.

28. The Commission's action does not by any means reduce adults to hearing only what is fit for children. Cf. *Butler v. Michigan* [Ch. 1, IV, B supra]. Adults who feel the need may purchase tapes and records or go to theatres and nightclubs to hear these words. In fact, the Commission has not unequivocally closed even broadcasting to speech of this sort; whether broadcast audi- ences in the late evening contain so few children that playing this monologue would be permissible is an issue neither the Commission nor this Court has decided. [Would the rationale based on supporting parental authority rule out banning Carlin's mono- logue in the early evening? See Baker, *The Evening Hours During Pacifica Standard Time,* 3 Vill. Sports & Ent. L.J. 45 (1996)].

[T]he language employed is, to most people, vulgar and offensive. It was chosen specifically for this quality, and it was repeated over and over as a sort of verbal shock treatment. The Commission did not err in characterizing the narrow category of language used here as "patently offensive" to most people regardless of age.

The issue, however, is whether the Commission may impose civil sanctions on a licensee radio station for broadcasting the monologue at two o'clock in the afternoon. The Commission's primary concern was to prevent the broadcast from reaching the ears of unsupervised children who were likely to be in the audience at that hour. In essence, the Commission sought to "channel" the monologue to hours when the fewest unsupervised children would be exposed to it. In my view, this consideration provides strong support for the Commission's holding.

[The] Commission properly held that the speech from which society may attempt to shield its children is not limited to that which appeals to the youthful prurient interest. The language involved in this case is as potentially degrading and harmful to children as representations of many erotic acts.

In most instances, the dissemination of this kind of speech to children may be limited without also limiting willing adults' access to it. Sellers of printed and recorded matter and exhibitors of motion pictures and live performances may be required to shut their doors to children, but such a requirement has no effect on adults' access. See *Ginsberg*. The difficulty is that such a physical separation of the audience cannot be accomplished in the broadcast media. During most of the broadcast hours, both adults and unsupervised children are likely to be in the broadcast audience, and the broadcaster cannot reach willing adults without also reaching children. This, as the Court emphasizes, is one of the distinctions between the broadcast and other media to which we often have adverted as justifying a different treatment of the broadcast media for First Amendment purposes. In my view, the Commission was entitled to give substantial weight to this difference in reaching its decision in this case.

[Another difference] is that broadcasting—unlike most other forms of communication—comes directly into the home, the one place where people ordinarily have the right not to be assaulted by uninvited and offensive sights and sounds. *Erznoznik; Cohen; Rowan*. Although the First Amendment may require unwilling adults to absorb the first blow of offensive but protected speech when they are in public before they turn away, see, e.g., *Erznoznik*, but cf. *Rosenfeld* (Powell, J., dissenting), a different order of values obtains in the home. "That we are often 'captives' outside the sanctuary of the home and subject to objectionable speech and other sound does not mean we must be captives everywhere." *Rowan*. The Commission also was entitled to give this factor appropriate weight in the circumstances of the instant case. This is not to say, however, that the Commission has an unrestricted license to decide what speech, protected in other media, may be banned from the airwaves in order to protect unwilling adults from momentary exposure to it in their homes.[2] * * *

The Commission's holding does not prevent willing adults from purchasing Carlin's record, from attending his performances, or, indeed, from reading the transcript reprinted as an appendix to the Court's opinion. On its face, it does not prevent respondent from broadcasting the monologue during late evening hours when fewer children are likely to be in the audience, nor from broadcasting discussions of the contemporary use of language at any time during the day. The Commission's holding, and certainly the Court's holding today, does not speak to cases involving the isolated use of a potentially offensive word in the course of a radio broadcast, as distinguished from the verbal shock treatment administered by respondent here. In short, I agree that on the facts of this case, the Commission's order did not violate respondent's First Amendment rights.

As the foregoing demonstrates, my views are generally in accord with what is said in Part IV(C) of opinion. I therefore join that portion of his opinion. I do not join Part IV(B), however, because I do not subscribe to the theory that the Justices of this Court are free generally to decide on the basis of its content which speech protected by the First Amendment is most "valuable" and hence deserving of the most protection, and which is less "valuable" and hence deserving of less protection.[3] In my view, the result in this case does not turn on whether Carlin's monologue, viewed as a whole, or the words that comprise it, have more or less "value" than a candidate's campaign speech. This is a judgment for each person to make, not one for the judges to impose upon him.[4]

The result turns instead on the unique characteristics of the broadcast media, combined with society's right to protect its children from speech generally agreed to be inappropriate for their years, and with the interest of unwilling adults in not being assaulted by such offensive speech in their homes. Moreover, I doubt whether today's decision will prevent any adult who wishes to receive Carlin's message in Carlin's own words from doing so,

---

2. It is true that the radio listener quickly may tune out speech that is offensive to him. In addition, broadcasters may preface potentially offensive programs with warnings. But such warnings do not help the unsuspecting listener who tunes in at the middle of a program. In this respect, too, broadcasting appears to differ from books and records, which may carry warnings on their faces, and from motion pictures and live performances, which may carry warnings on their marquees.

3. The Court has, however, created a limited exception to this rule in order to bring commercial speech within the protection of the First Amendment. See *Ohralik* [Ch. 3, II supra].

4. For much the same reason, I also do not join Part IV(A). I had not thought that

the application vel non of overbreadth analysis should depend on the Court's judgment as to the value of the protected speech that might be deterred. Except in the context of commercial speech, see *Bates* [Ch. 3, II supra], it has not in the past. See, e.g., *Lewis v. New Orleans; Gooding.*

As Justice Stevens points out, however, the Commission's order was limited to the facts of this case; "it did not purport to engage in formal rulemaking or in the promulgation of any regulations." In addition, since the Commission may be expected to proceed cautiously, as it has in the past, I do not foresee an undue "chilling" effect on broadcasters' exercise of their rights. I agree, therefore, that respondent's overbreadth challenge is meritless.

and from making for himself a value judgment as to the merit of the message and words. These are the grounds upon which I join the judgment of the Court as to Part IV.

MR. JUSTICE BRENNAN, with whom MR. JUSTICE MARSHALL joins, dissenting.

I agree with Justice Stewart that, under *Hamling,* the word "indecent" in 18 U.S.C.§ 1464 must be construed to prohibit only obscene speech. I would, therefore, normally refrain from expressing my views on any constitutional issues implicated in this case. However, I find the Court's misapplication of fundamental First Amendment principles so patent, and its attempt to impose *its* notions of propriety on the whole of the American people so misguided, that I am unable to remain silent.

For the second time in two years, see *Young v. American Mini Theatres* [Ch. 3, I supra], the Court refuses to embrace the notion, completely antithetical to basic First Amendment values, that the degree of protection the First Amendment affords protected speech varies with the social value ascribed to that speech by five Members of this Court. See opinion of Justice Powell. Moreover, [all] Members of the Court agree that [the monologue] does not fall within one of the categories of speech, such as "fighting words," or obscenity, that is totally without First Amendment protection. [Yet] despite the Court's refusal to create a sliding scale of First Amendment protection calibrated to this Court's perception of the worth of a communication's content, and despite our unanimous agreement that the Carlin monologue is protected speech, a majority of the Court[1] nevertheless finds that, on the facts of this case, the FCC is not constitutionally barred from imposing sanctions on Pacifica for its airing of the Carlin monologue. This majority apparently believes that the FCC's disapproval of Pacifica's afternoon broadcast of Carlin's "Dirty Words" recording is a permissible time, place, and manner regulation. [The opinions of both Stevens and Powell, JJ.,] rely principally on two factors in reaching this conclusion: (1) the capacity of a radio broadcast to intrude into the unwilling listener's home, and (2) the presence of children in the listening audience. Dispassionate analysis, removed from individual notions as to what is proper and what is not, starkly reveals that these justifications, whether individually or together, simply do not support even the professedly moderate degree of governmental homogenization of radio communications—if, indeed, such homogenization can ever be moderate given the pre-eminent status of the right of free speech in our constitutional scheme—that the Court today permits.

[In] finding [the privacy interests of an individual in his home] sufficient to justify the content regulation of protected speech, [the] Court commits two errors. First, it misconceives the nature of the privacy interests involved where an individual voluntarily chooses to admit radio communications into

---

1. Where I refer without differentiation to the actions of "the Court," my reference is to this majority, which consists of my Brothers Powell and Stevens and those Members of the Court joining their separate opinions.

his home. Second, it ignores the constitutionally protected interests of both those who wish to transmit and those who desire to receive broadcasts that many—including the FCC and this Court—might find offensive.

[A]n individual's actions in switching on and listening to communications transmitted over the public airways and directed to the public at-large do not implicate fundamental privacy interests, even when engaged in within the home. Instead, because the radio is undeniably a public medium, these actions are more properly viewed as a decision to take part, if only as a listener, in an ongoing public discourse. Although an individual's decision to allow public radio communications into his home undoubtedly does not abrogate all of his privacy interests, the residual privacy interests he retains vis-à-vis the communication he voluntarily admits into his home are surely no greater than those of the people present in the corridor of the Los Angeles courthouse in *Cohen* who bore witness to the words "Fuck the Draft" emblazoned across Cohen's jacket. Their privacy interests were held insufficient to justify punishing Cohen for his offensive communication.

Even if an individual who voluntarily opens his home to radio communications retains privacy interests of sufficient moment to justify a ban on protected speech if those interests are "invaded in an essentially intolerable manner," *Cohen,* the very fact that those interests are threatened only by a radio broadcast precludes any intolerable invasion of privacy; for unlike other intrusive modes of communication, such as sound trucks, "[t]he radio can be turned off"—and with a minimum of effort. As Judge Bazelon aptly observed below, "having elected to receive public airwaves, the scanner who stumbles onto an offensive program is in the same position as the unsuspected passers-by in *Cohen* and *Erznoznik;* he can avert his attention by changing channels or turning off the set." Whatever the minimal discomfort suffered by a listener who inadvertently tunes into a program he finds offensive during the brief interval before he can simply extend his arm and switch stations or flick the "off" button, it is surely worth the candle to preserve the broadcaster's right to send, and the right of those interested to receive, a message entitled to full First Amendment protection. To reach a contrary balance, as does the Court, is clearly, to follow Justice Stevens' reliance on animal metaphors, "to burn the house to roast the pig."

The Court's balance, of necessity, fails to accord proper weight to the interests of listeners who wish to hear broadcasts the FCC deems offensive. It permits majoritarian tastes completely to preclude a protected message from entering the homes of a receptive, unoffended minority. No decision of this Court supports such a result. Where the individuals comprising the offended majority may freely choose to reject the material being offered, we have never found their privacy interests of such moment to warrant the suppression of speech on privacy grounds. [In] *Rowan,* the Court upheld a statute, permitting householders to require that mail advertisers stop sending them lewd or offensive materials and remove their names from mailing lists. Unlike the situation here, householders who wished to receive the sender's communications were not prevented from doing so. Equally important, the determination of offensiveness vel non under the statute involved in *Rowan* was completely within the hands of the individual householder; no governmental evaluation of the worth of the mail's content stood between the mailer and the householder. In contrast, the visage of the censor is all too discernable here.

[Although] the government unquestionably has a special interest in the well-being of children and consequently "can adopt more stringent controls on communicative materials available to youths than on those available to adults," *Erznoznik*, the Court has accounted for this societal interest by adopting a "variable obscenity" standard that permits the prurient appeal of material available to children to be assessed in terms of the sexual interests of minors. *Ginsberg*. [But] we have made it abundantly clear that "under any test of obscenity as to minors [to] be obscene 'such expression must be, in some significant way, erotic.' "

Because the Carlin monologue is obviously not an erotic appeal to the prurient interests of children, the Court, for the first time, allows the government to prevent minors from gaining access to materials that are not obscene, and are therefore protected, as to them.[2] It thus ignores our recent admonition that "[s]peech that is neither obscene as to youths nor subject to some other legitimate proscription cannot be suppressed solely to protect the young from ideas or images that a legislative body thinks unsuitable for them." *Erznoznik*.[3] The Court's refusal to follow its own pronouncements is especially lamentable since it has the anomalous subsidiary effect, at least in the radio context at issue here, of making completely unavailable to adults material which may not constitutionally be kept even from children. This result violates in spades the principle of *Butler v. Michigan*. [Powell, J.'s opinion] acknowledges that there lurks in today's decision a potential for " 'reduc[ing] the adult population [to] [hearing] only what is fit for children,' " but expresses faith that the FCC will vigilantly prevent this potential from ever becoming a reality. I am far less certain than [he] that such faith in the Commission is warranted; and even if I shared it, I could not so easily shirk the responsibility assumed by each Member of this Court jealously to guard against encroachments on First Amendment freedoms.

---

2. Even if the monologue appealed to the prurient interest of minors, it would not be obscene as to them unless, as to them, "the work, taken as a whole, lacks serious literary, artistic, political, or scientific value." *Miller*.

3. It may be that a narrowly drawn regulation prohibiting the use of offensive language on broadcasts directed specifically at younger children constitutes one of the "other legitimate proscription[s]" alluded to in *Erznoznik*. This is so both because of the difficulties inherent in adapting the *Miller* formulation to communications re-ceived by young children, and because such children are "not possessed of that full capacity for individual choice which is the presupposition of the First Amendment guarantees." *Ginsberg*. (Stewart, J., concurring). I doubt, as my Brother Stevens suggests, that such a limited regulation amounts to a regulation of speech based on its content, since, by hypothesis, the only persons at whom the regulated communication is directed are incapable of evaluating its content. To the extent that such a regulation is viewed as a regulation based on content, it marks the outermost limits to which content regulation is permissible.

[T]he opinions of Justices Powell and Stevens both stress the time-honored right of a parent to raise his child as he sees fit—a right this Court has consistently been vigilant to protect. Yet this principle supports a result directly contrary to that reached by the Court. *Yoder* and *Pierce,* [Part 2, Ch. 12, I], hold that parents, *not* the government, have the right to make certain decisions regarding the upbringing of their children. As surprising as it may be to individual Members of this Court, some parents may actually find Mr. Carlin's unabashed attitude towards the seven "dirty words" healthy, and deem it desirable to expose their children to the manner in which Mr. Carlin defuses the taboo surrounding the words. Such parents may constitute a minority of the American public, but the absence of great numbers willing to exercise the right to raise their children in this fashion does not alter the right's nature or its existence. Only the Court's regrettable decision does that.[4]

As demonstrated above, neither of the factors relied on by both [Powell and Stevens, JJ.]—the intrusive nature of radio and the presence of children in the listening audience—can, when taken on its own terms, support the FCC's disapproval of the Carlin monologue. These two asserted justifications are further plagued by a common failing: the lack of principled limits on their use as a basis for FCC censorship. No such limits come readily to mind, and neither of the opinions comprising the Court serve to clarify the extent to which the FCC may assert the privacy and children-in-the-audience rationales as justification for expunging from the airways protected communications the Commission finds offensive. Taken to their logical extreme, these rationales would support the cleansing of public radio of any "four-letter words" whatsoever, regardless of their context. The rationales could justify the banning from radio of a myriad of literary works, novels, poems, and plays by the likes of Shakespeare, Joyce, Hemingway, Ben Jonson, Henry Fielding, Robert Burns, and Chaucer; they could support the suppression of a good deal of political speech, such as the Nixon tapes; and they could even provide the basis for imposing sanctions for the broadcast of certain portions of the Bible.

In order to dispel the spectre of the possibility of so unpalatable a degree of censorship, and to defuse Pacifica's overbreadth challenge, the FCC insists that it desires only the authority to reprimand a broadcaster on facts analogous to those present in this case. [Justices Powell and Stevens] take the FCC at its word, and consequently do no more than permit the Commission to censor the afternoon broadcast of the "sort of verbal shock treatment," opinion of Justice Powell, involved here. To insure that the FCC's regulation of protected speech does not exceed these bounds, my Brother Powell is content to rely upon the judgment of the Commission while my Brother Stevens deems it prudent to rely on this Court's ability accurately to assess the worth of various kinds of speech.[6] For my own part,

---

4. The opinions of my Brothers Powell and Stevens rightly refrain from relying on the notion of "spectrum scarcity" to support their result. As Chief Judge Bazelon noted below, "although scarcity has justified *increasing* the diversity of speakers and speech, it has never been held to justify censorship." See *Red Lion.*

even accepting that this case is limited to its facts,[7] I would place the responsibility and the right to weed worthless and offensive communications from the public airways where it belongs and where, until today, it resided: in a public free to choose those communications worthy of its attention from a marketplace unsullied by the censor's hand.

The absence of any hesitancy in the opinions of my Brothers Powell and Stevens to approve the FCC's censorship of the Carlin monologue on the basis of two demonstrably inadequate grounds is a function of their perception that the decision will result in little, if any, curtailment of communicative exchanges protected by the First Amendment. Although the extent to which the Court stands ready to countenance FCC censorship of protected speech is unclear from today's decision, I find the reasoning by which my Brethren conclude that the FCC censorship they approve will not significantly infringe on First Amendment values both disingenuous as to reality and wrong as a matter of law.

My Brother Stevens, in reaching a result apologetically described as narrow, takes comfort in his observation that "[a] requirement that indecent language be avoided will have its primary effect on the form, rather than the content, of serious communication," and finds solace in his conviction that "[t]here are few, if any, thoughts that cannot be expressed by the use of less offensive language." The idea that the content of a message and its potential impact on any who might receive it can be divorced from the words that are the vehicle for its expression is transparently fallacious. A given word may have a unique capacity to capsule an idea, evoke an emotion, or conjure up an image. Indeed, for those of us who place an appropriately high value on our cherished First Amendment rights, the word "censor" is such a word. Mr. Justice Harlan, speaking for the Court, recognized the truism that a speaker's choice of words cannot surgically be separated from the ideas he desires to express when he warned that "we cannot indulge the facile assumption that one can forbid particular words without also running a substantial risk of suppressing ideas in the process." *Cohen.* Moreover, even if an alternative phrasing may communicate a speaker's abstract ideas as effectively as those words he is forbidden to use, it is doubtful that the

---

6. Although ultimately dependent upon the outcome of review in this Court, the approach taken by my Brother Stevens would not appear to tolerate the FCC's suppression of any speech, such as political speech, falling within the core area of First Amendment concern. The same, however, cannot be said of the approach taken by my Brother Powell, which, on its face, permits the Commission to censor even political speech if it is sufficiently offensive to community standards. A result more contrary to rudimentary First Amendment principles is difficult to imagine.

7. Having insisted that it seeks to impose sanctions on radio communications only in the limited circumstances present here, I believe that the FCC is estopped from using either this decision or its own orders in this case, as a basis for imposing sanctions on any public radio broadcast other than one aired during the daytime or early evening and containing the relentless repetition, for longer than a brief interval, of "language that describes, in terms patently offensive as measured by contemporary community standards for the broadcast medium, sexual or excretory activities and organs." For surely broadcasters are not now on notice that the Commission desires to regulate any offensive broadcast other than the type of "verbal shock treatment" condemned here, or even this "shock treatment" type of offensive broadcast during the late evening.

sterilized message will convey the emotion that is an essential part of so many communications. This, too, was apparent to Mr. Justice Harlan and the Court in *Cohen.*

[Stevens, J.] also finds relevant to his First Amendment analysis the fact that "[a]dults who feel the need may purchase tapes and records or go to theatres and nightclubs to hear [the tabooed] words." [Powell, J.,] agrees. [The] opinions of my Brethren display both a sad insensitivity to the fact that these alternatives involve the expenditure of money, time, and effort that many of those wishing to hear Mr. Carlin's message may not be able to afford, and a naive innocence of the reality that in many cases, the medium may well be the message.

The Court apparently believes that the FCC's actions here can be analogized to the zoning ordinances upheld in *American Mini Theatres.* For two reasons, it is wrong. First, the zoning ordinances found to pass constitutional muster [had] valid goals other than the channeling of protected speech. No such goals are present here. Second, and crucial to the opinions of my Brothers Powell and Stevens in *American Mini Theatres*—opinions, which, as they do in this case, supply the bare five-person majority of the Court—the ordinances did not restrict the access of distributors or exhibitors to the market or impair the viewing public's access to the regulated material. Again, this is not the situation [here.]

It is quite evident that I find the Court's attempt to unstitch the warp and woof of First Amendment law in an effort to reshape its fabric to cover the patently wrong result the Court reaches in this case dangerous as well as lamentable. Yet there runs throughout the opinions of my Brothers Powell and Stevens another vein I find equally disturbing: a depressing inability to appreciate that in our land of cultural pluralism, there are many who think, act, and talk differently from the Members of this Court, and who do not share their fragile sensibilities. It is only an acute ethnocentric myopia that enables the Court to approve the censorship of communications solely because of the words they [contain.]

Today's decision will thus have its greatest impact on broadcasters desiring to reach, and listening audiences comprised of, persons who do not share the Court's view as to which words or expressions are acceptable and who, for a variety of reasons, including a conscious desire to flout majoritarian conventions, express themselves using words that may be regarded as offensive by those from different socio-economic backgrounds.[8] In this context, the Court's decision may be seen for what, in the broader perspective, it really is: another of the dominant culture's inevitable efforts to force those

---

8. Under the approach taken by my Brother Powell, the availability of broadcasts *about* groups whose members comprise such audiences might also be affected. Both news broadcasts about activities involving these groups and public affairs broadcasts about their concerns are apt to contain interviews, statements, or remarks by group leaders and members which may contain offensive language to an extent my Brother Powell finds unacceptable.

groups who do not share its mores to conform to its way of thinking, acting, and speaking.

Pacifica, in response to an FCC inquiry about its broadcast of Carlin's satire on "the words you couldn't say on the public airwaves," explained that "Carlin is not mouthing obscenities, he is merely using words to satirize as harmless and essentially silly our attitudes towards those words." In confirming Carlin's prescience as a social commentator by the result it reaches today, the Court evinces an attitude towards the "seven dirty words" that many others besides Mr. Carlin and Pacifica might describe as "silly." Whether today's decision will similarly prove "harmless" remains to be seen. One can only hope that it will.

MR. JUSTICE STEWART, with whom MR. JUSTICE BRENNAN, MR. JUSTICE WHITE, and MR. JUSTICE MARSHALL join, dissenting.

[The Court today] disregards [the] need to construe an Act of Congress so as to avoid, if possible, passing upon its constitutionality. It is apparent that the constitutional questions raised by the order of the Commission in this case are substantial. Before deciding them, we should be certain that it is necessary to do so.

[T]he clear holding of *Hamling* is that "indecent" as used in 18 U.S.C. § 1461 [prohibiting the mailing of "obscene, lewd, lascivious, indecent, filthy or vile article[s]"] has the same meaning as "obscene" as that term was defined in the *Miller* case.

Nothing requires the conclusion that the word "indecent" has any meaning in § 1464 other than that ascribed to the same word in § 1461. Indeed, although the legislative history is largely silent, such indications as there are support the view that §§ 1461 and 1464 should be construed similarly. * * *

I would hold, therefore, that Congress intended by using the word "indecent" in § 1464, to prohibit nothing more than obscene speech. Under that reading of the statute, the Commission's order in this case was not authorized, and on that basis I would affirm the judgment [below].

Notes and Questions

1.   Consider Shiffrin, *The First Amendment, Democracy, and Romance* 80 (1990): "Most people with any first amendment bones in their bodies are troubled by [*Pacifica*]. But the nub of the first amendment insult has little to do with self-government or with the marketplace of ideas. The concern does not flow from a worry that voters will be deprived of valuable information. Concern that the truth about vulgar language might not emerge in the marketplace of ideas may be well placed, but is not a sufficient concern to explain the widespread outrage against the decision. Again, the decision is an affront to a notion of content neutrality, but there are many of those. The *Pacifica* case produces heat precisely because Carlin's speech is considered by many to be precisely what the first amendment is *supposed* to protect.

Carlin is attacking conventions; assaulting the prescribed orthodoxy; mocking the stuffed shirts; Carlin *is* the prototypical dissenter.

"It matters not at all whether the target of his invective is society at large or a public official. The outrage is that the stuffed shirts are in a position to silence Carlin, or at least in a position to keep him from 'offending' the mass audience."

2. *Implications for broadcasting.* Consider Krattenmaker & Powe, *Televised Violence: First Amendment Principles and Social Science Theory,* 64 Va.L.Rev. 1123, 1228 (1978): *Pacifica* "marks the first time any theory other than scarcity has received the official imprimatur of the Court. [S]carcity could not have authorized the result in *Pacifica* because regardless of whether one thinks the incredible abundance of radio stations in the United States (and especially in New York City) is insufficient, scarcity supports adding voices not banning them." What is the significance of the Court's comment that "the broadcast media have established a uniquely pervasive presence in the lives of all Americans"? Consider Brenner, *Censoring the Airwaves: The Supreme Court's Pacifica Decision* in Free But Regulated: Conflicting Traditions in Media Law 175, 177 & 79 (1982): "[N]ewspapers, drive-in movies, direct mail advertisements and imprinted T-shirts are media that have also 'established a uniquely pervasive presence' in our lives, in and out of [home]. Offhand comments about broadcasting enjoying 'the most limited' First Amendment protection—What of comic books? Playing cards? Chinese cookie fortunes?—are not simply harmless baffle; they constitute Delphic pronouncements made at a watershed period in the development of electronic media." See also Powe, supra fn. a, at 210–11.

Is the Court suggesting that the broadcast media are uniquely powerful? If so, should that factor cut for or against government regulation?[b] See Powe, supra, at 211–15; Powe, *"Or of the [Broadcast] Press,"* 55 Tex.L.Rev. 39, 58–62 (1976). Does *Pacifica* support regulation of sex and violence on television, of "offensive" commercials, of advertising directed toward children? See generally Spitzer, *Seven Dirty Words and Six Other Stories* (1986) (criticizing *Pacifica's* distinctions between print and broadcast).

3. FCC v. LEAGUE OF WOMEN VOTERS, 468 U.S. 364, 104 S.Ct. 3106, 82 L.Ed.2d 278 (1984), per BRENNAN, J., invalidated a federal law prohibiting editorializing on public broadcast stations: "As our cases attest, [broadcast restrictions] have been upheld only when we were satisfied that the restriction is narrowly tailored to further a substantial governmental interest, such as ensuring adequate and balanced coverage of public issues.[13]"

b. See Powe, supra, at 211–15; Powe, *"Or of the [Broadcast] Press,"* 55 Tex. L.Rev. 39, 58–62 (1976). On the various justifications for broadcast regulation, see Balkin, *Media Filters, the V–Chip, and the*

Foundations of Broadcast Regulation, 45 Duke L.J. 1131 (1996).

13. [*Pacifica*] is consistent with the approach taken in our other broadcast cases. There, the Court focused on certain physi-

4. *Public/private.* Consider Cole, *Playing by Pornography's Rules: The Regulation of Sexual Expression,* 143 U.Pa.L.Rev. 111, 140 (1994): "The Court's sexual expression decisions can be organized along a similar public/private axis. The Court's zoning decisions allow communities to demand that when sexually explicit speech appears in public, it must be regulated to dark and distant parts of town. The Court's affirmance of the FCC's 'indecency' regulation permits the zoning of sexual speech to less 'public' times of day. And while private possession of obscenity cannot be regulated, the state is free to regulate obscenity in a public place even if it is enjoyed only by consenting adults, and even where it is only being transported through public channels for private home use. What is immune from regulation in private becomes suppressible in public, even if the very same speakers, listeners, and speech are involved."

5. *Anti-abortion advertising.* Is graphic anti-abortion advertising indecent? Should it be channeled to the late evening hours? From the perspective of Stevens, J.? Powell, J.? See Levi, *The FCC, Indecency, and Anti–Abortion Political Advertising,* 3 Vill.Spts. & Ent.L.J. 85 (1996).

6. *Telephonic "indecency" compared.* SABLE COMMUNICATIONS v. FCC, 492 U.S. 115, 109 S.Ct. 2829, 106 L.Ed.2d 93 (1989), per WHITE, J., invalidated a congressional ban on "indecent" interstate commercial telephone messages, i.e., "dial-a-porn."[c] The Court thought *Pacifica* was "readily distinguishable from this case, most obviously because it did not involve a total ban on broadcasting indecent material. [Second,] there is no 'captive audience' problem here; callers will generally not be unwilling listeners. [Third,] the congressional record contains no legislative findings that would justify us in concluding that there is no constitutionally acceptable less restrictive means, short of a total ban, to achieve the Government's interest in protecting minors."

———

Cable operators are required under federal law to reserve channels for commercial lease ("leased access channels") and are routinely required by

cal characteristics of broadcasting—specifically, that the medium's uniquely pervasive presence renders impossible any prior warning for those listeners who may be offended by indecent language, and, second, that the case with which children may gain access to the medium, especially during daytime hours, creates a substantial risk that they may be exposed to such offensive expression without parental supervision. The governmental interest in reduction of those risks through Commission regulation of the timing and character of such "indecent broadcasting" was thought sufficiently substantial to outweigh the broadcaster's First Amendment interest in controlling the presentation of its programming. In this case, by contrast, we are faced not with indecent expression, but rather with expression that is at the core of First Amendment protections, and no claim is made by the Government that the expression of editorial opinion by noncommercial stations will create a substantial "nuisance" of the kind addressed in *Pacifica.*

c. The Court upheld a ban on "obscene" interstate commercial telephonic messages. Scalia, J., concurring, noted: "[W]hile we hold the Constitution prevents Congress from banning indecent speech in this fashion, we do not hold that the Constitution requires public utilities to carry it." Brennan, J., joined by Marshall and Stevens, JJ., concurred on the indecency issue and dissented on the obscenity issue.

their franchise agreements with municipalities to reserve channels for public, educational, and governmental access ("public access channels" or "pegs"). For some years federal law prevented cable operators from employing any editorial control over the content of leased access or public access channels. The Cable Television Consumer Protection and Competition of 1992, however, permitted cable operators to prohibit the broadcast of material that the cable operator "reasonably believes describes or depicts sexual or excretory activities or organs in a patently offensive manner" on leased access channels (47 U.S.C. § 10(a)) and public access channels (47 U.S.C. § 10(c)). In addition, if the cable operator did not prohibit such material from being broadcast on leased access channels, the Act required the cable operator to provide a separate channel for the material, to scramble or otherwise block its presentation, and to permit its viewing only upon written request (47 U.S.C. § 10(b))(the "block and segregate requirements"). After the adoption of § 10(b), Congress passed block and segregate requirements for channels primarily dedicated to sexual programming and required cable operators to honor a subscriber's request to block any undesired programs.

DENVER AREA EDUCATIONAL TELECOMMUNICATIONS CONSORTIUM, INC. v. FCC, 518 U.S. 727, 116 S.Ct. 2374, 135 L.Ed.2d 888 (1996) upheld the constitutionality of § 10(a), but invalidated §§ 10(b) and (c). BREYER, J., joined by Stevens, O'Connor, Kennedy, and Souter, JJ., held that the segregate and block requirements (§ 10(b)) were invalid: "We agree with the Government that protection of children is a 'compelling interest.' But we do not agree that the 'segregate and block' requirements properly accommodate the speech restrictions they impose and the legitimate objective they seek to attain. Nor need we here determine whether, or the extent to which, *Pacifica* does, or does not, impose some lesser standard of review where indecent speech is at issue, compare (opinion of Stevens, J.)(indecent materials enjoy lesser First Amendment protection), with (Powell, J., concurring in part and concurring in judgment)(refusing to accept a lesser standard for nonobscene, indecent material). That is because once one examines this governmental restriction, it becomes apparent that, not only is it not a 'least restrictive alternative,' and is not 'narrowly tailored' to meet its legitimate objective, it also seems considerably 'more extensive than necessary.' That is to say, it fails to satisfy this Court's formulations of the First Amendment's 'strictest,' as well as its somewhat less 'strict,' requirements. * * *

"The record does not explain why, under the new Act, blocking alone—without written access-requests—adequately protects children from exposure to regular sex-dedicated channels, but cannot adequately protect those children from programming on similarly sex-dedicated channels that are leased. It does not explain why a simple subscriber blocking request system, perhaps a phone-call based system, would adequately protect children from 'patently offensive' material broadcast on ordinary non-sex-dedicated channels (i.e., almost all channels) but a far more restrictive segregate/block/written-access system is needed to protect children from similar broadcasts on what (in the absence of the segregation requirement) would be non-sex-dedicated channels that are leased. Nor is there any indication Congress thought the new ordinary channel protections less than adequate."

In a portion of his opinion joined by Stevens, O'Connor, and Souter, JJ., Breyer, J., concluded that § 10(a) was valid, but, in a portion of his opinion joined by Stevens and Souter, JJ., he concluded that § 10(c) was invalid. As to § 10(a), Breyer, J., observed: "Justices Kennedy and Thomas would have us decide this case simply by transferring and applying literally categorical standards this Court has developed in other contexts. For Justice Kennedy, leased access channels are like a common carrier, cablecast is a protected medium, strict scrutiny applies, § 10(a) fails this test, and, therefore, § 10(a) is invalid. For Justice Thomas, the case is simple because the cable operator who owns the system over which access channels are broadcast, like a bookstore owner with respect to what it displays on the shelves, has a predominant First Amendment interest. Both categorical approaches suffer from the same flaws: they import law developed in very different contexts into a new and changing environment, and they lack the flexibility necessary to allow government to respond to very serious practical problems without sacrificing the free exchange of ideas the First Amendment is designed to protect. * * *

"Over the years, this Court has restated and refined [basic] First Amendment principles, adopting them more particularly to the balance of competing interests and the special circumstances of each field of application. [This] tradition teaches that the First Amendment embodies an overarching commitment to protect speech from Government regulation through close judicial scrutiny, thereby enforcing the Constitution's constraints, but without imposing judicial formulae so rigid that they become a straightjacket that disables Government from responding to serious problems. This Court, in different contexts, has consistently held that the Government may directly regulate speech to address extraordinary problems, where its regulations are appropriately tailored to resolve those problems without imposing an unnecessarily great restriction on speech. Justices Kennedy and Thomas would have us further declare which, among the many applications of the general approach that this Court has developed over the years, we are applying here. But no definitive choice among competing analogies (broadcast, common carrier, bookstore) allows us to declare a rigid single standard, good for now and for all future media and purposes. That is not to say that we reject all the more specific formulations of the standard—they appropriately cover the vast majority of cases involving Government regulation of speech. Rather, aware as we are of the changes taking place in the law, the technology, and the industrial structure, related to telecommunications, we believe it unwise and unnecessary definitively to pick one analogy or one specific set of words now.

"[W]e can decide this case more narrowly, by closely scrutinizing § 10(a) to assure that it properly addresses an extremely important problem, without imposing, in light of the relevant interests, an unnecessarily great restriction on speech. The importance of the interest at stake here—protecting children from exposure to patently offensive depictions of sex; the accommodation of the interests of programmers in maintaining access channels and of cable operators in editing the contents of their channels; the similarity of the problem and its solution to those at issue in *Pacifica*; and the flexibility inherent in an approach that permits private cable operators to make editorial decisions, lead us to conclude that § 10(a) is a sufficiently tailored response to an extraordinarily important problem. * * *

"[W]e part company with Justice Kennedy on two issues. First, Justice Kennedy's focus on categorical analysis forces him to disregard the cable system operators' interests. We, on the other hand, recognize that in the context of cable broadcast that involves an access requirement (here, its partial removal), and unlike in most cases where we have explicitly required 'narrow tailoring,' the expressive interests of cable operators do play a legitimate role. Cf. *Turner*. While we cannot agree with Justice Thomas that everything turns on the rights of the cable owner, we also cannot agree with Justice Kennedy that we must ignore the expressive interests of cable operators altogether. Second, Justice Kennedy's application of a very strict 'narrow tailoring' test depends upon an analogy with a category ('the public forum cases'), which has been distilled over time from the similarities of many cases. Rather than seeking an analogy to a category of cases, however, we have looked to the cases themselves. And, [we find] [*Pacifica*] provides the closest analogy. * * *

"The Court's distinction in *Turner* [between] cable and broadcast television, relied on the inapplicability of the spectrum scarcity problem to cable. While that distinction was relevant in *Turner* to the justification for structural regulations at issue there (the 'must carry' rules), it has little to do with a case that involves the effects of television viewing on children. Those effects are the result of how parents and children view television programming, and how pervasive and intrusive that programming is. In that respect, cable and broadcast television differ little, if at all.

"[I]f one wishes to view the permissive provisions before us through a 'public forum' lens, one should view those provisions as limiting the otherwise totally open nature of the forum that leased access channels provide for communication of other than patently offensive sexual material—taking account of the fact that the limitation was imposed in light of experience gained from maintaining a totally open 'forum.' One must still ask whether the First Amendment forbids the limitation. But unless a label alone were to make a critical First Amendment difference (and we think here it does not), the features of this case that we have already discussed—the government's interest in protecting children, the 'permissive' aspect of the statute, and the nature of the medium—sufficiently justify the 'limitation' on the availability of this forum."

Breyer, J., argued that the balance was different in § 10(c): "[C]able operators have traditionally agreed to reserve channel capacity for public, governmental, and educational channels as part of the consideration they give municipalities that award them cable franchises. [Thus], these are channels over which cable operators have not historically exercised editorial control. Unlike § 10(a) therefore, § 10(c) does not restore to cable operators editorial rights that they once had, and the countervailing First Amendment interest is nonexistent, or at least much diminished.

"[A] second difference is the institutional background that has developed as a result of the historical difference. When a 'leased channel' is made available by the operator to a private lessee, the lessee has total control of programming during the leased time slot. Public access channels, on the other hand, are normally subject to complex supervisory systems of various sorts, often with both public and private elements. [G]iven present supervisory mechanisms, the need for this particular provision, aimed directly at public access channels, is not obvious."

STEVENS, J., concurring, agreed with Breyer, J., that it was unwise to characterize leased channels as public fora: "When the Federal Government opens cable channels that would otherwise be left entirely in private hands, it deserves more deference than a rigid application of the public forum doctrine would allow. At this early stage in the regulation of this developing industry, Congress should not be put to an all or nothing-at-all choice in deciding whether to open certain cable channels to programmers who would otherwise lack the resources to participate in the marketplace of ideas."

With respect to § 10(c), Stevens, J., stated: "What is of critical importance to me, however, is that if left to their own devices, those authorities may choose to carry some programming that the Federal Government has decided to restrict. As I read § 10(c), the federal statute would disable local governments from making that choice. It would inject federally authorized private censors into forums from which they might otherwise be excluded, and it would therefore limit local forums that might otherwise be open to all constitutionally protected speech."[3]

SOUTER, J., concurred: "All of the relevant characteristics of cable are presently in a state of technological and regulatory flux. Recent and far-reaching legislation not only affects the technical feasibility of parental control over children's access to undesirable material but portends fundamental changes in the competitive structure of the industry and, therefore, the ability of individual entities to act as bottlenecks to the free flow of information. As cable and telephone companies begin their competition for control over the single wire that will carry both their services, we can hardly

---

3. Although in 1984 Congress essentially barred cable operators from exercising editorial control over PEG channels, see 47 U.S.C. § 531(e), Section 10(c) does not merely restore the status quo ante. Section 10(c) authorizes private operators to exercise editorial discretion over "indecent" programming even if the franchising authority objects. Under the pre–1984 practice, local franchising authorities were free to exclude operators from exercising any such control on PEG channels.

settle rules for review of regulation on the assumption that cable will remain a separable and useful category of First Amendment scrutiny. And as broadcast, cable, and the cyber-technology of the Internet and the World Wide Web approach the day of using a common receiver, we can hardly assume that standards for judging the regulation of one of them will not have immense, but now unknown and unknowable, effects on the others. * * *

"The upshot of appreciating the fluidity of the subject that Congress must regulate is simply to accept the fact that not every nuance of our old standards will necessarily do for the new technology, and that a proper choice among existing doctrinal categories is not obvious. Rather than definitively settling the issue now, Justice Breyer wisely reasons by direct analogy rather than by rule, concluding that the speech and the restriction at issue in this case may usefully be measured against the ones at issue in *Pacifica*. If that means it will take some time before reaching a final method of review for cases like this one, there may be consolation in recalling that 16 years passed, from *Roth* to *Miller*, before the modern obscenity rule jelled; that it took over 40 years, from *Hague v. CIO* to *Perry*, for the public forum category to settle out; and that a round half-century passed before the clear and present danger of *Schenck* evolved into the modern incitement rule of *Brandenburg*.

"I cannot guess how much time will go by until the technologies of communication before us today have matured and their relationships become known. But until a category of indecency can be defined both with reference to the new technology and with a prospect of durability, the job of the courts will be just what Justice Breyer does today: recognizing established First Amendment interests through a close analysis that constrains the Congress, without wholly incapacitating it in all matters of the significance apparent here, maintaining the high value of open communication, measuring the costs of regulation by exact attention to fact, and compiling a pedigree of experience with the changing subject. These are familiar judicial responsibilities in times when we know too little to risk the finality of precision, and attention to them will probably take us through the communications revolution. Maybe the judicial obligation to shoulder these responsibilities can itself be captured by a much older rule, familiar to every doctor of medicine: 'First, do no harm.' "

O'CONNOR, J., concurring in part and dissenting in part, agreed with Breyer, J's assessment that § 10(a) was valid and § 10(b) invalid. She argued, however, that Breyer, J.'s distinctions regarding § 10(c) were insufficiently weighty: "The interest in protecting children remains the same, whether on a leased access channel or a public access channel, and allowing the cable operator the option of prohibiting the transmission of indecent speech seems a constitutionally permissible means of addressing that interest. Nor is the fact that public access programming may be subject to supervisory systems in addition to the cable operator sufficient in my mind to render § 10(c) so ill-tailored to its goal as to be unconstitutional."

KENNEDY, J., joined by Ginsburg, J., concurring in part and dissenting in part, agreed that §§ 10(b) and (c) were invalid, but faulted the plurality opinion for its upholding of § 10(a): "The plurality opinion, insofar as it upholds § 10(a) [is] adrift. The opinion treats concepts such as public forum, broadcaster, and common carrier as mere labels rather than as categories with settled legal significance; it applies no standard, and by this omission loses sight of existing First Amendment doctrine. When confronted with a threat to free speech in the context of an emerging technology, we ought to have the discipline to analyze the case by reference to existing elaborations of constant First Amendment principles. This is the essence of the case-by-case approach to ensuring protection of speech under the First Amendment, even in novel settings. * * *

"The plurality begins its flight from standards with a number of assertions nobody disputes. I agree, of course, that it would be unwise 'to declare a rigid single standard, good for now and for all future media and purposes.' I do think it necessary, however, to decide what standard applies to discrimination against indecent programming on cable access channels in the present state of the industry. We owe at least that much to public and leased access programmers whose speech is put at risk nationwide by these laws. * * *

"The plurality claims its resistance to standards is in keeping with our case law, where we have shown a willingness to be flexible in confronting novel First Amendment problems. [W]e have developed specialized or more or less stringent standards when certain contexts demanded them; we did not avoid the use of standards altogether. Indeed, the creation of standards and adherence to them, even when it means affording protection to speech unpopular or distasteful, is the central achievement of our First Amendment jurisprudence. Standards are the means by which we state in advance how to test a law's validity, rather than letting the height of the bar be determined by the apparent exigencies of the day. They also provide notice and fair warning to those who must predict how the courts will respond to attempts to suppress their speech. Yet formulations like strict scrutiny, used in a number of constitutional settings to ensure that the inequities of the moment are subordinated to commitments made for the long run mean little if they can be watered down whenever they seem too strong. They mean still less if they can be ignored altogether when considering a case not on all fours with what we have seen before.

"The plurality seems distracted by the many changes in technology and competition in the cable industry. The laws challenged here, however, do not retool the structure of the cable industry or (with the exception of § 10(b)) involve intricate technologies. The straight-forward issue here is whether the Government can deprive certain speakers, on the basis of the content of their speech, of protections afforded all others. There is no reason to discard our existing First Amendment jurisprudence in answering this question.

"While it protests against standards, the plurality does seem to favor one formulation of the question in this case: namely, whether the Act 'properly addresses an extremely important problem, without imposing, in light of the relevant interests, an unnecessarily great restriction on speech.' [This] description of the question accomplishes little, save to clutter our First Amendment case law by adding an untested rule with an uncertain relationship to the others we use to evaluate laws restricting speech. * * *

"Justice Souter recommends to the Court the precept 'First, do no harm.' The question, though, is whether the harm is in sustaining the law or striking it down. If the plurality is concerned about technology's direction, it ought to begin by allowing speech, not suppressing it. We have before us an urgent claim for relief against content-based discrimination, not a dry run.

"The constitutionality under *Turner Broadcasting* of requiring a cable operator to set aside leased access channels is not before us. For purposes of this case, we should treat the cable operator's rights in these channels as extinguished, and address the issue these petitioners present: namely, whether the Government can discriminate on the basis of content in affording protection to certain programmers. I cannot agree with Justice Thomas that the cable operator's rights inform this analysis.

"Laws requiring cable operators to provide leased access are the practical equivalent of making them common carriers, analogous in this respect to telephone companies: They are obliged to provide a conduit for the speech of others. [Laws] removing common-carriage protection from a single form of speech based on its content should be reviewed under the same standard as content-based restrictions on speech in a public forum. Making a cable operator a common carrier does not create a public forum in the sense of taking property from private control and dedicating it to public use; rather, regulations of a common carrier dictate the manner in which private control is exercised. A common-carriage mandate, nonetheless, serves the same function as a public forum. It ensures open, nondiscriminatory access to the means of communication.

"*Pacifica* did not purport, however, to apply a special standard for indecent broadcasting. Emphasizing the narrowness of its holding, the Court in *Pacifica* conducted a context-specific analysis of the FCC's restriction on indecent programming during daytime hours. It relied on the general rule that 'broadcasting has received the most limited First Amendment protection.' We already have rejected the application of this lower broadcast standard of review to infringements on the liberties of cable operators, even though they control an important communications medium. *Turner.* * * *

"[Indecency] often is inseparable from the ideas and viewpoints conveyed, or separable only with loss of truth or expressive power. Under our traditional First Amendment jurisprudence, factors perhaps justifying some restriction on indecent cable programming may all be taken into account without derogating this category of protected speech as marginal.

"Congress does have, however, a compelling interest in protecting children from indecent speech. So long as society gives proper respect to parental choices, it may, under an appropriate standard, intervene to spare children exposure to material not suitable for minors. This interest is substantial enough to justify some regulation of indecent speech even under, I will assume, the [strict scrutiny standard].

"Sections 10(a) and (c) nonetheless are not narrowly tailored to protect children from indecent programs on access channels. First, to the extent some operators may allow indecent programming, children in localities those operators serve will be left unprotected. Partial service of a compelling interest is not narrow tailoring. Put another way, the interest in protecting children from indecency only at the caprice of the cable operator is not compelling. Perhaps Congress drafted the law this way to avoid the clear constitutional difficulties of banning indecent speech from access channels, but the First Amendment does not permit this sort of ill fit between a law restricting speech and the interest it is said to serve.

"Second, to the extent cable operators prohibit indecent programming on access channels, not only children but adults will be deprived of it."

THOMAS, J., joined by Rehnquist, C.J., and Scalia, J., concurring in part and dissenting in part, argued that §§ 10(a), (b), and (c) validly protected the constitutional rights of cable operators: "The question petitioners pose is whether §§ 10(a) and (c) are improper restrictions on their free speech rights, but *Turner* strongly suggests that the proper question is whether the leased and public access requirements (with §§ 10(a) and (c)) are improper restrictions on the operators' free speech rights. In my view, the constitutional presumption properly runs in favor of the operators' editorial discretion, and that discretion may not be burdened without a compelling reason for doing so. Petitioners' view that the constitutional presumption favors their asserted right to speak on access channels is directly contrary to Turner and our established precedents.

"It is one thing to compel an operator to carry leased and public access speech, in apparent violation of *Tornillo*, but it is another thing altogether to say that the First Amendment forbids Congress to give back part of the operators' editorial discretion, which all recognize as fundamentally protected, in favor of a broader access right. It is no answer to say that leased and public access are content neutral and that §§ 10(a) and (c) are not, for that does not change the fundamental fact, which petitioners never address, that it is the operators' journalistic freedom that is infringed, whether the challenged restrictions be content neutral or content based.

"Because the access provisions are part of a scheme that restricts the free speech rights of cable operators, and expands the speaking opportunities of access programmers, who have no underlying constitutional right to speak through the cable medium, I do not believe that access programmers can challenge the scheme, or a particular part of it, as an abridgment of their 'freedom of speech.' Outside the public forum doctrine, government intervention that grants access programmers an opportunity to speak that they would not otherwise enjoy—and which does not directly limit programmers' underlying speech rights—cannot be an abridgement of the same programmers' First Amendment rights, even if the new speaking opportunity is content-based.

"The permissive nature of §§ 10(a) and (c) is important in this regard. If Congress had forbidden cable operators to carry indecent programming on leased and public access channels, that law would have burdened the programmer's right, recognized in *Turner* to compete for space on an operator's system. The Court would undoubtedly strictly scrutinize such a law. * * *

"Petitioners argue that public access channels are public fora in which they have First Amendment rights to speak and that § 10(c) is invalid because it imposes content-based burdens on those rights. * * *

"Cable systems are not public property. Cable systems are privately owned and privately managed, and petitioners point to no case in which we have held that government may designate private property as a public forum.

"Pursuant to federal and state law, franchising authorities require cable operators to create public access channels, but nothing in the record suggests that local franchising authorities take any formal easement or other property interest in those channels that would permit the government to designate that property as a public forum.

"Public access channels are not public fora, and, therefore, petitioners' attempt to redistribute cable speech rights in their favor must fail. For this reason, and the other reasons articulated earlier, I would sustain both § 10(a) and § 10(c).

"Unlike §§ 10(a) and (c), § 10(b) clearly implicates petitioners' free speech rights. Though § 10(b) by no means bans indecent speech, it clearly places content-based restrictions on the transmission of private speech by requiring cable operators to block and segregate indecent programming that the operator has agreed to carry. Consequently, § 10(b) must be subjected to strict scrutiny and can be upheld only if it furthers a compelling governmental interest by the least restrictive means available.

"The Court strikes down § 10(b) by pointing to alternatives, such as reverse-blocking [that] it says are less restrictive than segregation and blocking. Though these methods attempt to place in parents' hands the ability to permit their children to watch as little, or as much, indecent programming as the parents think proper, they do not effectively support parents' authority to direct the moral upbringing of their children. The FCC recognized that leased-access programming comes 'from a wide variety of independent sources, with no single editor controlling [its] selection and presentation.' Thus, indecent programming on leased access channels is 'especially likely to be shown randomly or intermittently between non-indecent programs.' Rather than being able to simply block out certain channels at certain times, a subscriber [must] carefully monitor all leased-access programming. [The Court's alternative is] largely ineffective."

Notes and Questions

1. Consider Benkler, *Free as the Air to Common Use: First Amendment Constraints on Enclosure of the Public Domain*, 74 N.Y.U. L. Rev. 354 (1999): "Beneath the veneer of an indecency case, *Denver Area* was a case about access rights. [A] majority of the justices acknowledged that access rights to the cable medium served the First Amendment by permitting many and diverse sources to reach viewers over this concentrated medium. These justices treated decisions by cable operators not to carry programming as 'censorial,' and acknowledged that the availability of access to the medium was a question of constitutional moment. Only the partial dissent by Justice Thomas thought that government intervention by requiring access rights was the relevant constitutional concern."

Compare Barron, *The Electronic Media and the Flight From First Amendment Doctrine: Justice Breyer's New Balancing Approach*, 31 U. Mich. J.L. Ref. 817, 868, 870 (1998): "Justice Breyer's [balancing] approach [provided] specific consideration to the access for expression dimension of the cable regulations under review in *Denver Area*. Access rights must be weighed against the free speech rights of the cable operator. For Justice Thomas, no First Amendment rights conflicted in *Denver Area* because the only rights asserted that merit First Amendment status were those of the cable operator. [Thomas] noted that the rationale behind the plurality was not 'intuitively obvious' as to why programmers and viewers have any First Amendment rights. In reality, however, it is not intuitively obvious that cable operators enjoy the whole panoply of First Amendment rights either. * * * To say that mandatory public access and leased access channels violate *Tornillo* would be an extravagant statement. If the rights of the communications entity's owners were intended to trump all other claims to First Amendment protection for all media, *Tornillo* would have been the ideal occasion to make that statement. The *Tornillo* Court instead directed itself to the print media alone and did not so much as cite *Red Lion*, the most obvious contrary electronic media precedent then extant."

2. Consider Weinberg, *Cable TV, Indecency and the Court*, 21 Colum.–VLA J.L. & Arts 95, 128 (1997): "[*Pacificas*] reasoning and jurisprudential approach are back. This is disturbing. The history of First Amendment decision making in this century suggests that rules are more effective than ad hoc analysis in protecting speech from the fears and repression of the

moment. Justice Breyer, in the *Denver Area* plurality opinion, attributed his contextual approach to 'the changes taking place in the law, the technology, and the industrial structure,' which, he said, made any attempt to enunciate abstract doctrine premature. The deeper message of the plurality opinion, though, is that no matter how technology evolves, *Pacifica's* contextual approach—not the law of rules—will continue to guide content-based regulation of media that feel like television."

3. § 505 of the Telecommunications Act of 1996 requires that cable television operators who provide channels "primarily dedicated to sexually-oriented programming" either "fully scramble or otherwise fully block" the channels so that non-subscribers to the programming would not be able to hear or see it. The art of scrambling has not been perfected, however. "Signal bleed" occurs on many channels, allowing some of the visual and audio aspects of the programming to be heard or seen. In the case of signal bleed, the act requires that the programming be blocked except during hours when children are unlikely to be viewing. The F.C.C.'s regulations provide that those hours are between 10 p.m. and 6 a.m ("the safe harbor provision"). § 504 of the same act required operators to block other programming upon a subscriber's request. A cable television programmer challenged § 505.

UNITED STATES v. PLAYBOY ENTERTAINMENT GROUP, 529 U.S. 803, 120 S.Ct. 1878, 146 L.Ed.2d 865 (2000), per KENNEDY, J., declared the restriction to be content-based with a serious impact on protected speech and held that it did not survive strict scrutiny. Kennedy, J., doubted that signal bleed was sufficiently substantial to imperil children and argued that the government had not demonstrated that a requirement to block upon request with notice of the option provided to the subscriber could not be an effective, but less restrictive alternative: A When the statute became operative, most cable operators had 'no practical choice but to curtail [the targeted] programming during the [regulated] sixteen hours or risk the penalties imposed . . . if any audio or video signal bleed occur[red] during [those] times.' The majority of operators—[in one survey, 69%]—complied with § 505 by time channeling the targeted programmers. Since '30 to 50% of all adult programming is viewed by households prior to 10 p.m.,' the result was a significant restriction of communication, with a corresponding reduction in Playboy's revenues. * * *

"Our zoning cases * * * are irrelevant to the question here. We have made clear that the lesser scrutiny afforded regulations targeting the secondary effects of crime or declining property values has no application to content-based regulations targeting the primary effects of protected speech. The statute now before us burdens speech because of its content; it must receive strict scrutiny.

"[A] key difference between cable television and the broadcasting media [is] the point on which this case turns: Cable systems have the capacity to block unwanted channels on a household-by-household basis. The option to block reduces the likelihood, so concerning to the Court in *Pacifica*, that traditional First Amendment scrutiny would deprive the Government of all authority to address this sort of problem. The corollary, of course, is that targeted blocking enables the Government to support parental authority without affecting the First Amendment interests of speakers and willing listeners—listeners for whom, if the speech is unpopular or indecent, the privacy of their own homes may be the optimal place of receipt. Simply put, targeted blocking is less restrictive than banning, and the Government cannot ban speech if targeted blocking is a feasible and effective means of furthering its compelling interests. [When] a plausible, less restrictive alternative is offered to a content-based speech restriction, it is the Government's obligation to prove that the alternative will be ineffective to achieve its goals. The Government has not met that burden here."

Stevens, J., concurred: "Because Justice Scalia has advanced an argument that the parties have not addressed, a brief response is in order. Relying on *Ginzburg v. United States*, Justice Scalia would treat programs whose content is, he assumes, protected by the First Amendment as though they were obscene because of the way they are advertised. The [*Ginzburg*] theory of obscenity is a legal fiction premised upon a logical bait-and-switch; advertising a bareheaded dancer as 'topless' might be deceptive, but it would not make her performance obscene."[a]

Scalia, J., dissenting, thought that obscenity law was relevant even if none of the programming was obscene: "We have recognized that commercial entities which engage in 'the sordid business of pandering' by 'deliberately emphasiz[ing] the sexually provocative aspects of [their nonobscene products], in order to catch the salaciously disposed,' engage in constitutionally unprotected behavior. *Ginzburg* . We are more permissive of government regulation in these circumstances because it is clear from the context in which exchanges between such businesses and their customers occur that neither the merchant nor the buyer is interested in the work's literary, artistic, political, or scientific value.

"Section 505 regulates just this sort of business. [It] is conceivable, I suppose, that a channel which is primarily dedicated to sex might not hold itself forth as primarily dedicated to sex—in which case its productions which contain 'serious literary, artistic, political, or scientific value' (if any) would be as entitled to First Amendment protection as the statuary rooms of the National Gallery. But in the competitive world of cable programming, the possibility that a channel devoted to sex would not advertise itself as such is sufficiently remote, and the number of such channels sufficiently small (if not indeed nonexistent), as not to render the provision substantially overbroad."[2]

a. Thomas, J., concurring, indicated that the case would be different if the government had proceeded against aspects of the programming that were obscene.

2. Justice Stevens misapprehends in several respects the nature of the test I would apply. First, he mistakenly believes that the nature of the advertising controls the obscenity analysis, regardless of the nature of the material being advertised. I entirely agree with him that "advertising a bareheaded dancer as 'topless' might be de-

BREYER, J., joined by Rehnquist, C.J., O'Connor and Scalia, JJ., dissenting, argued that the section was justified by the compelling interest in protecting children. He maintained that the suggested alternative of having subscribers ask for blocking if they wished was impractical: "As the majority observes, during the 14 months the Government was enjoined from enforcing § 505, 'fewer than 0.5% of cable subscribers requested full blocking' under § 504. The majority describes this public reaction as 'a collective yawn,' adding that the Government failed to prove that the 'yawn' reflected anything other than the lack of a serious signal bleed problem or a lack of notice which better information about § 504 might cure. The record excludes the first possibility—at least in respect to exposure, as discussed above. And I doubt that the public, though it may well consider the viewing habits of adults a matter of personal choice, would 'yawn' when the exposure in question concerns young children, the absence of parental consent, and the sexually explicit material here at issue.

"Neither is the record neutral in respect to the curative power of better notice. [An] opt-out right works only when parents (1) become aware of their [rights], (2) discover that their children are watching sexually-explicit signal 'bleed,' (3) reach their cable operator and ask that it block the sending of its signal to their home, (4) await installation of an individual blocking device, and, perhaps (5) (where the block fails or the channel number changes) make a new request. Better notice of [blocking rights] does little to help parents discover their children's viewing habits (step two). And it does nothing at all in respect to steps three through five. Yet the record contains considerable evidence that those problems matter, i.e., evidence of endlessly delayed phone call responses, faulty installations, blocking failures, and other mishaps, leaving those steps as significant [obstacles]."

———

Two provisions of the Communications Decency Act ("CDA") seek to protect minors from material on the Internet. 47 U.S.C. § 223(a) prohibits the knowing transmission of indecent messages to any recipient under 18 years of age. 47 U.S.C. § 223(d) prohibits the knowing sending or displaying of patently offensive messages in a manner that is available to a person under 18 years of age. Patently offensive is defined as any "image or other communication that in context, depicts or describes, in terms patently offensive as measured by contemporary community standards, sexual or excretory activities or organs * * *"

RENO v. AMERICAN CIVIL LIBERTIES UNION, 521 U.S. 844, 117 S.Ct. 2329, 138 L.Ed.2d 874 (1997), per STEVENS, J., held that both provisions were too vague and overbroad to withstand first amendment

ceptive, but it would not make her performance obscene." I believe, however, that if the material is 'patently offensive' and it is being advertised as such, we have little reason to think it is being proffered for its socially redeeming value. * * *

scrutiny.[a] After providing a lengthy description of the Internet focusing on e-mail, automatic mailing list services, newsgroups, chatrooms, and the WORLD Wide Web, Stevens, J., distinguished prior cases:

"In four important respects, the statute upheld in *Ginsberg* was narrower than the CDA. First, we noted in *Ginsberg* that 'the prohibition against sales to minors does not bar parents who so desire from purchasing the magazines for their children.' Under the CDA, by contrast, neither the parents' consent—nor even their participation—in the communication would avoid the application of the statute.[32] Second, the New York statute applied only to commercial transactions, whereas the CDA contains no such limitation. Third, the New York statute cabined its definition of material that is harmful to minors with the requirement that it be 'utterly without redeeming social importance for minors.' The CDA fails to provide us with any definition of the term 'indecent' as used in § 223(a)(1) and, importantly, omits any requirement that the 'patently offensive' material covered by § 223(d) lack serious literary, artistic, political, or scientific value. Fourth, the New York statute defined a minor as a person under the age of 17, whereas the CDA, in applying to all those under 18 years, includes an additional year of those nearest majority. * * *

"[S]ome of our cases have recognized special justifications for regulation of the broadcast media that are not applicable to other speakers. In these cases, the Court relied on the history of extensive government regulation of the broadcast medium, see, e.g., *Red Lion;* the scarcity of available frequencies at its inception, see, e.g., *Turner Broadcasting System, Inc. v. FCC;* and its 'invasive' nature, see *Sable Communications of Cal., Inc. v. FCC.*

"Those factors are not present in cyberspace. Neither before nor after the enactment of the CDA have the vast democratic fora of the Internet been subject to the type of government supervision and regulation that has attended the broadcast industry. Moreover, the Internet is not as 'invasive' as radio or television. The District Court specifically found that '[c]ommunications' over the Internet do not 'invade' an individual's home or appear on one's computer screen unbidden. Users seldom encounter content 'by accident.' It also found that '[a]lmost all sexually explicit images are preceded by warnings as to the content,' and cited testimony that '"odds are slim'" that a user would come across a sexually explicit sight by accident.' * * *

"Finally, unlike the conditions that prevailed when Congress first authorized regulation of the broadcast spectrum, the Internet can hardly be considered a 'scarce' expressive commodity. It provides relatively unlimited,

---

a. The CDA also prohibited obscenity on the Internet. That portion of the statute was not challenged, and the Court specifically noted that it had not struck down that part of the statute.

32. Given the likelihood that many E-mail transmissions from an adult to a mi-

nor are conversations between family members, it is therefore incorrect for the dissent to suggest that the provisions of the CDA, even in this narrow area, "are no different from the law we sustained in *Ginsberg.*"

low-cost capacity for communication of all kinds. The Government estimates that '[a]s many as 40 million people use the Internet today, and that figure is expected to grow to 200 million by 1999.' This dynamic, multifaceted category of communication includes not only traditional print and news services, but also audio, video, and still images, as well as interactive, real-time dialogue. Through the use of chat rooms, any person with a phone line can become a town crier with a voice that resonates farther than it could from any soapbox. Through the use of Web pages, mail exploders, and newsgroups, the same individual can become a pamphleteer. As the District Court found, 'the content on the Internet is as diverse as human thought.' We agree with its conclusion that our cases provide no basis for qualifying the level of First Amendment scrutiny that should be applied to this medium.

"Regardless of whether the CDA is so vague that it violates the Fifth Amendment, the many ambiguities concerning the scope of its coverage render it problematic for purposes of the First Amendment. For instance, each of the two parts of the CDA uses a different linguistic form. The first uses the word 'indecent,' 47 U.S.C.A. § 223(a), while the second speaks of material that 'in context, depicts or describes, in terms patently offensive as measured by contemporary community standards, sexual or excretory activities or organs,' § 223(d). Given the absence of a definition of either term,[35] this difference in language will provoke uncertainty among speakers about how the two standards relate to each other and just what they mean.[37] Could a speaker confidently assume that a serious discussion about birth control practices, homosexuality, the First Amendment issues raised by the Appendix to our *Pacifica* opinion, or the consequences of prison rape would not violate the CDA? This uncertainty undermines the likelihood that the CDA has been carefully tailored to the congressional goal of protecting minors from potentially harmful materials.

"The vagueness of the CDA is a matter of special concern for two reasons. First, the CDA is a content-based regulation of speech. [Second,] the CDA is a criminal statute. In addition to the opprobrium and stigma of a criminal conviction, the CDA threatens violators with penalties including up to two years in prison for each act of violation. The severity of criminal sanctions may well cause speakers to remain silent rather than communicate even arguably unlawful words, ideas, and images. As a practical matter, this increased deterrent effect, coupled with the 'risk of discriminatory enforcement' of vague regulations, poses greater First Amendment concerns than

---

35. "Indecent" does not benefit from any textual embellishment at all. "Patently offensive" is qualified only to the extent that it involves "sexual or excretory activities or organs" taken "in context" and "measured by contemporary community standards."

37. The statute does not indicate whether the "patently offensive" and "indecent" determinations should be made with respect to minors or the population as a whole. The Government asserts that the appropriate standard is "what is suitable material for minors." But the Conferees expressly rejected amendments that would have imposed such a "harmful to minors" standard.

those implicated by the civil regulation reviewed in *Denver Area Ed. Tele-communications Consortium, Inc. v. FCC.* * * *

"Because the CDA's 'patently offensive' standard (and, we assume arguendo, its synonymous 'indecent' standard) is one part of the three-prong *Miller* test, the Government reasons, it cannot be unconstitutionally vague. [The] Government's assertion is incorrect as a matter of fact. The second prong of the *Miller* test—the purportedly analogous standard—contains a critical requirement that is omitted from the CDA: that the proscribed material be 'specifically defined by the applicable state law.' This requirement reduces the vagueness inherent in the open-ended term 'patently offensive' as used in the CDA. Moreover, the *Miller* definition is limited to 'sexual conduct,' whereas the CDA extends also to include (1) 'excretory activities' as well as (2) 'organs' of both a sexual and excretory nature.

"The Government's reasoning is also flawed. Just because a definition including three limitations is not vague, it does not follow that one of those limitations, standing by itself, is not vague. Each of *Miller's* additional two prongs—(1) that, taken as a whole, the material appeal to the 'prurient' interest, and (2) that it 'lac[k] serious literary, artistic, political, or scientific value'—critically limits the uncertain sweep of the obscenity definition. The second requirement is particularly important because, unlike the 'patently offensive' and 'prurient interest' criteria, it is not judged by contemporary community standards. This 'societal value' requirement, absent in the CDA, allows appellate courts to impose some limitations and regularity on the definition by setting, as a matter of law, a national floor for socially redeeming value. The Government's contention that courts will be able to give such legal limitations to the CDA's standards is belied by *Miller's* own rationale for having juries determine whether material is 'patently offensive' according to community standards: that such questions are essentially ones of fact.

"In contrast to *Miller* and our other previous cases, the CDA thus presents a greater threat of censoring speech that, in fact, falls outside the statute's scope. Given the vague contours of the coverage of the statute, it unquestionably silences some speakers whose messages would be entitled to constitutional protection. That danger provides further reason for insisting that the statute not be overly broad. The CDA's burden on protected speech cannot be justified if it could be avoided by a more carefully drafted statute. * * *

"It is true that we have repeatedly recognized the governmental interest in protecting children from harmful materials. But that interest does not justify an unnecessarily broad suppression of speech addressed to adults. [In] arguing that the CDA does not so diminish adult communication, the Government relies on the incorrect factual premise that prohibiting a transmission whenever it is known that one of its recipients is a minor would not interfere with adult-to-adult communication. The findings of the District Court make clear that this premise is untenable. Given the size of the potential audience for most messages, in the absence of a viable age verification process, the sender must be charged with knowing that one or more minors will likely view it. Knowledge that, for instance, one or more members of a 100–person chat group will be [a] minor—and therefore that it would be a crime to send the group an indecent message—would surely burden communication among adults.[42]

"The District Court found that at the time of trial existing technology did not include any effective method for a sender to prevent minors from obtaining access to its communications on the Internet without also denying access to adults. The Court found no effective way to determine the age of a user who is accessing material through e-mail, mail exploders, newsgroups, or chatrooms. As a practical matter, the Court also found that it would be prohibitively expensive for noncommercial—as well as some commercial—speakers who have Web sites to verify that their users are adults. These limitations must inevitably curtail a significant amount of adult communication on the Internet. By contrast, the District Court found that '[d]espite its limitations, currently available user-based software suggests that a reasonably effective method by which parents can prevent their children from accessing sexually explicit and other material which parents may believe is inappropriate for their children will soon be widely available.'

"The breadth of the CDA's coverage is wholly unprecedented. Unlike the regulations upheld in *Ginsberg* and *Pacifica,* the scope of the CDA is not limited to commercial speech or commercial entities. Its open-ended prohibitions embrace all nonprofit entities and individuals posting indecent messages or displaying them on their own computers in the presence of minors. The general, undefined terms 'indecent' and 'patently offensive' cover large amounts of nonpornographic material with serious educational or other value. Moreover, the 'community standards' criterion as applied to the Internet means that any communication available to a nation-wide audience will be judged by the standards of the community most likely to be offended by the message. The regulated subject matter includes any of the seven 'dirty words' used in the *Pacifica* monologue, the use of which the Government's expert acknowledged could constitute a felony. It may also extend to discussions about prison rape or safe sexual practices, artistic images that include nude subjects, and arguably the card catalogue of the Carnegie Library.

"For the purposes of our decision, we need neither accept nor reject the Government's submission that the First Amendment does not forbid a blanket prohibition on all 'indecent' and 'patently offensive' messages communicated to a 17–year-old—no matter how much value the message may contain and regardless of parental approval. It is at least clear that the strength of the Government's interest in protecting minors is not equally strong throughout the coverage of this broad statute. Under the CDA, a parent allowing her 17–year-old to use the family computer to obtain

---

42. The Government agrees that these provisions are applicable whenever "a sender transmits a message to more than one recipient, knowing that at least one of the specific persons receiving the message is a minor."

information on the Internet that she, in her parental judgment, deems appropriate could face a lengthy prison term. Similarly, a parent who sent his 17–year-old college freshman information on birth control via e-mail could be incarcerated even though neither he, his child, nor anyone in their home community, found the material 'indecent' or 'patently offensive,' if the college town's community thought otherwise.

. "The breadth of this content-based restriction of speech imposes an especially heavy burden on the Government to explain why a less restrictive provision would not be as effective as the CDA. It has not done so. The arguments in this Court have referred to possible alternatives such as requiring that indecent material be 'tagged' in a way that facilitates parental control of material coming into their homes, making exceptions for messages with artistic or educational value, providing some tolerance for parental choice, and regulating some portions of the Internet—such as commercial web sites—differently than others, such as chat rooms. Particularly in the light of the absence of any detailed findings by the Congress, or even hearings addressing the special problems of the CDA, we are persuaded that the CDA is not narrowly tailored if that requirement has any meaning at all."

O'CONNOR, J., joined by Rehnquist, C.J., concurred in the judgment in part and dissented in part: * * * "Given the present state of cyberspace, I agree with the Court that the 'display' provision cannot pass muster. Until gateway technology is available throughout cyberspace, and it is not in 1997, a speaker cannot be reasonably assured that the speech he displays will reach only adults because it is impossible to confine speech to an 'adult zone.' Thus, the only way for a speaker to avoid liability under the CDA is to refrain completely from using indecent speech. But this forced silence impinges on the First Amendment right of adults to make and obtain this speech and, for all intents and purposes, 'reduce[s] the adult population [on the Internet] to reading only what is fit for children.'

"The 'indecency transmission' and 'specific person' provisions present a closer issue, for they are not unconstitutional in all of their applications. [T]he 'indecency transmission' provision makes it a crime to transmit knowingly an indecent message to a person the sender knows is under 18 years of age. The 'specific person' provision proscribes the same conduct, although it does not as explicitly require the sender to know that the intended recipient of his indecent message is a minor. Appellant urges the Court to construe the provision to impose such a knowledge requirement, and I would do so.

"So construed, both provisions are constitutional as applied to a conversation involving only an adult and one or more minors—e.g., when an adult speaker sends an e-mail knowing the addressee is a minor, or when an adult and minor converse by themselves or with other minors in a chat room. In this context, these provisions are no different from the law we sustained in *Ginsberg*. Restricting what the adult may say to the minors in no way restricts the adult's ability to communicate with other adults. He is not prevented from speaking indecently to other adults in a chat room (because there are no other adults participating in the conversation) and he remains free to send indecent e-mails to other adults. The relevant universe contains only one adult, and the adult in that universe has the power to refrain from using indecent speech and consequently to keep all such speech within the room in an 'adult' zone.

"The analogy to *Ginsberg* breaks down, however, when more than one adult is a party to the conversation. If a minor enters a chat room otherwise occupied by adults, the CDA effectively requires the adults in the room to stop using indecent speech. If they did not, they could be prosecuted under the 'indecency transmission' and 'specific person' provisions for any indecent statements they make to the group, since they would be transmitting an indecent message to specific persons, one of whom is a minor. The CDA is therefore akin to a law that makes it a crime for a bookstore owner to sell pornographic magazines to anyone once a minor enters his store. Even assuming such a law might be constitutional in the physical world as a reasonable alternative to excluding minors completely from the store, the absence of any means of excluding minors from chat rooms in cyberspace restricts the rights of adults to engage in indecent speech in those rooms. The 'indecency transmission' and 'specific person' provisions share this defect. * * *

"Whether the CDA substantially interferes with the First Amendment rights of minors, and thereby runs afoul of the second characteristic of valid zoning laws, presents a closer question. [The] Court neither 'accept[s]' nor reject[s]' the argument that the CDA is facially overbroad because it substantially interferes with the First Amendment rights of minors. [In] my view, the universe of speech constitutionally protected as to minors but banned by the CDA—i.e., the universe of material that is 'patently offensive,' but which nonetheless has some redeeming value for minors or does not appeal to their prurient interest—is a very small one. Appellees cite no examples of speech falling within this universe and do not attempt to explain why that universe is substantial 'in relation to the statute's plainly legitimate sweep.' That the CDA might deny minors the right to obtain material that has some 'value' is largely beside the point. While discussions about prison rape or nude art may have some redeeming education value for adults, they do not necessarily have any such value for minors, and under *Ginsberg*, minors only have a First Amendment right to obtain patently offensive material that has 'redeeming social importance for minors.' There is also no evidence in the record to support the contention that 'many [e]-mail transmissions from an adult to a minor are conversations between family members,' and no support for the legal proposition that such speech is absolutely immune from regulation. Accordingly, in my view, the CDA does not burden a substantial amount of minors' constitutionally protected speech. I would reject it.

"Thus, the constitutionality of the CDA as a zoning law hinges on the extent to which it substantially interferes with the First Amendment rights of adults. Because the rights of adults are infringed only by the 'display' provision and by the 'indecency transmission' and 'specific person' provisions as applied to communications involving more than one adult, I would invalidate the CDA only to that extent. Insofar as the 'indecency transmission' and 'specific person' provisions prohibit the use of indecent speech in communications between an adult and one or more minors, however, they can and should be sustained. The Court reaches a contrary conclusion, and from that holding that I respectfully dissent."[b]

Notes and Questions

1.   Consider Heins, *Indecency: The Ongoing American Debate Over Sex, Children, Free Speech, and Dirty Words* (1997): "It remains to be see whether *Reno v. ACLU* will prove an idiosycratically broad response to a broadly drafted law, or whether its recognition of the positive value of some speech about some speech, even for minors, will mark the beginning of a long-overdue process of actually examining the presumption that sexual explicitness or crude language is intrinsically harmful to the young."[c]

2.   Was it a mistake for the Court to suggest that a heavy burden on protected speech might be salvaged if a compelling governmental interest test could be satisfied? To what extent does first amendment doctrine permit substantial burdens on otherwise protected speech? See Volokh, *Freedom of Speech, Shielding Children, and Transcending Balancing*, 1997 Sup.Ct.Rev. 141.

3.   Are the application of obscenity laws to the internet problematic since the manager of a website can not discern from what jurisdiction a person is seeking to gain access. Does this force sexually oriented speech to comply with the most conservative jurisdiction and substantially burden protected speech?[d]

4.   Suppose a public library installs software on its computers designed to block websites with material that could be harmful to children. If a patron wishes to gain access to an excluded site, the librarian would decide if the material was age appropriate. Constitutional?[e]

5.   Suppose the government outlawed filter software. Would this be constitutional as "a market-structuring device designed content-neutrally to

---

b. Stevens, J., argued that Congress had not provided guidance as to where lines should be drawn if the statute were otherwise to be struck down. Lacking guidance, he declined to find that the statute was readily subject to a narrowing construction.

c. See generally Ross, *Anything Goes: Examining the State's Interest in Protecting Children From Controversial Speech*, 53 Vand. L.Rev. 427 (2000).

d. Hardy, *The Proper Legal Regime for "Cyberspace,"* 55 U.Pitt.L.Rev. 993, 1012–13 (1994).

e. *Mainstream Loudoun v. Board of Trustees*, 2 F.Supp.2d 783 (E.D.Va.1998); see also Lessig, *What Things Regulate Speech: CDA 2.0 vs. Filtering*, 38 Jurimetrics J. 629 (1998); Wagner, *Library Filters and the First Amendment*, 83 Minn. L.Rev. 755 (1999); Weinberg, *Rating the Net*, 19 Hastings Comm/Ent L.J. 453 (1997); Note, *Burning Cyberbooks in Public Libraries: Internet Filtering Software v. the First Amendment*, 52 Stan.L.Rev. 509 (2000).

make unrated fare more competitive and available to a wider variety of households, akin to the cable must-carry regulations upheld in *Turner.*" Sullivan, *First Amendment Intermediaries in the Age of Cyberspace,* 45 UCLA L.Rev. 1653, 1678 (1998).

6.   The Child Online Protection Act prohibits any person with commercial purposes from knowingly causing material that is obscene for children to be placed on the World Wide Web. It is a defense under the act that the defendant has required proof of age by credit card or adult verification screens, or any reasonable measure that is feasible under available technology. Constitutional? Would blocking software installed by parents be a less restrictive alternative? See *American Civil Liberties Union v. Reno,* 31 F.Supp.2d 473 (1999).[f] Would the best solution be to require that net browsers provide a preference that, if elected, would signal to web sites that the recipient is a child?[g] How serious is it that children might evade this by using a computer at a friend's house?[h]

f. See Strossen, *Children's Rights v. Adult Free Speech: Can They Be Reconciled?,* 29 Conn. L.Rev. 873, 876 (1997).

g. Lessig & Resnick, *Zoning Speech on the Internet: A Legal and Technical Model,* 98 Mich. L.Rev 395 (1999).

h. Volokh, *Freedom of Speech in Cyberspace From the Listener's Perspective: Private Speech Restrictions, Libel State Action, Harassment, and Sex,* 1996 U.Chi. Legal F. 377, 434 (1996).

Chapter 9

THE RIGHT NOT TO SPEAK, THE RIGHT TO ASSOCIATE, AND THE RIGHT NOT TO ASSOCIATE

NAACP v. Alabama ex rel. Patterson, 357 U.S. 449, 78 S.Ct. 1163, 2 L.Ed.2d 1488 (1958), per Harlan, J., held that the first amendment barred Alabama from compelling production of NAACP membership lists. The opinion used the phrase freedom of association repeatedly, "elevat[ing] freedom of association to an independent right, possessing an equal status with the other rights specifically enumerated in the first amendment." Emerson, *Freedom of Association and Freedom of Expression,* 74 Yale L.J. 1, 2 (1964).

From the materials on advocacy of illegal action (Ch. 1, I supra) onward, it has been evident that individuals have rights to join with others for expressive purposes. This section explores other aspects of the freedom to associate and its corollary, the freedom not to associate. First, we explore cases which the Court bases on a right not to speak, but might better be understood as establishing a right not to be associated with particular ideas. Second, we explore aspects of free association in the employment context—in particular the claims of employees not to be associated with a political party, or a union or its policies. Those claims are to some extent derived from the cases establishing a right not to be associated with particular ideas. Third, instead of persons resisting forced membership in a group, we confront groups resisting members. Finally, the section explores conflicts between rights of association in political parties and election regulations.

I. THE RIGHT NOT TO BE ASSOCIATED WITH PARTICULAR IDEAS

"If there is any fixed star in our constitutional constellation, it is that no official, high or petty, can prescribe what shall be orthodox in politics, nationalism, religion, or other matter of opinion or force citizens to confess by word or act their faith therein."

West Virginia State Bd. of Educ. v. Barnette, Ch. 12, I infra (Jackson, J.) (upholding right of public school students to refuse to salute flag).

New Hampshire required that noncommercial vehicles bear license plates embossed with the state motto, "Live Free or Die." "Refus[ing] to be coerced by the State into advertising a slogan which I find morally, ethically, religiously and politically abhorrent," appellee, a Jehovah's Witness, covered up the motto on his license plate, a misdemeanor under state law. After being convicted several times of violating the misdemeanor statute, appellee sought federal injunctive and declaratory relief. WOOLEY v. MAYNARD, 430 U.S. 705, 97 S.Ct. 1428, 51 L.Ed.2d 752 (1977), per Burger, C.J., held that requiring appellee to display the motto on his license plates violated his first amendment right to "refrain from speaking": "[T]he freedom of thought protected by the First Amendment [includes] both the right to speak freely and the right to refrain from speaking at all. See *Barnette.* The right to speak and the right to refrain from speaking are complementary components of the broader concept of 'individual freedom of mind.' This is illustrated [by] *Miami Herald Publishing Co. v. Tornillo* [Ch. 8, I supra], where we held unconstitutional a Florida statute placing an affirmative duty upon newspapers to publish the replies of political candidates whom they had criticized.

" * * * Compelling the affirmative act of a flag salute [the situation in *Barnette*] involved a more serious infringement upon personal liberties than the passive act of carrying the state motto on a license plate, but the difference is essentially one of degree.[a] Here, as in *Barnette,* we are faced with a state measure which forces an individual as part of his daily life— indeed constantly while his automobile is in public view—to be an instrument for fostering public adherence to an ideological point of view he finds unacceptable. In doing so, the State 'invades the sphere of intellect and spirit which it is the purpose of the First Amendment [to] reserve from all official control.' *Barnette.*

"New Hampshire's statute in effect requires that appellees use their private property as a 'mobile billboard' for the State's ideological message— or suffer a penalty, as Maynard already has. [The] fact that most individuals agree with the thrust of [the] motto is not the test; most Americans also find the flag salute acceptable. The First Amendment protects the right of individuals to hold a point of view different from the majority and to refuse to foster, in the way New Hampshire commands, an idea they find morally objectionable."

---

a. If a teacher leads a class in the pledge of allegiance, is psychological coercion involved even in the absence of a legal requirement? Is psychological coercion suffi- cient to trigger a free speech violation. See Greene, *The Pledge of Allegiance Problem,* 64 Fordham L.Rev. 451 (1995).

The Court next considered whether "the State's countervailing interest" was "sufficiently compelling" to justify appellees to display the motto on their license plates. The two interests claimed by the state were (1) facilitating the identification of state license plates from those of similar colors of other states and (2) promoting "appreciation of history, state pride, [and] individualism." As to (1), the record revealed that these state license plates were readily distinguishable from others without reference to the state motto and, in any event, the state's purpose could be achieved by "less drastic means," i.e., by alternative methods less restrictive of first amendment freedoms. As to (2), where the State's interest is to communicate an "official view" as to history and state pride or to disseminate any other "ideology," "such interest cannot outweigh an individual's First Amendment right to avoid becoming the courier for such message."

REHNQUIST, J., joined by Blackmun, J., dissented, not only agreeing with what he called "the Court's implicit recognition that there is no protected 'symbolic speech' in this case," but maintaining that "that conclusion goes far to undermine the Court's ultimate holding that there is an element of protected expression here. The State has not forced appellees to 'say' anything; and it has not forced them to communicate ideas with nonverbal actions reasonably likened to 'speech,' such as wearing a lapel button promoting a political candidate or waving a flag as a symbolic gesture.[b] The State has simply required that *all* noncommercial automobiles bear license tags with the state motto. [Appellees] have not been forced to affirm or reject that motto; they are simply required by the State [to] carry a state auto license tag for identification and registration purposes. [The] issue, unconfronted by the Court, is whether appellees, in displaying, as they are required to do, state license tags, the format of which is known to all as having been prescribed by the State, would be considered to be advocating political or ideological views.

"[H]aving recognized the rather obvious differences between [*Barnette* and this case], the Court does not explain why the same result should obtain. The Court suggests that the test is whether the individual is forced 'to be an instrument for fostering public adherence to an ideological point of view he finds unacceptable,' [but] these are merely conclusory words. [For] example, were New Hampshire to erect a multitude of billboards, each proclaiming 'Live Free or Die,' and tax all citizens for the cost of erection and maintenance, clearly the message would be 'fostered' by the individual citizen-taxpayers and just as clearly those individuals would be 'instruments' in that communication. Certainly, however, that case would not fall within the ambit of *Barnette*. In that case, as in this case, there is no *affirmation* of belief. For First Amendment principles to be implicated, the State must

---

b. Does *compelled* expression have to be understood by others to be "speech" or does it suffice that Maynard *subjectively believed* that he was being forced to make an expression? See note 1 following this case. Should compelled speech cases be characterized as personhood or autonomy cases rather than free speech cases? See Greene, supra note a.

place the citizen in the position of either appearing to, or actually, 'asserting as true' the message. This was the focus of *Barnette,* and clearly distinguishes this case from that one."[c]

Notes and Questions

1. Consider Tribe, *The Curvature of Constitutional Space: What Lawyers Can Learn From Modern Physics,* 103 Harv.L.Rev. 1, 22 (1989): "[T]he very existence of the challenged New Hampshire Law in a sense *protected* free speech rights. For it was well known that people had no choice about whether the state motto was to appear on their license plates. [Ironically], by requiring the state to give people the option whether or not to have its motto displayed on their license plates, the *Wooley* Court forced people into a symbolic expression."

2. *Use of private property as a forum for the speech of others.*

(a) Appellees sought to enjoin a shopping center from denying them access to the center's central courtyard in order to solicit signatures from passersby for petitions opposing a U.N. resolution. The California Supreme Court held they were entitled to conduct their activity at the center, construing the state constitution to protect "speech and petitioning, reasonably exercised, in shopping centers, even [when] privately owned." PRUNE-YARD SHOPPING CENTER v. ROBINS, 447 U.S. 74, 100 S.Ct. 2035, 64 L.Ed.2d 741 (1980) per Rehnquist, J., affirmed, rejecting, inter alia, the argument, based on *Wooley,* that "a State may not constitutionally require an individual to participate in the dissemination of an ideological message by displaying it on his private property [so] that it be observed and read by the public":

"[In *Wooley*] the government itself prescribed the message, required it to be displayed openly on appellee's personal property that was used 'as part of his daily life,' and refused to permit him [to] cover up the motto even though the Court found that the display of the motto served no important state interest. Here, by contrast, there are a number of distinguishing factors. Most important, [the center] is not limited to the personal use of appellants, [but is] a business establishment that is open to the public to come and go as they please. The views expressed by members of the public in passing out pamphlets or seeking signatures for a petition thus will not likely be identified with those of the owner. Second, no specific message is dictated by the State to be displayed on appellants' property. There consequently is no danger of government discrimination for or against a particular message. Finally, [it appears] appellants can expressly disavow any connection with the message by simply posting signs in the area where the speakers or handbillers stand."

c. White, J., joined by Blackmun and Rehnquist, JJ., dissented on procedural grounds.

The Court also found appellants' reliance on *Barnette* and *Tornillo* misplaced: Unlike *Barnette,* appellants "are not [being] compelled to affirm their belief in any governmentally prescribed position or view, and they are free to publicly dissociate themselves from the views of the speakers or handbillers. [*Tornillo*] rests on the principle that the State cannot tell a newspaper what it must print. [There was also a danger in *Tornillo* that the invalidated statute requiring a newspaper to publish a political candidate's reply to previously published criticism would deter] editors from publishing controversial political [statements]. Thus, the statute was found to be an 'intrusion into the function of editors.' These concerns obviously are not present here."[d]

POWELL, J., joined by White, J., concurring in part and in the judgment, agreed that "the owner of this shopping center has failed to establish a cognizable First Amendment claim," but maintained that "state action that transforms privately owned property into a forum for the expression of the public's views could raise serious First Amendment questions": "I do not believe that the result in *Wooley* would have changed had [the state] directed its citizens to place the slogan 'Live Free or Die' in their shop windows rather than on their automobiles. [The *Wooley* principle] on its face protects a person who refuses to allow use of his property as a market place for the ideas of others. [One] who has merely invited the public onto his property for commercial purposes cannot fairly be said to have relinquished his right 'to decline to be an instrument for fostering public adherence to an ideological point of view he finds unacceptable.' *Wooley.*

"[E]ven when [as here] no particular message is mandated by the State, First Amendment interests are affected by state action that forces a property owner to admit third-party speakers. [A] right of access [may be] no less intrusive than speech compelled by the State itself. For example, a law requiring that a newspaper permit others to use its columns imposes an unacceptable burden upon the newspaper's First Amendment right to select material for publication. *Tornillo.*

"[If] a state law mandated public access to the bulletin board of a freestanding store [or] small shopping center [or allowed soliciting or pamphleteering in the entrance area of a store], customers might well conclude that the messages reflect the view of the proprietor. [He] either could permit his customers to receive a mistaken impression [or] disavow the messages. Should he take the first course, he effectively has been compelled to affirm someone else's belief. Should he choose the second, he has been forced to speak when he would prefer to remain silent. In short, he has lost control over his freedom to speak or not to speak on certain issues. The mere fact

---

d. Could *PruneYard* be extended to parts of the Internet? To America Online? To Netscape? Are parts of the Internet already public fora. For various views, see Tribe, *The Constitution in Cyberspace,* The Humanist, Sept.–Oct. 1991, at 15; Di Lello, *Functional Equivalency and Its Application to Freedom of Speech on Computer Bulletin* *Boards,* 26 Colum. J.L. & Soc. Probs. 199 (1993); Note, *Sidewalks in Cyberspace: Making Space for Public Forums in the Electronic Environment,* 12 Harv. J.L. & Tech. 149 (1998); Note, *Is Cyberspace a Public Forum? Computer Bulletin Boards, Free Speech, and State Action,* 81 Geo.L.J. 409 (1992).

that he is free to dissociate himself from the views expressed on his property cannot restore his 'right to refrain from speaking at all.' *Wooley.*

"A property owner may also be faced with speakers who wish to use his premises as a platform for views that he finds morally repugnant[, for example, a] minority-owned business confronted with leafleteers from the American Nazi Party or the Ku Klux Klan, [or] a church-operated enterprise asked to host demonstrations in favor of abortion. [The] strong emotions evoked by speech in such situations may virtually compel the proprietor to respond.

"The pressure to respond is particularly apparent [in the above cases, but] an owner who strongly objects to some of the causes to which the state-imposed right of access would extend may oppose ideological activities 'of *any* sort' that are not related to the purposes for which he has invited the public onto his property. See *Abood.* To require the owner to specify the particular ideas he finds objectionable enough to compel a response would force him to relinquish his 'freedom to maintain his own beliefs without public disclosure.' *Abood.* Thus, the right to control one's own speech may be burdened impermissibly even when listeners will not assume that the messages expressed on private property are those of the owner.

"[On this record] I cannot say that customers of this vast center [occupying several city blocks and containing more than 65 shops] would be likely to assume that appellees' limited speech activity expressed the views of [the center]. [Moreover, appellants] have not alleged that they object to [appellees' views, nor asserted] that some groups who reasonably might be expected to speak at [the center] will express views that are so objectionable as to require a response even when listeners will not mistake their source. [Thus,] I join the judgment of the Court, [but] I do not interpret our decision today as a blanket approval for state efforts to transform privately owned commercial property into public forums."[e]

(b) PACIFIC GAS & ELECTRIC CO. v. PUBLIC UTILITIES COMM'N, 475 U.S. 1, 106 S.Ct. 903, 89 L.Ed.2d 1 (1986), per POWELL, J., joined by Burger, C.J., and Brennan and O'Connor, JJ., together with MARSHALL, J., concurring, struck down a commission requirement that a private utility company include in its billing envelope materials supplied by a public interest group that were critical of some of the company's positions.[f] Was the result required by *Tornillo?* Consistent with *PruneYard?*

3. *Paraders' rights.* The City of Boston gave authorization to the South Boston Allied War Veterans Council to conduct the St. Patrick's Day—

---

e. For commentary, see Berger, *Prune-yard Revisited: Political Activity on Private Lands,* 66 N.Y.U.L.Rev. 633 (1991); Levinson, *Freedom of Speech and the Right of Access to Private Property Under State Constitutional Law* in Developments in State Constitutional Law 51 (McGraw ed. 1985).

f. Burger, C.J., filed a concurring opinion; Rehnquist, J., joined by White and Stevens, JJ., dissented; Stevens, J., filed a separate dissent; Blackmun, J., took no part.

Evacuation parade (commemorating the evacuation of British troops from the city in 1776). The Veterans Council refused to let the Irish–American Gay, Lesbian and Bisexual Group of Boston march in the parade, but the Massachusetts courts ruled that the Council's refusal violated a public accommodations law in that the parade was an "open recreational event." HURLEY v. IRISH–AMERICAN GAY, LESBIAN AND BISEXUAL GROUP OF BOSTON, 515 U.S. 557, 115 S.Ct. 2338, 132 L.Ed.2d 487 (1995), per SOUTER, J., held that the use of the public accommodations law in this circumstance violated the expressive rights of the Council: "[T]his use of the State's power violates the fundamental rule of protection under the First Amendment, that a speaker has the autonomy to choose the content of his own message. * * *

"[The Council's] claim to the benefit of this principle of autonomy to control one's own speech is as sound as the South Boston parade is expressive. Rather like a composer, the Council selects the expressive units of the parade from potential participants, and though the score may not produce a particularized message, each contingent's expression in the Council's eyes comports with what merits celebration on that day. Even if this view gives the Council credit for a more considered judgment than it actively made, the Council clearly decided to exclude a message it did not like from the communication it chose to make, and that is enough to invoke its right as a private speaker to shape its expression by speaking on one subject while remaining silent on another. * * *

"Unlike the programming offered on various channels by a cable network, the parade does not consist of individual, unrelated segments that happen to be transmitted together for individual selection by members of the audience. Although each parade unit generally identifies itself, each is understood to contribute something to a common theme, and accordingly there is no customary practice whereby private sponsors disavow any 'identity of viewpoint' between themselves and the selected participants. Practice follows practicability here, for such disclaimers would be quite curious in a moving parade.

"[W]e found in [*PruneYard*] that the proprietors were running 'a business establishment that is open to the public to come and go as they please,' that the solicitations would 'not likely be identified with those of the owner,' and that the proprietors could 'expressly disavow any connection with the message by simply posting signs in the area where the speakers or handbillers stand.' "[g]

4. *Economic pressure to engage in political activity.* NAACP v. CLAIBORNE HARDWARE CO., 458 U.S. 886, 102 S.Ct. 3409, 73 L.Ed.2d 1215 (1982): The NAACP had organized a consumer boycott whose principal objective was, according to the lower court, "to force the white merchants [to] bring pressure upon [the government] to grant defendants' demands or, in the alternative, to suffer economic ruin." Mississippi characterized the boycott as a tortious and malicious interference with the plaintiffs' busi-

g. For incisive pre-*Hurley* commentary, see Yackle, *Parading Ourselves: Freedom of*   *Speech at the Feast of St. Patrick,* 73 B.U.L.Rev. 791 (1993).

nesses. The Court, per Stevens, J., held that the NAACP boycott was immune from state prohibition: Although labor boycotts organized for economic ends had long been subject to prohibition, "speech to protest racial discrimination" was "essential political speech lying at the core of the First Amendment" and was therefore distinguishable. Is the boycott protected association? Are there association rights on the other side? Does the state have a legitimate interest in protecting merchants from being forced to support political change they would otherwise oppose? Cf. *NLRB v. Retail Store Employees Union,* 447 U.S. 607, 100 S.Ct. 2372, 65 L.Ed.2d 377 (1980) (ban on labor picketing encouraging consumer boycott of neutral employer upheld). Are the white merchants neutral?[h] For commentary, compare Harper, *The Consumer's Emerging Right to Boycott: NAACP v. Claiborne Hardware and Its Implications for American Labor Law,* 93 Yale L.J. 409 (1984) with Schwarzschild & Alexander, *Consumer Boycotts and Freedom of Association: Comment on a Recently Proposed Theory,* 22 San Diego L.Rev. 555 (1985).

5. *Orthodoxy and commercial advertising.* ZAUDERER v. OFFICE OF DISCIPLINARY COUNSEL, 471 U.S. 626, 105 S.Ct. 2265, 85 L.Ed.2d 652 (1985), per White, J., upheld an Ohio requirement that an attorney advertising availability on a contingency basis must disclose in the ad that the clients would have to pay costs if their lawsuits should prove unsuccessful whenever that is the proposed financial arrangement: "[T]he interests at stake in this case are not of the same order as those discussed in *Wooley, Tornillo,* and *Barnette.* Ohio has not attempted to 'prescribe what shall be orthodox in politics, nationalism, religion, or other matters of opinion or force citizens to confess by word or act their faith therein.' The State has attempted only to prescribe what shall be orthodox in commercial advertising, and its prescription has taken the form of a requirement that appellant include in his advertising purely factual and uncontroversial[i] information about the terms under which his services will be available. Because the

h. Stevens, J., also argued in *Claiborne* that the boycott was protected as a right to petition the government. Are the white merchants the government?

i. What if the requested disclosures are controverted? Do cigarette companies have first amendment grounds to resist forced disclosures?

Do doctors have a first amendment right to resist state mandated disclosures to patients regarding abortion? Consider joint opinion of O'Connor, Kennedy, and Souter, JJ., in *Planned Parenthood v. Casey,* 505 U.S. 833, 112 S.Ct. 2791, 120 L.Ed.2d 674 (1992): "[A] requirement that a doctor give a woman certain information as part of obtaining her consent to an abortion is, for constitutional purposes, no different from a requirement that a doctor give certain specific information about any medical procedure. All that is left of petitioners' argument is an asserted First Amendment right of a physician not to provide information about the risks of abortion, and childbirth, in a manner mandated by the State. To be sure, the physician's First Amendment rights not to speak are implicated, see *Wooley v. Maynard,* but only as part of the practice of medicine, subject to reasonable licensing and regulation by the State. We see no constitutional infirmity in the requirement that the physician provide the information mandated by the State here."

Can professional fundraisers be required to disclose their professional status before soliciting funds? The percentage of charitable contributions that have been turned over to charity in the past 12 months? See *Riley v. National Federation of the Blind,* Ch. 4, III supra (the former can be required, but not the latter). On compelled commercial speech, see generally Note, *Can the Budweiser Frogs Be Forced to Sing A New Tune?,* 84 Va. L.Rev. 1195 (1998).

extension of First Amendment protection to commercial speech is justified principally by the value to consumers of the information such speech provides, *Virginia Pharmacy,* appellant's constitutionally protected interest in *not* providing any particular factual information in his advertising is minimal. * * *

"We do not suggest that disclosure requirements do not implicate the advertiser's First Amendment rights at all. We recognize that unjustified or unduly burdensome disclosure requirements might offend the First Amendment by chilling protected commercial speech. But we hold that an advertiser's rights are adequately protected as long as disclosure requirements are reasonably related to the State's interest in preventing deception of consumers."

The Court stated that the first amendment interests "implicated by disclosure requirements are substantially weaker than those at stake when speech is actually suppressed." Accordingly it rejected any requirement that the advertisement in question be shown to be deceptive absent the disclosure or that the state meet a "least restrictive means" analysis.

BRENNAN, J., joined by Marshall, J., dissenting on this issue, conceded that the distinction between disclosure and suppression "supports some differences in analysis," but thought the Court had exaggerated the importance of the distinction: "We have noted in traditional First Amendment cases that an affirmative publication requirement 'operates as a command in the same sense as a statute or regulation forbidding [someone] to publish specified matter,' and that a compulsion to publish that which 'reason tells [one] should not be published' therefore raises substantial first amendment concerns. *Tornillo.*" Accordingly, he would have required a demonstration that the advertising was inherently likely to deceive or record evidence that the advertising was in fact deceptive, or a showing that another substantial interest was directly advanced by state action extending only as far as the interest served. Applying this standard, Brennan, J., agreed with the Court that a state may require an advertising attorney to include a costs disclaimer, but concluded that the state had provided Zauderer with inadequate notice of what he was required to include in the advertisement.

6. *A right not to speak? Wooley* and succeeding cases establish a right not to be associated with ideas to which one is ideologically opposed. Yet individuals are forced to speak in a wide variety of situations. Does it violate the first amendment to compel witnesses to speak in court or legislative proceedings? Should such compulsion have limits? Consider *Barenblatt v. United States,* 360 U.S. 109, 79 S.Ct. 1081, 3 L.Ed.2d 1115 (1959)(witness can be compelled before Congress to testify about his political connections with the Communist Party if he does not invoke the fifth amendment). Other cases are more sympathetic to those who choose to remain silent.

(a) *Anonymous political speech.* McINTYRE v. OHIO ELECTIONS COMM'N, 514 U.S. 334, 115 S.Ct. 1511, 131 L.Ed.2d 426 (1995), per STEVENS, J., held that Ohio's prohibition against the distribution of anonymous campaign literature was unconstitutional: "Under our Constitution, anonymous pamphleteering is not a pernicious, fraudulent practice, but an honorable tradition of advocacy and of dissent. * * * The State may and does punish fraud directly. But it cannot seek to punish fraud indirectly by indiscriminately outlawing a category of speech, based on its content, with no necessary relationship to the danger sought to be prevented."[j]

THOMAS, J., concurred, but argued that instead of asking whether " 'an honorable tradition' of free speech has existed throughout American history * * *." [We] should seek the original understanding when we interpret the Speech and Press clauses, just as we do when we read the Religion Clauses of the First Amendment." According to Thomas, J., the original understanding approach also protected anonymous speech.

SCALIA, joined by Rehnquist, C.J., dissenting, asserted that it was the "Court's (and society's) traditional view that the Constitution bears its original meaning and is unchanging." Applying that approach, he concluded that anonymous political speech is not protected under the first amendment.

(b). *Compelled election disclosures.* BROWN v. SOCIALIST WORKERS, 459 U.S. 87, 103 S.Ct. 416, 74 L.Ed.2d 250 (1982), per MARSHALL, J., held that an Ohio statute requiring every political party to report the names and addresses of campaign contributors and recipients of campaign disbursements could not be applied to the Socialist Workers Party. Citing *Buckley v. Valeo,* Ch. 10 infra, the Court held that the " 'evidence offered [by a minor party] need show only a reasonable probability that the compelled disclosure [of] names will subject them to threats, harassment, or reprisals from either Government officials or private parties.' " Consider Stone & Marshall, *Brown v. Socialist Workers: Inequality As A Command of the First Amendment,* 1983 Sup.Ct.Rev. 583, 592: "[I]n *Brown* the Court expressly exempted particular political parties from an otherwise content-neutral regulation for reasons directly related to the content of their expression. [The] constitutionally compelled exemption substitutes a content-based law for one that is content neutral. It stands the presumption in favor of 'content neutrality' on its head." Is the decision, nonetheless, consistent with first amendment values? See Stone & Marshall, supra.

---

j. Ginsburg, J., concurred. *Buckley v. American Constitutional Law Foundation,* 525 U.S. 182, 119 S.Ct. 636, 142 L.Ed.2d 599 (1999), per Ginsburg, J., held unconstitutional a Colorado statute requiring that circulators of initiatives wear identification badges bearing their names and that sponsors of the initiative report the names and addresses of all paid circulators. By contrast, the Court was satisfied that the requirement of the filing of an affidavit containing the name and address of the circulator of petitions was consistent with the first amendment.

For broad-ranging commentary on the relationship between privacy and disclosure, see Kreimer, *Sunlight, Secrets, and Scarlet Letter: The Tension Between Privacy and Disclosure in Constitutional Law,* 140 U.Pa. L.Rev. 1, 70 (1991).

II. FREEDOM OF ASSOCIATION AND EMPLOYMENT

ELROD v. BURNS, 427 U.S. 347, 96 S.Ct. 2673, 49 L.Ed.2d 547 (1976), (Stevens, J., not participating) declared unconstitutional the dismissal of nonpolicymaking and nonconfidential state and local government employees solely on the ground that they were not affiliated with or sponsored by a particular political party. (The newly elected Democratic Sheriff of Cook County, Illinois, had sought to replace noncivil-service employees in his office, all Republicans, with members of his own party. The employees who brought suit were process servers and a juvenile court bailiff). BRENNAN, J., announced the judgment and an opinion joined by White and Marshall, JJ.: "The cost of the practice of patronage is the restraint it places on freedoms of belief and association. [The] free functioning of the electoral process also suffers. Conditioning political employment on partisan support prevents support of competing public interests. [As] government employment, state or federal, becomes more pervasive, the greater the dependence on it becomes, and therefore the greater becomes the power to starve political [opposition]. Patronage thus tips the electoral process in favor of the incumbent party.

"[P]olitical belief and association constitute the core of those activities protected by the First Amendment. Regardless of the nature of the inducement, whether it be by the denial of public employment or, as in *Barnette,* by the influence of a teacher over students, '[no government official] can prescribe what shall be orthodox in politics [or] other matters of opinion or force citizens to confess by word or act their faith therein.' Ibid. And, though freedom of belief is central, '[t]he First Amendment protects political association as well as political expression.' *Buckley v. Valeo* [Ch. 10 infra]. * * *

"The Court recognized in *United Public Workers v. Mitchell,* 330 U.S. 75, 100, 67 S.Ct. 556, 569, 91 L.Ed. 754 (1947), that 'Congress may not "enact a regulation providing that no Republican, Jew or Negro shall be appointed to federal office."' This principle was reaffirmed in *Wieman v. Updegraff,* 344 U.S. 183, 73 S.Ct. 215, 97 L.Ed. 216 (1952), which held that a State could not require its employees to establish their loyalty by extracting an oath denying past affiliation with Communists. And in *Cafeteria Workers v. McElroy,* 367 U.S. 886, 898, 81 S.Ct. 1743, 1750, 6 L.Ed.2d 1230 (1961), the Court recognized again that the government could not deny employment because of previous membership in a particular party.[11]

"Particularly pertinent to the constitutionality of the practice of patronage dismissals are *Keyishian v. Board of Regents,* 385 U.S. 589, 87 S.Ct. 675, 17 L.Ed.2d 629 (1967), and *Perry v. Sindermann,* 408 U.S. 593, 92 S.Ct.

---

11. Protection of First Amendment interests has not been limited to invalidation of conditions on government employment requiring allegiance to a particular political party. This Court's decisions have prohibited conditions on public benefits, in the form of jobs or otherwise, which dampen the exercise generally of First Amendment rights, however slight the inducement to the individual to forsake those rights.

[T]he First Amendment prohibits limiting the grant of a tax exemption to only those who affirm their loyalty to the State granting the exemption. *Speiser v. Randall,* 357 U.S. 513, 78 S.Ct. 1332, 2 L.Ed.2d 1460 (1958).

2694, 33 L.Ed.2d 570 (1972). In *Keyishian,* the Court invalidated New York statutes barring employment merely on the basis of membership in 'subversive' organizations. *Keyishian* squarely held that political association alone could not, consistently with the First Amendment, constitute an adequate ground for denying public employment.[12] In *Perry,* the Court broadly rejected the validity of limitations on First Amendment rights as a condition to the receipt of a governmental benefit, stating that the government 'may not deny a benefit to a person on a basis that infringes his constitutionally protected interests—especially, his interest in freedom of speech. For if the government could deny a benefit to a person because of his constitutionally protected speech or associations, his exercise of those freedoms would in effect be penalized and inhibited. This would allow the government to "produce a result which [it] could not command directly." *Speiser v. Randall.* Such interference with constitutional rights is impermissible.' * * *[13]"

If the practice is to survive constitutional challenge, "it must further some vital government end by a means that is least restrictive of freedom of belief and association in achieving that end, and the benefit gained must outweigh the loss of constitutionally protected rights." The plurality then considered and rejected three interests offered in justification of patronage—(1) "the need to insure effective government"; (2) "the need for political loyalty of employees" to assure implementation of the new administration's policies; and (3) "the preservation of the democratic process" and the continued vitality of "party politics":

As to (1), the argument fails, inter alia, "because it is doubtful that the mere difference of political persuasion motivates poor performance; nor do we think it legitimately may be used for imputing such behavior. [At] all events, less drastic means for insuring [this interest] are available"—discharge for good cause, "such as insubordination or poor job performance, when those bases exist."

"[Moreover] the lack of any justification for patronage dismissals as a means of furthering government effectiveness and efficiency distinguishes

12. Thereafter, *United States v. Robel,* 389 U.S. 258, 88 S.Ct. 419, 19 L.Ed.2d 508 (1967), similarly held that mere membership in the Communist Party could not bar a person from employment in private defense establishments important to national security.

13. The increasingly pervasive nature of public employment provides officials with substantial power through conditioning jobs on partisan support, particularly in this time of high unemployment. Since the government however, may not seek to achieve an unlawful end either directly or indirectly, the inducement afforded by placing conditions on a benefit need not be particularly great in order to find that rights have been violated. Rights are infringed both where the government fines a person a penny for

being a Republican and where it withholds the grant of a penny for the same reason.

Petitioners contend that even though the government may not provide that public employees may retain their jobs only if they become affiliated with or provide support for the in-party, respondents here have waived any objection to such requirements. The difficulty with this argument is that it completely swallows the rule. Since the qualification may not be constitutionally imposed absent an appropriate justification, to accept the waiver argument is to say that the government may do what it may not do. A finding of waiver in this case, therefore, would be contrary to our view that a partisan job qualification abridges the First Amendment.

this case from *U.S. Civil Service Comm'n v. Letter Carriers,* 413 U.S. 548, 93 S.Ct. 2880, 37 L.Ed.2d 796 (1973), and *Mitchell.* In both of those cases, legislative restraints on political management and campaigning by public employees were upheld despite their encroachment on First Amendment rights because, inter alia, they did serve in a necessary manner to foster and protect efficient and effective government. Interestingly, the activities that were restrained by the legislation involved in those cases are characteristic of patronage practices. As the Court observed in *Mitchell,* 'The conviction that an actively partisan governmental personnel threatens good administration has deepened since [1882]. Congress recognizes danger to the service in that political rather than official effort may earn advancement and to the public in that governmental favor may be channeled through political connections.' "

As for the second interest, the need for political loyalty and implementation of new policies "may be adequately met" by limiting patronage dismissals to "policymaking positions." As for the third interest—one "premised on the centrality of partisan politics in the democratic process"—"we are not persuaded [that] the interdiction of patronage dismissals [will cause] the demise of party politics." Political parties existed prior to active patronage and they have survived substantial reduction in their patronage power through the establishment of the merit system.

"Patronage dismissals thus are not the least restrictive alternative to achieving the contributions they may make to the democratic process. The process functions as well without the practice, perhaps even better, for patronage dismissals clearly also retard that practice. [U]nlike the gain to representative government provided by the Hatch Act in *Letter Carriers* and *Mitchell,* the gain to representative government provided by [the practice], if any, would be insufficient to justify its sacrifice of First Amendment rights.

"To be sure, *Letter Carriers* and *Mitchell* upheld Hatch Act restraints sacrificing political campaigning and management, activities themselves protected by the First Amendment. But in those cases it was the Court's judgment that congressional subordination of those activities was permissible to safeguard the core interests of individual belief and association. Subordination of some First Amendment activity was permissible to protect other such activity. Today, we hold that subordination of other First Amendment activity, that is, patronage dismissals, not only is permissible, but also is mandated by the First Amendment. And since patronage dismissals fall within the category of political campaigning and management, this conclusion irresistibly flows from *Mitchell* and *Letter Carriers.* For if the First Amendment did not place individual belief and association above political campaigning and management, at least in the setting of public employment, the restraints on those latter activities could not have been judged permissible in *Mitchell* and *Letter Carriers.* "

STEWART, J., joined by Blackmun, J., concurred: "This case does not require us to consider the broad contours of the so-called patronage system, with all its variations and permutations. In particular, it does not require us to consider the constitutional validity of a system that confines the hiring of some governmental employees to those of a particular political party, and I would intimate no views whatever on that question.

"The single substantive question involved in this case is whether a nonpolicymaking, nonconfidential government employee can be discharged or threatened with discharge from a job that he is satisfactorily performing upon the sole ground of his political beliefs. I agree with the plurality that he cannot. See *Perry v. Sindermann*."

POWELL, J., joined by Burger, C.J., and Rehnquist, J., dissented: "[Here, we have] complaining employees who apparently accepted patronage jobs knowingly and willingly, while fully familiar with the 'tenure' practices long prevailing in the Sheriff's Office. Such employees have *benefitted* from their political beliefs and activities; they have not been penalized for them. In these circumstances, I am inclined to [the view that they] may not be heard to challenge [the patronage system] when it comes their turn to be replaced."

Beyond waiver, he complained that the Court "unnecessarily constitutionalizes another element of American life—an element not without its faults but one which generations have accepted on balance as having merit." Powell, J., stressed the importance of political parties and their dependency upon patronage: "History and long prevailing practice across the country support the view that patronage hiring practices make a sufficiently substantial contribution to the practical functioning of our democratic system to support their relatively modest intrusion on First Amendment interests. * * *

"It is difficult to disagree with the view, as an abstract proposition, that government employment ordinarily should not be conditioned upon one's political beliefs or activities. But we deal here with a highly practical and rather fundamental element of our political system, not the theoretical abstraction of a political science seminar. [T]he plurality seriously underestimates the strength of the government interest—especially at the local level—in allowing some patronage hiring practices, and it exaggerates the perceived burden on First Amendment rights. * * *

"It is naive to think that [local political activity supporting parties is] motivated [by] some academic interest in 'democracy' or other public service impulse. For the most part, the hope of some reward generates a major portion of [such activity]. It is difficult to overestimate the contributions to our system by the major political parties, fortunately limited in number compared to the fractionalization that has made the continued existence of democratic government doubtful in some other countries. * * *

"It is against decades of experience to the contrary, then, that the plurality opinion concludes that patronage hiring practices interfere with the 'free functioning of the electoral process.' This *ad hoc* judicial judgment runs counter to the judgments of the representatives of the people in state and local governments, representatives who have chosen, in most instances, to retain some patronage practices in combination with a merit-oriented civil service. One would think that elected representatives of the people are better equipped than we to weigh the need for some continuation of patronage practices in light of the interests above identified,[9] and particularly in view of local conditions. *Letter Carriers; Mitchell.*"[a]

Notes and Questions

1. BRANTI v. FINKEL, 445 U.S. 507, 100 S.Ct. 1287, 63 L.Ed.2d 574 (1980), per STEVENS, J., applied *Elrod* to "protect an assistant public defender who is satisfactorily performing his job from discharge solely because of his political beliefs."[b] The Court rejected the argument that even if party sponsorship is an unconstitutional condition for retaining low-level public employees it is a permissible requirement for an assistant public defender: "[P]arty affiliation is not necessarily relevant to every policymaking or confidential position. The coach of a state university's football team formulates policy, but no one could seriously claim that Republicans make better coaches than Democrats, or vice versa, no matter which party is in control of the state government. On the other hand, it is equally clear that the governor of a state may appropriately believe that the official duties of various assistants who help him write speeches, explain his views to the press, or communicate with the legislature cannot be performed effectively unless those persons share his political beliefs and party commitments. In sum, the ultimate inquiry is not whether the label 'policymaker' or 'confidential' fits a particular position; rather, the question is whether the hiring

---

9. The plurality might be taken to concede some promotion of the democratic process by patronage hiring practices but to conclude that in net effect such practices will reduce political debate impermissibly by affecting some employees or potential employees and thereby depriving society of the 'unfettered judgment of each citizen on matters of political concern.' In the past the Court has upheld congressional actions designed to increase the overall level of political discourse but affecting adversely the First Amendment interests of some individuals. In *Letter Carriers* we indicated specifically that the First Amendment freedoms of federal employees could be limited in an effort to further the functioning of the democratic process. I do not believe that local legislative judgments as to what will further the democratic process in light of local conditions should receive less weight than these congressional judgments. Surely that

should be the case until we have a record, if one could be created, showing the fears of the plurality to be justified.

a. Burger, C.J., dissented, contending that the decision "represents a significant intrusion into the area of legislative and policy concerns."

b. The Court noted that in *Elrod,* as in the instant case, "the only practice at issue was the *dismissal* of public employees for partisan reasons" and thus there was "no occasion to address petitioner's argument that there is a compelling governmental interest in maintaining a political sponsorship system for *filling vacancies* in the public defender's office." (Emphasis added.) Should *Elrod* and *Branti* be extended to independent contractors? See *O'Hare Truck Service v. City of Northlake*, 518 U.S. 712, 116 S.Ct. 2353, 135 L.Ed.2d 874 (1996).

authority can demonstrate that party affiliation is an appropriate requirement for the effective performance of the public office involved."

The Court concluded that neither the policymaking of an assistant public defender nor the access of client's confidential information had any bearing on partisan political considerations.

2. RUTAN v. REPUBLICAN PARTY OF ILLINOIS, 497 U.S. 62, 110 S.Ct. 2729, 111 L.Ed.2d 52 (1990), per BRENNAN, J., extended *Elrod* and *Branti* not only to promotion, transfer, recall decisions, but also to hiring decisions: "It is unnecessary here to consider whether not being hired is less burdensome than being discharged because the government is not pressed to do *either* on the basis of political affiliation."[c]

STEVENS, J., concurring, argued that "[T]he entire rationale for patronage hiring [rests] on the assumption that the patronage employee filling the government position must be paid a premium to reward him for his partisan services. * * * This defense of patronage [assumes] that governmental power and public resources—in this case employment opportunities—may appropriately be used to subsidize partisan activities[4] even when the political affiliation of the employee or the job applicant is entirely unrelated to his or her public service. The premise on which this position rests would justify the use of public funds to compensate party members for their campaign work, or conversely, a legislative enactment denying public employment to nonmembers of the majority party. If such legislation is unconstitutional—as it clearly would be—an equally pernicious rule promulgated by the Executive must also be invalid."

---

c. The opinion excepted employment decisions where party affiliation or support was an "appropriate requirement for the position involved." Illinois, according to the complaint, however, was operating a wholesale patronage system out of the governor's office that functioned broadly to limit state hiring to those supported by the Republican Party.

4. Although Justice Scalia's defense of patronage turns on the benefits of fostering the two-party system, his opinion is devoid of reference to meaningful evidence that patronage practices have played a significant role in the preservation of the two-party system. In each of the examples that he cites—"the Boss Tweeds, the Tammany Halls, the Pendergast Machines, the Byrd Machines and the Daley Machines," patronage practices were used solely to protect the power of an entrenched majority. See Laycock, *Notes on the Role of Judicial Review, the Expansion of Federal Power, and the Structure of Constitutional Rights*, 99 Yale L.J. 1711, 1722 (1990) (describing the

"hopelessness of contesting elections" in Chicago's "one-party system" when "half a dozen employees of the city and of city contractors were paid with public funds to work [a precinct] for the other side"); Johnson, *Successful Reform Litigation: The Shakman Patronage Case,* 64 Chi.–Kent L.Rev. 479, 481 (1988) (the "massive Democratic patronage employment system" maintained a "noncompetitive political system" in Cook County in the 1960's).

Without repeating the Court's studied rejection of the policy arguments for patronage practices in *Elrod*, I note only that many commentators agree more with Justice Scalia's admissions of the systemic costs of patronage practices—the "financial corruption, such as salary kickbacks and partisan political activity on government-paid time," the reduced efficiency of government, and the undeniable constraint upon the expression of views by employees than with his belief that patronage is necessary to political stability and integration of powerless groups. * * *

SCALIA, J., joined by Rehnquist, C.J., and Kennedy, J., and in part[d] by O'Connor, J., dissenting, argued that *Elrod* and *Branti* were wrongly decided and opposed their extension: "As the merit principle [for government employment] has been extended and its effects increasingly felt; as the Boss Tweeds, the Tammany Halls, the Pendergast Machines, the Byrd Machines and the Daley Machines have faded into history; we find that political leaders at all levels increasingly complain of the helplessness of elected government, unprotected by 'party discipline,' before the demands of small and cohesive interest-groups.

"The choice between patronage and the merit principle—or, to be more realistic about it, the choice between the desirable mix of merit and patronage principles in widely varying federal, state, and local political contexts—is not so clear that I would be prepared, as an original matter, to chisel a single, inflexible prescription into the Constitution. * * *

"The provisions of the Bill of Rights were designed to restrain transient majorities from impairing long-recognized personal liberties. They did not create by implication novel individual rights overturning accepted political norms. Thus, when a practice not expressly prohibited by the text of the Bill of Rights bears the endorsement of a long tradition of open, wide-spread, and unchallenged use that dates back to the beginning of the Republic, we have no proper basis for striking it down.[1] Such a venerable and accepted tradition is not to be laid on the examining table and scrutinized for its conformity to some abstract principle of First–Amendment adjudication devised by this Court. To the contrary, such traditions are themselves the stuff out of which the Court's principles are to be formed. They are, in these uncertain areas, the very points of reference by which the legitimacy or illegitimacy of *other* practices are to be figured out. When it appears that the latest 'rule,' or 'three-part test,' or 'balancing test' devised by the Court has placed us on a collision course with such a landmark practice, it is the former that must be recalculated by us, and not the latter that must be abandoned by our citizens. I know of no other way to formulate a constitutional jurisprudence that reflects, as it should, the principles adhered to, over time, by the American people, rather than those favored by the personal (and necessarily shifting) philosophical dispositions of a majority of this Court.

d. O'Connor, J., did not join the sections of Scalia, J.'s opinion quoted infra, but did join sections arguing that *Elrod* and *Branti* were wrongly decided.

1. The customary invocation of *Brown v. Board of Education* as demonstrating the dangerous consequences of this principle, (Stevens, J., concurring), is unsupportable. I argue for the role of tradition in giving content only to *ambiguous* constitutional text; no tradition can supersede the Constitution. In my view the Fourteenth Amendment's requirement of "equal protection of the laws," combined with the Thirteenth Amendment's abolition of the institution of black slavery, leaves no room for doubt that laws treating people differently because of their race are invalid. Moreover, even if one does not regard the Fourteenth Amendment as crystal clear on this point, a tradition of *unchallenged* validity did not exist with respect to the practice in *Brown*. To the contrary, in the 19th century the principle of "separate-but-equal" had been vigorously opposed on constitutional grounds, litigated up to this Court, and upheld only over the dissent of one of our historically most respected Justices. See *Plessy v. Ferguson* (Harlan, J., dissenting).

"I will not describe at length the claim of patronage to landmark status as one of our accepted political traditions. Justice Powell discussed it in his dissenting opinions in *Elrod* and *Branti*. Suffice it to say that patronage was, without any thought that it could be unconstitutional, a basis for government employment from the earliest days of the Republic until *Elrod*—and has continued unabated since *Elrod*, to the extent still permitted by that unfortunate decision. Given that unbroken tradition regarding the application of an ambiguous constitutional text, there was in my view no basis for holding that patronage-based dismissals violated the First Amendment—much less for holding, as the Court does today, that even patronage hiring does so.²"ᵉ

3.   Might Communists be treated differently from Republican or Democrats for some confidential employment? Consider White, J., dissenting in *Robel* (cited in Brennan, J.'s *Elrod* opinion fn. 12): "[D]enying the opportunity to be employed in some defense plants is a much smaller deterrent to the exercise of associational rights than [a] criminal penalty attached solely to membership, and the Government's interest in keeping potential spies and saboteurs from defense plants is much greater than its interest [in] committing all Party members to prison." Compare Israel, *Elfbrandt v. Russell: The Demise of the Oath?*, 1966 Sup.Ct.Rev. 193, 201–07 and O'Neil, *Unconstitutional Conditions*, 54 Calif.L.Rev. 443 (1966) with Van Alstyne, *The Constitutional Rights of Employees*, 16 U.C.L.A.L.Rev. 751 (1969).

COLE v. RICHARDSON, 405 U.S. 676, 92 S.Ct. 1332, 31 L.Ed.2d 593 (1972), per BURGER, C.J. (over the dissents of Douglas, J., and Marshall, J.,

---

2.   Justice Stevens seeks to counteract this tradition by relying upon the supposed "unequivocal repudiation" of the right-privilege distinction. That will not do. If the right-privilege distinction was once used to explain the practice, and if that distinction is to be repudiated, then one must simply devise some other theory to explain it. The order of precedence is that a constitutional theory must be wrong if its application contradicts a clear constitutional tradition; not that a clear constitutional tradition must be wrong if it does not conform to the current constitutional theory. On Justice Stevens' view of the matter, this Court examines a historical practice, endows it with an intellectual foundation, and later, by simply undermining that foundation, relegates the constitutional tradition to the dustbin of history. That is not how constitutional adjudication works. I am not sure, in any event, that the right-privilege distinction has been as unequivocally rejected as Justice Stevens supposes. It has certainly been recognized that the fact that the government need not confer a certain benefit does not mean that it can attach any conditions whatever to the conferral of that benefit. But it remains true that certain conditions can be attached to benefits that cannot be imposed as pre-

scriptions upon the public at large. If Justice Stevens chooses to call this something other than a right-privilege distinction, that is fine and good—but it is in any case what explains the nonpatronage restrictions upon federal employees that the Court continues to approve, and there is no reason why it cannot support patronage restrictions as well.

e.   In addition to the arguments referred to in footnotes 1 and 2 of Scalia, J.'s opinion, Stevens, J., maintained in response:

"The tradition that is relevant in this case is the American commitment to examine and reexamine past and present practices against the basic principles embodied in the Constitution. The inspirational command by our President in 1961 is entirely consistent with that tradition: 'Ask not what your country can do for you—ask what you can do for your country.' This case involves a contrary command: 'Ask not what job applicants can do for the State—ask what they can do for our party.' Whatever traditional support may remain for a command of that ilk, it is plainly an illegitimate excuse for the practices rejected by the Court today."

joined by Brennan, J.), upheld the dismissal of Richardson's employment at a state hospital for refusing to sign a loyalty oath calling in part for an affirmation that "I will oppose the overthrow of the government [by] force, violence, or by any illegal or unconstitutional method": "Since there is no constitutionally protected right to overthrow a government by force, violence, or illegal or unconstitutional means, no constitutional right is infringed by an oath to abide by the constitutional system in the future."[f] Should the first amendment permit requiring public employees to oppose that which they have a right to advocate? Is *Cole* consistent with the cases cited in *Elrod*'s plurality opinion? With *Robel*? With *Wooley*?

4. The *Elrod* plurality argues that its conclusion flows irresistibly from *Mitchell* and *Letter Carriers*? Were these cases rightly decided? Is a ban on active participation in political campaigns by government employees necessary (as the Court thought in *Letter Carriers*) to avoid the impression that the government practices "political justice" or to prevent the government work force from becoming a "peaceful, invincible, and perhaps corrupt political machine"? Would prohibitions against coercion (such as those commanded by *Elrod*) be sufficient? If not, is the concern about coercion relevant only to participation on behalf of incumbents? See Blasi, *The Checking Value in First Amendment Theory*, 1977 Am.B.Found.Res.J. 521, 634–35. Is it of major import that the restrictions are "not aimed at particular parties, groups or points of [view]"? *Letter Carriers.* Does an emphasis on this factor, denigrate the liberty and associational interests of government employees? See Redish, *The Content Distinction in First Amendment Analysis,* 34 Stan.L.Rev. 113 (1981). See also Note, *"Un–Hatching" Federal Employee Political Endorsements,* 134 U.Pa.L.Rev. 1497 (1986) (criticizing Hatch Act policies).

5. *Beyond loyalty and partisanship.* A provision of the Ethics in Government Act prohibited receipt of honoraria for speeches or writings by federal employees. UNITED STATES v. NATIONAL TREASURY EMPLOYEES UNION, 513 U.S. 454, 115 S.Ct. 1003, 130 L.Ed.2d 964 (1995), per STEVENS, J., invalidated that provision as applied to lower level executive branch employees, the only parties before the Court.

O'CONNOR, J., concurring and dissenting, would have upheld the provision as applied to *work related* speeches and writings, by lower level executive branch employees (the majority thought this would rewrite the statute).[g]

_____

When District Attorney Connick proposed to transfer Assistant D.A. Myers to a different section of the criminal court, she strongly opposed it. Shortly thereafter, Myers prepared and distributed to the other assistants a questionnaire concerning office transfer policy, office morale, the need for a

f. Powell and Rehnquist, JJ., took no part.

g. Rehnquist, C.J., joined by Scalia & Thomas, JJ., dissented.

grievance committee and two questions Connick particularly objected to—the level of confidence in various supervisors and whether employees felt pressured to work in political campaigns. Connick then told Myers that she was being terminated for refusal to accept the transfer and that he considered distribution of the questionnaire an act of insubordination. Myers filed suit under 42 U.S.C. § 1983, contending that she was wrongfully discharged because she had exercised her right of free speech. The district court agreed. It found that the questionnaire was the real reason for Myers' termination, and that the state had not "clearly demonstrated" that the survey "substantially interfered" with the operation of the District Attorney's office. The Fifth Circuit affirmed. But CONNICK v. MYERS, 461 U.S. 138, 103 S.Ct. 1684, 75 L.Ed.2d 708 (1983), per WHITE, J., held that respondent's discharge did not offend the first amendment:

"For most of this century, the unchallenged dogma was that a public employee had no right to object to conditions placed upon the terms of employment—including those which restricted the exercise of constitutional rights. The classic formulation of this position was Justice Holmes', who, when sitting on the Supreme Judicial Court of Massachusetts, observed: 'A policeman may have a constitutional right to talk politics, but he has no constitutional right to be a policeman.' *McAuliffe v. Mayor,* 155 Mass. 216, 220, 29 N.E. 517, 517 (1892). For many years, Holmes' epigram expressed this Court's law. *Adler v. Bd. of Educ.,* 342 U.S. 485, 72 S.Ct. 380, 96 L.Ed. 517 (1952); *Garner v. Bd. of Pub. Works,* 341 U.S. 716, 71 S.Ct. 909, 95 L.Ed. 1317 (1951)."

The Court proceeded, however, to recount a series of cases in which it had subsequently repudiated Holmes' epigram.[a] Indeed, for some two decades it had become wholly impermissible to deny freedom of expression "by the denial of or placing of conditions upon a benefit or a privilege." As the Court characterized the public employee cases, they were all rooted in the rights of public employees to participate in public affairs.[b] In particular, the Court focused upon *Pickering v. Board of Educ.,* 391 U.S. 563, 88 S.Ct. 1731, 20 L.Ed.2d 811 (1968): "In *Pickering,* we stated that a public employee does not relinquish First Amendment rights to comment on matters of public interest by virtue of government employment. [The] repeated emphasis in *Pickering* on the right of a public employee 'as a citizen, in commenting upon matters of public concern,' was not accidental. This language, reiterated in all of *Pickering's* progeny, reflects both the historical evolvement of the rights of public employees, and the common sense realization that government offices could not function if every employment decision became a constitutional matter.[5] * * *

a. Most of the cases involved the right of public employees to associate.

b. But see *Letter Carriers,* Ch. 9, II supra.

5. The question of whether expression is of a kind that is of legitimate concern to the public is also the standard in determining whether a common-law action for invasion of privacy is present. See *Restatement (Second) of Torts,* § 652D. See also *Cox Broadcasting Co. v. Cohn* (action for invasion of privacy cannot be maintained when the subject-matter of the publicity is matter

"*Pickering* [held] impermissible under the First Amendment the dismissal of a high school teacher for openly criticizing the Board of Education on its allocation of school funds between athletics and education and its methods of informing taxpayers about the need for additional revenue. Pickering's subject was a matter of legitimate public concern upon which free and open debate is vital to informed decision-making by the electorate. [Most] recently, in *Givhan v. Western Line Cons. School Dist.*, 439 U.S. 410, 99 S.Ct. 693, 58 L.Ed.2d 619 (1979), we held that First Amendment protection applies when a public employee arranges to communicate privately with his employer rather than to express his views publicly. Although the subject-matter of Mrs. Givhan's statements were not the issue before the Court, it is clear that her statements concerning the school district's allegedly racially discriminatory policies involved a matter of public concern.

"*Pickering*, its antecedents and progeny, lead us to conclude that if Myers' questionnaire cannot be fairly characterized as constituting speech on a matter of public concern, it is unnecessary for us to scrutinize the reasons for her discharge. When employee expression cannot be fairly considered as relating to any matter of political, social, or other concern to the community, government officials should enjoy wide latitude in managing their offices, without intrusive oversight by the judiciary in the name of the First Amendment.[c] * * * We do not suggest, however, that Myers' speech, even if not touching upon a matter of public concern, is totally beyond the protection of the First Amendment. * * * [We] in no sense suggest that speech on private matters falls into one of the narrow and well-defined classes of expression which carries so little social value, such as obscenity, that the state can prohibit and punish such expression by all persons in its jurisdiction. See *Chaplinsky; Roth; Ferber.* For example, an employee's false criticism of his employer on grounds not of public concern may be cause for his discharge but would be entitled to the same protection in a libel action accorded an identical statement made by a man on the street. We hold only that when a public employee speaks not as a citizen upon matters of public concern, but instead as an employee upon matters only of personal interest, absent the most unusual circumstances, a federal court is not the appropriate forum in which to review the wisdom of a personnel decision taken by a public agency allegedly in reaction to the employee's behavior. Our responsibility is to ensure that citizens are not deprived of fundamental rights by virtue of working for the government; this does not require a grant of immunity for employee grievances not afforded by the First Amendment to those who do not work for the state.

of public record); *Time, Inc. v. Hill.* [Should *Pickering* be extended to independent contractors? See *Board of County Commissioners v. Umbehr*, 518 U.S. 668, 116 S.Ct. 2342, 135 L.Ed.2d 843 (1996)].

c. If there is dispute about what an employee said, does the first amendment permit an employee to be fired for a statement that was never made? Does the first amendment require the trier of fact to determine that the statement was made or is it enough that the employer reasonably thought the statement was made? See *Waters v. Churchill*, 511 U.S. 661, 114 S.Ct. 1878, 128 L.Ed.2d 686 (1994) (enough that the employer reasonably thought the statement was made).

"Whether an employee's speech addresses a matter of public concern must be determined by the content, form, and context of a given statement, as revealed by the whole record. In this case, with but one exception, the questions posed by Myers to her coworkers do not fall under the rubric of matters of 'public concern.' We view the questions pertaining to the confidence and trust that Myers' coworkers possess in various supervisors, the level of office morale, and the need for a grievance committee as mere extensions of Myers' dispute over her transfer to another section of the criminal court. * * * Indeed, the questionnaire, if released to the public, would convey no information at all other than the fact that a single employee is upset with the status quo. [T]he focus of Myers' questions is not to evaluate the performance of the office but rather to gather ammunition for another round of controversy with her superiors. These questions reflect one employee's dissatisfaction with a transfer and an attempt to turn that displeasure into a cause célèbre.[8] * * *

"One question in Myers' questionnaire, however, does touch upon a matter of public concern. Question 11 inquires if assistant district attorneys 'ever feel pressured to work in political campaigns on behalf of office supported candidates.' [This issue] is a matter of interest to the community upon which it is essential that public employees be able to speak out freely without fear of retaliatory dismissal.

"Because one of the questions in Myers' survey touched upon a matter of public concern, and contributed to her discharge we must determine whether Connick was justified in discharging Myers. Here the District Court again erred in imposing an unduly onerous burden on the state to justify Myers' discharge. The District Court viewed the issue of whether Myers' speech was upon a matter of 'public concern' as a threshold inquiry, after which it became the government's burden to 'clearly demonstrate' that the speech involved 'substantially interfered' with official responsibilities. Yet *Pickering* unmistakably states, and respondent agrees, that the state's burden in justifying a particular discharge varies depending upon the nature of the employee's expression. Although such particularized balancing is difficult, the courts must reach the most appropriate possible balance of the competing interests. * * *

"We agree with the District Court that there is no demonstration here that the questionnaire impeded Myers' ability to perform her responsibilities. The District Court was also correct to recognize that 'it is important to the efficient and successful operation of the District Attorney's office for

---

8. This is not a case like *Givhan,* where an employee speaks out as a citizen on a matter of general concern, not tied to a personal employment dispute, but arranges to do so privately. Mrs. Givhan's right to protest racial discrimination—a matter inherently of public concern—is not forfeited by her choice of a private forum. Here, however, a questionnaire not otherwise of public concern does not attain that status because its subject matter could, in different circumstances, have been the topic of a communication to the public that might be of general interest. The dissent's analysis of whether discussions of office morale and discipline could be matters of public concern is beside the point—it does not answer whether *this* questionnaire is such speech.

Assistants to maintain close working relationships with their superiors.' Connick's judgment, and apparently also that of his first assistant [who] characterized Myers' actions as causing a 'mini-insurrection', was that Myers' questionnaire was an act of insubordination which interfered with working relationships. When close working relationships are essential to fulfilling public responsibilities, a wide degree of deference to the employer's judgment is appropriate. Furthermore, we do not see the necessity for an employer to allow events to unfold to the extent that the disruption of the office and the destruction of working relationships is manifest before taking action. We caution that a stronger showing may be necessary if the employee's speech more substantially involved matters of public concern. * * *

"Also relevant is the manner, time, and place in which the questionnaire was distributed. '[When] a government employee personally confronts his immediate superior, the employing agency's institutional efficiency may be threatened not only by the content of the employee's message but also by the manner, time, and place in which it is delivered.' Here the questionnaire was prepared, and distributed at the office; the manner of distribution required not only Myers to leave her work but for others to do the same in order that the questionnaire be completed.[13] Although some latitude in when official work is performed is to be allowed when professional employees are involved, and Myers did not violate announced office policy, the fact that Myers, unlike Pickering, exercised her rights to speech at the office supports Connick's fears that the functioning of his office was endangered.

"Finally, the context in which the dispute arose is also significant. This is not a case where an employee, out of purely academic interest, circulated a questionnaire so as to obtain useful research. Myers acknowledges that it is no coincidence that the questionnaire followed upon the heels of the transfer notice. When employee speech concerning office policy arises from an employment dispute concerning the very application of that policy to the speaker, additional weight must be given to the supervisor's view that the employee has threatened the authority of the employer to run the office. Although we accept the District Court's factual finding that Myers' reluctance to accede to the transfer order was not a sufficient cause in itself for her dismissal, [this] does not render irrelevant the fact that the questionnaire emerged after a persistent dispute between Myers and Connick and his deputies over office transfer policy.

"Myers' questionnaire touched upon matters of public concern in only a most limited sense; her survey, in our view, is most accurately characterized as an employee grievance concerning internal office policy. The limited First Amendment interest involved here does not require that Connick tolerate action which he reasonably believed would disrupt the office, undermine his

---

13. The record indicates that some, though not all, of the questionnaires were distributed during lunch. Employee speech which transpires entirely on the employee's own time, and in non-work areas of the office, bring different factors into the *Pickering* calculus, and might lead to a different conclusion.

authority, and destroy close working relationships. Myers' discharge therefore did not offend the First Amendment. * * *

"Our holding today is grounded in our long-standing recognition that the First Amendment's primary aim is the full protection of speech upon issues of public concern, as well as the practical realities involved in the administration of a government office. Although today the balance is struck for the government, this is no defeat for the First Amendment. For it would indeed be a Pyrrhic victory for the great principles of free expression if the Amendment's safeguarding of a public employee's right, as a citizen, to participate in discussions concerning public affairs were confused with the attempt to constitutionalize the employee grievance that we see presented here."

BRENNAN, J., joined by Marshall, Blackmun and Stevens, JJ., dissented: "It is hornbook law [that] speech about 'the manner in which government is operated or should be operated' is an essential part of the communications necessary for self-governance the protection of which was a central purpose of the First Amendment. Because the questionnaire addressed such matters and its distribution did not adversely affect the operations of the District Attorney's Office or interfere with Myers' working relationship with her fellow employees, I dissent. * * *

"The balancing test articulated in *Pickering* comes into play only when a public employee's speech implicates the government's interests as an employer. When public employees engage in expression unrelated to their employment while away from the work place, their First Amendment rights are, of course, no different from those of the general public. Thus, whether a public employee's speech addresses a matter of public concern is relevant to the constitutional inquiry only when the statements at issue—by virtue of their content or the context in which they were made—may have an adverse impact on the government's ability to perform its duties efficiently.

"The Court's decision today is flawed in three respects. First, the Court distorts the balancing analysis required under *Pickering* by suggesting that one factor, the context in which a statement is made, is to be weighed *twice*—first in determining whether an employee's speech addresses a matter of public concern and then in deciding whether the statement adversely affected the government's interest as an employer. Second, in concluding that the effect of respondent's personnel policies on employee morale and the work performance of the District Attorney's Office is not a matter of public concern, the Court impermissibly narrows the class of subjects on which public employees may speak out without fear of retaliatory dismissal. Third, the Court misapplies the *Pickering* balancing test in holding that Myers could constitutionally be dismissed for circulating a questionnaire addressed to at least one subject that *was* 'a matter of interest to the community,' in the absence of evidence that her conduct disrupted the efficient functioning of the District Attorney's Office.

"[Based] on its own narrow conception of which matters are of public concern, the Court implicitly determines that information concerning employee morale at an important government office will not inform public debate. To the contrary, the First Amendment protects the dissemination of such information so that the people, not the courts may evaluate its usefulness. The proper means to ensure that the courts are not swamped with routine employee grievances mischaracterized as First Amendment cases is not to restrict artificially the concept of 'public concern,' but to require that adequate weight be given to the public's important interests in the efficient performance of governmental functions and in preserving employee discipline and harmony sufficient to achieve that end.

"The District Court weighed all of the relevant factors identified by our cases. It found that petitioner failed to establish that Myers violated either a duty of confidentiality or an office policy. Noting that most of the questionnaires were distributed during lunch, it rejected the contention that the distribution of the questionnaire impeded Myers' performance of her duties, and it concluded that 'Connick has not shown *any* evidence to indicate that the plaintiff's work performance was adversely affected by her expression.' (emphasis supplied).

"The Court accepts all of these findings. It concludes, however, that the District Court failed to give adequate weight to the context in which the questionnaires were distributed and to the need to maintain close working relationships in the District Attorney's Office. In particular, the Court suggests the District Court failed to give sufficient weight to the disruptive potential of Question 10, which asked whether the Assistants had confidence in the word of five named supervisors. The District Court, however, explicitly recognized that this was petitioner's 'most forceful argument'; but after hearing the testimony of four of the five supervisors named in the question, it found that the question had no adverse effect on Myers' relationship with her superiors.

"To this the Court responds that an employer need not wait until the destruction of working relationships is manifest before taking action. In the face of the District Court's finding that the circulation of the questionnaire had no disruptive effect, the Court holds that respondent may be dismissed because petitioner 'reasonably believed [the action] would disrupt the office, undermine his authority and destroy close working relationships.' Even though the District Court found that the distribution of the questionnaire did not impair Myers' working relationship with her supervisors, the Court bows to petitioner's judgment because '[w]hen close working relationships are essential to fulfilling public responsibilities, a wide degree of deference to the employer's judgment is appropriate.'

"Such extreme deference to the employer's judgment is not appropriate when public employees voice critical views concerning the operations of the agency for which they work. Although an employer's determination that an employee's statements have undermined essential working relationships must be carefully weighed in the *Pickering* balance, we must bear in mind that 'the threat of dismissal from public employment is [a] potent means of inhibiting speech.' If the employer's judgment is to be controlling, public employees will not speak out when what they have to say is critical of their supervisors. In order to protect public employees' First Amendment right to voice critical views on issues of public importance, the courts must make their own appraisal of the effects of the speech in question.

"[T]he District Court found that 'it cannot be said that the defendant's interest in promoting the efficiency of the public services performed through his employees was either adversely affected or substantially impeded by plaintiff's distribution of the questionnaire.' Based on these findings the District Court concluded that the circulation of the questionnaire was protected by the First Amendment. The District Court applied the proper legal standard and reached an acceptable accommodation between the competing interests. * * *

"The Court's decision today inevitably will deter public employees from making critical statements about the manner in which government agencies are operated for fear that doing so will provoke their dismissal. As a result, the public will be deprived of valuable information with which to evaluate the performance of elected officials. Because protecting the dissemination of such information is an essential function of the First Amendment, I dissent."

Notes and Questions

1. *Holmes' epigram.* Does the Court reject Holmes' epigram with one hand and embrace it with the other? Does it to some extent hold that because there is no right to hold a government job, its retention is a revocable privilege? Consider Tribe, *Constitutional Choices* 208 (1985): "*Connick* resurrects the right-privilege doctrine for 'private' speech by government employees. By hinging protection on the distinction between public and private speech, the Court has embarked on a difficult definitional course. The stated test, which includes the 'content, form, and context' of the expression, provides little guidance. As Justice Brennan pointed out in dissent, the Court significantly narrowed the concept of a public issue in holding that criticism of governmental officials is not necessarily of public concern, but provided no clear alternative formulation. The mere fact that expression constitutes an employee grievance surely cannot be decisive, since the Court found that pressure upon employees to work on political campaigns was of public concern. Nor can the absence of partisan political concerns be determinative, since an employee grievance criticizing hiring and personnel management policies is of public concern if based upon a claim of racial discrimination. What is clear is that, at least until the precise reach of *Connick* is determined, public employees, who often possess unique information, will be discouraged from adding their voices to the debate on government performance."[d]

FREEDOM OF EXPRESSION & ASSOCIATION Pt. 1

2. Consider the tension between *Letter Carriers* and *Pickering* or *Connick.* Consider also the relationship between *Pickering, Connick,* and *Elrod.* Suppose a deputy sheriff is discharged for meeting with a political opponent of the incumbent sheriff. Does *Elrod* apply or *Pickering–Connick?*[e] What is the difference? For discussion, see Note, *Politics and the Non–Civil Service Public Employee: A Categorical Approach to First Amendment Protection,* 85 Colum.L.Rev. 558 (1985).

3. Does *Connick* provide less protection for the public employee than is afforded to the school child in *Tinker,* Ch. 7, II supra? Does the public/private distinction distinguish *Tinker?* If *Tinker's* black arm band symbolized criticism of the school principal, would the outcome have been different?

4. After hearing of an assassination attempt on the life of the President, a clerical employee in a county constable's office remarked to a friend in the office, "If they go after him again, I hope they get him." Free speech? See *Rankin v. McPherson,* 483 U.S. 378, 107 S.Ct. 2891, 97 L.Ed.2d 315 (1987). For discussion, see Shiffrin, *The First Amendment, Democracy, and Romance* (1990); Massaro, *Significant Silences: Freedom of Speech in the Public Sector Workplace,* 61 S.Cal.L.Rev. 1, 68–76 (1987).[f]

———

A 1981 amendment to the Food Stamp Act provides that no family shall become eligible to participate in the program during the time that any member of the household is on strike nor shall receive any increase in food stamp allotments by virtue of decreased income of the striking member. LYNG v. UAW, 485 U.S. 360, 108 S.Ct. 1184, 99 L.Ed.2d 380 (1988), per WHITE, J., stated that associational rights included the "combination of workers together in order better to assert their lawful rights" but found no interference with such association: "[The statute] does not 'order' appellees not to associate together for the purpose of conducting a strike, or for any other purpose, and it does not 'prevent'

d. For recent commentary on the right-privilege distinction with substantial attention to first amendment issues, see Kreimer, *Allocational Sanctions: The Problem of Negative Rights in a Positive State,* 132 U.Pa.L.Rev. 1293 (1984).

e. Should the standards for public teachers, professors, professionals, and non-professional employees each be controlled by *Connick?* Should academic freedom apply to "intramural" speech in ways that permit freer speech than that available to other public employees? For discussion, see Finkin, *Intramural Speech, Academic Freedom, and the First Amendment,* 66 Texas L.Rev. 1323 (1988); Yudof, *Intramural Musings on Academic Freedom,* 66 Texas L.Rev.

1351 (1988); Brest, *Protecting Academic Freedom Through the First Amendment,* 66 Texas L.Rev. 1359 (1988).

f. For discussion of *Connick,* see e.g., Shiffrin, supra, Massaro, supra, Lieberwitz, *Freedom of Speech in Public Sector Employment: The Deconstitutionalization of the Public Sector Workplace,* 19 U.C.Davis L.Rev. 597 (1986); Post, *Between Governance and Management,* 34 UCLA L.Rev. 1713, 1813–16 (1987); Comment, *The Public Employee's Right of Free Speech,* 55 U.Cin.L.Rev. 449 (1986). For relevant pre-*Connick* commentary, see Schauer, *"Private" Speech and the "Private" Forum: Givhan v. Western Line School District,* 1979 Sup.Ct.Rev. 217.

them from associating together or burden their ability to do so in any significant manner. [I]t seems 'exceedingly unlikely' that this statute will prevent individuals from continuing to associate together in unions to promote their lawful objectives.[a] [A] 'legislature's decision not to subsidize the exercise of a fundamental right does not infringe the right.' *Regan.*"[b]

MARSHALL, J., joined by Brennan and Blackmun, JJ., dissenting, saw no need to reach the first amendment issue (although he was "unconvinced" by the Court's treatment of the issue) because, he argued, the statute failed to meet even the most deferential scrutiny. In light of a variety of statutory benefits easing management's burden in labor disputes, he concluded: "Altering the backdrop of governmental support in this one-sided and devastating way amounts to a penalty on strikers, not neutrality."[c]

———

In ABOOD v. DETROIT BD. OF EDUC., 431 U.S. 209, 97 S.Ct. 1782, 52 L.Ed.2d 261 (1977), a Michigan statute permitted an "agency shop" arrangement, whereby all local governmental employees represented by a union, even though not themselves union members, must, as a condition of employment, pay to the union "service charges" equal in amount to union dues. Alleging that they were unwilling to pay union dues, that (1) they opposed public sector collective bargaining and that (2) the union was engaged in non-collective bargaining political-ideological activities which they disapproved, public school teachers challenged the validity of the agency-shop clause in a collective bargaining agreement between the Board of Education and the union. The Court, per STEWART, J., rejected plaintiffs' first contention, but sustained the second—the union's expenditure of a part of such "service charges" "to contribute to political candidates and to express political views unrelated to its duties as exclusive bargaining representative" violates the first amendment rights of non-union employees who oppose such causes.

"To compel employees financially to support their collective-bargaining representative has an impact upon their First Amendment interests. An employee may very well have ideological objections to a wide variety of activities undertaken by the union in its role as exclusive representative. His moral or religious views about the desirability of abortion may not square with the union's policy in negotiating a medical benefits plan. One individual might disagree with a union policy of negotiating limits on the right to strike, believing that to be the road to serfdom for the working class, while

a. Should a penalty for the exercise of a right be unconstitutional even if it does not inhibit the exercise of that right?

b. How does one distinguish the mere failure to subsidize from a penalty? Is participation in a strike protected association? For commentary discussing and ranging be-

yond *Lyng*, see Sullivan, *Unconstitutional Conditions*, 102 Harv.L.Rev. 1413, 1428–56, 1474 (1989).

c. The government had argued that the statute was justified by the interest of governmental neutrality in private labor disputes.

another might have economic or political objections to unionism itself. An employee might object to the union's wage policy because it violates guidelines designed to limit inflation, or might object to the union's seeking a clause in the collective-bargaining agreement proscribing racial discrimination. The examples could be multiplied. To be required to help finance the union as a collective-bargaining agent might well be thought, therefore, to interfere in some way with an employee's freedom to associate for the advancement of ideas, or to refrain from doing so, as he sees fit. But the judgment clearly made in [*Railway Employees' Dep't v. Hanson,* 351 U.S. 225, 76 S.Ct. 714, 100 L.Ed. 1112 (1956), upholding against first amendment challenge a union-shop clause, authorized by the Railway Labor Act (RLA), requiring financial support of the union by every member of the bargaining unit, and *International Ass'n of Machinists v. Street,* 367 U.S. 740, 81 S.Ct. 1784, 6 L.Ed.2d 1141 (1961), avoiding serious constitutional issues by construing RLA to prohibit the use of compulsory union dues for political purposes] is that such interference as exists is constitutionally justified by the legislative assessment of the important contribution of the union shop to the system of labor relations established by the Congress. '[As long as the union leadership acts] to promote the cause which justified bringing the group together, the individual cannot withdraw his financial support merely because he disagrees with the group's strategy.' *Street* (Douglas, J., concurring).

"[The] desirability of labor peace is no less important in the public sector, nor is the risk of 'free riders' any smaller. [Thus], insofar as the service charge is used to finance expenditures by the union for the purposes of collective bargaining, contract administration, and grievance adjustment, [*Hanson* and *Street*] appear to require validation of the agency-shop agreement before us."

In agreeing with plaintiffs' contention that they fall within the protection of *Elrod* and other cases guaranteeing the freedom to associate for the purpose of advancing ideas and forbidding the government to require one to relinquish first amendment rights as a condition of public employment "because they have been prohibited not from actively associating, but rather from refusing to associate," and in ruling that plaintiffs could constitutionally prevent the union's spending a part of their required service fees for political and ideological purposes unrelated to collective bargaining, the Court pointed out: "The fact that [plaintiffs] are compelled to make, rather than prohibited from making, contributions for political purposes works no less an infringement of their constitutional rights. For at the heart of the First Amendment is the notion that an individual should be free to believe as he will, and that in a free society one's beliefs should be shaped by his mind and his conscience rather than coerced by the State. See [*Elrod.*]

"These principles prohibit a State from compelling an individual [to] associate with a political party, *Elrod,* as a condition of employment. They are no less applicable to the case at bar, and they thus prohibit the [union] from requiring any [plaintiff] to contribute to the support of an ideological cause he may oppose as a condition of holding a job as a public school teacher.

"We do not hold that a union cannot constitutionally spend funds for the expression of political views, on behalf of political candidates, or towards the advancement of other ideological causes not germane to its duties as collective bargaining representative. Rather, the Constitution requires only that expenditures be financed from [charges] paid by employees who do not object to advancing those ideas and who are not coerced into doing so against their will by the threat of loss of government employment."

The Court remanded to devise an appropriate "way of preventing subsidization of ideological activity by employees who object thereto without restricting the union's ability to require every employee to contribute to the cost of collective-bargaining activities."[a]

Powell, J., joined by Burger, C.J., and Blackmun, J., agreed that a state cannot constitutionally compel public employees to contribute to union political activities which they oppose and thus joined the Court's judgment remanding the case for further proceedings, but balked at the Court's apparent ruling "that public employees can be compelled by the State to pay full union dues to a union with which they disagree, subject only to a possible rebate or deduction if they are willing to step forward, declare their opposition to the union, and initiate a proceeding to establish that some portion of their dues has been spent on 'ideological activities unrelated to collective bargaining.' Such a sweeping limitation of First Amendment rights by the Court is not only unnecessary on this record; it [is] unsupported by either precedent or reason. * * *

"The Court's extensive reliance on *Hanson* and *Street* requires it to rule that there is no constitutional distinction between what the Government can require of its own employees and what it can permit private employees to do. To me the distinction is fundamental. Under the First Amendment the Government may authorize private parties to enter into voluntary agreements whose terms it could not adopt as its own.

"[The] collective-bargaining agreement to which a public agency is a party is not merely analogous to legislation; it has all of the attributes of legislation for the subjects [e.g., residency requirements for state employees] with which it deals. [The] State in this case has not merely authorized union-shop agreements between willing parties; it has negotiated and adopted such an agreement itself. [It] has undertaken to compel employees to pay full dues [to] a union as a condition of employment. Accordingly, the [Board of Education's] collective-bargaining agreement, like any other enactment of state law, is fully subject to the constraints that the Constitution imposes on coercive governmental regulation.

a. For procedural aspects of the implementation, see *Chicago Teachers Union v.* *Hudson,* 475 U.S. 292, 106 S.Ct. 1066, 89 L.Ed.2d 232 (1986).

"[I] would make it more explicit [than has the majority] that compelling a government employee to give financial support to a union in the public sector—regardless of the use to which the union puts the contribution—impinges seriously upon interests in free speech and association protected by the First Amendment.

"In *Buckley* [we held that] limitations on political contributions 'impinge on protected associational freedoms.' [That] *Buckley* dealt with a contribution limitation requirement does not alter its importance for this case. An individual can no more be required to affiliate with a candidate by making a contribution than he can be prohibited from such affiliation. The only question after *Buckley* is whether a union in the public sector is sufficiently distinguishable from a political candidate or committee to remove the withholding of financial contributions from First Amendment protection. In my view no principled distinction exists.

"The ultimate objective of a union in the public sector, like that of a political party, is to influence public decisionmaking in accordance with the views and perceived interests of the membership. [In this sense], the public sector union is indistinguishable from the traditional political party in this country.

"[It] is possible that paramount governmental interests may be found—at least with respect to certain narrowly defined subjects of bargaining—that would support this restriction on First Amendment rights. But 'the burden is on the government to show the existence of such an interest.' *Elrod*. Because this appeal reaches this Court on a motion to dismiss, the record is barren of any demonstration by the State that excluding minority views from the processes by which governmental policy is made is necessary to serve overriding governmental objectives. * * *

"Before today it had been well established that when state law intrudes upon protected speech, the State itself must shoulder the burden of proving that its action is justified by overriding state interests. See *Elrod; Speiser v. Randall*. The Court, for the first time in a First Amendment case, simply reverses this principle. Under today's decision, a nonunion employee who would vindicate his First Amendment rights apparently must initiate a proceeding to prove that the union has allocated some portion of its budget to 'ideological activities unrelated to collective bargaining.' I would adhere to established First Amendment principles and require the State to come forward and demonstrate, as to each union expenditure for which it would exact support from minority employees, that the compelled contribution is necessary to serve overriding governmental objectives."[b]

b. Reading *Elrod* and *Abood* together, Powell, J., maintains that public employees may be forced to support a political party, but not the union which represents them in collective bargaining. For revealing commentary, see Kahn, *The Court, the Community and the Judicial Balance: The Jurisprudence of Justice Powell*, 97 Yale L.J. 1, 45–47 (1987).

REHNQUIST, J., concurring, noted that had he joined the *Elrod* plurality, he "would find it virtually impossible to join the Court's opinion in this case." He did not "read the Court's opinion as leaving intact the 'unfettered judgment of each citizen on matters of political concern' [*Elrod*] when it holds that Michigan [may] require an objecting member of a public employees' union to contribute to the funds necessary for the union to carry out its bargaining activities. Nor does the Court's opinion leave such a member free 'to believe as he will and to act and associate according to his beliefs' [*Elrod*]." He was "unable to see a constitutional distinction between a governmentally imposed requirement that a public employee be a Democrat or Republican or else lose his job, and a similar requirement that a public employee contribute to the collective-bargaining expenses of a labor union."[c]

Notes and Questions

1.   How should the *Abood* rules apply to forced employee payments for union conventions, union newsletters, union social activities or union organizing? See *Lehnert v. Ferris Faculty Ass'n*, 500 U.S. 507, 111 S.Ct. 1950, 114 L.Ed.2d 572 (1991); *Ellis v. Brotherhood of Railway, Airline & Steamship Clerks*, 466 U.S. 435, 104 S.Ct. 1883, 80 L.Ed.2d 428 (1984). See also *Communications Workers v. Beck*, 487 U.S. 735, 108 S.Ct. 2641, 101 L.Ed.2d 634 (1988) (forced expenditures for purposes other than collective bargaining including non-germane-non-ideological activities violates National Labor Relations Act). For exploration of the issues raised by *Abood,* see Cantor, *Forced Payments to Service Institutions and Constitutional Interests in Ideological Non–Association,* 36 Rut.L.Rev. 3 (1984).

2.   Does *Abood* exaggerate the first amendment interests? See generally, Gaebler, *First Amendment Protection Against Government Compelled Expression and Association* 23 B.C.L.R. 995 (1982). If Michigan subsidized unions directly, would dissenting taxpayers have a first amendment claim? Suppose Michigan taxed those most likely to benefit from union activity, i.e., the employees? Are compelled contributions different from government taxation? See Shiffrin, *Government Speech,* 27 U.C.L.A.L.Rev. 565, 594 (1980). Suppose the union contract provided for a direct payment from the

c.   Stevens, J., also filed a brief concurrence: "The Court's opinion does not foreclose the argument that the Union should not be permitted to exact a service fee from nonmembers without first establishing a procedure which will avoid the risk that their funds will be used, even temporarily, to finance ideological activities unrelated to collective bargaining." For light on the application of *Abood* to a mandatory university student activity fee, see Board of Regents v. Southworth, 529 U.S. 217, 120 S.Ct. 1346, 146 L.Ed.2d 193 (2000)(no refund appropriate so long as allocation of funding is viewpoint neutral; interest in stimulating diverse ideas on campus outweighs the interests of objecting students). For light on the application of *Abood* to a mandatory university student activity fee, see Board of Regents v. Southworth, 529 U.S. 217, 120 S.Ct. 1346, 146 L.Ed.2d 193 (2000)(no refund required so long as allocation of funding is viewpoint neutral; interest in stimulating diverse ideas on campus outweighs the interests of objecting students).

employer and that union dues were not required of employees? Would this arrangement affect the rules set out in *Abood*?

3.   Although *Abood* limits the sources of funding for union speech, it does not question union rights of free speech and association. Such rights include not only the endorsement of political candidates and causes, but also associational rights to pursue legal claims. Even as against state bar regulations, for example, unions are free to recommend attorneys to their members and to hire or engage in contracts with attorneys to represent individual union members. See *United Transportation Union v. State Bar,* 401 U.S. 576, 91 S.Ct. 1076, 28 L.Ed.2d 339 (1971): "[C]ollective activity undertaken to obtain meaningful access to the courts is a fundamental right within the protection of the First Amendment. [T]hat right would be a hollow promise if courts could deny associations of workers or others the means of enabling their members to meet the costs of legal representation."

4.   Suppose the state declared the dues gathering body to be a governmental agency? California requires all attorneys to join and pay dues to the State Bar. Under California law the State Bar is a regulated state agency authorized not only to examine prospective attorneys and to recommend bar admission or discipline, but also to use compulsory dues for a broad range of lobbying and amicus curiae activities. The state believes that the input of the bar organization is valuable. It also believes that ad hoc decisionmaking about which legislation is or is not an appropriate concern of the bar is unworkable.

KELLER v. STATE BAR OF CALIFORNIA, 496 U.S. 1, 110 S.Ct. 2228, 110 L.Ed.2d 1 (1990), per REHNQUIST, C.J., unanimously held that compulsory bar dues could only be used if "reasonably incurred for the purpose of regulating the legal profession or improving the quality of the legal service available to the people of the State." Recognizing that difficult line-drawing questions could arise, the Court observed that the case presented clear ends of a spectrum: "Compulsory dues may not be expended to endorse or advance a gun control or nuclear weapons freeze initiative; at the other end of the spectrum petitioners have no valid constitutional objection to their compulsory dues being spent for activities connected with disciplining members of the bar or proposing ethical codes for the profession. * * *

"Of course the Supreme Court of California is the final authority on the 'governmental' status of the State Bar of California for purposes of state law. But its determination that respondent is a 'government agency,' and therefore entitled to the treatment accorded a governor, a mayor or a State Tax Commission, for instance, is not binding on us when such a determination is essential to the decision of a federal question. The State Bar of California is a good deal different from most other entities that would be regarded in common parlance as 'governmental agencies.' Its principal funding comes not from appropriations made to it by the legislature, but from dues levied on its members by the Board of Governors. Only lawyers admitted to practice in the State of California are members of the State Bar, and all

122,000 lawyers admitted to practice in the State must be members. Respondent undoubtedly performs important and valuable services for the State by way of governance of the profession, but those services are essentially advisory in nature. The State Bar does not admit anyone to the practice of law, it does not finally disbar or suspend anyone, nor does it ultimately establish ethical codes of conduct. All of those functions are reserved by California law to the State Supreme Court. * * *

"The State Bar of California was created, not to participate in the general government of the State, but to provide specialized professional advice to those with the ultimate responsibility of governing the legal profession. Its members and officers are such not because they are citizens or voters, but because they are lawyers. We think that these differences between the State Bar, on the one hand, and traditional government agencies and officials, on the other hand, render unavailing respondent's argument that it is not subject to the same constitutional rule with respect to the use of compulsory dues as are labor unions representing public and private employees."

5.   The Agricultural Marketing Agreement Act of 1937 enables committees of producers appointed by the Secretary of Agriculture to issue certain marketing orders without violating the antitrust laws provided that two thirds of the producers who market at least two thirds of the volume of a product approve. The purpose of such orders is to establish and maintain orderly marketing conditions and fair prices for agricultural commodities. Such orders, which are restricted to the smallest practicable production area, range from price fixing, joint research projects, standardized packaging, and joint advertising. Expenses of administering an order are paid from funds collected pursuant to the marketing order. Some producers of California nectarines, plums, and peaches brought a proceeding challenging marketing orders requiring them to pay for generic advertising. They invoked a first amendment right not to be compelled to subsidize the speech of others.

GLICKMAN v. WILEMAN BROTHERS & ELLIOTT, INC., 521 U.S. 457, 117 S.Ct. 2130, 138 L.Ed.2d 585 (1997), per Stevens, J., held that the compelled funding of generic advertising did not violate the first amendment: "The legal question that we address is whether being compelled to fund this advertising raises a First Amendment issue for us to resolve, or rather is simply a question of economic policy for Congress and the Executive to resolve.

"Three characteristics of the regulatory scheme at issue distinguish it from laws that we have found to abridge the freedom of speech protected by the First Amendment. First, the marketing orders impose no restraint on the freedom of any producer to communicate any message to any audience. Second, they do not compel any person to engage in any actual or symbolic speech. Third, they do not compel the producers to endorse or to finance any political or ideological views. Indeed, since all of the respondents are engaged in the business of marketing California nectarines, plums, and peaches, it is fair to presume that they agree with the central message of the speech that is generated by the generic program.[d] Thus, none of our First Amendment jurisprudence provides any support for the suggestion that the promotional regulations should be scrutinized under a different standard than that applicable to the other anticompetitive features of the marketing orders. * * *

"None of the advertising in this record promotes any particular message other than encouraging consumers to buy California tree fruit. Neither the fact that respondents may prefer to foster that message independently in order to promote and distinguish their own products, nor the fact that they think more or less money should be spent fostering it, makes this case comparable to those in which an objection rested on political or ideological disagreement with the content of the message. The mere fact that objectors believe their money is not being well spent 'does not mean [that] they have a First Amendment complaint.' "

THOMAS, J., joined by Scalia, J., dissenting observed: "What we are now left with, if we are to take the majority opinion at face value, is one of two disturbing consequences: Either (1) paying for advertising is not speech at all, while such activities as draft card burning, flag burning, armband wearing, public sleeping, and nude dancing are, or (2) compelling payment for third party communication does not implicate speech, and thus the Government would be free to force payment for a whole variety of expressive conduct that it could not restrict. In either case, surely we have lost our way."[e]

III. INTIMATE ASSOCIATION AND EXPRESSIVE ASSOCIATION

ROBERTS v. UNITED STATES JAYCEES, 468 U.S. 609, 104 S.Ct. 3244, 82 L.Ed.2d 462 (1984): Appellee U.S. Jaycees, a nonprofit national membership corporation whose objective is to pursue educational and charitable purposes that promote the growth and development of young men's civic organizations, limits regular membership to young men between the ages of 18 and 35. Associate membership is available to women and older men. An associate member may not vote or hold local or national office. Two local chapters in Minnesota violated appellee's bylaws by admitting women as regular members. When they learned that revocation of their charters was to be considered, members of both chapters filed discrimination charges with the Minnesota Department of Human Rights, alleging that the exclusion of women from full membership violated the Minnesota Human Rights Act (Act), which makes it an

---

d. The producers objected to the content of some of the advertisements. Stevens, J., stated that these concerns might call into question portions of the program, but had no bearing on the entire program. He also stated that these concerns were more properly addressed to the Secretary.

e. Souter, J., joined by Rehnquist, C.J., and Scalia and Thomas, JJ., also dissented.

"unfair discriminatory practice" to deny anyone "the full and equal enjoyment of goods, services, facilities, privileges, advantages, and accommodations of a place of accommodation" because, inter alia, of sex.

Before a hearing on the state charge took place, appellee brought federal suit, alleging that requiring it to accept women as regular members would violate the male members' constitutional "freedom of association." A state hearing officer decided against appellee and the federal district court certified to the Minnesota Supreme Court the question whether appellee is "a place of public accommodation" within the meaning of the Act. With the record of the administrative hearing before it, the state supreme court answered that question in the affirmative. The U.S. Court of Appeals held that application of the Act to appellee's membership policies would violate its freedom of association.[a]

In rejecting appellee's claims,[b] the Court, per BRENNAN, J., pointed out that the Constitution protects " 'freedom of association' in two distinct senses," what might be called "freedom of intimate association" and "freedom of expressive association": "In one line of decisions, the Court has concluded that choices to enter into and maintain certain intimate human relationships must be secured against undue intrusion by the State because of the role of such relationships in safeguarding the individual freedom that is central to our constitutional scheme. In this respect, freedom of association receives protection as a fundamental element of personal liberty. In another set of decisions, the Court has recognized a right to associate for the purpose of engaging in those activities protected by the First Amendment— speech, assembly, petition for the redress of grievances, and the exercise of religion. The Constitution guarantees freedom of association of this kind as an indispensable means of preserving other individual liberties."

The freedom of intimate association was deemed important because, "certain kinds of personal bonds have played a critical role in the culture and traditions of the Nation by cultivating and transmitting shared ideals and beliefs; they thereby foster diversity and act as critical buffers between the individual and the power of the State. Moreover, the constitutional shelter afforded such relationships reflects the realization that individuals draw much of their emotional enrichment from close ties with others. Protecting these relationships from unwarranted state interference therefore safeguards the ability independently to define one's identity that is central to any concept of liberty.

"The personal affiliations that exemplify these considerations [are] distinguished by such attributes as relative smallness, a high degree of

---

a. When the state supreme court held that appellee was "a place of public accommodation" within the meaning of the Act, it suggested that, unlike appellee, the Kiwanis Club might be sufficiently "private" to be outside the scope of the Act. Appellee then amended its complaint to allege that the state court's interpretation of the Act rendered it unconstitutionally vague. The Eighth Circuit so held, but the Supreme Court reversed.

b. There was no dissent. Rehnquist, J., concurred in the judgment. O'Connor, J., joined part of the Court's opinion and concurred in the judgment. See infra. Burger, C.J., and Blackmun, J., took no part.

selectivity in decisions to begin and maintain the affiliation, and seclusion from others in critical aspects of the relationship. As a general matter, only relationships with these sorts of qualities are likely to reflect the considerations that have led to an understanding of freedom of association as an intrinsic element of personal liberty. Conversely, an association lacking these qualities—such as a large business enterprise—seems remote from the concerns giving rise to this constitutional protection. * * *

"Between these poles, of course, lies a broad range of human relationships that may make greater or lesser claims to constitutional protection from particular incursions by the State. [We] need not mark the potentially significant points on this terrain with any precision. We note only that factors that may be relevant include size, purpose, policies, selectivity, congeniality, and other characteristics that in a particular case may be pertinent. In this case, however, several features of the Jaycees clearly place the organization outside of the category of relationships worthy of this kind of constitutional protection.

"The undisputed facts reveal that the local chapters of the Jaycees are large and basically unselective groups. * * * Apart from age and sex, neither the national organization nor the local chapters employs any criteria for judging applicants for membership, and new members are routinely recruited and admitted with no inquiry into their backgrounds. In fact, a local officer testified that he could recall no instance in which an applicant had been denied membership on any basis other than age or sex. Furthermore, despite their inability to vote, hold office, or receive certain awards, women affiliated with the Jaycees attend various meetings, participate in selected projects, and engage in many of the organization's social functions. Indeed, numerous non-members of both genders regularly participate in a substantial portion of activities central to the decision of many members to associate with one another, including many of the organization's various community programs, awards ceremonies, and recruitment meetings.

"[Thus], we conclude that the Jaycees chapters lack the distinctive characteristics that might afford constitutional protection to the decision of its members to exclude women. We turn therefore to consider the extent to which application of the Minnesota statute to compel the Jaycees to accept women infringes the group's freedom of expressive association. * * *

"Government actions that may unconstitutionally infringe upon [freedom of expressive association] can take a number of forms. Among other things, government may seek to impose penalties or withhold benefits from individuals because of their membership in a disfavored group; it may attempt to require disclosure of the fact of membership in a group seeking anonymity; and it may try to interfere with the internal organization or affairs of the group. By requiring the Jaycees to admit women as full voting members, the Minnesota Act works an infringement of the last type. There can be no clearer example of an intrusion into the internal structure or affairs of an association than a regulation that forces the group to accept members it does not desire. Such a regulation may impair the ability of the original members to express only those views that brought them together. Freedom of association therefore plainly presupposes a freedom not to associate. See *Abood.*

"The right to associate for expressive purposes is not, however, absolute. Infringements on that right may be justified by regulations adopted to serve compelling state interests, unrelated to the suppression of ideas, that cannot be achieved through means significantly less restrictive of associational freedoms. We are persuaded that Minnesota's compelling interest in eradicating discrimination against its female citizens justifies the impact that application of the statute to the Jaycees may have on the male members' associational freedoms.

"[I]n upholding Title II of the Civil Rights Act of 1964, which forbids race discrimination in public accommodations, we emphasized that its 'fundamental object [was] to vindicate "the deprivation of personal dignity that surely accompanies denials of equal access to public establishments.' " *Heart of Atlanta Motel.* That stigmatizing injury, and the denial of equal opportunities that accompanies it, is surely felt as strongly by persons suffering discrimination on the basis of their sex as by those treated differently because of their race.

"Nor is the state interest in assuring equal access limited to the provision of purely tangible goods and services. A State enjoys broad authority to create rights of public access on behalf of its citizens. *PruneYard.* Like many States and municipalities, Minnesota has adopted a functional definition of public accommodations that reaches various forms of public, quasi-commercial conduct. This expansive definition reflects a recognition of the changing nature of the American economy and of the importance, both to the individual and to society, of removing the barriers to economic advancement and political and social integration that have historically plagued certain disadvantaged groups, including women. * * *

"In applying the Act to the Jaycees, the State has advanced those interests through the least restrictive means of achieving its ends. Indeed, the Jaycees have failed to demonstrate that the Act imposes any serious burdens on the male members' freedom of expressive association. See *Hishon v. King & Spalding,* 467 U.S. 69, 104 S.Ct. 2229, 81 L.Ed.2d 59 (1984) (law firm 'has not shown how its ability to fulfill [protected] function[s] would be inhibited by a requirement that it consider [a woman lawyer] for partnership on her merits'). To be sure, a 'not insubstantial part' of the Jaycees' activities constitutes protected expression on political, economic, cultural, and social affairs. [There] is, however, no basis in the record for concluding that admission of women as full voting members will impede the organization's ability to engage in these protected activities or to disseminate its preferred views. The Act requires no change in the Jaycees' creed of promoting the interests of young men, and it imposes no restrictions on the organization's ability to exclude individuals with ideologies or philosophies different from those of its existing members. Moreover, the Jaycees already invite women to share the group's views and philosophy and to participate in much of its training and community activities. Accordingly, any claim that admission of women as full voting members will impair a symbolic message conveyed by the very fact that women are not permitted to vote is attenuated at best.

"[In] claiming that women might have a different attitude about such issues as the federal budget, school prayer, voting rights, and foreign relations, or that the organization's public positions would have a different effect if the group were not 'a purely young men's association,' the Jaycees rely solely on unsupported generalizations about the relative interests and perspectives of men and women. Although such generalizations may or may not have a statistical basis in fact with respect to particular positions adopted by the Jaycees, we have repeatedly condemned legal decisionmaking that relies uncritically on such assumptions. In the absence of a showing far more substantial than that attempted by the Jaycees, we decline to indulge in the sexual stereotyping that underlies appellee's contention that, by allowing women to vote, application of the Minnesota Act will change the content or impact of the organization's speech.

"In any event, even if enforcement of the Act causes some incidental abridgement of the Jaycees' protected speech, that effect is no greater than is necessary to accomplish the State's legitimate purposes. [A]cts of invidious discrimination in the distribution of publicly available goods, services, and other advantages cause unique evils that government has a compelling interest to prevent—wholly apart from the point of view such conduct may transmit. Accordingly, like violence or other types of potentially expressive activities that produce special harms distinct from their communicative impact, such practices are entitled to no constitutional protection."[c]

O'CONNOR, J., concurring, joined the Court's opinion except for its analysis of freedom of expressive association. She maintained that "the Court has adopted a test that unadvisedly casts doubt on the power of States to pursue the profoundly important goal of ensuring nondiscriminatory access to commercial opportunities" yet "accords insufficient protection to expressive associations and places inappropriate burdens on groups claiming the protection of the First Amendment":

"The Court analyzes Minnesota's attempt to regulate the Jaycees' membership using a test that I find both over-protective of activities unde-

---

c. For cases following or extending *Roberts*, see *Board of Directors of Rotary International v. Rotary Club of Duarte*, 481 U.S. 537, 107 S.Ct. 1940, 95 L.Ed.2d 474 (1987); *New York State Club Ass'n v. New York*, 487 U.S. 1, 108 S.Ct. 2225, 101 L.Ed.2d 1 (1988) (upholding city ordinance against facial challenge that prohibits discrimination based on race, creed, or sex by institutions (except benevolent orders or religious corporations) with more than 400 members that provide regular meal service and receive payment from nonmembers for the furtherance of trade or business); *Dallas v. Stanglin*, 490 U.S. 19, 109 S.Ct. 1591, 104 L.Ed.2d 18 (1989) (upholding ordinance restricting admission to certain dance halls to persons between the ages of 14 and 18).

serving of constitutional shelter and under-protective of important First Amendment concerns. The Court declares that the Jaycees' right of association depends on the organization's making a 'substantial' showing that the admission of unwelcome members 'will change the message communicated by the group's speech.' I am not sure what showing the Court thinks would satisfy its requirement of proof of a membership-message connection, but whatever it means, the focus on such a connection is objectionable.

"Imposing such a requirement, especially in the context of the balancing-of-interests test articulated by the Court, raises the possibility that certain commercial associations, by engaging occasionally in certain kinds of expressive activities, might improperly gain protection for discrimination. The Court's focus raises other problems as well. [W]ould the Court's analysis of this case be different if, for example, the Jaycees membership had a steady history of opposing public issues thought (by the Court) to be favored by women? It might seem easy to conclude, in the latter case, that the admission of women to the Jaycees' ranks would affect the content of the organization's message, but I do not believe that should change the outcome of this case. Whether an association is or is not constitutionally protected in the selection of its membership should not depend on what the association says or why its members say it.

"The Court's readiness to inquire into the connection between membership and message reveals a more fundamental flaw in its analysis. The Court pursues this inquiry as part of its mechanical application of a 'compelling interest' test, under which the Court weighs the interests of the State of Minnesota in ending gender discrimination against the Jaycees' First Amendment right of association. The Court entirely neglects to establish at the threshold that the Jaycees is an association whose activities or purposes should engage the strong protections that the First Amendment extends to expressive associations.

"On the one hand, an association engaged exclusively in protected expression enjoys First Amendment protection of both the content of its message and the choice of its members. Protection of the message itself is judged by the same standards as protection of speech by an individual. Protection of the association's right to define its membership derives from the recognition that the formation of an expressive association is the creation of a voice, and the selection of members is the definition of that voice. [A] ban on specific group voices on public affairs violates the most basic guarantee of the First Amendment—that citizens, not the government, control the content of public discussion.

"On the other hand, there is only minimal constitutional protection of the freedom of *commercial* association. There are, of course, some constitutional protections of commercial speech—speech intended and used to promote a commercial transaction with the speaker. But the State is free to impose any rational regulation on the commercial transaction itself. The Constitution does not guarantee a right to choose employees, customers, suppliers, or those with whom one engages in simple commercial transactions, without restraint from the State. A shopkeeper has no constitutional right to deal only with persons of one sex.

"[A]n association should be characterized as commercial, and therefore subject to rationally related state regulation of its membership and other associational activities, when, and only when, the association's activities are not predominantly of the type protected by the First Amendment. It is only when the association is predominantly engaged in protected expression that state regulation of its membership will necessarily affect, change, dilute, or silence one collective voice that would otherwise be heard. An association must choose its market. Once it enters the marketplace of commerce in any substantial degree it loses the complete control over its membership that it would otherwise enjoy if it confined its affairs to the marketplace of ideas.

"[N]otwithstanding its protected expressive activities, [appellee] is, first and foremost, an organization that, at both the national and local levels, promotes and practices the art of solicitation and management. The organization claims that the training it offers its members gives them an advantage in business, and business firms do indeed sometimes pay the dues of individual memberships for their employees. Jaycees members hone their solicitation and management skills, under the direction and supervision of the organization, primarily through their active recruitment of new members. * * *

"Recruitment and selling are commercial activities, even when conducted for training rather than for profit. The 'not insubstantial' volume of protected Jaycees activity found by the Court of Appeals is simply not enough to preclude state regulation of the Jaycees' commercial activities. The State of Minnesota has a legitimate interest in ensuring nondiscriminatory access to the commercial opportunity presented by membership in the Jaycees. The members of the Jaycees may not claim constitutional immunity from Minnesota's anti-discrimination law by seeking to exercise their First Amendment rights through this commercial organization."

Notes and Questions

1. *Freedom of intimate association.* The reference to the freedom of intimate association is the first in the Court's history, but the notion that the concept should serve as an organizing principle is found in Karst, *Freedom of Intimate Association,* 89 Yale L.J. 624 (1980). To what extent should freedom of intimate association itself be regarded as a first amendment right? Compare Karst with Baker, *Scope of the First Amendment Freedom of Speech,* 25 U.C.L.A.L.Rev. 964 (1978) and Raggi, *An Independent Right to Freedom of Association,* 12 Harv.Civ.Rts.—Civ.Lib.L.Rev. 1 (1977).

2. Is Brennan, J.'s conception of association's value too narrowly conceived? Consider Kateb, *The Value of Association* in *Freedom of Associa-*

tion 35, 49 (Gutmann ed. 1998): "The intrinsic value of association cannot be exclusively confined to close, intimate, or personal relationships, any more than pleasure or experience or adventure is found only in such relationships. If intrinsic value is present wherever a significant contribution to identity is present, then many relationships that are not close or intimate or deeply personal may have intrinsic value. Distant or formal or mediated or even abstract relationships contribute to the process of self-discovery and self-expression; so may chance or casual encounters or dealings with strangers; they can all help to shape or reshape an identity. It is an unattractive romanticism to believe that a self discloses or enhances itself only amid loving immediacy. * * *

"Different people will, of course, vary in the proportions of intimate and unintimate relationships they want; and many choices are made without reference to a concern to achieve or maintain or reform identity. [They] may think that by serving as a national or state officer of the Jaycees, or by being a member of a local chapter that excludes women as full members, they are engaged in a relationship of association that means a great deal to them. They may prefer to imagine that they are reduced in their identities by being told their choices are illegal, rather than constitutionally protected. We may—I do—think that it is unadult, bigoted, silly, to think as they do, and to wish to remain constitutionally free to choose to do what they want in this particular instance. I do not believe, however, that the Court should have interfered with the internal organization of an association on the grounds (partly) that such an association consisted of relationships that lacked intrinsic value * * *."[d] Does the concept of intimate association have "important implications for other private associations with discriminatory membership policies." Linder, *Freedom of Association After Roberts v. United States Jaycees,* 82 Mich.L.Rev. 1878, 1885 (1984). What are (should be) the implications for golf and country clubs, fraternal societies, athletic clubs and downtown or city clubs? Consider Comment, *Discrimination in Private Social Clubs: Freedom of Association and Right to Privacy,* 1970 Duke L.J. 1181, 1222: "Whether this society is capable of free evolution to social equality seems irrelevant in light of the influence of the social club in perpetuating general racial and religious economic and social inferiority and in light of the urgent need for reversal of racial polarization. Many private social clubs have become so affected with the public interest that some regulation of their membership practices is not only a proper but also a necessary exercise of legislative power."[e] Would such sentiments allow equality to run roughshod over other values? Consider Rosenblum, *Compelled Association* in *Freedom of Association* 75, 98, 101 (Gutmann ed. 1998): "Regardless of an association's purpose or members' intentions, selective groups will be seen as advancing some claim to preference, privilege, or desert, and they will provoke accusations that they violate the public ethos of

d. On the value of association, see generally Rosenblum, *Membership and Morals* (1998).

e. See generally Burns, *The Exclusion of Women From Influential Men's Clubs: The*

Inner Sanctum and the Myth of Full Equality, 18 Harv.Civ.Rts.-Civ.Lib.L.Rev. 321 (1983).

democratic equality. As *Roberts* demonstrates, egalitarian opposition to restrictive secular associations is endemic in the United States. [In] liberal democracy, romantic aloofness is as insufferable as exclusive groups; it too is perceived as aristocratic self-distancing, and generally despised. Nonetheless, romantic individualism points up the dark underside of gregariousness: dependence, craving for the good opinion of others, hypocrisy, and the desire of those excluded to join together and inflict the same on others. These are not just incidental accompaniments of voluntary association; they are among its sources.''

———

James Dale's position as an assistant scoutmaster of a New Jersey troop of the Boy Scouts of America was revoked when the Boy Scouts learned that he, an Eagle Scout, was gay, the co-President of the Rutgers University Lesbian/Gay Alliance, who had been publicly quoted on the importance in his own life on the need for gay role models. Dale sued, and the New Jersey Supreme Court ultimately held that New Jersey's anti-discrimination public accommodation law required that the Scouts readmit him.

BOY SCOUTS OF AMERICA v. DALE, 530 U.S. 640, 120 S.Ct. 2446, 147 L.Ed.2d 554 (2000), per REHNQUIST, C.J., held that the New Jersey accommodations law violated the expressive association rights of the Boy Scouts: "To determine whether a group is protected by the First Amendment's expressive associational right, we must determine whether the group engages in 'expressive association.' The First Amendment's protection of expressive association is not reserved for advocacy groups. But to come within its ambit, a group must engage in some form of expression, whether it be public or private.

"Because this is a First Amendment case where the ultimate conclusions of law are virtually inseparable from findings of fact, we are obligated to independently review the factual record to ensure that the state court's judgment does not unlawfully intrude on free expression. The record reveals the following. The Boy Scouts is a private, nonprofit organization. According to its mission statement:

"It is the mission of the Boy Scouts of America to serve others by helping to instill values in young people and, in other ways, to prepare them to make ethical choices over their lifetime in achieving their full potential.

"The values we strive to instill are based on those found in the Scout Oath and Law"

Rehnquist, C.J., cited a portion of the Scout Oath requiring Scouts to be "morally straight" and a portion of Scout law requiring Scouts to be "Clean": "Thus, the general mission of the Boy Scouts is clear: '[T]o instill values in young people.' The Boy Scouts seeks to instill these values by having its adult leaders spend time with the youth members, instructing and engaging them in activities like camping, archery, and fishing. During the time spent with the youth members, the scoutmasters and assistant scoutmasters inculcate them with the Boy Scouts' values—both expressly and by example. It seems indisputable that an association that seeks to transmit such a system of values engages in expressive activity. * * *

"Obviously, the Scout Oath and Law do not expressly mention sexuality or sexual orientation. And the terms 'morally straight' and 'clean' are by no means self-defining. Different people would attribute to those terms very different meanings. For example, some people may believe that engaging in homosexual conduct is not at odds with being 'morally straight' and 'clean.' And others may believe that engaging in homosexual conduct is contrary to being 'morally straight' and 'clean.' The Boy Scouts says it falls within the latter category.

"The Boy Scouts asserts that it 'teach[es] that homosexual conduct is not morally straight,' Brief for Petitioners 39, and that it does 'not want to promote homosexual conduct as a legitimate form of behavior,' Reply Brief for Petitioners 5. We accept the Boy Scouts' assertion. We need not inquire further to determine the nature of the Boy Scouts' expression with respect to homosexuality. But because the record before us contains written evidence of the Boy Scouts' viewpoint, we look to it as instructive, if only on the question of the sincerity of the professed beliefs."

Rehnquist, C.J., recounted a 1978 position statement to the Boy Scouts' Executive Committee, signed by the President of the Boy Scouts and the Chief Scout Executive, expressing the 'official position' that openly declared homosexuals could not be Scout leaders, a 1991 public position statement (issued after Dale's membership revocation, but before the litigation) asserting that homosexual conduct was inconsistent with being morally straight and clean, a 1993 public position statement maintaining that homosexual role models did not reflect the expectations that scouting families have had for the organization, and the Scouts' participation in litigation throughout the 80's and the 90's defending its position in litigation: "We cannot doubt that the Boy Scouts sincerely holds this view. We must then determine whether Dale's presence as an assistant scoutmaster would significantly burden the Boy Scouts' desire to not 'promote homosexual conduct as a legitimate form of behavior.' As we give deference to an association's assertions regarding the nature of its expression, we must also give deference to an association's view of what would impair its expression. [That] is not to say that an expressive association can erect a shield against antidiscrimination laws simply by asserting that mere acceptance of a member from a particular group would impair its message. But here Dale, by his own admission, is one of a group of gay Scouts who have 'become leaders in their community and are open and honest about their sexual orientation.' Dale was the copresident of a gay and lesbian organization at college and remains a gay rights activist. Dale's presence in the Boy Scouts would, at the very least, force the organization to send a message, both to the youth members and the world, that the Boy Scouts accepts homosexual conduct as a legitimate form of behavior. * * *

"*Hurley* is illustrative on this point. There we considered whether the application of Massachusetts' public accommodations law to require the organizers of a private St. Patrick's Day parade to include among the marchers an Irish—American gay, lesbian, and bisexual group, GLIB, violated the parade organizers' First Amendment rights. We noted that the parade organizers did not wish to exclude the GLIB members because of their sexual orientations, but because they wanted to march behind a GLIB banner. We observed:

> '[A] contingent marching behind the organization's banner would at least bear witness to the fact that some Irish are gay, lesbian, or bisexual, and the presence of the organized marchers would suggest their view that people of their sexual orientations have as much claim to unqualified social acceptance as heterosexuals. * * * The parade's organizers may not believe these facts about Irish sexuality to be so, or they may object to unqualified social acceptance of gays and lesbians or have some other reason for wishing to keep GLIB's message out of the parade. But whatever the reason, it boils down to the choice of a speaker not to propound a particular point of view, and that choice is presumed to lie beyond the government's power to control.'

"Here, we have found that the Boy Scouts believes that homosexual conduct is inconsistent with the values it seeks to instill in its youth members; it will not 'promote homosexual conduct as a legitimate form of behavior.' Reply Brief for Petitioners 5. As the presence of GLIB in Boston's St. Patrick's Day parade would have interfered with the parade organizers' choice not to propound a particular point of view, the presence of Dale as an assistant scoutmaster would just as surely interfere with the Boy Scout's choice not to propound a point of view contrary to its beliefs.

"[A]ssociations do not have to associate for the 'purpose' of disseminating a certain message in order to be entitled to the protections of the First Amendment. An association must merely engage in expressive activity that could be impaired in order to be entitled to protection. For example, the purpose of the St. Patrick's Day parade in Hurley was not to espouse any views about sexual orientation, but we held that the parade organizers had a right to exclude certain participants nonetheless.

"[E]ven if the Boy Scouts discourages Scout leaders from disseminating views on sexual issues—a fact that the Boy Scouts disputes with contrary evidence—the First Amendment protects the Boy Scouts' method of expression. If the Boy Scouts wishes Scout leaders to avoid questions of sexuality and teach only by example, this fact does not negate the sincerity of its belief discussed above. * * *

"Dale makes much of the claim that the Boy Scouts does not revoke the membership of heterosexual Scout leaders that openly disagree with the Boy

Scouts' policy on sexual orientation. But if this is true, it is irrelevant. The presence of an avowed homosexual and gay rights activist in an assistant scoutmaster's uniform sends a distinctly different message from the presence of a heterosexual assistant scoutmaster who is on record as disagreeing with Boy Scouts policy. The Boy Scouts has a First Amendment right to choose to send one message but not the other. The fact that the organization does not trumpet its views from the housetops, or that it tolerates dissent within its ranks, does not mean that its views receive no First Amendment protection. * * *

"We recognized in cases such as *Roberts* and *Duarte* that States have a compelling interest in eliminating discrimination against women in public accommodations. But in each of these cases we went on to conclude that the enforcement of these statutes would not materially interfere with the ideas that the organization sought to express. * * *

"Dale contends that we should apply the intermediate standard of review enunciated in *O'Brien* to evaluate the competing interests. [But] New Jersey's public accommodations law directly and immediately affects associational rights, in this case associational rights that enjoy First Amendment protection. Thus, *O'Brien* is inapplicable.

"In *Hurley*, we applied traditional First Amendment analysis to hold that the application of the Massachusetts public accommodations law to a parade violated the First Amendment rights of the parade organizers. Although we did not explicitly deem the parade in Hurley an expressive association, the analysis we applied there is similar to the analysis we apply here. We have already concluded that a state requirement that the Boy Scouts retain Dale as an assistant scoutmaster would significantly burden the organization's right to oppose or disfavor homosexual conduct. The state interests embodied in New Jersey's public accommodations law do not justify such a severe intrusion on the Boy Scouts' rights to freedom of expressive association. That being the case, we hold that the First Amendment prohibits the State from imposing such a requirement through the application of its public accommodations law."

STEVENS, J., joined by Souter, Ginsburg, and Breyer, J., dissenting, argued that nothing in the Scout Oath or Scout Law spoke of sexual orientation even in the definitions of morally straight and clean. Moreover, he observed that Scoutmasters are instructed not to instruct Scouts in any formalized manner regarding sex because it is not "Scouting's proper area" and they are advised to steer questions about sexual matters to spiritual leaders, family, or doctors, if possible, otherwise "you may just have to do the best you can." Stevens, J., observed that the 1978 statement (made before Dale entered scouting) was never distributed to the public and itself stated that termination of an individual because of homosexuality should ensue unless a law to the contrary existed. In that case the Scouts should obey the law. Stevens, J., added that statements issued in 1991 and a similar statement in 1992 about the relationship between homosexuality and morality and cleanliness was abandoned by the 1993 statement focusing on family expectations and could not ground an adequate claim of expressive association: "[E]ven during the brief period in 1991 and 1992, when BSA tried to connect its exclusion of homosexuals to its definition of terms found in the Oath and Law, there is no evidence that Scouts were actually taught anything about homosexuality's alleged inconsistency with those principles. Beyond the single sentence in these policy statements, there is no indication of any shared goal of teaching that homosexuality is incompatible with being 'morally straight' and 'clean.' Neither BSA's mission statement nor its official membership policy was altered; no Boy Scout or Scoutmaster Handbook was amended to reflect the policy statement; no lessons were imparted to Scouts; no change was made to BSA's policy on limiting discussion of sexual matters; and no effort was made to restrict acceptable religious affiliations to those that condemn homosexuality. In short, there is no evidence that this view was part of any collective effort to foster beliefs about homosexuality.

"[BSA] never took any clear and unequivocal position on homosexuality. Though the 1991 and 1992 policies state one interpretation of 'morally straight' and 'clean,' the group's published definitions appearing in the Boy Scout and Scoutmaster Handbooks take quite another view. And BSA's broad religious tolerance combined with its declaration that sexual matters are not its 'proper area' render its views on the issue equivocal at best and incoherent at worst. We have never held, however, that a group can throw together any mixture of contradictory positions and then invoke the right to associate to defend any one of those views. At a minimum, a group seeking to prevail over an antidiscrimination law must adhere to a clear and unequivocal view.

"[A]t most the 1991 and 1992 statements declare only that BSA believed 'homosexual conduct is inconsistent with the requirement in the Scout Oath that a Scout be morally straight and in the Scout Law that a Scout be clean in word and deed.' But New Jersey's law prohibits discrimination on the basis of sexual *orientation*. And when Dale was expelled from the Boy Scouts, BSA said it did so because of his sexual orientation, not because of his sexual conduct.

"It is clear, then, that nothing in these policy statements supports BSA's claim. The only policy written before the revocation of Dale's membership was an equivocal, undisclosed statement that evidences no connection between the group's discriminatory intentions and its expressive interests. The later policies demonstrate a brief—though ultimately abandoned— attempt to tie BSA's exclusion to its expression, but other than a single sentence, BSA fails to show that it ever taught Scouts that homosexuality is not 'morally straight' or 'clean,' or that such a view was part of the group's collective efforts to foster a belief. Furthermore, BSA's policy statements fail to establish any clear, consistent, and unequivocal position on homosexuality. Nor did BSA have any reason to think Dale's sexual conduct, as opposed to his orientation, was contrary to the group's values. * * *

"It speaks volumes about the credibility of BSA's claim to a shared goal that homosexuality is incompatible with Scouting that since at least 1984 it had been aware of this issue—indeed, concerned enough to twice file amicus briefs before this Court—yet it did nothing in the intervening six years (or even in the years after Dale's expulsion) to explain clearly and openly why the presence of homosexuals would affect its expressive activities, or to make the view of 'morally straight' and 'clean' taken in its 1991 and 1992 policies a part of the values actually instilled in Scouts through the Handbook, lessons, or otherwise.

"Several principles are made perfectly clear by *Jaycees* and *Rotary Club*. First, to prevail on a claim of expressive association in the face of a State's antidiscrimination law, it is not enough simply to engage in *some kind* of expressive activity. Both the Jaycees and the Rotary Club engaged in expressive activity protected by the First Amendment, yet that fact was not dispositive. Second, it is not enough to adopt an openly avowed exclusionary membership policy. Both the Jaycees and the Rotary Club did that as well. Third, it is not sufficient merely to articulate *some* connection between the group's expressive activities and its exclusionary policy. The Rotary Club, for example, justified its male-only membership policy by pointing to the 'aspect of fellowship ... that is enjoyed by the [exclusively] male membership' and by claiming that only with an exclusively male membership could it 'operate effectively' in foreign countries.

"Rather, in *Jaycees*, we asked whether Minnesota's Human Rights Law requiring the admission of women 'impose[d] any *serious burdens*' on the group's 'collective effort on behalf of [its] *shared goals*.' Notwithstanding the group's obvious publicly stated exclusionary policy, we did not view the inclusion of women as a 'serious burden' on the Jaycees' ability to engage in the protected speech of its choice. Similarly, in *Rotary Club*, we asked whether California's law would 'affect in any *significant* way the existing members' ability' to engage in their protected speech, or whether the law would require the clubs 'to abandon their basic goals.' * * *

"The evidence before this Court makes it exceptionally clear that BSA has, at most, simply adopted an exclusionary membership policy and has no shared goal of disapproving of homosexuality. BSA's mission statement and federal charter say nothing on the matter; its official membership policy is silent; its Scout Oath and Law—and accompanying definitions—are devoid of any view on the topic; its guidance for Scouts and Scoutmasters on sexuality declare that such matters are 'not construed to be Scouting's proper area,' but are the province of a Scout's parents and pastor; and BSA's posture respecting religion tolerates a wide variety of views on the issue of homosexuality. Moreover, there is simply no evidence that BSA otherwise teaches anything in this area, or that it instructs Scouts on matters involving homosexuality in ways not conveyed in the Boy Scout or Scoutmaster Handbooks. In short, Boy Scouts of America is simply silent on homosexuality. There is no shared goal or collective effort to foster a belief about homosexuality at all—let alone one that is significantly burdened by admitting homosexuals. * * *

"The majority pretermits this entire analysis. It finds that BSA in fact 'teach[es] that homosexual conduct is not morally straight.' 'This conclusion, remarkably, rests entirely on statements in BSA's briefs. Moreover, the majority insists that we must 'give deference to an association's assertions regarding the nature of its expression' and 'we must also give deference to an association's view of what would impair its expression.' So long as the record 'contains written evidence' to support a group's bare assertion, '[w]e need not inquire further.' Once the organization 'asserts' that it engages in particular expression, '[w]e cannot doubt' the truth of that assertion.

"This is an astounding view of the law. I am unaware of any previous instance in which our analysis of the scope of a constitutional right was determined by looking at what a litigant asserts in his or her brief and inquiring no further. It is even more astonishing in the First Amendment area, because, as the majority itself acknowledges, 'we are obligated to independently review the factual record.' It is an odd form of independent review that consists of deferring entirely to whatever a litigant claims. But the majority insists that our inquiry must be 'limited' because 'it is not the role of the courts to reject a group's expressed values because they disagree with those values or find them internally inconsistent.'

"But nothing in our cases calls for this Court to do any such thing. An organization can adopt the message of its choice, and it is not this Court's place to disagree with it. But we must inquire whether the group is, in fact, expressing a message (whatever it may be) and whether that message (if one is expressed) is significantly affected by a State's antidiscrimination law. More critically, that inquiry requires our *independent* analysis, rather than deference to a group's litigating posture. Reflection on the subject dictates that such an inquiry is required. * * *

"If this Court were to defer to whatever position an organization is prepared to assert in its briefs, there would be no way to mark the proper boundary between genuine exercises of the right to associate, on the one hand, and sham claims that are simply attempts to insulate nonexpressive private discrimination, on the other hand. Shielding a litigant's claim from judicial scrutiny would, in turn, render civil rights legislation a nullity, and turn this important constitutional right into a farce. Accordingly, the Court's prescription of total deference will not do. * * *

"In its briefs, BSA implies, even if it does not directly argue, that Dale would use his Scoutmaster position as a 'bully pulpit' to convey immoral messages to his troop, and therefore his inclusion in the group would compel BSA to include a message it does not want to impart. Even though the majority does not endorse that argument, I think it is important to explain why it lacks merit, before considering the argument the majority does accept. BSA has not contended, nor does the record support, that Dale had ever advocated a view on homosexuality to his troop before his membership was revoked. Accordingly, BSA's revocation could only have been based on an assumption that he would do so in the future. * * *

"But there is no basis for BSA to presume that a homosexual will be unable to comply with BSA's policy not to discuss sexual matters any more than it would presume that politically or religiously active members could not resist the urge to proselytize or politicize during troop meetings. As BSA itself puts it, its rights are 'not implicated unless a prospective leader presents himself as a role model inconsistent with Boy Scouting's understanding of the Scout Oath and Law.'

"The majority, though, does not rest its conclusion on the claim that Dale will use his position as a bully pulpit. Rather, it contends that Dale's mere presence among the Boy Scouts will itself force the group to convey a message about homosexuality—even if Dale has no intention of doing so. The majority holds that '[t]he presence of an avowed homosexual and gay rights activist in an assistant scoutmaster's uniform sends a distinc[t] . . . message,' and, accordingly, BSA is entitled to exclude that message. In particular, 'Dale's presence in the Boy Scouts would, at the very least, force the organization to send a message, both to the youth members and the world, that the Boy Scouts accepts homosexual conduct as a legitimate form of behavior.'

"The majority's argument relies exclusively on *Hurley*. [Though] *Hurley* has a superficial similarity to the present case, a close inspection reveals a wide gulf between that case and the one before us today.

"First, it was critical to our analysis that GLIB was actually conveying a message by participating in the parade—otherwise, the parade organizers could hardly claim that they were being forced to include any unwanted message at all. Our conclusion that GLIB was conveying a message was inextricably tied to the fact that GLIB wanted to march in a parade, as well as the manner in which it intended to march. * * * Indeed, we expressly distinguished between the members of GLIB, who marched as a unit to express their views about their own sexual orientation, on the one hand, and homosexuals who might participate as individuals in the parade without intending to express anything about their sexuality by doing so.

"Second, we found it relevant that GLIB's message 'would likely be perceived' as the parade organizers' own speech. That was so because '[p]arades and demonstrations * * * are not understood to be so neutrally presented or selectively viewed' as, say, a broadcast by a cable operator, who is usually considered to be 'merely "a conduit" for the speech' produced by others. Rather, parade organizers are usually understood to make the 'customary determination about a unit admitted to the parade.'

"Dale's inclusion in the Boy Scouts is nothing like the case in *Hurley*. His participation sends no cognizable message to the Scouts or to the world. Unlike GLIB, Dale did not carry a banner or a sign; he did not distribute any fact sheet; and he expressed no intent to send any message. If there is any kind of message being sent, then, it is by the mere act of joining the Boy Scouts. Such an act does not constitute an instance of symbolic speech under the First Amendment.

"It is true, of course, that some acts are so imbued with symbolic meaning that they qualify as 'speech' under the First Amendment. At the same time, however, '[w]e cannot accept the view that an apparently limitless variety of conduct can be labeled 'speech' whenever the person engaging in the conduct intends thereby to express an idea.' *O'Brien*. [Indeed], if merely joining a group did constitute symbolic speech; and such speech were attributable to the group being joined; and that group has the right to exclude that speech (and hence, the right to exclude that person from joining), then the right of free speech effectively becomes a limitless right to exclude for every organization, whether or not it engages in any expressive activities. That cannot be, and never has been, the law.

"The only apparent explanation for the majority's holding, then, is that homosexuals are simply so different from the rest of society that their presence alone—unlike any other individual's—should be singled out for special First Amendment treatment. Under the majority's reasoning, an openly gay male is irreversibly affixed with the label 'homosexual.' That label, even though unseen, communicates a message that permits his exclusion wherever he goes. His openness is the sole and sufficient justification for his ostracism. Though unintended, reliance on such a justification is tantamount to a constitutionally prescribed symbol of inferiority. As counsel for the Boy Scouts remarked, Dale 'put a banner around his neck when he * * * got himself into the newspaper * * * He created a reputation. * * * He can't take that banner off. He put it on himself and, indeed, he has continued to put it on himself.'

"Another difference between this case and *Hurley* lies in the fact that *Hurley* involved the parade organizers' claim to determine the content of the message they wish to give at a particular time and place. The standards governing such a claim are simply different from the standards that govern BSA's claim of a right of expressive association. Generally, a private person or a private organization has a right to refuse to broadcast a message with which it disagrees, and a right to refuse to contradict or garble its own specific statement at any given place or time by including the messages of others. An expressive association claim, however, normally involves the avowal and advocacy of a consistent position on some issue over time. This is why a different kind of scrutiny must be given to an expressive association claim, lest the right of expressive association simply turn into a right to discriminate whenever some group can think of an expressive object that would seem to be inconsistent with the admission of some person as a member or at odds with the appointment of a person to a leadership position in the group."[a]

a. Souter, J., joined by Ginsburg, J., and Breyer, J., also dissented.

IV. POLITICAL ASSOCIATION AND POLITICAL PARTIES

Minnesota's "antifusion" laws prohibit political candidates from appearing on the ballot as candidates for more than one party. Twin Cities Area New Party ("New Party") named a candidate for state representative, Andy Dawkins, who also was a candidate of the Minnesota–Democratic–Farmer–Labor Party ("DFL"). Dawkins signed an affidavit for the New Party, but local election officials refused to accept it since his affidavit of candidacy for DFL had already been filed.[a] The New Party brought suit maintaining that the antifusion laws violated the party's rights of association.

TIMMONS v. TWIN CITIES AREA NEW PARTY, 520 U.S. 351, 117 S.Ct. 1364, 137 L.Ed.2d 589 (1997), per REHNQUIST, C.J., upheld the antifusion laws: "The First Amendment protects the right of citizens to associate and to form political parties for the advancement of common political goals and ideas. * * * [On] the other hand, it is also clear that States may, and inevitably must, enact reasonable regulations of parties, elections, and ballots to reduce election-and campaign-related disorder. * * * When deciding whether a state election law violates First and Fourteenth Amendment associational rights, we weigh the 'character and magnitude' of the burden the State's rule imposes on those rights against the interests the State contends justify that burden, and consider the extent to which the State's concerns make the burden necessary. Regulations imposing severe burdens on plaintiffs' rights must be narrowly tailored and advance a compelling state interest. Lesser burdens, however, trigger less exacting review, and a State's 'important regulatory interests' will usually be enough to justify 'reasonable, nondiscriminatory restrictions.' No bright line separates permissible election-related regulation from unconstitutional infringements on First Amendment freedoms.

"The New Party's claim that it has a right to select its own candidate is uncontroversial, so far as it goes. That is, the New Party, and not someone else, has the right to select the New Party's 'standard bearer.' It does not follow, though, that a party is absolutely entitled to have its nominee appear on the ballot as that party's candidate. A particular candidate might be ineligible for office, unwilling to serve, or, as here, another party's candidate. That a particular individual may not appear on the ballot as a particular party's candidate does not severely burden that party's association rights.

"The New Party relies on *Eu v. San Francisco County Democratic Central Comm.*, 489 U.S. 214, 109 S.Ct. 1013, 103 L.Ed.2d 271 (1989)[b] and *Tashjian v. Republican Party of Conn.*, 479 U.S. 208, 107 S.Ct. 544, 93

---

a. The DFL did not object.

b. For commentary, see Lowenstein, *Associational Rights of Major Political Par-*

ties: A Skeptical Inquiry, 71 Tex. L.Rev. 1741 (1993).

L.Ed.2d 514 (1986). In *Eu,* we struck down California election provisions that prohibited political parties from endorsing candidates in party primaries and regulated parties' internal affairs and structure. And in *Tashjian,* we held that Connecticut's closed-primary statute, which required voters in a party primary to be registered party members, interfered with a party's associational rights by limiting 'the group of registered voters whom the Party may invite to participate in the basic function of selecting the Party's candidates.'[c] But while *Tashjian* and *Eu* involved regulation of political parties' internal affairs and core associational activities,[d] Minnesota's fusion ban does not. The ban, which applies to major and minor parties alike, simply precludes one party's candidate from appearing on the ballot, as that party's candidate, if already nominated by another party. Respondent is free to try to convince Representative Dawkins to be the New Party's, not the DFL's, candidate. * * *

"The New Party contends that the fusion ban burdens its 'right . . . to communicate its choice of nominees on the ballot on terms equal to those offered other parties, and the right of the party's supporters and other voters to receive that information,' and insists that communication on the ballot of a party's candidate choice is a 'critical source of information for the great majority of voters [who] rely upon party "labels" as a voting guide.'

"It is true that Minnesota's fusion ban prevents the New Party from using the ballot to communicate to the public that it supports a particular candidate who is already another party's candidate. In addition, the ban shuts off one possible avenue a party might use to send a message to its preferred *candidate* because, with fusion, a candidate who wins an election on the basis of two parties' votes will likely know more—if the parties' votes are counted separately—about the particular wishes and ideals of his constituency. We are unpersuaded, however, by the Party's contention that it has a right to use the ballot itself to send a particularized message, to its candidate and to the voters, about the nature of its support for the candidate. Ballots serve primarily to elect candidates, not as fora for political expression. Like all parties in Minnesota, the New Party is able to use the ballot to communicate information about itself and its candidate to the voters, so long as that candidate is not already someone else's candidate. * * *

"In sum, Minnesota's laws do not restrict the ability of the New Party and its members to endorse, support, or vote for anyone they like. The laws do not directly limit the Party's access to the ballot. They are silent on parties' internal structure, governance, and policy-making. Instead, these

---

c. *California Democratic Party v. Jones,* 530 U.S. 567, 120 S.Ct. 2402, 147 L.Ed.2d 502 (2000) invalidated California's "blanket primary" which required parties to permit citizens to vote in the primary of any party for any office regardless of their party membership.

d. But see *Morse v. Republican Party of Virginia,* 517 U.S. 186, 116 S.Ct. 1186, 134

L.Ed.2d 347 (1996)(requiring preclearance by Attorney General for fee requirement to become a delegate to a state nominating convention under the Voting Rights Act does not violate freedom of association rights).

provisions reduce the universe of potential candidates who may appear on the ballot as the Party's nominee only by ruling out those few individuals who both have already agreed to be another party's candidate and also, if forced to choose, themselves prefer that other party. They also limit, slightly, the Party's ability to send a message to the voters and to its preferred candidates. We conclude that the burdens Minnesota imposes on the Party's First and Fourteenth Amendment associational rights—though not trivial—are not severe.

"[Therefore,] the State's asserted regulatory interests need only be 'sufficiently weighty to justify the limitation' imposed on the Party's rights. Nor do we require elaborate, empirical verification of the weightiness of the State's asserted justifications. * * *

"Minnesota argues here that its fusion ban is justified by its interests in avoiding voter confusion, promoting candidate competition (by reserving limited ballot space for opposing candidates), preventing electoral distortions and ballot manipulations, and discouraging party splintering and 'unrestrained factionalism.' States certainly have an interest in protecting the integrity, fairness, and efficiency of their ballots and election processes as means for electing public officials. Petitioners contend that a candidate or party could easily exploit fusion as a way of associating his or its name with popular slogans and catch phrases. For example, members of a major party could decide that a powerful way of 'sending a message' via the ballot would be for various factions of that party to nominate the major party's candidate as the candidate for the newly-formed 'No New Taxes,' 'Conserve Our Environment,' and 'Stop Crime Now' parties. In response, an opposing major party would likely instruct its factions to nominate that party's candidate as the 'Fiscal Responsibility,' 'Healthy Planet,' and 'Safe Streets' parties' candidate.

"Whether or not the putative 'fusion' candidates' names appeared on one or four ballot lines, such maneuvering would undermine the ballot's purpose by transforming it from a means of choosing candidates to a billboard for political advertising. The New Party responds to this concern, ironically enough, by insisting that the State could avoid such manipulation by adopting more demanding ballot-access standards rather than prohibiting multiple-party nomination. However, [because] the burdens the fusion ban imposes on the Party's associational rights are not severe, the State need not narrowly tailor the means it chooses to promote ballot integrity. The Constitution does not require that Minnesota compromise the policy choices embodied in its ballot-access requirements to accommodate the New Party's fusion strategy.

"Relatedly, petitioners urge that permitting fusion would undercut Minnesota's ballot-access regime by allowing minor parties to capitalize on the popularity of another party's candidate, rather than on their own appeal to the voters, in order to secure access to the ballot. That is, voters who might not sign a minor party's nominating petition based on the party's own views and candidates might do so if they viewed the minor party as just another way of nominating the same person nominated by one of the major parties. * * * The State surely has a valid interest in making sure that minor and third parties who are granted access to the ballot are bona fide and actually supported, on their own merits, by those who have provided the statutorily required petition or ballot support.

"States also have a strong interest in the stability of their political systems.[10] This interest does not permit a State to completely insulate the two-party system from minor parties' or independent candidates' competition and influence, nor is it a paternalistic license for States to protect political parties from the consequences of their own internal disagreements. That said, the States' interest permits them to enact reasonable election regulations that may, in practice, favor the traditional two-party system, and that temper the destabilizing effects of party-splintering and excessive factionalism. The Constitution permits the Minnesota Legislature to decide that political stability is best served through a healthy two-party system. And while an interest in securing the perceived benefits of a stable two-party system will not justify unreasonably exclusionary restrictions, States need not remove all of the many hurdles third parties face in the American political arena today.

"In *Storer v. Brown,* 415 U.S. 724, 94 S.Ct. 1274, 39 L.Ed.2d 714 (1974), we upheld a California statute that denied ballot positions to independent candidates who had voted in the immediately preceding primary elections or had a registered party affiliation at any time during the year before the same primary elections.[11] After surveying the relevant caselaw, we 'ha[d] no hesitation in sustaining' the party-disaffiliation provisions. We recognized that the provisions were part of a 'general state policy aimed at maintaining the integrity of [the] ballot,' and noted that the provision did not discriminate against independent candidates. We concluded that while a 'State need not take the course California [has], California apparently believes with the Founding Fathers that splintered parties and unrestrained factionalism may do significant damage to the fabric of government. It appears obvious to us that the one-year disaffiliation provision furthers the State's interest in the stability of its political system.'[12]

10. The dissents state that we may not consider "what appears to be the true basis for [our] holding—the interest in preserving the two-party system," because Minnesota did not defend this interest in its briefs and "expressly rejected" it at oral argument. In fact, at oral argument, the State contended that it has an interest in the stability of its political system and that, even if certain election-related regulations, such as those requiring single-member districts, tend to work to the advantage of the traditional two-party system, the "States do have a permissible choice [there], as long as they don't go so far as to close the door to minor part[ies]." We agree.

11. A similar provision applied to party candidates, and imposed a "flat disqualification upon any candidate seeking to run in a party primary if he has been 'registered as affiliated with a political party other than that political party the nomination of which he seeks within 12 months immediately prior to the filing of the declaration.' " Another provision stated that "no person may file nomination papers for a party nomination and an independent nomination for the same office * * *."

12. The dissent insists that New York's experience with fusion politics undermines Minnesota's contention that its fusion ban promotes political stability. California's ex-

"Our decision in *Burdick v. Takushi,* 504 U.S. 428, 112 S.Ct. 2059, 119 L.Ed.2d 245 (1992) is also relevant. There, we upheld Hawaii's ban on write-in voting against a claim that the ban unreasonably infringed on citizens' First and Fourteenth Amendment rights. In so holding, we rejected the petitioner's argument that the ban 'deprive[d] him of the opportunity to cast a meaningful ballot,' emphasizing that the function of elections is to elect candidates and that 'we have repeatedly upheld reasonable, politically neutral regulations that have the effect of channeling expressive activit[ies] at the polls.'

"Minnesota's fusion ban is far less burdensome than the disaffiliation rule upheld in *Storer,* and is justified by similarly weighty state interests. By reading *Storer* as dealing only with 'sore-loser candidates,' the dissent, in our view, fails to appreciate the case's teaching. Under the California disaffiliation statute at issue in *Storer, any* person affiliated with a party at any time during the year leading up to the primary election was absolutely precluded from appearing on the ballot as an independent or as the candidate of another party. Minnesota's fusion ban is not nearly so restrictive; the challenged provisions say nothing about the previous party affiliation of would-be candidates but only require that, in order to appear on the ballot, a candidate not be the nominee of more than one party. California's disaffiliation rule limited the field of candidates by thousands; Minnesota's precludes only a handful who freely choose to be so limited. It is also worth noting that while California's disaffiliation statute absolutely banned many candidacies, Minnesota's fusion ban only prohibits a candidate from being named twice.

"We conclude that the burdens Minnesota's fusion ban imposes on the New Party's associational rights are justified by 'correspondingly weighty' valid state interests in ballot integrity and political stability.[13] In deciding that Minnesota's fusion ban does not unconstitutionally burden the New Party's First and Fourteenth Amendment rights, we express no views on the New Party's policy-based arguments concerning the wisdom of fusion. It may well be that, as support for new political parties increase, these arguments will carry the day in some States' legislatures. But the Constitution does not require Minnesota, and the approximately 40 other States that do not permit fusion, to allow it."[e]

periment with cross-filing, on the other hand, provides some justification for Minnesota's concerns. In 1946, for example, Earl Warren was the nominee of both major parties, and was therefore able to run unopposed in California's general election. It appears to be widely accepted that California's cross-filing system stifled electoral competition and undermined the role of distinctive political parties.

13. The dissent rejects the argument that Minnesota's fusion ban serves its alleged paternalistic interest in "avoiding voter confusion." Although this supposed interest was discussed below, and in the parties' briefs before this Court, it plays no part in our analysis today.

e. For relevant commentary, see Pope, *Fusion, Timmons v. Twin Cities Area New Party, and the Future of Third Parties in the United States,* 50 Rutgers. L.Rev. 473 (1998); Note, *Fusion Candidacies, Disaggregation, and Freedom of Association,* 109 Harv. L.Rev. 1302 (1996); Note, *Fusion and the Associational Rights of Minor Political Parties,* 95 Colum. L.Rev. 683 (1995).

STEVENS, J., joined in part by Ginsburg and Souter, JJ., dissented: "The Court's conclusion that the Minnesota statute prohibiting multiple-party candidacies is constitutional rests on three dubious premises: (1) that the statute imposes only a minor burden on the Party's right to choose and to support the candidate of its choice; (2) that the statute significantly serves the State's asserted interests in avoiding ballot manipulation and factionalism; and (3) that, in any event, the interest in preserving the two-party system justifies the imposition of the burden at issue in this case. I disagree with each of these premises. * * *

"The members of a recognized political party unquestionably have a constitutional right to select their nominees for public office and to communicate the identity of their nominees to the voting public. Both the right to choose and the right to advise voters of that choice are entitled to the highest respect.

"The Minnesota statutes place a significant burden on both of those rights. The Court's recital of burdens that the statute does not inflict on the Party does nothing to minimize the severity of the burdens that it does impose. The fact that the Party may nominate its second choice surely does not diminish the significance of a restriction that denies it the right to have the name of its first choice appear on the ballot. Nor does the point that it may use some of its limited resources to publicize the fact that its first choice is the nominee of some other party provide an adequate substitute for the message that is conveyed to every person who actually votes when a party's nominees appear on the ballot.[1] [T]he right to be on the election ballot is precisely what separates a political party from any other interest group.

"The majority rejects as unimportant the limits that the fusion ban may impose on the Party's ability to express its political views, relying on our decision in *Burdick v. Takushi,* in which we noted that 'the purpose of casting, counting, and recording votes is to elect public officials, not to serve as a general forum for political expression.' But in *Burdick* we concluded simply that an individual voter's interest in expressing his disapproval of the single candidate running for office in a particular election did not require the State to finance and provide a mechanism for tabulating write-in votes. Our conclusion that the ballot is not principally a forum for the individual expression of political sentiment through the casting of a vote does not justify the conclusion that the ballot serves no expressive purpose for the

---

1. The burden on the Party's right to nominate its first-choice candidate, by limiting the Party's ability to convey through its nominee what the Party represents, risks impinging on another core element of any political party's associational rights—the right to "broaden the base of public participation in and support for its activities." A fusion ban burdens the right of a minor party to broaden its base of support because of the political reality that the dominance of the major parties frequently makes a vote for a minor party or independent candidate a "wasted" vote. When minor parties can nominate a candidate also nominated by a major party, they are able to present their members with an opportunity to cast a vote for a candidate who will actually be elected. Although this aspect of a party's effort to broaden support is distinct from the ability to nominate the candidate who best represents the party's views, it is important to note that the party's right to broaden the base of its support is burdened in both ways by the fusion ban.

parties who place candidates on the ballot. Indeed, the long-recognized right to choose a 'standard bearer who best represents the party's ideologies and preferences,' *Eu*, is inescapably an expressive right. 'To the extent that party labels provide a shorthand designation of the views of party candidates on matters of public concern, the identification of candidates with particular parties plays a role in the process by which voters inform themselves for the exercise of the franchise.' *Tashjian v. Republican Party of Conn.*

"In this case, and presumably in most cases, the burden of a statute of this kind is imposed upon the members of a minor party, but its potential impact is much broader. Popular candidates like Andy Dawkins sometimes receive nation-wide recognition. Fiorello LaGuardia, Earl Warren, Ronald Reagan, and Franklin D. Roosevelt, are names that come readily to mind as candidates whose reputations and political careers were enhanced because they appeared on election ballots as fusion candidates. A statute that denied a political party the right to nominate any of those individuals for high office simply because he had already been nominated by another party would, in my opinion, place an intolerable burden on political expression and association.

"[E]ven accepting the majority's view that the burdens imposed by the law are not weighty, the State's asserted interests must at least bear some plausible relationship to the burdens it places on political parties. Although the Court today suggests that the State does not have to support its asserted justifications for the fusion ban with evidence that they have any empirical validity, we have previously required more than a bare assertion that some particular state interest is served by a burdensome election requirement.

"While the State describes some imaginative theoretical sources of voter confusion that could result from fusion candidacies, in my judgment the argument that the burden on First Amendment interests is justified by this concern is meritless and severely underestimates the intelligence of the typical voter. We have noted more than once that '[a] State's claim that it is enhancing the ability of its citizenry to make wise decisions by restricting the flow of information to them must be viewed with some skepticism.' *Eu*; *Tashjian.*

"The State's concern about ballot manipulation, readily accepted by the majority, is similarly farfetched. The possibility that members of the major parties will begin to create dozens of minor parties with detailed, issue-oriented titles for the sole purpose of nominating candidates under those titles is entirely hypothetical.[3] The majority dismisses out-of-hand the

---

3. [T]he parade of horribles that the majority appears to believe might visit Minnesota should fusion candidacies be allowed is fantastical, given the evidence from New York's experience with fusion. Thus, the evidence that actually is available diminishes, rather than strengthens, Minne- sota's claims. The majority asserts that California's cross-filing system, in place during the first half of this century, provides a compelling counter-example. But cross-filing, which "allowed candidates to file in the primary of any or all parties without specifying party affiliation." D. Mazmanian,

Party's argument that the risk of this type of ballot manipulation and crowding is more easily averted by maintaining reasonably stringent requirements for the creation of minor parties. In fact, though, the Party's point merely illustrates the idea that a State can place some kinds—but not every kind—of limitation on the abilities of small parties to thrive. If the State wants to make it more difficult for any group to achieve the legal status of being a political party, it can do so within reason and still not run up against the First Amendment. 'The State has the undoubted right to require candidates to make a preliminary showing of substantial support in order to qualify for a place on the ballot, because it is both wasteful and confusing to encumber the ballot with the names of frivolous candidates.' *Anderson,* 460 U.S., at 788–789, n. 9, 103 S.Ct., at 1570, n. 9. See also *Jenness v. Fortson,* 403 U.S. 431, 442, 91 S.Ct. 1970, 1976, 29 L.Ed.2d 554 (1971). But once the State has established a standard for achieving party status, forbidding an acknowledged party from putting on the ballot its chosen candidate clearly frustrates core associational rights.[5]

"The State argues that the fusion ban promotes political stability by preventing intra-party factionalism and party raiding. States do certainly have an interest in maintaining a stable political system. But the State has not convincingly articulated how the fusion ban will prevent the factionalism it fears. Unlike the law at issue in *Storer v. Brown,* for example, this law would not prevent sore-loser candidates from defecting with a disaffected segment of a major party and running as an opposition candidate for a newly formed minor party. Nor does this law, like those aimed at requiring parties to show a modicum of support in order to secure a place on the election ballot, prevent the formation of numerous small parties. Indeed, the activity banned by Minnesota's law is the formation of coalitions, not the division and dissension of 'splintered parties and unrestrained factionalism' * * *

"[The interest in preserving the two-party system is not] sufficient to justify the fusion ban.[e] In most States, perhaps in all, there are two and only two major political parties. It is not surprising, therefore, that most States have enacted election laws that impose burdens on the development and growth of third parties. The law at issue in this case is undeniably such a law. The fact that the law was both intended to disadvantage minor parties

Third Parties in Presidential Elections 132–133 (1974) is simply not the same as fusion politics, and the problems suffered in California do not provide empirical support for Minnesota's position.

5. A second "ballot manipulation" argument accepted by the majority is that minor parties will attempt to "capitalize on the popularity of another party's candidate, rather than on their own appeal to the voters, in order to secure access to the ballot." What the majority appears unwilling to accept is that *Andy Dawkins was the*

New Party's chosen candidate. The Party was not trying to capitalize on his status as someone else's candidate, but to identify him as their own choice.

e. Stevens, J., maintained that the majority should not have considered the interest in maintaining the two-party system because it was not argued in the briefs and was rejected by the state at oral arguments. Ginsburg and Souter, JJ., did not join the section of Stevens, J.'s opinion about the two-party system.

and has had that effect is a matter that should weigh against, rather than in favor of, its constitutionality.

"Our jurisprudence in this area reflects a certain tension: on the one hand, we have been clear that political stability is an important state interest and that incidental burdens on the formation of minor parties are reasonable to protect that interest, see *Storer;* on the other, we have struck down state elections laws specifically because they give 'the two old, established parties a decided advantage over any new parties struggling for existence,' *Williams v. Rhodes,* 393 U.S. 23, 89 S.Ct. 5, 21 L.Ed.2d 24 (1968).[7] * * *[f]

"Nothing in the Constitution prohibits the States from maintaining single-member districts with winner-take-all voting arrangements. And these elements of an election system do make it significantly more difficult for third parties to thrive. But these laws are different in two respects from the fusion bans at issue here. First, the method by which they hamper third-party development is not one that impinges on the associational rights of those third parties; minor parties remain free to nominate candidates of their choice, and to rally support for those candidates. The small parties' relatively limited likelihood of ultimate success on election day does not deprive them of the right to try. Second, the establishment of single-member districts correlates directly with the States' interests in political stability. Systems of proportional representation, for example, may tend toward factionalism and fragile coalitions that diminish legislative effectiveness. In the context of fusion candidacies, the risks to political stability are extremely attenuated.[8] Of course, the reason minor parties so ardently support fusion politics is because it allows the parties to build up a greater base of support, as potential minor party members realize that a vote for the smaller party candidate is not necessarily a 'wasted' vote. Eventually, a minor party might gather sufficient strength that—were its members so inclined—it could successfully run a candidate not endorsed by any major party, and legislative coalition-building will be made more difficult by the presence of third party legislators. But the risks to political stability in that scenario are speculative at best. * * *

---

7. In *Anderson v. Celebrezze,* 460 U.S. 780, 103 S.Ct. 1564, 75 L.Ed.2d 547 (1983) the State argued that its interest in political stability justified the early filing deadline for presidential candidates at issue in the case. We recognized that the 'asserted interest in political stability amounts to a desire to protect existing political parties from competition,' and rejected that interest.

f. *Williams* dealt with ballot access requirements making it virtually impossible for new political parties, even ones with hundreds of thousands of members, to gain access to the ballot. In Presidential elections, for example, Ohio had required new

parties to submit petitions totaling 15% of the number of ballots cast in the prior gubernatorial election. (Most states require less than 1% of the ballots cast). The result was to confine the ballot to the two major parties. The Court struck down the statute on equal protection grounds: "There is, of course, no reason why two parties should retain a permanent monopoly on the right to have people vote for or against them."

8. Even in a system that allows fusion, a candidate for election must assemble majority support, so the State's concern cannot logically be about risks to political stability in the particular election in which the fusion candidate is running.

"The strength of the two-party system—and of each of its major components—is the product of the power of the ideas, the traditions, the candidates, and the voters that constitute the parties. It demeans the strength of the two-party system to assume that the major parties need to rely on laws that discriminate against independent voters and minor parties in order to preserve their positions of power.[12] Indeed, it is a central theme of our jurisprudence that the entire electorate, which necessarily includes the members of the major parties, will benefit from robust competition in ideas and governmental policies that ' "is at the core of our electoral process and of the First Amendment freedoms." ' "

Souter, J., dissenting, was willing to "judge the challenged statutes only on the interests the State has raised in their defense and would hold them unconstitutional. [Surely] the majority is right that States 'have a strong interest in the stability of their political systems,' that is, in preserving a political system capable of governing effectively. If it could be shown that the disappearance of the two-party system would undermine that interest, and that permitting fusion candidacies poses a substantial threat to the two-party scheme, there might well be a sufficient predicate for recognizing the constitutionality of the state action presented by this case. Right now, however, no State has attempted even to make this argument, and I would therefore leave its consideration for another day."

12. The experience in New York with fusion politics provides considerable evidence that neither political stability nor the ultimate strength of the two major parties is truly risked by the existence of successful minor parties.

Chapter 10

WEALTH AND THE POLITICAL PROCESS: CONCERNS FOR EQUALITY

The idea of equality has loomed large throughout this casebook. Some feel it should be a central concern of the first amendment. See Tribe, *Constitutional Choices* 188–220 (1985); Karst, *Equality as a Central Principle in the First Amendment,* 43 U.Chi.L.Rev. 20 (1975). Equality has been championed by those who seek access to government property and to media facilities. It has been invoked in support of content regulation and against it. This section considers government efforts to prevent the domination of the political process by wealthy individuals and business corporations. In the end, it would be appropriate to reconsider the arguments for and against a marketplace conception of the first amendment, to ask whether the Court's interpretations overall (e.g., taking the public forum materials, the media materials, and the election materials together) have adequately considered the interest in equality, and to inquire generally about the relationship between liberty and equality in the constitutional scheme.

BUCKLEY v. VALEO

424 U.S. 1, 96 S.Ct. 612, 46 L.Ed.2d 659 (1976).

Per Curiam.

[In this portion of a lengthy opinion dealing with the validity of the Federal Election Campaign Act of 1971, as amended in 1974, the Court considers those parts of the Act limiting *contributions* to a candidate for federal office (all sustained), and those parts limiting *expenditures* in support of such candidacy (all held invalid).]

A. *General Principles.* The Act's contribution and expenditure limitations operate in an area of the most fundamental First Amendment activities. Discussion of public issues and debate on the qualifications of candidates are integral to the operation of the system of government established by our Constitution.

[Appellees] contend that what the Act regulates is conduct, and that its effect on speech and association is incidental at most. Appellants respond that contributions and expenditures are at the very core of political speech, and that the Act's limitations thus constitute restraints on First Amendment liberty that are both gross and [direct.]

We cannot share the view [that] the present Act's contribution and expenditure limitations are comparable to the restrictions on conduct upheld in *O'Brien.* The expenditure of money simply cannot be equated with such conduct as destruction of a draft card. Some forms of communication made possible by the giving and spending of money involve speech alone, some involve conduct primarily, and some involve a combination of the two. Yet this Court has never suggested that the dependence of a communication on the expenditure of money operates itself to introduce a non-speech element or to reduce the exacting scrutiny required by the First Amendment. * * *

Even if the categorization of the expenditure of money as conduct were accepted, the limitations challenged here would not meet the *O'Brien* test because the governmental interests advanced in support of the Act involve "suppressing communication." The interests served by the Act include restricting the voices of people and interest groups who have money to spend and reducing the overall scope of federal election campaigns. [Unlike] *O'Brien,* where [the] interest in the preservation of draft cards was wholly unrelated to their use as a means of communication, it is beyond dispute that the interest in regulating the alleged "conduct" of giving or spending money "arises in some measure because the communication allegedly integral to the conduct is itself thought to be harmful."

Nor can the Act's contribution and expenditure limitations be sustained, as some of the parties suggest, by reference to the constitutional principles reflected in such decisions as *Cox v. Louisiana, Adderley,* and *Kovacs.* [The] critical difference between this case and those time, place and manner cases is that the present Act's contribution and expenditure limitations impose direct quantity restrictions on political communication and association by persons, groups, candidates and political parties in addition to any reasonable time, place, and manner regulations otherwise imposed.

A restriction on the amount of money a person or group can spend on political communication during a campaign necessarily reduces the quantity of expression by restricting the number of issues discussed, the depth of their exploration, and the size of the audience reached. This is because virtually every means of communicating ideas in today's mass society requires the expenditure of [money].

The expenditure limitations contained in the Act represent substantial rather than merely theoretical restraints on the quantity and diversity of political speech. The $1,000 ceiling on spending "relative to a clearly identified candidate," 18 U.S.C. § 608(e)(1), would appear to exclude all citizens and groups except candidates, political parties and the institutional press from any significant use of the most effective modes of communication.[20] * * *

By contrast with a limitation upon expenditures for political expression, a limitation [on] the amount of money a person may give to a candidate or campaign organization [involves] little direct restraint on his political communication, for it permits the symbolic expression of support evidenced by a contribution but does not in any way infringe the contributor's freedom to discuss candidates and issues. While contributions may result in political expression if spent by a candidate or an association to present views to the voters, the transformation of contributions into political debate involves speech by someone other than the contributor.

[There] is no indication [that] the contribution limitations imposed by the Act would have any dramatic adverse effect on the funding of campaigns and political associations.[23] The overall effect of the Act's contribution ceilings is merely to require candidates and political committees to raise funds from a greater number of persons and to compel people who would otherwise contribute amounts greater than the statutory limits to expend such funds on direct political expression, rather than to reduce the total amount of money potentially available to promote political expression. * * *

In sum, although the Act's contribution and expenditure limitations both implicate fundamental First Amendment interests, its expenditure ceilings impose significantly more severe restrictions on protected freedoms of political expression and association than do its limitations on financial contributions.

B. *Contribution Limitations.* [Section] 608(b) provides, with certain limited exceptions, that "no person shall make contributions to any candidate with respect to any election for Federal office which, in the aggregate, exceeds $1,000."[a] * * *

Appellants contend that the $1,000 contribution ceiling unjustifiably burdens First Amendment freedoms, employs overbroad dollar limits, and discriminates against candidates opposing incumbent officeholders and against minor-party candidates in violation of the Fifth Amendment.

20. The record indicates that, as of January 1, 1975, one full-page advertisement in a daily edition of a certain metropolitan newspaper costs $6,971.04—almost seven times the annual limit on expenditures "relative to" a particular candidate imposed on the vast majority of individual citizens and associations by § 608(e)(1).

23. Statistical findings agreed to by the parties reveal that approximately 5.1% of the $73,483,613 raised by the 1161 candidates for Congress in 1974 was obtained in amounts in excess of $1,000. In 1974, two major-party senatorial candidates, Ramsey Clark and Senator Charles Mathias, Jr., operated large-scale campaigns on contributions raised under a voluntarily imposed $100 contribution limitation.

a. As defined, "person" includes "an individual, partnership, committee, association, corporation or any other organization or group." The limitation applies to: (1) anything of value, such as gifts, loans, advances, and promises to give, (2) contributions made direct to the candidate or to an intermediary, or a committee authorized by the candidate, (3) the aggregate amounts contributed to the candidate for each election, treating primaries, run-off elections and general elections separately and all Presidential primaries within a single calendar year as one election.

[In] view of the fundamental nature of the right to associate, governmental "action which may have the effect of curtailing the freedom to associate is subject to the closest scrutiny." Yet, it is clear that "[n]either the right to associate nor the right to participate in political activities is absolute." *Letter Carriers* [Ch. 9, II supra]. Even a " 'significant interference' with protected rights of political association" may be sustained if the State demonstrates a sufficiently important interest and employs means closely drawn to avoid unnecessary abridgment of associational freedoms.
* * *

It is unnecessary to look beyond the Act's primary purpose—to limit the actuality and appearance of corruption resulting from large individual financial contributions—in order to find a constitutionally sufficient justification for the $1,000 contribution limitation. [The] increasing importance of the communications media and sophisticated mass mailing and polling operations to effective campaigning make the raising of large sums of money an ever more essential ingredient of an effective candidacy. To the extent that large contributions are given to secure political quid pro quos from current and potential office holders, the integrity of our system of representative democracy is undermined. Although the scope of such pernicious practices can never be reliably ascertained, the deeply disturbing examples surfacing after the 1972 election demonstrate that the problem is not an illusory one.

Of almost equal concern as the danger of actual quid pro quo arrangements is the impact of the appearance of corruption stemming from public awareness of the opportunities for abuse inherent in a regime of large individual financial contributions. In *Letter Carriers,* the Court found that the danger to "fair and effective government" posed by partisan political conduct on the part of federal employees charged with administering the law was a sufficiently important concern to justify broad restrictions on the employees' right of partisan political association. Here, as there, Congress could legitimately conclude that the avoidance of the appearance of improper influence "is also critical [if] confidence in the system of representative Government is not to be eroded to a disastrous extent."[29]

Appellants contend that the contribution limitations must be invalidated because bribery laws and narrowly-drawn disclosure requirements constitute a less restrictive means of dealing with "proven and suspected quid pro quo arrangements." But laws [against] bribes deal with only the most blatant and specific attempts of those with money to influence governmental action. [And] Congress was surely entitled to conclude that disclosure was only a partial measure, and that contribution ceilings were a necessary legislative concomitant to deal with the reality or appearance of corruption inherent in a system permitting unlimited financial contributions, even when the identi-

---

29. Although the Court in *Letter Carriers* found that this interest was constitutionally sufficient to justify legislation prohibiting federal employees from engaging in certain partisan political activities, it was careful to emphasize that the limitations did not restrict an employee's right to express his views on political issues and candidates.

ties of the contributors and the amounts of their contributions are fully disclosed.

The Act's $1,000 contribution limitation focuses precisely on the problem of large campaign contributions—the narrow aspect of political association where the actuality and potential for corruption have been identified—while leaving persons free to engage in independent political expression, to associate actively through volunteering their services. [The] Act's contribution limitations [do] not undermine to any material degree the potential for robust and effective discussion of candidates and campaign [issues].

We find that, under the rigorous standard of review established by our prior decisions, the weighty interests served by restricting the size of financial contributions to political candidates are sufficient to justify the limited effect upon First Amendment freedoms caused by the $1,000 contribution ceiling.[b]

C. *Expenditure Limitations.* [1.] Section 608(e)(1) provides that "[n]o person may make any expenditure [relative] to a clearly identified candidate during a calendar year which, when added to all other expenditures made by such person during the year advocating the election or defeat of such candidate, exceeds $1,000." [Its] plain effect [is] to prohibit all individuals, who are neither candidates nor owners of institutional press facilities, and all groups, except political parties and campaign organizations, from voicing their views "relative to a clearly identified candidate" through means that entail aggregate expenditures of more than $1,000 during a calendar year. The provision, for example, would make it a federal criminal offense for a person or association to place a single one-quarter page advertisement "relative to a clearly identified candidate" in a major metropolitan newspaper.

[Although] "expenditure," "clearly identified," and "candidate" are defined in the Act, there is no definition clarifying what expenditures are "relative to" a candidate. [But the "when" clause in § 608(e)(1)] clearly

---

b. The Court rejected the challenges that the $1,000 limit was overbroad because (1) most large contributors do not seek improper influence over a candidate, and (2) much more than $1,000 would still not be enough to influence improperly a candidate or office holder. With respect to (1), "Congress was justified in concluding that the interest in safeguarding against the appearance of impropriety requires that the opportunity for abuse inherent in the process of raising large monetary contributions be eliminated." With respect to (2), "As the Court of Appeals observed, '[a] court has no scalpel to probe, whether, say, a $2,000 ceiling might not serve as well as $1,000.' Such distinctions in degree become significant only when they can be said to amount to differences in kind."

The Court also rejected as without support in the record the claims that the contribution limitations worked invidious discrimination between incumbents and challengers to whom the same limitations applied.

The Court then upheld (1) exclusion from the $1,000 limit of the value of unpaid volunteer services and of certain expenses paid by the volunteer up to a maximum of $500; (2) the higher limit of $5,000 for contributions to a candidate by established, registered political committees with at least 50 contributing supporters and fielding at least five candidates for federal office; and (3) the $25,000 limit on total contributions to all candidates by one person in one calendar year.

permits, if indeed it does not require, the phrase "relative to" a candidate to be read to mean "advocating the election or defeat of" a candidate.

But while such a construction of § 608(e)(1) refocuses the vagueness question, [it hardly] eliminates the problem of unconstitutional vagueness altogether. For the distinction between discussion of issues and candidates and advocacy of election or defeat of candidates may often dissolve in practical application. Candidates, especially incumbents, are intimately tied to public issues involving legislative proposals and governmental actions. Not only do candidates campaign on the basis of their positions on various public issues, but campaigns themselves generate issues of public interest.

[Constitutionally deficient uncertainty which "compels the speaker to hedge and trim"] can be avoided only by reading § 608(e)(1) as limited to communications that include explicit words of advocacy of election or defeat of a candidate, much as the definition of "clearly identified" in § 608(e)(2) requires that an explicit and unambiguous reference to the candidate appear as part of the communication. This is the reading of the provision suggested by the non-governmental appellees in arguing that "[f]unds spent to propagate one's views on issues without expressly calling for a candidate's election or defeat are thus not covered." We agree that in order to preserve the provision against invalidation on vagueness grounds, § 608(e)(1) must be construed to apply only to expenditures for communications that in express terms advocate the election or defeat of a clearly identified candidate for federal office.[c]

We turn then to the basic First Amendment question—whether § 608(e)(1), even as thus narrowly and explicitly construed, impermissibly burdens the constitutional right of free expression. * * *

We find that the governmental interest in preventing corruption and the appearance of corruption is inadequate to justify § 608(e)(1)'s ceiling on independent expenditures. First, assuming arguendo that large independent expenditures pose the same dangers of actual or apparent quid pro quo arrangements as do large contributions, § 608(e)(1) does not provide an answer that sufficiently relates to the elimination of those dangers. Unlike the contribution limitations' total ban on the giving of large amounts of money to candidates, § 608(e)(1) prevents only some large expenditures. So long as persons and groups eschew expenditures that in express terms advocate the election or defeat of a clearly identified candidate, they are free to spend as much as they want to promote the candidate and his views. The exacting interpretation of the statutory language necessary to avoid unconstitutional vagueness thus undermines the limitation's effectiveness as a loophole-closing provision by facilitating circumvention by those seeking to exert improper influence upon a candidate or office-holder. It would naively

---

c. On the issues raised by this interpretation, see Briffault, *Issue Advocacy: Redrawing the Elections/Politics Line,* 77 Texas L.Rev. 1751 (1999); Hayward, *When Does an Advertisement about Issues Become an* *"Issues" Ad,* 49 Cath. U.L.Rev. 63 (1999); Moramarco, *Beyond "Magic Words": Using Self–Disclosure to Regulate Electioneering,* 49 Cath. U.L.Rev. 107 (1999).

underestimate the ingenuity and resourcefulness of persons and groups desiring to buy influence to believe that they would have much difficulty devising expenditures that skirted the restriction on express advocacy of election or defeat but nevertheless benefited the candidate's campaign. * * *

Second, [the] independent advocacy restricted by the provision does not presently appear to pose dangers of real or apparent corruption comparable to those identified with large campaign contributions. The parties defending § 608(e)(1) contend that it is necessary to prevent would-be contributors from avoiding the contribution limitations by the simple expedient of paying directly for media advertisements or for other portions of the candidate's campaign activities. [Section] 608(b)'s contribution ceilings rather than § 608(e)(1)'s independent expenditure limitation prevent attempts to circumvent the Act through prearranged or coordinated expenditures amounting to disguised contributions.[53] By contrast, § 608(e)(1) limits expenditures for express advocacy of candidates made totally independently of the candidate and his campaign. [The] absence of prearrangement and coordination of an expenditure with the candidate or his agent not only undermines the value of the expenditure to the candidate, but also alleviates the danger that expenditures will be given as a quid pro quo for improper commitments from the candidate. Rather than preventing circumvention of the contribution limitations, § 608(e)(1) severely restricts all independent advocacy despite its substantially diminished potential for abuse.

While the independent expenditure ceiling thus fails to serve any substantial governmental interest in stemming the reality or appearance of corruption in the electoral process, it heavily burdens core First Amendment expression. [Advocacy] of the election or defeat of candidates for federal office is no less entitled to protection under the First Amendment than the discussion of political policy generally or advocacy of the passage or defeat of legislation.

It is argued, however, that the ancillary governmental interest in equalizing the relative ability of individuals and groups to influence the outcome of elections serves to justify the limitation on express advocacy of the election or defeat of candidates imposed by § 608(e)(1)'s expenditure ceiling. But the concept that government may restrict the speech of some elements of our society in order to enhance the relative voice of others[d] is

---

53. Section 608(e)(1) does not apply to expenditures "on behalf of a candidate within the meaning of" § 608(2)(B). That section provides that expenditures "authorized or requested by the candidate, an authorized committee of the candidate, or an agent of the candidate" are to be treated as expenditures of the candidate and contributions by the person or group making the expenditure. [In] view of [the] legislative history and the purposes of the Act, we find that the "authorized or requested" stan-

dard of the Act operates to treat all expenditures placed in cooperation with or with the consent of a candidate, his agents, or an authorized committee of the candidate as contributions subject to the limitations set forth in § 608(b). [Eds. Subsequent cases have held that group expenditures on behalf of a candidate that are not coordinated with the candidate may not constitutionally be restricted. FEC v. National Conservative Political Action Comm., 470 U.S. 480, 105 S.Ct. 1459, 84 L.Ed.2d 455 (1985)].

wholly foreign to the First Amendment, which was designed "to secure 'the widest possible dissemination of information from diverse and antagonistic sources,' " and " 'to assure unfettered interchange of ideas for the bringing about of political and social changes desired by the people.' " *New York Times Co. v. Sullivan.* The First Amendment's protection against governmental abridgement of free expression cannot properly be made to depend on a person's financial ability to engage in public discussion.[55]

[*Mills*] *v. Alabama,* 384 U.S. 214, 86 S.Ct. 1434, 16 L.Ed.2d 484 (1966), held that legislative restrictions on advocacy of the election or defeat of political candidates are wholly at odds with the guarantees of the First Amendment. [Yet] the prohibition on election day editorials invalidated in *Mills* is clearly a lesser intrusion on constitutional freedom than a $1,000 limitation on the amount of money any person or association can spend *during an entire election year* in advocating the election or defeat of a candidate for public office.

For the reasons stated, we conclude that § 608(e)(1)'s independent expenditure limitation is unconstitutional under the First Amendment. * * *e

2. [The] Act also sets limits on expenditures by a candidate "from his personal funds, or the personal funds of his immediate family, in connection with his campaigns during any calendar year." § 608(a)(1).[f]

The ceiling on personal expenditures by candidates on their own behalf [imposes] a substantial restraint on the ability of persons to engage in protected First Amendment expression. The candidate, no less than any other person, has a First Amendment right to engage in the discussion of public issues and vigorously and tirelessly to advocate his own election and the election of other candidates. Indeed, it is of particular importance that candidates have the unfettered opportunity to make their views known so that the electorate may intelligently evaluate the candidates' personal qualities and their positions on vital public issues before choosing among them on

---

d. For sustained defense of this aspect of *Buckley,* see Redish & Kaludis, *The Right of Expressive Access in First Amendment Theory: Redistributive Values and the Democratic Dilemma,* 93 Nw.U.L.Rev. 1083 (1999). On the other hand, the lower court characterized the issue somewhat differently. Can "the wealthy few [claim] a constitutional guarantee to a stronger political voice than the unwealthy many because they are able to give and spend more money, and because the amounts they give and spend cannot be limited"? 519 F.2d 821, 841 (D.C.Cir.1975).

55. Neither the voting rights cases [Ch. 10, Sec. 4, I, A] nor the Court's decision upholding the FCC's fairness doctrine [p. 938 supra] lends support to appellees' position that the First Amendment permits Congress to abridge the rights of some persons to engage in political expression in order to enhance the relative voice of other segments of our [society].

e. The Court invalidated restrictions on the amount of personal funds candidates could spend on their own behalf and on the amount of overall campaign expenditures by federal candidates. The anti-corruption rationale did not apply in the former instance and was already served by the act's contribution and disclosure provisions. On the other hand, the Court also stated that, "[A]cceptance of federal funding entails voluntary acceptance of an expenditure ceiling."

f. $50,000 for Presidential or Vice Presidential candidates; $35,000 for Senate candidates; $25,000 for most candidates for the House of Representatives.

election day. [Section] 608(a)'s ceiling on personal expenditures by a candidate in furtherance of his own candidacy thus clearly and directly interferes with constitutionally protected freedoms.

The primary governmental interest served by the Act—the prevention of actual and apparent corruption of the political process—does not support the limitation on the candidate's expenditure of his own personal funds. [Indeed], the use of personal funds reduces the candidate's dependence on outside contributions and thereby counteracts the coercive pressures and attendant risks of abuse to which the Act's contribution limitations are directed.

The ancillary interest in equalizing the relative financial resources of candidates competing for elective office, therefore, provides the sole relevant rationale for Section 608(a)'s expenditure ceiling. That interest is clearly not sufficient to justify the provision's infringement of fundamental First Amendment rights. First, the limitation may fail to promote financial equality among candidates. [Indeed], a candidate's personal wealth may impede his [fundraising efforts]. Second, and more fundamentally, the First Amendment simply cannot tolerate § 608(a)'s restriction upon the freedom of a candidate to speak without legislative limit on behalf of his own candidacy. We therefore hold that § 608(a)'s restrictions on a candidate's personal expenditures is unconstitutional.

3. [Section] 608(c) of the Act places limitations on overall campaign expenditures by candidates [seeking] election to federal office. [For Presidential candidates the ceiling is $10,000,000 in seeking nomination and $20,000,000 in the general election campaign; for House of Representatives candidates it is $70,000 for each campaign—primary and general; for candidates for Senator the ceiling depends on the size of the voting age population.]

No governmental interest that has been suggested is sufficient to justify [these restrictions] on the quantity of political expression. [The] interest in alleviating the corrupting influence of large contributions is served by the Act's contribution limitations and disclosure provisions rather than by § 608(c)'s campaign expenditure ceilings. [There] is no indication that the substantial criminal penalties for violating the contribution ceilings combined with the political repercussion of such violations will be insufficient to police the contribution provisions. Extensive reporting, auditing, and disclosure requirements applicable to both contributions and expenditures by political campaigns are designed to facilitate the detection of illegal contributions. * * *

The interest in equalizing the financial resources of candidates competing for federal office is no more convincing a justification for restricting the scope of federal election campaigns. Given the limitation on the size of outside contributions, the financial resources available to a candidate's campaign, like the number of volunteers recruited, will normally vary with the size and intensity of the candidate's support. There is nothing invidious, improper, or unhealthy in permitting such funds to be spent to carry the candidate's message to the electorate. Moreover, the equalization of permissible campaign expenditures might serve not to equalize the opportunities of all candidates but to handicap a candidate who lacked substantial name recognition or exposure of his views before the start of the campaign.

The campaign expenditure ceilings appear to be designed primarily to serve the governmental interests in reducing the allegedly skyrocketing costs of political campaigns. [But the] First Amendment denies government the power to determine that spending to promote one's political views is wasteful, excessive, or unwise. In the free society ordained by our Constitution it is not the government but the people individually as citizens and candidates and collectively as associations and political committees who must retain control over the quantity and range of debate on public issues in a political campaign.[65]

For these reasons we hold that § 608(c) is constitutionally invalid. * * *

CHIEF JUSTICE BURGER, concurring in part and dissenting in part.

[I] agree fully with that part of the Court's opinion that holds unconstitutional the limitations the Act puts on campaign expenditures. [Yet] when it approves similarly stringent limitations on contributions, the Court ignores the reasons it finds so persuasive in the context of expenditures. For me contributions and expenditures are two sides of the same First Amendment coin.

[Limiting] contributions, as a practical matter, will limit expenditures and will put an effective ceiling on the amount of political activity and debate that the Government will permit to take place.[5]

The Court attempts to separate the two communicative aspects of political contributions—the "moral" support that the gift itself conveys, which the Court suggests is the same whether the gift is of $10 or $10,000,[6] and the fact that money translates into communication. The Court dismisses

65. [Congress] may engage in public financing of election campaigns and may condition acceptance of public funds on an agreement by the candidate to abide by specified expenditure limitations. Just as a candidate may voluntarily limit the size of the contributions he chooses to accept he may decide to forgo private fundraising and accept public funding. [Ed. On the merits and demerits of public financing, compare Briffault, *Public Funding and Democratic Elections,* 148 U.Pa.L.Rev. 563 (1999) with Smith, *Some Problems with Taxpayer-funded Political Campaigns, id.* at 591].

5. The Court notes that 94.9% of the funds raised by congressional candidates in 1974 came in contributions of less than $1,000, n. 27, and suggests that the effect of the contribution limitations will be minimal. This logic ignores the disproportionate

influence large contributions may have when they are made early in a campaign; "seed money" can be essential, and the inability to obtain it may effectively end some candidacies before they begin. Appellants have excerpted from the record data on nine campaigns to which large, initial contributions were critical. Campaigns such as these will be much harder, and perhaps impossible, to mount under the Act.

6. Whatever the effect of the limitation, it is clearly arbitrary—Congress has imposed the same ceiling on contributions to a New York or California senatorial campaign that it has put on House races in Alaska or Wyoming. Both the strength of support conveyed by the gift of $1,000 *and* the gift's potential for corruptly influencing the recipient will vary enormously from place to place. * * *

the effect of the limitations on the second aspect of contributions: "[T]he transformation of contributions into political debate involves speech by someone other than the contributor." On this premise—that contribution limitations restrict only the speech of "someone other than the contributor"—rests the Court's justification for treating contributions differently from expenditures. The premise is demonstrably flawed; the contribution limitations will, in specific instances, limit exactly the same political activity that the expenditure ceilings limit, and at least one of the "expenditure" limitations the Court finds objectionable operates precisely like the "contribution" limitations.[8]

The Court's attempt to distinguish the communication inherent in political *contributions* from the speech aspects of political *expenditures* simply will not wash. We do little but engage in word games unless we recognize that people—candidates and contributors—spend money on political activity because they wish to communicate ideas, and their constitutional interest in doing so is precisely the same whether they or someone else utter the words.

[T]he restrictions are hardly incidental in their effect upon particular campaigns. Judges are ill-equipped to gauge the precise impact of legislation, but a law that impinges upon First Amendment rights requires us to make the attempt. It is not simply speculation to think that the limitations on contributions will foreclose some candidacies.[9] The limitations will also alter the nature of some electoral contests drastically.[10]

[In] striking down the limitations on campaign expenditures, the Court relies in part on its conclusion that other means—namely, disclosure and contribution ceilings—will adequately serve the statute's aim. It is not clear why the same analysis is not also appropriate in weighing the need for contribution ceilings in addition to disclosure requirements. Congress may well be entitled to conclude that disclosure was a "partial measure," but I had not thought until today that Congress could enact its conclusions in the First Amendment area into laws immune from the most searching review by this Court. * * *[g]

8. The Court treats the Act's provisions limiting a candidate's spending from his *personal resources* as *expenditure* limits, as indeed the Act characterizes them, and holds them unconstitutional. As Mr. Justice Marshall points out, infra, by the Court's logic these provisions could as easily be treated as limits on *contributions*, since they limit what the candidate can give to his own campaign.

9. Candidates who must raise large initial contributions in order to appeal for more funds to a broader audience will be handicapped. See n. 5, supra. It is not enough to say that the contribution ceilings "merely require candidates [to] raise funds from a greater number of persons," where

the limitations will effectively prevent candidates without substantial personal resources from doing just that.

10. Under the Court's holding, candidates with personal fortunes will be free to contribute to their own campaigns as much as they like, since the Court chooses to view the Act's provisions in this regard as unconstitutional "expenditure" limitations rather than "contribution" limitations. See n. 8, supra.

g. Blackmun, J., also dissented separately from that part of the Court's opinion upholding the Act's restrictions on campaign contributions, unpersuaded that "a principled constitutional distinction" could

JUSTICE WHITE, concurring in part and dissenting in part. * * *

I [agree] with the Court's judgment upholding the limitations on contributions. I dissent [from] the Court's view that the expenditure limitations [violate] the First Amendment. [This] case depends on whether the nonspeech interests of the Federal Government in regulating the use of money in political campaigns are sufficiently urgent to justify the incidental effects that the limitations visit upon the First Amendment interests of candidates and their supporters.

[The Court] accepts the congressional judgment that the evils of unlimited contributions are sufficiently threatening to warrant restriction regardless of the impact of the limits on the contributor's opportunity for effective speech and in turn on the total volume of the candidate's political communications by reason of his inability to accept large sums from those willing to give.

The congressional judgment, which I would also accept, was that other steps must be taken to counter the corrosive effects of money in federal election campaigns. One of these steps is § 608(e), which [limits] what a contributor may independently spend in support or denigration of one running for federal office. Congress was plainly of the view that these expenditures also have corruptive potential; but the Court strikes down the provision, strangely enough claiming more insight as to what may improperly influence candidates than is possessed by the majority of Congress that passed this Bill and the President who signed it. Those supporting the Bill undeniably included many seasoned professionals who have been deeply involved in elective processes and who have viewed them at close range over many years.

It would make little sense to me, and apparently made none to Congress, to limit the amounts an individual may give to a candidate or spend with his approval but fail to limit the amounts that could be spent on his behalf. Yet the Court permits the former while striking down the latter limitation. [I] would take the word of those who know—that limiting independent expenditures is essential to prevent transparent and widespread evasion of the contribution limits. * * *

The Court also rejects Congress' judgment manifested in § 608(c) that the federal interest in limiting total campaign expenditures by individual candidates justifies the incidental effect on their opportunity for effective political speech. I disagree both with the Court's assessment of the impact on speech and with its narrow view of the values the limitations will serve.

[M]oney is not always equivalent to or used for speech, even in the context of political campaigns. [There are] many expensive campaign activities that are not themselves communicative or remotely related to speech. Furthermore, campaigns differ among themselves. Some seem to spend much less money than others and yet communicate as much or more than those supported by enormous bureaucracies with unlimited financing. The

be made between the contribution and expenditure limitations involved.

record before us no more supports the conclusion that the communicative efforts of congressional and Presidential candidates will be crippled by the expenditure limitations than it supports the contrary. The judgment of Congress was that reasonably effective campaigns could be conducted within the limits established by the Act and that the communicative efforts of these campaigns would not seriously suffer. In this posture of the case, there is no sound basis for invalidating the expenditure limitations, so long as the purposes they serve are legitimate and sufficiently substantial, which in my view they are.

[E]xpenditure ceilings reinforce the contribution limits and help eradicate the hazard of corruption. [Without] limits on total expenditures, campaign costs will inevitably and endlessly escalate. Pressure to raise funds will constantly build and with it the temptation to resort in "emergencies" to those sources of large sums, who, history shows, are sufficiently confident of not being caught to risk flouting contribution [limits.]

The ceiling on candidate expenditures represents the considered judgment of Congress that elections are to be decided among candidates none of whom has overpowering advantage by reason of a huge campaign war chest. At least so long as the ceiling placed upon the candidates is not plainly too low, elections are not to turn on the difference in the amounts of money that candidates have to spend. This seems an acceptable purpose and the means chosen a common sense way to achieve [it.]

I also disagree with the Court's judgment that § 608(a), which limits the amount of money that a candidate or his family may spend on his campaign, violates the Constitution. Although it is true that this provision does not promote any interest in preventing the corruption of candidates, the provision does, nevertheless, serve salutary purposes related to the integrity of federal campaigns. By limiting the importance of personal wealth, § 608(a) helps to assure that only individuals with a modicum of support from others will be viable candidates. This in turn would tend to discourage any notion that the outcome of elections is primarily a function of money. Similarly, § 608(a) tends to equalize access to the political arena, encouraging the less wealthy, unable to bankroll their own campaigns, to run for political office.[h]

h. Marshall, J., dissented from that part of the Court's opinion invalidating the limitation on the amount a candidate or his family may spend on his campaign. He considered "the interest in promoting the reality and appearance of equal access to the political arena" sufficient to justify the limitation: "[T]he wealthy candidate's immediate access to a substantial personal fortune may give him an initial advantage that his less wealthy opponent can never overcome. [With the option of large contributions re-moved by § 608(b)], the less wealthy candidate is without the means to match the large initial expenditures of money of which the wealthy candidate is capable. In short, the limitations on contributions put a premium on a candidate's personal wealth. [Section 608(a) then] emerges not simply as a device to reduce the natural advantage of the wealthy candidate, but as a provision providing some symmetry to a regulatory scheme that otherwise enhances the natural advantage of the wealthy."

Notes and Questions

1. *Equality and Democracy.* Is it "foreign" to the first amendment to curb the spending of the wealthy in an effort to preserve the integrity of the elections process? Would it have been "foreign" to first amendment doctrine to engage in some type of balancing? Does the Court's expenditure ruling denigrate the interests in equality and democracy?[i] Even if the concept of political equity is a "legitimizing myth," is *Buckley* flawed because it underestimates the necessity of promoting political leadership that is autonomous and independent of pluralistic forces? Is government autonomy necessary for minimally adequate regulation of the economy? See Blum, *The Divisible First Amendment: A Critical Functionalist Approach to Freedom of Speech and Electoral Campaign Spending,* 58 N.Y.U.L.Rev. 1273, 1369–78 (1983). Alternatively, would it be better to solve the wealth problem by redistribution (and control of corporate power), while holding fast to a strong liberty principle?[j]

2. To what extent are campaign finance laws likely to advance equality values?[k] Aren't they most likely to benefit incumbents? See Epstein, *Modern Republicanism—Or the Flight From Substance,* 97 Yale L.J. 1633, 1643–45 (1988); Macey, *The Missing Element in the Republican Revival,* 97 Yale L.J. 1673, 1680–81 (1988). Do incumbents possess ordinarily insuperable advantages apart from the campaign finance system? Would campaign finance legislation free incumbents from the need to rely on interest group funding and improve the quality of representation? Blasi, *Free Speech and the Widening Gyre of Fund–Raising,* 94 Columbia L.Rev. 1281 (1994). Is increased legislative autonomy desirable?[l]

3. *Varying scrutiny.* (a) Did *Buckley* apply less exacting scrutiny to impairment of associational freedoms by contribution limits than to impairment of free expression by expenditure limits? Cf. 90 Harv.L.Rev. 178–79 (1976). "Granted that freedom of association is merely ancillary to speech, a

---

i. See, e.g., Tribe, *Constitutional Choices* 193–94 (1985); Fiss, *Money and Politics,* 97 Colum. L.Rev. 2470 (1997; Neuborne, *Toward a Democracy–Centered Reading of the First Amendment,* 93 Nw.U.L.Rev. 1055 (1999); Nicholson, *Buckley v. Valeo: The Constitutionality of the Federal Election Campaign Act Amendments of 1974,* 1977 Wis.L.Rev. 323, 336; Wright, *Money and the Pollution of Politics: Is the First Amendment an Obstacle to Political Equality?,* 82 Colum.L.Rev. 609 (1982).

j. See Baker, *Realizing Self–Realization: Corporate Political Expenditures and Redish's The Value of Free Speech,* 130 U.Pa. L.Rev. 646, 652 (1982); Baker, *Scope of the First Amendment Freedom of Speech,* 25 U.C.L.A.L.Rev. 964, 983–90 (1978).

k. Consider Brest, *Further Beyond the Republican Revival,* 97 Yale L.J. 1623, 1627 (1988): " 'Those who are better off partici-

pate more, and by participating more they exercise more influence on government officials.' Unequal resources produce unequal influence in determining which issues get on the political [agenda]. Campaign finance regulations barely begin to remedy the systematic ways in which inequalities of wealth distort the political process." But see Foley, *Equal–Dollars–Per Voter: A Constitutional Principle of Campaign Finance,* 94 Colum.L.Rev. 1204 (1994); Raskin & Bonifaz, *Equal Protection and the Wealth Primary,* 11 Yale L. & Pol'y Rev. 273 (1993). For a variety of views, see *Symposium on Campaign Finance Reform,* 94 Colum.L.Rev. 1125 (1994).

l. Compare Sunstein, *Beyond the Republican Revival,* 97 Yale L.J. 1539 (1988) with Fitts, *Look Before You Leap,* 97 Yale L.J. 1651 (1988); Fitts, *The Vices of Virtue,* 136 U.Pa.L.Rev. 1567 (1988).

means of amplifying and effectuating communication but logically secondary to speech," is this also "true of expenditures of money in aid of speech"? See Polsby, *Buckley v. Valeo: The Special Nature of Political Speech,* 1976 Sup.Ct.Rev. 1, 22. Can a lesser degree of scrutiny be justified for contributions? Or were the differing results based on the Court's perceiving a greater threat to first amendment interests in the expenditure limits and less risk of corruption and undue influence in unlimited independent expenditures? Cf. Nicholson, note 1 supra, at 340–45. For a defense of strict scrutiny across the board, see BeVier, *Money and Politics: A Perspective on the First Amendment and Campaign Finance Reform,* 73 Calif.L.Rev. 1045 (1985). For the argument that strict scrutiny is inappropriate in institutionally bounded contexts and that elections are such contexts, see Baker, *Campaign Expenditures and Free Speech,* 33 Harv. C.R.-C.L.Rev. 1 (1998).[m]

(b) *The O'Brien analogy.* May the Court's rejection of the less-exacting *O'Brien* standard on the ground that the expenditure of money did not introduce a non-speech element fairly be criticized for asking the wrong question: whether "*pure speech* can be regulated where there is some incidental effect on *money,*" rather than whether "the use of *money* can be regulated, by analogy to such conduct as draft-card burning, where there is an undoubted incidental effect on *speech*"? See Wright, *Politics and the Constitution: Is Money Speech?,* 85 Yale L.J. 1001, 1007 (1976). But compare Balkin, *Some Realism About Pluralism: Legal Realist Approaches to the First Amendment,* 1990 Duke L.J. 375, 414: "I suspect that the slogan 'money is not speech' is attractive because it appeals to a certain humanistic vision— that there is something quite different between the situation of a lone individual expressing her views and the purchase of hired mouths using hired expressions created by hired minds to saturate the airwaves with ideological drivel. Yet in one sense, this humanistic vision really turns upon a set of unstated egalitarian assumptions about economic and social power. Certainly we would have no objection to a person with a speech impediment hiring someone to do her talking for her; that is because we think that, under these circumstances, it is fair for such a person to boost her communicative powers. Modern political campaigns seem a far cry from this example because of the massive amounts of economic power expended to get the message across. I think we should isolate the egalitarian assumptions implicit in the 'money is not speech' position and put them to their best use—the justification of campaign finance reforms on the ground that gross inequalities of economic power destroy the integrity of the political process. [G]ov-

---

m. For similar views, see Briffault, *Issue Advocacy: Redrawing the Elections/Politics Line,* 77 Texas L.Rev. 1751 (1999); Schauer & Pildes, *Electoral Exceptionalism and the First Amendment,* 77 Texas L. Rev. 1803 (1999); and Neuborne, *The Supreme Court and Free Speech: Love and A Question,* 42 St.Louis U.L.J. 789, 800 (1998): "If we can conceive of an election campaign as a great deliberative assembly of the people, why shouldn't we allow ourselves to establish a content-neutral, meta-Roberts' Rules of Order to help assure that our elections are preceded by debate calculated to permit our democratic institutions to perform at an acceptable level, an electoral debate where political discourse is not completely dominated by the wealthy?" But see Sullivan, *Against Campaign Finance Reform,* 1998 Utah L.Rev. 311, 318–20 (1998); Post, *Commentary: Regulating Election Speech Under the First Amendment,* 77 Texas L.Rev 1837 (1999).

ernment is responsible for inequalities in access to the means of communication because it has created the system of property rights that makes such inequalities possible. Therefore, it is not only wrong but also incoherent for opponents of campaign finance reform to contend that the government should not regulate access to the political process. Government already regulates access to the political process—the first amendment simply demands that it do so fairly.''

4. *Expenditure limitations and political parties.* COLORADO REPUBLICAN FEDERAL CAMPAIGN COMMITTEE v. FEDERAL ELECTION COMMISSION, 518 U.S. 604, 116 S.Ct. 2309, 135 L.Ed.2d 795 (1996) ruled that the Federal Election Campaign Act's limitation on independent expenditures by political parties was unconstitutional. BREYER, J., joined by O'Connor and Souter, JJ., announced the judgment of the Court, but did not reach the question whether the limitation of expenditures coordinated with the candidate were similarly unconstitutional.

KENNEDY, J., joined by Scalia, J., concurring in part and dissenting in part, argued that the limitation on coordinated expenditures between political parties and their candidates was also unconstitutional: "We have a constitutional tradition of political parties and their candidates engaging in joint first amendment activity. [Congress] may have authority, consistent with the first amendment, to restrict undifferentiated political party contributions [as discussed in] *Buckley*, but that type of regulation is not at issue here." Kennedy, J., dissented from the judgment's failure to reach the question of coordinated expenditures.[n]

STEVENS, J., joined by Ginsburg, J., dissenting, maintained that independent expenditures by parties were contributions and that federal limits were justified by the need to level "the electoral playing field," and to avoid corruption or its appearance.

5. Under existing law, individuals, groups (with the exception of profit-organizations or unions) or political parties can spend unlimited sums in support of or against a federal candidate so long as there expenditures are not coordinated with the candidate, and profit-organizations or unions may do the same so long as they do not explicitly urge the candidate's election or defeat. Such advertising often takes the form of attack ads. In addition, parties may engage in voter registration and get out the vote campaigns that assist candidates. Unlimited contributions to parties and advocacy organizations may be made for some of these purposes and arguably for all of them. Commentators widely agree that loopholes such as these drastically undercut the effectiveness of the act. They disagree whether it is constitutional, wise or even possible effectively to close the loopholes.[o] If it is not possible to close

n. Thomas, J., joined by Rehnquist, C.J., and Scalia, J., would also have reached the question, arguing that *Buckley*'s anticorruption rationale did not apply to associations between political parties and candidates. Thomas, J., on his own, additionally argued that the distinction between contributions and expenditures was generally unsatisfactory and that both should receive first amendment protection.

the loopholes, or so long as they remain, should the contributions limitations be stricken on the ground that they are ineffective and/or that campaigns are better run by parties and candidates?

NIXON v. SHRINK MISSOURI GOVERNMENT PAC, 528 U.S. 377, 120 S.Ct. 897, 145 L.Ed.2d 886 (2000), per SOUTER, J., joined by Rehnquist, C.J., and Stevens, O'Connor, Ginsburg, and Breyer, JJ., reaffirmed *Buckley,* and upheld a Missouri scheme for restricting campaign contributions despite the fact that the limits were lower in real dollar value than those upheld in *Buckley:* "Precision about the relative rigor of the standard to review contribution limits was not a pretense of the *Buckley* per curiam opinion. [While] we did not then say in so many words that different standards might govern expenditure and contribution limits affecting associational rights, [i]t has [been] plain ever since *Buckley* that contribution limits would more readily clear the hurdles before them. * * * While the record does not show that the Missouri Legislature relied on the evidence and findings accepted in *Buckley,* the evidence introduced into the record by respondents or cited by the lower courts in this action is enough to show that the substantiation of the congressional concerns reflected in *Buckley* has its counterpart supporting the Missouri law. * * *

"Each dissenter would overrule *Buckley* and thinks we should do the same. The answer is that we are supposed to decide this case. [The plaintiffs] did not request that *Buckley* be overruled; the furthest reach of their arguments about the law was that subsequent decisions already on the books had enhanced the State's burden of justification beyond what *Buckley* required, a proposition we [reject] as mistaken."

STEVENS, J., concurred: "Money is property; it is not speech. [Because] I did not participate in the Court's decision in Buckley, I did not have the opportunity to suggest then that [property] and liberty concerns adequately explain the Court's decision to invalidate the expenditure limitations in the 1974 Act. * * *

"The right to use one's own money to hire gladiators, or to fund 'speech by proxy,' certainly merits significant constitutional protection. These property rights, however, are not entitled to the same protection as the right to say what one pleases."

BREYER, J., joined by Ginsburg, J., concurred: "The dissenters accuse the Court of weakening the First Amendment. [But] this is a case where constitutionally protected interests lie on both sides of the legal equation.

o. For a sampling, see Ansolabehere & Snyder, Jr., *Money and Institutional Power,* 77 Texas L.Rev. 1673 (1999); Briffault, *Issue Advocacy: Redrawing the Elections/Politics Line,* 77 Texas L.Rev. 1751 (1999); Issacharoff & Karlan, *The Hydraulics of Campaign Finance Reform,* 77 Texas L.Rev. 1705 (1999); Lochner & Cain, *Equity* *and Efficacy in the Enforcement of Campaign Finance Laws,* 77 Texas L. Rev. 1891 (1999); Lowenstein, *Election Law Miscellany,* 77 Texas L.Rev. 2001 (1999); Ortiz, Commentary: Water, Water Everywhere, 77 Texas L.Rev. 1837 (1999); Sullivan, *Against Campaign Finance Reform,* 1998 Utah L.Rev. 311, 318–20 (1998).

For that reason there is no place for a strong presumption against constitutionality, of the sort often thought to accompany the words 'strict scrutiny.'

"On the one hand, a decision to contribute money to a campaign is a matter of First Amendment concern—not because money is speech (it is not); but because it enables speech. Through contributions the contributor associates himself with the candidate's cause, helps the candidate communicate a political message with which the contributor agrees, and helps the candidate win by attracting the votes of similarly minded voters. *Buckley*. Both political association and political communication are at stake.

"On the other hand, restrictions upon the amount any one individual can contribute to a particular candidate seek to protect the integrity of the electoral process—the means through which a free society democratically translates political speech into concrete governmental action. Moreover, by limiting the size of the largest contributions, such restrictions aim to democratize the influence that money itself may bring to bear upon the electoral process. In doing so, they seek to build public confidence in that process and broaden the base of a candidate's meaningful financial support, encouraging the public participation and open discussion that the First Amendment itself presupposes. * * *

"I would uphold the statute essentially for the reasons stated by the Court. [But] what if [*Buckley*] denies the political branches sufficient leeway to enact comprehensive solutions to the problems posed by campaign finance. If so, like Justice Kennedy, I believe the Constitution would require us to reconsider *Buckley*. With that understanding I join the Court's opinion."

KENNEDY, J., dissented: "The plain fact is that the compromise the Court invented in *Buckley* set the stage for a new kind of speech to enter the political system. It is covert speech. The Court has forced a substantial amount of political speech underground, as contributors and candidates devise ever more elaborate methods of avoiding contribution limits, limits which take no account of rising campaign costs. The preferred method has been to conceal the real purpose of the speech. Soft money may be contributed to political parties in unlimited amounts, and is used often to fund so-called issue advocacy, advertisements that promote or attack a candidate's positions without specifically urging his or her election or defeat. Briffault, *Issue Advocacy: Redrawing the Elections/Politics Line*, 77 Tex. L.Rev. 1751, 1752–1753 (1999). Issue advocacy, like soft money, is unrestricted, while straightforward speech in the form of financial contributions paid to a candidate, speech subject to full disclosure and prompt evaluation by the public, is not. Thus has the Court's decision given us covert speech. This mocks the First Amendment. I would overrule *Buckley* and then free Congress or state legislatures to attempt some new reform, if, based upon their own considered view of the First Amendment, it is possible to do so. * * * The First Amendment ought to be allowed to take its own course without further obstruction from the artificial system we have imposed. It suffices here to say that the law in question does not come even close to passing any serious scrutiny."

THOMAS, J., joined by Scalia, J., dissented: "For nearly half a century, this Court has extended First Amendment protection to a multitude of forms of 'speech,' such as making false defamatory statements, filing lawsuits, dancing nude, exhibiting drive-in movies with nudity, burning flags, and wearing military uniforms. Not surprisingly, the Courts of Appeals have followed our lead and concluded that the First Amendment protects, for example, begging, shouting obscenities, erecting tables on a sidewalk, and refusing to wear a necktie. In light of the many cases of this sort, today's decision is a most curious anomaly. Whatever the proper status of such activities under the First Amendment, I am confident that they are less integral to the functioning of our Republic than campaign contributions. Yet the majority today, rather than going out of its way to protect political speech, goes out of its way to avoid protecting it. * * *

"Because the Court [fails] to strictly scrutinize the inhibition of political speech and competition, I respectfully dissent."

FIRST NAT'L. BANK v. BELLOTTI, 435 U.S. 765, 98 S.Ct. 1407, 55 L.Ed.2d 707 (1978), per POWELL, J., held invalid under the first and fourteenth amendments a Massachusetts criminal statute prohibiting banks or business corporations from making contributions or expenditures to influence the vote in certain initiative campaigns: "The speech proposed by appellants is at the heart of the first amendment's protection. [If] the speakers here were not corporations, no one would suggest that the state could silence their proposed speech. It is the type of speech indispensable to decision making in a democracy, and this is no less true because the speech comes from a corporation rather than an individual. The inherent worth of the speech in terms of its capacity for informing the public does not depend upon the identity of its source, whether corporation, association, union or individual.

"[Nonetheless,] preserving the integrity of the electoral process, preventing corruption, and 'sustain[ing] the active, alert responsibility of the individual citizen in a democracy for the wise conduct of government' are interests of the highest importance. *Buckley*. Preservation of the individual citizen's confidence in government is equally important.

"[Appellee's arguments] that these interests are endangered by corporate participation in discussion of a referendum [issue] hinge upon the assumption that such participation would exert an undue influence on the outcome of a referendum vote, and—in the end—destroy the confidence of the people in the democratic process and the integrity of government. According to appellee, corporations are wealthy and powerful and their views may drown out other points of view. If appellee's arguments were supported by record or legislative findings that corporate advocacy threatened imminently to undermine democratic processes, thereby denigrating rather than serving First Amendment interests,[a] these arguments would merit our consideration.[b] Cf. *Red Lion*. But there has been no showing that the relative voice of corporations has been overwhelming or even significant in influencing referenda in Massachusetts, or that there has been any threat to the confidence of the citizenry in government.

"[Referenda] are held on issues, not candidates for public office. The risk of corruption perceived in cases involving candidate elections simply is not present in a popular vote on a public issue. To be sure, corporate advertising may influence the outcome of the vote; this would be its purpose. But the fact that advocacy may persuade the electorate is hardly a reason to suppress [it]. [T]he people in our democracy are entrusted with the responsibility for judging and evaluating the relative merits of conflicting arguments. They may consider, in making their judgment, the source and credibility of the advocate. But if there be any danger that the people cannot evaluate the information and arguments advanced by appellants, it is a danger contemplated by the Framers of the First Amendment."[c]

WHITE, J., joined by Brennan and Marshall, JJ., dissented, arguing among other things, a proposition that was taken up by the Court in *Austin,* infra: "The statute was designed to protect first amendment rights by preventing institutions which have been permitted to amass wealth as a result of special advantages extended by the State for certain economic purposes from using that wealth to acquire an unfair advantage in the political process."

Notes and Questions

1. *Protecting the privileged.* Consider Tushnet, *An Essay on Rights,* 62 Tex.L.Rev. 1363, 1387 (1984): "The first amendment has replaced the due process clause as the primary guarantor of the privileged. [Even] in its heyday the due process clause stood in the way only of specific legislation designed to reduce the benefits of privilege. Today, in contrast, the first amendment stands as a general obstruction to all progressive legislative efforts. To protect their positions of privilege, the wealthy can make prudent investments either in political action or, more conventionally, in factories or stocks. But since the demise of substantive due process, their investments in

a. Legislatures wishing to support such findings need not look far. See, e.g., Lowenstein, *Campaign Spending and Ballot Propositions: Recent Experience, Public Choice Theory and the First Amendment,* 29 U.C.L.A. L.Rev. 505 (1982); Schockley, *Direct Democracy, Campaign Finance, and the Courts: Can Corruption, Undue Influence, and Declining Voter Confidence Be Found?,* 39 U.Miami L.Rev. 377 (1985).

b. "[I]f *Tornillo* and *Buckley* slammed the door on excessive power arguments,

[*Bellotti*] opened a window. [The] Court did not pause, however, to explain why factors found in *Buckley* and *Tornillo* to be foreign to the first amendment would have 'merited consideration' in *Bellotti*." Shiffrin, *Government Speech,* 27 U.C.L.A. L.Rev. 565, 598–99 (1980).

c. Burger, C.J., concurred; Rehnquist, J., dissented.

factories and stocks can be regulated by legislatures. Under *Buckley* and *Bellotti,* however, their investments in politics—or politicians—cannot be regulated significantly. Needless to say, careful investment in politics may prevent effective regulation of traditional investments." See also Tushnet, *Corporations and Free Speech* in The Politics of Law 253 (Kairys ed. 1982).[d] Compare Levinson, *Book Review,* 83 Mich.L.Rev. 939, 945 (1985): "Overtly, justifying restriction of campaign spending by reference to the idea of fair access to the public forum may seem content neutral. However, it is worth considering to what extent we in fact support such restrictions because of tacit assumptions about the contents of the views held by the rich, who would obviously feel most of the burden of the restrictions. If both political views and the propensity to spend money on politics were distributed randomly among the entire populace, it is hard to see why anyone would be very excited about the whole issue of campaign finance."

Does Levinson's observation shortchange participatory values? Consider Sunstein, *Beyond the Republican Revival,* 97 Yale L.J. 1539, 1577 (1988): "[R]epublican understandings would point toward large reforms of the electoral process in an effort to improve political deliberation and to promote political equality and citizenship." Is it reasonable to take the views of the rich into account? See Neuborne, *Is Money Different?,* 77 Texas L.Rev. 1609, 1612–13 (1999).

2. *Protecting listeners.* Is *Bellotti* justifiable because of listeners' rights? See Redish, *Self-Realization, Democracy, and Freedom of Expression: A Reply to Professor Baker,* 130 U.Pa.L.Rev. 678–79 (1982). But see Note, *Statutory Limitations on Corporate Spending in Ballot Measure Campaigns: The Case for Constitutionality,* 36 Hast.L.J. 433 (1985) (legal and market limitations on corporate speech inherently negate its value for listeners). Reconsider the arguments for and against the marketplace of ideas argument, Sec. 1, I supra.

d. For suggestions that the first amendment may be generally harmful from a progressive perspective, see Balkin, *Some Realism About Pluralism: Legal Realist Approaches to the First Amendment,* 1990 Duke L.J. 375; Becker, *The Politics of Women's Wrongs and the Bill of "Rights": A Bicentennial Perspective,* 59 U.Chi.L.Rev. 453, 486–94 (1992); Becker, *Conservative Free Speech and the Uneasy Case for Judicial Review,* 64 U.Colo.L.Rev. 975 (1993); Delgado, *Comments About Mary Becker,* 64 U.Colo.L.Rev. 1051 (1993); Horwitz, *Rights,* 23 Harv. CR–CL L.Rev. 393, 397–98, 402–03 (1988); Schauer, *The Political Incidence of the Free Speech Principle,* 64 U.Colo.L.Rev. 935 (1993); Tushnet, *An Essay on Rights,* 62 Tex.L.Rev. 1363, 1386–92 (1984). For contrary considerations, see Rabban, *Free Speech in its Forgotten Years* 388–93 (1997); Shiffrin, *Dissent, Injustice and the Meanings of America* ch. 5 (1999); Neuborne, *Blues for the Left Hand,* 62 U.Chi.L.Rev. 423 (1995); Sullivan, *Discrimination, Distribution and Free Speech,* 37 Ariz.L.Rev. 439 (1995); Sullivan, *Free Speech and Unfree Markets,* 42 U.C.L.A.L.Rev. 949 (1995); Sullivan, *Resurrecting Free Speech,* 63 Ford.L.Rev. 971 (1995); Sullivan, *Free Speech Wars,* 48 S.M.U.L.Rev. 203 (1994). See also Graber, *Old Wine in New Bottles,* 48 Vand.L.Rev. 349 (1995). For discussion on a broad range of issues concerning the relationship between speech values and property values in Burger Court decisions, see Dorsen & Gara, *Free Speech, Property, and the Burger Court: Old Values, New Balances,* 1982 Sup.Ct.Rev. 195.

3.   *Post–Bellotti initiative cases.* The city of Berkeley placed a $250 limitation on contributions to committees formed to support or oppose ballot measures submitted to popular vote. Constitutional? See *Citizens Against Rent Control v. Berkeley,* 454 U.S. 290, 102 S.Ct. 434, 70 L.Ed.2d 492 (1981)(invalidating statute).[e]

Colorado made it a felony to pay persons to circulate initiative or referendum petitions. The purposes of the provision were to assure that a ballot measure had a sufficiently broad base of popular support to warrant its placement on the ballot and to eliminate an incentive to produce fraudulent signatures. Constitutional? See *Meyer v. Grant,* 486 U.S. 414, 108 S.Ct. 1886, 100 L.Ed.2d 425 (1988) (invalidating statute).[f]

Michigan law prohibits corporations, profit or nonprofit, from making contributions to candidates or independent expenditures on behalf of or opposed to candidates. The law entitles such corporations, however, to solicit contributions for allowable expenditures from a segregated fund. The Michigan State Chamber of Commerce, a nonprofit corporation with more than 8,000 members (three quarters of whom are profit corporations), sought to place a newspaper advertisement in support of a Congressional candidate and argued that Michigan's prohibition of such corporate ads was unconstitutional. AUSTIN v. MICHIGAN CHAMBER OF COMMERCE, 494 U.S. 652, 110 S.Ct. 1391, 108 L.Ed.2d 652 (1990), per MARSHALL, J., upheld the scheme as applied to these facts: "[T]he political advantage of corporations is unfair because '[t]he resources in the treasury of a business corporation [are] not an indication of popular support for the corporation's political ideas. They reflect instead the economically motivated decisions of investors and customers. The availability of these resources may make a corporation a formidable political presence, even though the power of the corporation may be no reflection of the power of its ideas.' *FEC v. Massachusetts Citizens for Life, Inc.,* 479 U.S. 238, 107 S.Ct. 616, 93 L.Ed.2d 539 (1986) [MCFL]. * * *

"The Chamber argues that this concern about corporate domination of the political process is insufficient to justify restrictions on independent expenditures. Although this Court has distinguished these expenditures from direct contributions in the context of federal laws regulating individual donors, it has also recognized that a legislature might demonstrate a danger of real or apparent corruption posed by such expenditures when made by corporations to influence candidate elections, *Bellotti,* n. 26. Regardless of whether this danger of 'financial quid pro quo' corruption may be sufficient

---

e. For commentary, see Tribe, Constitutional Choices 195–97 (1985); Lowenstein, fn. a supra, at 584–602; Nicholson, *The Constitutionality of Contribution Limitations in Ballot Measure Elections,* 9 Ecol. L.Q. 683 (1981).

f. For criticism, see Lowenstein & Stern, *The First Amendment and Paid Ini-* *tiative Petition Circulators: A Dissenting View and a Proposal,* 17 Hastings Con.L.Q. 175 (1989). But see *Buckley v. American Constitutional Law Foundation,* 525 U.S. 182, 119 S.Ct. 636, 142 L.Ed.2d 599 (1999) (extending *Meyer* to a requirement that paid circulators be registered voters).

to justify a restriction on independent expenditures, Michigan's regulation aims at a different type of corruption in the political arena: the corrosive and distorting effects of immense aggregations of wealth that are accumulated with the help of the corporate form and that have little or no correlation to the public's support for the corporation's political ideas. The Act does not attempt 'to equalize the relative influence of speakers on elections'; rather, it ensures that expenditures reflect actual public support for the political ideas espoused by corporations. We emphasize that the mere fact that corporations may accumulate large amounts of wealth is not the justification for [the statute]; rather, the unique state-conferred corporate structure that facilitates the amassing of large treasuries warrants the limit on independent expenditures. [We] therefore hold that the State has articulated a sufficiently compelling rationale to support its restriction on independent expenditures by corporations.

"We next turn to the question whether the Act is sufficiently narrowly tailored to achieve its goal. We find that the Act is precisely targeted to eliminate the distortion caused by corporate spending while also allowing corporations to express their political views. [T]he Act does not impose an *absolute* ban on all forms of corporate political spending but permits corporations to make independent political expenditures through separate segregated funds. Because persons contributing to such funds understand that their money will be used solely for political purposes, the speech generated accurately reflects contributors' support for the corporation's political views.

"[Although] some closely held corporations, just as some publicly held ones, may not have accumulated significant amounts of wealth, they receive from the State the special benefits conferred by the corporate structure and present the potential for distorting the political process. This potential for distortion justifies § 54(1)'s general applicability to all corporations. The section therefore is not substantially overbroad.

"The Chamber contends that [the Act] cannot be applied to a nonprofit ideological corporation like a chamber of commerce. [The Chamber relied on *MCFL,* per Brennan, J., which held that 2 U.S.C. § 441b, prohibiting corporations from using their treasury funds for the purpose of influencing any election for public office, was unconstitutional as applied to the expenditures of a nonprofit, nonstock corporation. Specifically, MCFL an anti-abortion organization had printed and distributed some 100,000 'newsletters' advocating the election of a number of candidates. Rehnquist, C.J., joined by White, Blackmun, and Stevens, JJ., dissenting, argued that organizations opting for a corporate form could be barred from using treasury funds for election purposes.][a] In *MCFL,* we held that the nonprofit organization there had 'features more akin to voluntary political associations than business firms, and therefore should not have to bear burdens on independent spending solely because of [its] incorporated status.' In reaching that

---

a. For commentary on *MCFL,* see Seidman, *Reflections on Context and the Constitution,* 73 Minn.L.Rev. 73, 80–84 (1988).

conclusion, we enumerated three characteristics of the corporation that were 'essential' to our holding. * * *

"The first characteristic of MCFL that distinguished it from ordinary business corporations was that the organization 'was formed for the express purpose of promoting political ideas, and cannot engage in business activities.' [MCFL's] narrow political focus thus 'ensure[d] that [its] political resources reflect[ed] political support.'

"In contrast, the Chamber's bylaws set forth more varied purposes, several of which are not inherently political. For instance, the Chamber compiles and disseminates information relating to social, civic, and economic conditions, trains and educates its members, and promotes ethical business practices. Unlike MCFL's, the Chamber's educational activities are not expressly tied to political goals; many of its seminars, conventions, and publications are politically neutral and focus on business and economic issues. The Chamber's President and Chief Executive Officer stated that one of the corporation's main purposes is to provide 'service to [its] membership that includes everything from group insurance to educational seminars, [and] litigation activities on behalf of the business community.' * * *

"We described the second feature of MCFL as the absence of 'shareholders or other persons affiliated so as to have a claim on its assets or earnings. This ensures that persons connected with the organization will have no economic disincentive for disassociating with it if they disagree with its political activity.' Although the Chamber also lacks shareholders, many of its members may be similarly reluctant to withdraw as members even if they disagree with the Chamber's political expression, because they wish to benefit from the Chamber's nonpolitical [programs].[2]

"The final characteristic upon which we relied in *MCFL* was [that] the organization [was] not established by, and had a policy of not accepting contributions from, business corporations. Thus it could not 'serv[e] as [a] condui[t] for the type of direct spending that creates a threat to the political marketplace.' In striking contrast, more than three-quarters of the Chamber's members are business corporations, whose political contributions and expenditures can constitutionally be regulated by the [State].[3] Because the Chamber accepts money from for-profit corporations, it could, absent application of § 54(1), serve as a conduit for corporate political spending. * * *

2. A requirement that the Chamber disclose the nature and extent of its political activities would not eliminate the possible distortion of the political process inherent in independent expenditures from general corporate funds. Given the significant incentive for members to continue their financial support for the Chamber in spite of their disagreement with its political agenda, disclosure will not ensure that the funds in the Chamber's treasury correspond to members' support for its ideas.

3. A nonprofit corporation's segregated fund, on the other hand, apparently cannot receive contributions from corporations. * * *

"The Chamber also attacks § 54(1) as underinclusive because it does not regulate the independent expenditures of unincorporated labor unions.[4] Whereas unincorporated unions, and indeed individuals, may be able to amass large treasuries, they do so without the significant state-conferred advantages of the corporate structure; corporations are 'by far the most prominent example of entities that enjoy legal advantages enhancing their ability to accumulate wealth.' The desire to counterbalance those advantages unique to the corporate form is the State's compelling interest in this case * * *.

"[We now] address the Chamber's contention that the provision infringes its rights under the Fourteenth Amendment. The Chamber argues [that] the State should also restrict the independent expenditures of [corporations] engaged in the media business.[5] [But] media corporations differ significantly from other corporations in that their resources are devoted to the collection of information and its dissemination to the public. We have consistently recognized the unique role that the press plays in 'informing and educating the public, offering criticism, and providing a forum for discussion and debate.' *Bellotti.* See also *Mills v. Alabama* ('[T]he press serves and was designed to serve as a powerful antidote to any abuses of power by governmental officials and as a constitutionally chosen means for keeping officials elected by the people responsible to all the people whom they were selected to serve'). [The] media exception ensures that the Act does not hinder or prevent the institutional press from reporting on and publishing editorials about newsworthy events. Cf. 15 U.S.C. §§ 1801–1804 (enacting a limited exemption from the antitrust laws for newspapers in part because of the recognition of the special role of the press). [Although] the press' unique societal role may not entitle the press to greater protection under the Constitution, it does provide a compelling reason for the State to exempt media corporations from the scope of political expenditure limitations. We therefore hold that the Act does not violate the Equal Protection Clause."

BRENNAN, J., joined the Court's opinion, but referring to himself as "one of the 'Orwellian' 'censors' derided by the dissents and as the author of [*MCFL*]," also concurred to express his views: "The requirement that corporate independent expenditures be financed through a segregated fund or political action committee [may] be unconstitutional as applied to some corporations because they do not present the dangers at which expenditure

---

4. The Federal Election Campaign Act restricts the independent expenditures of labor organizations as well as those of corporations. 2 U.S.C. § 441b(a).

5. The Federal Election Campaign Act contains a similar exemption that excludes from the definition of expenditure "any news story, commentary, or editorial distributed through the facilities of any broadcasting station, newspaper, magazine, or other periodical publication, unless such facilities are owned or controlled by any political party, political committee, or candidate." 2 U.S.C. § 431(9)(B)(I). [Ed. For discussion, see Hasen, *Campaign Finance Laws and the Rupert Murdoch Problem,* 77 Texas L.Rev. 1627 (1999); Powe, Jr., *Boiling Blood,* 77 Texas L.Rev. 1667 (1999)].

634 FREEDOM OF EXPRESSION & ASSOCIATION Pt. 1

limitations are aimed. Indeed, we determined that [MCFL] fell into this category.[3][4]

"The Michigan law is concededly 'underinclusive' insofar as it does not ban other types of political expenditures to which a dissenting Chamber member or corporate shareholder might object. [A] corporation remains free, for example, to use general treasury funds to support an initiative proposal in a state referendum. See *Bellotti.*

"I do not find this underinclusiveness fatal, for several reasons.[8] First, as the dissents recognize, discussions on candidate elections lie 'at the heart of political debate.' But just as speech interests are at their zenith in this area, so too are the interests of unwilling Chamber members and corporate shareholders forced to subsidize that speech. The State's decision to focus on this especially sensitive context is a justifiable one. Second, in light of our decisions in *Bellotti, Consolidated Edison Co. v. Public Service Comm'n,* and related cases, a State cannot prohibit corporations from making many other types of political expenditures. [T]o the extent that the Michigan statute is 'underinclusive' only because it does not regulate corporate expenditures in referenda or other corporate expression (besides merely commercial speech), this reflects the requirements of our decisions rather than the lack of an important state interest on the part of Michigan in regulating expenditures in *candidate* elections. In this sense, the Michigan law is not 'underinclusive' at all. Finally, the provision in Michigan corporate law authorizing share-holder actions against corporate waste might serve as a remedy for other types of political expenditures that have no legitimate connection to the corporation's business."

STEVENS, J., joined the Court's opinion and concurred: "[T]he distinction between individual expenditures and individual contributions that the Court identified in *Buckley,* should have little, if any, weight in reviewing corporate

---

3. [Whether] an organization presents the threat at which the campaign finance laws are aimed has to do with the particular characteristics of the organization at issue and not with the content of its speech. Of course, if a correlation between the two factors could be shown to exist, a group would be free to mount a First Amendment challenge on that basis. * * *

4. According to Justice Kennedy's dissent, the majority holds that "it is now a felony in Michigan for the Sierra Club, or the American Civil Liberties Union" to make independent expenditures. This characterization [overlooks] the central lesson of *MCFL* that the First Amendment may require exemptions, on an as-applied basis, from expenditure restrictions. * * *

8. [In] the context of labor unions, [r]ather than assuming that an employee accepts as "the deal," that the union will use his dues for any purpose that will advance the interests of the bargaining unit,

including political contributions and expenditures, we have determined that "the authority to impose dues and fees [is] restricted at least to the 'extent of denying the unions the right, over the employee's objection, to use his money to support political causes which he opposes,' even though Congress was well aware that *unions had historically expended funds in the support of political candidates and issues.*" *Ellis v. Railway Clerks* [Ch. 9, II supra].

Given the extensive state regulation of corporations, shareholder expectations are always a function of *state law.* It is circular to say, as does Justice Scalia, that *if* a State did not protect shareholders, they would have no expectation of being protected, and therefore that the State has no legitimate interest in protecting them. [I] believe it entirely proper for a State to decide to promote the ability of investors to purchase stock in corporations without fear that their money will be used to support candidates with whom they do not agree.

participation in candidate elections. In that context, I believe the danger of either the fact, or the appearance, of quid pro quo relationships provides an adequate justification for state regulation of both expenditures and contributions. Moreover, as we recognized in *Bellotti*, there is a vast difference between lobbying and debating public issues on the one hand, and political campaigns for election to public office on the other.''

SCALIA, J., dissented: '' 'Attention all citizens. To assure the fairness of elections by preventing disproportionate expression of the views of any single powerful group, your Government has decided that the following associations of persons shall be prohibited from speaking or writing in support of any candidate: _____'. In permitting Michigan to make private corporations the first object of this Orwellian announcement, the Court today endorses the principle that too much speech is an evil that the democratic majority can proscribe. I dissent because that principle is contrary to our case law and incompatible with the absolutely central truth of the First Amendment: that government cannot be trusted to assure, through censorship, the 'fairness' of political debate.

"The Court's opinion says that political speech of corporations can be regulated because '[s]tate law grants [them] special advantages' and because this 'unique state-conferred corporate structure * * * facilitates the amassing of large treasuries.' This analysis seeks to create one good argument by combining two bad ones. Those individuals who form that type of voluntary association known as a corporation are, to be sure, given special advantages—notably, the immunization of their personal fortunes from liability for the actions of the association—that the State is under no obligation to confer. But so are other associations and private individuals given all sorts of special advantages that the State need not confer, ranging from tax breaks to contract awards to public employment to outright cash subsidies. It is rudimentary that the State cannot exact as the price of those special advantages the forfeiture of First Amendment rights. The categorical suspension of the right of any person, or of any association of persons, to speak out on political matters must be justified by a compelling state need. Which is why the Court puts forward its second bad argument, the fact [t]hat corporations 'amas[s] large treasuries' [is] also not sufficient justification for the suppression of political speech, unless one thinks it would be lawful to prohibit men and women whose net worth is above a certain figure from endorsing political candidates. Neither of these two flawed arguments is improved by combining them.

"In *FCC v. League of Women Voters of California*, [Ch. 8, II supra], striking down a congressionally imposed ban upon editorializing by noncommercial broadcasting stations that receive federal funds, the *only* respect in which we considered the receipt of that 'special advantage' relevant was in determining whether the speech limitation could be justified under Congress' spending power, as a means of assuring that the subsidy was devoted only to the purposes Congress intended, which did not include political editorializing. We held it could not be justified on that basis, since 'a noncommercial educational station that receives only 1% of its overall income from [federal] grants is barred absolutely from all editorializing. [The] station has no way of limiting the use of its federal funds to all noneditorializing activities, and, more importantly, it is barred from using even wholly private funds to finance its editorial activity.' Of course the same is true here, even assuming that tax exemptions and other benefits accorded to incorporated associations constitute an exercise of the spending power. It is not just that portion of the corporation's assets attributable to the gratuitously conferred 'special advantages' that is prohibited from being used for political endorsements, but *all* of the corporation's [assets.] Commercial corporations may not have a public persona as sympathetic as that of public broadcasters, but they are no less entitled to this Court's concern.[b]

"As for the second part of the Court's argumentation, [c]ertain uses of 'massive wealth' in the electoral process—whether or not the wealth is the result of 'special advantages' conferred by the State—pose a substantial risk of corruption which constitutes a compelling need for the regulation of speech. Such a risk plainly exists when the wealth is given directly to the political candidate, to be used under his direction and control. [But the] "contention that prohibiting overt advocacy for or against a political candidate satisfies a 'compelling need' to avoid 'corruption' is easily dismissed. As we said in *Buckley*, '[i]t would naively underestimate the ingenuity and resourcefulness of persons and groups desiring to buy influence to believe that they would have much difficulty devising expenditures that skirted the restriction on express advocacy of election or defeat but nevertheless benefited the candidate's campaign.' Independent advocacy, moreover, unlike contributions, 'may well provide little assistance to the candidate's campaign and indeed may prove counterproductive,' thus reducing the danger that it will be exchanged 'as a quid pro quo for improper commitments from the candidate.' The latter point seems even more plainly true with respect to corporate advocates than it is with respect to individuals. I expect I could count on the fingers of one hand the candidates who would generally welcome, much less negotiate for, a formal endorsement by AT & T or General Motors. The advocacy of such entities that have 'amassed great wealth' will be effective only to the extent that it brings to the people's attention *ideas* which—despite the invariably self-interested and probably uncongenial source—strike them as true.

"The Court does not try to defend the proposition that independent advocacy poses a substantial risk of political 'corruption,' as English-speakers understand that term. Rather, [its] opinion ultimately rests upon that proposition whose violation constitutes the New Corruption: expenditures must 'reflect actual public support for the political ideas espoused.' This illiberal free-speech principle of 'one man, one minute' was proposed and

b. Scalia, J., also argued that *Buckley* had decided the question of independent corporate political expenditures. He observed that *Buckley* had included corporate plaintiffs. Those plaintiffs apparently were the New York Civil Liberties Union, Inc. and Human Events, Inc. Can *Buckley* be distinguished?

soundly rejected in *Buckley*. [And the Court's limitation of this principle to corporations] is of course entirely irrational. Why is it perfectly all right if advocacy by an individual billionaire is out of proportion with 'actual public support' for his positions? * * *

"Justice Brennan's concurrence would have us believe that the prohibition [is] a paternalistic measure to protect the corporate shareholder of America. [But] the Michigan [statute] permits corporations to take as many ideological and political positions as they please, so long as they are not 'in assistance of, or in opposition to, the nomination or election of a candidate.' That is indeed the Court's sole basis for distinguishing *Bellotti*, which invalidated restriction of a corporation's general political speech. The Michigan law appears to be designed, in other words, neither to protect shareholders, nor even (impermissibly) to 'balance' general political debate, but to protect political candidates. * * *

"But even if the object of the prohibition could plausibly be portrayed as the protection of shareholders (which the Court's opinion, at least, does not even assert), that would not suffice as a 'compelling need' to support this blatant restriction upon core political speech. A person becomes a member of that form of association known as a for-profit corporation in order to pursue economic objectives. [In] joining such an association, the shareholder knows that management may take any action that is ultimately in accord with what the majority (or a specified supermajority) of the shareholders wishes, so long as that action is designed to make a profit. That is the deal. The corporate actions to which the shareholder exposes himself, therefore, include many things that he may find politically or ideologically uncongenial: investment in South Africa, operation of an abortion clinic, publication of a pornographic magazine, or even publication of a newspaper that adopts absurd political views and makes catastrophic political endorsements. His only protections against such assaults upon his ideological commitments are (1) his ability to persuade a majority (or the requisite minority) of his fellow shareholders that the action should not be taken, and ultimately (2) his ability to sell his stock. (The latter course, by the way, does not ordinarily involve the severe psychic trauma or economic disaster that Justice Brennan's opinion suggests.) It seems to me entirely fanciful, in other words, to suggest that the Michigan statute makes any significant contribution towards insulating the exclusively profit-motivated shareholder from the rude world of politics and ideology.

"But even if that were not fanciful, it would be fanciful to think, as Justice Brennan's opinion assumes, that there is any difference between for-profit and not-for-profit corporations insofar as the need for protection of the individual member's ideological psyche is concerned. Would it be any more upsetting to a shareholder of General Motors that it endorsed the election of Henry Wallace (to stay comfortably in the past) than it would be to a member of the American Civil Liberties Union that it endorsed the election of George Wallace?

"Finally, a few words are in order concerning the Court's approval of the Michigan law's exception for 'media corporations.' [I]f one believes in the Court's rationale of 'compelling state need' to prevent amassed corporate wealth from skewing the political debate, surely that 'unique role' of the press does not give Michigan justification for *excluding* media corporations from coverage, but provides especially strong reason to *include* them. Amassed corporate wealth that regularly sits astride the ordinary channels of information is much more likely to produce the New Corruption (too much of one point of view) than amassed corporate wealth that is generally busy making money elsewhere. Such media corporations not only have vastly greater power to perpetrate the evil of overinforming, they also have vastly greater opportunity. General Motors, after all, will risk a stockholder suit if it makes a political endorsement that is not plausibly tied to its ability to make money for its shareholders. But media corporations make money *by* making political commentary, including endorsements. * * *

"Members of the institutional press, despite the Court's approval of their illogical exemption from the Michigan law, will find little reason for comfort in today's decision. The theory of New Corruption it espouses is a dagger at their throat. The Court today holds merely that media corporations *may* be excluded from the Michigan law, not that they *must* be."[c]

Notes and Questions

1. *Distinguishing wealthy individuals.* Does *Austin* adequately distinguish spending by business corporations from that of wealthy individuals? Can the two be distinguished because (a) corporations in spending shareholders' money do not represent the overall interests of particular shareholders, but only their economic interests in the corporation; (b) the managers of corporations may lobby for structures that benefit managers at the expense of shareholders; and (c) the damage to equality interests is more pervasive? To what extent is spending by unions subject to these concerns? To a greater or lesser degree? See generally Issacharoff & Ortiz, *Governing Through Intermediaries,* 85 Va.L.Rev. 1627 (1999).

2. *Distinguishing media corporations.* BURGER, C.J., concurring in *Bellotti,* addressed the difficulty of distinguishing media corporations from business corporations: "A disquieting aspect of Massachusetts' position is that it may carry the risk of impinging on the First Amendment rights of

---

c. Kennedy, J., joined by O'Connor and Scalia, JJ., also dissented. For valuable commentary relevant to the issues raised in *Austin,* see Baker, *Turner Broadcasting: Content–Based Regulation of Persons and Presses,* 1994 Sup.Ct.Rev. 57; Brudney, *Association, Advocacy, and the First Amendment,* 4 Wm. & Mary Bill of Rts.J. 3 (1995); Eule, *Promoting Speaker Diversity: Austin and Metro Broadcasting,* 1990 Sup.Ct.Rev. 105; Fisch, *Frankenstein's Monster Hits the Campaign Trail: An Approach to Regulation of Corporate Political Expenditures,* 32 Wm. & Mary L.Rev. 587 (1991); Lowenstein, *A Patternless Mosaic,* 21 Capital U.L.Rev. 381 (1992); Stark, *Strange Bedfellows: Two Paradoxes in Constitutional Discourse Over Corporate and Individual Political Activity,* 14 Cardozo L.Rev. 1347 (1993).

those who employ the corporate form—as most do—to carry on the business of mass communications, particularly the large media conglomerates. This is so because of the difficulty, and perhaps impossibility, of distinguishing, either as a matter of fact or constitutional law, media corporations from corporations such as appellants.

"Making traditional use of the corporate form, some media enterprises have amassed vast wealth and power and conduct many activities, some directly related—and some not—to their publishing and broadcasting activities. Today, a corporation might own the dominant newspaper in one or more large metropolitan centers, television and radio stations in those same centers and others, a newspaper chain, news magazines with nationwide circulation, national or worldwide wire news services, and substantial interests in book publishing and distribution enterprises. Corporate ownership may extend, vertically, to pulp mills and pulp timberlands to insure an adequate, continuing supply of newsprint and to trucking and steamship lines for the purpose of transporting the newsprint to the presses. Such activities would be logical economic auxiliaries to a publishing conglomerate. Ownership also may extend beyond to business activities unrelated to the task of publishing newspapers and magazines or broadcasting radio and television programs. Obviously, such far-reaching ownership would not be possible without the state-provided corporate form and its 'special rules relating to such matters as limited liability, perpetual life, and the accumulation, distribution, and taxation of assets.'

"In terms of 'unfair advantage in the political process' and 'corporate domination of the electoral process,' it could be argued that such media conglomerates as I describe pose a much more realistic threat to valid interests than do appellants and similar entities not regularly concerned with shaping popular opinion on public issues."

Consider Nicholson, *The Constitutionality of the Federal Restrictions on Corporate and Union Campaign Contributions and Expenditures,* 65 Corn. L.Rev. 945, 959 (1980): "A solution may be to focus on the distinction between media activities and other activities. A diversified corporation, partially involved in the media, would be entitled to full first amendment protection for its media-related operations. Under this approach, a newspaper would not lose its first amendment rights because it purchased a pulp mill, but it could not extend these rights to its pulp mill operations. An oil company that purchased a newspaper would not gain first amendment rights for its oil operations, but it would be able to assert these first amendment rights in the operation of its newspaper. The problem is not, to paraphrase Chief Justice Burger, the impracticability of making a distinction, but rather the difficulty of finding a theory that will justify a distinction."

Can self-expression serve as a distinguishing factor? See id. at 959–60. Is there more freedom "to choose and create the content of the delivered speech in the communications industry than in other industries"? Does the communication industry "display less allegiance to the profit motive than other industries''? Does it matter that the communications industry's product is speech? Can a fourth estate theory distinguish the press? On that premise, is there no reason to expand the definition of the press to include business corporations? [d]

3. *Distinguishing non-profit advocacy corporations.* 2 U.S.C.A. § 441(b) prohibits corporations or unions from making contributions or expenditures in connection with federal elections, but allows corporations and unions to establish and pay the expenses of segregated funds to be used for political purposes during federal elections. It prohibits corporations from soliciting contributions from persons other than its "stockholders and their families and its executive or administrative personnel and their families." In lieu of shareholders, corporations without capital stock are permitted to solicit contributions for such a fund from their "members." FEC v. NATIONAL RIGHT TO WORK COMM., 459 U.S. 197, 103 S.Ct. 552, 74 L.Ed.2d 364 (1982), per REHNQUIST, J., characterized these provisions as sufficiently tailored to prevent corruption or its appearance and to protect corporate contributors as to negate any judgment that restriction on associational interests was "undue." The National Right to Work Committee is an advocacy group organized as a nonprofit corporation without capital stock. It conceded that it was required to set up a segregated fund under § 441(b) but argued that it was entitled to solicit contributions from anyone that had previously responded to any of its prior mass mailings. The Court unanimously held that this conception of membership would render the statutory corporation "meaningless." Without requiring any evidentiary showing, the Court stated that the interest in avoiding corruption or its appearance justified "treating unions, corporations, and similar organizations differently from individuals."

FEC v. National Conservative Political Action Comm., supra, per REHNQUIST, J., characterized *National Right to Work Comm.* as proceeding from the premise that "in return for the special advantages that the State confers on the corporate form, individuals acting jointly through corporations forgo some of the rights they have as individuals." But he suggested that the question of whether a corporation could constitutionally be restricted in making independent expenditures to influence elections for public office was still open. Should advocacy groups organized in corporate form be treated like business corporations?

4. *Protecting shareholders.* After *Bellotti,* could government "authorize management to make some kinds of corporate speech, such as commercial speech, but not others, such as political or noncommercial speech, without the approval or express consent of stockholders"? See generally Victor Brudney, *Business Corporations and Stockholders' Rights Under the First Amendment,* 91 Yale L.J. 235 (1981).

d. See generally Baker, *Human Liberty and Freedom of Speech,* Chs. 10, 11 (1989); Baker, *Commercial Speech: A Problem in the Theory of Freedom,* 62 Iowa L.Rev. 1, 25–40 (1976); Baker, *Press Rights and Government Power to Structure the Press,* 34 U.Miami L.Rev. 819, 822–36 (1980).

5.   After *Austin* and *Bellotti,* could a state prevent non-voters including corporations and out of state citizens from make contributions to candidate or to initiatives within its state? See Note, *"Foreign" Campaign Contributions and the First Amendment,* 110 Harv. L.Rev. 1886 (1997)(discussing permanent resident aliens and American subsidiaries of foreign corporations).

*

Part 2

FREEDOM OF RELIGION

This part concerns the "religion clauses" of the first amendment, commonly known as the "establishment clause" (forbidding laws "respecting an establishment of religion") and the "free exercise clause" (forbidding laws "prohibiting the free exercise thereof"). It is difficult to explore either clause in isolation from the other. The extent to which the clauses interact may be illustrated by the matter of public financial aid to parochial schools, the subject of Ch. 11, Sec. II. On the one hand, does such aid violate the establishment clause? On the other hand, does a state's failure to provide such aid violate the free exercise clause? Another example of the potential conflict between the clauses—also considered in the materials below—is whether, on the one hand, a state's exemption of church buildings from property taxes contravenes the establishment clause or whether, on the other hand, a state's taxing these buildings contravenes the free exercise clause.

Despite this interrelationship of the two clauses, Ch. 11 deals almost exclusively with the establishment clause. Ch. 12, Sec. I then considers conventional problems under the free exercise clause. Ch. 12, Sec. II examines the complex issues of defining "religion" for purposes of the first amendment and determining the bona fides of an asserted "religious" belief—both matters usually presumed in the cases decided by the Supreme Court and the former never specifically addressed by a majority of the justices. Issues under each clause having been explored in some detail, Ch. 13 presents the subject of preference among religions that has both establishment and free exercise ramifications, and, finally, Ch. 14 discusses problems presented by government action that attempts to accommodate the seemingly opposing demands of the two religion clauses.[a]

a. For discussion of the various "articulated justifications for the special constitutional place of religion" by the Justices, see Michael E. Smith, *The Special Place of Religion in the Constitution,* 1983 Sup.Ct.Rev. 83.

Chapter 11

ESTABLISHMENT CLAUSE

I. INTRODUCTION

It is generally agreed that the establishment clause seeks to assure the separation of church and state in a nation characterized by religious pluralism. Prior to 1947, only two decisions concerning the establishment clause produced any significant consideration by the Court. *Bradfield v. Roberts*, 175 U.S. 291, 20 S.Ct. 121, 44 L.Ed. 168 (1899) upheld federal appropriations to a hospital in the District of Columbia, operated by the Catholic Church, for ward construction and care of indigent patients. *Quick Bear v. Leupp*, 210 U.S. 50, 28 S.Ct. 690, 52 L.Ed. 954 (1908) upheld federal disbursement of funds, held in trust for the Sioux Indians, to Catholic schools designated by the Sioux for payment of tuition costs.

In the Court's first modern decision, *Everson v. Board of Educ.* (1947), Part II infra, Rutledge, J., observed that "no provision of the Constitution is more closely tied to or given content by its generating history than the religious clause of the First Amendment." Black, J., writing for the majority, recounted that the religion clauses "reflected in the minds of early Americans a vivid mental picture of conditions and practices which they fervently wished to stamp out in order to preserve liberty for themselves and for their posterity." Black, J., detailed the history of religious persecution in Europe "before and contemporaneous with the colonization of America" and the "repetition of many of the old world practices" in the colonies. For example, in Massachusetts, Quakers, Baptists, and other religious minorities suffered harshly and were taxed for the established Congregational Church. In 1776, the Maryland "Declaration of Rights" stated that "only persons professing the Christian religion" were entitled to religious freedom, and not until 1826 were Jews permitted to hold public office. The South Carolina Constitution of 1778 stated that "the Christian Protestant religion shall be deemed [the] established religion of this state." Black, J., explained that "abhorrence" of these practices "reached its dramatic climax in Virginia in 1785–86" when "Madison wrote his great Memorial and Remonstrance" against renewal of "Virginia's tax levy for support of the established church" and the Virginia Assembly "enacted the famous 'Virginia Bill for Religious Liberty' originally

644

written by Thomas Jefferson. [T]he provisions of the First Amendment, in the drafting and adoption of which Madison and Jefferson played such leading roles, had the same objective and were intended to provide the same protection against governmental intrusion on religious liberty as the Virginia statute."

Still, the specific historical record suggests that rather than disclosing a coherent "intent of the Framers," those who influenced the framing of the First Amendment were animated by several distinct and sometimes conflicting goals. Thus, Jefferson believed that the integrity of government could be preserved only by erecting "a wall of separation" between church and state. A sharp division of authority was essential, in his view, to insulate the democratic process from ecclesiastical depradations and excursions. Madison shared this view, but also perceived church-state separation as benefiting religious institutions.[a] Even more strongly, Roger Williams, one of the earliest colonial proponents of religious freedom, posited an evangelical theory of separation, believing it vital to protect the sanctity of the church's "garden" from the "wilderness" of the state. Finally, there is evidence that one purpose of the establishment clause was to protect the existing state-established churches from the newly ordained national government.[b] (Indeed, although disestablishment was then well under way, the epoch of state-sponsored churches did not close until 1833 when Massachusetts separated church and state.)

The varied ideologies that prompted the founders do, however, disclose a dominant theme: according constitutional status to the integrity of individual conscience. Moreover, as revealed in Virginia's Bill for Religious Liberty, one practice seen by many as anathema to religious freedom was forcing the people to support religion through compulsory taxation, although there was a division of opinion as to whether non-preferential aid to religion violated liberty of conscience.[c]

A final matter involving the history of the establishment clause concerns *Everson*'s unanimous ruling that it was "made applicable to the states" by the fourteenth amendment.[d]

a. For the view that "the Constitution was written on the assumption [that] government is a threat to human liberty [and] not the other way around [i.e.,] the First Amendment constrains Congress, not churches," see Douglas Laycock, *Continuity and Change in the Threat to Religious Liberty: The Reformation Era and the Late Twentieth Century*, 80 Minn.L.Rev. 1047 (1996).

b. For the view that "the religion clauses amounted to a decision by the national government not to address substantive questions concerning the proper relationship between religion and government," but rather "did no more and no less than confirm the constitutional allocation of jurisdic-

tion over religion to the states," see Steven D. Smith, *Foreordained Failure: The Quest for a Constitutional Principle of Religious Freedom* (1995). Compare Kurt T. Lash, *The Second Adoption of the Establishment Clause: The Rise of the Nonestablishment Principle*, 27 Ariz.St.L.J. 1085 (1995) (this understanding had changed by the time of the fourteenth amendment).

c. The view that did not do so was endorsed by Rehnquist, J., in *Wallace v. Jaffree*, Part III, and in *Rosenberger v. University of Virginia*, Part II infra, Thomas, J., found "much to commend" this position.

d. *Application of the establishment clause to the states.* Is nonestablishment as "implicit in the concept of ordered liberty"

II. AID TO RELIGION

EVERSON v. BOARD OF EDUC., 330 U.S. 1, 67 S.Ct. 504, 91 L.Ed. 711 (1947), involved one of the major areas of controversy under the establishment clause: public financial assistance to church-related institutions (mainly parochial schools). A New Jersey township reimbursed parents for the cost of sending their children "on regular buses operated by the public transportation system," to and from schools, including nonprofit private and parochial schools. The Court, per BLACK, J., rejected a municipal taxpayer's

as the freedoms of speech, press, religious exercise, and assembly? See *Palko v. Connecticut*, 302 U.S. 319, 58 S.Ct. 149. Is it "fundamental to the American scheme"? See *Duncan v. Louisiana*, Ch. 6, Sec. 1, I.

Brennan, J., stated: "It has been suggested [that] absorption of the First Amendment's ban against congressional legislation 'respecting an establishment of religion' is conceptually impossible because the Framers meant the Establishment Clause also to foreclose any attempt by Congress to disestablish the existing official state churches. [But] the last of the formal state establishments was dissolved more than three decades before the Fourteenth Amendment was ratified, and thus the problem of protecting official state churches from federal encroachments could hardly have been any concern of those who framed the post-Civil War Amendments. [T]he Fourteenth Amendment created a panoply of new federal rights for the protection of citizens of the various States. And among those rights was freedom from such state governmental involvement in the affairs of religion as the Establishment Clause had originally foreclosed on the part of Congress.

"It has also been suggested that the 'liberty' guaranteed by the Fourteenth Amendment logically cannot absorb the Establishment Clause because that clause is not one of the provisions of the Bill of Rights which in terms protects a 'freedom' of the individual. The fallacy in this contention, I think, is that it underestimates the role of the Establishment Clause as a coguarantor, with the Free Exercise Clause, of religious liberty. * * *

"Finally, it has been contended that absorption of the Establishment Clause is precluded by the absence of any intention on the part of the Framers of the Fourteenth Amendment to circumscribe the residual powers of the States to aid religious activities and institutions in ways which fell short of formal establishments. That argument relies in part upon the express terms of the abortive Blaine Amendment—proposed several years after the adoption of the Fourteenth Amendment—which would

have added to the First Amendment a provision that '[n]o state shall make any law respecting an establishment of religion.' Such a restriction would have been superfluous, it is said, if the Fourteenth Amendment had already made the Establishment Clause binding upon the States.

"The argument proves too much, for the Fourteenth Amendment's protection of the free exercise of religion can hardly be questioned; yet the Blaine Amendment would also have added an explicit protection against state laws abridging that liberty." *School Dist. v. Schempp*, Part III infra (concurring opinion).

Consider Mark D. Howe, *The Constitutional Question*, in Religion and the Free Society 49, 55 (1958): "The Court did not seem to be aware [that] some legislative enactments respecting an establishment of religion affect most remotely, if at all, the personal rights of religious liberty. [If the Court] reexamined its own interpretations of history [it might allow] the states to take such action in aid of religion as does not appreciably affect the religious or other constitutional rights of individuals."

Compare Jesse H. Choper, *The Establishment Clause and Aid to Parochial Schools*, 56 Calif.L.Rev. 260, 274–75 (1968): "[Howe] assumes that while the fourteenth amendment prevents infringements of liberty which 'significantly affect' the individual, the first amendment forbids abridgements which do not do so. [A] central design of the establishment clause was that it [prevent] government generally from coercing religious belief and specifically from compulsorily taxing individuals for strictly religious purposes. If nonsecular federal action involves either of these consequences, [it] has seemingly violated the fourteenth amendment by 'significantly' affecting personal liberty. However, if federal action involves neither consequence, then [the] establishment clause itself—as a matter of constitutional construction—has probably not been breached." See also Note, *Toward a Uniform Valuation of the Religion Guarantees*, 80 Yale L.J. 77 (1970).

contention that payment for Catholic parochial school students violated the establishment clause:

"The 'establishment of religion' clause of the First Amendment means at least this: Neither a state nor the Federal Government can set up a church. Neither can pass laws which aid one religion, aid all religions, or prefer one religion over another. Neither can force nor influence a person to go to or to remain away from church against his will or force him to profess a belief or disbelief in any religion. No person can be punished for entertaining or professing religious beliefs or disbeliefs, for church attendance or non-attendance. No tax in any amount, large or small can be levied to support any religious activities or institutions, whatever they may be called, or whatever form they may adopt to teach or practice religion. Neither a state nor the Federal Government can, openly or secretly, participate in the affairs of any religious organizations or groups and vice versa. In the words of Jefferson, the clause against establishment of religion by law was intended to erect 'a wall of separation between Church and State.'

"We must [not invalidate the New Jersey statute] if it is within the state's constitutional power even though it approaches the verge of that power. New Jersey [cannot] contribute tax-raised funds to the support of an institution which teaches the tenets and faith of any church. On the other hand, other language of the amendment commands that New Jersey cannot hamper its citizens in the free exercise of their own religion. Consequently, it cannot exclude individual Catholics, Lutherans, Mohammedans, Baptists, Jews, Methodists, Non-believers, Presbyterians, or the members of any other faith, *because of their faith, or lack of it,* from receiving the benefits of public welfare legislation. While we do not mean to intimate that a state could not provide transportation only to children attending public schools, we must be careful, in protecting the citizens of New Jersey against state-established churches, to be sure that we do not inadvertently prohibit New Jersey from extending its general State law benefits to all its citizens without regard to their religious belief."

Noting that "the New Jersey legislature has decided that a public purpose will be served" by having children "ride in public buses to and from schools rather than run the risk of traffic and other hazards incident to walking or 'hitchhiking,' " the Court conceded "that children are helped to get to church schools. There is even a possibility that some of the children might not be sent to the church schools if the parents were compelled to pay their children's bus fares out of their own pockets when transportation to a public school would have been paid for by the State. [But] state-paid policemen, detailed to protect children going to and from church schools from the very real hazards of traffic, would serve much the same [purpose]. Similarly, parents might be reluctant to permit their children to attend schools which the state had cut off from such general government services as ordinary police and fire protection, connections for sewage disposal, public highways and sidewalks. Of course, cutting off church schools from these services, so separate and so indisputably marked off from the religious function, would make it far more difficult for the schools to operate. But such is obviously not the purpose of the First Amendment. That Amendment requires the state to be a neutral in its relations with groups of religious believers and non-believers; it does not require the state to be their adversary. * * *

"This Court had said that parents may, in the discharge of their duty under state compulsory education laws, send their children to a religious rather than a public school if the school meets the secular educational requirements which the state has power to impose. See *Pierce v. Society of Sisters,* Ch. 7, II. It appears that these parochial schools meet New Jersey's requirements. The State contributes no money to the schools. [Its] legislation, as applied, does no more than provide a general program to help parents get their children, regardless of their religion, safely and expeditiously to and from accredited schools.

"The First Amendment has erected a wall between church and state. That wall must be kept high and impregnable. We could not approve the slightest breach. New Jersey has not breached it here."

RUTLEDGE, J., joined by Frankfurter, Jackson and Burton, JJ., filed the principal dissent, arguing that the statute aided children "in a substantial way to get the very thing which they are sent to the particular school to secure, namely, religious training and teaching. * * * Commingling the religious with the secular teaching does not divest the whole of its religious permeation and emphasis or make them of minor part, if proportion were material. Indeed, on any other view, the constitutional prohibition always could be brought to naught by adding a modicum of the secular. [Transportation] cost is as much a part of the total expense, except at times in amount, as the cost of textbooks, of school lunches, of athletic equipment, of writing and other [materials]. Payment of transportation is [no] less essential to education, whether religious or secular, than payment for tuitions, for teachers' salaries, for buildings, equipment and necessary materials. [No] rational line can be drawn between payment for such larger, but not more necessary, items and payment for transportation. [Now], as in Madison's time, not the amount but the principle of assessment is wrong.

" * * * Public money devoted to payment of religious costs, educational or other, brings the quest for more. It brings too the struggle of sect against sect for the larger share or for any. Here one by numbers alone will benefit most, there another. That is precisely the history of societies which have had an established religion and dissident groups. It is the very thing Jefferson and Madison experienced and sought to guard against, whether in its blunt or in its more screened forms. The end of such strife cannot be other than to destroy the cherished liberty. The dominating group will achieve the dominant benefit; or all will embroil the state in their dissensions. * * *

"Nor is the case comparable to one of furnishing fire or police protection, or access to public highways. These things are matters of common right, part of the general need for safety. Certainly the fire department must not stand idly by while the church burns."

———

The Court did not again confront the subject of aid to parochial schools for more than two decades.[a] During the intervening years, however, the Court continued to develop its establishment clause rationale in cases involving other issues, emphasizing the "purpose and primary effect" of the challenged government action (see Part III infra).

WALZ v. TAX COMM'N, 397 U.S. 664, 90 S.Ct. 1409, 25 L.Ed.2d 697 (1970), per BURGER, C.J., upheld state tax exemption for "real or personal property used exclusively for religious, educational or charitable purposes": "The legislative purpose of a property tax exemption is neither the advancement nor the inhibition of religion; it is neither sponsorship nor hostility. New York, in common with the other states, has determined that certain entities that exist in a harmonious relationship to the community at large, and that foster its 'moral or mental improvement,' should not be inhibited in their activities by property taxation or the hazard of loss of those properties for nonpayment of taxes. It [has] granted exemption to all houses of religious worship within a broad class of property owned by nonprofit, quasi-public corporations which include hospitals, libraries, playgrounds, scientific, professional, historical and patriotic groups. * * *

"We find it unnecessary to justify the tax exemption on the social welfare services or 'good works' that some churches perform for parishioners and others—family counselling, aid to the elderly and the infirm, and to children. [To] give emphasis to so variable an aspect of the work of religious bodies would introduce an element of governmental evaluation and standards as to the worth of particular social welfare programs, thus producing a kind of continuing day-to-day relationship which the policy of neutrality seeks to minimize. * * * We must also be sure that the end result—the effect—is not an excessive government entanglement with religion. The test is inescapably one of degree. * * * Elimination of exemption would tend to expand the involvement of government by giving rise to tax valuation of church property, tax liens, tax foreclosures, and the direct confrontations and conflicts that follow in the train of those legal processes.

"Granting tax exemptions to churches necessarily operates to afford an indirect economic benefit and also gives rise to some, but yet a lesser, involvement than taxing them. * * * Obviously a direct money subsidy would be a relationship pregnant with involvement and, as with most governmental grant programs, could encompass sustained and detailed administrative relationships for enforcement of statutory or administrative standards, but that is not this case. * * *

a. See *Board of Educ. v. Allen*, 392 U.S. 236, 88 S.Ct. 1923, 20 L.Ed.2d 1060 (1968), upholding a program for lending state approved secular textbooks to all schoolchildren, including those attending church-related schools.

"It is obviously correct that no one acquires a vested or protected right in violation of the Constitution by long use * * *. Yet an unbroken practice of according the exemption to churches [is] not something to be lightly cast aside."

BRENNAN, J., concurred: "Tax exemptions and general subsidies [both] provide economic assistance, [but a] subsidy involves the direct transfer of public monies to the subsidized enterprise and uses resources exacted from taxpayers as a whole. An exemption, on the other hand, involves no such transfer.[b] It assists the exempted enterprise only passively." Harlan, J., also concurred.

DOUGLAS, J., dissented: "If history be our guide, then tax exemption of church property in this country is indeed highly suspect, as it arose in the early days when the church was an agency of the state. [The] financial support rendered here is to the church, the place of worship. A tax exemption is a subsidy."

Notes and Questions

1. *Size of government.* Consider William W. Van Alstyne, *Constitutional Separation of Church and State: The Quest for a Coherent Position,* 57 Am.Pol.Sci.Rev. 865, 881 (1963): "To finance expanding government services, [taxes] may gradually divert an increasing fraction of total personal income, necessarily leaving proportionately less money in the private sector to each person to spend according to his individual choice, in support of religion or other undertakings. To the extent that the tax revenues thus collected may not be spent by government to support religious enterprises, but must be used exclusively for secular purposes, the net effect, arguably, is to reduce the relative supply of funds available to religion." Does this warrant tax exemption for "religion"? Does it "warrant the judicial junking of the establishment clause"? Id. Is it "equally arguable that government fiscal activity, far from reducing disposable personal income, actually increases it"? Id. See also Alan Schwarz, *The Nonestablishment Principle: A Reply to Professor Giannella,* 81 Harv.L.Rev. 1465, 1469–70 (1968).

2. *"Neutrality" and "endorsement."* TEXAS MONTHLY, INC. v. BULLOCK, 489 U.S. 1, 109 S.Ct. 890, 103 L.Ed.2d 1 (1989), held violative of the establishment clause a Texas sales tax exemption for books and "periodicals that are published or distributed by a religious faith and that consist wholly of writings promulgating the teaching of the faith." BRENNAN, J., joined by Marshall and Stevens, JJ., referred to several important themes in the Court's developing establishment clause rationale:[c] "[*Walz*] emphasized that the benefits derived by religious organizations flowed to a large number

---

b. What of the fact that exemption for churches augments the tax bills of others? For the view that there is a constitutional distinction between tax exemptions ("a standing arrangement open to a wide array of organizations") and annual appropriations, see Edward A. Zelinsky, *Are Tax*

"Benefits" Constitutionally Equivalent to Direct Expenditures, 112 Harv.L.Rev. 379 (1998).

c. In addition to "neutrality" and "endorsement," a third theme—"coercion"—is discussed more fully in Section IV infra.

of nonreligious groups as [well]. However, when government directs a subsidy exclusively to religious organizations [that] either burdens nonbeneficiaries markedly or cannot reasonably be seen as removing a significant state-imposed deterrent to the free exercise of religion, as Texas has done, it 'provide[s] unjustifiable awards of assistance to religious organizations' and cannot but 'conve[y] a message of endorsement' to slighted members of the community. This is particularly true where, as here, the subsidy is targeted at writings that *promulgate* the teachings of religious faiths. It is difficult to view Texas' narrow exemption as anything but state sponsorship of religious belief [which] lacks a secular objective."

BLACKMUN, J., joined by O'Connor, J., concurred: "[A] tax exemption *limited* to the sale of religious literature * * * offends our most basic understanding of what the establishment clause is all about." White, J., concurred on freedom of press grounds. Scalia, J., joined by Rehnquist, C.J., and Kennedy, J., dissented from Brennan, J.'s distinction of *Walz*.

———

In 1971, LEMON v. KURTZMAN, 403 U.S. 602, 91 S.Ct. 2105, 29 L.Ed.2d 745, per BURGER C.J., which invalidated state salary supplements to teachers of secular subjects in nonpublic schools, articulated a three-part test for judging establishment clause issues. This test is most frequently invoked by the lower courts and—as the materials that follow indicate—formally (if not operatively) has yet to be overruled: "First, the statute must have a secular legislative purpose; second, its principal or primary effect must be one that neither advances nor inhibits religion,[d] finally, the statute must not foster "an excessive government entanglement with religion." During the next fifteen years, the Court, using the *Lemon* test, invalidated a large number of aid programs for elementary and secondary schools, even though it found that virtually all had a "secular" purpose.[e] The *Lemon* Court began with a critical premise: the mission of church related elementary and

d. Compare Douglas Laycock, *Towards a General Theory of the Religion Clauses: The Case of Church Labor Relations and the Right to Church Autonomy*, 81 Colum.L.Rev. 1373, 1381, 1384 (1981): "The 'inhibits' language is at odds with the constitutional text and with the Court's own statements of the origins and purposes of [the] clause. Government support for religion is an element of every establishment claim, just as a burden or restriction on religion is an element of every free exercise claim. Regulation that burdens religion, enacted because of the government's general interest in regulation, is simply not establishment."

e. "This reflects, at least in part, our reluctance to attribute unconstitutional motives to the states, particularly when a plausible secular purpose for the state's program may be discerned from the face of the statute." *Mueller v. Allen*, cited infra. *Mueller* added: "A state's decision to defray the cost of educational expenses incurred by parents—regardless of the type of schools their children attend—evidences a purpose that is both secular and understandable. An educated populace is essential to the political and economic health of any community, and a state's efforts to assist parents in meeting the rising cost of educational expenses plainly serves this secular purpose of ensuring that the state's citizenry is well-educated. Similarly, [states] could conclude that there is a strong public interest in assuring the continued financial health of private schools, both sectarian and non-sectarian. By educating a substantial number of students such schools relieve public schools of a correspondingly great burden—

secondary schools is to teach religion, and all subjects either are, or carry the potential of being, permeated with religion. Thus, states would have to engage in a "comprehensive, discriminating, and continuing state surveillance" to prevent misuse of tax funds for religious purposes, which would be impermissibly entangling, and "pregnant with dangers of excessive government direction of church schools and hence of churches."[f] Furthermore, state assistance risked another sort of entanglement: "divisive political potential" along religious lines.[g]

The case that follows reviews the important subsequent decisions and, although there is no opinion for the Court, brings the matter up to date.

MITCHELL v. HELMS

530 U.S. 793, 120 S.Ct. 2530, 147 L.Ed.2d 660 (2000).

JUSTICE THOMAS announced the judgment of the Court and delivered an opinion, in which THE CHIEF JUSTICE, JUSTICE SCALIA, and JUSTICE KENNEDY join. * * *

to the benefit of all taxpayers. In addition, private schools may serve as a benchmark for public schools."

f. White, J., dissenting in *Lemon,* accused the Court of "creat[ing] an insoluble paradox for the State and the parochial schools. The State cannot finance secular instruction if it permits religion to be taught in the same classroom; but if it exacts a promise that religion not be so taught—a promise the school and its teachers are quite willing and on this record able to give—and enforces it, it is then entangled in the 'no entanglement' aspect of the Court's Establishment Clause jurisprudence."

g. *Lemon* reasoned: "In a community where such a large number of pupils are served by church-related schools, it can be assumed that state assistance will entail considerable political activity [by partisans and opponents]. Candidates will be forced to declare and voters to choose. It would be unrealistic to ignore the fact that many people confronted with issues of this kind will find their votes aligned with their faith.

"Ordinarily political debate and division, however vigorous or even partisan, are normal and healthy manifestations of our democratic system of government, but political division along religious lines was one of the principal evils against which the First Amendment was intended to protect. Paul A. Freund, *Public Aid to Parochial Schools,* 82 Harv.L.Rev. 1680, 1692 (1969)."

Compare Alan Schwarz, *No Imposition of Religion: The Establishment Clause Value,*

77 Yale L.J. 692, 711 (1968): "If avoidance of strife were an independent [establishment clause] value, no legislation could be adopted on any subject which aroused strong and divided [religious] feelings." See Jesse H. Choper, *The Establishment Clause and Aid to Parochial Schools,* 56 Calif.L.Rev. 260, 273 (1968): "Nor would a denial of aid to parochial schools largely diminish the extent of religious political activity. In fact, it 'might lead to greater political ruptures caused by the alienation of segments of the religious community.' Those who send their children to parochial schools might intensify opposition to increased governmental aid to public education." Contrast William D. Valente & William A. Stanmeyer, *Public Aid to Parochial Schools—A Reply to Professor Freund,* 59 Geo.L.J. 59, 70 n. 46 (1970): "[O]ne's assessment of the accuracy of the views of Professors Freund, Schwartz, and Choper as to likely political repercussions is itself a political judgment and not judicial, and [the] weighing of political reactions is a function of legislatures and not of courts." For the view that the historical evidence shows "that it is misguided to interpret the first amendment as prohibiting legislative consideration of an issue affecting religion on the ground that the very act of consideration will spawn impermissible religious division," see Peter M. Schotten, *The Establishment Clause and Excessive Governmental–Religious Entanglement,* 15 Wake For.L.Rev. 207, 225 (1979).

Chapter 2 of the Education Consolidation and Improvement Act of 1981, has its origins in the Elementary and Secondary Education Act of 1965 (ESEA), and is a close cousin of the provision of the ESEA that we recently considered in *Agostini v. Felton*, 521 U.S. 203, 117 S.Ct. 1997, 138 L.Ed.2d 391 (1997). [Chapter 2 lends educational materials (mainly for libraries and computers)—which may not "supplant funds from non-Federal sources"—to elementary and secondary schools, both public and private. The "services, materials, and equipment" for participating private schools (which were required to be nonprofit) must be "secular, neutral and nonideological."] It appears that, in an average year, about 30% of Chapter 2 funds spent in Jefferson Parish [La.] are allocated for private schools. [Since 1986, 46 private schools participated.] Of these 46, 34 were Roman Catholic; 7 were otherwise religiously affiliated; and 5 were not religiously affiliated.

Respondents filed suit in December 1985, alleging, among other things, that Chapter 2, as applied in Jefferson Parish, violated the Establishment Clause. The case's tortuous history over the next 15 years indicates well the degree to which our Establishment Clause jurisprudence has shifted in recent times.[a] [In] 1990, after extended discovery, Chief Judge Heebe of the District Court for the Eastern District of Louisiana granted summary judgment in favor of respondents [because] under the second part of our three-part test in *Lemon*, the program had the primary effect of advancing religion. Chapter 2 had such effect, in his view, because the materials and equipment loaned to the Catholic schools were direct aid to those schools and because the Catholic schools [were] "pervasively sectarian." Chief Judge Heebe relied primarily on *Meek v. Pittenger*, 421 U.S. 349, 95 S.Ct. 1753, 44 L.Ed.2d 217 (1975), and *Wolman v. Walter*, 433 U.S. 229, 97 S.Ct. 2593, 53 L.Ed.2d 714 (1977), in which we held unconstitutional programs that provided many of the same sorts of materials and equipment as does Chapter 2.

[Six] years later, Chief Judge Heebe having retired, Judge Livaudais [upheld] Chapter 2, pointing [to] our 1993 decision in *Zobrest v. Catalina Foothills School Dist.*, 509 U.S. 1, 113 S.Ct. 2462, 125 L.Ed.2d 1, in which we held that a State could, as part of a federal program for the disabled, provide a sign-language interpreter to a deaf student at a Catholic high school. Judge Livaudais [also] invoked *Rosenberger v. Rector and Visitors of Univ. of Va.*, 515 U.S. 819, 115 S.Ct. 2510, 132 L.Ed.2d 700 (1995), in [which], we held that the Establishment Clause does not require a public university to exclude a student-run religious publication from assistance available to numerous other student-run publications.[b] [While respondents'] appeal was

---

a. As early as *Lemon* in 1971, the Court observed that, on the issue of financial assistance to sectarian schools, "we can only dimly perceive the lines of demarcation in this extraordinarily sensitive area of constitutional law." *Committee for Pub. Educ. v. Regan*, 444 U.S. 646, 100 S.Ct. 840, 63 L.Ed.2d 94 (1980)—holding that states may reimburse parochial schools for the cost of routine recordkeeping and administering state-prepared tests—observed that the "decisions have tended to avoid categorical imperatives and absolutist approaches at either end of the range of possible outcomes. This course sacrifices clarity and predictability for flexibility."

pending, we decided *Agostini*, in which we approved a program [that] provided public employees to teach remedial classes at private schools, including religious schools. In so holding, we overruled *Aguilar v. Felton*, 473 U.S. 402, 105 S.Ct. 3232, 87 L.Ed.2d 290 (1985), and partially overruled *School Dist. of Grand Rapids v. Ball*, 473 U.S. 373, 105 S.Ct. 3248, 87 L.Ed.2d 267 (1985), both of which had involved such a program. [*Agostini*] acknowledged that our cases discussing excessive entanglement had applied many of the same considerations as had our cases discussing primary effect, and we therefore recast *Lemon's* entanglement inquiry as simply one criterion relevant to determining a statute's effect. We also acknowledged that our cases had pared somewhat the factors that could justify a finding of excessive entanglement. * * *

In this case, our inquiry under *Agostini's* purpose and effect test is a narrow one. Because respondents do not challenge the District Court's holding that Chapter 2 has a secular purpose, [we] will consider only Chapter 2's effect. Further, in determining that effect, we will consider only the first two *Agostini* criteria, since [respondents agree] that Chapter 2 does not create an excessive entanglement. Considering Chapter 2 in light of our more recent case law, we conclude that it neither results in religious indoctrination by the government nor defines its recipients by reference to religion. [For] the same reason, Chapter 2 also "cannot reasonably be viewed as an endorsement of religion," *Agostini*. [We] therefore hold that Chapter 2 is not a "law respecting an establishment of religion." In so holding, we acknowledge [that] *Meek* and *Wolman* are anomalies [and] therefore conclude that they are no longer good law.

As we indicated in *Agostini*, [the] question whether governmental aid to religious schools results in governmental indoctrination is ultimately a question whether any religious indoctrination that occurs in those schools could reasonably be attributed to governmental action. We have also indicated that the answer to the question of indoctrination will resolve the question whether a program of educational aid 'subsidizes' religion, as our religion cases use that term.

In distinguishing between indoctrination that is attributable to the State and indoctrination that is not, we have consistently turned to the principle of neutrality. [If] the religious, irreligious, and areligious are all alike eligible for governmental aid, no one would conclude that any indoctrination that any particular recipient conducts has been done at the behest of the government. [To] put the point differently, if the government, seeking to further some legitimate secular purpose, offers aid on the same terms, without regard to religion, to all who adequately further that purpose, then it is fair to say that any aid going to a religious recipient only has the effect

b. The student publication "offered a Christian perspective on both personal and community issues." Souter, J., joined by Stevens, Ginsburg and Breyer, JJ., dissenting, described the magazine as "straightfor-ward exhortation to enter into a relationship with God as revealed in Jesus Christ, and to satisfy a series of moral obligations derived from the teachings of Jesus Christ."

of furthering that secular purpose. The government, in crafting such an aid program, has had to conclude that a given level of aid is necessary to further that purpose among secular recipients and has provided no more than that same level to religious recipients.

As a way of assuring neutrality, we have repeatedly considered whether any governmental aid that goes to a religious institution does so "only as a result of the genuinely independent and private choices of individuals." [For] if numerous private choices, rather than the single choice of a government, determine the distribution of aid pursuant to neutral eligibility criteria, then a government cannot, or at least cannot easily, grant special favors that might lead to a religious establishment. Private choice also helps guarantee neutrality by mitigating the preference for pre-existing recipients that is arguably inherent in any governmental aid program, and that could lead to a program inadvertently favoring one religion or favoring religious private schools in general over nonreligious ones. * * *

The principles of neutrality and private choice, and their relationship to each other, were prominent not only in *Agostini*, but also in *Zobrest, Witters* [*v. Washington Dept. of Servs. for Blind*, 474 U.S. 481, 488–489, 106 S.Ct. 748, 88 L.Ed.2d 846 (1986)], and *Mueller* [*v. Allen*, 463 U.S. 388, 397, 103 S.Ct. 3062, 77 L.Ed.2d 721 (1983)]. The heart of our reasoning in *Zobrest,* [was that] neutrality and private choices together eliminated any possible attribution to the government even when the interpreter translated classes on Catholic doctrine.

Witters and *Mueller* employed similar reasoning. In *Witters*, we held that the Establishment Clause did not bar a State from including within a neutral program providing tuition payments for vocational rehabilitation a blind person studying at a Christian college to become a pastor, missionary, or youth director.[6]c

The [state income] tax deduction for educational expenses [incurred at any nonprofit elementary or secondary school] that we upheld in *Mueller* was, in these respects, the same as the tuition grant in *Witters*. We upheld it chiefly because it "neutrally provides state assistance to a broad spectrum of citizens," and because "numerous, private choices of individual parents of school-age children," determined which schools would benefit from the deductions. * * *

Agostini's [second] criterion requires a court to consider whether an aid program "define[s] its recipients by reference to religion" [—i.e.] whether

6. The majority opinion also noted that only a small portion of the overall aid under the State's program would go to religious education, [but more] recently, in *Agostini*, we held that the proportion of aid benefiting students at religious schools pursuant to a neutral program involving private choices was irrelevant to the constitutional inquiry.

c. On remand, the state court held that the aid in this case would violate the Washington constitution's provision that "no public money [shall] be appropriated for [any] religious instruction." *Witters v. State Commission for the Blind*, 112 Wash.2d 363, 771 P.2d 1119, cert. denied, 493 U.S. 850 (1989).

the criteria for allocating the aid "creat[e] a financial incentive to undertake religious indoctrination." [*Agostini* made] clear the close relationship between this rule, incentives, and private choice. For to say that a program does not create an incentive to choose religious schools is to say that the private choice is truly "independent." When such an incentive does exist, there is a greater risk that one could attribute to the government any indoctrination by the religious schools.

We hasten to add, what should be obvious from the rule itself, that simply because an aid program offers private schools, and thus religious schools, a benefit that they did not previously receive does not mean that the program, by reducing the cost of securing a religious education, creates, under *Agostini's* second criterion, an "incentive" for parents to choose such an education for their children. For *any* aid will have some such effect.

Respondents [argue] first, and chiefly, that "direct, nonincidental" aid to the primary educational mission of religious schools is always impermissible.[7]

Although some of our earlier cases [did] emphasize the distinction between direct and indirect aid, the purpose of this distinction was merely to prevent "subsidization" of religion. [O]ur more recent cases address this purpose not through the direct/indirect distinction but rather through the principle of private choice. [If] aid to schools, even "direct aid," is neutrally available and, before reaching or benefiting any religious school, first passes through the hands (literally or figuratively) of numerous private citizens who are free to direct the aid elsewhere, the government has not provided any "support of religion." [It] was undeniable in *Witters* that the aid (tuition) would ultimately go to the Inland Empire School of the Bible and would support religious education. We viewed this arrangement, however, as no different from a government issuing a paycheck to one of its employees knowing that the employee would direct the funds to a religious institution. Both arrangements would be valid * * *. Whether one chooses to label this program "direct" or "indirect" is a rather arbitrary choice, one that does not further the constitutional analysis.

Of course, we have seen "special Establishment Clause dangers," *Rosenberger*, when money is given to religious schools or entities directly[d] rather than, as in *Witters* and *Mueller*, indirectly.[8] But direct payments of money

---

7. Respondents also contend that Chapter 2 aid supplants, rather than supplements, the core educational function of parochial schools and therefore has the effect of furthering religion. Our case law does provide some indication that this distinction may be relevant to determining whether aid results in governmental indoctrination, but we have never delineated the distinction's contours or held that it is constitutionally required. Nor, [do] we need to resolve the distinction's constitutional status today, [for] Chapter 2 itself requires that aid may only be supplemental. * * *

d. The *Rosenberger* majority, which consisted of the *Mitchell* plurality and O'Connor, J., noted that its decision "cannot be read as addressing an expenditure from a general tax fund." Rather, the money came from a "special student activities fund from which any group of students with [recognized] status can draw for purposes consistent with the University's educational mission." As in *Lamb's Chapel*, fn. 9 infra, "a

are not at issue in this case, and we refuse to allow a "special" case to create a rule for all cases.

Respondents also contend that the Establishment Clause requires that aid to religious schools not be impermissibly religious in nature or be divertible to religious use. We agree with the first part of this argument but not the second. Respondents' "no divertibility" rule is inconsistent with our more recent case law and is unworkable. So long as the governmental aid is not itself "unsuitable for use in the public schools because of religious content," and eligibility for aid is determined in a constitutionally permissible manner, any use of that aid to indoctrinate cannot be attributed to the government and is thus not of constitutional concern [discussing *Zobrest, Witters* and *Mueller*]. [J]ust as a government interpreter does not herself inculcate a religious message—even when she is conveying one—so also a government computer or overhead projector does not itself inculcate a religious message, even when it is conveying one.[9] * * *

public university may maintain its own computer facility and give student groups access to that facility, including the use of the printers, on a religion neutral, say first-come-first-served, basis." This is no different than "a school paying a third-party contractor to operate the facility on its behalf. The latter occurs here." Since the University made payments for publication costs directly to the printing companies, "we do not confront a case where, even under a neutral program that includes nonsectarian recipients, the government is making direct money payments to an institution or group that is engaged in religious activity." Moreover, "the student publication is not a religious institution, at least in the usual sense of that term as used in our case law."

In a separate concurrence, O'Connor, J., noted that "unlike monies dispensed from state or federal treasuries, the Student Activities Fund is collected from students who themselves administer the fund." Thus, there is a "possibility that the student fee is susceptible to a Free Speech Clause challenge by an objecting student that she should not be compelled to pay for speech with which she disagrees. See, e.g., *Keller; Abood* [Ch. 9, II]. The existence of such an opt-out possibility not available to citizens generally, provides a potential basis for distinguishing proceeds of the student fees in this case from proceeds of the general assessments in support of religion that lie at the core of the prohibition against religious funding, and from government funds generally."

The dissenters distinguished cases like *Lamb's Chapel* as based "on the recognition that all speakers are entitled to use the

street corner (even though the State paves the roads and provides police protection to everyone on the street) and on the analogy between the public street corner and open classroom space. [T]he cases cannot be lifted to a higher plane of generalization without admitting that new economic benefits are being extended directly to religion in clear violation of the principle barring direct aid."

8. The reason for such concern is not that the form per se is bad, but that such a form creates special risks that governmental aid will have the effect of advancing religion (or, even more, a purpose of doing so). An indirect form of payment reduces these risks. It is arguable, however, at least after *Witters*, that the principles of neutrality and private choice would be adequate to address those special risks, for it is hard to see the basis for deciding *Witters* differently simply if the State had sent the tuition check directly to whichever school Witters chose to attend. Similarly, we doubt it would be unconstitutional if, to modify *Witters*'s hypothetical, a government employer directly sent a portion of an employee's paycheck to a religious institution designated by that employee pursuant to a neutral charitable program. [Finally,] at least some of our prior cases striking down direct payments involved serious concerns about whether the payments were truly neutral. See, e.g., *Committee for Pub. Educ. v. Nyquist*, 413 U.S. 756, 93 S.Ct. 2955, 37 L.Ed.2d 948 (1973) [involving a state partial tuition tax credit to parents who sent their children to nonpublic schools. For parents too poor to be liable for income taxes and therefore unable to benefit from a tax credit, the state gave an outright grant of up to fifty percent of tuition].

A concern for divertibility, as opposed to improper content, is misplaced not only because it fails to explain why the sort of aid that we have allowed is permissible, but also because it is boundless—enveloping all aid, no matter how trivial—and thus has only the most attenuated (if any) link to any realistic concern for preventing an "establishment of religion." Presumably, for example, government-provided lecterns, chalk, crayons, pens, paper, and paintbrushes would have to be excluded from religious schools under respondents' proposed rule. But we fail to see how indoctrination by means of (i.e., diversion of) such aid could be attributed to the government. In fact, the risk of improper attribution is less when the aid lacks content, for there is no risk (as there is with books), of the government inadvertently providing improper content. See *Allen* (Douglas, J., dissenting). Finally, any aid, with or without content, is "divertible" in the sense that it allows schools to "divert" resources. Yet we have "not accepted the recurrent argument that all aid is forbidden because aid to one aspect of an institution frees it to spend its other resources on religious ends."

It is perhaps conceivable that courts could take upon themselves the task of distinguishing among the myriad kinds of possible aid based on the ease of diverting each kind. But it escapes us how a court might coherently draw any such line. * * *

The dissent serves up a smorgasbord of 11 factors that, depending on the facts of each case "in all its particularity," could be relevant to the constitutionality of a school-aid program. [The] dissent resurrects the concern for political divisiveness that once occupied the Court but that post-*Aguilar* cases have rightly disregarded. As Justice O'Connor explained in dissent in *Aguilar*: "It is curious indeed to base our interpretation of the Constitution on speculation as to the likelihood of a phenomenon which the parties may create merely by prosecuting a lawsuit." * * *

One of the dissent's factors deserves special mention: whether a school that receives aid (or whose students receive aid) is pervasively sectarian. The dissent is correct that there was a period when this factor mattered, particularly if the pervasively sectarian school was a primary or secondary school. But that period [is] thankfully long past [discussing *Witters*, *Zobrest* and *Agostini*. The] religious nature of a recipient should not matter to the constitutional analysis, so long as the recipient adequately furthers the

---

9. The dissent would find an establishment of religion if a government-provided projector were used in a religious school to show a privately purchased religious film, even though a public school that possessed the same kind of projector would likely be constitutionally barred from refusing to allow a student bible club to use that projector in a classroom to show the very same film, where the classrooms and projectors were generally available to student groups.

See *Lamb's Chapel v. Center Moriches Union Free School Dist.*, 508 U.S. 384, 113 S.Ct. 2141, 124 L.Ed.2d 352 (1993), [holding that a school district did not violate the establishment clause in permitting a church's after-hours use of school facilities to show a religiously oriented film series on family values when the school district also permitted presentation of views on the subject by nonreligious groups].

government's secular purpose. If a program offers permissible aid to the religious (including the pervasively sectarian), the areligious, and the irreligious, it is a mystery which view of religion the government has established, and thus a mystery what the constitutional violation would be. The pervasively sectarian recipient has not received any special favor, and it is most bizarre that the Court would, as the dissent seemingly does, reserve special hostility for those who take their religion seriously * * *.

[T]he inquiry into the recipient's religious views required by a focus on whether a school is pervasively sectarian is not only unnecessary but also offensive.[e] It is well established, in numerous other contexts, that courts should refrain from trolling through a person's or institution's religious beliefs. [In] addition, and related, the application of the "pervasively sectarian" factor collides with our decisions that have prohibited governments from discriminating in the distribution of public benefits based upon religious status or sincerity. See *Rosenberger*; *Lamb's Chapel*.[19]

Finally, hostility to aid to pervasively sectarian schools has a shameful pedigree * * *. Opposition to aid to "sectarian" schools acquired prominence in the 1870's with Congress's consideration (and near passage) of the Blaine Amendment, which would have amended the Constitution to bar any aid to sectarian institutions. Consideration of the amendment arose at a time of pervasive hostility to the Catholic Church and to Catholics in general, and it was an open secret that "sectarian" was code for "Catholic." Notwithstanding its history, of course, "sectarian" could, on its face, describe the school of any religious sect, but the Court eliminated this possibility of confusion when [it] coined the term "pervasively sectarian"—a term which, at that time, could be applied almost exclusively to Catholic parochial schools and which even today's dissent exemplifies chiefly by reference to such schools. [This] doctrine, born of bigotry, should be buried now. * * *

[W]e agree with the dissent that there is evidence of actual diversion [in this case] and that, were the safeguards anything other than anemic, there would almost certainly be more such evidence. In any event, for reasons we discussed supra, the evidence of actual diversion and the weakness of the safeguards against actual diversion are not relevant to the constitutional inquiry * * *.

Respondents do, however, point to some religious books that [were] improperly allowed to be loaned to several religious schools, and they contend that the monitoring programs [are] insufficient to prevent such errors. The evidence, however, establishes just the opposite, for the improper

---

e. For the view that "the possibilities for misunderstandings, spiritual insensitivity, and outright sectarian bigotry wrought by the 'pervasively sectarian' test is breathtaking," see Carl H. Esbeck, *Myths, Miscues, and Misconceptions: No–Aid Separationism and the Establishment Clause,* 13 Not.D.J.L. Eth. & Pub.Pol. 285 (1999).

19. Indeed, [to] require exclusion of religious schools from such a program would raise serious questions under the Free Exercise Clause. See, e.g., *Church of Lukumi Babalu Aye, Inc. v. Hialeah*, [Ch. 12, I infra]; *Everson*.

lending of library books occurred—and was discovered and remedied—before this litigation began almost 15 years [ago]. We are unwilling to elevate scattered de minimis statutory violations, discovered and remedied by the relevant authorities themselves prior to any litigation, to such a level as to convert an otherwise unobjectionable parishwide program into a law that has the effect of advancing religion. * * *

JUSTICE O'CONNOR, with whom JUSTICE BREYER joins, concurring in the judgment.

* * * I believe that *Agostini* likewise controls the constitutional inquiry respecting Title II. [To] the extent our decisions in *Meek* and *Wolman* are inconsistent with the Court's judgment today, I agree that those decisions should be overruled. * * *

I write separately because, in my view, the plurality announces a rule of unprecedented breadth for the evaluation of Establishment Clause challenges to government school-aid programs. Reduced to its essentials, the plurality's rule states that government aid to religious schools does not have the effect of advancing religion so long as the aid is offered on a neutral basis and the aid is secular in content. [First,] the plurality's treatment of neutrality comes close to assigning that factor singular importance in the future adjudication of Establishment Clause challenges to government school-aid programs. Second, the plurality's approval of actual diversion of government aid to religious indoctrination is in tension with our precedents and, in any event, unnecessary to decide the instant case.

[W]e have never held that a government-aid program passes constitutional muster solely because of the neutral criteria it employs as a basis for distributing aid. For example, in *Agostini,* neutrality was only one of several factors we considered * * * (noting lack of evidence of inculcation of religion by Title I instructors, legal requirement that Title I services be supplemental to regular curricula, and that no Title I funds reached religious schools' coffers). Indeed, given that the aid in *Agostini* had secular content and was distributed on the basis of wholly neutral criteria, our consideration of additional factors demonstrates that the plurality's rule does not accurately describe our recent Establishment Clause jurisprudence. See also *Zobrest,* (noting that no government funds reached religious school's coffers, aid did not relieve school of expense it otherwise would have assumed, and aid was not distributed to school but to the child).

[At] least two of the decisions at the heart of today's case demonstrate that we have long been concerned that secular government aid not be diverted to the advancement of religion. [See] *Agostini,* ("[N]o evidence has ever shown that any New York City Title I instructor teaching on parochial school premises attempted to inculcate religion in students"); *Allen* ("Nothing in this record supports the proposition that all textbooks, whether they deal with mathematics, physics, foreign languages, history, or literature, are used by the parochial schools to teach religion"). * * *

The plurality bases its holding that actual diversion is permissible on *Witters* and *Zobrest*. Those decisions, however, rested [on] the understanding that the aid was provided directly to the individual student who, in turn, made the choice of where to put that aid to [use.] This characteristic of both programs made them less like a direct subsidy, which would be impermissible under the Establishment Clause, and more akin to the government issuing a paycheck to an employee who, in turn, donates a portion of that check to a religious institution. [Like] Justice Souter, I do not believe that we should treat a per-capita-aid program the same as the true private-choice programs considered in *Witters* and *Zobrest*. First, when the government provides aid directly to the student beneficiary, that student can attend a religious school and yet retain control over whether the secular government aid will be applied toward the religious education. The fact that aid flows to the religious school and is used for the advancement of religion is therefore *wholly* dependent on the student's private decision.

Second, [i]n terms of public perception, a government program of direct aid to religious schools based on the number of students attending each school differs meaningfully from the government distributing aid directly to individual students who, in turn, decide to use the aid at the same religious schools. In the former example, if the religious school uses the aid to inculcate religion in its students, it is reasonable to say that the government has communicated a message of endorsement. Because the religious indoctrination is supported by government assistance, the reasonable observer would naturally perceive the aid program as *government* support for the advancement of religion. That the amount of aid received by the school is based on the school's enrollment does not separate the government from the endorsement of the religious message. The aid formula does not—and could not—indicate to a reasonable observer that the inculcation of religion is endorsed only by the individuals attending the religious school, who each affirmatively choose to direct the secular government aid to the school and its religious mission. No such choices have been made. In contrast, when government aid supports a school's religious mission only because of independent decisions made by numerous individuals to guide their secular aid to that [school,] endorsement of the religious message is reasonably attributed to the individuals who select the path of the aid.[a]

[If,] as the plurality contends, a per-capita-aid program is identical in relevant constitutional respects to a true private-choice program, then there is no reason that, under the plurality's reasoning, the government should be precluded from providing direct money payments to religious organizations (including churches) based on the number of persons belonging to each organization. And, because actual diversion is permissible under the plurality's holding, the participating religious organizations (including churches) could use that aid to support religious indoctrination. * * *

---

a. The "endorsement" theme—highly influential in the present Court's reasoning—is considered in further detail in Section IV infra.

Our school-aid cases often pose difficult questions at the intersection of the [principle of government neutrality and the prohibition of state funding of religious activities] and therefore defy simple categorization under either rule. As I explained in *Rosenberger*, "[r]esolution instead depends on the hard task of judging—sifting through the details and determining whether the challenged program offends the Establishment Clause. Such judgment requires courts to draw lines, sometimes quite fine, based on the particular facts of each case."

[Under *Agostini*], we need ask only whether the [Jefferson Parish] program results in governmental indoctrination or defines its recipients by reference to religion. * * *

Respondents [claim] that the presumption that religious schools will use instructional materials and equipment [as in *Meek* and *Wolman*] to inculcate religion is sound because such materials and equipment, unlike textbooks [as in *Allen*] are reasonably divertible to religious uses. For example, no matter what secular criteria the government employs in selecting a film projector to lend to a religious school, school officials can always divert that projector to religious instruction. [But *Wolman*] never justified the inconsistent treatment it accorded the lending of textbooks and the lending of instructional materials and equipment based on the items' reasonable divertibility. * * *

In any event, [the] divertibility rationale urged by respondents and Justice Souter, [does] not provide a logical distinction between the lending of textbooks and the lending of instructional materials and equipment. An educator can use virtually any instructional tool, whether it has ascertainable content or not, to teach a religious message. [For] example, even a publicly financed lunch would apparently be unconstitutional under a divertibility rationale because religious-school officials conceivably could use the lunch to lead the students in a blessing over the bread. * * *

Because divertibility fails to explain the distinction our cases have drawn between textbooks and instructional materials and equipment,[b] there remains the question of which of the two irreconcilable strands of our Establishment Clause jurisprudence we should now follow. Between the two, I would adhere to the rule that we have applied in the context of textbook lending programs: To establish a First Amendment violation, plaintiffs must prove that the aid in question actually is, or has been, used for religious purposes. [In] *Agostini*, we repeatedly emphasized [that] plaintiffs raising an Establishment Clause challenge must present evidence that the government aid in question has resulted in religious indoctrination. * * *

b. O'Connor, J.'s opinion stated further: "[T]he most important reason for according special treatment to direct money grants is that this form of aid falls precariously close to the original object of the Establishment Clause's prohibition. Statements concerning the constitutionally suspect status of direct cash aid, accordingly, provide no justification for applying an absolute rule against divertibility when the aid consists instead of instructional materials and equipment."

Respondents note that in *Agostini* we did not overrule that portion of *Grand Rapids* holding the Community Education program unconstitutional. Under that program, the government paid religious-school teachers to operate as part-time public teachers at their religious schools by teaching secular classes at the conclusion of the regular school day. Relying on both the majority opinion and my separate opinion in *Grand Rapids*, respondents therefore contend that we must presume that religious-school teachers will inculcate religion in their students. If that is so, they argue, we must also presume that religious-school teachers will be unable to follow secular restrictions on the use of instructional materials and equipment lent to their schools by the government.

I disagree, however, that the latter proposition follows from the former. [When] a religious school receives textbooks or instructional materials and equipment lent with secular restrictions, the school's teachers need not refrain from teaching religion altogether. Rather, the instructors need only ensure that any such religious teaching is done without the instructional aids provided by the government. We have always been willing to assume that religious-school instructors can abide by such restrictions when the aid consists of textbooks. [The] same assumption should extend to instructional materials and equipment.

For the same reason, my position in *Grand Rapids* is distinguishable. [In] that context, I was willing to presume that the religious-school teacher who works throughout the day to advance the school's religious mission would also do so, at least to some extent, during the supplemental classes provided at the end of the day. Because the government financed the entirety of such classes, any religious indoctrination taking place therein would be directly attributable to the government. In the instant case, because the Chapter 2 aid concerns only teaching tools that must remain supplementary, the aid comprises only a portion of the teacher's educational efforts during any single class.* * *

The plurality and Justice Souter [proceed] from the premise that, so long as actual diversion presents a constitutional problem, the government must have a failsafe mechanism capable of detecting any instance of diversion. We rejected that very assumption, however, in *Agostini*. There, we explained that because we had "abandoned the assumption that properly instructed public employees will fail to discharge their duties faithfully, we must also discard the assumption that pervasive monitoring of Title I teachers is required." Because I believe that the Court should abandon the presumption adopted in *Meek* and *Wolman* respecting the use of instructional materials and equipment by religious-school teachers, I see no constitutional need for pervasive monitoring under the Chapter 2 program. * * *

Justice Souter contends that *any* evidence of actual diversion requires the Court to declare the Chapter 2 program unconstitutional as applied in Jefferson Parish [but] I know of no case in which we have declared an entire aid program unconstitutional on Establishment Clause grounds solely because of violations on the miniscule scale of those at issue here. * * *

JUSTICE SOUTER, with whom JUSTICE STEVENS and JUSTICE GINSBURG join, dissenting.

The First Amendment's Establishment Clause [bars] the use of public funds for religious aid. * * *

In all the years of its effort, the Court has isolated no single test of constitutional sufficiency, and the question in every case addresses the substantive principle of no aid: what reasons are there to characterize this benefit as aid to the sectarian school in discharging its religious mission? Particular factual circumstances control, and the answer is a matter of judgment.

[The] Court's decisions demonstrate its repeated attempts to isolate considerations relevant in classifying particular benefits as between those that do not discernibly support or threaten support of a school's religious mission, and those that cross or threaten to cross the line into support for religion.[a]

The most deceptively familiar of those considerations is "neutrality" * * *.

There is, of course, good reason for considering the generality of aid and the evenhandedness of its distribution in making close calls between benefits that in purpose or effect support a school's religious mission and those that do not. [O]n the face of it aid distributed generally and without a religious criterion is less likely to be meant to aid religion than a benefit going only to religious institutions or people. [And,] evenhandedness is a way of asking whether a benefit can reasonably be seen to aid religion in fact; we do not regard the postal system as aiding religion, even though parochial schools get mail. Given the legitimacy of considering evenhandedness, then, there is no reason to avoid the term "neutrality" to refer to it. But one crucial point must be borne in mind. [I]f we looked no further than evenhandedness, and failed to ask what activities the aid might support, or in fact did support, religious schools could be blessed with government funding as massive as expenditures made for the benefit of their public school counterparts, and religious missions would thrive on public money. This is why the consideration of less than universal neutrality has never been recognized as dispositive and has always been teamed with attention to other facts bearing on the substantive prohibition of support for a school's religious objective.

At least three main lines of enquiry addressed particularly to school aid have emerged to complement evenhandedness neutrality. First, we have noted that two types of aid recipients heighten Establishment Clause con-

---

a. See Marshall, J., joined by Brennan, Blackmun and Stevens, JJ., dissenting in *Mueller*: "While 'services such as police and fire protection, sewage disposal, highways, and sidewalks,' may be provided to parochial schools in common with other institu- tions, because this type of assistance is clearly 'marked off from the religious function' of those schools, unrestricted financial assistance, such as grants for the maintenance and construction of parochial schools, may not be provided."

cern: pervasively religious schools[6] and primary and secondary religious schools.[b] Second, we have identified two important characteristics of the method of distributing aid: directness or indirectness of distribution and distribution by genuinely independent choice. Third, we have found relevance in at least five characteristics of the aid itself: its religious content; its cash form; its divertibility or actual diversion to religious support;[13] its supplantation of traditional items of religious school expense; and its substantiality. * * *

The plurality, however, would reject that lesson. The majority misapplies it. * * *

First, the plurality treats an external observer's attribution of religious support to the government as the sole impermissible effect of a government aid scheme. While perceived state endorsement of religion is undoubtedly a relevant concern under the Establishment Clause, it is certainly not the only [one.] State aid not attributed to the government would still violate a taxpayer's liberty of conscience, threaten to corrupt religion, and generate disputes over aid.* * *[19]

Second, the plurality apparently assumes as a fact that equal amounts of aid to religious and nonreligious schools will have exclusively secular and equal effects, on both external perception and on incentives to attend different schools. But there is no reason to believe that this will be the case; the effects of same-terms aid may not be confined to the secular sphere at all.* * *

Third, the plurality assumes that per capita distribution rules safeguard the same principles as independent, private choices. But [n]ot the least of the significant differences [is] the right and genuine opportunity of the recipient to choose not to give the aid. To hold otherwise would be to license the government to donate funds to churches based on the number of their members, on the patent fiction of independent private choice. * * *

6. In fact, religious education in Roman Catholic schools is defined as part of required religious practice; aiding it is thus akin to aiding a church service. See 1983 *Code of Canon Law*, Canon 798 (directing parents to entrust children to Roman Catholic schools or otherwise provide for Roman Catholic education) * * *.

b. Aid to higher education is considered 1(a)infra.

13. I reject the plurality's argument that divertibility is a boundless principle. Our long experience of evaluating this consideration demonstrates its practical limits. Moreover, the Establishment Clause charges us with making such enquiries, regardless of their difficulty. Finally, the First Amendment's rule permitting only aid with fixed secular content seems no more difficult to apply than the plurality's rule prohibiting only aid with fixed religious content.

19. Adopting the plurality's rule would permit practically any government aid to religion so long as it could be supplied on terms ostensibly comparable to the terms under which aid was provided to nonreligious recipients. As a principle of constitutional sufficiency, the manipulability of this rule is breathtaking. A legislature would merely need to state a secular objective in order to legalize massive aid to all religions, one religion, or even one sect, to which its largess could be directed through the easy exercise of crafting facially neutral terms under which to offer aid favoring that religious group. Short of formally replacing the Establishment Clause, a more dependable key to the public fisc or a cleaner break with prior law would be difficult to imagine.

The plurality's conception of evenhandedness does not, however, control [this case]. The facts most obviously relevant to the Chapter 2 scheme in Jefferson Parish are those showing divertibility and actual diversion in the circumstance of pervasively sectarian religious schools [and] the lack of effective safeguards. [First,] the record shows actual diversion in the library book program. [D]iscovery revealed that under Chapter 2, nonpublic schools requested and the government purchased at least 191 religious books with taxpayer funds by December 1985. Books such as *A Child's Book of Prayers* and *The Illustrated Life of Jesus* were discovered among others that had been ordered under the program.

The evidence persuasively suggests that other aid was actually diverted as well. The principal of one religious school testified, for example, that computers lent with Chapter 2 funds were joined in a network with other non-Chapter 2 computers in some schools, and [that] the Chapter 2 computer took over the support of the computing system whenever there was a breakdown of the master computer purchased with the religious school's own funds. [Moreover,] film projectors and videotape machines purchased with public funds were [seemingly] used in religious indoctrination over a period of at least seven years. [The] Court has no choice but to hold that the program as applied violated the Establishment Clause.[28]

The plurality would break with the law. [Its] choice to employ imputations of bigotry and irreligion as terms in the Court's debate makes one point clear: that in rejecting the principle of no aid to a school's religious mission the plurality is attacking the most fundamental assumption underlying the Establishment Clause * * *.

Notes and Questions

1. *Direct payments to religious institutions.* (a) *Higher education.* TILTON v. RICHARDSON, 403 U.S. 672, 91 S.Ct. 2091, 29 L.Ed.2d 790 (1971) and ROEMER v. BOARD OF PUB. WORKS, 426 U.S. 736, 96 S.Ct. 2337, 49 L.Ed.2d 179 (1976), upheld direct government grants to church-related colleges and universities as part of general programs for construction of buildings and other activities not involving sectarian activities. *Roemer* noted "what is crucial to a nonentangling aid program: the ability of the State to identify and subsidize separate secular functions carried out at the school, without on-the-site inspections being necessary to prevent diversion of the funds to sectarian purposes." *Tilton* added: "There are generally significant differences between the religious aspects of church-related institutions of higher learning and parochial elementary and secondary schools. The 'affirmative, if not dominant, policy' of the instruction in pre-college church-schools is 'to assure future adherents to a particular faith by having control of their total education at an early age.' There is substance to the contention

---

28. Since the divertibility and diversion require a finding of unconstitutionality, I will not explore other grounds, beyond noting the likelihood that unconstitutional supplantation occurred as well. * * *

that college students are less impressionable and less susceptible to religious indoctrination. [Further], by their very nature, college and postgraduate courses tend to limit the opportunities for sectarian influence by virtue of their own internal disciplines. Many church-related colleges and universities are characterized by a high degree of academic freedom and seek to evoke free and critical responses from their students."

Brennan, J., dissented in *Tilton:* "[A] sectarian university is the equivalent in the realm of higher education of the Catholic elementary [schools]; it is an educational institution in which the propagation and advancement of a particular religion is a primary function of the institution. [It] is not that religion 'permeates' the secular education that is provided. Rather, it is that the secular education is provided within the environment of religion; the institution is dedicated to two goals, secular education *and* religious instruction. When aid flows directly to the institution, both functions benefit."

(b) *Social welfare programs.* BOWEN v. KENDRICK, 487 U.S. 589, 108 S.Ct. 2562, 101 L.Ed.2d 520 (1988), per Rehnquist, C.J., held that the Adolescent Family Life Act (AFLA)—which grants funds to a variety of public and private agencies (including religious organizations) to provide counseling for prevention of adolescent sexual relations and care for pregnant adolescents and adolescent parents—did not, on its face, violate the establishment clause. "As in *Tilton* and *Roemer*, we do not think the possibility that AFLA grants may go to religious institutions that can be considered 'pervasively sectarian' is sufficient to conclude that no grants whatsoever can be given under the statute to religious organizations."[a] It was to be determined on remand "whether in particular cases AFLA aid has been used to fund 'specifically religious activit(ies) in an otherwise substantially secular setting,' [for example], whether [grantees] use materials that have an explicitly religious content or are designed to inculcate the views of a particular religious faith."[b]

(c) *Burden of proof.* After *Mitchell*, is a *majority* now willing to apply the approach of the above decisions to elementary and secondary schools? If "plaintiffs must prove that the aid in question [is] used for religious purposes" ("O'Connor, J.), is a majority now willing *at least* to uphold previously invalidated programs on a showing that religion no more "permeates the secular education" in primary and secondary parochial schools than it does in church-related colleges?

(d) "*Endorsement.*" Consider Tribe 2d ed., at 1221: "Another reason that religious colleges are treated differently from parochial schools is the *public's* view of the aid programs. Aid for secular programs in all colleges, including those with church affiliation, is generally perceived as assistance to

---

a. Prior to *Mitchell*, in *Columbia Union College v. Clarke*, 527 U.S. 1013, 119 S.Ct. 2357, 144 L.Ed.2d 252 (1999), Thomas J., dissented from the Court's denial of certiorari from a decision excluding a "pervasively sectarian" Seventh-day Adventist college from a state aid program.

b. The 5–4 majority included O'Connor, Scalia and Kennedy, JJ.

non-religious activities. But the moment aid is sent to a parochial school as such, it is widely seen as aid to religion. The number of dollars released for religious purposes may be identical; the symbolism is not."

2. *Vouchers.* After *Mitchell*, would an "education voucher" plan pass muster if the vouchers were given to *all* parents for use in *any* school?

(a) *"Endorsement."* Consider Kathleen M. Sullivan, *Parades, Public Squares and Voucher Payments: Problems of Government Neutrality*, 28 Conn.L.Rev. 243, 255–58 (1996): "Public education [is] a form of government speech in which government is exercising a massive degree of content control. [The] Establishment Clause operates as a unique gag order on government speech and symbolism. Government itself may espouse any viewpoint a democratic majority wishes *except* a religious viewpoint. Thus, if [a] state extended its voucher system to religious schools, the Court still would, and should, strike it down." Compare Abner S. Greene, *Why Vouchers are Unconstitutional, and Why They're Not*, 13 Not.D.J.L.Eth. & Pub.Pol. 397, 400 (1999): "The generality of voucher programs, combined with the fact that each family, and not the government, decides how to use the voucher money, belies Sullivan's argument. [The] reasonable observer would not attribute to the government the message of any school benefited by voucher money. Rather, such an observer would assume that the government is funding all schools, and thus is supporting the message of none." Contrast Eugene Volokh, *Equal Treatment Is Not Establishment*, id. at 341, 368–70: "Under the endorsement test, the government may not express endorsement *or disapproval* of religion [citing, inter alia, *Wallace v. Jaffree*, Sec. III infra]. [I]f giving special benefits to religion [is] endorsement, then discriminating against religion [is] disapproval."

(b) *"Neutrality."* Do vouchers for religious schools violate "neutrality" because of the government support of "religious values"? Consider Volokh, supra, at 346: "The religious schools do teach a religious value system—just as secular schools teach a secular value system. There's [no] reason why the government is obligated to discriminate against one or the other system, and thus against the parents who choose to teach their children one or the other system. Just as we wouldn't tolerate discrimination against atheistic schools, or discrimination against secular schools, so we shouldn't assume that the Constitution requires discrimination against religious schools."

(c) *"Private choice."* Would a voucher be "no different from a government issuing a paycheck to one of its employees knowing that the employee would direct the funds to a religious institution" (Thomas, J.)? Consider Ira C. Lupu, *The Increasingly Anachronistic Case Against School Vouchers*, id. at 375, 379–80: "When the state pays its employees a wage, they can spend the money for any lawful purpose, including for the advancement of religion. In such circumstances, the state cannot be held responsible for any religious benefit arising from the unfettered spending choices of its employees. By contrast, when the state constrains the benefit in certain ways—for example, a state income tax deduction for all charitable contributions—the probability and forseeability of a boost to religion are markedly increased. Contemporary voucher programs tend to constrain yet further, limiting parents to the mix of participating schools, in which sectarian institutions will be heavily represented, at least in the short run." If a voucher program is the same as a charitable tax deduction, what follows?

(d) *"Religious purpose."* If at least *some* voucher funds might be used to support "religious indoctrination," would the program fail O'Connor, J.'s burden of proof standard in note 1(c) supra. If so, what of *Witters* (and the GI Bill)?

3. *"Neutrality" and political divisiveness.* To what extent does a "broad class" of beneficiary groups affect this criterion? Consider Note, *The Constitutionality of Tax Relief for Parents of Children Attending Public and Nonpublic Schools,* 67 Minn.L.Rev. 793, 820–21 (1983): "Legislation that primarily aids sectarian education disrupts political equality and promotes rivalry among religious sects by favoring those groups that emphasize private primary and secondary education. [In] contrast, aid which broadly benefits secular as well as sectarian groups is less likely to generate inter-faith rivalries or imbalances of power. Even if only some sects receive aid directly, members of other faiths will probably benefit as members of the broader legislative class. Because particular religious groups will not be perceived as the primary beneficiaries of state aid, competition among sects for government funds will also be reduced." Compare Laura Underkuffler–Freund, *The Separation of the Religious and the Secular,* 36 Wm. & M.L.Rev. 837, 975 (1995): "The concerns of reformers—that governmental financial support of religious institutions would promote their involvement in government, their meddling with laws, their grasping for money, and their attempts to protect governmentally-bestowed privileges and emoluments—are presented no less by the public funding of all religious institutions than by the funding of few. Rather, the answer becomes [one] of degree: while incidental public support for sectarian institutions (on a basis equal to public institutions and to each other) probably presents little danger of institutional alliance of church and state, extensive funding may pose significant danger."

4. *Other approaches.* Commentators have proposed various "tests" to measure the validity of public aid to church-related schools. In evaluating those that follow, what results would they produce in the decided cases?

(a) Jesse H. Choper, *The Establishment Clause and Aid to Parochial Schools,* 56 Calif.L.Rev. 260, 265–66 (1968): "[G]overnmental financial aid may be extended directly or indirectly to support parochial schools [so] long as such aid does not exceed the value of the secular educational service rendered by the school."[c] Would such aid have "a secular legislative purpose

c. For further analysis, see Michael W. McConnell & Richard Posner, *An Economic*

and a primary effect that neither advances nor inhibits religion"? Compare Harold D. Hammett, *The Homogenized Wall,* 53 A.B.A.J. 929, 932–33 (1967): "If the net effect of the financial aid is to increase proportionally the influence of both the church and the state, so that their influence relative to each other remains at the same original ratio, the 'primary' effect on religion has been neutral." Contrast Stephen D. Sugarman, *New Perspectives on "Aid" to Private School Users,* in Nonpublic School Aid 64, 66 (West ed. 1976): "Even if the [effect] principle were limited to cases in which there was (or the legislature knew there would be) a *large* beneficial impact on religion, it would intolerably inhibit secular government action. For example, perhaps building roads and running public transportation on Sunday may be shown to have large beneficial impacts on religion. [For] me the concerns underlying the Establishment clause could be satisfied with an affirmative answer to this hypothetical question: Would the legislature have acted as it did were there no interdependency with religion involved? If so, then I think it would be fair to say that there is no subsidy of religion, that the religious benefits are constitutionally permitted side effects."[d]

(b) Ira C. Lupu, *To Control Faction and Protect Liberty: A General Theory of the Religion Clauses,* 7 J.Contemp.Leg.Issues 357, 373 (1996): "The worry expressed so widely [about] coercive taxation to support religious teaching is a holdover relic from the Virginia story of coercive assessments earmarked for the support of Christian ministers and teachers. Such an exaction, taking from all to support a few on religious grounds and for religious ends, of course violates the Establishment Clause. [When] the state, however, makes funds available in a religion-neutral way for secular ends ["such as educational attainment, health care, or social services"], those objections quickly become attenuated. Such programs should survive, unless the challenger can persuasively demonstrate that the program (despite facially neutral criteria) is in essence a cover for sectarian discrimination."

III. RELIGION AND PUBLIC SCHOOLS

WALLACE v. JAFFREE

472 U.S. 38, 105 S.Ct. 2479, 86 L.Ed.2d 29 (1985).

JUSTICE STEVENS delivered the opinion of the Court.

[In 1978, Alabama enacted § 16–1–20 authorizing a one-minute period of silence in all public schools "for meditation"; in 1981, it enacted § 16–1–20.1 authorizing a period of silence "for meditation or voluntary prayer." Appellees, parents of second graders,] have not questioned the holding that § 16–1–20 is valid. Thus, the narrow question for decision [concerns § 16–1–20.1].

Approach to Issues of Religious Freedom, 56 U.Chi.L.Rev. 1 (1989); Note, *The Supreme Court, Effect Inquiry, and Aid to Parochial Education,* 37 Stan.L.Rev. 219 (1984).

d. Problems under the free exercise clause raised by the exclusion of parochial schools from public aid programs are considered in note 2, p. 736.

[T]he Court has unambiguously concluded that the individual freedom of conscience protected by the First Amendment embraces the right to select any religious faith or none at all. This conclusion derives [from] the conviction that religious beliefs worthy of respect are the product of free and voluntary choice by the faithful, and from recognition of the fact that the political interest in forestalling intolerance extends beyond intolerance among Christian sects—or even intolerance among "religions"—to encompass intolerance of the disbeliever and the uncertain. * * *

[Under *Lemon*,] even though a statute that is motivated in part by a religious purpose may satisfy the first criterion, the First Amendment requires that a statute must be invalidated if it is entirely motivated by a purpose to advance religion.

In applying the purpose test, it is appropriate to ask "whether government's actual purpose is to endorse or disapprove of religion."[42] In this case, the answer to that question is dispositive. * * *

The sponsor of the bill that became § 16–1–20.1, Senator Donald Holmes, inserted into the legislative record—apparently without dissent—a statement indicating that the legislation was an "effort to return voluntary prayer" to the public schools. Later Senator Holmes confirmed this purpose before the District Court. In response to the question whether he had any purpose for the legislation other than returning voluntary prayer to public schools, he stated: "No, I did not have no other purpose in mind."[44] The State did not present evidence of *any* secular purpose. * * *

The legislative intent to return prayer to the public schools is, of course, quite different from merely protecting every student's right to engage in voluntary prayer during an appropriate moment of silence during the schoolday. The 1978 statute already protected that right, containing nothing that prevented any student from engaging in voluntary prayer during a silent minute of meditation. [The] legislature enacted § 16–1–20.1, despite the existence of § 16–1–20 for the sole purpose of expressing the State's endorsement of prayer activities for one minute at the beginning of each schoolday. The addition of "or voluntary prayer" indicates that the State intended to characterize prayer as a favored practice. Such an endorsement is not consistent with the established principle that the government must pursue a course of complete neutrality toward religion.

42. *Lynch v. Donnelly,* [Section IV infra] (O'Connor, J., concurring) ("The purpose prong of the *Lemon* test asks whether government's actual purpose is to endorse or disapprove of religion. The effect prong asks whether, irrespective of government's actual purpose, the practice under review in fact conveys a message of endorsement or disapproval. An affirmative answer to either question should render the challenged practice invalid").

44. [The] evidence presented to the District Court elaborated on the express admission of the Governor of Alabama (then Fob James) that the enactment of § 16–1–20.1 was intended to "clarify [the State's] intent to have prayer as part of the daily classroom activity," and that the "expressed legislative purpose in enacting Section 16–1–20.1 (1981) was to 'return voluntary prayer to public schools.' "

The importance of that principle does not permit us to treat this as an inconsequential case involving nothing more than a few words of symbolic speech on behalf of the political majority.[51] For whenever the State itself speaks on a religious subject, one of the questions that we must ask is "whether the government intends to convey a message of endorsement or disapproval of religion." * * *

JUSTICE O'CONNOR concurring in the judgment.

* * * Although a distinct jurisprudence has enveloped each of [the Religion] Clauses, their common purpose is to secure religious liberty. On these principles the Court has been and remains unanimous. [O]ur goal should be "to frame a principle for constitutional adjudication that is not only grounded in the history and language of the first amendment, but one that is also capable of consistent application to the relevant problems." Jesse H. Choper, *Religion in the Public Schools: A Proposed Constitutional Standard,* 47 Minn.L.Rev. 329, 332–333 (1963). Last Term, I proposed a refinement of the *Lemon* test with this goal in mind. *Lynch v. Donnelly* (concurring opinion).

The *Lynch* concurrence suggested that the religious liberty protected by the Establishment Clause is infringed when the government makes adherence to religion relevant to a person's standing in the political community. Direct government action endorsing religion or a particular religious practice is invalid under this approach because it "sends a message to nonadherents that they are outsiders, not full members of the political community, and an accompanying message to adherents that they are insiders, favored members of the political community." [In] this country, church and state must necessarily operate within the same community. Because of this coexistence, it is inevitable that the secular interests of government and the religious interests of various sects and their adherents will frequently intersect, conflict, and combine. A statute that ostensibly promotes a secular interest often has an incidental or even a primary effect of helping or hindering a sectarian belief. Chaos would ensue if every such statute were invalid under the Establishment Clause. For example, the State could not criminalize murder for fear that it would thereby promote the Biblical command against killing.[a] The task for the Court is to sort out those statutes and government

51. As this Court stated in *Engel v. Vitale,* [infra]: "The Establishment Clause, unlike the Free Exercise Clause, does not depend upon any showing of direct governmental compulsion and is violated by the enactment of laws which establish an official religion whether those laws operate directly to coerce nonobserving individuals or not." Moreover, this Court has noted that "[w]hen the power, prestige and financial support of government is placed behind a particular religious belief, the indirect coercive pressure upon religious minorities to conform to the prevailing officially approved religion is plain." Id. This comment has special force in the public-school context where attendance is mandatory. Justice Frankfurter acknowledged this reality in *McCollum v. Board of Education,* [note 1(a) infra] (concurring opinion): "That a child is offered an alternative may reduce the constraint; it does not eliminate the operation of influence by the school in matters sacred to conscience and outside the school's domain. The law of imitation operates, and non-conformity is not an outstanding characteristic of children." * * *

a. On this analysis, *McGowan v. Maryland,* 366 U.S. 420, 81 S.Ct. 1101, 6 L.Ed.2d 393 (1961), per Warren, C.J., held that the "present purpose and effect" of Maryland's Sunday Closing Laws were not religious and did not violate the establishment

practices whose purpose and effect go against the grain of religious liberty protected by the First Amendment.

The endorsement test does not preclude government from acknowledging religion or from taking religion into account in making law and policy. It does preclude government from conveying or attempting to convey a message that religion or a particular religious belief is favored or preferred. Such an endorsement infringes the religious liberty of the nonadherent. * * *.

Twenty-five states permit or require public school teachers to have students observe [a] moment of silence at the beginning of the schoolday during which students may meditate, pray, or reflect on the activities of the day. * * * Relying on this Court's decisions disapproving vocal prayer and Bible reading in the public schools, see *School Dist. v. Schempp*, 374 U.S. 203, 83 S.Ct. 1560, 10 L.Ed.2d 844 (1963); *Engel v. Vitale*, 370 U.S. 421, 82 S.Ct. 1261, 8 L.Ed.2d 601 (1962), the courts that have struck down the moment of silence statutes generally conclude that their purpose and effect are to encourage prayer in public schools.

The *Engel* and *Schempp* decisions are not dispositive. [In] *Engel,* a New York statute required teachers to lead their classes in a vocal prayer.[b] The Court concluded that "it is no part of the business of government to compose official prayers for any group of the American people to recite as part of a religious program carried on by the government." In *Schempp,* the Court addressed Pennsylvania and Maryland statutes that authorized morning Bible readings in public schools.[c] The Court reviewed the purpose and effect of the statutes, concluded that they required religious exercises, and therefore found them to violate the Establishment Clause. Under all of these statutes, a student who did not share the religious beliefs expressed in the course of the exercise was left with the choice of participating, thereby

---

clause. Although "the original laws which dealt with Sunday labor were motivated by religious forces," the Court showed that secular emphases in language and interpretation have come about, that recent "legislation was supported by labor groups and trade associations," and that "secular justifications have been advanced for making Sunday a day of rest, a day when people may recover from the labors of the week just passed and may physically and mentally prepare for the week's work to come. [It] would seem unrealistic for enforcement purposes and perhaps detrimental to the general welfare to require a State to choose a common day of rest other than that which most persons would select of their own accord."

Douglas, J., dissented: "No matter how much is written, no matter what is said," Sunday is a Christian holiday. "There is an 'establishment' of religion in the constitutional sense if any practice of any religious group has the sanction of law behind it."

b. The prayer, composed by the N.Y. Board of Regents, provided: "Almighty God, we acknowledge our dependence upon Thee, and we beg Thy blessings upon us, our parents, our teachers and our country."

c. The reading of the Bible, without comment, was followed by recitation of the Lord's Prayer. In Pennsylvania, various students read passages they selected from any version of the Bible. Plaintiff father testified that "specific religious doctrines purveyed by a literal reading of the Bible" were contrary to the family's Unitarian religious beliefs; one expert testified that "portions of the New Testament were offensive to Jewish tradition" and, if "read without explanation, they could [be] psychologically harmful to the child and had caused a divisive force within the social media of the school"; a defense expert testified "that the Bible [was] non-sectarian within the Christian faiths."

compromising the nonadherent's beliefs, or withdrawing, thereby calling attention to his or her nonconformity. The decisions acknowledged the coercion implicit under the statutory schemes, see *Engel*,[d] but they expressly turned only on the fact that the government was sponsoring a manifestly religious exercise.[e]

A state-sponsored moment of silence in the public schools is different from state-sponsored vocal prayer or Bible reading. First, a moment of silence [unlike] prayer or Bible reading, need not be associated with a religious exercise. Second, [d]uring a moment of silence, a student who objects to prayer is left to his or her own thoughts, and is not compelled to listen to the prayers or thoughts of others. [It] is difficult to discern a serious threat to religious liberty from a room of silent, thoughtful schoolchildren.

By mandating a moment of silence, a State does not necessarily endorse any activity that might occur during the period. Even if a statute specifies that a student may choose to pray silently during a quiet moment, the State has not thereby encouraged prayer over other specified alternatives. Nonetheless, it is also possible that a moment of silence statute, either as drafted or as actually implemented, could effectively favor the child who prays over the child who does not. For example, the message of endorsement would seem inescapable if the teacher exhorts children to use the designated time to pray. Similarly, the fact of the statute or its legislative history may clearly establish that it seeks to encourage or promote voluntary prayer over other alternatives, rather than merely provide a quiet moment that may be dedicated to prayer by those so inclined. The crucial question is whether the State has conveyed or attempted to convey the message that children should use the moment of silence for prayer.[2] This question cannot be answered in the abstract, but instead requires courts to examine the history, language, and administration of a particular statute to determine whether it operates as an endorsement of religion.

---

d. See fn. 51 in the Court's opinion, supra.

e. *Engel* distinguished "the fact that school children and others are officially encouraged to express love for our country by reciting historical documents such as the Declaration of Independence which contain references to the Deity or by singing officially espoused anthems which include the composer's professions of faith in a Supreme Being, or with the fact that there are many manifestations in our public life of belief in God. Such patriotic or ceremonial occasions bear no true resemblance to the unquestioned religious exercise that the State of New York has sponsored in this instance."

2. Appellants argue that *Zorach v. Clauson*, [note 1(b) infra], suggests there is no constitutional infirmity in a State's encouraging a child to pray during a moment of silence. [There] the Court stated that "[w]hen the state encourages religious instruction—[by] *adjusting the schedule of public events to sectarian needs,* it follows the best of our traditions." When the State provides a moment of silence during which prayer may occur at the election of the student, it can be said to be adjusting the schedule of public events to sectarian needs. But when the State also encourages the student to pray during a moment of silence, it converts an otherwise inoffensive moment of silence into an effort by the majority to use the machinery of the State to encourage the minority to participate in a religious exercise.

[T]he inquiry into the purpose of the legislature in enacting a moment of silence law should be deferential and limited. In determining whether the government intends a moment of silence statute to convey a message of endorsement or disapproval of religion, a court has no license to psychoanalyze the legislators. If a legislature expresses a plausible secular purpose for a moment of silence statute in either the text or the legislative history, or if the statute disclaims an intent to encourage prayer over alternatives during a moment of silence, then courts should generally defer to that stated intent. It is particularly troublesome to denigrate an expressed secular purpose due to postenactment testimony by particular legislators or by interested persons who witnessed the drafting of the statute.[f] Even if the text and official history of a statute express no secular purpose, the statute should be held to have an improper purpose only if it is beyond purview that endorsement of religion or a religious belief "was and is the law's reason for existence." *Epperson v. Arkansas,* [note 3(b) infra]. Since there is arguably a secular pedagogical value to a moment of silence in public schools, courts should find an improper purpose behind such a statute only if the statute on its face, in its official legislative history, or in its interpretation by a responsible administrative agency suggests it has the primary purpose of endorsing prayer.

[It] is of course possible that a legislature will enunciate a sham secular purpose for a statute. I have little doubt that our courts are capable of distinguishing a sham secular purpose from a sincere one, or that the *Lemon* inquiry into the effect of an enactment would help decide those close cases where the validity of an expressed secular purpose is in doubt. [T]he *Lynch* concurrence suggested that the effect of a moment of silence law is not entirely a question of [fact]. The relevant issue is whether an objective observer, acquainted with the text, legislative history, and implementation of the statute, would perceive it as a state endorsement of prayer in public schools. A moment of silence law that is clearly drafted and implemented so as to permit prayer, meditation, and reflection within the prescribed period, without endorsing one alternative over the others, should pass this test.

The analysis above suggests that moment of silence laws in many States should pass Establishment Clause scrutiny because they do not favor the child who chooses to pray during a moment of silence over the child who chooses to meditate or reflect. § 16–1–20.1 does not stand on the same footing. However deferentially one examines its text and legislative history, however objectively one views the message attempted to be conveyed to the public, the conclusion is unavoidable that the purpose of the statute is to endorse prayer in public [schools.][5] * * * *[g]

f. For further discussion of this point, see Burger, C.J.'s opinion infra.

5. The Chief Justice suggests that one consequence of the Court's emphasis on the difference between § 16–1–20.1 and its predecessor statute might be to render the Pledge of Allegiance unconstitutional because Congress amended it in 1954 to add the words "under God". I disagree. In my view, the words "under God" in the Pledge serve as an acknowledgement of religion with "the legitimate secular purposes of

CHIEF JUSTICE BURGER dissenting.

* * * Today's decision recalls the observations of Justice Goldberg: "[U]ntutored devotion to the concept of neutrality can lead to invocation or approval of results which partake not simply of that noninterference and noninvolvement with the religious which the Constitution commands, but of a brooding and pervasive dedication to the secular and a passive, or even active, hostility to the religious. Such results are not only not compelled by the Constitution, but, it seems to me, are prohibited by it." *Schempp* (concurring opinion). * * *

Curiously, the opinions do not mention that *all* of the sponsor's statements relied upon—including the statement "inserted" into the Senate Journal—were made *after* the legislature had passed the statute; [there] is not a shred of evidence that the legislature as a whole shared the sponsor's motive or that a majority in either house was even aware of the sponsor's view of the bill when it was [passed.]

Even if an individual legislator's after-the-fact statements could rationally be considered relevant, all of the opinions fail to mention that the sponsor also testified that one of his purposes in drafting and sponsoring the moment-of-silence bill was to clear up a widespread misunderstanding that a schoolchild is legally *prohibited* from engaging in silent, individual prayer once he steps inside a public school building. That testimony is at least as important as the statements the Court relies upon, and surely that testimony manifests a permissible purpose. * * *

The several preceding opinions conclude that the principal difference between § 16–1–20.1 and its predecessor statute proves that the sole purpose behind the inclusion of the phrase "or voluntary prayer" in § 16–1–20.1 was to endorse and promote prayer. This reasoning is simply a subtle way of focusing exclusively on the religious component of the statute rather than examining the statute as a whole. Such logic—if it can be called that—would lead the Court to hold, for example, that a state may enact a statute that provides reimbursement for bus transportation to the parents of all schoolchildren, but may not *add* parents of parochial school students to an existing program providing reimbursement for parents of public school students. Congress amended the statutory Pledge of Allegiance 31 years ago to add the words "under God." Do the several opinions in support of the judgment today render the Pledge unconstitutional? [3]

solemnizing public occasions, [and] expressing confidence in the future." *Lynch* (concurring opinion).

g. Powell, J., who was the fifth justice to join the Court's opinion, also separately concurred, agreeing "fully with Justice O'Connor's assertion that some moment-of-silence statutes may be constitutional, a suggestion set forth in the Court's opinion as well."

3. The House Report on the legislation amending the Pledge states that the purpose of the amendment was to affirm the principle that "our people and our Government [are dependent] upon the moral directions of the Creator." If this is simply "acknowledgement," not "endorsement," of religion, the distinction is far too infinitesimal for me to grasp.

[Compare Jefferson B. Fordham, *The Implications of the Supreme Court Decisions*

* * * Without pressuring those who do not wish to pray, the statute simply creates an opportunity to think, to plan, or to pray if one wishes—as Congress does by providing chaplains and chapels. [If] the government may not accommodate religious needs when it does so in a wholly neutral and noncoercive manner, the "benevolent neutrality" that we have long considered the correct constitutional standard will quickly translate into the "callous indifference" that the Court has consistently held the Establishment Clause does not require. * * *

JUSTICE REHNQUIST, dissenting.

[There] is simply no historical foundation for the proposition that the Framers intended to build the "wall of separation" that was constitutionalized in *Everson*. [And the "purpose and effect" tests] are in no way based on either the language or intent of the drafters. [If] the purpose prong is intended to void those aids to sectarian institutions accompanied by a stated legislative purpose to aid religion, the prong will condemn nothing so long as the legislature utters a secular purpose and says nothing about aiding religion. * * *

However, if the purpose prong is aimed to void all statutes enacted with the intent to aid sectarian institutions, whether stated or not, then most statutes providing any aid, such as textbooks or bus rides for sectarian school children, will fail because one of the purposes behind every statute, whether stated or not, is to aid the target of its largesse. * * *

If a constitutional theory has no basis in the history of the amendment it seeks to interpret, is difficult to apply and yields unprincipled results, I see little use in it. [It] would come as much of a shock to those who drafted the Bill of Rights as it will to a large number of thoughtful Americans today to learn that the Constitution, as construed by the majority, prohibits the Alabama Legislature from "endorsing" prayer. George Washington himself, at the request of the very Congress which passed the Bill of Rights, proclaimed a day of "public thanksgiving and prayer, to be observed by acknowledging with grateful hearts the many and signal favors of Almighty God." History must judge whether it was the Father of his Country in 1789, or a majority of the Court today, which has strayed from the meaning of the Establishment Clause. * * *

Notes and Questions

1. *Released time.* (a) McCOLLUM v. BOARD OF EDUC., 333 U.S. 203, 68 S.Ct. 461, 92 L.Ed. 649 (1948), per BLACK, J., held that a public school released time program violated the establishment clause. Privately employed religious teachers held weekly classes, on public school premises, in their respective religions, for students whose parents signed request cards, while

Dealing with Religious Practices in the Public Schools, 6 J. of Chur. & St. 44, 56 (1964): "In view of the patriotic element here, one may suggest that the likelihood of indirect compulsion is much greater than in the simple prayer case. Here the individual dissenter is made to stand out as one unwilling to engage in a patriotic act and recital."]

[handwritten margin note: ?? look back @ his reference to Jefferson...]

non-attending students pursued secular studies in other parts of the building: "Here not only are the state's tax-supported public school buildings used for the dissemination of religious doctrines. The State also affords sectarian groups an invaluable aid in that it helps to provide pupils for their religious classes through use of the state's compulsory public school machinery."[a]

(b) ZORACH v. CLAUSON, 343 U.S. 306, 72 S.Ct. 679, 96 L.Ed. 954 (1952), per DOUGLAS, J., upheld a released time program in which the religious classes were held in church buildings: "[This] program involves neither religious instruction in public school classrooms nor the expenditure of public funds. All costs, including the application blanks, are paid by the religious organizations. The case is therefore unlike *McCollum*.

"[The] nullification of this law would have wide and profound effects. A Catholic student applies to his teacher for permission to leave the school during hours on a Holy Day of Obligation to attend a mass. A Jewish student asks his teacher for permission to be excused for Yom Kippur. A Protestant wants the afternoon off for a family baptismal ceremony. In each case the teacher requires parental consent in writing. In each case the teacher, in order to make sure the student is not a truant, goes further and requires a report from the priest, the rabbi, or the minister. The teacher in other words cooperates in a religious program to the extent of making it possible for her students to participate in it. Whether she does it occasionally for a few students, regularly for one, or pursuant to a systematized program designed to further the religious needs of all the students does not alter the character of the act.

"We are a religious people whose institutions presuppose a Supreme Being. We guarantee the freedom to worship as one chooses. [When] the state encourages religious instruction or cooperates with religious authorities by adjusting the schedule of public events to sectarian needs, [it] respects the religious nature of our people and accommodates the public service to their spiritual needs. To hold that it may not would [be] preferring those who believe in no religion over those who do believe. [The] problem, like many problems in constitutional law, is one of degree."

JACKSON, J., dissented: "If public education were taking so much of the pupils' time as to [encroach] upon their religious opportunity, simply shortening everyone's school day would facilitate voluntary and optional attendance at Church classes. But that suggestion is rejected upon the ground that if they are made free many students will not go to the Church. [Here] schooling is more or less suspended during the 'released time' so the nonreligious attendants will not forge ahead of the churchgoing absentees. But it serves as a temporary jail for a pupil who will not go to Church. It takes more subtlety of mind than I possess to deny that this is governmental constraint in support of religion."[b]

a. Frankfurter and Jackson, JJ., each filed concurrences. Reed, J., dissented.

b. Black and Frankfurter, JJ., also filed separate dissents.

(c) *Cost.* Brennan, J., has distinguished the cases "not [because] of the difference in public expenditures involved. True, the *McCollum* program involved the regular use of school facilities, classrooms, heat and light and time from the regular school day—even though the actual incremental cost may have been negligible. [But the] deeper difference was that the *McCollum* program placed the religious instructor in the public school classroom in precisely the position of authority held by the regular teachers of secular subjects, while the *Zorach* program did not. [This] brought government and religion into that proximity which the Establishment Clause forbids." *Schempp* (concurring opinion).

(d) *Coercion.* *Zorach* found "no evidence [that] the system involves the use of coercion to get public school students into religious classrooms. [If] it were established that any one or more teachers were using their office to persuade or force students to take the religious instruction, a wholly different case would be presented.[7]" Would the *Zorach* plan be inherently coercive, and therefore unconstitutional, if it were shown that most children found religious instruction more appealing than remaining in the public schools? Even if the alternative for those remaining was secular instruction with academic credit? If so, would it be permissible to excuse children from classes to enable them to attend special religious services of their faith? Would the first amendment forbid attendance at parochial schools, as an alternative to public schools, on the ground that this was simply one hundred per cent released time?

Under this analysis, would a program of "dismissed time" as described by Jackson, J., in *Zorach* (all children released early permitting those who so wish to attend religious schools) be unconstitutional? Would "dismissed time" be nonetheless invalid if it could be shown that the *purpose* for the early school closing was to facilitate religious education? Or is this merely an accommodation "adjusting the schedule of public events to sectarian needs"?

What of the argument that the *Zorach* program is inherently coercive, and therefore unconstitutional, because, as Frankfurter, J., contended in *McCollum,* "the law of imitation operates" placing "an obvious pressure upon children to attend" religious classes? Under this analysis, what result in the case of excusing students to attend a religious service? In the case of parochial schools? In the case of "dismissed time"? Do you agree with Jackson, J.'s assertion in *McCollum* that "it may be doubted whether the Constitution [protects] one from the embarrassment that always attends nonconformity, whether in religion, politics, behavior or dress"?

For a description of the interaction of the justices in fashioning the *Everson, McCollum* and *Zorach* opinions, see Note, *The "Released Time" Cases Revisited: A Study of Group Decisionmaking by the Supreme Court,* 83 Yale L.J. 1202 (1974).

7. [The] only allegation in the complaint that bears on the issue is that the operation of the program "has resulted and inevitably results in the exercise of pressure and coercion upon parents and children to secure attendance by the children for religious instruction." But this charge does not even implicate the school authorities. * * *

(e) *Use of public property.* Is the use of public school classrooms for religious education during nonschool hours distinguishable from *McCollum?* Consider Tribe 2d ed., at 1175: "Religious instructors will no longer stand in 'the position of authority held by the regular teachers,' because the activities lie outside the mandatory school day. Although coercion is conceivable, it is not inherent, as it probably is with official school prayer; students who do not want to take part in the religious activities may take part in other activities or leave the campus. [Thus,] the state neither lends power to religion, nor borrows legitimacy from religion. Permitting a religious group to use school facilities during non-school hours, accordingly, conveys no message of endorsement."

2. *School prayer and the relevance of coercion.* (a) Should *Engel* and *Schempp* (and *McCollum*) have been explicitly based on "the coercion implicit under the statutory schemes"? Consider Stewart, J., dissenting in *Schempp:* "[T]he duty laid upon government in connection with religious exercises in the public schools is that of refraining from so structuring the school environment as to put any kind of pressure on a child to participate in those exercises; it is not that of providing an atmosphere in which children are kept scrupulously insulated from any awareness that some of their fellows may want to open the school day with prayer, or of the fact that there exist in our pluralistic society differences of religious belief. [A] law which provided for religious exercises during the school day and which contained no excusal provision would obviously be unconstitutionally coercive upon those who did not wish to participate. And even under a law containing an excusal provision, if the exercises were held during the school day, and no equally desirable alternative were provided by the school authorities, the likelihood that children might be under at least some psychological compulsion to participate would be great. [Here,] the record shows no more than a subjective prophecy by a parent of what he thought would happen if a request were made to be excused from participation in the exercises under the amended statute. * * * I think we must not assume that school boards so lack the qualities of inventiveness and good will as to make impossible the achievement of that goal."

What evidence of coercion does Stewart, J. require? That the objectors first ask to be excused from participation and then show that social pressures were brought to bear on them? Would this force an objector to surrender his rights in order to vindicate them? Or would Stewart, J., accept the testimony of social scientists that the program was coercive? Could this be judicially noticed? Or would he require a showing that these particular objectors were coerced? Were likely to be coerced? If so, is this a desirable test?

(b) *Establishment vs. free exercise.* If the decisions *should* turn on the element of coercion, would it have been preferable to base them on "the narrower ground of freedom of religion or of conscience, explaining why the considerations advanced in support of the prayer were outweighed by the rights of the objectors, and why under the circumstances the feature of voluntary participation did not sufficiently protect the interests of objectors"? Paul Kauper, *Prayer, Public Schools and the Supreme Court,* 61 Mich.L.Rev. 1031, 1065–66 (1963). Would this analysis permit prayer in an elementary school where every child was willing to participate? In *any* high school? Consider Louis Pollak, *Public Prayers in Public Schools,* 77 Harv. L.Rev. 62, 70 (1963): "[T]o have pitched the decision [on the free exercise clause] would presumably have meant that the prayer programs were constitutionally unobjectionable unless and until challenged, and, therefore, that school boards would have been under no discernible legal obligation, as assuredly they now are, to suspend ongoing prayer programs on their own initiative. [Indeed,] the hypothetical schoolchild plaintiff, whose free exercise rights would thus be enforced, would have to be a child with the gumption not only to disassociate himself from the prayer program but to prefer litigation to the relatively expeditious exit procedure contemplated by the excusal proviso."

3. *Secular purpose.* Several decisions, in addition to *Jaffree,* have invalidated public school practices because their "purpose" has been found to be "religious":

(a) STONE v. GRAHAM, 449 U.S. 39, 101 S.Ct. 192, 66 L.Ed.2d 199 (1980), per curiam, held that a Kentucky statute—requiring "the posting of a copy of the Ten Commandments, purchased with private contributions, on the wall of each public classroom in the State," with the notation at the bottom that "The secular application of the Ten Commandments is clearly seen in its adoption as the fundamental legal code of Western Civilization and the Common Law of the United States"—had "no secular legislative purpose": "The Ten Commandments is undeniably a sacred text in the Jewish and Christian faiths, and no legislative recitation of a supposed secular purpose can blind us to that [fact]. Posting of religious texts on the wall serves [no] educational function. If the posted copies of the Ten Commandments are to have any effect at all, it will be to induce the school children to read, meditate upon, perhaps to venerate and obey, the Commandments. However desirable this might be as a matter of private devotion, it is not a permissible state objective under the Establishment Clause."

REHNQUIST, J., dissented: "The Court's summary rejection of a secular purpose articulated by the legislature and confirmed by the state court is without precedent in Establishment Clause jurisprudence. [This] Court has recognized that 'religion has been closely identified with our history and government,' *Schempp,* and that 'the history of man is inseparable from the history of religion,' *Engel.* Kentucky has decided to make students aware of this fact by demonstrating the secular impact of the Ten Commandments."[a]

(b) EPPERSON v. ARKANSAS, 393 U.S. 97, 89 S.Ct. 266, 21 L.Ed.2d 228 (1968), per FORTAS, J., held that an "anti-evolution" statute, forbidding

---

a. Stewart, J., also dissented. Burger, C.J., and Blackmun, J., dissented from not giving the case plenary consideration.

teachers in public schools "to teach the theory or doctrine that mankind ascended or descended from a lower order of animals," violated both religion clauses: "Arkansas' law selects from the body of knowledge a particular segment which it proscribes for the sole reason that it is deemed to conflict with a particular religious doctrine." Citing newspaper advertisements and letters supporting adoption of the statute in 1928, the Court found it "clear that fundamentalist sectarian conviction was and is the law's reason for existence. [The] law cannot be defended as an act of religious neutrality. Arkansas did not seek to excise from the curricula of its schools and universities all discussion of the origin of man."

BLACK, J., concurring on the ground of "vagueness," found the first amendment questions "troublesome": "Since there is no indication that the literal Biblical doctrine of the origin of man is included in the curriculum of Arkansas schools, does not the removal of the subject of evolution leave the State in a neutral position. [It] is plain that a state law prohibiting all teaching of human development or biology is constitutionally quite different from a law that compels a teacher to teach as true only one theory of a given doctrine. It would be difficult to make a First Amendment case out of a state law eliminating the subject of higher mathematics, or astronomy, or biology from its curriculum. [T]here is no reason I can imagine why a State is without power to withdraw from its curriculum any subject deemed too emotional and controversial for its public schools."[b]

(c) EDWARDS v. AGUILLARD, 482 U.S. 578, 107 S.Ct. 2573, 96 L.Ed.2d 510 (1987), per BRENNAN, J., held that a Louisiana statute, which forebade "the teaching of the theory of evolution in public schools unless accompanied by instruction in 'creation science,'" had "no clear secular purpose": "True, the Act's stated purpose is to protect academic freedom. [While] the Court is normally deferential to a State's articulation of a secular purpose, it is required that the statement of such purpose be sincere and not a sham. See *Jaffree; Stone; Schempp.* [It] is clear from the legislative history [that] requiring schools to teach creation science with evolution does not advance academic freedom. The Act does not grant teachers a flexibility that they did not already possess to supplement the present science curriculum with the presentation of theories, besides evolution, about the origin of life. [While] requiring that curriculum guides be developed for creation science, the Act says nothing of comparable guides for evolution. [The] Act forbids school boards to discriminate against anyone who 'chooses to be a creation-scientist' or to teach 'creationism,' but fails to protect those who choose to teach evolution or any other non-creation science theory, or who refuse to teach creation science.

"If the Louisiana legislature's purpose was solely to maximize the comprehensiveness and effectiveness of science instruction, it would have

b. Harlan, J., concurred in the Court's "establishment of religion" rationale. Stewart, J., concurred on the ground of vagueness.

encouraged the teaching of all scientific theories about the origins of human-kind. But [the] legislative history documents that the Act's primary purpose was to change the science curriculum of public schools in order to provide persuasive advantage to a particular religious doctrine that rejects the factual basis of evolution in its entirety [and that] embodies the religious belief that a supernatural creator was responsible for the creation of human-kind. * * *

"[T]eaching a variety of scientific theories about the origins of human-kind to school children might be validly done with the clear secular intent of enhancing the effectiveness of science instruction. But because the primary purpose of the Creationism Act is to endorse a particular religious doctrine, the Act furthers religion in violation of the Establishment Clause."[a]

SCALIA, J., joined by Rehnquist, C.J., dissented: "Even if I agreed with the questionable premise that legislation can be invalidated under the Establishment Clause on the basis of its motivation alone, without regard to its effects, I would still find no justification for today's decision. [The] Legislature explicitly set forth its secular purpose ('protecting academic freedom') [which] meant: *students'* freedom from *indoctrination.* The legisla-ture wanted to ensure that students would be free to decide for themselves how life began, based upon a fair and balanced presentation of the scientific evidence. [The] legislature did not care *whether* the topic of origins was taught; it simply wished to ensure that *when* the topic was taught, [it] be 'taught as a theory, rather than as proven scientific fact' and that scientific evidence inconsistent with the theory of evolution (viz., 'creation science') be taught as well. [The law] treats the teaching of creation the same way. It does *not* mandate instruction in creation science; *forbids* teachers to present creation science 'as proven scientific fact'; and *bans* the teaching of creation science unless the theory [is] 'discredit[ed] at every turn' with the teaching of evolution. It surpasses understanding how the Court can see in this a purpose 'to restructure the science curriculum to conform with a particular religious viewpoint,' 'to provide a persuasive advantage to a particular religious doctrine,' 'to promote the theory of creation science which embod-ies a particular religious tenet,' and 'to endorse a particular religious doctrine.'

"[The] Louisiana legislators had been told repeatedly that creation scientists were scorned by most educators and scientists, who themselves had an almost religious faith in evolution. It is hardly surprising, then, that in seeking to achieve a balanced, 'nonindoctrinating' curriculum, the legisla-tors protected from discrimination only those teachers whom they thought were *suffering* from discrimination. [In] light of the unavailability of works on creation science suitable for classroom use (a fact appellees concede) and the existence of ample materials on evolution, it was entirely reasonable for

---

a. Powell, J., joined by O'Connor, J., joined the Court's opinion but wrote sepa-rately "to emphasize that nothing in the Court's opinion diminishes the traditionally broad discretion accorded state and local school officials in the selection of the public school curriculum." White, J., concurred only in the judgment.

the Legislature to conclude that science teachers attempting to implement the Act would need a curriculum guide on creation science, but not on evolution. * * *

"It is undoubtedly true that what prompted the Legislature to direct its attention to the misrepresentation of evolution in the schools (rather than the inaccurate presentation of other topics) was its awareness of the tension between evolution and the religious beliefs of many children. But [a] valid secular purpose is not rendered impermissible simply because its pursuit is prompted by concern for religious sensitivities.[b] [I] am astonished by the Court's unprecedented readiness to [disbelieve] the secular purpose set forth in the Act [and to conclude] that it is a sham. [I] can only attribute [this] to an intellectual predisposition [and] an instinctive reaction that any governmentally imposed requirements bearing upon the teaching of evolution must be a manifestation of Christian fundamentalist repression. In this case, however, it seems to me the Court's position is the repressive one. [Perhaps] what the Louisiana Legislature has done is unconstitutional because there *is* no [scientific] evidence, and the scheme they have established will amount to no more than a presentation of the Book of Genesis. But we cannot say that on the evidence before us in this summary judgment context, which includes ample uncontradicted testimony that 'creation science' is a body of scientific knowledge rather than revealed belief.[c] *Infinitely less* can we say (or should we say) that the scientific evidence for evolution is so conclusive that no one could be gullible enough to believe that there is any real scientific evidence to the contrary, so that the legislation's stated purpose must be a lie. Yet that illiberal judgment, that *Scopes*-in-reverse, is ultimately the basis on which the Court's facile rejection of the Louisiana Legislature's purpose must rest. * * *

"I [think the *Lemon* 'purpose' test] is 'a constitutional theory [that] has no basis in the history of the amendment it seeks to interpret, is difficult to apply and yields unprincipled results.' *Jaffree* (Rehnquist, J., dissenting).

"[D]iscerning the subjective motivation of those enacting the statute [is] almost always an impossible task. The number of possible motivations [is] not binary, or indeed even finite. In the present case, for example, a particular legislator need not have voted for the Act either because he

b. See also Scalia, J., joined by Rehnquist, C.J., and Thomas, J., dissenting from denial of certiorari in *Tangipahoa Parish Board of Educ. v. Freiler*, 530 U.S. 1251, 120 S.Ct. 2706, 147 L.Ed.2d 974 (2000), which invalidated, as "not sufficiently neutral," a policy that when "the scientific theory of evolution" is taught, a statement of "disclaimer from endorsement of such theory" shall be made "to inform students of the scientific concept and not intended to influence or dissuade the Biblical version of Creation," and urging students "to exercise critical thinking and gather all information

possible and closely examine each alternative."

c. "The only evidence in the record [defining] 'creation science' is found in five affidavits filed by appellants. In those affidavits, two scientists, a philosopher, a theologian, and an educator, all of whom claim extensive knowledge of creation science, swear that it is essentially a collection of scientific data supporting the theory that the physical universe and life within it appeared suddenly and have not changed substantially since appearing."

wanted to foster religion or because he wanted to improve education. He may have thought the bill would provide jobs for his district, or may have wanted to make amends with a faction of his party he had alienated on another vote, or he may have been a close friend of the bill's sponsor, or he may have been repaying a favor he owed the Majority Leader, or he may have hoped the Governor would appreciate his vote and make a fundraising appearance for him, or he may have been pressured to vote for a bill he disliked by a wealthy contributor or by a flood of constituent mail, or he may have been seeking favorable publicity, or he may have been reluctant to hurt the feelings of a loyal staff member who worked on the bill, or he may have been settling an old score with a legislator who opposed the bill, or he may have been mad at his wife who opposed the bill, or he may have been intoxicated and utterly *un*motivated when the vote was called, or he may have accidentally voted 'yes' instead of 'no,' or, of course, he may have had (and very likely did have) a combination of some of the above and many other motivations. To look for *the sole purpose* of even a single legislator is probably to look for something that does not exist."

(d) Is it meaningful to distinguish between *secular* vs. *religious* purposes? Consider Phillip E. Johnson, *Concepts and Compromise in First Amendment Religious Doctrine,* 72 Calif.L.Rev. 817, 827 (1984): "Governments usually act out of secular motives, even when they are directly aiding a particular religious sect. An atheistic ruler might well create an established church because he thinks it a useful way of raising money, or of ensuring that the clergy do not preach seditious doctrines. In democratic societies, elected officials have an excellent secular reason to accommodate (or at least to avoid offending) groups and individuals who are religious, as well as groups and individuals who are not. They wish to be re-elected, and they do not want important groups to feel that the community does not honor their values."

(e) If the "purpose" of government action is found to be "religious," *should* that alone be enough to invalidate it under the establishment clause? If so, what result in *Zorach?* For a public school "dismissed time" program implemented to facilitate religious education?[d] Consider Tribe 2d ed., at 1211: "The secular purpose requirement [might] be used to strike down laws whose effects are utterly secular. A legislature might, for example, vote to increase welfare benefits because individual legislators feel religiously compelled to do so. So too, when a legislature passes a neutral moment-of-silence statute, many legislators may hope that students will use the time for prayer. However improper these purposes may be, it is hard to see a meaningful establishment clause problem so long as the statute's effects are completely secular. A visible religious purpose may independently convey a message of endorsement or exclusion, but such a message, standing alone, should rarely if ever suffice to transform a secular action into an establishment clause violation. A religious message may be conveyed by the legislative

d. For use of this test to invalidate the "religiously motivated" Utah firing squad, see Martin R. Gardner, *Illicit Legislative* *Motivation as a Sufficient Condition for Unconstitutionality Under the Establishment Clause,* 1979 Wash.U.L.Q. 435.

debates concerning a bill, but the same result is possible from debates that lead to no legislation; it can hardly be said that the debates themselves establish a religion."

See also Jesse H. Choper, *The Religion Clauses of the First Amendment: Reconciling the Conflict,* 41 U.Pitt.L.Rev. 673, 686–87 (1980): "[I]t is only when religious purpose is coupled with threatened impairment of religious freedom that government action should be held to violate the Establishment Clause. [Conceding] that the [*Epperson*] statute had a solely religious purpose, [there] was no evidence that religious beliefs were either coerced, compromised or influenced. That is, it was not shown, nor do I believe that it could be persuasively argued, that the anti-evolution law either (1) induced children of fundamentalist religions to accept the biblical theory of creation, or (2) conditioned other children for conversion to fundamentalism. [Thus, it] should have survived the Establishment Clause challenge." Similarly, "I would find that the creation science law had a religious purpose [to] placate those religious fundamentalists whose beliefs rejected the Darwinian theory of evolution. But [so] long as the theory of creation science is taught in an objective rather than a proselytizing fashion, it does not seem to me to pose a danger to religious liberty [and] should not be held to violate the Establishment Clause." Jesse H. Choper, *Church, State and the Supreme Court: Current Controversy,* 29 Ariz.L.Rev. 551, 557 (1987).

4. *Purpose, primary effect, and "neutrality."* BOARD OF EDUC. v. MERGENS, 496 U.S. 226, 110 S.Ct. 2356, 110 L.Ed.2d 191 (1990), interpreted the Equal Access Act, passed by Congress in 1984, to apply to public secondary schools that (a) receive federal financial assistance, and (b) give official recognition to noncurriculum related student groups (e.g., chess club and scuba diving club in contrast to Latin club and math club) in such ways as allowing them to meet on school premises during noninstructional time. The Act prohibited these schools from denying equal access to, or otherwise discriminating against, student groups "on the basis of the religious, political, philosophical, or other content of the speech at [their] meetings." O'CONNOR, J., joined by Rehnquist, C.J., and White and Blackmun, JJ., held that the establishment clause did not forbid Westside High School from including within its thirty recognized student groups a Christian club "to read and discuss the Bible, to have fellowship and to pray together": "In *Widmar v. Vincent,* 454 U.S. 263, 102 S.Ct. 269, 70 L.Ed.2d 440 (1981), we applied the three-part *Lemon* test to hold that an 'equal access' policy, at the university level, does not violate the Establishment Clause. We concluded that 'an open-forum policy, including nondiscrimination against religious speech, would have a secular purpose,' and would in fact *avoid* entanglement with religion. See id. ("[T]he University would risk greater 'entanglement' by attempting to enforce its exclusion of 'religious worship' and 'religious speech"). We also found that although incidental benefits accrued to religious groups who used university facilities, this result did not amount to an establishment of religion. First, we stated that a university's forum does not 'confer any imprimatur of state approval on religious sects or practices.'

Indeed, the message is one of neutrality rather than endorsement; if a State refused to let religious groups use facilities open to others, then it would demonstrate not neutrality but hostility toward religion. Second, we noted that '[t]he [University's] provision of benefits to [a] broad spectrum of groups'—both nonreligious and religious speakers—was 'an important index of secular effect.'

"We think the logic of *Widmar* applies [here.] Congress' avowed purpose—to prevent discrimination against religious and other types of speech—is undeniably secular. Even if some legislators were motivated by a conviction that religious speech in particular was valuable and worthy of protection, that alone would not invalidate the Act, because what is relevant is the legislative *purpose* of the statute, not the possibly religious *motives* of the legislators who enacted the law. Because the Act on its face grants equal access to both secular and religious speech, we think it clear that the Act's purpose was not to 'endorse or disapprove of religion,' *Jaffree* (O'Connor, J., concurring).

"Petitioners' principal contention is that the Act has the primary effect of advancing religion. Specifically, petitioners urge that, because the student religious meetings are held under school aegis, and because the state's compulsory attendance laws bring the students together (and thereby provide a ready-made audience for student evangelists), an objective observer in the position of a secondary school student will perceive official school support for such religious meetings.

"We disagree. First, [there] is a crucial difference between *government* speech endorsing religion, which the Establishment Clause forbids, and *private* speech endorsing religion, which the Free Speech and Free Exercise Clauses protect. We think that secondary school students are mature enough and are likely to understand that a school does not endorse or support student speech that it merely permits on a nondiscriminatory basis. * * *

"Second, we note that the Act expressly limits participation by school officials at meetings of student religious groups, and that any such meetings must be held during 'noninstructional time.' The Act therefore avoids the problems of 'the students' emulation of teachers as role models' and 'mandatory attendance requirements,' *Aguillard;* see also *McCollum.* To be sure, the possibility of *student* peer pressure remains, but there is little if any risk of official state endorsement or coercion where no formal classroom activities are involved and no school officials actively participate. * * *

"Third, the broad spectrum of officially recognized student clubs at Westside, and the fact that Westside students are free to initiate and organize additional student clubs counteract any possible message of official endorsement of or preference for religion or a particular religious belief.'"

KENNEDY, J., joined by Scalia, J., concurred, emphasizing his disagreement with the plurality's "endorsement test" developed further in *Allegheny*

County v. ACLU, Section IV infra: "I should think it inevitable that a public high school 'endorses' a religious club, in a common-sense use of the term, if the club happens to be one of many activities that the school permits students to choose in order to further the development of their intellect and character in an extracurricular setting. But no constitutional violation occurs if the school's action is based upon a recognition of the fact that membership in a religious club is one of many permissible ways for a student to further his or her own personal enrichment. The inquiry with respect to coercion must be whether the government imposes pressure upon a student to participate in a religious activity. This inquiry, of course, must be undertaken with sensitivity to the special circumstances that exist in a secondary school where the line between voluntary and coerced participation may be difficult to draw. No such coercion, however, has been shown to exist as a necessary result of this statute, either on its face [or] on the facts of this case."

MARSHALL, J., joined by Brennan, J., concurred "to emphasize the steps Westside must take to avoid appearing to endorse the Christian Club's goals."

STEVENS, J., dissented: "Under the Court's interpretation of the Act, Congress has imposed a difficult choice on public high schools receiving federal financial assistance. If such a school continues to allow students to participate in such familiar and innocuous activities as a school chess or scuba diving club, it must also allow religious groups to make use of school facilities. [This] comes perilously close to an outright command to allow organized prayer [on] school premises."[a]

5. *Military chaplains.* In rejecting the argument that Bible reading and prayer exercises in public schools furthered "the majority's right to free exercise of religion," *Schempp* did "not pass upon a situation such as military service, where the Government regulates the temporal and geographic environment of individuals to a point that, unless it permits voluntary religious services to be conducted with the use of government facilities, military personnel would be unable to engage in the practice of their faiths." Might it be that, while free exercise considerations may justify government provision for opportunity to worship, the establishment clause nonetheless bars a government subsidized ministry? "Could the governmental interest be satisfied merely by allowing free time for the serviceman to seek non-military worship or by merely giving the religious orders the right to come into the military environment, at their own expense, to provide the opportunity for worship?" M. Albert Figinski, *Military Chaplains—A Constitutionally Permissible Accommodation Between Church and State,* 24 Md.L.Rev. 377, 409 (1964). Or might it be "that the Government need not necessarily provide chapels and chaplains to those of its armed personnel who are *not*

---

a. May elementary or secondary schools permit their facilities to be used for instruction by religious groups if they also permit instruction by outside teachers of art, music, crafts, dance, etc. (cf. *McCollum*)? May they post the Ten Commandments if they also post the symbols of other civic or charitable groups (cf. *Stone*)? See Douglas Laycock, *Equal Access and Moments of Silence: The Equal Status of Religious Speech by Private Speakers,* 81 Nw.U.L.Rev. 1, 33–35 (1986).

cut off from civilian church facilities"? Klaus J. Herrmann, *Some Considerations on the Constitutionality of the United States Military Chaplaincy,* 14 Am.U.L.Rev. 24, 34 (1964). For fuller consideration of the "conflict" between the religion clauses, see Chapter 14 infra.

6. *Public school secularism. Schempp* emphasized that "it might well be said that one's education is not complete without a study of comparative religion or the history of religion and its relationship to the advancement of civilization. It certainly may be said that the Bible is worthy of study for its literary and historic qualities. Nothing we have said here indicates that such study of the Bible or of religion, when presented objectively as part of a secular program of education, may not be [effected]." May public schools inculcate "fundamental civic and democratic" values? Consider William H. Clune, *The Constitution and Vouchers for Religious Schools: The Demise of Separatism and the Rise of Non-discrimination as Measures of State Neutrality,* Working Paper No. 31 of the Earl Warren Legal Institute, Law School, University of California–Berkeley (1999): "The idea of brainwashing in religious schools only makes sense if it is contrasted with a supposed condition of free choice in secular public education. [But principles] of secularism and secular humanism, that the child should be able to choose among ultimate values on the basis of individual rational choice (as that faculty gradually matures) now seems just as much a value position and a value choice by parents and society as the opposite view that certain values have absolute priority and should be strongly socialized into the child's value system. Indeed the idea that individuals should choose values according to 'rational' criteria operates conceptually as the ultimate value position of secular humanism, just as the idea that individuals should choose values on the basis of religious criteria operates as the ultimate value in religious education." If government requires that public employees be of "good moral character," is this a "religious test" for public office? Contrast Stewart, J., dissenting in *Schempp:* "[A] compulsory state educational system so structures a child's life that if religious exercises are held to be an impermissible activity in schools, [this] is seen, not as the realization of state neutrality, but rather as the establishment of a religion of secularism, or at the least, as government support of the beliefs of those who think that religious exercises should be conducted only in private."

IV.   OFFICIAL ACKNOWLEDGMENT
OF RELIGION

ALLEGHENY COUNTY v. ACLU

492 U.S. 573, 109 S.Ct. 3086, 106 L.Ed.2d 472 (1989).

JUSTICE BLACKMUN announced the judgment of the Court and delivered the opinion of the Court with respect to Parts III–A, IV, and V, an opinion with respect to Parts I and II, in which JUSTICE O'CONNOR and JUSTICE STEVENS join, an opinion with respect to Part III–B, in which JUSTICE STEVENS joins, and an opinion with respect to Part VI.

This litigation concerns the constitutionality of two recurring holiday displays located on public property in downtown Pittsburgh. The first is a crèche placed on the Grand Staircase of the Allegheny County Courthouse. The second is a Chanukah menorah placed just outside the City–County Building, next to a Christmas tree and a sign saluting liberty. The Court of Appeals for the Third Circuit ruled that each display violates the Establishment Clause [because] each has the impermissible effect of endorsing religion. We agree that the crèche display has that unconstitutional effect but reverse the Court of Appeals' judgment regarding the menorah display.

I.A. [The] crèche [is] a visual representation of the scene in the manger in Bethlehem shortly after the birth of Jesus, as described in the Gospels of Luke and Matthew. The crèche includes [an] angel bearing a banner that proclaims "Gloria in Excelsis Deo!"

[III.A.] Although "the myriad, subtle ways in which Establishment Clause values can be eroded," are not susceptible to a single verbal formulation, this Court has attempted to encapsulate the essential precepts of the Establishment Clause. Thus, in *Everson,* the Court gave this often-repeated summary [stating the first ¶ on p. 647]. In *Lemon,* the Court sought to refine these principles by focusing on three "tests." [In] recent years, we have paid particularly close attention to whether the challenged governmental practice either has the purpose or effect of "endorsing" religion * * *.

Of course, the word "endorsement" is not self-defining. Rather, it derives its meaning from other words that this Court has found useful over the years in interpreting the Establishment Clause. [Whether] the key word is "endorsement," "favoritism," or "promotion," the essential principle remains the same. The Establishment Clause, at the very least, prohibits government from appearing to take a position on questions of religious belief or from "making adherence to a religion relevant in any way to a person's standing in the political community." *Lynch v. Donnelly,* 465 U.S. 668, 687, 104 S.Ct. 1355, 1386, 79 L.Ed.2d 604 (1984) (O'Connor, J., concurring).

B. [In *Lynch,*] we considered whether the city of Pawtucket, R.I., had violated the Establishment Clause by including a crèche in its annual Christmas display, located in a private park within the downtown shopping district.[a] By a 5–4 decision in that difficult case, the Court [held] that the inclusion of the crèche did not have the impermissible effect of advancing or promoting religion. [First,] the opinion states that the inclusion of the crèche in the display was "no more an advancement or endorsement of religion" than other "endorsements" this Court has approved in the past—but the

---

a. "[Ten years ago], when [the] crèche was acquired, it cost the City $1365; it now is valued at $200. The erection and dismantling of the crèche costs the City about $20 per year; nominal expenses are incurred in lighting the crèche. No money has been expended on its maintenance for the past 10 years."

opinion offers no discernible measure for distinguishing between permissible and impermissible endorsements. Second, the opinion observes that any benefit the government's display of the crèche gave to religion was no more than "indirect, remote, and incidental"—without saying how or why.

Although Justice O'Connor joined the majority opinion in *Lynch,* she wrote a concurrence [that] provides a sound analytical framework for evaluating governmental use of religious symbols.

First and foremost, the concurrence [recognizes] any endorsement of religion as "invalid," because it "sends a message to nonadherents that they are outsiders, not full members of the political community, and an accompanying message to adherents that they are insiders, favored members of the political community."

Second, the concurrence articulates a method for determining whether the government's use of an object with religious meaning has the effect of endorsing religion[:] the question is "what viewers may fairly understand to be the purpose of the display." That inquiry, of necessity, turns upon the context in which the contested object appears: "a typical museum setting, though not neutralizing the religious content of a religious painting, negates any message of endorsement of that content." * * *

The concurrence applied this mode of analysis to the Pawtucket crèche, seen in the context of that city's holiday celebration as a whole. In addition to the crèche the city's display contained: a Santa Claus House with a live Santa distributing candy, reindeer pulling Santa's sleigh; a live 40–foot Christmas tree strung with lights; statues of carolers in old-fashioned dress; candy-striped poles; a "talking" wishing well; a large banner proclaiming "SEASONS GREETINGS"; a miniature "village" with several houses and a church, and various "cut-out" figures, including those of a clown, a dancing elephant, a robot, and a teddy bear. The concurrence concluded that both because the crèche is "a traditional symbol" of Christmas, a holiday with strong secular elements, and because the crèche was "displayed along with purely secular symbols," the crèche's setting "changes what viewers may fairly understand to be the purpose of the display" and "negates any message of endorsement" of "the Christian beliefs represented by the crèche."

The four *Lynch* dissenters agreed with the concurrence that the controlling question was "whether Pawtucket ha[d] run afoul of the Establishment Clause by endorsing religion through its display of the crèche." The dissenters also agreed with the [relevance of] context [but] concluded that the other elements of the Pawtucket display did not negate the endorsement of Christian faith caused by the presence of the crèche. * * *

Thus, despite divergence at the bottom line, the five Justices in concurrence and dissent in *Lynch* agreed upon the relevant constitutional principles [which] are sound, and have been adopted by the Court in subsequent cases. [*Grand Rapids.*]

IV. We turn first to the county's crèche display. [U]nlike *Lynch*, nothing in the context of the display detracts from the crèche's religious message. [Furthermore,] the crèche sits on the Grand Staircase, the "main" and "most beautiful part" of the building that is the seat of county government. No viewer could reasonably think that it occupies this location without the support and approval of the government [which] has chosen to celebrate Christmas in a way that has the effect of endorsing a patently Christian message: Glory to God for the birth of Jesus Christ. * * *

V. Justice Kennedy and the three Justices who join him would find the display of the crèche consistent with the Establishment Clause. [The] reasons for deciding otherwise are so far-reaching in their implications that they require a response in some depth:

A. In *Marsh v. Chambers*, 463 U.S. 783, 103 S.Ct. 3330, 77 L.Ed.2d 1019 (1983) [upholding the practice of legislative prayer], the Court relied specifically on the fact that Congress authorized legislative prayer at the same time that it produced the Bill of Rights.[b] Justice Kennedy, however, argues that *Marsh* legitimates all "practices with no greater potential for an establishment of religion" than those "accepted traditions dating back to the Founding." Otherwise, the Justice asserts, such practices as our national motto ("In God We Trust") and our Pledge of Allegiance (with the phrase "under God," added in 1954) are in danger of invalidity.

Our previous opinions have considered in dicta the motto and the pledge, characterizing them as consistent with the proposition that government may not communicate an endorsement of religious belief. We need not return to the subject of "ceremonial deism,"[c] because there is an obvious

---

b. *Marsh* also pointed, inter alia, to the practice in the colonies (including Virginia after adopting its Declaration of Rights which has been "considered the precursor of both the Free Exercise and Establishment Clauses"), to the opening invocations in federal courts (including the Supreme Court), and in the Continental Congress and First Congress: "[T]he practice of opening sessions with prayer has continued without interruption ever since that early session of Congress. It has also been followed consistently in most of the states." Brennan, Marshall and Stevens, JJ., dissented.

Of what relevance is it that, subsequently, "Madison acknowledged that he had been quite mistaken in approving—as a member of the House, in 1789—bills for the payment of congressional chaplains"? William W. Van Alstyne, *Trends in the Supreme Court: Mr. Jefferson's Crumbling Wall*, 1984 Duke L.J. 770, 776.

c. Brennan, J., joined by Marshall, Blackmun and Stevens, JJ., dissenting in *Lynch* "suggest[ed] that such practices as

the designation of 'In God We Trust' as our national motto, or the references to God contained in the Pledge of Allegiance can best be understood [as] a form of 'ceremonial deism,' protected from Establishment Clause scrutiny chiefly because they have lost through rote repetition any significant religious content."

For the view that "secularizing religious practices conveniently preserves the inclusion of symbols and practices that many Americans understand as fundamental to American identity, [but] it also threatens the purity and integrity of both government and religion. In addition, such strained legal justification jeopardizes the historically neutral relationship between religion and the state," see Alexandra D. Furth, *Secular Idolatry and Sacred Traditions: A Critique of the Supreme Court's Secularization Analysis.* 146 U.Pa.L.Rev. 579 (1998). See also Steven B. Epstein, *Rethinking the Constitutionality of Ceremonial Deism*, 96 Colum.L.Rev. 2083 (1996) (extensive review concluding that most forms "violate a core purpose of the Establishment Clause").

distinction between crèche displays and references to God in the motto and the pledge. However history may affect the constitutionality of nonsectarian references to religion by the government,[52] history cannot legitimate practices that demonstrate the government's allegiance to a particular sect or creed. [The] history of this Nation, it is perhaps sad to say, contains numerous examples of official acts that endorsed Christianity specifically [but] this heritage of official discrimination against non-Christians has no place in the jurisprudence of the Establishment Clause. * * *

C.   Although Justice Kennedy repeatedly accuses the Court of harboring a "latent hostility" or "callous indifference" toward religion, nothing could be further from the truth. [The] government does not discriminate against any citizen on the basis of the citizen's religious faith if the government is secular in its functions and operations. On the contrary, the Constitution mandates that the government remain secular, rather than affiliating itself with religious beliefs or institutions, precisely in order to avoid discriminating among citizens on the basis of their religious faiths.

A secular state, it must be remembered, is not the same as an atheistic or antireligious state. A secular state establishes neither atheism nor religion as its official creed. * * *[59]

VI.   The display of the Chanukah menorah in front of the City–County Building may well present a closer [issue. The] relevant question for Establishment Clause purposes is whether the combined display of the tree, the sign, and the menorah has the effect of endorsing both Christian and Jewish faiths, or rather simply recognizes that both Christmas and Chanukah are part of the same winter-holiday season, which has attained a secular status in our society. Of the two interpretations of this particular display, the latter seems far more plausible and is also in line with *Lynch.*[64]

---

52.   It is worth noting that just because *Marsh* sustained the validity of legislative prayer, it does not necessarily follow that practices like proclaiming a National Day of Prayer are constitutional. Legislative prayer does not urge citizens to engage in religious practices, and on that basis could well be distinguishable from an exhortation from government to the people that they engage in religious conduct. But, as this practice is not before us, we express no judgment about its constitutionality.

59.   In his attempt to legitimate the display of the crèche on the Grand Staircase, Justice Kennedy repeatedly characterizes it as an "accommodation" of religion. But an accommodation of religion, in order to be permitted under the Establishment Clause, must lift "an identifiable burden *on the exercise of religion.*" *Corporation of Presid-*

ing Bishop v. Amos, [Ch. 14 infra]. Prohibiting the display of a crèche at this location [does] not impose a burden on the practice of Christianity (except to the extent some Christian sect seeks to be an officially approved religion), and therefore permitting the display is not an "accommodation" of religion in the conventional sense.

["Accommodation" of religion and the relationship between the establishment and free exercise clauses is considered in detail in Ch. 13 infra.]

64.   [The] conclusion that Pittsburgh's combined Christmas–Chanukah display cannot be interpreted as endorsing Judaism alone does not mean, however, that it is implausible, as a general matter, for a city like Pittsburgh to endorse a minority faith. The display of a menorah alone might well have that effect.

The Christmas tree, unlike the menorah, is not itself a religious symbol. [The] widely accepted view of the Christmas tree as the preeminent secular symbol of the Christmas holiday season serves to emphasize the secular component of the message communicated by other elements of an accompanying holiday display, including the Chanukah menorah.[66]

The tree, moreover, is clearly the predominant element in the city's display. The 45–foot tree occupies the central position [in] the City–County Building; the 18–foot menorah is positioned to one side. Given this configuration, it is much more sensible to interpret the meaning of the menorah in light of the tree, rather than vice versa. * * *

Although the city has used a symbol with religious meaning as its representation of Chanukah, this is not a case in which the city has reasonable alternatives that are less religious in nature. [Where] the government's secular message can be conveyed by two symbols, only one of which carries religious meaning, an observer reasonably might infer from the fact that the government has chosen to use the religious symbol that the government means to promote religious faith. See *Schempp* (Brennan, J., concurring) (Establishment Clause forbids use of religious means to serve secular ends when secular means suffice). But where, as here, no such choice has been made, this inference of endorsement is not present.[68]

The Mayor's sign further diminishes the possibility that the tree and the menorah will be interpreted as a dual endorsement of Christianity and Judaism. The sign states that during the holiday season the city salutes liberty. Moreover, the sign draws upon the theme of light, common to both Chanukah and Christmas as winter festivals, and links that theme with this Nation's legacy of freedom, which allows an American to celebrate the holiday season in whatever way he wishes, religiously or otherwise. [While] an adjudication of the display's effect must take into account the perspective of one who is neither Christian nor Jewish, as well as of those who adhere to either of these religions, the constitutionality of its effect must also be judged according to the standard of a "reasonable observer." When measured against this standard, the menorah need not be excluded from this particular display.

---

66. Although the Christmas tree represents the secular celebration of Christmas, its very association with Christmas (a holiday with religious dimensions) makes it conceivable that the tree might be seen as representing Christian religion when displayed next to an object associated with Jewish religion. For this reason, I agree with Justice Brennan and Justice Stevens that one must ask whether the tree and the menorah together endorse the *religious* beliefs of Christians and Jews. For the reasons stated in the text, however, I conclude the city's overall display does not have this impermissible effect.

68. In *Lynch,* in contrast, there was no need for Pawtucket to include a crèche in order to convey a secular message about Christmas. (Blackmun, J., dissenting). [In] displaying the menorah next to the tree, the city has demonstrated no preference for the *religious* celebration of the holiday season. This conclusion, however, would be untenable had the city substituted a crèche for its Christmas tree or if the city had failed to substitute for the menorah an alternative, more secular, representation of Chanukah.

The conclusion [here] does not foreclose the possibility that the display of the menorah might violate either the "purpose" or "entanglement" prong of the *Lemon* analysis. These issues [may] be considered [on] remand. * * *

JUSTICE KENNEDY, with whom THE CHIEF JUSTICE, JUSTICE WHITE, and JUSTICE SCALIA join, concurring in the judgment in part and dissenting in part. * * *

I. In keeping with the usual fashion of recent years, the majority applies the *Lemon* [test]. Persuasive criticism of *Lemon* has emerged. See *Aguillard* (Scalia, J., dissenting); *Aguilar v. Felton* (O'Connor, J., dissenting); *Jaffree* (Rehnquist, J., dissenting); *Roemer* (White, J., concurring in judgment). Our cases often question its utility in providing concrete answers to Establishment Clause questions, calling it but a "helpful signpos[t]" or "guidelin[e]", to assist our deliberations rather than a comprehensive test. *Mueller;* See *Lynch* ("we have repeatedly emphasized our unwillingness to be confined to any single test or criterion in this sensitive area").[d] Substantial revision of our Establishment Clause doctrine may be in order,[e] but it is unnecessary to undertake that task today, for even the *Lemon* test, when applied with proper sensitivity to our traditions and our caselaw, supports the conclusion that both the crèche and the menorah are permissible displays in the context of the holiday season. * * *

Rather than requiring government to avoid any action that acknowledges or aids religion, the Establishment Clause permits government some latitude in recognizing and accommodating the central role religion plays in our society. *Lynch; Walz.* Any approach less sensitive to our heritage would border on latent hostility toward religion, as it would require government in all its multifaceted roles to acknowledge only the secular, to the exclusion and so to the detriment of the religious. A categorical approach would install

d. In *Marsh,* Brennan, J., joined by Marshall, J. dissenting, noted that "the Court makes no pretense of subjecting Nebraska's practice of legislative prayer to any of the formal 'tests' that have traditionally structured our inquiry under the Establishment Clause": "I have no doubt that, if any group of law students were asked to apply the principles of *Lemon* to the question of legislative prayer, they would nearly unanimously find the practice to be unconstitutional. [W]e are faced here with the regularized practice of conducting official prayers, on behalf of the entire legislature, as part of the order of business constituting the formal opening of every single session of the legislative term."

e. Four year later, concurring in *Lamb's Chapel,* Scalia, J., joined by Thomas, J., noted that six "of the currently sitting Justices" have disagreed with *Lemon*—Rehnquist, C.J., and White, O'Connor, and Kennedy, JJ., in addition to themselves: "For my part, I agree with the long list of constitutional scholars who have criticized *Lemon* and bemoaned the strange Establishment Clause geometry of crooked lines and wavering shapes its intermittent use has produced. See, e.g., Jesse H. Choper, *The Establishment Clause and Aid to Parochial Schools—An Update,* 75 Cal.L.Rev. 5 (1987); William P. Marshall, *"We Know It When We See It": The Supreme Court and Establishment,* 59 S.Cal.L.Rev. 495 (1986); Michael W. McConnell, *Accommodation of Religion,* 1985 S.Ct.Rev. 1; Philip B. Kurland, *The Religion Clauses and the Burger Court,* 34 Cath.U.L.Rev. 1 (1984); Robert Cord, *Separation of Church and State* (1982); Jesse H. Choper, *The Religion Clauses of the First Amendment: Reconciling the Conflict,* 41 U.Pitt.L.Rev. 673 (1980). I will decline to apply *Lemon*—whether it validates or invalidates the government action in question—and therefore cannot join the opinion of the Court today."

federal courts as jealous guardians of an absolute "wall of separation," sending a clear message of disapproval. [In this century, as the modern administrative state expands to touch the lives of its citizens in such diverse ways and redirects their financial choices through programs of its own, it is difficult to maintain the fiction that requiring government to avoid all assistance to religion can in fairness be viewed as serving the goal of neutrality.] * * *

The ability of the organized community to recognize and accommodate religion in a society with a pervasive public sector requires diligent observance of the border between accommodation and establishment. Our cases disclose two limiting principles: government may not coerce anyone to support or participate in any religion or its exercise; and it may not, in the guise of avoiding hostility or callous indifference, give direct benefits to religion in such a degree that it in fact "establishes a [state] religion or religious faith, or tends to do so." *Lynch*. These two principles, while distinct, are not unrelated, for it would be difficult indeed to establish a religion without some measure of more or less subtle coercion, be it in the form of taxation to supply the substantial benefits that would sustain a state-established faith, direct compulsion to observance, or governmental exhortation to religiosity that amounts in fact to proselytizing.

[The] freedom to worship as one pleases without government interference or oppression is the great object of both the Establishment and the Free Exercise Clauses. Barring all attempts to aid religion through government coercion goes far toward attainment of this object. [S]ome of our recent cases reject the view that coercion is the sole touchstone of an Establishment Clause violation. See *Engel* (dictum) (rejecting, without citation of authority, proposition that coercion is required to demonstrate an Establishment Clause violation); *Schempp; Nyquist*. That may be true if by "coercion" is meant *direct* coercion in the classic sense of an establishment of religion that the Framers knew. But coercion need not be a direct tax in aid of religion or a test oath. Symbolic recognition or accommodation of religious faith may violate the Clause in an extreme case.[1] I doubt not, for example, that the Clause forbids a city to permit the permanent erection of a large Latin cross on the roof of city hall. This is not because government speech about religion is per se suspect, as the majority would have it, but because such an obtrusive year-round religious display would place the government's weight behind an obvious effort to proselytize on behalf of a particular religion. Speech may coerce in some circumstances, but this does not justify a ban on all government recognition of religion. As Chief Justice Burger wrote for the Court in *Walz:* "[W]e will not tolerate either governmentally established religion or governmental interference with religion. Short of those expressly proscribed governmental acts there is room for play in the joints productive

---

1. [The] prayer invalidated in *Engel* was unquestionably coercive in an indirect manner, as the *Engel* Court itself recognized * * *.

[*Marsh* noted that "here, the individual claiming injury by the practice is an adult, presumably not readily susceptible to 'religious indoctrination,' see *Tilton,* or peer pressure, compare *Schempp* (Brennan, J., concurring)."]

of a benevolent neutrality which will permit religious exercise to exist without sponsorship and without interference." * * * Absent coercion, the risk of infringement of religious liberty by passive or symbolic accommodation is minimal. [In] determining whether there exists an establishment, or a tendency toward one, we refer to the other types of church-state contacts that have existed unchallenged throughout our history, or that have been found permissible in our caselaw [discussing *Lynch* and *Marsh*].

II.   These principles are not difficult to apply to the facts of the case before us. [If] government is to participate in its citizens' celebration of a holiday that contains both a secular and a religious component, enforced recognition of only the secular aspect would signify the callous indifference toward religious faith that our cases and traditions do not require; [the] government would be refusing to acknowledge the plain fact, and the historical reality, that many of its citizens celebrate its religious aspects as well. [The] Religion Clauses do not require government to acknowledge these holidays or their religious component; but our strong tradition of government accommodation and acknowledgment permits government to do so.

There is no suggestion here that the government's power to coerce has been used to further the interests of Christianity or Judaism in any way. No one was compelled to observe or participate in any religious ceremony or activity. Neither the city nor the county contributed significant amounts of tax money to serve the cause of one religious faith. The crèche and the menorah are purely passive symbols of religious holidays. Passersby who disagree with the message conveyed by these displays are free to ignore them, or even to turn their backs, just as they are free to do when they disagree with any other form of government speech.

[Crucial] to the Court's conclusion [in *Lynch* was] the simple fact that, when displayed by government during the Christmas season, a crèche presents no realistic danger of moving government down the forbidden road toward an establishment of religion. Whether the crèche be surrounded by poinsettias, talking wishing wells, or carolers, the conclusion remains the same, for the relevant context is not the items in the display itself but the season as a whole. * * *

[III.] Even if *Lynch* did not control, I would not commit this Court to the test applied by the majority today. The notion that cases arising under the Establishment Clause should be decided by an inquiry into whether a " 'reasonable observer' " may " 'fairly understand' " government action to " 'sen[d] a message to nonadherents that they are outsiders, not full members of the political community,' " is a recent, and in my view most unwelcome, addition to our tangled Establishment Clause jurisprudence. * * *

[A.] *Marsh* stands for the proposition, not that specific practices common in 1791 are an exception to the otherwise broad sweep of the Establishment Clause, but rather that the meaning of the Clause is to be determined by reference to historical practices and understandings.[7] Whatever test we choose to apply must permit not only legitimate practices two centuries old but also any other practices with no greater potential for an establishment of religion. [Few] of our traditional practices recognizing the part religion plays in our society can withstand scrutiny under a faithful application [the endorsement test].

Some examples suffice to make plain my concerns. Since the Founding of our Republic, American Presidents have issued Thanksgiving Proclamations establishing a national day of celebration and prayer. The first such proclamation was issued by President Washington at the request of the First Congress [and] the forthrightly religious nature of these proclamations has not waned with the years. President Franklin D. Roosevelt went so far as to "suggest a nationwide reading of the Holy Scriptures during the period from Thanksgiving Day to Christmas" so that "we may bear more earnest witness to our gratitude to Almighty God." It requires little imagination to conclude that these proclamations would cause nonadherents to feel excluded, yet they have been a part of our national heritage from the beginning.[9]

The Executive has not been the only Branch of our Government to recognize the central role of religion in our society. [T]his Court opens its sessions with the request that "God save the United States and this honorable Court." [The] Legislature has gone much further, not only employing legislative chaplains, but also setting aside a special prayer room in the Capitol for use by Members of the House and Senate. The room is decorated with a large stained glass panel that depicts President Washington kneeling in prayer; around him is etched the first verse of the 16th Psalm: "Preserve me, O God, for in Thee do I put my trust." * * * Congress has directed the President to "set aside and proclaim a suitable day each year [as] a National Day of Prayer, on which the people of the United States may turn to God in prayer and meditation at churches, in groups, and as individuals." [Also] by statute, the Pledge of Allegiance to the Flag describes the United States as "one Nation under God." To be sure, no one is obligated to recite this phrase, see *West Virginia State Bd. of Educ. v. Barnette*, [Ch. 12, I infra] but it borders on sophistry to suggest that the " 'reasonable' " atheist would not feel less than a " 'full membe[r] of the political community' " every time his fellow Americans recited, as part of their expression of patriotism and love for country, a phrase he believed to be false. Likewise, our national motto, "In God we trust," which is prominently engraved in the wall above the Speaker's dias in the Chamber of the House of Representatives and is reproduced on every coin minted and every dollar printed by the Federal Government, must have the same effect.

---

7. [T]he relevant historical practices are those conducted by governmental units which were subject to the constraints of the Establishment Clause. Acts of "official discrimination against non-Christians" perpetrated in the eighteenth and nineteenth centuries by States and municipalities are of course irrelevant to this inquiry, but the practices of past Congresses and Presidents are highly informative.

9. Similarly, our presidential inaugurations have traditionally opened with a request for divine blessing. * * *

If the intent of the Establishment Clause is to protect individuals from mere feelings of exclusion, then legislative prayer cannot escape invalidation. It has been argued that "[these] government acknowledgments of religion serve, in the only ways reasonably possible in our culture, the legitimate secular purposes of solemnizing public occasions, expressing confidence in the future, and encouraging the recognition of what is worthy of appreciation in society." *Lynch* (O'Connor, J., concurring). I fail to see why prayer is the only way to convey these messages; appeals to patriotism, moments of silence, and any number of other approaches would be as effective, were the only purposes at issue the ones described by the *Lynch* concurrence. [No] doubt prayer is "worthy of appreciation," but that is most assuredly not because it is secular. Even accepting the secular-solemnization explanation at face value, moreover, it seems incredible to suggest that the average observer of legislative prayer who either believes in no religion or whose faith rejects the concept of God would not receive the clear message that his faith is out of step with the political norm.[10]

[B.] If there be such a person as the "reasonable observer," I am quite certain that he or she will take away a salient message from our holding in this case: the Supreme Court of the United States has concluded that the First Amendment creates classes of religions based on the relative numbers of their adherents. Those religions enjoying the largest following must be consigned to the status of least-favored faiths so as to avoid any possible risk of offending members of minority religions. I would be the first to admit that many questions arising under the Establishment Clause do not admit of easy answers, but whatever the Clause requires, it is not the result reached by the Court today.

[IV.] The case before us is admittedly a troubling one. It must be conceded that, however neutral the purpose of the city and county, the eager proselytizer may seek to use these symbols for his own ends. The urge to use them to teach or to taunt is always present. It is also true that some devout adherents of Judaism or Christianity may be as offended by the holiday display as are nonbelievers, if not more so. To place these religious symbols in a common hallway or sidewalk, where they may be ignored or even insulted, must be distasteful to many who cherish their meaning.

For these reasons, I might have voted against installation of these particular displays were I a local legislative official. But [the] principles of the Establishment Clause and our Nation's historic traditions of diversity

10. If the majority's test were to be applied logically, it would lead to the elimination of all nonsecular Christmas caroling in public buildings or, presumably, anywhere on public property. It is difficult to argue that lyrics like "Good Christian men, rejoice," "Joy to the world! the Savior reigns," "This, this is Christ the King," "Christ, by highest heav'n adored," and "Come and behold Him, Born the King of angels," have acquired such a secular nature that nonadherents would not feel "left out" by a government-sponsored or approved program that included these carols. [Like] Thanksgiving Proclamations, the reference to God in the Pledge of Allegiance, and invocations to God in sessions of Congress and of this Court, they constitute practices that the Court will not proscribe, but that the Court's reasoning today does not explain.

and pluralism allow communities to make reasonable judgments respecting the accommodation or acknowledgment of holidays with both cultural and religious aspects. No constitutional violation occurs when they do so by displaying a symbol of the holiday's religious origins. * * *

Justice O'Connor with whom Justice Brennan and Justice Stevens join as to Part II, concurring in part and concurring in the judgment. * * *

II.   In his separate opinion, Justice Kennedy asserts that the endorsement test "is flawed in its fundamentals and unworkable in practice." * * *

An Establishment Clause standard that prohibits only "coercive" practices or overt efforts at government proselytization, but fails to take account of the numerous more subtle ways that government can show favoritism to particular beliefs or convey a message of disapproval to others, would not, in my view, adequately protect the religious liberty or respect the religious diversity of the members of our pluralistic political community. Thus, this Court has never relied on coercion alone as the touchstone of Establishment Clause analysis. To require a showing of coercion, even indirect coercion, as an essential element of an Establishment Clause violation would make the Free Exercise Clause a redundancy. [Moreover,] as even Justice Kennedy recognizes, any Establishment Clause test limited to "*direct* coercion" clearly would fail to account for forms of "[s]ymbolic recognition or accommodation of religious faith" that may violate the Establishment Clause.

[To] be sure, the endorsement test depends on a sensitivity to the unique circumstances and context of a particular challenged practice and, like any test that is sensitive to context, it may not always yield results with unanimous agreement at the margins. But that is true of many standards in constitutional law, and even the modified coercion test offered by Justice Kennedy involves judgment and hard choices at the margin. He admits as much by acknowledging that the permanent display of a Latin cross at city hall would violate the Establishment Clause, as would the display of symbols of Christian holidays alone. Would the display of a Latin cross for six months have such an unconstitutional effect, or the display of the symbols of most Christian holidays and one Jewish holiday? Would the Christmas-time display of a crèche inside a courtroom be "coercive" if subpoenaed witnesses had no opportunity to "turn their backs" and walk away? Would displaying a crèche in front of a public school violate the Establishment Clause under Justice Kennedy's test? * * *

Justice Kennedy submits that the endorsement test [would] invalidate many traditional practices recognizing the role of religion in our society. * * * Historical acceptance of a practice does not in itself validate that practice under the Establishment Clause if the practice violates the values protected by that Clause, just as historical acceptance of racial or gender based discrimination does not immunize such practices from scrutiny under the 14th Amendment.[f] [On] the contrary, the "history and ubiquity" of a practice is relevant because it provides part of the context in which a reasonable observer evaluates whether a challenged governmental practice conveys a message of endorsement of religion. [Thus,] the celebration of Thanksgiving as a public holiday, despite its religious origins, is now generally understood as a celebration of patriotic values rather than particular religious beliefs.[g] * * *

III.   For reasons which differ somewhat from those set forth in Part VI of Justice Blackmun's opinion, I also conclude that the city of Pittsburgh's combined holiday display [does] not have the effect of conveying an endorsement of religion. [In] my view, Justice Blackmun's new rule that an inference of endorsement arises every time government uses a symbol with religious meaning if a "more secular alternative" is available, is too blunt an instrument for Establishment Clause analysis, which depends on sensitivity to the context and circumstances presented by each case. * * *

JUSTICE BRENNAN, with whom JUSTICE MARSHALL and JUSTICE STEVENS join, concurring in part and dissenting in part.

* * * I continue to believe that the display of an object that "retains a specifically Christian [or other] religious meaning," is incompatible with the separation of church and state demanded by our Constitution. I therefore agree with the Court that Allegheny County's display of a crèche at the county courthouse signals an endorsement of the Christian faith in violation of the Establishment Clause, and join Parts III–A, IV, and V of the Court's opinion. I cannot agree, however, [with] the decision as to the menorah [which] rests on three premises: the Christmas tree is a secular symbol; Chanukah is a holiday with secular dimensions, symbolized by the menorah; and the government may promote pluralism by sponsoring or condoning displays having strong religious associations on its property. None of these is sound.

[I.] Even though the tree alone may be deemed predominantly secular, it can hardly be so characterized when placed next to such a forthrightly

---

f. In contending that "specific historical practice should [not] override [the] clear constitutional imperative," Brennan, J., joined by Marshall, J., dissenting in *Marsh,* noted that "the sort of historical argument made by the Court should be advanced with some hesitation in light of certain other skeletons in the congressional closet. See, e.g., An Act for the Punishment of certain Crimes against the United States (1790) (enacted by the First Congress and requiring that persons convicted of certain theft offenses 'be publicly whipped, not exceeding thirty-nine stripes'); Act of July 23, 1866 (reaffirming the racial segregation of the public schools in the District of Columbia; enacted exactly one week after Congress proposed Fourteenth Amendment to the States)."

Brennan, J., concurring in *Schempp,* further observed that "today the Nation is far more heterogeneous religiously, including as it does substantial minorities not only of Catholics and Jews but as well of those who worship according to no version of the Bible and those who worship no God at all. In the face of such profound changes, practices which may have been objectionable to no one in the time of Jefferson and Madison may today be highly offensive to many persons, the deeply devout and the non-believers alike. [Thus], our use of the history of their time must limit itself to broad purposes, not specific practices."

g. Brennan, J.'s dissent in *Lynch* expressed a similar view.

religious symbol. Consider a poster featuring a star of David, a statue of Buddha, a Christmas tree, a mosque, and a drawing of Krishna. There can be no doubt that, when found in such company, the tree serves as an unabashedly religious symbol. * * *

[II.] The menorah is indisputably a religious symbol, used ritually in a celebration that has deep religious significance. That, in my view, is all that need be said. Whatever secular practices the holiday of Chanukah has taken on in its contemporary observance are beside the [point.] Pittsburgh's secularization of an inherently religious symbol [recalls] the effort in *Lynch* to render the crèche a secular symbol. As I said then: "To suggest, as the Court does, that such a symbol is merely 'traditional' and therefore no different from Santa's house or reindeer is not only offensive to those for whom the crèche has profound significance, but insulting to those who insist for religious or personal reasons that the story of Christ is in no sense a part of 'history' nor an unavoidable element of our national 'heritage.'" * * *

III. Justice Blackmun, in his acceptance of the city's message of "diversity," and, even more so, Justice O'Connor, in her approval of the "message of pluralism and freedom to choose one's own beliefs," appear to believe that, where seasonal displays are concerned, more is better. * * * I know of no principle under the Establishment Clause, however, that permits us to conclude that governmental promotion of religion is acceptable so long as one religion is not favored. We have, on the contrary, interpreted that Clause to require neutrality, not just among religions, but between religion and nonreligion. * * *

The uncritical acceptance of a message of religious pluralism also ignores the extent to which even that message may offend. Many religious faiths are hostile to each other, and indeed, refuse even to participate in ecumenical services designed to demonstrate the very pluralism Justices Blackmun and O'Connor extol. * * *

JUSTICE STEVENS, with whom JUSTICE BRENNAN and JUSTICE MARSHALL join, concurring in part and dissenting in part. * * *

In my opinion the Establishment Clause should be construed to create a strong presumption against the display of religious symbols on public property. There is always a risk that such symbols will offend nonmembers of the faith being advertised as well as adherents who consider the particular advertisement disrespectful. [Even] though "[p]assersby who disagree with the message conveyed by these displays are free to ignore them, or even turn their backs," displays of this kind inevitably have a greater tendency to emphasize sincere and deeply felt differences among individuals than to achieve an ecumenical goal. The Establishment Clause does not allow public bodies to foment such disagreement.

Application of a strong presumption against the public use of religious symbols scarcely will "require a relentless extirpation of all contact between government and religion," (Kennedy, J., concurring and dissenting), for it will prohibit a display only when its message, evaluated in the context in which it is presented, is nonsecular. For example, a carving of Moses holding the Ten Commandments, if that is the only adornment on a courtroom wall, conveys an equivocal message, perhaps of respect for Judaism, for religion in general, or for law. The addition of carvings depicting Confucius and Mohammed may honor religion, or particular religions, to an extent that the First Amendment does not tolerate any more than it does "the permanent erection of a large Latin cross on the roof of city hall." Placement of secular figures such as Caesar Augustus, William Blackstone, Napoleon Bonaparte, and John Marshall alongside these three religious leaders, however, signals respect not for great proselytizers but for great lawgivers. It would be absurd to exclude such a fitting message from a courtroom,[13] as it would to exclude religious paintings by Italian Renaissance masters from a public museum.[h] Far from "border[ing] on latent hostility toward religion," this careful consideration of context gives due regard to religious and nonreligious members of our society. * * *

Notes and Questions

1. *Secular purpose under the "Lemon" test. Lynch* found that "Pawtucket has *a* secular purpose for its display": "The City [has] principally taken note of a significant historical religious event long celebrated in the Western World. [Were] the test that the government must have 'exclusively secular' objectives, much of the conduct and legislation this Court has approved in the past would have been invalidated."

Brennan, J.'s dissent in *Lynch,* reasoned: "When government decides to recognize Christmas day as a public holiday, it does no more than accommodate the calendar of public activities to the plain fact that many Americans will expect on that day to spend time visiting with their families, attending religious services, and perhaps enjoying some respite from preholiday activities. [If] public officials go further and participate in the *secular* celebration of Christmas—by, for example, decorating public places with such secular images as wreaths, garlands or Santa Claus figures—they move closer to the limits of their constitutional power but nevertheless remain within the boundaries set by the Establishment Clause. But when those officials participate in or appear to endorse the distinctively religious elements of this otherwise secular event, they encroach upon First Amendment freedoms. [The] Court seems to assume that forbidding Pawtucket from displaying a crèche would be tantamount to forbidding a state college from including the Bible or Milton's *Paradise Lost* in a course on English literature. But in those cases the religiously-inspired materials are being considered solely as literature. [In] this case, by contrast, the crèche plays no comparable secular

---

13. All these leaders, of course, appear in friezes on the walls of our courtroom.

h. As an example of government "reference to our religious heritage," *Lynch* noted that "the National Gallery in Washington, maintained with Government support [has] long exhibited masterpieces with religious messages, notably the Last Supper, and paintings depicting the Birth of Christ, the Crucifixion, and the Resurrection, among many others with explicit Christian themes and messages."

role. [It] would be another matter if the crèche were displayed in a museum setting, in the company of other religiously-inspired artifacts, as an example, among many, of the symbolic representation of religious myths. In that setting, we would have objective guarantees that the crèche could not suggest that a particular faith had been singled out for public favor and recognition."

Does the dissent's approach require that government have "exclusively secular" objectives? If so, is this inconsistent with the Court's subsequent opinion in *Jaffree* (joined by all the *Lynch* dissenters) that "a statute that is motivated in part by a religious purpose may satisfy the first [*Lemon*] criterion."

2. *Differing interpretations of the "coercion" test.* LEE v. WEISMAN, 505 U.S. 577, 112 S.Ct. 2649, 120 L.Ed.2d 467 (1992), per KENNEDY, J., held violative of the establishment clause the practice of public school officials inviting members of the clergy to offer invocation and benediction prayers at graduation ceremonies: "We can decide the case without reconsidering the general constitutional framework [in *Lemon*. The] school district's supervision and control of a high school graduation ceremony places public pressure, as well as peer pressure, on attending students to stand as a group or, at least, maintain respectful silence during the Invocation and Benediction. This pressure, though subtle and indirect, can be as real as any overt compulsion. * * *

"Finding no violation under these circumstances would place objectors in the dilemma of participating, with all that implies, or protesting. * * * Research in psychology supports the common assumption that adolescents are often susceptible to pressure from their peers towards conformity, and that the influence is strongest in matters of social convention.[a] [That] the intrusion was in the course of promulgating religion that sought to be civic or nonsectarian rather than pertaining to one sect does not lessen the offense or isolation to the objectors. At best it narrows their number, at worst increases their sense of isolation and affront.

"[I]n our society and in our culture high school graduation is one of life's most significant occasions. A school rule which excuses attendance is beside the point. Attendance may not be required by official decree, yet it is apparent that a student is not free to absent herself from the graduation exercise in any real sense of the term 'voluntary,' for absence would require forfeiture of these intangible benefits which have motivated the student through youth and all her high school years.[b] [To] say that a student must

a. For criticism of the psychological evidence relied on by the Court, see Donald N. Bersoff & David J. Glass, *The Not–So Weisman: The Supreme Court's Continuing Misuse of Social Science Research*, 2 U.Chi.L.S.Roundtable 279 (1995).

b. Consider Steven G. Gey, *Religious Coercion and the Establishment Clause*,

1994 U.Ill.L.Rev. 463, 503: "But a citizen of Allegheny County may also be compelled to transact business in the county courthouse, which would inevitably require that person to pass by the prominent display of the birth of the Christian savior. If the Allegheny County citizen is not coerced by being required to respectfully pass by the

remain apart from the ceremony at the opening invocation and closing benediction is to risk compelling conformity in an environment analogous to the classroom setting, where we have said the risk of compulsion is especially high. See *Engel* and *Schempp*. * * *

"Inherent differences between the public school system and a session of a State Legislature distinguish this case from *Marsh*. [The] atmosphere at the opening of a session of a state legislature where adults are free to enter and leave with little comment and for any number of reasons cannot compare with the constraining potential of the one school event most important for the student to attend. * * *

"We do not hold that every state action implicating religion is invalid if one or a few citizens find it offensive. People may take offense at all manner of religious as well as nonreligious messages, but offense alone does not in every case show a violation. We know too that sometimes to endure social isolation or even anger may be the price of conscience or nonconformity. But, by any reading of our cases, the conformity required of the student in this case was too high an exaction to withstand the test of the Establishment Clause."

BLACKMUN, J., joined by Stevens and O'Connor, JJ., who joined the Court's opinion, concurred: "[I]t is not enough that the government restrain from compelling religious practices: it must not engage in them either. [To] that end, our cases have prohibited government endorsement of religion, its sponsorship, and active involvement in religion, whether or not citizens were coerced to conform."

SOUTER, J., (who also joined the Court's opinion), joined by Stevens and O'Connor, JJ., concurred: "The Framers adopted the Religion Clauses in response to a long tradition of coercive state support for religion, particularly in the form of tax assessments, but their special antipathy to religious coercion did not exhaust their hostility to the features and incidents of establishment. Indeed, Jefferson and Madison opposed any political appropriation of religion, [and] saw that even without the tax collector's participation, an official endorsement of religion can impair religious liberty. [O]ne can call any act of endorsement a form of coercion, but only if one is willing to dilute the meaning of 'coercion' until there is no meaning left. * * *

"Religious students cannot complain that omitting prayers from their graduation ceremony would, in any realistic sense, 'burden' their spiritual callings. To be sure, many of them invest this rite of passage with spiritual significance, but they may express their religious feelings about it before and after the ceremony. They may even organize a privately sponsored baccalaureate if they desire the company of likeminded students. Because they accordingly have no need for the machinery of the State to affirm their

religious display, why is the Providence student coerced by respectfully remaining silent during a one-minute prayer? Conversely, if 'the act of standing or remaining silent' during a graduation prayer is 'an ex-pression of participation' in the prayer, why is walking by an overtly Christian display in respectful silence not also 'an expression of participation' in the display?"

beliefs, the government's sponsorship of prayer at the graduation ceremony is most reasonably understood as an official endorsement of religion and, in this instance, of theistic religion."

SCALIA, J., joined by Rehnquist, C.J., and White and Thomas, JJ., dissented: "Three terms ago, I joined an opinion recognizing that 'the meaning of the [Establishment] Clause is to be determined by reference to historical practices and understandings.' * * * *Allegheny County* (Kennedy, J., concurring in judgment in part and dissenting in part).

"These views of course prevent me from joining today's opinion, which is conspicuously bereft of any reference to history [and] lays waste a tradition that is as old as public-school graduation ceremonies themselves, and that is a component of an even more longstanding American tradition of nonsectarian prayer to God at public celebrations generally.

"[Since] the Court does not dispute that students exposed to prayer at graduation ceremonies retain (despite 'subtle coercive pressures,') the free will to sit, there is absolutely no basis for the Court's decision. It is fanciful enough to say that 'a reasonable dissenter,' standing head erect in a class of bowed heads, 'could believe that the group exercise signified her own participation or approval of it.' It is beyond the absurd to say that she could entertain such a belief while pointedly declining to rise.

"But let us assume the very worst, that the nonparticipating graduate is 'subtly coerced' * * * to stand! Even that half of the disjunctive does not remotely establish a 'participation' (or an 'appearance of participation') in a religious exercise. * * *

"The deeper flaw in the Court's opinion does not lie in its wrong answer to the question whether there was state-induced 'peer-pressure' coercion; it lies, rather, in the Court's making violation of the Establishment Clause hinge on such a precious question. The coercion that was a hallmark of historical establishments of religion was coercion of religious orthodoxy and of financial support by force of *law and threat of penalty.* [I] concede that our constitutional tradition [has,] ruled out of order government-sponsored endorsement of religion—even when no legal coercion is present, and indeed even when no ersatz, 'peer-pressure' psycho-coercion is present—where the endorsement is sectarian, in the sense of specifying details upon which men and women who believe in a benevolent, omnipotent Creator and Ruler of the world, are known to differ (for example, the divinity of Christ). But there is simply no support for the proposition that the officially sponsored nondenominational invocation and benediction read by Rabbi Gutterman—with no one legally coerced to recite them—violated the Constitution of the United States.[c] To the contrary, they are so characteristically American they could have come from the pen of George Washington or Abraham Lincoln himself.

---

c. Compare Gey, supra, at 507: "If dissenting audience members at a state-sponsored public event may walk away from the affair without subjecting themselves to legal penalties, it should not matter whether a prayer given at that function incorporates the tenets of a particular sect, or comments unfavorably on the tenets of another sect. It should not matter even if the government sponsors a prayer overtly hostile to one or more faiths, so long as the dissenters are

"The Court relies on our 'school prayer' cases, *Engel* and *Schempp*. But whatever the merit of those cases, they do not support, much less compel, the Court's psycho-journey. In the first place, *Engel* and *Schempp* do not constitute an exception to the rule, distilled from historical practice, that public ceremonies may include prayer; rather, they simply do not fall within the scope of the rule (for the obvious reason that school instruction is not a public ceremony). Second, we have made clear our understanding that school prayer occurs within a framework in which legal coercion to attend school (i.e., coercion under threat of penalty) provides the ultimate backdrop. * * * Voluntary prayer at graduation—a one-time ceremony at which parents, friends and relatives are present—can hardly be thought to raise the same concerns."[d]

3. *Prayer at other school activities—issues of government purpose and involvement.* SANTA FE IND. SCHOOL DIST. v. DOE, 530 U.S. 290, 120 S.Ct. 2266, 147 L.Ed.2d 295 (2000), per STEVENS, J., relied on *Lee* to hold "invalid on its face" the school district's policy authorizing a student election (1) to determine whether to have a student "deliver a brief invocation and/or message [at] varsity football games to solemnize the event, to promote good sportsmanship and student safety, and to establish the appropriate environment for the competition," and (2) to select "a student volunteer who is [to] decide what statement or invocation to deliver, consistent with the goals and purposes of this policy. Any message and/or invocation delivered by a student must be nonsectarian and nonproselytizing." The Court found "the evolution of the current policy [to be] most striking," pointing to the earlier practice of having an elected "Student Chaplain [deliver] a prayer over the public address system before each varsity football game," and to the title—"Prayer at Football Games"—of the most recent preceding policy, which was similar to the school's policy for prayer at graduations. The Court also emphasized the parties' stipulation that "students voted to determine whether a student would deliver prayer at varsity football games," all of which led the Court "to infer that the specific purpose of the policy was to preserve a popular 'state-sponsored religious practice.'"[a]

allowed to ignore the government's advice and practice their own beliefs freely."

d. How would the *Lee* Court—with Souter, J. replacing Brennan, J. and Thomas, J. replacing Marshall, J.—have decided the crèche issue in *Allegheny County*? See Jesse H. Choper, *Separation of Church and State: "New" Directions by the "New" Supreme Court,* 34 J. Church & State 363 (1992); Suzanna Sherry, *Lee v. Weisman: Paradox Redux,* 1992 Sup.Ct.Rev. 123.

a. "[Further], the policy, by its terms, invites and encourages religious messages. The policy itself states that the purpose of the message is 'to solemnize the event.' A religious message is the most obvious method of solemnizing an event. Moreover, the requirements that the message 'promote good citizenship' and 'establish the appropriate environment for competition' further narrow the types of message deemed appropriate, suggesting that a solemn, yet nonreligious, message, such as commentary on United States foreign policy, would be prohibited. Indeed, the only type of message that is expressly endorsed in the text is an 'invocation'—a term that primarily describes an appeal for divine assistance. In fact, as used in the past at Santa Fe High School, an 'invocation' has always entailed a focused religious message."

"[T]he District first argues that [the] messages are private student speech, not public speech. [But] these invocations are authorized by a government policy and take place on government property at government-sponsored school-related events. [Unlike] the type of forum discussed in [*Rosenberger* and similar cases, here,] the school allows only one student, the same student for the entire season, to give the invocation. [T]he majoritarian process implemented by the District guarantees, by definition, that minority candidates will never prevail and that their views will be effectively silenced. [This] encourages divisiveness along religious lines in a public school setting, a result at odds with the Establishment Clause. [And, in the context of a] broadcast over the school's public address system [at all varsity football games,] the members of the listening audience must perceive the pregame message as a public expression of the views of the majority of the student body delivered with the approval of the school administration."

As for "coercion," "we may assume [that] the informal pressure to attend an athletic event is not as strong as a senior's desire to attend her own graduation ceremony. [But] to assert that [many] high school students do not feel immense social pressure, or have a truly genuine desire, to be involved in the extracurricular event that is American high school football is 'formalistic in the extreme.'"

REHNQUIST, C.J., joined by Scalia and Thomas, JJ., dissented: "Even if it were appropriate to apply the *Lemon* test here, the district's student-message policy should not be invalidated on its face. [I]t is possible that the students might vote not to have a pregame speaker, in which case there would be no threat of a constitutional violation. It is also possible that the election would not focus on prayer, but on public speaking ability or social popularity. And if student campaigning did begin to focus on prayer, the school might decide to implement reasonable campaign restrictions.[b]

"[A]ny speech that may occur as a result of the election process here would be private, not government, speech. [Unlike *Lee*, the] elected student, not the government, would choose what to say. [A] newly elected prom king or queen, could use opportunities for public speaking to say prayers. Under the Court's view, the mere grant of power to the students to vote for such offices, in light of the fear that those elected might publicly pray, violates the Establishment Clause.[c]

b. The Court responded: "Under the *Lemon* standard, a court must invalidate a statute if it lacks 'a secular legislative purpose.' [E]ven if no Santa Fe High School student were ever to offer a religious message, [the] attempt by the District to encourage prayer is also at issue. Government efforts to endorse religion cannot evade constitutional reproach based solely on the remote possibility that those attempts may fail."

c. The Court responded: "If instead of a choice between an invocation and no pre-

game message, the first election determined whether a political speech should be made, and the second election determined whether the speaker should be a Democrat or a Republican, it would be rather clear that the public address system was being used to deliver a partisan message reflecting the viewpoint of the majority rather than a random statement by a private individual.

"The fact that the District's policy provides for the election of the speaker only after the majority has voted on her message identifies an obvious distinction between

"[T]he Court dismisses the [policy's "plausible secular purpose"] of solemnization.[d] [But] it is easy to think of solemn messages that are not religious in nature, for example urging that a game be fought fairly. And sporting events often begin with a solemn rendition of our national anthem, with its concluding verse 'And this be our motto: "In God is our trust." Under the Court's logic, a public school that sponsors the singing of the national anthem before football games violates the Establishment Clause."

4. *Differing interpretations of the "endorsement" test.* (a) CAPITOL SQUARE REVIEW & ADVISORY BOARD v. PINETTE, 515 U.S. 753, 115 S.Ct. 2440, 132 L.Ed.2d 650 (1995), per SCALIA, J., relying on *Widmar* and *Lamb's Chapel,* held that petitioner's permitting the Ku Klux Klan to place a Latin cross in Capitol Square—"A 10–acre, state-owned plaza surrounding the Statehouse in Columbus, Ohio"—when it had also permitted such other unattended displays as "a State-sponsored lighted tree during the Christmas season, a privately-sponsored menorah during Chanukah, a display showing the progress of a United Way fundraising campaign, and booths and exhibits during an arts festival," did not violate the establishment clause: "The State did not sponsor respondents' expression, the expression was made on government property that had been opened to the public for speech, and permission was requested through the same application process and on the same terms required of other private groups."

The seven-justice majority divided, however, on the scope of the "endorsement" test. SCALIA, J., joined by Rehnquist, C.J., and Kennedy and Thomas, JJ., rejected petitioners' claim based on "the forum's proximity to the seat of government, which, they contend, may produce the perception that the cross bears the State's approval": "[W]e have consistently held that it is no violation for government to enact neutral policies that happen to benefit religion. Where we have tested for endorsement of religion, the subject of the test was either expression by the government itself, *Lynch,* or else government action alleged to discriminate in favor of private religious expression or activity, *Allegheny County.* The test petitioners propose, which would attribute to a neutrally behaving government private religious expression, has no antecedent in our jurisprudence. [O]ne can conceive of a case in which a governmental entity manipulates its administration of a public forum close to the seat of government (or within a government building) in such a manner that only certain religious groups take advantage of it,

this case and the typical election of a 'student body president, or even a newly elected prom king or queen.' "

"After *Lee,* what result if the class valedictorian begins her speech with a prayer? See Alan E. Brownstein, *Prayer and Religious Expression at High School Graduation: Constitutional Etiquette in a Pluralistic Society,* 5 Nexus 61 (2000).

d. The Court responded: "When a governmental entity professes a secular purpose for an arguably religious policy, the government's characterization is, of course, entitled to some deference. But it is nonetheless the duty of the courts to 'distinguis[h] a sham secular purpose from a sincere one.' (O'Connor, J., concurring in judgment)."

creating an impression of endorsement that is in fact accurate. But those situations, which involve governmental favoritism, do not exist here. * * *

"The contrary view, most strongly espoused by Justice Stevens [infra], but endorsed by Justice Souter and Justice O'Connor [and Breyer, J.] as well, [infra], exiles private religious speech to a realm of less-protected expression. [It] is no answer to say that the Establishment Clause tempers religious speech. By its terms that Clause applies only to the words and acts of government. It was never meant, and has never been read by this Court, to serve as an impediment to purely private religious speech connected to the State only through its occurrence in a public forum."[a]

O'CONNOR, J., joined by Souter and Breyer, JJ., concurred in part: "Where the government's operation of a public forum has the effect of endorsing religion, even if the governmental actor neither intends nor actively encourages that result, the Establishment Clause is violated [because] the State's own actions (operating the forum in a particular manner and permitting the religious expression to take place therein), and their relationship to the private speech at issue, actually convey a message of endorsement."[b]

STEVENS, J., dissented: "[W]hile this unattended, freestanding wooden cross was unquestionably a religious symbol, observers may well have received completely different messages from that symbol. Some might have perceived it as a message of love, others as a message of hate, still others as a message of exclusion—a Statehouse sign calling powerfully to mind their outsider status. [It] is especially important to take account of the perspective of a reasonable observer who may not share the particular religious belief it expresses. A paramount purpose of the Establishment Clause is to protect such a person from being made to feel like an outsider in matters of faith, and a stranger in the political community. If a reasonable person could perceive a government endorsement of religion from a private display, then the State may not allow its property to be used as a forum for that display. No less stringent rule can adequately protect non-adherents from a well-grounded perception that their sovereign supports a faith to which they do not subscribe.[c],[5]

---

a. Thomas, J., filed a brief concurrence, emphasizing that "a cross erected by the Ku Klux Klan [is] a political act, not a Christian one."

b. Souter, J., joined by O'Connor and Breyer, JJ., concurred "in large part because of the possibility of affixing a sign to the cross adequately disclaiming any government sponsorship or endorsement of it.

"[As] long as the governmental entity does not 'manipulat[e]' the forum in such a way as to exclude all other speech, the plurality's opinion would seem to [invite] government encouragement [of religion], even when the result will be the domination of the forum by religious displays and religious speakers. * * *

"Something of the sort, in fact, may have happened here. Immediately after the District Court issued the injunction ordering petitioners to grant the Klan's permit, a local church council [invited] all local churches to erect crosses, and the Board granted 'blanket permission' for 'all churches friendly to or affiliated with' the council to do so. The end result was that a part of the square was strewn with crosses, and while the effect in this case may have provided more embarrassment than suspicion of endorsement, the opportunity for the latter is clear."

c. O'Connor, J., responded: "Under such an approach, a religious display is necessarily precluded so long as some pass-

"[The] very fact that a sign is installed on public property implies official recognition and reinforcement of its message. That implication is especially strong when the sign stands in front of the seat of the government itself. The 'reasonable observer' of any symbol placed unattended in front of any capitol in the world will normally assume that the sovereign [has] sponsored and facilitated its message. [Even] if the disclaimer at the foot of the cross (which stated that the cross was placed there by a private organization) were legible, that inference would remain, because a property owner's decision to allow a third party to place a sign on her property conveys the same message of endorsement as if she had erected it herself. [This] clear image of endorsement was lacking in *Widmar* and *Lamb's Chapel,* in which the issue was access to government facilities. Moreover, there was no question in those cases of an unattended display; private speakers, who could be distinguished from the state, were present. * * *

"The battle over the Klan cross underscores the power of such symbolism. The menorah prompted the Klan to seek permission to erect an anti-semitic symbol, which in turn not only prompted vandalism but also motivated other sects to seek permission to place their own symbols in the Square. These facts illustrate the potential for insidious entanglement that flows from state-endorsed proselytizing."

GINSBURG, J., also dissented, reserving the question of whether an unequivocal disclaimer, "legible from a distance," "that Ohio did not endorse the display's message" would suffice: "Near the stationary cross were the government's flags and the government's statues. No human speaker was present to disassociate the religious symbol from the State. No other private display was in sight. No plainly visible sign informed the public that the cross belonged to the Klan and that Ohio's government did not endorse the display's message."

(b) *"Reasonable observer."* Consider William P. Marshall, *"We Know It When We See It," The Supreme Court and Establishment,* 59 So.Cal.L.Rev. 495, 537 (1986): "Is the objective observer (or average person) a religious person, an agnostic, a separationist, a person sharing the predominate

ersby would perceive a governmental endorsement thereof. In my view, however, [the] reasonable observer in the endorsement inquiry must be deemed aware of the history and context of the community and forum in which the religious display appears. [An] informed member of the community will know how the public space in question has been used in the past—and it is that fact, not that the space may meet the legal definition of a public forum, which is relevant to the endorsement inquiry. [The] reasonable observer would recognize the distinction between speech the government supports and speech that it merely allows in a place that traditionally has been open to a range of private speakers accompanied, if necessary, by an appropriate disclaimer."

5. [O'Connor, J.'s] 'reasonable person' comes off as a well-schooled jurist, a being finer than the tort-law model. With respect, I think this enhanced tort-law standard is singularly out of place in the Establishment Clause context. It strips of constitutional protection every reasonable person whose knowledge happens to fall below some 'ideal' standard. * * * Justice O'Connor's argument that 'there is always someone' who will feel excluded by any particular governmental action, ignores the requirement that such an apprehension be objectively reasonable. A person who views an exotic cow at the zoo as a symbol of the Government's approval of the Hindu religion cannot survive this test.

religious sensibility of the community, or one holding a minority view? Is there any 'correct' perception?" Compare Note, *Religion and the State,* 100 Harv.L.Rev. 1606, 1648 (1987): "[If the test] is governed by the perspective of the majority, it will be inadequately sensitive. [If] the establishment clause is to prohibit government from sending the message to religious minorities or nonadherents that the state favors certain beliefs and that as nonadherents they are not fully members of the political community, its application must turn on the message received *by the minority or nonadherent.*"

(c) *Ambiguities.* (i) Consider Steven D. Smith, *Symbols, Perceptions, and Doctrinal Illusions: Establishment Neutrality and the "No Endorsement" Test,* 86 Mich.L.Rev. 266, 283, 301–03, 310–12 (1987): "[E]vidence of the test's indeterminate character appears in [Arnold H. Loewy, *Rethinking Government Neutrality Towards Religion Under the Establishment Clause: The Untapped Potential of Justice O'Connor's Insight,* 64 N.C.L.Rev. 1049 (1986).] Loewy likes the 'no endorsement' test. In applying that test to particular controversies, however, he concludes that Pawtucket's sponsorship of a nativity scene violated the establishment clause, that Alabama's 'moment of silence' law probably did *not* violate the clause, and that ceremonial invocations of deity, such as those occurring in the Pledge of Allegiance or the opening of a Supreme Court session, *do* violate the 'no endorsement' test. In each instance, Justice O'Connor would disagree. [From] the Continental Congress[139] through the framing of the Bill of Rights[140] and on down to the present day, government and government officials—including Presidents [not] to mention the Supreme Court itself[141]— have frequently expressed approval of religion and religious ideas. Such history [at] least demonstrates that many Americans, including some of our early eminent statesmen, have *believed* such approval was proper. That fact alone is sufficient to show that the 'no endorsement' principle is controversial, not easily self-evident. [If] public institutions employ religious symbols, persons who do not adhere to the predominant religion may feel like 'outsiders.'[d] But if religious symbols are banned from such contexts, some religious people will feel that their most central values and concerns—and thus, in an important sense, they themselves—have been excluded from a public culture devoted purely to secular concerns. [We] might conclude, however, that any alienation felt by [the latter] groups, although perfectly sincere, should be disregarded because their dissatisfaction actually results not from particular governmental actions but rather from the very meaning of the establishment clause." Contrast Jesse H. Choper, *Securing Religious*

---

139. [The] Continental Congress "sprinkled its proceedings liberally with the mention of God, Jesus Christ, the Christian religion, and many other religious references."

140. Shortly after approving the Bill of Rights, which of course included the establishment clause, the first Congress resolved to observe a day of thanksgiving and prayer in appreciation of "the many signal favors of Almighty God."

141. See, e.g., *Zorach* ("We are a religious people whose institutions presuppose a Supreme Being."); *Church of the Holy Trinity v. United States,* 143 U.S. 457, 471, 12 S.Ct. 511, 516, 36 L.Ed. 226 (1892) (asserting that "this is a Christian nation").

d. For support of O'Connor, J.'s approach in this setting, see Steven G. Gey, *When Is Religious Speech Not "Free Speech"?* 2000 U.Ill.L.Rev. 379.

Liberty: Principles for Judicial interpretation of the Religion Clauses 28–29 (1995): "[T]his would grant something that I find too close to a self-interested veto for the minority. [An] effective solution here would be to entrust this 'perspective-dependent' inquiry to an independent judiciary * * *. Although justices of the Supreme Court 'cannot become someone else,' they should, with their own solicitude for the values of religious liberty, either assume the view of a reasonable member of the political community who is faithful to the Constitution's protection of individual rights or ask whether a *reasonable minority observer,* who would be 'acquainted with the text, legislative history, and implementation of the [challenged state action],' *should feel* less than a full member of the political community.[112]"

(ii) Do government accommodations for religion (such as exempting the sacramental use of wine during Prohibition) violate the endorsement test? Consider Mark Tushnet, "Of Church and State and the Supreme Court": Kurland Revisited, 1989 Sup.Ct.Rev. 373, 395 n. 73: "They use religion as a basis for government classification, and they do [so] precisely in order to confer a benefit on some religions that does not flow either to nonbelievers or to all religions. [It] is difficult to avoid the conclusion that permissible accommodations, with their necessarily disparate impact, indicate some degree of government approval of the practices." Compare Michael W. McConnell, *Religious Freedom at a Crossroads,* 59 U.Chi.L.Rev. 115, 150 (1992): "Any action the government takes on issues of this sort inevitably sends out messages, and it is not surprising that reasonable observers from different legal and religious perspectives respond to these messages in different ways. These examples raise some of the most important and most often litigated issues under the Establishment Clause, and the concept of endorsement does not help to resolve them."

(d) *None* of the opinions in *Capitol Square* invoked the *Lemon* test, which was barely mentioned. How would the *Capitol Square* Court have decided the crèche issue in *Allegheny*?

---

112. Although this process is basically normative rather than empirical, the Court's judgment should obviously be influenced by the perception (if fairly discerni- ble) of 'average' members of minority religious faiths and should be more strongly affected if their response is very widely shared.

Chapter 12

FREE EXERCISE CLAUSE AND RELATED PROBLEMS

I. CONFLICT WITH STATE REGULATION

The most common problem respecting free exercise of religion has involved a generally applicable government regulation, whose purpose is nonreligious, that either makes illegal (or otherwise burdens) conduct that is dictated by some religious belief, or requires (or otherwise encourages) conduct that is forbidden by some religious belief. REYNOLDS v. UNITED STATES, 98 U.S. 145, 25 L.Ed. 244 (1878), the first major decision on the free exercise clause, upheld a federal law making polygamy illegal as applied to a Mormon whose religious duty was to practice polygamy: "Congress was deprived of all legislative power over mere opinion, but was left free to reach actions which were in violation of social duties or subversive of good order." CANTWELL v. CONNECTICUT, 310 U.S. 296, 60 S.Ct. 900, 84 L.Ed. 1213 (1940), reemphasized this distinction between religious opinion or belief, on the one hand, and action taken because of religion, on the other, although the Court this time spoke more solicitously about the latter: "Freedom of conscience and freedom to adhere to such religious organization or form of worship as the individual may choose cannot be restricted by law. [Free exercise] embraces two concepts,—freedom to believe and freedom to act. The first is absolute but, in the nature of things, the second cannot be. [The] freedom to act must have appropriate definition to preserve the enforcement of that protection [although] the power to regulate must be so exercised as not, in attaining a permissible end, unduly to infringe the protected freedom."

Beginning with *Cantwell*—which first held that the fourteenth amendment made the free exercise guarantee applicable to the states—a number of cases invalidated application of state laws to conduct undertaken pursuant to religious beliefs. Like *Cantwell,* these decisions, a number of which are set forth in Ch. 8,[a] rested in whole or in part on the freedom of expression

---

a. E.g., *Schneider v. Irvington,* Ch. 6, I, A; *Lovell v. Griffin,* Ch. 4, I, A (involving distribution of religious literature). See also *Marsh v. Alabama,* Ch. 6, III.

protections of the first and fourteenth amendments. Similarly, WEST VIR-
GINIA STATE BD. OF EDUC. v. BARNETTE, 319 U.S. 624, 63 S.Ct. 1178,
87 L.Ed. 1628 (1943),[b] held that compelling a flag salute by public school
children whose religious scruples forbade it violated the first amendment:
"[The] freedoms of speech and of press, of assembly, and of worship [are]
susceptible of restriction only to prevent grave and immediate danger to
interests which the state may lawfully protect. [The] freedom asserted by
these appellees does not bring them into collision with rights asserted by any
other individual. It is such conflicts which most frequently require intervention of the State to determine where the rights of one end and those of
another begin. [T]he compulsory flag salute and pledge requires *affirmation
of a belief* and an *attitude of mind*. [If] there is any fixed star in our
constitutional constellation, it is that no official, high or petty, can prescribe
what shall be orthodox in politics, nationalism or other matters of opinion or
force citizens to confess by word or act their faith therein."

It was not until 1963, in *Sherbert v. Verner* (discussed below), that the
Court held conduct protected by the free exercise clause alone.

HOBBIE v. UNEMPLOYMENT APPEALS COMM'N

480 U.S. 136, 107 S.Ct. 1046, 94 L.Ed.2d 190 (1987).

JUSTICE BRENNAN delivered the opinion of the Court.

Appellant's employer discharged her when she refused to work certain
scheduled hours because of sincerely-held religious convictions adopted after
beginning employment. [Under] our precedents, the [Florida] Appeals Commission's disqualification of appellant from receipt of [unemployment com-
pensation] benefits violates the Free Exercise [Clause]. *Sherbert v. Verner*,
374 U.S. 398, 83 S.Ct. 1790, 10 L.Ed.2d 965 (1963); *Thomas v. Review
Board*, 450 U.S. 707, 101 S.Ct. 1425, 67 L.Ed.2d 624 (1981). In *Sherbert* we
considered South Carolina's denial of unemployment compensation benefits
to a Sabbatarian who, like Hobbie, refused to work on Saturdays. The Court
held that the State's disqualification of Sherbert "force[d] her to choose
between following the precepts of her religion and forfeiting benefits, on the
one hand, and abandoning one of the precepts of her religion in order to
accept work, on the other hand. Governmental imposition of such a choice
puts the same kind of burden upon the free exercise of religion as would a
fine imposed against [her] for her Saturday worship." * * *

In *Thomas*, [a] Jehovah's Witness, held religious beliefs that forbade his
participation in the production of armaments. He was forced to leave his job
when the employer closed his department and transferred him to a division
that fabricated turrets for tanks. Indiana then denied Thomas unemployment compensation benefits. * * *

b. Overruling *Minersville School Dist. v.
Gobitis,* 310 U.S. 586, 60 S.Ct. 1010, 84
L.Ed. 1375 (1940).

We see no meaningful distinction among the situations of Sherbert, Thomas, and Hobbie. We again affirm, as stated in *Thomas:* "Where the state conditions receipt of an important benefit upon conduct proscribed by a religious faith, *or where it denies such a benefit because of conduct mandated by religious belief, thereby putting substantial pressure on an adherent to modify his behavior and to violate his beliefs,* a burden upon religion exists. While the compulsion may be indirect, the infringement upon free exercise is nonetheless substantial" (emphasis added).

Both *Sherbert* and *Thomas* held that such infringements must be subjected to strict scrutiny and could be justified only by proof by the State of a compelling interest. The Appeals Commission does not seriously contend that its denial of benefits can withstand strict scrutiny;[a] rather it urges that we hold that its justification should be determined under the less rigorous standard articulated in Chief Justice Burger's opinion in *Bowen v. Roy:* "the Government meets its burden when it demonstrates that a challenged requirement for governmental benefits, neutral and uniform in its application, is a reasonable means of promoting a legitimate public interest."[b] 476 U.S. 693, 707–08, 106 S.Ct. 2147, 2156, 90 L.Ed.2d 735 (1986). Five Justices expressly rejected this argument in *Roy.* We reject the argument again today. As Justice O'Connor pointed out in *Roy,* "[s]uch a test has no basis in precedent and relegates a serious First Amendment value to the barest level of minimal scrutiny that the Equal Protection Clause already provides." See also *Wisconsin v. Yoder,* 406 U.S. 205, 215, 92 S.Ct. 1526, 1533, 32 L.Ed.2d 15 (1972)[c] ("[O]nly those interests of the highest order and those not

a. In *Sherbert,* the state "suggest[ed] no more than a possibility that the filing of fraudulent claims by unscrupulous claimants feigning religious objections to Saturday work [might] dilute the unemployment compensation fund [but] there is no proof whatever to warrant such fears of malingering or deceit [and] it is highly doubtful whether such evidence would be sufficient to warrant a substantial infringement of religious liberties. For [it] would plainly be incumbent upon the [state] to demonstrate that no alternative forms of regulation would combat such abuses without infringing First Amendment rights."

b. Burger, C.J., joined by Powell and Rehnquist, JJ., prefaced this statement in *Roy* as follows: "[G]overnment regulation that indirectly and incidentally calls for a choice between securing a governmental benefit and adherence to religious beliefs is wholly different from government [action] that criminalizes religiously inspired activity or inescapably compels conduct that some find objectionable for religious reasons. Although the denial of governmental benefits over religious objection can raise serious Free Exercise problems, these two very different forms of government action are not governed by the same constitutional standard. * * * Absent proof of an intent to

discriminate against particular religious beliefs or against religion in general, the Government meets its burden [etc.]"

c. *Yoder* invalidated a law compelling school attendance to age 16 as applied to Amish parents who refused on religious grounds to send their children to high school, noting no "showing that upon leaving the Amish community Amish children, with their practical agricultural training and habits of industry and self-reliance, would become burdens on society because of educational shortcomings. [The] independence and successful social functioning of the Amish community for a period approaching almost three centuries [is] strong evidence that there is at best a speculative gain, in terms of meeting the duties of citizenship, from an additional one or two years of compulsory formal education."

Only Douglas, J., dissented: If parents "are allowed a religious exemption, the inevitable effect is to impose the parents' notions of religious duty upon their children. Where the child is mature enough to express potentially conflicting desires, it would be an invasion of the child's rights to permit such an imposition without canvassing his views."

On the question of "whether children should be afforded rights of religious exer-

otherwise served can overbalance legitimate claims to the free exercise of religion''). * * *

The Appeals Commission also attempts to distinguish this case by arguing that [in] *Sherbert* and *Thomas,* the employees held their respective religious beliefs at the time of hire; subsequent changes in the conditions of employment made *by the employer* caused the conflict between work and belief. In this case, Hobbie's beliefs changed during the course of her employment, creating a conflict between job and faith that had not previously existed. * * *

In effect, the Appeals Commission asks us to single out the religious convert for different, less favorable treatment. * * * We decline to do so. * * *

Finally, we reject the Appeals Commission's argument that the awarding of benefits to Hobbie would violate the Establishment Clause. This Court has long recognized that the government may (and sometimes must) accommodate religious practices and that it may do so without violating the Establishment Clause.[10] See e.g., *Yoder* (judicial exemption of Amish children from compulsory attendance at high school); *Walz* (tax exemption for churches). * * *

Reversed.[d]

CHIEF JUSTICE REHNQUIST, dissenting.

I adhere to the views I stated in dissent in *Thomas* [where Rehnquist, J., stated: "As to the proper interpretation of the Free Exercise Clause, I would accept the decision of *Braunfeld v. Brown,* 366 U.S. 599, 81 S.Ct. 1144, 6 L.Ed.2d 563 (1961), and the dissent in *Sherbert.* In *Braunfeld,* we held that Sunday closing laws do not violate the First Amendment rights of Sabbatarians. Chief Justice Warren explained that the statute did not make unlawful any religious practices of appellants; it simply made the practice of their religious beliefs more expensive. We concluded that '[t]o strike down, without the most critical scrutiny, legislation which imposes only an indirect burden on the exercise of religion, i.e., legislation which does not make unlawful the religious practice itself, would radically restrict the operating latitude of the legislature.'[e] Likewise in this case, it cannot be said that the State discriminated against Thomas on the basis of his religious beliefs or

---

cise independent of their parents," see Emily Buss, *What Does Frieda Yoder Believe?*, 2 U.Pa.J.Con.L. 53 (1999).

10. In the unemployment benefits context, the majorities *and* those dissenting have concluded that, were a state voluntarily to provide benefits to individuals in Hobbie's situation, such an accommodation would not violate the Establishment Clause. See *Thomas* (Rehnquist, J., dissenting); *Sherbert* (Harlan, J., dissenting). [The conflict between the establishment and free exercise clauses is considered in Ch. 14 infra.]

d. The opinions of Powell and Stevens, JJ., concurring in the judgment, are omitted.

e. *Braunfeld* continued: "Statutes which tax income and limit the amount which may be deducted for religious contributions impose an indirect economic burden on the observance of the religion of the citizen whose religion requires him to donate a greater amount to his church; statutes which require the courts to be closed on Saturday and Sunday impose a similar indirect burden on the observance of the religion of the trial lawyer whose religion

that he was denied benefits *because* he was a Jehovah's Witness.[1] Where, as here, a State has enacted a general statute, the purpose and effect of which is to advance the State's secular goals, the Free Exercise Clause does not in my view require the State to conform that statute to the dictates of religious conscience of any group."]

Notes and Questions

1. *Scope of decisions.* After *Sherbert, Thomas* and *Hobbie,* may a state deny unemployment benefits (a) to member of a pacifist religion who agreed to produce tanks as a condition of employment and who was fired for subsequently refusing to do so because of religious beliefs, see *Employment Division, Oregon Dep't of Human Resources v. Smith,* 485 U.S. 660, 108 S.Ct. 1444, 99 L.Ed.2d 753 (1988); (b) to a Sabbatarian who is dismissed from a job in the post office for refusal to work on Saturday because to grant an exemption would require paying overtime to another employee?[a] May (c) a state deny worker's compensation to the widow of an employee who, after being injured at work, died because of his refusal on religious grounds to accept a blood transfusion?

2. *Other forms of government largesse.* If a state fluoridates drinking water, must it supply nonfluoridated water to persons whose religion forbids such "medicinal aids"? Consider Tribe 2d ed., at 1274: "Presumably the government could provide subsidized loans to beef producers without facing a colorable free exercise claim brought by people whose religion requires them to raise and eat only vegetables; or provide tax benefits to medical or military professionals without facing a claim brought by people whose religious tenets forbid such work. But the principles underlying [the distinctions between these policies and that in *Sherbert, Thomas* and *Hobbie*] resist ready definition."

3. *Rejections of free exercise claims.* (a) *Taxation.* (i) JIMMY SWAGGART MINISTRIES v. BOARD OF EQUAL., 493 U.S. 378, 110 S.Ct. 688, 107 L.Ed.2d 796 (1990), per O'CONNOR, J., unanimously held that the free exercise clause does not prohibit imposing a sales and use tax on the sale of religious materials by a religious organization. The Court distinguished *Murdock v. Pennsylvania,* 319 U.S. 105, 63 S.Ct. 870, 87 L.Ed. 1292 (1943) and *Follett v. McCormick,* 321 U.S. 573, 64 S.Ct. 717, 88 L.Ed. 938 (1944),

---

requires him to rest on a weekday. The list of legislation of this nature is nearly limitless."

Query: If a statute makes a religious practice unlawful but the maximum penalty is a fine, does this impose a "direct" or "indirect" burden?

1. [T]he Indiana Supreme Court *has* construed the State's unemployment statute to make every personal subjective reason for leaving a job a basis for disqualification. [Because] Thomas left his job for a personal reason, the State of Indiana should not be prohibited from disqualifying him from receiving benefits.

a. See also *TWA v. Hardison,* 432 U.S. 63, 97 S.Ct. 2264, 53 L.Ed.2d 113 (1977), interpreting the Civil Rights Act prohibition against religious discrimination in employment as permitting dismissal of a Sabbatarian if accommodating his work schedule would require "more than a de minimis cost" by the employer. Brennan and Marshall, JJ., dissented.

which had invalidated license taxes for sellers as applied to Jehovah's Witnesses who went from house to house selling religious pamphlets, because of the "particular nature of the challenged taxes—flat license taxes that operated as a prior restraint on the exercise of religious liberty": "[T]o the extent that imposition of a generally applicable tax merely decreases the amount of money appellant has to spend on its religious activities, any such burden is not constitutionally significant. * * *

"Finally, because appellant's religious beliefs do not forbid payment of the sales and use tax, appellant's reliance on *Sherbert* and its progeny is misplaced. [Although] it is of course possible to imagine that a more onerous tax, even if generally applicable, might effectively choke off an adherent's religious practices, cf. *Murdock* (the burden of a flat tax could render itinerant evangelism 'crushed and closed out by the sheer weight of the toll or tribute which is exacted town by town'), we face no such situation in this case."

(ii) UNITED STATES v. LEE, 455 U.S. 252, 102 S.Ct. 1051, 71 L.Ed.2d 127 (1982), per Burger, C.J., held that the free exercise clause does not require an exemption for members of the Old Order Amish from payment of social security taxes even though "both payment and receipt of social security benefits is forbidden by the Amish faith": "The state may justify a limitation on religious liberty by showing that it is essential to accomplish an overriding governmental interest [and] mandatory participation is indispensable to the fiscal vitality of the social security system. [To] maintain an organized society that guarantees religious freedom to a great variety of faiths requires that some religious practices yield to the common good. [The] tax system could not function if denominations were allowed to challenge the tax system because tax payments were spent in a manner that violates their religious belief."

Stevens, J., concurred in the judgment: "As a matter of fiscal policy, an enlarged exemption probably would benefit the social security system because the nonpayment of these taxes by the Amish would be more than offset by the elimination of their right to collect benefits.[b] * * * Nonetheless, I agree with the Court's conclusion that the difficulties associated with processing other claims to tax exemption on religious grounds justify a rejection of this claim.[2]"

(b) *Conscription.* (i) GILLETTE v. UNITED STATES, 401 U.S. 437, 91 S.Ct. 828, 28 L.Ed.2d 168 (1971), per Marshall, J., held that the free exercise

---

b. Stevens, J., found the distinction between this case and *Yoder* "unconvincing because precisely the same religious interest is implicated in both cases and Wisconsin's interest in requiring its children to attend school until they reach the age of 16 is surely not inferior to the federal interest in collecting these social security taxes."

2. [T]he principal reason for adopting a strong presumption against such claims is not a matter of administrative convenience. It is the overriding interest in keeping the government—whether it be the legislature or the courts—out of the business of evaluating the relative merits of differing religious claims. The risk that governmental approval of some and disapproval of others will be perceived as favoring one religion over another is an important risk the Establishment Clause was designed to preclude.

clause does not forbid Congress from "conscripting persons who oppose a particular war on grounds of conscience and religion. * * *[23]": "The conscription laws [are] not designed to interfere with any religious ritual or practice, and do not work a penalty against any theological position. The incidental burdens felt by persons in petitioners' position are strictly justified by substantial governmental interests that relate directly to the very impacts questioned. And more broadly, of course, there is the Government's interest in procuring the manpower necessary for military purposes * * *."

DOUGLAS, J., dissented: "[M]y choice is the dicta of Chief Justice Hughes who, dissenting in *Macintosh,* spoke for Holmes, Brandeis, and Stone: '[Among] the most eminent statesmen here and abroad have been those who condemned the action of their country in entering into wars they thought to be unjustified. [If] the mere holding of religious or conscientious scruples against all wars should not disqualify a citizen from holding office in this country, or an applicant otherwise qualified from being admitted to citizenship, there would seem to be no reason why a reservation of religious or conscientious objection to participation in wars believed to be unjust should constitute such a disqualification.' "[d]

(ii) In JOHNSON v. ROBISON, 415 U.S. 361, 94 S.Ct. 1160, 39 L.Ed.2d 389 (1974), a federal statute granted educational benefits for veterans who served on active duty but disqualified conscientious objectors who performed alternate civilian service. The Court, per BRENNAN, J., found a "rational basis" for the classification and thus no violation of equal protection, because the "disruption caused by military service is quantitatively greater" and "qualitatively different." Further, the statute "involves only an incidental burden upon appellee's free exercise of religion—if, indeed, any burden exists at all.[19] [T]he Government's substantial interest in raising and supporting armies is of 'a kind and weight' clearly sufficient to sustain the

---

23. We are not faced with the question whether the Free Exercise Clause itself would require exemption of any class other than objectors to particular wars. * * * We note that the Court has previously suggested that relief for conscientious objectors is not mandated by the Constitution. See *Hamilton v. Regents,* 293 U.S. 245, 55 S.Ct. 197, 79 L.Ed. 343 (1934); *United States v. Macintosh,* 283 U.S. at 623–24, 51 S.Ct. at 574–75, 75 L.Ed. 1302 (1931).

d. Did *Gillette* discard the "alternative means" approach found in *Sherbert?* Consider Tribe 2d ed., at 1266: "In light of the relative ease with which the conscientious-objector exemption has been administered throughout our history without placing a noticeable burden on the country's military manpower needs, a court might well require a concrete showing of threat to such needs

in order to justify abolition of the exemption. The use of conscientious objectors—even selective conscientious objectors—in paramedical or other non-military roles could meet both the personnel argument and the morale argument well enough to constitute a required alternative under *Sherbert."*

19. * * * Congress has bestowed relative benefits upon conscientious objectors by permitting them to perform their alternate service obligation as civilians. Thus, Congress' decision to grant educational benefits to military servicemen might arguably be viewed as an attempt to equalize the burdens of military service and civilian alternate service, rather than an effort [to] place a relative burden upon a conscientious objector's free exercise of religion.

challenged legislation, for the burden upon appellee's free exercise [is] not nearly of the same order or magnitude as" in *Gillette*. Douglas, J., dissented.

(c) *Tax exemption*. BOB JONES UNIV. v. UNITED STATES, 461 U.S. 574, 103 S.Ct. 2017, 76 L.Ed.2d 157 (1983), per BURGER, C.J., held that IRS denial of tax exempt status to private schools that practice racial discrimination on the basis of sincerely held religious beliefs does not violate the free exercise clause: "[T]he Government has a fundamental, overriding interest in eradicating racial discrimination in education [which] substantially outweighs whatever burden denial of tax benefits places on petitioners' exercise of their religious beliefs. The interests asserted by petitioners cannot be accommodated with that compelling governmental interest, see *Lee;* and no "less restrictive means' are available to achieve the governmental interest."[e] Rehnquist, J., agreeing with the Court's free exercise analysis, dissented on the ground that Congress had not authorized the IRS denial of tax exemption.[f]

(d) *Internal government affairs*. LYNG v. NORTHWEST INDIAN CEMETERY PROTECTIVE ASS'N, 485 U.S. 439, 108 S.Ct. 1319, 99 L.Ed.2d 534 (1988), per O'CONNOR, J., held the federal government's building a road and allowing timber harvesting in a national forest did not violate the free exercise rights of American Indian tribes even though this would "virtually destroy the Indians' ability to practice their religion" because it would irreparably damage "sacred areas which are an integral and necessary part of [their] belief systems": "In *Bowen v. Roy,* we considered a challenge to a federal statute that required the States to use Social Security numbers in administering certain welfare programs. Two applicants for benefits under these programs contended that their religious beliefs prevented them from acceding to the use of a Social Security number [that had been assigned to] their two-year-old daughter because the use of a numerical identifier would ' "rob the spirit" of [their] daughter and prevent her from attaining greater spiritual power.' [The] Court rejected this kind of challenge in *Roy:* 'The Free Exercise Clause simply cannot be understood to require the Government to conduct its own internal affairs in ways that comport with the religious beliefs of particular citizens. Just as the Government may not insist that [the Roys] engage in any set form of religious observance, so [they] may not demand that the Government join in their chosen religious practices by refraining from using a number to identify their daughter. [The] Free Exercise Clause affords an individual protection from certain forms of governmental compulsion; it does not afford an individual a right to dictate the conduct of the Government's internal procedures.'

e. Contra, Douglas Laycock, *Tax Exemptions for Racially Discriminatory Religious Schools,* 60 Tex.L.Rev. 259 (1982); Mayer G. Freed & Daniel D. Polsby, *Race, Religion, and Public Policy: Bob Jones University v. United States,* 1983 Sup.Ct.Rev. 1, 20–30.

f. Four justices also rejected the claim that Nebraska's denial of a driver's license

to a person whose sincerely held religious beliefs—pursuant to the Second Commandment prohibition of "graven images"—forbade her to be photographed, violated the free exercise clause. *Quaring v. Peterson,* 728 F.2d 1121 (8th Cir.1984) (free exercise violation), affirmed by an equally divided Court, 472 U.S. 478, 105 S.Ct. 3492, 86 L.Ed.2d 383 (1985).

"The building of a road or the harvesting of timber on publicly owned land cannot meaningfully be distinguished from the use of a Social Security number in *Roy*. In both cases, the challenged government action would interfere significantly with private persons' ability to pursue spiritual fulfillment according to their own religious beliefs. In neither case, however, would the affected individuals be coerced by the Government's action into violating their religious beliefs; nor would either governmental action penalize religious activity by denying any person an equal share of the rights, benefits, and privileges. [However] much we might wish that it were otherwise, government simply could not operate if it were required to satisfy every citizen's religious needs and desires. A broad range of government activities—from social welfare programs to foreign aid to conservation projects—will always be considered essential to the spiritual well-being of some citizens, often on the basis of sincerely held religious beliefs. Others will find the very same activities deeply offensive, and perhaps incompatible with their own search for spiritual fulfillment and with the tenets of their religion. The First Amendment must apply to all citizens alike, and it can give to none of them a veto over public programs that do not prohibit the free exercise of religion. * * *

"[The] dissent now offers to distinguish [*Roy*] by saying that the Government was acting there 'in a purely internal manner,' whereas land-use decisions 'are likely to have substantial external effects.' [But robbing] the spirit of a child, and preventing her from attaining greater spiritual power, is both a 'substantial external effect' and one that is remarkably similar to the injury claimed [today]."[g]

Brennan, J., joined by Marshall and Blackmun, JJ., dissented: "[R]espondents have claimed—and proved—that the desecration of the high country will prevent religious leaders from attaining the religious power or medicine indispensable to the success of virtually all their rituals and ceremonies. [T]oday's ruling sacrifices a religion at least as old as the Nation itself, along with the spiritual well-being of its approximately 5,000 adherents, so that the Forest Service can build a six-mile segment of road that two lower courts found had only the most marginal and speculative utility, both to the Government itself and to the private lumber interests that might conceivably use it." Kennedy, J., did not participate.

EMPLOYMENT DIVISION v. SMITH

494 U.S. 872, 110 S.Ct. 1595, 108 L.Ed.2d 876 (1990).

Justice Scalia delivered the opinion of the Court. * * *

g. *Nature of remedy.* Is there a difference between the remedy needed to satisfy the free exercise claim in *Roy* and that in *Lyng?* If so, what about the required remedy in the other instances in which the Court has sustained the free exercise claim?

Respondents Alfred Smith and Galen Black were fired from their jobs with a private drug rehabilitation organization because they ingested peyote for sacramental purposes at a ceremony of the Native American Church, of which both are members. When respondents applied to petitioner Employment Division for unemployment compensation, they were determined to be ineligible for benefits because they had been discharged for work-related "misconduct." [We believe] that "if a State has prohibited through its criminal laws certain kinds of religiously motivated conduct without violating the First Amendment, it certainly follows that it may impose the lesser burden of denying unemployment compensation benefits to persons who engage in that conduct." * * *

[The] free exercise of religion means, first and foremost, the right to believe and profess whatever religious doctrine one desires. Thus, the First Amendment obviously excludes all "governmental regulation of religious *beliefs* as such." The government may not compel affirmation of religious belief, see *Torcaso v. Watkins,* [Part II infra], punish the expression of religious doctrines it believes to be false, *United States v. Ballard,* [Part II infra], impose special disabilities on the basis of religious views or religious status, see *McDaniel v. Paty,* 435 U.S. 618, 98 S.Ct. 1322, 55 L.Ed. 2d 593 (1978) [state rule disqualifying clergy from being legislators]; cf. *Larson v. Valente,* [Sec. 3 infra] or lend its power to one or the other side in controversies over religious authority or dogma, see *Presbyterian Church v. Hull Church,* [Sec. 3 infra].

But the "exercise of religion" often involves not only belief and profession but the performance of (or abstention from) physical acts: assembling with others for a worship service, participating in sacramental use of bread and wine, proselytizing, abstaining from certain foods or certain modes of transportation. It would be true, we think (though no case of ours has involved the point), that a state would be "prohibiting the free exercise [of religion]" if it sought to ban such acts or abstentions only when they are engaged in for religious reasons, or only because of the religious belief that they display. It would doubtless be unconstitutional, for example, to ban the casting of "statues that are to be used for worship purposes," or to prohibit bowing down before a golden calf.

Respondents in the present case, however, seek to carry the meaning of "prohibiting the free exercise [of religion]" one large step further. They contend that their religious motivation for using peyote places them beyond the reach of a criminal law that is not specifically directed at their religious practice, and that is concededly constitutional as applied to those who use the drug for other reasons. [As] a textual matter, we do not think the words must be given that meaning. It is no more necessary to regard the collection of a general tax, for example, as "prohibiting the free exercise [of religion]" by those citizens who believe support of organized government to be sinful, than it is to regard the same tax as "abridging the freedom [of] the press" of those publishing companies that must pay the tax as a condition of staying in business. It is a permissible reading of the text, in the one case as in the other, to say that if prohibiting the exercise of religion (or burdening the activity of printing) is not the object of the tax but merely the incidental effect of a generally applicable and otherwise valid provision, the First Amendment has not been offended. Compare *Citizen Publishing Co. v. United States,* 394 U.S. 131, 89 S.Ct. 927, 22 L.Ed.2d 148 (1969) (upholding application of antitrust laws to press), with *Grosjean v. American Press Co.,* [p. ___ supra] (striking down license tax applied only to newspapers with weekly circulation above a specified level); see generally *Minneapolis Star & Tribune Co. v. Minnesota Commissioner of Revenue* [p. ___ supra].

Our decisions reveal that the latter reading is the correct one. We have never held that an individual's religious beliefs excuse him from compliance with an otherwise valid law prohibiting conduct that the State is free to regulate. [In] *Prince v. Massachusetts,* 321 U.S. 158, 64 S.Ct. 438, 88 L.Ed. 645 (1944), we held that a mother could be prosecuted under the child labor laws for using her children to dispense literature in the streets, her religious motivation notwithstanding. [The opinion also discusses *Braunfeld, Gillette,* and *Lee.*]

The only decisions in which we have held that the First Amendment bars application of a neutral, generally applicable law to religiously motivated action have involved not the Free Exercise Clause alone, but the Free Exercise Clause in conjunction with other constitutional protections, such as freedom of speech and of the press, see *Cantwell* (invalidating a licensing system for religious and charitable solicitations under which the administrator had discretion to deny a license to any cause he deemed nonreligious); *Murdock; Follett,* or the right of parents, acknowledged in *Pierce v. Society of Sisters* [Ch. 7, II supra] to direct the education of their children, see *Yoder.*[1] Some of our cases prohibiting compelled expression, decided exclusively upon free speech grounds, have also involved freedom of religion, cf. *Wooley v. Maynard* [Ch. 9, I] (invalidating compelled display of a license plate slogan that offended individual religious beliefs); *Barnette.* And it is easy to envision a case in which a challenge on freedom of association grounds would likewise be reinforced by Free Exercise Clause concerns. Cf. *Roberts v. United States Jaycees* [Ch. 9, III] ("An individual's freedom to speak, to worship, and to petition the government for the redress of grievances could not be vigorously protected from interference by the State [if] a correlative freedom to engage in group effort toward those ends were not also guaranteed."). * * *

Respondents argue that even though exemption from generally applicable criminal laws need not automatically be extended to religiously motivated actors, at least the claim for a religious exemption must be evaluated under the balancing test set forth in *Sherbert.* Under the *Sherbert* test, governmental actions that substantially burden a religious practice must be

---

1. [*Yoder*] said that "the Court's holding in *Pierce* stands as a charter of the rights of parents to direct the religious upbringing of their children. And, when the interests of parenthood are combined with a free exercise claim of the nature revealed by this record, more than merely a 'reasonable relation to some purpose within the competency of the State' is required to sustain the validity of the State's requirement under the First Amendment."

justified by a compelling governmental interest. [We] have never invalidated any governmental action on the basis of the *Sherbert* test except the denial of unemployment compensation. Although we have sometimes purported to apply the *Sherbert* test in contexts other than that, we have always found the test satisfied, see *Lee, Gillette.* In recent years we have abstained from applying the *Sherbert* test (outside the unemployment compensation field) at all [discussing *Roy* and *Lyng*]. In *Goldman v. Weinberger,* 475 U.S. 503, 106 S.Ct. 1310, 89 L.Ed.2d 478 (1986), we rejected application of the *Sherbert* test to military dress regulations that forbade the wearing of yarmulkes. In *O'Lone v. Shabazz,* 482 U.S. 342, 107 S.Ct. 2400, 96 L.Ed.2d 282 (1987), we sustained, without mentioning the *Sherbert* test, a prison's refusal to excuse inmates from work requirements to attend worship services.[a]

Even if we were inclined to breathe into *Sherbert* some life beyond the unemployment compensation field, we would not apply it to require exemptions from a generally applicable criminal law. The *Sherbert* test, it must be recalled, was developed in a context that lent itself to individualized governmental assessment of the reasons for the relevant conduct. [As] the plurality pointed out in *Roy,* our decisions in the unemployment cases stand for the proposition that where the State has in place a system of individual exemptions, it may not refuse to extend that system to cases of "religious hardship" without compelling reason.[b]

Whether or not the decisions are that limited, they at least have nothing to do with an across-the-board criminal prohibition on a particular form of conduct. [We] conclude today that the sounder approach, and the approach in accord with the vast majority of our precedents, is to hold the test

---

a. For a careful review of the cases, both in the Supreme Court and in the U.S. courts of appeals for ten years preceding *Smith,* concluding that "despite the apparent protection afforded claimants by the language of the compelling interest test, courts overwhelmingly sided with the government when applying that test," see James E. Ryan, *Smith and the Religious Freedom Restoration Act: An Iconoclastic Assessment,* 78 Va.L.Rev. 1407 (1992). See also Jesse H. Choper, *The Rise and Decline of the Constitutional Protection of Religious Liberty,* 70 Neb.L.Rev. 651, 659–70 (1991).

b. For the view that the system of discretionary hearings involved in the unemployment cases presents "a fertile ground for the undervaluation of minority religious interests" and is therefore "vulnerable to a distinct constitutional objection," see Christopher L. Eisgruber & Lawrence G. Sager, *The Vulnerability of Conscience: The Constitutional Basis for Protecting Religious Conduct,* 61 U.Chi.L.Rev. 1245 (1994). For an empirical study reaching an opposite conclusion, see Prabha S. Bhandari, *The Fail-*

ure of Equal Regard to Explain the Sherbert Quartet, 72 N.Y.U.L.Rev. 97 (1997).

See also Ira C. Lupu, *The Case Against Legislative Codification of Religious Liberty,* 21 Card.L.Rev. 565, 573 (1999): "Long prior to *Smith,* our civil liberties tradition had recognized the dangers of permitting local officials to exercise licensing authority over expressive activity without the benefit of determinate criteria. The absence of such criteria invites discriminatory treatment of groups disfavored by local decision makers. Identical concerns [favor] aggressive implementation of [the] anti-discrimination principle of free exercise with the individual assessment principle which *Smith* purports to preserve."

For review of lower court decisions that have attempted to "evade" *Smith* through the "individual exemptions" analysis and the "hybrid rights exemption," see Carol M. Kaplan, *The Devil is in the Details: Neutral, Generally Applicable Laws and Exceptions from Smith,* 75 N.Y.U.L.Rev. 1045 (2000).

inapplicable to such challenges. [To] make an individual's obligation to obey such a law contingent upon the law's coincidence with his religious beliefs, except where the State's interest is "compelling"—permitting him, by virtue of his beliefs, "to become a law unto himself," *Reynolds*—contradicts both constitutional tradition and common sense.[2]

The "compelling government interest" requirement seems benign, because it is familiar from other fields. But using it as the standard that must be met before the government may accord different treatment on the basis of race, see [Ch. 9, Sec. 2, I], or before the government may regulate the content of speech, is not remotely comparable to using it for the purpose asserted here. What it produces in those other fields—equality of treatment, and an unrestricted flow of contending speech—are constitutional norms; what it would produce here—a private right to ignore generally applicable laws—is a constitutional anomaly.[3]

Nor is it possible to limit the impact of respondents' proposal by requiring a "compelling state interest" only when the conduct prohibited is "central" to the individual's religion. It is no more appropriate for judges to determine the "centrality" of religious beliefs before applying a "compelling interest" test in the free exercise field, than it would be for them to determine the "importance" of ideas before applying the "compelling interest" test in the free speech field. What principle of law or logic can be brought to bear to contradict a believer's assertion that a particular act is "central" to his personal faith? [I]n many different contexts, we have warned that courts must not presume to determine the place of a particular belief in a religion or the plausibility of a religious claim. See, e.g., *Thomas* [Sec. II infra]; *Jones v. Wolf,* [Ch. 13 infra]; *Ballard.*[4]

2. Justice O'Connor seeks to distinguish *Lyng* and *Roy* on the ground that those cases involved the government's conduct of "its own internal affairs." [But] it is hard to see any reason in principle or practicality why the government should have to tailor its health and safety laws to conform to the diversity of religious belief, but should not have to tailor its management of public lands, *Lyng,* or its administration of welfare programs, *Roy.*

3. [Just] as we subject to the most exacting scrutiny laws that make classifications based on race or on the content of speech, so too we strictly scrutinize governmental classifications based on religion, see *McDaniel;* see also *Torcaso.* But we have held that race-neutral laws that have the *effect* of disproprotionately disadvantaging a particular racial group do not thereby become subject to compelling-interest analysis under the Equal Protection Clause, see *Washington v. Davis* 426 U.S. 229, 96 S.Ct. 2040 (1976) (police employment examination); and we have held that generally applicable laws unconcerned with regulating speech that have the *effect* of interfering with speech do not thereby become subject to compelling-interest analysis under the First Amendment, see *Citizen Publishing Co. v. United States* (antitrust laws). Our conclusion that generally applicable, religion-neutral laws that have the effect of burdening a particular religious practice need not be justified by a compelling governmental interest is the only approach compatible with these precedents.

4. [In] any case, dispensing with a "centrality" inquiry is utterly unworkable. It would require, for example, the same degree of "compelling state interest" to impede the practice of throwing rice at church weddings as to impede the practice of getting married in church. There is no way out of the difficulty that, if general laws are to be subjected to a "religious practice" exception, *both* the importance of the law at issue *and* the centrality of the practice at issue must reasonably be considered. * * *

[For the conclusion that "the Court has never required that the claimant establish either centrality or compulsion in order to

If the "compelling interest" test is to be applied at all, then, it must be applied across the board, to all actions thought to be religiously commanded. Moreover, if "compelling interest" really means what it says (and watering it down here would subvert its rigor in the other fields where it is applied), many laws will not meet the test. Any society adopting such a system would be courting anarchy, but that danger increases in direct proportion to the society's diversity of religious beliefs, and its determination to coerce or suppress none of them.[c] Precisely because "we are a cosmopolitan nation made up of people of almost every conceivable religious preference," and precisely because we value and protect that religious divergence, we cannot afford the luxury of deeming *presumptively invalid,* as applied to the religious objector, every regulation of conduct that does not protect an interest of the highest order. The rule respondents favor would open the prospect of constitutionally required religious exemptions from civic obligations of almost every conceivable kind—ranging from compulsory military service, see, e.g., *Gillette,* to the payment of taxes, see, e.g., *Lee,* to health and safety regulation such as manslaughter and child neglect laws, compulsory vaccination laws, drug laws, and traffic laws, to social welfare legislation such as minimum wage laws, see *Tony and Susan Alamo Foundation v. Secretary of Labor,* 471 U.S. 290, 105 S.Ct. 1953, 85 L.Ed.2d 278 (1985), child labor laws, see *Prince;* animal cruelty laws, see, e.g., *Church of the Lukumi Babalu Aye Inc. v. Hialeah,* [note 1 infra], environmental protection laws, and laws providing for equality of opportunity for the races, see e.g., *Bob Jones University.* The First Amendment's protection of religious liberty does not require this.[5]

[A] number of States have made an exception to their drug laws for sacramental peyote use. But to say that a nondiscriminatory religious-practice exemption is permitted, or even that it is desirable, is not to say that it is constitutionally required, and that the appropriate occasions for its creation can be discerned by the courts. It may fairly be said that leaving

receive protection under the First Amendment," see Steven C. Seeger, *Restoring Rights to Rites: The Religious Motivation Test and the Religious Freedom Restoration Act,* 95 Mich.L.Rev. 1472 (1997).]

c. Contra, Gary Simson, *Endangering Religious Liberty,* 84 Calif.L.Rev. 441, 461 (1996): "[I]t is far from clear that the government's ability to govern effectively would be seriously undermined as a result. After all, since the legislative process generally makes allowance for the needs of adherents of mainstream religions, court-ordered exemptions typically would be limited in scope to affected members of relatively small groups."

5. Justice O'Connor contends that the "parade of horribles" in the text only "demonstrates [that] courts have been quite capable of strik[ing] sensible balances between religious liberty and competing

state interests." But the cases we cite have struck "sensible balances" only because they have all applied the general laws, despite the claims for religious exemption. In any event, Justice O'Connor mistakes the purpose of our parade: it is not to suggest that courts would necessarily permit harmful exemptions from these laws (though they might), but to suggest that courts would constantly be in the business of determining whether the "severe impact" of various laws on religious practice (to use Justice Blackmun's terminology) or the "constitutiona[l] significan[ce]" of the "burden on the particular plaintiffs" (to use Justice O'Connor's terminology) suffices to permit us to confer an exemption. It is a parade of horribles because it is horrible to contemplate that federal judges will regularly balance against the importance of general laws the significance of religious practice.

accommodation to the political process will place at a relative disadvantage those religious practices that are not widely engaged in; but that unavoidable consequence of democratic government must be preferred to a system in which each conscience is a law unto itself or in which judges weigh the social importance of all laws against the centrality of all religious beliefs. * * *

JUSTICE O'CONNOR, with whom JUSTICE BRENNAN, JUSTICE MARSHALL, and JUSTICE BLACKMUN join as to [Part II], concurring in the judgment. * * *

II. [A] law that prohibits certain conduct—conduct that happens to be an act of worship for someone—manifestly does prohibit that person's free exercise of his religion [regardless] of whether the law prohibits the conduct only when engaged in for religious reasons, only by members of that religion, or by all persons.

[If] the First Amendment is to have any vitality, it ought not be construed to cover only the extreme and hypothetical situation in which a State directly targets a religious practice. [*Yoder*] expressly rejected the interpretation the Court now adopts: "[T]o agree that religiously grounded conduct must often be subject to the broad police power of the State is not to deny that there are areas of conduct protected by the Free Exercise Clause of the First Amendment and thus beyond the power of the State to control, *even under regulations of general applicability.* [A] regulation neutral on its face may, in its application, nonetheless offend the constitutional requirement for government neutrality if it unduly burdens the free exercise of religion."

The Court endeavors to escape from our decisions in *Cantwell* and *Yoder* by labeling them "hybrid" decisions but there is no denying that both cases expressly relied on the Free Exercise Clause and that we have consistently regarded those cases as part of the mainstream of our free exercise jurisprudence. Moreover, in each of the other cases cited by the Court to support its categorical rule, we rejected the particular constitutional claims before us only after carefully weighing the competing interests. [That] we rejected the free exercise claims in those cases hardly calls into question the applicability of First Amendment doctrine * * *. [I]t is surely unusual to judge the vitality of a constitutional doctrine by looking to the win-loss record of the plaintiffs who happen to come before us.

[W]e have never distinguished between cases in which a State conditions receipt of a benefit on conduct prohibited by religious beliefs and cases in which a State affirmatively prohibits such conduct. The *Sherbert* compelling interest test applies in both kinds of cases. [A] neutral criminal law prohibiting conduct that a State may legitimately regulate is, if anything, *more* burdensome than a neutral civil statute placing legitimate conditions on the award of a state benefit.

[Even] if, as an empirical matter, a government's criminal laws might usually serve a compelling interest in health, safety, or public order, the First Amendment at least requires a case-by-case determination of the question, sensitive to the facts of each particular claim. Given the range of conduct that a State might legitimately make criminal, we cannot assume, merely because a law carries criminal sanctions and is generally applicable, that the First Amendment *never* requires the State to grant a limited exemption for religiously motivated conduct.

Moreover, we have not "rejected" or "declined to apply" the compelling interest test in our recent cases. See, e.g., *Hobbie*. The cases cited by the Court signal no retreat from our consistent adherence to the compelling interest test. In both *Roy* and *Lyng,* for example, we expressly distinguished *Sherbert* on the ground that the First Amendment does not "require the Government *itself* to behave in ways that the individual believes will further his or her spiritual development. * * * " This distinction makes sense because "the Free Exercise Clause is written in terms of what the government cannot do to the individual, not in terms of what the individual can exact from the government." *Sherbert* (Douglas, J., concurring).[a] Because the case sub judice, like the other cases in which we have applied *Sherbert,* plainly falls into the former category, I would apply those established precedents to the facts of this case.

Similarly, the other cases cited by the Court for the proposition that we have rejected application of the *Sherbert* test outside the unemployment compensation field are distinguishable because they arose in the narrow, specialized contexts in which we have not traditionally required the government to justify a burden on religious conduct by articulating a compelling interest. See *Goldman v. Weinberger* ("Our review of military regulations challenged on First Amendment grounds is far more deferential than constitutional review of similar laws or regulations designed for civilian society"); *O'Lone v. Shabazz* ("[P]rison regulations alleged to infringe constitutional rights are judged under a 'reasonableness' test less restrictive than that ordinarily applied to alleged infringements of fundamental constitutional rights"). That we did not apply the compelling interest test in these cases says nothing about whether the test should continue to apply in paradigm free exercise cases such as the one presented here.[b]

[As] the language of the Clause itself makes clear, an individual's free exercise of religion is a preferred constitutional activity. A law that makes

---

a. For the view that the *Lyng* approach, which "seems to involve neither social science nor theology," attracts the Court because it functions to "reduce the number of claims that must be afforded the searching inquiry demanded by the free exercise clause" and to permit the Court to avoid resolving the difficult issues of "cognizability of the asserted burden, the sincerity of the claimant, and religiosity of the claim," see Ira C. Lupu, *Where Rights Begin: The Problem of Burdens on The Free Exercise of Religion,* 102 Harv.L.Rev. 933 (1989).

b. See also Michael W. McConnell, *Free Exercise Revisionism and the Smith Deci-*

sion, 57 U.Chi.L.Rev. 1109, 1127 (1990): "The Court also failed to point out that in [*Roy*], five Justices expressed the view that adherents to a traditional Abenaki religion under which computer-generated numbers are deemed to rob the individual's spirit of its power were entitled to an exemption from the requirement that welfare recipients provide a social security number on their application. This did not become a holding of the Court because one of the five Justices supporting the result concluded that this aspect of the case had become moot."

criminal such an activity therefore triggers constitutional concern—and heightened judicial scrutiny—even if it does not target the particular religious conduct at issue. Our free speech cases similarly recognize that neutral regulations that affect free speech values are subject to a balancing, rather than categorical, approach. See, e.g., *United States v. O'Brien*, [Ch. 2]; *Renton v. Playtime Theatres, Inc.*, [Ch. 3, I]; cf. *Anderson v. Celebrezze*, 460 U.S. 780, 103 S.Ct. 1564, 75 L.Ed.2d 547 (1983) (generally applicable laws may impinge on free association concerns). * * *

Finally, the Court today suggests that the disfavoring of minority religions is an "unavoidable consequence" under our system of government and that accommodation of such religions must be left to the political process. In my view, however, the First Amendment was enacted precisely to protect the rights of those whose religious practices are not shared by the majority and may be viewed with hostility. The history of our free exercise doctrine amply demonstrates the harsh impact majoritarian rule has had on unpopular or emerging religious groups such as the Jehovah's Witnesses and the Amish.[c] [The] compelling interest test reflects the First Amendment's mandate of preserving religious liberty to the fullest extent possible in a pluralistic society. For the Court to deem this command a "luxury," is to denigrate "[t]he very purpose of a Bill of Rights."

III. The Court's holding today not only misreads settled First Amendment precedent; it appears to be unnecessary to this case. I would reach the same result applying our established free exercise jurisprudence.

There is no dispute that Oregon's criminal prohibition of peyote places a severe burden on the ability of respondents to freely exercise their religion. Peyote is a sacrament of the Native American Church and is regarded as vital to respondents' ability to practice their religion. * * *

---

c. See also Douglas Laycock, *Formal, Substantive, and Disaggregated Neutrality Toward Religion*, 39 De Paul L.Rev. 993, 1016 (1990): "Of course, inadvertence can interact with hostility, or with an insensitivity that borders on hostility. Consider what might happen when Frances Quaring [fn. f supra] writes her legislator. She may get a sympathetic response and a legislated exemption. But her legislator may find it so impossible to empathize with her belief that he never seriously considers whether an exemption would be workable. Even if he empathizes, the legislative calendar is crowded, and the original statute having been enacted, all the burdens of legislative inertia now work against an exemption."

Compare Eisengruber & Sager, supra, at 1304: "[After *Lyng,*] the political process responded to interests the judiciary had not protected, and the Bureau of Land Management relocated the road. [After *Lee,*] Congress accommodated churches that had religious objections to participating in the social security system. [After *Goldman,*] Congress granted relief. And [after *Smith,*] Oregon legislated an exemption to its law," and Congress protected religious use of peyote in all states. But contrast Dhananjai Shivakumar, *Neutrality and the Religion Clauses*, 33 Harv. Civ. Rts.—Civ. Lib. L. Rev. 505, 512 n. 28 (1998): "The rejection of meaningful judicial review will deprive free exercise claimants of one historically effective way of eliciting attention and public support in cases where substantial burdens are borne, namely, litigation. Many well-known examples of political accommodation were preceded by lengthy, well-publicized free exercise litigation."

There is also no dispute that Oregon has a significant interest in enforcing laws that control the possession and use of controlled substances by its citizens. [Indeed,] under federal law (incorporated by Oregon law in relevant part), peyote is specifically regulated as a Schedule I controlled substance, which means that Congress has found that it has a high potential for abuse, that there is no currently accepted medical use, and that there is a lack of accepted safety for use of the drug under medical supervision. In light of our recent decisions holding that the governmental interests in the collection of income tax, *Hernandez,* a comprehensive social security system, see *Lee,* and military conscription, see *Gillette,* are compelling, respondents do not seriously dispute that Oregon has a compelling interest in prohibiting the possession of peyote by its citizens.

[Although] the question is close, I would conclude that uniform application of Oregon's criminal prohibition is "essential to accomplish," *Lee,* its overriding interest in preventing the physical harm caused by the use of a Schedule I controlled substance. [Because] the health effects caused by the use of controlled substances exist regardless of the motivation of the user, the use of such substances, even for religious purposes, violates the very purpose of the laws that prohibit them. Moreover, in view of the societal interest in preventing trafficking in controlled substances, uniform application of the criminal prohibition at issue is essential to the effectiveness of Oregon's stated interest in preventing any possession of peyote. * * *

Respondents contend that any incompatibility is belied by the fact that the Federal Government and several States provide exemptions for the religious use of peyote. But other governments may surely choose to grant an exemption without Oregon, with its specific asserted interest in uniform application of its drug laws, being *required* to do so by the First Amendment. Respondents also note that the sacramental use of peyote is central to the tenets of the Native American Church, but I agree with the Court [that] "[i]t is not within the judicial ken to question the centrality of particular beliefs or practices to a faith." [This] does not mean, of course, that courts may not make factual findings as to whether a claimant holds a sincerely held religious belief that conflicts with, and thus is burdened by, the challenged law. The distinction between questions of centrality and questions of sincerity and burden is admittedly fine, but it is one that is an established part of our free exercise doctrine * * *.[d]

d. In *Boerne v. Flores,* p. 734 infra, O'Connor, J., joined by Breyer, J., argued that "the historical evidence [bears] out the conclusion that, at the time the Bill of Rights was ratified, it was accepted that government should, when possible, accommodate religious practice." Scalia, J., joined by Stevens, J., disagreed: "The historical evidence put forward by the dissent does nothing to undermine the conclusion we reached in *Smith.*" For an extensive review, see Michael W. McConnell, *Freedom From Persecution or Protection of the Rights of Conscience?: A Critique of Justice Scalia's Historical Arguments,* 39 Wm. & M. L. Rev. 819 (1998). For support at the time of the fourteenth amendment for O'Connor, J.'s position, see Kurt T. Lash, *The Second Adoption of the Free Exercise Clause: Religious Exemptions Under the Fourteenth*

JUSTICE BLACKMUN, with whom JUSTICE BRENNAN and JUSTICE MARSHALL join, dissenting.

This Court over the years painstakingly has developed a consistent and exacting standard to test the constitutionality of a state statute that burdens the free exercise of religion. Such a statute may stand only if the law in general, and the State's refusal to allow a religious exemption in particular, are justified by a compelling interest that cannot be served by less restrictive means.

[I]t is important to articulate in precise terms the state interest involved. It is not the State's broad interest in fighting the critical "war on drugs" that must be weighed against respondents' claim, but the State's narrow interest in refusing to make an exception for the religious, ceremonial use of peyote. [The] State cannot plausibly assert that unbending application of a criminal prohibition is essential to fulfill any compelling interest, if it does not, in fact, attempt to enforce that prohibition. * * * Oregon has never sought to prosecute respondents, and does not claim that it has made significant enforcement efforts against other religious users of peyote. The State's asserted interest thus amounts only to the symbolic preservation of an unenforced prohibition. * * *

Similarly, this Court's prior decisions have not allowed a government to rely on mere speculation about potential harms, but have demanded evidentiary support for a refusal to allow a religious exception. [In] this case, the State [offers] no evidence that the religious use of peyote has ever harmed anyone. The factual findings of other courts cast doubt on the State's assumption that religious use of peyote is harmful. See *State v. Whittingham,* 19 Ariz.App. 27, 30, 504 P.2d 950, 953 (1973) ("the State failed to prove that the quantities of peyote used in the sacraments of the Native American Church are sufficiently harmful to the health and welfare of the participants so as to permit a legitimate intrusion under the State's police power"); *People v. Woody,* 61 Cal.2d 716, 722–723, 40 Cal.Rptr. 69, 74, 394 P.2d 813, 818 (1964) ("as the Attorney General [admits,] the opinion of scientists and other experts is 'that peyote [works] no permanent deleterious injury to the Indian' ").

The fact that peyote is classified as a Schedule I controlled substance does not, by itself, show that any and all uses of peyote, in any circumstance, are inherently harmful and dangerous. The Federal Government [does] not find peyote so dangerous as to preclude an exemption for religious use.[5] Moreover, other Schedule I drugs have lawful uses. See *Olsen v. Drug Enforcement Administration,* 878 F.2d 1458 (D.C.Cir.1989) (medical and research uses of marijuana).

Amendment, 88 Nw.U.L.Rev. 1106, 1149–55 (1994).

5. [Moreover,] 23 States, including many that have significant Native American populations, have statutory or judicially crafted exemptions in their drug laws for religious use of peyote.

The carefully circumscribed ritual context in which respondents used peyote is far removed from the irresponsible and unrestricted recreational use of unlawful drugs.[6] * * *[7]

Moreover, just as in *Yoder,* the values and interests of those seeking a religious exemption in this case are congruent, to a great degree, with those the State seeks to promote through its drug laws. See *Yoder* (since the Amish accept formal schooling up to 8th grade, and then provide "ideal" vocational education, State's interest in enforcing its law against the Amish is "less substantial than [for] children generally"). Not only does the Church's doctrine forbid nonreligious use of peyote; it also generally advocates self-reliance, familial responsibility, and abstinence from alcohol. There is considerable evidence that the spiritual and social support provided by the Church has been effective in combatting the tragic effects of alcoholism on the Native American population. * * *

The State also seeks to support its refusal to make an exception [by] invoking its interest in abolishing drug trafficking. There is, however, practically no illegal traffic in peyote. Also, the availability of peyote for religious use, even if Oregon were to allow an exemption from its criminal laws, would still be strictly controlled by federal regulations, see 21 U.S.C. §§ 821–823 (registration requirements for distribution of controlled substances); and by the State of Texas, the only State in which peyote grows in significant quantities. Peyote simply is not a popular drug; its distribution for use in religious rituals has nothing to do with the vast and violent traffic in illegal narcotics that plagues this country.

Finally, the State argues that, [if] it grants an exemption for religious peyote use, a flood of other claims to religious exemptions will follow. It would then be placed in a dilemma, it says, between allowing a patchwork of exemptions that would hinder its law enforcement efforts, and risking a violation of the Establishment Clause by arbitrarily limiting its religious exemptions. [But almost] half the States, and the Federal Government, have maintained an exemption for religious peyote use for many years, and apparently have not found themselves overwhelmed by claims to other religious exemptions.[8] Allowing an exemption for religious peyote use would not necessarily oblige the State to grant a similar exemption to other religious groups. The unusual circumstances that make the religious use of peyote compatible with the State's interests in health and safety and in preventing drug trafficking would not apply to other religious claims. Some

---

6. In this respect, respondents' use of peyote seems closely analogous to the sacramental use of wine by the Roman Catholic Church. During Prohibition, the Federal Government exempted such use of wine from its general ban on possession and use of alcohol. However compelling the Government's then general interest in prohibiting the use of alcohol may have been, it could not plausibly have asserted an interest sufficiently compelling to outweigh Catholics' right to take communion.

7. The use of peyote is, to some degree, self-limiting. The peyote plant is extremely bitter, and eating it is an unpleasant experience, which would tend to discourage casual or recreational use.

8. Over the years, various sects have raised free exercise claims regarding drug use. In no reported case, except those involving claims of religious peyote use, has the claimant prevailed.

religions, for example, might not restrict drug use to a limited ceremonial context, as does the Native American Church. See, e.g., *Olsen* ("the Ethiopian Zion Coptic Church [teaches] that marijuana is properly smoked 'continually all day' "). Some religious claims involve drugs such as marijuana and heroin, in which there is significant illegal traffic, with its attendant greed and violence, so that it would be difficult to grant a religious exemption without seriously compromising law enforcement efforts.[9] [Though] the State must treat all religions equally, and not favor one over another, this obligation is fulfilled by the uniform application of the "compelling interest" *test* to all free exercise claims, not by reaching uniform *results* as to all claims. * * *

Respondents believe, and their sincerity has *never* been at issue, that the peyote plant embodies their deity, and eating it is an act of worship and communion. Without peyote, they could not enact the essential ritual of their religion. [This] potentially devastating impact must be viewed in light of the federal policy—reached in reaction to many years of religious persecution and intolerance—of protecting the religious freedom of Native Americans. See American Indian Religious Freedom Act. * * *[a]

Notes and Questions

1. *Discrimination.* (a) CHURCH OF THE LUKUMI BABALU AYE, INC. v. HIALEAH, 508 U.S. 520, 113 S.Ct. 2217, 124 L.Ed.2d 472 (1993), per KENNEDY, J., held that city ordinances barring ritual animal sacrifice violated the free exercise clause: "[I]f the object of a law is to infringe upon or restrict practices because of their religious motivation, the law is not neutral, see *Smith;* and it is invalid unless it is justified by a compelling interest and is narrowly tailored to advance that interest. [The] ordinances had as their object the suppression of [the Santeria] religion. The [record] discloses animosity to Santeria adherents and their religious practices; the ordinances by their own terms target this religious exercise; the texts of the ordinances were gerrymandered with care to proscribe religious killings of animals but to exclude almost all secular killings; and the ordinances suppress much more religious conduct than is necessary in order to achieve the legitimate

---

9. Thus, this case is distinguishable from *Lee,* in which the Court concluded that there was "no principled way" to distinguish other exemption claims, and the "tax system could not function if denominations were allowed to challenge the tax system because tax payments were spent in a manner that violates their religious belief."

a. In 1993, Congress passed the Religious Freedom Restoration Act which effectively reinstated the *Sherbert-Yoder* test for generally applicable laws that burden religious practices. RFRA was held unconstitu-

tional in *Boerne v. Flores*, 521 U.S. 507, 117 S.Ct. 2157 (1997).

For the view that the "core meaning of the Establishment Clause" prevents congressional efforts "to regulate matters of faith directly or to tell states what relation their laws must have to the fostering of one or all religions," which "means that Congress may not try to dictate church-state relations even to vindicate religious toleration or free exercise," see Jed Rubenfeld, *Antidisestablishmentarianism: Why RFRA Really Was Unconstitutional*, 95 Mich. L.Rev. 2347 (1997).

ends asserted in their defense. [A] law that targets religious conduct for distinctive treatment or advances legitimate governmental interests only against conduct with a religious motivation will survive strict scrutiny only in rare cases. It follows from what we have already said that these ordinances cannot withstand this scrutiny."

SOUTER, J., concurred specially "for I have doubts whether the *Smith* rule merits adherence": Because "*Smith* refrained from overruling prior free-exercise cases that [are] fundamentally at odds with the rule *Smith* declared, [in] a case presenting the issue, the Court should re-examine the rule *Smith* declared."

BLACKMUN, J., joined by O'Connor, J., concurred only in the judgment: "I continue to believe that *Smith* was wrongly decided, because it ignored the value of religious freedom as an affirmative individual liberty and treated the Free Exercise Clause as no more than an antidiscrimination principle." Moreover, "when a law discriminates against religion as such, as do the ordinances in this case, it automatically will fail strict scrutiny [because] a law that targets religious practice for disfavored treatment both burdens the free exercise of religion and, by definition, is not precisely tailored to a compelling governmental interest.[a]

"[This] case does not present [the] question whether the Free Exercise Clause would require a religious exemption from a law that sincerely pursued the goal of protecting animals from cruel treatment. [That] is not a concern to be treated lightly."

(b) *Scope.* Does the *Smith-Lukumi* rule bar only those laws whose "object is suppression" of a religious practice, or that "target religious conduct"? After *Lukumi*, what result in *Smith* if Oregon had permitted the medicinal use of peyote (or marijuana) in designated circumstances to relieve pain? Would the law barring other uses of peyote (including sacramental use) be "generally applicable"? Would it "target religious conduct"? Of what relevance is *Smith's* reaffirmation of *Sherbert's* "individualized governmental assessment" context? Consider Frederick M. Gedicks, *The Normalized Free Exercise Clause: Three Abnormalities*, 75 Ind. L.J. 77, 117–120 (2000): "[T]he free exercise of religion is a fundamental right, the protection of which is specified by the constitutional text [but] the Court is not treating free exercise rights like privacy, speech, travel, and other fundamental rights. [What] fundamental rights/equal protection analysis [Ch. 9, Sec. 5] requires in the context of incidental burdens on religion is that religious conduct be exempted from a law whenever exemption of such conduct would not present a substantially greater threat to the purpose of the law than already-exempt secular conduct. Fundamental rights/equal protection analysis makes clear that any law or government action that excuses—by adminis-

---

a. See also James D. Gordon III, *The New Free Exercise Clause*, 26 Cap.U.L.Rev. 65, 89, 92 (1997): "[I]f a law restricts only religious conduct, it exempts nonreligious conduct that produces the same harm. The government cannot have a compelling interest in denying a religious exemption, because it already has shown its willingness to exempt everyone else. [Therefore,] the compelling interest test adds nothing to the analysis."

trative exemption, legislative exemption, or otherwise—one or more secular activities but not *comparable* religious practices creates a classification that impermissibly burdens the fundamental right of free exercise of religion, and thus should normally be subject to strict scrutiny."

What result under the *Smith-Lukumi* rule if a state prohibits *all* polygamous marriages after a religious group that engages in the practice becomes active in the state? See Garrett Epps, *What We Talk About When We Talk About Free Exercise*, 30 Ariz.St.L.J. 563 (1998). Is this any different than Hialeah's ordinances? For the view that there should be no free exercise violation if a law serves "a substantial secular purpose" regardless of its motivation, see Lino A. Graglia, *Church of the Lukumi Babalu Aye: Of Animal Sacrifice and Religious Persecution*, 85 Geo.L.J. 1 (1996): "[Hialeah's] only complaint against the church was that it conducted animal slaughtering exhibitions, and there is no reason to doubt the district judge's finding [that] the ordinances were 'not targeted at the Church of the Lukumi Babalu Aye, [but] meant to prohibit all animal sacrifice, whether it be practiced by an individual, a religion, or a cult.' [I]t applied equally [to] all other exhibitionistic killings, like those that are sometimes performed by entertainers or as part of college fraternity or other initiation ceremonies."

If a state bars ingestion of all alcoholic beverages but exempts sacramental use, may it bar ingestion of all hallucinogenic substances without exempting sacramental use? See Michael J. Perry, *Freedom of Religion in the United States: Fin de Siècle Sketches*, 75 Ind.L.J. 295, 305 (2000).

2. *Aid to parochial schools.* Is the Court's statement, that denial of financial benefits to parochial schools does not infringe the free exercise rights of attending children,[b] consistent with *Sherbert, Thomas* and *Hobbie*? With *Smith* and *Lukumi*? Could a student bus transportation program include all nonprofit private schools except parochial schools? See *Luetkemeyer v. Kaufmann*, 419 U.S. 888, 95 S.Ct. 167, 42 L.Ed.2d 134 (1974). Would affording aid to *all* schools (public and nonpublic) *except* those that are church-related "target religious conduct" (*Lukumi*)? Consider Jesse H. Choper, *Federal Constitutional Issues*, in School Choice and Social Controversy 235, 249 (Sugarman & Kemerer eds. 1999): "First, such a program would plainly discriminate on its face against 'some or all religious beliefs,' violating the basic protections of the Free Exercise Clause, unless justified after strict scrutiny. Second, since all schools teach values, the state could be fairly seen as discriminating against religious viewpoints, much as the University of Virginia had done in *Rosenberger*, and would also be subject to strict scrutiny under the Free Speech Clause [see Ch.7, Sec. 1]. Unless Establishment Clause concerns with providing support to parochial schools are found to present a compelling government interest, both *Lukumi* and *Rosenberger* would appear to compel the inclusion of religious schools in any

b. See the dictum in *Sloan v. Lemon*, 413 U.S. 825, 93 S.Ct. 2982, 37 L.Ed.2d 939 (1973): "[V]alid aid to nonpublic, nonsecta-rian schools would provide no lever for aid to their sectarian counterparts."

voucher program or other plan of aid to education that included nonreligious private schools."

Indeed, might it be argued that *Sherbert* would require aid for parochial schools even though public support was given only to public schools? If some religions impose a duty on parents to send children to religious schools, may these parents argue that, since they must pay public school taxes, the state's failure to support parochial as well as public schools imposes a serious financial burden on their exercise of religion? That "conditioning the availability of benefits upon their willingness to violate a cardinal principle of their religious faith effectively penalizes the free exercise of their constitutional liberties" (*Sherbert*); that there is no "compelling state interest to justify the substantial infringement of their First Amendment rights"? May these parents further argue that their position is stronger than *Sherbert, Thomas* and *Hobbie* because the purpose of granting an exemption in that case was *solely* to aid religion whereas there is a wholly nonreligious purpose in giving aid to all nonpublic schools—improving the quality of the secular education? What result after *Smith*? See Choper, supra, at 246–48.

3. *Balancing process.* Of what significance is it that all the decisions sustaining free exercise claims against government regulations of conduct (*Sherbert—Thomas—Hobbie, Yoder* and *Roy*) involved religious refusal to engage in conduct required by government rather than religiously dictated action forbidden by the state? What results in respect to the religiously mandated *inaction* in the following: (a) Citing for contempt person who refuses to serve on jury. See *In re Jenison,* 265 Minn. 96, 120 N.W.2d 515 (1963), vacated, 375 U.S. 14, 84 S.Ct. 63, 11 L.Ed.2d 39 (1963), reversed, 267 Minn. 136, 125 N.W.2d 588 (1963); (b) Statute requiring smallpox vaccination applied to person whose religion forbids medicinal aids. See *Jacobson v. Massachusetts,* 197 U.S. 11, 25 S.Ct. 358, 49 L.Ed. 643 (1905); (c) Court order of blood transfusion, to save life of pregnant mother and child, for woman of Jehovah's Witness faith which obligates adherents to "abstain from blood." Suppose the woman were not pregnant but had infant children? See *Application of Georgetown College, Inc.,* 331 F.2d 1000 (D.C.Cir.1964), cert. denied, 377 U.S. 978, 84 S.Ct. 1883, 12 L.Ed.2d 746 (1964). Suppose the woman were neither pregnant nor had any children? Suppose there were only a slight chance that the transfusion would save the life? That the woman is a brilliant scientist whose work is vital to national security? Suppose the transfusion is thought necessary not to preserve life but to bring back to good health? (d) School board's refusal to exempt children of "born again Christian" parents from using textbooks with subjects—such as "secular humanism," "pacifism," "magic," and "women's achievements outside the home"—that were contrary to their religious beliefs. See *Mozert v. Hawkins County Bd. of Educ.,* 827 F.2d 1058 (6th Cir. 1987), cert. denied, 484 U.S. 1066 (1988), discussed in Stephen L. Carter, *Culture of Disbelief* 168–76, 191–92 (1993). If the subject matter in a textbook (or a course) is contrary to children's religious beliefs, does *exposure* to the material (in the textbook or the course) impose a "substantial" enough burden to trigger the

free exercise clause? See Gary J. Simson & Erika A. Sussman, *Keeping the Sex in Sex Education: The First Amendment's Religion Clauses and the Sex Education Debate*, 9 S.Cal. Rev. L. & Women's Studies 265 (2000).

4. *Willingness of others.* In the case of *action* due to religious beliefs, should a distinction be drawn between action that is requested by the people affected and action that is imposed on others? Should the conviction of a religious Spiritualist for fortune telling be sustained despite the fact that fortunes were told only upon request? If not, how do you distinguish the polygamy cases?[c]

II. UNUSUAL RELIGIOUS BELIEFS AND PRACTICES

1. *Validity and sincerity.* In UNITED STATES v. BALLARD, 322 U.S. 78, 64 S.Ct. 882, 88 L.Ed. 1148 (1944), defendant was indicted for mail fraud. He had solicited funds for the "I Am" movement, asserting, inter alia, that he had been selected as a divine messenger, had the divine power of healing incurable diseases, and had talked with Jesus and would transmit these conversations to mankind. The Court, per DOUGLAS, J., held that the first amendment barred submitting to the jury the question of whether these religious beliefs were true: "Men may believe what they cannot [prove.] Religious experiences which are as real as life to some may be incomprehensible to others. [The] miracles of the New Testament, the Divinity of Christ, life after death, the power of prayer are deep in the religious convictions of many. If one could be sent to jail because a jury in a hostile environment found those teachings false, little indeed would be left of religious freedom."

(a) *Ballard* permits the prosecution to prove that, irrespective of whether the incidents described by defendant happened, he did not honestly believe that they had? If so, may the prosecution introduce evidence that the incidents did not in fact happen and that therefore defendant could not honestly believe that they did? Should this line of proof be permitted in the prosecution of an official of the Catholic church for soliciting funds to construct a shrine commemorating the Miracle of Fatima in 1930?

(b) Is it relevant that in *Ballard* the alleged divine revelation was made to defendant himself? Would it be material if the experiences had allegedly occurred at a definite time and place? Many Biblical happenings are so identified. Could the prosecution introduce evidence that Ballard was not physically present at the alleged place at the alleged time? If Protestant, Catholic or Jewish clergy were prosecuted and there was overwhelming

c. For several recent approaches that evaluate a wide range of factors in considering religious exemptions from generally applicable laws, see Eugene Volokh, *A Common–Law Model for Religious Exemptions*, 46 UCLA L.Rev. 1465 (1999); Eugene Volokh, *Intermediate Questions of Religious Exemptions—A Research Agenda with Test Suites*, 21 Card.L.Rev. 595 (1999); Jesse H. Choper, *Securing Religious Liberty* ch. 3 (1995).

scientific evidence disputing the Biblical doctrine, what would the jury be likely to find as to the honesty of the beliefs? Should the first amendment permit people to obtain money in the name of religion by knowingly making false statements? See Tribe 2d ed., at 1243–47.

(c) Should the prosecution be able to prove that defendant had stated on many occasions that he believed none of his representations but that by saying that he did he was amassing great wealth? Suppose it can be shown that a priest or rabbi is *somewhat* skeptical as to the truth of certain Biblical occurrences? See John T. Noonan, Jr., *How Sincere Do You Have to Be to Be Religious,* 1988 U.Ill.L.Rev. 713. Could Ballard be convicted on the ground that fraudulent procurement of money, just like polygamy, is conduct which may be constitutionally prohibited even if done in the name of religion?

2.   *What is "religion"?* May the Court determine that asserted religious beliefs and practices do not constitute a valid religion? Consider Jonathan Weiss, *Privilege, Posture and Protection—"Religion" in the Law,* 73 Yale L.J. 593, 604 (1964): "[A]ny definition of religion would seem to violate religious freedom in that it would dictate to religions, present and future, what they must [be]. Furthermore, an attempt to define religion, even for purposes of increasing freedom for religions, would run afoul of the 'establishment' clause as excluding some religions, or even as establishing a notion respecting religion."

Is it relevant that the beliefs of a group do not include the existence of God? TORCASO v. WATKINS, per Black, J., 367 U.S. 488, 81 S.Ct. 1680, 6 L.Ed.2d 982 (1961), invalidating a Maryland provision requiring a declaration of belief in the existence of God as a test for public office, stated: "Neither [a state nor the federal government can] impose requirements which aid all religions as against nonbelievers, and neither can aid those religions based on a belief in the existence of God as against those religions founded on different beliefs." The Court noted that "among religions in this country which do not teach what would generally be considered a belief in the existence of God are Buddhism, Taoism, Ethical Culture, Secular Humanism and others."

What if the Communist Party claimed religious status? Consider Paul G. Kauper, *Religion and the Constitution* 31 (1964): "What makes secular humanism a religion? Is it because it is an ideology or system of belief that attempts to furnish a rationale of life? But if any ideology, creed, or philosophy respecting man and society is a religion, then must not democracy, fascism, and communism also qualify as religions? It is not uncommon to refer to these as secular or quasi religions, for some find in these systems an adequate explanation of the meaning and purpose of life and the source of values that command faith and devotion. Certainly in the case of communism, with its discipline, its cultus, its sense of community, and its obligation to duties owing to the system, the resemblance to religion in the conventional sense is [clear]."

May a single person establish his or her own religion? Consider Milton Konvitz, *Religious Liberty and Conscience* 84 (1968): "[Many religions] had their origin in a 'private and personal' religious experience. Mohammed did not take over an on-going, established religion; the history of Islam records the names of his first three converts. John Wesley is given credit as the founder of Methodism. Mrs. Mary Baker Eddy was the founder of the Christian Science church. Menno Simons organized a division of Anabaptists that in due course became the sect known as the Mennonites. Jacob Ammon broke away from the Mennonites and founded the sect known as the Amish."

How important is it that the group has regular weekly services? Designated leaders who conduct these services? Ceremonies for naming, marrying and burying members? Does the first amendment extend only to those groups that conform to the "conventional" concept of religion? Consider Harvey Cox (Harvard Divinity School), N.Y. Times 25 (Feb. 16, 1977): "[C]ourts [often] turn to some vague 'man-in-the-street' idea of what 'religion' should be. [But] a man-in-the-street approach would surely have ruled out early Christianity, which seemed both subversive and atheistic to the religious Romans of the day. The truth is that one man's 'bizarre cult' is another's true path to salvation, and the Bill of Rights was designed to safeguard minorities from the man-on-the-street's uncertain capacity for tolerance. The new challenge to our pluralism often comes from Oriental religious movements, because their views of religion differ so fundamentally from ours." To what extent should a group's "brainwashing," mental coercion techniques affect its constitutional status as a "religion"? Compare Richard Delgado, *Religious Totalism: Gentle and Ungentle Persuasion Under the First Amendment,* 51 So.Cal.L.Rev. 1 (1977) with Note, *Conservatorship and Religious Cults: Divining A Theory of Free Exercise,* 53 N.Y.U.L.Rev. 1247 (1978).

Suppose that a group has certain characteristics of "traditional" religions, such as a holy book, ministers, houses of worship, prescribed prayers, a strict moral code, a belief in the hereafter and an appeal to faith, but also has announced social and economic tenets? (Methodism developed originally out of social concerns.) Consider Note, *Toward a Constitutional Definition of Religion,* 91 Harv.L.Rev. 1056, 1069 (1978): "[A] spokesman for the new 'liberation theology' within Catholicism argues that true religion is to be found in liberation 'as the creation of a new social consciousness and as a social appropriation not only of the means of production, but also of the political processes.' The church, he says, seeks 'the abolition of the exploitation of man by man.' The views of these and other significant Christian theologians coalesce around one important theme: the Christian church will find itself only by discarding what until now has been perceived to be religious and by immersing itself in the secular world." Does the first amendment encompass any political, philosophical, moral or social doctrine that some group honestly espouses as its religion?

UNITED STATES v. SEEGER, 380 U.S. 163, 85 S.Ct. 850, 13 L.Ed.2d 733 (1965), interpreted § 6(j) of the Universal Military Training and Service Act, which exempted from combat any person "who, by reason of religious training and belief, is conscientiously opposed to participation in war in any form. Religious training and belief in this connection means an individual's belief in a relation to a Supreme Being involving duties superior to those arising from any human relation, but does not include essentially political, sociological or philosophical views or a merely personal moral code."[a] The Court, per CLARK, J., avoided constitutional questions and upheld claims for exemption of three conscientious objectors. One declared "that he preferred to leave the question as to his belief in a Supreme Being open, [and] that his was a 'belief in and devotion to goodness and virtue for their own sakes, and a religious faith in a purely ethical creed.' " another said "that he felt it a violation of his moral code to take human life and that he considered this belief superior to his obligation to the state. As to whether his conviction was religious, he quoted with approval Reverend John Haynes Holmes' definition of religion as 'the consciousness of some power manifest in nature which helps man in the ordering of his life in harmony with its demands * * *; it is man thinking his highest, feeling his deepest, and living his best.' The source of his conviction he attributed to reading and meditation 'in our democratic American culture, with its values derived from the western religious and philosophical tradition.' As to his belief in a supreme being, Peter stated that he supposed 'you could call that a belief in the Supreme Being or God. These just do not happen to be the words I use.' "

The Court "concluded that Congress, in using the expression 'Supreme Being' rather than the designation 'God,' was merely clarifying the meaning of religious training and belief so as to embrace all religions and to exclude essentially political, sociological, or philosophical views [and that] the test of belief 'in a relation to a Supreme Being' is whether a given belief that is sincere and meaningful occupies a place in the life of its possessor parallel to that filled by the orthodox belief in God of one who clearly qualifies for the exemption. [No] party claims to be an atheist * * *. We do not deal with or intimate any decision on that situation in these cases. [The] use by Congress of the words 'merely personal' seems to us to restrict the exception to a moral code which [is] in no way related to a Supreme Being. [Congress did] not distinguish between externally and internally derived beliefs. Such a determination [would] prove impossible as a practical matter."

In WELSH v. UNITED STATES, 398 U.S. 333, 90 S.Ct. 1792, 26 L.Ed.2d 308 (1970), petitioner, in his application for exemption, "struck the

---

a. The statute was subsequently amended to omit the "belief in a Supreme Being" element. For the view that "religion" under the first amendment "involves some conception of God," see Michael S. Paulsen, *God is Great, Garvey is Good: Making Sense of Religious Freedom*, 72 Not. D.L.Rev. 1597, 1623 (1997): "Text and historical evidence of original meaning should settle the matter. If this seems illiberal today, that is unfortunate, but irrelevant to the task of textual interpretation of the constitutional provision the framers wrote."

word 'religious' entirely and later characterized his beliefs as having been formed 'by reading in the fields of history and sociology.' " BLACK, J., joined by Douglas, Brennan and Marshall, JJ., held that, under *Seeger,* "if an individual deeply and sincerely holds beliefs which are purely ethical or moral in source and content but that nevertheless impose upon him a duty of conscience to refrain from participating in any war at any time, those beliefs certainly occupy in the life of that individual 'a place parallel to that filled [by] God' in traditionally religious persons." "Although [Welsh] originally characterized his beliefs as nonreligious, he later upon reflection wrote a long and thoughtful letter to his Appeal Board in which he declared that his beliefs were 'certainly religious in the ethical sense of that word.' * * * § 6(j)'s exclusion of those persons with 'essentially political, sociological, or philosophical views or a merely personal moral code' should [not] be read to exclude those who hold strong beliefs about our domestic and foreign affairs or even those whose conscientious objection to participation in all wars is founded to a substantial extent upon considerations of public policy. The two groups of registrants which obviously do fall within these exclusions from the exemption are those whose beliefs are not deeply held and those whose objection to war does not rest at all upon moral, ethical, or religious principle but instead rests solely upon considerations of policy, pragmatism, or expediency."[b]

3. *What is "religious belief"?* (a) Of what significance is it that the practice is an "age-old form" of religious conduct (*Murdock*)? Is a "cardinal principle" of the asserted religious faith (*Sherbert*)? Consider Laycock, fn. d, p. 651 at 1390–91: "Many activities that obviously are exercises of religion are not required by conscience or doctrine. Singing in the church choir and saying the Roman Catholic rosary are two common examples. Any activity engaged in by a church as a body is an exercise of religion. [Indeed,] many would say that an emphasis on rules and obligations misconceives the essential nature of some religions." Compare Donald Giannella, *Religious Liberty, Nonestablishment, and Doctrinal Developments—Part I. The Religious Liberty Guarantee,* 80 Har.L.Rev. 1381, 1427–28 (1967): "Personal alienation from one's Maker, frustration of one's ultimate mission in life, and violation of the religious person's integrity are all at stake when the right to worship is threatened. Although the seeker of new psychological worlds [through use of hallucinogens] may feel equally frustrated when deprived of his gropings for a higher reality, there is not the same sense of acute loss—the loss of the Be-all and End-all of life. [A] different problem presents itself when an individual who does not believe in a supernatural or personal God asserts conscientious objection to certain conduct because of its

b. In separate opinions, Harlan, J., and White, J., (joined by Burger, C.J., and Stewart, J.) dissented on the issue of statutory construction. For their views on the constitutional issue, see Ch. 14 infra.

injurious effects on his fellow man. [T]his ethical belief may be held with such a degree of intensity that its violation

occasions the same interior revulsion and anguish as does violation of the law of God to the pious." Under this approach, on what evidence should these factual questions be determined? Suppose a drug-use defendant claims "that its use was essential to attain a unique level of spiritual consciousness [and] compared the effect of depriving him of marihuana with that of forbidding a Catholic to celebrate the Mass"? Joel J. Finer, *Psychedelics and Religious Freedom,* 19 Hast.L.J. 667, 692 (1968).

For the view that "belief [in] 'extratemporal consequences'—whether the effects of actions taken pursuant or contrary to the dictates of a person's beliefs extend in some meaningful way beyond his lifetime—is a sensible and desirable criterion (albeit plainly far short of ideal) for determining when the free exercise clause should trigger judicial consideration of whether an exemption from general government regulations of conduct is constitutionally required," see Jesse H. Choper, *Defining "Religion" in the First Amendment,* 1982 U.Ill.L.Rev. 579, 599, 603–04:[c] "It may be persuasively argued that *all* beliefs that invoke a transcendent reality—and especially those that provide their adherents with glimpses of meaning and truth that make them so important and so uncompromisable—should be encompassed by the special constitutional protection granted 'religion' by the free exercise clause. [In] many ways, however, transcendental explanations of worldly realities are essentially no different [than] conventional exegeses for temporal outcomes that are based on such 'rational' disciplines as economics, political science, sociology, or psychology, or even such 'hard' sciences [as] physics. When justifying competing government policies on such varied matters as social welfare, the economy, and military and foreign affairs, there is at bedrock only a gossamer line between 'rational' and 'supernatural' causation—the former really being little more capable of 'scientific proof' than the latter. [Therefore, government's] plenary authority to regulate the worldly affairs of society [should] not be restricted because of the nature of the causes, which are all basically unverifiable, that different groups believe will produce consequences that the state seeks to achieve."[d] Compare Kent Greenawalt, *Religion as a Concept in Constitutional Law,* 72 Calif.L.Rev. 753, 763, 815 (1984): "No specification of essential conditions will capture all and only the beliefs, practices, and organizations that are regarded as religious in modern culture and should be treated as such under the Constitution. [Rather, determining] whether questionable beliefs, practices, and organizations are religious by seeing how closely they resemble what is undeniably religious is a method that has been implicitly used by courts in difficult borderline cases [and] is consonant with Supreme Court decisions."[e]

c. For criticism of this view, see Stanley Ingber, *Religion or Ideology: A Needed Clarification of the Religion Clauses,* 41 Stan.L.Rev. 233, 274–77 (1989); Note, *Religion and Morality Legislation: A Reexamination of Establishment Clause Analysis,* 59 N.Y.U.L.Rev. 301, 346–52 (1984); Note, *Defining "Religion" in the First Amendment: A Functional Approach,* 74 Corn.L.Rev. 532 (1989).

d. For the view that religion should be defined as dealing only with "quintessentially religious questions," "addressing the profound questions of human existence," "such as God's existence or the proper definition of life and death," see Tom Stacy, *Death, Privacy, and the Free Exercise of Religion,* 77 Corn.L.Rev. 490 (1992).

(b) *Judicial role.* In THOMAS v. REVIEW BD., Sec. I supra, petitioner testified that, although his religious convictions forbade him to manufacture weapons, "he could, in good conscience, engage indirectly in the production, [for] example, as an employee of a raw material supplier." The state court, viewing petitioner's positions as inconsistent, ruled that "Thomas had made a merely 'personal philosophical choice rather than a religious choice.' " The Court, per BURGER, C.J. reversed: "The determination of what is a 'religious' belief or practice is more often than not a difficult and delicate task, [but] resolution of that question is not to turn upon a judicial perception of the particular belief or practice in question; religious beliefs need not be acceptable, logical, consistent, or comprehensible to others in order to merit First Amendment protection. * * * Thomas drew a line and it is not for us to say that the line he drew was an unreasonable one. Courts should not undertake to dissect religious beliefs because the believer admits that he is 'struggling' with his position or because his beliefs are not articulated with the clarity and precision that a more sophisticated person might employ.

"The Indiana court also appears to have given significant weight to the fact that another Jehovah's Witness had no scruples about working on tank turrets; for that other Witness, at least, such work was 'scripturally' acceptable. Intra-faith differences of that kind are not uncommon [and] the judicial process is singularly ill equipped to resolve such differences in relation to the Religion Clauses. [The] narrow function of a reviewing court in this context is to determine whether there was an appropriate finding that petitioner terminated his work because of an honest conviction that such work was forbidden by his religion."

4. *Variable definition.* May "religion" be defined differently for purposes of the establishment clause than the free exercise clause? Consider Marc S. Galanter, *Religious Freedom in the United States: A Turning Point?* 1966 Wis.L.Rev. 217, 266–67: "[For purposes of the establishment clause, the] effect and purpose of government action are not to be assessed by the religious sensibilities of the person who is complaining of the alleged establishment. It must be essentially religious in some widely shared public understanding. [But, for the free exercise clause, the] claimants' view of religion controls the characterization of their objection as a religious one." Does this analysis solve the dilemma of Leonard F. Manning, The Douglas concept of God in Government, 39 Wash.L.Rev. 47, 66 (1964): "If religion need not be predicated on a belief in God or even in a god and if it may not be tested by the common consensus of what reasonable men would reasonably call religion, if it is so private that—so long as it does not inflict injury

e. Accord, George C. Freeman, III, *The Misguided Search for the Constitutional Definition of "Religion,"* 71 Geo.L.J. 1519 (1983). See also Eduardo Peñalver, *The Concept of Religion,* 107 Yale L.J. 791 (1997) (supporting "analogical" approach that "takes into account the evolutionary nature of language" and "tries to minimize the scope for [western] judicial bias").

on society—it is immured from governmental interference and from judicial inquiry, [might] not a group of gymnasts proclaiming on their trampolines that physical culture is their religion be engaged in a religious exercise? And if Congress, in a particular Olympic year, appropriated funds to subsidize their calisthenics would this not [be] an establishment of religion?'' See generally Note, *Transcendental Meditation and the Meaning of Religion Under the Establishment Clause,* 62 Minn.L.Rev. 887 (1978).

Chapter 13

PREFERENCE AMONG RELIGIONS

In BOARD OF EDUC. OF KIRYAS JOEL v. GRUMET, 512 U.S. 687, 114 S.Ct. 2481, 129 L.Ed.2d 546 (1994), a New York statute constituted the Village of Kiryas Joel—"a religious enclave of Satmar Hasidim, practitioners of a strict form of Judaism"—as a separate school district. Most of the children attend pervasively religious private schools. The newly created district "currently runs only a special education program for handicapped [Satmar] children" who reside both inside and outside the village. The statute was passed "to enable the village's handicapped children to receive a secular, public-school education" because when they previously attended public schools in the larger school district outside the village, they suffered "panic, fear and trauma [in] leaving their own community and being with people whose ways were so different." The Court, per SOUTER, J., invoked "a principle at the heart of the Establishment Clause, that government should not prefer one religion to another, or religion to irreligion. Because the religious community of Kiryas Joel did not receive its new governmental authority simply as one of many communities eligible for equal treatment under a general law, we have no assurance that the next similarly situated group seeking a school district of its own will receive one; [and] a legislature's failure to enact a special law is itself unreviewable.[a] [Here] the benefit flows only to a single sect, [and] whatever the limits of permissible legislative

***

a. Kennedy, J., disagreed, arguing that if another religious community were denied special legislative help, it "could sue the State of New York, contending that New York's discriminatory treatment of the two religious communities violated the Establishment Clause. To resolve this claim, the court would have only to determine whether the community does indeed bear the same burden on its religious practice as did the Satmars in Kiryas Joel. See *Olsen v. Drug Enforcement Admin.,* 878 F.2d 1458 (D.C.Cir.1989) (R.B. Ginsburg, J.) (rejecting claim that the members of the Ethiopian Zion Coptic Church were entitled to an exemption from the marijuana laws on the same terms as the peyote exemption for the Native American Church). While a finding of discrimination would then raise a difficult question of relief, compare *Olsen* ('Faced with the choice between invalidation and extension of any controlled-substances religious exemption, which would the political branches choose? It would take a court bolder than this one to predict [that] extension, not invalidation, would be the probable choice'), with *Califano v. Westcott,* [443 U.S. 76, 99 S.Ct. 2655, 61 L.Ed.2d 382 (1979) infra] (curing gender discrimination in the AFDC program by extending benefits to children of unemployed mothers instead of denying benefits to children of unemployed fathers), the discrimination itself would not be beyond judicial remedy."

accommodations may be, it is clear that neutrality as among religions must be honored.[b] [The statute] therefore crosses the line from permissible accommodation to impermissible establishment."[c]

KENNEDY, J., concurred in the judgment: "[G]overnment may not use religion as a criterion to draw political or electoral lines. Whether or not the purpose is accommodation and whether or not the government provides similar gerrymanders to people of all religious faiths, the Establishment Clause forbids the government to use religion as a line-drawing criterion."[d]

SCALIA, J., joined by Rehnquist, C.J., and Thomas, J., dissented: "[A]ll the residents of the Kiryas Joel Village School District are Satmars. But all its residents also wear unusual dress, have unusual civic customs, and have not much to do with people who are culturally different from them. [I]t was not theology but dress, language, and cultural alienation that posed the educational problem for the children [and caused the Legislature to] provide a public education for these students, in the same way it addressed, by a similar law, the unique needs of children institutionalized in a hospital. "[T]he creation of a special, one-culture school district for the benefit of [children whose] parents were nonreligious commune dwellers, or American Indians, or gypsies [would] pose no problem. The neutrality demanded by the Religion Clauses requires the same indulgence towards cultural characteristics that are accompanied by religious belief."[e]

Notes and Questions

1. *Delegation of government power:* In *Kiryas Joel,* SOUTER, J., joined by Blackmun, Stevens and Ginsburg, JJ., found an additional ground for invalidating the statute: "delegating the State's discretionary authority over public schools to a group defined by its character as a religious community,

b. Compare Thomas C. Berg, *Slouching Towards Secularism,* 44 Emory L.J. 433 (1995): "[T]he legislature specifically accommodated the Satmars [because] their plight was unique: no other group of children was being denied effective special education because they were traumatized by the atmosphere of the mainstream public schools. [Even] if the children of other groups had been harmed by the public school ethos, few if any such groups live together communally so as to permit the solution of a geographically based school district such as that drawn for the Satmars." But see Ira C. Lupu, *The Lingering Death of Separationism,* 62 Geo.Wash. L.Rev. 230 (1994): "Is it imaginable that New York State would create a new public school district at the behest of an insular group of Branch Davidians or members of the Unification Church, whose children—

like the Hasidim—may suffer panic, fear, and trauma at encountering those outside their own community?"

c. Within ten days of *Kiryas Joel,* the New York legislature passed a new law allowing "any municipality situated wholly within a single school district" to form its own district if it meets designated criteria regarding population, enrollment and property wealth. Constitutional when used by the Village of Kiryas Joel?

d. For discussion of similarities and differences between the use of religion and race in drawing political districts, see Abner S. Greene, *Kiryas Joel and Two Mistakes About Equality,* 96 Colum.L.Rev. 1 (1996).

e. Is this persuasive when there is total congruence between a religion and distinctive cultural needs *and* the cultural distinctiveness is defined by the religion?

in a legal and historical context that gives no assurance that governmental power has been or will be exercised neutrally." They relied on LARKIN v. GRENDEL'S DEN, INC., 459 U.S. 116, 103 S.Ct. 505, 74 L.Ed.2d 297 (1982), per BURGER, C.J., which held that a Massachusetts law (§ 16C), giving churches and schools the power "to veto applications for liquor licenses within a five hundred foot radius of the church or school, violates the Establishment Clause": "§ 16C is not simply a legislative exercise of zoning power [because it] delegates * * * discretionary governmental powers [to] religious bodies.

"[The] valid secular objectives [of protecting] spiritual, cultural, and educational centers from the 'hurly-burly' associated with liquor outlets [can] be readily accomplished by [an] absolute legislative ban on liquor outlets within reasonable prescribed distances from churches, schools, hospitals and like institutions, or by ensuring a hearing for the views of affected institutions at licensing proceedings. [But the] churches' power under the statute is standardless [and] may therefore be used [for] explicitly religious goals, for example, favoring liquor licenses for members of that congregation or adherents of that faith. [In] addition, the mere appearance of a joint exercise of legislative authority by Church and State provides a significant symbolic benefit to religion in the minds of some by reason of the power conferred. It does not strain our prior holdings to say that the statute can be seen as having a 'primary' and 'principal' effect of advancing religion. [Finally, § 16C] enmeshes churches in the processes of government and creates the danger of 'political fragmentation and divisiveness along religious lines.'"

REHNQUIST, J., dissented in *Grendel's Den:* A "flat ban [on] the grant of an alcoholic beverages license to any establishment located within 500 feet of a church or a [school], which the majority concedes is valid, is more protective of churches and more restrictive of liquor sales than the present § 16C. * * * Nothing in the Court's opinion persuades me why the more rigid prohibition would be constitutional, but the more flexible not. [It] does not sponsor or subsidize any religious group or activity. It does not encourage, much less compel, anyone to participate in religious activities or to support religious institutions. [If] a church were to seek to advance the interests of its members [by favoring them for licenses], there would be an occasion to determine whether it had violated any right of an unsuccessful applicant for a liquor license. But our ability to discern a risk of such abuse does not render § 16C violative of the Establishment Clause."

Scalia, J., joined by Rehnquist, C.J., and Thomas, J., dissenting in *Kiryas Joel,* argued that *Grendel's Den* had ruled that "a state may not delegate its civil authority *to a church,*" and did not involve delegation to "groups of people sharing a common religious and cultural heritage": "If the conferral of governmental power upon a religious institution *as such* (rather than upon American citizens who belong to the religious institution) is not the test of *Grendel's Den* invalidity, there is no reason why giving power to a body that is overwhelmingly dominated by the members of one sect would not suffice to invoke the Establishment Clause. That might have made the entire States of Utah and New Mexico unconstitutional at the time of their admission to the Union."

2. *"Excessive government entanglement" in ecclesiastical disputes.* (a) In JONES v. WOLF, 443 U.S. 595, 99 S.Ct. 3020, 61 L.Ed.2d 775 (1979), a majority of the Vineville Presbyterian Church of Macon, Ga. voted to separate from the Presbyterian Church in the United States (PCUS). A commission of PCUS, acting pursuant to the PCUS constitution (called the Book of Church Order), declared the Vineville minority to be "the true congregation." The minority sued to establish its right to the local church property. The state court applied "the 'neutral principles of law' method for resolving church property disputes. The court examined the deeds to the properties, the state statutes dealing with implied trusts, and the Book of Church Order, to determine whether there was any basis for a trust in favor of the general church. Finding nothing that would give rise to a trust in any of these documents, the court awarded the property on the basis of legal title, which was in the local church, or in the names of trustees for the local church. [Without] further analysis or elaboration, [it] further decreed that the local congregation was represented by the majority faction, respondents herein."

The Court, per BLACKMUN, J., stated the established principle that "the First Amendment prohibits civil courts from resolving church property disputes on the basis of religious doctrine and practice. *Presbyterian Church v. Hull Church,* 393 U.S. 440, 89 S.Ct. 601, 21 L.Ed.2d 658 (1969). As a corollary to this commandment, the Amendment requires that civil courts defer to the resolution of issues of religious doctrine or polity by the highest court of a hierarchical church organization. *Serbian Eastern Orthodox Diocese v. Milivojevich,* 426 U.S. 696, 96 S.Ct. 2372, 49 L.Ed.2d 151 (1976)[a] Subject to these limitations, [however,] 'a State may adopt *any* of various approaches for settling church property disputes so long as it involves no consideration of doctrinal matters, whether the ritual and liturgy of worship or the tenets of faith.' *Maryland & Virginia Eldership v. Sharpsburg Church,* 396 U.S. 367, 90 S.Ct. 499, 24 L.Ed.2d 582 (1970) (Brennan, J., concurring).

"[W]e think the 'neutral principles of law' approach is consistent with the foregoing constitutional principles. [It] relies extensively on objective, well-established concepts of trust and property law familiar to lawyers and

---

a. *Serbian,* per Brennan, J., reversed a state court decision that the Mother Church's removal of respondent as bishop of the American–Canadian diocese was "procedurally and substantively defective under the internal regulations of the Mother Church and were therefore arbitrary and invalid": "[W]hether or not there is room for 'marginal civil court review' under the narrow rubrics of 'fraud' or 'collusion' when church tribunals act in bad faith for secular purposes, no 'arbitrariness' exception—in the sense of an inquiry whether the decisions of the highest ecclesiastical tribunal of a hierarchical church complied with church laws and regulations—is consistent with the constitutional mandate that civil courts are bound to accept the decisions of the highest judicatories of a religious organization of hierarchical polity on matters of discipline, faith, internal organization, or ecclesiastical rule, custom or law. [I]t is the essence of religious faith that ecclesiastical decisions are reached and are to be accepted as matters of faith whether or not rational or measurable by objective criteria."

Rehnquist and Stevens, JJ., dissented.

judges. It thereby promises to free civil courts completely from entanglement in questions of religious doctrine, polity, and practice. Furthermore, the neutral principles analysis [affords] flexibility in ordering private rights and obligations to reflect the intentions of the parties. Through appropriate reversionary clauses and trust provisions, religious societies can specify what is to happen to church property in the event of a particular contingency, or what religious body will determine the ownership in the event of a schism or doctrinal controversy. In this manner, a religious organization can ensure that a dispute over the ownership of church property will be resolved in accord with the desires of the members.

"[The] neutral principles method [does require] a civil court to examine certain religious documents, such as a church constitution, for language of trust in favor of the general church. [A] civil court must take special care to scrutinize the document in purely secular terms, and not to rely on religious precepts in determining whether the document indicates that the parties have intended to create a trust. In addition, there may be cases where the deed, the corporate charter, or the constitution of the general church incorporates religious concepts in the provisions relating to the ownership of property. If in such a case the interpretation of the instruments of ownership would require the civil court to resolve a religious controversy, then the court must defer to the resolution of the doctrinal issue by the authoritative ecclesiastical body. *Serbian.*"

The Court vacated the judgment, however, since "the grounds for the decision that respondents represent the Vineville church remain unarticulated": "If in fact Georgia has adopted a presumptive rule of majority representation, defeasible upon a showing that the identity of the local church is to be determined by some other means, we think this would be consistent with [the] First Amendment. Majority rule is generally employed in the governance of religious societies. Furthermore, the majority faction generally can be identified without resolving any question of religious doctrine or polity. [Most] importantly, any rule of majority representation can always be overcome, under the neutral principles approach, either by providing, in the corporate charter or the constitution of the general church, that the identity of the local church is to be established in some other way, or by providing that the church property is held in trust for the general church and those who remain loyal to it. Indeed, the State may adopt any method of overcoming the majoritarian presumption, so long as the use of that method does not impair free exercise rights or entangle the civil courts in matters of religious controversy.

"[But] there are at least some indications that under Georgia law the process of identifying the faction that represents the Vineville church [must] be determined according to terms of the Book of Church Order. [That] would appear to require a civil court to pass on questions of religious doctrine. [Therefore,] if Georgia law provides that the identity of the Vineville church is to be determined according to the 'laws and regulations' of the PCUS, then the First Amendment requires that the Georgia courts give deference to the presbyterial commission's determination of that church's identity."

POWELL, J., joined by Burger, C.J., and Stewart and White, JJ., dissented, finding that the neutral principles "approach inevitably will increase the involvement of civil courts in church controversies": "Until today, [the] first question presented in a case involving an intrachurch dispute over church property was where within the religious association the rules of polity, accepted by its members before the schism, had placed ultimate authority over the use of the church property. The courts, in answering this question have recognized two broad categories of church government. One is congregational, in which authority over questions of church doctrine, practice, and administration rests entirely in the local congregation or some body within it [and] the civil courts enforce the authoritative resolution of the controversy within the local church itself. *Watson v. Jones,* 80 U.S. (13 Wall.) 679, 20 L.Ed. 666 (1871). The second is hierarchical, in which the local church is but an integral and subordinate part of a larger church and is under the authority of the general church. [Here], this Court has held that the civil courts must give effect to the duly made decisions of the highest body within the hierarchy that has considered the dispute. [By] doing so, the [civil] court avoids two equally unacceptable departures from the genuine neutrality mandated by the First Amendment. First, it refrains from direct review and revision of decisions of the church on matters of religious doctrine and practice that underlie the church's determination of intrachurch controversies, including those that relate to control of church property.[b] Equally important, by recognizing the authoritative resolution reached within the religious association, the civil court avoids interfering indirectly with the religious governance of those who have formed the association and submitted themselves to its authority."[c]

(b) *Scope of the decision.* After *Jones v. Wolf,* what results in the following situations: (i) A donor who made a bequest "to the First Methodist Church" seeks return of the money because subsequently a majority of the

---

b. In response, the Court pointed out that, under the dissent's approach, "civil courts would always be required to examine the polity and administration of a church to determine which unit of government has ultimate control over church property. In some cases, [the] locus of control would be ambiguous, and 'a careful examination of the constitutions of the general and local church, as well as other relevant documents, [would] be necessary to ascertain the form of governance adopted by the members of the religious association.' In such cases, the suggested rule would appear to require 'a searching and therefore impermissible inquiry into church polity.' *Serbian.* The neutral principles approach, in contrast, obviates entirely the need for an analysis or examination of ecclesiastical polity or doctrine in settling church property disputes."

c. In response, the Court contended that "the neutral principles approach cannot be said to 'inhibit' the free exercise of religion, any more than do other neutral provisions of state law governing the manner in which churches own property, hire employees, or purchase goods. Under the neutral principles approach, the outcome of a church property dispute is not foreordained. At any time before the dispute erupts, the parties can ensure, if they so desire, that the faction loyal to the hierarchical church will retain the church property" by using reversionary clauses, trust provisions, etc.

church's members decided to affiliate with another denomination. Suppose the bequest had been "to the First Methodist Church so long as it does not substantially deviate from existing doctrine"? (ii) A state statute makes it a crime for sellers to falsely represent food to be "kosher." See Kent Greenawalt, *Religious Law and Civil Law: Using Secular Law to Assure Observance of Practices with Religious Significance*, 71 So.Cal.L.Rev. 781 (1998). (iii) An adult sues a member of the clergy for "malpractice" based on consensual sexual acts with the plaintiff. See Scott C. Idleman, *Tort Liability, Religious Entities, and the Decline of Constitutional Protection*, 75 Ind. L.J., 219 (2000).

(c) *Proposed approach.* "The solution most of the time is to honor internal church agreements, just as a court would honor the internal agreements of a secular organization. Only when doctrinal decisions[d] or the imposition of external policies are involved[e] need a court refrain from deciding a dispute. This approach serves both organizational autonomy and the other interests of the church and its members, while preserving the religious neutrality demanded by the first amendment." Ira M. Ellman, *Driven from the Tribunal: Judicial Resolution of Internal Church Disputes*, 69 Calif.L.Rev. 1378, 1444 (1981).[f]

———

LARSON v. VALENTE, 456 U.S. 228, 102 S.Ct. 1673, 72 L.Ed.2d 33 (1982), involved a challenge by the Unification Church ("Moonies") to "a Minnesota statute, imposing certain registration and reporting requirements upon only those religious organizations that solicit more than fifty per cent of their funds from nonmembers." The Court, per BRENNAN, J., noting that "the clearest command of the establishment clause is that one religious denomination cannot be officially preferred over another, [*Everson*]," and that the "constitutional prohibition of denominational preferences is inextricably connected with the continuing vitality of the Free Exercise Clause,"

d. "Few [cases] present the problem of governmental determination of religious doctrine. [More] common are a second group of cases in which the court is asked to determine which religious doctrine the embattled parties agreed to follow. This kind of question is very different and need not present the first amendment difficulties inherent in the first group of cases." Id. at 1414.

e. "[T]he application of judge-made rules of procedural fairness in associational governance, and the use of charitable trust rules of charitable assets [are issues that] present the potential for courts to impose government-created policies on religious organizations [rather than rules seeking to fulfill the parties' intentions]." Id. at 1421.

f. For the view that "freedom of church groups" should be preferred to "freedom of individual members," and therefore the rule of "deference" to church decisions should prevail over the "neutral principles" approach, see John H. Garvey, *Churches and the Free Exercise of Religion*, 4 Notre D.J.L.Eth & Pub.Pol. 567 (1990).

For the view that the Court should adopt "a framework based on neutral principles"; that "national churches should specify the range of authority of their highest courts in documents clearly designed for recognition under civil law"; and that "civil courts should await the determinations of those religious courts and then accept their determinations, unless those determinations are undercut by some gross failure of the religious courts to comply with their own rules," see Kent Greenawalt, *Hands Off! Civil Court Involvement in Conflicts Over Religious Property*, 98 Colum.L.Rev. 1843 (1998).

held that the statute violated the establishment clause because it did not survive "strict scrutiny."[a] Assuming that the state's "valid secular purpose [in] protecting its citizens from abusive practices in the solicitation of funds for charity" is "compelling," the state "failed to demonstrate that the fifty per cent rule [is] 'closely fitted'" to furthering that interest. Moreover, the statute failed the third *Lemon* "test": "The fifty per cent [rule] effects the *selective* legislative imposition of burdens and advantages upon particular denominations. The 'risk of politicizing religion' that inheres in such legislation is obvious, and indeed is confirmed by the provision's legislative history [which] demonstrates that the provision was drafted with the explicit intention of including particular religious denominations and excluding others."

WHITE, J., joined by Rehnquist, J., dissented,[b] disagreeing with the Court's view "that the rule on its face represents an explicit and deliberate preference for some religious beliefs over others": "The rule [names] no churches or denominations. [Some] religions will qualify and some will not, but this depends on the source of their contributions, not on their brand of religion. [The Court's assertion] that the limitation might burden the less well-organized denominations [is contrary to the state's claim] that both categories include not only well-established, but also not so well-established organizations." Further, "I cannot join the Court's easy rejection of the state's submission that a valid secular purpose justifies basing the exemption on the percentage of external funding."[c]

Notes and Questions

1. *The Gillette rationale.* (a) Should the existence of a "neutral, secular basis" justify government preference—de jure or de facto—among religions?

a. The Court rejected the argument that the statute was merely "a law based upon secular criteria which may not identically affect all religious organizations." This "is not simply a facially neutral statute, the provisions of which happen to have a 'disparate impact' upon different religious organizations. On the contrary [it] makes explicit and deliberate distinctions between different religious organizations [and] effectively distinguishes between 'well-established churches' that have 'achieved strong but not total financial support from their members,' on the one hand, and 'churches which are new and lacking in a constituency, or, which, as a matter of policy, may favor public solicitation over general reliance on financial support from members,' on the other hand."

The Court found *Gillette v. United States,* Ch. 12, I supra, "readily distinguishable": "In that case, we rejected an Establishment Clause attack upon § 6(j) of the Military

Selective Service Act of 1967, which afforded 'conscientious objector' status to any person who, 'by reason of religious training and belief,' was 'conscientiously opposed to participation in war in any form * * *.' Section 6(j) 'focused on individual conscientious belief, not on sectarian affiliation.' Under § 6(j), conscientious objector status was available on an equal basis to both the Quaker and the Roman Catholic, despite the distinction drawn by the latter's church between 'just' and 'unjust' wars. [In] contrast, the statute challenged in the case before us focuses precisely and solely upon religious organizations."

b. Rehnquist, J., joined by Burger, C.J. and White and O'Connor, JJ., also dissented on the ground that appellee Unification Church had no standing.

c. *Gillette* held that there was no religious "gerrymander" if there was "a neutral, secular basis for the lines government has drawn."

Consider Kent Greenawalt, *All or Nothing at All: The Defeat of Selective Conscientious Objection,* 1971 Sup.Ct.Rev. 31, 71: "If a sociological survey indicated that Protestants generally work harder than Catholics, the government might simplify its hiring problems by interviewing only Protestants. If the doctors of Catholic hospitals were determined to be on the average more qualified than those at Lutheran hospitals, aid might be limited to the Catholic hospitals. It is, of course, inconceivable that such legislation would be passed and its unconstitutionality is [apparent]." How significant was the Court's observation that the *Gillette* law "attempts to accommodate free exercise values"?

(b) Was the Draft Act of 1917, which exempted only conscientious objectors affiliated with some "well-recognized religious sect" whose principles forbade participation in war, also valid under the *Gillette* rationale? Consider 48 Minn.L.Rev. 776–77 (1964): "Since pacifism often arises from religious beliefs, a workable method for ascertaining sincerity may have to be couched in terms of those beliefs. Such a test should be permissible, even though it may theoretically 'prefer' some sincere conscientious objectors over others, if it reasonably advances the [statute's] purpose by aiding local draft boards in administering the act. For example, since membership in an organized pacifist sect may be better evidence of sincerity than the mere assertion of pacificist beliefs, a requirement to that effect should be permissible."

2. *The Larson rationale.* (a) Consider Jesse H. Choper, *The Free Exercise Clause: A Structural Overview and An Appraisal of Recent Developments,* 27 Wm. & M.L.Rev. 943, 958–61 (1986): "*Larson* should be seen as a free exercise clause decision parading in an establishment clause disguise. [The] major thrust of the Court's opinion [used] classic free exercise clause analysis[:] strict scrutiny. [Even if] the Minnesota statute did not specifically give preference to some religions over others, it did expressly deal with the subject of religion, and it resulted in favoring some and disfavoring others. In my view, it should have been as vulnerable—that is, subject to the same level of scrutiny—as a general, neutral law that says nothing about religion but that happens to have an adverse impact on some faiths, [as] in *Yoder.* The problem is that when the [pre-*Smith*] Court has invoked the establishment clause, it has applied a much more lenient test to laws that expressly deal with religion and subject some faiths to discriminatory treatment than it has applied under the free exercise clause to general, neutral laws that come into conflict with religious beliefs. [In] reality, I believe that the Selective Service Act survived strict scrutiny in *Gillette* [because of the] powerful government interest in raising an army and the difficulties in administering a draft exemption based on 'just war' beliefs. [In] sum, the doctrine in *Gillette,* that a valid secular basis for de facto religious discrimination is enough to sustain it under the establishment clause, plainly supports Justice White's dissent in *Larson.* The *Gillette* doctrine, however, effectively has been abandoned, and rightly so."

(b) HERNANDEZ v. COMMISSIONER, 490 U.S. 680, 109 S.Ct. 2136, 104 L.Ed.2d 766 (1989), per MARSHALL, J., found no violation of the establishment clause in not permitting federal taxpayers to deduct as "charitable contributions" payments to the Church of Scientology for "auditing" and "training" sessions. A central tenet of the Church requires "fixed donations" for these sessions to study the faith's tenets and to increase spiritual awareness. The proceeds are the Church's primary source of income:

Larson was distinguished on the ground that IRS disallowance for payments made "with some expectation of a quid pro quo in terms of goods or services [makes] no 'explicit and deliberate distinctions between different religious organizations.' [It] may be that a consequence of the quid pro quo orientation of the 'contribution or gift' requirement is to impose a disparate burden on those charitable and religious groups that rely on sales of commodities or services as a means of fund-raising, relative to those groups that raise funds primarily by soliciting unilateral donations. But a statute primarily having a secular effect does not violate the Establishment Clause merely because it 'happens to coincide or harmonize with the tenets of some or all religions.' *McGowan*."

Because of the absence of "a proper factual record," the Court did not consider the contention of O'CONNOR, J., joined by Scalia, J., dissenting, that "at least some of the fixed payments which the IRS has treated as charitable deductions [are as much a 'quid pro quo exchange'] as the payments [here]": "In exchange for their payment of pew rents, Christians receive particular seats during worship services. Similarly, in some synagogues attendance at the worship services for Jewish High Holy Days is often predicated upon the purchase of a general admission ticket or a reserved seat ticket. Religious honors such as publicly reading from Scripture are purchased or auctioned periodically in some synagogues of Jews from Morocco and Syria. Mormons must tithe ten percent of their income as a necessary but not sufficient condition to obtaining a 'temple recommend,' i.e., the right to be admitted into the temple. A Mass stipend—a fixed payment given to a Catholic priest, in consideration of which he is obliged to apply the fruits of the Mass for the intention of the donor—has similar overtones of exchange. [Thus, the case] involves the differential application of a standard based on constitutionally impermissible differences drawn by the Government among religions." Brennan and Kennedy, JJ., did not participate.

3. *Preference for "religious" objectors.* Is Congress' limitation of draft exemption to "religious" conscientious objectors valid? Consider John H. Mansfield, *Conscientious Objection—1964 Term,* 1965 Relig. & Pub.Or. 3, 76: "[T]here are really no convincing reasons why the religious objector should be exempt and not the non-religious conscientious objector. [T]he religious objector's opposition rests on somewhat more fundamental grounds [and] makes reference to realities that can more easily be described as spiritual. But the non-religious conscientious objector's opposition does rest on basic propositions about the nature of reality and the significance of human existence; this is what distinguishes it from objection that is not even conscientious." Does the "religious" exemption result in more or less government "entanglement" with religion than an exemption for *all* conscientious objectors?

Chapter 14

CONFLICT BETWEEN THE CLAUSES

The decision in *Employment Division v. Smith* appeared to have relieved some of the tension that had existed between the doctrines that the Court had developed under the establishment and free exercise clauses. But substantial questions remained, e.g., do (a) the decisions in *Sherbert (Thomas, Hobbie), Yoder* and *Roy,* and (b) statutes granting religious exemptions from laws of general applicability violate the establishment clause because they impermissibly aid religion?

CORPORATION OF THE PRESIDING BISHOP OF THE CHURCH OF JESUS CHRIST OF LATTER–DAY SAINTS v. AMOS

483 U.S. 327, 107 S.Ct. 2862, 97 L.Ed.2d 273 (1987).

JUSTICE WHITE delivered the opinion of the Court.

Section 702 of the Civil Rights Act of 1964 exempts religious organizations from Title VII's prohibition against discrimination in employment on the basis of religion. [The] Deseret Gymnasium (Gymnasium) in Salt Lake City, Utah, is a nonprofit facility, open to the public, run by [an] unincorporated religious association sometimes called the Mormon or LDS Church. Appellee Mayson worked at the Gymnasium for some 16 years as an assistant building engineer and then building engineer. He was discharged in 1981 because he failed to qualify for a temple recommend, that is, a certificate that he is a member of the Church and eligible to attend its temples. Mayson [contended] that if construed to allow religious employers to discriminate on religious grounds in hiring for nonreligious jobs, § 702 violates the Establishment Clause. * * *

"This Court has long recognized that the government may (and sometimes must) accommodate religious practices and that it may do so without violating the Establishment Clause." It is well established, too, that "[t]he limits of permissible state accommodation to religion are by no means co-extensive with the noninterference mandated by the Free Exercise Clause."

756

Walz.[a] [At] some point, accommodation may devolve into "an unlawful fostering of religion," but this is not such a case, in our view. * * *

Lemon requires [a] "secular legislative purpose." This does not mean that the law's purpose must be unrelated to religion. [Rather,] *Lemon*'s "purpose" requirement aims at preventing the relevant governmental decisionmaker—in this case, Congress—from abandoning neutrality and acting with the intent of promoting a particular point of view in religious matters.

Under the *Lemon* analysis, it is a permissible legislative purpose to alleviate significant governmental interference with the ability of religious organizations to define and carry out their religious missions.[b] Appellees argue that there is no such purpose here because § 702 provided adequate protection for religious employers prior to the 1972 amendment, when it exempted only the religious activities of such employers from the statutory ban on religious discrimination. We may assume for the sake of argument that the pre–1972 exemption was adequate in the sense that the Free Exercise Clause required no more. Nonetheless, it is a significant burden on a religious organization to require it, on pain of substantial liability, to predict which of its activities a secular court will consider religious. The line is hardly a bright one, and an organization might understandably be concerned that a judge would not understand its religious tenets and sense of mission. Fear of potential liability might affect the way an organization carried out what it understood to be its religious mission. * * *

The second requirement under *Lemon* is that the law in question have "a principal or primary effect [that] neither advances nor inhibits religion." Undoubtedly, religious organizations are better able now to advance their purposes than they were prior to the 1972 amendment to § 702. But religious groups have been better able to advance their purposes on account of many laws that have passed constitutional muster: for example, the property tax exemption at issue in *Walz,* or the loans of school books to school children, including parochial school students, upheld in *Allen.* A law is

a. Consider Michael W. McConnell, *Accommodation of Religion,* 1985 Sup.Ct.Rev. 1, 34: "[S]ome government employees may view attendance at religious services on a holy day a sacred duty; they could make out a plausible free exercise case if the government refused them leave. Others may view attendance at services as no more than a spiritually wholesome activity; their free exercise claim would be much weaker. It is not unreasonable for the government to disregard these distinctions—to implement a general policy permitting leave for employees on the holy days of their faith. * * * Religious liberty is not enhanced by a rule confining government accommodations to the minimum compelled under the Constitution."

b. See also Wilbur Katz, *Note on the Constitutionality of Shared Time,* 1964 Relig. & Pub.Or. 85, 88: "It is no violation of neutrality for the government to express its concern for religious freedom by measures which merely neutralize what would otherwise be restrictive effects of government action. Provision for voluntary worship in the armed forces is constitutional, not because government policy may properly favor religion, but because the government is not required to exercise its military powers in a manner restrictive of religious freedom. Affirmative government action to maintain religious freedom in these instances serves the secular purpose of promoting a constitutional right, the free exercise of religion."

not unconstitutional simply because it *allows* churches to advance religion, which is their very purpose. For a law to have forbidden "effects" under *Lemon,* it must be fair to say that the *government itself* has advanced religion through its own activities and influence. [Moreover,] we find no persuasive evidence in the record before us that the Church's ability to propagate its religious doctrine through the Gymnasium is any greater now than it was prior to the passage of the Civil Rights Act in 1964. In such circumstances, we do not see how any advancement of religion achieved by the Gymnasium can be fairly attributed to the Government, as opposed to the Church.[15]

We find unpersuasive the District Court's reliance on the fact that § 702 singles out religious entities for a benefit. [The Court] has never indicated that statutes that give special consideration to religious groups are per se invalid. That would run contrary to the teaching of our cases that there is ample room for accommodation of religion under the Establishment Clause. Where, as here, government acts with the proper purpose of lifting a regulation that burdens the exercise of religion, we see no reason to require that the exemption come packaged with benefits to secular entities. * * * *Larson* indicates that laws discriminating *among* religions are subject to strict scrutiny, and that laws "affording a uniform benefit to *all* religions" should be analyzed under *Lemon.* In a case such as this, where a statute is neutral on its face and motivated by a permissible purpose of limiting governmental interference with the exercise of religion, we see no justification for applying strict scrutiny to a statute that passes the *Lemon* test. * * * § 702 is rationally related to the legitimate purpose of alleviating significant governmental interference with the ability of religious organizations to define and carry out their religious missions. * * *

JUSTICE BRENNAN, with whom JUSTICE MARSHALL joins, concurring in the judgment.

[Any] exemption from Title VII's proscription on religious discrimination [says] that a person may be put to the choice of either conforming to certain religious tenets or losing a job opportunity, a promotion, or, as in this case, employment itself. The potential for coercion created by such a provision is in serious tension with our commitment to individual freedom of conscience in matters of religious belief.

At the same time, religious organizations have an interest in autonomy in ordering their internal affairs * * *. Determining that certain activities are in furtherance of an organization's religious mission, and that only those committed to that mission should conduct them, is thus a means by which a religious community defines itself. Solicitude for a church's ability to do so reflects the idea that furtherance of the autonomy of religious organizations often furthers individual religious freedom as well.[a] * * *

---

15. Undoubtedly, Mayson's freedom of choice in religious matters was impinged upon, but it was the Church [and] not the Government, who put him to the choice of changing his religious practices or losing his [job.]

a. For the view that the establishment clause requires an exemption from a neu-

This rationale suggests that, ideally, religious organizations should be able to discriminate on the basis of religion *only* with respect to religious activities [because] the infringement on religious liberty that results from conditioning performance of *secular* activity upon religious belief cannot be defended as necessary for the community's self-definition. Furthermore, the authorization of discrimination in such circumstances is not an accommodation that simply enables a church to gain members by the normal means of prescribing the terms of membership for those who seek to participate in furthering the mission of the community. Rather, it puts at the disposal of religion the added advantages of economic leverage in the secular realm. * * *

What makes the application of a religious-secular distinction difficult is that the character of an activity is not self-evident. As a result, determining whether an activity is religious or secular requires a searching case-by-case analysis. This results in considerable ongoing government entanglement in religious affairs. Furthermore, this prospect of government intrusion raises concern that a religious organization may be chilled in its Free Exercise activity. * * *

The risk [is] most likely to arise with respect to *nonprofit* activities. The fact that an operation is not organized as a profit-making commercial enterprise makes colorable a claim that it is not purely secular in orientation. * * *

Sensitivity to individual religious freedom dictates that religious discrimination be permitted only with respect to employment in religious activities. Concern for the autonomy of religious organizations demands that we avoid the entanglement and the chill on religious expression that a case-by-case determination would produce. We cannot escape the fact that these aims are in tension. Because of the nature of nonprofit activities, I believe that a categorical exemption for such enterprises appropriately balances these competing concerns. * * *

Justice Blackmun, concurring in the judgment.

Essentially for the reasons set forth in Justice O'Connor's opinion, * * * I too, concur in the judgment of the Court. * * *

Justice O'Connor, concurring in the judgment. * * *

In *Jaffree,* I noted a tension in the Court's use of the *Lemon* test to evaluate an Establishment Clause challenge to government efforts to accommodate the free exercise of religion: "On the one hand, a rigid application of the *Lemon* test would invalidate legislation exempting religious observers from generally applicable government obligations. By definition, such legislation has a religious purpose and effect in promoting the free exercise of religion.[b] On the other hand, judicial deference to all legislation that pur-

---

tral, generally applicable law that "interferes with the relationship between clergy and church" or "intrudes on religious organizations' sphere of autonomy," see Carl H. Esbeck, *The Establishment Clause as a*

Structural Restraint on Governmental Power, 84 Ia.L.Rev. 1 (1998).

b. In her *Jaffree* concurrence, O'Connor, J., added: "Indeed, the statute at issue in *Lemon* [can] be viewed as an accommo-

ports to facilitate the free exercise of religion would completely vitiate the Establishment Clause. Any statute pertaining to religion can be viewed as an 'accommodation' of free exercise rights."[c]

In my view, the opinion for the Court leans toward the second of the two unacceptable options described [above.] Almost any government benefit to religion could be recharacterized as simply "allowing" a religion to better advance itself, unless perhaps it involved actual proselytization by government agents. In nearly every case of a government benefit to religion, the religious mission would not be advanced if the religion did not take advantage of the benefit; even a direct financial subsidy to a religious organization

dation of the religious beliefs of parents who choose to send their children to religious schools."

In this connection, consider Phillip Kurland, *Religion and the Law* 112 (1962): "The [free exercise and establishment] clauses should be read as stating a single precept: that government cannot utilize religion as a standard for action or inaction because these clauses, read together as they should be, prohibit classification in terms of religion either to confer a benefit or to impose a burden." For thoughtful comment, see Paul Kauper, *Book Review,* 41 Texas L.Rev. 467 (1963); Leo Pfeffer, *Religion–Blind Government,* 15 Stan.L.Rev. 389 (1963); John Mansfield, *Book Review,* 52 Calif.L.Rev. 212 (1964). For consideration of "the extent to which equality, as a constitutional value, constrains our understanding of religious guarantees," see Laura S. Underkuffler–Freund, *Yoder and the Question of Equality,* 25 Cap.U.L.Rev. 789 (1996).

Similarly, for the view that the free exercise clause should generally only guarantee "equality of treatment for those who act out of sincere religious belief" and should afford special protection only for acts of "worship," as defined, see Fernandez, *The Free Exercise of Religion,* 36 So.Calif.L.Rev. 546 (1963). For the view that free exercise claims should be treated "no differently than free expression claims," see Marshall, *Solving the Free Exercise Dilemma: Free Exercise as Expression,* 67 Minn.L.Rev. 545 (1983).

c. In *Jaffree,* O'Connor, J. added: "It [is] difficult to square any notion of 'complete neutrality' with the mandate of the Free Exercise Clause that government must sometimes exempt a religious observer from an otherwise generally applicable obligation. [The] solution [lies] in identifying workable limits to the Government's license to promote the free exercise of religion. [O]ne can plausibly assert that government pursues free exercise clause values when it

lifts a government-imposed burden on the free exercise of religion. If a statute falls within this category, then the standard Establishment Clause test should be modified accordingly. [T]he Court should simply acknowledge that the religious purpose of such a statute is legitimated by the Free Exercise Clause."

See also Abner S. Greene, *The Political Balance of the Religion Clauses,* 102 Yale L.J. 1611, 1644 (1993): "[I]f we construe the Establishment Clause to prohibit legislation enacted for the express purpose of advancing religious values, then the predicate for universal obedience to law has been removed. A religious conscientious objector may legitimately claim that because she was thwarted from offering her values for majority acceptance as law, she should have at least a prima facie right of exemption from law that conflicts with her religion. The Free Exercise Clause works as a counterweight to the Establishment Clause; it gives back what the Establishment Clause takes away." Compare Sherry, fn. d, p. 707 supra, at 145: "This formulation can also be reversed: protecting the values of the Establishment Clause should constitute a compelling government interest sufficient to justify the impact of neutral laws on religious exercise. Whichever clause serves as the compelling interest trumps the other. Which formulation one prefers depends solely on whether one places a higher priority on the values of the Establishment Clause or on those of the Free Exercise Clause."

For the view that "there is much to be said for allowing broad interpretations of both clauses to remain in a symbiotic relationship, in dynamic 'tension,' thereby maximizing the goal of religious liberty for all Americans," see Derek H. Davis, *Resolving Not to Resolve the Tension between the Establishment and Free Exercise Clauses,* 38 J.Ch. & St. 245 (1996).

would not advance religion if for some reason the organization failed to make any use of the funds. * * *

The necessary first step in evaluating an Establishment Clause challenge to a government action lifting from religious organizations a generally applicable regulatory burden is to recognize that such government action *does* have the effect of advancing religion. The necessary second step is to separate those benefits to religion that constitutionally accommodate the free exercise of religion from those that provide unjustifiable awards of assistance to religious organizations. As I have suggested in earlier opinions, the inquiry framed by the *Lemon* test should be "whether government's purpose is to endorse religion and whether the statute actually conveys a message of endorsement." [T]he relevant issue is how it would be perceived by an objective observer, acquainted with the text, legislative history, and implementation of the statute.[d] [This] case involves a government decision to lift from a nonprofit activity of a religious organization the burden of demonstrating that the particular nonprofit activity is religious as well as the burden of refraining from discriminating on the basis of religion. Because there is a probability that a nonprofit activity of a religious organization will itself be involved in the organization's religious mission, in my view the objective observer should perceive the government action as an accommodation of the exercise of religion rather than as a government endorsement of religion.

[U]nder the holding of the Court, and under my view of the appropriate Establishment Clause analysis, the question of the constitutionality of the § 702 exemption as applied to for-profit activities of religious organizations remains open.

Notes and Questions

1. *Draft exemption.* Did the statute in *Gillette,* exempting only "religious" conscientious objectors, impermissibly prefer religion over nonreligion? In WELSH v. UNITED STATES, Sec. 2, II supra, four justices addressed the issue. WHITE, J., joined by Burger, C.J., and Stewart, J., found it valid: "First, § 6(j) may represent a purely practical judgment that religious objectors, however admirable, would be of no more use in combat

---

d. In *Jaffree,* O'Connor, J., added: "[C]ourts should assume that the 'objective observer,' is acquainted with the Free Exercise Clause and the values it promotes. Thus individual perceptions, or resentment that a religious observer is exempted from a particular government requirement, would be entitled to little weight if the Free Exercise Clause strongly supported the exemption."

Compare William P. Marshall, *The Religious Freedom Restoration Act: Establishment, Equal Protection and Free Speech Concerns,* 56 Mont.L.Rev. 227, 236 (1995):

"Prior to *Smith,* one could argue that the Constitution demanded some accommodation from general laws of neutral applicability for free exercise interests. Legislative exemptions from neutral laws, which provided this accommodation, could therefore be defended as in accord with this constitutional mandate. The denial of the free exercise right in *Smith,* however, suggests that exempting religion from neutral laws is no longer based upon a constitutional requirement. Accordingly, after *Smith,* the strength of the state interest supporting the legislative exemption is necessarily diminished."

than many others unqualified for military service. [On] this basis, the exemption has neither the primary purpose nor the effect of furthering religion. * * *

"Second, Congress may have [believed that] to deny the exemption would violate the Free Exercise Clause or at least raise grave problems in this respect. [If] it is 'favoritism' and not 'neutrality' to exempt religious believers from the draft, is it 'neutrality' and not 'inhibition' of religion to compel religious believers to fight * * * ? It cannot be ignored that the First Amendment itself contains a religious classification [and the free exercise clause] protects conduct as well as religious belief and speech. [It] was not suggested [in *Braunfeld*] that the Sunday closing laws in 21 States exempting Sabbatarians and others violated the Establishment Clause because no provision was made for others who claimed nonreligious reasons for not working on some particular day of the week. Nor was it intimated in *Zorach* that the no-establishment holding might be infirm because only those pursuing religious studies for designated periods were released from the public school routine; neither was it hinted that a public school's refusal to institute a released time program would violate the Free Exercise Clause. The Court in *Sherbert* construed the Free Exercise Clause to require special treatment for Sabbatarians under the State's unemployment compensation law. But the State could deal specially with Sabbatarians whether the Free Exercise Clause required it or not * * *."

HARLAN, J., disagreed, believing that "having chosen to exempt, [Congress] cannot draw the line between theistic or nontheistic religious beliefs on the one hand and secular beliefs on the other. [I]t must encompass the class of individuals it purports to exclude, those whose beliefs emanate from a purely moral, ethical, or philosophical source.[9] The common denominator must be the intensity of moral conviction with which a belief is [held]. *Everson, McGowan* and *Allen,* all sustained legislation on the premise that it was neutral in its application and thus did not constitute an establishment, notwithstanding the fact that it may have assisted religious groups by giving them the same benefits accorded to nonreligious groups.[12] To the extent that *Zorach* and *Sherbert* stand for the proposition that the Government may (*Zorach*), or must (*Sherbert*), shape its secular programs to accommodate the beliefs and tenets of religious groups, I think these cases unsound.[13]"

---

9. * * * I suggested [in *Sherbert*] that a State could constitutionally create exceptions to its program to accommodate religious scruples. [But] any such exception in order to satisfy the Establishment Clause [would] have to be sufficiently broad so as to be religiously neutral. This would require creating an exception for anyone who, as a matter of conscience, could not comply with the statute. * * *

12. [I] fail to see how [§ 6(j)] has "any substantial legislative purpose" apart from

honoring the conscience of individuals who oppose war on only religious grounds. * * *

13. [At] the very least the Constitution requires that the State not excuse students early for the purpose of receiving religious instruction when it does not offer to nonreligious students the opportunity to use school hours for spiritual or ethical instruction of a nonreligious nature. Moreover, whether a released-time program cast in terms of improving "conscience" to the exclusion of artistic or cultural pursuits, would be "neutral" and consistent with the

2. *Unemployment compensation.* (a) Did the Court's decisions in *Sherbert, Thomas* and *Hobbie* impermissibly prefer religion? In THOMAS v. REVIEW BD., Sec. 2 supra, REHNQUIST, J., dissented, finding the result "inconsistent with many of our prior Establishment Clause cases"[2]: "If Indiana were to legislate what the Court today requires—an unemployment compensation law which permitted benefits to be granted to those persons who quit their jobs for religious reasons—the statute would 'plainly' violate the Establishment Clause as interpreted in such cases as [*Lemon*]. First, [the] proviso would clearly serve only a religious purpose. It would grant financial benefits for the sole purpose of accommodating religious beliefs. Second, there can be little doubt that the primary effect of the proviso would be to 'advance' religion by facilitating the exercise of religious belief. Third, any statute including such a proviso would surely 'entangle' the State in religion far more than the mere grant of tax exemptions, as in [*Walz*]. By granting financial benefits to persons solely on the basis of their religious beliefs, the State must necessarily inquire whether the claimant's belief is 'religious' and whether it is sincerely [held.] I believe that Justice Stewart, dissenting in *Schempp,* accurately stated the reach of the Establishment Clause [as] limited to 'government support of proselytizing activities of religious sects by throwing the weight of secular authorities behind the dissemination of religious tenets.' See *McCollum* (Reed, J., dissenting) (impermissible aid is only 'purposeful assistance directly to the church itself or to some religious [group] performing ecclesiastical functions'). Conversely, governmental assistance which does not have the effect of 'inducing' religious belief, but instead merely 'accommodates' or implements an independent religious choice does not impermissibly involve the government in religious choices and therefore does not violate the Establishment [Clause]. I would think that in this case, as in *Sherbert,* had the state voluntarily chosen to pay unemployment compensation benefits to persons who left their jobs for religious reasons, such aid would be constitutionally permissible because it redounds directly to the benefit of the individual."

(b) *Accommodation vs. inducement vs. imposition vs. coercion.* Consider Alan Schwarz, *No Imposition of Religion: The Establishment Clause Value,*

requirement of "voluntarism," is by no means an easy question. * * *

2. To the extent *Sherbert* was correctly decided, it might be argued that cases such as *McCollum, Engel, Schempp, Lemon,* and *Nyquist* were wrongly decided. The "aid" rendered to religion in these latter cases may not be significantly different, in kind or degree, than the "aid" afforded Mrs. Sherbert or Thomas. For example, if the State in *Sherbert* could not deny compensation to one refusing work for religious reasons, it might be argued that a State may not deny reimbursement to students who choose for religious reasons to attend parochial schools. The argument would be that although a State need not allocate any funds to education, once it has done so, it may not require any person to sacrifice his religious beliefs in order to obtain an equal education. There can be little doubt that to the extent secular education provides answers to important moral questions without reference to religion or teaches that there are no answers, a person in one sense sacrifices his religious belief by attending secular schools. And even if such "aid" were not constitutionally compelled by the Free Exercise Clause, Justice Harlan may well be right in *Sherbert* when he finds sufficient flexibility in the Establishment Clause to permit the States to voluntarily choose to grant such benefits to individuals.

77 Yale L.J. 692, 693, 723, 728 (1968): "[T]he establishment clause [should] be read to prohibit only aid which has as its motive or substantial effect the imposition of religious belief or practice * * *. Exemption of Mrs. Sherbert [represents] a judgment that the exercise of Seventh-day Adventism is more worthy than bowling on Saturdays, but the exemption has no significant effect and arguably no effect at all upon whether someone becomes a Seventh-day Adventist. Similarly, the Sabbatarian exemption from Sunday closing laws does not induce one to become a Jew; draft exemption to conscientious objectors does not normally induce one to become a Quaker; closing the public schools on all religious holidays or on every Wednesday at 2 P.M. does not induce the adoption of religion; and compulsory Sunday closing, while implementing an independent desire to attend church services, has no substantial effect upon the creation of such desire. The availability of preferential aid to religious exercise may, to be sure, induce false claims of religious belief, but the establishment clause is not concerned with false claims of belief, only with induced belief." Does this distinguish *McCollum, Engel* and *Schempp* from *Sherbert?* Do you agree with all of the *factual* assumptions made? Under this analysis, what result in *Epperson?* What of a small governmental payment to all persons who would lose salary because they have to be absent from their jobs in order to attend religious services? Would the state's failure to provide Mrs. Sherbert with unemployment compensation be the same as its not having on-premises released time and school prayer in that all of these actions simply "make the practice of religious beliefs more expensive"?

Compare Jesse H. Choper, *The Religion Clauses of the First Amendment: Reconciling the Conflict,* 41 U.Pitt.L.Rev. 673, 691, 697–700 (1980): "My proposal for resolving the conflict between the two Religion Clauses seeks to implement their historically and contemporarily acknowledged common goal: to safeguard religious liberty. [I]t is only when an accommodation would jeopardize religious liberty—when it would coerce, compromise, or influence religious choice—that it would fail. [For example, in *Yoder,* unless] it could be shown that relieving the Amish [would] tend to coerce, compromise, or influence religious choice—and it is extremely doubtful that it could—the exemption was permissible under the Establishment Clause. In contrast, in *Sherbert,* [the] exemption results in impairment of religious liberty because compulsorily raised tax funds must be used to subsidize Mrs. Sherbert's exercise of religion.[b] [In the draft exemption cases], draftees seeking exemption would have to formulate a statement of personal doctrine that would pass muster. This endeavor would involve deep and careful thought, and perhaps reading in philosophy and religion. Some undoubtedly would be persuaded by what they read. Moreover, the theory of 'cognitive

b. See also Jesse H. Choper, *The Free Exercise Clause,* 27 Wm. & M.L.Rev. 943, 951 n. 25 (1986): "Under Justice Rehnquist's [and Professor Schwarz's] rationale, if a municipally-owned bus company wanted to waive the fare to take people to churches, it could do so. According to Justice Rehnquist, the waiver would not 'induce' religion, but would simply 'accommodate' a religious choice that already had been made. That may be true, but the waiver also would result in what the religion clauses protect against—the use of tax funds for exclusively religious purposes."

dissonance'—which posits that to avoid madness we tend to become what we hold ourselves to be and what others believe us to be—also suggests that some initially fraudulent claims of belief in a personal religion would develop into true belief. Thus, a draft exemption for religious objectors threatens values of religious freedom by encouraging the adoption of religious beliefs by those who seek to qualify for the benefit."

(c) *Breadth of exemption.* In TEXAS MONTHLY, INC. v. BULLOCK, Sec. 2, II supra, SCALIA, J., joined by Rehnquist, C.J., and Kennedy, J., charged that according to Brennan, J.'s plurality opinion, "no law is constitutional whose 'benefits [are] confined to religious organizations,' except, of course, those laws that are unconstitutional *unless* they contain benefits confined to religious organizations. [But] 'the limits of permissible state accommodation to religion are by no means co-extensive with the noninterference mandated by the Free Exercise Clause.' Breadth of coverage is essential to constitutionality whenever a law's benefiting of religious activity is sought to be defended [as] merely the incidental consequence of seeking to benefit *all* activity that achieves a particular secular goal. But that is a different rationale—more commonly invoked than accommodation of religion but, as our cases show, not preclusive of it. Where accommodation of religion is the justification, by definition religion is being singled out." Finally, "the proper lesson to be drawn from" the fact that the free exercise clause may not require the Texas sales tax exemption and "that *Murdock* and *Follett* are narrowly distinguishable" is that "if the exemption comes so close to being a constitutionally required accommodation, there is no doubt that it is at least a permissible one."[c]

BRENNAN, J., joined by Marshall and Stevens, JJ., responded: "Contrary to the dissent's claims, we in no way suggest that *all* benefits conferred exclusively upon religious groups or upon individuals on account of their religious beliefs are forbidden by the Establishment Clause unless they are mandated by the Free Exercise Clause. Our decisions in *Zorach* and *Amos* offer two examples. Similarly, if the Air Force provided a sufficiently broad exemption from its dress requirements for servicemen whose religious faiths commanded them to wear certain headgear or other attire, see *Goldman v. Weinberger,* that exemption presumably would not be invalid under the Establishment Clause even though this Court has not found it to be required by the Free Exercise Clause.

"All of these cases, however, involve legislative exemptions that did not or would not impose substantial burdens on nonbeneficiaries while allowing others to act according to their religious beliefs, or that were designed to alleviate government intrusions that might significantly deter adherents of a particular faith from conduct protected by the Free Exercise Clause. New York City's decision to release students from public schools so that they

---

c. Why didn't Texas' exemption violate the establishment clause test articulated by Kennedy, J. (joined by Rehnquist, C.J., and White and Scalia, JJ.) in *Allegheny County v. ACLU,* Ch. 11, IV supra, because it gave "direct benefits to religion" and involved "subtle coercion [in] the form of taxation"?

might obtain religious instruction elsewhere, which we upheld in *Zorach,* was found not to coerce students who wished to remain behind to alter their religious beliefs, nor did it impose monetary costs on their parents or other taxpayers who opposed or were indifferent to the religious instruction given to students who were released. The hypothetical Air Force uniform exemption also would not place a monetary burden on those required to conform to the dress code or subject them to any appreciable privation. And the application of Title VII's exemption for religious organizations that we approved in *Amos* though it had some adverse effect on those holding or seeking employment with those organizations (if not on taxpayers generally), prevented potentially serious encroachments on protected religious freedoms.

"Texas' tax exemption, by contrast, does not remove a demonstrated and possible grave imposition on religious activity sheltered by the Free Exercise Clause. Moreover, it burdens nonbeneficiaries by increasing their tax bills by whatever amount is needed to offset the benefit bestowed on subscribers to religious publications."

3. *Sabbath observance.* THORNTON v. CALDOR, INC., 472 U.S. 703, 105 S.Ct. 2914, 86 L.Ed.2d 557 (1985), per BURGER, C.J., held that a Connecticut law—which provided "that those who observe a Sabbath any day of the week as a matter of religious conviction must be relieved of the duty to work on that day, no matter what burden or inconvenience this imposes on the employer or fellow workers"—"has a primary effect that impermissibly advances a particular religious practice" and thus violates the establishment clause: "The statute arms Sabbath observers with an absolute and unqualified right not to work on whatever day they designate as their Sabbath [and thus] goes beyond having an incidental or remote effect of advancing religion."[d]

O'CONNOR, J., joined by Marshall, J., concurred, distinguishing "the religious accommodation provisions of Title VII of the Civil Rights Act [which] require private employers to reasonably accommodate the religious practices of employees unless to do so would cause undue hardship to the employer's business": "In my view, a statute outlawing employment discrimination based on race, color, religion, sex or national origin has the valid secular purpose of assuring employment opportunity to all groups in our pluralistic society. Since Title VII calls for reasonable rather than absolute accommodation and extends that requirement to all religious beliefs and practices rather than protecting only the Sabbath observance, I believe an

---

d. Rehnquist, J., dissented without opinion.

Consider Richard A. Epstein, *Religious Liberty in the Welfare State*, 31 Wm. & M.L.Rev. 375, 406 (1990): "[It would plainly be unconstitutional] if the state offered to pay a small sum out of public funds to the employer to defray the additional costs it had to bear to keep the religious worker on its payroll. [If] a public subsidy of religious workers is not acceptable under the estab-

lishment clause, then a public mandate of a private subsidy is unacceptable as well."

For the view that since "securing individual constitutional rights often (or almost always) imposes impediments to the smooth functioning of our system, if accommodations for religion impose only imprecise social/economic costs, then these prices of religious tolerance are permitted to be paid," see Jesse H. Choper, *Securing Religious Liberty*, 123–126 (1995).

objective observer would perceive it as an anti-discrimination law rather than an endorsement of religion or a particular religious practice."

Was the purpose or effect of the *Caldor* statute any different than that of the *Amos* statute or the Court's decisions in *Sherbert, Thomas, Hobbie, Roy* and *Yoder? Amos* distinguished *Caldor* on the ground that in *Amos,* "appellee was not legally obligated to take the steps necessary to qualify for a temple recommend, and his discharge was not required by statute." Should it make a difference that, unlike the other cases, the Caldor statute sought to alleviate burdens on religion posed by private parties rather than the state?

Does the *Caldor* statute "promote" and "endorse" a particular "religion" or "religious belief" or "religious practice" any moreso than the Court's decisions in *Sherbert, Thomas, Hobbie, Yoder* and *Roy,* or than the statutory exemptions from the draft or Sunday Closing Laws? *Hobbie* distinguished *Caldor* as follows: "Florida's provision of unemployment benefits to religious observers does not single out a particular class of such persons for favorable treatment and thereby have the effect of implicitly endorsing a particular religious belief. Rather, the provision of unemployment benefits generally available within the State to religious observers who must leave their employment due to an irreconcilable conflict between the demands of work and conscience neutrally accommodates religious beliefs and practices, without endorsement."

In *Kiryas Joel,* Sec. 3 supra, SCALIA, J., joined by Rehnquist, C.J., and Thomas, J., disagreed with the Court's conclusion that New York had impermissibly preferred one religion: "[M]ost efforts at accommodation seek to solve a problem that applies to members of only one or a few religions. Not every religion uses wine in its sacraments, but that does not make an exemption from Prohibition for sacramental wine-use impermissible, nor does it require the State granting such an exemption to explain in advance how it will treat every other claim for dispensation from its controlled-substances laws. Likewise, not every religion uses peyote in its services, but we have suggested that legislation which exempts the sacramental use of peyote from generally applicable drug laws is not only permissible, but desirable, see *Smith,* without any suggestion that some 'up front' legislative guarantee of equal treatment for sacramental substances used by other sects must be provided."

Kennedy, J., expressed a similar view: "It is normal for legislatures to respond to problems as they arise—no less so when the issue is religious accommodation. Most accommodations cover particular religious practices."

Is a *general* rule for free exercise exemptions—as under *Sherbert-Yoder,* or the Religious Freedom Restoration Act (fn. a after *Smith*)—preferable to a specific exemption for religion (as the statutes in *Texas Monthly* and *Caldor*)? Consider Thomas C. Berg, *The New Attacks on Religious Freedom Legislation, and Why They are Wrong,* 21 Card.L.Rev. 415, 435–36 (1999): "Requiring the same standard for all religious freedom claims, in the less political forum of the courts, serves the goal of religious equality by minimizing the chance that only politically powerful groups will get accommodations, while individuals or very small groups without a lobbyist will escape the legislature's attention altogether.[89]"

4. *School prayer.* In *Jaffree,* O'CONNOR, J., applied her "solution"[e] to Alabama's moment of silence law: "No law prevents a student who is so inclined from praying silently in public schools. [Of] course, the State might argue that § 16–1–20.1 protects not silent prayer, but rather group silent prayer under State sponsorship. Phrased in these terms, the burden lifted by the statute is not one imposed by the State of Alabama, but by the Establishment Clause as interpreted in *Engel* and *Schempp.* In my view, it is beyond the authority of the State of Alabama to remove burdens imposed by the Constitution itself."

5. *Reconciling the conflict.* Assuming the validity of the distinction between *McCollum, Engel, Schempp* and *Jaffree* on the one hand, and the programs such as that in *Amos* and exemption from the draft etc. on the other, are the above approaches nonetheless undesirable because they result not merely in protection of free exercise (or neutrality or accommodation) but in relieving persons with certain religious beliefs of significant burdens from which many other persons strongly desire to be exempted? That, in this sense, there is "preference" for minority religions and "discrimination" against the other persons because of their religion or lack of it?[f]

Might religious exemptions be seen as "restorative or equalizing" (Galanter, note 4, Ch. 12, II supra)? Consider Gordon, fn. a in *Lukumi,* at 91–92: "In a democracy, laws inevitably will reflect the majority's values, and consequently, laws will tend to burden minority religions but not majority ones. Therefore, majority religions generally have a kind of inherent exemption from the force of law. In addition, politically powerful minority religions often are able to obtain express exemptions from legislation. Therefore, powerless minority religions will be the only religions without exemptions. The accommodation principle provides powerless minority religions with some measure of the same protection that other religions already enjoy in the democratic process." What about exemptions (accommodations) for majority (mainstream) religions? Consider Greene, fn. d in *Kiryas Joel,* at 74: "When a majority pushes for governmentally organized prayer in public schools or for the placement of its favored religious symbols in the halls of government, it is wrong to call such actions 'accommodation.' [But] when the effect of the majority's actions is to make life easier for a minority, there is no concern about an 'Establishment' of religion. It also seems wrong to

89. See Ira C. Lupu, *Reconstructing the Establishment Clause: The Case Against Discretionary Accommodation of Religion,* 140 U.Pa.L.Rev. 555 (1991) (claiming that statute-by-statute legislative accommodations are unconstitutional because they reflect the varying political power of different religious groups).

e. See fn. c in *Amos.*

f. Should the Court "either suggest or require that an alternative burden be imposed on individuals who would otherwise qualify for religious exemptions"? Choper, fn. d supra, at 92.

say that accommodation of minority religions constitutes a symbolic endorsement of those religions; rather, accommodation in this context suggests that the majority is coming to the aid of a burdened minority, not that the majority agrees with the minority on any matter of religious truth." Compare Ira C. Lupu, *Uncovering the Village of Kiryas Joel*, 96 Colum.L.Rev. 104, 117–18 (1996): "If Jews are a relatively small minority in New York State but a sizable minority or a majority in some New York City area suburbs, may the state close public schools on Yom Kippur while the suburb is forbidden from doing likewise? May Pennsylvania accommodate Mormon traditions, while Utah may not?"

Index

References are to Pages

771